O E C D

S T A T I S T I C S

NATIONAL ACCOUNTS
MAIN AGGREGATES 1960-1997

COMPTES NATIONAUX
PRINCIPAUX AGRÉGATS 1960-1997

1999 EDITION V O L U M E I **ÉDITION 1999**

ORGANISATION FOR ECONOMIC CO-OPERATION AND DEVELOPMENT

ORGANISATION DE COOPÉRATION ET DE DÉVELOPPEMENT ÉCONOMIQUES

ORGANISATION FOR ECONOMIC CO-OPERATION AND DEVELOPMENT

ORGANISATION DE COOPÉRATION ET DE DÉVELOPPEMENT ÉCONOMIQUES

Pursuant to Article 1 of the Convention signed in Paris on 14th December 1960, and which came into force on 30th September 1961, the Organisation for Economic Co-operation and Development (OECD) shall promote policies designed:

- to achieve the highest sustainable economic growth and employment and a rising standard of living in Member countries, while maintaining financial stability, and thus to contribute to the development of the world economy;
- to contribute to sound economic expansion in Member as well as non-member countries in the process of economic development; and
- to contribute to the expansion of world trade on a multilateral, non-discriminatory basis in accordance with international obligations.

The original Member countries of the OECD are Austria, Belgium, Canada, Denmark, France, Germany, Greece, Iceland, Ireland, Italy, Luxembourg, the Netherlands, Norway, Portugal, Spain, Sweden, Switzerland, Turkey, the United Kingdom and the United States. The following countries became Members subsequently through accession at the dates indicated hereafter: Japan (28th April 1964), Finland (28th January 1969), Australia (7th June 1971), New Zealand (29th May 1973), Mexico (18th May 1994), the Czech Republic (21st December 1995), Hungary (7th May 1996), Poland (22nd November 1996) and the Republic of Korea (12th December 1996). The Commission of the European Communities takes part in the work of the OECD (Article 13 of the OECD Convention).

En vertu de l'article 1er de la Convention signée le 14 décembre 1960, à Paris, et entrée en vigueur le 30 septembre 1961, l'Organisation de Coopération et de Développement Économiques (OCDE) a pour objectif de promouvoir des politiques visant :

- à réaliser la plus forte expansion de l'économie et de l'emploi et une progression du niveau de vie dans les pays Membres, tout en maintenant la stabilité financière, et à contribuer ainsi au développement de l'économie mondiale ;
- à contribuer à une saine expansion économique dans les pays Membres, ainsi que les pays non membres, en voie de développement économique ;
- à contribuer à l'expansion du commerce mondial sur une base multilatérale et non discriminatoire conformément aux obligations internationales.

Les pays Membres originaires de l'OCDE sont : l'Allemagne, l'Autriche, la Belgique, le Canada, le Danemark, l'Espagne, les États-Unis, la France, la Grèce, l'Irlande, l'Islande, l'Italie, le Luxembourg, la Norvège, les Pays-Bas, le Portugal, le Royaume-Uni, la Suède, la Suisse et la Turquie. Les pays suivants sont ultérieurement devenus Membres par adhésion aux dates indiquées ci-après : le Japon (28 avril 1964), la Finlande (28 janvier 1969), l'Australie (7 juin 1971), la Nouvelle-Zélande (29 mai 1973), le Mexique (18 mai 1994), la République tchèque (21 décembre 1995), la Hongrie (7 mai 1996), la Pologne (22 novembre 1996) et la République de Corée (12 décembre 1996). La Commission des Communautés européennes participe aux travaux de l'OCDE (article 13 de la Convention de l'OCDE).

INTRODUCTION

National Accounts is published in two separate volumes.

VOLUME I

The **first volume** gives for each country the main aggregates calculated according to either the 1968 System of National Accounts (1968 SNA)[1] or the former[2] Systems of National Accounts. After a summary of the definitions of these main aggregates, this volume is divided into eight parts.

Part one contains graphs for each country showing the growth in real terms of Gross domestic product and expenditure.

Part two gives for each zone (OECD-Total, OECD-Europe and EU15) the main aggregates in US dollars using either exchange rates or purchasing power parities.

Part three gives for each country the main aggregates in national currencies.

Parts four and **five** give for zones and individual countries "growth triangles" for the main components of final expenditure. These triangles are made up of geometric average annual rates of change in per cent between any two years within the period shown.

Part six gives a set of comparative tables based on **exchange rates** (US dollars, volume and price indices). The national accounts data have been converted into US dollars using market or official exchange rates[3]. It must be emphasized that these rates do not necessarily reflect the relationships between the internal purchasing powers of currencies and may consequently distort intercountry comparisons of GDP and its components.

Part seven contains a set of comparative tables based on **purchasing power parities**. These tables enable direct comparisons to be made of the volumes of final goods and services produced in the Member countries.

Part eight gives three tables referring to population, exchange rates and purchasing power parities (PPPs) for GDP.

VOLUME II

The **second volume** gives detailed national accounts for each country. To the extent that data are available, the following tables are shown:

1. Main aggregates.
2. Private final consumption expenditure by type and purpose (current and constant prices).
3. Gross fixed capital formation by kind of activity of owner (current and constant prices).
4. Gross fixed capital formation by type of good and owner (current and constant prices).
5. Total government outlays by function and type.

6. Accounts for general government.
6.1 Accounts for central government.
6.2 Accounts for state or provincial government.
6.3 Accounts for local government.

Les Comptes nationaux sont publiés en deux volumes séparés.

VOLUME I

Le **premier volume** présente pour chaque pays les principaux agrégats de comptabilité nationale évalués conformément soit au Système de Comptabilité Nationale de 1968 (SCN de 1968)[1] soit à l'ancien[2] Système de Comptabilité Nationale. Après un rappel sommaire des définitions de ces principaux agrégats, ce volume se divise en huit parties.

La **première partie** présente, sous forme de graphiques, l'évolution en termes de volume du Produit intérieur brut et de ses emplois.

La **deuxième partie** comprend pour chaque zone (OCDE-Total, OCDE-Europe et UE15) les principaux agrégats en dollars des États-Unis en utilisant ou bien les taux de change ou les parités de pouvoir d'achat.

La **troisième partie** comprend pour chaque pays les données en monnaies nationales des principaux agrégats.

Les **quatrième** et **cinquième parties** présentent pour les zones et les pays individuels des « triangles de croissance » pour les principales composantes de la demande. Ces triangles de croissance sont composés de moyennes géométriques de pourcentages annuels de variation enregistrés entre deux années quelconques de la période montrée.

La **sixième partie** fournit un ensemble de tableaux comparatifs basés sur **les taux de change** (dollars, indices de volume et de prix). Les données des comptes nationaux ont été converties en dollars des États-Unis en utilisant le taux de change du marché ou le taux de change officiel[3]. Il faut souligner que ces taux ne reflètent pas nécessairement les rapports entre les pouvoirs d'achat intérieurs des monnaies et peuvent rendre donc inexacts les comparaisons entre le PIB et ses composantes d'un pays à l'autre.

La **septième partie** comprend un ensemble de tableaux comparatifs basés sur **les parités de pouvoir d'achat**. Ces tableaux permettent des comparaisons directes entre les volumes de biens et services finals produits dans les pays Membres.

La **huitième partie** fournit trois tableaux concernant la population, les taux de change et les parités de pouvoir d'achat (PPA) du PIB.

VOLUME II

Le **deuxième volume** présente les statistiques détaillées de chaque pays. Dans la mesure de la disponibilité des données, les tableaux montrés sont les suivants :

1. Principaux agrégats.
2. Consommation finale privée par catégorie de dépenses et par fonction (prix courants et prix constants).
3. Formation brute de capital fixe par genre d'activité du propriétaire (prix courants et prix constants).
4. Formation brute de capital selon la nature des biens et par propriétaire (prix courants et prix constants).
5. Dépenses des administrations publiques par fonction et par nature.

6. Comptes des administrations publiques.
6.1 Comptes des administrations centrales.
6.2 Comptes des administrations provinciales.
6.3 Comptes des administrations locales.

6.4 Accounts for social security funds.

7. Accounts for non-financial and financial corporate and quasi-corporate enterprises.

7.1 Accounts for non-financial corporate and quasi-corporate enterprises.

7.2 Accounts for financial institutions.

8. Accounts for households and private unincorporated enterprises.

9. Accounts for private non-profit institutions serving households.

10. External transactions, current and capital accumulation accounts.

11. Capital finance accounts.

12. Gross domestic product by kind of activity (current and constant prices).

13. Cost components of value added by kind of activity.

14. Profit shares and rates of return on capital.

15. Employment by kind of activity.

A table on page 8 of Volume II shows which of these data are available for each country. The explanatory notes to the tables appear at the end of each country section.

Two annexes are included at the end of Volume II. **Annex I** is a glossary of the technical terms used in the present System of National Accounts (SNA); **Annex II** gives a full set of English and French translations of the item descriptions in the detailed country tables.

The national accounts in both volumes have been prepared from statistics reported to the OECD by Member countries in their answers to successive *National Accounts Questionnaires*. These questionnaires are designed to collect internationally comparable data according to either the 1968 SNA or the *Former* SNA. Although Member countries have all agreed to adopt 1968 SNA a number are still using the earlier system or can give data for only a few years according to the 1968 SNA. The country tables in both volumes indicate the system used by each country. There are numerous differences between the 1968 SNA and the earlier system as regards valuation, classifications and definitions, and these must be taken into account when comparing data compiled according to different systems.

The following signs and abbreviations are used:

* : Secretariat estimates
.. : not available
- : nil or negligible
. : decimal point
billion : thousand million
n.e.c. : not elsewhere classified
c.i.f. : cost, insurance and freight
f.o.b. : free on board

EU15: European Union (15 countries): Austria, Belgium, Denmark, Finland, France, Germany, Greece, Ireland, Italy, Luxembourg, Netherlands, Portugal, Spain, Sweden and the United Kingdom.
OECD-Europe: All European Member countries of OECD with the exception of the Czech Republic, Hungary and Poland, *i.e.* countries in EU15 plus Iceland, Norway, Switzerland and Turkey.
OECD-Total: All Member countries of OECD with the exception of the Czech Republic, Hungary, Poland and Korea, *i.e.* countries of OECD-Europe plus Canada, Mexico, United States, Japan, Australia and New Zealand.

---

1. *A System of National Accounts* (Series F. No. 2, Rev 3) New York, United Nations, 1968.
2. *A System of National Accounts and Supporting Tables* (Series F, No. 2, Rev 2) New York, United Nations, 1964.
3. The rates used are the monthly average market rates/par or central rates shown in *International Financial Statistics* published by the International Monetary Fund.

6.4 Comptes des administrations de sécurité sociale.

7. Comptes des sociétés et quasi-sociétés, non financières et financières.

7.1 Comptes des sociétés et quasi-sociétés non financières.

7.2 Comptes institutions financières.

8. Comptes des ménages et des entreprises individuelles.

9. Comptes des institutions privées sans but lucratif au services des ménages.

10. Transactions extérieures, compte courant et compte d'accumulation de capital.

11. Compte de financement de capital par secteur.

12. Produit intérieur brut par genre d'activité (prix courants et prix constants).

13. Coûts constitutifs de la valeur ajoutée par genre d'activité.

14. Part des bénéfices et taux de rendement.

15. Emploi par genre d'activité.

La disponibilité de ces données est précisée dans le tableau page 8, et les notes explicatives relatives aux tableaux apparaissent à la fin du chapitre du pays.

Deux annexes sont à la fin du volume II. **L'annexe I** est un glossaire des termes techniques utilisés dans le nouveau Système de Comptabilité Nationale (SCN); l'**annexe II** comprend les traductions anglaise et française des rubriques des tableaux par pays.

Les deux volumes des comptes nationaux sont préparés à l'aide de l'information statistique fournie à l'OCDE par les pays Membres dans leurs réponses aux *Questionnaires des comptes nationaux* des dernières années. Ces questionnaires sont destinés à rassembler des données comparables au niveau international et conformes soit au SCN de 1968 ou à l'*ancien* SCN. Bien que tous les pays Membres aient été d'accord pour adopter le SCN de 1968, un certain nombre utilisent encore le système précédent ou ne peuvent fournir des données que pour quelques années suivant le SCN de 1968. Les pages de couvertures des tableaux par pays dans les deux volumes spécifient le système utilisé par chaque pays. Il existe de nombreuses différences entre le SCN de 1968 et le système précédent en ce qui concernent les évaluations, les classifications et les définitions et il faut en tenir compte lorsqu'on compare des données compilées selon des systèmes différents.

Les signes et abréviations utilisés sont les suivants :

* : estimations du Secrétariat
.. : non disponible
- : nul ou négligeable
. : point décimal
billion : mille millions
n.d.a. : non défini ailleurs
c.a.f. : coût, assurance et fret
f.a.b. : franco à bord

UE15 : Union européenne (15 pays) : Autriche, Belgique, Danemark, Finlande, France, Allemagne, Grèce, Irlande, Italie, Luxembourg, Pays-Bas, Portugal, Espagne, Suède et Royaume-Uni.
OCDE-Europe : Ensemble des pays européens Membres de l'OCDE à l'exception de la République tchèque, de la Hongrie et de la Pologne, *i.e.* les pays de l'UE15 plus Islande, Norvège, Suisse et Turquie.
OCDE-Total : Ensemble des pays Membres de l'OCDE à l'exception de la République tchèque, de la Hongrie, de la Pologne et de la Corée, *i.e.* les pays de l'OCDE-Europe plus Canada, Mexique, États-Unis, Japon, Australie et Nouvelle-Zélande.

---

1. *Système de Comptabilité nationale* (série F, n° 2, Rev 3) Nations Unies, New York, 1970.
2. *Systèmes de Comptes nationaux et tableaux connexes* (série F, n° 2, Rev 2) Nations Unies, New York, 1964.
3. Les taux utilisés sont les moyennes mensuelles des taux du marché/parité ou taux central montré dans *International Financial Statistics* publié par le Fonds Monétaire International.

TABLE OF CONTENTS – TABLE DES MATIÈRES

DEFINITION OF MAIN AGGREGATES
DÉFINITION DES PRINCIPAUX AGRÉGATS

1. Government Final Consumption Expenditure

The value of goods and services produced by governments for their own use on current account, that is the value of their gross output *less* the sum of the value of their commodity and non-commodity sales and the value of their own-account capital formation. The value of their gross output is equal to the sum of the value of their intermediate consumption of goods and services, compensation of employees, consumption of fixed capital and indirect taxes.

2. Private Final Consumption Expenditure

This is the sum of two items:

i) The outlays of resident households on new durable and non-durable goods and services *less* their net sales of second-hand goods, scraps and wastes.

ii) The value of goods and services produced by private non-profit institutions for own use on current account, that is the value of their gross output reduced by the sum of the value of their commodity and non-commodity sales. The value of their gross output is equal to the sum of the value of their intermediate consumption of goods and services, compensation of employees, consumption of fixed capital and indirect taxes.

3. Increase in stocks

In principle, the market value at the owning establishment of the physical change during a period of account in stocks of materials, supplies, work-in-progress except on construction projects, finished products, livestock raised for slaughter and merchandise held by resident industries, and in stocks of strategic materials and emergency stocks of important products held by government services.

In practice, the closest feasible approximation may be the difference between the levels of these stocks at the beginning and end of the period, both valued at approximate average prices ruling over the period, perhaps valuing commodities processed internally at explicit costs.

1. Consommation finale des administrations publiques

Valeur des biens et services produits par les branches non marchandes des administrations publiques pour leur propre usage courant. La consommation finale des services des administrations publiques est égale à leur production moins la somme de leurs ventes de biens et services marchands, de leurs ventes de biens et services non marchands et de leur formation de capital pour compte propre, lorsque la production d'auto-équipement n'est pas isolée comme branche d'activité marchande. La valeur de la production des branches non marchandes des administrations publiques est égale à la somme de leur consommation intermédiaire de biens et services, augmentée de la rémunération des salariés, de la consommation de capital fixe et des impôts indirects.

2. Consommation finale privée

Ce flux est la somme de:

i) Achats de services et de biens neufs de consommation durables, semi-durables, et non durables par les ménages résidents diminués de leurs ventes – nettes de leurs achats – de biens d'occasion, de rebuts et de déchets.

ii) Valeur des biens et services produits par les branches non marchandes des institutions privées sans but lucratif pour leur propre usage courant. La consommation finale de ces institutions est égale à la production de leurs branches non marchandes, moins la somme de leurs ventes de biens et services marchands et de biens et services non marchands. La valeur de la production des branches non marchandes des institutions privées sans but lucratif au service des ménages est égale à la somme de leur consommation intermédiaire de biens et services augmentée de la rémunération des salariés, de la consommation de capital fixe et des impôts indirects.

3. Variation des stocks

En principe, la variation des stocks au cours d'une période comptable est égale à la différence entre les entrées en stocks et les sorties de stocks évaluées au cours du jour, chez le propriétaire. Les stocks comprennent : les stocks de matières premières, de produits semi-ouvrés, de travaux en cours, à l'exclusion des travaux de construction, les stocks de produits finis, le bétail élevé pour la boucherie et les stocks de marchandises importées, détenus par les unités de production résidentes, les stocks de matières stratégiques et les stocks d'urgence, détenus par les producteurs des services rendus par les administrations publiques.

En pratique, la meilleure approximation de la règle d'évaluation théorique peut être de calculer la différence entre les niveaux des stocks à la fin et au début de la période et de l'évaluer aux prix moyens approximatifs de la période, les biens provenant de la production interne de l'entreprise pouvant éventuellement être évalués au prix de revient.

4. Gross Fixed Capital Formation

The outlays (purchases and own-account production) of industries, producers of government services and producers of private non-profit services to households, on additions of new durable goods (commodities) to their stocks of fixed assets *less* their net sales of similar second-hand and scrapped goods. Excluded are the outlays of government services on durable goods for military use. Included are acquisitions of reproducible and non-reproducible durable goods, except land, mineral deposits, timber tracts and the like, for civilian use; work-in-progress on construction projects; capital repairs; outlays on the improvement of land and on the development and extension of timber tracts, plantations, vineyards, etc. which take considerably more than a year to become productive, until they become productive; the acquisition of breeding stock, draught animals, dairy cattle and the like; and the transfer costs in connexion with purchases and sales of land, mineral deposits, timber tracts, etc.

5. Exports of goods and services

In principle, all transfers of the ownership of goods from residents of a country to non-residents and services provided by resident producers of the country to non-residents. In practice, the exports of goods may consist of the outward movement of merchandise across the customs frontier of a country and of other goods across the boundaries of her domestic territory, including the direct purchases in the country of extra-territorial organisations and non-resident persons. Since the imports of merchandise into a country are to be valued at c.i.f., the exports of services of the country should also include the charges in respect of the imports for the transport and insurance services provided by resident producers of the given country.

6. Imports of goods and services

In principle, all transfers of the ownership of goods from non-residents of a country to residents and services provided by non-resident producers to residents of the country. In practice, the imports of goods may consist of the inward movement of merchandise across the customs frontier of a country and of other goods across the boundaries of her domestic territory, including the direct purchases of the government services and residents of the country abroad. Since imports of merchandise are valued c.i.f., imports also include the charges of resident producers for transport and insurance services in respect of these imports.

7. Gross Domestic Product

The Gross Domestic Product is equal to the total of the gross expenditure on the final uses of the domestic supply of goods and services valued at purchasers' values *less* imports of goods and services valued c.i.f.; or the sum of the compensation of employees, consumption of fixed capital, operating surplus and indirect taxes, net, of resident producers and import duties.

8. Indirect taxes

Taxes assessed on producers in respect of the production, sale, purchase or use of goods and services, which they charge to the expenses of production. Also included are import duties and the operating surplus, reduced by the normal margin of profits of business units, of fiscal and similar monopolies of government.

4. Formation brute de capital fixe

Dépenses (achats et production pour compte propre) des branches d'activité marchande, des branches non marchandes des administrations publiques et des branches non marchandes des institutions privées sans but lucratif, ayant pour but d'ajouter des biens durables neufs à leur capital fixe, diminuées des ventes de ces branches, nettes de leurs achats, de biens analogues d'occasion ou de rebuts. Les dépenses des administrations publiques au titre de biens durables à usage militaire sont exclues de la formation brute de capital fixe. Les acquisitions à usage civil de biens durables, reproductibles ou non, à l'exception des terres, des gisements de minéraux, des zones boisées et des biens analogues, la valeur des travaux du bâtiment et des travaux publics et la valeur du gros entretien effectué sont incluses dans la formation brute de capital fixe. De même, on inclura dans la formation brute de capital fixe les dépenses de mise en valeur et d'amélioration des terres et les dépenses engagées pour développer et étendre les zones boisées, les plantations, les vignobles, etc., jusqu'à ce qu'ils deviennent productifs, lorsque le délai qui les sépare de l'entrée en production est largement supérieur à un an, et les acquisitions d'animaux pour la reproduction, d'animaux de trait, de bétail laitier, etc., ainsi que les frais de mutation relatifs aux achats et aux ventes de terrains, de gisements minéraux, de zones boisées, etc.

5. Exportations de biens et services

En principe, on enregistre dans les exportations d'un pays tous les transferts de propriété des biens et des services fournis par les producteurs résidents de ce pays à des non-résidents. En pratique on peut saisir les exportations de biens de la manière suivante : au passage des frontières douanières, s'il s'agit de marchandises, à la sortie du territoire économique s'il s'agit d'autres biens, en y incluant les achats directs à l'intérieur des organismes extra-territoriaux et des particuliers non résidents. Étant donné que les importations d'un pays doivent être évaluées c.a.f., les exportations de services de ce pays doivent inclure la valeur des services de transport et d'assurance des marchandises importées fournis par des producteurs résidents.

6. Importations de biens et services

En principe, on enregistre dans les importations d'un pays tous les transferts de propriété des biens et des services fournis par les producteurs non résidents à des résidents de ce pays. En pratique on peut saisir les importations de la manière suivante: au passage des frontières du pays s'il s'agit de marchandises, à l'entrée du territoire économique s'il s'agit des autres biens et services; ces derniers comprennent les achats directs courants à l'extérieur des administrations publiques et des particuliers résidents. Comme les importations de marchandises d'un pays sont évaluées c.a.f., leur valeur inclut la valeur des services de transports et d'assurance fournis par les producteurs résidents sur les marchandises importées.

7. Produit intérieur brut

Le produit intérieur brut est égal au total des emplois finals de biens et services aux prix d'acquisition diminué des importations c.a.f. On peut encore définir le produit intérieur brut comme la somme de la rémunération des salariés, de la consommation de capital fixe, de l'excédent net d'exploitation, des impôts indirects – nets des subventions d'exploitation – des producteurs résidents et des droits et taxes sur importations.

8. Impôts indirects

Impôts payés par les producteurs, figurant dans leur coût de production et assis sur la production, la vente, l'achat ou l'utilisation de biens ou de services. Ces impôts comprennent les droits et taxes sur importations ainsi que les excédents d'exploitation des monopoles fiscaux et autres monopoles publics diminués de la marge bénéficiaire normale.

9. Subsidies

All grants on current account made by government to private industries and public corporations; and grants made by the public authorities to government enterprises in compensation for operating losses when these losses are clearly the consequence of the policy of the government to maintain prices at a level below costs of production.

10. Consumption of fixed capital

The value, at current replacement cost, of the reproducible fixed assets except the roads, dams and other forms of construction other than structures of the producers of government services used up during a period of account as a result of normal wear and tear, foreseen obsolescence and the normal rate of accidental damage. Unforeseen obsolescence, main catastrophies and the depletion of natural resources are not taken into account.

11. Compensation of employees paid by resident producers

All payments by resident producers of wages and salaries to their employees, in kind and in cash, and of contributions, paid or imputed, in respect of their employees to social security schemes and to private pension, family allowance, casualty insurance, life insurance and similar schemes.

12. Operating surplus

Gross output at producers' values *less* the sum of intermediate consumption, compensation of employees, consumption of fixed capital and indirect taxes reduced by subsidies. It includes the earnings of self-employed persons.

13. Net saving

The difference between current receipts and current disbursements of the nation. It is derived by deducting government and private final consumption from National Disposable Income.

14. Surplus of the nation on current transactions

The excess of receipts on current account over disbursements on current account in respect of the transactions of a country with the rest of the world. It is equal to exports *less* imports of goods and services, *plus* net factor income and net current transfers from the rest of the world.

15. Net factor income from the rest of the world

Receipts (*less* payments) of compensation of employees and entrepreneurial and property income from the rest of the world.

16. Net current transfers from the rest of the world

Net transfers of income between residents and the rest of the world. The transfers are made from the current income of the payer and add to the current income of the recipient for such purposes as consumption expenditure. They may include transfers in cash or in kind between governments, migrants' remittances, transfers of immigrants personal and household goods, and transfers in cash and in kind between resident and non-resident households.

9. Subventions d'exploitation

Tous les transferts courants de l'administration aux unités de production marchande du secteur privé et aux sociétés publiques et les transferts des pouvoirs publics aux unités de production marchandes gérées par l'administration pour compenser leurs pertes d'exploitation lorsque celles-ci sont manifestement la conséquence de la politique des pouvoirs publics visant à maintenir des prix à un niveau inférieur aux coûts de production.

10. Consommation de capital fixe

Valeur, aux prix courants de remplacement, du capital fixe reproductible consommé au cours de la période, du fait de l'usure normale, de l'obsolescence prévisible et des dommages accidentels probables. On ne calcule pas de consommation de capital fixe pour les routes, les barrages, et les constructions autres que les bâtiments des producteurs de services rendus par les administrations publiques. L'obsolescence imprévisible, les grands catastrophes, l'épuisement des ressources naturelles ne sont pas pris en compte dans le calcul de la consommation de capital fixe.

11. Rémunération des salariés payée par les producteurs résidents

Paiements en espèces et en nature des producteurs résidents à leur personnel de salaries et de traitements ainsi que leurs contributions effectives ou imputées aux régimes de sécurité sociale et aux régimes privés de retraite, d'allocations familiales, d'assurance-dommages, d'assurance-vie, etc.. pour le compte de leur personnel.

12. Excédent net d'exploitation

Différence entre la production aux prix départ-usine et la somme de la consommation intermédiaire, de la rémunération des salariés, de la consommation de capital fixe et des impôts indirects diminués des subventions d'exploitation. Il comprend le revenu des entreprises individuelles.

13. Épargne nette

Différence entre les ressources courantes et les emplois courants de la nation. Elle est obtenue comme la différence entre le Revenu national disponible et la consommation finale privée et celle des administrations publiques.

14. Solde des opérations courantes avec le reste du monde

Excédent du compte des opérations courantes d'un pays avec le reste du monde. Il est égal aux exportations (*moins* importations) de biens et services, *plus* le revenu net des facteurs reçu du reste du monde et les transferts courants nets reçus du reste du monde.

15. Revenu net des facteurs reçu du reste du monde

La rémunération des salariés et le revenu de la propriété et de l'entreprise reçus du reste du monde *moins* les paiements au reste du monde.

16. Transferts courants nets reçus du reste du monde

Transferts nets de revenus entre les résidents et le reste du monde. Ils s'opèrent par prélèvement sur le revenu courant du payeur et s'ajoutent au revenu courant du bénéficiaire pour financer ses dépenses courantes, en particulier ses dépenses de consommation. Il peut s'agir de transferts en espèce ou en nature entre des gouvernements, des envois de fonds des émigrés, des transferts de biens personnels et ménagers des émigrants, et des transferts en espèce ou en nature entre ménages résidents et non-résidents.

Graphs
Graphiques

The statistics for Germany in this publication refer to Germany after unification. Official data for Germany after unification are available only from 1991 onwards. In this publication, the secretariat has estimated some national accounts aggregates for the whole of Germany back to 1960 in order to calculate the various zones totals. These estimates are based on statistics published by Deutsches Institut für Wirtschaftsforschung for period 1989-90 and by the East German Statistical Office in 1990 for period 1980-89. They are also based on the ratios of the aggregates of West Germany and the whole of Germany.

Les statistiques concernant l'Allemagne dans cette publication se réfèrent à l'Allemagne après l'unification. Des données officielles pour l'Allemagne après l'unification ne sont disponibles qu'à partir de 1991. Dans cette publication, le secrétariat a estimé certains agrégats des comptes nationaux pour l'Allemagne dans son ensemble depuis 1960 afin de calculer les différentes zones. Ces estimations sont basées sur des statistiques publiées par Deutsches Institut für Wirtschaftsforschung pour la période 1989-90 et par l'Office Statistique de l'Allemagne de l'Est en 1990 pour la période 1980-89. Elles sont aussi basées sur les rapports des agrégats de l'Allemagne occidentale et de l'Allemagne dans son ensemble.

This part contains graphs for each country and groups of countries showing the growth from 1960 to 1997 in reals terms of Gross Domestic Product, consumption expenditure, and fixed capital formation.

Cette partie présente, sous forme de graphiques, l'évolution de 1960 à 1997 en termes de volume du Produit Intérieur Brut, de la consommation finale, et de la formation brute de capital fixe.

Volume indices

1990 = 100
(Semi–logarithmic scale)

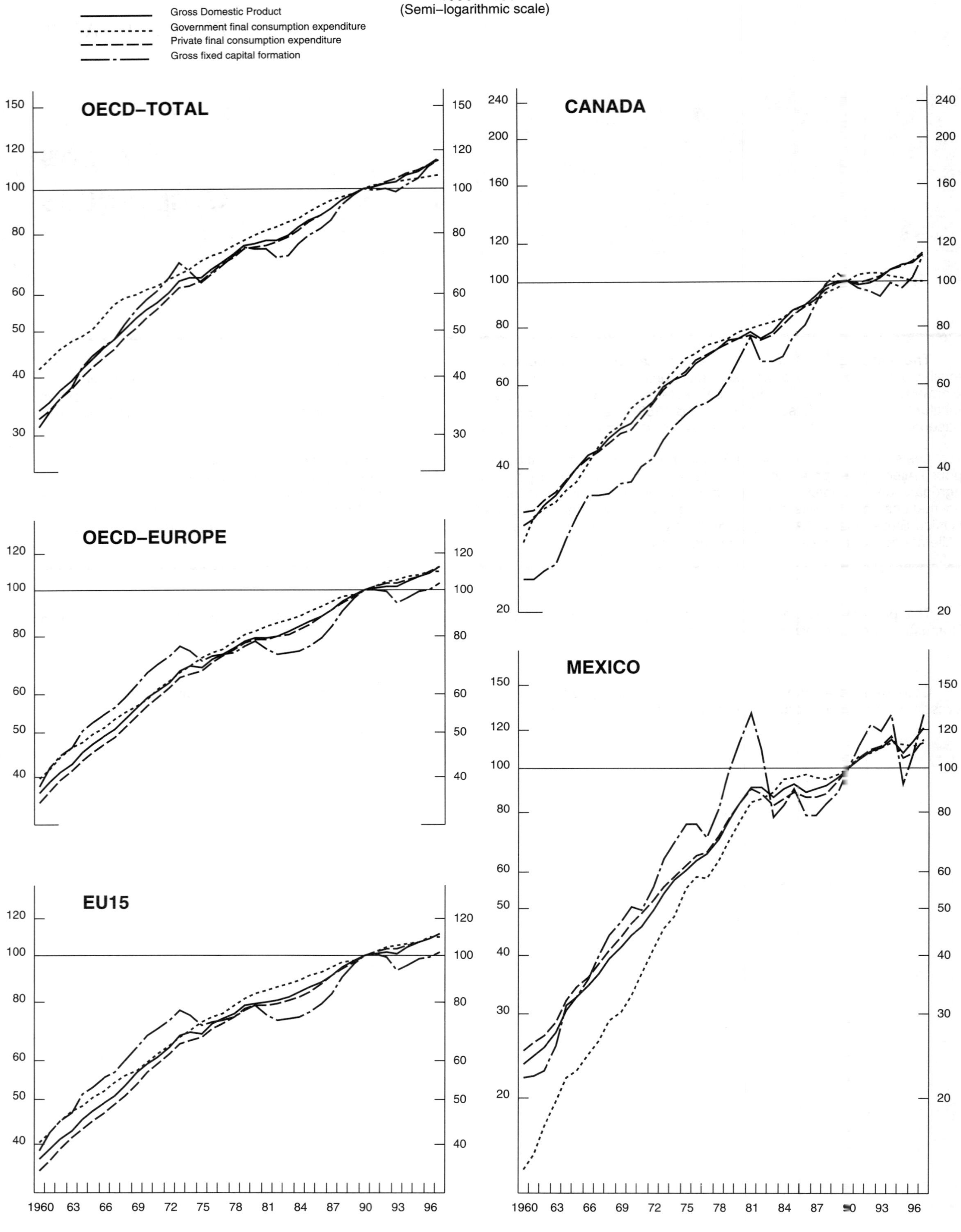

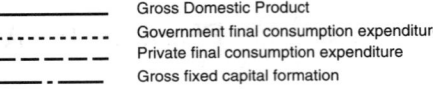

——————— Gross Domestic Product
················· Government final consumption expenditure
– – – – – Private final consumption expenditure
–·–·–·– Gross fixed capital formation

OECD–TOTAL

OECD–EUROPE

EU15

CANADA

MEXICO

Volume indices

1990 = 100
(Semi–logarithmic scale)

Gross Domestic Product
Government final consumption expenditure
Private final consumption expenditure
Gross fixed capital formation

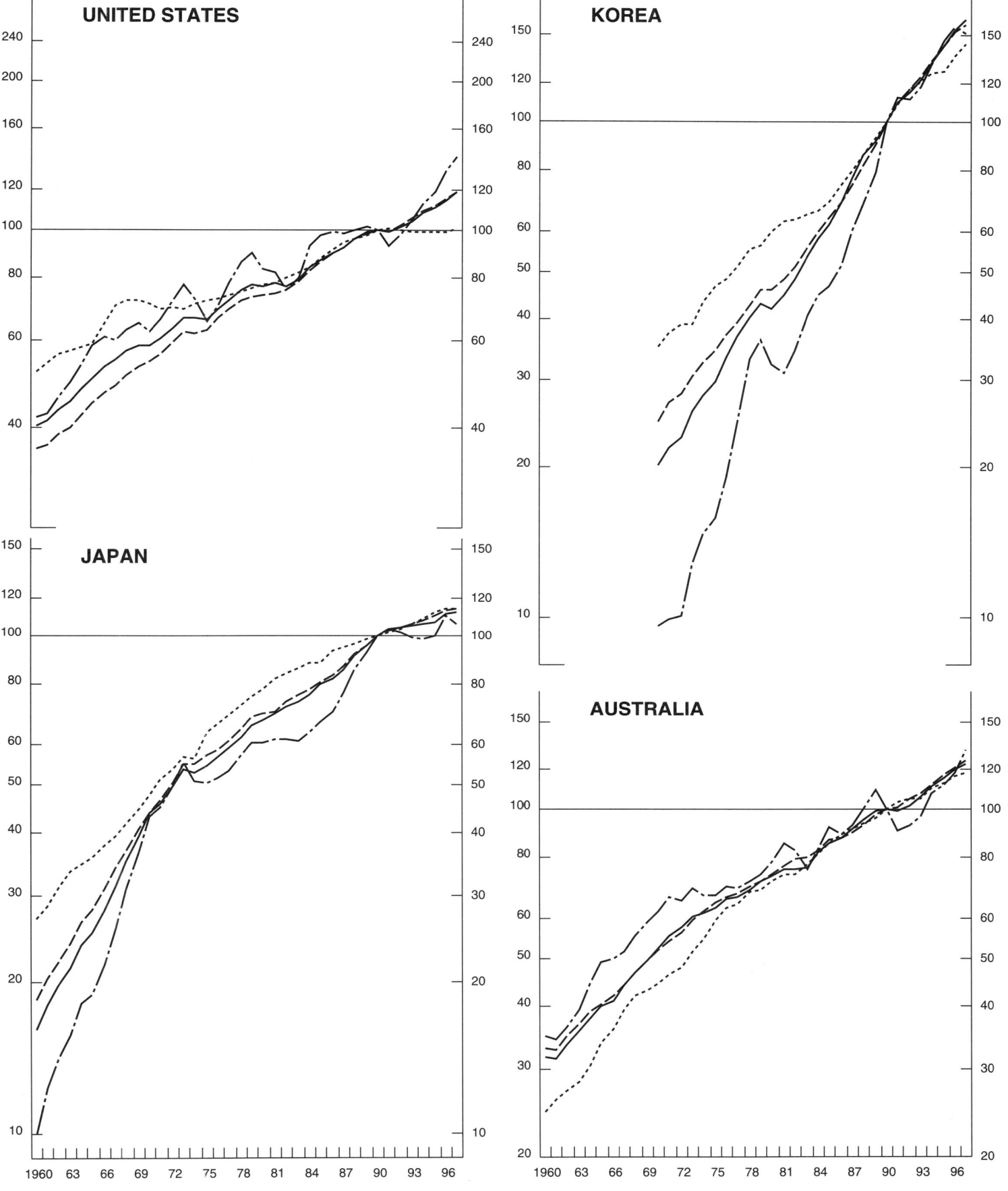

UNITED STATES

KOREA

JAPAN

AUSTRALIA

11

Volume indices

1990 = 100
(Semi–logarithmic scale)

Gross Domestic Product
Government final consumption expenditure
Private final consumption expenditure
Gross fixed capital formation

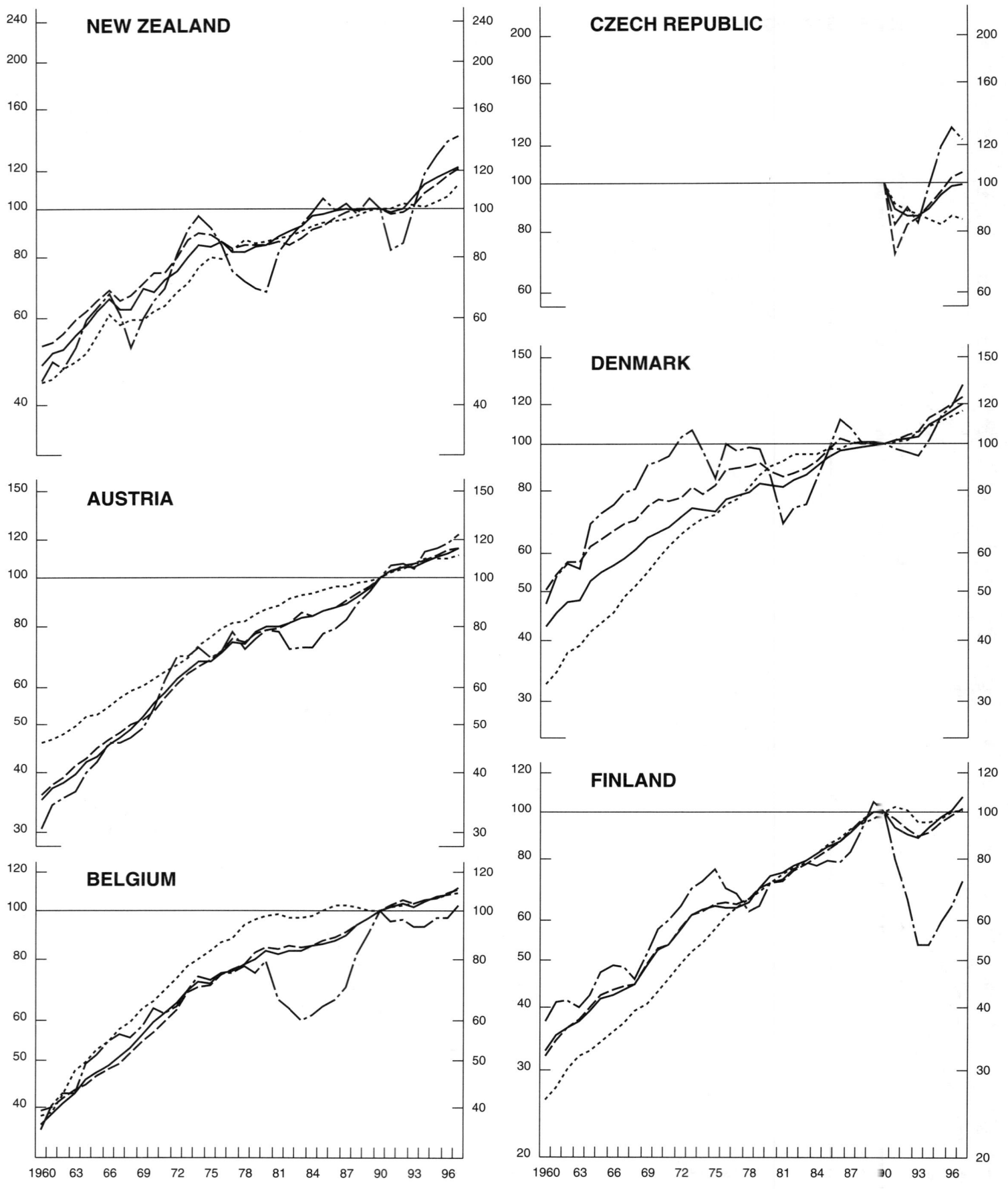

NEW ZEALAND

CZECH REPUBLIC

AUSTRIA

DENMARK

BELGIUM

FINLAND

Volume indices

1990 = 100
(Semi–logarithmic scale)

Gross Domestic Product
.... Government final consumption expenditure
- - - - - Private final consumption expenditure
-·-·-·- Gross fixed capital formation

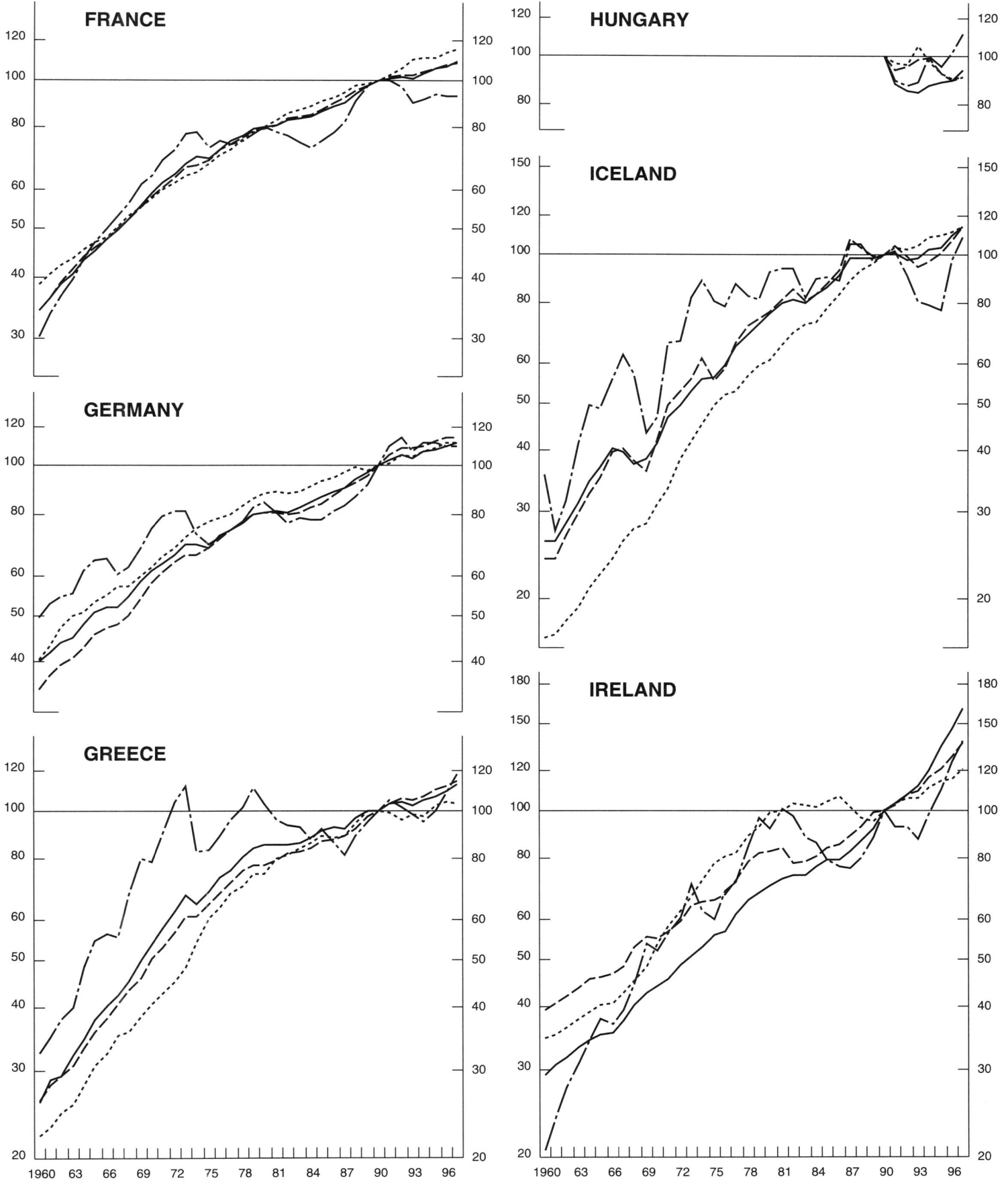

FRANCE

GERMANY

GREECE

HUNGARY

ICELAND

IRELAND

Volume indices

1990 = 100
(Semi–logarithmic scale)

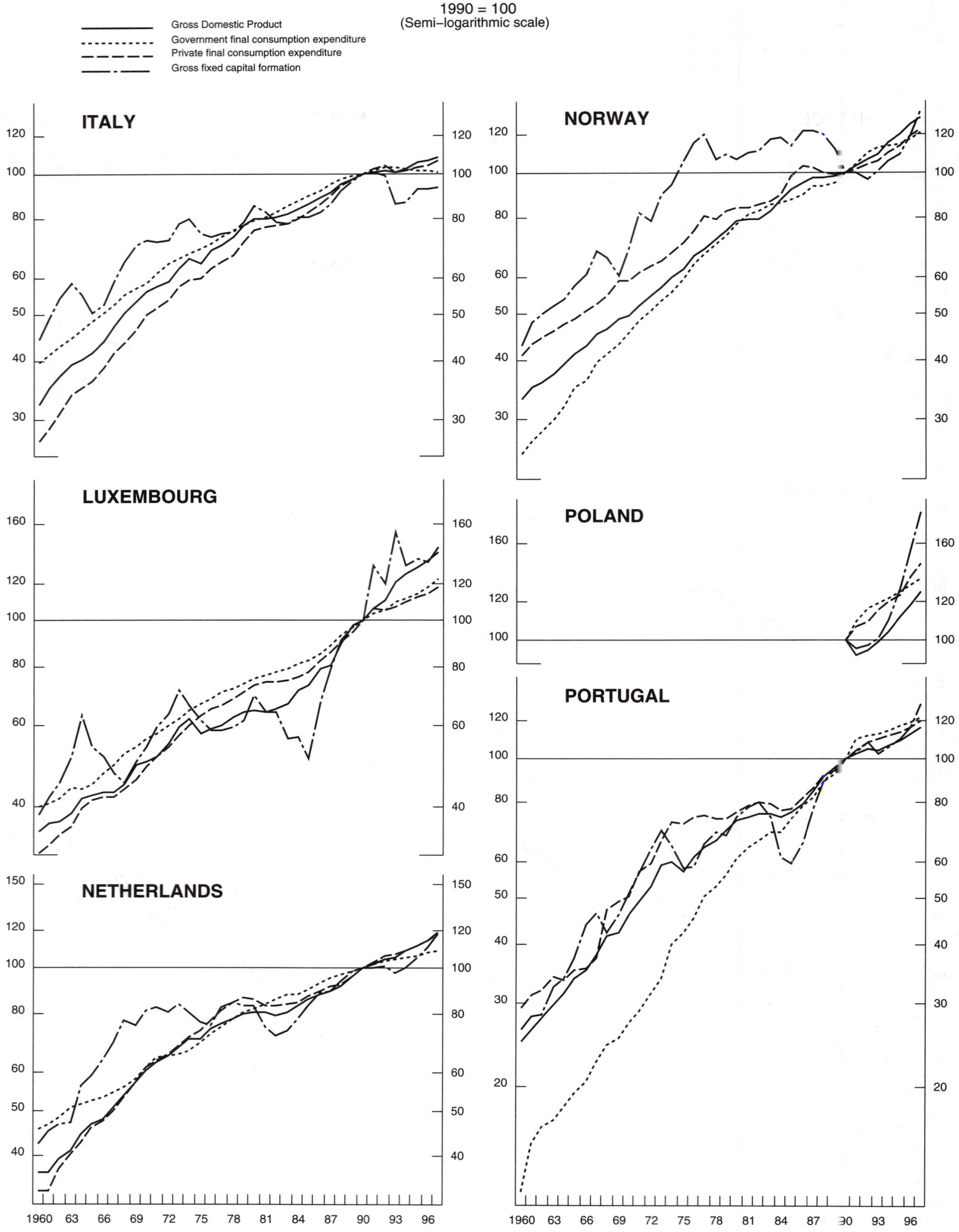

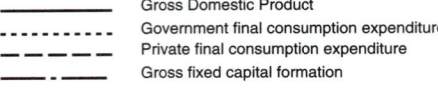

Gross Domestic Product
Government final consumption expenditure
Private final consumption expenditure
Gross fixed capital formation

ITALY

NORWAY

LUXEMBOURG

POLAND

PORTUGAL

NETHERLANDS

1960 63 66 69 72 75 78 81 84 87 90 93 96

1960 63 66 69 72 75 78 81 84 87 90 93 96

Volume indices

1990 = 100
(Semi–logarithmic scale)

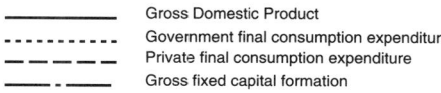

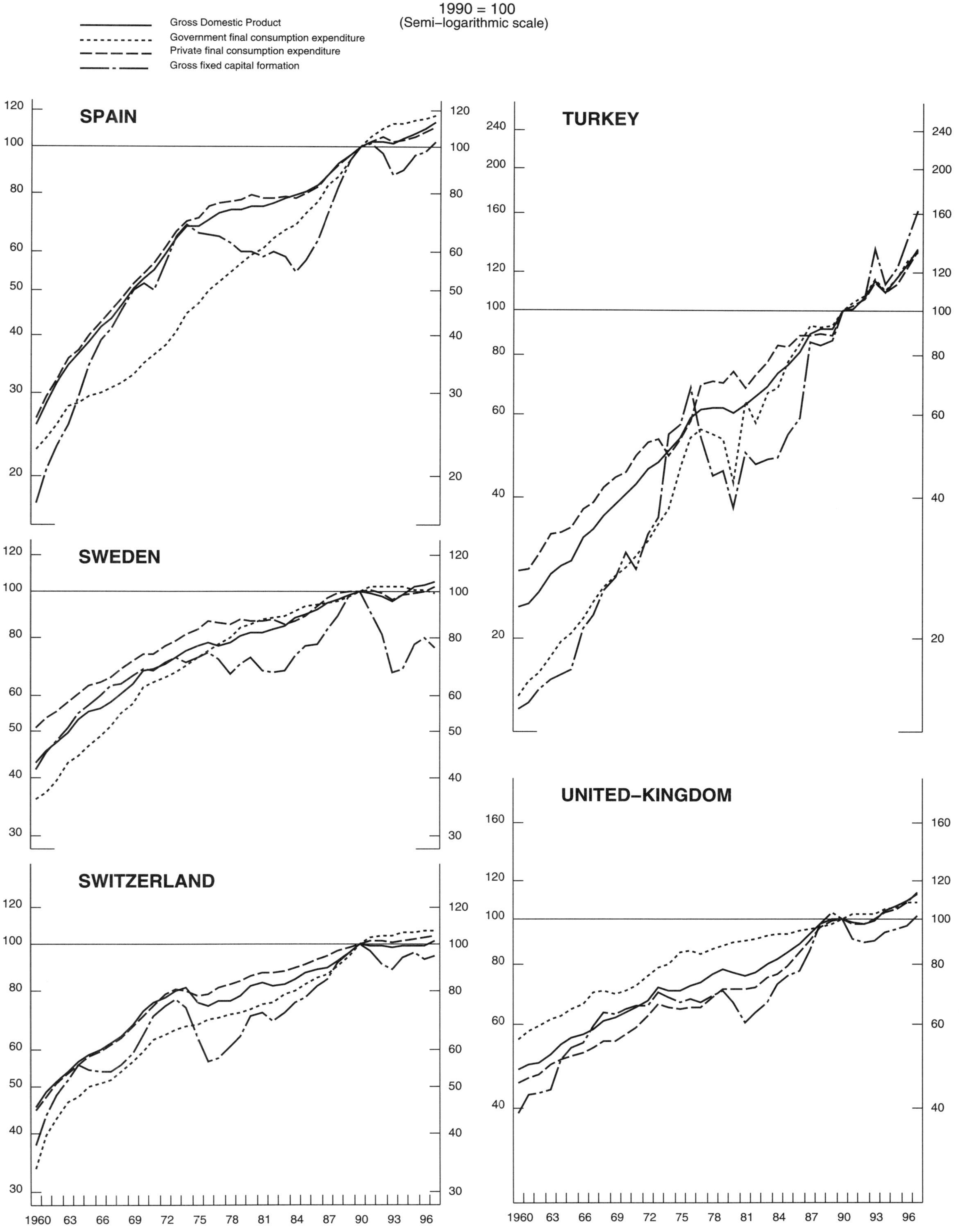
Gross Domestic Product
Government final consumption expenditure
Private final consumption expenditure
Gross fixed capital formation
SPAIN
TURKEY
SWEDEN
SWITZERLAND
UNITED–KINGDOM
1960 63 66 69 72 75 78 81 84 87 90 93 96

Main aggregates: Zones
Principaux agrégats : Zones

The statistics for Germany in this publication refer to Germany after unification. Official data for Germany after unification are available only from 1991 onwards. In this publication, the secretariat has estimated some national accounts aggregates for the whole of Germany back to 1960 in order to calculate the various zones totals. These estimates are based on statistics published by Deutsches Institut für Wirtschaftsforschung for period 1989-90 and by the East German Statistical Office in 1990 for period 1980-89. They are also based on the ratios of the aggregates of West Germany and the whole of Germany.

Les statistiques concernant l'Allemagne dans cette publication se réfèrent à l'Allemagne après l'unification. Des données officielles pour l'Allemagne après l'unification ne sont disponibles qu'à partir de 1991. Dans cette publication, le secrétariat a estimé certains agrégats des comptes nationaux pour l'Allemagne dans son ensemble depuis 1960 afin de calculer les différentes zones. Ces estimations sont basées sur des statistiques publiées par Deutsches Institut für Wirtschaftsforschung pour la période 1989-90 et par l'Office Statistique de l'Allemagne de l'Est en 1990 pour la période 1980-89. Elles sont aussi basées sur les rapports des agrégats de l'Allemagne occidentale et de l'Allemagne dans son ensemble.

This part presents for each zone (OECD-Total, OECD-Europe and EU15), in US dollars, the following tables:
– Expenditure on the gross domestic product, at current and constant prices.
– Cost components of G.D.P.
– Capital transactions of the nation.
– Relations among national accounting aggregates.

a) The first three tables, referring to OECD-Total, OECD-Europe and EU15 are based on *exchange rates*. The data for the individual countries in each group have been converted into US dollars using 1990 exchange rates. The use of constant exchange rates throughout ensures that year to year movements depend only on movements in the current price data for the countries concerned, and are not affected by fluctuations in exchange rates from one year to the next.

b) The last three tables, referring also to OECD-Total, OECD-Europe and EU15 are based on *Purchasing Power parities*. The data for the individual countries in each group have been converted into US dollars using the general GDP PPPs and not the PPPs specific to each aggregate. 1990 PPPs are used to calculate constant dollars series.

Data for Korea, Czech Republic, Hungary and Poland have not been included in area total.

Cette partie fournit pour chaque zone (OCDE-Total, OCDE-Europe et UE15), en dollars des É-U les tableaux suivants :
– Produit intérieur brut et ses emplois aux prix courants et aux prix constants.
– Répartition du P.I.B.
– Opérations en capital de la nation.
– Relations entre les principaux agrégats de la Comptabilité nationale.

a) Les trois premiers tableaux concernant l'OCDE-Total, l'OCDE-Europe et l'UE15 sont basés sur les *taux de change*. Les données des pays composant chaque groupe de pays ont été convertis en dollars É-U en utilisant les taux de change de 1990. L'utilisation de taux de change constant sur toute la période assure le fait que les variations d'une année à l'autre dépendent uniquement des mouvements des données à prix courants des pays concernés et ne sont pas affectées par les fluctuations des taux de change d'une année à l'autre.

b) Les trois derniers tableaux concernant l'OCDE-Total, l'OCDE-Europe et l'UE15 sont basés sur *les parités de pouvoir d'achat*. Les données des pays composant chaque zone ont été converties en dollars É-U en utilisant la PPA du PIB et non les PPA spécifiques de chaque agrégat. Les PPA de 1990 ont été utilisées pour calculer les séries en dollars constants.

Les données de la Corée, de la République tchèque, de la Hongrie et de la Pologne n'ont pas été intégrées aux totaux par zones.

OECD-TOTAL[1]

Main aggregates based on exchange rates

billions of US dollars

	1960	1969	1970	1971	1972	1973	1974	1975	1976	1977	1978	1979	1980	1981	1982
EXPENDITURE ON THE G.D.P.															
At current prices and 1990 exchange rates															
1. Government final consumption expenditure	161.35	369.58	410.18	457.43	507.42	572.83	672.96	781.59	863.28	950.65	1047.48	1163.16	1318.34	1471.79	1609.49
2. Private final consumption expenditure	692.88	1433.95	1572.51	1732.17	1930.96	2187.81	2474.98	2792.26	3142.16	3502.09	3876.05	4322.81	4798.07	5269.04	5710.09
3. Households	..	..	..	..	..	..	..	..	..	..	..	..	..	..	..
4. Private non-profit institutions serving households	..	..	..	..	..	..	..	..	..	..	..	..	..	..	..
5. Increase in stocks	21.17	47.51	45.17	29.86	28.79	55.42	71.70	-9.48	54.98	53.80	50.62	74.12	38.57	37.92	-15.43
6. Gross fixed capital formation	238.92	572.83	650.30	720.76	808.26	949.83	1041.36	1078.95	1193.80	1337.06	1513.45	1720.53	1879.42	2009.60	2039.35
7. **Total Domestic Expenditure**	1114.31	2423.87	2678.16	2940.22	3275.43	3765.88	4261.01	4643.33	5254.23	5843.59	6487.59	7280.62	8034.40	8788.35	9343.50
8. Exports of goods and services	143.13	337.91	389.73	431.02	474.75	575.68	772.28	800.70	929.10	1023.73	1100.90	1283.32	1505.05	1707.52	1795.96
9. *Less:* Imports of goods and services	134.38	318.76	370.37	403.55	445.64	553.65	774.32	769.53	918.67	1014.22	1069.30	1318.00	1562.56	1709.83	1780.42
10. Statistical discrepancy	2.26	4.88	3.63	3.09	5.66	6.21	5.91	4.28	2.60	2.92	5.03	5.84	4.97	1.88	2.27
11. **Gross Domestic Product**	1125.32	2447.90	2701.15	2970.78	3310.20	3794.12	4264.87	4678.77	5267.26	5856.02	6524.23	7251.77	7981.86	8787.92	9361.32
At the price levels and exchange rates of 1990															
1. Government final consumption expenditure	1158.98	1671.66	1710.65	1742.06	1790.15	1832.30	1884.11	1966.96	2009.91	2051.24	2117.15	2169.92	2218.67	2266.94	2310.99
2. Private final consumption expenditure	3397.78	5325.49	5565.06	5799.95	6141.05	6478.32	6524.06	6686.11	6973.14	7211.84	7490.99	7760.60	7855.67	7942.92	8051.28
3. Households	..	..	..	..	..	..	..	..	..	..	..	..	..	..	..
4. Private non-profit institutions serving households	..	..	..	..	..	..	..	..	..	..	..	..	..	..	..
5. Increase in stocks	71.21	101.16	109.55	69.49	55.62	127.79	163.02	-15.34	109.90	100.45	84.46	117.87	68.59	53.06	-4.08
6. Gross fixed capital formation	1149.65	2050.81	2149.22	2246.24	2395.52	2572.31	2464.12	2343.30	2429.09	2523.47	2656.53	2776.86	2754.22	2738.38	2627.15
7. **Total Domestic Expenditure**	5777.62	9149.13	9534.48	9857.74	10382.35	11010.72	11035.31	10981.03	11522.03	11886.99	12349.14	12825.25	12897.15	13001.31	12985.33
8. Exports of goods and services	522.65	1027.03	1122.64	1192.46	1285.04	1425.48	1534.45	1489.38	1623.78	1711.35	1807.47	1921.98	2001.96	2091.21	2087.09
9. *Less:* Imports of goods and services	534.45	1089.74	1207.70	1270.09	1380.89	1532.45	1568.32	1456.48	1624.99	1681.93	1764.33	1910.83	1924.43	1932.88	1913.98
10. Statistical discrepancy	-23.59	-19.79	-26.56	-28.87	-22.06	-34.75	-38.31	-31.32	-43.38	-42.42	-40.44	-41.00	-35.66	-27.65	-18.60
11. **Gross Domestic Product**	5742.22	9066.62	9422.86	9751.24	10264.43	10869.00	10963.13	10982.61	11477.43	11873.99	12351.83	12795.41	12939.02	13131.98	13139.85
COST COMPONENTS OF THE G.D.P.[2]															
1. Indirect taxes	117.92	258.90	281.39	309.97	342.40	383.79	421.15	456.06	513.25	576.10	631.03	706.88	792.42	892.51	954.22
2. *Less:* Subsidies	8.49	31.34	33.28	36.02	44.18	49.63	61.96	73.68	81.14	92.86	107.44	119.02	134.92	146.59	159.89
3. Consumption of fixed capital	106.39	249.18	284.30	318.07	358.39	407.02	476.48	537.95	594.86	664.85	740.37	836.91	955.31	1082.62	1183.92
4. Compensation of employees paid by resident producers	582.90	1303.88	1462.38	1625.91	1819.84	2101.69	2425.77	2698.05	3027.27	3363.32	3726.29	4137.93	4590.82	5041.30	5380.86
5. Operating surplus	319.87	649.21	686.08	723.74	809.78	932.18	971.63	1016.62	1161.76	1288.95	1474.13	1620.29	1712.56	1865.51	1966.22
6. Statistical discrepancy	6.73	18.08	20.28	29.11	23.95	19.07	31.81	43.78	51.27	55.64	59.86	68.78	65.68	52.56	35.93
7. **Gross Domestic Product**	1125.32	2447.91	2701.16	2970.79	3310.19	3794.12	4264.88	4678.78	5267.26	5856.00	6524.23	7251.77	7981.86	8787.92	9361.32
CAPITAL TRANSACTIONS OF THE NATION[2]															
Finance of Gross Capital Formation															
1. Consumption of fixed capital	106.39	249.18	284.30	318.07	358.39	407.02	476.48	537.95	594.86	664.85	740.37	836.91	955.31	1082.62	1183.92
2. Net saving	161.10	383.83	419.03	439.52	497.55	623.01	622.71	532.36	632.57	700.29	822.64	894.06	870.00	915.63	813.82
3. *Less:* Surplus of the nation on current transactions	-0.27	0.54	7.92	16.59	15.08	1.36	-43.16	0.27	-10.44	-12.59	-0.77	-15.96	-16.51	-4.18	-32.59
4. Statistical discrepancy	-7.86	-11.93	-0.35	9.08	-3.81	-23.16	-28.40	-0.01	11.72	12.76	0.44	47.94	76.81	46.40	-5.79
5. **Finance of Gross Capital Formation**	259.90	620.53	695.06	750.08	837.05	1005.51	1113.95	1070.03	1249.59	1390.48	1564.22	1794.87	1918.63	2048.84	2024.54
Gross capital formation															
6. Increase in stocks	21.17	47.51	45.17	29.86	28.79	55.42	71.70	-9.48	54.98	53.80	50.62	74.12	38.57	37.92	-15.43
7. Gross fixed capital formation	238.92	572.83	650.30	720.76	808.26	949.83	1041.36	1078.95	1193.80	1337.06	1513.45	1720.53	1879.42	2009.60	2039.35
8. Statistical discrepancy	-0.19	0.18	-0.41	-0.54	0.00	0.26	0.88	0.56	0.81	-0.37	0.15	0.21	0.64	1.32	0.62
9. **Gross Capital Formation**	259.90	620.52	695.06	750.08	837.05	1005.51	1113.95	1070.03	1249.59	1390.48	1564.22	1794.87	1918.63	2048.84	2024.54
RELATIONS AMONG NATIONAL ACCOUNTING AGGREGATES[2]															
1. **Gross Domestic Product**	1125.32	2447.91	2701.16	2970.79	3310.20	3794.12	4264.88	4678.77	5267.25	5856.01	6524.23	7251.77	7981.86	8787.92	9361.32
2. *Plus:* Net factor income from the rest of the world	4.45	8.19	8.65	10.42	13.18	18.43	18.84	15.07	19.78	19.80	24.84	38.88	34.57	22.49	14.32
3. Factor income from the rest of the world	..	..	..	..	..	..	..	..	..	..	..	..	..	..	..
4. Factor income paid to the rest of the world	..	..	..	..	..	..	..	..	..	..	..	..	..	..	..
5. *Equals:* **Gross National Product**	1129.77	2456.10	2709.81	2981.21	3323.28	3812.44	4283.73	4693.84	5287.04	5875.81	6549.07	7290.66	8016.44	8810.40	9375.64
6. *Less:* Consumption of fixed capital	106.39	249.18	284.30	318.07	358.39	407.02	476.48	537.95	594.86	664.85	740.37	836.91	955.31	1082.62	1183.92
7. *Plus:* Statistical discrepancy	-6.47	-12.23	-12.06	-14.96	-10.09	-5.42	-14.61	-19.78	-17.18	-23.49	-25.73	-24.97	-26.05	-27.04	-26.94
8. *Equals:* **National Income**	1016.92	2194.69	2413.46	2648.28	2954.89	3400.01	3792.63	4136.21	4674.98	5187.47	5782.98	6428.78	7034.98	7700.84	8164.78
9. *Plus:* Net current transfers from the rest of the world	-4.89	-8.92	-10.11	-12.11	-14.04	-12.77	-14.18	-15.89	-13.77	-14.84	-15.73	-17.94	-19.59	-28.02	-32.61
10. Current transfers from the rest of the world	..	..	..	..	..	..	..	..	..	..	..	..	..	..	..
11. Current transfers paid to the rest of the world	..	..	..	..	..	..	..	..	..	..	..	..	..	..	..
12. *Equals:* **National Disposable Income**	1012.13	2185.78	2403.35	2636.07	2940.85	3387.23	3778.45	4120.32	4661.21	5172.62	5767.35	5410.94	7015.48	7672.82	8132.18
13. *Less:* Final consumption	854.45	1803.78	1982.85	2189.11	2438.95	2760.45	3146.50	3571.74	4000.85	4450.61	4921.48	5485.54	6115.03	6738.27	7318.62
14. *Plus:* Statistical discrepancy	3.41	1.92	-1.57	-7.54	-4.36	-3.87	-9.25	-16.12	-27.81	-21.63	-23.22	-31.34	-30.35	-18.91	0.36
15. *Equals:* **Net Saving**	161.10	383.83	419.03	439.52	497.55	623.01	622.71	532.36	632.55	700.29	822.64	894.06	870.00	915.63	813.82
16. *Less:* Surplus of the nation on current transactions	-0.27	0.54	7.92	16.59	15.08	1.36	-43.16	0.27	-10.44	-12.59	-0.77	-15.96	-16.51	-4.18	-32.59
17. *Plus:* Statistical discrepancy	-7.69	-12.21	0.17	9.61	-3.71	-23.32	-29.29	-0.67	10.91	13.13	0.28	47.83	76.07	45.18	-6.51
18. *Equals:* **Net Capital Formation**	153.67	371.16	411.17	432.54	478.65	598.23	636.48	531.42	653.90	726.11	823.70	957.74	962.68	964.89	839.91

1. Excluding Korea, Czech Republic, Hungary and Poland.
2. At current prices and 1990 exchange rates.

Principaux Agrégats basés sur les taux de change

milliards de dollars É-U

DÉPENSES IMPUTÉES AU P.I.B.

Aux prix courants et taux de change de 1990

1983	1984	1985	1986	1987	1988	1989	1990	1991	1992	1993	1994	1995	1996	1997	
1735.34	1856.51	2000.89	2131.82	2267.65	2405.10	2557.17	2784.23	2990.75	3178.11	3328.16	3501.77	3771.85	4244.92	5042.18	1. Consommation finale des administrations publiques
6194.23	6693.82	7220.81	7701.41	8247.14	8932.69	9668.93	10435.01	11120.46	11896.38	12645.24	13771.36	15442.81	17887.87	22362.74	2. Consommation finale privée
..	..	..	..	..	..	..	..	..	..	..	..	..	..	..	3. Ménages
..	..	..	..	..	..	..	..	..	..	..	..	..	..	..	4. Institutions privées sans but lucratif au service des ménages
−4.35	102.64	64.45	50.95	54.76	73.23	121.50	72.36	45.70	23.85	15.19	62.84	171.65	67.33	60.78	5. Variations des stocks
2126.60	2326.84	2496.29	2639.79	2825.45	3132.21	3435.60	3681.65	3770.10	3892.42	3987.59	4330.32	4858.24	5838.55	7543.46	6. Formation brute de capital fixe
10051.82	10979.82	11782.44	12523.97	13395.00	14543.23	15783.20	16973.24	17927.00	18990.76	19976.18	21666.28	24244.55	28038.67	35009.16	7. **Demande intérieure totale**
1893.45	2168.72	2321.03	2231.84	2334.69	2585.39	2924.77	3117.91	3237.09	3410.49	3586.49	4142.14	4955.68	5937.54	7946.78	8. Exportations de biens et services
1865.10	2152.60	2289.37	2181.08	2332.49	2588.92	2949.03	3154.09	3226.60	3383.68	3513.20	4029.78	4923.05	6109.93	8388.95	9. *Moins*: Importations de biens et services
1.78	8.74	6.86	7.09	4.19	8.37	6.24	4.06	−8.79	−18.78	−34.53	−62.87	−63.05	164.14	47.46	10. Divergence statistique
10081.95	11004.68	11820.96	12581.81	13401.39	14548.07	15765.17	16941.12	17928.70	18998.70	20014.95	21715.77	24214.14	28030.43	34614.45	11. **Produit intérieur brut**

Aux niveaux de prix et taux de change de 1990

1983	1984	1985	1986	1987	1988	1989	1990	1991	1992	1993	1994	1995	1996	1997	
2359.18	2407.40	2481.40	2558.67	2622.94	2678.32	2717.98	2784.23	2829.05	2861.92	2871.68	2897.11	2917.82	2952.45	2970.75	1. Consommation finale des administrations publiques
8273.11	8531.08	8832.96	9155.56	9463.78	9845.58	10161.86	10435.01	10552.84	10786.47	10930.73	11196.80	11426.99	11726.74	12033.51	2. Consommation finale privée
..	..	..	..	..	..	..	..	..	..	..	..	..	..	..	3. Ménages
..	..	..	..	..	..	..	..	..	..	..	..	..	..	..	4. Institutions privées sans but lucratif au service des ménages
7.82	113.55	78.08	66.16	68.59	80.28	118.03	72.36	37.99	30.44	23.68	110.56	102.04	65.63	137.87	5. Variations des stocks
2651.95	2811.20	2934.62	3024.10	3162.10	3383.25	3571.90	3681.65	3648.98	3670.97	3621.99	3742.32	3860.39	4103.17	4235.76	6. Formation brute de capital fixe
13292.06	13863.23	14327.05	14804.48	15317.41	15987.42	16569.76	16973.24	17068.87	17349.80	17448.09	17946.79	18307.25	18847.99	19377.89	7. **Demande intérieure totale**
2131.83	2319.67	2417.81	2450.77	2556.82	2748.89	2968.09	3117.91	3204.54	3350.15	3436.78	3734.04	4070.03	4350.17	4804.86	8. Exportations de biens et services
1963.49	2177.83	2283.20	2397.48	2561.03	2777.92	3007.62	3154.09	3206.51	3344.11	3372.65	3676.59	3974.68	4266.43	4694.27	9. *Moins*: Importations de biens et services
−13.24	−0.77	−1.50	2.53	4.61	6.03	2.29	4.06	1.41	−0.71	0.03	−1.20	−2.72	−7.58	−12.42	10. Divergence statistique
13447.16	14004.30	14460.16	14860.30	15317.81	15964.43	16532.53	16941.12	17068.31	17355.13	17512.25	18003.04	18399.87	18924.16	19476.06	11. **Produit intérieur brut**

RÉPARTITION DU P.I.B.[2]

1983	1984	1985	1986	1987	1988	1989	1990	1991	1992	1993	1994	1995	1996	1997	
1035.93	1141.57	1225.75	1308.73	1423.04	1538.99	1653.43	1779.03	1911.74	2035.24	2149.93	2350.79	2619.80	3076.59	3837.70	1. Impôts indirects
181.57	199.73	206.34	221.22	235.25	237.97	234.35	252.52	262.16	269.05	297.67	314.94	317.02	392.54	485.86	2. *Moins*: Subventions
1267.89	1348.88	1442.10	1536.48	1636.11	1764.56	1918.24	2057.75	2200.28	2331.18	2432.78	2603.50	2808.97	3096.58	3556.60	3. Consommation de capital fixe
5710.58	6146.53	6569.24	6975.01	7426.34	7989.83	8568.36	9283.40	9857.92	10411.29	10852.70	11405.01	12157.63	13371.57	15284.06	4. Rémunération des salariés payée par les producteurs résidents
2169.47	2512.46	2735.17	2904.00	3118.67	3492.93	3798.47	4030.75	4213.40	4445.17	4820.20	5651.72	6975.61	8950.24	12498.95	5. Excédent net d'exploitation
79.65	54.98	55.05	78.83	32.48	−0.28	61.01	42.70	7.52	44.97	57.00	19.68	−30.85	−72.01	−77.00	6. Divergence statistique
10081.95	11004.68	11820.96	12581.82	13401.40	14548.07	15765.17	16941.12	17928.69	18998.80	20014.95	21715.77	24214.13	28030.43	34614.45	7. **Produit intérieur brut**

OPÉRATIONS EN CAPITAL DE LA NATION[2]

Financement de la formation brute de capital

1983	1984	1985	1986	1987	1988	1989	1990	1991	1992	1993	1994	1995	1996	1997	
1267.89	1348.88	1442.10	1536.48	1636.11	1764.56	1918.24	2057.75	2200.28	2331.18	2432.78	2603.50	2808.97	3096.57	3556.60	1. Consommation de capital fixe
805.49	1049.52	1090.63	1112.54	1202.29	1425.40	1530.84	1545.78	1540.60	1422.62	1421.14	1653.57	2084.47	2770.66	3754.96	2. Épargne nette
−17.39	−49.69	−75.78	−122.91	−168.81	−192.10	−248.39	−243.78	−58.82	−98.91	−57.82	−53.84	−104.62	−275.27	−417.56	3. *Moins*: Solde des opérations courantes de la nation
30.74	−19.27	−47.69	−81.68	−128.11	−175.08	−140.05	−93.29	16.11	62.26	89.51	81.22	32.35	−236.81	−124.39	4. Divergence statistique
2121.50	2428.82	2560.82	2690.25	2879.10	3206.97	3557.43	3754.02	3815.81	3914.96	4001.26	4392.14	5030.40	5905.70	7604.74	5. **Financement de la formation brute de capital**

Formation brute de capital

1983	1984	1985	1986	1987	1988	1989	1990	1991	1992	1993	1994	1995	1996	1997	
−4.35	102.64	64.45	50.95	54.76	73.23	121.50	72.36	45.70	23.85	15.19	62.84	171.65	67.33	60.78	6. Variations des stocks
2126.60	2326.84	2496.29	2639.79	2825.45	3132.21	3435.60	3681.65	3770.10	3892.42	3987.59	4330.32	4858.24	5838.55	7543.46	7. Formation brute de capital fixe
−0.74	−0.66	0.08	−0.49	−1.12	1.54	0.33	0.02	0.01	−1.31	−1.52	−1.02	0.51	−0.18	0.50	8. Divergence statistique
2121.50	2428.82	2560.82	2690.25	2879.10	3206.97	3557.43	3754.02	3815.81	3914.96	4001.25	4392.14	5030.40	5905.70	7604.74	9. **Formation brute de capital**

RELATIONS ENTRE LES PRINCIPAUX AGRÉGATS[2]

1983	1984	1985	1986	1987	1988	1989	1990	1991	1992	1993	1994	1995	1996	1997	
10081.95	11004.68	11820.96	12581.81	13401.40	14548.07	15765.17	16941.12	17928.70	18998.79	20014.95	21715.77	24214.14	28030.42	34614.46	1. **Produit intérieur brut**
19.64	17.57	7.91	−2.77	−2.86	−9.22	−11.92	−28.50	−32.31	−36.43	−32.66	−62.93	−46.93	−7.60	118.28	2. *Plus*: Revenu net des facteurs reçu du reste du monde
..	..	..	..	..	..	..	..	..	..	..	..	..	..	..	3. Revenu des facteurs reçu du reste du monde
..	..	..	..	..	..	..	..	..	..	..	..	..	..	..	4. Revenu des facteurs payé au reste du monde
10101.59	11022.25	11828.86	12579.04	13398.54	14538.85	15753.24	16917.38	17896.39	18962.27	19982.39	21652.84	24167.21	28022.83	34732.75	5. *Égal*: **Produit national brut**
1267.89	1348.88	1442.10	1536.48	1636.11	1764.56	1918.24	2057.75	2200.28	2331.18	2432.78	2603.50	2808.97	3096.57	3556.60	6. *Moins*: Consommation de capital fixe
−28.52	−33.33	−34.08	−32.10	−22.34	−17.56	−14.50	−17.39	2.80	0.01	−4.77	..	3.11	11.62	10.17	7. *Plus*: Divergence statistique
8805.08	9640.04	10352.69	11010.46	11740.09	12756.73	13820.51	14842.14	15698.91	16631.21	17545.60	19044.57	21361.35	24937.78	31186.32	8. *Égal*: **Revenu national**
−33.02	−33.11	−37.96	−41.40	−38.41	−40.74	−50.26	−59.62	−37.00	−89.29	−98.46	−103.38	−90.43	−95.29	−93.68	9. *Plus*: Transferts courants nets reçus du reste du monde
..	..	..	..	..	..	..	..	..	..	..	..	..	..	..	10. Transferts courants reçus du reste du monde
..	..	..	..	..	..	..	..	..	..	..	..	..	..	..	11. Transferts courants payés au reste du monde
8772.07	9606.93	10314.73	10969.07	11701.68	12715.99	13770.24	14782.51	15661.91	16541.92	17447.14	18941.30	21270.93	24842.49	31092.64	12. *Égal*: **Revenu national disponible**
7928.27	8551.29	9221.70	9833.23	10514.79	11337.89	12226.20	13219.34	14111.20	15074.50	15973.41	17273.12	19214.66	22134.52	27407.34	13. *Moins*: Consommation finale
−38.21	−6.22	−2.40	−23.30	15.40	47.30	−13.20	−17.40	−10.10	−44.80	−52.60	−14.60	28.20	62.69	69.77	14. *Plus*: Divergence statistique
805.49	1049.52	1090.63	1112.54	1202.29	1425.40	1530.84	1545.88	1540.60	1422.62	1421.14	1653.57	2084.47	2770.66	3754.96	15. *Égal*: **Épargne nette**
−17.39	−49.69	−75.78	−122.91	−168.81	−192.10	−248.39	−243.78	−58.82	−98.91	−57.82	−53.84	−104.62	−275.27	−417.56	16. *Moins*: Solde des opérations courantes de la nation
31.29	−18.61	−47.67	−81.19	−127.10	−176.72	−140.48	−93.50	16.10	63.67	91.03	82.24	31.84	−236.73	−124.99	17. *Plus*: Divergence statistique
854.26	1080.61	1118.74	1154.26	1244.11	1440.87	1638.75	1696.15	1615.42	1585.20	1569.99	1789.66	2220.82	2809.31	4047.64	18. *Égal*: **Formation nette de capital**

1. Non compris la Corée, la République tchèque, la Hongrie et la Pologne.
2. Aux prix courants et taux de change de 1990.

OECD-EUROPE [1]

Main aggregates based on exchange rates

billions of US dollars

	1960	1969	1970	1971	1972	1973	1974	1975	1976	1977	1978	1979	1980	1981	1982
EXPENDITURE ON THE G.D.P.															
At current prices and 1990 exchange rates															
1. Government final consumption expenditure	61.27	146.58	166.25	194.59	218.29	251.01	297.22	347.98	389.02	428.98	478.77	536.14	614.14	688.57	754.62
2. Private final consumption expenditure	270.05	552.11	610.26	677.41	755.46	849.94	958.19	1082.17	1220.48	1360.87	1497.91	1680.20	1889.28	2089.75	2300.61
3. Households	..	..	..	..	..	..	..	..	..	..	..	..	..	..	..
4. Private non-profit institutions serving households	..	..	..	..	..	..	..	..	..	..	..	..	..	..	..
5. Increase in stocks	12.72	22.35	24.93	12.59	9.79	23.60	29.28	−7.72	27.93	19.16	14.59	38.28	32.91	−7.54	−4.37
6. Gross fixed capital formation	104.24	225.08	266.36	301.34	330.10	368.57	399.39	414.34	457.26	504.80	554.09	627.96	717.76	751.70	789.94
7. **Total Domestic Expenditure**	448.28	946.12	1067.79	1185.93	1313.64	1493.11	1684.08	1836.77	2094.69	2313.80	2545.36	2882.57	3254.09	3522.48	3840.80
8. Exports of goods and services	96.74	221.82	253.99	280.30	310.75	371.26	480.80	489.50	575.54	641.25	692.56	796.16	903.47	1038.80	1134.67
9. *Less:* Imports of goods and services	91.61	210.44	246.32	269.45	294.16	354.44	471.96	470.35	569.71	626.60	657.17	792.70	933.52	1036.61	1118.53
10. Statistical discrepancy	2.41	4.74	4.27	3.74	5.53	5.54	4.39	3.87	2.26	3.74	5.30	6.58	4.71	1.15	3.20
11. **Gross Domestic Product**	455.82	962.25	1079.74	1200.53	1335.75	1515.46	1697.30	1859.79	2102.79	2332.19	2586.06	2892.61	3228.75	3525.83	3860.14
At the price levels and exchange rates of 1990															
1. Government final consumption expenditure	527.94	753.61	783.52	817.66	852.27	886.94	915.17	954.84	982.70	999.64	1036.63	1068.79	1092.92	1117.62	1133.82
2. Private final consumption expenditure	1509.97	2309.09	2432.99	2538.89	2666.28	2797.94	2836.79	2890.73	3007.34	3098.66	3193.33	3305.54	3365.54	3371.94	3407.08
3. Households	..	..	..	..	..	..	..	..	..	..	..	..	..	..	..
4. Private non-profit institutions serving households	..	..	..	..	..	..	..	..	..	..	..	..	..	..	..
5. Increase in stocks	43.71	44.85	65.32	23.39	11.72	59.11	77.24	−17.31	57.46	39.69	20.06	61.53	44.97	−15.85	−1.69
6. Gross fixed capital formation	597.28	988.96	1046.37	1086.68	1129.24	1188.94	1164.11	1108.78	1130.34	1139.86	1151.35	1191.79	1215.23	1168.00	1142.90
7. **Total Domestic Expenditure**	2678.90	4096.52	4328.20	4466.62	4659.51	4932.93	4993.30	4937.03	5177.84	5277.84	5401.36	5627.65	5718.66	5641.72	5682.10
8. Exports of goods and services	361.05	708.13	769.34	819.28	884.01	975.99	1041.75	1001.78	1096.59	1156.48	1215.52	1288.32	1307.84	1363.55	1383.88
9. *Less:* Imports of goods and services	346.19	706.36	796.10	839.15	908.74	1005.37	1027.43	972.64	1079.95	1105.71	1140.98	1247.72	1275.16	1246.76	1263.70
10. Statistical discrepancy	−15.25	−14.35	−16.45	−19.41	−13.48	−23.35	−26.59	−20.16	−31.50	−25.81	−23.05	−23.08	−20.20	−12.98	−7.86
11. **Gross Domestic Product**	2678.50	4083.94	4284.99	4427.34	4621.30	4880.20	4981.04	4946.02	5162.98	5302.80	5452.85	5645.17	5731.13	5745.54	5794.43
COST COMPONENTS OF THE G.D.P. [2]															
1. Indirect taxes	57.36	130.30	137.68	152.12	169.50	189.21	204.13	223.25	256.27	288.31	321.04	366.10	412.00	450.81	494.78
2. *Less:* Subsidies	6.34	21.25	21.76	23.66	28.62	34.35	40.39	48.83	56.08	63.58	74.34	83.17	90.32	97.72	107.23
3. Consumption of fixed capital	41.50	95.59	111.37	126.75	142.50	160.86	188.66	212.98	238.23	267.58	297.48	333.90	384.11	434.45	481.29
4. Compensation of employees paid by resident producers	217.61	489.73	565.69	640.71	717.10	823.52	948.24	1064.90	1193.54	1321.14	1456.75	1622.23	1828.10	1995.79	2156.27
5. Operating surplus	136.33	249.99	268.07	283.73	312.48	351.25	369.74	379.33	437.87	486.49	547.96	614.22	657.57	706.05	796.64
6. Statistical discrepancy	9.37	17.89	18.70	20.90	22.77	24.97	26.93	28.17	32.96	32.24	37.16	39.34	37.29	36.45	38.39
7. **Gross Domestic Product**	455.82	962.25	1079.74	1200.55	1335.73	1515.46	1697.31	1859.80	2102.78	2332.18	2586.06	2892.61	3228.75	3525.83	3860.14
CAPITAL TRANSACTIONS OF THE NATION [2]															
Finance of Gross Capital Formation															
1. Consumption of fixed capital	41.50	95.59	111.37	126.75	142.50	160.86	188.66	212.98	238.23	267.58	297.48	333.90	384.11	434.45	481.29
2. Net saving	78.21	158.62	180.66	188.67	206.49	240.34	235.22	195.23	232.60	250.61	286.86	317.63	313.11	275.44	275.82
3. *Less:* Surplus of the nation on current transactions	−2.36	−5.40	−1.42	2.24	4.24	−7.80	−37.42	−14.07	−21.42	−16.75	−7.02	2.85	−5.60	−4.57	−33.28
4. Statistical discrepancy	−5.10	−12.17	−2.15	0.76	−4.86	−16.84	−32.63	−15.66	−7.06	−10.99	−22.69	17.56	47.85	29.70	−4.83
5. **Finance of Gross Capital Formation**	116.96	247.44	291.29	313.93	339.89	392.16	428.67	406.61	485.19	523.96	568.68	666.23	750.67	744.17	785.57
Gross capital formation															
6. Increase in stocks	12.72	22.35	24.93	12.59	9.79	23.60	29.28	−7.72	27.93	19.16	14.59	38.28	32.91	−7.54	−4.37
7. Gross fixed capital formation	104.24	225.08	266.36	301.34	330.10	368.57	399.39	414.34	457.26	504.80	554.09	627.96	717.76	751.70	789.94
8. Statistical discrepancy	..	..	..	..	..	..	..	..	..	..	..	..	..	..	..
9. **Gross Capital Formation**	116.96	247.44	291.29	313.93	339.89	392.16	428.67	406.61	485.19	523.96	568.68	666.23	750.67	744.16	785.57
RELATIONS AMONG NATIONAL ACCOUNTING AGGREGATES [2]															
1. **Gross Domestic Product**	455.82	962.25	1079.75	1200.54	1335.75	1515.46	1697.31	1859.80	2102.78	2332.19	2586.06	2892.61	3228.75	3525.83	3860.14
2. *Plus:* Net factor income from the rest of the world	1.80	3.96	4.32	4.66	5.49	6.66	6.00	4.28	6.33	3.24	6.85	10.05	6.37	1.75	−6.11
3. Factor income from the rest of the world	..	..	..	..	..	..	..	..	..	..	..	..	..	..	..
4. Factor income paid to the rest of the world	..	..	..	..	..	..	..	..	..	..	..	..	..	..	..
5. *Equals:* **Gross National Product**	457.62	966.20	1084.07	1205.20	1341.24	1522.12	1703.32	1864.07	2109.11	2335.42	2592.90	2902.66	3235.13	3527.58	3854.04
6. *Less:* Consumption of fixed capital	41.50	95.59	111.37	126.75	142.50	160.86	188.66	212.98	238.25	267.58	297.48	333.90	384.11	434.45	431.29
7. *Plus:* Statistical discrepancy	−5.64	−10.64	−12.28	−12.85	−13.21	−14.73	−15.24	−16.27	−18.67	−18.30	−21.03	−23.73	−25.17	−25.84	−26.92
8. *Equals:* **National Income**	410.48	859.98	960.42	1065.61	1185.52	1346.53	1499.42	1634.82	1852.19	2049.55	2274.39	2545.03	2825.85	3067.29	3345.82
9. *Plus:* Net current transfers from the rest of the world	−0.96	−2.84	−3.42	−4.08	−4.67	−4.96	−6.49	−7.43	−6.71	−7.68	−7.67	−8.35	−7.94	−12.07	−13.59
10. Current transfers from the rest of the world	..	..	..	..	..	..	..	..	..	..	..	..	..	..	..
11. Current transfers paid to the rest of the world	..	..	..	..	..	..	..	..	..	..	..	..	..	..	..
12. *Equals:* **National Disposable Income**	409.53	857.14	957.00	1061.52	1180.86	1341.58	1492.93	1627.39	1845.49	2041.87	2266.72	2536.69	2817.91	3055.21	3332.24
13. *Less:* Final consumption	331.53	698.94	776.67	871.41	974.31	1100.77	1253.96	1428.15	1605.00	1787.83	1974.74	2215.91	2502.05	2775.76	3054.28
14. *Plus:* Statistical discrepancy	0.21	0.42	0.33	−1.44	−0.06	−0.47	−3.75	−4.02	−7.91	−3.43	−5.12	−3.14	−2.75	−4.01	−2.14
15. *Equals:* **Net Saving**	78.21	158.62	180.66	188.66	206.49	240.34	235.23	195.23	232.57	250.61	286.86	317.63	313.11	275.44	275.82
16. *Less:* Surplus of the nation on current transactions	−2.36	−5.40	−1.42	2.24	4.24	−7.80	−37.42	−14.07	−21.42	−16.75	−7.02	2.85	−5.60	−4.57	−33.28
17. *Plus:* Statistical discrepancy	−5.22	−12.17	−2.15	0.76	−4.86	−16.84	−32.63	−15.66	−7.06	−10.99	−22.69	17.56	47.85	29.70	−4.83
18. *Equals:* **Net Capital Formation**	75.34	151.85	179.92	187.18	197.38	231.30	240.01	193.64	246.94	256.37	271.19	332.34	366.56	309.71	304.28

1. Excluding Czech Republic, Hungary and Poland.
2. At current prices and 1990 exchange rates.

Principaux Agrégats basés sur les taux de change

milliards de dollars É-U

1983	1984	1985	1986	1987	1988	1989	1990	1991	1992	1993	1994	1995	1996	1997	
															DÉPENSES IMPUTÉES AU P.I.B.
															Aux prix courants et taux de change de 1990
819.08	876.02	939.34	999.91	1067.49	1137.44	1211.50	1331.38	1456.94	1587.18	1695.16	1824.03	2033.96	2441.87	3181.42	1. Consommation finale des administrations publiques
2503.74	2706.11	2924.15	3139.46	3364.75	3627.88	3944.04	4281.89	4682.49	5080.24	5487.49	6243.75	7545.31	9521.11	13472.23	2. Consommation finale privée
..	..	..	..	..	..	..	..	..	..	..	..	..	..	..	3. Ménages
..	..	..	..	..	..	..	..	..	..	..	..	..	..	..	4. Institutions privées sans but lucratif au service des ménages
−3.13	21.22	15.52	21.82	20.47	39.47	50.10	37.22	15.73	−1.56	−23.31	−14.83	103.32	−16.04	−86.75	5. Variations des stocks
842.90	898.31	965.68	1040.35	1129.58	1274.81	1428.83	1563.54	1650.87	1706.45	1740.23	1974.81	2420.22	3170.57	4735.32	6. Formation brute de capital fixe
4162.59	4501.66	4844.70	5201.53	5582.29	6079.60	6634.47	7214.03	7806.04	8372.32	8899.58	10027.76	12102.82	15117.52	21302.21	7. **Demande intérieure totale**
1231.95	1415.02	1545.66	1486.33	1535.38	1666.53	1893.87	1992.69	2054.26	2159.99	2300.30	2737.27	3292.45	4080.75	5872.15	8. Exportations de biens et services
1191.99	1358.73	1473.29	1389.53	1468.37	1618.88	1861.07	1965.24	2056.29	2144.48	2213.37	2570.15	3242.49	4208.51	6256.49	9. *Moins :* Importations de biens et services
3.67	8.01	8.40	8.04	6.22	5.93	3.56	1.34	−6.99	−14.42	−30.36	−60.78	−64.11	164.42	46.64	10. Divergence statistique
4206.23	4565.96	4925.46	5306.37	5655.52	6133.18	6670.84	7242.83	7797.02	8373.41	8956.15	10134.10	12088.68	15154.19	20964.51	11. **Produit intérieur brut**
															Aux niveaux de prix et taux de change de 1990
1155.69	1173.54	1201.83	1229.30	1260.12	1286.77	1299.44	1331.38	1361.11	1390.03	1403.27	1418.68	1431.47	1459.45	1463.34	1. Consommation finale des administrations publiques
3458.07	3516.89	3609.40	3755.92	3889.66	4034.95	4160.16	4281.89	4375.74	4443.97	4436.59	4501.80	4583.70	4684.97	4789.90	2. Consommation finale privée
..	..	..	..	..	..	..	..	..	..	..	..	..	..	..	3. Ménages
..	..	..	..	..	..	..	..	..	..	..	..	..	..	..	4. Institutions privées sans but lucratif au service des ménages
−2.55	19.78	18.37	32.14	29.03	40.63	46.43	37.22	14.12	6.01	−20.11	30.30	53.74	19.42	54.33	5. Variations des stocks
1148.49	1161.95	1191.77	1240.62	1312.26	1414.37	1505.71	1563.54	1571.69	1553.58	1466.55	1498.53	1552.71	1572.77	1620.85	6. Formation brute de capital fixe
5759.70	5872.16	6021.37	6257.97	6491.07	6776.73	7011.74	7214.03	7322.66	7393.58	7286.31	7449.31	7621.63	7736.60	7928.43	7. **Demande intérieure totale**
1425.76	1535.09	1606.43	1621.84	1680.96	1779.65	1916.88	1992.69	2015.97	2089.37	2121.83	2306.50	2483.08	2614.94	2869.58	8. Exportations de biens et services
1281.40	1359.70	1420.95	1493.14	1602.49	1726.63	1869.01	1965.24	2024.18	2092.77	2043.47	2188.31	2349.44	2454.04	2680.44	9. *Moins :* Importations de biens et services
−3.35	4.72	3.64	3.76	6.01	3.19	0.58	1.34	2.62	4.04	5.09	4.21	3.49	4.18	2.26	10. Divergence statistique
5900.72	6052.27	6210.49	6390.43	6575.56	6832.93	7060.19	7242.83	7317.06	7394.23	7369.76	7571.71	7758.76	7901.68	8119.82	11. **Produit intérieur brut**
															RÉPARTITION DU P.I.B. [2]
545.58	598.10	640.49	697.56	752.69	813.72	874.12	938.37	1024.97	1094.56	1175.01	1321.99	1544.92	1942.50	2638.67	1. Impôts indirects
119.11	136.78	143.79	154.78	164.04	167.28	168.76	176.12	187.97	195.26	218.56	240.56	240.69	315.91	408.26	2. *Moins :* Subventions
526.00	568.83	611.96	650.26	692.71	747.82	809.81	879.57	947.58	1006.30	1073.87	1175.59	1316.39	1522.66	1904.88	3. Consommation de capital fixe
2303.04	2450.46	2623.05	2799.83	2976.43	3169.37	3440.29	3780.17	4088.13	4354.15	4541.56	4804.94	5268.48	6156.14	7636.87	4. Rémunération des salariés payée par les producteurs résidents
909.48	1036.77	1141.94	1260.66	1343.68	1492.99	1661.36	1796.75	1923.99	2113.48	2383.88	3071.73	4199.12	5849.38	9192.98	5. Excédent net d'exploitation
41.24	48.59	51.80	52.84	54.06	56.56	54.02	24.08	0.31	0.18	0.40	0.41	0.46	−0.59	−0.63	6. Divergence statistique
4206.23	4565.96	4925.46	5306.37	5655.52	6133.18	6670.84	7242.83	7797.02	8373.41	8956.15	10134.10	12088.68	15154.19	20964.51	7. **Produit intérieur brut**
															OPÉRATIONS EN CAPITAL DE LA NATION [2]
															Financement de la formation brute de capital
526.00	568.83	611.96	650.26	692.71	747.82	809.81	879.57	947.58	1006.30	1073.87	1175.59	1316.39	1522.66	1904.88	1. Consommation de capital fixe
312.84	366.44	397.69	464.89	481.08	564.48	646.67	671.19	623.92	600.06	592.35	766.52	1107.99	1622.44	2505.63	2. Épargne nette
−9.78	−8.44	−23.95	−55.57	−83.33	−119.51	−167.15	−159.41	−88.11	−84.12	−20.35	42.92	−35.06	−174.92	−285.85	3. *Moins :* Solde des opérations courantes de la nation
−8.86	−24.18	−52.39	−108.56	−107.06	−117.54	−144.70	−109.41	6.98	14.42	30.36	60.78	64.11	−165.48	−47.80	4. Divergence statistique
839.77	919.53	981.21	1062.16	1150.05	1314.27	1478.93	1600.76	1666.60	1704.89	1716.93	1959.98	2523.55	3154.54	4648.57	5. **Financement de la formation brute de capital**
															Formation brute de capital
−3.13	21.22	15.52	21.82	20.47	39.47	50.10	37.22	15.73	−1.56	−23.31	−14.83	103.32	−16.04	−86.75	6. Variations des stocks
842.90	898.31	965.68	1040.35	1129.58	1274.81	1428.83	1563.54	1650.87	1706.45	1740.23	1974.81	2420.22	3170.57	4735.32	7. Formation brute de capital fixe
..	..	..	..	..	..	..	..	..	..	..	..	..	..	..	8. Divergence statistique
839.77	919.53	981.21	1062.16	1150.05	1314.27	1478.93	1600.76	1666.60	1704.89	1716.93	1959.98	2523.55	3154.53	4648.56	9. **Formation brute de capital**
															RELATIONS ENTRE LES PRINCIPAUX AGRÉGATS [2]
4206.23	4565.96	4925.46	5306.37	5655.52	6133.18	6670.84	7242.83	7797.02	8373.41	8956.15	10134.10	12088.68	15154.19	20964.51	1. **Produit intérieur brut**
−4.30	−4.34	−6.12	−6.66	−6.98	−3.39	−13.18	−33.67	−36.20	−42.79	−46.90	−58.83	−23.88	15.16	161.64	2. *Plus :* Revenu net des facteurs reçu du reste du monde
..	..	..	..	..	..	..	..	..	..	..	..	..	..	..	3. Revenu des facteurs reçu du reste du monde
..	..	..	..	..	..	..	..	..	..	..	..	..	..	..	4. Revenu des facteurs payé au reste du monde
4201.93	4561.62	4919.34	5299.71	5648.55	6119.79	6657.66	7213.92	7760.82	8330.62	8909.25	10075.27	12064.80	15169.35	21126.16	5. *Égal :* **Produit national brut**
526.00	568.83	611.96	650.26	692.71	747.82	809.81	879.57	947.58	1006.30	1073.87	1175.59	1316.39	1522.66	1904.88	6. *Moins :* Consommation de capital fixe
−27.31	−32.06	−33.32	−28.98	−28.77	−26.99	−20.70	−16.17	0.00	0.00	0.00	0.00	0.00	0.00	0.00	7. *Plus :* Divergence statistique
3648.62	3960.73	4274.05	4620.47	4927.07	5344.97	5827.15	6318.18	6813.23	7324.32	7835.38	8899.68	10748.41	13646.69	19221.28	8. *Égal :* **Revenu national**
−13.14	−10.09	−12.88	−16.21	−13.75	−15.17	−24.94	−33.71	−49.88	−56.84	−60.37	−65.37	−61.15	−62.32	−63.15	9. *Plus :* Transferts courants nets reçus du reste du monde
..	..	..	..	..	..	..	..	..	..	..	..	..	..	..	10. Transferts courants reçus du reste du monde
..	..	..	..	..	..	..	..	..	..	..	..	..	..	..	11. Transferts courants payés au reste du monde
3635.48	3950.65	4261.17	4604.26	4913.32	5329.80	5802.21	6284.46	6763.35	7267.49	7775.00	8834.31	10687.27	13584.37	19158.13	12. *Égal :* **Revenu national disponible**
3321.52	3582.99	3863.49	4139.37	4432.24	4765.32	5155.54	5613.28	6139.43	6667.43	7182.65	8067.79	9579.27	11964.72	16656.06	13. *Moins :* Consommation finale
−1.11	−1.22	0.00	0.00	0.00	0.00	0.00	0.00	0.00	0.00	0.00	0.00	0.00	2.79	3.57	14. *Plus :* Divergence statistique
312.84	366.44	397.69	464.89	481.08	564.48	646.67	671.19	623.92	600.06	592.35	766.52	1107.99	1622.44	2505.63	15. *Égal :* **Épargne nette**
−9.78	−8.44	−23.95	−55.57	−83.33	−119.51	−167.15	−159.41	−88.11	−84.12	−20.35	42.92	−35.06	−174.92	−285.85	16. *Moins :* Solde des opérations courantes de la nation
−8.86	−24.18	−52.39	−108.56	−107.06	−117.54	−144.70	−109.41	6.98	14.42	30.36	60.78	64.11	−165.48	−47.80	17. *Plus :* Divergence statistique
313.76	350.71	369.24	411.90	457.34	566.45	669.12	721.18	719.02	698.60	643.06	784.38	1207.16	1631.88	2743.68	18. *Égal :* **Formation nette de capital**

1. Non compris la République tchèque, la Hongrie et la Pologne.
2. Aux prix courants et taux de change de 1990.

Main aggregates based on exchange rates

billions of US dollars

	1960	1969	1970	1971	1972	1973	1974	1975	1976	1977	1978	1979	1980	1981	1982
EXPENDITURE ON THE G.D.P.															
At current prices and 1990 exchange rates															
1. Government final consumption expenditure	58.06	138.16	156.80	183.42	205.70	236.54	280.82	329.77	369.11	408.11	456.57	512.56	588.38	659.71	722.88
2. Private final consumption expenditure	249.24	508.87	562.88	624.38	695.58	782.95	884.43	1004.19	1138.25	1273.25	1406.98	1582.95	1783.27	1974.63	2176.01
3. Households	..	..	..	..	..	..	..	..	..	..	..	..	..	..	..
4. Private non-profit institutions serving households	..	..	..	..	..	..	..	..	..	..	..	..	..	..	..
5. Increase in stocks	11.24	20.36	20.49	9.10	7.27	20.74	23.65	−7.64	26.66	18.51	14.60	35.98	27.20	−9.57	−5.32
6. Gross fixed capital formation	95.23	205.53	242.92	272.88	297.93	332.61	361.68	378.77	423.18	468.31	516.38	587.80	671.91	700.74	736.73
7. **Total Domestic Expenditure**	413.78	872.92	983.08	1089.77	1206.48	1372.84	1550.58	1705.09	1957.20	2168.18	2394.53	2719.26	3070.77	3325.52	3630.29
8. Exports of goods and services	86.66	197.95	227.25	251.49	278.58	334.49	438.13	447.83	529.95	590.53	640.22	738.94	836.57	963.83	1057.59
9. *Less:* Imports of goods and services	81.46	187.73	218.53	239.27	261.62	316.87	427.12	430.42	525.43	575.91	607.75	735.88	865.26	964.43	1045.28
10. Statistical discrepancy	2.42	4.62	4.50	4.05	5.68	5.77	4.80	3.62	1.99	3.55	4.63	6.18	4.71	1.15	3.20
11. **Gross Domestic Product**	421.41	887.76	996.31	1106.04	1229.13	1396.23	1566.40	1726.13	1963.71	2186.35	2431.62	2728.53	3046.79	3326.07	3645.81
At the price levels and exchange rates of 1990															
1. Government final consumption expenditure	508.43	720.43	748.63	780.70	813.79	846.80	873.64	910.86	935.84	951.58	987.49	1018.82	1043.36	1063.02	1079.70
2. Private final consumption expenditure	1398.19	2140.78	2258.72	2354.20	2471.87	2598.77	2640.73	2691.78	2799.54	2872.73	2964.16	3073.90	3125.73	3136.50	3165.75
3. Households	..	..	..	..	..	..	..	..	..	..	..	..	..	..	..
4. Private non-profit institutions serving households	..	..	..	..	..	..	..	..	..	..	..	..	..	..	..
5. Increase in stocks	40.98	42.92	57.97	18.82	11.21	57.84	68.80	−17.44	56.77	42.00	25.62	63.88	40.27	−16.29	−1.67
6. Gross fixed capital formation	557.93	927.56	978.18	1011.94	1051.30	1105.86	1075.54	1022.82	1042.01	1054.87	1070.74	1108.35	1130.96	1077.79	1055.22
7. **Total Domestic Expenditure**	2505.53	3831.68	4043.49	4165.67	4348.18	4609.27	4658.71	4608.03	4834.15	4921.18	5048.01	5264.95	5340.32	5261.02	5298.99
8. Exports of goods and services	330.10	651.19	709.31	757.11	816.25	902.42	968.04	930.26	1017.29	1073.35	1127.07	1198.13	1213.68	1263.43	1283.97
9. *Less:* Imports of goods and services	317.41	652.23	734.10	772.93	839.11	928.43	949.17	898.13	996.06	1017.05	1054.94	1158.30	1176.95	1148.48	1163.87
10. Statistical discrepancy	−18.33	−18.19	−19.21	−21.07	−16.12	−25.61	−29.34	−21.77	−31.16	−23.67	−22.24	−22.11	−18.91	−11.85	−7.00
11. **Gross Domestic Product**	2499.90	3812.46	3999.49	4128.77	4309.20	4557.65	4648.25	4618.39	4824.21	4953.81	5097.91	5282.67	5358.14	5364.12	5412.08
COST COMPONENTS OF THE G.D.P. [1]															
1. Indirect taxes	54.56	124.07	130.50	144.17	160.37	179.28	193.54	212.05	244.07	274.83	306.67	350.96	394.90	432.06	474.42
2. *Less:* Subsidies	5.84	20.09	20.57	22.22	26.95	32.53	37.94	46.18	53.00	60.03	70.29	79.04	85.79	93.02	101.75
3. Consumption of fixed capital	36.40	83.81	97.72	111.25	124.82	141.61	167.70	192.61	217.24	244.51	273.26	308.93	356.89	404.51	448.61
4. Compensation of employees paid by resident producers	200.82	451.38	522.62	590.59	660.23	758.76	875.69	988.54	1114.47	1238.40	1368.83	1529.65	1727.12	1884.99	2035.97
5. Operating surplus	125.98	230.40	246.85	260.91	287.31	323.62	340.03	350.88	408.18	456.45	515.86	578.72	616.41	661.12	750.22
6. Statistical discrepancy	9.50	18.20	19.20	21.35	23.32	25.48	27.38	28.24	32.75	32.18	37.28	39.30	37.26	36.42	38.33
7. **Gross Domestic Product**	421.42	887.77	996.31	1106.05	1229.11	1396.23	1566.40	1726.13	1963.71	2186.34	2431.62	2728.53	3046.79	3326.07	3645.81
CAPITAL TRANSACTIONS OF THE NATION [1]															
Finance of Gross Capital Formation															
1. Consumption of fixed capital	36.40	83.81	97.72	111.25	124.82	141.61	167.70	192.61	217.24	244.51	273.26	308.93	356.89	404.51	448.61
2. Net saving	72.46	146.39	165.92	172.01	188.05	219.50	212.57	175.66	213.87	233.34	267.55	297.01	287.78	246.18	247.78
3. *Less:* Surplus of the nation on current transactions	−2.30	−5.66	−1.25	2.61	4.22	−7.66	−36.78	−13.13	−19.76	−14.36	−6.35	3.41	−6.60	−10.79	−39.85
4. Statistical discrepancy	−4.69	−9.98	−1.48	1.33	−3.46	−15.42	−31.73	−10.27	−1.02	−5.40	−16.18	21.25	47.85	29.70	−4.83
5. **Finance of Gross Capital Formation**	106.48	225.89	263.41	281.98	305.19	353.34	385.33	371.13	449.84	486.81	530.98	623.78	699.12	691.18	731.41
Gross capital formation															
6. Increase in stocks	11.24	20.36	20.49	9.10	7.27	20.74	23.65	−7.64	26.66	18.51	14.60	35.98	27.20	−9.57	−5.32
7. Gross fixed capital formation	95.23	205.53	242.92	272.88	297.93	332.61	361.68	378.77	423.18	468.31	516.38	587.80	671.91	700.74	736.73
8. Statistical discrepancy	..	..	..	..	..	..	..	..	..	..	..	..	..	..	..
9. **Gross Capital Formation**	106.48	225.89	263.41	281.98	305.19	353.34	385.33	371.13	449.84	486.81	530.98	623.78	699.12	691.17	731.41
RELATIONS AMONG NATIONAL ACCOUNTING AGGREGATES [1]															
1. **Gross Domestic Product**	421.41	887.76	996.31	1106.05	1229.12	1396.23	1566.40	1726.13	1963.71	2186.35	2431.62	2728.53	3046.79	3326.07	3645.81
2. *Plus:* Net factor income from the rest of the world	1.21	2.20	2.07	2.27	2.90	3.63	2.42	1.37	3.08	−0.38	3.84	6.76	2.84	−3.17	−10.69
3. Factor income from the rest of the world	..	..	..	..	..	..	..	..	..	..	..	..	..	..	..
4. Factor income paid to the rest of the world	..	..	..	..	..	..	..	..	..	..	..	..	..	..	..
5. *Equals:* **Gross National Product**	422.62	889.97	998.39	1108.32	1232.03	1399.85	1568.83	1727.50	1966.78	2185.97	2435.46	2735.29	3049.63	3322.90	3635.12
6. *Less:* Consumption of fixed capital	36.40	83.81	97.72	111.25	124.82	141.61	167.70	192.61	217.26	244.51	273.26	308.93	356.89	404.51	448.61
7. *Plus:* Statistical discrepancy	−5.64	−10.61	−12.43	−12.97	−13.40	−14.92	−15.46	−16.67	−18.94	−18.53	−21.20	−23.80	−25.17	−25.84	−26.92
8. *Equals:* **National Income**	380.59	795.54	888.24	984.09	1093.80	1243.33	1385.67	1518.22	1730.58	1922.92	2141.00	2402.56	2667.57	2892.55	3159.58
9. *Plus:* Net current transfers from the rest of the world	−0.82	−2.28	−2.81	−3.44	−3.85	−4.05	−5.55	−6.59	−5.96	−6.81	−6.73	−7.33	−6.77	−10.58	−11.74
10. Current transfers from the rest of the world	..	..	..	..	..	..	..	..	..	..	..	..	..	..	..
11. Current transfers paid to the rest of the world	..	..	..	..	..	..	..	..	..	..	..	..	..	..	..
12. *Equals:* **National Disposable Income**	379.77	793.26	885.43	980.66	1089.95	1239.27	1380.12	1511.63	1724.62	1916.11	2134.27	2395.24	2660.80	2881.98	3147.84
13. *Less:* Final consumption	307.52	647.29	719.84	807.21	901.85	1019.31	1163.80	1331.95	1502.86	1679.35	1861.59	2095.09	2370.28	2631.79	2897.93
14. *Plus:* Statistical discrepancy	0.21	0.42	0.33	−1.44	−0.06	−0.47	−3.75	−4.02	−7.91	−3.43	−5.12	−3.14	−2.75	−4.01	−2.14
15. *Equals:* **Net Saving**	72.46	146.39	165.92	172.01	188.05	219.49	212.57	175.66	213.84	233.34	267.55	297.01	287.78	246.18	247.78
16. *Less:* Surplus of the nation on current transactions	−2.30	−5.66	−1.25	2.61	4.22	−7.66	−36.78	−13.13	−19.76	−14.36	−6.35	3.41	−6.60	−10.79	−39.85
17. *Plus:* Statistical discrepancy	−4.81	−9.98	−1.48	1.33	−3.46	−15.42	−31.73	−10.27	−1.02	−5.40	−16.18	21.25	47.85	29.70	−4.83
18. *Equals:* **Net Capital Formation**	69.96	142.07	165.69	170.73	180.37	211.73	217.63	178.52	232.58	242.30	257.73	314.85	342.23	286.67	282.80

1. At current prices and 1990 exchange rates.

Principaux Agrégats basés sur les taux de change

milliards de dollars É-U

1983	1984	1985	1986	1987	1988	1989	1990	1991	1992	1993	1994	1995	1996	1997	
															DÉPENSES IMPUTÉES AU P.I.B.
															Aux prix courants et taux de change de 1990
784.50	839.32	899.37	956.63	1020.43	1085.73	1151.50	1257.88	1365.10	1467.70	1529.54	1582.57	1642.89	1713.81	1751.96	1. Consommation finale des administrations publiques
2370.73	2563.10	2766.92	2969.34	3180.42	3425.06	3706.56	3986.79	4306.50	4574.22	4741.70	4978.62	5217.56	5468.55	5700.44	2. Consommation finale privée
..	..	..	..	..	..	..	..	..	..	..	..	..	..	..	3. Ménages
0.00	19.38	12.96	18.11	17.90	39.02	46.87	30.45	17.59	-0.93	-30.90	31.75	49.87	10.55	52.21	4. Institutions privées sans but lucratif au service des ménages
785.19	836.39	899.05	965.50	1047.56	1179.49	1322.07	1441.12	1505.69	1524.63	1456.52	1523.29	1623.18	1660.75	1721.05	5. Variations des stocks
3940.43	4258.20	4578.29	4909.58	5266.31	5729.30	6227.00	6716.23	7194.87	7565.62	7696.86	8116.24	8533.50	8853.66	9225.66	6. Formation brute de capital fixe
1149.67	1321.05	1440.98	1387.41	1432.60	1551.19	1756.42	1840.78	1885.44	1961.70	2053.42	2273.13	2549.52	2696.95	2973.73	7. **Demande intérieure totale**
1115.14	1271.20	1375.56	1289.21	1364.30	1504.36	1725.98	1815.72	1893.80	1951.10	1944.73	2141.05	2386.54	2493.90	2740.31	8. Exportations de biens et services
3.67	8.01	8.40	8.04	6.11	4.61	0.81	0.74	0.00	-0.60	0.43	-0.52	-1.25	0.85	2.47	9. *Moins :* Importations de biens et services
3978.63	4316.06	4652.12	5015.82	5340.71	5780.74	6258.26	6742.04	7186.52	7575.62	7805.97	8247.80	8695.24	9057.56	9461.55	10. Divergence statistique
															11. **Produit intérieur brut**
															Aux niveaux de prix et taux de change de 1990
1098.50	1115.55	1140.87	1165.83	1193.86	1219.41	1229.97	1257.88	1284.84	1311.56	1322.76	1338.12	1349.65	1374.71	1376.94	1. Consommation finale des administrations publiques
3209.62	3258.73	3344.95	3480.66	3611.92	3755.31	3879.03	3986.79	4074.63	4138.14	4121.42	4189.24	4262.67	4349.89	4439.89	2. Consommation finale privée
..	..	..	..	..	..	..	..	..	..	..	..	..	..	..	3. Ménages
2.16	20.02	16.81	25.24	24.55	42.31	45.42	30.45	15.08	7.53	-21.34	35.10	46.80	16.31	52.57	4. Institutions privées sans but lucratif au service des ménages
1057.37	1068.22	1095.97	1138.50	1198.70	1297.44	1387.31	1441.12	1450.97	1435.52	1339.40	1374.11	1422.82	1435.64	1471.75	5. Variations des stocks
5367.65	5462.53	5598.60	5810.22	6029.03	6314.47	6541.73	6716.23	6825.53	6892.75	6762.23	6936.56	7081.94	7176.55	7341.16	6. Formation brute de capital fixe
1321.87	1421.38	1485.18	1500.68	1554.28	1643.00	1770.91	1840.78	1862.29	1928.44	1956.09	2130.58	2300.99	2417.62	2652.95	7. **Demande intérieure totale**
1177.72	1246.51	1303.55	1366.91	1470.66	1592.99	1729.08	1815.72	1877.20	1946.34	1885.45	2030.35	2175.95	2266.21	2469.45	8. Exportations de biens et services
-2.42	5.11	3.76	4.49	5.07	1.52	-0.85	0.74	2.42	2.87	5.07	4.25	2.83	4.57	2.50	9. *Moins :* Importations de biens et services
5509.37	5642.50	5784.00	5948.48	6117.72	6366.01	6582.71	6742.04	6813.04	6877.71	6837.95	7041.04	7209.81	7332.52	7527.16	10. Divergence statistique
															11. **Produit intérieur brut**
															RÉPARTITION DU P.I.B. [1]
523.25	573.77	612.17	666.16	718.39	777.08	833.78	889.73	964.16	1013.19	1052.22	1122.34	1175.49	1235.46	1300.75	1. Impôts indirects
113.41	130.63	137.09	147.68	156.59	158.94	159.28	165.10	173.65	175.14	193.22	194.27	193.87	204.99	202.82	2. *Moins :* Subventions
490.84	531.17	570.49	605.68	643.10	691.78	746.46	809.65	867.68	913.70	962.04	1003.36	1055.67	1096.80	1135.15	3. Consommation de capital fixe
2175.82	2315.81	2477.32	2641.02	2803.70	3001.17	3231.95	3537.53	3795.90	3998.97	4082.07	4196.69	4371.03	4536.72	4698.70	4. Rémunération des salariés payée par les producteurs résidents
861.00	977.44	1077.55	1198.01	1278.10	1413.21	1551.55	1646.49	1732.43	1824.91	1902.87	2119.67	2286.92	2394.63	2530.93	5. Excédent net d'exploitation
41.13	48.50	51.67	52.65	54.00	56.45	53.80	23.74	0.00	0.00	0.00	0.00	0.00	-1.06	-1.15	6. Divergence statistique
3978.63	4316.06	4652.12	5015.82	5340.71	5780.74	6258.26	6742.04	7186.52	7575.62	7805.97	8247.80	8695.24	9057.56	9461.55	7. **Produit intérieur brut**
															OPÉRATIONS EN CAPITAL DE LA NATION [1]
															Financement de la formation brute de capital
490.84	531.17	570.49	605.68	643.10	691.78	746.46	809.65	867.68	913.70	962.04	1003.36	1055.67	1096.80	1135.15	1. Consommation de capital fixe
284.76	328.75	357.02	427.79	442.99	517.46	588.98	604.19	556.84	513.69	455.99	550.39	654.83	648.49	752.06	2. Épargne nette
-18.47	-20.02	-36.89	-58.70	-86.32	-125.50	-175.46	-166.54	-98.76	-95.71	-8.03	-0.77	38.71	72.08	110.34	3. *Moins :* Solde des opérations courantes de la nation
-8.86	-24.18	-52.39	-108.56	-106.95	-116.23	-141.95	-108.81	0.00	0.60	-0.43	0.52	1.25	-1.91	-3.62	4. Divergence statistique
785.20	855.77	912.01	983.61	1065.46	1218.51	1368.95	1471.57	1523.27	1523.70	1425.62	1555.05	1673.05	1671.30	1773.25	5. **Financement de la formation brute de capital**
															Formation brute de capital
0.00	19.38	12.96	18.11	17.90	39.02	46.87	30.45	17.59	-0.93	-30.90	31.75	49.87	10.55	52.21	6. Variations des stocks
785.19	836.39	899.05	965.50	1047.56	1179.49	1322.07	1441.12	1505.69	1524.63	1456.52	1523.29	1623.18	1660.75	1721.05	7. Formation brute de capital fixe
..	..	..	..	..	..	..	..	..	..	..	..	..	..	..	8. Divergence statistique
785.20	855.77	912.01	983.61	1065.46	1218.51	1368.95	1471.57	1523.27	1523.70	1425.62	1555.05	1673.05	1671.30	1773.25	9. **Formation brute de capital**
															RELATIONS ENTRE LES PRINCIPAUX AGRÉGATS [1]
3978.63	4316.06	4652.12	5015.82	5340.71	5780.74	6258.26	6742.04	7186.52	7575.62	7805.97	8247.80	8695.24	9057.56	9461.55	1. **Produit intérieur brut**
-9.42	-11.43	-14.21	-13.45	-13.72	-21.11	-21.74	-41.38	-43.92	-53.44	-60.58	-72.65	-68.49	-73.41	-64.79	2. *Plus :* Revenu net des facteurs reçu du reste du monde
..	..	..	..	..	..	..	..	..	..	..	..	..	..	..	3. Revenu des facteurs reçu du reste du monde
..	..	..	..	..	..	..	..	..	..	..	..	..	..	..	4. Revenu des facteurs payé au reste du monde
3969.21	4304.63	4637.91	5002.38	5326.99	5759.64	6236.52	6705.42	7142.60	7522.18	7745.39	8175.15	8626.75	8984.15	9396.77	5. *Égal :* **Produit national brut**
490.84	531.17	570.49	605.68	643.10	691.78	746.46	809.65	867.68	913.70	962.04	1003.36	1055.67	1096.80	1135.15	6. *Moins :* Consommation de capital fixe
-27.31	-32.06	-33.32	-28.98	-28.77	-26.99	-20.70	-16.17	0.00	0.00	0.00	0.00	0.00	0.00	0.00	7. *Plus :* Divergence statistique
3451.07	3741.40	4034.10	4367.72	4655.12	5040.87	5469.36	5879.60	6274.92	6608.49	6783.35	7171.79	7571.08	7887.35	8261.62	8. *Égal :* **Revenu national**
-11.27	-8.13	-10.79	-13.96	-11.29	-12.62	-22.32	-30.74	-46.48	-52.88	-56.13	-60.21	-55.79	-57.56	-58.30	9. *Plus :* Transferts courants nets reçus du reste du monde
..	..	..	..	..	..	..	..	..	..	..	..	..	..	..	10. Transferts courants reçus du reste du monde
..	..	..	..	..	..	..	..	..	..	..	..	..	..	..	11. Transferts courants payés au reste du monde
3439.80	3733.26	4023.31	4353.77	4643.83	5028.25	5447.04	5848.86	6228.44	6555.61	6727.22	7111.58	7515.28	7829.79	8203.32	12. *Égal :* **Revenu national disponible**
3153.94	3403.29	3666.29	3925.97	4200.84	4510.79	4858.05	5244.67	5671.60	6041.92	6271.24	6561.19	6860.45	7184.09	7454.82	13. *Moins :* Consommation finale
-1.11	-1.22	0.00	0.00	0.00	0.00	0.00	0.00	0.00	0.00	0.00	0.00	0.00	2.79	3.57	14. *Plus :* Divergence statistique
284.76	328.75	357.02	427.79	442.99	517.46	588.98	604.19	556.84	513.69	455.99	550.39	654.83	648.49	752.06	15. *Égal :* **Épargne nette**
-18.47	-20.02	-36.89	-58.70	-86.32	-125.50	-175.46	-166.53	-98.76	-95.71	-8.03	-0.77	38.71	72.08	110.34	16. *Moins :* Solde des opérations courantes de la nation
-8.86	-24.18	-52.39	-108.56	-106.95	-116.23	-141.95	-108.81	0.00	0.60	-0.43	0.52	1.25	-1.91	-3.62	17. *Plus :* Divergence statistique
294.36	324.60	341.51	377.93	422.36	526.73	622.49	661.91	655.60	610.00	463.58	551.68	617.38	574.50	638.10	18. *Égal :* **Formation nette de capital**

1. Aux prix courants et taux de change de 1990.

OECD-TOTAL [1]

Main aggregates based on PPPs

billions of US dollars

	1960	1969	1970	1971	1972	1973	1974	1975	1976	1977	1978	1979	1980	1981	1982
EXPENDITURE ON THE G.D.P.															
At current prices and current PPPs															
1. Government final consumption expenditure	..	..	401.46	443.06	487.32	539.97	617.59	713.43	782.31	858.51	949.18	1064.65	1208.15	1375.71	1492.07
2. Private final consumption expenditure	..	..	1570.71	1719.66	1893.46	2109.40	2330.40	2601.27	2889.45	3193.19	3551.36	4005.90	4473.43	4991.29	5367.72
3. Households	..	..	..	..	..	..	..	..	..	..	..	..	..	..	..
4. Private non-profit institutions serving households	..	..	..	..	..	..	..	..	..	..	..	..	..	..	..
5. Increase in stocks	..	..	39.49	28.40	26.40	54.75	73.19	−3.64	56.41	58.18	54.97	73.04	49.56	55.66	−1.26
6. Gross fixed capital formation	..	..	594.53	652.26	726.12	838.80	902.46	941.91	1036.91	1156.42	1316.81	1520.55	1670.70	1839.85	1854.04
7. **Total Domestic Expenditure**	..	..	2606.19	2843.38	3133.31	3542.92	3923.64	4252.98	4765.08	5266.30	5872.32	6664.15	7401.84	8262.51	8712.58
8. Exports of goods and services	..	..	358.37	393.00	429.53	514.83	662.01	684.69	785.11	869.69	956.30	1133.57	1323.15	1520.55	1603.77
9. *Less:* Imports of goods and services	..	..	349.10	377.04	415.42	513.58	702.14	683.80	807.75	891.48	954.07	1176.24	1395.22	1561.36	1603.67
10. Statistical discrepancy	..	..	0.10	−1.11	2.30	1.55	0.29	−0.77	−3.27	−2.09	−0.77	0.39	−0.67	−3.06	−2.77
11. **Gross Domestic Product**	..	..	2615.57	2858.22	3149.71	3545.72	3883.79	4253.10	4739.17	5242.42	5873.78	6621.86	7329.10	8218.64	8709.90
At the price levels and PPPs of 1990															
1. Government final consumption expenditure	..	..	1536.72	1559.60	1600.77	1635.50	1682.98	1756.01	1793.34	1829.04	1886.05	1931.31	1973.14	2018.70	2057.59
2. Private final consumption expenditure	..	..	5036.64	5250.27	5558.76	5861.48	5901.39	6049.96	6316.56	6539.55	6797.81	7037.54	7131.73	7217.11	7307.90
3. Households	..	..	..	..	..	..	..	..	..	..	..	..	..	..	..
4. Private non-profit institutions serving households	..	..	..	..	..	..	..	..	..	..	..	..	..	..	..
5. Increase in stocks	..	..	95.32	66.07	55.56	122.41	153.69	−3.70	105.93	102.54	91.12	114.91	76.86	76.40	8.18
6. Gross fixed capital formation	..	..	1877.43	1959.54	2095.13	2252.73	2167.93	2060.26	2142.12	2225.01	2348.31	2458.26	2432.88	2431.10	2317.68
7. **Total Domestic Expenditure**	..	..	8546.10	8835.48	9310.23	9872.12	9905.99	9862.52	10357.96	10696.14	11123.29	11542.02	11614.61	11743.31	11691.35
8. Exports of goods and services	..	..	963.10	1022.16	1103.04	1226.85	1316.58	1279.85	1393.54	1465.54	1552.72	1654.57	1722.79	1798.19	1796.76
9. *Less:* Imports of goods and services	..	..	1045.60	1098.65	1197.75	1328.68	1360.98	1261.96	1407.81	1456.50	1531.73	1659.27	1682.13	1702.85	1669.18
10. Statistical discrepancy	..	..	−26.60	−28.64	−23.17	−36.47	−38.34	−31.61	−42.15	−42.39	−40.75	−41.16	−36.65	−29.75	−22.01
11. **Gross Domestic Product**	..	..	8437.01	8730.35	9192.35	9733.82	9823.25	9848.80	10301.54	10662.78	11103.52	11496.17	11618.61	11808.90	11796.93
COST COMPONENTS OF THE G.D.P. [2]															
1. Indirect taxes	..	..	275.54	300.11	325.70	358.49	385.93	416.58	463.99	516.82	566.27	640.07	726.22	832.94	890.02
2. *Less:* Subsidies	..	..	30.53	33.35	39.79	43.61	54.69	67.05	72.67	82.46	95.55	108.38	123.48	138.79	151.88
3. Consumption of fixed capital	..	..	262.86	291.20	323.17	360.07	413.70	472.07	518.35	577.45	647.83	742.56	850.71	980.57	1070.64
4. Compensation of employees paid by resident producers	..	..	1408.87	1548.03	1715.04	1939.63	2177.33	2414.17	2681.16	2957.06	3296.61	3712.53	4129.10	4614.14	4892.60
5. Operating surplus	..	..	689.28	734.74	813.19	922.65	943.26	990.56	1113.64	1238.19	1419.88	1586.70	1700.01	1896.61	1989.92
6. Statistical discrepancy	..	..	9.56	17.51	12.39	8.49	18.27	26.77	34.70	35.34	38.75	48.39	46.55	33.17	18.60
7. **Gross Domestic Product**	..	..	2615.57	2858.23	3149.70	3545.71	3883.80	4253.10	4739.17	5242.41	5873.78	6621.86	7329.10	8218.64	8709.90
CAPITAL TRANSACTIONS OF THE NATION [2]															
Finance of Gross Capital Formation															
1. Consumption of fixed capital	..	..	262.86	291.20	323.17	360.07	413.70	472.07	518.35	577.45	647.83	742.56	850.71	980.57	1070.64
2. Net saving	..	..	378.76	395.61	444.69	547.32	521.17	448.22	526.84	592.01	704.30	792.19	777.23	839.64	739.66
3. *Less:* Surplus of the nation on current transactions	..	..	5.69	13.69	11.32	−1.28	−53.99	−12.74	−30.38	−29.42	−12.85	−22.88	−39.31	−44.97	−49.96
4. Statistical discrepancy	..	..	−2.33	6.97	−4.02	−14.84	−12.35	5.77	18.50	15.38	6.94	36.17	53.59	31.54	−6.91
5. **Finance of Gross Capital Formation**	..	..	633.60	680.09	752.53	893.82	976.50	938.80	1094.07	1214.25	1371.92	1593.80	1720.84	1896.72	1853.34
Gross capital formation															
6. Increase in stocks	..	..	39.49	28.40	26.40	54.75	73.19	−3.64	56.41	58.18	54.97	73.04	49.56	55.66	−1.26
7. Gross fixed capital formation	..	..	594.53	652.26	726.13	838.80	902.46	941.91	1036.91	1156.42	1316.81	1520.55	1670.70	1839.85	1854.04
8. Statistical discrepancy	..	..	−0.43	−0.57	0.00	0.27	0.85	0.53	0.75	−0.35	0.14	0.20	0.59	1.21	0.55
9. **Gross Capital Formation**	..	..	633.60	680.09	752.53	893.82	976.50	938.80	1094.07	1214.25	1371.92	1593.80	1720.84	1896.72	1853.34
RELATIONS AMONG NATIONAL ACCOUNTING AGGREGATES [2]															
1. **Gross Domestic Product**	..	..	2615.57	2858.23	3149.71	3545.71	3883.80	4253.10	4739.16	5242.41	5873.78	6621.86	7329.10	8218.64	8709.90
2. *Plus:* Net factor income from the rest of the world	..	..	7.71	9.55	11.65	17.42	18.41	12.09	13.74	14.06	16.56	29.89	25.04	9.44	−7.77
3. Factor income from the rest of the world	..	..	..	..	..	..	..	..	..	..	..	..	..	..	..
4. Factor income paid to the rest of the world	..	..	..	..	..	..	..	..	..	..	..	..	..	..	..
5. *Equals:* **Gross National Product**	..	..	2623.28	2867.77	3161.26	3563.03	3902.21	4265.19	4752.90	5256.47	5890.34	6651.75	7354.14	8228.08	8702.14
6. *Less:* Consumption of fixed capital	..	..	262.86	291.20	323.17	360.07	413.70	472.07	518.35	577.45	647.83	742.56	850.71	980.57	1070.64
7. *Plus:* Statistical discrepancy	..	..	−2.00	−3.24	0.93	4.45	−1.30	−5.71	−3.93	−6.85	−6.59	−5.66	−5.31	−6.99	−11.93
8. *Equals:* **National Income**	..	..	2358.42	2573.43	2839.12	3207.42	3487.20	3787.51	4230.61	4672.16	5235.93	5903.53	6498.02	7240.62	7619.57
9. *Plus:* Net current transfers from the rest of the world	..	..	−6.02	−7.29	−8.21	−6.92	−8.61	−9.51	−7.58	−8.46	−9.27	−9.50	−10.12	−17.52	−21.28
10. Current transfers from the rest of the world	..	..	..	..	..	..	..	..	..	..	..	..	..	..	..
11. Current transfers paid to the rest of the world	..	..	..	..	..	..	..	..	..	..	..	..	..	..	..
12. *Equals:* **National Disposable Income**	..	..	2352.40	2566.04	2830.90	3200.50	3478.59	3778.00	4223.03	4663.70	5226.75	5894.13	6488.00	7223.09	7598.29
13. *Less:* Final consumption	..	..	1972.49	2161.70	2381.81	2649.04	2945.50	3311.63	3665.53	4049.02	4498.04	5070.06	5680.09	6364.26	6858.78
14. *Plus:* Statistical discrepancy	..	..	−1.26	−8.83	−4.40	−4.25	−11.92	−18.05	−30.68	−22.57	−24.41	−31.88	−30.57	−19.19	0.25
15. *Equals:* **Net Saving**	..	..	378.76	395.61	444.69	547.31	521.17	448.22	526.82	592.01	704.30	792.19	777.23	839.64	739.66
16. *Less:* Surplus of the nation on current transactions	..	..	5.69	13.69	11.32	−1.28	−53.99	−12.74	−30.38	−29.42	−12.85	−22.88	−39.31	−44.97	−49.96
17. *Plus:* Statistical discrepancy	..	..	−1.80	7.54	−3.92	−15.01	−13.21	5.14	17.75	15.72	6.80	36.07	52.91	30.44	−7.57
18. *Equals:* **Net Capital Formation**	..	..	371.16	389.46	429.36	533.49	561.85	466.10	574.95	637.25	723.95	851.03	869.54	914.94	782.05

1. Excluding Korea, Czech Republic, Hungary and Poland.
2. At current prices and current PPPs.

Principaux Agrégats basés sur les PPA

milliards de dollars É-U

DÉPENSES IMPUTÉES AU P.I.B.

Aux prix et PPA courants

1983	1984	1985	1986	1987	1988	1989	1990	1991	1992	1993	1994	1995	1996	1997	
1591.83	1700.25	1825.44	1924.04	2042.67	2160.72	2295.83	2491.61	2649.21	2815.07	2892.99	2976.00	3104.38	3216.01	3308.42	1. Consommation finale des administrations publiques
5772.93	6244.52	6702.85	7080.51	7570.85	8169.82	8818.82	9469.01	9949.13	10624.81	11058.88	11612.51	12253.07	12819.30	13471.03	2. Consommation finale privée
..	..	..	..	..	..	..	..	..	..	..	..	..	..	..	3. Ménages
..	..	..	..	..	..	..	..	..	..	..	..	..	..	..	4. Institutions privées sans but lucratif au service des ménages
16.78	113.25	75.79	50.96	63.93	71.98	122.01	74.95	45.65	29.22	19.90	95.51	115.41	80.04	159.14	5. Variations des stocks
1907.62	2091.91	2245.62	2354.16	2512.75	2776.74	3022.40	3216.36	3248.37	3366.13	3382.67	3553.34	3765.29	4002.46	4190.96	6. Formation brute de capital fixe
9289.16	10149.93	10849.70	11409.68	12190.20	13179.26	14259.06	15251.92	15892.36	16835.23	17354.43	18237.36	19238.16	20117.82	21129.55	7. **Demande intérieure totale**
1692.85	1927.72	2037.38	1956.63	2069.62	2277.99	2555.84	2712.89	2785.67	2949.68	3044.19	3366.21	3867.56	4133.57	4564.21	8. Exportations de biens et services
1667.80	1928.49	2038.48	1953.76	2098.51	2318.68	2615.89	2782.66	2805.41	2958.43	3003.48	3323.59	3769.09	4036.61	4452.27	9. *Moins :* Importations de biens et services
-5.30	4.28	2.81	4.84	1.39	11.41	10.22	4.00	-9.69	-14.23	-17.06	-15.30	-7.09	11.54	4.60	10. Divergence statistique
9308.89	10153.44	10851.41	11417.39	12162.70	13149.98	14209.22	15186.15	15862.93	16812.25	17378.09	18264.67	19329.55	20226.33	21246.09	11. **Produit intérieur brut**

Aux niveaux de prix et PPA de 1990

1983	1984	1985	1986	1987	1988	1989	1990	1991	1992	1993	1994	1995	1996	1997	
2102.35	2146.74	2216.16	2286.58	2345.20	2393.73	2430.86	2491.61	2531.49	2558.11	2566.18	2586.70	2603.82	2633.59	2652.82	1. Consommation finale des administrations publiques
7507.40	7753.50	8030.02	8315.72	8586.04	8929.59	9215.06	9469.01	9567.57	9790.97	9942.90	10189.35	10382.40	10663.49	10968.73	2. Consommation finale privée
..	..	..	..	..	..	..	..	..	..	..	..	..	..	..	3. Ménages
..	..	..	..	..	..	..	..	..	..	..	..	..	..	..	4. Institutions privées sans but lucratif au service des ménages
17.96	116.38	82.13	64.42	72.23	80.73	115.59	74.95	41.72	44.38	44.39	118.59	101.25	74.38	141.39	5. Variations des stocks
2330.24	2480.39	2593.99	2663.45	2782.94	2968.37	3125.79	3216.36	3179.60	3217.17	3197.34	3308.94	3402.18	3629.55	3778.71	6. Formation brute de capital fixe
11957.95	12497.00	12922.29	13330.16	13786.41	14372.42	14887.30	15251.92	15320.37	15610.63	15750.81	16203.58	16489.66	17001.01	17541.65	7. **Demande intérieure totale**
1836.19	1998.27	2076.46	2112.73	2216.43	2389.53	2578.95	2712.89	2795.04	2928.08	3010.84	3281.40	3599.26	3871.66	4284.41	8. Exportations de biens et services
1709.14	1908.47	2002.51	2101.04	2249.03	2443.22	2643.44	2782.66	2832.79	2974.69	3021.51	3295.38	3549.20	3834.97	4247.26	9. *Moins :* Importations de biens et services
-17.43	-5.21	-6.56	-1.09	2.26	5.07	2.76	4.00	1.25	0.72	0.02	-0.70	-4.45	-12.04	-17.17	10. Divergence statistique
12067.55	12581.59	12989.69	13340.75	13756.07	14323.79	14825.57	15186.15	15283.87	15564.74	15740.16	16188.91	16535.27	17025.66	17561.64	11. **Produit intérieur brut**

RÉPARTITION DU P.I.B. [2]

1983	1984	1985	1986	1987	1988	1989	1990	1991	1992	1993	1994	1995	1996	1997	
956.55	1047.92	1121.41	1182.43	1284.47	1376.57	1473.44	1576.50	1675.27	1785.19	1841.75	1950.51	2058.65	2153.94	2264.70	1. Impôts indirects
170.63	184.49	188.36	197.53	207.02	206.23	202.02	213.72	219.28	225.22	242.63	239.79	239.61	250.27	249.82	2. *Moins :* Subventions
1143.73	1211.88	1288.77	1365.97	1453.12	1559.48	1685.64	1797.97	1904.57	2027.12	2091.53	2201.57	2335.07	2432.55	2532.74	3. Consommation de capital fixe
5136.39	5528.01	5892.56	6198.26	6609.06	7115.99	7632.85	8252.39	8687.78	9216.98	9503.90	9876.43	10408.39	10843.91	11398.69	4. Rémunération des salariés payée par les producteurs résidents
2177.89	2510.36	2698.33	2806.49	3003.21	3316.10	3569.24	3736.10	3806.48	3963.10	4127.30	4457.21	4797.63	5116.71	5375.65	5. Excédent net d'exploitation
64.96	39.75	38.70	61.77	19.87	-11.92	50.07	36.91	8.11	45.10	56.23	18.74	-30.58	-70.51	-75.87	6. Divergence statistique
9308.89	10153.44	10851.41	11417.39	12162.71	13149.98	14209.22	15186.15	15862.93	16812.26	17378.09	18264.68	19329.54	20226.33	21246.09	7. **Produit intérieur brut**

OPÉRATIONS EN CAPITAL DE LA NATION [2]

Financement de la formation brute de capital

1983	1984	1985	1986	1987	1988	1989	1990	1991	1992	1993	1994	1995	1996	1997	
1143.73	1211.88	1288.77	1365.97	1453.12	1559.48	1685.64	1797.97	1904.57	2027.12	2091.53	2201.57	2335.07	2432.55	2532.74	1. Consommation de capital fixe
722.64	939.44	969.80	941.63	1048.72	1243.29	1326.28	1324.30	1299.48	1191.17	1165.79	1309.03	1523.80	1682.85	1859.67	2. Épargne nette
-25.63	-67.60	-98.39	-145.35	-171.79	-195.30	-242.33	-238.16	-72.29	-117.87	-72.33	-104.39	-45.58	-49.52	-38.45	3. *Moins :* Solde des opérations courantes de la nation
31.74	-14.37	-35.47	-48.27	-97.95	-147.97	-109.54	-69.11	17.70	58.01	71.51	32.91	-23.25	-82.58	-80.27	4. Divergence statistique
1923.74	2204.56	2321.49	2404.68	2575.68	2850.09	3144.70	3291.32	3294.03	3394.16	3401.16	3647.90	3881.20	4082.33	4350.59	5. **Financement de la formation brute de capital**

Formation brute de capital

1983	1984	1985	1986	1987	1988	1989	1990	1991	1992	1993	1994	1995	1996	1997	
16.78	113.25	75.79	50.96	63.93	71.98	122.01	74.95	45.65	29.22	19.90	95.51	115.41	80.04	159.14	6. Variations des stocks
1907.62	2091.91	2245.62	2354.16	2512.75	2776.74	3022.40	3216.36	3248.37	3366.13	3382.67	3553.34	3765.29	4002.46	4190.96	7. Formation brute de capital fixe
-0.66	-0.59	0.07	-0.44	-1.00	1.37	0.29	0.02	0.01	-1.20	-1.40	-0.95	0.50	-0.18	0.50	8. Divergence statistique
1923.73	2204.56	2321.48	2404.68	2575.68	2850.09	3144.70	3291.32	3294.04	3394.16	3401.16	3647.90	3881.20	4082.33	4350.59	9. **Formation brute de capital**

RELATIONS ENTRE LES PRINCIPAUX AGRÉGATS [2]

1983	1984	1985	1986	1987	1988	1989	1990	1991	1992	1993	1994	1995	1996	1997	
9308.89	10153.44	10851.41	11417.39	12162.71	13149.98	14209.22	15186.15	15862.93	16812.25	17378.09	18264.68	19329.54	20226.32	21246.09	1. **Produit intérieur brut**
-5.09	-7.34	-14.56	-25.72	-22.25	-22.77	-21.46	-32.03	-33.83	-37.61	-33.51	-61.81	-67.94	-62.52	-64.77	2. *Plus :* Revenu net des facteurs reçu du reste du monde
..	..	..	..	..	..	..	..	..	..	..	..	..	..	..	3. Revenu des facteurs reçu du reste du monde
..	..	..	..	..	..	..	..	..	..	..	..	..	..	..	4. Revenu des facteurs payé au reste du monde
9303.80	10146.10	10836.85	11391.67	12140.46	13127.21	14187.76	15157.81	15829.10	16774.55	17344.68	18202.87	19261.61	20163.80	21181.33	5. *Égal :* **Produit national brut**
1143.73	1211.88	1288.77	1365.97	1453.12	1559.48	1685.64	1797.97	1904.57	2027.12	2091.53	2201.57	2335.07	2432.55	2532.74	6. *Moins :* Consommation de capital fixe
-14.12	-20.72	-22.04	-28.34	-16.02	-13.28	-11.31	-13.42	2.10	-0.17	-3.36	-3.95	2.73	10.14	9.06	7. *Plus :* Divergence statistique
8145.85	8913.49	9526.05	9997.35	10671.31	11554.45	12490.81	13346.33	13926.63	14747.36	15249.79	15997.35	16929.28	17741.30	18657.66	8. *Égal :* **Revenu national**
-21.44	-22.10	-25.56	-27.87	-24.47	-27.82	-36.58	-43.91	-18.72	-71.51	-79.53	-85.30	-76.22	-83.96	-85.63	9. *Plus :* Transferts courants nets reçus du reste du monde
..	..	..	..	..	..	..	..	..	..	..	..	..	..	..	10. Transferts courants reçus du reste du monde
..	..	..	..	..	..	..	..	..	..	..	..	..	..	..	11. Transferts courants payés au reste du monde
8124.40	8891.39	9500.49	9969.48	10646.84	11526.63	12454.23	13302.42	13907.91	14675.85	15170.26	15912.14	16853.05	17657.34	18572.03	12. *Égal :* **Revenu national disponible**
7363.40	7945.78	8528.29	9004.55	9613.52	10330.63	11114.75	11960.72	12598.33	13439.88	13951.87	14588.51	15357.46	16036.83	16781.55	13. *Moins :* Consommation finale
-38.26	-6.27	-2.40	-23.30	15.40	47.30	-13.20	-17.40	-10.10	-44.80	-52.60	-14.60	28.20	62.34	69.30	14. *Plus :* Divergence statistique
722.64	939.44	969.80	941.63	1048.72	1243.29	1326.28	1324.40	1299.48	1191.17	1165.79	1309.03	1523.80	1682.85	1859.67	15. *Égal :* **Épargne nette**
-25.63	-67.60	-98.39	-145.35	-171.79	-195.30	-242.33	-238.16	-72.29	-117.87	-72.33	-104.39	-45.58	-49.52	-38.45	16. *Moins :* Solde des opérations courantes de la nation
32.20	-13.77	-35.45	-47.83	-97.05	-149.44	-109.94	-69.32	17.69	59.31	72.91	33.85	-23.75	-82.51	-80.87	17. *Plus :* Divergence statistique
780.56	993.27	1032.74	1039.15	1123.56	1289.25	1458.67	1493.24	1389.36	1368.34	1311.04	1447.28	1545.53	1649.96	1817.36	18. *Égal :* **Formation nette de capital**

1. Non compris la Corée, la République tchèque, la Hongrie et la Pologne.
2. Aux prix et PPA courants.

OECD-EUROPE[1]

Main aggregates based on PPPs

billions of US dollars

	1960	1969	1970	1971	1972	1973	1974	1975	1976	1977	1978	1979	1980	1981	1982
EXPENDITURE ON THE G.D.P.															
At current prices and current PPPs															
1. Government final consumption expenditure	..	..	164.75	188.55	208.48	234.57	271.84	315.48	349.00	383.20	426.67	482.30	548.73	630.31	676.12
2. Private final consumption expenditure	..	..	652.44	713.75	781.08	871.32	974.31	1077.92	1191.89	1308.29	1437.09	1621.91	1820.14	2028.11	2182.31
3. Households	..	..	..	..	..	..	..	..	..	..	..	..	..	..	..
4. Private non-profit institutions serving households	..	..	..	..	..	..	..	..	..	..	..	..	..	..	..
5. Increase in stocks	..	..	23.14	11.40	8.75	24.77	35.59	−5.25	28.84	20.16	14.59	32.74	32.91	−0.90	1.64
6. Gross fixed capital formation	..	..	264.88	290.02	314.76	358.36	395.30	409.10	447.05	484.29	524.72	596.05	673.72	720.21	740.17
7. **Total Domestic Expenditure**	..	..	1105.21	1203.73	1313.07	1489.02	1677.05	1797.26	2016.79	2195.94	2403.07	2733.00	3075.50	3377.73	3600.24
8. Exports of goods and services	..	..	235.21	257.82	280.88	331.51	420.87	425.72	494.90	552.89	602.90	700.57	787.17	919.19	988.85
9. *Less:* Imports of goods and services	..	..	232.61	250.65	272.27	333.56	447.92	430.90	513.35	556.45	580.49	704.43	829.85	938.36	998.51
10. Statistical discrepancy	..	..	1.55	0.37	2.86	1.37	−0.82	−0.35	−2.87	−0.59	0.10	1.76	−0.52	−3.28	2.31
11. **Gross Domestic Product**	..	..	1109.35	1211.27	1324.54	1488.33	1649.18	1791.73	1995.46	2191.79	2425.58	2730.90	3032.29	3355.28	3592.88
At the price levels and PPPs of 1990															
1. Government final consumption expenditure	..	..	645.32	673.30	702.15	731.15	754.99	789.29	813.08	826.91	856.72	882.52	900.59	923.83	936.43
2. Private final consumption expenditure	..	..	2051.54	2144.48	2254.17	2367.47	2397.18	2444.52	2545.27	2630.26	2711.24	2803.47	2857.72	2858.22	2892.47
3. Households	..	..	..	..	..	..	..	..	..	..	..	..	..	..	..
4. Private non-profit institutions serving households	..	..	..	..	..	..	..	..	..	..	..	..	..	..	..
5. Increase in stocks	..	..	51.75	17.60	8.98	51.10	64.71	−15.17	46.35	32.94	16.87	49.05	36.20	−11.42	−0.67
6. Gross fixed capital formation	..	..	867.14	898.36	936.00	987.90	973.29	928.10	949.61	953.37	961.50	994.08	1009.46	973.88	953.60
7. **Total Domestic Expenditure**	..	..	3615.75	3733.74	3901.29	4137.61	4190.16	4146.73	4354.31	4443.48	4546.33	4729.12	4803.97	4744.52	4781.83
8. Exports of goods and services	..	..	628.07	670.49	723.61	799.48	851.60	820.38	898.66	945.92	995.15	1055.57	1069.45	1115.50	1134.39
9. *Less:* Imports of goods and services	..	..	651.78	688.16	748.08	830.05	847.89	801.46	888.96	910.04	937.45	1024.82	1049.67	1028.33	1044.30
10. Statistical discrepancy	..	..	−13.60	−16.30	−11.17	−21.21	−22.61	−16.58	−26.46	−21.38	−18.81	−18.76	−16.76	−10.69	−5.62
11. **Gross Domestic Product**	..	..	3578.43	3699.78	3865.65	4085.83	4171.27	4149.07	4337.55	4457.98	4585.20	4741.11	4807.00	4821.01	4866.30
COST COMPONENTS OF THE G.D.P.[2]															
1. Indirect taxes	..	..	140.44	151.26	163.60	179.94	192.59	206.69	234.44	262.01	289.36	332.54	374.82	417.46	449.41
2. *Less:* Subsidies	..	..	20.56	22.51	26.15	30.61	38.28	47.47	52.58	58.88	68.40	77.86	85.02	94.69	100.81
3. Consumption of fixed capital	..	..	109.09	121.29	133.66	150.35	176.31	199.02	219.88	244.61	271.09	306.04	349.28	399.94	432.07
4. Compensation of employees paid by resident producers	..	..	561.78	623.23	686.46	776.86	883.69	992.05	1093.47	1194.40	1313.58	1475.13	1648.04	1824.82	1928.89
5. Operating surplus	..	..	309.70	326.87	355.35	399.80	419.32	425.36	480.25	531.12	597.05	670.28	721.75	783.39	856.78
6. Statistical discrepancy	..	..	8.92	11.14	11.62	11.98	15.55	16.08	20.01	18.52	22.90	24.78	23.42	24.35	26.55
7. **Gross Domestic Product**	..	..	1109.36	1211.28	1324.54	1488.33	1649.19	1791.73	1995.46	2191.78	2425.58	2730.91	3032.29	3355.28	3592.88
CAPITAL TRANSACTIONS OF THE NATION[2]															
Finance of Gross Capital Formation															
1. Consumption of fixed capital	..	..	109.09	121.29	133.66	150.35	176.31	199.02	219.88	244.61	271.09	306.04	349.28	399.94	432.07
2. Net saving	..	..	184.17	187.54	203.28	236.35	223.45	190.58	223.39	244.84	279.04	313.72	306.00	277.50	268.78
3. *Less:* Surplus of the nation on current transactions	..	..	2.17	7.96	8.50	−7.07	−44.54	−18.37	−29.69	−18.16	0.87	2.72	−20.68	−20.08	−42.06
4. Statistical discrepancy	..	..	−3.07	0.56	−4.93	−10.64	−13.40	−4.11	2.93	−3.16	−9.94	11.74	30.67	21.79	−1.10
5. **Finance of Gross Capital Formation**	..	..	288.02	301.43	323.51	383.13	430.90	403.86	475.90	504.45	539.31	628.79	706.63	719.31	741.81
Gross capital formation															
6. Increase in stocks	..	..	23.15	11.40	8.75	24.77	35.59	−5.25	28.84	20.16	14.59	32.74	32.91	−0.90	1.64
7. Gross fixed capital formation	..	..	264.88	290.02	314.76	358.36	395.30	409.10	447.05	484.29	524.72	596.05	673.72	720.21	740.17
8. Statistical discrepancy	..	..	..	..	..	..	..	..	..	..	..	..	..	..	..
9. **Gross Capital Formation**	..	..	288.02	301.43	323.51	383.13	430.90	403.86	475.90	504.45	539.31	628.79	706.63	719.31	741.81
RELATIONS AMONG NATIONAL ACCOUNTING AGGREGATES[2]															
1. **Gross Domestic Product**	..	..	1109.36	1211.27	1324.54	1488.33	1649.19	1791.73	1995.46	2191.79	2425.58	2730.90	3032.29	3355.27	3592.88
2. *Plus:* Net factor income from the rest of the world	..	..	4.22	4.92	5.50	7.52	6.85	3.22	3.15	1.23	3.38	7.91	4.16	−1.83	−9.62
3. Factor income from the rest of the world	..	..	..	..	..	..	..	..	..	..	..	..	..	..	..
4. Factor income paid to the rest of the world	..	..	..	..	..	..	..	..	..	..	..	..	..	..	..
5. *Equals:* **Gross National Product**	..	..	1113.57	1216.19	1330.04	1495.85	1656.05	1794.95	1998.61	2193.02	2428.96	2738.81	3036.45	3353.44	3583.26
6. *Less:* Consumption of fixed capital	..	..	109.09	121.29	133.66	150.35	176.31	199.02	219.90	244.61	271.09	306.04	349.28	399.94	432.07
7. *Plus:* Statistical discrepancy	..	..	−3.91	−3.90	−3.26	−3.37	−4.99	−7.58	−8.85	−8.39	−9.23	−10.84	−11.19	−13.36	−19.24
8. *Equals:* **National Income**	..	..	1000.58	1091.00	1193.12	1342.13	1474.75	1588.36	1769.87	1940.02	2148.64	2421.93	2675.98	2940.14	3131.95
9. *Plus:* Net current transfers from the rest of the world	..	..	0.46	0.45	0.85	0.63	−1.21	−1.40	−0.96	−1.89	−1.94	−0.81	0.37	−2.66	−3.50
10. Current transfers from the rest of the world	..	..	..	..	..	..	..	..	..	..	..	..	..	..	..
11. Current transfers paid to the rest of the world	..	..	..	..	..	..	..	..	..	..	..	..	..	..	..
12. *Equals:* **National Disposable Income**	..	..	1001.04	1091.45	1193.97	1342.76	1473.54	1586.95	1768.91	1938.13	2146.71	2421.13	2676.36	2937.48	3128.45
13. *Less:* Final consumption	..	..	817.51	901.19	990.59	1105.56	1243.67	1390.43	1534.76	1688.91	1861.36	2103.72	2367.38	2655.69	2857.42
14. *Plus:* Statistical discrepancy	..	..	0.64	−2.73	−0.10	−0.85	−6.42	−5.95	−10.78	−4.37	−6.31	−3.68	−2.97	−4.29	−2.25
15. *Equals:* **Net Saving**	..	..	184.17	187.53	203.28	236.35	223.45	190.58	223.37	244.84	279.04	313.72	306.00	277.50	268.78
16. *Less:* Surplus of the nation on current transactions	..	..	2.17	7.96	8.50	−7.07	−44.54	−18.37	−29.69	−18.16	0.87	2.72	−20.68	−20.08	−42.06
17. *Plus:* Statistical discrepancy	..	..	−3.07	0.56	−4.93	−10.64	−13.40	−4.11	2.93	−3.16	−9.94	11.74	30.67	21.79	−1.10
18. *Equals:* **Net Capital Formation**	..	..	178.93	180.13	189.85	232.77	254.59	204.84	256.00	259.84	268.22	322.75	357.35	319.37	309.74

1. Excluding Czech Republic, Hungary and Poland.
2. At current prices and current PPPs.

Principaux Agrégats basés sur les PPA

milliards de dollars É-U

1983	1984	1985	1986	1987	1988	1989	1990	1991	1992	1993	1994	1995	1996	1997	
															DÉPENSES IMPUTÉES AU P.I.B.
															Aux prix et PPA courants
721.48	763.17	807.45	843.17	897.05	953.88	1015.27	1106.85	1187.64	1293.20	1323.65	1358.60	1418.43	1479.39	1520.85	1. Consommation finale des administrations publiques
2318.93	2479.78	2629.10	2760.76	2957.66	3165.03	3411.60	3654.96	3887.33	4169.41	4244.34	4422.11	4667.18	4866.20	5092.09	2. Consommation finale privée
..	..	..	..	..	..	..	..	..	..	..	..	..	..	..	3. Ménages
..	..	..	..	..	..	..	..	..	..	..	..	..	..	..	4. Institutions privées sans but lucratif au service des ménages
−0.83	18.21	14.38	19.68	20.30	33.67	42.99	32.41	13.27	−0.27	−21.22	15.21	48.90	9.87	40.02	5. Variations des stocks
766.99	804.63	856.32	906.97	984.92	1108.94	1223.47	1320.24	1360.64	1390.75	1327.04	1372.64	1468.86	1505.96	1576.87	6. Formation brute de capital fixe
3806.57	4065.78	4307.25	4530.58	4859.92	5261.52	5693.33	6114.46	6448.88	6853.08	6873.81	7168.57	7603.36	7861.41	8229.83	7. **Demande intérieure totale**
1061.47	1216.60	1310.35	1237.98	1288.94	1400.20	1578.00	1647.86	1672.48	1767.16	1817.23	2018.01	2261.78	2397.62	2658.18	8. Exportations de biens et services
1045.66	1185.93	1264.37	1172.21	1250.22	1376.18	1570.83	1646.26	1687.12	1763.00	1741.35	1901.03	2137.88	2248.45	2483.75	9. *Moins :* Importations de biens et services
2.70	8.21	8.04	6.80	6.02	9.20	7.79	1.49	−7.99	−10.19	−13.14	−13.32	−8.13	11.81	3.78	10. Divergence statistique
3825.09	4104.66	4361.27	4603.15	4904.66	5294.75	5708.29	6117.55	6426.24	6847.06	6936.55	7272.22	7719.13	8022.39	8408.04	11. **Produit intérieur brut**
															Aux niveaux de prix et PPA de 1990
956.25	970.87	995.26	1019.13	1045.76	1067.84	1079.36	1106.85	1132.51	1156.41	1169.15	1180.79	1192.80	1217.21	1221.62	1. Consommation finale des administrations publiques
2940.11	2993.29	3069.23	3196.47	3309.52	3436.39	3542.20	3654.96	3733.27	3794.35	3798.57	3847.10	3919.97	4014.58	4115.01	2. Consommation finale privée
..	..	..	..	..	..	..	..	..	..	..	..	..	..	..	3. Ménages
..	..	..	..	..	..	..	..	..	..	..	..	..	..	..	4. Institutions privées sans but lucratif au service des ménages
−1.75	14.87	14.40	26.19	25.03	34.37	39.34	32.41	10.95	6.79	−13.57	20.37	46.32	15.61	41.15	5. Variations des stocks
957.03	966.35	992.84	1034.06	1104.07	1191.50	1268.01	1320.24	1327.11	1315.92	1254.21	1273.03	1321.17	1344.23	1392.71	6. Formation brute de capital fixe
4851.64	4945.38	5071.73	5275.84	5484.38	5730.11	5928.92	6114.46	6203.84	6273.48	6208.36	6321.30	6480.27	6591.64	6770.49	7. **Demande intérieure totale**
1170.53	1263.24	1320.61	1334.40	1388.57	1471.61	1583.69	1647.86	1669.71	1734.15	1762.69	1918.91	2067.53	2183.56	2398.87	8. Exportations de biens et services
1060.73	1127.15	1175.22	1235.04	1332.73	1433.55	1558.61	1646.26	1694.40	1758.29	1727.55	1838.25	1979.37	2075.88	2273.54	9. *Moins :* Importations de biens et services
−2.80	4.80	3.54	3.39	6.96	4.21	1.90	1.49	1.67	3.67	3.53	3.08	2.99	2.95	1.61	10. Divergence statistique
4958.64	5086.27	5220.66	5378.59	5547.19	5767.38	5955.90	6117.55	6180.81	6253.01	6247.04	6405.05	6571.41	6702.26	6897.44	11. **Produit intérieur brut**
															RÉPARTITION DU P.I.B. [2]
487.15	526.86	556.28	599.08	646.30	696.43	741.51	787.88	842.69	898.17	916.68	970.41	1026.68	1078.21	1138.15	1. Impôts indirects
108.56	122.76	126.09	131.42	136.91	139.27	139.75	144.26	151.70	156.66	168.34	170.06	167.25	178.50	177.95	2. *Moins :* Subventions
461.19	493.42	523.49	544.90	581.60	626.40	672.49	722.52	764.64	813.40	837.69	873.42	923.29	954.47	990.23	3. Consommation de capital fixe
2018.93	2124.70	2243.34	2345.11	2493.25	2671.88	2877.35	3139.33	3333.89	3554.57	3563.55	3631.27	3802.96	3943.09	4098.90	4. Rémunération des salariés payée par les producteurs résidents
937.60	1047.15	1126.84	1207.32	1280.71	1396.85	1515.25	1593.47	1636.52	1737.45	1786.69	1966.89	2133.10	2225.69	2359.32	5. Excédent net d'exploitation
28.78	35.29	37.41	38.15	39.70	42.46	41.44	18.61	0.21	0.13	0.28	0.28	0.35	−0.57	−0.61	6. Divergence statistique
3825.09	4104.66	4361.27	4603.15	4904.66	5294.75	5708.29	6117.55	6426.24	6847.06	6936.55	7272.22	7719.13	8022.39	8408.04	7. **Produit intérieur brut**
															OPÉRATIONS EN CAPITAL DE LA NATION [2]
															Financement de la formation brute de capital
461.19	493.42	523.49	544.90	581.60	626.40	672.49	722.52	764.64	813.40	837.69	873.42	923.29	954.47	990.23	1. Consommation de capital fixe
291.31	331.22	360.55	415.33	432.65	508.38	567.01	574.47	522.67	494.25	448.21	518.43	620.54	630.32	723.09	2. Épargne nette
−18.36	−14.37	−23.44	−44.05	−69.83	−100.78	−142.99	−140.77	−78.61	−72.63	−6.78	17.33	34.20	56.23	91.64	3. *Moins :* Solde des opérations courantes de la nation
−4.70	−16.17	−36.78	−77.63	−78.88	−92.95	−116.04	−85.12	7.99	10.19	13.14	13.32	8.13	−12.73	−4.78	4. Divergence statistique
766.16	822.84	870.70	926.65	1005.21	1142.61	1266.46	1352.65	1373.91	1390.48	1305.82	1387.85	1517.76	1515.83	1616.89	5. **Financement de la formation brute de capital**
															Formation brute de capital
−0.83	18.21	14.38	19.68	20.30	33.67	42.99	32.41	13.27	−0.27	−21.22	15.21	48.90	9.87	40.02	6. Variations des stocks
766.99	804.63	856.32	906.97	984.92	1108.94	1223.47	1320.24	1360.64	1390.75	1327.04	1372.64	1468.86	1505.96	1576.87	7. Formation brute de capital fixe
..	..	..	..	..	..	..	..	..	..	..	..	..	..	..	8. Divergence statistique
766.16	822.84	870.70	926.65	1005.21	1142.61	1266.46	1352.65	1373.91	1390.48	1305.82	1387.85	1517.76	1515.83	1616.89	9. **Formation brute de capital**
															RELATIONS ENTRE LES PRINCIPAUX AGRÉGATS [2]
3825.09	4104.66	4361.27	4603.15	4904.66	5294.75	5708.29	6117.55	6426.24	6847.06	6936.55	7272.22	7719.13	8022.39	8408.04	1. **Produit intérieur brut**
−9.23	−8.93	−9.63	−8.84	−8.54	−14.59	−11.35	−27.96	−30.14	−35.51	−39.02	−50.47	−42.53	−44.21	−32.52	2. *Plus :* Revenu net des facteurs reçu du reste du monde
															3. Revenu des facteurs reçu du reste du monde
..	..	..	..	..	..	..	..	..	..	..	..	..	..	..	4. Revenu des facteurs payé au reste du monde
3815.86	4095.74	4351.64	4594.31	4896.12	5280.15	5696.94	6093.27	6396.11	6811.55	6897.53	7221.75	7676.60	7978.18	8375.52	5. *Égal :* **Produit national brut**
461.19	493.42	523.49	544.90	581.60	626.40	672.49	722.52	764.64	813.40	837.69	873.42	923.29	954.47	990.23	6. *Moins :* Consommation de capital fixe
−20.00	−25.23	−27.09	−22.73	−22.22	−20.25	−15.88	−12.51	0.00	0.00	0.00	0.00	0.00	0.00	0.00	7. *Plus :* Divergence statistique
3334.67	3577.09	3801.06	4026.68	4292.30	4633.50	5008.57	5358.24	5631.47	5998.16	6059.84	6348.33	6753.31	7023.71	7385.30	8. *Égal :* **Revenu national**
−3.15	−0.75	−3.95	−7.41	−4.94	−6.20	−14.69	−21.95	−33.83	−41.29	−43.64	−49.18	−47.16	−48.72	−50.27	9. *Plus :* Transferts courants nets reçus du reste du monde
..	..	..	..	..	..	..	..	..	..	..	..	..	..	..	10. Transferts courants reçus du reste du monde
..	..	..	..	..	..	..	..	..	..	..	..	..	..	..	11. Transferts courants payés au reste du monde
3331.52	3576.33	3797.10	4019.26	4287.36	4627.30	4993.88	5336.28	5597.64	5956.86	6016.20	6299.15	6706.15	6974.98	7335.03	12. *Égal :* **Revenu national disponible**
3039.05	3243.84	3436.55	3603.93	3854.71	4118.92	4426.87	4761.81	5074.97	5462.61	5567.99	5780.72	6085.60	6347.10	6615.04	13. *Moins :* Consommation finale
−1.16	−1.27	0.00	0.00	0.00	0.00	0.00	0.00	0.00	0.00	0.00	0.00	0.00	2.44	3.10	14. *Plus :* Divergence statistique
291.31	331.22	360.55	415.33	432.65	508.38	567.01	574.47	522.67	494.25	448.21	518.43	620.54	630.32	723.09	15. *Égal :* **Épargne nette**
−18.36	−14.37	−23.44	−44.05	−69.83	−100.78	−142.99	−140.77	−78.61	−72.63	−6.78	17.33	34.20	56.23	91.64	16. *Moins :* Solde des opérations courantes de la nation
−4.70	−16.17	−36.78	−77.63	−78.88	−92.95	−116.04	−85.12	7.99	10.19	13.14	13.32	8.13	−12.73	−4.78	17. *Plus :* Divergence statistique
304.97	329.41	347.21	381.75	423.61	516.21	593.97	630.13	609.27	577.08	468.13	514.43	594.47	561.36	626.67	18. *Égal :* **Formation nette de capital**

1. Non compris la République tchèque, la Hongrie et la Pologne.
2. Aux prix et PPA courants.

EU15

Main aggregates based on PPPs

billions of US dollars

	1960	1969	1970	1971	1972	1973	1974	1975	1976	1977	1978	1979	1980	1981	1982
EXPENDITURE ON THE G.D.P.															
At current prices and current PPPs															
1. Government final consumption expenditure	..	..	156.44	178.87	197.50	222.01	258.00	298.82	329.13	360.24	402.92	456.78	523.77	598.92	643.82
2. Private final consumption expenditure	..	..	603.47	658.87	720.68	806.06	900.10	994.88	1099.83	1204.60	1322.19	1494.47	1674.35	1873.29	2012.46
3. Households	..	..	..	..	..	..	..	..	..	..	..	..	..	..	..
4. Private non-profit institutions serving households	..	..	..	..	..	..	..	..	..	..	..	..	..	..	..
5. Increase in stocks	..	..	20.50	9.32	7.45	23.16	31.19	−7.09	27.61	20.23	16.03	33.69	28.37	−4.99	0.40
6. Gross fixed capital formation	..	..	246.46	269.18	291.78	332.70	366.80	378.38	411.54	445.38	486.57	553.28	628.99	665.27	682.24
7. **Total Domestic Expenditure**	..	..	1026.86	1116.24	1217.41	1383.93	1556.10	1664.99	1868.12	2030.46	2227.71	2538.22	2855.47	3132.48	3338.92
8. Exports of goods and services	..	..	219.26	240.73	262.17	309.99	396.10	400.94	466.68	521.81	568.88	661.84	739.17	860.92	924.56
9. *Less:* Imports of goods and services	..	..	215.71	231.81	252.29	310.70	419.26	402.65	481.31	519.59	545.41	663.26	775.33	877.54	933.62
10. Statistical discrepancy	..	..	1.66	0.53	2.91	1.48	−0.58	−0.36	−2.86	−0.56	−0.24	1.55	−0.52	−3.28	2.31
11. **Gross Domestic Product**	..	..	1032.07	1125.69	1230.20	1384.70	1532.36	1662.92	1850.63	2032.13	2250.95	2538.35	2818.79	3112.58	3332.18
At the price levels and PPPs of 1990															
1. Government final consumption expenditure	..	..	617.90	644.25	671.71	699.16	721.56	752.75	773.34	786.03	815.43	840.94	861.06	877.22	891.36
2. Private final consumption expenditure	..	..	1889.00	1970.65	2070.52	2179.91	2216.31	2257.12	2346.45	2406.80	2484.15	2575.76	2620.09	2629.81	2654.91
3. Households	..	..	..	..	..	..	..	..	..	..	..	..	..	..	..
4. Private non-profit institutions serving households	..	..	..	..	..	..	..	..	..	..	..	..	..	..	..
5. Increase in stocks	..	..	46.59	14.31	8.65	49.68	57.00	−17.63	45.47	35.22	22.32	52.64	32.38	−13.62	−1.00
6. Gross fixed capital formation	..	..	812.01	840.00	873.56	921.10	895.97	851.49	867.17	878.68	893.14	923.45	941.23	897.28	879.69
7. **Total Domestic Expenditure**	..	..	3365.50	3469.21	3624.44	3849.85	3890.84	3843.72	4032.43	4106.73	4215.03	4392.79	4454.76	4390.69	4424.96
8. Exports of goods and services	..	..	586.35	626.88	675.84	747.19	799.75	769.57	841.64	888.55	933.16	992.85	1004.45	1043.52	1059.74
9. *Less:* Imports of goods and services	..	..	607.11	640.28	696.96	772.93	789.54	744.45	824.65	843.02	875.28	961.03	975.59	952.75	966.66
10. Statistical discrepancy	..	..	−15.62	−17.44	−13.01	−22.79	−25.28	−18.07	−26.71	−19.03	−17.83	−17.81	−15.07	−9.17	−4.85
11. **Gross Domestic Product**	..	..	3329.13	3438.37	3590.31	3801.32	3875.78	3850.78	4022.71	4133.23	4255.09	4406.81	4468.55	4472.29	4513.19
COST COMPONENTS OF THE G.D.P. [1]															
1. Indirect taxes	..	..	133.61	143.57	154.79	170.62	182.20	195.03	221.14	246.98	273.44	315.67	355.96	395.88	427.54
2. *Less:* Subsidies	..	..	19.48	21.33	24.87	29.29	36.35	45.24	49.69	55.06	63.77	72.67	79.81	88.73	94.78
3. Consumption of fixed capital	..	..	100.02	111.25	122.60	138.61	163.02	185.26	204.74	227.48	252.44	285.70	326.70	374.38	404.50
4. Compensation of employees paid by resident producers	..	..	529.45	586.95	646.52	732.65	834.49	937.08	1031.96	1127.34	1240.06	1392.90	1560.62	1728.27	1826.64
5. Operating surplus	..	..	279.31	293.94	319.35	359.97	373.31	374.76	422.69	467.06	525.97	592.16	632.09	678.61	741.96
6. Statistical discrepancy	..	..	9.16	11.31	11.81	12.15	15.70	16.02	19.79	18.32	22.81	24.59	23.24	24.16	26.32
7. **Gross Domestic Product**	..	..	1032.07	1125.69	1230.19	1384.69	1532.36	1662.92	1850.63	2032.12	2250.95	2538.35	2818.79	3112.58	3332.18
CAPITAL TRANSACTIONS OF THE NATION [1]															
Finance of Gross Capital Formation															
1. Consumption of fixed capital	..	..	100.02	111.25	122.60	138.61	163.02	185.26	204.74	227.48	252.44	285.70	326.70	374.38	404.50
2. Net saving	..	..	171.85	174.64	189.12	219.21	204.79	172.44	203.42	226.80	260.04	292.68	283.48	243.11	235.09
3. *Less:* Surplus of the nation on current transactions	..	..	2.30	8.32	8.39	−7.86	−43.05	−15.34	−25.52	−12.12	3.22	5.15	−16.51	−21.00	−44.16
4. Statistical discrepancy	..	..	−2.61	0.93	−4.09	−9.81	−12.86	−1.75	5.49	−0.78	−6.67	13.73	30.67	21.79	−1.10
5. **Finance of Gross Capital Formation**	..	..	266.96	278.50	299.23	355.86	397.99	371.29	439.16	465.62	502.60	586.97	657.35	660.28	632.64
Gross capital formation															
6. Increase in stocks	..	..	20.50	9.32	7.45	23.16	31.19	−7.09	27.61	20.23	16.03	33.69	28.37	−4.99	0.40
7. Gross fixed capital formation	..	..	246.46	269.18	291.78	332.70	366.80	378.38	411.54	445.38	486.57	553.28	628.99	665.27	682.24
8. Statistical discrepancy	..	..	..	..	..	..	..	..	..	..	..	..	..	..	..
9. **Gross Capital Formation**	..	..	266.96	278.50	299.23	355.86	397.99	371.29	439.16	465.62	502.60	586.97	657.35	660.28	682.64
RELATIONS AMONG NATIONAL ACCOUNTING AGGREGATES [1]															
1. **Gross Domestic Product**	..	..	1032.07	1125.69	1230.20	1384.69	1532.36	1662.92	1850.62	2032.12	2250.95	2538.35	2818.79	3112.57	3332.18
2. *Plus:* Net factor income from the rest of the world	..	..	2.88	3.02	3.23	4.41	3.62	0.52	0.92	−1.17	1.43	5.66	1.07	−6.26	−13.50
3. Factor income from the rest of the world	..	..	..	..	..	..	..	..	..	..	..	..	..	..	..
4. Factor income paid to the rest of the world	..	..	..	..	..	..	..	..	..	..	..	..	..	..	..
5. *Equals:* **Gross National Product**	..	..	1034.95	1128.71	1233.43	1389.11	1535.99	1663.44	1851.54	2030.95	2252.38	2544.01	2819.86	3106.32	3318.68
6. *Less:* Consumption of fixed capital	..	..	100.02	111.25	122.60	138.61	163.02	185.26	204.74	227.48	252.44	285.70	326.70	374.38	404.50
7. *Plus:* Statistical discrepancy	..	..	−4.09	−4.07	−3.47	−3.61	−5.26	−7.89	−9.05	−8.48	−9.32	−10.88	−11.19	−13.36	−19.24
8. *Equals:* **National Income**	..	..	930.84	1013.39	1107.36	1246.89	1367.70	1470.29	1637.74	1795.00	1990.62	2247.43	2481.98	2718.57	2894.94
9. *Plus:* Net current transfers from the rest of the world	..	..	0.59	0.60	1.07	0.91	−0.87	−1.17	−0.74	−1.56	−1.56	−0.31	1.11	−1.70	−2.33
10. Current transfers from the rest of the world	..	..	..	..	..	..	..	..	..	..	..	..	..	..	..
11. Current transfers paid to the rest of the world	..	..	..	..	..	..	..	..	..	..	..	..	..	..	..
12. *Equals:* **National Disposable Income**	..	..	931.43	1014.00	1108.43	1247.79	1366.82	1469.12	1637.00	1793.44	1989.07	2247.12	2483.08	2716.87	2892.61
13. *Less:* Final consumption	..	..	760.23	836.62	919.21	1027.74	1155.62	1290.73	1422.82	1562.26	1722.71	1950.76	2196.63	2469.47	2655.27
14. *Plus:* Statistical discrepancy	..	..	0.64	−2.73	−0.10	−0.85	−6.42	−5.95	−10.78	−4.37	−6.31	−3.68	−2.97	−4.29	−2.25
15. *Equals:* **Net Saving**	..	..	171.85	174.64	189.12	219.21	204.79	172.44	203.40	226.80	260.04	292.68	283.48	243.11	235.09
16. *Less:* Surplus of the nation on current transactions	..	..	2.30	8.32	8.39	−7.86	−43.05	−15.34	−25.52	−12.12	3.22	5.15	−16.51	−21.00	−44.16
17. *Plus:* Statistical discrepancy	..	..	−2.61	0.93	−4.09	−9.81	−12.86	−1.75	5.49	−0.78	−6.67	13.73	30.67	21.79	−1.10
18. *Equals:* **Net Capital Formation**	..	..	166.94	167.26	176.64	217.25	234.97	186.03	234.40	238.14	250.16	301.27	330.66	285.90	278.15

1. At current prices and current PPPs.

Principaux Agrégats basés sur les PPA

milliards de dollars É-U

1983	1984	1985	1986	1987	1988	1989	1990	1991	1992	1993	1994	1995	1996	1997	
															DÉPENSES IMPUTÉES AU P.I.B.
															Aux prix et PPA courants
684.98	726.15	767.53	799.69	852.01	906.41	960.55	1041.58	1114.04	1211.14	1235.61	1275.07	1332.88	1386.09	1419.28	1. Consommation finale des administrations publiques
2133.72	2275.30	2415.68	2536.23	2710.66	2915.79	3145.00	3352.04	3562.27	3820.55	3868.33	4045.79	4261.60	4447.48	4638.99	2. Consommation finale privée
..	..	..	..	..	..	..	..	..	..	..	..	..	..	..	3.　Ménages
1.76	17.68	12.17	15.84	16.90	35.22	39.79	25.63	15.79	0.02	−24.46	25.21	40.01	9.19	41.50	4.　Institutions privées sans but lucratif au service des ménages
															5. Variations des stocks
704.49	736.67	779.10	816.10	885.70	993.91	1115.45	1203.99	1239.40	1265.68	1184.31	1235.94	1325.99	1350.87	1403.53	6. Formation brute de capital fixe
3524.95	3755.79	3974.48	4167.86	4465.25	4856.33	5260.78	5623.24	5931.50	6297.39	6263.80	6582.02	6960.49	7193.63	7503.30	7. **Demande intérieure totale**
991.00	1132.05	1217.25	1150.82	1193.98	1291.57	1461.98	1528.79	1548.35	1632.89	1676.19	1850.74	2089.07	2204.75	2432.33	8. Exportations de biens et services
974.57	1101.09	1172.35	1080.48	1150.22	1270.13	1453.57	1521.59	1563.69	1631.49	1595.88	1750.71	1963.24	2049.03	2250.52	9. *Moins :* Importations de biens et services
2.70	8.21	8.04	6.80	5.16	3.34	0.49	0.45	0.00	−0.36	0.27	−0.33	−0.81	0.94	2.13	10. Divergence statistique
3544.08	3794.96	4027.42	4245.00	4514.18	4881.11	5269.68	5630.89	5916.15	6298.42	6344.38	6681.72	7085.51	7350.29	7687.24	11. **Produit intérieur brut**
															Aux niveaux de prix et PPA de 1990
907.49	921.36	942.09	963.05	986.42	1007.98	1018.02	1041.58	1064.80	1086.60	1096.34	1109.14	1118.96	1139.65	1142.03	1. Consommation finale des administrations publiques
2692.38	2732.11	2804.60	2919.32	3031.10	3155.55	3261.50	3352.04	3423.41	3477.68	3465.48	3522.79	3584.17	3658.66	3737.61	2. Consommation finale privée
..	..	..	..	..	..	..	..	..	..	..	..	..	..	..	3.　Ménages
1.73	15.52	13.07	20.90	21.12	36.81	37.95	25.63	13.40	7.24	−16.73	28.77	38.99	14.70	42.83	4.　Institutions privées sans but lucratif au service des ménages
															5. Variations des stocks
880.47	887.96	911.00	946.46	999.00	1084.65	1159.55	1203.99	1211.77	1199.83	1121.52	1150.35	1191.04	1202.77	1235.56	6. Formation brute de capital fixe
4482.07	4556.95	4670.76	4849.72	5037.64	5284.99	5477.02	5623.24	5713.38	5771.34	5666.61	5811.04	5933.16	6015.78	6158.02	7. **Demande intérieure totale**
1091.88	1175.17	1228.04	1242.65	1289.47	1362.79	1468.98	1528.79	1548.67	1605.94	1629.44	1774.95	1917.09	2015.83	2210.84	8. Exportations de biens et services
978.30	1035.44	1082.10	1136.94	1227.01	1332.69	1447.35	1521.59	1572.87	1634.06	1584.85	1704.80	1826.31	1904.92	2076.29	9. *Moins :* Importations de biens et services
−1.29	5.82	4.32	4.68	5.47	1.73	−0.38	0.45	1.32	1.37	3.24	2.49	1.27	2.66	1.14	10. Divergence statistique
4594.35	4702.51	4821.03	4960.11	5316.81	5316.81	5498.27	5630.89	5690.50	5744.60	5714.44	5883.69	6025.21	6129.36	6293.71	11. **Produit intérieur brut**
															RÉPARTITION DU P.I.B. [1]
461.59	500.34	526.07	563.71	606.99	656.16	700.43	740.51	790.97	841.62	853.90	908.86	958.62	1002.59	1057.02	1. Impôts indirects
101.65	115.05	118.56	124.09	130.39	132.13	131.89	135.42	140.55	142.78	154.58	154.90	155.57	164.02	162.86	2. *Moins :* Subventions
431.42	461.23	488.36	506.96	536.81	576.70	620.67	668.19	706.42	750.94	773.02	804.88	853.85	883.62	916.15	3. Consommation de capital fixe
1909.55	2008.90	2119.17	2210.30	2344.21	2511.60	2702.51	2939.30	3109.83	3313.67	3311.51	3395.88	3562.92	3685.68	3824.91	4. Rémunération des salariés payée par les producteurs résidents
814.64	904.43	975.16	1050.19	1116.94	1225.43	1336.69	1399.94	1449.48	1534.97	1560.54	1727.00	1865.69	1943.34	2053.01	5. Excédent net d'exploitation
28.53	35.12	37.22	37.91	39.63	42.36	41.26	18.37	0.00	0.00	0.00	0.00	0.00	−0.92	−1.00	6. Divergence statistique
3544.08	3794.96	4027.42	4245.00	4514.18	4881.11	5269.68	5630.89	5916.15	6298.42	6344.38	6681.72	7085.51	7350.29	7687.24	7. **Produit intérieur brut**
															OPÉRATIONS EN CAPITAL DE LA NATION [1]
															Financement de la formation brute de capital
431.42	461.23	488.36	506.96	536.81	576.70	620.67	668.19	706.42	750.94	773.02	804.88	853.85	883.62	916.15	1. Consommation de capital fixe
259.84	291.15	310.47	360.20	375.74	433.14	495.50	505.65	466.08	434.66	380.13	454.05	540.72	532.60	617.59	2. Épargne nette
−19.69	−18.14	−29.22	−42.40	−68.06	−106.39	−147.81	−139.85	−82.69	−79.73	−6.98	−1.90	29.38	54.29	85.58	3. *Moins :* Solde des opérations courantes de la nation
−4.70	−16.17	−36.78	−77.63	−78.02	−87.10	−108.74	−84.07	0.00	0.36	−0.27	0.33	0.81	−1.87	−3.13	4. Divergence statistique
706.25	754.34	791.27	831.94	902.59	1034.13	1155.24	1229.62	1255.19	1265.70	1159.86	1261.01	1366.01	1360.07	1445.03	5. **Financement de la formation brute de capital**
															Formation brute de capital
1.76	17.68	12.17	15.84	16.90	35.22	39.79	25.63	15.79	0.02	−24.46	25.21	40.01	9.19	41.50	6. Variations des stocks
704.49	736.67	779.10	816.10	885.70	998.91	1115.45	1203.99	1239.40	1265.68	1184.31	1235.94	1325.99	1350.88	1403.53	7. Formation brute de capital fixe
..	..	..	..	..	..	..	..	..	..	..	..	..	..	..	8. Divergence statistique
706.25	754.34	791.27	831.94	902.59	1034.13	1155.24	1229.62	1255.19	1265.70	1159.86	1261.16	1366.01	1360.06	1445.03	9. **Formation brute de capital**
															RELATIONS ENTRE LES PRINCIPAUX AGRÉGATS [1]
3544.08	3794.96	4027.42	4245.00	4514.18	4881.11	5269.68	5630.89	5916.15	6298.42	6344.38	6681.72	7085.51	7350.29	7687.24	1. **Produit intérieur brut**
−12.36	−14.22	−15.65	−13.21	−13.37	−19.23	−19.06	−34.54	−35.67	−42.46	−46.49	−56.22	−52.96	−55.94	−49.31	2. *Plus :* Revenu net des facteurs reçu du reste du monde
															3.　Revenu des facteurs reçu du reste du monde
..	..	..	..	..	..	..	..	..	..	..	..	..	..	..	4.　Revenu des facteurs payé au reste du monde
3531.72	3780.75	4011.77	4231.79	4500.82	4861.87	5250.62	5600.03	5880.49	6255.96	6297.89	6625.50	7032.55	7294.35	7637.94	5. *Égal :* **Produit national brut**
431.42	461.23	488.36	506.96	536.81	576.70	620.67	668.19	706.42	750.94	773.02	804.88	853.85	883.62	916.15	6. *Moins :* Consommation de capital fixe
−20.00	−25.23	−27.09	−22.73	−22.22	−20.25	−15.88	−12.51	0.00	0.00	0.00	0.00	0.00	0.00	0.00	7. *Plus :* Divergence statistique
3080.31	3294.29	3496.32	3702.09	3941.78	4264.92	4614.07	4919.33	5174.07	5505.02	5524.87	5820.62	6178.70	6410.73	6721.79	8. *Égal :* **Revenu national**
−1.96	0.48	−2.64	−5.97	−3.38	−4.58	−13.02	−20.06	−31.68	−38.67	−40.80	−45.71	−43.49	−45.48	−46.93	9. *Plus :* Transferts courants nets reçus du reste du monde
..	..	..	..	..	..	..	..	..	..	..	..	..	..	..	10.　Transferts courants reçus du reste du monde
..	..	..	..	..	..	..	..	..	..	..	..	..	..	..	11.　Transferts courants payés au reste du monde
3078.35	3294.77	3493.68	3696.12	3938.40	4260.34	4601.05	4899.27	5142.39	5466.35	5484.07	5774.91	6135.21	6365.25	6674.86	12. *Égal :* **Revenu national disponible**
2817.35	3002.35	3183.21	3335.92	3562.66	3822.20	4105.55	4393.62	4676.31	5031.69	5103.94	5320.86	5594.48	5835.08	6060.36	13. *Moins :* Consommation finale
−1.16	−1.27	0.00	0.00	0.00	0.00	0.00	0.00	0.00	0.00	0.00	0.00	0.00	2.44	3.10	14. *Plus :* Divergence statistique
259.84	291.15	310.47	360.20	375.74	438.14	495.50	505.65	466.09	434.66	380.13	454.05	540.72	532.60	617.59	15. *Égal :* **Épargne nette**
−19.69	−18.14	−29.22	−42.40	−68.06	−106.39	−147.81	−139.85	−82.69	−79.73	−6.98	−1.90	29.38	54.29	85.58	16. *Moins :* Solde des opérations courantes de la nation
−4.70	−16.17	−36.78	−77.63	−78.02	−87.10	−108.74	−84.07	0.00	0.36	−0.27	0.33	0.81	−1.87	−3.13	17. *Plus :* Divergence statistique
274.83	293.12	302.91	324.98	365.78	457.43	534.57	561.43	548.78	514.76	386.84	456.27	512.15	476.45	528.88	18. *Égal :* **Formation nette de capital**

1. Aux prix et PPA courants.

Main aggregates: Countries
Principaux agrégats : Pays

The statistics for Germany in this publication refer to Germany after unification. Official data for Germany after unification are available only from 1991 onwards. In this publication, the secretariat has estimated some national accounts aggregates for the whole of Germany back to 1960 in order to calculate the various zones totals. These estimates are based on statistics published by Deutsches Institut für Wirtschaftsforschung for period 1989-90 and by the East German Statistical Office in 1990 for period 1980-89. They are also based on the ratios of the aggregates of West Germany and the whole of Germany.

Les statistiques concernant l'Allemagne dans cette publication se réfèrent à l'Allemagne après l'unification. Des données officielles pour l'Allemagne après l'unification ne sont disponibles qu'à partir de 1991. Dans cette publication, le secrétariat a estimé certains agrégats des comptes nationaux pour l'Allemagne dans son ensemble depuis 1960 afin de calculer les différentes zones. Ces estimations sont basées sur des statistiques publiées par Deutsches Institut für Wirtschaftsforschung pour la période 1989-90 et par l'Office Statistique de l'Allemagne de l'Est en 1990 pour la période 1980-89. Elles sont aussi basées sur les rapports des agrégats de l'Allemagne occidentale et de l'Allemagne dans son ensemble.

This part presents for each country, in national currency, the following tables:

– Expenditure on the gross domestic product, at current and constant prices.
– Cost components of G.D.P.
– Capital transactions of the nation.
– Relations among national accounting aggregates.

To facilitate inter-country comparisons the constant price data are shown at the price levels of 1990. For countries that do not use 1990 as the base year calculating their constant price series, the constant price data for each aggregate have been scaled up by the ratio in 1990 of the current value of that aggregate to its value at the prices of the base year used by the country concerned. This scaling procedure in no way alters the fact that the constant price series concerned still reflect the *relative* prices of the years actually used. The base years used are given in the tables when they differ from 1990.

Cette partie fournit pour chaque pays, en monnaie nationale, les tableaux suivants :

– Produit intérieur brut et ses emplois aux prix courants et aux prix constants.
– Répartition du P.I.B.
– Opérations en capital de la nation.
– Relations entre les principaux agrégats de la Comptabilité nationale.

Pour faciliter les comparaisons entre pays, les séries à prix constants sont montrées, aux niveaux de prix de 1990. Pour les pays n'utilisant pas 1990 comme année de base de leurs séries à prix constants, les données à prix constants de chaque agrégat ont été multipliées par le rapport en 1990 de la valeur courante de cet agrégat à sa valeur aux prix de l'année de base utilisée par le pays concerné. Cette procédure ne modifie pas le fait que les séries ainsi rebasées aux prix de 1990 reflètent toujours les prix *relatifs* de l'année de base réellement utilisée. Les années de base utilisées sont précisées dans les tableaux lorsqu'elles diffèrent de 1990.

CANADA
1993 SNA

Main aggregates

millions of Canadian dollars

	1960	1969	1970	1971	1972	1973	1974	1975	1976	1977	1978	1979	1980	1981	1982
EXPENDITURE ON THE G.D.P.															
At current prices															
1. Government final consumption expenditure	5649*	15896	18459	20365	22584	25612	31058	37738	43326	49122	53436	59047	67024	76408	86928
2. Private final consumption expenditure	25124*	46925	49435	53797	60209	68885	80260	92797	105639	117844	131690	147194	165469	187050	200698
3. Households	..	..	..	..	..	..	..	..	..	..	..	..	..	..	..
4. Private non-profit institutions serving households	..	..	..	..	..	..	..	..	..	..	..	..	..	..	..
5. Increase in stocks	413*	1479	240	370	781	1866	3592	1368	2331	1864	952	4794	−679	973	−9947
6. Gross fixed capital formation	8946*	18281	19166	21732	24025	28977	36015	41995	46835	50394	54975	63829	72938	87511	82060
7. **Total Domestic Expenditure**	40132*	82581	87300	96264	107599	125340	150925	173898	198131	219224	241053	274864	304752	351942	359739
8. Exports of goods and services	6741*	17818	20124	21023	23710	29738	37593	38763	44072	50955	60985	74708	87689	96288	96640
9. *Less:* Imports of goods and services	7287*	17732	17831	19405	22726	27938	37411	41875	45576	51449	60214	73332	82169	94029	82383
10. Statistical discrepancy	−181*	208	−481	−626	−2	305	1032	649	941	−435	177	250	743	1540	723
11. **Gross Domestic Product**	39405*	82875	89112	97256	108581	127445	152139	171435	197568	218295	242001	276490	311015	355741	374719
At 1990 price levels[1]															
1. Government final consumption expenditure	42416*	75083	81651	85017	87621	91762	97478	104175	106191	111062	112908	114259	118117	119912	122472
2. Private final consumption expenditure	122546*	179964	182942	194140	207431	221708	233152	243024	256029	263425	272298	279502	285147	289767	282424
3. Households	..	..	..	..	..	..	..	..	..	..	..	..	..	..	..
4. Private non-profit institutions serving households	..	..	..	..	..	..	..	..	..	..	..	..	..	..	..
5. Increase in stocks	61*	4173	325	799	1786	4113	7819	2190	4128	2638	1550	7896	−888	703	−12177
6. Gross fixed capital formation	33150*	52740	52965	57026	59347	64898	69304	73090	76319	77914	80554	87213	95798	107824	95084
7. **Total Domestic Expenditure**	198173*	311960	317883	336982	356185	382481	407753	422479	442667	455039	467310	488870	498174	518206	487803
8. Exports of goods and services	26329*	58201	63648	66434	72101	79694	77620	72596	80345	86525	95847	99186	100772	104404	102714
9. *Less:* Imports of goods and services	23767*	47238	46391	49441	56558	64770	72005	70555	76136	76867	81184	87816	92274	101974	85712
10. Statistical discrepancy	2952*	2580	−1227	−1467	−594	307	590	−1210	−381	−3197	−1809	−118	143	1913	1828
11. **Gross Domestic Product**	203687*	325503	333913	352508	371134	397712	413958	423310	446495	461500	480164	500122	506815	522549	506633
COST COMPONENTS OF THE G.D.P.															
1. Indirect taxes	4984*	11518	12228	13332	15007	17055	21300	22000	25678	28248	30225	33053	37375	48753	51253
2. *Less:* Subsidies	336*	732	785	860	929	1178	2920	4371	3984	4078	4146	5686	8628	9934	9635
3. Consumption of fixed capital	4861*	9485	10335	11241	12207	14203	17182	19676	22462	24905	27808	32073	37212	42443	46009
4. Compensation of employees paid by resident producers	20133*	45065	48851	53555	60109	69243	82571	96306	111412	123390	134216	150946	170642	196716	210085
5. Operating surplus	9536*	17747	18001	19362	22185	28427	35038	38474	42941	45394	54075	66355	75158	79303	77730
6. Statistical discrepancy	227*	−208	482	626	2	−305	−1032	−650	−941	436	−177	−251	−744	−1540	−723
7. **Gross Domestic Product**	39405*	82875	89112	97256	108581	127445	152139	171435	197568	218295	242001	276490	311015	355741	374719
CAPITAL TRANSACTIONS OF THE NATION															
Finance of Gross Capital Formation															
1. Consumption of fixed capital	4861*	9485	10335	11241	12207	14203	17182	19676	22462	24905	27808	32073	37212	42443	46009
2. Net saving	2803*	9538	8944	9702	11997	17153	22296	19029	23367	21185	22953	30750	33765	39559	28937
3. *Less:* Surplus of the nation on current transactions	−1260*	−1153	836	93	−598	−97	−2193	−5957	−5219	−5297	−5520	−6301	−2769	−9562	1387
4. Statistical discrepancy	218*	−208	482	626	2	−305	−1032	−650	−941	436	−177	−251	−744	−1540	−723
5. **Finance of Gross Capital Formation**	9142*	19968	18925	21476	24804	31148	40639	44012	50107	51823	56104	68873	73002	90024	72836
Gross capital formation															
6. Increase in stocks	413*	1479	240	370	781	1866	3592	1368	2331	1864	952	4794	−679	973	−9947
7. Gross fixed capital formation	8946*	18281	19166	21732	24025	28977	36015	41995	46835	50394	54975	63829	72938	87511	82060
8. Statistical discrepancy	−217*	208	−481	−626	−2	305	1032	649	941	−435	177	250	743	1540	723
9. **Gross Capital Formation**	9142*	19968	18925	21476	24804	31148	40639	44012	50107	51823	56104	68873	73002	90024	72836
RELATIONS AMONG NATIONAL ACCOUNTING AGGREGATES															
1. **Gross Domestic Product**	39406*	82875	89112	97256	108581	127445	152139	171435	197568	218295	242001	276490	311015	355741	374719
2. *Plus:* Net factor income from the rest of the world	−616*	−1165	−1350	−1456	−1463	−1797	−2276	−2586	−3539	−4573	−5949	−7444	−8243	−11781	−12711
3. Factor income from the rest of the world	255*	1085	1347	1473	1577	2327	3322	3194	2820	3240	4649	7068	7558	11227	11831
4. Factor income paid to the rest of the world	871*	2250	2697	2929	3040	4124	5598	5780	6359	7813	10598	14512	15801	23008	24542
5. *Equals:* **Gross National Product**	38790*	81710	87762	95800	107118	125648	149863	168849	194029	213722	236052	269046	302772	343960	362008
6. *Less:* Consumption of fixed capital	4861*	9485	10335	11241	12207	14203	17182	19676	22462	24905	27808	32073	37212	42443	46009
7. *Plus:* Statistical discrepancy	−423*	208	−482	−626	−2	305	1032	650	941	−436	177	251	744	1540	723
8. *Equals:* **National Income**	33506*	72433	76945	83933	94909	111750	133713	149823	172508	188381	208421	237224	266304	303057	316722
9. *Plus:* Net current transfers from the rest of the world	70*	−86	−116	−69	−119	−100	−99	−259	−176	−230	−342	−233	−46	−40	−159
10. Current transfers from the rest of the world	126*	331	383	443	458	541	663	722	779	863	964	1214	1532	1659	1804
11. Current transfers paid to the rest of the world	191*	417	499	512	577	641	762	981	955	1093	1306	1447	1578	1699	1963
12. *Equals:* **National Disposable Income**	33576*	72347	76829	83864	94790	111650	133614	149564	172332	188151	208079	236991	266258	303017	316563
13. *Less:* Final consumption	30773*	62821	67894	74162	82793	94497	111318	130535	148965	166966	185126	206241	232493	263458	287626
14. *Plus:* Statistical discrepancy	..	..	..	..	..	..	..	..	..	..	..	..	..	..	..
15. *Equals:* **Net Saving**	2803*	9538	8944	9702	11997	17153	22296	19029	23367	21185	22953	30750	33765	39559	28937
16. *Less:* Surplus of the nation on current transactions	−1260*	−1153	836	93	−598	−97	−2193	−5957	−5219	−5297	−5520	−6301	−2769	−9562	1387
17. *Plus:* Statistical discrepancy	435*	−416	963	1252	4	−610	−2064	−1299	−1882	871	−354	−501	−1487	−3080	−1446
18. *Equals:* **Net Capital Formation**	4498*	10263	9063	10861	12599	16640	22425	23686	26704	27354	28119	36549	35046	46041	26104

1. At 1992 relative prices for period 1992-1997, at 1986 relative prices for period 1986-1991, at 1981 relative prices for period 1981-1985, at 1971 relative prices for period 1971-1980 and at 961 relative prices for period 1961-1970.

Principaux Agrégats

millions de dollars canadiens

1983	1984	1985	1986	1987	1988	1989	1990	1991	1992	1993	1994	1995	1996	1997	
															DÉPENSES IMPUTÉES AU P.I.B.
															Aux prix courants
93362	98117	106065	111482	117964	127982	138578	151546	162311	168806	170251	169130	170570	168356	167907	1. Consommation finale des administrations publiques
219941	239826	261727	282936	306047	331304	358140	377860	390135	402705	419405	435062	449018	466108	493322	2. Consommation finale privée
..	..	..	..	..	..	..	..	..	..	..	..	..	..	..	3. Ménages
..	..	..	..	..	..	..	..	..	..	..	..	..	..	..	4. Institutions privées sans but lucratif au service des ménages
−2612	3970	3480	2655	2651	3467	4063	−2660	−5882	−6562	561	2142	8164	1043	7256	5. Variations des stocks
82608	86624	96256	103317	118410	133662	145676	140996	130343	127045	125447	137850	135342	141178	158566	6. Formation brute de capital fixe
393299	**428537**	**467528**	**500390**	**545072**	**596415**	**646457**	**667742**	**676907**	**691994**	**715664**	**744184**	**763094**	**776685**	**827051**	7. **Demande intérieure totale**
103700	127664	136223	141562	148823	162800	167739	174438	170995	188586	218885	260483	300849	319456	342066	8. Exportations de biens et services
90905	112419	125592	137228	142723	158577	168139	174019	175401	191673	219462	252998	277529	288356	328276	9. *Moins :* Importations de biens et services
−869	−772	95	−572	−1304	1795	387	20	13	−1532	−1774	−1187	595	−210	583	10. Divergence statistique
405225	**443010**	**478254**	**504152**	**549868**	**602433**	**646444**	**668181**	**672514**	**687375**	**713313**	**750482**	**787009**	**807575**	**841424**	11. **Produit intérieur brut**
															Aux niveaux de prix de 1990 [1]
124640	126110	131581	134079	135985	142234	146207	151546	155851	157462	157051	154298	153655	151637	151539	1. Consommation finale des administrations publiques
290971	304184	319857	332405	345768	360763	373125	377860	372542	379206	386259	398210	404865	414253	431354	2. Consommation finale privée
..	..	..	..	..	..	..	..	..	..	..	..	..	..	..	3. Ménages
..	..	..	..	..	..	..	..	..	..	..	..	..	..	..	4. Institutions privées sans but lucratif au service des ménages
−3554	3892	4215	2491	2621	1960	3960	−2660	−6721	−7508	−127	2443	7240	353	6635	5. Variations des stocks
95380	97754	107780	113603	125796	138106	146316	140996	136018	134287	130456	139659	135720	142264	158440	6. Formation brute de capital fixe
507437	**531940**	**563433**	**582578**	**610170**	**643063**	**669608**	**667742**	**657690**	**663447**	**673639**	**694610**	**701480**	**708507**	**747968**	7. **Demande intérieure totale**
109699	130353	137673	145030	150038	164569	166376	174438	178461	192614	215859	241514	263815	279017	301464	8. Exportations de biens et services
95199	112516	122573	133070	140589	160083	170146	174019	179590	190834	206364	225328	240474	252833	286825	9. *Moins :* Importations de biens et services
−558	1497	2547	1764	995	3229	689	20	−1140	−3839	−5036	−6148	−5235	−6253	−7254	10. Divergence statistique
521379	**551274**	**581080**	**596302**	**620614**	**650778**	**666527**	**668181**	**655421**	**661388**	**678098**	**704648**	**719586**	**728438**	**755353**	11. **Produit intérieur brut**
															RÉPARTITION DU P.I.B.
53780	58503	62470	68734	75966	84020	92507	96415	102508	106588	109386	112351	115208	117686	122574	1. Impôts indirects
10487	12295	12129	11174	11028	10611	9818	10052	12854	12323	10488	9426	8637	7742	8073	2. *Moins :* Subventions
48795	52291	57154	61237	64627	68592	73742	79701	83019	86424	90279	95323	100737	105935	110722	3. Consommation de capital fixe
220282	237248	255826	272755	296442	325248	350743	368891	379091	387788	395047	405163	419096	429601	445804	4. Rémunération des salariés payée par les producteurs résidents
91985	106491	115029	112028	122556	136979	139654	133246	120764	117365	127314	145884	161200	161884	170981	5. Excédent net d'exploitation
870	772	−96	572	1305	−1795	−388	−20	−14	1533	1775	1187	−595	211	−584	6. Divergence statistique
405225	**443010**	**478254**	**504152**	**549868**	**602433**	**646444**	**668181**	**672514**	**687375**	**713313**	**750482**	**787009**	**807575**	**841424**	7. **Produit intérieur brut**
															OPÉRATIONS EN CAPITAL DE LA NATION
															Financement de la formation brute de capital
48795	52291	57154	61237	64627	68592	73742	79701	83019	86424	90279	95323	100737	105935	110722	1. Consommation de capital fixe
30206	37590	38044	30739	41945	56004	53292	34193	13411	1852	6157	21736	39607	40404	43768	2. Épargne nette
744	831	−4729	−12852	−11880	−16123	−23480	−24482	−28058	−29142	−26023	−20559	−4352	4539	−12499	3. *Moins :* Solde des opérations courantes de la nation
870	772	−96	572	1305	−1795	−388	−20	−14	1533	1775	1187	−595	211	−584	4. Divergence statistique
79127	**89822**	**99831**	**105400**	**119757**	**138924**	**150126**	**138356**	**124474**	**118951**	**124234**	**138805**	**144101**	**142011**	**166405**	5. **Financement de la formation brute de capital**
															Formation brute de capital
−2612	3970	3480	2655	2651	3467	4063	−2660	−5882	−6562	561	2142	8164	1043	7256	6. Variations des stocks
82608	86624	96256	103317	118410	133662	145676	140996	130343	127045	125447	137850	135342	141178	158566	7. Formation brute de capital fixe
−869	−772	95	−572	−1304	1795	387	20	13	−1532	−1774	−1187	595	−210	583	8. Divergence statistique
79127	**89822**	**99831**	**105400**	**119757**	**138924**	**150126**	**138356**	**124474**	**118951**	**124234**	**138805**	**144101**	**142011**	**166405**	9. **Formation brute de capital**
															RELATIONS ENTRE LES PRINCIPAUX AGRÉGATS
405225	**443010**	**478254**	**504152**	**549868**	**602433**	**646444**	**668181**	**672514**	**687375**	**713313**	**750482**	**787009**	**807575**	**841424**	1. **Produit intérieur brut**
−11635	−13571	−14405	−16804	−16808	−19299	−21930	−23974	−22380	−24919	−24679	−27548	−27469	−26823	−26881	2. *Plus :* Revenu net des facteurs reçu du reste du monde
10326	12482	12489	11855	11891	15554	14710	16692	15623	13496	14496	16786	21247	21622	24448	3. Revenu des facteurs reçu du reste du monde
21961	26053	26894	28659	28699	34853	36640	40666	38003	38415	39175	44334	48716	48445	51329	4. Revenu des facteurs payé au reste du monde
393590	**429439**	**463849**	**487348**	**533060**	**583134**	**624514**	**644207**	**650134**	**662456**	**688634**	**722934**	**759540**	**780752**	**814543**	5. *Égal :* **Produit national brut**
48795	52291	57154	61237	64627	68592	73742	79701	83019	86424	90279	95323	100737	105935	110722	6. *Moins :* Consommation de capital fixe
−870	−772	96	−572	−1305	1795	388	20	14	−1533	−1775	−1187	595	−211	584	7. *Plus :* Divergence statistique
343925	**376376**	**406791**	**425539**	**467128**	**516337**	**551160**	**564526**	**567129**	**574499**	**596580**	**626424**	**659398**	**674606**	**704405**	8. *Égal :* **Revenu national**
−416	−843	−955	−382	−1172	−1047	−1150	−927	−1272	−1136	−767	−496	−203	262	592	9. *Plus :* Transferts courants nets reçus du reste du monde
1679	1680	1686	2597	2212	2730	2640	2955	2905	3100	3339	3576	3817	4484	4866	10. Transferts courants reçus du reste du monde
2095	2523	2641	2979	3384	3777	3790	3882	4177	4236	4106	4072	4020	4222	4274	11. Transferts courants payé au reste du monde
343509	**375533**	**405836**	**425157**	**465956**	**515290**	**550010**	**563599**	**565857**	**573363**	**595813**	**625928**	**659195**	**674868**	**704997**	12. *Égal :* **Revenu national disponible**
313303	337943	367792	394418	424011	459286	496718	529406	552446	571511	589656	604192	619588	634464	661229	13. *Moins :* Consommation finale
..	..	..	..	..	..	..	..	..	..	..	..	..	..	..	14. *Plus :* Divergence statistique
30206	**37590**	**38044**	**30739**	**41945**	**56004**	**53292**	**34193**	**13411**	**1852**	**6157**	**21736**	**39607**	**40404**	**43768**	15. *Égal :* **Épargne nette**
744	831	−4729	−12852	−11880	−16123	−23480	−24482	−28058	−29142	−26023	−20559	−4352	4539	−12499	16. *Moins :* Solde des opérations courantes de la nation
1739	1544	−191	1144	2609	−3590	−775	−40	−27	3065	3549	2374	−1190	421	−1167	17. *Plus :* Divergence statistique
31202	**38303**	**42581**	**44735**	**56435**	**68537**	**75996**	**58635**	**41441**	**34060**	**35730**	**44669**	**42769**	**36287**	**55099**	18. *Égal :* **Formation nette de capital**

1. Aux prix relatifs de 1992 pour la période 1992-1997, aux prix relatifs de 1986 pour la période 1986-1991, aux prix relatifs de 1981 pour la période 1981-1985, aux prix relatifs de 1971 pour la période 1971-1980 et aux prix relatifs de 1961 pour la période 1961-1970.

MEXICO
1968 SNA

Main aggregates

millions of new pesos

	1960	1969	1970	1971	1972	1973	1974	1975	1976	1977	1978	1979	1980	1981	1982
EXPENDITURE ON THE G.D.P.															
At current prices															
1. Government final consumption expenditure	9.6*	29.0*	32.5*	37.6*	49.1*	63.9*	82.8*	114.2*	151.9*	200.3*	256.9*	336.5*	465.9*	685.2*	1065.0*
2. Private final consumption expenditure	130.8*	307.8*	364.2*	408.9*	462.3*	555.1*	716.2*	861.6*	1063.9*	1397.5*	1759.7*	2252.1*	3022.2*	4098.8*	6271.6*
3. Households	..	..	..	..	..	..	..	..	..	..	..	..	..	..	..
4. Private non-profit institutions serving households	..	..	..	..	..	..	..	..	..	..	..	..	..	..	..
5. Increase in stocks	7.3*	14.2*	22.7*	21.2*	18.8*	29.2*	51.5*	51.1*	46.6*	103.2*	115.1*	157.5*	295.7*	319.0*	339.0*
6. Gross fixed capital formation	28.0*	79.9*	97.4*	96.8*	117.7*	146.5*	196.5*	258.9*	316.9*	399.2*	541.0*	789.4*	1134.9*	1657.9*	2306.0*
7. **Total Domestic Expenditure**	175.6*	430.9*	516.7*	564.5*	647.8*	794.7*	1047.1*	1285.8*	1579.2*	2100.2*	2672.7*	3535.5*	4918.7*	6760.8*	9981.5*
8. Exports of goods and services	17.6*	38.8*	38.8*	42.2*	51.3*	65.5*	85.3*	85.5*	131.2*	215.0*	275.8*	386.9*	605.5*	806.9*	1900.6*
9. *Less:* Imports of goods and services	24.6*	48.8*	55.8*	55.6*	64.9*	85.1*	123.7*	137.6*	176.0*	245.8*	335.6*	496.8*	751.5*	1027.0*	1309.7*
10. Statistical discrepancy	−0.8*	−3.1*	−4.6*	−5.0*	−4.9*	−5.1*	−5.9*	−7.7*	−6.6*	−8.5*	−8.0*	−6.9*	−6.6*	−7.4*	−125.8*
11. **Gross Domestic Product**	167.7*	417.8*	495.1*	546.1*	629.4*	770.0*	1002.7*	1226.0*	1527.9*	2061.0*	2605.0*	3418.7*	4766.1*	6533.4*	10446.6*
At 1990 price levels[1]															
1. Government final consumption expenditure	8731*	18791*	20351*	22514*	25534*	28097*	29873*	34095*	36263*	35853*	39415*	43193*	47310*	52170*	53229*
2. Private final consumption expenditure	129012*	224860*	239183*	251679*	268667*	286487*	301260*	318466*	332929*	339717*	367401*	399898*	430053*	461759*	450342*
3. Households	..	..	..	..	..	..	..	..	..	..	..	..	..	..	..
4. Private non-profit institutions serving households	..	..	..	..	..	..	..	..	..	..	..	..	..	..	..
5. Increase in stocks	25753*	23700*	24524*	21221*	22327*	26096*	38683*	36767*	33194*	39507*	41191*	45588*	64767*	72276*	41150*
6. Gross fixed capital formation	29117*	61856*	66868*	65723*	73764*	84642*	91331*	99793*	100241*	93511*	107699*	129507*	148852*	173010*	143958*
7. **Total Domestic Expenditure**	192612*	329206*	350925*	361138*	390292*	425322*	461147*	489121*	502627*	508587*	555705*	618185*	690983*	759215*	688680*
8. Exports of goods and services	13835*	26691*	29075*	30220*	35185*	39998*	40075*	36507*	42573*	48812*	54466*	61077*	64808*	72306*	88062*
9. *Less:* Imports of goods and services	26428*	40094*	43659*	41655*	45911*	53573*	64437*	64716*	65356*	58694*	71520*	92894*	122512*	144220*	89629*
10. Statistical discrepancy	−5947*	−9881*	−10331*	−10094*	−11132*	−12330*	−12959*	−13307*	−13263*	−16064*	−16194*	−16080*	−15519*	−15214*	−19778*
11. **Gross Domestic Product**	174071*	305923*	326010*	339610*	368434*	399417*	423826*	447604*	466580*	482642*	522457*	570289*	617760*	672086*	667334*
COST COMPONENTS OF THE G.D.P.															
1. Indirect taxes	7.2*	20.0*	24.5*	27.8*	32.7*	41.5*	56.2*	78.3*	95.1*	137.8*	173.4*	257.5*	429.7*	576.3*	1129.3*
2. *Less:* Subsidies	1.0*	2.9*	3.5*	5.0*	5.8*	7.9*	17.1*	18.2*	26.6*	36.0*	41.5*	59.8*	89.2*	121.7*	277.3*
3. Consumption of fixed capital	16.8*	41.6*	39.4*	42.2*	49.3*	58.5*	77.3*	98.8*	125.5*	176.5*	225.2*	295.0*	391.2*	537.8*	975.5*
4. Compensation of employees paid by resident producers	59.5*	161.9*	200.8*	220.3*	264.3*	314.1*	418.8*	530.8*	699.5*	910.7*	1122.3*	1466.3*	1954.2*	2784.5*	4185.3*
5. Operating surplus	88.1*	206.6*	243.2*	270.0*	301.9*	377.1*	486.4*	565.0*	678.4*	927.2*	1190.9*	1542.6*	2167.6*	2894.0*	4507.6*
6. Statistical discrepancy	−2.8*	−9.5*	−9.2*	−9.3*	−13.0*	−13.3*	−19.0*	−28.7*	−44.0*	−55.3*	−65.3*	−83.0*	−87.6*	−137.5*	−173.7*
7. **Gross Domestic Product**	167.7*	417.8*	495.2*	546.1*	629.4*	770.0*	1002.7*	1226.0*	1527.9*	2061.0*	2605.0*	3418.7*	4766.1*	6533.4*	10446.6*
CAPITAL TRANSACTIONS OF THE NATION															
Finance of Gross Capital Formation															
1. Consumption of fixed capital	16.8*	41.6*	39.4*	42.2*	49.3*	58.5*	77.3*	98.8*	125.5*	176.5*	225.2*	295.0*	391.2*	537.8*	975.5*
2. Net saving	16.8*	51.1*	67.9*	66.7*	78.8*	102.3*	137.2*	164.8*	196.2*	296.4*	377.1*	539.8*	867.3*	1123.0*	1769.9*
3. *Less:* Surplus of the nation on current transactions	−6.8*	−10.7*	−24.2*	−19.9*	−19.7*	−29.5*	−59.6*	−83.5*	−82.1*	−67.5*	−110.9*	−200.3*	−274.3*	−447.2*	−61.5*
4. Statistical discrepancy	−5.1*	−9.4*	−11.4*	−10.9*	−11.4*	−14.6*	−26.0*	−37.0*	−40.4*	−38.0*	−57.1*	−88.2*	−102.2*	−131.1*	−161.9*
5. **Finance of Gross Capital Formation**	35.3*	94.1*	120.1*	118.0*	136.5*	175.7*	248.1*	310.0*	363.5*	502.4*	656.2*	946.8*	1430.6*	1976.8*	2544.9*
Gross capital formation															
6. Increase in stocks	7.3*	14.2*	22.7*	21.2*	18.8*	29.2*	51.5*	51.1*	46.6*	103.2*	115.1*	157.5*	295.7*	319.0*	339.0*
7. Gross fixed capital formation	28.0*	79.9*	97.4*	96.8*	117.7*	146.5*	196.5*	258.9*	316.9*	399.2*	541.0*	789.4*	1134.9*	1657.9*	2306.0*
8. Statistical discrepancy	..	..	..	..	..	..	..	..	..	..	..	..	..	..	..
9. **Gross Capital Formation**	35.3*	94.1*	120.1*	118.0*	136.5*	175.7*	248.1*	310.0*	363.5*	502.4*	656.2*	946.8*	1430.6*	1976.8*	2544.9*
RELATIONS AMONG NATIONAL ACCOUNTING AGGREGATES															
1. **Gross Domestic Product**	167.7*	417.8*	495.1*	546.1*	629.4*	770.0*	1002.7*	1226.0*	1527.9*	2061.0*	2605.0*	3418.7*	4766.1*	6533.4*	10446.6*
2. *Plus:* Net factor income from the rest of the world	−0.9*	−4.0*	−6.9*	−7.9*	−9.0*	−12.2*	−18.3*	−21.8*	−35.2*	−52.3*	−63.9*	−93.9*	−142.7*	−240.7*	−518.8*
3. Factor income from the rest of the world	1.1*	2.4*	2.7*	2.5*	3.0*	3.4*	3.4*	4.1*	6.4*	10.8*	17.6*	21.2*	29.6*	41.7*	85.3*
4. Factor income paid to the rest of the world	2.1*	6.5*	9.5*	10.3*	11.9*	15.5*	21.4*	25.7*	41.2*	62.5*	81.0*	114.2*	170.8*	279.6*	695.7*
5. *Equals:* **Gross National Product**	166.8*	413.8*	488.3*	538.2*	620.4*	757.8*	984.4*	1204.2*	1492.7*	2008.7*	2541.1*	3324.8*	4623.4*	6292.6*	9827.7*
6. *Less:* Consumption of fixed capital	16.8*	41.6*	39.4*	42.2*	49.3*	58.5*	77.3*	98.8*	125.5*	176.5*	225.2*	295.0*	391.2*	537.8*	975.5*
7. *Plus:* Statistical discrepancy	6.6*	15.2*	14.8*	16.3*	18.1*	20.7*	27.2*	33.1*	41.8*	57.3*	72.3*	92.3*	115.7*	143.6*	234.3*
8. *Equals:* **National Income**	156.6*	387.4*	463.7*	512.3*	589.2*	720.0*	934.4*	1138.5*	1409.0*	1889.5*	2388.2*	3122.2*	4347.9*	5898.5*	9086.6*
9. *Plus:* Net current transfers from the rest of the world	0.5*	0.5*	0.8*	0.9*	1.0*	1.2*	1.9*	2.1*	3.0*	4.7*	5.5*	6.3*	7.6*	8.5*	19.9*
10. Current transfers from the rest of the world	0.7*	0.8*	1.1*	1.1*	1.1*	1.5*	2.1*	2.4*	3.3*	5.4*	6.3*	7.2*	8.7*	10.1*	21.2*
11. Current transfers paid to the rest of the world	0.2*	0.2*	0.2*	0.1*	0.1*	0.2*	0.2*	0.2*	0.3*	0.6*	0.7*	0.8*	1.0*	1.4*	1.1*
12. *Equals:* **National Disposable Income**	157.1*	387.9*	464.5*	513.2*	590.2*	721.2*	936.2*	1140.6*	1412.0*	1894.2*	2393.7*	3128.4*	4355.4*	5906.9*	9106.5*
13. *Less:* Final consumption	140.3*	336.8*	396.6*	446.5*	511.3*	618.9*	799.0*	975.9*	1215.8*	1597.8*	2016.6*	2588.6*	3488.1*	4784.0*	7336.5*
14. *Plus:* Statistical discrepancy	..	..	..	..	..	..	..	..	..	..	..	..	..	..	..
15. *Equals:* **Net Saving**	16.8*	51.1*	67.9*	66.7*	78.8*	102.3*	137.2*	164.8*	196.2*	296.4*	377.1*	539.8*	867.3*	1123.0*	1769.9*
16. *Less:* Surplus of the nation on current transactions	−6.8*	−10.7*	−24.2*	−19.9*	−19.7*	−29.5*	−59.6*	−83.5*	−82.1*	−67.5*	−110.9*	−200.3*	−274.3*	−447.2*	−61.5*
17. *Plus:* Statistical discrepancy	−5.1*	−9.4*	−11.4*	−10.9*	−11.4*	−14.6*	−26.0*	−37.0*	−40.4*	−38.0*	−57.1*	−88.2*	−102.2*	−131.1*	−161.9*
18. *Equals:* **Net Capital Formation**	18.5*	52.4*	80.7*	75.8*	87.2*	117.2*	170.8*	211.2*	237.9*	326.0*	431.0*	651.8*	1039.4*	1439.1*	1669.5*

1. At 1993 relative prices for 1988-1997, at 1980 relative prices for 1980-1987 and at 1970 relative prices for 1960-1979.

Principaux Agrégats

millions de nouveaux pesos

1983	1984	1985	1986	1987	1988	1989	1990	1991	1992	1993	1994	1995	1996	1997	
															DÉPENSES IMPUTÉES AU P.I.B.
															Aux prix courants
1634*	2825*	4541*	7483*	17644*	35028	45383	61949	86163	111752	138565	164161	191981	243706	266213	1. Consommation finale des administrations publiques
11306*	19315*	31768*	56323*	132232*	281569	377907	514117	669159	808120	903174	1016129	1232003	1624278	2079991	2. Consommation finale privée
..	..	..	..	..	..	..	..	..	..	..	..	..	..	..	3. Ménages
..	..	..	..	..	..	..	..	..	..	..	..	..	..	..	4. Institutions privées sans but lucratif au service des ménages
1156*	1476*	2547*	1494*	7303*	16812	31254	38879	44379	41563	30597	33538	67391	132477	214251	5. Variations des stocks
3217*	5422*	9278*	15806*	36573*	77110	94670	132113	177044	220545	233179	274861	296708	449949	622853	6. Formation brute de capital fixe
17312*	29038*	48134*	81107*	193752*	410518	549214	747059	976745	1181981	1305515	1488689	1788083	2450411	3183308	7. **Demande intérieure totale**
4299*	6481*	9243*	17375*	47691*	82961	104266	137441	155327	171476	191540	238965	558798	812854	963215	8. Exportations de biens et services
2183*	3648*	6346*	13786*	33532*	77174	104622	145603	182924	228123	240859	307494	509862	759451	964196	9. Moins : Importations de biens et services
–366*	–448*	–501*	–261*	–1800*	..	..	..	..	..	..	..	..	..	..	10. Divergence statistique
19063*	31423*	50530*	84435*	206112*	416305	548858	738898	949148	1125334	1256196	1420159	1837019	2503814	3182327	11. **Produit intérieur brut**
															Aux niveaux de prix de 1990[1]
54678*	58280*	58808*	59679*	58959*	58662	59950	61949	65310	66525	68124	70067	69146	68638	69895	1. Consommation finale des administrations publiques
426208*	440089*	455761*	442845*	442249*	450270	483064	514117	538171	563352	571607	597795	540922	552924	587983	2. Consommation finale privée
..	..	..	..	..	..	..	..	..	..	..	..	..	..	..	3. Ménages
..	..	..	..	..	..	..	..	..	..	..	..	..	..	..	4. Institutions privées sans but lucratif au service des ménages
30905*	32400*	40107*	23253*	30675*	40474	36500	38879	41360	50498	52840	61358	30103	49246	63419	5. Variations des stocks
103246*	109882*	118511*	104528*	104400*	110435	116786	132113	146637	162531	158422	171715	121913	141900	171601	6. Formation brute de capital fixe
615038*	640651*	673186*	630304*	636283*	659841	696301	747059	791479	842905	850994	900936	762083	812708	892898	7. **Demande intérieure totale**
100013*	105719*	101012*	106669*	116793*	123523	130517	137441	144409	151607	163875	193042	251329	297110	335677	8. Exportations de biens et services
59339*	69909*	77589*	71704*	75394*	103075	121595	145603	167702	200599	204329	247754	210489	258487	315442	9. Moins : Importations de biens et services
–17045*	–14805*	–16611*	–10798*	–11065*	–5370	–1968	0	1909	4126	3065	3305	–5785	–12923	–15999	10. Divergence statistique
638666*	661655*	679998*	654472*	666617*	674919	703254	738898	770096	798040	813606	849529	797139	838407	897133	11. **Produit intérieur brut**
															RÉPARTITION DU P.I.B.
1914*	3147*	5658*	8496*	23399*	42323	56052	74857	93900	112508	119862	131036	178982	234049	297470*	1. Impôts indirects
598*	789*	1261*	2222*	4795*	6937	8455	8660	7743	9039	10816	9875	13094	17338	22040*	2. Moins : Subventions
2220*	3426*	5438*	11089*	25791*	47700	55120	68039	84911	100204	113388	129563	210842	273082	347080*	3. Consommation de capital fixe
6366*	10244*	16485*	27422*	62933*	123951	162130	218203	293064	370021	436483	501897	570936	728989	926540*	4. Rémunération des salariés payée par les producteurs résidents
9278*	15543*	24437*	40041*	99015*	209268	284011	386459	485016	551640	597279	667538	889354	1285030	1633280*	5. Excédent net d'exploitation
–117*	–149*	–228*	–390*	–231*	..	..	..	..	..	..	..	..	..	..	6. Divergence statistique
19063*	31423*	50530*	84435*	206112*	416305	548858	738898	949148	1125334	1256196	1420159	1837019	2503814	3182330	7. **Produit intérieur brut**
															OPÉRATIONS EN CAPITAL DE LA NATION
															Financement de la formation brute de capital
2220*	3426*	5438*	11089*	25791*	47700	55120	68039	84911	100204	113388	129563	210842	273082	347080*	1. Consommation de capital fixe
3199*	4660*	7604*	5031*	24657*	41005	56571	82253	92256	86279	76370	80450	143495	295904	404090*	2. Épargne nette
862*	938*	754*	–357*	6494*	–5217	–14233	–20701	–44256	–75625	–74019	–98386	–9762	–13440	–85930*	3. Moins : Solde des opérations courantes de la nation
–184*	–251*	–463*	824*	–78*	..	..	..	..	..	..	..	..	..	..	4. Divergence statistique
4372*	6897*	11825*	17300*	43877*	93922	125924	170993	221423	262109	263777	308399	364099	582426	837100	5. **Financement de la formation brute de capital**
															Formation brute de capital
1156*	1476*	2547*	1494*	7303*	16812	31254	38879	44379	41563	30597	33538	67391	132477	214251	6. Variations des stocks
3217*	5422*	9278*	15806*	36573*	77110	94670	132113	177044	220545	233179	274861	296708	449949	622853	7. Formation brute de capital fixe
..	..	..	..	..	..	..	..	..	..	..	..	..	..	..	8. Divergence statistique
4372*	6897*	11825*	17300*	43877*	93922	125924	170993	221423	262109	263777	308399	364099	582426	837104	9. **Formation brute de capital**
															RELATIONS ENTRE LES PRINCIPAUX AGRÉGATS
19063*	31423*	50530*	84435*	206112*	416305	548858	738898	949148	1125334	1256196	1420159	1837019	2503814	3182330	1. **Produit intérieur brut**
–1169*	–1794*	–2353*	–4718*	–9811*	–16174	–20190	–23927	–25683	–29457	–35859	–42266	–84091	–101266	–128710*	2. Plus : Revenu net des facteurs reçu du reste du monde
222*	440*	655*	1161*	3414*	6985	7875	9522	10854	8897	8805	11084	24706	31586	..	3. Revenu des facteurs reçu du reste du monde
1378*	2219*	2991*	5838*	13187*	23159	28065	33449	36537	38354	44664	53350	108797	132852	..	4. Revenu des facteurs payé au reste du monde
17893*	29629*	48177*	79717*	196300*	400131	528668	714971	923465	1095877	1220337	1377893	1752929	2402547	3053620*	5. Égal : **Produit national brut**
2220*	3426*	5438*	11089*	25791*	47700	55120	68039	84911	100204	113388	129563	210842	273082	347080*	6. Moins : Consommation de capital fixe
411*	506*	780*	–833*	1232*	..	..	..	..	..	..	..	..	..	..	7. Plus : Divergence statistique
16085*	26709*	43519*	67795*	171742*	352431	473548	646932	838554	995673	1106949	1248330	1542086	2129465	2706540*	8. Égal : **Revenu national**
54*	91*	394*	1042*	2791*	5170	6313	11388	9025	10478	11160	12410	25393	34423	43750*	9. Plus : Transferts courants nets reçus du reste du monde
60*	96*	402*	1051*	2819*	5204	6352	11428	9082	10538	11212	12539	25614	34651	..	10. Transferts courants reçus du reste du monde
5*	4*	8*	8*	26*	34	39	40	57	59	52	130	221	228	..	11. Transferts courants payés au reste du monde
16139*	26801*	43912*	68837*	174533*	357601	479860	658320	847578	1006151	1118109	1260740	1567479	2163888	2750290*	12. Égal : **Revenu national disponible**
12940*	22141*	36308*	63807*	149876*	316596	423290	576067	755322	919872	1041738	1180290	1423984	1867984	2346200	13. Moins : Consommation finale
..	..	..	..	..	..	..	..	..	..	..	..	..	..	..	14. Plus : Divergence statistique
3199*	4660*	7604*	5031*	24657*	41005	56571	82253	92256	86279	76370	80450	143495	295904	404090*	15. Égal : **Épargne nette**
862*	938*	754*	–357*	6494*	–5217	–14233	–20701	–44256	–75625	–74019	–98386	–9762	–13440	–85930*	16. Moins : Solde des opérations courantes de la nation
–184*	–251*	–463*	824*	–78*	..	..	..	..	..	..	..	..	..	..	17. Plus : Divergence statistique
2152*	3471*	6387*	6211*	18085*	46222	70804	102954	136512	161905	150389	178836	153257	309344	490020*	18. Égal : **Formation nette de capital**

1. Aux prix relatifs de 1993 pour la période 1988-1997, aux prix relatifs de 1980 pour la période 1980-1987 et aux prix relatifs de 1970 pour la période 1960-1979.

UNITED STATES
1968 SNA

Main aggregates

billions of dollars

	1960	1969	1970	1971	1972	1973	1974	1975	1976	1977	1978	1979	1980	1981	1982
EXPENDITURE ON THE G.D.P.															
At current prices															
1. Government final consumption expenditure	84.9	174.3	186.4	196.4	212.5	229.1	256.5	287.9	311.2	339.4	370.4	410.3	463.2	516.9	567.8
2. Private final consumption expenditure	327.8	595.5	637.3	690.2	757.2	836.8	914.0	1008.4	1126.6	1252.6	1396.8	1556.9	1720.6	1902.4	2034.6
3. Households	..	..	..	..	..	..	..	..	..	..	..	..	..	..	..
4. Private non-profit institutions serving households	..	..	..	..	..	..	..	..	..	..	..	..	..	..	..
5. Increase in stocks	3.4	10.2	1.8	8.2	9.5	16.8	13.6	−6.0	17.1	23.6	28.0	17.2	−5.6	33.4	−10.6
6. Gross fixed capital formation	91.7	177.2	180.1	201.3	230.6	263.0	276.1	281.1	319.9	383.2	461.6	529.2	547.3	603.2	590.1
7. **Total Domestic Expenditure**	**507.8**	**957.2**	**1005.6**	**1096.1**	**1209.8**	**1345.7**	**1460.2**	**1571.4**	**1774.8**	**1998.8**	**2256.8**	**2513.6**	**2725.5**	**3055.9**	**3181.9**
8. Exports of goods and services	26.8	51.4	59.1	62.3	70.1	93.7	124.9	137.0	147.8	157.5	184.6	227.0	277.3	301.1	280.3
9. *Less:* Imports of goods and services	22.8	50.5	55.8	62.3	74.2	91.2	127.5	122.7	151.1	182.4	212.3	252.7	293.8	317.8	303.2
10. Statistical discrepancy	−0.1	0.0	0.0	0.0	0.1	0.1	0.0	−0.2	−0.1	−0.1	−0.1	0.1	0.0	0.1	−0.1
11. **Gross Domestic Product**	**511.7**	**958.1**	**1008.9**	**1096.1**	**1205.8**	**1348.3**	**1457.6**	**1585.5**	**1771.4**	**1973.8**	**2229.0**	**2488.0**	**2709.0**	**3039.3**	**3158.9**
At 1990 price levels[1]															
1. Government final consumption expenditure	504.0	701.9	695.4	677.9	680.1	673.3	689.9	704.1	707.7	719.7	734.1	743.7	755.8	765.3	784.3
2. Private final consumption expenditure	1344.7	1972.2	2022.8	2092.6	2211.8	2314.1	2301.9	2349.6	2472.6	2569.6	2676.8	2741.3	2744.0	2786.0	2813.4
3. Households	..	..	..	..	..	..	..	..	..	..	..	..	..	..	..
4. Private non-profit institutions serving households	..	..	..	..	..	..	..	..	..	..	..	..	..	..	..
5. Increase in stocks	8.7	27.1	3.0	22.0	21.8	36.4	29.3	−16.0	27.2	33.3	40.6	18.0	−7.6	31.9	−13.6
6. Gross fixed capital formation	392.3	603.7	581.8	613.4	672.2	723.5	679.1	611.2	657.4	730.6	804.0	837.0	776.4	769.8	707.3
7. **Total Domestic Expenditure**	**2249.7**	**3304.9**	**3303.0**	**3405.9**	**3585.9**	**3747.3**	**3700.2**	**3648.9**	**3864.9**	**4053.2**	**4255.5**	**4340.0**	**4268.6**	**4353.0**	**4291.4**
8. Exports of goods and services	104.3	171.5	186.4	188.8	204.9	240.4	263.7	262.8	270.9	274.6	300.9	327.5	357.8	362.5	329.4
9. *Less:* Imports of goods and services	117.4	224.1	231.8	242.4	266.4	278.1	269.4	235.3	279.8	306.7	334.0	338.4	323.3	339.7	339.4
10. Statistical discrepancy	−3.6	−4.9	−3.2	−4.3	−5.3	−8.2	−7.8	−4.9	−5.5	−6.5	−8.8	−9.7	−8.6	−8.8	−2.9
11. **Gross Domestic Product**	**2233.0**	**3247.4**	**3254.4**	**3348.0**	**3519.1**	**3701.4**	**3686.7**	**3671.5**	**3850.5**	**4014.6**	**4213.6**	**4319.4**	**4294.5**	**4367.0**	**4278.5**
COST COMPONENTS OF THE G.D.P.															
1. Indirect taxes	45.5	86.6	94.3	103.6	111.4	121.0	129.3	140.0	151.6	165.5	177.8	188.7	212.0	249.3	256.4
2. *Less:* Subsidies	1.2	4.7	5.0	5.0	7.0	5.6	3.7	5.0	5.7	7.7	9.4	9.2	10.6	12.2	15.5
3. Consumption of fixed capital	47.1	85.0	93.2	102.2	112.2	123.0	143.7	168.3	184.5	205.7	233.7	270.2	310.7	357.5	391.0
4. Compensation of employees paid by resident producers	296.9	579.2	619.1	660.3	727.5	814.7	893.8	952.1	1062.4	1181.8	1338.5	1503.1	1653.6	1827.4	1927.8
5. Operating surplus	126.7	213.4	205.5	228.9	257.4	291.8	289.0	318.0	358.8	410.3	470.4	507.0	515.8	602.4	601.7
6. Statistical discrepancy	−3.3	−1.4	1.8	6.1	4.3	3.4	5.5	12.1	19.8	18.2	18.0	28.2	27.5	14.9	−2.5
7. **Gross Domestic Product**	**511.7**	**958.1**	**1008.9**	**1096.1**	**1205.8**	**1348.3**	**1457.6**	**1585.5**	**1771.4**	**1973.8**	**2229.0**	**2488.0**	**2709.0**	**3039.3**	**3158.9**
CAPITAL TRANSACTIONS OF THE NATION															
Finance of Gross Capital Formation															
1. Consumption of fixed capital	47.1	85.0	93.2	102.2	112.2	123.0	143.7	168.3	184.5	205.7	233.7	270.2	310.7	357.5	391.0
2. Net saving	54.5	105.6	90.9	101.8	120.1	162.2	147.6	116.0	141.5	173.9	227.4	249.5	214.7	270.6	184.8
3. *Less:* Surplus of the nation on current transactions	3.2	1.8	4.0	0.6	−3.6	8.7	7.1	21.4	8.9	−9.0	−10.4	1.4	11.4	6.3	−6.1
4. Statistical discrepancy	−3.3	−1.4	1.8	6.1	4.2	3.3	5.5	12.2	19.9	19.9	18.2	18.1	28.1	27.7	−2.4
5. **Finance of Gross Capital Formation**	**95.1**	**187.4**	**181.9**	**209.5**	**240.1**	**279.8**	**289.7**	**275.1**	**337.0**	**406.8**	**489.6**	**546.4**	**541.7**	**636.6**	**579.5**
Gross capital formation															
6. Increase in stocks	3.4	10.2	1.8	8.2	9.5	16.8	13.6	−6.0	17.1	23.6	28.0	17.2	−5.6	33.4	−10.6
7. Gross fixed capital formation	91.7	177.2	180.1	201.3	230.6	263.0	276.1	281.1	319.9	383.2	461.6	529.2	547.3	603.2	590.1
8. Statistical discrepancy	..	..	..	..	..	..	..	..	..	..	..	..	..	..	..
9. **Gross Capital Formation**	**95.1**	**187.4**	**181.9**	**209.5**	**240.1**	**279.8**	**289.7**	**275.1**	**337.0**	**406.8**	**489.6**	**546.4**	**541.7**	**636.6**	**579.5**
RELATIONS AMONG NATIONAL ACCOUNTING AGGREGATES															
1. **Gross Domestic Product**	511.7	958.1	1008.9	1096.1	1205.8	1348.3	1457.6	1585.5	1771.4	1973.8	2229.0	2488.0	2709.0	3039.3	3158.9
2. *Plus:* Net factor income from the rest of the world	3.4	6.7	7.0	8.2	9.3	13.6	16.9	14.7	18.5	22.2	23.9	35.0	37.7	37.0	34.1
3. Factor income from the rest of the world	5.0	11.9	13.0	14.1	16.4	23.8	30.3	28.2	32.9	37.9	47.4	70.4	81.8	95.6	96.9
4. Factor income paid to the rest of the world	1.6	5.3	6.0	5.9	7.1	10.3	13.3	13.4	14.3	15.7	23.5	35.4	44.1	58.6	62.8
5. *Equals:* **Gross National Product**	515.1	964.8	1015.9	1104.3	1215.0	1361.8	1474.5	1600.2	1789.9	1996.0	2252.9	2523.0	2746.7	3076.3	3193.0
6. *Less:* Consumption of fixed capital	47.1	85.0	93.2	102.2	112.2	123.0	143.7	168.3	184.5	205.7	233.7	270.2	310.7	357.5	391.0
7. *Plus:* Statistical discrepancy	..	..	..	..	..	..	..	..	..	..	..	..	..	..	..
8. *Equals:* **National Income**	468.0	879.8	922.7	1002.2	1102.9	1238.8	1330.8	1432.0	1605.4	1790.3	2019.2	2252.8	2435.9	2718.9	2802.0
9. *Plus:* Net current transfers from the rest of the world	−4.1	−5.8	−6.3	−7.6	−8.8	−7.4	−7.2	−7.6	−6.3	−6.2	−6.7	−8.0	−9.8	−14.1	−17.2
10. Current transfers from the rest of the world	0.4	0.8	0.8	0.8	1.0	1.1	1.1	1.2	1.5	1.7	2.2	2.5	3.1	2.9	3.0
11. Current transfers paid to the rest of the world	4.5	6.6	7.1	8.4	9.8	8.5	8.3	8.8	7.8	7.9	8.8	10.5	12.9	17.0	20.2
12. *Equals:* **National Disposable Income**	464.0	874.0	916.4	994.5	1094.1	1231.4	1323.6	1424.4	1599.1	1784.1	2012.6	2244.9	2426.2	2704.8	2784.8
13. *Less:* Final consumption	412.7	769.8	823.7	886.7	969.7	1065.9	1170.5	1296.2	1437.7	1591.9	1767.1	1967.2	2183.8	2419.3	2602.4
14. *Plus:* Statistical discrepancy	3.2	1.5	−1.9	−6.1	−4.3	−3.4	−5.5	−12.1	−19.9	−18.2	−18.1	−28.2	−27.6	−14.9	2.5
15. *Equals:* **Net Saving**	54.5	105.6	90.9	101.8	120.1	162.2	147.6	116.0	141.5	173.9	227.4	249.5	214.7	270.6	184.8
16. *Less:* Surplus of the nation on current transactions	3.2	1.8	4.0	0.6	−3.6	8.7	7.1	21.4	8.9	−9.0	−10.4	1.4	11.4	6.3	−6.1
17. *Plus:* Statistical discrepancy	−3.2	−1.5	1.9	6.1	4.3	3.4	5.5	12.1	19.9	18.2	18.1	28.2	27.6	14.9	−2.5
18. *Equals:* **Net Capital Formation**	**48.1**	**102.4**	**88.7**	**107.3**	**127.9**	**156.8**	**145.9**	**106.7**	**152.5**	**201.2**	**255.9**	**276.2**	**231.0**	**279.1**	**188.4**

1. At 1992 relative prices.

Principaux Agrégats

milliards de dollars

1983	1984	1985	1986	1987	1988	1989	1990	1991	1992	1993	1994	1995	1996	1997	
															DÉPENSES IMPUTÉES AU P.I.B.
															Aux prix courants
612.2	658.5	719.5	767.7	819.7	860.2	907.2	974.9	1016.8	1043.3	1062.7	1089.9	1124.6	1163.0	1206.1*	1. Consommation finale des administrations publiques
2226.7	2432.3	2633.7	2803.9	2998.6	3247.4	3486.7	3720.5	3844.5	4079.8	4318.4	4569.4	4802.4	5043.0	5311.8*	2. Consommation finale privée
..	..	..	..	..	..	..	..	..	..	..	..	..	..	..	3. Ménages
0.2	67.8	29.6	16.3	24.5	4.1	31.3	6.6	−2.4	6.5	20.4	60.8	29.9	25.0	60.5*	4. Institutions privées sans but lucratif au service des ménages
629.5	734.5	785.5	818.2	835.5	881.6	924.6	932.5	882.1	937.5	1011.7	1106.4	1176.9	1269.3	1359.5*	5. Variations des stocks
3468.6	3893.1	4168.3	4406.1	4678.3	4993.3	5349.8	5634.5	5741.0	6067.1	6413.2	6826.5	7133.8	7500.3	7937.9*	6. Formation brute de capital fixe
272.9	298.3	297.0	314.1	357.7	438.7	500.9	548.2	592.2	629.5	647.8	708.5	804.2	856.0	945.7*	7. **Demande intérieure totale**
328.6	405.1	417.2	452.2	507.9	553.2	589.7	628.6	622.3	669.0	719.3	812.1	904.5	965.7	1059.6*	8. Exportations de biens et services
0.0	0.1	0.1	0.1	0.0	0.0	−0.1	0.0	0.0	0.1	−0.1	0.0	0.1	0.0	0.0	9. *Moins :* Importations de biens et services
															10. Divergence statistique
3412.9	3786.4	4048.2	4268.1	4528.1	4878.8	5260.9	5554.1	5710.9	6027.7	6341.6	6722.9	7033.6	7390.6	7824.0*	11. **Produit intérieur brut**
															Aux niveaux de prix de 1990[1]
800.4	820.9	858.7	891.9	919.1	935.2	951.9	974.9	978.4	974.1	964.0	966.2	963.8	965.8	978.5*	1. Consommation finale des administrations publiques
2940.5	3083.9	3222.5	3340.9	3439.9	3575.5	3660.8	3720.5	3696.2	3803.9	3919.9	4055.9	4169.3	4292.5	4438.0*	2. Consommation finale privée
..	..	..	..	..	..	..	..	..	..	..	..	..	..	..	3. Ménages
															4. Institutions privées sans but lucratif au service des ménages
3.2	70.6	28.6	15.3	22.7	3.1	29.8	6.6	−5.7	4.3	17.8	55.4	23.6	19.9	53.0*	5. Variations des stocks
751.3	862.7	908.6	921.0	914.2	933.7	948.7	932.5	867.6	916.9	974.2	1048.7	1113.7	1227.8	1315.4*	6. Formation brute de capital fixe
4495.4	4838.1	5018.4	5169.1	5295.9	5447.5	5591.2	5634.5	5536.5	5699.2	5876.5	6126.2	6270.4	6506.0	6784.9*	7. **Demande intérieure totale**
312.7	332.6	336.8	359.4	394.6	456.7	508.6	548.2	581.3	619.1	638.8	695.8	791.5	888.1	1001.7*	8. Exportations de biens et services
382.5	476.1	509.1	542.9	571.2	591.1	609.7	628.6	620.3	665.2	725.3	816.9	902.3	1012.9	1153.6*	9. *Moins :* Importations de biens et services
−1.3	−2.7	−0.2	1.5	2.0	1.2	−1.0	0.0	1.0	0.1	0.4	−0.6	−0.8	−2.5	−3.5	10. Divergence statistique
4424.3	4691.9	4845.9	4987.1	5121.3	5314.3	5489.1	5554.1	5498.5	5653.2	5790.4	6004.5	6158.8	6378.7	6629.5*	11. **Produit intérieur brut**
															RÉPARTITION DU P.I.B.
280.1	309.5	329.6	344.7	364.8	385.5	414.7	442.6	478.1	505.6	532.5	568.5	582.8	604.8	625.5*	1. Impôts indirects
22.8	22.7	23.1	26.8	32.7	31.9	29.0	28.5	29.0	32.3	37.0	33.7	34.0	33.5	32.9*	2. *Moins :* Subventions
409.7	426.2	448.5	476.7	502.9	537.4	578.8	602.0	627.8	660.0	672.9	721.6	740.1	773.7	810.7*	3. Consommation de capital fixe
2044.4	2247.2	2415.8	2563.1	2749.7	2968.7	3147.5	3351.5	3456.5	3644.2	3820.3	4020.5	4228.3	4437.6	4717.6*	4. Rémunération des salariés payée par les producteurs résidents
664.4	821.2	875.1	887.1	958.9	1066.5	1135.7	1169.1	1167.5	1205.4	1300.3	1431.5	1544.6	1667.8	1769.3*	5. Excédent net d'exploitation
37.1	5.0	2.3	23.3	−15.5	−47.4	13.2	17.4	10.0	44.8	52.6	14.5	−28.2	−59.8	−66.2*	6. Divergence statistique
3412.9	3786.4	4048.2	4268.1	4528.1	4878.8	5260.9	5554.1	5710.9	6027.7	6341.6	6722.9	7033.6	7390.6	7824.0*	7. **Produit intérieur brut**
															OPÉRATIONS EN CAPITAL DE LA NATION
															Financement de la formation brute de capital
409.7	426.2	448.5	476.7	502.9	537.4	578.8	602.0	627.8	660.0	672.9	721.6	740.1	773.7	810.7*	1. Consommation de capital fixe
145.4	279.6	247.4	191.6	216.0	277.4	271.4	240.9	249.1	188.8	228.0	311.0	380.5	447.5	518.3*	2. Épargne nette
−37.3	−91.5	−116.9	−142.9	−156.4	−118.1	−92.4	−78.6	7.3	−50.5	−78.6	−120.0	−114.4	−132.9	−157.1*	3. *Moins :* Solde des opérations courantes de la nation
37.3	5.0	2.3	23.3	−15.3	−47.2	13.3	17.6	10.1	44.7	52.6	14.6	−28.2	−59.8	−66.1*	4. Divergence statistique
629.7	802.3	815.1	834.5	860.0	885.7	955.9	939.1	879.7	944.0	1032.1	1167.2	1206.8	1294.3	1420.0*	5. **Financement de la formation brute de capital**
															Formation brute de capital
0.2	67.8	29.6	16.3	24.5	4.1	31.3	6.6	−2.4	6.5	20.4	60.8	29.9	25.0	60.5*	6. Variations des stocks
629.5	734.5	785.5	818.2	835.5	881.6	924.6	932.5	882.1	937.5	1011.7	1106.4	1176.9	1269.3	1359.5*	7. Formation brute de capital fixe
..	..	..	..	..	..	..	..	..	..	..	..	..	..	..	8. Divergence statistique
629.7	802.3	815.1	834.5	860.0	885.7	955.9	939.1	879.7	944.0	1032.1	1167.2	1206.8	1294.3	1420.0*	9. **Formation brute de capital**
															RELATIONS ENTRE LES PRINCIPAUX AGRÉGATS
3412.9	3786.4	4048.2	4268.1	4528.1	4878.8	5260.9	5554.1	5710.9	6027.7	6341.6	6722.9	7033.6	7390.6	7824.0*	1. **Produit intérieur brut**
36.3	36.0	26.4	19.5	17.0	21.6	22.6	30.3	25.7	22.0	30.6	21.5	19.7	17.0	−2.3*	2. *Plus :* Revenu net des facteurs reçu du reste du monde
97.6	118.7	108.1	106.5	116.0	⁺44.7	169.0	177.5	156.2	137.9	150.8	176.5	222.8	234.3	264.1*	3. Revenu des facteurs reçu du reste du monde
61.4	82.7	81.6	87.0	99.0	⁻23.1	146.3	147.2	130.4	115.9	120.2	154.9	203.1	217.3	266.4*	4. Revenu des facteurs payé au reste du monde
3449.2	3822.4	4074.6	4287.6	4545.1	4900.4	5283.5	5584.4	5736.6	6049.6	6372.3	6744.4	7053.3	7407.6	7821.7*	5. *Égal :* **Produit national brut**
409.7	426.2	448.5	476.7	502.9	537.4	578.8	602.0	627.8	660.0	672.9	721.6	740.1	773.7	810.7*	6. *Moins :* Consommation de capital fixe
..	..	..	..	..	..	..	..	..	..	..	..	..	..	..	7. *Plus :* Divergence statistique
3039.4	3396.2	3626.1	3810.9	4042.2	4363.0	4704.7	4982.3	5108.8	5389.7	5699.4	6022.8	6313.2	6633.8	7011.0*	8. *Égal :* **Revenu national**
−17.9	−20.8	−23.1	−24.4	−23.3	−25.2	−26.1	−28.5	11.7	−33.0	−37.7	−38.0	−33.9	−40.2	−40.9*	9. *Plus :* Transferts courants nets reçus du reste du monde
2.9	3.3	3.8	4.1	4.7	5.7	6.5	16.3	54.2	9.1	7.9	8.8	9.2	9.0	..	10. Transferts courants reçus du reste du monde
20.8	24.1	27.0	28.5	28.0	30.9	32.7	44.8	42.5	42.1	45.6	46.8	43.0	49.2	..	11. Transferts courants payés au reste du monde
3021.5	3375.4	3603.0	3786.5	4018.9	4337.8	4678.6	4953.8	5120.5	5356.7	5661.7	5984.9	6279.3	6593.6	6970.1*	12. *Égal :* **Revenu national disponible**
2838.9	3090.9	3353.2	3571.6	3818.3	4107.7	4394.0	4695.5	4861.3	5123.1	5381.1	5659.3	5927.0	6206.0	6517.9*	13. *Moins :* Consommation finale
−37.1	−5.0	−2.4	−23.3	15.4	47.3	−13.2	−17.4	−10.1	−44.8	−52.6	−14.6	28.2	59.9	66.2*	14. *Plus :* Divergence statistique
145.4	279.6	247.4	191.6	216.0	277.4	271.4	241.0	249.1	188.8	228.0	311.0	380.5	447.5	518.3*	15. *Égal :* **Épargne nette**
−37.3	−91.5	−116.9	−142.9	−156.4	−118.1	−92.4	−78.6	7.3	−50.5	−78.6	−120.0	−114.4	−132.9	−157.1*	16. *Moins :* Solde des opérations courantes de la nation
37.1	5.0	2.4	23.3	−15.4	−47.3	13.2	17.4	10.1	44.8	52.6	14.6	−28.2	−59.9	−66.2*	17. *Plus :* Divergence statistique
219.9	376.1	366.7	357.8	357.1	348.3	377.0	337.0	251.8	284.1	359.2	445.6	466.6	520.6	609.3*	18. *Égal :* **Formation nette de capital**

1. Aux prix relatifs de 1992.

JAPAN
1968 SNA

Main aggregates

billions of yen

	1960	1969	1970	1971	1972	1973	1974	1975	1976	1977	1978	1979	1980	1981	1982
EXPENDITURE ON THE G.D.P.															
At current prices															
1. Government final consumption expenditure	1282	4558	5455	6421	7537	9336	12240	14890	16417	18243	19753	21486	23568	25585	26796
2. Private final consumption expenditure	9395	33300	38333	43230	49901	60308	72912	84763	95784	107076	117923	130078	141324	149997	160834
3. Households	9218	32725	37805	42687	49302	59651	72108	83920	94846	105870	116643	128558	139506	147988	153854
4. Private non-profit institutions serving households	178	575	528	543	599	657	804	843	938	1206	1280	1520	1818	2008	1980
5. Increase in stocks	623	1938	2573	1215	1299	1885	3396	476	1092	1280	1027	1813	1613	1424	1187
6. Gross fixed capital formation	4638	21441	26043	27637	31524	40938	46695	48136	51945	55982	62147	70171	75821	78908	79735
7. **Total Domestic Expenditure**	**15938**	**61237**	**72404**	**78503**	**90260**	**112468**	**135243**	**148265**	**165238**	**182582**	**200850**	**223548**	**242326**	**255913**	**263551**
8. Exports of goods and services	1714	6558	7926	9452	9779	11291	18258	18982	22582	24308	22729	25627	32887	37977	39391
9. *Less:* Imports of goods and services	1641	5567	6985	7254	7645	11261	19257	18919	21247	21267	19174	27629	35036	35927	37341
10. Statistical discrepancy	..	..	..	..	..	..	..	..	..	..	..	..	..	..	..
11. **Gross Domestic Product**	**16011**	**62228**	**73345**	**80701**	**92394**	**112498**	**134244**	**148327**	**166573**	**185622**	**204404**	**221547**	**240176**	**257963**	**270601**
At 1990 price levels[1]															
1. Government final consumption expenditure	10398	17205	18428	19910	20899	22028	21936	24698	25742	26817	28214	29399	30314	31677	32600
2. Private final consumption expenditure	46242	101808	109352	115360	125716	136787	136672	142691	146840	152763	160787	171216	173032	175577	183228
3. Households	44911	99342	107347	113516	123911	135093	135044	141149	145302	150947	158926	169143	170742	173109	180841
4. Private non-profit institutions serving households	1384	2542	2038	1864	1816	1692	1624	1529	1523	1811	1853	2069	2297	2482	2391
5. Increase in stocks	1019	2296	4355	2140	2204	2673	4050	724	1279	1451	1254	1731	1262	1327	1224
6. Gross fixed capital formation	13625	50136	58593	61352	67538	75349	68939	68470	70456	72464	78206	82818	84383	84200	
7. **Total Domestic Expenditure**	**71284**	**171444**	**190729**	**198763**	**216357**	**236837**	**231597**	**236583**	**244317**	**253494**	**268461**	**285163**	**287107**	**292965**	**301252**
8. Exports of goods and services	2566	9522	11189	12979	13513	14221	17512	17345	20225	22597	22540	23511	27503	30952	31242
9. *Less:* Imports of goods and services	3650	11491	14119	15114	16701	20765	21633	19407	20702	21549	23038	26013	23994	24093	23499
10. Statistical discrepancy	−706	150	−9	−14	−14	−16	−19	−33	−30	−30	−32	−36	−28	−23	−28
11. **Gross Domestic Product**	**69493**	**169625**	**187790**	**196614**	**213156**	**230278**	**227457**	**234489**	**243809**	**254513**	**267931**	**282625**	**290588**	**299801**	**303966**
COST COMPONENTS OF THE G.D.P.															
1. Indirect taxes	1353	4253	5202	5712	6491	7890	9254	9736	10870	12890	13912	16188	17688	19455	20285
2. *Less:* Subsidies	85	657	805	904	1066	1180	2123	2207	2181	2469	2713	2930	3593	3745	3780
3. Consumption of fixed capital	1751	8275	9730	10911	12825	15296	17766	19025	20704	23012	24999	27644	30701	34059	36216
4. Compensation of employees paid by resident producers	6453	26453	31895	37817	44026	55180	70010	81581	92020	102795	111079	120062	130398	141490	149559
5. Operating surplus	6470	23648	27415	26937	30569	36622	39298	39602	45256	48693	56422	60368	64757	66332	63217
6. Statistical discrepancy	68	257	−91	228	−450	−1309	39	590	−97	702	706	215	225	373	104
7. **Gross Domestic Product**	**16010**	**62229**	**73345**	**80701**	**92394**	**112498**	**134244**	**148327**	**166573**	**185622**	**204404**	**221547**	**240176**	**257963**	**270601**
CAPITAL TRANSACTIONS OF THE NATION															
Finance of Gross Capital Formation															
1. Consumption of fixed capital	1751	8275	9730	10911	12825	15296	17766	19025	20704	23012	24999	27644	30701	34059	36216
2. Net saving	3522	15651	19722	19748	22524	28847	31001	28845	33547	36416	40974	42230	44026	47152	46486
3. *Less:* Surplus of the nation on current transactions	80	803	744	2036	2077	11	−1285	−152	1117	2867	3504	−1896	−2481	1251	1885
4. Statistical discrepancy	68	257	−91	228	−450	−1309	39	590	−97	702	706	215	225	373	104
5. **Finance of Gross Capital Formation**	**5261**	**23380**	**28616**	**28852**	**32823**	**42824**	**50091**	**48612**	**53037**	**57262**	**63174**	**71984**	**77434**	**80332**	**80921**
Gross capital formation															
6. Increase in stocks	623	1938	2573	1215	1299	1885	3396	476	1092	1280	1027	1813	1613	1424	1187
7. Gross fixed capital formation	4638	21441	26043	27637	31524	40938	46695	48136	51945	55982	62147	70171	75821	78908	79735
8. Statistical discrepancy	..	..	..	..	..	..	..	..	..	..	..	..	..	..	..
9. **Gross Capital Formation**	**5261**	**23379**	**28616**	**28852**	**32822**	**42824**	**50091**	**48612**	**53037**	**57262**	**63174**	**71984**	**77434**	**80332**	**80921**
RELATIONS AMONG NATIONAL ACCOUNTING AGGREGATES															
1. **Gross Domestic Product**	**16010**	**62229**	**73345**	**80701**	**92394**	**112498**	**134244**	**148327**	**166573**	**185622**	**204404**	**221547**	**240176**	**257963**	**270601**
2. *Plus:* Net factor income from the rest of the world	−12	−163	−157	−110	7	21	−247	−157	−156	−92	70	278	−78	−546	69
3. Factor income from the rest of the world	60	260	347	443	598	841	1189	1273	1257	1254	1376	2276	2820	3837	5088
4. Factor income paid to the rest of the world	72	423	503	552	592	820	1436	1430	1414	1346	1306	1998	2898	4384	5019
5. *Equals:* **Gross National Product**	**15998**	**62066**	**73188**	**80592**	**92401**	**112519**	**133997**	**148170**	**166417**	**185530**	**204475**	**221825**	**240098**	**257417**	**270669**
6. *Less:* Consumption of fixed capital	1751	8275	9730	10911	12825	15296	17766	19025	20704	23012	24999	27644	30701	34059	36216
7. *Plus:* Statistical discrepancy	−68	−257	91	−228	450	1309	−39	−590	97	−702	−706	−215	−225	−373	−104
8. *Equals:* **National Income**	**14180**	**53534**	**63550**	**69453**	**80026**	**98532**	**116192**	**128555**	**145809**	**161816**	**178770**	**193966**	**209172**	**222985**	**234350**
9. *Plus:* Net current transfers from the rest of the world	19	−26	−40	−53	−64	−41	−39	−57	−62	−81	−121	−172	−254	−252	−233
10. Current transfers from the rest of the world	22	31	35	45	42	41	55	59	68	70	62	80	87	97	117
11. Current transfers paid to the rest of the world	4	56	75	98	106	81	94	115	129	151	183	252	342	349	350
12. *Equals:* **National Disposable Income**	**14199**	**53509**	**63510**	**69400**	**79962**	**98492**	**116153**	**128498**	**145748**	**161735**	**178649**	**193794**	**208918**	**222733**	**234116**
13. *Less:* Final consumption	10677	37858	43788	49651	57438	69644	85152	99653	112201	125319	137676	151564	164892	175582	187630
14. *Plus:* Statistical discrepancy	..	..	..	..	..	..	..	..	..	..	..	..	..	..	..
15. *Equals:* **Net Saving**	**3522**	**15651**	**19722**	**19748**	**22524**	**28847**	**31001**	**28845**	**33547**	**36416**	**40974**	**42230**	**44026**	**47152**	**46486**
16. *Less:* Surplus of the nation on current transactions	80	803	744	2036	2077	11	−1285	−152	1117	2867	3504	−1896	−2481	1251	1885
17. *Plus:* Statistical discrepancy	68	257	−91	228	−450	−1309	39	590	−97	702	706	215	225	373	104
18. *Equals:* **Net Capital Formation**	**3510**	**15105**	**18887**	**17941**	**19998**	**27527**	**32324**	**29587**	**32333**	**34250**	**38175**	**44340**	**46733**	**46273**	**44705**

1. At 1990 relative prices for 1970-1997 and at 1980 relative prices for 1960-1969.

Principaux Agrégats

milliards de yens

DÉPENSES IMPUTÉES AU P.I.B.

Aux prix courants

	1983	1984	1985	1986	1987	1988	1989	1990	1991	1992	1993	1994	1995	1996	1997
1. Consommation finale des administrations publiques	27996	29449	30685	32387	32975	34183	36275	38807	41356	43262	44771	45743	47419	48353	48895
2. Consommation finale privée	169687	178631	188760	196712	205956	217840	232890	249289	261891	272294	278703	286154	290524	299281	307448
3. Ménages	167509	176267	186235	194051	203342	214992	229831	246154	258332	268677	274696	282354	286455	295020	..
4. Institutions privées sans but lucratif au service des ménages	2179	2364	2525	2661	2614	2848	3060	3135	3559	3618	4007	3799	4069	4261	..
5. Variations des stocks	187	1011	2159	1560	661	2676	2976	2430	3453	1489	620	50	546	1227	1072
6. Formation brute de capital fixe	78881	83251	88040	91499	99152	110856	122274	136467	143998	143525	140433	137291	137611	148322	143547
7. **Demande intérieure totale**	276751	292343	309643	322158	338745	365555	394415	426992	450698	460571	464527	469237	476099	497183	500961
8. Exportations de biens et services	39275	45066	46307	38090	36210	37483	42352	45920	46722	47341	44197	44410	45393	49700	56332
9. *Moins :* Importations de biens et services	34258	36866	35532	24791	25195	29065	36768	42872	39121	36891	33343	34387	38272	47022	50316
10. Divergence statistique	..	..	..	..	..	..	..	..	..	..	..	..	..	..	..
11. **Produit intérieur brut**	281767	300543	320419	335457	349760	373973	399998	430040	458299	471021	475381	479260	483220	499861	506977

Aux niveaux de prix de 1990[1]

	1983	1984	1985	1986	1987	1988	1989	1990	1991	1992	1993	1994	1995	1996	1997
1. Consommation finale des administrations publiques	33429	34215	34314	36078	36642	37497	38237	38807	39580	40355	41304	42291	43688	44358	44291
2. Consommation finale privée	189347	194317	200762	207794	216543	227997	238846	249289	255563	260864	263902	268962	274533	282524	285534
3. Ménages	186775	191592	197891	204807	213616	224888	235626	246154	252092	257385	259994	265331	270630	278482	..
4. Institutions privées sans but lucratif au service des ménages	2582	2740	2888	3006	2937	3121	3231	3135	3484	3490	3939	3644	3926	4067	..
5. Variations des stocks	174	775	1960	1464	703	2801	3135	2430	3486	1481	825	15	864	1106	1085
6. Formation brute de capital fixe	83281	86842	91177	95554	104286	116242	125805	136467	140938	138759	136051	135027	137380	150496	145185
7. **Demande intérieure totale**	306231	316149	328212	340889	358175	384536	406022	426992	439567	441458	442082	446295	456465	478484	476095
8. Exportations de biens et services	32727	37570	39614	37359	37158	39362	42958	45920	48329	50715	51398	53757	56673	58655	65010
9. *Moins :* Importations de biens et services	22785	25170	24818	25302	27710	33511	39735	42872	41537	41246	41139	44782	51162	57048	56952
10. Divergence statistique	−32	−25	−14	−22	−20	−12	−10	0	12	6	−3	−15	−25	−17	−14
11. **Produit intérieur brut**	316141	328525	342993	352924	367602	390375	409235	430040	446372	450933	452339	455255	461952	480074	484139

RÉPARTITION DU P.I.B.

	1983	1984	1985	1986	1987	1988	1989	1990	1991	1992	1993	1994	1995	1996	1997
1. Impôts indirects	20631	22943	24900	25213	28379	30878	32158	35212	34968	37301	37199	38003	39348	41062	43100*
2. *Moins :* Subventions	3968	3807	3650	3678	3419	3409	3104	4644	3852	3304	3471	3466	3658	3587	3551*
3. Consommation de capital fixe	38426	40778	43615	46205	48930	52398	58081	62987	68541	72823	74383	75605	77153	79850	80986*
4. Rémunération des salariés payée par les producteurs résidents	157357	166120	173892	181278	187757	198284	212422	230313	248301	256885	262899	269534	273964	279433	287406*
5. Excédent net d'exploitation	69233	74395	81501	86101	89142	96965	101293	105992	110744	107509	104012	99041	96790	104813	100436*
6. Divergence statistique	89	114	161	338	−1030	−1143	−851	179	−403	−192	360	543	−377	−1709	−1400*
7. **Produit intérieur brut**	281767	300543	320419	335457	349760	373973	399998	430040	458299	471021	475381	479260	483220	499861	506977

OPÉRATIONS EN CAPITAL DE LA NATION

Financement de la formation brute de capital

	1983	1984	1985	1986	1987	1988	1989	1990	1991	1992	1993	1994	1995	1996	1997
1. Consommation de capital fixe	38426	40778	43615	46205	48931	52398	58081	62987	68541	72823	74383	75605	77153	79849	80986*
2. Épargne nette	45636	51838	58082	60822	64610	72642	76120	81368	89732	86640	80982	74574	71805	78567	76540*
3. *Moins :* Solde des opérations courantes de la nation	5083	8467	11660	14306	12697	10364	8100	5638	10419	14256	14672	13381	10425	7158	11507*
4. Divergence statistique	89	114	161	338	−1030	−1143	−851	179	−403	−192	360	543	−377	−1710	−1400*
5. **Financement de la formation brute de capital**	79067	84263	90198	93059	99814	113533	125250	138897	147451	145014	141053	137341	138157	149549	144619

Formation brute de capital

	1983	1984	1985	1986	1987	1988	1989	1990	1991	1992	1993	1994	1995	1996	1997
6. Variations des stocks	187	1011	2159	1560	661	2676	2976	2430	3453	1489	620	50	546	1227	1072
7. Formation brute de capital fixe	78881	83251	88040	91499	99152	110856	122274	136467	143998	143525	140433	137291	137611	148322	143547
8. Divergence statistique	..	..	..	..	..	..	..	..	..	..	..	..	..	..	..
9. **Formation brute de capital**	79067	84262	90198	93059	99813	113532	125250	138897	147451	145014	141053	137341	138157	149549	144619

RELATIONS ENTRE LES PRINCIPAUX AGRÉGATS

	1983	1984	1985	1986	1987	1988	1989	1990	1991	1992	1993	1994	1995	1996	1997
1. **Produit intérieur brut**	281767	300543	320419	335457	349760	373973	399998	430040	458299	471021	475381	479260	483220	499861	506977
2. *Plus :* Revenu net des facteurs reçu du reste du monde	311	505	1137	1229	2054	2302	2849	2932	3190	4268	4381	3942	3991	5457	6491
3. Revenu des facteurs reçu du reste du monde	4211	4953	5768	5338	7607	10124	14761	18520	19767	19052	17381	16765	19131	25675	28463
4. Revenu des facteurs payé au reste du monde	3900	4448	4631	4108	5553	7822	11911	15588	16577	14784	13001	12823	15140	20218	21972
5. *Égal :* **Produit national brut**	282078	301048	321556	336686	351814	376275	402848	432972	461489	475289	479762	483202	487212	505318	513468
6. *Moins :* Consommation de capital fixe	38426	40778	43615	46205	48930	52398	58081	62987	68541	72823	74383	75605	77153	79849	80986*
7. *Plus :* Divergence statistique	−89	−114	−161	−338	1030	1143	851	−179	403	192	−360	−543	377	1709	1400*
8. *Égal :* **Revenu national**	243564	260157	277780	290143	303914	325021	345618	369805	393351	402658	405019	407053	410435	427178	433882*
9. *Plus :* Transferts courants nets reçus du reste du monde	−245	−239	−253	−222	−372	−356	−333	−343	−372	−462	−563	−583	−688	−977	−1000*
10. Transferts courants reçus du reste du monde	114	134	102	70	92	141	142	149	191	212	175	187	187	655	..
11. Transferts courants payés au reste du monde	359	373	355	292	463	497	475	491	563	674	738	771	875	1632	..
12. *Égal :* **Revenu national disponible**	243320	259918	277527	289921	303542	324665	345285	369463	392979	402196	404457	406470	409747	426201	432882*
13. *Moins :* Consommation finale	197684	208080	219445	229099	238932	252023	269165	288095	303247	315557	323475	331896	337942	347634	356343
14. *Plus :* Divergence statistique	..	..	..	..	..	..	..	..	..	..	..	..	..	..	..
15. *Égal :* **Épargne nette**	45636	51838	58082	60822	64610	72642	76120	81368	89732	86640	80982	74574	71805	78567	76540*
16. *Moins :* Solde des opérations courantes de la nation	5083	8467	11660	14306	10364	10364	8100	5638	10419	14256	14672	13381	10425	7158	11507*
17. *Plus :* Divergence statistique	89	114	161	338	−1030	−1143	−851	179	−403	−192	360	543	−377	−1710	−1400*
18. *Égal :* **Formation nette de capital**	40642	43485	46583	46854	50883	61135	67169	75910	78910	72191	66670	61735	61004	69700	63633*

1. Aux prix relatifs de 1990 pour la période 1970-1997 et aux prix relatifs de 1980 pour la période 1960-1969.

KOREA
1968 SNA

Main aggregates

billions of won

	1960	1969	1970	1971	1972	1973	1974	1975	1976	1977	1978	1979	1980	1981	1982
EXPENDITURE ON THE G.D.P.															
At current prices															
1. Government final consumption expenditure	..	..	261.8	333.4	425.9	457.1	741.0	1134.3	1537.7	1945.7	2542.0	3130.1	4416.2	5555.5	6313.5
2. Private final consumption expenditure	..	..	2069.0	2586.3	3103.6	3770.1	5391.9	7263.8	9221.2	11250.3	14785.6	19366.9	24584.7	30649.4	34629.9
3. Households	..	..	2049.3	2555.4	3073.1	3736.7	5348.1	7202.8	9141.6	11147.0	14643.5	19181.9	24343.0	30356.5	34276.7
4. Private non-profit institutions serving households	..	..	19.8	30.8	30.5	33.4	43.8	61.0	79.5	103.3	142.1	185.0	241.7	292.9	353.3
5. Increase in stocks	..	..	-3.7	93.2	21.6	78.3	380.3	189.8	164.5	43.7	106.6	679.2	-170.5	650.5	38.2
6. Gross fixed capital formation	..	..	695.6	768.6	871.4	1298.3	2068.6	2744.8	3593.7	5107.0	7923.5	10573.4	12229.9	13368.8	15586.3
7. **Total Domestic Expenditure**	..	..	3022.7	3781.5	4422.5	5603.8	8581.8	11332.7	14517.1	18346.7	25357.7	33749.6	41060.3	50224.2	56567.9
8. Exports of goods and services	..	..	389.7	527.7	838.6	1598.7	2131.6	2859.1	4369.7	5706.9	7227.0	8738.5	12943.6	17340.6	18769.3
9. *Less:* Imports of goods and services	..	..	658.7	878.9	1033.0	1757.2	2972.8	3727.6	4621.6	5812.6	8063.3	10831.5	15774.0	19718.7	20173.7
10. Statistical discrepancy	..	..	17.5	-6.8	-16.3	-23.8	-76.9	-168.7	-177.3	-177.7	-133.1	-263.2	-81.5	-189.4	-442.5
11. **Gross Domestic Product**	..	..	2771.2	3423.5	4211.8	5421.5	7663.7	10295.5	14087.9	18063.3	24388.3	31393.4	38148.4	47656.7	54721.0
At 1990 price levels[1]															
1. Government final consumption expenditure	..	..	6398.0	6821.1	7109.1	7084.2	7868.4	8494.2	8756.0	9263.4	10107.2	10215.0	10898.8	11426.3	11522.2
2. Private final consumption expenditure	..	..	23931.2	26029.1	27295.0	29595.6	31591.9	33209.0	35951.0	37858.5	41063.2	44379.7	44188.8	46304.7	49218.5
3. Households	..	..	23694.2	25707.9	27001.5	29289.8	31279.4	32864.8	35578.1	37431.4	40569.8	43849.5	43645.1	45784.5	48668.9
4. Private non-profit institutions serving households	..	..	237.0	321.2	293.5	305.8	312.5	344.2	372.9	427.1	493.4	530.2	543.7	520.2	549.6
5. Increase in stocks	..	..	872.8	1449.5	737.9	1061.2	2757.4	1494.6	1477.5	1464.6	1218.2	2875.2	47.2	1208.5	790.1
6. Gross fixed capital formation	..	..	6390.7	6583.2	6670.2	8513.6	9775.1	10523.4	12731.8	16381.0	22009.4	24141.1	21561.6	20757.6	23050.0
7. **Total Domestic Expenditure**	..	..	37592.7	40882.9	41812.2	46254.6	51992.8	53721.2	58916.3	64967.5	74398.0	81611.0	76696.4	79697.1	84580.8
8. Exports of goods and services	..	..	2996.7	3658.9	4972.1	7672.8	7640.4	9073.2	12557.0	15174.3	17358.5	17637.2	19046.8	21953.0	22954.6
9. *Less:* Imports of goods and services	..	..	4879.9	5849.9	5913.7	8023.2	9442.3	9710.1	12091.2	14596.6	18637.0	20814.8	19803.5	20953.1	21522.0
10. Statistical discrepancy	..	..	596.8	698.3	416.8	667.6	139.0	586.2	600.9	627.0	-735.1	-886.4	-474.1	-547.4	217.4
11. **Gross Domestic Product**	..	..	36306.3	39390.2	41287.4	46571.8	50329.9	53670.5	59983.0	66172.2	72384.4	77547.0	75465.6	80149.6	86230.8
COST COMPONENTS OF THE G.D.P.															
1. Indirect taxes	..	..	267.4	317.7	356.3	464.3	764.2	1150.3	1628.9	2124.9	2948.9	3867.7	4919.8	6075.1	7042.9
2. *Less:* Subsidies	..	..	9.6	10.2	16.8	45.7	144.4	148.3	170.8	233.0	301.0	342.1	326.7	343.8	347.8
3. Consumption of fixed capital	..	..	197.3	251.4	310.1	434.9	609.8	768.9	1092.5	1419.9	1810.3	2509.8	3132.6	3990.8	5046.0
4. Compensation of employees paid by resident producers	..	..	936.2	1156.9	1406.0	1831.8	2474.8	3345.0	4720.1	6344.1	9034.2	12044.1	15097.5	18545.1	21475.9
5. Operating surplus	..	..	1380.1	1707.6	2156.3	2736.1	3959.2	5179.5	6817.3	8407.4	10895.9	13314.0	15325.2	19389.5	21504.0
6. Statistical discrepancy	..	..	..	..	..	..	..	..	..	..	..	..	..	..	..
7. **Gross Domestic Product**	..	..	2771.4	3423.4	4211.9	5421.4	7663.6	10295.4	14088.0	18063.3	24388.3	31393.5	38148.4	47656.7	54721.0
CAPITAL TRANSACTIONS OF THE NATION															
Finance of Gross Capital Formation															
1. Consumption of fixed capital	..	..	197.3	251.4	310.1	434.9	609.8	768.9	1092.5	1419.9	1810.3	2509.8	3132.6	3990.8	5046.0
2. Net saving	..	..	316.7	307.8	425.8	798.8	948.3	1086.5	2339.2	3577.9	5569.3	6467.6	5647.7	6754.1	8159.7
3. *Less:* Surplus of the nation on current transactions	..	..	-195.5	-295.8	-140.8	-119.1	-813.9	-910.4	-149.3	24.7	-517.3	-2012.0	-3197.7	-3085.0	-1976.3
4. Statistical discrepancy	..	..	..	..	..	..	..	..	..	..	..	..	..	..	..
5. **Finance of Gross Capital Formation**	..	..	709.5	855.0	876.7	1352.8	2372.0	2765.8	3581.0	4973.1	7896.9	10989.4	11978.0	13829.9	15182.0
Gross capital formation															
6. Increase in stocks	..	..	-3.7	93.2	21.6	78.3	380.3	189.8	164.5	43.7	106.6	679.2	-170.5	650.5	38.2
7. Gross fixed capital formation	..	..	695.6	768.6	871.4	1298.3	2068.6	2744.8	3593.7	5107.0	7923.5	10573.4	12229.9	13368.8	15586.3
8. Statistical discrepancy	..	..	17.5	-6.8	-16.3	-23.8	-76.9	-168.7	-177.3	-177.7	-133.1	-263.2	-81.5	-189.4	-442.5
9. **Gross Capital Formation**	..	..	709.4	855.0	876.7	1352.8	2372.0	2765.9	3580.9	4973.0	7897.0	10989.4	11977.9	13829.9	15182.0
RELATIONS AMONG NATIONAL ACCOUNTING AGGREGATES															
1. **Gross Domestic Product**	..	..	2771.3	3423.4	4211.9	5421.5	7663.7	10295.5	14088.0	18063.3	24388.2	31393.4	38148.4	47656.7	54721.0
2. *Plus:* Net factor income from the rest of the world	..	..	17.1	-4.3	-18.4	-44.0	-72.0	-166.3	-188.3	-267.5	-325.5	-521.3	-1291.4	-1953.8	-2260.5
3. Factor income from the rest of the world	..	..	42.6	41.3	48.9	47.5	71.5	69.1	83.3	122.2	213.0	274.0	433.2	628.9	699.9
4. Factor income paid to the rest of the world	..	..	25.5	45.6	67.3	91.5	143.5	235.4	271.6	389.7	538.5	795.3	1724.6	2582.7	2960.4
5. *Equals:* **Gross National Product**	..	..	2788.4	3419.1	4193.5	5377.5	7591.7	10129.2	13899.7	17795.8	24062.7	30872.1	36857.0	45702.9	52460.5
6. *Less:* Consumption of fixed capital	..	..	197.3	251.4	310.1	434.9	609.8	768.9	1092.5	1419.9	1810.3	2509.8	3132.6	3990.8	5046.0
7. *Plus:* Statistical discrepancy	..	..	..	..	..	..	..	..	..	..	..	..	..	..	..
8. *Equals:* **National Income**	..	..	2591.1	3167.7	3883.4	4942.6	6981.8	9360.2	12807.2	16375.9	22252.4	28362.3	33724.5	41712.1	47414.5
9. *Plus:* Net current transfers from the rest of the world	..	..	56.4	59.7	72.0	83.4	99.3	124.4	290.9	397.9	644.5	602.3	924.1	1246.9	1688.6
10. Current transfers from the rest of the world	..	..	67.1	71.6	88.9	124.5	138.0	179.1	379.0	518.5	743.7	731.1	1151.0	1495.0	1984.4
11. Current transfers paid to the rest of the world	..	..	10.7	11.9	16.9	41.1	38.7	54.7	88.1	120.6	99.2	128.8	226.9	248.1	295.8
12. *Equals:* **National Disposable Income**	..	..	2647.5	3227.4	3955.4	5026.0	7081.1	9484.6	13098.1	16773.8	22896.9	28964.6	34648.6	42959.0	49103.1
13. *Less:* Final consumption	..	..	2330.8	2919.7	3529.6	4227.2	6132.9	8398.2	10758.9	13195.9	17327.6	22497.0	29000.9	36205.0	40943.4
14. *Plus:* Statistical discrepancy	..	..	..	..	..	..	..	..	..	..	..	..	..	..	..
15. *Equals:* **Net Saving**	..	..	316.7	307.8	425.8	798.8	948.3	1086.5	2339.2	3577.9	5569.3	6467.6	5647.7	6754.1	8159.7
16. *Less:* Surplus of the nation on current transactions	..	..	-195.5	-295.8	-140.8	-119.1	-813.9	-910.4	-149.3	24.7	-517.3	-2012.0	-3197.7	-3085.0	-1976.3
17. *Plus:* Statistical discrepancy	..	..	..	..	..	..	..	..	..	..	..	..	..	..	..
18. *Equals:* **Net Capital Formation**	..	..	512.2	603.6	566.6	917.9	1762.2	1996.9	2488.5	3553.2	6086.6	8479.6	8845.4	9839.1	10136.0

1. At 1990 relative prices.

Principaux Agrégats

milliards de wons

DÉPENSES IMPUTÉES AU P.I.B.

Aux prix courants

1983	1984	1985	1986	1987	1988	1989	1990	1991	1992	1993	1994	1995	1996	1997	
6935.2	7353.7	8304.5	9574.9	10843.2	12659.8	15237.4	18187.0	22169.5	26110.3	28745.9	32424.7	36086.4	41722.6	46887.4	1. Consommation finale des administrations publiques
38892.2	43442.8	48026.8	52822.1	59030.9	67963.3	79424.0	96387.7	115042.8	129735.2	143721.7	164356.4	186413.0	209818.0	225772.4	2. Consommation finale privée
38405.4	42806.2	47236.2	51973.9	58076.3	66793.0	78075.2	94772.2	113161.8	127491.6	141353.7	161688.2	183349.7	206341.8	221907.4	3. Ménages
486.8	636.6	790.6	848.1	954.6	1170.3	1348.8	1615.5	1880.9	2243.6	2367.9	2668.2	3063.2	3476.2	3865.0	4. Institutions privées sans but lucratif au service des ménages
−345.9	778.3	849.0	504.6	840.8	1531.7	2538.7	−270.0	973.0	35.2	−2511.7	935.5	1737.1	6089.9	−126.6	5. Variations des stocks
18944.4	21381.2	23434.9	26969.2	32587.2	39424.6	47625.3	66568.7	82946.5	87907.0	96218.5	109379.2	128663.5	143688.7	147340.2	6. Formation brute de capital fixe
64425.9	72956.0	80615.2	89870.8	103302.1	121979.4	144825.4	180873.4	221131.8	243787.7	266174.4	307095.8	352900.0	401319.2	419873.4	7. **Demande intérieure totale**
22748.5	26126.1	27968.3	36034.2	45050.9	51132.1	48828.7	53467.0	60735.0	69432.7	78162.6	92121.3	116360.0	126236.6	160466.8	8. Exportations de biens et services
23048.8	26039.5	26922.6	30365.5	36356.0	40566.5	44784.8	54417.2	66049.7	71840.0	76970.7	94359.8	120086.4	141649.3	163512.6	9. *Moins :* Importations de biens et services
71.0	562.5	401.1	196.9	133.3	589.2	295.4	−384.3	−82.6	−988.2	−220.4	1112.8	2801.1	3907.0	4159.1	10. Divergence statistique
64196.6	73605.1	82062.0	95736.4	112130.3	133134.2	149164.7	179538.9	215734.5	240392.2	267145.9	305970.1	351974.3	389813.5	420986.7	11. **Produit intérieur brut**

Aux niveaux de prix de 1990[1]

1983	1984	1985	1986	1987	1988	1989	1990	1991	1992	1993	1994	1995	1996	1997	
11857.9	12006.6	12581.0	13639.5	14473.8	15632.8	16969.5	18187.0	19725.0	21222.8	21868.5	22788.1	23023.6	24827.4	26248.9	1. Consommation finale des administrations publiques
53745.0	57965.8	61701.4	66700.7	72131.7	78606.4	87108.8	96387.7	105526.2	112501.4	118883.3	127864.7	138461.0	147869.4	152480.0	2. Consommation finale privée
53027.0	57055.7	60618.2	65577.9	70915.6	77215.9	85612.9	94772.2	103799.8	110628.4	117041.3	125938.9	136445.2	145787.0	150316.8	3. Ménages
718.0	910.1	1083.2	1122.8	1216.1	1390.5	1495.9	1615.5	1726.4	1873.0	1842.0	1925.8	2015.8	2082.4	2163.2	4. Institutions privées sans but lucratif au service des ménages
85.3	1292.5	1212.7	545.0	665.3	2027.5	2893.7	−270.0	1147.4	153.2	−1890.7	1189.8	94.5	3243.7	−6922.2	5. Variations des stocks
27029.3	29725.8	31018.2	34315.8	40141.6	45646.3	52885.0	66568.7	74973.2	74375.9	78279.1	87484.2	97717.3	104641.3	100947.0	6. Formation brute de capital fixe
92717.5	100990.7	106513.3	115201.0	127412.4	141913.0	159857.0	180873.4	201371.8	208253.3	217140.2	239326.8	259296.4	280581.8	272753.7	7. **Demande intérieure totale**
27416.0	29531.9	30882.1	39078.2	47542.6	53506.9	51335.6	53467.0	59785.7	66351.2	73857.2	86039.6	106675.4	120544.9	149014.2	8. Exportations de biens et services
24085.2	25867.7	25717.6	30329.3	36259.2	40954.3	47613.6	54417.2	64890.0	68207.8	72777.1	88578.8	108036.5	124032.3	128694.1	9. *Moins :* Importations de biens et services
97.7	−166.3	−347.9	243.9	−196.6	−354.5	371.2	−384.3	−331.8	−536.5	−521.5	−412.6	−434.1	−1403.3	−2185.6	10. Divergence statistique
96146.0	104488.6	111329.9	124193.8	138499.2	154111.1	163950.2	179538.9	195935.7	205860.2	217698.8	236375.1	257501.2	275691.1	290888.2	11. **Produit intérieur brut**

RÉPARTITION DU P.I.B.

1983	1984	1985	1986	1987	1988	1989	1990	1991	1992	1993	1994	1995	1996	1997	
8641.8	9330.5	9895.4	11422.7	13068.2	15211.5	16762.8	21519.1	24857.2	28915.8	32548.6	39152.3	45912.3	53564.3	59346.0	1. Impôts indirects
462.3	578.0	488.1	550.3	520.3	390.5	631.3	956.3	1250.5	1573.2	2041.2	2146.9	2322.3	1572.0	752.7	2. *Moins :* Subventions
6114.4	7291.4	8205.4	9466.6	11590.8	14052.0	15687.5	18586.9	21589.8	23925.9	26963.8	29910.3	35543.5	40606.0	44080.3	3. Consommation de capital fixe
25898.1	29650.9	32904.1	37726.4	45386.4	55714.0	66368.0	81740.4	101360.3	113876.0	125164.8	141766.0	164695.5	186787.6	200791.4	4. Rémunération des salariés payée par les producteurs résidents
24004.4	27910.4	31545.2	37671.2	42605.3	48547.2	50977.6	58648.9	69177.6	75247.7	84509.9	97288.5	108145.7	110427.4	117521.8	5. Excédent net d'exploitation
..	..	..	..	..	..	..	..	..	..	..	..	..	..	..	6. Divergence statistique
64196.4	73605.2	82062.0	95736.4	112130.4	133134.2	149164.6	179539.0	215734.4	240392.2	267145.9	305970.2	351974.7	389813.3	420986.8	7. **Produit intérieur brut**

OPÉRATIONS EN CAPITAL DE LA NATION

Financement de la formation brute de capital

1983	1984	1985	1986	1987	1988	1989	1990	1991	1992	1993	1994	1995	1996	1997	
6114.4	7291.4	8205.4	9466.6	11590.8	14052.0	15687.5	18586.9	21589.8	23925.9	26963.8	29910.3	35543.5	40606.0	44080.3	1. Consommation de capital fixe
11345.1	14332.4	15721.4	22224.6	29979.7	38103.7	38114.3	45716.3	55838.5	59522.3	66825.9	77835.1	90780.2	93837.4	99893.7	2. Épargne nette
−1209.9	−1098.2	−758.2	4020.4	8009.1	10210.2	3342.4	−1611.3	−6408.6	−3505.8	303.2	−3682.2	−6878.0	−19242.1	−7398.7	3. *Moins :* Solde des opérations courantes de la nation
..	..	..	..	..	..	..	..	..	..	..	..	..	..	..	4. Divergence statistique
18669.4	22722.0	24685.0	27670.8	33561.4	41945.5	50459.4	65914.5	83836.9	86954.0	93486.5	111427.6	133201.7	153685.5	151372.7	5. **Financement de la formation brute de capital**

Formation brute de capital

1983	1984	1985	1986	1987	1988	1989	1990	1991	1992	1993	1994	1995	1996	1997	
−345.9	778.3	849.0	504.6	840.8	1931.7	2538.7	−270.0	973.0	35.2	−2511.7	935.5	1737.1	6089.9	−126.6	6. Variations des stocks
18944.4	21381.2	23434.9	26969.2	32587.2	39424.6	47625.3	66568.7	82946.5	87907.0	96218.5	109379.2	128663.5	143688.7	147340.2	7. Formation brute de capital fixe
71.0	562.5	401.1	196.9	133.3	589.2	295.4	−384.3	−82.6	−988.2	−220.4	1112.8	2801.1	3907.0	4159.1	8. Divergence statistique
18669.5	22722.0	24685.0	27670.7	33561.3	41945.5	50459.4	65914.4	83836.9	86954.0	93486.4	111427.5	133201.7	153685.6	151372.7	9. **Formation brute de capital**

RELATIONS ENTRE LES PRINCIPAUX AGRÉGATS

1983	1984	1985	1986	1987	1988	1989	1990	1991	1992	1993	1994	1995	1996	1997	
64196.5	73605.1	82062.1	95736.4	112130.3	133134.2	149164.7	179539.0	215734.4	240392.2	267146.0	305970.2	351974.7	389813.4	420986.7	1. **Produit intérieur brut**
−2110.5	−2560.5	−2761.0	−2827.1	−2403.8	−1762.9	−1223.1	−1276.9	−1494.5	−1687.6	−1628.1	−2197.6	−2995.4	−3375.2	−4968.8	2. *Plus :* Revenu net des facteurs reçu du reste du monde
712.8	882.8	1039.7	1159.6	1028.0	1096.7	1530.9	2118.5	2360.0	2538.9	2296.0	2372.9	3141.3	3327.7	4616.9	3. Revenu des facteurs reçu du reste du monde
2823.3	3443.3	3800.7	3986.7	3431.8	2859.6	2754.0	3395.4	3854.5	4226.5	3924.1	4570.5	6136.7	6702.9	9585.7	4. Revenu des facteurs payé au reste du monde
62086.0	71044.6	79301.1	92909.3	109726.5	131371.3	147941.6	178262.1	214239.9	238704.6	265517.9	303772.6	348979.3	386438.2	416017.9	5. *Égal :* **Produit national brut**
6114.4	7291.4	8205.4	9466.6	11590.8	14052.0	15687.5	18586.9	21589.8	23925.9	26963.8	29910.3	35543.5	40606.0	44080.3	6. *Moins :* Consommation de capital fixe
..	..	..	..	..	..	..	..	..	..	..	..	..	..	..	7. *Plus :* Divergence statistique
55971.5	63753.2	71095.7	83442.8	98135.7	117319.3	132254.1	159675.2	192650.1	214778.7	238554.0	273862.3	313435.8	345832.2	371937.7	8. *Égal :* **Revenu national**
1200.9	1375.7	957.1	1178.8	1718.0	1407.5	521.6	615.8	400.6	589.1	739.4	753.9	−156.2	−454.2	615.9	9. *Plus :* Transferts courants nets reçus du reste du monde
1503.8	1678.6	1306.9	1466.7	2110.5	1950.1	1493.0	1897.4	2249.0	2681.2	2987.3	3171.4	3357.6	3641.9	5403.4	10. Transferts courants reçus du reste du monde
302.9	302.9	349.8	287.9	392.5	542.6	971.4	1281.6	1848.4	2092.2	2247.9	2417.5	3513.8	4096.1	4787.5	11. Transferts courants payés au reste du monde
57172.5	65128.9	72052.8	84621.6	99853.7	118726.8	132775.7	160291.0	193050.7	215367.8	239293.4	274616.2	313279.6	345378.0	372553.6	12. *Égal :* **Revenu national disponible**
45827.3	50796.5	56331.3	62397.0	69874.1	80623.1	94661.5	114574.7	137212.2	155845.5	172467.6	196781.1	222499.4	251540.6	272659.9	13. *Moins :* Consommation finale
..	..	..	..	..	..	..	..	..	..	..	..	..	..	..	14. *Plus :* Divergence statistique
11345.1	14332.4	15721.4	22224.6	29979.7	38103.7	38114.3	45716.3	55838.5	59522.3	66825.9	77835.1	90780.2	93837.4	99893.7	15. *Égal :* **Épargne nette**
−1209.9	−1098.2	−758.2	4020.4	8009.1	10210.2	3342.4	−1611.3	−6408.6	−3505.8	303.2	−3682.2	−6878.0	−19242.1	−7398.7	16. *Moins :* Solde des opérations courantes de la nation
..	..	..	..	..	..	..	..	..	..	..	..	..	..	..	17. *Plus :* Divergence statistique
12555.0	15430.6	16479.6	18204.2	21970.6	27893.5	34771.9	47327.6	62247.1	63028.1	66522.7	81517.3	97658.2	113079.5	107292.4	18. *Égal :* **Formation nette de capital**

1. Aux prix relatifs de 1990.

AUSTRALIA [1]
1968 SNA

Main aggregates

millions of Australian dollars, fiscal years

	1960	1969	1970	1971	1972	1973	1974	1975	1976	1977	1978	1979	1980	1981	1982
EXPENDITURE ON THE G.D.P.															
At current prices															
1. Government final consumption expenditure	1747	4296	4899	5591	6357	7954	10780	13333	15394	17272	19099	21394	25075	28639	32474
2. Private final consumption expenditure	9634	18837	20837	23170	26001	30730	37446	44790	51171	56933	64228	72532	82871	94412	105965
3. Households	..	..	..	..	..	..	..	..	..	..	..	..	..	..	..
4. Private non-profit institutions serving households	..	..	..	..	..	..	..	..	..	..	..	..	..	..	..
5. Increase in stocks	478	440	441	17	−270	1166	1025	159	1129	−430	1343	845	465	1559	−2437
6. Gross fixed capital formation	3718	8209	9131	10113	10996	12930	15138	18440	21009	22649	25984	28844	35192	41456	41105
7. **Total Domestic Expenditure**	15577	31782	35308	38891	43084	52780	64389	76722	88703	96424	110654	123615	143603	166066	177107
8. Exports of goods and services	2165	4754	5076	5683	7017	7890	10107	11217	13402	14236	16893	21993	22539	23631	25540
9. *Less:* Imports of goods and services	2590	4733	5093	5242	5392	7893	10379	10921	13934	15179	17978	21105	25075	29023	29062
10. Statistical discrepancy	56	10	−180	−44	84	833	633	−417	−577	−173	−1110	−1219	−452	−1952	−1109
11. **Gross Domestic Product**	15208	31813	35111	39288	44793	53610	64750	76601	87594	95308	108459	123284	140615	158722	172476
At 1990 price levels [2]															
1. Government final consumption expenditure	16939	29107	30187	31606	32638	35097	38049	40822	42293	43753	45458	46321	48477	48885	50174
2. Private final consumption expenditure	75887	116950	121887	127002	134044	141230	145875	150796	154447	157348	162883	166755	173568	180715	182966
3. Households	..	..	..	..	..	..	..	..	..	..	..	..	..	..	..
4. Private non-profit institutions serving households	..	..	..	..	..	..	..	..	..	..	..	..	..	..	..
5. Increase in stocks	3696	2558	2603	−222	−1223	4590	4400	407	3623	−1188	3775	2309	1173	2791	−3574
6. Gross fixed capital formation	29937	52606	55247	57195	57939	59869	56716	59335	60411	59767	63494	64065	70309	74912	66746
7. **Total Domestic Expenditure**	126459	201221	209924	215581	223398	240786	245040	251360	260774	259680	275610	279450	293527	307303	296543
8. Exports of goods and services	12184	22965	25101	27544	28302	26643	28609	29767	31798	32511	34525	37102	35261	36132	36160
9. *Less:* Imports of goods and services	16395	27808	27369	26607	26700	34287	35158	33012	36656	35191	38162	37997	41512	46194	42248
10. Statistical discrepancy	−422	−555	−923	816	1645	2616	1737	−1207	−1811	−416	−2791	−3277	−2383	−5883	−3681
11. **Gross Domestic Product**	121826	195823	206733	217334	226645	235758	240228	246908	254105	256584	269182	275278	284893	291358	286543
COST COMPONENTS OF THE G.D.P.															
1. Indirect taxes	1639	3284	3579	4099	4572	5695	6969	8873	10054	10848	12679	14975	17297	19711	22686
2. *Less:* Subsidies	77	296	346	433	466	592	760	850	1026	1292	1591	1839	2235	2569	3180
3. Consumption of fixed capital	1869	4069	4571	5164	5849	6910	9049	10914	12631	14341	16077	18430	21207	24300	27801
4. Compensation of employees paid by resident producers	7634	16452	18884	21077	23562	28894	37160	42830	48316	53066	57085	63616	74054	85566	94949
5. Operating surplus	4143	8304	8423	9381	11276	12703	12332	14834	17619	18345	24209	28102	30292	31714	30220
6. Statistical discrepancy	..	..	..	..	..	..	..	..	..	..	..	..	..	..	..
7. **Gross Domestic Product**	15208	31813	35111	39288	44793	53610	64750	76601	87594	95308	108459	123284	140615	158722	172476
CAPITAL TRANSACTIONS OF THE NATION															
Finance of Gross Capital Formation															
1. Consumption of fixed capital	1869	4069	4571	5164	5849	6910	9049	10914	12631	14341	16077	18430	21207	24300	27801
2. Net saving	1741	4105	4291	4823	5948	7430	6770	6393	7050	5295	7200	8853	9188	8223	2462
3. *Less:* Surplus of the nation on current transactions	−642	−485	−530	−99	987	−589	−977	−875	−1880	−2410	−2940	−1187	−4810	−8540	−7296
4. Statistical discrepancy	−56	−10	180	44	−84	−833	−633	417	577	173	1110	1219	452	1952	1109
5. **Finance of Gross Capital Formation**	4196	8649	9572	10130	10726	14096	16163	18599	22138	22219	27327	29689	35657	43015	38668
Gross capital formation															
6. Increase in stocks	478	440	441	17	−270	1166	1025	159	1129	−430	1343	845	465	1559	−2437
7. Gross fixed capital formation	3718	8209	9131	10113	10996	12930	15138	18440	21009	22649	25984	28844	35192	41456	41105
8. Statistical discrepancy	..	..	..	..	..	..	..	..	..	..	..	..	..	..	..
9. **Gross Capital Formation**	4196	8649	9572	10130	10726	14096	16163	18599	22138	22219	27327	29689	35657	43015	38668
RELATIONS AMONG NATIONAL ACCOUNTING AGGREGATES															
1. **Gross Domestic Product**	15208	31813	35111	39288	44793	53610	64750	76601	87594	95308	108459	123284	140615	158722	172476
2. *Plus:* Net factor income from the rest of the world	−195	−494	−485	−514	−550	−406	−505	−845	−1050	−1210	−1515	−1940	−2134	−2956	−3579
3. Factor income from the rest of the world	49	127	152	210	302	493	565	343	344	378	432	559	682	761	1175
4. Factor income paid to the rest of the world	244	621	637	724	852	899	1070	1188	1394	1588	1947	2499	2816	3717	4754
5. *Equals:* **Gross National Product**	15013	31319	34626	38774	44243	53204	64245	75756	86544	94098	106944	121344	138481	155766	168897
6. *Less:* Consumption of fixed capital	1869	4069	4571	5164	5849	6910	9049	10914	12631	14341	16077	18430	21207	24300	27801
7. *Plus:* Statistical discrepancy	..	..	..	..	..	..	..	..	..	..	..	..	..	..	..
8. *Equals:* **National Income**	13144	27250	30055	33610	38394	46294	55196	64842	73913	79757	90867	102914	117274	131466	141096
9. *Plus:* Net current transfers from the rest of the world	−22	−12	−28	−26	−88	−180	−200	−326	−298	−257	−340	−135	−140	−192	−195
10. Current transfers from the rest of the world	83	283	294	354	383	376	427	410	446	606	621	833	986	1138	1320
11. Current transfers paid to the rest of the world	105	295	322	380	471	556	627	736	744	863	961	968	1126	1330	1515
12. *Equals:* **National Disposable Income**	13122	27238	30027	33584	38306	46114	54996	64516	73615	79500	90527	102779	117134	131274	140901
13. *Less:* Final consumption	11381	23133	25736	28761	32358	38684	48226	58123	66565	74205	83327	93926	107946	123051	138439
14. *Plus:* Statistical discrepancy	..	..	..	..	..	..	..	..	..	..	..	..	..	..	..
15. *Equals:* **Net Saving**	1741	4105	4291	4823	5948	7430	6770	6393	7050	5295	7200	8853	9188	8223	2462
16. *Less:* Surplus of the nation on current transactions	−642	−485	−530	−99	987	−589	−977	−875	−1880	−2410	−2940	−1187	−4810	−8540	−7296
17. *Plus:* Statistical discrepancy	−56	−10	180	44	−84	−833	−633	417	577	173	1110	1219	452	1952	1109
18. *Equals:* **Net Capital Formation**	2327	4580	5001	4966	4877	7186	7114	7685	9507	7878	11250	11259	14450	18715	10867

1. Fiscal years beginning on 1st July.
2. At 1989-90 relative prices for 1984-1997, at 1984-85 relative prices for 1974-1983, at 1979-80 relative prices for 1969-1973, at 1974-75 relative prices for 1966-1968 and at 1966-67 relative prices for 1960-1965.

Principaux Agrégats

millions dollars australiens, années fiscales

DÉPENSES IMPUTÉES AU P.I.B.

Aux prix courants

	1983	1984	1985	1986	1987	1988	1989	1990	1991	1992	1993	1994	1995	1996	1997
1. Consommation finale des administrations publiques	35860	40188	44859	49043	52497	56662	61482	66602	71682	74599	76954	79449	83645	87062	90690
2. Consommation finale privée	116722	128163	143680	157323	175656	196362	218273	231462	243825	256062	268987	286270	306316	318454	336802
3. Ménages	..	..	..	..	..	..	..	..	..	..	..	..	..	..	..
4. Institutions privées sans but lucratif au service des ménages	..	..	..	..	..	..	..	..	..	..	..	..	..	..	..
5. Variations des stocks	1376	1013	828	-1634	574	3502	5203	-1550	-2179	487	1237	2557	2233	-1528	2032
6. Formation brute de capital fixe	44325	51016	59265	64360	72300	85089	89584	81468	77660	83223	89317	98862	101845	107754	116965
7. **Demande intérieure totale**	198283	220380	248632	269092	301027	341615	374542	377982	390988	414371	436495	467138	494039	511742	546547
8. Exportations de biens et services	28773	35566	38772	44031	51468	55110	60625	65988	69774	76488	82557	87121	98589	104730	113315
9. *Moins :* Importations de biens et services	31304	39650	45985	47894	52578	60734	67007	65220	67453	77410	83507	95693	99114	101706	116414
10. Divergence statistique	78	834	-922	-614	-207	3916	3332	1985	-3876	-5151	-2543	1709	-1143	1616	1233
11. **Produit intérieur brut**	195830	217130	240497	264615	299710	339907	371492	380735	389433	408298	433002	460275	492371	516382	544681

Aux niveaux de prix de 1990[2]

	1983	1984	1985	1986	1987	1988	1989	1990	1991	1992	1993	1994	1995	1996	1997
1. Consommation finale des administrations publiques	52322	55273	57874	59849	61560	62814	64863	66602	68766	69804	71180	73597	75876	77408	79377
2. Consommation finale privée	187665	194348	202656	203996	210999	219762	229443	231462	237605	244621	253045	266001	277256	283799	296959
3. Ménages	..	..	..	..	..	..	..	..	..	..	..	..	..	..	..
4. Institutions privées sans but lucratif au service des ménages	..	..	..	..	..	..	..	..	..	..	..	..	..	..	..
5. Variations des stocks	2701	1714	608	-2433	306	3315	4834	-1550	-2697	315	603	1814	1215	-2807	489
6. Formation brute de capital fixe	68760	75078	78546	77617	82486	91020	90751	81468	78099	81818	86591	95843	98709	107579	116482
7. **Demande intérieure totale**	311448	326413	339684	339029	355351	376911	389891	377982	381773	396558	411419	437255	453056	465979	493307
8. Exportations de biens et services	38818	44734	46408	51153	55346	56068	59158	65988	71965	76323	81853	87405	96894	106701	111335
9. *Moins :* Importations de biens et services	44439	51349	51329	47991	52816	65464	68921	65220	67692	72775	78398	92544	98255	110366	124376
10. Divergence statistique	-2154	-807	-1634	-1027	-239	4382	3477	1985	-3739	-4671	-1763	2428	105	3086	2932
11. **Produit intérieur brut**	303673	318991	333129	341164	357642	371897	383605	380735	382307	395435	415111	434544	451800	465400	483198

RÉPARTITION DU P.I.B.

	1983	1984	1985	1986	1987	1988	1989	1990	1991	1992	1993	1994	1995	1996	1997
1. Impôts indirects	26001	29758	32860	36367	41532	45817	49056	50412	50225	51937	57216	62416	66864	70471	74380
2. *Moins :* Subventions	3523	3918	4345	4721	4545	4616	4638	5770	6013	6372	6491	6240	6171	7019	6811
3. Consommation de capital fixe	29940	32539	37478	42592	46733	51372	55997	58294	59814	62779	65166	66799	69530	72407	75406
4. Rémunération des salariés payée par les producteurs résidents	100621	110983	122250	133478	146826	163744	182279	190386	194510	201673	212211	225362	241208	258484	272052
5. Excédent net d'exploitation	42791	47768	52254	56900	69165	83590	88797	87413	90897	98283	104900	111939	120941	122039	129653
6. Divergence statistique	..	..	..	..	..	..	..	..	..	..	..	..	..	..	..
7. **Produit intérieur brut**	195830	217130	240497	264616	299711	339907	371491	380735	389433	408300	433002	460276	492372	516382	544680

OPÉRATIONS EN CAPITAL DE LA NATION

Financement de la formation brute de capital

	1983	1984	1985	1986	1987	1988	1989	1990	1991	1992	1993	1994	1995	1996	1997
1. Consommation de capital fixe	29940	32539	37478	42592	46733	51372	55997	58294	59814	62779	65166	66799	69530	72407	75406
2. Épargne nette	8784	9925	7290	8139	15966	23862	20386	8970	701	1798	8347	11943	17207	22331	24719
3. *Moins :* Solde des opérations courantes de la nation	-7055	-10399	-14403	-11382	-9968	-17273	-21735	-14639	-11091	-13984	-14498	-24386	-16198	-13104	-20104
4. Divergence statistique	-78	-834	922	614	207	-3916	-3332	-1985	3876	5151	2543	-1709	1143	-1616	-1233
5. **Financement de la formation brute de capital**	45701	52029	60093	62727	72874	88591	94786	79918	75482	83712	90554	101419	104078	106226	118996

Formation brute de capital

	1983	1984	1985	1986	1987	1988	1989	1990	1991	1992	1993	1994	1995	1996	1997
6. Variations des stocks	1376	1013	828	-1634	574	3502	5203	-1550	-2179	487	1237	2557	2233	-1528	2032
7. Formation brute de capital fixe	44325	51016	59265	64360	72300	85089	89584	81468	77660	83223	89317	98862	101845	107754	116965
8. Divergence statistique	..	..	..	..	..	..	..	..	..	..	..	..	..	..	..
9. **Formation brute de capital**	45701	52029	60093	62726	72874	88591	94787	79918	75481	83710	90554	101419	104078	106226	118997

RELATIONS ENTRE LES PRINCIPAUX AGRÉGATS

	1983	1984	1985	1986	1987	1988	1989	1990	1991	1992	1993	1994	1995	1996	1997
1. **Produit intérieur brut**	195830	217130	240497	264616	299711	339907	371491	380735	389433	408300	433002	460276	492371	516382	544680
2. *Plus :* Revenu net des facteurs reçu du reste du monde	-4639	-6513	-7636	-8617	-10206	-13521	-17329	-17550	-15357	-13316	-13509	-15826	-16696	-17577	-18153
3. Revenu des facteurs reçu du reste du monde	1508	1555	1663	1960	1935	2259	3418	3899	3969	4191	3999	3809	5403	5274	6242
4. Revenu des facteurs payé au reste du monde	6147	8068	9299	10577	12141	15780	20747	21449	19326	17507	17508	19635	22099	22851	24395
5. *Égal :* **Produit national brut**	191191	210617	232861	255999	289505	326386	354162	363185	374076	394984	419493	444450	475675	498805	526527
6. *Moins :* Consommation de capital fixe	29940	32539	37478	42592	46733	51372	55997	58294	59814	62779	65166	66799	69530	72407	75406
7. *Plus :* Divergence statistique	..	..	..	..	..	..	..	..	..	..	..	..	..	..	..
8. *Égal :* **Revenu national**	161251	178078	195383	213407	242772	275014	298165	304891	314262	332205	354327	377651	406145	426398	451121
9. *Plus :* Transferts courants nets reçus du reste du monde	115	198	446	1098	1348	1872	1976	2143	1945	254	-39	12	1023	1449	1148
10. Transferts courants reçus du reste du monde	1758	1952	2485	2971	3509	4168	4443	4667	4406	2820	2922	3025	3792	4137	4127
11. Transferts courants payés au reste du monde	1643	1754	2039	1873	2161	2296	2467	2524	2461	2566	2961	3013	2769	2688	2979
12. *Égal :* **Revenu national disponible**	161366	178276	195829	214505	244120	276886	300141	307034	316207	332459	354288	377663	407168	427847	452269
13. *Moins :* Consommation finale	152582	168351	188539	206366	228153	253024	279755	298064	315507	330661	345941	365719	389961	405516	427550
14. *Plus :* Divergence statistique	..	..	..	..	..	..	..	..	..	..	..	..	..	..	..
15. *Égal :* **Épargne nette**	8784	9925	7290	8139	15966	23862	20386	8970	701	1798	8347	11943	17207	22331	24719
16. *Moins :* Solde des opérations courantes de la nation	-7055	-10399	-14403	-11382	-9968	-17273	-21735	-14639	-11091	-13984	-14498	-24386	-16198	-13104	-20104
17. *Plus :* Divergence statistique	-78	-834	922	614	207	-3916	-3332	-1985	3876	5151	2543	-1709	1143	-1616	-1233
18. *Égal :* **Formation nette de capital**	15761	19490	22615	20134	26141	37219	38790	21624	15667	20931	25388	34620	34548	33819	43591

1. Années fiscales commençant le 1er juillet.
2. Aux prix relatifs de 1989-90 pour la période 1984-1997, aux prix relatifs de 1984-85 pour la période 1974-1983, aux prix relatifs de 1979-80 pour la période 1969-1973, aux prix relatifs de 1974-75 pour la période 1966-1968 et aux prix relatifs de 1966-67 pour la période 1960-1965.

NEW ZEALAND[1]
1968 SNA

Main aggregates

millions of N. Z. dollars, fiscal years

	1960	1969	1970	1971	1972	1973	1974	1975	1976	1977	1978	1979	1980	1981	1982
EXPENDITURE ON THE G.D.P.															
At current prices															
1. Government final consumption expenditure	300	643	770	886	1023	1176	1443	1732	1937	2363	2882	3314	4134	4989	5566
2. Private final consumption expenditure	1930*	3344	3742	4225	4768	5479	6229	7127	8196	9149	10324	12053	14169	16633	19018
3. Households	..	..	..	4163	4708	5411	6150	7039	8078	9022	10178	11879	13961	16360	18726
4. Private non-profit institutions serving households	..	..	..	62	61	67	80	88	119	128	147	173	208	272	292
5. Increase in stocks	85	116	109	163	−39	274	752	−179	121	133	−246	470	−33	165	248
6. Gross fixed capital formation	607	1073	1302	1514	1880	2188	2695	3246	3538	3545	3880	4067	4754	6597	7774
7. **Total Domestic Expenditure**	2922*	5176	5923	6788	7632	9117	11119	11926	13792	15190	16840	19904	23024	28384	32606
8. Exports of goods and services	628	1263	1296	1560	1946	2241	2117	2666	3765	4125	4687	5996	7003	8249	9266
9. *Less:* Imports of goods and services	691	1142	1472	1505	1710	2233	3344	3430	4057	4378	4647	6256	7272	9168	10318
10. Statistical discrepancy	−4*	−170	−19	−104	−160	−100	−45	−56	12	34	78	150	237	426	−145
11. **Gross Domestic Product**	2855*	5127	5728	6739	7708	9025	9847	11106	13512	14971	16958	19794	22992	27891	31409
At 1990 price levels [2]															
1. Government final consumption expenditure	5484*	7348*	7656*	7840*	8317*	8654*	9368*	9825*	9749*	10146*	10619*	10479*	10574*	10768*	10829
2. Private final consumption expenditure	24213*	32324*	33839*	33990*	36390*	39466*	41050*	40746*	39413*	38134*	38815*	38632*	38540*	39327*	38785
3. Households	..	..	..	..	..	..	..	..	..	..	..	..	..	..	38441
4. Private non-profit institutions serving households	..	..	..	..	..	..	..	..	..	..	..	..	..	..	405
5. Increase in stocks	599*	1128*	529*	683*	−458*	1541*	3930*	−974*	630*	497*	−605*	940*	289*	346*	423
6. Gross fixed capital formation	6201*	8271*	8995*	9529*	11182*	12521*	13374*	12651*	11625*	10359*	9851*	9497*	9358*	11291*	12075
7. **Total Domestic Expenditure**	36497*	49071*	51019*	52042*	55431*	62182*	67722*	62248*	61417*	59136*	58680*	59548*	58761*	61732*	62112
8. Exports of goods and services	5681*	9554*	9625*	10327*	10540*	10334*	10054*	11337*	12593*	12587*	12891*	13458*	13884*	14205*	14426
9. *Less:* Imports of goods and services	6343*	8386*	10041*	9846*	10767*	13062*	14796*	11601*	11427*	11564*	11753*	13226*	12313*	13665*	13864
10. Statistical discrepancy	−955*	−365*	−1435*	−807*	−1271*	−1690*	−1777*	−1485*	−608*	−1204*	−624*	620*	484*	1496*	2287
11. **Gross Domestic Product**	34880*	49874*	49168*	51716*	53933*	57764*	61203*	60499*	61975*	58955*	59194*	60400*	60816*	63768*	64961
COST COMPONENTS OF THE G.D.P.															
1. Indirect taxes	285	482	577	662	754	850	917	1103	1300	1469	1725	1998	2344	2913	3440
2. *Less:* Subsidies	32	26	59	108	129	163	238	391	243	277	428	352	348	578	756
3. Consumption of fixed capital	203	450	505	549	609	689	799	943	1077	1167	1297	1468	1672	1926	2247
4. Compensation of employees paid by resident producers	1223	2382	2870	3403	3827	4514	5439	6278	7072	8102	9415	10977	13066	15754	17248
5. Operating surplus	1176*	1839	1834	2233	2647	3135	2930	3173	4306	4509	4948	5704	6257	7876	9231
6. Statistical discrepancy	..	..	..	..	..	..	..	..	..	1	1	−1	1	..	−1
7. **Gross Domestic Product**	2855*	5127	5727	6739	7708	9025	9847	11106	13512	14971	16958	19794	22992	27891	31409
CAPITAL TRANSACTIONS OF THE NATION															
Finance of Gross Capital Formation															
1. Consumption of fixed capital	203	450	505	549	609	689	799	943	1077	1167	1297	1468	1672	1926	2247
2. Net saving	406*	636	661	1063	1298	1690	1313	1163	2045	1960	2013	2511	2546	3760	3832
3. *Less:* Surplus of the nation on current transactions	−79	67	−226	39	226	17	−1290	−905	−549	−584	−402	−709	−740	−1502	−1799
4. Statistical discrepancy	4*	170	19	104	160	100	45	56	−12	−33	−78	−151	−237	−426	145
5. **Finance of Gross Capital Formation**	692	1189	1411	1677	1841	2462	3447	3067	3659	3678	3634	4537	4721	6762	8023
Gross capital formation															
6. Increase in stocks	85	116	109	163	−39	274	752	−179	121	133	−246	470	−33	165	248
7. Gross fixed capital formation	607	1073	1302	1514	1880	2188	2695	3246	3538	3545	3880	4067	4754	6597	7774
8. Statistical discrepancy	..	..	..	..	..	..	..	..	..	..	..	..	..	..	..
9. **Gross Capital Formation**	692	1189	1411	1677	1841	2462	3447	3067	3659	3678	3634	4537	4721	6762	8022
RELATIONS AMONG NATIONAL ACCOUNTING AGGREGATES															
1. **Gross Domestic Product**	2855*	5127	5728	6739	7708	9025	9847	11106	13512	14970	16958	19795	22992	27891	31409
2. *Plus:* Net factor income from the rest of the world	−14	−41	−41	−46	−54	−37	−82	−165	−265	−336	−409	−460	−511	−615	−858
3. Factor income from the rest of the world	..	..	..	39	57	79	73	75	70	87	83	79	93	188	210
4. Factor income paid to the rest of the world	..	..	..	85	111	116	155	240	335	423	492	539	604	803	1068
5. *Equals:* **Gross National Product**	2841*	5086	5687	6693	7654	8988	9765	10941	13247	14634	16549	19335	22481	27276	30551
6. *Less:* Consumption of fixed capital	203	450	505	549	609	689	799	943	1077	1167	1297	1468	1672	1926	2247
7. *Plus:* Statistical discrepancy	..	..	..	..	..	..	..	..	..	..	..	..	..	..	..
8. *Equals:* **National Income**	2638*	4636	5182	6144	7045	8299	8966	9998	12170	13467	15252	17867	20809	25350	28304
9. *Plus:* Net current transfers from the rest of the world	−3	−13	−9	30	44	46	19	24	8	5	−33	11	40	32	112
10. Current transfers from the rest of the world	..	..	..	84	105	123	124	143	142	163	166	223	302	343	325
11. Current transfers paid to the rest of the world	..	..	..	54	61	77	105	119	134	158	199	212	262	311	214
12. *Equals:* **National Disposable Income**	2635*	4623	5173	6174	7089	8345	8985	10022	12178	13472	15219	17878	20849	25382	28416
13. *Less:* Final consumption	2230*	3987	4512	5111	5791	6655	7672	8859	10133	11512	13206	15367	18303	21622	24584
14. *Plus:* Statistical discrepancy	..	..	..	..	..	..	..	..	..	..	..	..	..	..	..
15. *Equals:* **Net Saving**	406*	636	661	1063	1298	1690	1313	1163	2045	1960	2013	2511	2546	3760	3832
16. *Less:* Surplus of the nation on current transactions	−79	67	−226	39	226	17	−1290	−905	−549	−584	−402	−709	−740	−1502	−1799
17. *Plus:* Statistical discrepancy	4*	170	19	104	160	100	45	56	−12	−33	−78	−151	−237	−426	145
18. *Equals:* **Net Capital Formation**	489	739	906	1128	1232	1773	2648	2124	2582	2511	2337	3069	3049	4836	5776

1. Fiscal years beginning on 1st April.
2. At 1991-92 relative prices.

NOUVELLE-ZÉLANDE[1]

SCN de 1968

Principaux Agrégats

millions dollars N. Z., années fiscales

1983	1984	1985	1986	1987	1988	1989	1990	1991	1992	1993	1994	1995	1996	1997	
															DÉPENSES IMPUTÉES AU P.I.B.
															Aux prix courants
5858	6334	7345	8930	10128	11023	11733	12291	12269	12682	12578	12535	13218	13760	14928	1. Consommation finale des administrations publiques
20718	23582	27869	32962	37432	40523	43455	45760	45810	46680	49026	52943	56576	59849	62337	2. Consommation finale privée
20429	23260	27493	32475	36863	39899	42734	44938	44924	45796	48043	51954	55566	58568	..	3. Ménages
289	322	375	487	569	625	720	822	886	883	945	984	1094	1174	..	4. Institutions privées sans but lucratif au service des ménages
375	1111	−154	588	−381	−62	1406	−116	85	757	1729	1438	1161	571	880	5. Variations des stocks
8612	9994	11978	12363	13382	12892	14303	13795	11536	12280	14768	17607	19251	20120	19531	6. Formation brute de capital fixe
35563	41021	47038	54843	60561	64376	70897	71730	69700	72399	78101	84523	90206	94300	97676	7. **Demande intérieure totale**
10507	13229	13947	15122	16663	16060	19151	19960	21680	23889	25311	27173	27423	27545	28172	8. Exportations de biens et services
11063	14539	15311	15240	15635	15582	18938	19441	19104	21709	22588	25139	26169	26713	27723	9. *Moins* : Importations de biens et services
−168	−364	−391	0	51	−401	−338	0	0	0	0	0	0	74	121	10. Divergence statistique
34839	39347	45283	54725	61640	66453	70772	72249	72276	74579	80824	86557	91460	95206	98246	11. **Produit intérieur brut**
															Aux niveaux de prix de 1990[2]
11124	11327	11523	11601	11764	11900	12204	12291	12285	12653	12516	12399	12750	13037	13825	1. Consommation finale des administrations publiques
39986	41542	42111	43869	44939	45725	45877	45760	44845	44982	46426	49249	51268	53348	55113	2. Consommation finale privée
39620	41129	41642	43270	44248	45015	45117	44938	43960	44075	45468	48227	50127	52119	53834	3. Ménages
422	457	501	593	688	707	760	822	897	911	963	1021	1151	1242	1245	4. Institutions privées sans but lucratif au service des ménages
322	1296	−260	252	−633	−347	909	−116	−79	408	1183	1152	562	237	398	5. Variations des stocks
12860	13582	14524	13692	14175	13539	14556	13795	11366	11782	13925	16321	17817	18973	19524	6. Formation brute de capital fixe
64292	67747	67898	69414	70245	70817	73546	71730	68417	69825	74050	79121	82397	85595	88860	7. **Demande intérieure totale**
15304	16739	17017	17799	19100	19234	18763	19960	21817	22371	24148	26185	26871	27901	28666	8. Exportations de biens et services
13754	15341	15575	15891	17268	17133	19512	19441	18708	20091	21692	24785	26574	28405	29765	9. *Moins* : Importations de biens et services
899	887	1232	729	272	−852	−120	0	−162	110	273	392	1139	1038	339	10. Divergence statistique
66741	70032	70572	72051	72349	72066	72677	72249	71364	72215	76779	80913	83833	86129	88100	11. **Produit intérieur brut**
															RÉPARTITION DU P.I.B.
3874	4524	4854	6735	9081	9398	10848	11135	10837	10888	11408	12170	12810	13447	13682	1. Impôts indirects
660	598	362	292	271	180	206	205	241	313	304	319	313	318	319	2. *Moins* : Subventions
2689	3241	3826	4492	5230	5764	6168	6525	6884	7403	7700	8185	8661	9152	9590	3. Consommation de capital fixe
17589	19250	22675	27095	30458	31869	32959	33368	33001	33785	35263	37523	39753	42190	43721	4. Rémunération des salariés payée par les producteurs résidents
11347	12929	14289	16695	17144	19603	21004	21425	21795	22815	26757	28997	30550	30735	31573	5. Excédent net d'exploitation
..	1	1	..	−2	−1	−1	1	..	1	..	1	−1	..	−1	6. Divergence statistique
34839	39347	45283	54725	61640	66453	70772	72249	72276	74579	80824	86557	91460	95206	98246	7. **Produit intérieur brut**
															OPÉRATIONS EN CAPITAL DE LA NATION
															Financement de la formation brute de capital
2689	3241	3826	4492	5230	5764	6168	6525	6884	7403	7700	8185	8661	9152	9590	1. Consommation de capital fixe
4422	4378	3912	5853	5814	6033	4892	3554	3006	4838	7834	7897	7344	5124	4596	2. Épargne nette
−1708	−3122	−3695	−2606	−2009	−633	−4312	−3600	−1731	−795	−963	−2962	−4407	−6488	−6346	3. *Moins* : Solde des opérations courantes de la nation
168	365	392	0	−52	400	337	1	−1	1	0	1	0	−74	−122	4. Divergence statistique
8987	11106	11825	12951	13001	12830	15709	13680	11620	13037	16497	19045	20411	20690	20410	5. **Financement de la formation brute de capital**
															Formation brute de capital
375	1111	−154	588	−381	−62	1406	−116	85	757	1729	1438	1161	571	880	6. Variations des stocks
8612	9994	11978	12363	13382	12892	14303	13795	11536	12280	14768	17607	19251	20120	19531	7. Formation brute de capital fixe
..	..	..	..	..	..	..	..	..	..	..	..	..	..	..	8. Divergence statistique
8987	11105	11824	12951	13001	12830	15709	13679	11621	13037	16497	19045	20412	20691	20411	9. **Formation brute de capital**
															RELATIONS ENTRE LES PRINCIPAUX AGRÉGATS
34839	39346	45282	54725	61641	66454	70773	72248	72277	74578	80824	86556	91460	95205	98246	1. **Produit intérieur brut**
−1275	−2002	−2520	−2767	−3270	−3318	−4770	−4243	−4424	−3064	−3957	−5177	−5820	−8066	−7285	2. *Plus* : Revenu net des facteurs reçu du reste du monde
238	150	418	608	788	611	644	1033	853	795	778	593	1213	893	1151	3. Revenu des facteurs reçu du reste du monde
1513	2152	2938	3375	4058	3929	5414	5276	5277	3859	4735	5770	7033	8959	8436	4. Revenu des facteurs payé au reste du monde
33564	37344	42762	51958	58371	63136	66003	68005	67853	71514	76867	81379	85640	87139	90961	5. *Égal* : **Produit national brut**
2689	3241	3826	4492	5230	5764	6168	6525	6884	7403	7700	8185	8661	9152	9590	6. *Moins* : Consommation de capital fixe
..	..	..	..	..	..	..	..	..	..	..	..	..	..	..	7. *Plus* : Divergence statistique
30875	34103	38936	47466	53141	57372	59835	61480	60969	64111	69167	73194	76979	77987	81371	8. *Égal* : **Revenu national**
123	191	190	279	233	207	245	125	116	89	271	181	159	746	490	9. *Plus* : Transferts courants nets reçus du reste du monde
335	402	426	484	463	487	537	513	531	523	775	884	790	1375	1174	10. Transferts courants reçus du reste du monde
212	212	237	205	231	279	292	389	414	434	504	704	631	630	684	11. Transferts courants payés au reste du monde
30998	34294	39126	47745	53374	57579	60080	61605	61085	64200	69438	73375	77138	78733	81861	12. *Égal* : **Revenu national disponible**
26576	29916	35214	41892	47560	51546	55188	58051	58079	59362	61604	65478	69794	73609	77265	13. *Moins* : Consommation finale
..	..	..	..	..	..	..	..	..	..	..	..	..	..	..	14. *Plus* : Divergence statistique
4422	4378	3912	5853	5814	6033	4892	3554	3006	4838	7834	7897	7344	5124	4596	15. *Égal* : **Épargne nette**
−1708	−3122	−3695	−2606	−2009	−633	−4312	−3600	−1731	−795	−963	−2962	−4407	−6488	−6346	16. *Moins* : Solde des opérations courantes de la nation
168	365	392	0	−52	400	337	1	−1	1	0	1	0	−74	−122	17. *Plus* : Divergence statistique
6298	7865	7999	8459	7771	7066	9541	7155	4736	5634	8797	10860	11750	11538	10820	18. *Égal* : **Formation nette de capital**

1. Années fiscales commençant le 1er avril.
2. Aux prix relatifs de 1991-92.

AUSTRIA
1968 SNA

Main aggregates

millions of schilling

	1960	1969	1970	1971	1972	1973	1974	1975	1976	1977	1978	1979	1980	1981	1982
EXPENDITURE ON THE G.D.P.															
At current prices															
1. Government final consumption expenditure	21893*	52328*	57241*	64248*	72666*	84908*	100996*	117188*	132467	143889	157967	171651	184796	201524	221096
2. Private final consumption expenditure	99112*	193590*	209500*	234716*	265138*	297763*	337389*	375811*	418591	466780	477526	519611	559756	605458	657560
3. Households	..	..	..	..	..	..	..	..	409074	456160	466109	507136	546038	590910	641337
4. Private non-profit institutions serving households	..	..	..	..	..	..	..	..	9517	10620	11417	12475	13718	14548	16243
5. Increase in stocks [2]	8248*	12996*	21766*	16279*	12386*	24138*	29799*	8074*	22797	24767	28958	37793	45611	30262	10772
6. Gross fixed capital formation	38632*	79763*	92333*	111069*	137682*	147241*	166956*	166196*	179294	206969	202045	220739	245394	258451	253217
7. **Total Domestic Expenditure**	167885*	338677*	380840*	426312*	487872*	554050*	635140*	667269*	753149	842405	866496	949794	1035557	1095695	1142665
8. Exports of goods and services	39510*	95020*	116750*	128640*	146440*	165890*	204210*	209020*	236292	256937	280757	327688	366244	404512	425438
9. *Less:* Imports of goods and services	40760*	91010*	113070*	125660*	143710*	163890*	206290*	204810*	247341	278398	280430	331588	385659	418470	406938
10. Statistical discrepancy	156*	336*	361*	375*	421*	424*	313*	343*	..	..	..	..	..	..	..
11. **Gross Domestic Product**	166791*	343023*	384881*	429667*	491023*	556474*	633373*	671822*	742100	820944	866823	945894	1016142	1081737	1161165
At 1990 price levels [1]															
1. Government final consumption expenditure	154982*	203741*	210456*	217353*	226298*	233048*	246337*	256138*	267047	274623	276810	286419	292526	298024	307116
2. Private final consumption expenditure	363353*	522526*	544285*	580851*	616168*	649268*	668694*	690409*	721790	761490	749112	781779	794054	800752	821206
3. Households	..	..	..	..	..	..	..	..	701482	740689	728108	760268	771890	778536	798223
4. Private non-profit institutions serving households	..	..	..	..	..	..	..	..	20477	20903	21171	21635	22329	22365	23160
5. Increase in stocks [2]	25063*	30587*	45008*	21755*	17791*	45812*	37884*	10954*	37178	30470	32655	50109	57456	19454	10631
6. Gross fixed capital formation	128616*	208487*	228949*	260521*	292143*	293163*	304797*	289704*	300765	328488	303487	317984	330591	327736	303562
7. **Total Domestic Expenditure**	672014*	965341*	1028698*	1080480*	1152400*	1221291*	1257712*	1247205*	1326780	1395071	1362064	1436291	1474627	1445966	1442515
8. Exports of goods and services	93682*	189593*	220871*	235025*	258868*	272953*	302188*	294938*	327557	342308	368544	412290	433842	455806	463057
9. *Less:* Imports of goods and services	104571*	199295*	233091*	247746*	277838*	304380*	325398*	310271*	364314	386843	387221	432397	459075	455535	434274
10. Statistical discrepancy	−22620*	−11272*	−4844*	−4400*	−4057*	−5295*	−3216*	−5048*	−7048	−7567	−5287	−5095	−5653	−3932	−1478
11. **Gross Domestic Product**	638505*	944367*	1011634*	1063359*	1129373*	1184569*	1231286*	1226824*	1282975	1342969	1338100	1411089	1443741	1442305	1469820
COST COMPONENTS OF THE G.D.P.															
1. Indirect taxes	24000*	55190*	61680*	70000*	82490*	97230*	106920*	111530*	119550	135872	139301	151202	162828	174395	184984
2. *Less:* Subsidies	2983*	6391*	6440*	7468*	7804*	9088*	12752*	18748*	20553	23012	26249	26619	29732	31743	34285
3. Consumption of fixed capital	18790*	39420*	43850*	49520*	56200*	62370*	71470*	77420*	82508	90609	97618	104268	116098	128514	140763
4. Compensation of employees paid by resident producers	70046*	153111*	167580*	193667*	220059*	257708*	300266*	337028*	390834	432868	475680	507826	548992	592865	620892
5. Operating surplus	61022*	106010*	124244*	128449*	144925*	150839*	169737*	162975*	169761	184607	180473	209217	217956	217706	248811
6. Statistical discrepancy	−4084*	−4319*	−6033*	−4501*	−4848*	−2586*	−2268*	1617*	..	..	..	..	..	..	..
7. **Gross Domestic Product**	166791*	343021*	384881*	429667*	491022*	556473*	633373*	671822*	742100	820944	866823	945894	1016142	1081737	1161165
CAPITAL TRANSACTIONS OF THE NATION															
Finance of Gross Capital Formation															
1. Consumption of fixed capital	18790*	39420*	43850*	49520*	56200*	62370*	71470*	77420*	82508	90609	97618	104268	116098	128514	140763
2. Net saving	26432*	57694*	73132*	80444*	95266*	108263*	120196*	96800*	103269	112191	127158	145219	148479	138791	135080
3. *Less:* Surplus of the nation on current transactions	−1750*	3920*	2260*	1980*	630*	−1610*	−5900*	−370*	−16314	−28936	−6227	−9045	−26428	−21408	11854
4. Statistical discrepancy	−92*	−435*	−623*	−636*	−768*	−864*	−811*	−320*	..	..	..	..	..	..	..
5. **Finance of Gross Capital Formation**	46880*	92759*	114099*	127348*	150068*	171379*	196755*	174270*	202091	231736	231003	258532	291005	288713	263989
Gross capital formation															
6. Increase in stocks [2]	8248*	12996*	21766*	16279*	12386*	24138*	29799*	8074*	22797	24767	28958	37793	45611	30262	10772
7. Gross fixed capital formation	38632*	79763*	92333*	111069*	137682*	147241*	166956*	166196*	179294	206969	202045	220739	245394	258451	253217
8. Statistical discrepancy	..	..	..	..	..	..	..	..	..	..	..	..	..	..	..
9. **Gross Capital Formation**	46880*	92759*	114099*	127348*	150068*	171379*	196755*	174270*	202091	231736	231003	258532	291005	288713	263989
RELATIONS AMONG NATIONAL ACCOUNTING AGGREGATES															
1. **Gross Domestic Product**	166791*	343022*	384881*	429668*	491023*	556474*	633372*	671821*	742100	820944	866823	945894	1016142	1081737	1161165
2. *Plus:* Net factor income from the rest of the world	−330*	−1670*	−1970*	−1900*	−2700*	−3380*	−2970*	−3620*	−5043	−6873	−8378	−7813	−8353	−8758	−8426
3. Factor income from the rest of the world	550*	2620*	3530*	4230*	4090*	5120*	10181*	10621*	11371	12350	14499	21088	32847	50941	54194
4. Factor income paid to the rest of the world	880*	4291*	5511*	6141*	6802*	8502*	13153*	14233*	16414	19223	22877	28901	41200	59699	62620
5. *Equals:* **Gross National Product**	166461*	341352*	382911*	427768*	488323*	553094*	630402*	668201*	737057	814071	858445	938081	1007789	1072979	1152739
6. *Less:* Consumption of fixed capital	18790*	39420*	43850*	49520*	56200*	62370*	71470*	77420*	82508	90609	97618	104268	116098	128514	140763
7. *Plus:* Statistical discrepancy	−54*	100*	262*	260*	347*	440*	499*	−12*	..	..	..	..	..	..	..
8. *Equals:* **National Income**	147617*	302032*	339323*	378508*	432470*	491164*	559431*	590769*	654549	723462	760827	833813	891691	944465	1011976
9. *Plus:* Net current transfers from the rest of the world	−180*	1580*	550*	900*	600*	−230*	−850*	−970*	−222	−602	1824	2668	1340	1308	1780
10. Current transfers from the rest of the world	1470*	3380*	3730*	4540*	5130*	6000*	6910*	7190*	8328	8838	10146	12250	12947	14120	14575
11. Current transfers paid to the rest of the world	1650*	1800*	3180*	3640*	4530*	6230*	7760*	8160*	8550	9440	8322	9582	11607	12812	12795
12. *Equals:* **National Disposable Income**	147437*	303612*	339873*	379408*	433070*	490934*	558581*	589799*	654327	722860	762651	836481	893031	945773	1013756
13. *Less:* Final consumption	121005*	245918*	266741*	298964*	337804*	382671*	438385*	492999*	551058	610669	635493	691262	744552	806982	878676
14. *Plus:* Statistical discrepancy	..	..	..	..	..	..	..	..	..	..	..	..	..	..	..
15. *Equals:* **Net Saving**	26432*	57694*	73132*	80444*	95266*	108263*	120196*	96800*	103269	112191	127158	145219	148479	138791	135080
16. *Less:* Surplus of the nation on current transactions	−1750*	3920*	2260*	1980*	630*	−1610*	−5900*	−370*	−16314	−28936	−6227	−9045	−26428	−21408	11854
17. *Plus:* Statistical discrepancy	−92*	−435*	−623*	−636*	−768*	−864*	−811*	−320*	..	..	..	..	..	..	..
18. *Equals:* **Net Capital Formation**	28090*	53339*	70249*	77828*	93868*	109009*	125285*	96850*	119583	141127	133385	154264	174907	160199	123226

1. At 1983 relative prices for 1976-1997, at 1976 relative prices for 1970-1975 and at 1964 relative prices for 1960-1969.
2. Including statistical discrepancy.

Principaux Agrégats

millions de schillings

DÉPENSES IMPUTÉES AU P.I.B.

Aux prix courants

1983	1984	1985	1986	1987	1988	1989	1990	1991	1992	1993	1994	1995	1996	1997	
235490	248025	264298	281858	292480	302489	319601	338117	367799	398258	429574	454957	469322	478304	487200	1. Consommation finale des administrations publiques
716954	744752	783706	813986	843921	886040	943288	1012961	1073004	1147677	1194057	1254605	1310245	1375415	1412500	2. Consommation finale privée
699402	726791	764361	793414	822108	863268	919359	986375	1043736	1115792	1160149	1218044	1271569	1335662	..	3. Ménages
17552	17961	19345	20572	21813	22772	23929	26586	29268	31885	33908	36561	38676	39753	..	4. Institutions privées sans but lucratif au service des ménages
6240	34047	23671	21388	24434	14930	11505	16978	22027	8245	2713	833	10320	4120	25600	5. Variations des stocks[2]
262637	270372	294745	309108	327813	354112	386060	421989	466285	483440	485099	533348	554070	576791	607800	6. Formation brute de capital fixe
1221321	**1297196**	**1366420**	**1426340**	**1488648**	**1557571**	**1660454**	**1790045**	**1929115**	**2037620**	**2111443**	**2243743**	**2343957**	**2434630**	**2533100**	7. **Demande intérieure totale**
444417	491364	542580	516675	522948	590759	669618	728312	774706	791618	786507	838841	900905	988783	1061300	8. Exportations de biens et services
428358	489552	539905	503971	517471	582559	653395	704875	757999	771967	772607	842963	910504	1001790	1077500	9. *Moins :* Importations de biens et services
..	..	..	..	..	..	..	..	..	..	..	..	..	..	..	10. Divergence statistique
1237380	**1299008**	**1369095**	**1439044**	**1494125**	**1565771**	**1676677**	**1813482**	**1945822**	**2057271**	**2125343**	**2239621**	**2334358**	**2421623**	**2516900**	11. **Produit intérieur brut**

Aux niveaux de prix de 1990[1]

1983	1984	1985	1986	1987	1988	1989	1990	1991	1992	1993	1994	1995	1996	1997	
312397	314853	319037	324876	325538	329237	333901	338117	345688	352658	362278	371238	371067	371493	374760	1. Consommation finale des administrations publiques
862011	850665	866811	885678	911501	941655	976311	1012961	1041781	1072726	1080268	1099162	1130762	1158131	1166254	2. Consommation finale privée
838470	827489	843325	861674	885828	916665	950765	986375	1014362	1044070	1051978	1069900	1101182	1128109	..	3. Ménages
23655	23281	23578	24098	25889	25024	25536	26586	27428	28718	28283	29312	29568	29975	..	4. Institutions privées sans but lucratif au service des ménages
13359	44522	31383	31690	30061	24048	11331	16978	18307	6251	14327	19515	23482	11435	29292	5. Variations des stocks[2]
304739	305036	326149	334047	348687	372546	395883	421989	448624	449140	440214	477163	486374	498276	516336	6. Formation brute de capital fixe
1492506	**1515076**	**1543380**	**1576291**	**1615787**	**1667486**	**1717426**	**1790045**	**1854400**	**1880812**	**1897087**	**1967078**	**2011685**	**2039335**	**2086642**	7. **Demande intérieure totale**
479901	510297	546526	533692	550243	606459	675196	728312	771479	784339	774157	817754	870704	951940	1016782	8. Exportations de biens et services
458987	505115	536207	520599	548954	605917	656668	704875	750349	763822	758852	821740	878875	955383	1016750	9. *Moins :* Importations de biens et services
-2379	-4203	-3629	-3032	-4055	-3901	-1481	0	48	-590	-1903	-4040	-4159	-3823	-2884	10. Divergence statistique
1511041	**1516055**	**1550070**	**1586352**	**1613021**	**1664127**	**1734473**	**1813482**	**1875578**	**1900739**	**1910489**	**1959052**	**1999355**	**2032069**	**2083790**	11. **Produit intérieur brut**

RÉPARTITION DU P.I.B.

1983	1984	1985	1986	1987	1988	1989	1990	1991	1992	1993	1994	1995	1996	1997	
197080	216087	225931	234044	245154	254887	271413	287880	305779	325823	340005	356603	367337	387463	410500	1. Impôts indirects
35666	36418	40323	47366	48872	48265	48467	51532	60462	62878	67630	50835	50393	53450	55500*	2. *Moins :* Subventions
149238	158193	167526	176195	183870	194114	205630	218486	235159	252567	270078	288691	306784	324700	344200	3. Consommation de capital fixe
644681	680180	721231	765733	797421	826879	879607	949140	1030150	1098620	1145579	1189018	1230698	1244973	1269800*	4. Rémunération des salariés payée par les producteurs résidents
282047	280966	294730	310438	316552	338156	368494	409508	435196	443139	437311	456144	479932	517937	547900*	5. Excédent net d'exploitation
..	..	..	..	..	..	..	..	..	..	..	..	..	..	..	6. Divergence statistique
1237380	**1299008**	**1369095**	**1439044**	**1494125**	**1565771**	**1676677**	**1813482**	**1945822**	**2057271**	**2125343**	**2239621**	**2334358**	**2421623**	**2516900**	7. **Produit intérieur brut**

OPÉRATIONS EN CAPITAL DE LA NATION

Financement de la formation brute de capital

1983	1984	1985	1986	1987	1988	1989	1990	1991	1992	1993	1994	1995	1996	1997	
149238	158193	167526	176195	183870	194114	205630	218486	235159	252567	270078	288691	306784	324700	344200	1. Consommation de capital fixe
123953	142143	148778	157685	165937	171986	195212	234116	253973	237490	209489	224873	216290	206371	235800*	2. Épargne nette
4314	-4083	-2112	3384	-2440	-2942	3277	13635	820	-1628	-8245	-20617	-41316	-49840	-53400*	3. *Moins :* Solde des opérations courantes de la nation
..	..	..	..	..	..	..	..	..	..	..	..	..	..	..	4. Divergence statistique
268877	**304419**	**318416**	**330496**	**352247**	**369042**	**397565**	**438967**	**488312**	**491685**	**487812**	**534181**	**564390**	**580911**	**633400**	5. **Financement de la formation brute de capital**

Formation brute de capital

1983	1984	1985	1986	1987	1988	1989	1990	1991	1992	1993	1994	1995	1996	1997	
6240	34047	23671	21388	24434	14930	11505	16978	22027	8245	2713	833	10320	4120	25600	6. Variations des stocks[2]
262637	270372	294745	309108	327813	354112	386060	421989	466285	483440	485099	533348	554070	576791	607800	7. Formation brute de capital fixe
..	..	..	..	..	..	..	..	..	..	..	..	..	..	..	8. Divergence statistique
268877	**304419**	**318416**	**330496**	**352247**	**369042**	**397565**	**438967**	**488312**	**491685**	**487812**	**534181**	**564390**	**580911**	**633400**	9. **Formation brute de capital**

RELATIONS ENTRE LES PRINCIPAUX AGRÉGATS

1983	1984	1985	1986	1987	1988	1989	1990	1991	1992	1993	1994	1995	1996	1997	
1237380	1299008	1369094	1439043	1494124	1565770	1676677	1813481	1945821	2057271	2125343	2239621	2334358	2421623	2516900	1. **Produit intérieur brut**
-8807	-8570	-7074	-11933	-12903	-8467	-8915	-7278	-13092	-9660	-9429	-8237	-7624	-7614	-3400	2. *Plus :* Revenu net des facteurs reçu du reste du monde
47137	58288	66433	58403	57287	66912	88239	100230	104997	103072	108008	102157	115346	135686	..	3. Revenu des facteurs reçu du reste du monde
55944	66858	73507	70336	70190	75379	97154	107508	118089	112732	117437	110394	122970	143300	..	4. Revenu des facteurs payé au reste du monde
1228573	1290438	1362020	1427110	1481221	1557303	1667762	1806203	1932729	2047611	2115914	2231384	2326734	2414009	2513600	5. *Égal :* **Produit national brut**
149238	158193	167526	176195	183870	194114	205630	218486	235159	252567	270078	288691	306784	324700	344200	6. *Moins :* Consommation de capital fixe
..	..	..	..	..	..	..	..	..	..	..	..	..	..	..	7. *Plus :* Divergence statistique
1079335	1132245	1194494	1250915	1297351	1363189	1462132	1587717	1697570	1795044	1845836	1942693	2019950	2089309	2169400	8. *Égal :* **Revenu national**
-2938	2675	2287	2613	4986	-2675	-4031	-2524	-2795	-11619	-12716	-8258	-24093	-29219	-33800*	9. *Plus :* Transferts courants nets reçus du reste du monde
14389	15383	16122	16641	17703	12965	14281	16556	20518	17052	17559	23076	35828	38036	..	10. Transferts courants reçus du reste du monde
17327	12708	13835	14028	12717	15640	18312	19080	23313	28671	30275	31334	59921	67255	..	11. Transferts courants payés au reste du monde
1076397	1134920	1196781	1253528	1302337	1360514	1458101	1585193	1694775	1783425	1833120	1934435	1995857	2060090	2135600*	12. *Égal :* **Revenu national disponible**
952444	992777	1048004	1095844	1136401	1188529	1262889	1351078	1440803	1545935	1623631	1709562	1779567	1853719	1899700	13. *Moins :* Consommation finale
..	..	..	..	..	..	..	..	..	..	..	..	..	..	..	14. *Plus :* Divergence statistique
123953	142143	148778	157685	165937	171986	195212	234116	253973	237490	209489	224873	216290	206371	235800*	15. *Égal :* **Épargne nette**
4314	-4083	-2112	3384	-2440	-2942	3277	13635	820	-1628	-8245	-20617	-41316	-49840	-53400*	16. *Moins :* Solde des opérations courantes de la nation
..	..	..	..	..	..	..	..	..	..	..	..	..	..	..	17. *Plus :* Divergence statistique
119639	146226	150890	154301	168377	174928	191935	220481	253153	239118	217734	245490	257606	256211	289200	18. *Égal :* **Formation nette de capital**

1. Aux prix relatifs de 1983 pour la période 1976-1997, aux prix relatifs de 1976 pour la période 1970-1975 et aux prix relatifs de 1964 pour la période 1960-1969.
2. Y compris une divergence statistique.

BELGIUM
1968 SNA

Main aggregates

millions of francs

	1960	1969	1970	1971	1972	1973	1974	1975	1976	1977	1978	1979	1980	1981	1982
EXPENDITURE ON THE G.D.P.															
At current prices															
1. Government final consumption expenditure	69309	154503	169406	194660	224282	255264	302339	373592	423388	467281	520144	561057	616437	669168	706535
2. Private final consumption expenditure	386916	708049	758225	837733	937129	1072859	1243549	1410361	1597707	1757064	1877948	2051485	2241091	2414669	2643699
3. Households	..	..	..	..	..	..	..	..	..	..	..	..	..	..	..
4. Private non-profit institutions serving households	..	..	..	..	..	..	..	..	..	..	..	..	..	..	..
5. Increase in stocks	−334	21845	20784	19024	7417	22431	45121	−12512	5304	10013	5485	25048	27294	−4217	6462
6. Gross fixed capital formation	107741	241297	286177	304806	329746	375579	467370	511147	568732	602958	647527	661101	735427	661481	675405
7. **Total Domestic Expenditure**	563632	1125694	1234592	1356223	1498574	1726133	2058379	2282588	2595131	2837316	3051104	3298691	3620249	3741101	4032101
8. Exports of goods and services	213900	561600	648600	691800	781000	965700	1247300	1198300	1440200	1524000	1576500	1839400	1998730	2265900	2625200
9. *Less:* Imports of goods and services	218800	551200	620000	664100	730300	931500	1241000	1195900	1438300	1552600	1611300	1912100	2110600	2351800	2700200
10. Statistical discrepancy	..	..	..	..	..	..	..	..	..	..	..	..	..	..	..
11. **Gross Domestic Product**	558732	1136094	1263192	1383923	1549274	1760333	2064679	2284988	2597031	2808716	3016304	3225991	3508379	3655201	3957101
At 1990 price levels [1]															
1. Government final consumption expenditure	352537	582594	600630	633858	671185	707019	731124	764056	792198	810213	859154	880469	897516	903539	891324
2. Private final consumption expenditure	1639523	2266025	2365334	2481691	2628591	2842820	2922545	2947554	3097410	3178911	3258267	3425463	3506712	3496391	3560274
3. Households	..	..	..	..	..	..	..	..	..	..	..	..	..	..	..
4. Private non-profit institutions serving households	..	..	..	..	..	..	..	..	..	..	..	..	..	..	..
5. Increase in stocks	−4279	51299	51443	49159	20439	63921	101097	−24480	14650	21871	17602	43834	47721	−9249	8548
6. Gross fixed capital formation	477037	775886	841280	825291	853308	913239	976601	958365	996637	997055	1024616	996733	1052908	882809	846730
7. **Total Domestic Expenditure**	2464818	3675804	3858687	3989999	4173523	4526999	4731367	4645495	4900895	5008050	5159639	5351499	5504857	5273490	5306876
8. Exports of goods and services	768015	1685319	1840852	1923780	2136482	2438223	2528571	2319069	2617464	2673476	2734581	2925897	2907900	3012700	3088400
9. *Less:* Imports of goods and services	804252	1693871	1812564	1878624	2058391	2440974	2548778	2317288	2604296	2728545	2801351	3052237	2966500	2907900	2941100
10. Statistical discrepancy	−4997	14429	22675	21225	17955	6718	10090	11323	7875	−225	640	−12408	0	0	0
11. **Gross Domestic Product**	2423584	3681681	3909650	4056380	4269569	4530966	4721250	4658599	4921938	4952756	5093509	5212751	5446257	5378290	5454176
COST COMPONENTS OF THE G.D.P.															
1. Indirect taxes	64961	155170	167885	181263	191239	213959	246204	266526	321060	353895	381129	412109	433557	454964	501572
2. *Less:* Subsidies	9344	31105	34562	36878	45859	58273	60240	71929	95850	110466	120027	136859	129070	136536	146841
3. Consumption of fixed capital	56286	108861	124569	133834	148993	161636	193201	212444	231274	262291	281399	302497	312145	332471	362803
4. Compensation of employees paid by resident producers	256177	560720	629532	716665	821339	945434	1140099	1308990	1510487	1642613	1762758	1884590	2083572	2166910	2276726
5. Operating surplus	190652	342448	375768	389039	433562	497577	545415	568957	630060	660383	711045	763654	808175	837392	962841
6. Statistical discrepancy	..	..	..	..	..	..	..	..	..	..	..	..	..	..	..
7. **Gross Domestic Product**	558732	1136094	1263192	1383923	1549274	1760333	2064679	2284988	2597031	2808716	3016304	3225991	3508379	3655201	3957101
CAPITAL TRANSACTIONS OF THE NATION															
Finance of Gross Capital Formation															
1. Consumption of fixed capital	56286	108861	124569	133834	148993	161636	193201	212444	231274	262291	281399	302497	312145	332471	362803
2. Net saving	52121	173181	217987	221920	244649	274025	329289	283840	348426	316311	331714	287815	291779	179446	159422
3. *Less:* Surplus of the nation on current transactions	1000	18900	35595	31924	56479	37651	9999	−2351	5664	−34369	−39899	−95837	−158797	−145347	−159642
4. Statistical discrepancy	..	..	..	..	..	..	..	..	..	..	..	..	..	..	..
5. **Finance of Gross Capital Formation**	107407	263142	306961	323830	337163	398010	512491	498635	574036	612971	653012	686149	762721	657264	681867
Gross capital formation															
6. Increase in stocks	−334	21845	20784	19024	7417	22431	45121	−12512	5304	10013	5485	25048	27294	−4217	6462
7. Gross fixed capital formation	107741	241297	286177	304806	329746	375579	467370	511147	568732	602958	647527	661101	735427	661481	675405
8. Statistical discrepancy	..	..	..	..	..	..	..	..	..	..	..	..	..	..	..
9. **Gross Capital Formation**	107407	263142	306961	323830	337163	398010	512491	498635	574036	612971	653012	686149	762721	657264	681867
RELATIONS AMONG NATIONAL ACCOUNTING AGGREGATES															
1. **Gross Domestic Product**	558732	1136094	1263192	1383923	1549274	1760333	2064679	2284988	2597031	2808716	3016304	3225991	3508379	3655201	3957101
2. *Plus:* Net factor income from the rest of the world	7200	13300	17200	17000	19500	19200	22300	24400	28500	23100	21300	7800	−6400	−7900	−32100
3. Factor income from the rest of the world	15300	44300	62200	54300	55900	65800	102000	104900	106200	111800	129300	149400	228700	472800	552600
4. Factor income paid to the rest of the world	8100	31000	45000	37300	36400	46600	79700	80500	77700	88700	108000	141600	235100	480700	584700
5. *Equals:* **Gross National Product**	565932	1149394	1280392	1400923	1568774	1779533	2086979	2309388	2625531	2831816	3037604	3233791	3501979	3647301	3925001
6. *Less:* Consumption of fixed capital	56286	108861	124569	133834	148993	161636	193201	212444	231274	262291	281399	302497	312145	332471	362803
7. *Plus:* Statistical discrepancy	..	..	..	..	..	..	..	..	..	..	..	..	..	..	..
8. *Equals:* **National Income**	509646	1040533	1155823	1267089	1419781	1617897	1893778	2096944	2394257	2569525	2756205	2931294	3189834	3314830	3562198
9. *Plus:* Net current transfers from the rest of the world	−1300	−4800	−10205	−12776	−13721	−15749	−18601	−29151	−24736	−28869	−26399	−30937	−40527	−51547	−52542
10. Current transfers from the rest of the world	..	..	19920	23269	25581	31427	26930	29416	39365	46144	56612	63625	58428	63816	77982
11. Current transfers paid to the rest of the world	..	..	30125	36045	39302	47176	45531	58567	64101	75013	83011	94562	98955	115363	130524
12. *Equals:* **National Disposable Income**	508346	1035733	1145618	1254313	1406060	1602148	1875177	2067793	2369521	2540656	2729806	2900357	3149307	3263283	3509656
13. *Less:* Final consumption	456225	862552	927631	1032393	1161411	1328123	1545888	1783953	2021095	2224345	2398092	2612542	2857528	3083837	3350234
14. *Plus:* Statistical discrepancy	..	..	..	..	..	..	..	..	..	..	..	..	..	..	..
15. *Equals:* **Net Saving**	52121	173181	217987	221920	244649	274025	329289	283840	348426	316311	331714	287815	291779	179446	159422
16. *Less:* Surplus of the nation on current transactions	1000	18900	35595	31924	56479	37651	9999	−2351	5664	−34369	−39899	−95837	−158797	−145347	−159642
17. *Plus:* Statistical discrepancy	..	..	..	..	..	..	..	..	..	..	..	..	..	..	..
18. *Equals:* **Net Capital Formation**	51121	154281	182392	189996	188170	236374	319290	286191	342762	350680	371613	383652	450576	324793	319064

1. At 1990 relative prices for 1980-1997, at 1980 relative prices for 1970-1979 and at 1970 relative prices for 1960-1969.

Principaux Agrégats

millions de francs

1983	1984	1985	1986	1987	1988	1989	1990	1991	1992	1993	1994	1995	1996	1997	
															DÉPENSES IMPUTÉES AU P.I.B.
															Aux prix courants
728460	765015	820280	852550	856475	857185	884036	917652	987397	1027608	1088344	1139453	1181921	1205417	1251591	1. Consommation finale des administrations publiques
2802235	2989480	3224095	3324731	3477779	3633172	3919071	4166130	4423563	4629464	4714894	4924045	5071235	5282002	5488027	2. Consommation finale privée
..	..	..	..	..	..	..	..	..	..	..	..	..	..	..	3. Ménages
..	..	..	..	..	..	..	..	..	..	..	..	..	..	..	4. Institutions privées sans but lucratif au service des ménages
−27163	16333	−34834	−29543	8397	16148	19599	−2889	5737	7431	1403	24020	32567	21513	2822	5. Variations des stocks
662069	705914	760140	795812	853727	1013666	1178651	1327982	1292651	1347960	1321085	1349068	1430212	1449812	1539944	6. Formation brute de capital fixe
4165601	**4476742**	**4769681**	**4943550**	**5196378**	**5520171**	**6001357**	**6408875**	**6709348**	**7012463**	**7125726**	**7436586**	**7715935**	**7958744**	**8282384**	7. **Demande intérieure totale**
2887900	3330100	3432400	3293100	3322100	3758100	4347600	4464400	4573000	4677800	4591700	5042600	5394600	5649400	6326400	8. Exportations de biens et services
2864700	3294200	3367700	3151800	3199800	3588800	4181600	4318900	4413400	4461700	4312200	4710300	5042400	5303000	5933300	9. *Moins :* Importations de biens et services
..	..	..	..	..	..	..	..	..	..	..	..	..	..	..	10. Divergence statistique
4188801	**4512642**	**4834381**	**5084850**	**5318678**	**5689471**	**6167357**	**6554375**	**6868948**	**7228563**	**7405226**	**7768886**	**8068135**	**8305144**	**8675484**	11. **Produit intérieur brut**
															Aux niveaux de prix de 1990[1]
893659	899218	921468	938690	939874	931249	922345	917652	937685	941027	952791	968825	975164	988750	996997	1. Consommation finale des administrations publiques
3529088	3552022	3622806	3696948	3780484	3902833	4046881	4166130	4285205	4380880	4322356	4392581	4430343	4510223	4603343	2. Consommation finale privée
..	..	..	..	..	..	..	..	..	..	..	..	..	..	..	3. Ménages
..	..	..	..	..	..	..	..	..	..	..	..	..	..	..	4. Institutions privées sans but lucratif au service des ménages
−30473	32494	−39364	−27082	13783	27406	17691	−2889	6491	12508	3336	21338	16328	2391	−20484	5. Variations des stocks
797138	817212	849466	879352	934434	1087298	1211131	1327982	1265724	1282357	1236436	1235103	1286688	1293083	1363089	6. Formation brute de capital fixe
5189412	**5300946**	**5354376**	**5487908**	**5668575**	**5948786**	**6198048**	**6408875**	**6495105**	**6616772**	**6514919**	**6617847**	**6708523**	**6794447**	**6942945**	7. **Demande intérieure totale**
3166300	3373200	3383200	3473300	3625200	3955900	4280900	4464400	4605000	4765500	4734100	5130800	5437900	5556600	5953300	8. Exportations de biens et services
2901900	3085600	3092800	3232200	3429500	3763600	4117500	4318900	4440900	4623700	4589300	4917600	5155700	5270100	5602700	9. *Moins :* Importations de biens et services
0	0	0	0	0	0	0	0	0	0	0	0	0	0	0	10. Divergence statistique
5453812	**5588546**	**5644776**	**5729008**	**5864275**	**6141086**	**6361448**	**6554375**	**6659205**	**6758572**	**6659719**	**6831047**	**6990723**	**7080947**	**7293545**	11. **Produit intérieur brut**
															RÉPARTITION DU P.I.B.
537221	561736	589824	603799	653943	689439	749421	801449	832827	876474	918707	988660	992125	1052710	1111240	1. Impôts indirects
169255	175882	181172	182623	172180	175672	158487	186645	202613	192387	195352	187799	196106	199695	176100	2. *Moins :* Subventions
398532	423312	455805	478624	508423	565642	602702	657487	681115	732112	738276	769176	808029	820769	863694	3. Consommation de capital fixe
2370662	2528227	2668512	2786859	2857477	2974232	3124942	3389242	3639760	3827573	3919667	4058039	4179692	4256213	4391557	4. Rémunération des salariés payée par les producteurs résidents
1051641	1175249	1301412	1398191	1471015	1635830	1848779	1892842	1917859	1984791	2023928	2140810	2284395	2375147	2485093	5. Excédent net d'exploitation
..	..	..	..	..	..	..	..	..	..	..	..	..	..	..	6. Divergence statistique
4188801	**4512642**	**4834381**	**5084850**	**5318678**	**5689471**	**6167357**	**6554375**	**6868948**	**7228563**	**7405226**	**7768886**	**8068135**	**8305144**	**8675484**	7. **Produit intérieur brut**
															OPÉRATIONS EN CAPITAL DE LA NATION
															Financement de la formation brute de capital
398532	423312	455805	478624	508423	565642	602702	657487	681115	732112	738276	769176	808029	820769	863694	1. Consommation de capital fixe
168167	246044	242295	350070	403070	544640	680058	715780	704082	735253	828476	906247	1007700	985390	1078466	2. Épargne nette
−68207	−52891	−27206	62425	49369	80468	84510	48174	86809	111974	244264	302335	352950	334834	399394	3. *Moins :* Solde des opérations courantes de la nation
..	..	..	..	..	..	..	..	..	..	..	..	..	..	..	4. Divergence statistique
634906	**722247**	**725306**	**766269**	**862124**	**1029814**	**1198250**	**1325093**	**1298388**	**1355391**	**1322488**	**1373088**	**1462779**	**1471325**	**1542766**	5. **Financement de la formation brute de capital**
															Formation brute de capital
−27163	16333	−34834	−29543	8397	16148	19599	−2889	5737	7431	1403	24020	32567	21513	2822	6. Variations des stocks
662069	705914	760140	795812	853727	1013666	1178651	1327982	1292651	1347960	1321085	1349068	1430212	1449812	1539944	7. Formation brute de capital fixe
..	..	..	..	..	..	..	..	..	..	..	..	..	..	..	8. Divergence statistique
634906	**722247**	**725306**	**766269**	**862124**	**1029814**	**1198250**	**1325093**	**1298388**	**1355391**	**1322488**	**1373088**	**1462779**	**1471325**	**1542766**	9. **Formation brute de capital**
															RELATIONS ENTRE LES PRINCIPAUX AGRÉGATS
4188801	**4512642**	**4834381**	**5084850**	**5318678**	**5689471**	**6167357**	**6554375**	**6868948**	**7228563**	**7405226**	**7768886**	**8068135**	**8305144**	**8675484**	1. **Produit intérieur brut**
−37100	−34900	−49500	−31800	−19200	−13700	−11000	−34100	−800	−14400	58400	76400	107300	125600	141100	2. *Plus :* Revenu net des facteurs reçu du reste du monde
521500	620900	734700	665600	645300	773300	1132000	1250800	1465400	1665000	1676800	1793300	1807600	1576600	1470700	3. Revenu des facteurs reçu du reste du monde
558600	655800	784200	697400	664500	789000	1143000	1284900	1466200	1679400	1618400	1716900	1700300	1451000	1329600	4. Revenu des facteurs payé au reste du monde
4151701	**4477742**	**4784881**	**5053050**	**5299478**	**5670771**	**6156357**	**6520275**	**6868148**	**7214163**	**7463626**	**7845286**	**8175435**	**8430744**	**8816584**	5. *Égal :* **Produit national brut**
398532	423312	455805	478624	508423	565642	602702	657487	681115	732112	738276	769176	808029	820769	863694	6. *Moins :* Consommation de capital fixe
..	..	..	..	..	..	..	..	..	..	..	..	..	..	..	7. *Plus :* Divergence statistique
3753169	**4054430**	**4329076**	**4574426**	**4791055**	**5105129**	**5553655**	**5862788**	**6187033**	**6482051**	**6725350**	**7076110**	**7367406**	**7609975**	**7952890**	8. *Égal :* **Revenu national**
−54307	−53891	−42406	−47075	−53731	−70132	−70490	−63226	−71991	−89726	−93636	−106365	−106550	−137166	−134806	9. *Plus :* Transferts courants nets reçus du reste du monde
87798	98503	118977	110607	115451	115718	121495	167862	175090	156555	159473	153381	181040	189576	207097	10. Transferts courants reçus du reste du monde
142105	152394	161383	157682	169182	185850	191985	231088	247081	246281	253109	259746	287590	326742	341903	11. Transferts courants payés au reste du monde
3698862	**4000539**	**4286670**	**4527351**	**4737324**	**5034997**	**5483165**	**5799562**	**6115042**	**6392325**	**6631714**	**6969745**	**7260856**	**7472809**	**7818084**	12. *Égal :* **Revenu national disponible**
3530695	3754495	4044375	4177281	4334254	4490357	4803107	5083782	5410960	5657072	5803238	6063498	6253156	6487419	6739618	13. *Moins :* Consommation finale
..	..	..	..	..	..	..	..	..	..	..	..	..	..	..	14. *Plus :* Divergence statistique
168167	**246044**	**242295**	**350070**	**403070**	**544640**	**680058**	**715780**	**704082**	**735253**	**828476**	**906247**	**1007700**	**985390**	**1078466**	15. *Égal :* **Épargne nette**
−68207	−52891	−27206	62425	49369	80468	84510	48174	86809	111974	244264	302335	352950	334834	399394	16. *Moins :* Solde des opérations courantes de la nation
..	..	..	..	..	..	..	..	..	..	..	..	..	..	..	17. *Plus :* Divergence statistique
236374	**298935**	**269501**	**287645**	**353701**	**464172**	**595548**	**667606**	**617273**	**623279**	**584212**	**603912**	**654750**	**650556**	**679072**	18. *Égal :* **Formation nette de capital**

1. Aux prix relatifs de 1990 pour la période 1980-1997, aux prix relatifs de 1980 pour la période 1970-1979 et aux prix relatifs de 1970 pour la période 1960-1969.

CZECH REPUBLIC

1968 SNA

Main aggregates

billions of koruny

	1960	1969	1970	1971	1972	1973	1974	1975	1976	1977	1978	1979	1980	1981	1982
EXPENDITURE ON THE G.D.P.															
At current prices															
1. Government final consumption expenditure	..	..	..	..	..	..	..	..	..	..	..	..	..	..	..
2. Private final consumption expenditure	..	..	..	..	..	..	..	..	..	..	..	..	..	..	..
3. Households	..	..	..	..	..	..	..	..	..	..	..	..	..	..	..
4. Private non-profit institutions serving households	..	..	..	..	..	..	..	..	..	..	..	..	..	..	..
5. Increase in stocks	..	..	..	..	..	..	..	..	..	..	..	..	..	..	..
6. Gross fixed capital formation	..	..	..	..	..	..	..	..	..	..	..	..	..	..	..
7. **Total Domestic Expenditure**	..	..	..	..	..	..	..	..	..	..	..	..	..	..	..
8. Exports of goods and services	..	..	..	..	..	..	..	..	..	..	..	..	..	..	..
9. *Less:* Imports of goods and services	..	..	..	..	..	..	..	..	..	..	..	..	..	..	..
10. Statistical discrepancy	..	..	..	..	..	..	..	..	..	..	..	..	..	..	..
11. **Gross Domestic Product**	..	..	..	..	..	..	..	..	..	..	..	..	..	..	..
At 1990 price levels[1]															
1. Government final consumption expenditure	..	..	..	..	..	..	..	..	..	..	..	..	..	..	..
2. Private final consumption expenditure	..	..	..	..	..	..	..	..	..	..	..	..	..	..	..
3. Households	..	..	..	..	..	..	..	..	..	..	..	..	..	..	..
4. Private non-profit institutions serving households	..	..	..	..	..	..	..	..	..	..	..	..	..	..	..
5. Increase in stocks	..	..	..	..	..	..	..	..	..	..	..	..	..	..	..
6. Gross fixed capital formation	..	..	..	..	..	..	..	..	..	..	..	..	..	..	..
7. **Total Domestic Expenditure**	..	..	..	..	..	..	..	..	..	..	..	..	..	..	..
8. Exports of goods and services	..	..	..	..	..	..	..	..	..	..	..	..	..	..	..
9. *Less:* Imports of goods and services	..	..	..	..	..	..	..	..	..	..	..	..	..	..	..
10. Statistical discrepancy	..	..	..	..	..	..	..	..	..	..	..	..	..	..	..
11. **Gross Domestic Product**	..	..	..	..	..	..	..	..	..	..	..	..	..	..	..
COST COMPONENTS OF THE G.D.P.															
1. Indirect taxes	..	..	..	..	..	..	..	..	..	..	..	..	..	..	..
2. *Less:* Subsidies	..	..	..	..	..	..	..	..	..	..	..	..	..	..	..
3. Consumption of fixed capital	..	..	..	..	..	..	..	..	..	..	..	..	..	..	..
4. Compensation of employees paid by resident producers	..	..	..	..	..	..	..	..	..	..	..	..	..	..	..
5. Operating surplus	..	..	..	..	..	..	..	..	..	..	..	..	..	..	..
6. Statistical discrepancy	..	..	..	..	..	..	..	..	..	..	..	..	..	..	..
7. **Gross Domestic Product**	..	..	..	..	..	..	..	..	..	..	..	..	..	..	..
CAPITAL TRANSACTIONS OF THE NATION															
Finance of Gross Capital Formation															
1. Consumption of fixed capital	..	..	..	..	..	..	..	..	..	..	..	..	..	..	..
2. Net saving	..	..	..	..	..	..	..	..	..	..	..	..	..	..	..
3. *Less:* Surplus of the nation on current transactions	..	..	..	..	..	..	..	..	..	..	..	..	..	..	..
4. Statistical discrepancy	..	..	..	..	..	..	..	..	..	..	..	..	..	..	..
5. **Finance of Gross Capital Formation**	..	..	..	..	..	..	..	..	..	..	..	..	..	..	..
Gross capital formation															
6. Increase in stocks	..	..	..	..	..	..	..	..	..	..	..	..	..	..	..
7. Gross fixed capital formation	..	..	..	..	..	..	..	..	..	..	..	..	..	..	..
8. Statistical discrepancy	..	..	..	..	..	..	..	..	..	..	..	..	..	..	..
9. **Gross Capital Formation**	..	..	..	..	..	..	..	..	..	..	..	..	..	..	..
RELATIONS AMONG NATIONAL ACCOUNTING AGGREGATES															
1. **Gross Domestic Product**	..	..	..	..	..	..	..	..	..	..	..	..	..	..	..
2. *Plus:* Net factor income from the rest of the world	..	..	..	..	..	..	..	..	..	..	..	..	..	..	..
3. Factor income from the rest of the world	..	..	..	..	..	..	..	..	..	..	..	..	..	..	..
4. Factor income paid to the rest of the world	..	..	..	..	..	..	..	..	..	..	..	..	..	..	..
5. *Equals:* **Gross National Product**	..	..	..	..	..	..	..	..	..	..	..	..	..	..	..
6. *Less:* Consumption of fixed capital	..	..	..	..	..	..	..	..	..	..	..	..	..	..	..
7. *Plus:* Statistical discrepancy	..	..	..	..	..	..	..	..	..	..	..	..	..	..	..
8. *Equals:* **National Income**	..	..	..	..	..	..	..	..	..	..	..	..	..	..	..
9. *Plus:* Net current transfers from the rest of the world	..	..	..	..	..	..	..	..	..	..	..	..	..	..	..
10. Current transfers from the rest of the world	..	..	..	..	..	..	..	..	..	..	..	..	..	..	..
11. Current transfers paid to the rest of the world	..	..	..	..	..	..	..	..	..	..	..	..	..	..	..
12. *Equals:* **National Disposable Income**	..	..	..	..	..	..	..	..	..	..	..	..	..	..	..
13. *Less:* Final consumption	..	..	..	..	..	..	..	..	..	..	..	..	..	..	..
14. *Plus:* Statistical discrepancy	..	..	..	..	..	..	..	..	..	..	..	..	..	..	..
15. *Equals:* **Net Saving**	..	..	..	..	..	..	..	..	..	..	..	..	..	..	..
16. *Less:* Surplus of the nation on current transactions	..	..	..	..	..	..	..	..	..	..	..	..	..	..	..
17. *Plus:* Statistical discrepancy	..	..	..	..	..	..	..	..	..	..	..	..	..	..	..
18. *Equals:* **Net Capital Formation**	..	..	..	..	..	..	..	..	..	..	..	..	..	..	..

1. At 1994 relative prices.

RÉPUBLIQUE TCHÈQUE

SCN de 1968

Principaux Agrégats

milliards de couronnes tchèques

DÉPENSES IMPUTÉES AU P.I.B.

Aux prix courants

1983	1984	1985	1986	1987	1988	1989	1990	1991	1992	1993	1994	1995	1996	1997	
..	..	..	..	..	..	..	111.5*	134.2*	163.1	221.6	255.5	281.5	323.6	334.0	1. Consommation finale des administrations publiques
..	..	..	..	..	..	..	308.1*	344.3*	442.8	496.3	571.5	667.6	771.9	847.2	2. Consommation finale privée
..	..	..	..	..	..	..			439.2	490.5	564.0	658.0	760.3	834.1	3. Ménages
..	..	..	..	..	..	..			3.5	5.8	7.5	9.6	11.6	13.1	4. Institutions privées sans but lucratif au service des ménages
..	..	..	..	..	..	..	−15.9*	34.2*	−15.0	−11.7	6.2	16.9	39.0	52.0	5. Variations des stocks
..	..	..	..	..	..	..	159.6*	176.7*	241.3	285.8	339.9	442.5	505.5	506.9	6. Formation brute de capital fixe
..	..	..	..	..	..	..	**563.3***	**689.4***	**832.2**	**992.0**	**1173.2**	**1408.4**	**1640.0**	**1740.1**	7. **Demande intérieure totale**
..	..	..	..	..	..	..	341.7*	428.3*	465.2	523.6	608.0	755.9	818.8	949.4	8. Exportations de biens et services
..	..	..	..	..	..	..	325.7*	368.1*	450.6	511.5	632.5	815.6	926.2	1040.0	9. *Moins :* Importations de biens et services
..	..	..	..	..	..	..	..	..	..	..	..	..	..	..	10. Divergence statistique
..	..	..	..	..	..	..	**579.3***	**749.6***	**846.8**	**1004.1**	**1148.7**	**1348.7**	**1532.6**	**1649.5**	11. **Produit intérieur brut**

Aux niveaux de prix de 1990[1]

1983	1984	1985	1986	1987	1988	1989	1990	1991	1992	1993	1994	1995	1996	1997	
..	..	..	..	..	..	..	111.5*	101.4*	98.3*	96.6*	94.1*	92.2*	96.0*	93.9*	1. Consommation finale des administrations publiques
..	..	..	..	..	..	..	308.1*	220.4*	253.7*	262.8*	277.0*	296.3*	317.3*	322.8*	2. Consommation finale privée
..	..	..	..	..	..	..	..	..	..	..	..	..	..	..	3. Ménages
..	..	..	..	..	..	..	..	..	..	..	..	..	..	..	4. Institutions privées sans but lucratif au service des ménages
..	..	..	..	..	..	..	−15.9*	9.9*	−18.5*	−5.2*	−4.8*	−2.5*	5.4*	10.7*	5. Variations des stocks
..	..	..	..	..	..	..	159.6*	131.4*	143.0*	132.0*	157.1*	190.1*	206.6*	196.5*	6. Formation brute de capital fixe
..	..	..	..	..	..	..	**563.3***	**463.1***	**476.6***	**486.3***	**523.5***	**576.1***	**625.3***	**624.0***	7. **Demande intérieure totale**
..	..	..	..	..	..	..	341.7*	326.7*	348.8*	375.1*	375.7*	436.1*	459.7*	506.7*	8. Exportations de biens et services
..	..	..	..	..	..	..	325.7*	270.1*	329.5*	364.0*	392.3*	478.8*	540.5*	576.8*	9. *Moins :* Importations de biens et services
..	..	..	..	..	..	..	0.0*	−6.9*	0.0*	1.3*	7.9*	14.0*	24.3*	20.6*	10. Divergence statistique
..	..	..	..	..	..	..	**579.3***	**512.8***	**495.9***	**498.7***	**514.8***	**547.4***	**568.9***	**574.4***	11. **Produit intérieur brut**

RÉPARTITION DU P.I.B.

1983	1984	1985	1986	1987	1988	1989	1990	1991	1992	1993	1994	1995	1996	1997	
..	..	..	..	..	..	..	..	..	124.5	151.6	172.8	195.1	220.2*	..	1. Impôts indirects
..	..	..	..	..	..	..	..	..	43.5	33.4	41.6	42.6	47.1*	..	2. *Moins :* Subventions
..	..	..	..	..	..	..	..	..	179.8	217.0	261.6	262.9	298.7*	..	3. Consommation de capital fixe
..	..	..	..	..	..	..	..	..	377.6	462.4	549.7	654.1	772.8*	..	4. Rémunération des salariés payée par les producteurs résidents
..	..	..	..	..	..	..	..	..	208.5	206.5	206.1	279.1	288.0*	..	5. Excédent net d'exploitation
..	..	..	..	..	..	..	..	..	..	..	..	..	..	..	6. Divergence statistique
..	..	..	..	..	..	..	..	..	**846.8**	**1004.1**	**1148.7**	**1348.7**	**1532.6**	..	7. **Produit intérieur brut**

OPÉRATIONS EN CAPITAL DE LA NATION

Financement de la formation brute de capital

1983	1984	1985	1986	1987	1988	1989	1990	1991	1992	1993	1994	1995	1996	1997	
..	..	..	..	..	..	..	..	..	179.8	217.0	261.6	262.9	298.7*	..	1. Consommation de capital fixe
..	..	..	..	..	..	..	..	..	67.6	68.2	62.6	144.8	147.5*	..	2. Épargne nette
..	..	..	..	..	..	..	..	..	21.0	11.0	−21.9	−51.6	−98.3*	..	3. *Moins :* Solde des opérations courantes de la nation
..	..	..	..	..	..	..	..	..	..	..	..	..	..	..	4. Divergence statistique
..	..	..	..	..	..	..	..	..	**226.3**	**274.1**	**346.1**	**459.4**	**544.5**	..	5. **Financement de la formation brute de capital**

Formation brute de capital

1983	1984	1985	1986	1987	1988	1989	1990	1991	1992	1993	1994	1995	1996	1997	
..	..	..	..	..	..	..	..	..	−15.0	−11.7	6.2	16.9	39.0	52.0	6. Variations des stocks
..	..	..	..	..	..	..	..	..	241.3	285.8	339.9	442.5	505.5	506.9	7. Formation brute de capital fixe
..	..	..	..	..	..	..	..	..	..	..	..	..	..	..	8. Divergence statistique
..	..	..	..	..	..	..	..	..	**226.3**	**274.1**	**346.1**	**459.4**	**544.5**	**558.9**	9. **Formation brute de capital**

RELATIONS ENTRE LES PRINCIPAUX AGRÉGATS

1983	1984	1985	1986	1987	1988	1989	1990	1991	1992	1993	1994	1995	1996	1997	
..	..	..	..	..	..	..	..	..	**846.8**	**1004.1**	**1148.7**	**1348.7**	**1532.6**	**1649.5**	1. **Produit intérieur brut**
..	..	..	..	..	..	..	..	..	5.6	−4.3	−0.8	−7.1	−8.1	..	2. *Plus :* Revenu net des facteurs reçu du reste du monde
..	..	..	..	..	..	..	..	..	16.1	17.0	24.6	32.1	..	..	3. Revenu des facteurs reçu du reste du monde
..	..	..	..	..	..	..	..	..	10.5	21.2	25.5	39.3	..	..	4. Revenu des facteurs payé au reste du monde
..	..	..	..	..	..	..	..	..	**852.5**	**999.8**	**1147.8**	**1341.6**	**1524.5***	..	5. *Égal :* **Produit national brut**
..	..	..	..	..	..	..	..	..	179.8	217.0	261.6	262.9	298.7*	..	6. *Moins :* Consommation de capital fixe
..	..	..	..	..	..	..	..	..	..	..	..	..	..	..	7. *Plus :* Divergence statistique
..	..	..	..	..	..	..	..	..	**672.7**	**782.8**	**886.2**	**1078.7**	**1225.8***	..	8. *Égal :* **Revenu national**
..	..	..	..	..	..	..	..	..	0.8	3.2	3.5	15.2	17.2*	..	9. *Plus :* Transferts courants nets reçus du reste du monde
..	..	..	..	..	..	..	..	..	8.3	10.4	10.2	18.4	..	..	10. Transferts courants reçus du reste du monde
..	..	..	..	..	..	..	..	..	7.5	7.2	6.8	3.2	..	..	11. Transferts courants payés au reste du monde
..	..	..	..	..	..	..	..	..	**673.5**	**786.1**	**889.7**	**1093.9**	**1243.0***	..	12. *Égal :* **Revenu national disponible**
..	..	..	..	..	..	..	..	..	605.9	717.9	827.1	949.1	1095.5	1181.2	13. *Moins :* Consommation finale
..	..	..	..	..	..	..	..	..	..	..	..	..	..	..	14. *Plus :* Divergence statistique
..	..	..	..	..	..	..	..	..	**67.6**	**68.2**	**62.6**	**144.8**	**147.5***	..	15. *Égal :* **Épargne nette**
..	..	..	..	..	..	..	..	..	21.0	11.0	−21.9	−51.6	−98.3*	..	16. *Moins :* Solde des opérations courantes de la nation
..	..	..	..	..	..	..	..	..	..	..	..	..	..	..	17. *Plus :* Divergence statistique
..	..	..	..	..	..	..	..	..	**46.6**	**57.2**	**84.5**	**196.5**	**245.8***	..	18. *Égal :* **Formation nette de capital**

1. Aux prix relatifs de 1994.

DENMARK
1993 SNA

Main aggregates

millions of kroner

	1960	1969	1970	1971	1972	1973	1974	1975	1976	1977	1978	1979	1980	1981	1982
EXPENDITURE ON THE G.D.P.															
At current prices															
1. Government final consumption expenditure	5702*	21128*	24698*	29069*	33461*	38398*	47209*	55480*	63138*	69652*	79541*	90586*	104043*	118107*	136762*
2. Private final consumption expenditure	24641*	59626*	65806*	70724*	77753*	91059*	101713*	115940*	137391*	153598*	169055*	189280*	201847*	220940*	247109*
3. Households	..	59119*	65233*	70045*	76948*	90132*	100625*	114671*	135870*	151877*	166985*	186949*	199208*	218120*	244016*
4. Private non-profit institutions serving households	..	333*	389*	509*	646*	733*	895*	1062*	1283*	1464*	1868*	2111*	2474*	2607*	2829*
5. Increase in stocks	2223*	1828*	1618*	1181*	707*	3137*	3208*	–91*	3550*	3123*	–13*	2512*	–697*	–372*	1991*
6. Gross fixed capital formation	10414*	30875*	34302*	37193*	43348*	50146*	54424*	53401*	67563*	72227*	79062*	84891*	82362*	74754*	87401*
7. **Total Domestic Expenditure**	**42980***	**113457***	**126424***	**138167***	**155269***	**182740***	**206554***	**224730***	**271642***	**298600***	**327645***	**367269***	**387555***	**413429***	**473263***
8. Exports of goods and services	13761*	30603*	34423*	37626*	42464*	51281*	63934*	67643*	75343*	83672*	89966*	105490*	127132*	154986*	175660*
9. *Less:* Imports of goods and services	14519*	33535*	38718*	40770*	42184*	55556*	70926*	70844*	88865*	95743*	98480*	117490*	133287*	154246*	176295*
10. Statistical discrepancy	–161*	–828*	–874*	–998*	–1481*	–1773*	–1644*	–480*	–1340*	–1029*	–856*	–690*	668*	2656*	2128*
11. **Gross Domestic Product**	**42061***	**109697***	**121255***	**134025***	**154068***	**176692***	**197918***	**221049***	**256780***	**285500***	**318275***	**354579***	**382068***	**416825***	**474756***
At 1990 price levels[1]															
1. Government final consumption expenditure	68887*	115773*	123745*	130504*	138002*	143508*	148550*	151544*	158308*	162109*	172155*	182246*	190037*	195039*	201039*
2. Private final consumption expenditure	204316*	301295*	311862*	309509*	314621*	329872*	320430*	332210*	358355*	362239*	364951*	369973*	356338*	348109*	353152*
3. Households	..	298322*	308752*	306167*	311007*	326150*	316725*	328408*	354200*	357967*	360255*	365194*	351430*	343404*	348535*
4. Private non-profit institutions serving households	..	2108*	2232*	2611*	2993*	3032*	3085*	3138*	3467*	3617*	4252*	4339*	4653*	4408*	4229*
5. Increase in stocks	12753*	9873*	7517*	5753*	3825*	11633*	10472*	803*	9007*	7493*	226*	5123*	–750*	–562*	4499*
6. Gross fixed capital formation	78243*	150003*	153286*	156259*	170725*	176648*	161006*	141065*	165221*	161180*	162969*	162253*	141801*	114549*	122660*
7. **Total Domestic Expenditure**	**364199***	**576944***	**596410***	**602025***	**627173***	**661661***	**640458***	**625622***	**690891***	**693021***	**700301***	**719595***	**687426***	**657135***	**681350***
8. Exports of goods and services	65621*	115815*	122302*	129102*	136310*	146963*	152108*	149399*	155503*	161901*	163820*	177511*	186659*	201967*	207020*
9. *Less:* Imports of goods and services	75735*	148150*	161960*	160796*	163176*	184014*	177012*	168500*	194761*	194809*	195042*	204731*	190873*	187666*	194758*
10. Statistical discrepancy	–2889*	–11447*	–12790*	–11871*	–12381*	–15329*	–11955*	–6909*	–13205*	–11327*	–10711*	–10674*	–4524*	1213*	–653*
11. **Gross Domestic Product**	**351196***	**533162***	**543962***	**558460***	**587926***	**609281***	**603599***	**599612***	**638428***	**648786***	**658368***	**681701***	**678688***	**672649***	**692959***
COST COMPONENTS OF THE G.D.P.															
1. Indirect taxes	5023*	18413*	20464*	22913*	26197*	29105*	30803*	33528*	40758*	47823*	56762*	65696*	69524*	75005*	81961*
2. *Less:* Subsidies	264*	2849*	3113*	3625*	4256*	5282*	6737*	5912*	7569*	8608*	10315*	10989*	11588*	12190*	14725*
3. Consumption of fixed capital	4832*	12943*	14790*	16617*	18912*	21213*	26333*	31339*	35191*	40525*	45486*	50809*	57413*	64827*	72198*
4. Compensation of employees paid by resident producers	20879*	59241*	66666*	75290*	83749*	96376*	113889*	128137*	146633*	162663*	180396*	201618*	222071*	240167*	271369*
5. Operating surplus	10895*	20999*	21624*	22126*	28297*	33821*	32812*	33416*	40830*	42361*	45272*	47002*	44973*	49359*	63581*
6. Statistical discrepancy	696*	949*	844*	703*	1171*	1458*	819*	539*	936*	734*	672*	441*	–327*	–345*	372*
7. **Gross Domestic Product**	**42061***	**109696***	**121255***	**134024***	**154070***	**176691***	**197919***	**221047***	**256779***	**285498***	**318273***	**354577***	**382066***	**416823***	**474756***
CAPITAL TRANSACTIONS OF THE NATION															
Finance of Gross Capital Formation															
1. Consumption of fixed capital	4832*	12943*	14790*	16617*	18912*	21213*	26333*	31339*	35191*	40525*	45486*	50809*	57413*	64827*	72198*
2. Net saving	13888*	30357*	28998*	33224*	46238*	54173*	43658*	29755*	35590*	34732*	37371*	23168*	2363*	–26789*	–30998*
3. *Less:* Surplus of the nation on current transactions	–522*	–3450*	–5172*	–3614*	–601*	–3315*	–6822*	–3698*	–13935*	–12657*	–9652*	–18476*	–15454*	–13927*	–22328*
4. Statistical discrepancy	–6605*	–14047*	–13040*	–15081*	–21696*	–25418*	–19181*	–11482*	–13603*	–12564*	–13460*	–5050*	6435*	22417*	25864*
5. **Finance of Gross Capital Formation**	**12637***	**32703***	**35920***	**38374***	**44055***	**53283***	**57632***	**53310***	**71113***	**75350***	**79049***	**87403***	**81665***	**74382***	**89392***
Gross capital formation															
6. Increase in stocks	2223*	1828*	1618*	1181*	707*	3137*	3208*	–91*	3550*	3123*	–13*	2512*	–697*	–372*	1991*
7. Gross fixed capital formation	10414*	30875*	34302*	37193*	43348*	50146*	54424*	53401*	67563*	72227*	79062*	84891*	82362*	74754*	87401*
8. Statistical discrepancy	..	..	..	..	..	..	..	..	..	..	..	..	..	..	..
9. **Gross Capital Formation**	**12637***	**32703***	**35920***	**38374***	**44055***	**53283***	**57632***	**53310***	**71113***	**75350***	**79049***	**87403***	**81665***	**74382***	**89392***
RELATIONS AMONG NATIONAL ACCOUNTING AGGREGATES															
1. **Gross Domestic Product**	**42061***	**109697***	**121255***	**134024***	**154068***	**176691***	**197919***	**221048***	**256779***	**285498***	**318275***	**354577***	**382066***	**416825***	**474757***
2. *Plus:* Net factor income from the rest of the world	38*	–90*	–139*	–266*	–488*	–545*	–835*	–1089*	–1280*	–2007*	–3011*	–4310*	–6076*	–8304*	–11663*
3. Factor income from the rest of the world	..	1069*	1246*	1292*	1412*	1859*	2786*	2583*	2917*	3846*	4901*	6922*	9229*	13563*	13438*
4. Factor income paid to the rest of the world	..	950*	1157*	1374*	1784*	2209*	3337*	3545*	4074*	5830*	8077*	11491*	15793*	22313*	27028*
5. *Equals:* **Gross National Product**	**42099***	**109607***	**121116***	**133758***	**153580***	**176146***	**197084***	**219959***	**255499***	**283491***	**315264***	**350267***	**375990***	**408521***	**463094***
6. *Less:* Consumption of fixed capital	4832*	12943*	14790*	16617*	18912*	21213*	26333*	31339*	35191*	40525*	45486*	50809*	57413*	64827*	72198*
7. *Plus:* Statistical discrepancy	6974*	15887*	15137*	16775*	24442*	25774*	19572*	11510*	12559*	9938*	9333*	3434*	–9279*	–25031*	–28442*
8. *Equals:* **National Income**	**44241***	**112551***	**121463***	**133916***	**159110***	**180707***	**190323***	**200130***	**232867***	**252904***	**279111***	**302892***	**309298***	**318663***	**362454***
9. *Plus:* Net current transfers from the rest of the world	–10*	–1440*	–1961*	–899*	–1658*	2923*	2257*	1045*	3252*	5078*	6856*	142*	–1045*	–6405*	–9581*
10. Current transfers from the rest of the world	..	71*	109*	157*	127*	2171*	1966*	2095*	3048*	4472*	5218*	4148*	4303*	3164*	2777*
11. Current transfers paid to the rest of the world	..	926*	1282*	778*	1145*	2225*	2220*	3132*	3597*	5106*	5441*	7273*	8207*	9166*	10243*
12. *Equals:* **National Disposable Income**	**44231***	**111111***	**119502***	**133017***	**157452***	**183630***	**192580***	**201175***	**236119***	**257982***	**285967***	**303034***	**308253***	**312258***	**352873***
13. *Less:* Final consumption	30343*	80754*	90504*	99793*	111214*	129457*	148922*	171420*	200529*	223250*	248596*	279866*	305890*	339047*	383871*
14. *Plus:* Statistical discrepancy	..	..	..	..	..	..	..	..	..	..	..	..	..	..	..
15. *Equals:* **Net Saving**	**13888***	**30357***	**28998***	**33224***	**46238***	**54173***	**43658***	**29755***	**35590***	**34732***	**37371***	**23168***	**2363***	**–26789***	**–30998***
16. *Less:* Surplus of the nation on current transactions	–522*	–3450*	–5172*	–3614*	–601*	–3315*	–6822*	–3698*	–13935*	–12657*	–9652*	–18476*	–15454*	–13927*	–22328*
17. *Plus:* Statistical discrepancy	–6605*	–14047*	–13040*	–15081*	–21696*	–25418*	–19181*	–11482*	–13603*	–12564*	–13460*	–5050*	6435*	22417*	25864*
18. *Equals:* **Net Capital Formation**	**7805***	**19760***	**21130***	**21757***	**25143***	**32070***	**31299***	**21971***	**35922***	**34825***	**33563***	**36594***	**24252***	**9555***	**17194***

1. At 1995 relative prices for 1988-1997, at 1980 relative prices for 1966-1987 and at 1975 relative prices for 1960-1965.

Principaux Agrégats

millions de couronnes

1983	1984	1985	1986	1987	1988	1989	1990	1991	1992	1993	1994	1995	1996	1997	
															DÉPENSES IMPUTÉES AU P.I.B.
															Aux prix courants
146617*	152492*	162199*	166244*	183828*	196631	204568	210930	220530	229156	240918	250302	259705	272060	284628	1. Consommation finale des administrations publiques
270622*	297616*	325963*	354510*	365270*	375833	393255	404915	423030	439262	450158	493821	514487	537540	568919	2. Consommation finale privée
267165*	293641*	321536*	349579*	359968*	370247	387305	398573	416237	432115	442741	485491	505627	528066	558783	3. Ménages
3199*	3770*	4237*	4776*	5244*	5586	5950	6342	6793	7147	7417	8330	8860	9474	10136	4. Institutions privées sans but lucratif au service des ménages
515*	8960*	7051*	7162*	−4752*	−570	3184	1645	−1912	−220	−7931	1605	9730	6368	6517	5. Variations des stocks
96112*	113919*	134934*	162084*	161689*	154887	163175	165954	165591	160995	155735	168361	189231	202872	225296	6. Formation brute de capital fixe
513866*	**572987***	**630147***	**690000***	**706035***	**726781**	**764182**	**783444**	**807239**	**829193**	**838880**	**914089**	**973153**	**1018840**	**1085360**	7. **Demande intérieure totale**
193741*	215799*	234562*	222076*	228861*	248443	276653	295698	319090	324246	318577	342632	358383	376424	403917	8. Exportations de biens et services
186024*	211654*	236021*	228707*	218855*	226951	252236	253832	268677	265572	257305	291002	317896	328458	366302	9. *Moins :* Importations de biens et services
2314*	676*	12*	−2107*	−626*	..	..	..	..	..	..	..	..	..	..	10. Divergence statistique
523897*	**577808***	**628700***	**681262***	**715415***	**748273**	**788599**	**825310**	**857652**	**887867**	**900152**	**965719**	**1013640**	**1066806**	**1122975**	11. **Produit intérieur brut**
															Aux niveaux de prix de 1990[1]
200957*	200129*	205182*	206178*	211262*	213257	211459	210930	212327	214132	222866	229357	234759	240415	245614	1. Consommation finale des administrations publiques
362273*	374521*	393115*	415671*	409435*	405258	403904	404915	412091	422669	428618	458910	473689	486661	504165	2. Consommation finale privée
357359*	369237*	387482*	409656*	403389*	399151	397649	398573	405462	415799	421663	451324	465876	478609	495811	3. Ménages
4613*	5085*	5472*	5878*	5978*	6107	6255	6342	6629	6870	6955	7586	7813	8052	8354	4. Institutions privées sans but lucratif au service des ménages
2210*	11889*	10200*	7132*	−3702*	588	4217	1645	−1819	34	−7854	1645	5684	6296	4618	5. Variations des stocks
124931*	141030*	158745*	185895*	178891*	167002	167406	165954	161442	159844	156753	168368	189013	198004	218693	6. Formation brute de capital fixe
690371*	**727569***	**767242***	**814876***	**795886***	**786105**	**786986**	**783444**	**784041**	**796679**	**800383**	**858280**	**903145**	**931376**	**973090**	7. **Demande intérieure totale**
217073*	224603*	235745*	235817*	247790*	267069	278475	295698	316408	314901	315233	341052	357115	372118	388239	8. Exportations de biens et services
198185*	208990*	225912*	241163*	236335*	239876	250022	253832	263649	264094	260995	295536	327409	341000	366882	9. *Moins :* Importations de biens et services
1152*	−1587*	−3672*	−7954*	−3408*	0	0	0	0	0	0	0	0	0	0	10. Divergence statistique
710411*	**741595***	**773403***	**801576***	**803933***	**813298**	**815439**	**825310**	**836800**	**847486**	**854621**	**903796**	**932851**	**962494**	**994447**	11. **Produit intérieur brut**
															RÉPARTITION DU P.I.B.
91338*	102130*	112805*	130754*	135842*	139419	139533	140490	143267	147126	151793	166659	173406	185589	198778	1. Impôts indirects
16463*	18296*	18038*	19710*	21627*	24898	25980	27485	27584	33794	35051	35681	36283	36975	35936	2. *Moins :* Subventions
79503*	86566*	93292*	99502*	108536*	115646	123234	128959	135521	141857	143471	145953	155977	168830	179045	3. Consommation de capital fixe
295807*	319548*	345382*	371887*	405983*	424999	441382	458389	473555	487620	492177	509916	536482	560491	596714	4. Rémunération des salariés payée par les producteurs résidents
72913*	86166*	93278*	96851*	86713*	93108	110432	124957	132893	145058	147763	178870	184057	188873	184374	5. Excédent net d'exploitation
798*	1693*	1979*	1978*	−35*	..	..	..	..	..	..	..	..	..	..	6. Divergence statistique
523896*	**577807***	**628698***	**681262***	**715412***	**748274**	**788601**	**825310**	**857652**	**887867**	**900153**	**965717**	**1013639**	**1066808**	**1122975**	7. **Produit intérieur brut**
															OPÉRATIONS EN CAPITAL DE LA NATION
															Financement de la formation brute de capital
79503*	86566*	93292*	99502*	108536*	115646	123234	128959	135521	141857	143471	145953	155977	168830	179045	1. Consommation de capital fixe
−17023*	8088*	7968*	30963*	22608*	23003	30742	42067	35779	38007	29547	38828	50473	52409	55690	2. Épargne nette
−14972*	−20977*	−32112*	−40978*	−23312*	−10669	−12384	3427	7622	19089	25214	14815	7489	11998	2922	3. *Moins :* Solde des opérations courantes de la nation
19175*	7248*	8613*	−2197*	2481*	..	..	..	..	..	..	..	..	..	..	4. Divergence statistique
96627*	**122879***	**141985***	**169246***	**156937***	**154318**	**166360**	**167599**	**163678**	**160775**	**147804**	**169966**	**198961**	**209241**	**231813**	5. **Financement de la formation brute de capital**
															Formation brute de capital
515*	8960*	7051*	7162*	−4752*	−570	3184	1645	−1912	−220	−7931	1605	9730	6368	6517	6. Variations des stocks
96112*	113919*	134934*	162084*	161689*	154887	163175	165954	165591	160995	155735	168361	189231	202872	225296	7. Formation brute de capital fixe
..	..	..	..	..	..	..	..	..	..	..	..	..	..	..	8. Divergence statistique
96627*	**122879***	**141985***	**169246***	**156937***	**154317**	**166359**	**167599**	**163679**	**160775**	**147804**	**169966**	**198961**	**209240**	**231813**	9. **Formation brute de capital**
															RELATIONS ENTRE LES PRINCIPAUX AGRÉGATS
523896*	**577807***	**628698***	**681262***	**715414***	**748273**	**788599**	**825310**	**857652**	**887867**	**900152**	**965719**	**1013640**	**1066806**	**1122975**	1. **Produit intérieur brut**
−12065*	−15619*	−17132*	−17998*	−18046*	−18155	−21662	−24752	−26393	−22323	−15974	−16039	−11868	−13468	−14236	2. *Plus :* Revenu net des facteurs reçu du reste du monde
12706*	18428*	21642*	23331*	25460*	33859	40491	49269	63484	90916	119729	127281	120265	125048	127300	3. Revenu des facteurs reçu du reste du monde
27041*	36527*	41163*	43701*	45405*	52014	62153	74021	89877	113239	135703	143320	132133	138516	141536	4. Revenu des facteurs payé au reste du monde
511831*	**562188***	**611566***	**663264***	**697368***	**730118**	**766937**	**800558**	**831259**	**865544**	**884178**	**949680**	**1001772**	**1053338**	**1108739**	5. *Égal :* **Produit national brut**
79503*	86566*	93292*	99502*	108536*	115646	123234	128959	135521	141857	143471	145953	155977	168830	179045	6. *Moins :* Consommation de capital fixe
−19368*	−13031*	−11623*	1975*	−2695*	..	..	..	..	..	..	..	..	..	..	7. *Plus :* Divergence statistique
412392*	**462591***	**506651***	**565737***	**586137***	**614472**	**643703**	**671599**	**695738**	**723687**	**740707**	**803727**	**845795**	**884508**	**929694**	8. *Égal :* **Revenu national**
−12176*	−4395*	−10521*	−14020*	−14431*	−14005	−15138	−13687	−16399	−17262	−20084	−20776	−21130	−22499	−20457	9. *Plus :* Transferts courants nets reçus du reste du monde
3008*	5952*	5612*	7138*	6839*	8060	8332	10044	12660	11640	11540	10533	10894	11379	14778	10. Transferts courants reçus du reste du monde
12095*	12991*	15791*	20438*	20136*	22064	23469	23731	29058	28904	31624	31305	32024	33875	35231	11. Transferts courants payés au reste du monde
400216*	**458196***	**496130***	**551717***	**571706***	**600467**	**628565**	**657912**	**679339**	**706425**	**720623**	**782951**	**824665**	**862009**	**909237**	12. *Égal :* **Revenu national disponible**
417239*	450108*	488162*	520754*	549098*	572464	597823	615845	643560	668418	691076	744123	774192	809600	853547	13. *Moins :* Consommation finale
..	..	..	..	..	..	..	..	..	..	..	..	..	..	..	14. *Plus :* Divergence statistique
−17023*	**8088***	**7968***	**30963***	**22608***	**28003**	**30742**	**42067**	**35779**	**38007**	**29547**	**38828**	**50473**	**52409**	**55690**	15. *Égal :* **Épargne nette**
−14972*	−20977*	−32112*	−40978*	−23312*	−10669	−12384	3427	7622	19089	25214	14815	7489	11998	2922	16. *Moins :* Solde des opérations courantes de la nation
19175*	7248*	8613*	−2197*	2481*	..	..	..	..	..	..	..	..	..	..	17. *Plus :* Divergence statistique
17124*	**36313***	**48693***	**69744***	**48401***	**38672**	**43126**	**38640**	**28157**	**18918**	**4333**	**24013**	**42984**	**40411**	**52768**	18. *Égal :* **Formation nette de capital**

1. Aux prix relatifs de 1995 pour la période 1988-1997, aux prix relatifs de 1980 pour la période 1966-1987 et aux prix relatifs de 1975 pour la période 1960-1965.

FINLAND
1968 SNA

Main aggregates

millions of markkaa

	1960	1969	1970	1971	1972	1973	1974	1975	1976	1977	1978	1979	1980	1981	1982
EXPENDITURE ON THE G.D.P.															
At current prices															
1. Government final consumption expenditure	1931	5934	6613	7618	8959	10694	13686	17585	21019	23735	25941	29414	34392	40177	45840
2. Private final consumption expenditure	9857	23679	25901	28116	33042	39269	47812	57496	65714	72648	80377	91314	103551	117277	134225
3. Households	9576	22852	24989	27064	31847	37880	46149	55492	63401	70100	77639	88146	99873	112964	129260
4. Private non-profit institutions serving households	281	827	912	1052	1195	1389	1663	2004	2313	2548	2738	3168	3678	4313	4965
5. Increase in stocks	168	461	1594	1163	−347	−74	4258	2360	−1426	−1742	−2752	3731	6700	2060	2061
6. Gross fixed capital formation	4589	9768	12010	13817	16359	20566	26859	32483	32738	35026	34228	38532	48703	54782	61647
7. **Total Domestic Expenditure**	16545	39842	46118	50714	58013	70455	92615	109924	118045	129667	137794	162991	193346	214296	243773
8. Exports of goods and services	3640	9905	11745	12226	14946	18153	24799	24758	29537	36974	43037	52546	63489	72357	75801
9. *Less:* Imports of goods and services	3755	9517	12310	13139	14797	18603	28094	30923	31823	34727	37390	49948	65016	69250	73762
10. Statistical discrepancy	−231	756	190	456	463	1359	735	−585	885	−3369	−1152	−39	−443	−743	−2227
11. **Gross Domestic Product**	16199	40986	45743	50257	58625	71364	90055	103174	116644	128545	142289	165550	191376	216660	243585
At 1990 price levels[1]															
1. Government final consumption expenditure	28387	44359	46777	49474	53309	56290	58824	62881	66478	69283	71789	74441	77552	80721	83403
2. Private final consumption expenditure	86150	132680	142728	145120	157285	166643	169608	174947	176467	174691	178882	187838	191933	194487	204006
3. Households	82240	126548	136264	138259	150096	159285	162290	167710	169187	167336	171435	179985	183794	185961	195085
4. Private non-profit institutions serving households	3997	6292	6603	7074	7359	7474	7393	7237	7280	7355	7447	7853	8139	8526	8921
5. Increase in stocks	1630	3044	11021	7343	−2319	−684	16438	7585	−4342	−4372	−6671	8397	12522	3399	2926
6. Gross fixed capital formation	52500	71823	80771	83816	89285	96885	100268	106228	96926	94296	87485	89766	99657	100916	105098
7. **Total Domestic Expenditure**	168667	251906	281297	285753	297560	319134	345138	351641	335529	333898	331485	360442	381664	379523	396433
8. Exports of goods and services	27228	50664	55091	54400	62269	66804	66381	57109	63976	73942	81079	87733	95192	100180	99125
9. *Less:* Imports of goods and services	26922	47296	56894	56554	58933	66603	71061	71460	70297	69433	67281	79281	85908	82406	84226
10. Statistical discrepancy	160	−3709	−9136	−7594	−3828	−2341	−13864	−6930	−250	−8643	−8616	−8802	−11654	−10936	−12425
11. **Gross Domestic Product**	169133	251565	270358	276005	297068	316994	326594	330360	328958	329764	336667	360092	379294	386361	398907
COST COMPONENTS OF THE G.D.P.															
1. Indirect taxes	2131	5615	6020	6799	7930	9346	11152	12792	14517	17292	19572	22313	25593	29580	33091
2. *Less:* Subsidies	461	1216	1279	1374	1560	1626	2784	3955	4472	4731	4781	5818	6225	7264	7760
3. Consumption of fixed capital	1844	4763	5511	6442	7547	9318	12277	14476	16671	19406	21824	24511	28343	32219	35788
4. Compensation of employees paid by resident producers	7376	20117	22784	26268	30735	37537	47419	58981	68227	73679	77719	88920	104064	120469	133452
5. Operating surplus	5309	11707	12707	12122	13973	16789	21991	20880	21701	22899	27955	35624	39601	41656	49014
6. Statistical discrepancy	..	..	..	..	..	..	..	..	..	..	..	..	..	..	..
7. **Gross Domestic Product**	16199	40986	45743	50257	58625	71364	90055	103174	116644	128545	142289	165550	191376	216660	243585
CAPITAL TRANSACTIONS OF THE NATION															
Finance of Gross Capital Formation															
1. Consumption of fixed capital	1844	4763	5511	6442	7547	9318	12277	14476	16671	19406	21824	24511	28343	32219	35788
2. Net saving	2544	6222	7280	7566	8378	11187	15142	11969	11213	10085	11250	17241	21454	21676	20959
3. *Less:* Surplus of the nation on current transactions	−138	0	−1003	−1428	−550	−1346	−4433	−7813	−4313	−424	2750	−472	−5163	−2204	−4734
4. Statistical discrepancy	231	−756	−190	−456	−463	−1359	−735	585	−885	3369	1152	39	443	743	2227
5. **Finance of Gross Capital Formation**	4757	10229	13604	14980	16012	20492	31117	34843	31312	33284	31476	42263	55403	56842	63708
Gross capital formation															
6. Increase in stocks	168	461	1594	1163	−347	−74	4258	2360	−1426	−1742	−2752	3731	6700	2060	2061
7. Gross fixed capital formation	4589	9768	12010	13817	16359	20566	26859	32483	32738	35026	34228	38532	48703	54782	61647
8. Statistical discrepancy	..	..	..	..	..	..	..	..	..	..	..	..	..	..	..
9. **Gross Capital Formation**	4757	10229	13604	14980	16012	20492	31117	34843	31312	33284	31476	42263	55403	56842	63708
RELATIONS AMONG NATIONAL ACCOUNTING AGGREGATES															
1. **Gross Domestic Product**	16199	40986	45743	50257	58625	71364	90055	103174	116644	128545	142289	165550	191376	216660	243585
2. *Plus:* Net factor income from the rest of the world	−27	−369	−426	−496	−648	−815	−1042	−1525	−1858	−2476	−2692	−2773	−3242	−4405	−5347
3. Factor income from the rest of the world	33	118	174	238	253	329	569	512	544	609	943	1455	2007	3072	3544
4. Factor income paid to the rest of the world	60	487	600	734	901	1144	1611	2037	2402	3085	3635	4228	5249	7477	8891
5. *Equals:* **Gross National Product**	16172	40617	45317	49761	57977	70549	89013	101649	114786	126069	139597	162777	188134	212255	238238
6. *Less:* Consumption of fixed capital	1844	4763	5511	6442	7547	9318	12277	14476	16761	19406	21824	24511	28343	32219	35788
7. *Plus:* Statistical discrepancy	..	..	..	..	..	..	..	..	..	..	..	..	..	..	..
8. *Equals:* **National Income**	14328	35854	39806	43319	50430	61231	76736	87173	98025	106663	117773	138266	159791	180036	202450
9. *Plus:* Net current transfers from the rest of the world	4	−19	−12	−19	−51	−81	−96	−123	−169	−195	−205	−297	−394	−906	−1426
10. Current transfers from the rest of the world	65	206	248	296	301	321	358	489	547	640	721	956	1237	1725	1430
11. Current transfers paid to the rest of the world	61	225	260	315	352	402	454	612	716	835	926	1253	1631	2631	2856
12. *Equals:* **National Disposable Income**	14332	35835	39794	43300	50379	61150	76640	87050	97856	106468	117568	137969	159397	179130	201024
13. *Less:* Final consumption	11788	29613	32514	35734	42001	49963	61498	75081	86733	96383	106318	120728	137943	157454	80065
14. *Plus:* Statistical discrepancy	..	..	..	..	..	..	..	..	..	..	..	..	..	..	..
15. *Equals:* **Net Saving**	2544	6222	7280	7566	8378	11187	15142	11969	11123	10085	11250	17241	21454	21676	20959
16. *Less:* Surplus of the nation on current transactions	−138	0	−1003	−1428	−550	−1346	−4433	−7813	−4313	−424	2750	−472	−5163	−2204	−4734
17. *Plus:* Statistical discrepancy	−231	−756	−190	−456	−463	−1359	−735	585	−885	3369	1152	39	443	743	2227
18. *Equals:* **Net Capital Formation**	2451	5466	8093	8538	8465	11174	18840	20367	14551	13878	9652	17752	27060	24623	27920

1. At 1990 relative prices for 1975-1997 and at 1980 relative prices for 1960-1974.

Principaux Agrégats

millions de markkas

DÉPENSES IMPUTÉES AU P.I.B.

Aux prix courants

1983	1984	1985	1986	1987	1988	1989	1990	1991	1992	1993	1994	1995	1996	1997	
52451	58842	66967	72849	80046	87199	96019	108535	118719	118453	112190	114001	119795	126457	129996	1. Consommation finale des administrations publiques
149624	165149	180887	194007	211534	232580	254588	269754	274709	272114	275252	284425	298201	313690	329147	2. Consommation finale privée
144066	159140	174165	186830	203783	223918	245058	259157	263886	261136	264379	273649	287106	302013	316884	3. Ménages
5558	6009	6722	7177	7751	8662	9530	10597	10823	10978	10873	10776	11095	11677	12263	4. Institutions privées sans but lucratif au service des ménages
−116	1487	−440	−2211	−889	3006	6424	2924	−9498	−5833	−3880	7892	5396	−2169	2868	5. Variations des stocks
69546	73010	79423	82908	92541	109258	136148	139144	110061	87953	71194	74186	85089	92035	104847	6. Formation brute de capital fixe
271505	**298488**	**326837**	**347553**	**383232**	**432043**	**493179**	**520357**	**493991**	**472687**	**454756**	**480504**	**508481**	**530013**	**566858**	7. **Demande intérieure totale**
82735	94190	98034	95634	100048	108750	116702	118828	109289	128272	159438	182530	207242	218929	247678	8. Exportations de biens et services
81361	86137	94639	89898	97775	109866	125996	126600	112422	121878	133450	150043	161080	171555	192632	9. Moins : Importations de biens et services
−1272	−1944	1396	1705	1350	3414	3113	2845	10	−2303	1653	−1999	−4780	−3360	202	10. Divergence statistique
271607	**304597**	**331628**	**354994**	**386855**	**434341**	**486998**	**515430**	**490868**	**476778**	**482397**	**510992**	**549863**	**574027**	**622106**	11. **Produit intérieur brut**

Aux niveaux de prix de 1990 [1]

1983	1984	1985	1986	1987	1988	1989	1990	1991	1992	1993	1994	1995	1996	1997	
86507	88878	92900	95792	99878	102132	104526	108535	111256	108799	103028	102728	104645	108197	108995	1. Consommation finale des administrations publiques
210290	216906	225002	234000	246163	258821	269879	269754	260031	247363	240177	244761	255968	264872	273700	2. Consommation finale privée
201100	207739	215488	224238	236228	248631	259445	259157	249612	236968	230024	234728	245857	254584	263090	3. Ménages
9190	9167	9514	9762	9935	10190	10434	10597	10419	10395	10151	10033	10111	10288	10610	4. Institutions privées sans but lucratif au service des ménages
−138	1967	−577	−2620	−1321	2967	7978	2924	−9567	−6071	−3694	7491	6542	−2195	2662	5. Variations des stocks
109995	107729	110138	109707	115067	126370	145054	139144	110965	92237	74528	74650	83056	89548	100451	6. Formation brute de capital fixe
406654	**415480**	**427463**	**436879**	**459787**	**490290**	**527437**	**520357**	**472685**	**442328**	**414039**	**429630**	**450211**	**460422**	**485808**	7. **Demande intérieure totale**
101143	106215	107365	108673	111632	115761	117241	118828	110965	122059	142459	161376	174580	185360	209172	8. Exportations de biens et services
86811	88216	93868	96281	105175	116898	127311	126600	111755	112989	113842	128411	137327	143611	158689	9. Moins : Importations de biens et services
−11296	−11431	−4702	−2665	−1327	−1434	−2003	2845	7116	10605	13915	14745	14026	17151	14241	10. Divergence statistique
409690	**422048**	**436258**	**446606**	**464917**	**487719**	**515364**	**515430**	**479011**	**462003**	**456571**	**477340**	**501490**	**519322**	**550532**	11. **Produit intérieur brut**

RÉPARTITION DU P.I.B.

1983	1984	1985	1986	1987	1988	1989	1990	1991	1992	1993	1994	1995	1996	1997	
36848	43380	47639	52316	57388	66667	75595	78025	74730	71643	71556	74200	76678	83211	91080	1. Impôts indirects
8868	9794	10347	11308	11684	11271	13717	14756	17174	17028	16376	18177	16643	14714		2. Moins : Subventions
40487	44489	48516	52202	57102	63366	71813	79512	82170	81892	83819	85480	87027	87632	90974	3. Consommation de capital fixe
147913	164641	183327	196548	213873	236454	264582	288768	289775	273616	258075	263775	281440	293581	307743	4. Rémunération des salariés payée par les producteurs résidents
55227	61881	62493	65236	70176	79125	88725	83881	61367	66655	85323	103393	122895	126246	147023	5. Excédent net d'exploitation
..	..	..	..	..	..	..	..	..	..	..	..	..	..	..	6. Divergence statistique
271607	**304597**	**331628**	**354994**	**386855**	**434341**	**486998**	**515430**	**490868**	**476778**	**482397**	**510992**	**549863**	**574027**	**622106**	7. **Produit intérieur brut**

OPÉRATIONS EN CAPITAL DE LA NATION

Financement de la formation brute de capital

1983	1984	1985	1986	1987	1988	1989	1990	1991	1992	1993	1994	1995	1996	1997	
40487	44489	48516	52202	57102	63366	71813	79512	82170	81892	83819	85480	87027	87632	90974	1. Consommation de capital fixe
21369	27929	27180	26575	28351	40981	48998	38888	−8294	−24110	−21192	1226	21209	23847*	47966*	2. Épargne nette
−6302	−135	−4683	−3625	−7549	−11331	−24874	−26513	−26697	−22035	−6340	6627	22531	24973*	31023*	3. Moins : Solde des opérations courantes de la nation
1272	1944	−1396	−1705	−1350	−3414	−3113	−2845	−10	2303	−1653	1999	4780	3360	−202	4. Divergence statistique
69430	**74497**	**78983**	**80697**	**91652**	**112264**	**142572**	**142068**	**100563**	**82120**	**67314**	**82078**	**90485**	**89866**	**107715**	5. **Financement de la formation brute de capital**

Formation brute de capital

1983	1984	1985	1986	1987	1988	1989	1990	1991	1992	1993	1994	1995	1996	1997	
−116	1487	−440	−2211	−889	3006	6424	2924	−9498	−5833	−3880	7892	5396	−2169	2868	6. Variations des stocks
69546	73010	79423	82908	92541	109258	136148	139144	110061	87953	71194	74186	85089	92035	104847	7. Formation brute de capital fixe
..	..	..	..	..	..	..	..	..	..	..	..	..	..	..	8. Divergence statistique
69430	**74497**	**78983**	**80697**	**91652**	**112264**	**142572**	**142068**	**100563**	**82120**	**67314**	**82078**	**90485**	**89866**	**107715**	9. **Formation brute de capital**

RELATIONS ENTRE LES PRINCIPAUX AGRÉGATS

1983	1984	1985	1986	1987	1988	1989	1990	1991	1992	1993	1994	1995	1996	1997	
271607	**304597**	**331628**	**354994**	**386855**	**434341**	**486998**	**515430**	**490868**	**476778**	**482397**	**510992**	**549863**	**574027**	**622106**	1. **Produit intérieur brut**
−5794	−7104	−6708	−7584	−8013	−8367	−11096	−13936	−16569	−19817	−23217	−21538	−18903	−18260	−18196	2. *Plus :* Revenu net des facteurs reçu du reste du monde
3665	4883	6221	4976	5586	8497	11222	15024	14437	12674	13229	10469	12885	14824	15859	3. Revenu des facteurs reçu du reste du monde
9459	11987	12929	12560	13599	16864	22318	28960	31006	32491	36446	32007	31788	33084	34055	4. Revenu des facteurs payé au reste du monde
265813	**297493**	**324920**	**347410**	**378842**	**425974**	**475902**	**501494**	**474299**	**456961**	**459180**	**489454**	**530960**	**555767**	**603910**	5. *Égal :* **Produit national brut**
40487	44489	48516	52202	57102	63366	71813	79512	82170	81892	83819	85480	87027	87632	90974	6. *Moins :* Consommation de capital fixe
..	..	..	..	..	..	..	..	..	..	..	..	..	..	..	7. *Plus :* Divergence statistique
225326	**253004**	**276404**	**295208**	**321740**	**362608**	**404089**	**421982**	**392129**	**375069**	**375361**	**403974**	**443933**	**468135**	**512936**	8. *Égal :* **Revenu national**
−1882	−1084	−1370	−1777	−1809	−1848	−4484	−4805	−6995	−8612	−9111	−4322	−4728	−4141	−5827	9. *Plus :* Transferts courants nets reçus du reste du monde
2010	3695	3426	3440	3807	5453	2642	2176	902	−332	−587	4067	8641	8249	..	10. Transferts courants reçus du reste du monde
3892	4779	4796	5217	5616	7301	7126	6981	7897	8897	8524	8389	13369	14336	..	11. Transferts courants payés au reste du monde
223444	**251920**	**275034**	**293431**	**319931**	**360760**	**399605**	**417177**	**385134**	**366457**	**366250**	**399652**	**439205**	**463994**	**507109**	12. *Égal :* **Revenu national disponible**
202075	223991	247854	266856	291580	319779	350607	378289	393428	390567	387442	398426	417996	440147	459143	13. *Moins :* Consommation finale
..	..	..	..	..	..	..	..	..	..	..	..	..	..	..	14. *Plus :* Divergence statistique
21369	**27929**	**27180**	**26575**	**28351**	**40981**	**48998**	**38888**	**−8294**	**−24110**	**−21192**	**1226**	**21209**	**23847***	**47966***	15. *Égal :* **Épargne nette**
−6302	−135	−4683	−3625	−7549	−11331	−24874	−26513	−26697	−22035	−6340	6627	22531	24973*	31023*	16. *Moins :* Solde des opérations courantes de la nation
1272	1944	−1396	−1705	−1350	−3414	−3113	−2845	−10	2303	−1653	1999	4780	3360	−202	17. *Plus :* Divergence statistique
28943	**30008**	**30467**	**28495**	**34550**	**48898**	**70759**	**62556**	**18393**	**228**	**−16505**	**−3402**	**3458**	**2234**	**16741**	18. *Égal :* **Formation nette de capital**

1. Aux prix relatifs de 1990 pour la période 1975-1997 et aux prix relatifs de 1980 pour la période 1960-1974.

FRANCE

1968 SNA

Main aggregates

millions of francs

	1960	1969	1970	1971	1972	1973	1974	1975	1976	1977	1978	1979	1980	1981	1982
EXPENDITURE ON THE G.D.P.															
At current prices															
1. Government final consumption expenditure	42766*	103752*	116640	131926	146800	167688	200234	243436	287761	329533	383684	436653	509274	595028	701299
2. Private final consumption expenditure	179610*	419612*	459577	511128	570303	645005	749585	862260	993537	1117094	1263999	1442018	1653311	1907219	2200820
3. Households	178759*	417500*	457196	508440	567287	641563	745647	857794	988445	1111354	1257568	1434812	1645072	1897908	2190339
4. Private non-profit institutions serving households	838*	2102*	2381	2688	3016	3442	3938	4466	5092	5740	6431	7206	8239	9311	10481
5. Increase in stocks	8418*	17649*	20181	13258	16132	22108	30107	-9667	24503	29469	17410	32530	34326	-7501	18809
6. Gross fixed capital formation	62707*	173154*	192937	218274	244451	285188	336123	354310	407235	439349	488441	555074	645753	700530	774278
7. **Total Domestic Expenditure**	293501*	714167*	789335	874586	977686	1119989	1316049	1450339	1713036	1915445	2153534	2466275	2842664	3195276	3695206
8. Exports of goods and services	43579*	100232*	125428	145213	165138	198573	269637	279799	332954	392889	445463	526941	604422	714282	790351
9. *Less:* Imports of goods and services	37357*	103963*	121244	135613	154877	188727	282708	262254	345437	390531	416409	512119	638791	744754	859536
10. Statistical discrepancy	935*	65*	..	..	..	..	..	..	..	..	..	..	..	..	..
11. **Gross Domestic Product**	300658*	710501*	793519	884186	987947	1129835	1302978	1467884	1700553	1917803	2182588	2481097	2808295	3164804	3626021
At 1990 price levels[1]															
1. Government final consumption expenditure	451231*	648039*	675150	701741	726476	750997	760160	793473	826452	846128	889029	916133	938195	967002	1002459
2. Private final consumption expenditure	1328779*	2150141*	2241793	2346691	2456035	2575796	2607570	2673013	2796319	2871760	2974338	3057361	3089121	3145100	3246396
3. Households	1320113*	2139223*	2230579	2334709	2443500	2562642	2594645	2660098	2783025	2858072	2960351	3043100	3074726	3130619	3231864
4. Private non-profit institutions serving households	8899*	10938*	11214	11982	12535	13514	12925	12915	13294	13688	13987	14261	14395	14481	14532
5. Increase in stocks	17343*	23939*	23330	1066	-2036	27281	60341	-51716	17604	59334	3608	31802	28038	-41139	515
6. Gross fixed capital formation	420844*	852737*	892149	953347	1007660	1079911	1089105	1014493	1044789	1030196	1049264	1082589	1112642	1090972	1074086
7. **Total Domestic Expenditure**	2218198*	3674856*	3832422	4002845	4188135	4433985	4517176	4429263	4685164	4807418	4916239	5087885	5167996	5161935	5323456
8. Exports of goods and services	212324*	418865*	486388	536386	600325	666223	731975	728285	788157	852231	908859	974123	998993	1037372	1025764
9. *Less:* Imports of goods and services	186993*	462918*	491920	527157	598003	681732	701169	641261	761805	772296	802092	887664	923882	922580	955583
10. Statistical discrepancy	-17320*	-11344*	0	0	0	0	0	0	0	0	0	0	0	0	0
11. **Gross Domestic Product**	2226209*	3619459*	3826890	4012074	4190457	4418476	4547982	4516287	4711516	4887353	5023006	5174344	5243107	5276727	5393637
COST COMPONENTS OF THE G.D.P.															
1. Indirect taxes	48284*	113840*	119002	130967	147679	167175	186846	212990	254674	273914	318554	376633	428590	480076	559807
2. *Less:* Subsidies	4960*	17316*	15975	17395	19811	24535	27059	35366	41870	49589	54919	64955	71637	89924	98984
3. Consumption of fixed capital	26513*	58587*	72363	82981	95657	111102	138314	163602	192611	222144	253030	292432	346185	397229	456655
4. Compensation of employees paid by resident producers	133767*	345178*	391444	441486	493521	566401	678946	801764	932940	1061181	1203113	1363245	1575784	1792602	2054560
5. Operating surplus	97391*	211063*	226685	246147	270901	309692	325931	324894	362198	410153	462810	513742	529373	584821	553983
6. Statistical discrepancy	-337*	-851*	..	..	..	..	..	..	..	..	..	..	..	..	..
7. **Gross Domestic Product**	300658*	710501*	793519	884186	987947	1129835	1302978	1467884	1700553	1917803	2182588	2481097	2808295	3164804	3626021
CAPITAL TRANSACTIONS OF THE NATION															
Finance of Gross Capital Formation															
1. Consumption of fixed capital	26513*	58587*	72363	82981	95657	111102	138314	163602	192611	222144	253030	292432	346185	397229	456655
2. Net saving	51177*	129956*	147029	156560	174341	203417	211034	193445	224563	244855	283861	318339	317194	270525	259472
3. *Less:* Surplus of the nation on current transactions	6565*	-2260*	6274	8009	9415	7223	-16882	12404	-14564	-1819	31040	23167	-16700	-25275	-76960
4. Statistical discrepancy	..	..	..	..	..	..	..	..	..	..	..	..	..	..	..
5. **Finance of Gross Capital Formation**	71125*	190803*	213118	231532	260583	307296	366230	344643	431738	468818	505851	587604	680079	693029	793087
Gross capital formation															
6. Increase in stocks	8418*	17649*	20181	13258	16132	22108	30107	-9667	24503	29469	17410	32530	34326	-7501	18809
7. Gross fixed capital formation	62707*	173154*	192937	218274	244451	285188	336123	354310	407235	439349	488441	555074	645753	700530	774278
8. Statistical discrepancy	..	..	..	..	..	..	..	..	..	..	..	..	..	..	..
9. **Gross Capital Formation**	71125*	190803*	213118	231532	260583	307296	366230	344643	431738	468818	505851	587604	680079	693029	793087
RELATIONS AMONG NATIONAL ACCOUNTING AGGREGATES															
1. **Gross Domestic Product**	300658*	710501*	793519	884186	987947	1129835	1302978	1467884	1700553	1917803	2182588	2481097	2808295	3164804	3626021
2. *Plus:* Net factor income from the rest of the world	1574*	2940*	3299	2897	2105	2324	4138	2371	2910	3893	4755	8616	12587	10277	1980
3. Factor income from the rest of the world	3045*	8692*	11229	11556	12462	16461	26242	24668	28825	33056	42557	61742	92182	146949	70350
4. Factor income paid to the rest of the world	1359*	5689*	7930	8659	10357	14137	22104	22297	25915	29163	37802	53126	79595	136672	68370
5. *Equals:* **Gross National Product**	302232*	713441*	796818	887083	990052	1132159	1307116	1470255	1703463	1921696	2187343	2489713	2820882	3175081	3628001
6. *Less:* Consumption of fixed capital	26513*	58587*	72363	82981	95657	111102	138314	163602	192611	222144	253030	292432	346185	397229	456655
7. *Plus:* Statistical discrepancy	-1557*	-349*	..	..	..	..	..	..	..	..	..	..	..	..	..
8. *Equals:* **National Income**	274162*	654505*	724455	804102	894395	1021057	1168802	1306653	1510852	1699552	1934313	2197281	2474697	2777852	3171346
9. *Plus:* Net current transfers from the rest of the world	-609*	-1185*	-1209	-4488	-2951	-4947	-7949	-7512	-4991	-8070	-2769	-271	5082	-5080	-9755
10. Current transfers from the rest of the world	3540*	11139*	15009	16464	18649	22381	20850	26268	32780	35771	51329	61831	71518	75235	89001
11. Current transfers paid to the rest of the world	6071*	14032*	16218	20952	21600	27328	28799	33780	37771	43841	54098	62102	66436	80315	98756
12. *Equals:* **National Disposable Income**	273553*	653320*	723246	799614	891444	1016110	1160853	1299141	1505861	1691482	1931544	2197010	2479779	2772772	3161591
13. *Less:* Final consumption	222376*	523364*	576217	643054	717103	812693	949819	1105696	1281298	1446627	1647683	1878671	2162585	2502247	2902119
14. *Plus:* Statistical discrepancy	..	..	..	..	..	..	..	..	..	..	..	..	..	..	..
15. *Equals:* **Net Saving**	51177*	129956*	147029	156560	174341	203417	211034	193445	224563	244855	283861	318339	317194	270525	259472
16. *Less:* Surplus of the nation on current transactions	6565*	-2260*	6274	8009	9415	7223	-16882	12404	-14564	-1819	31040	23167	-16700	-25275	-76960
17. *Plus:* Statistical discrepancy	..	..	..	..	..	..	..	..	..	..	..	..	..	..	..
18. *Equals:* **Net Capital Formation**	44612*	132216*	140755	148551	164926	196194	227916	181041	239127	246674	252821	295172	333894	295800	336432

1. At 1990 relative prices for 1970-1997 and at 1970 relative prices for 1960-1969.

Principaux Agrégats

millions de francs

DÉPENSES IMPUTÉES AU P.I.B.

Aux prix courants

1983	1984	1985	1986	1987	1988	1989	1990	1991	1992	1993	1994	1995	1996	1997	
782134	854300	910315	959509	1004657	1058400	1106075	1170435	1238998	1320450	1402898	1438634	1476381	1539007	1573054	1. Consommation finale des administrations publiques
2435547	2651305	2871097	3062808	3249514	3444407	3671748	3878580	4055649	4208087	4309128	4461087	4605910	4783518	4877929	2. Consommation finale privée
2424143	2639171	2858393	3049520	3235582	3429508	3655793	3861322	4037525	4189535	4290741	4442335	4586648	4763486	4857296	3. Ménages
11404	12134	12704	13288	13932	14899	15955	17258	18124	18552	18387	18752	19262	20032	20633	4. Institutions privées sans but lucratif au service des ménages
-14054	-12416	-17871	17156	20679	40295	59270	70945	21061	-28972	-97933	-3223	23749	-28345	-22483	5. Variations des stocks
809601	840364	905291	977517	1054768	1188313	1314552	1391358	1436922	1405409	1311393	1332101	1374835	1372053	1388088	6. Formation brute de capital fixe
4013228	**4333553**	**4668832**	**5016990**	**5329618**	**5731415**	**6151645**	**6511318**	**6752630**	**6904974**	**6925486**	**7228599**	**7480875**	**7666233**	**7816588**	7. **Demande intérieure totale**
900658	1053328	1123930	1074095	1101383	1221304	1411087	1467972	1538062	1588103	1556368	1684130	1802974	1897678	2168498	8. Exportations de biens et services
907388	1024968	1092619	1021789	1094349	1217627	1403052	1469802	1514461	1493531	1404767	1523075	1621458	1692180	1848001	9. *Moins :* Importations de biens et services
..	..	..	..	..	..	..	..	..	..	..	..	..	..	..	10. Divergence statistique
4006498	**4361913**	**4700143**	**5069296**	**5336652**	**5735092**	**6159680**	**6509488**	**6776231**	**6999546**	**7077087**	**7389654**	**7662391**	**7871731**	**8137085**	11. **Produit intérieur brut**

Aux niveaux de prix de 1990[1]

1983	1984	1985	1986	1987	1988	1989	1990	1991	1992	1993	1994	1995	1996	1997	
1021953	1034040	1057152	1074494	1104059	1141154	1147283	1170435	1202511	1242613	1285434	1299942	1301324	1334325	1349077	1. Consommation finale des administrations publiques
3272049	3299791	3368969	3489966	3581912	3686443	3789116	3878580	3924209	3974878	3977349	4031525	4092612	4169107	4198630	2. Consommation finale privée
3257549	3285450	3354607	3475532	3566924	3670709	3772788	3861322	3906496	3957194	3960207	4014230	4075231	4151477	4180590	3. Ménages
14500	14341	14362	14434	14988	15734	16328	17258	17713	17684	17142	17295	17381	17630	18040	4. Institutions privées sans but lucratif au service des ménages
-22382	-16490	-13638	19790	32439	46558	56538	70945	25555	-7655	-78710	13803	43743	-3119	2996	5. Variations des stocks
1035904	1011232	1043295	1090181	1147097	1256680	1352295	1391358	1389369	1345537	1252735	1267401	1299875	1292432	1296395	6. Formation brute de capital fixe
5307524	**5328573**	**5455778**	**5674431**	**5865507**	**6130835**	**6345232**	**6511318**	**6541644**	**6555373**	**6436808**	**6612671**	**6737554**	**6792745**	**6847098**	7. **Demande intérieure totale**
1062981	1134968	1154395	1137877	1166368	1260300	1396505	1467972	1529282	1605083	1587062	1689226	1791419	1886800	2130588	8. Exportations de biens et services
934343	956529	1002689	1071354	1161867	1272304	1384391	1469802	1510751	1531021	1479969	1583047	1665129	1719030	1858798	9. *Moins :* Importations de biens et services
0	0	0	0	0	0	0	0	0	0	0	0	0	0	0	10. Divergence statistique
5436162	**5507012**	**5607484**	**5740954**	**5870008**	**6118831**	**6357346**	**6509488**	**6560175**	**6629435**	**6543901**	**6718850**	**6863844**	**6960515**	**7118888**	11. **Produit intérieur brut**

RÉPARTITION DU P.I.B.

1983	1984	1985	1986	1987	1988	1989	1990	1991	1992	1993	1994	1995	1996	1997	
619647	688426	742648	785542	836125	891710	934229	983429	995345	1015800	1035458	1102813	1155070	1221100	1275264	1. Impôts indirects
113645	133516	142752	157979	168705	144159	137504	136487	144242	154294	170136	172413	178482	212766	221939	2. *Moins :* Subventions
508546	551642	589380	631975	673500	725034	776143	828961	880117	905901	925815	954624	983997	1000996	1031616	3. Consommation de capital fixe
2259282	2425773	2582446	2708114	2821197	2976425	3161614	3371797	3531792	3668567	3738938	3829366	3980473	4115718	4221754	4. Rémunération des salariés payée par les producteurs résidents
732668	829588	928421	1101644	1174535	1286082	1425198	1461788	1513219	1563572	1547012	1675265	1721333	1746683	1830390	5. Excédent net d'exploitation
..	..	..	..	..	..	..	..	..	..	..	-1	..	..	..	6. Divergence statistique
4006498	**4361913**	**4700143**	**5069296**	**5336652**	**5735092**	**6159680**	**6509488**	**6776231**	**6999546**	**7077087**	**7389654**	**7662391**	**7871731**	**8137085**	7. **Produit intérieur brut**

OPÉRATIONS EN CAPITAL DE LA NATION

Financement de la formation brute de capital

1983	1984	1985	1986	1987	1988	1989	1990	1991	1992	1993	1994	1995	1996	1997	
508546	551642	589380	631975	673500	725034	776143	828961	880117	905901	925815	954624	983997	1000996	1031616	1. Consommation de capital fixe
255023	275821	300424	386574	392443	485822	565381	571005	540651	478827	359094	446628	529667	464254	596127	2. Épargne nette
-31978	-485	2384	23876	-9504	-17752	-32298	-62337	-37215	8291	71449	72374	115080	121542	262138	3. *Moins :* Solde des opérations courantes de la nation
..	..	..	..	..	..	..	..	..	..	..	..	..	..	..	4. Divergence statistique
795547	**827948**	**887420**	**994673**	**1075447**	**1228608**	**1373822**	**1462303**	**1457983**	**1376437**	**1213460**	**1328878**	**1398584**	**1343708**	**1365605**	5. **Financement de la formation brute de capital**

Formation brute de capital

1983	1984	1985	1986	1987	1988	1989	1990	1991	1992	1993	1994	1995	1996	1997	
-14054	-12416	-17871	17156	20679	40295	59270	70945	21061	-28972	-97933	-3223	23749	-28345	-22483	6. Variations des stocks
809601	840364	905291	977517	1054768	1188313	1314552	1391358	1436922	1405409	1311393	1332101	1374835	1372053	1388088	7. Formation brute de capital fixe
..	..	..	..	..	..	..	..	..	..	..	..	..	..	..	8. Divergence statistique
795547	**827948**	**887420**	**994673**	**1075447**	**1228608**	**1373822**	**1462303**	**1457983**	**1376437**	**1213460**	**1328878**	**1398584**	**1343708**	**1365605**	9. **Formation brute de capital**

RELATIONS ENTRE LES PRINCIPAUX AGRÉGATS

1983	1984	1985	1986	1987	1988	1989	1990	1991	1992	1993	1994	1995	1996	1997	
4006498	4361913	4700143	5069296	5336652	5735092	6159680	6509488	6776231	6999546	7077087	7389654	7662391	7871731	8137085	1. **Produit intérieur brut**
-11727	-23505	-25679	-16608	-12467	-11647	-9971	-32084	-38287	-57621	-56192	-52966	-30779	-28593	13813	2. *Plus :* Revenu net des facteurs reçu du reste du monde
158672	183267	201020	173526	171913	191330	237813	263783	329004	345528	395607	359227	374333	364131	454771	3. Revenu des facteurs reçu du reste du monde
170399	206772	226699	190134	184380	202977	247784	295867	367291	403149	451799	412193	405112	392724	440958	4. Revenu des facteurs payé au reste du monde
3994771	4338408	4674464	5052688	5324185	5723445	6149709	6477404	6737944	6941925	7020895	7336688	7631612	7843138	8150898	5. *Égal :* **Produit national brut**
508546	551642	589380	631975	673500	725034	776143	828961	880117	905901	925815	954624	983997	1000996	1031616	6. *Moins :* Consommation de capital fixe
..	..	..	..	..	..	..	..	..	..	..	..	..	..	..	7. *Plus :* Divergence statistique
3486225	3786766	4085084	4420713	4650685	4998411	5373566	5648443	5857827	6036024	6095080	6382064	6647615	6842142	7119282	8. *Égal :* **Revenu national**
-13521	-5340	-3248	-11822	-4071	-9782	-30362	-28423	-22529	-28660	-23960	-35715	-35657	-55363	-72172	9. *Plus :* Transferts courants nets reçus du reste du monde
98970	105188	119676	116887	133104	148960	130948	135558	171448	166897	186232	179259	183024	176827	169022	10. Transferts courants reçus du reste du monde
112491	110528	122924	128709	137175	158742	161310	163981	193977	195557	210192	214974	218681	232190	241194	11. Transferts courants payés au reste du monde
3472704	3781426	4081836	4408891	4646614	4988629	5343204	5620020	5835298	6007251	6071120	6346349	6611958	6786779	7047110	12. *Égal :* **Revenu national disponible**
3217681	3505605	3781412	4022317	4254171	4502807	4777823	5049015	5294647	5528537	5712026	5899721	6082291	6322525	6450983	13. *Moins :* Consommation finale
..	..	..	..	..	..	..	..	..	..	..	..	..	..	..	14. *Plus :* Divergence statistique
255023	275821	300424	386574	392443	485822	565381	571005	540651	478827	359094	446628	529667	464254	596127	15. *Égal :* **Épargne nette**
-31978	-485	2384	23876	-9504	-17752	-32298	-62337	-37215	8291	71449	72374	115080	121542	262138	16. *Moins :* Solde des opérations courantes de la nation
..	..	..	..	..	..	..	..	..	..	..	..	..	..	..	17. *Plus :* Divergence statistique
287001	**276306**	**298040**	**362698**	**401947**	**503574**	**597679**	**633342**	**577866**	**470536**	**287645**	**374254**	**414587**	**342712**	**333989**	18. *Égal :* **Formation nette de capital**

1. Aux prix relatifs de 1990 pour la période 1970-1997 et aux prix relatifs de 1970 pour la période 1960-1969.

GERMANY[1]

1968 SNA

Main aggregates

millions of DM

	1960	1969	1970	1971	1972	1973	1974	1975	1976	1977	1978	1979	1980	1981	1982
EXPENDITURE ON THE G.D.P.															
At current prices															
1. Government final consumption expenditure	..	..	..	..	..	..	..	..	..	..	..	..	..	..	..
2. Private final consumption expenditure	..	..	..	..	..	..	..	..	..	..	..	..	..	..	..
3. Households	..	..	..	..	..	..	..	..	..	..	..	..	..	..	..
4. Private non-profit institutions serving households	..	..	..	..	..	..	..	..	..	..	..	..	..	..	..
5. Increase in stocks	..	..	..	..	..	..	..	..	..	..	..	..	..	..	..
6. Gross fixed capital formation	..	..	..	..	..	..	..	..	..	..	..	..	..	..	..
7. **Total Domestic Expenditure**	..	..	..	..	..	..	..	..	..	..	..	..	..	..	..
8. Exports of goods and services	..	..	..	..	..	..	..	..	..	..	..	..	..	..	..
9. *Less:* Imports of goods and services	..	..	..	..	..	..	..	..	..	..	..	..	..	..	..
10. Statistical discrepancy	..	..	..	..	..	..	..	..	..	..	..	..	..	..	..
11. **Gross Domestic Product**	..	..	..	..	..	..	..	..	..	..	..	..	..	..	..
At 1990 price levels[2]															
1. Government final consumption expenditure	..	..	..	..	..	..	..	..	..	..	..	..	..	..	..
2. Private final consumption expenditure	..	..	..	..	..	..	..	..	..	..	..	..	..	..	..
3. Households	..	..	..	..	..	..	..	..	..	..	..	..	..	..	..
4. Private non-profit institutions serving households	..	..	..	..	..	..	..	..	..	..	..	..	..	..	..
5. Increase in stocks	..	..	..	..	..	..	..	..	..	..	..	..	..	..	..
6. Gross fixed capital formation	..	..	..	..	..	..	..	..	..	..	..	..	..	..	..
7. **Total Domestic Expenditure**	..	..	..	..	..	..	..	..	..	..	..	..	..	..	..
8. Exports of goods and services	..	..	..	..	..	..	..	..	..	..	..	..	..	..	..
9. *Less:* Imports of goods and services	..	..	..	..	..	..	..	..	..	..	..	..	..	..	..
10. Statistical discrepancy	..	..	..	..	..	..	..	..	..	..	..	..	..	..	..
11. **Gross Domestic Product**	..	..	..	..	..	..	..	..	..	..	..	..	..	..	..
COST COMPONENTS OF THE G.D.P.															
1. Indirect taxes	..	..	..	..	..	..	..	..	..	..	..	..	..	..	..
2. *Less:* Subsidies	..	..	..	..	..	..	..	..	..	..	..	..	..	..	..
3. Consumption of fixed capital	..	..	..	..	..	..	..	..	..	..	..	..	..	..	..
4. Compensation of employees paid by resident producers	..	..	..	..	..	..	..	..	..	..	..	..	..	..	..
5. Operating surplus	..	..	..	..	..	..	..	..	..	..	..	..	..	..	..
6. Statistical discrepancy	..	..	..	..	..	..	..	..	..	..	..	..	..	..	..
7. **Gross Domestic Product**	..	..	..	..	..	..	..	..	..	..	..	..	..	..	..
CAPITAL TRANSACTIONS OF THE NATION															
Finance of Gross Capital Formation															
1. Consumption of fixed capital	..	..	..	..	..	..	..	..	..	..	..	..	..	..	..
2. Net saving	..	..	..	..	..	..	..	..	..	..	..	..	..	..	..
3. *Less:* Surplus of the nation on current transactions	..	..	..	..	..	..	..	..	..	..	..	..	..	..	..
4. Statistical discrepancy	..	..	..	..	..	..	..	..	..	..	..	..	..	..	..
5. **Finance of Gross Capital Formation**	..	..	..	..	..	..	..	..	..	..	..	..	..	..	..
Gross capital formation															
6. Increase in stocks	..	..	..	..	..	..	..	..	..	..	..	..	..	..	..
7. Gross fixed capital formation	..	..	..	..	..	..	..	..	..	..	..	..	..	..	..
8. Statistical discrepancy	..	..	..	..	..	..	..	..	..	..	..	..	..	..	..
9. **Gross Capital Formation**	..	..	..	..	..	..	..	..	..	..	..	..	..	..	..
RELATIONS AMONG NATIONAL ACCOUNTING AGGREGATES															
1. **Gross Domestic Product**	..	..	..	..	..	..	..	..	..	..	..	..	..	..	..
2. *Plus:* Net factor income from the rest of the world	..	..	..	..	..	..	..	..	..	..	..	..	..	..	..
3. Factor income from the rest of the world	..	..	..	..	..	..	..	..	..	..	..	..	..	..	..
4. Factor income paid to the rest of the world	..	..	..	..	..	..	..	..	..	..	..	..	..	..	..
5. *Equals:* **Gross National Product**	..	..	..	..	..	..	..	..	..	..	..	..	..	..	..
6. *Less:* Consumption of fixed capital	..	..	..	..	..	..	..	..	..	..	..	..	..	..	..
7. *Plus:* Statistical discrepancy	..	..	..	..	..	..	..	..	..	..	..	..	..	..	..
8. *Equals:* **National Income**	..	..	..	..	..	..	..	..	..	..	..	..	..	..	..
9. *Plus:* Net current transfers from the rest of the world	..	..	..	..	..	..	..	..	..	..	..	..	..	..	..
10. Current transfers from the rest of the world	..	..	..	..	..	..	..	..	..	..	..	..	..	..	..
11. Current transfers paid to the rest of the world	..	..	..	..	..	..	..	..	..	..	..	..	..	..	..
12. *Equals:* **National Disposable Income**	..	..	..	..	..	..	..	..	..	..	..	..	..	..	..
13. *Less:* Final consumption	..	..	..	..	..	..	..	..	..	..	..	..	..	..	..
14. *Plus:* Statistical discrepancy	..	..	..	..	..	..	..	..	..	..	..	..	..	..	..
15. *Equals:* **Net Saving**	..	..	..	..	..	..	..	..	..	..	..	..	..	..	..
16. *Less:* Surplus of the nation on current transactions	..	..	..	..	..	..	..	..	..	..	..	..	..	..	..
17. *Plus:* Statistical discrepancy	..	..	..	..	..	..	..	..	..	..	..	..	..	..	..
18. *Equals:* **Net Capital Formation**	..	..	..	..	..	..	..	..	..	..	..	..	..	..	..

1. Data refer to Germany after unification.
2. At 1991 relative prices.

Principaux Agrégats

millions de DM

1983	1984	1985	1986	1987	1988	1989	1990	1991	1992	1993	1994	1995	1996	1997	
															DÉPENSES IMPUTÉES AU P.I.B.
															Aux prix courants
..	..	..	..	..	..	..	..	556720	616350	634860	658580	686550	705110	703400	1. Consommation finale des administrations publiques
..	..	..	..	..	..	..	..	1630330	1755510	1829260	1906020	1975310	2046350	2095230	2. Consommation finale privée
..	..	..	..	..	..	..	..	1592830	1712550	1782490	1856900	1920870	1986660	2034360	3. Ménages
..	..	..	..	..	..	..	..	37500	42960	46770	49120	54440	59690	60870	4. Institutions privées sans but lucratif au service des ménages
..	..	..	..	..	..	..	..	12810	−1720	−9210	16400	18270	5890	47580	5. Variations des stocks
..	..	..	..	..	..	..	..	656010	709360	691010	726170	735610	723440	722930	6. Formation brute de capital fixe
..	..	..	..	..	..	..	..	2855870	3079500	3145920	3307170	3415740	3480790	3569140	7. **Demande intérieure totale**
..	..	..	..	..	..	..	..	727120	732300	697570	756960	821240	866180	971790	8. Exportations de biens et services
..	..	..	..	..	..	..	..	729390	733200	679790	735930	794180	823470	916930	9. *Moins :* Importations de biens et services
..	..	..	..	..	..	..	..	..	..	..	..	..	..	..	10. Divergence statistique
..	..	..	..	..	..	..	..	2853600	3078600	3163700	3328200	3442800	3523500	3624000	11. **Produit intérieur brut**
															Aux niveaux de prix de 1990[2]
..	..	..	..	..	..	..	..	518609	539708	537165	548577	559420	574679	570785	1. Consommation finale des administrations publiques
..	..	..	..	..	..	..	..	1556539	1600505	1602720	1622063	1651889	1678001	1685801	2. Consommation finale privée
..	..	..	..	..	..	..	..	1520639	1562044	1563457	1583285	1609883	1633549	1641253	3. Ménages
..	..	..	..	..	..	..	..	35911	38477	39282	38793	42030	44481	44577	4. Institutions privées sans but lucratif au service des ménages
..	..	..	..	..	..	..	..	15647	3970	−419	21995	21204	7213	43610	5. Variations des stocks
..	..	..	..	..	..	..	..	628325	650603	614437	636131	635949	628382	628766	6. Formation brute de capital fixe
..	..	..	..	..	..	..	..	2719120	2794786	2753903	2828766	2868462	2888275	2928962	7. **Demande intérieure totale**
..	..	..	..	..	..	..	..	717351	715141	679398	732820	781202	821325	912365	8. Exportations de biens et services
..	..	..	..	..	..	..	..	712989	727329	684064	737016	790691	813771	879919	9. *Moins :* Importations de biens et services
..	..	..	..	..	..	..	..	1691	2548	2962	2405	2382	2198	412	10. Divergence statistique
..	..	..	..	..	..	..	..	2725173	2785146	2752199	2826975	2861355	2898027	2961820	11. **Produit intérieur brut**
															RÉPARTITION DU P.I.B.
..	..	..	..	..	..	..	..	358460	389840	409560	443820	447400	449540	459770	1. Impôts indirects
..	..	..	..	..	..	..	..	64950	59840	61900	69080	71490	70030	66860	2. *Moins :* Subventions
..	..	..	..	..	..	..	..	361150	393840	420610	435440	451710	460990	471500	3. Consommation de capital fixe
..	..	..	..	..	..	..	..	1607850	1739280	1776880	1823890	1884980	1904520	1909260	4. Rémunération des salariés payée par les producteurs résidents
..	..	..	..	..	..	..	..	591090	615480	618550	694130	730200	778480	850330	5. Excédent net d'exploitation
..	..	..	..	..	..	..	..	..	..	..	..	..	..	..	6. Divergence statistique
..	..	..	..	..	..	..	..	2853600	3078600	3163700	3328200	3442800	3523500	3624000	7. **Produit intérieur brut**
															OPÉRATIONS EN CAPITAL DE LA NATION
															Financement de la formation brute de capital
..	..	..	..	..	..	..	..	361150	393840	420610	435440	451710	460990	471500	1. Consommation de capital fixe
..	..	..	..	..	..	..	..	274270	279500	226210	259580	258370	233940	277750	2. Épargne nette
..	..	..	..	..	..	..	..	−33400	−34300	−34980	−47550	−43800	−34400	−21260	3. *Moins :* Solde des opérations courantes de la nation
..	..	..	..	..	..	..	..	..	..	..	..	..	..	..	4. Divergence statistique
..	..	..	..	..	..	..	..	668820	707640	681800	742570	753880	729330	770510	5. **Financement de la formation brute de capital**
															Formation brute de capital
..	..	..	..	..	..	..	..	12810	−1720	−9210	16400	18270	5890	47580	6. Variations des stocks
..	..	..	..	..	..	..	..	656010	709360	691010	726170	735610	723440	722930	7. Formation brute de capital fixe
..	..	..	..	..	..	..	..	..	..	..	..	..	..	..	8. Divergence statistique
..	..	..	..	..	..	..	..	668820	707640	681800	742570	753880	729330	770510	9. **Formation brute de capital**
															RELATIONS ENTRE LES PRINCIPAUX AGRÉGATS
..	..	..	..	..	..	..	..	2853600	3078600	3163700	3328200	3442800	3523500	3624000	1. **Produit intérieur brut**
..	..	..	..	..	..	..	..	28500	19000	5100	−8000	−16200	−26000	−23900	2. *Plus :* Revenu net des facteurs reçu du reste du monde
..	..	..	..	..	..	..	..	121890	127300	126990	123860	119200	113300	127980	3. Revenu des facteurs reçu du reste du monde
..	..	..	..	..	..	..	..	93390	108300	121890	131860	135400	139300	151880	4. Revenu des facteurs payé au reste du monde
..	..	..	..	..	..	..	..	2882100	3097600	3168800	3320200	3426600	3497500	3600100	5. *Égal :* **Produit national brut**
..	..	..	..	..	..	..	..	361150	393840	420610	435440	451710	460990	471500	6. *Moins :* Consommation de capital fixe
..	..	..	..	..	..	..	..	..	..	..	..	..	..	..	7. *Plus :* Divergence statistique
..	..	..	..	..	..	..	..	2520950	2703760	2748190	2884760	2974890	3036510	3128600	8. *Égal :* **Revenu national**
..	..	..	..	..	..	..	..	−59630	−52400	−57860	−60580	−54660	−51110	−52220	9. *Plus :* Transferts courants nets reçus du reste du monde
..	..	..	..	..	..	..	..	20880	21460	20130	22220	24560	26330	27620	10. Transferts courants reçus du reste du monde
..	..	..	..	..	..	..	..	80510	73860	77990	82800	79220	77440	79840	11. Transferts courants payés au reste du monde
..	..	..	..	..	..	..	..	2461320	2651360	2690330	2824180	2920230	2985400	3076380	12. *Égal :* **Revenu national disponible**
..	..	..	..	..	..	..	..	2187050	2371860	2464120	2564600	2661860	2751460	2798630	13. *Moins :* Consommation finale
..	..	..	..	..	..	..	..	0	0	0	0	0	0	0	14. *Plus :* Divergence statistique
..	..	..	..	..	..	..	..	274270	279500	226210	259580	258370	233940	277750	15. *Égal :* **Épargne nette**
..	..	..	..	..	..	..	..	−33400	−34300	−34980	−47550	−43800	−34400	−21260	16. *Moins :* Solde des opérations courantes de la nation
..	..	..	..	..	..	..	..	0	0	0	0	0	0	0	17. *Plus :* Divergence statistique
..	..	..	..	..	..	..	..	307670	313800	261190	307130	302170	268340	299010	18. *Égal :* **Formation nette de capital**

1. Les données se réfèrent à l'Allemagne après l'unification de l'Allemagne.
2. Aux prix relatifs de 1991.

WEST GERMANY[1]

1968 SNA

Main aggregates

millions of DM

	1960	1969	1970	1971	1972	1973	1974	1975	1976	1977	1978	1979	1980	1981	1982
EXPENDITURE ON THE G.D.P.															
At current prices															
1. Government final consumption expenditure	40450	93120	106470	126760	141040	163090	190110	210080	221860	235130	253090	273540	298020	318390	326440
2. Private final consumption expenditure	171840	330900	368850	408980	451960	495590	533640	583450	631870	682130	725940	781310	837020	883520	916100
3. Households	169390	325750	363130	402580	444690	487150	525080	574800	622100	670770	713390	767540	821690	866660	898330
4. Private non-profit institutions serving households	2450	5150	5720	6400	7270	8440	8560	8650	9770	11360	12550	13770	15330	16860	17770
5. Increase in stocks	9200	17300	14200	4470	4300	12380	3710	−6360	15680	6990	7230	23000	11770	−10550	−16040
6. Gross fixed capital formation	73580	138900	172050	196110	209170	219260	212710	209410	225650	242430	264900	301290	332080	331290	323450
7. **Total Domestic Expenditure**	295070	580220	661570	736320	806470	890320	940170	996580	1095060	1166680	1251160	1379140	1478890	1522650	1549950
8. Exports of goods and services	57490	129460	143000	155690	169780	200400	259960	253500	287820	304550	318290	348190	389140	441120	474390
9. *Less:* Imports of goods and services	49850	112730	129270	142260	153130	173470	216200	223450	262380	275940	285900	338890	395990	428800	436250
10. Statistical discrepancy	..	..	..	..	..	..	..	..	..	..	..	..	..	..	..
11. **Gross Domestic Product**	302710	596950	675300	749750	823120	917250	983930	1026630	1120500	1195290	1283550	1388440	1472040	1534970	1588090
At 1990 price levels[2]															
1. Government final consumption expenditure	180949	267628	279135	293316	305596	320817	333719	346591	351757	356398	370120	382582	392542	399723	396123
2. Private final consumption expenditure	470372	719541	774875	817456	855525	880753	885091	912970	948841	991913	1028488	1062537	1075744	1069266	1055105
3. Households	460236	706398	761220	803017	840032	863982	869612	898373	933141	974340	1009629	1042950	1054896	1047636	1033781
4. Private non-profit institutions serving households	10141	13167	13684	14470	15523	16797	15513	14642	15743	17611	18894	19622	20876	21652	21345
5. Increase in stocks	20661	21179	23881	1141	1509	20033	7685	−5221	27657	13052	9077	30866	9775	−13293	−14822
6. Gross fixed capital formation	255011	353629	385268	407970	418901	417737	377017	356786	369558	382693	398317	424853	434181	412548	390218
7. **Total Domestic Expenditure**	926993	1361977	1463159	1519883	1581531	1639340	1603512	1611126	1697813	1744056	1806002	1900838	1912242	1868244	1826624
8. Exports of goods and services	135218	264780	283022	295381	315568	348953	390886	366129	401468	417253	429207	447548	470706	504585	524298
9. *Less:* Imports of goods and services	102715	215995	265039	288812	305551	320451	321576	325675	359956	372166	392613	428703	443955	430259	425719
10. Statistical discrepancy	3050	3410	4258	4381	4353	4100	2392	2651	2979	2732	2989	3868	3424	1772	851
11. **Gross Domestic Product**	962546	1414172	1485400	1530833	1595901	1671942	1675214	1654231	1742304	1791875	1845585	1923551	1942417	1944342	1926054
COST COMPONENTS OF THE G.D.P.															
1. Indirect taxes	41780	88280	89050	98690	110180	121070	125040	130280	141920	152520	167560	183160	193470	198290	201680
2. *Less:* Subsidies	2520	11620	11780	12610	15780	18650	18860	20390	22130	24630	29700	31160	30650	29120	29250
3. Consumption of fixed capital	23630	58200	68030	78080	86730	95980	107780	117240	125770	134010	144390	157800	175000	190620	203690
4. Compensation of employees paid by resident producers	143160	302620	359290	406820	450560	512630	566600	591240	637940	685410	731740	791660	860880	902550	929750
5. Operating surplus	96660	159470	170710	178770	191430	206220	203370	208260	237000	247980	269560	286980	273340	272630	282220
6. Statistical discrepancy	..	..	..	..	..	..	..	..	..	..	..	..	..	..	..
7. **Gross Domestic Product**	302710	596950	675300	749750	823120	917250	983930	1026630	1120500	1195290	1283550	1388440	1472040	1534970	1588090
CAPITAL TRANSACTIONS OF THE NATION															
Finance of Gross Capital Formation															
1. Consumption of fixed capital	23630	58200	68030	78080	86730	95980	107780	117240	125770	134010	144390	157800	175000	190620	203690
2. Net saving	63900	106510	122000	125400	131600	149060	135610	98210	124830	125130	145960	159180	144080	120910	116840
3. *Less:* Surplus of the nation on current transactions	4750	8510	3780	2900	4860	13400	26970	12400	9270	9720	18220	−7310	−24770	−9210	13120
4. Statistical discrepancy	..	..	..	..	..	..	..	..	..	..	..	..	..	..	..
5. **Finance of Gross Capital Formation**	82780	156200	186250	200580	213470	231640	216420	203050	241330	249420	272130	324290	343850	320740	307410
Gross capital formation															
6. Increase in stocks	9200	17300	14200	4470	4300	12380	3710	−6360	15680	6990	7230	23000	11770	−10550	−16040
7. Gross fixed capital formation	73580	138900	172050	196110	209170	219260	212710	209410	225650	242430	264900	301290	332080	331290	323450
8. Statistical discrepancy	..	..	..	..	..	..	..	..	..	..	..	..	..	..	..
9. **Gross Capital Formation**	82780	156200	186250	200580	213470	231640	216420	203050	241330	249420	272130	324290	343850	320740	307410
RELATIONS AMONG NATIONAL ACCOUNTING AGGREGATES															
1. **Gross Domestic Product**	302710	596950	675300	749750	823120	917250	983930	1026630	1120500	1195290	1283550	1388440	1472040	1534970	1588090
2. *Plus:* Net factor income from the rest of the world	290	850	400	650	1480	1550	−230	1070	3300	310	5850	5360	5360	4630	2210
3. Factor income from the rest of the world	3190	7880	9930	11270	12080	13650	15950	16050	18720	19980	22910	26400	31520	40580	43300
4. Factor income paid to the rest of the world	2900	7030	9530	10620	10600	12100	16180	14980	15420	19670	17060	21040	26160	35950	41090
5. *Equals:* **Gross National Product**	303000	597800	675700	750400	824600	918800	983700	1027700	1123800	1195600	1289400	1393800	1477400	1539600	1590300
6. *Less:* Consumption of fixed capital	23630	58200	68030	78080	86730	95980	107780	117240	125770	134010	144390	157800	175000	190620	203690
7. *Plus:* Statistical discrepancy	..	..	..	..	..	..	..	..	..	..	..	..	..	..	..
8. *Equals:* **National Income**	279370	539600	607670	672320	737870	822820	875920	910460	998030	1061590	1145010	1236000	1302400	1348980	1386610
9. *Plus:* Net current transfers from the rest of the world	−3180	−9070	−10350	−11180	−13270	−15080	−16560	−18720	−19470	−19200	−20020	−21970	−23280	−26160	−27230
10. Current transfers from the rest of the world	240	1980	2420	3910	4100	5400	5690	5740	6960	9520	11330	11260	11340	10800	10970
11. Current transfers paid to the rest of the world	3420	11050	12770	15090	17370	20480	22250	24460	26430	28720	31350	33230	34620	36960	38200
12. *Equals:* **National Disposable Income**	276190	530530	597320	661140	724600	807740	859360	891740	978560	1042390	1124990	1214030	1279120	1322820	1359380
13. *Less:* Final consumption	212290	424020	475320	535740	593000	658680	723750	793530	853730	917260	979030	1054850	1135040	1201910	1242540
14. *Plus:* Statistical discrepancy	..	..	..	..	..	..	..	..	..	..	..	..	..	..	..
15. *Equals:* **Net Saving**	63900	106510	122000	125400	131600	149060	135610	98210	124830	125130	145960	159180	144080	120910	116840
16. *Less:* Surplus of the nation on current transactions	4750	8510	3780	2900	4860	13400	26970	12400	9270	9720	18220	−7310	−24770	−9210	13120
17. *Plus:* Statistical discrepancy	..	..	..	..	..	..	..	..	..	..	..	..	..	..	..
18. *Equals:* **Net Capital Formation**	59150	98000	118220	122500	126740	135660	108640	85810	115560	115410	127740	166490	168850	130120	103720

1. Federal Republic of Germany before the unification of Germany.
2. At 1991 relative prices.

ALLEMAGNE OCCIDENTALE[1]

SCN de 1968

Principaux Agrégats

millions de DM

1983	1984	1985	1986	1987	1988	1989	1990	1991	1992	1993	1994	1995	1996	1997	
															DÉPENSES IMPUTÉES AU P.I.B.
															Aux prix courants
336440	350440	365720	382550	397280	412380	418820	444070	467080	504840	512970	525110	..	..	..	1. Consommation finale des administrations publiques
959280	1001200	1036530	1066430	1108020	1153690	1220950	1320710	1446940	1536620	1587380	1647070	..	..	..	2. Consommation finale privée
940130	981230	1014740	1042340	1082150	1126620	1192120	1289980	1412650	1498420	1546350	1605040	..	..	..	3. Ménages
19150	19970	21790	24090	25870	27070	28830	30730	34290	38200	41030	42030	..	..	..	4. Institutions privées sans but lucratif au service des ménages
-1500	5320	1250	2920	-560	10300	16010	11490	17160	-1890	-14050	14260	..	..	..	5. Variations des stocks
340810	350670	355810	373480	385780	409900	448520	507780	564260	582650	538250	543320	..	..	..	6. Formation brute de capital fixe
1635030	1707630	1759310	1825380	1890520	1986270	2104300	2284050	2495440	2622220	2624550	2729760	..	..	..	7. **Demande intérieure totale**
479630	536320	592740	580540	576610	619830	701430	778900	888780	939670	922650	1003550	..	..	..	8. Exportations de biens et services
446120	493060	528870	480630	476650	510120	581290	636950	736260	748890	703100	767410	..	..	..	9. *Moins* : Importations de biens et services
..	..	..	..	..	..	..	..	..	..	..	..	..	..	..	10. Divergence statistique
1668540	1750890	1823180	1925290	1990480	2095980	2224440	2426000	2647960	2813000	2844100	2965900	..	..	..	11. **Produit intérieur brut**
															Aux niveaux de prix de 1990[2]
396906	406809	415203	425745	432305	441492	434377	444070	446028	464620	463379	469815	..	..	..	1. Consommation finale des administrations publiques
1070625	1089867	1108665	1147129	1186326	1218843	1253364	1320710	1394872	1424737	1423214	1436025	..	..	..	2. Consommation finale privée
1048321	1067084	1084140	1120383	1158140	1190140	1223722	1289980	1362032	1390157	1387939	1401621	..	..	..	3. Ménages
22322	22801	24534	26746	28183	28700	29638	30730	32837	34570	35260	34398	..	..	..	4. Institutions privées sans but lucratif au service des ménages
15	5713	89	1828	-2871	9114	14609	11490	13355	-1684	-9874	18285	..	..	..	5. Variations des stocks
402380	402943	400949	414246	421829	440458	468014	507780	538217	535222	481730	481177	..	..	..	6. Formation brute de capital fixe
1869926	1905332	1924906	1988948	2037589	2109640	2170364	2284050	2392472	2422895	2358449	2405302	..	..	..	7. **Demande intérieure totale**
520073	562678	605203	601462	603831	636950	701775	778900	877347	914434	892816	962932	..	..	..	8. Exportations de biens et services
431491	453787	474176	486796	507018	533012	577497	636950	720304	742482	705991	766119	..	..	..	9. *Moins* : Importations de biens et services
1427	866	64	607	909	972	452	0	-733	-1460	-2421	-2761	..	..	..	10. Divergence statistique
1959935	2015089	2055997	2104221	2135311	2214817	2295094	2426000	2548782	2593387	2542853	2599354	..	..	..	11. **Produit intérieur brut**
															RÉPARTITION DU P.I.B.
214390	226130	230310	236170	245500	257110	278330	302220	337530	365350	380620	408120	..	..	..	1. Impôts indirects
31720	36330	37940	41310	44800	47740	46780	44830	44770	43500	46270	50440	..	..	..	2. *Moins* : Subventions
214930	226370	235360	243690	252300	263090	279450	303010	332890	359700	379570	388560	..	..	..	3. Consommation de capital fixe
949030	983690	1021420	1074440	1119350	1163780	1216250	1315520	1430160	1529370	1544360	1569490	..	..	..	4. Rémunération des salariés payée par les producteurs résidents
321910	351030	374030	412300	418130	459740	497190	554080	592150	602080	585820	650170	..	..	..	5. Excédent net d'exploitation
..	..	..	..	..	..	..	..	..	..	..	..	..	..	..	6. Divergence statistique
1668540	1750890	1823180	1925290	1990480	2095980	2224440	2426000	2647960	2813000	2844100	2965900	..	..	..	7. **Produit intérieur brut**
															OPÉRATIONS EN CAPITAL DE LA NATION
															Financement de la formation brute de capital
214930	226370	235360	243690	252300	263090	279450	303010	332890	359700	379570	388560	..	..	..	1. Consommation de capital fixe
138750	153840	165620	214940	215250	246260	292100	301300	268120	257060	190410	222060	..	..	..	2. Épargne nette
14370	24220	43920	82230	82330	89150	107020	85040	19590	36000	45780	53040	..	..	..	3. *Moins* : Solde des opérations courantes de la nation
..	..	..	..	..	..	..	..	..	..	..	..	..	..	..	4. Divergence statistique
339310	355990	357060	376400	385220	420200	464530	519270	581420	580760	524200	557580	..	..	..	5. **Financement de la formation brute de capital**
															Formation brute de capital
-1500	5320	1250	2920	-560	10300	16010	11490	17160	-1890	-14050	14260	..	..	..	6. Variations des stocks
340810	350670	355810	373480	385780	409900	448520	507780	564260	582650	538250	543320	..	..	..	7. Formation brute de capital fixe
..	..	..	..	..	..	..	..	..	..	..	..	..	..	..	8. Divergence statistique
339310	355990	357060	376400	385220	420200	464530	519270	581420	580760	524200	557580	..	..	..	9. **Formation brute de capital**
															RELATIONS ENTRE LES PRINCIPAUX AGRÉGATS
1668540	1750890	1823180	1925290	1990480	2095980	2224440	2426000	2647960	2813000	2844100	2965900	..	..	..	1. **Produit intérieur brut**
7160	12410	11320	10810	12520	12020	24660	22600	20500	8200	-3200	-16100	..	..	..	2. *Plus* : Revenu net des facteurs reçu du reste du monde
42610	49480	51920	56480	60910	68040	86860	105490	123500	131020	133430	129620	..	..	..	3. Revenu des facteurs reçu du reste du monde
35450	37070	40600	45670	48390	56020	62200	82890	103000	122820	136630	145720	..	..	..	4. Revenu des facteurs payé au reste du monde
1675700	1763300	1834500	1936100	2003000	2108000	2249100	2448600	2668460	2821200	2840900	2949800	..	..	..	5. *Égal* : **Produit national brut**
214930	226370	235360	243690	252300	263090	279450	303010	332890	359700	379570	388560	..	..	..	6. *Moins* : Consommation de capital fixe
..	..	..	..	..	..	..	..	..	..	..	..	..	..	..	7. *Plus* : Divergence statistique
1460770	1536930	1599140	1692410	1750700	1844910	1969650	2145590	2335570	2461500	2461330	2561240	..	..	..	8. *Égal* : **Revenu national**
-26300	-31450	-31270	-28490	-30150	-32580	-37780	-79510	-153430	-162980	-170570	-167000	..	..	..	9. *Plus* : Transferts courants nets reçus du reste du monde
13670	13830	13840	16160	14830	18590	17860	21320	35260	41230	41600		..	..	..	10. Transferts courants reçus du reste du monde
39970	45280	45110	44650	44980	51170	55640	100830	185360	198910	206120		..	..	..	11. Transferts courants payés au reste du monde
1434470	1505480	1567870	1663920	1720550	1812330	1931870	2066080	2182140	2298520	2290760	2394240	..	..	..	12. *Égal* : **Revenu national disponible**
1295700	1351640	1402250	1448980	1505300	1566070	1639770	1764780	1914020	2041460	2100350	2172180	..	..	..	13. *Moins* : Consommation finale
..	..	..	..	..	..	..	..	..	..	..	..	..	..	..	14. *Plus* : Divergence statistique
138750	153840	165620	214940	215250	246260	292100	301300	268120	257060	190410	222060	..	..	..	15. *Égal* : **Épargne nette**
14370	24220	43920	82230	82330	89150	107020	85040	19590	36000	45780	53040	..	..	..	16. *Moins* : Solde des opérations courantes de la nation
..	..	..	..	..	..	..	..	..	..	..	..	..	..	..	17. *Plus* : Divergence statistique
124380	129620	121700	132710	132920	157110	185080	216260	248530	221060	144630	169020	..	..	..	18. *Égal* : **Formation nette de capital**

1. République Fédérale d'Allemagne avant l'unification de l'Allemagne.
2. Aux prix relatifs de 1991.

GREECE
1968 SNA

Main aggregates

billions of drachmae

	1960	1969	1970	1971	1972	1973	1974	1975	1976	1977	1978	1979	1980	1981	1982
EXPENDITURE ON THE G.D.P.															
At current prices															
1. Government final consumption expenditure	10.5*	29.0*	32.3*	35.5*	39.4*	47.5*	66.9*	87.4*	106.6*	131.9*	158.7*	200.2*	240.0*	315.9*	403.9*
2. Private final consumption expenditure	106.5*	232.6*	261.0*	283.3*	313.1*	387.5*	482.0*	572.9*	684.4*	801.1*	955.0*	1141.9*	1393.8*	1745.2*	2188.2*
3. Households	..	..	..	..	..	..	..	..	..	..	..	..	..	..	..
4. Private non-profit institutions serving households	..	..	..	..	..	..	..	..	..	..	..	..	..	..	..
5. Increase in stocks	-2.8*	-2.6*	10.5*	3.1*	-2.3*	36.6*	41.1*	41.5*	38.0*	21.2*	28.8*	43.7*	58.3*	37.7*	-16.2*
6. Gross fixed capital formation	29.8*	97.8*	105.4*	124.3*	156.4*	202.4*	187.2*	208.8*	261.1*	330.3*	414.7*	550.7*	617.1*	680.8*	766.0*
7. **Total Domestic Expenditure**	144.1*	356.9*	409.2*	446.1*	506.6*	674.1*	777.1*	910.6*	1090.1*	1284.5*	1557.2*	1936.5*	2309.2*	2779.6*	3341.9*
8. Exports of goods and services	9.0*	24.4*	28.2*	32.1*	41.7*	64.9*	85.5*	106.8*	136.7*	152.9*	192.5*	235.1*	336.9*	397.9*	445.6*
9. *Less:* Imports of goods and services	18.1*	51.3*	56.7*	62.8*	78.0*	125.8*	149.1*	186.1*	219.6*	250.7*	294.8*	371.9*	462.6*	573.1*	760.8*
10. Statistical discrepancy	-7.7*	-7.3*	-18.9*	-15.5*	-12.9*	-26.9*	-30.3*	-17.4*	-8.3*	-19.7*	-48.6*	-69.7*	-111.8*	-122.0*	90.9*
11. **Gross Domestic Product**	127.3*	322.6*	361.9*	399.9*	457.4*	586.2*	683.2*	813.9*	998.9*	1166.9*	1406.3*	1730.0*	2071.7*	2482.3*	3117.6*
At 1990 price levels [1]															
1. Government final consumption expenditure	445.4*	774.2*	819.9*	860.4*	909.2*	971.0*	1088.3*	1218.2*	1280.7*	1364.3*	1412.1*	1494.6*	1497.7*	1599.8*	1636.5*
2. Private final consumption expenditure	2520.0*	4443.3*	4834.2*	5102.9*	5459.2*	5875.7*	5915.0*	6238.3*	6569.8*	6870.5*	7261.1*	7452.2*	7464.5*	7616.7*	7912.5*
3. Households	..	..	..	..	..	..	..	..	..	..	..	..	..	..	..
4. Private non-profit institutions serving households	..	..	..	..	..	..	..	..	..	..	..	..	..	..	..
5. Increase in stocks	-131.1*	-149.9*	142.3*	-33.1*	-145.5*	430.0*	404.7*	360.6*	249.7*	73.8*	139.4*	183.9*	239.8*	-4.3*	-133.9*
6. Gross fixed capital formation	981.4*	2414.8*	2381.4*	2714.9*	3133.4*	3373.3*	2510.7*	2516.1*	2687.7*	2896.6*	3070.2*	3340.5*	3124.3*	2889.9*	2834.3*
7. **Total Domestic Expenditure**	3815.7*	7482.4*	8177.8*	8645.1*	9356.3*	10649.9*	9918.7*	10333.2*	10787.9*	11205.2*	11882.7*	12471.3*	12326.3*	12102.0*	12249.3*
8. Exports of goods and services	167.4*	412.4*	463.4*	518.4*	637.0*	785.8*	786.7*	870.4*	1013.0*	1030.9*	1199.9*	1279.7*	1368.6*	1287.4*	1194.8*
9. *Less:* Imports of goods and services	343.9*	934.5*	992.1*	1068.0*	1232.6*	1630.0*	1364.4*	1450.4*	1539.6*	1662.3*	1781.2*	1908.8*	1756.6*	1820.7*	1948.6*
10. Statistical discrepancy	-245.6*	-407.0*	-574.5*	-517.3*	-509.6*	-950.3*	-807.8*	-703.7*	-636.3*	-618.8*	-679.8*	-828.5*	-731.5*	-355.8*	-238.4*
11. **Gross Domestic Product**	3393.6*	6553.3*	7074.6*	7578.2*	8251.2*	8855.4*	8533.2*	9049.5*	9625.0*	9955.0*	10621.7*	11013.7*	11206.7*	11212.9*	11257.2*
COST COMPONENTS OF THE G.D.P.															
1. Indirect taxes	11.5*	38.1*	41.4*	44.7*	50.1*	61.9*	68.3*	91.6*	113.9*	140.9*	170.1*	206.9*	218.3*	264.0*	367.8*
2. *Less:* Subsidies	0.2*	2.7*	2.8*	4.4*	5.3*	9.9*	16.4*	18.9*	25.7*	31.8*	37.4*	36.9*	46.2*	96.3*	135.1*
3. Consumption of fixed capital	6.5*	17.6*	20.7*	24.1*	29.1*	37.5*	48.2*	58.2*	72.6*	88.9*	109.8*	137.8*	174.3*	215.3*	264.3*
4. Compensation of employees paid by resident producers	30.9*	85.3*	95.2*	105.8*	122.2*	147.5*	179.8*	220.8*	280.4*	351.3*	438.3*	546.7*	656.2*	810.5*	1046.9*
5. Operating surplus	86.4*	196.4*	221.7*	246.0*	279.6*	379.5*	437.6*	493.7*	591.6*	640.8*	745.0*	893.4*	1105.4*	1332.2*	1599.6*
6. Statistical discrepancy	-7.9*	-12.1*	-14.3*	-16.3*	-18.3*	-30.3*	-34.4*	-31.5*	-33.9*	-23.2*	-19.6*	-18.0*	-36.4*	-43.4*	-25.9*
7. **Gross Domestic Product**	127.3*	322.6*	361.9*	399.9*	457.4*	586.2*	683.2*	813.9*	998.9*	1166.9*	1406.3*	1730.0*	2071.7*	2482.3*	3117.6*
CAPITAL TRANSACTIONS OF THE NATION															
Finance of Gross Capital Formation															
1. Consumption of fixed capital	6.5*	17.6*	20.7*	24.1*	29.1*	37.5*	48.2*	58.2*	72.6*	88.9*	109.8*	137.8*	174.3*	215.3*	264.3*
2. Net saving	18.1*	70.8*	93.1*	108.9*	133.9*	199.8*	177.6*	175.8*	228.4*	263.7*	348.1*	469.5*	573.7*	530.8*	345.2*
3. *Less:* Surplus of the nation on current transactions	-3.2*	-11.4*	-9.9*	-5.3*	-5.0*	-19.7*	-16.8*	-26.4*	-16.7*	-19.7*	-16.7*	-28.5*	9.9*	-16.3*	-121.2*
4. Statistical discrepancy	-0.8*	-4.6*	-7.8*	-10.9*	-14.0*	-18.0*	-14.4*	-10.1*	-18.6*	-20.7*	-31.0*	-41.3*	-62.8*	-43.9*	19.2*
5. **Finance of Gross Capital Formation**	27.0*	95.3*	115.9*	127.3*	154.1*	239.0*	228.2*	250.3*	299.1*	351.5*	443.5*	594.5*	675.4*	718.5*	749.8*
Gross capital formation															
6. Increase in stocks	-2.8*	-2.6*	10.5*	3.1*	-2.3*	36.6*	41.1*	41.5*	38.0*	21.2*	28.8*	43.7*	58.3*	37.7*	-16.2*
7. Gross fixed capital formation	29.8*	97.8*	105.4*	124.3*	156.4*	202.4*	187.2*	208.8*	261.1*	330.3*	414.7*	550.7*	617.1*	680.8*	766.0*
8. Statistical discrepancy	..	..	..	..	..	..	..	..	..	..	..	..	..	..	..
9. **Gross Capital Formation**	27.0*	95.3*	115.9*	127.3*	154.1*	239.0*	228.2*	250.3*	299.1*	351.5*	443.5*	594.5*	675.4*	718.5*	749.8*
RELATIONS AMONG NATIONAL ACCOUNTING AGGREGATES															
1. **Gross Domestic Product**	127.3*	322.6*	361.9*	399.9*	457.4*	586.2*	683.2*	813.9*	998.9*	1166.9*	1406.3*	1730.0*	2071.7*	2482.3*	3117.6*
2. *Plus:* Net factor income from the rest of the world	0.6*	1.5*	1.7*	2.4*	2.9*	4.0*	5.5*	5.9*	7.6*	9.2*	9.9*	13.3*	17.3*	18.0*	17.7*
3. Factor income from the rest of the world	2.8*	8.6*	9.9*	13.7*	16.6*	22.4*	31.4*	34.0*	44.4*	51.6*	56.8*	75.7*	101.9*	139.3*	147.0*
4. Factor income paid to the rest of the world	0.3*	1.8*	2.4*	3.1*	3.6*	4.8*	7.3*	8.0*	10.5*	10.9*	12.9*	17.0*	24.9*	53.4*	61.1*
5. *Equals:* **Gross National Product**	127.9*	324.2*	363.6*	402.4*	460.3*	590.2*	688.6*	819.8*	1006.5*	1176.2*	1416.2*	1743.3*	2089.0*	2500.4*	3135.2*
6. *Less:* Consumption of fixed capital	6.5*	17.6*	20.7*	24.1*	29.1*	37.5*	48.2*	58.2*	72.6*	88.9*	109.8*	137.8*	174.3*	215.3*	264.3*
7. *Plus:* Statistical discrepancy	9.8*	15.1*	30.0*	31.0*	32.7*	53.6*	59.3*	43.8*	49.4*	66.8*	11.0*	151.8*	235.2*	228.5*	-57.5*
8. *Equals:* **National Income**	131.2*	321.7*	373.0*	409.3*	463.8*	606.4*	699.7*	805.4*	983.3*	1154.2*	1417.4*	1757.3*	2149.9*	2513.6*	2813.5*
9. *Plus:* Net current transfers from the rest of the world	4.0*	10.8*	13.4*	18.4*	22.5*	28.5*	26.8*	30.7*	36.1*	42.5*	44.3*	54.2*	57.7*	78.3*	123.8*
10. Current transfers from the rest of the world	..	..	..	..	..	..	..	..	..	..	..	..	..	..	..
11. Current transfers paid to the rest of the world	..	..	..	..	..	..	..	..	..	..	..	..	..	..	..
12. *Equals:* **National Disposable Income**	135.2*	332.4*	386.4*	427.6*	486.4*	634.8*	726.5*	836.1*	1019.4*	1196.6*	1461.8*	1811.5*	2207.6*	2591.8*	2937.3*
13. *Less:* Final consumption	117.1*	261.6*	293.3*	318.8*	352.5*	435.0*	548.9*	660.3*	791.0*	932.9*	1113.7*	1342.0*	1633.8*	2061.1*	2592.1*
14. *Plus:* Statistical discrepancy	..	..	..	..	..	..	..	..	..	..	..	..	..	..	..
15. *Equals:* **Net Saving**	18.1*	70.8*	93.1*	108.9*	133.9*	199.8*	177.6*	175.8*	228.4*	263.7*	348.1*	469.5*	573.7*	530.8*	345.2*
16. *Less:* Surplus of the nation on current transactions	-3.2*	-11.4*	-9.9*	-5.3*	-5.0*	-19.7*	-16.8*	-26.4*	-16.7*	-19.7*	-16.7*	-28.5*	9.9*	-16.3*	-121.2*
17. *Plus:* Statistical discrepancy	-0.8*	-4.6*	-7.8*	-10.9*	-14.0*	-18.0*	-14.4*	-10.1*	-18.6*	-20.7*	-31.0*	-41.3*	-62.8*	-43.9*	19.2*
18. *Equals:* **Net Capital Formation**	20.5*	77.7*	95.3*	103.2*	125.0*	201.5*	180.0*	192.1*	226.4*	262.7*	333.7*	456.6*	501.0*	503.2*	485.5*

1. At 1990 relative prices for 1988-1997 and at 1970 relative prices for 1960-1987.

Principaux Agrégats

milliards de drachmes

DÉPENSES IMPUTÉES AU P.I.B.

Aux prix courants

1983	1984	1985	1986	1987	1988	1989	1990	1991	1992	1993	1994	1995	1996	1997	
496.6*	636.6*	807.4*	914.7*	1049.8*	1311.0	1654.5	2007.0	2337.9	2613.9	3063.3	3345.4	4178.3	4332.6	4838.0	1. Consommation finale des administrations publiques
2591.2*	3105.9*	3817.6*	4692.5*	5496.8*	6502.0	7827.7	9627.7	11851.4	14033.5	15900.9	18012.1	20138.8	22219.6	24045.3	2. Consommation finale privée
..	..	..	..	..	6482.7	7794.1	9585.0	11787.8	13965.4	15828.0	17939.9	20052.6	22124.0	23940.2	3. Ménages
..	..	..	..	..	19.3	33.6	42.7	63.6	68.1	72.8	72.2	86.2	95.6	105.2	4. Institutions privées sans but lucratif au service des ménages
-1.8*	-28.3*	43.7*	-10.2*	-81.0*	53.5	-24.1	-39.4	153.0	-60.6	-75.5	25.8	42.2	19.4	15.3	5. Variations des stocks
930.8*	1048.5*	1313.3*	1518.7*	1603.2*	1966.7	2447.4	3027.0	3650.2	3983.7	4267.1	4453.5	4981.2	5728.8	6563.7	6. Formation brute de capital fixe
4016.9*	4762.7*	5982.0*	7115.8*	8068.7*	9833.2	11905.5	14622.3	17992.5	20570.6	23155.7	25836.8	29340.5	32300.3	35462.4	7. **Demande intérieure totale**
574.1*	776.8*	920.9*	1161.6*	1447.6*	1696.4	1982.8	2209.8	2620.7	3174.6	3355.6	3904.0	4258.2	4697.8	5143.7	8. Exportations de biens et services
953.6*	1173.9*	1559.7*	1755.2*	2054.3*	2360.6	2993.1	3689.0	4382.7	4979.1	5375.6	5757.2	6715.1	7300.4	7853.9	9. Moins : Importations de biens et services
91.0*	242.5*	248.3*	155.5*	132.4*	..	..	..	..	..	..	..	..	..	..	10. Divergence statistique
3728.5*	4608.2*	5591.6*	6677.6*	7594.5*	9169.0	10895.2	13143.1	16230.5	18766.1	21135.7	23983.6	26883.5	29697.7	32752.2	11. **Produit intérieur brut**

Aux niveaux de prix de 1990[1]

1983	1984	1985	1986	1987	1988	1989	1990	1991	1992	1993	1994	1995	1996	1997	
1681.5*	1732.7*	1787.9*	1773.3*	1789.0*	1891.7	1995.8	2007.0	1976.7	1916.3	1966.5	1945.3	2055.6	2075.5	2067.4	1. Consommation finale des administrations publiques
7933.9*	8068.8*	8383.8*	8438.9*	8542.8*	8847.0	9385.8	9627.7	9900.1	10137.5	10057.8	10262.4	10545.9	10743.3	11019.2	2. Consommation finale privée
..	..	..	..	..	8820.0	9345.5	9585.0	9843.2	10084.1	10008.0	10219.2	10498.8	10695.5	10970.2	3. Ménages
..	..	..	..	..	27.0	40.4	42.7	57.0	53.3	49.8	43.2	47.1	47.8	49.1	4. Institutions privées sans but lucratif au service des ménages
-119.1*	-173.6*	3.4*	-18.2*	-200.7*	89.6	-34.7	-39.4	119.4	-210.6	-200.5	-136.3	-31.8	-49.5	-88.2	5. Variations des stocks
2797.2*	2638.8*	2775.6*	2602.9*	2470.8*	2690.4	2882.6	3027.0	3171.9	3071.1	2963.5	2882.6	3004.8	3269.4	3584.6	6. Formation brute de capital fixe
12293.5*	12266.7*	12950.8*	12796.8*	12601.9*	13518.8	14229.5	14622.3	15168.2	14914.3	14953.9	14953.9	15574.5	16038.7	16583.0	7. **Demande intérieure totale**
1290.1*	1508.6*	1528.0*	1742.6*	2021.1*	2202.3	2303.0	2209.8	2291.3	2532.4	2442.9	2597.2	2620.8	2702.9	2844.5	8. Exportations de biens et services
2076.6*	2080.9*	2347.4*	2436.6*	2840.4*	3068.0	3392.9	3689.0	3911.1	3801.7	3808.4	3854.7	4213.1	4426.6	4659.2	9. Moins : Importations de biens et services
-204.7*	-81.0*	-155.5*	67.3*	331.2*	0.0	0.0	0.0	0.0	0.0	0.0	0.0	0.0	0.0	0.0	10. Divergence statistique
11302.4*	11613.5*	11975.9*	12170.1*	12113.8*	12653.1	13139.6	13143.1	13548.5	13645.1	13421.9	13696.4	13982.2	14315.0	14768.3	11. **Produit intérieur brut**

RÉPARTITION DU P.I.B.

1983	1984	1985	1986	1987	1988	1989	1990	1991	1992	1993	1994	1995	1996	1997	
468.2*	580.1*	711.1*	955.8*	1111.8*	1254.2	1347.5	1845.6	2396.1	2914.8	3150.1	3466.8	3856.2	4322.7	4755.7	1. Impôts indirects
160.9*	183.3*	294.0*	400.1*	413.0*	403.5	451.3	536.3	577.9	684.9	840.1	870.6	886.7	984.7	977.3	2. Moins : Subventions
334.5*	404.1*	494.5*	619.8*	709.2*	811.7	959.8	1132.0	1395.7	1640.0	1847.7	2117.2	2409.1	2770.7	3174.5	3. Consommation de capital fixe
1266.5*	1553.4*	1942.1*	2194.7*	2469.0*	3019.1	3816.7	4646.8	5316.1	5950.7	6679.4	7546.1	8709.7	9981.3	11142.6	4. Rémunération des salariés payée par les producteurs résidents
1823.5*	2259.3*	2736.8*	3315.8*	3710.0*	4487.4	5222.6	6054.9	7700.5	8945.5	10298.6	11724.1	12795.1	13607.8	14656.7	5. Excédent net d'exploitation
-3.2*	-5.5*	1.0*	-8.4*	7.4*	0.0	0.0	0.0	0.0	0.0	0.0	0.0	0.0	0.0	0.0	6. Divergence statistique
3728.5*	4608.2*	5591.6*	6677.6*	7594.5*	9169.0	10895.2	13143.1	16230.5	18766.1	21135.7	23983.6	26883.5	29697.7	32752.2	7. **Produit intérieur brut**

OPÉRATIONS EN CAPITAL DE LA NATION

Financement de la formation brute de capital

1983	1984	1985	1986	1987	1988	1989	1990	1991	1992	1993	1994	1995	1996	1997	
334.5*	404.1*	494.5*	619.8*	709.2*	811.7	959.8	1132.0	1395.7	1640.0	1847.7	2117.2	2409.1	2770.7	3174.5	1. Consommation de capital fixe
394.8*	412.9*	326.6*	478.2*	535.4*	1045.4	997.9	1232.3	1786.5	1906.7	1803.7	2247.7	1957.1	2264.1	2633.8	2. Épargne nette
-166.0*	-163.8*	-403.1*	-310.7*	-205.4*	-163.1	-465.6	-623.3	-621.0	-376.5	-540.1	-114.4	-657.1	-713.3	-770.7	3. Moins : Solde des opérations courantes de la nation
33.9*	39.4*	132.7*	99.8*	72.2*	..	..	..	..	..	..	..	..	..	..	4. Divergence statistique
929.1*	1020.2*	1357.0*	1508.6*	1522.2*	2020.2	2423.3	2987.6	3803.2	3923.2	4191.6	4479.3	5023.3	5748.1	6579.0	5. **Financement de la formation brute de capital**

Formation brute de capital

1983	1984	1985	1986	1987	1988	1989	1990	1991	1992	1993	1994	1995	1996	1997	
-1.8*	-28.3*	43.7*	-10.2*	-81.0*	53.5	-24.1	-39.4	153.0	-60.6	-75.5	25.8	42.2	19.4	15.3	6. Variations des stocks
930.8*	1048.5*	1313.3*	1518.7*	1603.2*	1966.7	2447.4	3027.0	3650.2	3983.7	4267.1	4453.5	4981.2	5728.8	6563.7	7. Formation brute de capital fixe
..	..	..	..	..	..	..	..	..	..	..	..	..	..	..	8. Divergence statistique
929.1*	1020.2*	1357.0*	1508.6*	1522.2*	2020.2	2423.3	2987.6	3803.2	3923.2	4191.6	4479.3	5023.3	5748.1	6579.0	9. **Formation brute de capital**

RELATIONS ENTRE LES PRINCIPAUX AGRÉGATS

1983	1984	1985	1986	1987	1988	1989	1990	1991	1992	1993	1994	1995	1996	1997	
3728.5*	4608.2*	5591.6*	6677.6*	7594.5*	9169.0	10895.2	13143.1	16230.5	18766.1	21135.7	23983.6	26883.5	29697.7	32752.2	1. **Produit intérieur brut**
9.3*	0.6*	-10.3*	-20.7*	-19.3*	-17.3	-29.3	105.1	196.5	249.8	137.8	212.1	242.4	197.7	189.5	2. Plus : Revenu net des facteurs reçu du reste du monde
147.0*	169.2*	185.2*	167.2*	196.7*	251.3	301.0	451.7	601.5	754.3	685.0	787.3	946.5	1011.1	1071.6	3. Revenu des facteurs reçu du reste du monde
90.0*	138.6*	189.6*	210.6*	230.3*	268.6	330.3	346.6	405.0	504.5	547.2	575.2	704.1	813.4	882.0	4. Revenu des facteurs payé au reste du monde
3737.8*	4608.7*	5581.2*	6656.9*	7575.1*	9151.7	10866.0	13248.1	16427.0	19015.9	21273.5	24195.7	27125.9	29895.4	32941.7	5. Égal : **Produit national brut**
334.5*	404.1*	494.5*	619.8*	709.2*	811.7	959.8	1132.0	1395.7	1640.0	1847.7	2117.2	2409.1	2770.7	3174.5	6. Moins : Consommation de capital fixe
-92.0*	-258.9*	-388.4*	-277.0*	-215.4*	..	..	..	..	..	..	..	..	..	..	7. Plus : Divergence statistique
3311.2*	3945.7*	4698.4*	5760.1*	6650.5*	8340.0	9906.2	12116.1	15031.3	17375.9	19425.8	22078.5	24716.7	27124.7	29767.2	8. Égal : **Revenu national**
171.3*	209.7*	253.3*	325.2*	431.4*	518.4	573.9	751.0	944.5	1178.2	1342.1	1526.6	1557.5	1691.6	1750.0	9. Plus : Transferts courants nets reçus du reste du monde
..	..	..	..	..	..	..	..	..	..	..	..	..	..	..	10. Transferts courants reçus du reste du monde
..	..	..	..	..	..	..	..	..	..	..	..	..	..	..	11. Transferts courants payés au reste du monde
3482.6*	4155.4*	4951.7*	6085.5*	7081.9*	8858.3	10480.1	12867.0	15975.8	18554.1	20767.9	23605.2	26274.3	28816.3	31517.2	12. Égal : **Revenu national disponible**
3087.8*	3742.5*	4625.1*	5607.3*	6546.5*	7813.0	9482.2	11634.7	14189.3	16647.4	18964.1	21357.5	24317.1	26552.2	28883.4	13. Moins : Consommation finale
..	..	..	..	..	..	..	..	..	..	..	..	..	..	..	14. Plus : Divergence statistique
394.8*	412.9*	326.6*	478.2*	535.4*	1045.4	997.9	1232.3	1786.5	1906.7	1803.7	2247.7	1957.1	2264.1	2633.8	15. Égal : **Épargne nette**
-166.0*	-163.8*	-403.1*	-310.7*	-205.4*	-163.1	-465.6	-623.3	-621.0	-376.5	-540.1	-114.4	-657.1	-713.3	-770.7	16. Moins : Solde des opérations courantes de la nation
33.9*	39.4*	132.7*	99.8*	72.2*	..	..	..	..	..	..	..	..	..	..	17. Plus : Divergence statistique
594.6*	616.1*	862.5*	888.8*	813.0*	1208.5	1463.5	1855.5	2407.5	2283.1	2343.9	2362.1	2614.2	2977.4	3404.5	18. Égal : **Formation nette de capital**

1. Aux prix relatifs de 1990 pour la période 1988-1997 et aux prix relatifs de 1970 pour la période 1960-1987.

HUNGARY
1968 SNA

Main aggregates

millions of forint

	1960	1969	1970	1971	1972	1973	1974	1975	1976	1977	1978	1979	1980	1981	1982
EXPENDITURE ON THE G.D.P.															
At current prices															
1. Government final consumption expenditure	..	..	..	..	..	..	..	..	..	..	..	..	..	..	..
2. Private final consumption expenditure	..	..	..	..	..	..	..	..	..	..	..	..	..	..	..
3. Households	..	..	..	..	..	..	..	..	..	..	..	..	..	..	..
4. Private non-profit institutions serving households	..	..	..	..	..	..	..	..	..	..	..	..	..	..	..
5. Increase in stocks	..	..	..	..	..	..	..	..	..	..	..	..	..	..	..
6. Gross fixed capital formation	..	..	..	..	..	..	..	..	..	..	..	..	..	..	..
7. **Total Domestic Expenditure**	..	..	..	..	..	..	..	..	..	..	..	..	..	..	..
8. Exports of goods and services	..	..	..	..	..	..	..	..	..	..	..	..	..	..	..
9. *Less:* Imports of goods and services	..	..	..	..	..	..	..	..	..	..	..	..	..	..	..
10. Statistical discrepancy	..	..	..	..	..	..	..	..	..	..	..	..	..	..	..
11. **Gross Domestic Product**	..	..	..	..	..	..	..	..	..	..	..	..	..	..	..
At 1990 price levels[1]															
1. Government final consumption expenditure	..	..	..	..	..	..	..	..	..	..	..	..	..	..	..
2. Private final consumption expenditure	..	..	..	..	..	..	..	..	..	..	..	..	..	..	..
3. Households	..	..	..	..	..	..	..	..	..	..	..	..	..	..	..
4. Private non-profit institutions serving households	..	..	..	..	..	..	..	..	..	..	..	..	..	..	..
5. Increase in stocks	..	..	..	..	..	..	..	..	..	..	..	..	..	..	..
6. Gross fixed capital formation	..	..	..	..	..	..	..	..	..	..	..	..	..	..	..
7. **Total Domestic Expenditure**	..	..	..	..	..	..	..	..	..	..	..	..	..	..	..
8. Exports of goods and services	..	..	..	..	..	..	..	..	..	..	..	..	..	..	..
9. *Less:* Imports of goods and services	..	..	..	..	..	..	..	..	..	..	..	..	..	..	..
10. Statistical discrepancy	..	..	..	..	..	..	..	..	..	..	..	..	..	..	..
11. **Gross Domestic Product**	..	..	..	..	..	..	..	..	..	..	..	..	..	..	..
COST COMPONENTS OF THE G.D.P.															
1. Indirect taxes	..	..	..	..	..	..	..	..	..	..	..	..	..	..	..
2. *Less:* Subsidies	..	..	..	..	..	..	..	..	..	..	..	..	..	..	..
3. Consumption of fixed capital	..	..	..	..	..	..	..	..	..	..	..	..	..	..	..
4. Compensation of employees paid by resident producers	..	..	..	..	..	..	..	..	..	..	..	..	..	..	..
5. Operating surplus	..	..	..	..	..	..	..	..	..	..	..	..	..	..	..
6. Statistical discrepancy	..	..	..	..	..	..	..	..	..	..	..	..	..	..	..
7. **Gross Domestic Product**	..	..	..	..	..	..	..	..	..	..	..	..	..	..	..
CAPITAL TRANSACTIONS OF THE NATION															
Finance of Gross Capital Formation															
1. Consumption of fixed capital	..	..	..	..	..	..	..	..	..	..	..	..	..	..	..
2. Net saving	..	..	..	..	..	..	..	..	..	..	..	..	..	..	..
3. *Less:* Surplus of the nation on current transactions	..	..	..	..	..	..	..	..	..	..	..	..	..	..	..
4. Statistical discrepancy	..	..	..	..	..	..	..	..	..	..	..	..	..	..	..
5. **Finance of Gross Capital Formation**	..	..	..	..	..	..	..	..	..	..	..	..	..	..	..
Gross capital formation															
6. Increase in stocks	..	..	..	..	..	..	..	..	..	..	..	..	..	..	..
7. Gross fixed capital formation	..	..	..	..	..	..	..	..	..	..	..	..	..	..	..
8. Statistical discrepancy	..	..	..	..	..	..	..	..	..	..	..	..	..	..	..
9. **Gross Capital Formation**	..	..	..	..	..	..	..	..	..	..	..	..	..	..	..
RELATIONS AMONG NATIONAL ACCOUNTING AGGREGATES															
1. **Gross Domestic Product**	..	..	..	..	..	..	..	..	..	..	..	..	..	..	..
2. *Plus:* Net factor income from the rest of the world	..	..	..	..	..	..	..	..	..	..	..	..	..	..	..
3. Factor income from the rest of the world	..	..	..	..	..	..	..	..	..	..	..	..	..	..	..
4. Factor income paid to the rest of the world	..	..	..	..	..	..	..	..	..	..	..	..	..	..	..
5. *Equals:* **Gross National Product**	..	..	..	..	..	..	..	..	..	..	..	..	..	..	..
6. *Less:* Consumption of fixed capital	..	..	..	..	..	..	..	..	..	..	..	..	..	..	..
7. *Plus:* Statistical discrepancy	..	..	..	..	..	..	..	..	..	..	..	..	..	..	..
8. *Equals:* **National Income**	..	..	..	..	..	..	..	..	..	..	..	..	..	..	..
9. *Plus:* Net current transfers from the rest of the world	..	..	..	..	..	..	..	..	..	..	..	..	..	..	..
10. Current transfers from the rest of the world	..	..	..	..	..	..	..	..	..	..	..	..	..	..	..
11. Current transfers paid to the rest of the world	..	..	..	..	..	..	..	..	..	..	..	..	..	..	..
12. *Equals:* **National Disposable Income**	..	..	..	..	..	..	..	..	..	..	..	..	..	..	..
13. *Less:* Final consumption	..	..	..	..	..	..	..	..	..	..	..	..	..	..	..
14. *Plus:* Statistical discrepancy	..	..	..	..	..	..	..	..	..	..	..	..	..	..	..
15. *Equals:* **Net Saving**	..	..	..	..	..	..	..	..	..	..	..	..	..	..	..
16. *Less:* Surplus of the nation on current transactions	..	..	..	..	..	..	..	..	..	..	..	..	..	..	..
17. *Plus:* Statistical discrepancy	..	..	..	..	..	..	..	..	..	..	..	..	..	..	..
18. *Equals:* **Net Capital Formation**	..	..	..	..	..	..	..	..	..	..	..	..	..	..	..

1. At 1991 relative prices.

Principaux Agrégats

millions de forint

1983	1984	1985	1986	1987	1988	1989	1990	1991	1992	1993	1994	1995	1996	1997	
															DÉPENSES IMPUTÉES AU P.I.B.
															Aux prix courants
..	..	..	..	..	..	..	491700*	641400	780600	1013500	1145400	1337300	1534700*	1854400*	1. Consommation finale des administrations publiques
..	..	..	..	..	..	..	1094500*	1370200	1696900	2117800	2533400	3007100	3587400*	4328000*	2. Consommation finale privée
..	..	..	..	..	..	..	..	1354100	1670800	2061500	2458300	2938600	3498800*	4206000*	3. Ménages
..	..	..	..	..	..	..	..	16100	26100	56300	75100	68500	90000*	126300*	4. Institutions privées sans but lucratif au service des ménages
..	..	..	..	..	..	..	119000*	−12000	−111700	38100	90100	279700	454000*	559500*	5. Variations des stocks
..	..	..	..	..	..	..	475000*	522900	584700	670000	878500	1059600	1389200*	1773900*	6. Formation brute de capital fixe
..	..	..	..	..	..	..	2180200*	2522500	2950500	3839400	4647400	5683700	6965300*	8515800*	7. **Demande intérieure totale**
..	..	..	..	..	..	..	637800*	818400	925300	937000	1262500	1914800	2474200*	3589000*	8. Exportations de biens et services
..	..	..	..	..	..	..	556800*	842600	933200	1228100	1545100	2036600	2615200*	3670300*	9. *Moins :* Importations de biens et services
..	..	..	..	..	..	..	..	..	..	..	..	..	5600*	27500*	10. Divergence statistique
..	..	..	..	..	..	..	2261200*	2498300	2942600	3548300	4364800	5561900	6829900*	8462000*	11. **Produit intérieur brut**
															Aux niveaux de prix de 1990 [1]
..	..	..	..	..	..	..	491700*	478493*	473420*	519904*	481478*	454020*	443500*	448872*	1. Consommation finale des administrations publiques
..	..	..	..	..	..	..	1094500*	1033766*	1048251*	1084390*	1086427*	1009698*	977181*	1000117*	2. Consommation finale privée
..	..	..	..	..	..	..	..	..	..	..	..	..	..	..	3. Ménages
..	..	..	..	..	..	..	..	..	..	..	..	..	..	..	4. Institutions privées sans but lucratif au service des ménages
..	..	..	..	..	..	..	119000*	20268*	−59217*	47109*	87367*	154093*	201566*	215635*	5. Variations des stocks
..	..	..	..	..	..	..	475000*	425450*	414221*	422683*	475407*	454822*	485415*	528130*	6. Formation brute de capital fixe
..	..	..	..	..	..	..	2180200*	1957977*	1876675*	2074086*	2130679*	2072633*	2107662*	2192754*	7. **Demande intérieure totale**
..	..	..	..	..	..	..	637800*	618235*	631228*	567244*	645052*	731547*	792736*	1016642*	8. Exportations de biens et services
..	..	..	..	..	..	..	556800*	586963*	588426*	707546*	770102*	764599*	815381*	1023459*	9. *Moins :* Importations de biens et services
..	..	..	..	..	..	..	0*	2907*	11677*	−13714*	−28943*	−33550*	−52114*	−59977*	10. Divergence statistique
..	..	..	..	..	..	..	2261200*	1992156*	1931154*	1920070*	1976686*	2006031*	2032903*	2125960*	11. **Produit intérieur brut**
															RÉPARTITION DU P.I.B.
..	..	..	..	..	..	..	..	..	..	..	..	..	..	..	1. Impôts indirects
..	..	..	..	..	..	..	..	..	..	..	..	..	..	..	2. *Moins :* Subventions
..	..	..	..	..	..	..	..	..	..	..	..	..	..	..	3. Consommation de capital fixe
..	..	..	..	..	..	..	..	..	..	..	..	..	..	..	4. Rémunération des salariés payée par les producteurs résidents
..	..	..	..	..	..	..	..	..	..	..	..	..	..	..	5. Excédent net d'exploitation
..	..	..	..	..	..	..	..	..	..	..	..	..	..	..	6. Divergence statistique
..	..	..	..	..	..	..	..	..	..	..	..	..	..	..	7. **Produit intérieur brut**
															OPÉRATIONS EN CAPITAL DE LA NATION
															Financement de la formation brute de capital
..	..	..	..	..	..	..	..	..	..	..	..	..	..	..	1. Consommation de capital fixe
..	..	..	..	..	..	..	..	..	..	..	..	..	..	..	2. Épargne nette
..	..	..	..	..	..	..	..	..	..	..	..	..	..	..	3. *Moins :* Solde des opérations courantes de la nation
..	..	..	..	..	..	..	..	..	..	..	..	..	..	..	4. Divergence statistique
..	..	..	..	..	..	..	..	..	..	..	..	..	..	..	5. **Financement de la formation brute de capital**
															Formation brute de capital
..	..	..	..	..	..	..	..	..	..	..	..	..	..	..	6. Variations des stocks
..	..	..	..	..	..	..	..	..	..	..	..	..	..	..	7. Formation brute de capital fixe
..	..	..	..	..	..	..	..	..	..	..	..	..	..	..	8. Divergence statistique
..	..	..	..	..	..	..	..	..	..	..	..	..	..	..	9. **Formation brute de capital**
															RELATIONS ENTRE LES PRINCIPAUX AGRÉGATS
..	..	..	..	..	..	..	..	..	..	..	..	..	..	..	1. **Produit intérieur brut**
..	..	..	..	..	..	..	..	..	..	..	..	..	..	..	2. *Plus :* Revenu net des facteurs reçu du reste du monde
..	..	..	..	..	..	..	..	..	..	..	..	..	..	..	3. Revenu des facteurs reçu du reste du monde
..	..	..	..	..	..	..	..	..	..	..	..	..	..	..	4. Revenu des facteurs payé au reste du monde
..	..	..	..	..	..	..	..	..	..	..	..	..	..	..	5. *Égal :* **Produit national brut**
..	..	..	..	..	..	..	..	..	..	..	..	..	..	..	6. *Moins :* Consommation de capital fixe
..	..	..	..	..	..	..	..	..	..	..	..	..	..	..	7. *Plus :* Divergence statistique
..	..	..	..	..	..	..	..	..	..	..	..	..	..	..	8. *Égal :* **Revenu national**
..	..	..	..	..	..	..	..	..	..	..	..	..	..	..	9. *Plus :* Transferts courants nets reçus du reste du monde
..	..	..	..	..	..	..	..	..	..	..	..	..	..	..	10. Transferts courants reçus du reste du monde
..	..	..	..	..	..	..	..	..	..	..	..	..	..	..	11. Transferts courants payés au reste du monde
..	..	..	..	..	..	..	..	..	..	..	..	..	..	..	12. *Égal :* **Revenu national disponible**
..	..	..	..	..	..	..	..	..	..	..	..	..	..	..	13. *Moins :* Consommation finale
..	..	..	..	..	..	..	..	..	..	..	..	..	..	..	14. *Plus :* Divergence statistique
..	..	..	..	..	..	..	..	..	..	..	..	..	..	..	15. *Égal :* **Épargne nette**
..	..	..	..	..	..	..	..	..	..	..	..	..	..	..	16. *Moins :* Solde des opérations courantes de la nation
..	..	..	..	..	..	..	..	..	..	..	..	..	..	..	17. *Plus :* Divergence statistique
..	..	..	..	..	..	..	..	..	..	..	..	..	..	..	18. *Égal :* **Formation nette de capital**

1. Aux prix relatifs de 1991.

ICELAND
1968 SNA

Main aggregates

millions of kronur

	1960	1969	1970	1971	1972	1973	1974	1975	1976	1977	1978	1979	1980	1981	1982
EXPENDITURE ON THE G.D.P.															
At current prices															
1. Government final consumption expenditure	9.47*	45.87*	59.45*	78.19*	108.96*	148.11*	239.73*	350.29*	469.53*	683.01*	1122.83*	1712.85*	2663	4227	6942
2. Private final consumption expenditure	58.13*	220.31*	283.93*	359.18*	442.06*	587.25*	890.91*	1252.12*	1714.34*	2468.98*	3854.97*	5799.11*	9326	14957	23864
3. Households	..	..	..	..	..	..	..	..	..	..	..	..	..	..	..
4. Private non-profit institutions serving households	..	..	..	..	..	..	..	..	..	..	..	..	..	..	..
5. Increase in stocks	−1.24*	2.05*	−2.89*	14.13*	−10.40*	−3.15*	25.34*	37.13*	−17.79*	66.01*	−38.57*	51.00*	80	253	913
6. Gross fixed capital formation	27.86*	93.28*	113.58*	174.24*	212.13*	325.17*	500.88*	696.29*	854.54*	1194.83*	1653.01*	2360.09*	4116	6214	9726
7. **Total Domestic Expenditure**	94.22*	361.51*	454.07*	625.74*	752.75*	1057.38*	1656.86*	2335.83*	3020.62*	4412.83*	6592.24*	9923.05*	16185	25652	41445
8. Exports of goods and services	37.14*	156.87*	204.41*	216.48*	254.41*	362.82*	466.41*	705.71*	1029.86*	1417.69*	2438.47*	3743.18*	5645	8561	12466
9. *Less:* Imports of goods and services	40.71*	149.64*	196.74*	253.85*	267.60*	383.87*	610.89*	883.48*	1019.31*	1452.00*	2242.00*	3631.00*	5648	8936	14329
10. Statistical discrepancy	0.04*	0.78*	0.60*	−0.01*	−0.32*	1.58*	−1.73*	−1.08*	2.57*	2.60*	4.14*	0.92*	..	..	..
11. **Gross Domestic Product**	90.69*	369.52*	462.34*	588.36*	739.24*	1037.91*	1510.65*	2156.98*	3033.74*	4381.12*	6792.85*	10036.15*	16182	25276	39582
At 1990 price levels[1]															
1. Government final consumption expenditure	11626*	19974*	21735*	23388*	26782*	29058*	31520*	34462*	36192*	36974*	39604*	41774*	42641	45833	48555
2. Private final consumption expenditure	54167*	80869*	93828*	109926*	117915*	124201*	136939*	123783*	130495*	147344*	160551*	165086*	170670	181199	190172
3. Households	..	..	..	..	..	..	..	..	..	..	..	..	..	..	..
4. Private non-profit institutions serving households	..	..	..	..	..	..	..	..	..	..	..	..	..	..	..
5. Increase in stocks	−3125*	−15*	−2299*	5324*	−7216*	−4718*	3008*	5071*	−6777*	550*	−4276*	−1361*	−1375	−44	2783
6. Gross fixed capital formation	25066*	30491*	32683*	46525*	46932*	57461*	62014*	56543*	55006*	61326*	57928*	56903*	64838	65606	65647
7. **Total Domestic Expenditure**	87734*	131319*	145947*	185163*	184413*	206002*	233481*	219859*	214916*	246194*	253807*	262402*	276774	292594	307157
8. Exports of goods and services	31783*	47214*	54989*	50463*	57782*	62789*	61117*	62719*	70915*	77236*	88943*	94518*	97069	100140	91184
9. *Less:* Imports of goods and services	26600*	40250*	51464*	64114*	64443*	77544*	87250*	76122*	73345*	88439*	91659*	93920*	96728	103611	103021
10. Statistical discrepancy	2800*	1678*	929*	−1468*	2797*	1590*	−3507*	−1298*	4898*	1571*	−296*	−15*	971	824	874
11. **Gross Domestic Product**	95717*	139961*	150401*	170044*	180549*	192837*	203841*	205158*	217384*	236562*	250795*	262985*	278086	289947	296194
COST COMPONENTS OF THE G.D.P.															
1. Indirect taxes	24.39*	69.74*	97.85*	133.83*	164.15*	234.98*	372.39*	539.81*	723.76*	1006.11*	1520.29*	2271.24*	3681	6126	9530
2. *Less:* Subsidies	8.42*	17.02*	19.47*	35.18*	38.72*	40.39*	71.21*	107.98*	109.73*	141.83*	254.01*	435.65*	572	973	1535
3. Consumption of fixed capital	12.03*	57.49*	64.77*	72.56*	92.92*	138.87*	190.71*	309.05*	401.37*	530.42*	819.88*	1237.74*	1964	3080	5076
4. Compensation of employees paid by resident producers	43.22*	179.85*	225.55*	294.02*	359.17*	500.37*	751.65*	1005.32*	1364.78*	2014.93*	3213.10*	4883.79*	7725	11990	18781
5. Operating surplus	16.51*	68.60*	80.79*	105.66*	140.40*	155.72*	185.26*	282.22*	436.73*	594.15*	820.32*	1109.50*	1972	3013	4255
6. Statistical discrepancy	2.95*	10.85*	12.86*	17.45*	21.30*	48.36*	81.87*	128.56*	216.83*	377.35*	673.28*	969.55*	1412	2041	3476
7. **Gross Domestic Product**	90.68*	369.51*	462.35*	588.34*	739.22*	1037.91*	1510.67*	2156.98*	3033.74*	4381.13*	6792.86*	10036.17*	16182	25276	39582
CAPITAL TRANSACTIONS OF THE NATION															
Finance of Gross Capital Formation															
1. Consumption of fixed capital	12.03*	57.49*	64.77*	72.56*	92.92*	138.87*	190.71*	309.05*	401.37*	530.42*	819.88*	1237.74*	1964	3080	5076
2. Net saving	10.45*	41.51*	52.11*	76.90*	90.70*	156.17*	179.35*	208.80*	389.93*	632.12*	871.56*	1103.03*	1912	2343	2425
3. *Less:* Surplus of the nation on current transactions	−4.14*	3.67*	6.19*	−38.90*	−18.10*	−26.99*	−156.16*	−215.56*	−45.45*	−98.30*	77.00*	−70.32*	−320	−1045	−3138
4. Statistical discrepancy	..	..	..	..	..	..	..	..	..	..	..	..	..	..	..
5. **Finance of Gross Capital Formation**	26.62*	95.33*	110.69*	188.36*	201.72*	322.03*	526.22*	733.41*	836.75*	1260.84*	1614.44*	2411.09*	4196	6467	10639
Gross capital formation															
6. Increase in stocks	−1.24*	2.05*	−2.89*	14.13*	−10.40*	−3.15*	25.34*	37.13*	−17.79*	66.01*	−38.57*	51.00*	80	253	913
7. Gross fixed capital formation	27.86*	93.28*	113.58*	174.24*	212.13*	325.17*	500.88*	696.29*	854.54*	1194.83*	1653.01*	2360.09*	4116	6214	9726
8. Statistical discrepancy	..	..	..	..	..	..	..	..	..	..	..	..	..	..	..
9. **Gross Capital Formation**	26.62*	95.33*	110.69*	188.37*	201.73*	322.02*	526.22*	733.42*	836.75*	1260.84*	1614.44*	2411.09*	4196	6467	10639
RELATIONS AMONG NATIONAL ACCOUNTING AGGREGATES															
1. **Gross Domestic Product**	90.68*	369.52*	462.35*	588.35*	739.23*	1037.91*	1510.66*	2156.98*	3033.74*	4381.13*	6792.86*	10036.16*	16182	25276	39582
2. *Plus:* Net factor income from the rest of the world	−0.93*	−4.62*	−3.63*	−3.84*	−6.72*	−8.89*	−14.45*	−36.70*	−54.96*	−66.63*	−121.50*	−184.37*	−310	−648	−1247
3. Factor income from the rest of the world	0.25*	4.14*	8.34*	8.51*	7.78*	11.55*	15.22*	9.01*	17.48*	24.38*	40.00*	105.91*	167	326	597
4. Factor income paid to the rest of the world	1.33*	7.77*	8.13*	8.48*	12.00*	16.38*	25.21*	52.22*	79.79*	98.01*	176.93*	286.50*	477	974	1844
5. *Equals:* **Gross National Product**	89.75*	364.90*	458.72*	584.51*	732.51*	1029.02*	1496.21*	2120.28*	2978.78*	4314.50*	6671.36*	9851.79*	15872	24629	38335
6. *Less:* Consumption of fixed capital	12.03*	57.49*	64.77*	72.56*	92.92*	138.87*	190.71*	309.05*	401.37*	530.42*	819.88*	1237.74*	1964	3080	5076
7. *Plus:* Statistical discrepancy	0.33*	0.52*	1.86*	2.62*	2.68*	2.02*	5.35*	1.74*	−2.06*	1.03*	−0.12*	5.94*	..	..	..
8. *Equals:* **National Income**	78.05*	307.93*	395.81*	514.57*	642.27*	892.17*	1310.85*	1812.97*	2575.35*	3785.11*	5851.36*	8619.99*	13909	21549	33259
9. *Plus:* Net current transfers from the rest of the world	0.00*	−0.24*	−0.32*	−0.30*	−0.55*	−0.64*	−0.86*	−1.76*	−1.55*	−1.00*	−2.00*	−5.00*	−7	−22	−28
10. Current transfers from the rest of the world	0.00*	0.00*	0.00*	0.00*	0.00*	0.00*	0.00*	0.00*	0.00*	0.00*	0.00*	0.00*	0	0	0
11. Current transfers paid to the rest of the world	0.00*	0.24*	0.32*	0.30*	0.55*	0.64*	0.86*	1.76*	1.55*	1.00*	2.00*	5.00*	7	22	28
12. *Equals:* **National Disposable Income**	78.05*	307.69*	395.49*	514.27*	641.72*	891.53*	1309.99*	1811.21*	2573.80*	3784.11*	5849.36*	8614.99*	13902	21527	33231
13. *Less:* Final consumption	67.60*	266.18*	343.38*	437.37*	551.02*	735.36*	1130.64*	1602.41*	2183.87*	3151.99*	4977.80*	7511.96*	11989	19184	30806
14. *Plus:* Statistical discrepancy	..	..	..	..	..	..	..	..	..	..	..	..	0	0	0
15. *Equals:* **Net Saving**	10.45*	41.51*	52.11*	76.90*	90.70*	156.17*	179.35*	208.80*	389.93*	632.12*	871.56*	1103.03*	1912	2343	2425
16. *Less:* Surplus of the nation on current transactions	−4.14*	3.67*	6.19*	−38.90*	−18.10*	−26.99*	−156.16*	−215.56*	−45.45*	−98.30*	77.00*	−70.32*	−320	−1045	−3138
17. *Plus:* Statistical discrepancy	0*	0*	0*	0*	0*	0*	0*	0*	0*	0*	0*	0*	0	0	0
18. *Equals:* **Net Capital Formation**	14.59*	37.84*	45.92*	115.80*	108.80*	183.16*	335.51*	424.36*	435.38*	730.42*	794.56*	1173.35*	2232	3388	5563

1. At 1990 relative prices for 1990-1997, at 1980 relative prices for 1977-1989, at 1969 relative prices for 1965-1976 and at 1960 relative prices for 1960-1964.

Principaux Agrégats

millions de couronnes

1983	1984	1985	1986	1987	1988	1989	1990	1991	1992	1993	1994	1995	1996	1997	
															DÉPENSES IMPUTÉES AU P.I.B.
															Aux prix courants
12050	14701	21130	28776	38981	50537	60341	69990	78157	80375	84818	89424	94080	100358	107304	1. Consommation finale des administrations publiques
41016	55872	77240	99196	133557	161068	190254	223176	248366	248339	248182	256949	272708	296840	320314	2. Consommation finale privée
..	..	..	..	..	..	..	..	..	..	..	..	..	..	..	3. Ménages
..	..	..	..	..	..	..	..	..	..	..	..	..	..	..	4. Institutions privées sans but lucratif au service des ménages
−1070	−661	−3111	−3748	−3779	−3080	−8143	−4247	−891	−486	1016	−26	2285	−1202	−5093	5. Variations des stocks
14839	19337	25528	30911	42639	50498	58698	70103	76173	69589	64177	65876	65950	86752	98666	6. Formation brute de capital fixe
66834	89249	120788	155135	211398	259023	301150	359022	401805	397817	398193	412223	435023	482748	521191	7. **Demande intérieure totale**
26683	33765	48774	61961	71681	81721	106282	124936	125671	121597	135694	157436	161250	176863	190945	8. Exportations de biens et services
25275	33871	48663	55880	73965	84100	99240	119556	130491	121782	122466	134631	144725	173727	187716	9. *Moins :* Importations de biens et services
..	..	..	..	..	..	..	..	..	..	..	..	..	..	..	10. Divergence statistique
68242	89144	120899	161217	209114	256645	308192	364402	396985	397632	411421	435028	451548	485884	524420	11. **Produit intérieur brut**
															Aux niveaux de prix de 1990[1]
50829	51126	54445	58393	62212	65109	67072	69990	72195	71582	73228	75938	76925	77694	79714	1. Consommation finale des administrations publiques
179465	186113	193972	207380	240911	231752	222092	223176	232386	222014	212052	216002	225142	239446	253813	2. Consommation finale privée
..	..	..	..	..	..	..	..	..	..	..	..	..	..	..	3. Ménages
..	..	..	..	..	..	..	..	..	..	..	..	..	..	..	4. Institutions privées sans but lucratif au service des ménages
−5415	−653	−3809	−5525	−4080	−983	−3319	−4247	1126	34	925	136	2528	48	−3335	5. Variations des stocks
57292	62660	63304	62322	74015	73863	68055	70103	71537	63479	56229	55637	54060	68400	76051	6. Formation brute de capital fixe
282171	299246	307912	322570	373058	369741	353900	359022	377244	357109	342434	347713	358655	385588	406243	7. **Demande intérieure totale**
101218	103653	115107	121952	125935	121396	124968	124936	117537	115269	123465	135763	132800	146064	154295	8. Exportations de biens et services
93032	101540	111105	112159	138253	131914	118383	119556	126361	116287	106313	110733	114903	133968	145422	9. *Moins :* Importations de biens et services
−535	430	−187	−1089	−1156	38	−295	0	0	0	0	0	0	0	0	10. Divergence statistique
289822	301789	311727	331274	359584	359261	360190	364402	368420	356091	359586	372743	376552	397684	415116	11. **Produit intérieur brut**
															RÉPARTITION DU P.I.B.
15094	20918	27638	35823	48320	61324	72152	79167	83943	83714	77009	79004	82373	89811	95509	1. Impôts indirects
2511	2866	4107	5273	5988	9107	12835	12953	12319	13225	10504	9607	9492	10054	10363	2. *Moins :* Subventions
9296	11382	15475	19668	23435	28905	37308	43692	47933	50881	54144	56452	57702	59911	62841	3. Consommation de capital fixe
29519	38359	56230	74425	109930	136181	153447	175063	201642	203831	203471	211092	224677	248774	266665	4. Rémunération des salariés payée par les producteurs résidents
10527	16265	18291	25345	29639	32830	45283	59835	57621	61754	64267	74213	69622	70084	79302	5. Excédent net d'exploitation
6317	5085	7373	11229	3779	6511	12836	19598	18164	10678	23034	23874	26665	27359	30465	6. Divergence statistique
68242	89144	120899	161217	209114	256645	308192	364402	396984	397633	411421	435028	451547	485885	524419	7. **Produit intérieur brut**
															OPÉRATIONS EN CAPITAL DE LA NATION
															Financement de la formation brute de capital
9296	11382	15475	19668	23435	28905	37308	43692	47933	50881	54144	56452	57702	59911	62841	1. Consommation de capital fixe
3181	3151	2240	8385	8418	9571	8785	14495	11374	8857	14245	18132	14249	17464	22224	2. Épargne nette
−1292	−4143	−4703	890	−7007	−8942	−4462	−7669	−15974	−9365	3196	8734	3717	−8176	−8507	3. *Moins :* Solde des opérations courantes de la nation
..	..	..	..	0	0	0	0	0	0	0	0	0	0	0	4. Divergence statistique
13769	18677	22418	27163	38860	47418	50555	65856	75281	69103	65193	65850	68234	85551	93572	5. **Financement de la formation brute de capital**
															Formation brute de capital
−1070	−661	−3111	−3748	−3779	−3080	−8143	−4247	−891	−486	1016	−26	2285	−1202	−5093	6. Variations des stocks
14839	19337	25528	30911	42639	50498	58698	70103	76173	69589	64177	65876	65950	86752	98666	7. Formation brute de capital fixe
..	..	..	..	..	..	..	..	..	..	..	..	..	..	..	8. Divergence statistique
13769	18677	22418	27163	38860	47418	50555	65856	75282	69103	65193	65850	68235	85550	93573	9. **Formation brute de capital**
															RELATIONS ENTRE LES PRINCIPAUX AGRÉGATS
68242	89144	120899	161217	209114	256645	308192	364402	396984	397632	411421	435028	451547	485884	524419	1. **Produit intérieur brut**
−2671	−4024	−4824	−5302	−4799	−6506	−11164	−12849	−10644	−8911	−9821	−13445	−12502	−10848	−11498	2. *Plus :* Revenu net des facteurs reçu du reste du monde
773	1027	1431	1740	2482	2955	3923	4471	4940	5771	5982	5503	5755	7501	8129	3. Revenu des facteurs reçu du reste du monde
3444	5051	6255	7042	7281	9461	15087	17320	15584	14682	15803	18948	18257	18349	19627	4. Revenu des facteurs payé au reste du monde
65571	85119	116075	155915	204315	250138	297028	351553	386341	388721	401600	421583	439045	475036	512921	5. *Égal :* **Produit national brut**
9296	11382	15475	19668	23435	23905	37308	43692	47933	50881	54144	56452	57702	59911	62841	6. *Moins :* Consommation de capital fixe
..	..	..	..	..	..	..	..	..	..	..	..	..	..	..	7. *Plus :* Divergence statistique
56275	73737	100600	136247	180880	221233	259720	307861	338408	337840	347456	365131	381343	415125	450080	8. *Égal :* **Revenu national**
−29	−13	11	111	76	−57	−340	−200	−510	−269	−211	−626	−306	−464	−238	9. *Plus :* Transferts courants nets reçus du reste du monde
0	0	0	0	0	0	0	0	0	0	0	0	0	0	0	10. Transferts courants reçus du reste du monde
29	13	−11	−111	−76	57	340	200	510	269	211	626	306	464	238	11. Transferts courants payés au reste du monde
56246	73724	100610	136358	180956	221176	259380	307661	337897	337571	347245	364505	381037	414661	449842	12. *Égal :* **Revenu national disponible**
53066	70573	98370	127972	172538	211605	250595	293166	326523	328714	333000	346373	366788	397198	427618	13. *Moins :* Consommation finale
0	0	0	0	0	0	0	0	0	0	0	0	0	0	0	14. *Plus :* Divergence statistique
3181	3151	2240	8385	8418	9571	8785	14495	11374	8857	14245	18132	14249	17464	22224	15. *Égal :* **Épargne nette**
−1292	−4143	−4703	890	−7007	−8942	−4462	−7669	−15974	−9365	3196	8734	3717	−8176	−8507	16. *Moins :* Solde des opérations courantes de la nation
0	0	0	0	0	0	0	0	0	0	0	0	0	0	0	17. *Plus :* Divergence statistique
4472	7295	6943	7495	15425	18513	13248	22164	27348	18222	11049	9398	10532	25640	30731	18. *Égal :* **Formation nette de capital**

1. Aux prix relatifs de 1990 pour la période 1990-1997, aux prix relatifs de 1980 pour la période 1977-1989, aux prix relatifs de 1969 pour la période 1965-1976 et aux prix relatifs de 1960 pour la période 1960-1964.

IRELAND
1968 SNA

Main aggregates

millions of irish pounds

	1960	1969	1970	1971	1972	1973	1974	1975	1976	1977	1978	1979	1980	1981	1982
EXPENDITURE ON THE G.D.P.															
At current prices															
1. Government final consumption expenditure	78.6*	194.6*	237.3*	282.5*	343.0*	422.8*	513.1*	705.3*	839.4*	972.9*	1155.8*	1431.3*	1860.2*	2260.3*	2646.2*
2. Private final consumption expenditure	519.0*	1077.2*	1198.2*	1353.8*	1560.9*	1866.3*	2194.9*	2611.1*	3223.2*	3927.8*	4626.3*	5551.3*	6611.2*	8041.7*	9590.5*
3. Households	..	..	..	..	..	..	..	..	..	..	..	..	..	..	..
4. Private non-profit institutions serving households	..	..	..	..	..	..	..	..	..	..	..	..	..	..	..
5. Increase in stocks	12.6*	35.1*	28.1*	6.2*	31.0*	42.5*	132.1*	22.9*	17.3*	181.0*	93.0*	201.1*	−75.0*	−148.8*	169.1*
6. Gross fixed capital formation	92.0*	338.5*	372.6*	443.1*	535.7*	689.9*	744.1*	871.5*	1177.1*	1428.2*	1889.9*	2441.2*	2707.3*	3406.0*	3587.3*
7. **Total Domestic Expenditure**	702.2*	1645.4*	1836.2*	2085.6*	2470.6*	3021.5*	3584.2*	4210.8*	5257.0*	6509.9*	7765.0*	9624.9*	11103.7*	13559.2*	14993.1*
8. Exports of goods and services	201.5*	538.2*	600.4*	670.8*	775.1*	1029.0*	1274.9*	1623.0*	2157.8*	2824.0*	3382.2*	3946.1*	4650.2*	5517.3*	6449.3*
9. *Less:* Imports of goods and services	236.8*	670.7*	733.5*	809.5*	899.3*	1219.4*	1720.2*	1861.8*	2539.6*	3359.8*	4071.3*	5271.3*	5940.6*	7166.4*	7465.7*
10. Statistical discrepancy	−7.9*	−11.5*	−11.8*	−12.4*	−10.7*	−11.5*	−20.2*	−13.5*	−17.5*	−20.2*	−22.4*	−35.2*	−41.5*	−52.4*	−6.8*
11. **Gross Domestic Product**	659.0*	1501.4*	1691.3*	1934.5*	2335.7*	2819.6*	3118.7*	3958.5*	4857.7*	5953.9*	7053.5*	8264.5*	9771.8*	11857.7*	13969.9*
At 1990 price levels[1]															
1. Government final consumption expenditure	1406.2*	1964.1*	2186.5*	2375.3*	2554.3*	2726.7*	2933.0*	3188.1*	3271.2*	3339.2*	3603.4*	3768.2*	4035.5*	4048.9*	4180.3*
2. Private final consumption expenditure	6306.0*	8913.9*	8822.5*	9108.1*	9577.0*	10264.5*	10433.1*	10519.1*	10816.8*	11549.0*	12601.3*	13160.0*	13216.4*	13440.9*	12492.3*
3. Households	..	..	..	..	..	..	..	..	..	..	..	..	..	..	..
4. Private non-profit institutions serving households	..	..	..	..	..	..	..	..	..	..	..	..	..	..	..
5. Increase in stocks	120.9*	185.7*	252.0*	85.8*	311.0*	346.4*	749.6*	−9.4*	103.8*	576.1*	317.7*	491.3*	−109.1*	−134.4*	300.2*
6. Gross fixed capital formation	1070.8*	2782.7*	2690.1*	2930.1*	3159.2*	3669.8*	3243.5*	3126.4*	3550.3*	3694.3*	4391.7*	4989.5*	4754.1*	5207.1*	5029.5*
7. **Total Domestic Expenditure**	8903.9*	13846.4*	13951.1*	14499.3*	15601.5*	17007.4*	17359.2*	16824.2*	17742.1*	19158.6*	20914.1*	22409.0*	21896.9*	22562.5*	22002.3*
8. Exports of goods and services	1421.1*	2962.4*	3519.0*	3663.2*	3795.1*	4209.4*	4239.1*	4559.2*	4929.3*	5620.9*	6313.4*	6721.8*	7148.9*	7288.7*	7692.1*
9. *Less:* Imports of goods and services	1857.4*	4346.3*	4719.5*	4939.4*	5189.5*	6177.3*	6036.0*	5419.7*	6214.9*	7039.3*	8144.9*	9273.9*	8857.0*	9008.4*	8727.6*
10. Statistical discrepancy	−416.5*	−635.1*	−608.5*	−659.7*	−828.4*	−1029.1*	−955.0*	−530.2*	−807.6*	−806.4*	−931.7*	−1148.2*	−904.2*	−916.9*	−585.9*
11. **Gross Domestic Product**	8051.1*	11827.4*	12142.1*	12563.4*	13378.7*	14010.4*	14607.3*	15433.5*	15648.9*	16933.8*	18150.9*	18708.7*	19284.6*	19925.9*	20380.9*
COST COMPONENTS OF THE G.D.P.															
1. Indirect taxes	100.6*	274.3*	314.7*	358.1*	414.5*	494.2*	532.1*	645.8*	891.3*	1016.2*	1116.8*	1229.8*	1571.2*	1980.6*	2423.2*
2. *Less:* Subsidies	18.1*	60.8*	69.3*	75.5*	83.0*	104.2*	136.5*	224.9*	261.3*	423.8*	556.2*	617.6*	648.9*	662.1*	749.4*
3. Consumption of fixed capital	41.6*	126.4*	138.6*	159.6*	189.6*	221.0*	265.6*	311.3*	404.5*	514.0*	674.9*	820.4*	1062.4*	1195.2*	1403.5*
4. Compensation of employees paid by resident producers	294.1*	724.8*	845.6*	980.0*	1145.4*	1394.4*	1688.4*	2159.6*	2568.7*	3035.3*	3624.5*	4499.5*	5590.3*	6624.6*	7558.7*
5. Operating surplus	243.6*	433.4*	454.3*	501.1*	660.7*	805.0*	747.0*	1057.2*	1234.2*	1837.9*	2240.3*	2354.1*	2144.0*	2639.1*	3249.9*
6. Statistical discrepancy	−2.7*	3.4*	7.5*	11.1*	8.6*	9.2*	22.1*	9.5*	20.1*	−25.7*	−46.8*	−21.6*	52.8*	80.4*	84.1*
7. **Gross Domestic Product**	659.1*	1501.5*	1691.4*	1934.4*	2335.8*	2819.6*	3118.7*	3958.5*	4857.5*	5953.9*	7053.5*	8264.6*	9771.8*	11857.8*	13970.0*
CAPITAL TRANSACTIONS OF THE NATION															
Finance of Gross Capital Formation															
1. Consumption of fixed capital	41.6*	126.4*	138.6*	159.6*	189.6*	221.0*	265.6*	311.3*	404.5*	514.0*	674.9*	820.4*	1062.4*	1195.2*	1403.5*
2. Net saving	56.1*	160.1*	177.1*	196.7*	295.5*	375.4*	283.0*	472.7*	487.9*	706.1*	762.5*	682.4*	423.0*	346.5*	843.6*
3. *Less:* Surplus of the nation on current transactions	−1.0*	−82.1*	−77.6*	−84.4*	−57.5*	−110.9*	−350.0*	−68.6*	−293.4*	−367.0*	−546.0*	−1258.4*	−1308.5*	−1990.4*	−1681.3*
4. Statistical discrepancy	5.9*	5.0*	7.4*	8.6*	24.1*	25.1*	−22.4*	41.8*	8.6*	22.1*	−0.5*	−118.9*	−161.6*	−274.9*	−172.0*
5. **Finance of Gross Capital Formation**	104.6*	373.6*	400.7*	449.3*	566.7*	732.4*	876.2*	894.4*	1194.4*	1609.2*	1982.9*	2642.3*	2632.3*	3257.2*	3756.4*
Gross capital formation															
6. Increase in stocks	12.6*	35.1*	28.1*	6.2*	31.0*	42.5*	132.1*	22.9*	17.3*	181.0*	93.0*	201.1*	−75.0*	−148.8*	169.1*
7. Gross fixed capital formation	92.0*	338.5*	372.6*	443.1*	535.7*	689.9*	744.1*	871.5*	1177.1*	1428.2*	1889.9*	2441.2*	2707.3*	3406.0*	3587.3*
8. Statistical discrepancy	..	..	..	..	..	..	..	..	..	..	..	..	..	..	..
9. **Gross Capital Formation**	104.6*	373.6*	400.7*	449.3*	566.7*	732.4*	876.2*	894.4*	1194.4*	1609.2*	1982.9*	2642.3*	2632.3*	3257.2*	3756.4*
RELATIONS AMONG NATIONAL ACCOUNTING AGGREGATES															
1. **Gross Domestic Product**	659.0*	1501.5*	1691.3*	1934.5*	2335.8*	2819.6*	3118.7*	3958.5*	4857.5*	5953.9*	7053.5*	8264.6*	9771.8*	11857.8*	13970.0*
2. *Plus:* Net factor income from the rest of the world	16.3*	29.2*	29.2*	27.4*	30.5*	12.9*	19.8*	4.4*	−37.1*	−111.7*	−235.1*	−291.6*	−369.0*	−520.0*	−956.0*
3. Factor income from the rest of the world	..	..	69.6*	74.5*	89.6*	121.3*	166.4*	183.7*	235.3*	241.6*	286.7*	348.2*	476.6*	581.7*	598.5*
4. Factor income paid to the rest of the world	..	..	41.9*	48.6*	60.9*	110.6*	149.7*	182.6*	276.4*	356.9*	525.4*	644.1*	851.7*	1108.6*	1558.8*
5. *Equals:* **Gross National Product**	675.3*	1530.7*	1720.5*	1961.9*	2366.3*	2832.5*	3138.5*	3962.9*	4820.4*	5842.2*	6818.4*	7973.0*	9402.8*	11337.8*	13014.0*
6. *Less:* Consumption of fixed capital	41.6*	126.4*	138.6*	159.6*	189.6*	221.0*	265.6*	311.3*	404.5*	514.0*	674.9*	820.4*	1062.4*	1195.2*	1403.5*
7. *Plus:* Statistical discrepancy	2.4*	−4.2*	−5.3*	−6.5*	−19.2*	−25.8*	−4.9*	−30.5*	−24.3*	−40.8*	−37.3*	−10.5*	35.6*	62.5*	−24.4*
8. *Equals:* **National Income**	636.1*	1400.1*	1576.6*	1795.8*	2157.5*	2585.7*	2868.0*	3621.1*	4391.6*	5287.4*	6106.2*	7142.1*	8376.0*	10205.1*	11586.1*
9. *Plus:* Net current transfers from the rest of the world	17.6*	31.8*	36.0*	37.2*	41.9*	78.8*	123.0*	168.0*	158.9*	319.4*	438.4*	522.9*	518.4*	443.4*	494.2*
10. Current transfers from the rest of the world	..	..	38.6*	40.3*	45.5*	89.3*	136.0*	202.3*	221.8*	404.5*	517.6*	619.0*	641.8*	598.0*	685.7*
11. Current transfers paid to the rest of the world	..	..	2.6*	3.1*	3.6*	10.5*	13.0*	34.3*	62.9*	85.1*	79.2*	96.1*	123.4*	154.6*	191.5*
12. *Equals:* **National Disposable Income**	653.7*	1431.9*	1612.6*	1833.0*	2199.4*	2664.5*	2991.0*	3789.1*	4550.5*	5606.8*	6544.6*	7665.0*	8894.4*	10648.5*	12080.3*
13. *Less:* Final consumption	597.6*	1271.8*	1435.5*	1636.3*	1903.9*	2289.1*	2708.0*	3316.4*	4062.6*	4900.7*	5782.1*	6932.6*	8471.4*	10302.0*	11236.7*
14. *Plus:* Statistical discrepancy	..	..	..	..	..	..	..	..	..	..	..	..	..	..	..
15. *Equals:* **Net Saving**	56.1*	160.1*	177.1*	196.7*	295.5*	375.4*	283.0*	472.7*	487.9*	706.1*	762.5*	682.4*	423.0*	346.5*	843.6*
16. *Less:* Surplus of the nation on current transactions	−1.0*	−82.1*	−77.6*	−84.4*	−57.5*	−110.9*	−350.0*	−68.6*	−293.4*	−367.0*	−546.0*	−1258.4*	−1308.5*	−1990.4*	−1681.3*
17. *Plus:* Statistical discrepancy	5.9*	5.0*	7.4*	8.6*	24.1*	25.1*	−22.4*	41.8*	8.6*	22.1*	−0.5*	−118.9*	−161.6*	−274.9*	−172.0*
18. *Equals:* **Net Capital Formation**	63.0*	247.2*	262.1*	289.7*	377.1*	511.4*	610.6*	583.1*	789.9*	1095.2*	1308.0*	1821.9*	1569.9*	2062.0*	2352.9*

1. At 1990 relative prices for 1987-1997 and at 1985 relative prices for 1960-1986.

Principaux Agrégats

millions de livres irlandaises

DÉPENSES IMPUTÉES AU P.I.B.

Aux prix courants

1983	1984	1985	1986	1987	1988	1989	1990	1991	1992	1993	1994	1995	1996	1997	
2857.3*	3066.6*	3300.9*	3541.9	3574.7	3539.5	3670.2	4066.9	4479.5	4842.7	5210.5	5569.6	5871.1	6124.9	6669.0	1. Consommation finale des administrations publiques
9463.1*	10362.8*	11378.3*	12138.4	12845.4	13936.7	15449.2	15991.8	16814.0	18047.2	18819.4	20553.9	21840.5	23487.0	25191.2	2. Consommation finale privée
..	..	..	..	..	..	..	..	..	..	..	..	..	..	..	3. Ménages
101.3*	217.8*	163.4*	142.0	11.3	−150.2	175.9	662.6	604.1	−195.7	−148.4	−171.0	347.5	345.7	481.5	4. Institutions privées sans but lucratif au service des ménages 5. Variations des stocks
3457.5*	3556.0*	3424.6*	3431.7	3469.5	3836.2	4468.0	5184.4	4928.9	5146.6	5099.9	5860.4	6788.1	8010.0	9505.0	6. Formation brute de capital fixe
15879.2*	17203.2*	18267.2*	19254.0	19900.9	21162.2	23763.3	25905.7	26826.5	27840.8	28981.4	31812.9	34847.2	37967.6	41846.7	7. **Demande intérieure totale**
7770.9*	9794.4*	10765.2*	10377.3	11855.1	13652.8	16159.0	16152.7	16958.0	18858.8	21988.1	25248.1	30755.3	34278.2	40539.9	8. Exportations de biens et services
8220.6*	9882.9*	10468.4*	9928.5	10681.3	11920.9	14359.5	14533.5	15084.1	15920.1	17631.0	20612.1	24670.6	27232.6	31490.4	9. *Moins :* Importations de biens et services
−1.3*	12.5*	7.1*													10. Divergence statistique
15428.2*	17127.2*	18571.1*	19702.8	21074.7	22894.1	25562.8	27524.9	28700.4	30779.5	33338.5	36448.9	40931.9	45013.2	50896.2	11. **Produit intérieur brut**

Aux niveaux de prix de 1990 [1]

1983	1984	1985	1986	1987	1988	1989	1990	1991	1992	1993	1994	1995	1996	1997	
4165.0*	4136.0*	4211.3*	4321.8	4112.3	3907.5	3857.8	4066.9	4186.2	4288.4	4303.8	4520.5	4638.8	4706.9	4930.6	1. Consommation finale des administrations publiques
12598.7*	12851.9*	13442.0*	13712.5	14168.4	14803.9	15768.9	15991.8	16331.8	17089.4	17496.3	18591.1	19345.1	20517.2	21812.2	2. Consommation finale privée
..	..	..	..	..	..	..	..	..	..	..	..	..	..	..	3. Ménages
195.6*	326.1*	265.6*	256.0	3.1	−157.9	152.3	662.6	621.3	−184.3	−140.5	−237.9	296.8	357.4	490.4	4. Institutions privées sans but lucratif au service des ménages 5. Variations des stocks
4562.5*	4447.7*	4104.6*	3989.9	3944.5	4151.0	4571.7	5184.4	4809.2	4804.5	4543.1	5094.8	5690.8	6466.7	7171.3	6. Formation brute de capital fixe
21521.8*	21761.7*	22023.5*	22280.2	22228.3	22704.5	24350.7	25905.7	25948.5	25998.0	26202.7	27968.5	29971.5	32048.2	34404.5	7. **Demande intérieure totale**
8496.2*	9905.7*	10557.4*	10862.1	12352.3	13467.0	14855.8	16152.7	17006.5	19311.1	21164.5	24165.1	28893.0	32303.1	37777.2	8. Exportations de biens et services
9134.8*	10035.0*	10360.5*	10943.6	11619.6	12189.4	13830.1	14533.5	14730.3	15739.9	16704.5	18993.6	21816.5	24246.7	27806.2	9. *Moins :* Importations de biens et services
−552.0*	−416.0*	−349.2*	−421.3	−168.1	0.0	0.0	0.0	0.0	0.0	0.0	0.0	0.0	0.0	0.0	10. Divergence statistique
20331.2*	21216.4*	21871.2*	21777.4	22792.9	23982.1	25376.4	27524.9	28224.7	29569.2	30662.7	33140.0	37048.0	40104.6	44375.5	11. **Produit intérieur brut**

RÉPARTITION DU P.I.B.

1983	1984	1985	1986	1987	1988	1989	1990	1991	1992	1993	1994	1995	1996	1997	
2794.4*	3113.5*	3269.6*	3475.2	3672.4	3965.4	4377.0	4445.9	4510.8	4781.3	4901.0	5589.7	6062.9	6637.6	7458.2	1. Impôts indirects
894.5*	1086.1*	1272.5*	1303.0	1374.7	1612.2	1179.7	1609.7	1644.8	1478.7	1682.5	1629.8	1686.6	2098.4	2010.0	2. *Moins :* Subventions
1569.9*	1640.3*	1770.9*	1885.1	2062.5	2140.2	2384.3	2615.4	2850.1	2997.6	3238.6	3612.0	4041.0	4463.3	5113.2	3. Consommation de capital fixe
8261.5*	8965.6*	9610.0*	10264.5	10796.6	11259.8	12019.0	12995.4	13846.4	14866.1	16073.3	17090.3	18421.3	20001.4	22040.6	4. Rémunération des salariés payée par les producteurs résidents
3617.0*	4464.1*	5214.7*	5380.9	5917.9	7140.9	7962.1	9077.9	9138.0	9613.3	10807.9	11786.9	14093.3	16009.4	18294.1	5. Excédent net d'exploitation
79.9*	29.7*	−21.6*													6. Divergence statistique
15428.2*	17127.1*	18571.1*	19702.7	21074.7	22894.1	25562.7	27524.9	28700.5	30779.6	33338.3	36449.1	40931.9	45013.3	50896.1	7. **Produit intérieur brut**

OPÉRATIONS EN CAPITAL DE LA NATION

Financement de la formation brute de capital

1983	1984	1985	1986	1987	1988	1989	1990	1991	1992	1993	1994	1995	1996	1997	
1569.9*	1640.3*	1770.9*	1885.1	2062.5	2140.2	2384.3	2615.4	2850.1	2997.6	3238.6	3612.0	4041.0	4463.3	5113.2	1. Consommation de capital fixe
880.0*	1068.0*	1015.0*	1046.5	1371.5	1683.6	1985.9	3183.4	3374.2	2941.6	3476.3	3360.4	4900.3	5985.8	6941.9	2. Épargne nette
−1208.3*	−1132.0*	−832.5*	−642.0	−46.8	137.8	−273.7	−48.1	691.3	988.3	1763.5	1283.0	1805.7	2093.4	2068.7	3. *Moins :* Solde des opérations courantes de la nation
−99.4*	−66.5*	−30.4*	0.1	0.0											4. Divergence statistique
3558.8*	3773.8*	3588.0*	3573.7	3480.8	3686.0	4643.9	5846.9	5533.0	4950.9	4951.4	5689.4	7135.6	8355.7	9986.4	5. **Financement de la formation brute de capital**

Formation brute de capital

1983	1984	1985	1986	1987	1988	1989	1990	1991	1992	1993	1994	1995	1996	1997	
101.3*	217.8*	163.4*	142.0	11.3	−150.2	175.9	662.6	604.1	−195.7	−148.4	−171.0	347.5	345.7	481.5	6. Variations des stocks
3457.5*	3556.0*	3424.6*	3431.7	3469.5	3836.2	4468.0	5184.4	4928.9	5146.6	5099.9	5860.4	6788.1	8010.0	9505.0	7. Formation brute de capital fixe
..	..	..	..	..	..	..	..	..	..	..	..	..	..	..	8. Divergence statistique
3558.8*	3773.8*	3588.0*	3573.7	3480.8	3686.0	4643.9	5847.0	5533.0	4950.9	4951.4	5689.4	7135.6	8355.7	9986.5	9. **Formation brute de capital**

RELATIONS ENTRE LES PRINCIPAUX AGRÉGATS

1983	1984	1985	1986	1987	1988	1989	1990	1991	1992	1993	1994	1995	1996	1997	
15428.2*	17127.1*	18571.1*	19702.7	21074.8	22894.0	25562.8	27524.9	28700.4	30779.5	33338.4	36449.0	40932.1	45013.2	50896.2	1. **Produit intérieur brut**
−1220.0*	−1688.7*	−2025.6*	−2016.6	−2112.4	−2543.2	−3108.9	−3079.5	−2791.1	−3195.7	−3902.1	−4508.7	−5389.0	−6305.9	−8270.4	2. *Plus :* Revenu net des facteurs reçu du reste du monde
564.6*	708.0*	811.6*	752.2	787.0	1185.2	1504.6	1834.1	1987.5	1877.5	1841.5	2169.3	2814.6	3147.6	4333.4	3. Revenu des facteurs reçu du reste du monde
1786.5*	2398.1*	2838.2*	2768.8	2899.4	3728.4	4613.5	4913.6	4778.5	5073.2	5743.6	6678.0	8203.6	9453.5	12603.9	4. Revenu des facteurs payé au reste du monde
14208.2*	15438.4*	16545.5*	17686.1	18962.4	20350.8	22453.9	24445.4	25909.4	27583.8	29436.3	31940.3	35543.0	38707.3	42625.7	5. *Égal :* **Produit national brut**
1569.9*	1640.3*	1770.9*	1885.1	2062.5	2140.0	2384.3	2615.4	2850.1	2997.6	3238.6	3612.0	4041.0	4463.3	5113.2	6. *Moins :* Consommation de capital fixe
−17.6*	−32.0*	−3.8*	0.0	−0.1	0.0	−0.1	0.0	0.0	0.0	0.0	0.1	0.0	0.1	0.0	7. *Plus :* Divergence statistique
12620.7*	13766.1*	14770.8*	15801.0	16899.8	18210.6	20069.5	21830.0	23059.3	24586.2	26197.6	28328.3	31502.0	34244.1	37512.5	8. *Égal :* **Revenu national**
579.7*	731.3*	923.4*	925.8	891.8	349.1	1035.8	1412.2	1608.5	1245.3	1308.6	1155.7	1110.0	1353.7	1289.7	9. *Plus :* Transferts courants nets reçus du reste du monde
831.3*	1014.4*	1235.9*	1299.5	1270.3	1312.1	1407.7	1851.1	2131.2	1777.3	1954.2	1883.4	1879.2	2194.1	..	10. Transferts courants reçus du reste du monde
251.6*	283.1*	312.5*	373.7	378.5	363.1	371.9	438.9	522.7	532.0	645.6	727.7	769.2	840.8	..	11. Transferts courants payés au reste du monde
13200.4*	14497.4*	15694.2*	16726.8	17791.6	19159.7	21105.3	23242.1	24667.7	25831.6	27506.2	29484.0	32612.0	35597.8	38802.2	12. *Égal :* **Revenu national disponible**
12320.4*	13429.4*	14679.2*	15680.3	16420.1	17476.1	19119.4	20058.7	21293.5	22889.9	24029.9	26123.6	27711.6	29611.9	31860.2	13. *Moins :* Consommation finale
..	..	..	..	..	..	..	..	..	..	..	..	..	..	..	14. *Plus :* Divergence statistique
880.0*	1068.0*	1015.0*	1046.5	1371.5	1683.6	1985.9	3183.4	3374.2	2941.6	3476.3	3360.4	4900.3	5985.8	6941.9	15. *Égal :* **Épargne nette**
−1208.3*	−1132.0*	−832.5*	−642.0	−46.8	137.8	−273.7	−48.1	691.3	988.3	1763.5	1283.0	1805.7	2093.4	2068.7	16. *Moins :* Solde des opérations courantes de la nation
−99.4*	−66.5*	−30.4*	0.1	0.0											17. *Plus :* Divergence statistique
1988.9*	2133.5*	1817.1*	1688.6	1418.3	1545.8	2259.6	3231.5	2682.9	1953.3	1712.8	2077.5	3094.6	3892.4	4873.2	18. *Égal :* **Formation nette de capital**

1. Aux prix relatifs de 1990 pour la période 1987-1997 et aux prix relatifs de 1985 pour la période 1960-1986.

ITALY
1968 SNA

Main aggregates

billions of lire

	1960	1969	1970	1971	1972	1973	1974	1975	1976	1977	1978	1979	1980	1981	1982
EXPENDITURE ON THE G.D.P.															
At current prices															
1. Government final consumption expenditure	3037*	8156*	8892	10832	12296	14180	17095	19882	23799	29924	36311	45523	57709	75085	88499
2. Private final consumption expenditure	14719*	35215*	39797	43506	47836	58283	73309	85792	106077	127740	148309	183103	234512	280819	332416
3. Households	14619*	35108*	39623	43297	47603	58041	72993	85413	105551	127187	147668	182331	233470	279622	330994
4. Private non-profit institutions serving households	84*	129*	174	209	233	242	316	379	526	553	641	772	1042	1197	1422
5. Increase in stocks	786*	859*	1773	605	484	1922	4939	−1480	5059	2540	3130	5114	9875	3985	6562
6. Gross fixed capital formation	6452*	14470*	16541	17489	18484	24049	31655	34564	41741	50304	57684	70880	94305	111024	121993
7. **Total Domestic Expenditure**	24994*	58700*	67003	72432	79100	98434	126998	138758	176676	210508	245434	304620	396401	470913	549470
8. Exports of goods and services	3237*	9882*	11093	12413	14175	16830	24673	28552	38607	49864	59402	75027	84349	107649	124031
9. *Less:* Imports of goods and services	3347*	9114*	10963	11842	13525	18663	29683	28720	40699	47665	53836	71824	95423	117511	131376
10. Statistical discrepancy	−108*	184*	..	..	..	..	..	..	..	..	..	..	..	..	..
11. **Gross Domestic Product**	24776*	59653*	67133	73003	79750	96601	121988	138590	174584	212707	251000	307823	385327	461051	542125
At 1990 price levels[1]															
1. Government final consumption expenditure	91240*	131184*	134554	141160	148016	152183	156030	159970	163632	168476	174083	178858	182546	186494	191067
2. Private final consumption expenditure	216341*	374662*	403160	417604	432526	461296	478653	482088	506414	522542	537645	574700	610301	619145	626203
3. Households	214922*	373639*	401541	415836	430697	459569	476673	479961	503988	520397	535448	572403	607760	616596	623604
4. Private non-profit institutions serving households	1145*	1263*	1619	1768	1829	1727	1980	2127	2426	2145	2197	2297	2541	2549	2599
5. Increase in stocks	8677*	3382*	12582	3075	3532	8111	17606	−11131	15413	5014	9159	14261	16539	4114	9886
6. Gross fixed capital formation	117679*	186973*	192652	191198	192824	209061	213132	198056	195977	198673	199840	210232	227850	220853	209952
7. **Total Domestic Expenditure**	433938*	696201*	742948	753037	776898	830651	865421	828983	881436	894705	920727	978051	1037236	1030606	1037108
8. Exports of goods and services	33063*	89878*	95112	101714	109587	115967	125611	127074	143051	157878	173676	186990	171505	180202	178819
9. *Less:* Imports of goods and services	34272*	85892*	99645	102349	112067	121538	127260	110825	124330	126413	133705	149844	157699	154786	155068
10. Statistical discrepancy	−8900*	992*	0	0	0	0	0	0	0	0	0	0	0	0	0
11. **Gross Domestic Product**	423829*	701179*	738415	752402	774418	825080	863772	845232	900157	926170	960698	1015197	1051042	1056022	1060859
COST COMPONENTS OF THE G.D.P.															
1. Indirect taxes	2789*	6349*	6977	7550	7795	8984	11103	11286	15338	20099	23129	26834	35846	41369	50208
2. *Less:* Subsidies	384*	1189*	1147	1474	1685	1803	2092	4392	5098	6556	7773	10216	13350	15765	20058
3. Consumption of fixed capital	2587*	6001*	6992	7569	8321*	10260*	13868*	17615*	21533*	26509*	30492*	36042*	44539	56461	67697
4. Compensation of employees paid by resident producers	9917*	26118*	30541	35012	39056	47051	58692	70854	86915	106315	123164	149607	184063	224032	250859
5. Operating surplus	9991*	22412*	23770*	24346*	26263*	32109*	40417*	43227*	55896*	66340*	81988*	105556*	134229	154954	133419
6. Statistical discrepancy	−124*	−39*	..	..	..	..	..	..	..	..	..	..	..	..	..
7. **Gross Domestic Product**	24775*	59653*	67133	73003	79750	96601	121988	138590	174584	212707	251000	307823	385327	461051	542125
CAPITAL TRANSACTIONS OF THE NATION															
Finance of Gross Capital Formation															
1. Consumption of fixed capital	2587*	6001*	6992*	7569*	8321*	10260*	13868*	17615*	21533*	26509*	30492*	36042*	44539	56461	67697
2. Net saving	4717*	10840*	11856*	11549*	11836*	14092*	17408*	15102*	22988*	28534*	35576*	44912*	50584	47517	51098
3. *Less:* Surplus of the nation on current transactions	136*	1099*	534	1024	1189	−1619	−5318	−367	−2279	2199	5254	4960	−9057	−11031	−9760
4. Statistical discrepancy	70*	−412*	..	..	..	..	..	..	..	..	..	..	..	..	..
5. **Finance of Gross Capital Formation**	7238*	15329*	18314	18094	18968	25971	36594	33084	46800	52844	60814	75994	104180	115009	128555
Gross capital formation															
6. Increase in stocks	786*	859*	1773	605	484	1922	4939	−1480	5059	2540	3130	5114	9875	3985	6562
7. Gross fixed capital formation	6452*	14470*	16541	17489	18484	24049	31655	34564	41741	50304	57684	70880	94305	111024	121993
8. Statistical discrepancy	..	..	..	..	..	..	..	..	..	..	..	..	..	..	..
9. **Gross Capital Formation**	7238*	15329*	18314	18094	18968	25971	36594	33084	46800	52844	60814	75994	104180	115009	128555
RELATIONS AMONG NATIONAL ACCOUNTING AGGREGATES															
1. **Gross Domestic Product**	24776*	59652*	67133	73003	79750	96601	121988	138590	174584	212707	251000	307823	385327	461051	542125
2. *Plus:* Net factor income from the rest of the world	71*	306*	287	318	300	143	−283	−448	−556	−243	11	971	961	−1998	−3521
3. Factor income from the rest of the world	180*	845*	998	1125	1243	1490	2185	1685	1752	2331	3253	4894	6623	8987	10410
4. Factor income paid to the rest of the world	113*	552*	711	807	943	1347	2468	2133	2308	2574	3242	3923	5662	10985	13931
5. *Equals:* **Gross National Product**	24846*	59958*	67420	73321	80050	96744	121705	138142	174028	212464	251011	308794	386288	459053	538604
6. *Less:* Consumption of fixed capital	2587*	6001*	6992*	7569*	8321*	10260*	13868*	17615*	21533*	26509*	30492*	36042*	44539	56461	67697
7. *Plus:* Statistical discrepancy	76*	20*	..	..	..	..	..	..	..	..	..	..	..	..	..
8. *Equals:* **National Income**	22336*	53977*	60428*	65752*	71729*	86484*	107837*	120527*	152495*	185955*	220519*	272752*	341749	402592	470907
9. *Plus:* Net current transfers from the rest of the world	137*	233*	117	135	239	71	−25	249	369	243	−323	786	1056	829	1106
10. Current transfers from the rest of the world	221*	515*	570	784	949	987	861	1287	1617	2081	2535	3333	4968	5881	7271
11. Current transfers paid to the rest of the world	52*	236*	453	649	710	916	886	1038	1248	1838	2858	3147	3912	5052	6165
12. *Equals:* **National Disposable Income**	22472*	54211*	60545*	65887*	71968*	86555*	107812*	120776*	152864*	186198*	220196*	273538*	342805	403421	472013
13. *Less:* Final consumption	17756*	43371*	48689	54338	60132	72463	90404	105674	129876	157664	184620	228626	292221	355904	420915
14. *Plus:* Statistical discrepancy	..	..	..	..	..	..	..	..	..	..	..	..	..	..	..
15. *Equals:* **Net Saving**	4717*	10840*	11856*	11549*	11836*	14092*	17408*	15102*	22988*	28534*	35576*	44912*	50584	47517	51098
16. *Less:* Surplus of the nation on current transactions	136*	1099*	534	1024	1189	−1619	−5318	−367	−2279	2199	5254	4960	−9057	−11031	−9760
17. *Plus:* Statistical discrepancy	70*	−412*	..	..	..	..	..	..	..	..	..	..	..	..	..
18. *Equals:* **Net Capital Formation**	4652*	9329*	11322*	10525*	10647*	15711*	22726*	15469*	25267*	26335*	30322*	39952*	59641	58548	60858

1. At 1990 relative prices for 1970-1997 and at 1970 relative prices for 1960-1969.

Principaux Agrégats

milliards de lires

DÉPENSES IMPUTÉES AU P.I.B.

Aux prix courants

	1983	1984	1985	1986	1987	1988	1989	1990	1991	1992	1993	1994	1995	1996	1997
1. Consommation finale des administrations publiques	104865	119474	134917	147636	165565	186034	200304	230163	251260	265418	273379	280474	284633	305995	318411
2. Consommation finale privée	383668	440474	496434	549170	603508	668195	738181	803619	882079	944094	961466	1014471	1089514	1149318	1205745
3. Ménages	382064	438495	494197	546774	601048	665527	735321	800412	878437	940367	957650	1010470	1085224	1144790	1201016
4. Institutions privées sans but lucratif au service des ménages	1604	1979	2237	2396	2460	2668	2860	3207	3642	3727	3816	4001	4290	4528	4729
5. Variations des stocks	5240	13004	14986	11643	15069	15410	14220	10361	11043	4910	−475	9695	16330	1897	17193
6. Formation brute de capital fixe	134697	152827	167564	177509	193658	219196	241161	266044	282647	288203	262765	272813	306869	317541	324914
7. **Demande intérieure totale**	628470	725779	813901	885958	977800	1088835	1193866	1310187	1427029	1502625	1497135	1577453	1697346	1774751	1866263
8. Exportations de biens et services	138895	164061	184848	181067	191016	207495	238437	262664	271428	295515	355486	399915	491571	499986	532957
9. *Moins :* Importations de biens et services	135755	167029	188668	168736	186053	206307	240342	262192	270886	295647	302325	338702	416663	402102	448540
10. Divergence statistique	..	..	..	..	..	..	..	..	..	..	..	..	..	..	..
11. **Produit intérieur brut**	631610	722811	810081	898289	982763	1090023	1191961	1310659	1427571	1502493	1550296	1638666	1772254	1872635	1950680

Aux niveaux de prix de 1990[1]

	1983	1984	1985	1986	1987	1988	1989	1990	1991	1992	1993	1994	1995	1996	1997
1. Consommation finale des administrations publiques	197050	201252	207528	212617	219424	225326	227396	230163	233978	236675	237748	236333	233786	234304	232588
2. Consommation finale privée	630391	646043	666113	693949	723972	756941	784281	803619	824974	836094	807864	814806	826597	836191	855904
3. Ménages	627748	643272	663305	691058	721039	753949	781215	800412	821653	832750	804506	811446	823129	832661	852283
4. Institutions privées sans but lucratif au service des ménages	2643	2771	2808	2891	2933	2992	3066	3207	3321	3344	3358	3360	3468	3530	3621
5. Variations des stocks	4494	8842	13827	14768	17419	10882	8861	10361	6147	7004	−517	7960	8196	3530	17083
6. Formation brute de capital fixe	207825	214923	215985	220371	230058	245872	256720	266044	268273	263361	229628	230785	247134	248117	249535
7. **Demande intérieure totale**	1039760	1071060	1103453	1141705	1190873	1239021	1277258	1310187	1333372	1343134	1274723	1289884	1315713	1322142	1355110
8. Exportations de biens et services	184565	199190	206150	207708	216863	227704	245208	262664	262990	280762	308303	339908	380865	378403	402887
9. *Moins :* Importations de biens et services	150542	168884	177290	184948	207213	219759	239561	262192	270780	290824	265358	283525	310718	305527	341942
10. Divergence statistique	0	0	0	0	0	0	0	0	0	0	0	0	0	0	0
11. **Produit intérieur brut**	1073783	1101366	1132313	1164465	1200523	1246966	1282905	1310659	1325582	1333072	1317668	1346267	1385860	1395018	1416055

RÉPARTITION DU P.I.B.

	1983	1984	1985	1986	1987	1988	1989	1990	1991	1992	1993	1994	1995	1996	1997
1. Impôts indirects	62084	72097	77636	89071	101141	117823	132464	148938	170552	178864	198094	204154	221301	233504	248454
2. *Moins :* Subventions	22447	26649	26414	30715	30558	31560	34614	32952	37191	35177	42435	39500	34738	37756	37147
3. Consommation de capital fixe	78001	88642	100146	107975	116878	128224	140643	154886	168539	180407	192379	203505	219765	232605	239390
4. Rémunération des salariés payée par les producteurs résidents	300156	334994	374051	404065	438837	482553	528340	592391	647792	681573	688223	698174	726045	769780	806110
5. Excédent net d'exploitation	213816	253727	284662	327893	356465	392983	425128	447396	477879	496826	514035	572333	639881	674502	693873
6. Divergence statistique	..	..	..	..	..	..	..	..	..	..	..	..	..	..	..
7. **Produit intérieur brut**	631610	722811	810081	898289	982763	1090023	1191961	1310659	1427571	1502493	1550296	1638666	1772254	1872635	1950680

OPÉRATIONS EN CAPITAL DE LA NATION

Financement de la formation brute de capital

	1983	1984	1985	1986	1987	1988	1989	1990	1991	1992	1993	1994	1995	1996	1997
1. Consommation de capital fixe	78001	88642	100146	107975	116878	128224	140643	154886	168539	180407	192379	203505	219765	232605	239390
2. Épargne nette	63079	71614	74320	84324	88661	97384	97272	100234	95083	76512	85133	101576	144452	150076	159207
3. *Moins :* Solde des opérations courantes de la nation	1143	−5575	−8084	3147	−3188	−8998	−17466	−21285	−30068	−36194	15222	22573	41018	63243	56490
4. Divergence statistique	..	..	..	..	..	..	..	..	..	..	..	..	..	..	..
5. **Financement de la formation brute de capital**	139937	165831	182550	189152	208727	234606	255381	276405	293690	293113	262290	282508	323199	319438	342107

Formation brute de capital

	1983	1984	1985	1986	1987	1988	1989	1990	1991	1992	1993	1994	1995	1996	1997
6. Variations des stocks	5240	13004	14986	11643	15069	15410	14220	10361	11043	4910	−475	9695	16330	1897	17193
7. Formation brute de capital fixe	134697	152827	167564	177509	193658	219196	241161	266044	282647	288203	262765	272813	306869	317541	324914
8. Divergence statistique	..	..	..	..	..	..	..	..	..	..	..	..	..	..	..
9. **Formation brute de capital**	139937	165831	182550	189152	208727	234606	255381	276405	293690	293113	262290	282508	323199	319438	342107

RELATIONS ENTRE LES PRINCIPAUX AGRÉGATS

	1983	1984	1985	1986	1987	1988	1989	1990	1991	1992	1993	1994	1995	1996	1997
1. **Produit intérieur brut**	631610	722811	810081	898289	982763	1090023	1191961	1310659	1427571	1502493	1550296	1638666	1772254	1872635	1950680
2. *Plus :* Revenu net des facteurs reçu du reste du monde	−4058	−4775	−5447	−6582	−6633	−7557	−10436	−17938	−22174	−26267	−26466	−27342	−26221	−23386	−20809
3. Revenu des facteurs reçu du reste du monde	9254	11760	13292	12270	11967	14453	20049	23329	26502	34136	48057	46355	56057	62093	78244
4. Revenu des facteurs payé au reste du monde	13312	16535	18739	18852	18600	22010	30485	41267	48676	60403	74523	73697	82278	85479	99053
5. *Égal :* **Produit national brut**	627552	718036	804634	891707	976130	1082466	1181525	1292721	1405397	1476226	1523830	1611324	1746033	1849249	1929871
6. *Moins :* Consommation de capital fixe	78001	88642	100146	107975	116878	128224	140643	154886	168539	180407	192379	203505	219765	232605	239390
7. *Plus :* Divergence statistique	..	..	..	..	..	..	..	..	..	..	..	..	..	..	..
8. *Égal :* **Revenu national**	549551	629394	704488	783732	859252	954242	1040882	1137835	1236858	1295819	1331451	1407819	1526268	1616644	1690481
9. *Plus :* Transferts courants nets reçus du reste du monde	2061	2168	1183	−2602	−1518	−2629	−5125	−3819	−8436	−9795	−11473	−11298	−7669	−11255	−7118
10. Transferts courants reçus du reste du monde	9112	10763	11072	10737	12244	14004	15595	15025	16087	15770	19464	17259	18691	19311	24254
11. Transferts courants payés au reste du monde	7051	8595	9889	13339	13762	16633	20720	18844	24523	25565	30937	28557	26360	30566	31372
12. *Égal :* **Revenu national disponible**	551612	631562	705671	781130	857734	951613	1035757	1134016	1228422	1286024	1319978	1396521	1518599	1605389	1683363
13. *Moins :* Consommation finale	488533	559948	631351	696806	769073	854229	938485	1033782	1133339	1209512	1234845	1294945	1374147	1455313	1524156
14. *Plus :* Divergence statistique	..	..	..	..	..	..	..	..	..	..	..	..	..	..	..
15. *Égal :* **Épargne nette**	63079	71614	74320	84324	88661	97384	97272	100234	95083	76512	85133	101576	144452	150076	159207
16. *Moins :* Solde des opérations courantes de la nation	1143	−5575	−8084	3147	−3188	−8998	−17466	−21285	−30068	−36194	15222	22573	41018	63243	56490
17. *Plus :* Divergence statistique	..	..	..	..	..	..	..	..	..	..	..	..	..	..	..
18. *Égal :* **Formation nette de capital**	61936	77189	82404	81177	91849	106382	114738	121519	125151	112706	69911	79003	103434	86833	102717

1. Aux prix relatifs de 1990 pour la période 1970-1997 et aux prix relatifs de 1970 pour la période 1960-1969.

LUXEMBOURG[1]
1968 SNA

Main aggregates

millions of francs

	1960	1969	1970	1971	1972	1973	1974	1975	1976	1977	1978	1979	1980	1981	1982
EXPENDITURE ON THE G.D.P.															
At current prices															
1. Government final consumption expenditure	2381*	4841*	5405*	6138*	6945*	8098*	10034*	12110*	13748*	15228*	16413*	18249*	20741*	23065*	24401*
2. Private final consumption expenditure	17350*	30909*	34210*	37819*	41671*	46213*	53138*	61667*	69525*	75172*	80009*	86932*	96081*	106131*	117825*
3. Households	..	..	..	..	..	..	..	..	..	..	..	..	..	..	..
4. Private non-profit institutions serving households	..	..	..	..	..	..	..	..	..	..	..	..	..	..	..
5. Increase in stocks	−386*	−2223*	−867*	−2042*	−2553*	−3637*	−6483*	−7521*	−5936*	−8282*	−3673*	−7337*	−8107*	−7054*	−6808*
6. Gross fixed capital formation	5466*	10472*	12721*	15921*	17589*	20987*	23032*	24096*	24893*	25744*	27030*	29822*	36090*	36075*	39732*
7. **Total Domestic Expenditure**	24811*	43999*	51469*	57836*	63652*	71661*	79721*	90352*	102230*	107862*	119779*	127666*	144805*	158217*	175150*
8. Exports of goods and services	24651*	43187*	53306*	53831*	57080*	74767*	104721*	87399*	95831*	97062*	102430*	121007*	128210*	133768*	153985*
9. *Less:* Imports of goods and services	20842*	35503*	45109*	51192*	52496*	63670*	82510*	82715*	88851*	91835*	99989*	114785*	128334*	137251*	155732*
10. Statistical discrepancy	186*	203*	1068*	1370*	1506*	2000*	1395*	674*	914*	75*	1598*	886*	1992*	1607*	1800*
11. **Gross Domestic Product**	28806*	51886*	60734*	61845*	69742*	84758*	103327*	95710*	110124*	113164*	123818*	134774*	146673*	156341*	175203*
At 1990 price levels[2]															
1. Government final consumption expenditure	18612*	24976*	26001*	26774*	27887*	28846*	29928*	30917*	31783*	32711*	33298*	34041*	35091*	35582*	36109*
2. Private final consumption expenditure	68129*	98887*	104947*	110844*	116214*	122903*	128433*	135206*	139452*	142639*	146846*	152033*	156308*	159027*	159653*
3. Households	..	..	..	..	..	..	..	..	..	..	..	..	..	..	..
4. Private non-profit institutions serving households	..	..	..	..	..	..	..	..	..	..	..	..	..	..	..
5. Increase in stocks	1532*	−5629*	−2116*	−2827*	−4927*	−7578*	−9470*	−9956*	−7139*	−14742*	−5363*	−12802*	−12361*	−8213*	−6765*
6. Gross fixed capital formation	31950*	41712*	44836*	49612*	53094*	59374*	55233*	51128*	48969*	48930*	49450*	51314*	57831*	53543*	53291*
7. **Total Domestic Expenditure**	120223*	159946*	173668*	184403*	192268*	203545*	204124*	207295*	213065*	209538*	224231*	224586*	236869*	239939*	242288*
8. Exports of goods and services	80892*	131328*	143186*	148729*	156584*	178334*	197498*	166556*	168131*	175252*	180068*	197469*	194611*	185225*	184645*
9. *Less:* Imports of goods and services	80677*	123129*	146516*	158201*	162404*	180685*	191263*	174026*	176032*	175334*	187583*	199606*	207368*	201428*	200839*
10. Statistical discrepancy	2125*	2153*	2861*	2885*	3103*	4115*	3597*	71*	−202*	−1276*	−53*	−704*	−503*	−1359*	−1200*
11. **Gross Domestic Product**	122563*	170298*	173199*	177816*	189551*	205309*	213956*	199896*	204962*	208180*	216663*	221745*	223609*	222377*	224894*
COST COMPONENTS OF THE G.D.P.															
1. Indirect taxes	2723*	4628*	5581*	6299*	7632*	9213*	10320*	11721*	13199*	14215*	16177*	16857*	19617*	21182*	24870*
2. *Less:* Subsidies	332*	791*	759*	812*	1041*	1372*	1897*	2694*	3668*	4578*	4830*	5207*	5447*	7285*	8279*
3. Consumption of fixed capital	4952*	10637*	11703*	12761*	13208*	16717*	18101*	18404*	18197*	17942*	19063*	21733*	23696*	25244*	27005*
4. Compensation of employees paid by resident producers	11567*	22240*	26385*	29599*	33703*	38628*	49332*	56586*	63084*	69603*	73477*	79438*	87813*	96436*	103137*
5. Operating surplus	10796*	17024*	19749*	15688*	17788*	23926*	29691*	12398*	19844*	15689*	19755*	22143*	20837*	20280*	28181*
6. Statistical discrepancy	−902*	−1852*	−1926*	−1690*	−1547*	−2355*	−2221*	−706*	−531*	292*	175*	−190*	156*	482*	290*
7. **Gross Domestic Product**	28804*	51886*	60733*	61845*	69743*	84757*	103326*	95709*	110125*	113163*	123817*	134774*	146672*	156339*	175204*
CAPITAL TRANSACTIONS OF THE NATION															
Finance of Gross Capital Formation															
1. Consumption of fixed capital	4952*	10637*	11703*	12761*	13208*	16717*	18101*	18404*	18197*	17942*	19063*	21733*	23696*	25244*	27005*
2. Net saving	4674*	7225*	11521*	9119*	12258*	17225*	25188*	17264*	24812*	24105*	28894*	30134*	33184*	37194*	58884*
3. *Less:* Surplus of the nation on current transactions	3067*	6176*	7995*	3482*	6260*	11880*	23286*	13860*	20185*	20849*	20726*	24888*	23638*	28299*	51262*
4. Statistical discrepancy	−1479*	−3437*	−3375*	−4519*	−4170*	−4712*	−3454*	−5233*	−3867*	−3736*	−3874*	−4494*	−5259*	−5118*	−1703*
5. **Finance of Gross Capital Formation**	5080*	8249*	11854*	13879*	15036*	17350*	16549*	16575*	18957*	17462*	23357*	22485*	27983*	29021*	32924*
Gross capital formation															
6. Increase in stocks	−386*	−2223*	−867*	−2042*	−2553*	−3637*	−6483*	−7521*	−5936*	−8282*	−3673*	−7337*	−8107*	−7054*	−6808*
7. Gross fixed capital formation	5466*	10472*	12721*	15921*	17589*	20987*	23032*	24096*	24893*	25744*	27030*	29822*	36090*	36075*	39732*
8. Statistical discrepancy	..	..	..	..	..	..	..	..	..	..	..	..	..	..	..
9. **Gross Capital Formation**	5080*	8249*	11854*	13879*	15036*	17350*	16549*	16575*	18957*	17462*	23357*	22485*	27983*	29021*	32924*
RELATIONS AMONG NATIONAL ACCOUNTING AGGREGATES															
1. **Gross Domestic Product**	28805*	51886*	60733*	61845*	69742*	84757*	103326*	95711*	110124*	113164*	123817*	134774*	146673*	156341*	175203*
2. *Plus:* Net factor income from the rest of the world	89*	364*	1731*	1996*	3084*	3145*	5128*	10710*	15043*	17550*	19219*	20926*	25270*	33018*	54282*
3. Factor income from the rest of the world	1066*	6729*	12744*	17475*	21972*	39881*	77961*	80335*	87335*	102086*	127944*	208904*	342925*	555294*	588504*
4. Factor income paid to the rest of the world	983*	6428*	11010*	15519*	18871*	36992*	73453*	69629*	71901*	84083*	108481*	188799*	320062*	527094*	537078*
5. *Equals:* **Gross National Product**	28894*	52250*	62464*	63841*	72826*	87902*	108454*	106421*	125167*	130714*	143036*	155700*	171943*	189359*	229485*
6. *Less:* Consumption of fixed capital	4952*	10637*	11703*	12761*	13208*	16717*	18101*	18404*	18197*	17942*	19063*	21733*	23696*	25244*	27005*
7. *Plus:* Statistical discrepancy	660*	2003*	1008*	2601*	1880*	963*	−1258*	3904*	2119*	3166*	2174*	2989*	3635*	4617*	1519*
8. *Equals:* **National Income**	24602*	43616*	51769*	53681*	61498*	72148*	89095*	91921*	109089*	115938*	126147*	136956*	151882*	168732*	203999*
9. *Plus:* Net current transfers from the rest of the world	−197*	−641*	−633*	−605*	−624*	−612*	−735*	−880*	−1004*	−1433*	−831*	−1641*	−1876*	−2342*	−2889*
10. Current transfers from the rest of the world	..	..	..	..	..	..	..	..	..	..	..	..	..	..	..
11. Current transfers paid to the rest of the world	..	..	..	..	..	..	..	..	..	..	..	..	..	..	..
12. *Equals:* **National Disposable Income**	24405*	42975*	51136*	53076*	60874*	71536*	88360*	91041*	108085*	114505*	125316*	135315*	150006*	166390*	201110*
13. *Less:* Final consumption	19731*	35750*	39615*	43957*	48616*	54311*	63172*	73777*	83273*	90400*	96422*	105181*	116822*	129196*	142226*
14. *Plus:* Statistical discrepancy	..	..	..	..	..	..	..	..	..	..	..	..	..	..	..
15. *Equals:* **Net Saving**	4674*	7225*	11521*	9119*	12258*	17225*	25188*	17264*	24812*	24105*	28894*	30134*	33184*	37194*	58884*
16. *Less:* Surplus of the nation on current transactions	3067*	6176*	7995*	3482*	6297*	11880*	23286*	13860*	20185*	20849*	20726*	24888*	23638*	28299*	51262*
17. *Plus:* Statistical discrepancy	−1479*	−3437*	−3375*	−4519*	−4133*	−4712*	−3454*	−5233*	−3867*	−3736*	−3874*	−4494*	−5259*	−5118*	−1703*
18. *Equals:* **Net Capital Formation**	128*	−2388*	151*	1118*	1828*	633*	−1552*	−1829*	760*	−480*	4294*	752*	4287*	3777*	5919*

1. In the National Accounts published by the Service Central de la Statistique et des Études Économiques of Luxembourg imputed bank services provided to non-residents are not deducted in calculating GDP. For this reason
estimates of GDP published by the Luxembourg authorities are somewhat higher than those shown here, particularly for recent years.
2. At 1985 relative prices for 1970-1997 and at 1975 relative prices for 1960-1969.

Principaux Agrégats

millions de francs

1983	1984	1985	1986	1987	1988	1989	1990	1991	1992	1993	1994	1995	1996	1997	
															DÉPENSES IMPUTÉES AU P.I.B.
															Aux prix courants
25766*	27823*	30207	32205	35654	37487	40903	46354	49499	53189	57498	60929	67151	71302	74795	1. Consommation finale des administrations publiques
128190*	138553*	148300	157489	167171	179704	195541	214558	234461	240210	254368	266582	278709	288670	299339	2. Consommation finale privée
..	..	146592	155569	164987	177213	192528	211177	230476	235850	249311	261394	272177	281716	..	3. Ménages
..	..	1708	1920	2184	2491	3013	3381	3985	4360	5057	5188	6532	6954	..	4. Institutions privées sans but lucratif au service des ménages
−1658*	1093*	−1578	−2710	−6964	−7753	−164	−3669	−1264	−1958	−8282	4513	8040	2518	1582	5. Variations des stocks
37151*	38879*	36320	49236	58076	69395	75628	83244	96578	92368	105202	99620	107962	109100	126544	6. Formation brute de capital fixe
189449*	206348*	213249	236220	253937	279333	311908	340487	379274	383809	408786	431644	461862	471590	502260	7. **Demande intérieure totale**
171750*	213316*	242879	247217	249873	285531	326649	338444	360433	383659	413300	457242	467591	478877	513929	8. Exportations de biens et services
170205*	208267*	229650	232688	244828	276954	311327	333193	367279	361780	377793	401215	419714	425077	452393	9. *Moins* : Importations de biens et services
1750*	2292*	−1	..	..	..	..	..	..	..	..	..	..	..	..	10. Divergence statistique
192744*	213689*	226477	250749	258982	287910	327230	345738	372428	405688	444293	487671	509739	525390	563796	11. **Produit intérieur brut**
															Aux niveaux de prix de 1990[2]
36793*	37594*	38334*	39369*	41218*	43250*	44945*	46354*	48151*	48878*	50673*	51685*	52843*	54581*	56713*	1. Consommation finale des administrations publiques
160439*	162759*	167086*	176594*	184696*	193184*	203001*	214558*	228108*	226004*	229802*	235391*	240950*	245525*	252397*	2. Consommation finale privée
..	..	..	..	..	..	..	..	..	..	..	..	..	..	..	3. Ménages
..	..	..	..	..	..	..	..	..	..	..	..	..	..	..	4. Institutions privées sans but lucratif au service des ménages
−2781*	−351*	471*	−1681*	−7058*	−8150*	1257*	−3669*	−15525*	−9860*	−7937*	2416*	4490*	7617*	7465*	5. Variations des stocks
47022*	47079*	42599*	55819*	65836*	75719*	81045*	83244*	109508*	99674*	127975*	108925*	112761*	110849*	119716*	6. Formation brute de capital fixe
241473*	247081*	248490*	270101*	284692*	304003*	330248*	340487*	370242*	364696*	400513*	398417*	411044*	418572*	436291*	7. **Demande intérieure totale**
194411*	229462*	251334*	259693*	271144*	302961*	327378*	338444*	360954*	378219*	388699*	405693*	423466*	433204*	453134*	8. Exportations de biens et services
203348*	231632*	247739*	257132*	276300*	298982*	318815*	333193*	363186*	360351*	370497*	369968*	384062*	387903*	408076*	9. *Moins* : Importations de biens et services
−922*	1036*	1038*	79*	−437*	117*	−374*	0*	−1016*	804*	−1941*	131*	279*	556*	259*	10. Divergence statistique
231614*	245947*	253123*	272741*	279099*	308099*	338437*	345738*	366994*	383368*	416774*	434273*	450727*	464429*	481608*	11. **Produit intérieur brut**
															RÉPARTITION DU P.I.B.
31071*	33655*	36253	38662	40227	44303	50761	55240	60333	66336	75711	82914	86225	92010	98740*	1. Impôts indirects
10542*	9831*	7892	8474	9090	9246	9242	10956	12221	12552	13293	14505	10989	12403	13310*	2. *Moins* : Subventions
30035*	33652*	35691	37216	38985	41172	45283	49086	53815	58623	61661	64384	67634	69710	74810*	3. Consommation de capital fixe
110056*	118838*	126169	137453	147646	158056	177266	195928	218176	236213	252959	270615	284310	297535	319280*	4. Rémunération des salariés payée par les producteurs résidents
31939*	37647*	36255	45893	41213	53625	63162	56440	52325	57068	67255	84263	82559	78538	84280*	5. Excédent net d'exploitation
184*	−273*	..	..	..	..	..	..	..	..	..	..	..	..	..	6. Divergence statistique
192743*	213688*	226476	250750	258981	287910	327230	345738	372428	405688	444293	487671	509739	525390	563800	7. **Produit intérieur brut**
															OPÉRATIONS EN CAPITAL DE LA NATION
															Financement de la formation brute de capital
30035*	33652*	35691	37216	38985	41172	45283	49086	53815	58623	61661	64384	67634	69710	74810*	1. Consommation de capital fixe
70777*	78290*	83392	93538	81862	94808	117270	125867	135259	137472	124703	128464	126654	127418	148890*	2. Épargne nette
64672*	71008*	84341	84228	69735	73838	87089	95378	93760	105685	89444	88715	78286	85510	95570*	3. *Moins* : Solde des opérations courantes de la nation
−647*	−962*	..	..	..	..	..	..	..	..	..	..	..	..	..	4. Divergence statistique
35493*	39972*	34742	46526	51112	62142	75464	79575	95314	90410	96920	104133	116002	111618	128130	5. **Financement de la formation brute de capital**
															Formation brute de capital
−1658*	1093*	−1578	−2710	−6964	−7753	−164	−3669	−1264	−1958	−8282	4513	8040	2518	1582	6. Variations des stocks
37151*	38879*	36320	49236	58076	69895	75628	83244	96578	92368	105202	99620	107962	109100	126544	7. Formation brute de capital fixe
..	..	..	..	..	..	..	..	..	..	..	..	..	..	..	8. Divergence statistique
35493*	39972*	34742	46526	51112	62142	75464	79575	95314	90410	96920	104133	116002	111618	128126	9. **Formation brute de capital**
															RELATIONS ENTRE LES PRINCIPAUX AGRÉGATS
192744*	213690*	226477	250749	258981	287910	327230	345738	372428	405688	444293	487671	509739	525390	563800	1. **Produit intérieur brut**
65150*	69236*	75388	75057	70876	72345	77239	96009	109495	91504	60698	41749	38092	38800	41640*	2. *Plus* : Revenu net des facteurs reçu du reste du monde
491537*	561392*	563217	511363	524179	594479	878596	1073126	1126487	1210417	1167863	1040070	1203488	1020042	..	3. Revenu des facteurs reçu du reste du monde
426463*	492845*	487829	436306	453303	522134	801357	977117	1016992	1118913	1107165	998321	1165396	981242	..	4. Revenu des facteurs payé au reste du monde
257894*	282926*	301865	325806	329857	360255	404469	441747	481923	497192	504991	529420	547831	564190	605440*	5. *Égal* : **Produit national brut**
30035*	33652*	35691	37216	38985	41172	45283	49086	53815	58623	61661	64384	67634	69710	74810*	6. *Moins* : Consommation de capital fixe
422*	−319*	..	..	..	..	..	..	..	..	..	..	..	..	..	7. *Plus* : Divergence statistique
228281*	248955*	266174	288590	290872	319083	359186	392661	428108	438569	443330	465036	480197	494480	530630*	8. *Égal* : **Revenu national**
−3548*	−4289*	−4275	−5358	−6185	−7084	−5472	−5882	−8889	−7698	−6761	−9061	−7683	−7089	−7610*	9. *Plus* : Transferts courants nets reçus du reste du monde
..	..	..	..	..	..	..	..	..	..	..	..	..	..	..	10. Transferts courants reçus du reste du monde
..	..	..	..	..	..	..	..	..	..	..	..	..	..	..	11. Transferts courants payés au reste du monde
224733*	244666*	261899	283232	284687	311999	353714	386779	419219	430871	436569	455975	472514	487390	523020*	12. *Égal* : **Revenu national disponible**
153956*	166376*	178507	189694	202825	217191	236444	260912	283960	293399	311866	327511	345860	359972	374130	13. *Moins* : Consommation finale
..	..	..	..	..	..	..	..	..	..	..	..	..	..	..	14. *Plus* : Divergence statistique
70777*	78290*	83392	93538	81862	94808	117270	125867	135259	137472	124703	128464	126654	127418	148890*	15. *Égal* : **Épargne nette**
64672*	71008*	84341	84228	69735	73838	87089	95378	93760	105685	89444	88715	78286	85510	95570*	16. *Moins* : Solde des opérations courantes de la nation
−647*	−962*	..	..	..	..	..	..	..	..	..	..	..	..	..	17. *Plus* : Divergence statistique
5458*	6320*	−949	9310	12127	20970	30181	30489	41499	31787	35259	39749	48368	41908	53320*	18. *Égal* : **Formation nette de capital**

1. Dans les Comptes Nationaux publiés par le Service Central de la Statistique et des Études Économiques du Luxembourg les services bancaires imputés fournis aux non-résidents ne sont pas déduits du PIB. Pour cette raison, le PIB publié par les autorités Luxembourgeoises est sensiblement plus élevé que celui montré ici, surtout pour les années récentes.
2. Aux prix relatifs de 1985 pour la période 1970-1997 et aux prix relatifs de 1975 pour la période 1960-1969.

NETHERLANDS
1968 SNA

Main aggregates

millions of guilders

	1960	1969	1970	1971	1972	1973	1974	1975	1976	1977	1978	1979	1980	1981	1982
EXPENDITURE ON THE G.D.P.															
At current prices															
1. Government final consumption expenditure	5502*	15908*	18301*	21430*	23960*	26893*	31826*	37515*	42634*	46930	51610	56310	59390	61880	64640
2. Private final consumption expenditure	26416*	64268*	72040*	80300*	89973*	101549*	115343*	131171*	150539*	167140	182140	195410	207900	214570	224360
3. Households	..	..	..	..	..	..	..	..	..	..	..	..	..	..	..
4. Private non-profit institutions serving households	..	..	..	..	..	..	..	..	..	..	..	..	..	..	..
5. Increase in stocks	1386*	2378*	2544*	1568*	759*	2576*	4797*	−975*	3074*	1600	1270	1230	2900	−1020	−1760
6. Gross fixed capital formation	11133*	27553*	32557*	35962*	37790*	42212*	45524*	48088*	50839*	60100	65530	68570	73050	70040	69500
7. **Total Domestic Expenditure**	44437*	110107*	125442*	139260*	152482*	173230*	197490*	215799*	247086*	275770	300550	321520	343240	345470	356740
8. Exports of goods and services	20852*	45187*	53457*	61057*	68322*	82115*	106106*	108016*	126475*	128710	131840	153240	174600	202680	208380
9. *Less:* Imports of goods and services	20099*	45492*	55617*	61553*	64235*	76667*	100873*	100902*	118245*	125610	131810	154820	176160	189950	192060
10. Statistical discrepancy	−133*	−266*	−365*	−278*	−99*	−115*	−81*	199*	223*	..	..	..	..	..	..
11. **Gross Domestic Product**	45057*	109536*	122917*	138486*	156470*	178563*	202642*	223112*	255539*	278870	300580	319940	341680	358200	373060
At 1990 price levels[1]															
1. Government final consumption expenditure	34173*	43690*	46328*	48355*	48736*	49127*	50211*	52267*	54414*	56260	58410	60450	61300	63000	64440
2. Private final consumption expenditure	102161*	173887*	186743*	192909*	199664*	207646*	215334*	222434*	234229*	245000	255690	261600	260610	252890	251720
3. Households	..	..	..	..	..	..	..	..	..	..	..	..	..	..	..
4. Private non-profit institutions serving households	..	..	..	..	..	..	..	..	..	..	..	..	..	..	..
5. Increase in stocks	4474*	6910*	7105*	5410*	3972*	6783*	9325*	1299*	7825*	5420	5110	4730	6120	1810	1000
6. Gross fixed capital formation	45906*	81318*	87447*	88779*	86744*	90374*	86756*	82976*	81167*	89080	91210	89830	89640	80750	77370
7. **Total Domestic Expenditure**	186714*	305805*	327623*	335453*	339116*	353930*	361626*	358976*	377635*	395760	410420	416610	417670	398450	394530
8. Exports of goods and services	49188*	98696*	110403*	122161*	134321*	150575*	154474*	149628*	164411*	161500	166870	179270	183160	186580	184960
9. *Less:* Imports of goods and services	47584*	105930*	121482*	128912*	135084*	149946*	148677*	142637*	157072*	161610	171790	181880	182440	171600	170840
10. Statistical discrepancy	2176*	−3260*	−4416*	−3397*	−2280*	−2730*	−1640*	−519*	−817*	−2590	−3170	−2710	−2140	710	670
11. **Gross Domestic Product**	190494*	295311*	312128*	325305*	336073*	351829*	365783*	365448*	384157*	393060	402330	411290	416250	414140	409320
COST COMPONENTS OF THE G.D.P.															
1. Indirect taxes	4596*	11695*	14138*	16186*	18723*	21000*	22330*	25096*	29992*	34930	37490	39940	41210	41570	43790
2. *Less:* Subsidies	947*	1821*	2378*	2065*	2599*	3689*	4084*	4559*	7054*	7970	9040	10010	10380	10120	11480
3. Consumption of fixed capital	4575*	10027*	11547*	13347*	14912*	16577*	19425*	22520*	25254*	27280	29890	32870	36310	40130	43010
4. Compensation of employees paid by resident producers	20980*	59892*	68429*	78525*	87897*	101823*	118378*	133628*	148624*	162530	175910	189150	201070	205080	211190
5. Operating surplus	15892*	29508*	31040*	32583*	37557*	42743*	46618*	46821*	58639*	62100	66330	67990	73470	81540	86550
6. Statistical discrepancy	−37*	237*	141*	−89*	−19*	109*	−24*	−393*	84*	..	..	..	..	..	..
7. **Gross Domestic Product**	45059*	109538*	122917*	138487*	156471*	178563*	202643*	223113*	255539*	278870	300580	319940	341680	358200	373060
CAPITAL TRANSACTIONS OF THE NATION															
Finance of Gross Capital Formation															
1. Consumption of fixed capital	4575*	10027*	11547*	13347*	14912*	16577*	19425*	22520*	25254*	27280	29890	32870	36310	40130	43010
2. Net saving	9169*	19899*	21546*	23518*	27817*	34641*	36909*	30430*	36386*	36810	34660	33310	35200	36910	36970
3. *Less:* Surplus of the nation on current transactions	1373*	290*	−1899*	−491*	4836*	7505*	6947*	6131*	8276*	2390	−2250	−3620	−4440	8020	12240
4. Statistical discrepancy	148*	295*	109*	174*	656*	1075*	934*	294*	549*	..	..	..	..	..	..
5. **Finance of Gross Capital Formation**	12519*	29931*	35101*	37530*	38549*	44788*	50321*	47113*	53913*	61700	66800	69800	75950	69020	67740
Gross capital formation															
6. Increase in stocks	1386*	2378*	2544*	1568*	759*	2576*	4797*	−975*	3074*	1600	1270	1230	2900	−1020	−1760
7. Gross fixed capital formation	11133*	27553*	32557*	35962*	37790*	42212*	45524*	48088*	50839*	60100	65530	68570	73050	70040	69500
8. Statistical discrepancy	..	..	..	..	..	..	..	..	..	..	..	..	..	..	..
9. **Gross Capital Formation**	12519*	29931*	35101*	37530*	38549*	44788*	50321*	47113*	53913*	61700	66800	69800	75950	69020	67740
RELATIONS AMONG NATIONAL ACCOUNTING AGGREGATES															
1. **Gross Domestic Product**	45058*	109538*	122917*	138487*	156471*	178563*	202643*	223112*	255540*	278870	300580	319940	341680	358200	373060
2. *Plus:* Net factor income from the rest of the world	147*	242*	171*	119*	214*	398*	511*	−6*	37*	150	−1020	−1140	−1340	−1870	−1150
3. Factor income from the rest of the world	1547*	3865*	4846*	5470*	5542*	7382*	10204*	9171*	9601*	10470	11560	16340	22970	30620	31250
4. Factor income paid to the rest of the world	1099*	3165*	4424*	5250*	4996*	6266*	8796*	9516*	9812*	10320	12580	17480	24310	32490	32400
5. *Equals:* **Gross National Product**	45205*	109780*	123088*	138606*	156685*	178961*	203154*	223106*	255577*	279020	299560	318800	340340	356330	371910
6. *Less:* Consumption of fixed capital	4575*	10027*	11547*	13347*	14912*	16577*	19425*	22520*	25254*	27280	29890	32870	36310	40130	43010
7. *Plus:* Statistical discrepancy	471*	470*	422*	203*	293*	816*	817*	−518*	−128*	..	..	..	..	..	..
8. *Equals:* **National Income**	41101*	100223*	111963*	125462*	142066*	163200*	184546*	200068*	230195*	251740	269670	285930	304030	316200	328900
9. *Plus:* Net current transfers from the rest of the world	−14*	−148*	−76*	−214*	−316*	−117*	−468*	−952*	−636*	−860	−1260	−900	−1540	−2840	−2930
10. Current transfers from the rest of the world	..	..	..	..	..	..	..	..	..	5440	6010	6830	6650	6080	6360
11. Current transfers paid to the rest of the world	..	..	..	..	..	..	..	..	..	6300	7270	7730	8190	8920	9290
12. *Equals:* **National Disposable Income**	41087*	100075*	111887*	125248*	141750*	163083*	184078*	199116*	229559*	250880	268410	285030	302490	313360	325970
13. *Less:* Final consumption	31918*	80176*	90341*	101730*	113933*	128442*	147169*	168686*	193173*	214070	233750	251720	267290	276450	289000
14. *Plus:* Statistical discrepancy	..	..	..	..	..	..	..	..	..	..	..	..	..	..	..
15. *Equals:* **Net Saving**	9169*	19899*	21546*	23518*	27817*	34641*	36909*	30430*	36386*	36810	34660	33310	35200	36910	36970
16. *Less:* Surplus of the nation on current transactions	1373*	290*	−1899*	−491*	4836*	7505*	6947*	6131*	8276*	2390	−2250	−3620	−4440	8020	12240
17. *Plus:* Statistical discrepancy	148*	295*	109*	174*	656*	1075*	934*	294*	549*	..	..	..	..	..	..
18. *Equals:* **Net Capital Formation**	7944*	19904*	23554*	24183*	23637*	28211*	30896*	24593*	28659*	34420	36910	36930	39640	28890	24730

1. At 1995 relative prices for 1990-1997, at 1990 relative prices for 1985-1989, at 1985 relative prices for 1980-1984, at 1980 relative prices for 1969-1979 and at 1975 relative prices for 1960-1968.

Principaux Agrégats

millions de florins

DÉPENSES IMPUTÉES AU P.I.B.

Aux prix courants

1983	1984	1985	1986	1987	1988	1989	1990	1991	1992	1993	1994	1995	1996	1997	
66270	65870	67070	67940	70040	70470	72040	75080	78600	83010	86210	88030	91800	93850	96910	1. Consommation finale des administrations publiques
232990	240330	252910	260230	267940	271640	284490	303100	322460	340920	351720	369450	382200	398690	419030	2. Consommation finale privée
..	..	..	..	..	..	..	..	..	..	..	..	..	..	..	3. Ménages
790	970	1440	3830	-420	310	5430	6520	5350	3140	-3770	2310	980	1160	1460	4. Institutions privées sans but lucratif au service des ménages
72210	77290	83690	89350	91580	97390	104080	107940	110460	113320	111620	115210	121950	130610	141880	5. Variations des stocks
372260	**384460**	**405110**	**421350**	**429140**	**439810**	**466040**	**492640**	**516870**	**540390**	**545780**	**575000**	**596930**	**624310**	**659280**	6. Formation brute de capital fixe
214680	242690	258730	221950	219260	240250	267670	279740	293090	294880	293180	314440	339570	360580	396720	7. **Demande intérieure totale**
199590	221450	238300	205440	207560	222380	248760	255830	267390	269170	257500	275170	296850	315540	347010	8. Exportations de biens et services
..	..	..	..	..	..	..	..	..	..	..	..	..	..	..	9. *Moins :* Importations de biens et services
387350	**405700**	**425540**	**437860**	**440840**	**457680**	**484950**	**516550**	**542570**	**566100**	**581460**	**614270**	**639650**	**669350**	**708990**	10. Divergence statistique
															11. **Produit intérieur brut**

Aux niveaux de prix de 1990[1]

1983	1984	1985	1986	1987	1988	1989	1990	1991	1992	1993	1994	1995	1996	1997	
65900	65900	67470	69890	71730	72750	73870	75080	76236	77513	78668	79111	79754	80736	81917	1. Consommation finale des administrations publiques
254110	257140	264380	271250	278670	281020	290820	303100	312495	320390	323604	330730	337494	346563	357018	2. Consommation finale privée
..	..	..	..	..	..	..	..	..	..	..	..	..	..	..	3. Ménages
..	..	..	..	..	..	..	..	..	..	..	..	..	..	..	4. Institutions privées sans but lucratif au service des ménages
3090	2690	3130	3860	-200	50	5290	6520	4892	2883	-4185	1356	1065	1008	1158	5. Variations des stocks
79330	83910	89810	95990	96850	101230	106230	107940	108154	108823	105793	108126	113330	119426	127521	6. Formation brute de capital fixe
402430	**409640**	**424790**	**440990**	**447050**	**455050**	**476210**	**492640**	**501776**	**509608**	**503881**	**519323**	**531643**	**547733**	**567614**	7. **Demande intérieure totale**
190820	205220	215680	219620	228500	249010	265570	279740	292879	301294	305896	326312	348030	366161	390769	8. Exportations de biens et services
177580	186390	198200	205220	213760	230010	245520	255830	266374	271868	266179	284078	305373	321431	344104	9. *Moins :* Importations de biens et services
650	1540	980	70	110	-70	-100	0	-1	-53	-512	-969	-1068	-1334	-1616	10. Divergence statistique
416320	**430010**	**443250**	**455460**	**461900**	**473980**	**496160**	**516550**	**528281**	**538981**	**543086**	**560588**	**573233**	**591129**	**612664**	11. **Produit intérieur brut**

RÉPARTITION DU P.I.B.

1983	1984	1985	1986	1987	1988	1989	1990	1991	1992	1993	1994	1995	1996	1997	
45800	49300	51620	55340	58620	60560	60370	63720	67370	72040	74980	78830	81970	88240	95390	1. Impôts indirects
12870	14290	15190	15830	19190	18350	16740	15730	17710	18050	17420	16050	12410	12400	15340	2. *Moins :* Subventions
44770	46630	48470	49650	51080	53580	56900	59720	62830	65910	68610	70980	73610	76880	80400	3. Consommation de capital fixe
213380	214300	221710	231570	239360	245740	252850	267740	283870	300240	308770	314790	325270	337400	354170	4. Rémunération des salariés payée par les producteurs résidents
96270	109760	118930	117130	110970	116650	131570	141100	146210	145960	146520	165720	170940	179230	194370	5. Excédent net d'exploitation
..	..	..	..	..	..	..	..	..	..	..	..	..	..	..	6. Divergence statistique
387350	**405700**	**425540**	**437860**	**440840**	**457680**	**484950**	**516550**	**542570**	**566100**	**581460**	**614270**	**639650**	**669350**	**708990**	7. **Produit intérieur brut**

OPÉRATIONS EN CAPITAL DE LA NATION

Financement de la formation brute de capital

1983	1984	1985	1986	1987	1988	1989	1990	1991	1992	1993	1994	1995	1996	1997	
44770	46630	48470	49650	51080	53580	56900	59720	62830	65910	68610	70980	73610	76880	80400	1. Consommation de capital fixe
40740	48890	54800	56920	48640	56980	69520	74490	71690	68320	67540	79840	84680	96180	111960	2. Épargne nette
12510	17260	18140	13390	8560	12860	16910	19750	18710	17770	28300	33300	35360	41290	49020	3. *Moins :* Solde des opérations courantes de la nation
..	..	..	..	..	..	..	..	..	..	..	..	..	..	..	4. Divergence statistique
73000	**78260**	**85130**	**93180**	**91160**	**97700**	**109510**	**114460**	**115810**	**116460**	**107850**	**117520**	**122930**	**131770**	**143340**	5. **Financement de la formation brute de capital**

Formation brute de capital

1983	1984	1985	1986	1987	1988	1989	1990	1991	1992	1993	1994	1995	1996	1997	
790	970	1440	3830	-420	310	5430	6520	5350	3140	-3770	2310	980	1160	1460	6. Variations des stocks
72210	77290	83690	89350	91580	97390	104080	107940	110460	113320	111620	115210	121950	130610	141880	7. Formation brute de capital fixe
..	..	..	..	..	..	..	..	..	..	..	..	..	..	..	8. Divergence statistique
73000	**78260**	**85130**	**93180**	**91160**	**97700**	**109510**	**114460**	**115810**	**116460**	**107850**	**117520**	**122930**	**131770**	**143340**	9. **Formation brute de capital**

RELATIONS ENTRE LES PRINCIPAUX AGRÉGATS

1983	1984	1985	1986	1987	1988	1989	1990	1991	1992	1993	1994	1995	1996	1997	
387350	405700	425540	437860	440840	457680	484950	516550	542570	566100	581460	614270	639650	669350	708990	1. **Produit intérieur brut**
-380	-1620	-40	-680	-1150	-3500	-200	-910	-940	-2250	-600	1740	910	5240	8170	2. *Plus :* Revenu net des facteurs reçu du reste du monde
26220	30150	32120	29260	30880	33230	48290	50310	52110	53060	52350	50780	52400	59330	..	3. Revenu des facteurs reçu du reste du monde
26600	31770	32160	29940	32030	36730	48490	51220	53050	55310	52950	49040	51840	54220	..	4. Revenu des facteurs payé au reste du monde
386970	**404080**	**425500**	**437180**	**439690**	**454180**	**484750**	**515640**	**541630**	**563850**	**580860**	**616010**	**640560**	**674590**	**717160**	5. *Égal :* **Produit national brut**
44770	46630	48470	49650	51080	53580	56900	59720	62830	65910	68610	70980	73610	76880	80400	6. *Moins :* Consommation de capital fixe
..	..	..	..	..	..	..	..	..	..	..	..	..	..	..	7. *Plus :* Divergence statistique
342200	**357450**	**377030**	**387530**	**388610**	**400600**	**427850**	**455920**	**478800**	**497940**	**512250**	**545030**	**566950**	**597710**	**636760**	8. *Égal :* **Revenu national**
-2200	-2360	-2250	-2440	-1990	-1510	-1800	-3250	-6050	-5690	-6780	-7710	-8270	-8990	-8860	9. *Plus :* Transferts courants nets reçus du reste du monde
7070	7970	8520	9090	10010	11070	11750	10910	10300	10390	10390	9980	9240	9880	..	10. Transferts courants reçus du reste du monde
9270	10330	10770	11530	12000	12580	13550	14160	16350	16080	17170	17690	17440	18330	..	11. Transferts courants payés au reste du monde
340000	**355090**	**374780**	**385090**	**386620**	**399090**	**426050**	**452670**	**472750**	**492250**	**505470**	**537320**	**558680**	**588720**	**627900**	12. *Égal :* **Revenu national disponible**
299260	306200	319980	328170	337980	342110	356530	378180	401060	423930	437930	457480	474000	492540	515940	13. *Moins :* Consommation finale
..	..	..	..	..	..	..	..	..	..	..	..	..	..	..	14. *Plus :* Divergence statistique
40740	**48890**	**54800**	**56920**	**48640**	**56980**	**69520**	**74490**	**71690**	**68320**	**67540**	**79840**	**84680**	**96180**	**111960**	15. *Égal :* **Épargne nette**
12510	17260	18140	13390	8560	12860	16910	19750	18710	17770	28300	33300	35360	41290	49020	16. *Moins :* Solde des opérations courantes de la nation
..	..	..	..	..	..	..	..	..	..	..	..	..	..	..	17. *Plus :* Divergence statistique
28230	**31630**	**36660**	**43530**	**40080**	**44120**	**52610**	**54740**	**52980**	**50550**	**39240**	**46540**	**49320**	**54890**	**62940**	18. *Égal :* **Formation nette de capital**

1. Aux prix relatifs de 1995 pour la période 1990-1997, aux prix relatifs de 1990 pour la période 1985-1989, aux prix relatifs de 1985 pour la période 1980-1984, aux prix relatifs de 1980 pour la période 1969-1979 et aux prix relatifs de 1975 pour la période 1960-1968.

NORWAY
1993 SNA

Main aggregates

millions of kroner

	1960	1969	1970	1971	1972	1973	1974	1975	1976	1977	1978	1979	1980	1981	1982
EXPENDITURE ON THE G.D.P.															
At current prices															
1. Government final consumption expenditure	4618*	12687*	14707*	17365*	19411*	22161*	25821*	31193*	37044*	41977*	47322	50818	58651	67978	76328
2. Private final consumption expenditure	21192*	42486*	46634*	51896*	56939*	63144*	71615*	84083*	96943*	112574*	119892	131481	146664	165794	186189
3. Households	..	..	..	..	..	..	..	..	..	..	113611	124551	138913	157007	176154
4. Private non-profit institutions serving households	..	..	..	..	..	..	..	..	..	..	6281	6930	7751	8787	10035
5. Increase in stocks	881*	1163*	4878*	3536*	1506*	3044*	6989*	4774*	5237*	2344*	−4080	−3768	4160	14	3819
6. Gross fixed capital formation	10548*	18584*	23353*	29144*	30082*	36087*	43638*	55963*	68315*	78312*	74601	78910	84411	96620	107619
7. **Total Domestic Expenditure**	37239*	74920*	89572*	101941*	107938*	124436*	148063*	176013*	207539*	235207*	237735	257441	293886	330406	373955
8. Exports of goods and services	13673*	29414*	33456*	35865*	40118*	48807*	60111*	62287*	70284*	76385*	87359	105147	135491	155411	164672
9. Less: Imports of goods and services	13698*	26774*	33092*	37235*	37761*	47355*	61294*	69333*	83051*	93003*	85652	98739	116136	128883	143934
10. Statistical discrepancy	−66*	446*	−176*	−438*	284*	−194*	−1099*	−1867*	−2941*	−3356*	3	..	..	..	..
11. **Gross Domestic Product**	37148*	78006*	89760*	100133*	110579*	125694*	145781*	167100*	191831*	215233*	239445	263849	313241	356934	394693
At 1990 price levels[1]															
1. Government final consumption expenditure	37959*	64709*	68769*	72915*	76223*	80380*	83612*	88978*	95541*	100254*	105613	110395	116488	122332	124454
2. Private final consumption expenditure	145759*	209799*	209779*	219389*	225881*	232415*	241377*	253746*	269166*	287824*	283140	295021	300918	301305	304454
3. Households	..	..	..	..	..	..	..	..	..	..	269413	280352	285794	285609	297974
4. Private non-profit institutions serving households	..	..	..	..	..	..	..	..	..	..	13727	14669	15124	15696	16480
5. Increase in stocks	8163*	9840*	21739*	15885*	6222*	8081*	22014*	15931*	17124*	6160*	−8892	−7914	7913	24	5927
6. Gross fixed capital formation	67011*	94009*	107991*	128238*	122985*	139759*	146886*	164393*	181033*	187626*	166594	169794	165919	172244	173537
7. **Total Domestic Expenditure**	258892*	378357*	408278*	436427*	431311*	460635*	493889*	523048*	562864*	581864*	546455	567296	591238	595905	608372
8. Exports of goods and services	55367*	101106*	101206*	102360*	116779*	126456*	127317*	131250*	146027*	151331*	164024	167913	175701	178723	178936
9. Less: Imports of goods and services	66750*	120183*	136502*	145263*	143792*	164550*	172309*	184298*	206993*	214106*	185115	188282	193341	196209	206339
10. Statistical discrepancy	−9361*	−7403*	−14072*	−18180*	−9561*	−11579*	−16588*	−19672*	−20900*	−20867*	−4523	−3567	−3324	−2658	−4214
11. **Gross Domestic Product**	238148*	351877*	358910*	375344*	394737*	410962*	432309*	450328*	480998*	498222*	520841	543360	570274	575761	576755
COST COMPONENTS OF THE G.D.P.															
1. Indirect taxes	4705*	11399*	14862*	16933*	18560*	20742*	23199*	26988*	31636*	37059*	38711	41730	49633	56817	61977
2. Less: Subsidies	1230*	2972*	3446*	3945*	4379*	5000*	6287*	7747*	9726*	11807*	13761	14019	16194	17485	20054
3. Consumption of fixed capital	5248*	11287*	13071*	14683*	15986*	18034*	22165*	25000*	31153*	36820*	41014	43623	48883	55228	62845
4. Compensation of employees paid by resident producers	17019*	39300*	43713*	51018*	57454*	64999*	75573*	89961*	104371*	117929*	129393	135168	151929	172068	192095
5. Operating surplus	12264*	19528*	22062*	21313*	22587*	26722*	31249*	32353*	33448*	33753*	44088	57347	78990	90306	97830
6. Statistical discrepancy	−857*	−534*	−501*	132*	372*	197*	−118*	546*	948*	1480*	..	..	..	..	..
7. **Gross Domestic Product**	37149*	78008*	89761*	100134*	110580*	125694*	145781*	167101*	191830*	215234*	239445	263849	313241	356934	394693
CAPITAL TRANSACTIONS OF THE NATION															
Finance of Gross Capital Formation															
1. Consumption of fixed capital	5248*	11287*	13068*	14683*	15985*	18034*	22165*	25000*	31153*	36820*	41014	43623	48883	55228	62845
2. Net saving	6753*	12160*	16742*	17489*	19308*	23873*	27140*	26839*	24200*	16831*	21932	26318	46972	53861	51998
3. Less: Surplus of the nation on current transactions	−519*	627*	−1190*	−2536*	−266*	−1379*	−4245*	−8740*	−14027*	−18456*	−7578	−5201	7284	12455	3405
4. Statistical discrepancy	−1091*	−3073*	−2769*	−2028*	−3971*	−4155*	−2923*	158*	4172*	8549*	−3	..	..	..	..
5. **Finance of Gross Capital Formation**	11429*	19747*	28231*	32680*	31588*	39131*	50627*	60737*	73552*	80656*	70521	75142	88571	96634	111438
Gross capital formation															
6. Increase in stocks	881*	1163*	4878*	3536*	1506*	3044*	6989*	4774*	5237*	2344*	−4080	−3768	4160	14	3819
7. Gross fixed capital formation	10548*	18584*	23353*	29144*	30082*	36087*	43638*	55963*	68315*	78312*	74601	78910	84411	96620	107619
8. Statistical discrepancy	..	..	..	..	..	..	..	..	..	..	..	..	..	..	..
9. **Gross Capital Formation**	11429*	19747*	28231*	32680*	31588*	39131*	50627*	60737*	73552*	80656*	70521	75142	88571	96634	111438
RELATIONS AMONG NATIONAL ACCOUNTING AGGREGATES															
1. **Gross Domestic Product**	37149*	78008*	89761*	100133*	110579*	125693*	145781*	167101*	191832*	215234*	239445	263849	313241	356934	394693
2. Plus: Net factor income from the rest of the world	−332*	−587*	−644*	−775*	−1065*	−1229*	−1914*	−1985*	−3159*	−4905*	−7443	−9395	−9628	−11003	−12877
3. Factor income from the rest of the world	193*	1020*	1106*	1047*	915*	1276*	2047*	1875*	1840*	1958*	2568	3460	5311	8764	11046
4. Factor income paid to the rest of the world	524*	1600*	1742*	1816*	1976*	2499*	3950*	3851*	4994*	6861*	10011	12855	14939	19767	23923
5. Equals: **Gross National Product**	36817*	77421*	89117*	99358*	109514*	124464*	143867*	165116*	188673*	210329*	232002	254454	303613	345931	381816
6. Less: Consumption of fixed capital	5248*	11287*	13068*	14683*	15985*	18034*	22165*	25000*	31153*	36820*	41014	43623	48883	55228	62845
7. Plus: Statistical discrepancy	833*	1231*	2110*	2076*	2248*	3010*	3408*	2790*	1702*	−629*	..	..	..	..	..
8. Equals: **National Income**	32402*	67365*	78159*	86751*	95777*	109440*	125110*	142906*	159222*	172880*	190988	210831	254730	290703	318971
9. Plus: Net current transfers from the rest of the world	161*	−32*	−76*	−1*	−119*	−262*	−534*	−791*	−1035*	−1498*	−1842	−2214	−2443	−3070	−4456
10. Current transfers from the rest of the world	230*	330*	361*	456*	445*	447*	469*	468*	468*	480*	489	496	628	636	645
11. Current transfers paid to the rest of the world	87*	382*	458*	486*	590*	733*	1023*	1276*	1515*	1983*	2331	2710	3071	3706	5101
12. Equals: **National Disposable Income**	32563*	67333*	78083*	86750*	95658*	109178*	124576*	142576*	158187*	171382*	189146	208617	252287	287633	314515
13. Less: Final consumption	25810*	55173*	61341*	69261*	76350*	85305*	97436*	115276*	133987*	154551*	167214	182299	205315	233772	262517
14. Plus: Statistical discrepancy	..	..	..	..	..	..	..	..	..	..	..	..	..	..	..
15. Equals: **Net Saving**	6753*	12160*	16742*	17489*	19308*	23873*	27140*	26839*	24200*	16831*	21932	26318	46972	53861	51998
16. Less: Surplus of the nation on current transactions	−519*	627*	−1190*	−2536*	−266*	−1379*	−4245*	−8740*	−14027*	−18456*	−7578	−5201	7284	12455	3405
17. Plus: Statistical discrepancy	−1091*	−3073*	−2769*	−2028*	−3971*	−4155*	−2923*	158*	4172*	8549*	−3	..	..	..	..
18. Equals: **Net Capital Formation**	6181*	8460*	15163*	17997*	15603*	21097*	28462*	35737*	42399*	43836*	29507	31519	39688	41406	48593

1. At t-1 relative prices for 1987-1997, at 1984 relative prices for 1985-1986, at 1980 relative prices for 1980-1984, at 1975 relative prices for 1975-1979 and at 1970 relative prices for 1960-1974.

Principaux Agrégats

millions de couronnes

1983	1984	1985	1986	1987	1988	1989	1990	1991	1992	1993	1994	1995	1996	1997	
															DÉPENSES IMPUTÉES AU P.I.B.
															Aux prix courants
84538	90764	98914	108251	124217	130754	139016	150099	161966	173583	179940	186576	194525	206871	218810	1. Consommation finale des administrations publiques
205619	225601	261243	292660	312868	325167	338778	357100	376275	394949	411637	433100	458492	486678	515747	2. Consommation finale privée
194651	213751	248471	278346	297092	308211	320913	338236	356054	373649	389987	410536	435247	462620	490949	3. Ménages
10968	11850	12772	14314	15776	16956	17865	18864	20221	21300	21650	22564	23245	24058	24798	4. Institutions privées sans but lucratif au service des ménages
−10075	1353	8968	22077	15445	5616	4297	11903	6068	5774	9634	14502	27438	22221	23741	5. Variations des stocks
121815	129962	134922	155389	170915	181428	175057	156210	157426	156340	168202	179371	192518	216503	249931	6. Formation brute de capital fixe
401897	**447680**	**504047**	**578377**	**623445**	**642965**	**657148**	**675312**	**701735**	**730646**	**769413**	**813549**	**872973**	**932273**	**1008229**	7. **Demande intérieure totale**
184515	213023	235046	194066	199787	213858	262658	293752	308046	300094	315960	333197	353426	414268	447582	8. Exportations de biens et services
149169	168408	194104	213294	213185	217232	237459	246359	246367	245806	261669	279183	297654	326488	371024	9. *Moins :* Importations de biens et services
..	..	..	..	..	..	..	..	..	..	..	..	..	..	1	10. Divergence statistique
437243	**492295**	**544989**	**559149**	**610047**	**639591**	**682347**	**722705**	**763414**	**784934**	**823704**	**867563**	**928745**	**1020053**	**1084788**	11. **Produit intérieur brut**
															Aux niveaux de prix de 1990[1]
127898	128892	131947	134464	140586	140435	143127	150099	156618	164990	168538	170865	171375	176901	182166	1. Consommation finale des administrations publiques
310093	319919	349845	367222	364223	356812	354582	357100	362297	370428	378417	393435	406869	425846	440417	2. Consommation finale privée
293382	303043	332906	349496	346326	338663	336131	338236	342779	350159	358096	372561	385994	404908	419415	3. Ménages
16711	16876	16939	17726	17897	18149	18451	18864	19518	20269	20321	20874	20875	20938	21002	4. Institutions privées sans but lucratif au service des ménages
−14605	1867	11725	27321	17465	6017	4433	11903	5930	5582	9241	13718	25251	20291	22010	5. Variations des stocks
182881	184624	177305	190863	191521	188072	175147	156210	155537	150735	157271	164370	169913	186299	209857	6. Formation brute de capital fixe
606267	**635302**	**670822**	**719870**	**713795**	**691336**	**677289**	**675312**	**680382**	**691735**	**713467**	**742398**	**773408**	**809337**	**854450**	7. **Demande intérieure totale**
191578	206669	221645	226610	229103	243687	270453	293752	311615	327853	338216	367714	383553	421302	445712	8. Exportations de biens et services
200044	211617	230469	257580	240896	235218	240301	246359	246794	248575	259600	272322	287706	311693	350103	9. *Moins :* Importations de biens et services
−607	1903	3245	159	1048	2456	1286	0	24	−1437	−1464	−3741	−3127	−5432	−5090	10. Divergence statistique
597194	**632257**	**665243**	**689059**	**703050**	**702261**	**708727**	**722705**	**745227**	**769576**	**790619**	**834039**	**866128**	**913514**	**944969**	11. **Produit intérieur brut**
															RÉPARTITION DU P.I.B.
69665	77626	92339	101074	107934	106704	107049	110849	116724	122212	130332	141231	152012	165003	174084	1. Impôts indirects
19809	20882	22738	24547	26063	28035	30001	32565	34176	34914	36322	36202	33916	34841	33641	2. *Moins :* Subventions
69338	75505	83365	92760	106617	117275	123189	124387	127670	131751	137622	142686	150270	157861	166278	3. Consommation de capital fixe
208102	227401	252148	284524	320081	339738	344185	357217	374035	388233	396224	415750	440140	472984	511120	4. Rémunération des salariés payée par les producteurs résidents
109947	132645	139875	105338	101478	103309	137925	162817	179161	177652	195848	204098	220239	259046	266946	5. Excédent net d'exploitation
..	..	..	..	..	..	..	..	..	..	..	..	..	..	..	6. Divergence statistique
437243	**492295**	**544989**	**559149**	**610047**	**639591**	**682347**	**722705**	**763414**	**784934**	**823704**	**867563**	**928745**	**1020053**	**1084787**	7. **Produit intérieur brut**
															OPÉRATIONS EN CAPITAL DE LA NATION
															Financement de la formation brute de capital
69338	75505	83365	92760	106617	117275	123189	124387	127670	131751	137622	142686	150270	157861	166278	1. Consommation de capital fixe
60241	82570	86627	50027	50416	43563	55516	62146	64234	58149	65201	77553	100538	149432	164170	2. Épargne nette
17839	26760	26102	−34681	−29327	−26206	−649	18420	28410	27786	24987	26366	30852	68569	56776	3. *Moins :* Solde des opérations courantes de la nation
..	..	..	−2	..	..	..	..	..	..	..	..	..	..	..	4. Divergence statistique
111740	**131315**	**143890**	**177466**	**186360**	**187044**	**179354**	**168113**	**163494**	**162114**	**177836**	**193873**	**219956**	**238724**	**273672**	5. **Financement de la formation brute de capital**
															Formation brute de capital
−10075	1353	8968	22077	15445	5616	4297	11903	6068	5774	9634	14502	27438	22221	23741	6. Variations des stocks
121815	129962	134922	155389	170915	181428	175057	156210	157426	156340	168202	179371	192518	216503	249931	7. Formation brute de capital fixe
..	..	..	..	..	..	..	..	..	..	..	..	..	..	..	8. Divergence statistique
111740	**131315**	**143890**	**177466**	**186360**	**187044**	**179354**	**168113**	**163494**	**162114**	**177836**	**193873**	**219956**	**238724**	**273672**	9. **Formation brute de capital**
															RELATIONS ENTRE LES PRINCIPAUX AGRÉGATS
437243	**492295**	**544989**	**559149**	**610047**	**639591**	**682347**	**722705**	**763414**	**784934**	**823704**	**867563**	**928745**	**1020053**	**1084787**	1. **Produit intérieur brut**
−13177	−13375	−9894	−9369	−9383	−16391	−19237	−21510	−25332	−17474	−19773	−15423	−11869	−9521	−9687	2. *Plus :* Revenu net des facteurs reçu du reste du monde
10555	13866	18616	20859	21207	21126	25464	26038	21347	16713	16882	24151	28761	30003	..	3. Revenu des facteurs reçu du reste du monde
23732	27241	28510	30228	30590	37517	44701	47548	46679	34187	36655	39574	40970	40739	..	4. Revenu des facteurs payé au reste du monde
424066	**478920**	**535095**	**549780**	**600664**	**623200**	**663110**	**701195**	**738082**	**767460**	**803931**	**852140**	**916876**	**1010532**	**1075100**	5. *Égal :* **Produit national brut**
69338	75505	83365	92760	106617	117275	123189	124387	127670	131751	137622	142686	150270	157861	166278	6. *Moins :* Consommation de capital fixe
..	..	..	..	..	..	..	..	..	..	..	..	..	..	..	7. *Plus :* Divergence statistique
354728	**403415**	**451730**	**457020**	**494047**	**505925**	**539921**	**576808**	**610412**	**635709**	**666309**	**709454**	**766606**	**852671**	**908822**	8. *Égal :* **Revenu national**
−4330	−4480	−4946	−6084	−6546	−6441	−6611	−7463	−7937	−9028	−9531	−12225	−13051	−9690	−10095	9. *Plus :* Transferts courants nets reçus du reste du monde
734	732	736	747	855	1087	1136	1358	1556	10429	10877	9120	8087	9123	9300	10. Transferts courants reçus du reste du monde
5064	5212	5682	6831	7401	7528	7747	8821	9493	19457	20408	21345	21138	18813	19395	11. Transferts courants payés au reste du monde
350398	**398935**	**446784**	**450938**	**487501**	**499484**	**533310**	**569345**	**602475**	**626681**	**656778**	**697229**	**753555**	**842981**	**898727**	12. *Égal :* **Revenu national disponible**
290157	316365	360157	400911	437085	455921	477794	507199	538241	568532	591577	619676	653017	693549	734557	13. *Moins :* Consommation finale
..	..	..	..	..	..	..	..	..	..	..	..	..	..	..	14. *Plus :* Divergence statistique
60241	**82570**	**86627**	**50027**	**50416**	**43563**	**55516**	**62146**	**64234**	**58149**	**65201**	**77553**	**100538**	**149432**	**164170**	15. *Égal :* **Épargne nette**
17839	26760	26102	−34681	−29327	−26206	−649	18420	28410	27786	24987	26366	30852	68569	56776	16. *Moins :* Solde des opérations courantes de la nation
..	..	..	−2	..	..	..	..	..	..	..	..	..	..	..	17. *Plus :* Divergence statistique
42402	**55810**	**60525**	**84706**	**79743**	**69769**	**56165**	**43726**	**35824**	**30363**	**40214**	**51187**	**69686**	**80863**	**107394**	18. *Égal :* **Formation nette de capital**

1. Aux prix relatifs de t-1 pour la période 1987-1997, aux prix relatifs de 1984 pour la période 1985-1986, aux prix relatifs de 1980 pour la période 1980-1984, aux prix relatifs de 1975 pour la période 1975-1979 et aux prix relatifs de 1970 pour la période 1960-1974.

POLAND

1968 SNA

Main aggregates

millions of zlotys

	1960	1969	1970	1971	1972	1973	1974	1975	1976	1977	1978	1979	1980	1981	1982
EXPENDITURE ON THE G.D.P.															
At current prices															
1. Government final consumption expenditure	..	..	..	..	..	..	..	..	..	..	..	..	..	..	..
2. Private final consumption expenditure	..	..	..	..	..	..	..	..	..	..	..	..	..	..	..
3. Households	..	..	..	..	..	..	..	..	..	..	..	..	..	..	..
4. Private non-profit institutions serving households	..	..	..	..	..	..	..	..	..	..	..	..	..	..	..
5. Increase in stocks	..	..	..	..	..	..	..	..	..	..	..	..	..	..	..
6. Gross fixed capital formation	..	..	..	..	..	..	..	..	..	..	..	..	..	..	..
7. **Total Domestic Expenditure**	..	..	..	..	..	..	..	..	..	..	..	..	..	..	..
8. Exports of goods and services	..	..	..	..	..	..	..	..	..	..	..	..	..	..	..
9. *Less:* Imports of goods and services	..	..	..	..	..	..	..	..	..	..	..	..	..	..	..
10. Statistical discrepancy	..	..	..	..	..	..	..	..	..	..	..	..	..	..	..
11. **Gross Domestic Product**	..	..	..	..	..	..	..	..	..	..	..	..	..	..	..
At 1990 price levels[1]															
1. Government final consumption expenditure	..	..	..	..	..	..	..	..	..	..	..	..	..	..	..
2. Private final consumption expenditure	..	..	..	..	..	..	..	..	..	..	..	..	..	..	..
3. Households	..	..	..	..	..	..	..	..	..	..	..	..	..	..	..
4. Private non-profit institutions serving households	..	..	..	..	..	..	..	..	..	..	..	..	..	..	..
5. Increase in stocks	..	..	..	..	..	..	..	..	..	..	..	..	..	..	..
6. Gross fixed capital formation	..	..	..	..	..	..	..	..	..	..	..	..	..	..	..
7. **Total Domestic Expenditure**	..	..	..	..	..	..	..	..	..	..	..	..	..	..	..
8. Exports of goods and services	..	..	..	..	..	..	..	..	..	..	..	..	..	..	..
9. *Less:* Imports of goods and services	..	..	..	..	..	..	..	..	..	..	..	..	..	..	..
10. Statistical discrepancy	..	..	..	..	..	..	..	..	..	..	..	..	..	..	..
11. **Gross Domestic Product**	..	..	..	..	..	..	..	..	..	..	..	..	..	..	..
COST COMPONENTS OF THE G.D.P.															
1. Indirect taxes	..	..	..	..	..	..	..	..	..	..	..	..	..	..	..
2. *Less:* Subsidies	..	..	..	..	..	..	..	..	..	..	..	..	..	..	..
3. Consumption of fixed capital	..	..	..	..	..	..	..	..	..	..	..	..	..	..	..
4. Compensation of employees paid by resident producers	..	..	..	..	..	..	..	..	..	..	..	..	..	..	..
5. Operating surplus	..	..	..	..	..	..	..	..	..	..	..	..	..	..	..
6. Statistical discrepancy	..	..	..	..	..	..	..	..	..	..	..	..	..	..	..
7. **Gross Domestic Product**	..	..	..	..	..	..	..	..	..	..	..	..	..	..	..
CAPITAL TRANSACTIONS OF THE NATION															
Finance of Gross Capital Formation															
1. Consumption of fixed capital	..	..	..	..	..	..	..	..	..	..	..	..	..	..	..
2. Net saving	..	..	..	..	..	..	..	..	..	..	..	..	..	..	..
3. *Less:* Surplus of the nation on current transactions	..	..	..	..	..	..	..	..	..	..	..	..	..	..	..
4. Statistical discrepancy	..	..	..	..	..	..	..	..	..	..	..	..	..	..	..
5. **Finance of Gross Capital Formation**	..	..	..	..	..	..	..	..	..	..	..	..	..	..	..
Gross capital formation															
6. Increase in stocks	..	..	..	..	..	..	..	..	..	..	..	..	..	..	..
7. Gross fixed capital formation	..	..	..	..	..	..	..	..	..	..	..	..	..	..	..
8. Statistical discrepancy	..	..	..	..	..	..	..	..	..	..	..	..	..	..	..
9. **Gross Capital Formation**	..	..	..	..	..	..	..	..	..	..	..	..	..	..	..
RELATIONS AMONG NATIONAL ACCOUNTING AGGREGATES															
1. **Gross Domestic Product**	..	..	..	..	..	..	..	..	..	..	..	..	..	..	..
2. *Plus:* Net factor income from the rest of the world	..	..	..	..	..	..	..	..	..	..	..	..	..	..	..
3. Factor income from the rest of the world	..	..	..	..	..	..	..	..	..	..	..	..	..	..	..
4. Factor income paid to the rest of the world	..	..	..	..	..	..	..	..	..	..	..	..	..	..	..
5. *Equals:* **Gross National Product**	..	..	..	..	..	..	..	..	..	..	..	..	..	..	..
6. *Less:* Consumption of fixed capital	..	..	..	..	..	..	..	..	..	..	..	..	..	..	..
7. *Plus:* Statistical discrepancy	..	..	..	..	..	..	..	..	..	..	..	..	..	..	..
8. *Equals:* **National Income**	..	..	..	..	..	..	..	..	..	..	..	..	..	..	..
9. *Plus:* Net current transfers from the rest of the world	..	..	..	..	..	..	..	..	..	..	..	..	..	..	..
10. Current transfers from the rest of the world	..	..	..	..	..	..	..	..	..	..	..	..	..	..	..
11. Current transfers paid to the rest of the world	..	..	..	..	..	..	..	..	..	..	..	..	..	..	..
12. *Equals:* **National Disposable Income**	..	..	..	..	..	..	..	..	..	..	..	..	..	..	..
13. *Less:* Final consumption	..	..	..	..	..	..	..	..	..	..	..	..	..	..	..
14. *Plus:* Statistical discrepancy	..	..	..	..	..	..	..	..	..	..	..	..	..	..	..
15. *Equals:* **Net Saving**	..	..	..	..	..	..	..	..	..	..	..	..	..	..	..
16. *Less:* Surplus of the nation on current transactions	..	..	..	..	..	..	..	..	..	..	..	..	..	..	..
17. *Plus:* Statistical discrepancy	..	..	..	..	..	..	..	..	..	..	..	..	..	..	..
18. *Equals:* **Net Capital Formation**	..	..	..	..	..	..	..	..	..	..	..	..	..	..	..

1. At 1990 relative prices.

Principaux Agrégats

millions de zlotys

1983	1984	1985	1986	1987	1988	1989	1990	1991	1992	1993	1994	1995	1996	1997	
															DÉPENSES IMPUTÉES AU P.I.B.
															Aux prix courants
..	..	..	..	..	..	..	10488	17690	23819	30407	37491	50802	63428	76824	1. Consommation finale des administrations publiques
..	..	..	..	..	..	..	27187	48643	71925	99627	137360	182034	236327	290239	2. Consommation finale privée
..	..	..	..	..	..	..	26867	48001	70955	98200	135389	179235	232856	286044	3. Ménages
..	..	..	..	..	..	..	320	642	970	1427	1971	2799	3471	4194	4. Institutions privées sans but lucratif au service des ménages
..	..	..	..	..	..	..	2590	328	−1860	−520	−715	3300	4428	5650	5. Variations des stocks
..	..	..	..	..	..	..	11761	15775	19297	24749	34078	48731	68764	94070	6. Formation brute de capital fixe
..	..	..	..	..	..	..	**52026**	**82436**	**113181**	**154263**	**208214**	**284867**	**372947**	**466783**	7. **Demande intérieure totale**
..	..	..	..	..	..	..	16051	19026	27242	35733	50583	74770	90092	112479	8. Exportations de biens et services
..	..	..	..	..	..	..	12050	20579	25479	34215	48389	70935	100224	134514	9. *Moins :* Importations de biens et services
..	..	..	..	..	..	..	..	..	..	−1	−1	−1	−1	1	10. Divergence statistique
..	..	..	..	..	..	..	**56027**	**80883**	**114944**	**155780**	**210407**	**288701**	**362814**	**444749**	11. **Produit intérieur brut**
															Aux niveaux de prix de 1990[1]
..	..	..	..	..	..	..	10488	11495	12178	12567*	12848*	13219*	13674*	14103*	1. Consommation finale des administrations publiques
..	..	..	..	..	..	..	27187	28991	29732	31332*	32722*	33894*	36821*	39424*	2. Consommation finale privée
..	..	..	..	..	..	..	26867	28572	29233	30753*	32072*	33223*	36119*	38683*	3. Ménages
..	..	..	..	..	..	..	320	419	499	592*	679*	700*	724*	761*	4. Institutions privées sans but lucratif au service des ménages
..	..	..	..	..	..	..	2590	222	−1531	−592*	−667*	336*	358*	370*	5. Variations des stocks
..	..	..	..	..	..	..	11761	11243	11505	11838*	12923*	15108*	18226*	21975*	6. Formation brute de capital fixe
..	..	..	..	..	..	..	**52026**	**51951**	**51884**	**55145***	**57826***	**62557***	**69079***	**75872***	7. **Demande intérieure totale**
..	..	..	..	..	..	..	16051	15786	17487	18054*	20417*	25228*	28370*	31373*	8. Exportations de biens et services
..	..	..	..	..	..	..	12050	15616	15881	17983*	20009*	24879*	31848*	37628*	9. *Moins :* Importations de biens et services
..	..	..	..	..	..	..	0	0	−1	306*	174*	−384*	709*	1236*	10. Divergence statistique
..	..	..	..	..	..	..	**56027**	**52121**	**53489**	**55522***	**58408***	**62522***	**66310***	**70853***	11. **Produit intérieur brut**
															RÉPARTITION DU P.I.B.
..	..	..	..	..	..	..	..	..	..	..	..	..	..	..	1. Impôts indirects
..	..	..	..	..	..	..	..	..	..	..	..	..	..	..	2. *Moins :* Subventions
..	..	..	..	..	..	..	..	..	..	..	..	..	..	..	3. Consommation de capital fixe
..	..	..	..	..	..	..	..	..	..	..	..	..	..	..	4. Rémunération des salariés payée par les producteurs résidents
..	..	..	..	..	..	..	..	..	..	..	..	..	..	..	5. Excédent net d'exploitation
..	..	..	..	..	..	..	..	..	..	..	..	..	..	..	6. Divergence statistique
..	..	..	..	..	..	..	..	..	..	..	..	..	..	..	7. **Produit intérieur brut**
															OPÉRATIONS EN CAPITAL DE LA NATION
															Financement de la formation brute de capital
..	..	..	..	..	..	..	..	..	..	..	..	..	..	..	1. Consommation de capital fixe
..	..	..	..	..	..	..	..	..	..	..	..	..	..	..	2. Épargne nette
..	..	..	..	..	..	..	..	..	..	..	..	..	..	..	3. *Moins :* Solde des opérations courantes de la nation
..	..	..	..	..	..	..	..	..	..	..	..	..	..	..	4. Divergence statistique
..	..	..	..	..	..	..	..	..	..	..	..	..	..	..	5. **Financement de la formation brute de capital**
															Formation brute de capital
..	..	..	..	..	..	..	..	..	..	..	..	..	..	..	6. Variations des stocks
..	..	..	..	..	..	..	..	..	..	..	..	..	..	..	7. Formation brute de capital fixe
..	..	..	..	..	..	..	..	..	..	..	..	..	..	..	8. Divergence statistique
..	..	..	..	..	..	..	..	..	..	..	..	..	..	..	9. **Formation brute de capital**
															RELATIONS ENTRE LES PRINCIPAUX AGRÉGATS
..	..	..	..	..	..	..	..	..	..	..	..	..	..	..	1. **Produit intérieur brut**
..	..	..	..	..	..	..	..	..	..	..	..	..	..	..	2. *Plus :* Revenu net des facteurs reçu du reste du monde
..	..	..	..	..	..	..	..	..	..	..	..	..	..	..	3. Revenu des facteurs reçu du reste du monde
..	..	..	..	..	..	..	..	..	..	..	..	..	..	..	4. Revenu des facteurs payé au reste du monde
..	..	..	..	..	..	..	..	..	..	..	..	..	..	..	5. *Égal :* **Produit national brut**
..	..	..	..	..	..	..	..	..	..	..	..	..	..	..	6. *Moins :* Consommation de capital fixe
..	..	..	..	..	..	..	..	..	..	..	..	..	..	..	7. *Plus :* Divergence statistique
..	..	..	..	..	..	..	..	..	..	..	..	..	..	..	8. *Égal :* **Revenu national**
..	..	..	..	..	..	..	..	..	..	..	..	..	..	..	9. *Plus :* Transferts courants nets reçus du reste du monde
..	..	..	..	..	..	..	..	..	..	..	..	..	..	..	10. Transferts courants reçus du reste du monde
..	..	..	..	..	..	..	..	..	..	..	..	..	..	..	11. Transferts courants payés au reste du monde
..	..	..	..	..	..	..	..	..	..	..	..	..	..	..	12. *Égal :* **Revenu national disponible**
..	..	..	..	..	..	..	..	..	..	..	..	..	..	..	13. *Moins :* Consommation finale
..	..	..	..	..	..	..	..	..	..	..	..	..	..	..	14. *Plus :* Divergence statistique
..	..	..	..	..	..	..	..	..	..	..	..	..	..	..	15. *Égal :* **Épargne nette**
..	..	..	..	..	..	..	..	..	..	..	..	..	..	..	16. *Moins :* Solde des opérations courantes de la nation
..	..	..	..	..	..	..	..	..	..	..	..	..	..	..	17. *Plus :* Divergence statistique
..	..	..	..	..	..	..	..	..	..	..	..	..	..	..	18. *Égal :* **Formation nette de capital**

1. Aux prix relatifs de 1990.

Comptes nationaux, Volume 1, OCDE, 1999

PORTUGAL
1968 SNA

Main aggregates

millions of escudos

	1960	1969	1970	1971	1972	1973	1974	1975	1976	1977	1978	1979	1980	1981	1982
EXPENDITURE ON THE G.D.P.															
At current prices															
1. Government final consumption expenditure	7972*	21864*	26018*	28497*	32816*	38243*	50641*	59759*	68147*	92963*	116057	145588*	193243*	239047*	292248*
2. Private final consumption expenditure	59245*	125275*	133002*	154222*	168791*	207668*	279772*	330161*	399081*	511078*	607515*	760591*	959480*	1186348*	1460529*
3. Households	..	..	..	..	..	..	..	..	..	504649*	599824*	750747*	945881*	1170271*	1441178*
4. Private non-profit institutions serving households	..	..	..	..	..	..	..	..	..	5641*	6835*	9144*	14752*	16231*	18779*
5. Increase in stocks	-2227*	-3961*	5513*	-2052*	-2252*	6446*	4898*	-38413*	-13985*	8507*	10202*	17943*	40681*	37232*	30847*
6. Gross fixed capital formation	20799*	45289*	51862*	61824*	78860*	95005*	110777*	122775*	147563*	208243*	276021*	331511*	450688*	581512*	721871*
7. **Total Domestic Expenditure**	85790*	188467*	216395*	242491*	278216*	347362*	446087*	474282*	600807*	820791*	1009795*	1255633*	1644091*	2044140*	2505496*
8. Exports of goods and services	13128*	41002*	45541*	52439*	66307*	79210*	95732*	80809*	85840*	121086*	166319*	282213*	361216*	409068*	513003*
9. *Less:* Imports of goods and services	17429*	47153*	56681*	65897*	76338*	98157*	147599*	127474*	149175*	215993*	264162*	388055*	544585*	699797*	858537*
10. Statistical discrepancy	317*	667*	-1671*	-1058*	-2717*	-5268*	-5721*	4305*	-605*	-9263*	-10490*	-12394*	-22465*	-34522*	-41130*
11. **Gross Domestic Product**	81805*	182983*	203584*	227976*	265468*	323147*	388499*	431922*	536868*	716620*	901462*	1137396*	1438257*	1718889*	2118832*
At 1990 price levels [1]															
1. Government final consumption expenditure	182924*	388818*	416016*	442706*	480834*	518339*	608091*	648345*	693730*	775579*	810069*	861909*	930810*	981997*	1018593*
2. Private final consumption expenditure	1823745*	3062602*	3143593*	3542249*	3684900*	4127929*	4529950*	4489867*	4647000*	4674877*	4579409*	4579298*	4750457*	4888274*	5003244*
3. Households	..	..	..	..	..	..	..	..	..	4614092*	4519797*	4517760*	4681841*	4820126*	4934481*
4. Private non-profit institutions serving households	..	..	..	..	..	..	..	..	..	49707*	48885*	54324*	69840*	64925*	63664*
5. Increase in stocks	-129571*	-204967*	20478*	-166350*	-169915*	-4926*	-34617*	-620732*	-352178*	-123791*	-125640*	30889*	74327*	38895*	18812*
6. Gross fixed capital formation	717487*	1249233*	1393140*	1530027*	1736713*	1902172*	1769871*	1569817*	1582694*	1772635*	1882800*	1857486*	2016034*	2126985*	2175000*
7. **Total Domestic Expenditure**	2594585*	4495686*	4973227*	5348632*	5732532*	6543514*	6873295*	6087297*	6571246*	7099300*	7146638*	7329582*	7771628*	8036151*	8215649*
8. Exports of goods and services	420306*	1038581*	1021694*	1122685*	1330938*	1386544*	1168732*	986533*	986533*	1044733*	1139732*	1515459*	1549036*	1480213*	1549321*
9. *Less:* Imports of goods and services	505349*	1283698*	1294939*	1482864*	1661346*	1871513*	1960604*	1466137*	1515988*	1697917*	1700931*	1914893*	2047340*	2095081*	2176119*
10. Statistical discrepancy	-59121*	-89016*	-159152*	-146491*	-172045*	-242662*	-199073*	18914*	-26935*	-94272*	-54729*	-31175*	-57734*	-88937*	-99932*
11. **Gross Domestic Product**	2450421*	4161553*	4540830*	4841962*	5230079*	5815883*	5882350*	5626607*	6014856*	6351844*	6530710*	6898973*	7215590*	7332346*	7488919*
COST COMPONENTS OF THE G.D.P.															
1. Indirect taxes	5693*	17341*	21020*	22383*	25250*	30343*	36974*	41710*	61635*	79240*	93890*	116295*	171913*	208992*	257611*
2. *Less:* Subsidies	634*	2055*	3108*	3130*	2985*	3952*	8596*	8699*	18969*	23797*	36158*	45026*	65505*	81594*	79765*
3. Consumption of fixed capital	4390*	9876*	10852*	12151*	14217*	15971*	18061*	20866*	23350*	31261*	42823*	51845*	64654*	74335*	95375*
4. Compensation of employees paid by resident producers	34128*	71297*	90477*	104595*	121206*	142864*	192603*	255804*	313241*	382990*	455541*	557947*	712300*	873637*	1067482*
5. Operating surplus	39363*	88434*	85437*	93214*	109388*	140352*	151238*	121300*	155307*	246669*	351686*	467167*	562610*	649677*	768576*
6. Statistical discrepancy	-1134*	-1910*	-1093*	-1238*	-1608*	-2431*	-1780*	941*	2304*	257*	-6321*	-10833*	-7715*	-6158*	-447*
7. **Gross Domestic Product**	81805*	182983*	203584*	227976*	265468*	323147*	388499*	431922*	536868*	716620*	901462*	1137396*	1438257*	1718889*	2118832*
CAPITAL TRANSACTIONS OF THE NATION															
Finance of Gross Capital Formation															
1. Consumption of fixed capital	4390*	9876*	10852*	12151*	14217*	15971*	18061*	20866*	23350*	31261*	42823*	51845*	64654*	74335*	95375*
2. Net saving	10617*	42194*	55341*	58831*	86834*	106158*	73828*	34904*	61153*	113600*	186216*	271946*	331427*	320779*	351975*
3. *Less:* Surplus of the nation on current transactions	-2944*	5859*	3457*	5131*	12956*	8770*	-21444*	-21387*	-38538*	-58871*	-45313*	-17345*	-75131*	-183584*	-252085*
4. Statistical discrepancy	622*	-4883*	-5362*	-6079*	-11487*	-11908*	2343*	7205*	10538*	13018*	11872*	8318*	20158*	40047*	53284*
5. **Finance of Gross Capital Formation**	18573*	41328*	57374*	59772*	76608*	101451*	115675*	84362*	133579*	216750*	286223*	349454*	491369*	618744*	752719*
Gross capital formation															
6. Increase in stocks	-2227*	-3961*	5513*	-2052*	-2252*	6446*	4898*	-38413*	-13985*	8507*	10202*	17943*	40681*	37232*	30847*
7. Gross fixed capital formation	20799*	45289*	51862*	61824*	78860*	95005*	110777*	122775*	147563*	208243*	276021*	331511*	450688*	581512*	721871*
8. Statistical discrepancy	..	..	..	..	..	..	..	..	..	..	..	..	..	..	..
9. **Gross Capital Formation**	18573*	41328*	57374*	59772*	76608*	101451*	115675*	84362*	133579*	216750*	286223*	349454*	491369*	618744*	752719*
RELATIONS AMONG NATIONAL ACCOUNTING AGGREGATES															
1. **Gross Domestic Product**	81805*	182983*	203584*	227976*	265468*	323147*	388499*	431922*	536868*	716620*	901462*	1137397*	1438257*	1718889*	2118832*
2. *Plus:* Net factor income from the rest of the world	114*	1396*	1327*	620*	863*	3149*	4896*	-551*	-6004*	-10260*	-20370*	-29002*	-42301*	-80750*	-137617*
3. Factor income from the rest of the world	..	..	..	..	..	..	..	..	..	..	3251*	4778*	8134*	10677*	14778*	15246*
4. Factor income paid to the rest of the world	..	..	..	..	..	..	..	..	..	13557*	25092*	37174*	52928*	94941*	150992*
5. *Equals:* **Gross National Product**	81919*	184379*	204911*	228595*	266331*	326296*	393395*	431371*	530864*	706360*	881092*	1103395*	1395957*	1638139*	1981215*
6. *Less:* Consumption of fixed capital	4390*	9876*	10852*	12151*	14217*	15971*	18061*	20866*	23350*	31261*	42823*	51845*	64654*	74335*	95375*
7. *Plus:* Statistical discrepancy	-1360*	2129*	4854*	4848*	11110*	13051*	-1017*	-13770*	-10313*	-3655*	-1119*	1971*	2088*	3242*	7247*
8. *Equals:* **National Income**	76169*	176632*	198913*	221292*	263225*	323376*	374317*	396735*	497201*	671445*	837150*	1053520*	1333391*	1567047*	1893086*
9. *Plus:* Net current transfers from the rest of the world	1665*	12702*	15448*	20259*	25217*	28693*	29923*	28089*	31180*	46197*	72638*	119605*	150759*	179128*	211666*
10. Current transfers from the rest of the world	..	..	..	..	..	..	..	..	..	51519*	79382*	125637*	155632*	182299*	218117*
11. Current transfers paid to the rest of the world	..	..	..	..	..	..	..	..	..	5480*	7139*	7145*	6524*	5371*	8805*
12. *Equals:* **National Disposable Income**	77834*	189334*	214362*	241551*	288441*	352069*	404241*	424824*	528381*	717641*	909788*	1178125*	1484149*	1746175*	2104752*
13. *Less:* Final consumption	67217*	147139*	159020*	182719*	201607*	245910*	330413*	389920*	467229*	604041*	723572*	906179*	1152723*	1425396*	1752777*
14. *Plus:* Statistical discrepancy	..	..	..	..	..	..	..	..	..	..	..	..	..	..	..
15. *Equals:* **Net Saving**	10617*	42194*	55341*	58831*	86834*	106158*	73828*	34904*	61153*	113600*	186216*	271946*	331427*	320779*	351975*
16. *Less:* Surplus of the nation on current transactions	-2944*	5859*	3457*	5131*	12956*	8770*	-21444*	-21387*	-38538*	-58871*	-45313*	-17345*	-75131*	-183584*	-252085*
17. *Plus:* Statistical discrepancy	622*	-4883*	-5362*	-6079*	-11487*	-11908*	2343*	7205*	10538*	13018*	11872*	8318*	20158*	40047*	53284*
18. *Equals:* **Net Capital Formation**	14182*	31452*	46522*	47621*	62392*	85481*	97614*	63496*	110228*	185489*	243400*	297609*	426715*	544409*	657344*

1. At 1990 relative prices for 1986-1997, at 1985 relative prices for 1977-1985 and at 1963 relative prices for 1960-1976.

Principaux Agrégats

millions d'escudos

DÉPENSES IMPUTÉES AU P.I.B. — Aux prix courants

1983	1984	1985	1986	1987	1988	1989	1990	1991	1992	1993	1994	1995	1996	1997	
368642*	447717*	578749*	718375	830736	1030749	1260757	1531961	1951000	2208286	2410437	2572342	2795006	3045500	3310300	1. Consommation finale des administrations publiques
1811341*	2258588*	2715801*	3263848	3778129	4503837	5229747	6221706	7239665	8281247	8957183	9666556	10262594	10896504	11452089	2. Consommation finale privée
1786212*	2228154*	2679310*	3219863	3729122	4451615	5170613	6151045	7147323	8167551	8834545	9533816	10118673	10739685	11281634	3. Ménages
26367*	30428*	36305*	43985	49007	52222	59134	70661	92342	113696	122638	132740	143921	156819	170455	4. Institutions privées sans but lucratif au service des ménages
−67381*	−87015*	−97258*	−49269	39232	141457	100836	101594	60030	111529	−17523	56450	114941	83306	88127	5. Variations des stocks
843367*	833555*	964505*	1227039	1590608	2026012	2316788	2717755	2964225	3191440	3139621	3432227	3734411	3996157	4451499	6. Formation brute de capital fixe
2955969*	3452845*	4161798*	5159993	6238705	7702055	8908128	10573016	12214920	13792502	14489718	15727575	16906952	18021467	19302015	7. **Demande intérieure totale**
757448*	1101273*	1381232*	1540193	1897157	2291645	2873409	3345441	3505273	3638992	3690468	4249285	4878817	5191477	5579896	8. Exportations de biens et services
1046549*	1312154*	1504295*	1638551	2207549	2909918	3409271	4063383	4404980	4672512	4717064	5348038	5968078	6427612	7125070	9. *Moins :* Importations de biens et services
−31263*	−17779*	−3597*	..	..	..	..	..	..	..	..	..	..	..	..	10. Divergence statistique
2635605*	3224185*	4035138*	5061635	5928313	7083782	8372266	9855074	11315213	12758982	13463122	14628822	15817691	16785332	17756841	11. **Produit intérieur brut**

Aux niveaux de prix de 1990 [1]

1983	1984	1985	1986	1987	1988	1989	1990	1991	1992	1993	1994	1995	1996	1997	
1057189*	1059519*	1127626*	1208401	1254617	1362462	1452839	1531961	1689497	1708192	1723271	1759422	1797726	1833700*	1879500*	1. Consommation finale des administrations publiques
4931488*	4786250*	4818607*	5088007	5358238	5726964	5877518	6221706	6449630	6724194	6824852	6977786	7089291	7268700*	7490100*	2. Consommation finale privée
4860108*	4717949*	4750459*	5015234	5285408	5658022	5808431	6151045	6367387	6624989	6720577	6874542	6983841	..	..	3. Ménages
72919*	68016*	66743*	72773	72830	68942	69087	70661	82243	99205	104275	103244	105450	..	..	4. Institutions privées sans but lucratif au service des ménages
−244892*	−255664*	−224633*	−151350	−5200	139956	108770	101594	61647	186959	103288	164860	226517	175100*	191600*	5. Variations des stocks
2019882*	1668700*	1609512*	1784478	2105635	2417356	2525425	2717755	2811602	2946781	2769469	2863033	3000444	3172500*	3532100*	6. Formation brute de capital fixe
7763667*	7258805*	7331112*	7929536	8713290	9647338	9964552	10573016	11012376	11566126	11420880	11765101	12113978	12450000*	13093300*	7. **Demande intérieure totale**
1760109*	1964900*	2095879*	2237469	2488357	2691385	3042515	3345441	3432153	3599509	3469496	3772682	4117381	4536000*	4915200*	8. Exportations de biens et services
2042451*	1951703*	1979220*	2313376	2846847	3358323	3565305	4063383	4358767	4826082	4665506	5083808	5479440	5892300*	6507200*	9. *Moins :* Importations de biens et services
−5370*	63406*	93574*	0	0	0	0	0	0	0	0	0	0	0	0	10. Divergence statistique
7475955*	7335408*	7541345*	7853629	8354800	8980500	9441762	9855074	10085762	10339553	10224870	10453975	10751919	11093700*	11501300*	11. **Produit intérieur brut**

RÉPARTITION DU P.I.B.

1983	1984	1985	1986	1987	1988	1989	1990	1991	1992	1993	1994	1995	1996	1997	
348371*	424412*	519058*	756187	863339	1075744	1204627	1413707	1622148	1938654	1933112	2203947	2361716	2506300*	2651400*	1. Impôts indirects
91984*	120346*	127388*	149655	148935	158644	151704	187316	221162	234506	270087	306643	304708	323400*	342100*	2. *Moins :* Subventions
118021*	145100*	181524*	227774	266774	318770	385124	463188	543130	625190	673156	746070	822520	872800*	923300*	3. Consommation de capital fixe
1300782*	1535294*	1849869*	2225899	2588732	3013538	3560689	4314586	5216265	5994443	6280655	6497578	6888832	7310400*	7733700*	4. Rémunération des salariés payée par les producteurs résidents
958256*	1247091*	1628578*	2001430	2358403*	2834374*	3373530*	3850909*	4154832*	4435201*	4846286*	5487870*	6049331*	6419200*	6790500*	5. Excédent net d'exploitation
2159*	−7366*	−16504*	..	..	..	..	..	..	..	..	..	..	..	..	6. Divergence statistique
2635606*	3224185*	4035138*	5061635	5928313	7083782	8372266	9855074	11315213	12758982	13463122	14628822	15817691	16785300	17756800	7. **Produit intérieur brut**

OPÉRATIONS EN CAPITAL DE LA NATION — Financement de la formation brute de capital

1983	1984	1985	1986	1987	1988	1989	1990	1991	1992	1993	1994	1995	1996	1997	
118021*	145100*	181524*	227774	266774	318770	385124	463188*	543130	625190*	673156	746070	822520*	872800*	923300*	1. Consommation de capital fixe
422791*	477450*	687902*	1055870	1382933*	1617291*	1972795*	2189873*	2167884*	2315581*	2104948*	2093371*	2301707*	2357300*	2480300*	2. Épargne nette
−191802*	−97235*	12512*	105874	19867	−231408	−59705	−166288	−313241	−362198	−343994	−649236	−725125	−849400*	−1136000*	3. *Moins :* Solde des opérations courantes de la nation
43372*	26755*	10333*	..	..	..	..	..	..	..	..	..	..	..	..	4. Divergence statistique
775985*	746540*	867248*	1177770	1629840	2167469	2417624	2819349	3024255	3302969	3122098	3488677	3849352	4079500	4539600	5. **Financement de la formation brute de capital**

Formation brute de capital

1983	1984	1985	1986	1987	1988	1989	1990	1991	1992	1993	1994	1995	1996	1997	
−67381*	−87015*	−97258*	−49269	39232	141457	100836	101594	60030	111529	−17523	56450	114941	83300	88100	6. Variations des stocks
843367*	833555*	964505*	1227039	1590608	2026012	2316788	2717755	2964225	3191440	3139621	3432227	3734411	3996200	4451500	7. Formation brute de capital fixe
..	..														8. Divergence statistique
775985*	746540*	867248*	1177770	1629840	2167469	2417624	2819349	3024255	3302969	3122098	3488677	3849352	4079500	4539600	9. **Formation brute de capital**

RELATIONS ENTRE LES PRINCIPAUX AGRÉGATS

1983	1984	1985	1986	1987	1988	1989	1990	1991	1992	1993	1994	1995	1996	1997	
2635606*	3224185*	4035138*	5061635	5928313	7083782	8372266	9855074	11315213	12758982	13463122	14628822	15817691	16785300	17756800	1. **Produit intérieur brut**
−160282*	−231102*	−255258*	−204783	−178459	−159926	−133487	−96210	−95682	−38887	−9441	−75614	−142201	−150500*	−159200*	2. *Plus :* Revenu net des facteurs reçu du reste du monde
22896*	36987*	56416*	54446	65771	90617	149449	236831	276328	381086	402029	376138	546394	..	..	3. Revenu des facteurs reçu du reste du monde
181448*	265944*	310671*	259229	244230	250543	282936	333041	372010	419973	411470	451752	688595	..	..	4. Revenu des facteurs payé au reste du monde
2475324*	2993083*	3779879*	4856852	5749854	6923856	8238779	9758864	11219531	12720095	13453681	14553208	15675490	16634800*	17597600*	5. *Égal :* **Produit national brut**
118021*	145100*	181524*	227774	266774	318770	385124	463188	543130	625190	673156	746070	822520*	872800*	923300*	6. *Moins :* Consommation de capital fixe
5209*	11929*	9873*	..	..											7. *Plus :* Divergence statistique
2362512*	2859912*	3608228*	4629078*	5483080*	6605086*	7853655*	9295676*	10676401*	12094905*	12780525*	13807138*	14852970*	15762000*	16674300*	8. *Égal :* **Revenu national**
240262*	323842*	374224*	409015	508718	546791	609644	647864	682148	710209	692043	525131	506337	537300*	568400*	9. *Plus :* Transferts courants nets reçus du reste du monde
250305*	337054*	390792*	471454	598310	662865	756886	818535	918192	984304	985339	880554	849216	..	..	10. Transferts courants reçus du reste du monde
12467*	16508*	20259*	62439	89592	116074	147242	170671	236044	274095	293296	355423	342879	..	..	11. Transferts courants payés au reste du monde
2602774*	3183755*	3982453*	5038093*	5991798*	7151877*	8463299*	9943540*	11358549*	12805114*	13472568*	14332269*	15359307*	16299300*	17242700*	12. *Égal :* **Revenu national disponible**
2179983*	2706305*	3294550*	3982223	4608865	5534586	6490504	7753667	9190665	10489533	11367620	12238898	13057600	13942000	14762400	13. *Moins :* Consommation finale
..	..														14. *Plus :* Divergence statistique
422791*	477450*	687902*	1055870	1382933*	1617291*	1972795*	2189873*	2167884*	2315581*	2104948*	2093371*	2301707*	2357300*	2480300*	15. *Égal :* **Épargne nette**
−191802*	−97235*	12512*	105874	19867	−23408	−59705	−166288	−313241	−362198	−343994	−649236	−725125	−849400*	−1136000*	16. *Moins :* Solde des opérations courantes de la nation
43372*	26755*	10333*	..	..											17. *Plus :* Divergence statistique
657965*	601440*	685723*	949996*	1363066*	1848699*	2032500*	2356161*	2481125*	2677779*	2448942*	2742607*	3026832*	3206700*	3616300*	18. *Égal :* **Formation nette de capital**

1. Aux prix relatifs de 1990 pour la période 1986-1997, aux prix relatifs de 1985 pour la période 1977-1985 et aux prix relatifs de 1963 pour la période 1960-1976.

SPAIN

1968 SNA

Main aggregates

billions of pesetas

	1960	1969	1970	1971	1972	1973	1974	1975	1976	1977	1978	1979	1980	1981	1982
EXPENDITURE ON THE G.D.P.															
At current prices															
1. Government final consumption expenditure	57.4	217.7	248.8	285.7	331.4	399.0	508.7	630.8	820.0	1059.4	1344.4	1638.9	1994.6	2355.6	2768.1
2. Private final consumption expenditure	476.7	1532.1	1701.1	1925.6	2245.3	2694.4	3332.9	3919.5	4817.1	6050.3	7272.4	8581.4	10129.6	11465.0	13123.2
3. Households	..	..	..	..	..	..	..	..	..	..	..	..	..	..	..
4. Private non-profit institutions serving households	..	..	..	..	..	..	..	..	..	..	..	..	..	..	..
5. Increase in stocks	−2.0	58.7	21.1	25.7	32.0	31.6	112.7	126.6	145.2	97.1	27.8	99.0	156.6	−0.6	115.7
6. Gross fixed capital formation	140.9	618.0	684.1	706.0	867.6	1108.0	1435.9	1592.5	1807.4	2201.5	2551.5	2842.4	3368.2	3728.8	4263.8
7. **Total Domestic Expenditure**	673.0	2426.5	2655.1	2943.0	3476.3	4233.0	5390.2	6269.4	7589.7	9408.3	11196.1	13161.7	15649.0	17548.8	20270.8
8. Exports of goods and services	60.9	287.3	348.3	421.7	507.3	610.8	740.3	815.9	997.0	1334.0	1710.1	1975.2	2386.4	3041.9	3630.6
9. *Less:* Imports of goods and services	50.2	332.6	373.6	396.7	500.3	644.3	987.8	1047.0	1320.3	1522.3	1621.3	1935.8	2740.8	3394.0	4006.7
10. Statistical discrepancy	..	..	..	..	..	..	..	..	..	..	..	..	..	..	..
11. **Gross Domestic Product**	683.7	2381.2	2629.8	2968.0	3483.3	4199.5	5142.7	6038.3	7266.4	9220.0	11284.9	13201.1	15294.6	17196.7	19894.7
At 1990 price levels[1]															
1. Government final consumption expenditure	1786.9	2569.3	2717.2	2834.0	2981.4	3172.2	3467.3	3647.6	3899.2	4051.3	4270.1	4449.3	4604.7	4768.9	5024.4
2. Private final consumption expenditure	8338.0	16109.9	16861.3	17721.3	19192.2	20689.1	21744.2	22135.7	23375.3	23725.9	23939.5	24250.7	24751.6	24458.2	24425.6
3. Households	..	..	..	..	..	..	..	..	..	..	..	..	..	..	..
4. Private non-profit institutions serving households	..	..	..	..	..	..	..	..	..	..	..	..	..	..	..
5. Increase in stocks	−14.8	482.0	223.3	265.7	319.9	291.1	620.6	586.9	564.7	318.3	81.0	249.5	396.6	−27.4	133.0
6. Gross fixed capital formation	2161.3	6113.8	6323.4	6133.6	7004.7	7915.2	8406.0	8027.7	7963.5	7891.8	7678.8	7340.9	7392.2	7205.7	7358.2
7. **Total Domestic Expenditure**	12271.4	25275.0	26125.2	26954.7	29498.2	32067.6	34238.1	34397.9	35802.7	35987.3	35969.4	36290.4	37145.1	36405.4	36941.2
8. Exports of goods and services	831.0	2117.0	2497.7	2852.4	3234.6	3558.1	3522.5	3508.4	3683.8	4129.5	4571.4	4827.4	4938.2	5344.5	5609.2
9. *Less:* Imports of goods and services	483.6	2448.4	2631.1	2649.6	3293.4	3843.4	4150.8	4113.4	4516.6	4268.2	4225.5	4707.3	4859.0	4654.3	4875.3
10. Statistical discrepancy	289.8	344.3	369.7	429.6	396.0	376.7	356.3	357.4	308.5	431.2	495.4	415.4	415.0	496.4	497.4
11. **Gross Domestic Product**	12908.5	25287.9	26361.4	27587.1	29835.4	32159.1	33966.0	34150.2	35278.5	36279.9	36810.6	36825.9	37639.3	37592.0	38172.5
COST COMPONENTS OF THE G.D.P.															
1. Indirect taxes	50.0	182.5	204.6	222.0	265.0	331.3	353.8	403.9	480.4	613.2	693.4	824.0	1002.6	1236.6	1513.9
2. *Less:* Subsidies	5.7	16.8	23.0	30.8	35.5	38.8	48.4	68.6	94.7	130.2	213.6	222.5	251.5	254.2	393.3
3. Consumption of fixed capital	78.3	246.9	283.3	317.0	351.7	412.6	523.1	638.7	767.3	970.5	1178.7	1440.2	1722.3	2058.4	2402.8
4. Compensation of employees paid by resident producers	278.0	1048.6	1186.0	1374.0	1669.0	2035.0	2525.0	3077.0	3785.0	4805.0	5892.0	6870.0	7784.0	8714.9	9853.2
5. Operating surplus	283.0	920.0	978.9	1085.8	1233.2	1459.3	1789.3	1987.2	2328.4	2961.4	3734.5	4289.4	5037.4	5441.0	6518.2
6. Statistical discrepancy	..	..	..	..	..	..	..	..	..	..	..	..	..	..	..
7. **Gross Domestic Product**	683.6	2381.2	2629.8	2968.0	3483.4	4199.4	5142.8	6038.2	7266.4	9219.9	11285.0	13201.1	15294.8	17196.7	19894.8
CAPITAL TRANSACTIONS OF THE NATION															
Finance of Gross Capital Formation															
1. Consumption of fixed capital	78.3	246.9	283.3	317.0	351.7	412.6	523.1	638.7	767.3	970.5	1178.7	1440.2	1722.3	2058.4	2402.8
2. Net saving	76.2	407.6	426.9	479.8	600.2	763.1	846.9	904.3	902.7	1169.2	1517.9	1566.7	1431.1	1206.4	1461.9
3. *Less:* Surplus of the nation on current transactions	15.6	−22.2	4.9	65.1	52.2	36.1	−178.6	−176.1	−282.6	−158.9	117.3	65.5	−371.5	−463.5	−514.8
4. Statistical discrepancy	..	..	..	..	..	..	..	..	..	..	..	..	..	..	..
5. **Finance of Gross Capital Formation**	138.9	676.7	705.3	731.7	899.7	1139.6	1548.6	1719.1	1952.6	2298.6	2579.3	2941.4	3524.9	3728.3	4379.5
Gross capital formation															
6. Increase in stocks	−2.0	58.7	21.2	25.7	32.0	31.6	112.7	126.6	145.2	97.1	27.8	99.0	156.6	−0.6	115.7
7. Gross fixed capital formation	140.9	618.0	684.1	706.0	867.7	1108.0	1435.9	1592.5	1807.4	2201.5	2551.5	2842.4	3368.2	3728.8	4263.8
8. Statistical discrepancy	..	..	..	..	..	..	..	..	..	..	..	..	..	..	..
9. **Gross Capital Formation**	138.9	676.7	705.3	731.7	899.7	1139.6	1548.6	1719.1	1952.6	2298.6	2579.3	2941.4	3524.8	3728.2	4379.5
RELATIONS AMONG NATIONAL ACCOUNTING AGGREGATES															
1. **Gross Domestic Product**	683.7	2381.2	2629.9	2968.0	3483.4	4199.4	5142.8	6038.2	7266.4	9219.9	11285.0	13201.1	15294.7	17196.6	19894.7
2. *Plus:* Net factor income from the rest of the world	−0.4	−15.8	−16.8	−15.4	−15.3	−10.8	0.4	−17.0	−38.5	−60.0	−84.2	−74.9	−127.5	−234.6	−280.3
3. Factor income from the rest of the world	0.8	3.7	4.9	9.1	14.4	23.6	43.1	37.0	31.3	34.7	58.6	94.5	129.6	194.7	216.1
4. Factor income paid to the rest of the world	1.1	19.5	21.7	24.5	29.7	34.4	42.7	54.0	69.8	94.6	142.7	169.4	257.1	429.3	496.4
5. *Equals:* **Gross National Product**	683.3	2365.4	2613.0	2952.6	3468.1	4188.6	5143.2	6021.2	7227.9	9159.9	11200.8	13126.2	15167.2	16962.0	19514.5
6. *Less:* Consumption of fixed capital	78.3	246.9	283.3	317.0	351.7	412.6	523.1	638.7	767.3	970.5	1178.7	1440.2	1722.3	2058.4	2402.8
7. *Plus:* Statistical discrepancy	..	..	..	..	..	..	..	..	..	..	..	..	..	..	..
8. *Equals:* **National Income**	605.0	2118.5	2329.7	2635.5	3116.4	3776.0	4620.1	5382.5	6460.6	8189.4	10022.2	11686.1	13445.0	14903.6	17211.6
9. *Plus:* Net current transfers from the rest of the world	5.3	38.9	47.1	55.5	60.4	80.3	68.5	72.1	79.2	89.5	112.6	100.9	110.3	123.3	141.6
10. Current transfers from the rest of the world	7.5*	39.4*	49.7*	59.7*	66.5*	88.5*	83.0*	88.5	106.9*	128.1*	154.2*	156.4*	146.8*	171.3*	197.3*
11. Current transfers paid to the rest of the world	0.7*	1.3*	3.5*	5.2*	7.2*	9.7*	16.0*	18.2*	29.8*	40.9*	44.5*	58.3*	35.1*	45.1*	51.4*
12. *Equals:* **National Disposable Income**	610.3	2157.4	2376.7	2691.0	3176.8	3856.3	4688.6	5454.5	6539.8	8278.9	10134.8	11787.0	13555.3	15026.9	17353.2
13. *Less:* Final consumption	534.1	1749.8	1949.9	2211.3	2576.7	3093.3	3841.6	4550.3	5637.1	7109.7	8616.8	10220.3	12124.2	13820.5	15891.4
14. *Plus:* Statistical discrepancy	..	..	..	..	..	..	..	..	..	..	..	..	..	..	..
15. *Equals:* **Net Saving**	76.1	407.6	426.8	479.7	600.2	763.0	847.0	904.3	902.7	1169.2	1517.9	1566.7	1431.1	1206.4	1461.9
16. *Less:* Surplus of the nation on current transactions	15.6	−22.2	4.9	65.1	52.2	36.1	−178.6	−176.1	−282.6	−158.9	117.3	65.5	−371.5	−463.5	−514.8
17. *Plus:* Statistical discrepancy	..	..	..	..	..	..	..	..	..	..	..	..	..	..	..
18. *Equals:* **Net Capital Formation**	60.5	429.8	421.9	414.6	548.0	726.9	1025.6	1080.3	1185.3	1328.1	1400.6	1501.2	1802.6	1669.9	1976.7

1. At 1986 relative prices.

Principaux Agrégats

milliards de pesetas

1983	1984	1985	1986	1987	1988	1989	1990	1991	1992	1993	1994	1995	1996	1997	
															DÉPENSES IMPUTÉES AU P.I.B.
															Aux prix courants
3263.0	3628.3	4151.7	4740.2	5451.8	5924.4	6831.3	7814.6	8881.9	10093.1	10700.5	10963.2	11650.2	12255.9	12584.7	1. Consommation finale des administrations publiques
14814.8	16549.7	18080.0	20437.7	22855.8	25179.6	28366.9	31303.4	34268.8	37277.1	38481.9	40723.5	43313.6	45668.2	48276.8	2. Consommation finale privée
..	..	..	..	..	..	..	..	..	..	..	..	..	..	..	3. Ménages
155.0	254.3	13.4	162.0	257.6	419.3	448.5	461.4	438.0	488.4	9.6	154.0	250.5	248.2	72.5	4. Institutions privées sans but lucratif au service des ménages
4686.0	4778.8	5408.7	6296.8	7518.1	9083.1	10867.6	12261.4	13066.5	12889.2	12100.1	12859.6	14494.2	14975.7	16028.7	5. Variations des stocks
22918.8	25211.1	27653.8	31636.7	36083.3	40606.4	46514.3	51840.8	56655.2	60747.8	61292.1	64700.3	69708.5	73148.0	76962.7	6. Formation brute de capital fixe
4666.2	5864.4	6407.2	6416.9	6995.8	7574.8	8150.4	8555.1	9409.4	10420.2	11840.8	14442.6	16731.7	18760.5	22106.1	7. **Demande intérieure totale**
4855.6	5323.9	5860.1	5729.7	6935.1	8022.5	9620.6	10250.7	11137.3	12063.1	12180.3	14331.4	16660.1	18165.2	21172.2	8. Exportations de biens et services
															9. *Moins :* Importations de biens et services
															10. Divergence statistique
22730.0	25751.6	28200.9	32323.9	36144.0	40158.7	45044.1	50145.2	54927.3	59104.9	60952.6	64811.5	69780.1	73743.3	77896.6	11. **Produit intérieur brut**
															Aux niveaux de prix de 1990[1]
5220.5	5349.1	5671.4	5976.8	6505.9	6768.5	7330.0	7814.6	8250.7	8584.1	8790.1	8760.6	8919.4	9004.0	9127.5	1. Consommation finale des administrations publiques
24480.2	24445.1	24929.7	25757.1	27249.5	28587.6	30203.6	31303.4	32208.0	32920.6	32190.9	32483.8	32999.3	33651.7	34697.3	2. Consommation finale privée
..	..	..	..	..	..	..	..	..	..	..	..	..	..	..	3. Ménages
222.6	292.1	−1.1	171.5	268.3	438.5	443.8	461.4	409.2	456.8	−29.1	109.2	189.8	180.8	18.4	4. Institutions privées sans but lucratif au service des ménages
7183.8	6686.3	7092.2	7794.4	8888.9	10123.7	11499.3	12261.4	12459.9	11906.0	10656.4	10926.1	11827.2	11981.9	12587.1	5. Variations des stocks
37107.0	36772.6	37692.2	39699.7	42912.6	45918.2	49476.7	51840.8	53328.0	53867.5	51608.4	52279.7	53935.7	54818.4	56430.4	6. Formation brute de capital fixe
6168.1	6889.1	7071.8	7202.9	7658.9	8047.4	8288.5	8555.1	9228.1	9909.7	10753.1	12551.5	13806.6	15271.4	17524.3	7. **Demande intérieure totale**
4860.3	4772.6	5155.7	5899.7	7086.2	8108.6	9509.5	10250.7	11174.3	11948.8	11327.0	12612.2	13998.0	15027.2	16865.1	8. Exportations de biens et services
583.4	693.4	645.4	538.8	400.2	293.3	81.4	0.0	−99.2	−193.4	−0.3	−36.1	−143.6	−166.1	−254.0	9. *Moins :* Importations de biens et services
															10. Divergence statistique
38998.3	39582.5	40253.8	41541.7	43885.5	46150.4	48337.1	50145.2	51282.6	51635.0	51034.2	52183.0	53600.6	54896.5	56835.5	11. **Produit intérieur brut**
															RÉPARTITION DU P.I.B.
1885.3	2258.0	2668.7	3490.4	3908.3	4394.2	4910.2	5356.2	5888.8	6658.5	6427.9	7106.2	7501.0	8027.7*	8479.8*	1. Impôts indirects
444.1	544.2	687.3	672.7	777.6	1110.7	1148.7	1269.4	1452.4	1527.7	1973.2	2070.2	2199.7	2140.3*	2260.8*	2. *Moins :* Subventions
2812.5	3230.1	3587.5	3857.9	4177.7	4599.8	5033.3	5545.2	6023.8	6451.5	6980.5	7428.1*	7953.2*	8404.9*	8878.3*	3. Consommation de capital fixe
11132.4	11876.2	13127.4	14795.9	16563.3	18533.2	20905.9	23977.9	26792.3	28946.9	30060.7	30764.1	32346.1	34183.3*	36108.5*	4. Rémunération des salariés payée par les producteurs résidents
7343.8	8931.6	9504.6	10852.5	12272.3	13742.2	15343.4	16535.3	17674.7	18575.9	19456.8	21583.2*	24179.4*	25267.7*	26690.8*	5. Excédent net d'exploitation
															6. Divergence statistique
22729.9	25751.7	28200.9	32324.0	36144.0	40158.7	45044.1	50145.2	54927.2	59105.1	60952.6	64811.5	69780.0	73743.3	77896.6	7. **Produit intérieur brut**
															OPÉRATIONS EN CAPITAL DE LA NATION
															Financement de la formation brute de capital
2812.5	3230.1	3587.5	3857.9	4177.7	4599.8	5033.3	5545.2	6023.8	6451.5	6980.5	7428.1*	7953.2*	8404.9*	8878.3*	1. Consommation de capital fixe
1631.4	2112.9	2232.0	3124.2	3630.4	4469.3	4828.9	5322.6	5510.4	4806.5	4530.2	4728.1*	6875.6*	6976.1*	7504.5*	2. Épargne nette
−397.1	309.9	397.3	523.3	32.3	−433.3	−1453.9	−1855.0	−1970.3	−2119.7	−599.0	−857.4*	84.1*	157.0*	281.5*	3. *Moins :* Solde des opérations courantes de la nation
															4. Divergence statistique
4841.0	5033.1	5422.2	6458.8	7775.8	9502.4	11316.1	12722.8	13504.5	13377.7	12109.7	13013.6	14744.7	15224.0	16101.3	5. **Financement de la formation brute de capital**
															Formation brute de capital
155.0	254.3	13.4	162.0	257.6	419.3	448.5	461.4	438.0	488.4	9.6	154.0	250.5	248.2	72.5	6. Variations des stocks
4686.0	4778.8	5408.7	6296.8	7518.1	9083.1	10867.6	12261.4	13066.5	12889.2	12100.1	12859.6	14494.2	14975.7	16028.7	7. Formation brute de capital fixe
															8. Divergence statistique
4841.0	5033.1	5422.1	6458.8	7775.7	9502.4	11316.1	12722.8	13504.5	13377.6	12109.7	13013.6	14744.7	15223.9	16101.2	9. **Formation brute de capital**
															RELATIONS ENTRE LES PRINCIPAUX AGRÉGATS
22729.9	25751.6	28200.9	32324.0	36144.0	40158.7	45044.1	50145.2	54927.3	59105.0	60952.6	64811.5	69780.0	73743.3	77896.6	1. **Produit intérieur brut**
−352.7	−391.4	−330.7	−296.4	−304.5	−410.6	−384.0	−451.8	−554.1	−708.4	−526.3	−1182.0	−603.6	−889.6	−1134.9	2. *Plus :* Revenu net des facteurs reçu du reste du monde
199.8	250.3	538.2	407.5	379.9	476.8	723.7	826.2	1172.2	1485.6	1558.1	1224.4	1751.2	1836.7	1976.5	3. Revenu des facteurs reçu du reste du monde
552.5	641.7	868.9	703.9	684.4	887.4	1107.7	1278.0	1726.3	2193.9	2084.4	2406.4	2354.8	2726.3	3111.4	4. Revenu des facteurs payé au reste du monde
22377.2	25360.2	27870.2	32027.6	35839.5	39748.2	44660.1	49693.4	54373.3	58396.6	60426.3	63629.5	69176.4	72853.7	76761.7	5. *Égal :* **Produit national brut**
2812.5	3230.1	3587.5	3857.9	4177.7	4599.8	5033.3	5545.2	6023.8	6451.5	6980.5	7428.1*	7953.2*	8404.9*	8878.3*	6. *Moins :* Consommation de capital fixe
															7. *Plus :* Divergence statistique
19564.7	22130.1	24282.7	28169.7	31661.8	35148.3	39626.8	44148.3	48349.4	51945.2	53445.8	56201.4*	61223.2*	64448.8*	67883.4*	8. *Égal :* **Revenu national**
144.4	160.8	180.9	132.4	276.2	425.0	400.3	292.3	311.6	231.6	266.9	213.4	616.2	451.4	482.6	9. *Plus :* Transferts courants nets reçus du reste du monde
221.9*	236.7*	295.0	346.8	545.1	793.5	866.0	840.4	1060.5	1169.0	1242.9	1306.6	1593.6	1575.9	1800.1	10. Transferts courants reçus du reste du monde
71.4*	69.7*	114.1	214.4	269.0	368.6	465.7	548.2	748.9	937.4	976.0	1093.3	977.4	1124.5	1317.5	11. Transferts courants payés au reste du monde
19709.2	22290.9	24463.6	28302.1	31937.9	35573.3	40027.1	44440.6	48661.0	52176.8	53712.7	56414.8*	61839.4*	64900.2*	68366.0*	12. *Égal :* **Revenu national disponible**
18077.8	20178.0	22231.7	25178.0	28307.6	31104.0	35198.2	39118.0	43150.6	47370.3	49182.5	51686.7	54963.8	57924.1	60861.5	13. *Moins :* Consommation finale
															14. *Plus :* Divergence statistique
1631.4	2112.9	2232.0	3124.2	3630.4	4469.3	4828.9	5322.6	5510.4	4806.5	4530.2	4728.1*	6875.6*	6976.1*	7504.5*	15. *Égal :* **Épargne nette**
−397.1	309.9	397.3	523.3	32.3	−433.3	−1453.9	−1855.0	−1970.3	−2119.7	−599.0	−857.4*	84.1*	157.0*	281.5*	16. *Moins :* Solde des opérations courantes de la nation
															17. *Plus :* Divergence statistique
2028.5	1803.0	1834.6	2600.9	3598.0	4902.5	6282.8	7177.6	7480.7	6926.2	5129.2	5585.5*	6791.5*	6819.1*	7223.0*	18. *Égal :* **Formation nette de capital**

1. Aux prix relatifs de 1986.

SWEDEN
1968 SNA

Main aggregates

millions of kronor

	1960	1969	1970	1971	1972	1973	1974	1975	1976	1977	1978	1979	1980	1981	1982
EXPENDITURE ON THE G.D.P.															
At current prices															
1. Government final consumption expenditure	11730*	32674*	37911*	42960*	47502*	52770*	60993*	73457*	86817*	104352*	118168*	134177*	155452	172001	187654
2. Private final consumption expenditure	43248*	85348*	92746*	99920*	109976*	121344*	138384*	157773*	182465*	200026*	221696*	245099*	273330	305552	340036
3. Households	..	..	91286*	98311*	108210*	119407*	136070*	154998*	179018*	195919*	216641*	239720*	267276	298244	331973
4. Private non-profit institutions serving households	..	..	1317*	1464*	1606*	1757*	2133*	2603*	3304*	4030*	5090*	5368*	6054	7308	8063
5. Increase in stocks	1903*	2004*	5285*	1990*	−178*	−1193*	6084*	10044*	7889*	−2406*	−7446*	965*	5923	−4073	−6286
6. Gross fixed capital formation	16424*	35869*	38928*	41049*	45420*	49817*	55230*	63180*	72324*	78372*	80432*	91942*	106427	109397	118089
7. **Total Domestic Expenditure**	73305*	155895*	174870*	185919*	202720*	222738*	260691*	304454*	349495*	380344*	412850*	472183*	541132	582877	639493
8. Exports of goods and services	16530*	34993*	41501*	45301*	49267*	62112*	82465*	84650*	94041*	101297*	116359*	140520*	156469	174107	204756
9. *Less:* Imports of goods and services	16977*	35591*	42485*	43177*	46217*	55885*	84465*	85277*	99785*	107525*	112191*	145220*	166547	175299	208234
10. Statistical discrepancy	88*	245*	294*	283*	298*	349*	341*	370*	305*	97*	109*	67*	..	..	..
11. **Gross Domestic Product**	72946*	155542*	174180*	188326*	206068*	229314*	259032*	304197*	344056*	374213*	417127*	467550*	531054	581685	636015
At 1990 price levels[1]															
1. Government final consumption expenditure	133461	215175	232555	237625	243440	249684	257366	269401	278906	287213	296686	310739	317636	324851	327940
2. Private final consumption expenditure	353232	493339	510581	511036	528574	542208	560515	576199	600146	593915	589712	603959	599129	597584	601895
3. Households	..	..	499926*	500229*	517384*	530499*	548548*	564113*	588465*	582144*	577657*	591559*	586321	583372	586946
4. Private non-profit institutions serving households	..	..	10545*	10723*	11103*	11666*	11896*	11972*	11393*	11526*	11880*	12230*	12720	14173	14932
5. Increase in stocks	10726	6285	22101	9565	−411	−6465	16430	24803	20310	−4716	−15350	−284	8332	−8234	−11083
6. Gross fixed capital formation	121847	193330	199619	198467	206736	212236	205805	212167	216106	209745	195395	204120	211178	198577	196816
7. **Total Domestic Expenditure**	619266	908129	964856	956693	978339	997663	1040116	1082570	1115468	1086157	1066443	1118534	1136275	1112778	1115568
8. Exports of goods and services	90422	173204	188184	197158	208719	237301	249898	226702	236492	239935	258652	274524	272780	278418	294554
9. *Less:* Imports of goods and services	111928	202390	223365	215947	224528	240079	263955	254797	277748	267322	252686	282054	283277	268092	276193
10. Statistical discrepancy	−14255	−16452	−11350	−10904	−14313	−9043	−8688	−11132	−19829	−21217	−16683	−14738	−11216	−8690	−8340
11. **Gross Domestic Product**	583505	862491	918325	927000	948217	985842	1017371	1043343	1054383	1037553	1055726	1096266	1114562	1114414	1125589
COST COMPONENTS OF THE G.D.P.															
1. Indirect taxes	7229*	20202*	21787*	27669*	28980*	32847*	34164*	41686*	49364*	56549*	57710*	62096*	71446	82758	89247
2. *Less:* Subsidies	979*	2970*	2870*	3453*	3910*	4332*	6098*	9285*	13475*	15406*	17452*	19879*	22827	26829	31249
3. Consumption of fixed capital	8012*	15919*	17717*	19480*	21434*	24060*	28643*	33090*	38096*	43901*	49803*	56045*	64386	71902	80562
4. Compensation of employees paid by resident producers	39669*	94542*	105839*	115754*	126692*	136296*	157629*	188775*	223939*	251817*	280382*	308161*	346317	378800	400577
5. Operating surplus	18027*	26791*	30480*	28161*	31965*	38942*	43276*	48563*	45919*	38798*	47823*	61369*	71732	75054	96878
6. Statistical discrepancy	988*	1059*	1226*	716*	907*	1501*	1418*	1368*	212*	−1447*	−1140*	−241*	..	..	..
7. **Gross Domestic Product**	72946*	155543*	174179*	188327*	206068*	229314*	259032*	304197*	344055*	374212*	417126*	467551*	531054	581685	636015
CAPITAL TRANSACTIONS OF THE NATION															
Finance of Gross Capital Formation															
1. Consumption of fixed capital	8012*	15919*	17717*	19480*	21434*	24060*	28643*	33090*	38096*	43901*	49803*	56045*	64386	71902	80562
2. Net saving	9276*	19609*	23473*	23795*	24924*	28955*	28713*	36500*	33542*	22778*	23677*	27349*	30010	18755	9894
3. *Less:* Surplus of the nation on current transactions	−391*	−972*	−1304*	1711*	2548*	5959*	−2327*	−1401*	−6795*	−9151*	−159*	−9669*	−17954	−14667	−21347
4. Statistical discrepancy	648*	1373*	1719*	1475*	1432*	1568*	1631*	2233*	1780*	136*	−653*	−156*	..	..	..
5. **Finance of Gross Capital Formation**	18327*	37873*	44213*	43039*	45242*	48624*	61314*	73224*	80213*	75966*	72986*	92907*	112350	105324	111803
Gross capital formation															
6. Increase in stocks	1903*	2004*	5285*	1990*	−178*	−1193*	6084*	10044*	7889*	−2406*	−7446*	965*	5923	−4073	−6286
7. Gross fixed capital formation	16424*	35869*	38928*	41049*	45420*	49817*	55230*	63180*	72324*	78372*	80432*	91942*	106427	109397	118089
8. Statistical discrepancy	..	..	..	..	..	..	..	..	..	..	..	..	..	..	..
9. **Gross Capital Formation**	18327*	37873*	44213*	43039*	45242*	48624*	61314*	73224*	80213*	75966*	72986*	92907*	112350	105324	111803
RELATIONS AMONG NATIONAL ACCOUNTING AGGREGATES															
1. **Gross Domestic Product**	72946*	155542*	174179*	188327*	206069*	229315*	259032*	304196*	344055*	374212*	417127*	467550*	531054	581685	636015
2. *Plus:* Net factor income from the rest of the world	95*	−82*	−43*	141*	277*	584*	544*	616*	352*	−526*	−1051*	−967*	−3073	−7849	−12125
3. Factor income from the rest of the world	365*	665*	958*	1338*	1653*	2376*	2839*	3236*	4272*	4503*	6680*	7522*	8870	12531	14850
4. Factor income paid to the rest of the world	202*	701*	912*	1011*	1114*	1358*	1823*	2083*	3354*	4710*	7342*	7983*	11943	20380	26975
5. *Equals:* **Gross National Product**	73041*	155460*	174136*	188468*	206346*	229899*	259576*	304812*	344407*	373686*	416076*	466583*	527981	573836	623890
6. *Less:* Consumption of fixed capital	8012*	15919*	17717*	19480*	21434*	24060*	28643*	33090*	38096*	43901*	49803*	56045*	64386	71902	80562
7. *Plus:* Statistical discrepancy	−675*	−1578*	−1941*	−1776*	−1744*	−1995*	−1649*	−2300*	−1598*	100*	285*	330*	..	..	..
8. *Equals:* **National Income**	64354*	137963*	154478*	167212*	183168*	203844*	229284*	269422*	304713*	329885*	366558*	410868*	463595	501934	543328
9. *Plus:* Net current transfers from the rest of the world	−100*	−332*	−348*	−537*	−766*	−775*	−1194*	−1692*	−1889*	−2729*	−3017*	−4243*	−4803	−5626	−5744
10. Current transfers from the rest of the world	173*	741*	887*	923*	1144*	1274*	1457*	1691*	2062*	2110*	2453*	2024*	2100	6360	9199
11. Current transfers paid to the rest of the world	273*	1073*	1235*	1460*	1910*	2049*	2651*	3383*	3951*	4839*	5470*	6267*	6903	11986	14943
12. *Equals:* **National Disposable Income**	64254*	137631*	154130*	166675*	182402*	203069*	228090*	267730*	302824*	327156*	363541*	406625*	458792	496308	537584
13. *Less:* Final consumption	54978*	118022*	130657*	142880*	157478*	174114*	199377*	231230*	269282*	304378*	339864*	379276*	428782	477553	527690
14. *Plus:* Statistical discrepancy	..	..	..	..	..	..	..	..	..	..	..	..	..	..	..
15. *Equals:* **Net Saving**	9276*	19609*	23473*	23795*	24924*	28955*	28713*	36500*	33542*	22778*	23677*	27349*	30010	18755	9894
16. *Less:* Surplus of the nation on current transactions	−391*	−972*	−1304*	1711*	2548*	5959*	−2327*	−1401*	−6795*	−9151*	−159*	−9669*	−17954	−14667	−21347
17. *Plus:* Statistical discrepancy	648*	1373*	1719*	1475*	1432*	1568*	1631*	2233*	1780*	136*	−653*	−156*	..	..	..
18. *Equals:* **Net Capital Formation**	10315*	21954*	26496*	23559*	23808*	24564*	32671*	40134*	42117*	32065*	23183*	36862*	47964	33422	31241

1. At 1991 relative prices for 1991-1997, at 1985 relative prices for 1985-1990, at 1980 relative prices for 1970-1984 and at 1975 relative prices for 1960-1969.

Principaux Agrégats

millions de couronnes

1983	1984	1985	1986	1987	1988	1989	1990	1991	1992	1993	1994	1995	1996	1997	
															DÉPENSES IMPUTÉES AU P.I.B.
															Aux prix courants
205717	223403	241754	260171	273408	290266	322630	372130	394394	402508	406071	416167	425668	443064	449298	1. Consommation finale des administrations publiques
369442	403775	443671	487328	537868	584354	632744	692668	771310	777324	796370	834502	863547	885067	922922	2. Consommation finale privée
360584	394530	433555	476119	525312	570687	617469	674870	751413	756662	775384	812173	839829	860281	897736	3. Ménages
8858	9245	10116	11209	12556	13667	15275	17798	19897	20662	20986	22329	23718	24786	25186	4. Institutions privées sans but lucratif au service des ménages
−10263	−7757	−484	−5840	−4764	−3559	−488	−2475	−21173	−6657	−13742	7178	14177	−3257	6825	5. Variations des stocks
132296	148792	166980	175503	197948	225105	271000	292525	280371	244603	205715	209220	240359	249594	237895	6. Formation brute de capital fixe
697192	**768213**	**851921**	**917162**	**1004460**	**1096166**	**1225886**	**1354848**	**1424902**	**1417778**	**1394414**	**1467067**	**1543751**	**1574468**	**1616940**	7. **Demande intérieure totale**
253260	289819	305866	311134	332449	359690	394467	406831	404184	401586	473292	557757	675372	675105	761405	8. Exportations de biens et services
238142	260699	291186	281033	313307	341354	387751	401800	381759	377641	421494	493722	569201	561373	639486	9. *Moins* : Importations de biens et services
..	..	..	..	..	..	..	..	..	..	..	..	..	..	..	10. Divergence statistique
712310	**797333**	**866601**	**947263**	**1023602**	**1114502**	**1232602**	**1359879**	**1447327**	**1441723**	**1446212**	**1531102**	**1649922**	**1688200**	**1738859**	11. **Produit intérieur brut**
															Aux niveaux de prix de 1990[1]
330656	337918	345361	349681	353033	355130	362653	372130	382424	382281	383003	380472	376864	376205	368449	1. Consommation finale des administrations publiques
589923	598613	614651	641860	671127	687452	695465	692668	699056	689265	668169	680077	685362	694257	708241	2. Consommation finale privée
574893	584397	600086	626711	655074	670941	678748	674870	680446	670709	649831	661143	665861	675225	689110	3. Ménages
15025	14177	14523	15103	16012	16472	16678	17798	18631	18585	18378	18984	19566	19072	19163	4. Institutions privées sans but lucratif au service des ménages
−17176	−10383	−1146	−8399	−7031	−6176	−3599	−2475	−21674	−6745	−13479	4746	10895	−4704	4962	5. Variations des stocks
198928	213117	224119	224849	243327	259440	288846	292525	266548	237674	196773	200612	225399	233805	222659	6. Formation brute de capital fixe
1102331	**1139265**	**1182985**	**1207991**	**1260456**	**1295846**	**1343365**	**1354848**	**1326354**	**1302475**	**1234466**	**1265907**	**1298520**	**1299563**	**1304311**	7. **Demande intérieure totale**
323372	345392	350275	363329	378795	388255	400320	406831	397407	406723	437801	498922	563339	597651	674095	8. Exportations de biens et services
278367	293246	313509	327578	352809	371665	399127	401800	382087	386432	376762	426310	469886	487327	544281	9. *Moins* : Importations de biens et services
−2023	255	−5094	−1219	−4840	−1983	−2963	0	3023	2813	637	864	212	−56	519	10. Divergence statistique
1145313	**1191666**	**1214657**	**1242523**	**1281602**	**1310453**	**1341595**	**1359879**	**1344697**	**1325579**	**1296142**	**1339383**	**1392185**	**1409831**	**1434644**	11. **Produit intérieur brut**
															RÉPARTITION DU P.I.B.
108262	125764	142565	158958	176860	182766	199786	233362	256806	235067	225954	228755	237106	279292	283570	1. Impôts indirects
36496	39510	43394	46111	48395	48919	55719	63268	72710	78634	84948	80781	84135	80977	74370	2. *Moins* : Subventions
91650	100342	109794	118284	128095	142137	160168	178929	191562	193291	203543	205560	207599	207557	210185	3. Consommation de capital fixe
434137	475004	517802	567510	614232	670708	756614	851189	895127	883597	867520	897346	935426	991113	1017957	4. Rémunération des salariés payée par les producteurs résidents
114757	135733	139834	148622	152810	167810	171753	159667	176542	208402	234143	280222	353926	291215	301517	5. Excédent net d'exploitation
..	..	..	..	..	..	..	..	..	..	..	..	..	..	..	6. Divergence statistique
712310	**797333**	**866601**	**947263**	**1023602**	**1114502**	**1232602**	**1359879**	**1447327**	**1441723**	**1446212**	**1531102**	**1649922**	**1688200**	**1738859**	7. **Produit intérieur brut**
															OPÉRATIONS EN CAPITAL DE LA NATION
															Financement de la formation brute de capital
91650	100342	109794	118284	128095	142137	160168	178929	191562	193291	203543	205560	207599	207557	210185	1. Consommation de capital fixe
22824	42771	41847	53383	58510	66900	76561	61689	37156	236	−31219	2427	67425	63382	70241	2. Épargne nette
−7559	2078	−14855	2004	−6579	−12509	−33783	−49432	−30480	−44419	−19649	−8411	20488	24602	35706	3. *Moins* : Solde des opérations courantes de la nation
..	..	..	..	..	..	..	..	..	..	..	..	..	..	..	4. Divergence statistique
122033	**141035**	**166496**	**169663**	**193184**	**221546**	**270512**	**290050**	**259198**	**237946**	**191973**	**216398**	**254536**	**246337**	**244720**	5. **Financement de la formation brute de capital**
															Formation brute de capital
−10263	−7757	−484	−5840	−4764	−3559	−488	−2475	−21173	−6657	−13742	7178	14177	−3257	6825	6. Variations des stocks
132296	148792	166980	175503	197948	225105	271000	292525	280371	244603	205715	209220	240359	249594	237895	7. Formation brute de capital fixe
..	..	..	..	..	..	..	..	..	..	..	..	..	..	..	8. Divergence statistique
122033	**141035**	**166496**	**169663**	**193184**	**221546**	**270512**	**290050**	**259198**	**237946**	**191973**	**216398**	**254536**	**246337**	**244720**	9. **Formation brute de capital**
															RELATIONS ENTRE LES PRINCIPAUX AGRÉGATS
712310	**797333**	**866601**	**947263**	**1023602**	**1114502**	**1232602**	**1359879**	**1447327**	**1441723**	**1446212**	**1531102**	**1649922**	**1688200**	**1738859**	1. **Produit intérieur brut**
−15997	−19578	−20568	−18665	−16618	−21215	−28855	−40621	−41438	−53036	−58472	−58717	−66079	−73122	−68288	2. *Plus :* Revenu net des facteurs reçu du reste du monde
14624	15940	20060	19537	21790	21175	31054	47448	58091	54215	62571	59288	75444	75841	84451	3. Revenu des facteurs reçu du reste du monde
30621	35518	40628	38202	38408	42390	59909	88069	99529	107251	121043	118005	141523	148963	152739	4. Revenu des facteurs payé au reste du monde
696313	**777755**	**846033**	**928598**	**1006984**	**1093287**	**1203747**	**1319258**	**1405889**	**1388687**	**1387740**	**1472385**	**1583843**	**1615078**	**1670571**	5. *Égal :* **Produit national brut**
91650	100342	109794	118284	128095	142137	160168	178929	191562	193291	203543	205560	207599	207557	210185	6. *Moins :* Consommation de capital fixe
..	..	..	..	..	..	..	..	..	..	..	..	..	..	..	7. *Plus :* Divergence statistique
604663	**677413**	**736239**	**810314**	**878889**	**951150**	**1043579**	**1140329**	**1214327**	**1195396**	**1184197**	**1266825**	**1376244**	**1407521**	**1460386**	8. *Égal :* **Revenu national**
−6680	−7464	−8967	−9432	−9103	−9630	−11644	−13842	−11467	−15328	−12975	−13729	−19604	−16008	−17925	9. *Plus :* Transferts courants nets reçus du reste du monde
9405	9447	11760	12511	13673	14609	15634	16230	19233	22503	18938	15099	16508	16906	..	10. Transferts courants reçus du reste du monde
16085	16911	20727	21943	22776	24239	27278	30072	30700	37831	31913	28828	36112	32914	..	11. Transferts courants payés au reste du monde
597983	**669949**	**727272**	**800882**	**869786**	**941520**	**1031935**	**1126487**	**1202860**	**1180068**	**1171222**	**1253096**	**1356640**	**1391513**	**1442461**	12. *Égal :* **Revenu national disponible**
575159	627178	685425	747499	811276	874620	955374	1064798	1165704	1179832	1202441	1250669	1289215	1328131	1372220	13. *Moins :* Consommation finale
..	..	..	..	..	..	..	..	..	..	..	..	..	..	..	14. *Plus :* Divergence statistique
22824	**42771**	**41847**	**53383**	**58510**	**66900**	**76561**	**61689**	**37156**	**236**	**−31219**	**2427**	**67425**	**63382**	**70241**	15. *Égal :* **Épargne nette**
−7559	2078	−14855	2004	−6579	−12509	−33783	−49432	−30480	−44419	−19649	−8411	20488	24602	35706	16. *Moins :* Solde des opérations courantes de la nation
..	..	..	..	..	..	..	..	..	..	..	..	..	..	..	17. *Plus :* Divergence statistique
30383	**40693**	**56702**	**51379**	**65089**	**79409**	**110344**	**111121**	**67636**	**44655**	**−11570**	**10838**	**46937**	**38780**	**34535**	18. *Égal :* **Formation nette de capital**

1. Aux prix relatifs de 1991 pour la période 1991-1997, aux prix relatifs de 1985 pour la période 1985-1990, aux prix relatifs de 1980 pour la période 1970-1984 et aux prix relatifs de 1975 pour la période 1960-1969.

SWITZERLAND

1968 SNA

Main aggregates

millions of francs

	1960	1969	1970	1971	1972	1973	1974	1975	1976	1977	1978	1979	1980	1981	1982
EXPENDITURE ON THE G.D.P.															
At current prices															
1. Government final consumption expenditure	3424*	8869*	9849*	11646*	13164*	15149*	17008*	18324*	19366*	19578*	20215*	21262*	22469	24447	26463
2. Private final consumption expenditure	24173*	50552*	55386*	62053*	70409*	78890*	86355*	89386*	92365*	96255*	98991*	104648*	112248	119763	127115
3. Households	..	..	..	..	..	..	..	..	..	..	..	..	107754	115023	122074
4. Private non-profit institutions serving households	..	..	..	..	..	..	..	..	..	..	..	..	4494	4740	5041
5. Increase in stocks	1860*	2515*	5079*	4074*	3167*	3296*	6267*	−1183*	602*	387*	898*	4054*	6975	2711	428
6. Gross fixed capital formation	10165*	23023*	27365*	33035*	37986*	41901*	42641*	36906*	32053*	33155*	35628*	37926*	44412	48385	48727
7. **Total Domestic Expenditure**	39622*	84959*	97679*	110808*	124726*	139236*	152271*	143433*	144386*	149375*	155732*	167890*	186104	195306	202733
8. Exports of goods and services	10955*	26630*	29710*	32059*	35769*	40224*	45904*	44029*	47699*	53444*	53224*	56014*	62579	69104	69553
9. *Less:* Imports of goods and services	11060*	25604*	31249*	33644*	36814*	41664*	48649*	40029*	43009*	49684*	49524*	55828*	68588	70923	68658
10. Statistical discrepancy	−6*	76*	−276*	−324*	−281*	−280*	−338*	757*	1023*	1011*	937*	559*	..	1	..
11. **Gross Domestic Product**	39511*	86061*	95864*	108899*	123400*	137516*	149188*	148190*	150099*	154146*	160369*	167635*	180095	193488	203628
At 1990 price levels[1]															
1. Government final consumption expenditure	14949*	24993*	26192*	27722*	28521*	29210*	29706*	29899*	30725*	30849*	31469*	31800*	32103	32909	33271
2. Private final consumption expenditure	81563*	122236*	128802*	134935*	142272*	146199*	145488*	141236*	142741*	147067*	150332*	152247*	156247	157896	158435
3. Households	..	..	..	..	..	..	..	..	..	..	..	..	150012	151617	152136
4. Private non-profit institutions serving households	..	..	..	..	..	..	..	..	..	..	..	..	6235	6279	6299
5. Increase in stocks	2223*	767*	4845*	2240*	−509*	−663*	3860*	−6401*	−3181*	−3557*	−3260*	1127*	3758	−1772	−1815
6. Gross fixed capital formation	32440*	50800*	55334*	60789*	63815*	65667*	62873*	54336*	48627*	49414*	52429*	55101*	60567	61668	59230
7. **Total Domestic Expenditure**	131175*	198796*	215173*	225686*	234099*	240413*	241927*	219070*	218912*	223773*	230970*	240275*	252675	250701	249121
8. Exports of goods and services	27600*	51704*	55236*	57384*	61037*	65834*	66512*	62143*	67925*	74525*	77296*	79201*	83217	86777	83161
9. *Less:* Imports of goods and services	21268*	42289*	48161*	51158*	54880*	58448*	57878*	48993*	55389*	60513*	67125*	71725*	76888	74387	72972
10. Statistical discrepancy	6766*	6891*	6571*	6235*	5511*	5464*	6386*	6014*	3441*	2821*	449*	−142*	0	1	1
11. **Gross Domestic Product**	144273*	215102*	228819*	238147*	245767*	253263*	256947*	238234*	234889*	240606*	241590*	247609*	259004	263092	259311
COST COMPONENTS OF THE G.D.P.															
1. Indirect taxes	2833*	6125*	6664*	7275*	8540*	9162*	9528*	9528*	9867*	10442*	11263*	11608*	12449	12966	13932
2. *Less:* Subsidies	426*	951*	887*	1114*	1348*	1423*	2001*	1960*	2118*	2298*	2549*	2584*	2625	2520	3028
3. Consumption of fixed capital	5924*	13846*	16051*	18257*	20999*	22728*	24181*	22721*	22206*	23831*	24487*	24889*	26767	29037	31019
4. Compensation of employees paid by resident producers	19537*	44522*	50097*	58247*	66205*	75476*	83913*	85994*	86529*	88559*	93098*	98057*	105687	114498	122854
5. Operating surplus	11630*	22828*	24517*	26892*	29858*	32322*	34165*	32119*	33539*	33872*	34250*	35631*	37817	39507	38851
6. Statistical discrepancy	14*	−309*	−579*	−657*	−853*	−748*	−597*	−210*	74*	−258*	−178*	34*	..	..	..
7. **Gross Domestic Product**	39512*	86061*	95863*	108900*	123401*	137517*	149189*	148192*	150097*	154148*	160371*	167635*	180095	193488	203628
CAPITAL TRANSACTIONS OF THE NATION															
Finance of Gross Capital Formation															
1. Consumption of fixed capital	5924*	13846*	16051*	18257*	20999*	22728*	24181*	22721*	22206*	23831*	24487*	24889*	26767	29037	31019
2. Net saving	6478*	14273*	16744*	19242*	21316*	23627*	25403*	21169*	20573*	20185*	21846*	22639*	24544	28062	26647
3. *Less:* Surplus of the nation on current transactions	39*	220*	32*	39*	89*	100*	64*	652*	819*	805*	769*	410*	−76	6003	8511
4. Statistical discrepancy	−338*	−2361*	−319*	−351*	−1073*	−1058*	−612*	−7515*	−9305*	−9669*	−9038*	−5138*	..	..	..
5. **Finance of Gross Capital Formation**	12025*	25538*	32444*	37109*	41153*	45197*	48908*	35723*	32655*	33542*	36526*	41980*	51387	51096	49155
Gross capital formation															
6. Increase in stocks	1860*	2515*	5079*	4074*	3167*	3296*	6267*	−1183*	602*	387*	898*	4054*	6975	2711	428
7. Gross fixed capital formation	10165*	23023*	27365*	33035*	37986*	41901*	42641*	36906*	32053*	33155*	35628*	37926*	44412	48385	48727
8. Statistical discrepancy	..	..	..	..	..	..	..	..	..	..	..	..	..	..	..
9. **Gross Capital Formation**	12025*	25538*	32444*	37109*	41153*	45197*	48908*	35723*	32655*	33542*	36526*	41980*	51387	51096	49155
RELATIONS AMONG NATIONAL ACCOUNTING AGGREGATES															
1. **Gross Domestic Product**	39512*	86061*	95863*	108900*	123401*	137516*	149189*	148190*	150099*	154148*	160371*	167634*	180095	193488	203628
2. *Plus:* Net factor income from the rest of the world	900*	2565*	3265*	3490*	3825*	4480*	5395*	4470*	5220*	6110*	5820*	6645*	7015	9220	9190
3. Factor income from the rest of the world	2379*	6297*	7891*	9000*	10311*	11946*	14333*	13046*	13791*	15224*	15499*	16964*	18210	24220	24280
4. Factor income paid to the rest of the world	1507*	3503*	4256*	5472*	6728*	7666*	9146*	9490*	8723*	8710*	9926*	10138*	11195	15000	15090
5. *Equals:* **Gross National Product**	40412*	88626*	99128*	112390*	127226*	141996*	154584*	152660*	155319*	160258*	166191*	174279*	187110	202708	212818
6. *Less:* Consumption of fixed capital	5924*	13346*	16051*	18257*	20999*	22728*	24181*	22721*	22206*	23831*	24487*	24889*	26767	29037	31019
7. *Plus:* Statistical discrepancy	−182*	−311*	−259*	−293*	−229*	−403*	−447*	−68*	−4*	460*	238*	88*	..	..	..
8. *Equals:* **National Income**	34306*	74469*	82818*	93840*	105998*	118865*	129956*	129871*	133109*	136887*	141942*	149478*	160343	173671	181799
9. *Plus:* Net current transfers from the rest of the world	−231*	−775*	−839*	−899*	−1109*	−1199*	−1190*	−992*	−805*	−869*	−890*	−929*	−1082	−1398	−1574
10. Current transfers from the rest of the world	402*	634*	673*	920*	804*	913*	998*	1315*	1438*	1384*	1454*	1570*	1941	2162	2317
11. Current transfers paid to the rest of the world	638*	1682*	1811*	2068*	2340*	2558*	2598*	2474*	2246*	2315*	2395*	2533*	3023	3560	3891
12. *Equals:* **National Disposable Income**	34075*	73694*	81979*	92941*	104889*	117666*	128766*	128879*	132304*	136018*	141052*	148549*	159261	172273	180225
13. *Less:* Final consumption	27597*	59421*	65235*	73699*	83573*	94039*	103363*	107710*	111731*	115833*	119206*	125910*	134717	144210	153578
14. *Plus:* Statistical discrepancy	..	..	..	..	..	..	..	..	..	..	..	..	..	..	..
15. *Equals:* **Net Saving**	6478*	14273*	16744*	19242*	21316*	23627*	25403*	21169*	20573*	20185*	21846*	22639*	24544	28062	26647
16. *Less:* Surplus of the nation on current transactions	39*	220*	32*	39*	89*	100*	64*	652*	819*	805*	769*	410*	−76	6003	8511
17. *Plus:* Statistical discrepancy	−338*	−2361*	−319*	−351*	−1073*	−1058*	−612*	−7515*	−9305*	−9669*	−9038*	−5138*	..	..	..
18. *Equals:* **Net Capital Formation**	6101*	11692*	16393*	18852*	20154*	22469*	24727*	13002*	10449*	9711*	12039*	17091*	24620	22059	18136

1. At 1990 relative prices for 1980-1997 and at 1970 relative prices for 1960-1979.

Principaux Agrégats

millions de francs

DÉPENSES IMPUTÉES AU P.I.B.

Aux prix courants

	1983	1984	1985	1986	1987	1988	1989	1990	1991	1992	1993	1994	1995	1996	1997
1. Consommation finale des administrations publiques	28217	29446	31406	32970	33777	36366	39750	44188	48308	50672	50688	51940	51993	52889	52108
2. Consommation finale privée	132667	138404	145327	150696	156284	162072	170774	181841	195983	204541	209561	214091	218923	222526	226558
3. Ménages	127390	132906	139577	144766	150128	155678	164001	174582	188140	196176	201052	204965	209499	212859	216288
4. Institutions privées sans but lucratif au service des ménages	5277	5498	5750	5930	6156	6394	6773	7259	7843	8365	8510	9126	9423	9667	10270
5. Variations des stocks	-2060	2326	1574	121	-138	112	2911	3786	-192	-3452	-3121	-3274	398	589	2821
6. Formation brute de capital fixe	51377	54490	57947	61971	65148	72974	80454	85854	84975	78627	75420	78717	77606	73526	72532
7. **Demande intérieure totale**	210201	224666	236254	245758	255071	271524	293889	315669	329074	330388	332548	341474	348920	349530	354019
8. Exportations de biens et services	71759	80550	89016	89112	90526	97991	110507	115049	116717	122166	125301	127004	127523	131527	147781
9. *Moins :* Importations de biens et services	71850	81153	88064	86378	88422	96790	111079	113415	112129	110191	108050	111015	112952	116294	131332
10. Divergence statistique	..	1	..	..	..	1	..	1	-1	..	-1	..	-1	..	..
11. **Produit intérieur brut**	210110	224064	237206	248492	257175	272726	293317	317304	333661	342363	349798	357463	363490	364763	370468

Aux niveaux de prix de 1990[1]

	1983	1984	1985	1986	1987	1988	1989	1990	1991	1992	1993	1994	1995	1996	1997
1. Consommation finale des administrations publiques	34527	35128	36288	37475	38063	39791	41906	44188	45684	46046	45949	46905	46795	47282	47165
2. Consommation finale privée	160286	162367	165021	168862	172559	175528	179642	181841	184925	185178	183533	185381	186384	187428	189674
3. Ménages	153919	155897	158456	162146	165701	168526	172471	174582	177458	177571	175910	177336	178175	179043	180849
4. Institutions privées sans but lucratif au service des ménages	6367	6470	6566	6716	6858	7002	7171	7259	7467	7606	7623	8045	8209	8384	8824
5. Variations des stocks	-2572	-118	-759	2562	1143	-1911	-444	3786	-376	-3983	-3304	-3002	391	1177	1155
6. Formation brute de capital fixe	61550	64442	66260	69866	72649	78514	82681	85854	83400	77899	75797	80755	82186	79927	81128
7. **Demande intérieure totale**	253791	261819	266810	278765	284414	291922	303785	315669	313633	305140	301975	310039	315756	315814	319122
8. Exportations de biens et services	83831	90109	97355	96952	99176	105665	112659	115049	112688	116052	117766	119835	121787	124845	136060
9. *Moins :* Importations de biens et services	76999	83415	86474	93507	99302	104456	110589	113415	111557	106826	106890	115356	121289	124526	133543
10. Divergence statistique	1	-1	1	1	-1	0	-1	1	0	0	1	0	0	0	0
11. **Produit intérieur brut**	260624	268512	277692	282211	284287	293131	305854	317304	314764	314366	312852	314518	316254	316133	321639

RÉPARTITION DU P.I.B.

	1983	1984	1985	1986	1987	1988	1989	1990	1991	1992	1993	1994	1995	1996	1997
1. Impôts indirects	14614	15261	16822	18019	18980	19708	20078	20797	21349	21035	22040	22480	25272	25562	25961*
2. *Moins :* Subventions	3296	3553	3786	3868	4078	4498	4964	5536	6504	7076	7283	7392	7444	8055	8181*
3. Consommation de capital fixe	32842	34641	37719	39406	41913	46018	51855	56230	60729	62633	63497	62861	60415	59644	58538
4. Rémunération des salariés payée par les producteurs résidents	128258	133288	141444	150398	158042	167994	180295	196680	211240	218002	219677	221611	226692	227597	231150*
5. Excédent net d'exploitation	37692	44427	45007	44537	42318	43504	46052	49134	46846	47770	51868	57902	58555	60015	63000*
6. Divergence statistique	..	..	..	..	..	..	..	..	..	..	..	..	..	..	..
7. **Produit intérieur brut**	210110	224064	237206	248492	257175	272726	293316	317305	333660	342364	349799	357462	363490	364763	370468

OPÉRATIONS EN CAPITAL DE LA NATION

Financement de la formation brute de capital

	1983	1984	1985	1986	1987	1988	1989	1990	1991	1992	1993	1994	1995	1996	1997
1. Consommation de capital fixe	32842	34641	37719	39406	41913	46018	51855	56230	60729	62633	63497	62861	60415	59644	58538
2. Épargne nette	24828	32688	34360	35215	34640	40689	43581	46174	40018	34450	37675	36700	43299	40984	48922*
3. *Moins :* Solde des opérations courantes de la nation	8353	10513	12557	12529	11543	13621	12072	12762	15964	21908	28872	24118	25710	26511	32106*
4. Divergence statistique	..	..	..	..	..	..	..	..	..	..	..	..	..	..	..
5. **Financement de la formation brute de capital**	49317	56816	59522	62092	65010	73086	83364	89642	84783	75175	72300	75443	78004	74117	75354

Formation brute de capital

	1983	1984	1985	1986	1987	1988	1989	1990	1991	1992	1993	1994	1995	1996	1997
6. Variations des stocks	-2060	2326	1574	121	-138	112	2911	3786	-192	-3452	-3121	-3274	398	589	2821
7. Formation brute de capital fixe	51377	54490	57947	61971	65148	72974	80454	85854	84975	78627	75420	78717	77606	73526	72532
8. Divergence statistique	..	..	..	..	..	..	..	..	..	..	..	..	..	..	..
9. **Formation brute de capital**	49317	56816	59521	62092	65010	73086	83365	89640	84783	75175	72299	75443	78004	74115	75353

RELATIONS ENTRE LES PRINCIPAUX AGRÉGATS

	1983	1984	1985	1986	1987	1988	1989	1990	1991	1992	1993	1994	1995	1996	1997
1. **Produit intérieur brut**	210110	224064	237206	248492	257175	272726	293316	317304	333661	342363	349799	357463	363490	364763	370469
2. *Plus :* Revenu net des facteurs reçu du reste du monde	10084	12831	13406	11576	11408	14538	14811	13598	14314	13428	15396	12572	15673	15734	20157
3. Revenu des facteurs reçu du reste du monde	23441	27698	28570	26997	27991	31492	39570	42254	42082	39785	40051	39901	40450	42327	50609
4. Revenu des facteurs payé au reste du monde	13357	14867	15164	15421	16583	16954	24759	28656	27767	26357	24655	27329	24777	26593	30452
5. *Égal :* **Produit national brut**	220194	236895	250612	260068	268583	287264	308127	330901	347975	355791	365195	370034	379163	380497	390626
6. *Moins :* Consommation de capital fixe	32842	34641	37719	39406	41913	46018	51855	56230	60729	62633	63497	62861	60415	59644	58538
7. *Plus :* Divergence statistique	..	..	..	..	..	..	..	..	..	..	..	..	..	..	..
8. *Égal :* **Revenu national**	187352	202254	212893	220662	226670	241246	256272	274671	287246	293158	301698	307173	318748	320853	332088
9. *Plus :* Transferts courants nets reçus du reste du monde	-1640	-1716	-1800	-1781	-1969	-2118	-2167	-2468	-2938	-3495	-3774	-4443	-4534	-4455	-4500*
10. Transferts courants reçus du reste du monde	2404	2580	2851	3137	3308	3603	3954	4282	4487	4642	4729	4481	4549	4666	..
11. Transferts courants payés au reste du monde	4044	4296	4651	4918	5277	5721	6121	6751	7426	8138	8502	8925	9083	9121	..
12. *Égal :* **Revenu national disponible**	185712	200538	211093	218881	224701	239128	254105	272203	284309	289663	297924	302730	314215	316398	327588*
13. *Moins :* Consommation finale	160884	167850	176733	183666	190061	198438	210523	226030	244290	255213	260249	266031	270915	275415	278666
14. *Plus :* Divergence statistique	..	..	..	..	..	..	..	..	..	..	..	..	..	..	..
15. *Égal :* **Épargne nette**	24828	32688	34360	35215	34640	40689	43581	46174	40018	34450	37675	36700	43299	40984	48922*
16. *Moins :* Solde des opérations courantes de la nation	8353	10513	12557	12529	11543	13621	12072	12762	15964	21908	28872	24118	25710	26511	32106*
17. *Plus :* Divergence statistique	..	..	..	..	..	..	..	..	..	..	..	..	..	..	..
18. *Égal :* **Formation nette de capital**	16475	22175	21803	22686	23097	27068	31509	33411	24054	12542	8802	12582	17589	14472	16816*

1. Aux prix relatifs de 1990 pour la période 1980-1997 et aux prix relatifs de 1970 pour la période 1960-1979.

TURKEY
1968 SNA

Main aggregates

billions cf liras

	1960	1969	1970	1971	1972	1973	1974	1975	1976	1977	1978	1979	1980	1981	1982
EXPENDITURE ON THE G.D.P.															
At current prices															
1. Government final consumption expenditure	5.0*	15.7*	19	25	32	43	53	77	107	152	199	328	440	861	994
2. Private final consumption expenditure	52.5*	131.5*	150	192	228	278	382	488	593	776	1205	2126	4230	5643	7691
3. Households	..	..	..	..	..	..	..	..	..	..	..	..	..	..	..
4. Private non-profit institutions serving households	..	..	..	..	..	..	..	..	..	..	..	..	..	..	..
5. Increase in stocks	–0.1*	–0.3*	2	2	1	2	16	18	5	–7	–24	–63	61	198	47
6. Gross fixed capital formation	10.6*	30.5*	38	43	53	69	97	133	198	246	302	549	831	1526	2021
7. **Total Domestic Expenditure**	67.9*	177.4*	209	262	314	392	548	716	903	1167	1682	2940	5562	8228	10753
8. Exports of goods and services	3.0*	6.7*	9	13	17	25	30	34	46	42	72	108	284	666	1274
9. *Less:* Imports of goods and services	3.8*	8.1*	12	20	26	34	58	76	92	113	122	197	615	993	1535
10. Statistical discrepancy	–0.6*	0.2*	..	..	..	..	..	..	..	..	..	..	..	..	..
11. **Gross Domestic Product**	66.5*	176.2*	206	255	305	383	520	674	857	1096	1632	2851	5231	7901	10492
At 1990 price levels[1]															
1. Government final consumption expenditure	6479*	11761*	12185	12917	13868	15052	16304	19937	23119	24001	23317	22756	18548	27607	24678
2. Private final consumption expenditure	75265*	118498*	121143	132055	140575	142618	131524	142492	156025	186650	190334	188054	199144	184015	196639
3. Households	..	..	..	..	..	..	..	..	..	..	..	..	..	..	..
4. Private non-profit institutions serving households	..	..	..	..	..	..	..	..	..	..	..	..	..	..	..
5. Increase in stocks	–309*	–501*	1116	851	9	1413	5445	5484	959	–1946	–4472	–4890	1958	4475	765
6. Gross fixed capital formation	12683*	24246*	27523	25292	30116	32593	49011	51156	61199	47991	39798	40893	34044	44813	42254
7. **Total Domestic Expenditure**	94118*	154004*	161968	171115	184569	191675	202284	219069	241302	256696	248977	246813	253695	260911	264337
8. Exports of goods and services	4405*	7202*	8232	9505	10890	12794	11579	12360	15282	10409	13245	12346	11790	19274	25832
9. *Less:* Imports of goods and services	6152*	9910*	12092	13265	15787	18914	19754	22161	25269	24476	17155	15906	26921	30286	32785
10. Statistical discrepancy	–908*	92*	687	280	411	403	2252	1178	1150	–2249	–1071	–780	–2022	–1872	–520
11. **Gross Domestic Product**	91463*	151388*	158794	167635	180084	185958	196361	210446	232465	240380	243996	242473	236542	248027	256864
COST COMPONENTS OF THE G.D.P.															
1. Indirect taxes	4.2*	14.1*	16	21	27	32	44	57	72	93	130	209	386	604	693
2. *Less:* Subsidies	0.2*	1.6*	2	2	2	2	5	7	12	22	38	73	112	189	199
3. Consumption of fixed capital	3.4*	10.3*	12	15	18	21	30	38	48	60	89	157	288	436	577
4. Compensation of employees paid by resident producers	19.5*	49.1*	60*	73*	87*	108*	136*	183*	242*	300*	447*	819*	1299*	1791*	2239*
5. Operating surplus	40.1*	104.3*	120*	148*	175*	224*	315*	403*	507*	665*	1004*	1739*	3370*	5259*	7182*
6. Statistical discrepancy	–0.5*	0.1*	..	..	..	..	..	..	..	..	..	..	..	..	..
7. **Gross Domestic Product**	66.5*	176.2*	206	255	305	383	520	674	857	1096	1632	2851	5231	7901	10492
CAPITAL TRANSACTIONS OF THE NATION															
Finance of Gross Capital Formation															
1. Consumption of fixed capital	3.4*	10.3*	12	15	18	21	30	38	48	60	89	157	288	436	577
2. Net saving	6.5*	18.8*	28	30	37	58	74	90	122	122	156	270	345	1083	1350
3. *Less:* Surplus of the nation on current transactions	0.0*	0.0*	0	0	1	8	–9	–23	–33	–57	–33	–59	–259	–205	–141
4. Statistical discrepancy	0.6*	1.1*	..	..	..	..	..	..	..	..	..	..	..	..	..
5. **Finance of Gross Capital Formation**	10.4*	30.3*	40	45	54	71	113	151	203	239	278	486	892	1724	2068
Gross capital formation															
6. Increase in stocks	–0.1*	–0.3*	2	2	1	2	16	18	5	–7	–24	–63	61	198	47
7. Gross fixed capital formation	10.6*	30.5*	38	43	53	69	97	133	198	246	302	549	831	1526	2021
8. Statistical discrepancy	..	..	..	..	..	..	..	..	..	..	..	..	..	..	..
9. **Gross Capital Formation**	10.4*	30.3*	40	45	54	71	113	151	203	239	278	486	892	1724	2068
RELATIONS AMONG NATIONAL ACCOUNTING AGGREGATES															
1. **Gross Domestic Product**	66.5*	176.2*	206	255	305	383	520	674	857	1096	1632	2851	5231	7901	10492
2. *Plus:* Net factor income from the rest of the world	–0.3*	0.4*	2	6	9	16	18	17	11	12	14	26	72	122	120
3. Factor income from the rest of the world	..	1.0*	3	7	11	17	20	19	16	18	26	60	160	285	378
4. Factor income paid to the rest of the world	..	0.6*	1	1	2	1	2	2	5	6	12	34	88	163	258
5. *Equals:* **Gross National Product**	66.2*	176.6*	208	261	314	399	538	691	868	1108	1646	2877	5303	8023	10612
6. *Less:* Consumption of fixed capital	3.4*	10.3*	12	15	18	21	30	38	48	60	89	157	288	436	577
7. *Plus:* Statistical discrepancy	0.0*	–0.7*	..	..	..	..	..	..	..	..	..	..	..	..	..
8. *Equals:* **National Income**	62.8*	165.5*	196	246	296	378	508	653	820	1048	1557	2720	5015	7587	10035
9. *Plus:* Net current transfers from the rest of the world	1.1*	0.5*	1	1	1	1	1	2	2	2	3	4	0	0	0
10. Current transfers from the rest of the world	..	0.6*	1	1	1	1	1	2	2	2	4	5	0	0	0
11. Current transfers paid to the rest of the world	..	0.0*	0	0	0	0	0	0	0	0	1	1	0	0	0
12. *Equals:* **National Disposable Income**	64.0*	166.0*	197	247	297	379	509	655	822	1050	1560	2724	5015	7587	10035
13. *Less:* Final consumption	57.5*	147.2*	169	217	260	321	435	565	700	928	1404	2454	4670	6504	8685
14. *Plus:* Statistical discrepancy	..	..	..	..	..	..	..	..	..	..	..	..	..	..	..
15. *Equals:* **Net Saving**	6.5*	18.8*	28	30	37	58	74	90	122	122	156	270	345	1083	1350
16. *Less:* Surplus of the nation on current transactions	0.0*	0.0*	0	0	1	8	–9	–23	–33	–57	–33	–59	–259	–205	–141
17. *Plus:* Statistical discrepancy	1*	1*	..	..	..	..	..	..	..	..	..	..	..	..	..
18. *Equals:* **Net Capital Formation**	7.1*	19.9*	28	30	36	50	83	113	155	179	189	329	604	1288	1491

1. At 1987 relative prices.

Principaux Agrégats

milliards de livres

DÉPENSES IMPUTÉES AU P.I.B.

Aux prix courants

1983	1984	1985	1986	1987	1988	1989	1990	1991	1992	1993	1994	1995	1996	1997	
1454	1964	3139	4592	5845	9837	21240	43083	77895	140584	258084	450605	837243	1709247	3535104	1. Consommation finale des administrations publiques
10324	16626	24930	34394	51019	82050	149140	269562	444871	760256	1369339	2706262	5457903	9937697	19619096	2. Consommation finale privée
..	..	..	..	..	..	..	..	..	..	..	..	..	..	..	3. Ménages
..	..	..	..	..	..	..	..	..	..	..	..	..	..	..	4. Institutions privées sans but lucratif au service des ménages
−56	−87	136	409	687	−1247	1522	5792	−6973	2454	21619	−121416	127149	−79656	−377455	5. Variations des stocks
2628	4168	7650	12745	18491	33738	51837	89892	150156	258406	525506	952322	1850288	3706404	7618372	6. Formation brute de capital fixe
14350	22671	35855	52140	76042	124378	223739	408329	665949	1161700	2174548	3987773	8272583	15273692	30395117	7. Demande intérieure totale
1814	3574	5762	7043	11642	24106	36833	52215	87215	157360	270997	826379	1544077	3182305	7088355	8. Exportations de biens et services
2258	4248	6522	8104	13269	22683	40420	69042	104819	189646	383358	788530	1890238	4110584	8762823	9. Moins : Importations de biens et services
..	..	..	..	306	3424	7172	1558	−18228	−36045	−80320	−157193	−163966	426698	115234	10. Divergence statistique
13906	21997	35095	51079	74721	129225	227324	393060	630117	1093369	1981867	3868429	7762456	14772111	28835883	11. Produit intérieur brut

Aux niveaux de prix de 1990[1]

1983	1984	1985	1986	1987	1988	1989	1990	1991	1992	1993	1994	1995	1996	1997	
28763	29310	33450	36542	39990	39566	39888	43083	44663	46285	50246	47469	50705	55056	57328	1. Consommation finale des administrations publiques
209888	226896	225516	238671	237925	240812	238326	269562	276851	285782	310330	293621	307840	333969	361978	2. Consommation finale privée
..	..	..	..	..	..	..	..	..	..	..	..	..	..	..	3. Ménages
..	..	..	..	..	..	..	..	..	..	..	..	..	..	..	4. Institutions privées sans but lucratif au service des ménages
−1118	−1161	778	2058	2449	−3242	1756	5792	−4330	1176	5522	−12586	6753	−2550	−6595	5. Variations des stocks
43349	43751	48767	52857	76705	75908	77576	89892	90282	96019	121323	101951	111272	126927	145756	6. Formation brute de capital fixe
280882	298796	308510	330128	357070	353044	357546	408329	407466	429261	487422	430454	476570	513402	558467	7. Demande intérieure totale
29220	36652	35944	34111	43109	51049	50919	52215	54163	60121	64742	74570	80524	98205	116987	8. Exportations de biens et services
38335	45896	42861	41347	50856	48560	51906	69042	65439	72583	98558	76999	99776	120254	147240	9. Moins : Importations de biens et services
−2140	−1827	−1665	−1923	2083	3328	3205	1558	515	3647	653	1449	3046	1258	1481	10. Divergence statistique
269627	287724	299928	320969	351406	358860	359763	393060	396705	420445	454259	429475	460363	492611	529694	11. Produit intérieur brut

RÉPARTITION DU P.I.B.

1983	1984	1985	1986	1987	1988	1989	1990	1991	1992	1993	1994	1995	1996	1997	
1102	1532	2574	4347	6700	11356	19680	38109	66132	118109	221174	416215	849230	1723626	3364602*	1. Impôts indirects
322	540	701	788	669	1212	2322	4198	10335	24049	36820	91371	93587	259246	506061*	2. Moins : Subventions
758	1206	1923	2784	5219	9617	14877	23019	39065	66775	112728	269255	501449	930442	1825918*	3. Consommation de capital fixe
2975*	4473*	6965*	9947*	15501	27810	54621	106936	200752	346264	611904	987853	1721977	3588860	7005630*	4. Rémunération des salariés payée par les producteurs résidents
9393*	15326*	24334*	34789*	47972	81654	140468	229193	334503	586269	1072881	2286478	4783386	8788429	17145794*	5. Excédent net d'exploitation
..	..	..	..	..	..	..	..	..	..	..	..	..	..	..	6. Divergence statistique
13906	21997	35095	51079	74723	129225	227324	393059	630117	1093368	1981867	3868430	7762455	14772111	28835883	7. Produit intérieur brut

OPÉRATIONS EN CAPITAL DE LA NATION

Financement de la formation brute de capital

1983	1984	1985	1986	1987	1988	1989	1990	1991	1992	1993	1994	1995	1996	1997	
758	1206	1923	2784	5219	9617	14877	23019	39065	66775	112728	269255	501449	930442	1825918*	1. Consommation de capital fixe
1397	2371	5358	9414	12936	27671	45113	61512	72562	135991	257172	461781	1058292	2400681	4413144*	2. Épargne nette
−417	−504	−505	−956	−1329	1374	−541	−12710	−13328	−22049	−96905	57323	−253730	−722322	−1117089	3. Moins : Solde des opérations courantes de la nation
..	..	..	..	−306	−3424	−7172	−1558	18228	36045	80320	157193	163966	−426698	−115234	4. Divergence statistique
2572	4081	7786	13154	19178	32490	53359	95683	143183	260860	547125	830906	1977437	3626747	7240917	5. Financement de la formation brute de capital

Formation brute de capital

1983	1984	1985	1986	1987	1988	1989	1990	1991	1992	1993	1994	1995	1996	1997	
−56	−87	136	409	687	−1247	1522	5792	−6973	2454	21619	−121416	127149	−79656	−377455	6. Variations des stocks
2628	4168	7650	12745	18491	33738	51837	89892	150156	258406	525506	952322	1850288	3706404	7618372	7. Formation brute de capital fixe
..	..	..	..	..	..	..	..	..	..	..	..	..	..	..	8. Divergence statistique
2572	4081	7786	13154	19178	32491	53359	95684	143183	260860	547125	830906	1977437	3626748	7240917	9. Formation brute de capital

RELATIONS ENTRE LES PRINCIPAUX AGRÉGATS

1983	1984	1985	1986	1987	1988	1989	1990	1991	1992	1993	1994	1995	1996	1997	
13906	21997	35095	51079	74722	129225	227324	393060	630117	1093369	1981867	3868429	7762456	14772110	28835883	1. Produit intérieur brut
27	170	255	105	297	−49	3046	4117	4276	10237	15456	19474	92431	205957	557379	2. Plus : Revenu net des facteurs reçu du reste du monde
378	771	1216	1590	2404	3972	9415	13083	19207	35307	58078	144523	305222	576587	1320452	3. Revenu des facteurs reçu du reste du monde
351	601	961	1485	2106	4022	6369	8965	14931	25070	42622	125049	212791	370630	763073	4. Revenu des facteurs payé au reste du monde
13933	22167	35350	51184	75019	129175	230370	397177	634393	1103606	1997323	3887903	7854887	14978067	29393262	5. Égal : Produit national brut
758	1206	1923	2784	5219	9617	14877	23020	39065	66775	112728	269255	501449	930442	1825918*	6. Moins : Consommation de capital fixe
..	..	..	..	..	..	..	..	..	..	..	..	..	..	..	7. Plus : Divergence statistique
13175	20961	33427	48400	69800	119558	215493	374157	595328	1036831	1884595	3618648	7353438	14047625	27567344*	8. Égal : Revenu national
0	0	0	0	0	0	0	0	0	0	0	0	0	0	0	9. Plus : Transferts courants nets reçus du reste du monde
0	0	0	0	0	0	0	0	0	0	0	0	0	0	0	10. Transferts courants reçus du reste du monde
0	0	0	0	0	0	0	0	0	0	0	0	0	0	0	11. Transferts courants payés au reste du monde
13175	20961	33427	48400	69800	119558	215493	374157	595328	1036831	1884595	3618648	7353438	14047625	27567344*	12. Égal : Revenu national disponible
11778	18590	28069	38986	56864	91887	170380	312645	522766	900840	1627423	3156867	6295146	11646944	23154200	13. Moins : Consommation finale
..	..	..	..	..	..	..	..	..	..	..	..	..	..	..	14. Plus : Divergence statistique
1397	2371	5358	9414	12936	27672	45113	61512	72562	135991	257172	461781	1058292	2400681	4413144*	15. Égal : Épargne nette
−417	−504	−505	−956	−1329	1374	−541	−12710	−13328	−22049	−96905	57323	−253730	−722322	−1117089	16. Moins : Solde des opérations courantes de la nation
..	..	..	..	−306	−3424	−7172	−1559	18228	36045	80320	157193	163966	−426698	−115234	17. Plus : Divergence statistique
1814	2875	5863	10370	13959	22874	38482	72663	104118	194085	434397	561651	1475988	2696306	5414999*	18. Égal : Formation nette de capital

1. Aux prix relatifs de 1987.

Main aggregates

millions of pounds sterling

	1960	1969	1970	1971	1972	1973	1974	1975	1976	1977	1978	1979	1980	1981	1982
EXPENDITURE ON THE G.D.P.															
At current prices															
1. Government final consumption expenditure	4241	8195	9249	10557	12068	13780	17157	23659	27708	30191	34141	39623	50003	56533	61665
2. Private final consumption expenditure	17057	29065	31666	35512	40173	45932	52977	65193	75768	86623	99920	118595	137819	153413	168326
3. Households	..	28739	31276	35086	39729	45431	52354	64405	74813	85572	98683	117147	136074	151282	165909
4. Private non-profit institutions serving households	..	326	390	427	444	501	623	789	956	1052	1237	1448	1745	2131	2417
5. Increase in stocks	562	537	382	114	25	1529	1045	-1354	901	1824	1804	2162	-2572	-2768	-1188
6. Gross fixed capital formation	4232	8832	9736	10894	11940	14726	17497	21035	24504	27036	31060	36925	41561	41304	44824
7. **Total Domestic Expenditure**	26092	46629	51033	57077	64206	75967	88676	108533	128881	145674	166925	197305	226811	248482	273562
8. Exports of goods and services	5414	10461	11916	13356	14021	17553	23442	27379	35676	43835	47949	55464	63097	67837	73184
9. *Less:* Imports of goods and services	5771	10236	11435	12518	14065	19340	27590	29182	37031	42715	45634	54706	57900	60607	68030
10. Statistical discrepancy	123	143	93	-332	316	-103	-817	-1131	-2535	-1137	-1097	-237	-775	-1439	-540
11. **Gross Domestic Product**	25858	46997	51607	57583	64478	74077	83711	105599	124991	145657	168143	197826	231233	254273	278241
At 1990 price levels [1]															
1. Government final consumption expenditure	63079*	78022	79404	81816	85431	89230	90840	95784	97033	95388	97480	99314	101041	101297	102183
2. Private final consumption expenditure	155759*	191370	196915	203145	215702	227506	224212	223448	224523	223750	235708	245989	245883	246138	248499
3. Households	..	189007	194550	200883	213600	225370	221901	221059	222050	221320	232718	242880	242802	242791	244950
4. Private non-profit institutions serving households	..	2404	2583	2511	2350	2383	2547	2624	2704	2662	2990	3109	3085	3347	3544
5. Increase in stocks	4438	3074	2290	727	-9	7953	3593	-4103	1955	4119	3458	4013	-4064	-3859	-1545
6. Gross fixed capital formation	41752	67568	69276	70556	70401	74991	73173	71720	72921	71618	73777	75840	71764	64888	68404
7. **Total Domestic Expenditure**	265028*	340034	347885	356244	371525	399680	391818	386849	396432	394875	410423	425156	414624	408464	417541
8. Exports of goods and services	38059*	59334	62556	66800	67362	75412	80632	78027	84860	90389	91853	95340	95195	94406	95293
9. *Less:* Imports of goods and services	40673*	58769	61788	64995	71099	79306	79948	74406	77938	79056	82038	89971	86845	84375	88539
10. Statistical discrepancy	916*	-242	-265	-2281	570	-2658	-4717	-3133	-7323	-1589	-1194	75	562	-479	193
11. **Gross Domestic Product**	263330*	340357	348388	355768	368358	393128	387785	387337	396031	404619	419044	430600	423536	418016	424488
COST COMPONENTS OF THE G.D.P.															
1. Indirect taxes	3316	7497	8115	8407	8931	9784	11107	13660	15865	19374	22291	29146	35802	41809	45637
2. *Less:* Subsidies	493	842	884	939	1160	1504	3113	3785	3600	3456	3900	4720	5773	6553	6003
3. Consumption of fixed capital	2164	4077	4618	5330	6131	7329	9088	11621	13976	16501	19378	22827	27952	31641	33653
4. Compensation of employees paid by resident producers	15205	27295	30627	33570	37945	43972	52503	68630	78196	86776	99050	116072	137970	149923	159060
5. Operating surplus	5663	9062	9223	10734	12283	14334	12833	14342	18634	25670	29537	32968	34507	36633	45231
6. Statistical discrepancy	2	-92	-92	481	348	162	1293	1131	1920	792	1787	1533	775	820	663
7. **Gross Domestic Product**	25857	46997	51607	57583	64478	74077	83711	105599	124991	145657	168143	197826	231233	254273	278241
CAPITAL TRANSACTIONS OF THE NATION															
Finance of Gross Capital Formation															
1. Consumption of fixed capital	2164	4077	4618	5330	6131	7329	9088	11621	13976	16501	19378	22827	27952	31641	33653
2. Net saving	2496	5821	6340	5889	5884	7217	3598	3663	5024	10419	11496	14792	12926	10936	12867
3. *Less:* Surplus of the nation on current transactions	-255	294	655	1024	82	-1444	-3746	-2135	-1950	-11	894	302	3439	6300	4087
4. Statistical discrepancy	-121	-235	-185	813	32	265	2110	2262	4455	1929	2884	1770	1550	2259	1203
5. **Finance of Gross Capital Formation**	4794	9369	10118	11008	11965	16255	18542	19681	25405	28860	32864	39087	38989	38536	43636
Gross capital formation															
6. Increase in stocks	562	537	382	114	25	1529	1045	-1354	901	1824	1804	2162	-2572	-2768	-1188
7. Gross fixed capital formation	4232	8832	9736	10894	11940	14726	17497	21035	24504	27036	31060	36925	41561	41304	44824
8. Statistical discrepancy	..	..	..	..	..	..	..	..	..	..	..	..	..	..	..
9. **Gross Capital Formation**	4794	9369	10118	11008	11965	16255	18542	19681	25405	28860	32864	39087	38989	38536	43636
RELATIONS AMONG NATIONAL ACCOUNTING AGGREGATES															
1. **Gross Domestic Product**	25858	46997	51607	57583	64478	74077	83711	105599	124991	145657	168143	197826	231233	254273	278241
2. *Plus:* Net factor income from the rest of the world	170	275	356	382	398	786	824	143	191	-3	370	1754	226	617	674
3. Factor income from the rest of the world	591	1062	1181	1221	2956	4107	5384	5722	6976	7580	9982	15948	22116	35570	42774
4. Factor income paid to the rest of the world	421	787	825	839	2558	3321	4560	5579	6785	7583	9612	14194	21890	34953	42100
5. *Equals:* **Gross National Product**	26028	47272	51963	57965	64876	74863	84537	105741	125182	145654	168513	199580	231460	254890	278917
6. *Less:* Consumption of fixed capital	2164	4077	4618	5330	6131	7329	9088	11621	13976	16501	19378	22827	27952	31641	33653
7. *Plus:* Statistical discrepancy	..	..	..	..	..	..	..	..	..	..	..	..	..	..	..
8. *Equals:* **National Income**	23864	43195	47345	52635	58745	67534	75447	94121	111206	129153	149135	176753	203507	223249	245262
9. *Plus:* Net current transfers from the rest of the world	-68	-206	-182	-196	-272	-443	-422	-475	-786	-1128	-1791	-2210	-1984	-1547	-1741
10. Current transfers from the rest of the world	117	206	230	246	264	388	495	773	821	987	1344	1482	1952	2983	3603
11. Current transfers paid to the rest of the world	185	412	412	442	536	831	917	1248	1607	2115	3135	3692	3936	4530	5344
12. *Equals:* **National Disposable Income**	23796	42989	47163	52439	58473	67091	75025	93646	110420	128025	147344	174543	201523	221702	243521
13. *Less:* Final consumption	21421	37403	41008	45737	52557	59609	69317	87721	100941	115677	132964	157981	187047	208507	229451
14. *Plus:* Statistical discrepancy	121	235	185	-813	-32	-265	-2110	-2262	-4455	-1929	-2884	-1770	-1550	-2259	-1203
15. *Equals:* **Net Saving**	2496	5821	6340	5889	5884	7217	3598	3663	5024	10419	11496	14792	12926	10936	12867
16. *Less:* Surplus of the nation on current transactions	-255	294	655	1024	82	-1444	-3746	-2135	-1950	-11	894	302	3439	6300	4087
17. *Plus:* Statistical discrepancy	-121	-235	-185	813	32	265	2110	2262	4455	1929	2884	1770	1550	2259	1203
18. *Equals:* **Net Capital Formation**	2630	5292	5500	5678	5834	8926	9454	8060	11429	12359	13486	16260	11037	6895	9983

1. At 1990 relative prices.

Principaux Agrégats

millions de livres sterling

DÉPENSES IMPUTÉES AU P.I.B.

Aux prix courants

1983	1984	1985	1986	1987	1988	1989	1990	1991	1992	1993	1994	1995	1996	1997	
67231	71229	75296	80943	87077	93675	101835	112974	124149	131915	137800	144117	149256	155780	158860*	1. Consommation finale des administrations publiques
184400	197503	215974	239956	263646	297722	325531	345650	363546	381487	404224	424799	443480	470679	502750*	2. Consommation finale privée
181653	194259	212087	235266	258366	291414	318722	337812	355610	373680	396254	416421	434387	461268	..	3. Ménages
2747	3247	3887	4690	5280	6308	6809	7838	7936	7807	7970	8378	9093	9411	..	4. Institutions privées sans but lucratif au service des ménages
1465	1296	821	682	1228	4333	2677	-1800	-4927	-1937	329	3708	4748	2917	2350*	5. Variations des stocks
48615	55181	60718	65032	75158	91530	105443	107577	97747	93642	94293	100252	108736	114623	122010*	6. Formation brute de capital fixe
301711	325209	352809	386613	427109	487260	535486	564401	580515	605107	636646	672876	706220	743999	785970*	7. **Demande intérieure totale**
80323	92161	102518	98362	106948	107866	122169	133870	135036	143263	161336	177572	200710	218365	224770*	8. Exportations de biens et services
77784	93013	99155	101343	112166	125366	143414	148885	141642	151360	169307	184018	205434	224079	228480*	9. *Moins :* Importations de biens et services
-731	485	0	0	0	0	0	0	0	0	0	0	0	975	1360*	10. Divergence statistique
303519	324842	356172	383632	421891	469760	514241	549386	573909	597010	628675	666430	701496	739260	783620*	11. **Produit intérieur brut**

Aux niveaux de prix de 1990[1]

1983	1984	1985	1986	1987	1988	1989	1990	1991	1992	1993	1994	1995	1996	1997	
104332	105213	105134	106864	107898	108653	110182	112974	115883	115764	115557	118115	119609	122445	122740*	1. Consommation finale des administrations publiques
259751	264991	275166	294012	309579	332859	343571	345650	338108	337791	346236	355871	362082	374652	391920*	2. Consommation finale privée
255922	260640	270206	288343	303379	325736	336260	337812	330752	330788	339362	348893	354670	367082	..	3. Ménages
3830	4349	4959	5669	6200	7123	7311	7838	7356	7003	6874	6978	7412	7570	..	4. Institutions privées sans but lucratif au service des ménages
1637	1307	990	1199	1652	5094	2704	-1800	-4631	-1699	312	2890	4119	2635	2190*	5. Variations des stocks
71845	78270	81575	83685	92339	105164	111470	107577	97403	95973	96586	100778	102249	104090	109520*	6. Formation brute de capital fixe
437565	449781	462865	485760	511468	551770	567927	564401	546763	547829	558691	577654	588059	603822	626370*	7. **Demande intérieure totale**
97180	103588	109645	114542	121192	121828	127538	133870	133012	138793	143632	156982	169134	180894	195330*	8. Exportations de biens et services
94120	103493	106066	113339	122513	138036	148232	148885	141251	150962	155639	164359	171226	185971	203080*	9. *Moins :* Importations de biens et services
-1063	670	0	0	0	0	0	0	0	0	0	0	0	795	1160*	10. Divergence statistique
439562	450546	466444	486963	510147	535562	547233	549386	538524	535660	546684	570277	585967	599540	619780*	11. **Produit intérieur brut**

RÉPARTITION DU P.I.B.

1983	1984	1985	1986	1987	1988	1989	1990	1991	1992	1993	1994	1995	1996	1997	
48451	51588	55282	61461	67697	74555	78455	76719	83765	85713	88070	93898	101099	105752	113730*	1. Impôts indirects
6404	7678	7322	6456	6603	6246	6050	6324	6223	6892	7238	7510	7674	9150	8120*	2. *Moins :* Subventions
36150	38758	41883	45085	48164	52636	56716	61261	63356	62485	65353	68298	73014	77372	79560*	3. Consommation de capital fixe
170094	181685	197168	212735	230605	256844	285278	315892	332359	342975	351875	365306	381574	400485	426680*	4. Rémunération des salariés payée par les producteurs résidents
55333	59319	69161	70807	82028	91971	99842	101838	100652	112729	130615	146438	153483	165396	172420*	5. Excédent net d'exploitation
-105	1170	0	0	0	0	0	0	0	0	0	0	0	-595	-650*	6. Divergence statistique
303519	324842	356172	383632	421891	469760	514241	549386	573909	597010	628675	666430	701496	739260	783620*	7. **Produit intérieur brut**

OPÉRATIONS EN CAPITAL DE LA NATION

Financement de la formation brute de capital

1983	1984	1985	1986	1987	1988	1989	1990	1991	1992	1993	1994	1995	1996	1997	
36150	38758	41883	45085	48164	52636	56716	61261	63356	62485	65353	68298	73014	77372	79560*	1. Consommation de capital fixe
15822	15976	20806	16472	19143	20062	22413	17877	14423	13638	13880	22825	27298	30602	37350*	2. Épargne nette
2518	-1058	1150	-4157	-9079	-23165	-28991	-26639	-15041	-15582	-15389	-12837	-13172	-11136	-9460*	3. *Moins :* Solde des opérations courantes de la nation
626	685	0	0	0	0	0	0	0	0	0	0	0	-1570	-2010*	4. Divergence statistique
50080	56477	61539	65714	76386	95863	108120	105777	92820	91705	94622	103960	113484	117540	124360*	5. **Financement de la formation brute de capital**

Formation brute de capital

1983	1984	1985	1986	1987	1988	1989	1990	1991	1992	1993	1994	1995	1996	1997	
1465	1296	821	682	1228	4333	2677	-1800	-4927	-1937	329	3708	4748	2917	2350*	6. Variations des stocks
48615	55181	60718	65032	75158	91530	105443	107577	97747	93642	94293	100252	108736	114623	122010*	7. Formation brute de capital fixe
..	..	..	..	..	..	..	..	..	..	..	..	..	..	..	8. Divergence statistique
50080	56477	61539	65714	76386	95863	108120	105777	92820	91705	94622	103960	113484	117540	124360*	9. **Formation brute de capital**

RELATIONS ENTRE LES PRINCIPAUX AGRÉGATS

1983	1984	1985	1986	1987	1988	1989	1990	1991	1992	1993	1994	1995	1996	1997	
303519	324842	356172	383632	421891	469760	514241	549386	573909	597010	628675	666430	701496	739260	783620*	1. **Produit intérieur brut**
1572	1524	898	981	-461	-2147	-3168	-6728	-7051	-2383	-2472	-1422	-1561	-791	-840*	2. *Plus :* Revenu net des facteurs reçu du reste du monde
40297	46807	47235	42865	40760	47880	64493	70472	70775	63290	64491	63766	77201	76829	..	3. Revenu des facteurs reçu du reste du monde
38725	45283	46337	41884	41221	50027	67661	77200	77826	65672	66963	65188	78762	77620	..	4. Revenu des facteurs payé au reste du monde
305090	326366	357070	384613	421430	467613	511073	542658	566858	594628	626203	665008	699935	738469	782780*	5. *Égal :* **Produit national brut**
36150	38758	41883	45085	48164	52636	56716	61261	63356	62485	65353	68298	73014	77372	79560*	6. *Moins :* Consommation de capital fixe
															7. *Plus :* Divergence statistique
268941	287608	315187	339528	373266	414977	454357	481397	503502	532143	560850	596710	626921	661097	703220*	8. *Égal :* **Revenu national**
-1593	-1730	-3111	-2157	-3400	-3518	-4578	-4896	-1383	-5102	-4946	-4969	-6887	-4631	-4910*	9. *Plus :* Transferts courants nets reçus du reste du monde
3911	4200	3648	4040	4301	4056	4178	4305	7043	5014	5601	5669	6203	7028	..	10. Transferts courants reçus du reste du monde
5504	5930	6759	6197	7701	7574	8756	9201	8426	10116	10547	10638	13090	11659	..	11. Transferts courants payés au reste du monde
267348	285878	312076	337371	369866	411459	449779	476501	502119	527041	555904	591741	620034	656466	698310*	12. *Égal :* **Revenu national disponible**
250900	269217	291270	320899	350723	391397	427366	458624	487695	513402	542024	568916	592736	627434	662970*	13. *Moins :* Consommation finale
-626	-685	0	0	0	0	0	0	0	0	0	0	0	1570	2010*	14. *Plus :* Divergence statistique
15822	15976	20806	16472	19143	20062	22413	17877	14424	13639	13880	22825	27298	30602	37350*	15. *Égal :* **Épargne nette**
2518	-1058	1150	-4157	-9079	-23165	-28991	-26638	-15041	-15582	-15389	-12837	-13172	-11136	-9460*	16. *Moins :* Solde des opérations courantes de la nation
626	685	0	0	0	0	0	0	0	0	0	0	0	-1570	-2010*	17. *Plus :* Divergence statistique
13930	17719	19656	20629	28222	43227	51404	44515	29465	29221	29269	35662	40470	40168	44800*	18. *Égal :* **Formation nette de capital**

1. Aux prix relatifs de 1990.

Growth triangles: Zones
Triangles de croissance : Zones

The statistics for Germany in this publication refer to Germany after unification. Official data for Germany after unification are available only from 1991 onwards. In this publication, the secretariat has estimated some national accounts aggregates for the whole of Germany back to 1960 in order to calculate the various zones totals. These estimates are based on statistics published by Deutsches Institut für Wirtschaftsforschung for period 1989-90 and by the East German Statistical Office in 1990 for period 1980-89. They are also based on the ratios of the aggregates of West Germany and the whole of Germany.

Les statistiques concernant l'Allemagne dans cette publication se réfèrent à l'Allemagne après l'unification. Des données officielles pour l'Allemagne après l'unification ne sont disponibles qu'à partir de 1991. Dans cette publication, le secrétariat a estimé certains agrégats des comptes nationaux pour l'Allemagne dans son ensemble depuis 1960 afin de calculer les différentes zones. Ces estimations sont basées sur des statistiques publiées par Deutsches Institut für Wirtschaftsforschung pour la période 1989-90 et par l'Office Statistique de l'Allemagne de l'Est en 1990 pour la période 1980-89. Elles sont aussi basées sur les rapports des agrégats de l'Allemagne occidentale et de l'Allemagne dans son ensemble.

This part presents for each zone growth triangles for the following aggregates:
– *Per capita* GDP (volume).
– *Per capita* private consumption (volume).
– GDP (volume and implicit price deflator).
– Private final consumption expenditure (volume and implicit price deflator).
– Government final consumption expenditure (volume and implicit price deflator).
– Gross fixed capital formation (volume and implicit price deflator).
– National disposable income (value).
– Compensation of employees (value).

Two sets of zones are presented: the first is based on exchange rates and the second on PPPs.

The price indices for zones based on exchange rates (or PPPs) are harmonic weighted averages of the component indices using as weights the current value of the aggregate expressed in US dollars at 1990 exchange rates (or 1990 PPPs).

Data for Korea, Czech Republic, Hungary and Poland have not been included in area total.

Cette partie fournit pour chaque zone des triangles de croissance pour les agrégats suivants :
– PIB par habitant (volume).
– Consommation finale privée par habitant (volume).
– PIB (volume et prix implicite).
– Consommation finale privée (volume et prix implicite).
– Consommation des administrations publiques (volume et prix implicite).
– Formation brute de capital fixe (volume et prix implicite).
– Revenu national disponible (valeur).
– Rémunération des salariés (valeur).

Deux ensembles de zones sont montrés : le premier basé sur les taux de change et l'autre sur les PPA.

Les indices de prix des zones basées sur les taux de change (ou les PPA) sont obtenus comme moyennes harmoniques des indices par pays pondérés par la valeur courante de l'agrégat exprimée en dollars É-U au taux de change de 1990 (ou PPA de 1990).

Les données de la Corée, de la République tchèque, de la Hongrie et de la Pologne n'ont pas été intégrées aux totaux par zones.

OECD-TOTAL[1]

Average per cent changes at annual rate

G.D.P. per head (volume) / P.I.B. par tête (volume)

	1985	1986	1987	1988	1989	1990	1991	1992	1993	1994	1995	1996	1997
1984	2.5	2.2	2.3	2.5	2.6	2.4	2.0	1.9	1.7	1.7	1.7	1.7	1.8
1985		2.0	2.1	2.6	2.6	2.4	2.0	1.8	1.6	1.6	1.6	1.6	1.7
1986			2.3	2.8	2.8	2.5	2.0	1.8	1.5	1.6	1.6	1.6	1.7
1987				3.4	3.0	2.5	1.9	1.7	1.4	1.5	1.5	1.5	1.6
1988					2.7	2.1	1.4	1.2	1.0	1.2	1.2	1.3	1.4
1989						1.6	0.7	0.7	0.6	0.9	0.9	1.1	1.3
1990							–0.1	0.3	0.2	0.7	0.8	1.0	1.2
1991								0.8	0.4	1.0	1.1	1.3	1.4
1992									0.1	1.0	1.1	1.4	1.6
1993										2.0	1.7	1.8	2.0
1994											1.4	1.7	1.9
1995												2.1	2.2
1996													2.3

Gross domestic product (volume) / Produit intérieur brut (volume)

	1985	1986	1987	1988	1989	1990	1991	1992	1993	1994	1995	1996	1997
1984	3.3	3.0	3.0	3.3	3.4	3.2	2.9	2.7	2.5	2.5	2.5	2.5	2.6
1985		2.8	2.9	3.4	3.4	3.2	2.8	2.6	2.4	2.5	2.4	2.5	2.5
1986			3.1	3.6	3.6	3.3	2.8	2.6	2.4	2.4	2.4	2.4	2.5
1987				4.2	3.9	3.4	2.7	2.5	2.3	2.3	2.3	2.4	2.4
1988					3.6	3.0	2.3	2.1	1.9	2.0	2.0	2.1	2.2
1989						2.5	1.6	1.6	1.4	1.7	1.8	1.9	2.1
1990							0.8	1.2	1.1	1.5	1.7	1.9	2.0
1991								1.7	1.3	1.8	1.9	2.1	2.2
1992									0.9	1.8	2.0	2.2	2.3
1993										2.8	2.5	2.6	2.7
1994											2.2	2.5	2.7
1995												2.8	2.9
1996													2.9

Private final consumption expenditure (volume) / Consommation finale privée (volume)

	1985	1986	1987	1988	1989	1990	1991	1992	1993	1994	1995	1996	1997
1984	3.5	3.6	3.5	3.6	3.6	3.4	3.1	3.0	2.8	2.8	2.7	2.7	2.7
1985		3.7	3.5	3.7	3.6	3.4	3.0	2.9	2.7	2.7	2.6	2.6	2.6
1986			3.4	3.7	3.5	3.3	2.9	2.8	2.6	2.5	2.5	2.5	2.5
1987				4.0	3.6	3.3	2.8	2.7	2.4	2.4	2.4	2.4	2.4
1988					3.2	2.9	2.3	2.3	2.1	2.2	2.2	2.2	2.3
1989						2.7	1.9	2.0	1.8	2.0	2.0	2.1	2.1
1990							1.1	1.7	1.6	1.8	1.8	2.0	2.1
1991								2.2	1.8	2.0	2.0	2.1	2.2
1992									1.3	1.9	1.9	2.1	2.2
1993										2.4	2.2	2.4	2.4
1994											2.1	2.3	2.4
1995												2.6	2.6
1996													2.6

Government final consumption expenditure (volume) / Consommation des administrations publiques (volume)

	1985	1986	1987	1988	1989	1990	1991	1992	1993	1994	1995	1996	1997
1984	3.1	3.1	2.9	2.7	2.5	2.5	2.3	2.2	2.0	1.9	1.8	1.7	1.6
1985		3.1	2.8	2.6	2.3	2.3	2.2	2.1	1.8	1.7	1.6	1.6	1.5
1986			2.5	2.3	2.0	2.1	2.0	1.9	1.7	1.6	1.5	1.4	1.4
1987				2.1	1.8	2.0	1.9	1.8	1.5	1.4	1.3	1.3	1.3
1988					1.5	2.0	1.8	1.7	1.4	1.3	1.2	1.2	1.2
1989						2.4	2.0	1.7	1.4	1.3	1.2	1.2	1.1
1990							1.6	1.4	1.0	1.0	0.9	1.0	0.9
1991								1.2	0.8	0.8	0.8	0.9	0.8
1992									0.3	0.6	0.6	0.8	0.7
1993										0.9	0.8	0.9	0.9
1994											0.7	1.0	0.8
1995												1.2	0.9
1996													0.6

Gross fixed capital formation (volume) / Formation brute de capital fixe (volume)

	1985	1986	1987	1988	1989	1990	1991	1992	1993	1994	1995	1996	1997
1984	4.4	3.7	4.0	4.7	4.9	4.6	3.8	3.4	2.9	2.9	2.9	3.2	3.2
1985		3.0	3.8	4.9	5.0	4.6	3.7	3.2	2.7	2.7	2.8	3.1	3.1
1986			4.6	5.8	5.7	5.0	3.8	3.3	2.6	2.7	2.7	3.1	3.1
1987				7.0	6.3	5.2	3.6	3.0	2.3	2.4	2.5	2.9	3.0
1988					5.6	4.3	2.6	2.1	1.4	1.7	1.9	2.4	2.5
1989						3.1	1.1	0.9	0.3	0.9	1.3	2.0	2.2
1990							–0.9	–0.1	–0.5	0.4	1.0	1.8	2.0
1991								0.6	–0.4	0.8	1.4	2.4	2.5
1992									–1.3	1.0	1.7	2.8	2.9
1993										3.3	3.2	4.2	4.0
1994											3.2	4.7	4.2
1995												6.3	4.7
1996													3.2

National disposable income (value) / Revenu national disponible (valeur)

	1985	1986	1987	1988	1989	1990	1991	1992	1993	1994	1995	1996	1997
1984	7.4	6.9	6.8	7.3	7.5	7.4	7.2	7.0	6.9	7.0	7.5	8.2	9.5
1985		6.3	6.5	7.2	7.5	7.5	7.2	7.0	6.8	7.0	7.5	8.3	9.6
1986			6.7	7.7	7.9	7.7	7.4	7.1	6.9	7.1	7.6	8.5	9.9
1987				8.7	8.5	8.1	7.6	7.2	6.9	7.1	7.8	8.7	10.3
1988					8.3	7.8	7.2	6.8	6.5	6.9	7.6	8.7	10.4
1989						7.4	6.6	6.3	6.1	6.6	7.5	8.8	10.7
1990							5.9	5.8	5.7	6.4	7.5	9.0	11.2
1991								5.6	5.5	6.5	8.0	9.7	12.1
1992									5.5	7.0	8.7	10.7	13.5
1993										8.6	10.4	12.5	15.5
1994											12.3	14.5	18.0
1995												16.8	20.9
1996													25.2

1. These growth triangles are derived from data based on exchange rates. OECD-Total excludes Korea, Czech Republic, Hungary and Poland.

OCDE-TOTAL[1]

Variations moyennes en pourcentage aux taux annuels

Private final consumption expenditure per head (volume) / Consommation finale privée par tête (volume)

	1985	1986	1987	1988	1989	1990	1991	1992	1993	1994	1995	1996	1997
1984	2.8	2.8	2.7	2.9	2.8	2.6	2.3	2.1	2.0	1.9	1.9	1.9	1.9
1985		2.9	2.7	2.9	2.7	2.6	2.2	2.0	1.9	1.8	1.8	1.8	1.8
1986			2.6	2.9	2.7	2.5	2.0	1.9	1.7	1.7	1.6	1.7	1.7
1987				3.2	2.8	2.4	1.9	1.8	1.6	1.6	1.5	1.6	1.6
1988					2.3	2.1	1.5	1.4	1.2	1.3	1.3	1.4	1.4
1989						1.8	1.0	1.1	1.0	1.1	1.1	1.2	1.3
1990							0.3	0.8	0.7	0.9	1.0	1.1	1.3
1991								1.3	0.9	1.2	1.2	1.3	1.4
1992									0.5	1.1	1.1	1.3	1.5
1993										1.7	1.4	1.6	1.7
1994											1.2	1.6	1.7
1995												1.9	2.0
1996													2.0

Gross domestic product (implicit price deflator) / Produit intérieur brut (prix implicite)

	1985	1986	1987	1988	1989	1990	1991	1992	1993	1994	1995	1996	1997
1984	4.0	3.8	3.6	3.8	3.9	4.1	4.2	4.2	4.3	4.4	4.8	5.4	6.5
1985		3.6	3.5	3.7	3.9	4.1	4.3	4.3	4.3	4.4	4.9	5.6	6.7
1986			3.3	3.7	4.0	4.2	4.4	4.4	4.3	4.5	5.0	5.8	7.0
1987				4.2	4.4	4.6	4.7	4.6	4.6	4.7	5.2	6.0	7.3
1988					4.6	4.8	4.9	4.7	4.6	4.8	5.4	6.3	7.7
1989						4.9	5.0	4.7	4.6	4.8	5.5	6.5	8.1
1990							5.0	4.6	4.6	4.8	5.6	6.8	8.6
1991								4.2	4.3	4.7	5.8	7.1	9.2
1992									4.4	5.0	6.3	7.9	10.2
1993										5.5	7.3	9.0	11.7
1994											9.1	10.8	13.8
1995												12.6	16.2
1996													20.0

Private final consumption expenditure (implicit price deflator) / Consommation finale privée (prix implicite)

	1985	1986	1987	1988	1989	1990	1991	1992	1993	1994	1995	1996	1997
1984	4.2	3.5	3.6	3.7	3.9	4.1	4.3	4.3	4.4	4.6	5.1	5.7	6.9
1985		2.9	3.2	3.5	3.9	4.1	4.3	4.4	4.4	4.6	5.2	5.8	7.1
1986			3.6	3.9	4.2	4.4	4.6	4.6	4.7	4.9	5.4	6.1	7.5
1987				4.1	4.5	4.7	4.9	4.8	4.8	5.0	5.6	6.4	7.9
1988					4.9	5.0	5.1	5.0	5.0	5.2	5.9	6.7	8.3
1989						5.1	5.2	5.0	5.0	5.3	6.0	7.0	8.7
1990							5.4	5.0	5.0	5.3	6.2	7.3	9.3
1991								4.7	4.8	5.3	6.4	7.7	9.9
1992									4.9	5.6	7.0	8.4	11.0
1993										6.3	8.1	9.7	12.6
1994											9.9	11.4	14.7
1995												12.9	17.3
1996													21.8

Government final consumption expenditure (implicit price deflator) / Consommation des administrations publiques (prix implicite)

	1985	1986	1987	1988	1989	1990	1991	1992	1993	1994	1995	1996	1997
1984	4.6	3.9	3.9	3.9	4.1	4.4	4.6	4.7	4.6	4.6	4.8	5.3	6.3
1985		3.3	3.5	3.7	3.9	4.4	4.6	4.7	4.6	4.6	4.8	5.4	6.4
1986			3.8	3.8	4.1	4.7	4.9	4.9	4.8	4.8	5.0	5.6	6.7
1987				3.9	4.3	5.0	5.2	5.1	5.0	4.9	5.2	5.8	7.0
1988					4.8	5.5	5.6	5.5	5.2	5.1	5.3	6.1	7.3
1989						6.3	6.0	5.7	5.4	5.1	5.4	6.2	7.7
1990							5.7	5.4	5.0	4.9	5.3	6.2	7.9
1991								5.0	4.7	4.6	5.2	6.3	8.2
1992									4.4	4.3	5.2	6.7	8.9
1993										4.3	5.6	7.4	10.0
1994											6.9	9.1	12.0
1995												11.2	14.6
1996													18.1

Gross fixed capital formation (implicit price deflator) / Formation brute de capital fixe (prix implicite)

	1985	1986	1987	1988	1989	1990	1991	1992	1993	1994	1995	1996	1997
1984	2.8	2.7	2.6	2.8	3.0	3.2	3.2	3.1	3.2	3.4	3.9	4.6	6.1
1985		2.6	2.5	2.9	3.1	3.3	3.3	3.2	3.3	3.5	4.0	4.8	6.4
1986			2.4	3.0	3.3	3.5	3.4	3.3	3.4	3.6	4.1	5.0	6.7
1987				3.6	3.8	3.8	3.7	3.5	3.5	3.8	4.4	5.3	7.1
1988					3.9	3.9	3.7	3.5	3.5	3.8	4.5	5.5	7.5
1989						4.0	3.6	3.3	3.4	3.8	4.6	5.8	8.0
1990							3.3	3.0	3.3	3.7	4.7	6.1	8.6
1991								2.6	3.2	3.8	5.1	6.6	9.5
1992									3.8	4.5	5.9	7.6	10.9
1993										5.1	6.9	8.9	12.8
1994											8.8	10.9	15.5
1995												13.1	19.0
1996													25.2

Compensation of employees (value) / Rémunération des salariés (valeur)

	1985	1986	1987	1988	1989	1990	1991	1992	1993	1994	1995	1996	1997
1984	6.9	6.5	6.5	6.8	6.9	7.1	7.0	6.8	6.5	6.4	6.4	6.7	7.3
1985		6.2	6.3	6.7	6.9	7.2	7.0	6.8	6.5	6.3	6.3	6.7	7.3
1986			6.5	7.0	7.1	7.4	7.2	6.9	6.5	6.3	6.4	6.7	7.4
1987				7.6	7.4	7.7	7.3	7.0	6.5	6.3	6.4	6.8	7.5
1988					7.2	7.8	7.3	6.8	6.3	6.1	6.2	6.6	7.5
1989						8.3	7.3	6.7	6.1	5.9	6.0	6.6	7.5
1990							6.2	5.9	6.3	5.3	5.5	6.3	7.4
1991								5.6	4.9	5.0	5.4	6.3	7.6
1992									4.2	4.7	5.3	6.5	8.0
1993										5.1	5.8	7.2	8.9
1994											6.6	8.3	10.3
1995												10.0	12.1
1996													14.3

1. Ces triangles de croissance sont calculés à partir de données basées sur les taux de change. OCDE-Total ne comprend pas la Corée, la République tchèque, la Hongrie et la Pologne.

OECD-EUROPE[1]

Average per cent changes at annual rate

G.D.P. per head (volume)
P.I.B. par tête (volume)

	1985	1986	1987	1988	1989	1990	1991	1992	1993	1994	1995	1996	1997
1984	2.2	2.3	2.3	2.6	2.6	2.5	2.2	1.9	1.6	1.7	1.7	1.7	1.7
1985		2.4	2.4	2.7	2.7	2.5	2.2	1.9	1.6	1.6	1.7	1.6	1.7
1986			2.4	2.9	2.8	2.6	2.1	1.8	1.4	1.5	1.6	1.5	1.6
1987				3.3	3.0	2.6	2.1	1.7	1.3	1.4	1.5	1.5	1.5
1988					2.7	2.3	1.6	1.3	0.9	1.1	1.2	1.2	1.3
1989						1.9	1.1	0.9	0.4	0.8	0.9	1.0	1.2
1990							0.4	0.4	−0.1	0.5	0.8	0.9	1.1
1991								0.4	−0.3	0.5	0.9	1.0	1.2
1992									−1.0	0.6	1.0	1.1	1.3
1993										2.2	2.1	1.8	1.9
1994											2.0	1.7	1.9
1995												1.4	1.8
1996													2.3

Gross domestic product (volume)
Produit intérieur brut (volume)

	1985	1986	1987	1988	1989	1990	1991	1992	1993	1994	1995	1996	1997
1984	2.6	2.8	2.8	3.1	3.1	3.0	2.7	2.5	2.2	2.3	2.3	2.2	2.3
1985		2.9	2.9	3.2	3.3	3.1	2.8	2.5	2.2	2.2	2.3	2.2	2.3
1986			2.9	3.4	3.4	3.2	2.7	2.5	2.1	2.1	2.2	2.1	2.2
1987				3.9	3.6	3.3	2.7	2.4	1.9	2.0	2.1	2.1	2.1
1988					3.3	3.0	2.3	2.0	1.5	1.7	1.8	1.8	1.9
1989						2.6	1.8	1.6	1.1	1.4	1.6	1.6	1.8
1990							1.0	1.0	0.6	1.1	1.4	1.5	1.6
1991								1.1	0.4	1.1	1.5	1.5	1.8
1992									−0.3	1.2	1.6	1.7	1.9
1993										2.7	2.6	2.4	2.5
1994											2.5	2.2	2.4
1995												1.8	2.3
1996													2.8

Private final consumption expenditure (volume)
Consommation finale privée (volume)

	1985	1986	1987	1988	1989	1990	1991	1992	1993	1994	1995	1996	1997
1984	2.6	3.3	3.4	3.5	3.4	3.3	3.2	3.0	2.6	2.5	2.4	2.4	2.4
1985		4.1	3.8	3.8	3.6	3.5	3.3	3.0	2.6	2.5	2.4	2.4	2.4
1986			3.6	3.6	3.5	3.3	3.1	2.8	2.4	2.3	2.2	2.2	2.2
1987				3.7	3.4	3.3	3.0	2.7	2.2	2.1	2.1	2.1	2.1
1988					3.1	3.0	2.7	2.4	1.9	1.8	1.8	1.9	1.9
1989						2.9	2.6	2.2	1.6	1.6	1.6	1.7	1.8
1990							2.2	1.9	1.2	1.3	1.4	1.5	1.6
1991								1.6	0.7	1.0	1.2	1.4	1.5
1992									−0.2	0.6	1.0	1.3	1.5
1993										1.5	1.6	1.8	1.9
1994											1.8	2.0	2.1
1995												2.2	2.2
1996													2.2

Government final consumption expenditure (volume)
Consommation des administrations publiques (volume)

	1985	1986	1987	1988	1989	1990	1991	1992	1993	1994	1995	1996	1997
1984	2.4	2.3	2.4	2.3	2.1	2.1	2.1	2.1	2.0	1.9	1.8	1.8	1.7
1985		2.3	2.4	2.3	2.0	2.1	2.1	2.1	2.0	1.9	1.8	1.8	1.7
1986			2.5	2.3	1.9	2.0	2.1	2.1	1.9	1.8	1.7	1.7	1.6
1987				2.1	1.5	1.9	1.9	2.0	1.8	1.7	1.6	1.6	1.5
1988					1.0	1.7	1.9	1.9	1.7	1.6	1.5	1.6	1.4
1989						2.5	2.3	2.3	1.9	1.8	1.6	1.7	1.5
1990							2.2	2.2	1.8	1.6	1.5	1.5	1.4
1991								2.1	1.5	1.4	1.3	1.4	1.2
1992									1.0	1.0	1.0	1.2	1.0
1993										1.1	1.0	1.3	1.1
1994											0.9	1.4	1.0
1995												2.0	1.1
1996													0.3

Gross fixed capital formation (volume)
Formation brute de capital fixe (volume)

	1985	1986	1987	1988	1989	1990	1991	1992	1993	1994	1995	1996	1997
1984	2.6	3.3	4.1	5.0	5.3	5.1	4.4	3.7	2.6	2.6	2.7	2.6	2.6
1985		4.1	4.9	5.9	6.0	5.6	4.7	3.9	2.6	2.6	2.7	2.6	2.6
1986			5.8	6.8	6.7	6.0	4.8	3.8	2.4	2.4	2.5	2.4	2.5
1987				7.8	7.1	6.0	4.6	3.4	1.9	1.9	2.1	2.0	2.1
1988					6.5	5.1	3.6	2.4	0.7	1.0	1.3	1.3	1.5
1989						3.8	2.2	1.0	−0.7	−0.1	0.5	0.6	0.9
1990							0.5	−0.3	−2.1	−1.1	−0.1	0.1	0.5
1991								−1.2	−3.4	−1.6	−0.3	0.0	0.5
1992									−5.6	−1.8	−0.0	0.3	0.9
1993										2.2	2.9	2.4	2.5
1994											3.6	2.4	2.7
1995												1.3	2.2
1996													3.1

National disposable income (value)
Revenu national disponible (valeur)

	1985	1986	1987	1988	1989	1990	1991	1992	1993	1994	1995	1996	1997
1984	7.9	8.0	7.5	7.8	8.0	8.0	8.0	7.9	7.8	8.4	9.5	10.8	12.9
1985		8.1	7.4	7.7	8.0	8.1	8.0	7.9	7.8	8.4	9.6	11.1	13.3
1986			6.7	7.6	8.0	8.1	8.0	7.9	7.8	8.5	9.8	11.4	13.8
1987				8.5	8.7	8.6	8.3	8.1	7.9	8.7	10.2	12.0	14.6
1988					8.9	8.6	8.3	8.1	7.8	8.8	10.4	12.4	15.3
1989						8.3	8.0	7.8	7.6	8.8	10.7	12.9	16.1
1990							7.6	7.5	7.4	8.9	11.2	13.7	17.3
1991								7.5	7.2	9.3	12.1	15.0	19.0
1992									7.0	10.3	13.7	16.9	21.4
1993										13.6	17.2	20.4	25.3
1994											21.0	24.0	29.4
1995												27.1	33.9
1996													41.0

1. These growth triangles are derived from data based on exchange rates. OECD-Europe excludes Czech Republic, Hungary and Poland.

OCDE-EUROPE[1]

Variations moyennes en pourcentage aux taux annuels

Private final consumption expenditure per head (volume)
Consommation finale privée par tête (volume)

	1985	1986	1987	1988	1989	1990	1991	1992	1993	1994	1995	1996	1997
1984	2.2	2.9	2.9	3.0	2.9	2.8	2.6	2.4	2.0	1.9	1.9	1.8	1.8
1985		3.6	3.3	3.3	3.1	2.9	2.7	2.4	2.0	1.9	1.8	1.8	1.8
1986			3.1	3.1	2.9	2.7	2.5	2.2	1.8	1.7	1.6	1.6	1.6
1987				3.2	2.8	2.6	2.3	2.0	1.6	1.5	1.4	1.5	1.5
1988					2.5	2.3	2.1	1.8	1.2	1.2	1.2	1.3	1.3
1989						2.2	1.9	1.5	0.9	0.9	1.0	1.1	1.2
1990							1.5	1.2	0.5	0.6	0.8	0.9	1.0
1991								0.9	0.0	0.3	0.6	0.8	1.0
1992									−0.8	0.0	0.5	0.8	1.0
1993										0.9	1.1	1.3	1.4
1994											1.3	1.5	1.6
1995												1.7	1.7
1996													1.8

Gross domestic product (implicit price deflator)
Produit intérieur brut (prix implicite)

	1985	1986	1987	1988	1989	1990	1991	1992	1993	1994	1995	1996	1997
1984	5.1	4.9	4.5	4.4	4.6	4.8	5.1	5.2	5.4	5.9	6.8	8.1	9.9
1985		4.7	4.1	4.2	4.5	4.7	5.0	5.2	5.5	6.0	7.0	8.4	10.3
1986			3.6	4.0	4.4	4.8	5.1	5.3	5.6	6.1	7.2	8.7	10.9
1987				4.4	4.8	5.2	5.5	5.7	5.9	6.5	7.7	9.3	11.6
1988					5.3	5.6	5.9	6.0	6.2	6.9	8.2	10.0	12.5
1989						5.8	6.2	6.2	6.5	7.2	8.7	10.6	13.4
1990							6.6	6.4	6.7	7.6	9.3	11.5	14.5
1991								6.3	6.8	7.9	10.0	12.5	15.9
1992									7.3	8.7	11.2	14.1	17.9
1993										10.1	13.2	16.4	20.7
1994											16.4	19.7	24.5
1995												23.1	28.7
1996													34.6

Private final consumption expenditure (implicit price deflator)
Consommation finale privée (prix implicite)

	1985	1986	1987	1988	1989	1990	1991	1992	1993	1994	1995	1996	1997
1984	5.3	4.2	4.0	4.0	4.3	4.5	4.8	5.1	5.4	6.1	7.2	8.4	10.5
1985		3.2	3.3	3.5	4.0	4.3	4.7	5.0	5.4	6.2	7.3	8.7	10.9
1986			3.5	3.7	4.3	4.6	5.1	5.4	5.8	6.5	7.8	9.3	11.7
1987				3.9	4.7	5.0	5.5	5.7	6.1	7.0	8.4	10.0	12.5
1988					5.4	5.5	6.0	6.2	6.6	7.5	9.0	10.7	13.5
1989						5.5	6.2	6.4	6.9	7.9	9.6	11.5	14.6
1990							7.0	6.9	7.3	8.5	10.5	12.5	15.9
1991								6.8	7.5	9.0	11.4	13.7	17.5
1992									8.2	10.1	12.9	15.5	19.7
1993										12.1	15.4	18.0	22.8
1994											18.7	21.0	26.6
1995												23.5	30.7
1996													38.4

Government final consumption expenditure (implicit price deflator)
Consommation des administrations publiques (prix implicite)

	1985	1986	1987	1988	1989	1990	1991	1992	1993	1994	1995	1996	1997
1984	4.7	4.4	4.3	4.3	4.5	5.0	5.3	5.5	5.5	5.6	6.0	7.0	8.6
1985		4.1	4.1	4.2	4.5	5.1	5.4	5.6	5.6	5.7	6.2	7.2	8.9
1986			4.1	4.2	4.7	5.3	5.6	5.8	5.8	5.9	6.4	7.5	9.3
1987				4.3	4.9	5.7	6.0	6.2	6.1	6.1	6.7	7.9	9.9
1988					5.5	6.4	6.6	6.6	6.4	6.4	7.0	8.3	10.5
1989						7.3	7.1	7.0	6.7	6.6	7.3	8.7	11.2
1990							7.0	6.9	6.5	6.5	7.3	9.0	11.7
1991								6.7	6.2	6.3	7.3	9.3	12.5
1992									5.8	6.1	7.6	10.0	13.7
1993										6.4	8.5	11.5	15.8
1994											10.5	14.1	19.1
1995												17.8	23.7
1996													29.9

Gross fixed capital formation (implicit price deflator)
Formation brute de capital fixe (prix implicite)

	1985	1986	1987	1988	1989	1990	1991	1992	1993	1994	1995	1996	1997
1984	4.8	4.1	3.6	3.9	4.2	4.4	4.5	4.5	4.9	5.5	6.6	8.3	10.8
1985		3.5	3.1	3.6	4.0	4.3	4.4	4.4	4.9	5.6	6.8	8.6	11.3
1986			2.6	3.7	4.2	4.5	4.6	4.6	5.1	5.8	7.1	9.2	12.0
1987				4.7	5.0	5.1	5.1	5.0	5.5	6.3	7.7	9.9	13.0
1988					5.3	5.3	5.2	5.1	5.7	6.5	8.1	10.6	14.0
1989						5.4	5.2	5.0	5.7	6.8	8.6	11.4	15.1
1990							5.0	4.8	5.9	7.1	9.3	12.4	16.6
1991								4.6	6.3	7.9	10.4	13.9	18.6
1992									8.0	9.5	12.4	16.4	21.6
1993										11.1	14.6	19.3	25.3
1994											18.3	23.7	30.4
1995												29.3	36.9
1996													44.9

Compensation of employees (value)
Rémunération des salariés (valeur)

	1985	1986	1987	1988	1989	1990	1991	1992	1993	1994	1995	1996	1997
1984	7.0	6.9	6.7	6.8	7.0	7.5	7.6	7.5	7.1	7.0	7.2	8.0	9.1
1985		6.7	6.5	6.7	7.0	7.6	7.7	7.5	7.1	7.0	7.2	8.1	9.3
1986			6.3	6.7	7.1	7.8	7.9	7.6	7.2	7.0	7.3	8.2	9.6
1987				7.2	7.5	8.3	8.3	7.9	7.3	7.1	7.4	8.4	9.9
1988					7.9	8.9	8.6	8.1	7.3	7.1	7.4	8.6	10.2
1989						9.9	9.0	8.2	7.2	6.9	7.4	8.7	10.5
1990							8.1	7.3	6.3	6.2	6.9	8.5	10.6
1991								6.5	5.4	5.5	6.5	8.5	11.0
1992									4.3	5.0	6.6	9.0	11.9
1993										5.8	7.7	10.7	13.9
1994											9.6	13.2	16.7
1995												16.8	20.4
1996													24.1

1. Ces triangles de croissance sont calculés à partir de données basées sur les taux de change. OCDE-Europe ne comprend pas la République tchèque, la Hongrie et la Pologne.

Average per cent changes at annual rate

G.D.P. per head (volume) / **P.I.B. par tête** (volume)

	1985	1986	1987	1988	1989	1990	1991	1992	1993	1994	1995	1996	1997
1984	2.3	2.5	2.5	2.8	2.9	2.7	2.4	2.2	1.8	1.9	1.9	1.9	1.9
1985		2.6	2.6	3.0	3.0	2.8	2.4	2.1	1.7	1.8	1.9	1.8	1.9
1986			2.6	3.2	3.1	2.8	2.4	2.1	1.6	1.7	1.8	1.7	1.8
1987				3.7	3.4	2.9	2.3	1.9	1.4	1.6	1.7	1.6	1.7
1988					3.0	2.5	1.8	1.5	1.0	1.3	1.4	1.4	1.5
1989						2.0	1.3	1.0	0.5	0.9	1.1	1.2	1.3
1990							0.6	0.5	–0.0	0.6	0.9	1.0	1.2
1991								0.5	–0.3	0.7	1.0	1.1	1.3
1992									–1.0	0.8	1.2	1.3	1.5
1993										2.6	2.4	2.0	2.1
1994											2.1	1.8	2.0
1995												1.4	1.9
1996													2.4

Gross domestic product (volume) / **Produit intérieur brut** (volume)

	1985	1986	1987	1988	1989	1990	1991	1992	1993	1994	1995	1996	1997
1984	2.5	2.7	2.7	3.1	3.1	3.0	2.7	2.5	2.2	2.2	2.3	2.2	2.2
1985		2.8	2.8	3.2	3.3	3.1	2.8	2.5	2.1	2.2	2.2	2.2	2.2
1986			2.8	3.4	3.4	3.2	2.8	2.4	2.0	2.1	2.2	2.1	2.2
1987				4.1	3.7	3.3	2.7	2.4	1.9	2.0	2.1	2.0	2.1
1988					3.4	2.9	2.3	2.0	1.4	1.7	1.8	1.8	1.9
1989						2.4	1.7	1.5	1.0	1.4	1.5	1.6	1.7
1990							1.1	1.0	0.5	1.1	1.4	1.4	1.6
1991								0.9	0.2	1.1	1.4	1.5	1.7
1992									–0.6	1.2	1.6	1.6	1.8
1993										3.0	2.7	2.4	2.4
1994											2.4	2.0	2.3
1995												1.7	2.2
1996													2.7

Private final consumption expenditure (volume) / **Consommation finale privée** (volume)

	1985	1986	1987	1988	1989	1990	1991	1992	1993	1994	1995	1996	1997
1984	2.6	3.3	3.5	3.6	3.5	3.4	3.2	3.0	2.6	2.5	2.5	2.4	2.4
1985		4.1	3.9	3.9	3.8	3.6	3.3	3.1	2.6	2.5	2.5	2.4	2.4
1986			3.8	3.9	3.7	3.5	3.2	2.9	2.4	2.3	2.3	2.3	2.2
1987				4.0	3.6	3.3	3.1	2.8	2.2	2.1	2.1	2.1	2.1
1988					3.3	3.0	2.8	2.5	1.9	1.8	1.8	1.9	1.9
1989						2.8	2.5	2.2	1.5	1.6	1.6	1.7	1.7
1990							2.2	1.9	1.1	1.2	1.3	1.5	1.5
1991								1.6	0.6	0.9	1.1	1.3	1.4
1992									–0.4	0.6	1.0	1.3	1.4
1993										1.6	1.7	1.8	1.9
1994											1.8	1.9	2.0
1995												2.0	2.1
1996													2.1

Government final consumption expenditure (volume) / **Consommation des administrations publiques** (volume)

	1985	1986	1987	1988	1989	1990	1991	1992	1993	1994	1995	1996	1997
1984	2.3	2.2	2.3	2.3	2.0	2.0	2.0	2.0	1.9	1.8	1.7	1.8	1.6
1985		2.2	2.3	2.2	1.9	2.0	2.0	2.0	1.9	1.8	1.7	1.7	1.6
1986			2.4	2.3	1.8	1.9	2.0	2.0	1.8	1.7	1.6	1.7	1.5
1987				2.1	1.5	1.8	1.9	1.9	1.7	1.6	1.5	1.6	1.4
1988					0.9	1.6	1.8	1.8	1.6	1.6	1.5	1.5	1.4
1989						2.3	2.2	2.2	1.8	1.7	1.6	1.6	1.4
1990							2.1	2.1	1.7	1.6	1.4	1.5	1.3
1991								2.1	1.5	1.4	1.2	1.4	1.2
1992									0.9	1.0	1.0	1.2	1.0
1993										1.2	1.0	1.3	1.0
1994											0.9	1.4	1.0
1995												1.9	1.0
1996													0.2

Gross fixed capital formation (volume) / **Formation brute de capital fixe** (volume)

	1985	1986	1987	1988	1989	1990	1991	1992	1993	1994	1995	1996	1997
1984	2.6	3.2	3.9	5.0	5.4	5.1	4.5	3.8	2.5	2.6	2.6	2.5	2.5
1985		3.9	4.6	5.8	6.1	5.6	4.8	3.9	2.5	2.5	2.6	2.5	2.5
1986			5.3	6.8	6.8	6.1	5.0	3.9	2.3	2.4	2.5	2.3	2.4
1987				8.2	7.6	6.3	4.9	3.7	1.9	2.0	2.2	2.0	2.1
1988					6.9	5.4	3.8	2.6	0.6	1.0	1.3	1.3	1.4
1989						3.9	2.3	1.1	–0.9	–0.2	0.4	0.5	0.7
1990							0.7	–0.2	–2.4	–1.2	–0.3	–0.1	0.3
1991								–1.1	–3.9	–1.8	–0.5	–0.2	0.2
1992									–6.7	–2.2	–0.3	0.0	0.5
1993										2.6	3.1	2.3	2.4
1994											3.5	2.2	2.3
1995												0.9	1.7
1996													2.5

National disposable income (value) / **Revenu national disponible** (valeur)

	1985	1986	1987	1988	1989	1990	1991	1992	1993	1994	1995	1996	1997
1984	7.8	8.0	7.5	7.7	7.8	7.8	7.6	7.3	6.8	6.7	6.6	6.4	6.2
1985		8.2	7.4	7.7	7.9	7.8	7.6	7.2	6.6	6.5	6.4	6.2	6.1
1986			6.7	7.5	7.8	7.7	7.4	7.1	6.4	6.3	6.3	6.0	5.9
1987				8.3	8.3	8.0	7.6	7.1	6.4	6.3	6.2	6.0	5.9
1988					8.3	7.9	7.4	6.9	6.0	5.9	5.9	5.7	5.6
1989						7.4	6.9	6.4	5.4	5.5	5.5	5.3	5.3
1990							6.5	5.9	4.8	5.0	5.1	5.0	5.0
1991								5.3	3.9	4.5	4.8	4.7	4.7
1992									2.6	4.2	4.7	4.5	4.6
1993										5.7	5.7	5.2	5.1
1994											5.7	4.9	4.9
1995												4.2	4.5
1996													4.8

1. These growth triangles are derived from data based on exchange rates.

Variations moyennes en pourcentage aux taux annuels

Private final consumption expenditure per head (volume) / **Consommation finale privée par tête** (volume)

	1985	1986	1987	1988	1989	1990	1991	1992	1993	1994	1995	1996	1997
1984	2.5	3.2	3.3	3.4	3.3	3.1	2.9	2.7	2.3	2.2	2.1	2.1	2.1
1985		3.8	3.7	3.7	3.5	3.3	3.0	2.7	2.3	2.2	2.1	2.1	2.0
1986			3.6	3.6	3.4	3.1	2.8	2.5	2.0	1.9	1.9	1.9	1.9
1987				3.6	3.3	3.0	2.6	2.3	1.8	1.7	1.7	1.7	1.7
1988					2.9	2.6	2.3	2.0	1.4	1.4	1.4	1.5	1.5
1989						2.3	2.0	1.7	1.1	1.1	1.2	1.2	1.3
1990							1.7	1.4	0.6	0.8	0.9	1.1	1.2
1991								1.1	0.1	0.5	0.7	0.9	1.1
1992									–0.9	0.2	0.6	0.9	1.1
1993										1.3	1.4	1.5	1.6
1994											1.4	1.6	1.7
1995												1.8	1.8
1996													1.8

Gross domestic product (implicit price deflator) / **Produit intérieur brut** (prix implicite)

	1985	1986	1987	1988	1989	1990	1991	1992	1993	1994	1995	1996	1997
1984	5.1	5.0	4.5	4.4	4.4	4.6	4.7	4.7	4.5	4.4	4.2	4.1	3.9
1985		4.8	4.2	4.1	4.3	4.5	4.6	4.6	4.5	4.3	4.1	4.0	3.8
1986			3.5	3.8	4.1	4.4	4.6	4.6	4.4	4.2	4.1	3.9	3.7
1987				4.0	4.4	4.6	4.8	4.8	4.6	4.3	4.1	3.9	3.7
1988					4.7	4.9	5.1	4.9	4.7	4.3	4.1	3.9	3.7
1989						5.2	5.3	5.0	4.7	4.3	4.0	3.8	3.6
1990							5.5	5.0	4.5	4.0	3.8	3.6	3.3
1991								4.4	4.0	3.6	3.4	3.2	3.0
1992									3.6	3.1	3.1	2.9	2.7
1993										2.6	2.8	2.7	2.4
1994											3.0	2.7	2.4
1995												2.4	2.1
1996													1.8

Private final consumption expenditure (implicit price deflator) / **Consommation finale privée** (prix implicite)

	1985	1986	1987	1988	1989	1990	1991	1992	1993	1994	1995	1996	1997
1984	5.2	4.1	3.8	3.8	4.0	4.1	4.3	4.3	4.3	4.2	4.1	4.0	3.8
1985		3.1	3.2	3.3	3.7	3.9	4.2	4.2	4.2	4.1	4.0	3.9	3.7
1986			3.2	3.4	3.9	4.1	4.4	4.4	4.4	4.2	4.1	4.0	3.8
1987				3.6	4.2	4.3	4.7	4.7	4.6	4.4	4.2	4.0	3.8
1988					4.8	4.7	5.0	4.9	4.8	4.5	4.3	4.1	3.9
1989						4.7	5.2	5.0	4.8	4.5	4.2	4.0	3.8
1990							5.7	5.1	4.8	4.4	4.1	3.9	3.6
1991								4.6	4.3	4.0	3.7	3.5	3.3
1992									4.1	3.7	3.5	3.3	3.0
1993										3.3	3.1	3.0	2.8
1994											3.0	2.9	2.6
1995												2.7	2.4
1996													2.1

Government final consumption expenditure (implicit price deflator) / **Consommation des administrations publiques** (prix implicite)

	1985	1986	1987	1988	1989	1990	1991	1992	1993	1994	1995	1996	1997
1984	4.8	4.4	4.3	4.3	4.5	4.9	5.1	5.1	4.9	4.6	4.5	4.3	4.1
1985		4.1	4.1	4.1	4.4	4.9	5.1	5.1	4.9	4.6	4.4	4.3	4.1
1986			4.2	4.2	4.5	5.1	5.3	5.3	5.0	4.7	4.5	4.3	4.1
1987				4.2	4.7	5.4	5.6	5.5	5.2	4.7	4.5	4.3	4.1
1988					5.1	6.0	6.1	5.9	5.4	4.8	4.6	4.3	4.0
1989						6.8	6.5	6.1	5.4	4.8	4.5	4.2	3.9
1990							6.2	5.8	5.0	4.3	4.0	3.7	3.5
1991								5.3	4.3	3.6	3.5	3.2	3.1
1992									3.3	2.8	2.8	2.7	2.6
1993										2.3	2.6	2.5	2.4
1994											2.9	2.7	2.5
1995												2.4	2.2
1996													2.1

Gross fixed capital formation (implicit price deflator) / **Formation brute de capital fixe** (prix implicite)

	1985	1986	1987	1988	1989	1990	1991	1992	1993	1994	1995	1996	1997
1984	4.8	4.1	3.7	3.8	4.0	4.2	4.1	3.9	3.7	3.5	3.5	3.3	3.1
1985		3.4	3.2	3.5	3.8	4.0	4.0	3.8	3.6	3.4	3.4	3.2	3.0
1986			3.1	3.5	4.0	4.2	4.1	3.8	3.6	3.4	3.4	3.2	3.0
1987				4.0	4.4	4.6	4.4	4.0	3.7	3.5	3.4	3.2	3.0
1988					4.8	4.9	4.5	4.0	3.6	3.4	3.3	3.1	2.8
1989						4.9	4.4	3.7	3.4	3.1	3.0	2.8	2.6
1990							3.8	3.1	2.8	2.6	2.7	2.5	2.3
1991								2.3	2.4	2.2	2.4	2.2	2.0
1992									2.4	2.2	2.4	2.2	1.9
1993										1.9	2.4	2.1	1.8
1994											2.9	2.2	1.8
1995												1.4	1.2
1996													1.1

Compensation of employees (value) / **Rémunération des salariés** (valeur)

	1985	1986	1987	1988	1989	1990	1991	1992	1993	1994	1995	1996	1997
1984	7.0	6.8	6.6	6.7	6.9	7.3	7.3	7.1	[illegible]	6.1	5.9	5.8	5.6
1985		6.6	6.4	6.6	6.9	7.4	7.4	7.1	[illegible]	6.0	5.8	5.7	5.5
1986			6.2	6.6	7.0	7.6	7.5	7.2	[illegible]	6.0	5.8	5.6	5.4
1987				7.0	7.4	8.1	7.9	7.4	[illegible]	5.9	5.7	5.5	5.3
1988					7.7	8.6	8.1	7.4	[illegible]	5.7	5.5	5.3	5.1
1989						9.5	8.4	7.4	[illegible]	5.4	5.2	5.0	4.8
1990							7.3	6.3	[illegible]	4.4	4.3	4.2	4.1
1991								5.3	[illegible]	3.4	3.6	3.6	3.6
1992									[illegible]	2.4	3.0	3.2	3.3
1993										2.8	3.5	3.6	3.6
1994											4.2	4.0	3.8
1995												3.8	3.7
1996													3.6

1. Ces triangles de croissance sont calculés à partir de données basées sur les taux de change.

OECD-TOTAL[1]

Average per cent changes at annual rate

G.D.P. per head (volume)
P.I.B. par tête (volume)

	1985	1986	1987	1988	1989	1990	1991	1992	1993	1994	1995	1996	1997
1984	2.5	2.2	2.2	2.5	2.5	2.4	2.0	1.9	1.7	1.7	1.7	1.7	1.8
1985		1.9	2.1	2.5	2.5	2.3	1.9	1.8	1.6	1.6	1.6	1.7	1.7
1986			2.3	2.8	2.8	2.4	1.9	1.7	1.5	1.6	1.6	1.6	1.7
1987				3.3	3.0	2.5	1.8	1.6	1.4	1.5	1.5	1.6	1.7
1988					2.6	2.1	1.3	1.2	1.0	1.2	1.2	1.3	1.5
1989						1.5	0.6	0.7	0.6	0.9	1.0	1.2	1.3
1990							−0.2	0.4	0.3	0.8	0.9	1.1	1.3
1991								1.0	0.6	1.1	1.2	1.4	1.6
1992									0.3	1.2	1.2	1.5	1.7
1993										2.1	1.7	1.9	2.0
1994											1.3	1.8	2.0
1995												2.2	2.4
1996													2.5

Gross domestic product (volume)
Produit intérieur brut (volume)

	1985	1986	1987	1988	1989	1990	1991	1992	1993	1994	1995	1996	1997
1984	3.2	3.0	3.0	3.3	3.3	3.2	2.8	2.7	2.5	2.6	2.5	2.6	2.6
1985		2.7	2.9	3.3	3.4	3.2	2.7	2.6	2.4	2.5	2.4	2.5	2.5
1986			3.1	3.6	3.6	3.3	2.8	2.6	2.4	2.4	2.4	2.5	2.5
1987				4.1	3.8	3.4	2.7	2.5	2.3	2.4	2.3	2.4	2.5
1988					3.5	3.0	2.2	2.1	1.9	2.1	2.1	2.2	2.3
1989						2.4	1.5	1.6	1.5	1.8	1.8	2.0	2.1
1990							0.6	1.2	1.2	1.6	1.7	1.9	2.1
1991								1.8	1.5	1.9	2.0	2.2	2.3
1992									1.1	2.0	2.0	2.3	2.4
1993										2.9	2.5	2.7	2.8
1994											2.1	2.6	2.8
1995												3.0	3.1
1996													3.1

Private final consumption expenditure (volume)
Consommation finale privée (volume)

	1985	1986	1987	1988	1989	1990	1991	1992	1993	1994	1995	1996	1997
1984	3.6	3.6	3.5	3.6	3.5	3.4	3.0	3.0	2.8	2.8	2.7	2.7	2.7
1985		3.6	3.4	3.6	3.5	3.4	3.0	2.9	2.7	2.7	2.6	2.6	2.6
1986			3.3	3.6	3.5	3.3	2.8	2.8	2.6	2.6	2.5	2.5	2.5
1987				4.0	3.6	3.3	2.7	2.7	2.5	2.5	2.4	2.4	2.5
1988					3.2	3.0	2.3	2.3	2.2	2.2	2.2	2.2	2.3
1989						2.8	1.9	2.0	1.9	2.0	2.0	2.1	2.2
1990							1.0	1.7	1.6	1.8	1.9	2.0	2.1
1991								2.3	1.9	2.1	2.1	2.2	2.3
1992									1.6	2.0	2.0	2.2	2.3
1993										2.5	2.2	2.4	2.5
1994											1.9	2.3	2.5
1995												2.7	2.8
1996													2.9

Government final consumption expenditure (volume)
Consommation des administrations publiques (volume)

	1985	1986	1987	1988	1989	1990	1991	1992	1993	1994	1995	1996	1997
1984	3.2	3.2	3.0	2.8	2.5	2.5	2.4	2.2	2.0	1.9	1.8	1.7	1.6
1985		3.2	2.9	2.6	2.3	2.4	2.2	2.1	1.8	1.7	1.6	1.6	1.5
1986			2.6	2.3	2.1	2.2	2.1	1.9	1.7	1.6	1.5	1.4	1.4
1987				2.1	1.8	2.0	1.9	1.8	1.5	1.4	1.3	1.3	1.2
1988					1.6	2.0	1.9	1.7	1.4	1.3	1.2	1.2	1.1
1989						2.5	2.0	1.7	1.4	1.3	1.2	1.2	1.1
1990							1.6	1.3	1.0	0.9	0.9	0.9	0.9
1991								1.1	0.7	0.7	0.7	0.8	0.8
1992									0.3	0.6	0.6	0.7	0.7
1993										0.8	0.7	0.9	0.8
1994											0.7	0.9	0.8
1995												1.1	0.9
1996													0.7

Gross fixed capital formation (volume)
Formation brute de capital fixe (volume)

	1985	1986	1987	1988	1989	1990	1991	1992	1993	1994	1995	1996	1997
1984	4.6	3.6	3.9	4.6	4.7	4.4	3.6	3.3	2.9	2.9	2.9	3.2	3.3
1985		2.7	3.6	4.6	4.8	4.4	3.5	3.1	2.6	2.7	2.7	3.1	3.2
1986			4.5	5.6	5.5	4.8	3.6	3.2	2.6	2.7	2.8	3.1	3.2
1987				6.7	6.0	4.9	3.4	2.9	2.3	2.5	2.5	3.0	3.1
1988					5.3	4.1	2.3	2.0	1.5	1.8	2.0	2.5	2.7
1989						2.9	0.9	1.0	0.6	1.1	1.4	2.2	2.4
1990							−1.1	0.0	−0.2	0.7	1.1	2.0	2.3
1991								1.2	0.3	1.3	1.7	2.7	2.9
1992									−0.6	1.4	1.9	3.1	3.3
1993										3.5	3.2	4.3	4.3
1994											2.8	4.7	4.5
1995												6.7	5.4
1996													4.1

National disposable income (values at current PPPs)
Revenu national disponible (valeurs en PPA courantes)

	1985	1986	1987	1988	1989	1990	1991	1992	1993	1994	1995	1996	1997
1984	6.9	5.9	6.2	6.7	7.0	6.9	6.6	6.5	6.1	6.0	6.0	5.9	5.8
1985		4.9	5.9	6.7	7.0	7.0	6.6	6.4	6.0	5.9	5.9	5.8	5.7
1986			6.8	7.5	7.7	7.5	6.9	6.7	6.2	6.0	6.0	5.9	5.8
1987				8.3	8.2	7.7	6.9	6.6	6.1	5.9	5.9	5.8	5.7
1988					8.0	7.4	6.5	6.2	5.6	5.5	5.6	5.5	5.4
1989						6.8	5.7	5.6	5.1	5.0	5.2	5.1	5.1
1990							4.6	5.0	4.5	4.6	4.8	4.8	4.9
1991								5.5	4.4	4.6	4.9	4.9	4.9
1992									3.4	4.1	4.7	4.7	4.8
1993										4.9	5.4	5.2	5.2
1994											5.9	5.3	5.3
1995												4.8	5.0
1996													5.2

1. These growth triangles are derived from data based on purchasing power parities. OECD-Total excludes Korea, Czech Republic, Hungary and Poland.

OCDE-TOTAL[1]

Variations moyennes en pourcentage aux taux annuels

Private final consumption expenditure per head (volume)
Consommation finale privée par tête (volume)

	1985	1986	1987	1988	1989	1990	1991	1992	1993	1994	1995	1996	1997
1984	2.8	2.8	2.7	2.8	2.7	2.6	2.2	2.1	2.0	1.9	1.9	1.9	1.9
1985		2.8	2.6	2.8	2.7	2.5	2.1	2.0	1.9	1.8	1.8	1.8	1.8
1986			2.5	2.8	2.7	2.5	2.0	1.9	1.7	1.7	1.7	1.7	1.7
1987				3.2	2.8	2.4	1.9	1.8	1.6	1.6	1.6	1.6	1.7
1988					2.3	2.1	1.4	1.4	1.3	1.4	1.3	1.4	1.5
1989						1.8	1.0	1.2	1.0	1.2	1.2	1.3	1.4
1990							0.2	0.8	0.8	1.0	1.0	1.2	1.3
1991								1.4	1.1	1.3	1.2	1.4	1.5
1992									0.7	1.2	1.2	1.4	1.5
1993										1.7	1.4	1.6	1.8
1994											1.1	1.5	1.8
1995												2.0	2.1
1996													2.3

Gross domestic product (implicit price deflator)
Produit intérieur brut (prix implicite)

	1985	1986	1987	1988	1989	1990	1991	1992	1993	1994	1995	1996	1997
1984	4.2	4.0	4.0	4.2	4.4	4.6	4.8	4.9	5.0	5.4	6.2	7.4	9.0
1985		3.8	3.8	4.2	4.5	4.7	4.9	5.0	5.1	5.5	6.4	7.6	9.4
1986			3.8	4.4	4.7	4.9	5.1	5.1	5.3	5.7	6.7	8.0	10.0
1987				5.0	5.1	5.3	5.4	5.4	5.5	6.0	7.1	8.5	10.6
1988					5.2	5.4	5.6	5.5	5.6	6.1	7.4	9.0	11.2
1989						5.6	5.7	5.6	5.7	6.3	7.7	9.5	12.0
1990							5.9	5.6	5.8	6.5	8.2	10.2	12.9
1991								5.3	5.7	6.7	8.8	11.0	14.2
1992									6.1	7.4	9.9	12.5	16.0
1993										8.8	11.9	14.7	18.7
1994											15.1	17.9	22.1
1995												20.7	25.8
1996													31.2

Private final consumption expenditure (implicit price deflator)
Consommation finale privée (prix implicite)

	1985	1986	1987	1988	1989	1990	1991	1992	1993	1994	1995	1996	1997
1984	4.4	3.9	4.0	4.3	4.5	4.7	5.0	5.1	5.3	5.7	6.6	7.7	9.5
1985		3.3	3.8	4.2	4.5	4.8	5.1	5.2	5.4	5.8	6.8	8.0	9.9
1986			4.3	4.7	5.0	5.2	5.4	5.5	5.7	6.2	7.2	8.5	10.6
1987				5.1	5.3	5.5	5.7	5.7	5.9	6.4	7.6	9.0	11.2
1988					5.5	5.7	5.9	5.9	6.0	6.7	8.0	9.5	11.9
1989						5.9	6.1	6.0	6.2	6.9	8.4	10.1	12.7
1990							6.3	6.1	6.3	7.1	8.9	10.8	13.8
1991								5.9	6.3	7.4	9.6	11.7	15.1
1992									6.7	8.2	10.8	13.2	17.0
1993										9.8	13.0	15.5	19.7
1994											16.3	18.4	23.2
1995												20.6	26.8
1996													33.4

Government final consumption expenditure (implicit price deflator)
Consommation des administrations publiques (prix implicite)

	1985	1986	1987	1988	1989	1990	1991	1992	1993	1994	1995	1996	1997
1984	4.7	4.0	4.0	4.1	4.3	4.7	4.9	5.1	5.2	5.3	5.8	6.8	8.4
1985		3.4	3.7	3.9	4.2	4.7	5.0	5.1	5.2	5.4	5.9	7.0	8.7
1986			4.0	4.2	4.5	5.0	5.3	5.4	5.5	5.6	6.2	7.3	9.2
1987				4.3	4.7	5.4	5.6	5.7	5.7	5.8	6.4	7.7	9.7
1988					5.1	5.9	6.0	6.0	6.0	6.1	6.7	8.1	10.3
1989						6.7	6.5	6.4	6.2	6.3	7.0	8.6	11.0
1990							6.3	6.2	6.1	6.2	7.1	8.9	11.6
1991								6.0	6.0	6.2	7.3	9.4	12.5
1992									5.9	6.2	7.7	10.3	13.8
1993										6.5	8.6	11.8	15.9
1994											10.7	14.5	19.2
1995												18.4	23.7
1996													29.2

Gross fixed capital formation (implicit price deflator)
Formation brute de capital fixe (prix implicite)

	1985	1986	1987	1988	1989	1990	1991	1992	1993	1994	1995	1996	1997
1984	2.8	3.0	2.9	3.3	3.5	3.6	3.7	3.7	4.0	4.5	5.5	6.8	9.0
1985		3.2	2.9	3.4	3.6	3.8	3.9	3.9	4.2	4.7	5.7	7.2	9.5
1986			2.6	3.6	3.8	4.0	4.0	4.0	4.3	4.9	6.0	7.6	10.1
1987				4.5	4.4	4.4	4.4	4.2	4.6	5.2	6.4	8.2	10.9
1988					4.3	4.4	4.3	4.2	4.6	5.3	6.7	8.6	11.6
1989						4.5	4.3	4.2	4.7	5.5	7.1	9.3	12.6
1990							4.2	4.0	4.8	5.8	7.7	10.1	13.8
1991								3.8	5.0	6.3	8.6	11.3	15.5
1992									6.3	7.6	10.2	13.3	18.0
1993										9.0	12.2	15.7	21.1
1994											15.5	19.2	25.4
1995												23.0	30.7
1996													38.9

Compensation of employees (values at current PPPs)
Rémunération des salariés (valeurs en PPA courantes)

	1985	1986	1987	1988	1989	1990	1991	1992	1993	1994	1995	1996	1997
1984	6.6	5.9	6.1	6.5	6.7	6.9	6.7	6.6	6.2	6.0	5.9	5.8	5.7
1985		5.2	5.9	6.5	6.7	7.0	6.7	6.6	6.2	5.9	5.9	5.7	5.7
1986			6.6	7.1	7.2	7.4	7.0	6.8	6.3	6.0	5.9	5.8	5.7
1987				7.7	7.5	7.7	7.1	6.9	6.2	5.9	5.8	5.7	5.6
1988					7.3	7.7	6.9	6.7	6.0	5.6	5.6	5.4	5.4
1989						8.1	6.7	6.5	5.6	5.3	5.3	5.1	5.1
1990							5.3	5.7	4.8	4.6	4.8	4.7	4.7
1991								6.1	4.6	4.4	4.6	4.5	4.6
1992									3.1	3.5	4.1	4.1	4.3
1993										3.9	4.7	4.5	4.6
1994											5.4	4.8	4.9
1995												4.2	4.6
1996													5.1

1. Ces triangles de croissance sont calculés à partir de données basées sur les parités de pouvoir d'achat. OCDE-Total ne comprend pas la Corée, la République tchèque, la Hongrie et la Pologne.

Average per cent changes at annual rate

G.D.P. per head / P.I.B. par tête (volume)

	1985	1986	1987	1988	1989	1990	1991	1992	1993	1994	1995	1996	1997
1984	2.2	2.4	2.5	2.7	2.7	2.6	2.3	2.0	1.7	1.7	1.8	1.7	1.8
1985		2.6	2.6	2.9	2.8	2.6	2.3	2.0	1.7	1.7	1.7	1.7	1.8
1986			2.7	3.0	2.9	2.7	2.2	1.9	1.5	1.6	1.6	1.6	1.7
1987				3.4	3.0	2.7	2.1	1.8	1.3	1.4	1.5	1.5	1.6
1988					2.6	2.3	1.7	1.4	0.9	1.1	1.2	1.3	1.4
1989						2.0	1.2	0.9	0.5	0.8	1.0	1.1	1.3
1990							0.4	0.4	0.0	0.5	0.8	0.9	1.1
1991								0.5	-0.1	0.6	0.9	1.1	1.3
1992									-0.8	0.6	1.1	1.2	1.4
1993										2.0	2.0	1.9	2.0
1994											2.1	1.8	2.0
1995												1.5	2.0
1996													2.4

Gross domestic product / Produit intérieur brut (volume)

	1985	1986	1987	1988	1989	1990	1991	1992	1993	1994	1995	1996	1997
1984	2.6	2.8	2.9	3.2	3.2	3.1	2.8	2.6	2.3	2.3	2.4	2.3	2.4
1985		3.0	3.1	3.4	3.3	3.2	2.9	2.6	2.3	2.3	2.3	2.3	2.3
1986			3.1	3.6	3.5	3.3	2.8	2.5	2.2	2.2	2.3	2.2	2.3
1987				4.0	3.6	3.3	2.7	2.4	2.0	2.1	2.1	2.1	2.2
1988					3.3	3.0	2.3	2.0	1.6	1.8	1.9	1.9	2.0
1989						2.7	1.9	1.6	1.2	1.5	1.7	1.7	1.9
1990							1.0	1.1	0.7	1.2	1.4	1.5	1.7
1991								1.2	0.5	1.2	1.5	1.6	1.8
1992									-0.1	1.2	1.7	1.7	2.0
1993										2.5	2.6	2.4	2.5
1994											2.6	2.3	2.5
1995												2.0	2.5
1996													2.9

Private final consumption expenditure / Consommation finale privée (volume)

	1985	1986	1987	1988	1989	1990	1991	1992	1993	1994	1995	1996	1997
1984	2.5	3.3	3.4	3.5	3.4	3.4	3.2	3.0	2.7	2.5	2.5	2.5	2.5
1985		4.1	3.8	3.8	3.6	3.6	3.3	3.1	2.7	2.5	2.5	2.5	2.5
1986			3.5	3.7	3.5	3.4	3.2	2.9	2.5	2.3	2.3	2.3	2.3
1987				3.8	3.5	3.4	3.1	2.8	2.3	2.2	2.1	2.2	2.2
1988					3.1	2.8	2.5	2.0	1.9	1.9	2.0	2.0	2.0
1989						3.2	2.7	2.3	1.8	1.7	1.7	1.8	1.9
1990							2.1	1.9	1.3	1.3	1.4	1.6	1.7
1991								1.6	0.9	1.0	1.2	1.5	1.6
1992									0.1	0.7	1.1	1.4	1.6
1993										1.3	1.6	1.9	2.0
1994											1.9	2.2	2.3
1995												2.4	2.5
1996													2.5

Government final consumption expenditure / Consommation des administrations publiques (volume)

	1985	1986	1987	1988	1989	1990	1991	1992	1993	1994	1995	1996	1997
1984	2.5	2.5	2.5	2.4	2.1	2.2	2.2	2.2	2.1	2.0	1.9	1.9	1.8
1985		2.4	2.5	2.4	2.0	2.1	2.2	2.2	2.0	1.9	1.8	1.8	1.7
1986			2.6	2.4	1.9	2.1	2.1	2.1	2.0	1.9	1.8	1.8	1.7
1987				2.1	1.6	1.9	2.0	2.0	1.9	1.7	1.7	1.7	1.6
1988					1.1	1.8	2.0	2.0	1.8	1.7	1.6	1.6	1.5
1989						2.5	2.4	2.3	2.0	1.8	1.7	1.7	1.6
1990							2.3	2.2	1.8	1.6	1.5	1.6	1.4
1991								2.1	1.6	1.4	1.3	1.5	1.3
1992									1.1	1.0	1.0	1.3	1.1
1993										1.0	1.0	1.4	1.1
1994											1.0	1.5	1.1
1995												2.0	1.2
1996													0.4

Gross fixed capital formation / Formation brute de capital fixe (volume)

	1985	1986	1987	1988	1989	1990	1991	1992	1993	1994	1995	1996	1997
1984	2.7	3.4	4.5	5.4	5.6	5.3	4.6	3.9	2.9	2.8	2.9	2.8	2.9
1985		4.2	5.5	6.3	6.3	5.9	5.0	4.1	3.0	2.8	2.9	2.8	2.9
1986			6.8	7.3	7.0	6.3	5.1	4.1	2.8	2.6	2.8	2.7	2.7
1987				7.9	7.2	6.1	4.7	3.6	2.1	2.1	2.3	2.2	2.3
1988					6.4	5.3	3.7	2.5	1.0	1.1	1.5	1.5	1.7
1989						4.1	2.3	1.2	-0.3	0.1	0.7	0.8	1.2
1990							0.5	-0.2	-1.7	-0.9	0.0	0.3	0.8
1991								-0.8	-2.8	-1.4	-0.1	0.3	0.8
1992									-4.7	-1.6	0.1	0.5	1.1
1993										1.5	2.6	2.3	2.7
1994											3.8	2.8	3.0
1995												1.7	2.7
1996													3.6

National disposable income / Revenu national disponible (values at current PPPs / valeurs en PPA courantes)

	1985	1986	1987	1988	1989	1990	1991	1992	1993	1994	1995	1996	1997
1984	6.2	6.0	6.2	6.7	6.9	6.9	6.6	6.6	5.9	5.8	5.9	5.7	5.7
1985		5.9	6.3	6.8	7.1	7.0	6.7	6.6	5.9	5.8	5.9	5.7	5.6
1986			6.7	7.3	7.5	7.3	6.8	6.8	5.9	5.8	5.9	5.7	5.6
1987				7.9	7.9	7.6	6.9	6.8	5.8	5.7	5.8	5.6	5.5
1988					7.9	7.4	6.6	6.5	5.4	5.3	5.4	5.3	5.3
1989						6.9	5.9	6.1	4.8	4.8	5.0	4.9	4.9
1990							4.9	5.7	4.1	4.2	4.7	4.6	4.6
1991								6.4	3.7	4.0	4.6	4.5	4.6
1992									1.0	2.8	4.0	4.0	4.3
1993										4.7	5.6	5.1	5.1
1994											6.5	5.2	5.2
1995												4.0	4.6
1996													5.2

Variations moyennes en pourcentage aux taux annuels

Private final consumption expenditure per head / Consommation finale privée par tête (volume)

	1985	1986	1987	1988	1989	1990	1991	1992	1993	1994	1995	1996	1997
1984	2.1	2.9	2.9	3.0	2.9	2.8	2.6	2.4	2.1	1.9	1.9	1.9	1.9
1985		3.7	3.4	3.3	3.1	3.0	2.7	2.5	2.1	1.9	1.9	1.9	1.9
1986			3.1	3.2	2.9	2.8	2.5	2.3	1.9	1.7	1.7	1.7	1.7
1987				3.3	2.9	2.7	2.4	2.1	1.7	1.5	1.5	1.6	1.6
1988					2.4	2.5	2.1	1.8	1.3	1.2	1.3	1.3	1.4
1989						2.5	2.0	1.6	1.1	1.0	1.1	1.2	1.3
1990							1.5	1.2	0.6	0.6	0.8	0.9	1.1
1991								0.9	0.2	0.4	0.6	0.9	1.1
1992									0.5	0.7	1.1	1.3	1.5
1993										0.7	1.1	1.3	1.5
1994											1.4	1.7	1.8
1995												1.9	2.0
1996													2.0

Gross domestic product / Produit intérieur brut (implicit price deflator / prix implicite)

	1985	1986	1987	1988	1989	1990	1991	1992	1993	1994	1995	1996	1997
1984	5.4	5.1	4.7	4.7	5.0	5.3	5.7	6.0	6.6	7.6	9.3	11.3	13.9
1985		4.9	4.3	4.5	4.9	5.3	5.7	6.1	6.7	7.8	9.7	11.9	14.7
1986			3.7	4.3	4.9	5.4	5.9	6.3	7.0	8.2	10.2	12.6	15.6
1987				4.9	5.5	5.9	6.4	6.8	7.5	8.9	11.0	13.6	16.9
1988					6.1	6.4	6.9	7.3	8.1	9.6	11.9	14.8	18.3
1989						6.8	7.3	7.7	8.6	10.3	12.9	16.1	19.9
1990							7.9	8.2	9.2	11.2	14.2	17.7	21.9
1991								8.5	9.8	12.3	15.9	19.7	24.4
1992									11.1	14.2	18.4	22.7	27.9
1993										17.3	22.3	26.9	32.4
1994											27.4	31.9	37.9
1995												36.6	43.4
1996													50.6

Private final consumption expenditure / Consommation finale privée (implicit price deflator / prix implicite)

	1985	1986	1987	1988	1989	1990	1991	1992	1993	1994	1995	1996	1997
1984	5.7	4.6	4.3	4.4	4.8	5.1	5.5	6.0	6.7	8.0	9.9	11.9	14.7
1985		3.5	3.7	4.0	4.6	4.9	5.5	6.1	6.8	8.2	10.3	12.4	15.5
1986			3.9	4.2	4.9	5.3	5.9	6.5	7.3	8.9	11.1	13.4	16.6
1987				4.5	5.4	5.8	6.5	7.0	7.9	9.6	12.0	14.5	18.0
1988					6.4	6.4	7.1	7.7	8.6	10.5	13.2	15.8	19.6
1989						6.5	7.5	8.1	9.1	11.3	14.3	17.2	21.3
1990							8.6	8.9	10.0	12.5	16.0	19.1	23.6
1991								9.3	10.8	13.9	17.9	21.3	26.3
1992									12.3	16.2	20.9	24.5	30.0
1993										20.3	25.5	28.9	34.9
1994											30.9	33.4	40.1
1995												36.0	45.0
1996													54.6

Government final consumption expenditure / Consommation des administrations publiques (implicit price deflator / prix implicite)

	1985	1986	1987	1988	1989	1990	1991	1992	1993	1994	1995	1996	1997
1984	4.8	4.5	4.4	4.5	4.8	5.3	5.7	6.0	6.3	6.8	7.7	9.4	11.9
1985		4.2	4.2	4.3	4.8	5.4	5.9	6.2	6.5	7.0	8.0	9.8	12.6
1986			4.2	4.4	5.0	5.7	6.2	6.6	6.9	7.3	8.4	10.4	13.4
1987				4.7	5.3	6.2	6.7	7.0	7.3	7.8	9.0	11.1	14.3
1988					6.0	7.0	7.4	7.6	7.8	8.3	9.6	12.0	15.4
1989						8.0	8.1	8.2	8.3	8.8	10.2	12.8	16.7
1990							8.2	8.3	8.4	9.0	10.6	13.7	18.0
1991								8.4	8.5	9.2	11.3	14.8	19.7
1992									8.6	9.7	12.2	16.4	22.1
1993										10.7	14.1	19.2	25.7
1994											17.6	23.7	31.1
1995												30.0	38.5
1996													47.5

Gross fixed capital formation / Formation brute de capital fixe (implicit price deflator / prix implicite)

	1985	1986	1987	1988	1989	1990	1991	1992	1993	1994	1995	1996	1997
1984	5.0	4.4	3.7	4.1	4.5	4.8	5.0	5.3	6.2	7.4	9.3	12.0	15.2
1985		3.8	3.0	3.8	4.4	4.7	5.0	5.3	6.3	7.7	9.8	12.6	16.1
1986			2.2	3.9	4.6	5.0	5.3	5.6	6.7	8.2	10.4	13.5	17.3
1987				5.5	5.7	5.9	6.1	6.3	7.5	9.1	11.5	14.9	18.9
1988					6.0	6.1	6.4	6.7	7.8	9.7	12.4	16.1	20.5
1989						6.2	6.4	6.6	8.3	10.5	13.5	17.6	22.4
1990							6.6	6.8	9.0	11.6	15.0	19.6	25.0
1991								7.0	10.3	13.3	17.2	22.4	28.3
1992									11.6	16.5	20.9	26.6	33.0
1993										19.5	24.6	31.3	38.4
1994											30.0	37.6	45.3
1995												45.6	53.7
1996													62.2

Compensation of employees / Rémunération des salariés (values at current PPPs / valeurs en PPA courantes)

	1985	1986	1987	1988	1989	1990	1991	1992	1993	1994	1995	1996	1997
1984	5.6	5.1	5.5	5.9	6.3	6.7	6.6	6.6	5.9	5.5	5.4	5.3	5.2
1985		4.5	5.4	6.0	6.4	7.0	6.8	6.8	6.0	5.5	5.4	5.3	5.2
1986			6.3	6.7	7.1	7.6	7.3	7.2	6.2	5.6	5.5	5.3	5.2
1987				7.2	7.4	8.0	7.5	7.4	6.1	5.5	5.4	5.2	5.1
1988					7.7	8.4	7.7	7.4	5.9	5.2	5.2	5.0	4.9
1989						9.1	7.6	7.3	5.5	4.8	4.8	4.6	4.5
1990							6.2	6.4	4.3	3.7	3.9	3.9	3.9
1991								6.6	3.4	2.9	3.3	3.4	3.5
1992									0.3	1.1	2.3	2.6	2.9
1993										1.9	3.3	3.4	3.5
1994											4.7	4.2	4.1
1995												3.7	3.8
1996													4.0

1. These growth triangles are derived from data based on purchasing power parities. OECD-Europe excludes Czech Republic, Hungary and Poland.

1. Ces triangles de croissance sont calculés à partir de données basées sur les parités de pouvoir d'achat. OCDE-Europe ne comprend pas la République tchèque, la Hongrie et la Pologne.

EU15[1]

UE15[1]

Average per cent changes at annual rate

Variations moyennes en pourcentage aux taux annuels

G.D.P. per head (volume) / P.I.B. par tête (volume)

	1985	1986	1987	1988	1989	1990	1991	1992	1993	1994	1995	1996	1997
1984	2.3	2.5	2.6	2.9	2.9	2.8	2.4	2.2	1.8	1.9	1.9	1.9	1.9
1985		2.7	2.7	3.1	3.1	2.8	2.5	2.2	1.8	1.9	1.9	1.8	1.9
1986			2.7	3.3	3.2	2.9	2.4	2.1	1.6	1.8	1.8	1.8	1.8
1987				3.8	3.4	2.9	2.3	2.0	1.5	1.6	1.7	1.7	1.7
1988					3.0	2.5	1.8	1.5	1.0	1.3	1.4	1.4	1.5
1989						2.0	1.3	1.0	0.5	0.9	1.1	1.2	1.3
1990							0.6	0.5	0.0	0.7	0.9	1.0	1.2
1991								0.5	–0.3	0.7	1.0	1.1	1.3
1992									–1.0	0.8	1.3	1.3	1.5
1993										2.6	2.4	2.1	2.1
1994											2.1	1.8	2.0
1995												1.4	1.9
1996													2.4

Private final consumption expenditure per head (volume) / Consommation finale privée par tête (volume)

	1985	1986	1987	1988	1989	1990	1991	1992	1993	1994	1995	1996	1997
1984	2.5	3.2	3.3	3.4	3.3	3.2	3.0	2.7	2.3	2.2	2.1	2.1	2.1
1985		3.9	3.7	3.8	3.6	3.3	3.0	2.8	2.3	2.2	2.1	2.1	2.1
1986			3.6	3.7	3.5	3.2	2.9	2.6	2.1	2.0	1.9	1.9	1.9
1987				3.8	3.4	3.0	2.7	2.4	1.8	1.7	1.7	1.7	1.7
1988					3.0	2.6	2.3	2.0	1.4	1.4	1.4	1.5	1.5
1989						2.3	2.0	1.7	1.1	1.1	1.2	1.3	1.3
1990							1.7	1.4	0.6	0.8	0.9	1.1	1.2
1991								1.1	0.1	0.5	0.8	1.0	1.1
1992									–0.8	0.2	0.6	0.9	1.1
1993										1.3	1.4	1.5	1.6
1994											1.4	1.6	1.7
1995												1.8	1.8
1996													1.9

Gross domestic product (volume) / Produit intérieur brut (volume)

	1985	1986	1987	1988	1989	1990	1991	1992	1993	1994	1995	1996	1997
1984	2.5	2.7	2.8	3.1	3.2	3.0	2.8	2.5	2.2	2.3	2.3	2.2	2.3
1985		2.9	2.9	3.3	3.3	3.2	2.8	2.5	2.1	2.2	2.3	2.2	2.2
1986			2.9	3.5	3.5	3.2	2.8	2.5	2.0	2.2	2.2	2.1	2.2
1987				4.1	3.8	3.3	2.7	2.4	1.9	2.0	2.1	2.1	2.1
1988					3.4	2.9	2.3	2.0	1.5	1.7	1.8	1.8	1.9
1989						2.4	1.7	1.5	1.0	1.4	1.5	1.6	1.7
1990							1.1	1.0	0.5	1.1	1.4	1.4	1.6
1991								1.0	0.2	1.1	1.4	1.5	1.7
1992									–0.5	1.2	1.6	1.6	1.8
1993										3.0	2.7	2.4	2.4
1994											2.4	2.1	2.3
1995												1.7	2.2
1996													2.7

Gross domestic product (implicit price deflator) / Produit intérieur brut (prix implicite)

	1985	1986	1987	1988	1989	1990	1991	1992	1993	1994	1995	1996	1997
1984	5.3	5.2	4.7	4.5	4.6	4.7	4.8	4.8	4.7	4.5	4.4	4.2	4.0
1985		5.0	4.3	4.3	4.4	4.6	4.8	4.7	4.6	4.4	4.3	4.1	3.9
1986			3.7	3.9	4.2	4.5	4.7	4.7	4.6	4.3	4.2	4.0	3.8
1987				4.2	4.5	4.8	5.0	4.9	4.7	4.4	4.3	4.1	3.8
1988					4.9	5.1	5.3	5.1	4.8	4.5	4.3	4.1	3.8
1989						5.3	5.5	5.2	4.8	4.4	4.2	3.9	3.7
1990							5.7	5.1	4.7	4.2	3.9	3.7	3.4
1991								4.6	4.2	3.7	3.5	3.3	3.1
1992									3.7	3.2	3.2	3.0	2.8
1993										2.7	2.9	2.8	2.5
1994											3.0	2.8	2.5
1995												2.5	2.2
1996													1.8

Private final consumption expenditure (volume) / Consommation finale privée (volume)

	1985	1986	1987	1988	1989	1990	1991	1992	1993	1994	1995	1996	1997
1984	2.7	3.4	3.5	3.7	3.6	3.5	3.3	3.1	2.7	2.6	2.5	2.5	2.4
1985		4.1	4.0	4.0	3.8	3.6	3.4	3.1	2.7	2.6	2.5	2.4	2.4
1986			3.8	4.0	3.8	3.5	3.2	3.0	2.5	2.4	2.3	2.3	2.3
1987				4.1	3.7	3.4	3.1	2.8	2.3	2.2	2.1	2.1	2.1
1988					3.4	3.1	2.8	2.5	1.9	1.9	1.8	1.9	1.9
1989						2.8	2.5	2.2	1.5	1.6	1.6	1.7	1.7
1990							2.1	1.9	1.1	1.2	1.3	1.5	1.6
1991								1.6	0.6	1.0	1.2	1.3	1.5
1992									–0.4	0.6	1.0	1.3	1.5
1993										1.7	1.7	1.8	1.9
1994											1.7	1.9	2.0
1995												2.1	2.1
1996													2.2

Private final consumption expenditure (implicit price deflator) / Consommation finale privée (prix implicite)

	1985	1986	1987	1988	1989	1990	1991	1992	1993	1994	1995	1996	1997
1984	5.3	4.3	4.0	3.9	4.1	4.2	4.5	4.5	4.5	4.4	4.3	4.1	4.0
1985		3.4	3.4	3.5	3.8	4.0	4.3	4.4	4.4	4.3	4.1	4.0	3.9
1986			3.4	3.5	4.0	4.2	4.5	4.6	4.5	4.4	4.2	4.1	3.9
1987				3.7	4.3	4.5	4.8	4.8	4.7	4.5	4.3	4.2	4.0
1988					4.9	4.9	5.2	5.1	4.9	4.6	4.4	4.2	4.0
1989						4.8	5.3	5.1	4.9	4.6	4.3	4.1	3.9
1990							5.9	5.3	4.9	4.5	4.3	4.0	3.7
1991								4.8	4.5	4.1	3.9	3.6	3.4
1992									4.2	3.8	3.6	3.4	3.1
1993										3.4	3.3	3.1	2.9
1994											3.1	3.0	2.7
1995												2.8	2.5
1996													2.2

Government final consumption expenditure (volume) / Consommation des administrations publiques (volume)

	1985	1986	1987	1988	1989	1990	1991	1992	1993	1994	1995	1996	1997
1984	2.2	2.2	2.3	2.3	2.0	2.1	2.1	2.1	2.0	1.9	1.8	1.8	1.7
1985		2.2	2.3	2.3	2.0	2.0	2.1	2.1	1.9	1.8	1.7	1.7	1.6
1986			2.4	2.3	1.9	2.0	2.0	2.0	1.9	1.8	1.7	1.7	1.6
1987				2.2	1.6	1.8	1.9	2.0	1.8	1.7	1.6	1.6	1.5
1988					1.0	1.7	1.8	1.9	1.7	1.6	1.5	1.5	1.4
1989						2.3	2.3	2.2	1.9	1.7	1.6	1.6	1.4
1990							2.2	2.1	1.7	1.6	1.4	1.5	1.3
1991								2.0	1.5	1.4	1.2	1.4	1.2
1992									0.9	1.0	1.0	1.2	1.0
1993										1.2	1.0	1.3	1.0
1994											0.9	1.4	1.0
1995												1.8	1.0
1996													0.2

Government final consumption expenditure (implicit price deflator) / Consommation des administrations publiques (prix implicite)

	1985	1986	1987	1988	1989	1990	1991	1992	1993	1994	1995	1996	1997
1984	4.9	4.6	4.5	4.4	4.6	5.0	5.2	5.2	5.0	4.8	4.6	4.4	4.3
1985		4.2	4.3	4.3	4.5	5.0	5.2	5.3	5.0	4.7	4.6	4.4	4.2
1986			4.3	4.3	4.6	5.2	5.4	5.4	5.2	4.8	4.6	4.4	4.2
1987				4.3	4.8	5.5	5.7	5.7	5.3	4.9	4.7	4.4	4.2
1988					5.3	6.1	6.2	6.0	5.5	5.0	4.7	4.4	4.2
1989						7.0	6.7	6.3	5.6	4.9	4.6	4.3	4.0
1990							6.4	6.0	5.1	4.4	4.1	3.9	3.6
1991								5.5	4.5	3.8	3.6	3.4	3.2
1992									3.5	2.9	3.0	2.8	2.7
1993										2.3	2.7	2.6	2.5
1994											3.0	2.8	2.6
1995												2.5	2.3
1996													2.2

Gross fixed capital formation (volume) / Formation brute de capital fixe (volume)

	1985	1986	1987	1988	1989	1990	1991	1992	1993	1994	1995	1996	1997
1984	2.6	3.2	4.0	5.1	5.5	5.2	4.5	3.8	2.6	2.6	2.7	2.6	2.6
1985		3.9	4.7	6.0	6.2	5.7	4.9	4.0	2.6	2.6	2.7	2.6	2.6
1986			5.6	7.1	7.0	6.2	5.1	4.0	2.5	2.5	2.6	2.4	2.5
1987				8.6	7.7	6.4	4.9	3.7	1.9	2.0	2.2	2.1	2.1
1988					6.9	5.4	3.8	2.6	0.7	1.0	1.3	1.3	1.5
1989						3.8	2.2	1.1	–0.8	–0.2	0.4	0.5	0.8
1990							0.6	–0.2	–2.3	–1.1	–0.2	–0.0	0.4
1991								–1.0	–3.8	–1.7	–0.4	–0.1	0.3
1992									–6.5	–2.1	–0.2	0.1	0.6
1993										2.6	3.1	2.4	2.5
1994											3.5	2.3	2.4
1995												1.0	1.9
1996													2.7

Gross fixed capital formation (implicit price deflator) / Formation brute de capital fixe (prix implicite)

	1985	1986	1987	1988	1989	1990	1991	1992	1993	1994	1995	1996	1997
1984	4.9	4.2	3.9	4.0	4.2	4.3	4.2	4.0	3.8	3.6	3.6	3.4	3.2
1985		3.6	3.4	3.6	4.0	4.2	4.1	3.9	3.7	3.5	3.5	3.3	3.1
1986			3.2	3.7	4.1	4.3	4.2	3.9	3.7	3.5	3.5	3.3	3.1
1987				4.2	4.6	4.7	4.5	4.1	3.8	3.5	3.5	3.3	3.1
1988					5.0	5.0	4.6	4.0	3.7	3.4	3.4	3.2	2.9
1989						5.0	4.4	3.7	3.4	3.1	3.1	2.9	2.7
1990							3.8	3.1	2.9	2.7	2.8	2.6	2.4
1991								2.4	2.4	2.3	2.5	2.3	2.1
1992									2.5	2.2	2.5	2.3	2.1
1993										2.0	2.6	2.2	2.0
1994											3.1	2.3	1.9
1995												1.5	1.4
1996													1.2

National disposable income (values at current PPPs) / Revenu national disponible (valeurs en PPA courantes)

	1985	1986	1987	1988	1989	1990	1991	1992	1993	1994	1995	1996	1997
1984	6.0	5.9	6.1	6.6	6.9	6.8	6.6	6.5	5.8	5.8	5.8	5.6	5.6
1985		5.8	6.2	6.8	7.1	7.0	6.7	6.6	5.8	5.7	5.8	5.6	5.5
1986			6.6	7.4	7.6	7.3	6.8	6.7	5.8	5.7	5.8	5.6	5.5
1987				8.2	8.1	7.5	6.9	6.8	5.7	5.6	5.7	5.5	5.4
1988					8.0	7.2	6.5	6.4	5.2	5.2	5.3	5.1	5.1
1989						6.5	5.7	5.9	4.5	4.6	4.9	4.7	4.8
1990							5.0	5.6	3.8	4.2	4.6	4.5	4.5
1991								6.3	3.3	3.9	4.5	4.4	4.4
1992									0.3	2.8	3.9	3.9	4.1
1993										5.3	5.8	5.1	5.0
1994											6.2	5.0	4.9
1995												3.7	4.3
1996													4.9

Compensation of employees (values at current PPPs) / Rémunération des salariés (valeurs en PPA courantes)

	1985	1986	1987	1988	1989	1990	1991	1992	1993	1994	1995	1996	1997
1984	5.5	4.9	5.3	5.7	6.1	6.5	6.4	6.5	5.7	5.4	5.3	5.2	5.1
1985		4.3	5.2	5.8	6.3	6.8	6.6	6.6	5.7	5.4	5.3	5.2	5.0
1986			6.1	6.6	6.9	7.4	7.1	7.0	5.9	5.5	5.4	5.2	5.1
1987				7.1	7.4	7.8	7.3	7.2	5.9	5.4	5.4	5.2	5.0
1988					7.6	8.2	7.4	7.2	5.7	5.2	5.1	4.9	4.8
1989						8.8	7.3	7.0	5.2	4.7	4.7	4.5	4.4
1990							5.8	6.2	4.1	3.7	3.9	3.8	3.8
1991								6.6	3.2	3.0	3.5	3.5	3.5
1992									–0.1	1.2	2.4	2.7	2.9
1993										2.5	3.7	3.6	3.7
1994											4.9	4.2	4.0
1995												3.4	3.6
1996													3.8

1. These growth triangles are derived from data based on purchasing power parities.

1. Ces triangles de croissance sont calculés à partir de données basées sur les parités de pouvoir d'achat.

Growth triangles: Countries
Triangles de croissance : Pays

The statistics for Germany in this publication refer to Germany after unification. Official data for Germany after unification are available only from 1991 onwards. In this publication, the secretariat has estimated some national accounts aggregates for the whole of Germany back to 1960 in order to calculate the various zones totals. These estimates are based on statistics published by Deutsches Institut für Wirtschaftsforschung for period 1989-90 and by the East German Statistical Office in 1990 for period 1980-89. They are also based on the ratios of the aggregates of West Germany and the whole of Germany.

Les statistiques concernant l'Allemagne dans cette publication se réfèrent à l'Allemagne après l'unification. Des données officielles pour l'Allemagne après l'unification ne sont disponibles qu'à partir de 1991. Dans cette publication, le secrétariat a estimé certains agrégats des comptes nationaux pour l'Allemagne dans son ensemble depuis 1960 afin de calculer les différentes zones. Ces estimations sont basées sur des statistiques publiées par Deutsches Institut für Wirtschaftsforschung pour la période 1989-90 et par l'Office Statistique de l'Allemagne de l'Est en 1990 pour la période 1980-89. Elles sont aussi basées sur les rapports des agrégats de l'Allemagne occidentale et de l'Allemagne dans son ensemble.

This part presents for each country growth triangles for the following aggregates:
– *Per capita* GDP (volume).
– *Per capita* private consumption (volume).
– GDP (volume and implicit price deflator).
– Private final consumption expenditure (volume and implicit price deflator).
– Government final consumption expenditure (volume and implicit price deflator).
– Gross fixed capital formation (volume and implicit price deflator).
– National disposable income (value).
– Compensation of employees (value).

Cette partie fournit pour chaque pays des triangles de croissance pour les agrégats suivants :
– PIB par habitant (volume).
– Consommation finale privée par habitant (volume).
– PIB (volume et prix implicite).
– Consommation finale privée (volume et prix implicite).
– Consommation des administrations publiques (volume et prix implicite).
– Formation brute de capital fixe (volume et prix implicite).
– Revenu national disponible (valeur).
– Rémunération des salariés (valeur).

CANADA

Average per cent changes at annual rate

Variations moyennes en pourcentage aux taux annuels

G.D.P. per head (volume) / P.I.B. par tête (volume)

	1985	1986	1987	1988	1989	1990	1991	1992	1993	1994	1995	1996	1997
1984	4.4	3.0	2.9	3.1	2.6	1.9	1.2	1.0	1.0	1.2	1.1	1.0	1.2
1985		1.6	2.2	2.6	2.1	1.4	0.7	0.5	0.6	0.8	0.8	0.7	0.9
1986			2.7	3.1	2.3	1.4	0.5	0.3	0.4	0.7	0.7	0.7	0.8
1987				3.5	2.1	0.9	–0.1	–0.2	0.0	0.4	0.5	0.4	0.6
1988					0.6	–0.3	–1.2	–1.1	–0.6	–0.1	0.1	0.1	0.3
1989						–1.2	–2.2	–1.6	–1.0	–0.2	–0.0	–0.0	0.3
1990							–3.1	–1.8	–0.9	0.0	0.2	0.2	0.5
1991								–0.6	0.3	1.1	1.0	0.8	1.1
1992									1.1	2.0	1.6	1.2	1.5
1993										2.8	1.8	1.2	1.6
1994											0.9	0.5	1.2
1995												0.0	1.3
1996													2.6

Private final consumption expenditure per head (volume) / Consommation finale privée par tête (volume)

	1985	1986	1987	1988	1989	1990	1991	1992	1993	1994	1995	1996	1997
1984	4.2	3.5	3.2	3.2	2.9	2.3	1.6	1.5	[illegible].3	1.4	1.3	1.3	1.4
1985		2.9	2.8	2.8	2.5	2.0	1.2	1.1	[illegible].0	1.1	1.0	1.0	1.2
1986			2.7	2.8	2.4	1.7	0.9	0.8	[illegible].7	0.9	0.8	0.9	1.1
1987				3.0	2.3	1.4	0.4	0.4	[illegible].4	0.6	0.6	0.7	0.9
1988					1.6	0.7	–0.4	–0.2	–[illegible].1	0.2	0.3	0.4	0.7
1989						–0.2	–1.4	–0.8	–[illegible].5	–0.0	0.1	0.2	0.6
1990							–2.6	–1.1	–[illegible].6	0.0	0.1	0.3	0.7
1991								0.3	[illegible].4	0.9	0.8	0.9	1.2
1992									[illegible].4	1.2	1.0	1.0	1.4
1993										2.0	1.2	1.2	1.6
1994											0.4	0.8	1.5
1995												1.1	2.1
1996													3.0

Gross domestic product (volume) / Produit intérieur brut (volume)

	1985	1986	1987	1988	1989	1990	1991	1992	1993	1994	1995	1996	1997
1984	5.4	4.0	4.0	4.2	3.9	3.3	2.5	2.3	2.3	2.5	2.5	2.3	2.5
1985		2.6	3.3	3.8	3.5	2.8	2.0	1.9	1.9	2.2	2.2	2.1	2.2
1986			4.1	4.5	3.8	2.9	1.9	1.7	1.9	2.1	2.1	2.0	2.2
1987				4.9	3.6	2.5	1.4	1.3	1.5	1.8	1.9	1.8	2.0
1988					2.4	1.3	0.2	0.4	0.8	1.3	1.4	1.4	1.7
1989						0.2	–0.8	–0.3	0.4	1.1	1.3	1.3	1.6
1990							–1.9	–0.5	0.5	1.3	1.5	1.4	1.8
1991								0.9	1.7	2.4	2.4	2.1	2.4
1992									2.5	3.2	2.9	2.4	2.7
1993										3.9	3.0	2.4	2.7
1994											2.1	1.7	2.3
1995												1.2	2.5
1996													3.7

Gross domestic product (implicit price deflator) / Produit intérieur brut (prix implicite)

	1985	1986	1987	1988	1989	1990	1991	1992	1993	1994	1995	1996	1997
1984	2.4	2.6	3.3	3.6	3.8	3.7	3.6	3.3	[illegible].0	2.9	2.8	2.7	2.5
1985		2.7	3.8	4.0	4.2	4.0	3.7	3.4	[illegible].1	2.9	2.9	2.7	2.6
1986			4.8	4.6	4.7	4.3	3.9	3.5	[illegible].2	2.9	2.9	2.7	2.5
1987				4.5	4.6	4.1	3.7	3.2	[illegible].9	2.7	2.7	2.5	2.3
1988					4.8	3.9	3.5	2.9	[illegible].6	2.4	2.4	2.3	2.1
1989						3.1	2.9	2.3	[illegible].1	1.9	2.0	1.9	1.7
1990							2.6	1.9	[illegible].7	1.6	1.8	1.7	1.6
1991								1.3	[illegible].3	1.3	1.6	1.6	1.4
1992									[illegible].2	1.2	1.7	1.6	1.4
1993										1.2	2.0	1.8	1.4
1994											2.7	2.0	1.5
1995												1.4	0.9
1996													0.5

Private final consumption expenditure (volume) / Consommation finale privée (volume)

	1985	1986	1987	1988	1989	1990	1991	1992	1993	1994	1995	1996	1997
1984	5.2	4.5	4.4	4.4	4.2	3.7	2.9	2.8	2.7	2.7	2.6	2.6	2.7
1985		3.9	4.0	4.1	3.9	3.4	2.6	2.5	2.4	2.5	2.4	2.4	2.5
1986			4.0	4.2	3.9	3.3	2.3	2.2	2.2	2.3	2.2	2.2	2.4
1987				4.3	3.9	3.0	1.9	1.9	1.9	2.0	2.0	2.0	2.2
1988					3.4	2.3	1.1	1.3	1.4	1.7	1.7	1.7	2.0
1989						1.3	–0.1	0.5	0.9	1.3	1.4	1.5	1.8
1990							–1.4	0.2	0.7	1.3	1.4	1.5	1.9
1991								1.8	1.8	2.2	2.1	2.1	2.5
1992									1.9	2.5	2.2	2.2	2.6
1993										3.1	2.4	2.4	2.8
1994											1.7	2.0	2.7
1995												2.3	3.2
1996													4.1

Private final consumption expenditure (implicit price deflator) / Consommation finale privée (prix implicite)

	1985	1986	1987	1988	1989	1990	1991	1992	1993	1994	1995	1996	1997
1984	3.8	3.9	3.9	3.9	4.0	4.0	4.1	3.8	[illegible].6	3.3	3.2	3.0	2.9
1985		4.0	4.0	3.9	4.1	4.1	4.2	3.8	[illegible].6	3.3	3.1	2.9	2.8
1986			4.0	3.9	4.1	4.1	4.2	3.8	[illegible].5	3.2	3.0	2.8	2.7
1987				3.8	4.1	4.2	4.3	3.7	[illegible].5	3.1	2.9	2.7	2.6
1988					4.5	4.4	4.5	3.7	[illegible].4	2.9	2.7	2.6	2.5
1989						4.2	4.5	3.4	[illegible].1	2.6	2.4	2.3	2.2
1990							4.7	3.1	[illegible].8	2.2	2.1	2.0	1.9
1991								1.4	[illegible].8	1.4	1.4	1.4	1.5
1992									[illegible].2	1.4	1.5	1.5	1.5
1993										0.6	1.1	1.2	1.3
1994											1.5	1.5	1.5
1995												1.5	1.5
1996													1.6

Government final consumption expenditure (volume) / Consommation des administrations publiques (volume)

	1985	1986	1987	1988	1989	1990	1991	1992	1993	1994	1995	1996	1997
1984	4.3	3.1	2.5	3.1	3.0	3.1	3.1	2.8	2.5	2.0	1.8	1.5	1.4
1985		1.9	1.7	2.6	2.7	2.9	2.9	2.6	2.2	1.8	1.6	1.3	1.2
1986			1.4	3.0	2.9	3.1	3.1	2.7	2.3	1.8	1.5	1.2	1.1
1987				4.6	3.7	3.7	3.5	3.0	2.4	1.8	1.5	1.2	1.1
1988					2.8	3.2	3.1	2.6	2.0	1.4	1.1	0.8	0.7
1989						3.7	3.2	2.5	1.8	1.1	0.8	0.5	0.4
1990							2.8	1.9	1.2	0.5	0.3	0.0	–0.0
1991								1.0	0.4	–0.3	–0.4	–0.5	–0.5
1992									–0.3	–1.0	–0.8	–0.9	–0.8
1993										–1.8	–1.1	–1.2	–0.9
1994											–0.4	–0.9	–0.6
1995												–1.3	–0.7
1996													–0.1

Government final consumption expenditure (implicit price deflator) / Consommation des administrations publiques (prix implicite)

	1985	1986	1987	1988	1989	1990	1991	1992	1993	1994	1995	1996	1997
1984	3.6	3.4	3.7	3.7	4.0	4.3	4.3	4.1	[illegible].8	3.5	3.3	3.0	2.8
1985		3.1	3.7	3.7	4.1	4.4	4.4	4.2	[illegible].8	3.5	3.3	3.0	2.7
1986			4.3	4.0	4.5	4.7	4.6	4.3	[illegible].9	3.5	3.3	2.9	2.6
1987				3.7	4.5	4.9	4.7	4.3	[illegible].8	3.4	3.1	2.8	2.5
1988					5.3	5.4	5.0	4.5	[illegible].8	3.3	3.0	2.7	2.3
1989						5.5	4.8	4.2	[illegible].4	3.0	2.7	2.3	2.0
1990							4.1	3.5	[illegible].7	2.3	2.1	1.8	1.5
1991								2.9	[illegible].0	1.7	1.6	1.3	1.0
1992									[illegible].1	1.1	1.2	0.9	0.7
1993										1.1	1.2	0.8	0.5
1994											1.3	0.6	0.4
1995												0.0	–0.1
1996													–0.2

Gross fixed capital formation (volume) / Formation brute de capital fixe (volume)

	1985	1986	1987	1988	1989	1990	1991	1992	1993	1994	1995	1996	1997
1984	10.3	7.8	8.8	9.0	8.4	6.3	4.8	4.0	3.3	3.6	3.0	3.2	3.8
1985		5.4	8.0	8.6	7.9	5.5	4.0	3.2	2.4	2.9	2.3	2.6	3.3
1986			10.7	10.3	8.8	5.5	3.7	2.8	2.0	2.6	2.0	2.3	3.1
1987				9.8	7.8	3.9	2.0	1.3	0.6	1.5	1.0	1.4	2.3
1988					5.9	1.0	–0.5	–0.7	–1.1	0.2	–0.2	0.4	1.5
1989						–3.6	–3.6	–2.8	–2.8	–0.9	–1.2	–0.4	1.0
1990							–3.5	–2.4	–2.6	–0.2	–0.8	0.1	1.7
1991								–1.3	–2.1	0.9	–0.1	0.9	2.6
1992									–2.9	2.0	0.4	1.5	3.4
1993										7.1	2.0	2.9	5.0
1994											–2.8	0.9	4.3
1995												4.8	8.0
1996													11.4

Gross fixed capital formation (implicit price deflator) / Formation brute de capital fixe (prix implicite)

	1985	1986	1987	1988	1989	1990	1991	1992	1993	1994	1995	1996	1997
1984	0.8	1.3	2.0	2.2	2.4	2.0	1.1	0.8	[illegible]	1.1	1.1	0.9	0.9
1985		1.8	2.7	2.7	2.8	2.3	1.2	0.8	[illegible]	1.1	1.1	1.0	1.0
1986			3.5	3.2	3.1	2.4	1.1	0.7	[illegible]	1.0	1.0	0.9	0.9
1987				2.8	2.8	2.0	0.4	0.1	[illegible]	0.7	0.7	0.6	0.6
1988					2.9	1.6	–0.3	–0.6	[illegible]	0.3	0.4	0.3	0.4
1989						0.4	–1.9	–1.7	[illegible]	–0.2	0.0	–0.0	0.1
1990							–4.2	–2.7	[illegible]	–0.3	–0.1	–0.1	0.0
1991								–1.3	[illegible]	1.0	1.0	0.7	0.7
1992									[illegible]	2.1	1.8	1.2	1.1
1993										2.6	1.8	1.1	1.0
1994											1.0	0.3	0.5
1995												–0.5	0.2
1996													0.8

National disposable income (value) / Revenu national disponible (valeur)

	1985	1986	1987	1988	1989	1990	1991	1992	1993	1994	1995	1996	1997
1984	8.1	6.4	7.5	8.2	7.9	7.0	6.0	5.4	5.3	5.2	5.2	5.0	5.0
1985		4.8	7.2	8.3	7.9	6.8	5.7	5.1	4.9	4.9	5.0	4.7	4.7
1986			9.6	10.1	9.0	7.3	5.9	5.1	4.9	5.0	5.0	4.7	4.7
1987				10.6	8.6	6.5	5.0	4.2	4.2	4.3	4.4	4.2	4.2
1988					6.7	4.6	3.2	2.7	2.9	3.3	3.6	3.4	3.5
1989						2.5	1.4	1.4	2.0	2.6	3.1	3.0	3.2
1990							0.4	0.9	1.9	2.7	3.2	3.0	3.2
1991								1.3	2.6	3.4	3.9	3.6	3.7
1992									3.9	4.5	4.8	4.2	4.2
1993										5.1	5.2	4.2	4.3
1994											5.3	3.8	4.0
1995												2.4	3.4
1996													4.5

Compensation of employees (value) / Rémunération des salariés (valeur)

	1985	1986	1987	1988	1989	1990	1991	1992	1993	1994	1995	1996	1997
1984	7.8	7.2	7.7	8.2	8.1	7.6	6.9	6.3	[illegible]	5.5	5.3	5.1	5.0
1985		6.6	7.6	8.3	8.2	7.6	6.8	6.1	[illegible]	5.2	5.1	4.8	4.7
1986			8.7	9.2	8.7	7.8	6.8	6.0	[illegible]	5.1	4.9	4.6	4.6
1987				9.7	8.8	7.6	6.3	5.5	[illegible]	4.6	4.4	4.2	4.2
1988					7.8	6.5	5.2	4.5	[illegible]	3.7	3.7	3.5	3.6
1989						5.2	4.0	3.4	[illegible]	2.9	3.0	2.9	3.0
1990							2.8	2.5	[illegible]	2.4	2.6	2.6	2.7
1991								2.3	[illegible]	2.2	2.5	2.5	2.7
1992									[illegible]	2.2	2.6	2.6	2.8
1993										2.6	3.0	2.8	3.1
1994											3.4	3.0	3.2
1995												2.5	3.1
1996													3.8

MEXICO

MEXIQUE

Average per cent changes at annual rate

Variations moyennes en pourcentage aux taux annuels

G.D.P. per head (volume)
P.I.B. par tête (volume)

	1985	1986	1987	1988	1989	1990	1991	1992	1993	1994	1995	1996	1997
1984	0.6	−2.6	−1.8	−1.6	−0.8	−0.2	0.2	0.4	0.4	0.6	−0.2	0.1	0.4
1985		−5.7	−3.0	−2.3	−1.2	−0.3	0.1	0.4	0.3	0.6	−0.3	0.0	0.4
1986			−0.2	−0.5	0.4	1.1	1.3	1.4	1.2	1.4	0.3	0.6	1.0
1987				−0.8	0.7	1.5	1.7	1.7	1.5	1.6	0.4	0.7	1.1
1988					2.2	2.6	2.5	2.4	1.9	2.1	0.5	0.9	1.4
1989						3.0	2.7	2.4	1.9	2.0	0.2	0.7	1.2
1990							2.4	2.1	1.5	1.8	−0.3	0.3	1.0
1991								1.9	1.0	1.6	−1.0	−0.1	0.8
1992									0.2	1.4	−1.9	−0.6	0.5
1993										2.7	−2.9	−0.9	0.6
1994											−8.3	−2.6	−0.0
1995												3.4	4.3
1996													5.2

Private final consumption expenditure per head (volume)
Consommation finale privée par tête (volume)

	1985	1986	1987	1988	1989	1990	1991	1992	1993	1994	1995	1996	1997
1984	1.4	−1.8	−1.9	−1.5	−0.2	0.6	0.9	1.1	1.0	1.2	−0.1	−0.0	0.3
1985		−4.8	−3.5	−2.4	−0.6	0.4	0.8	1.1	0.9	1.1	−0.2	−0.1	0.2
1986			−2.1	−1.2	0.9	1.8	2.0	2.1	1.8	1.9	0.3	0.3	0.7
1987				−0.2	2.5	3.1	3.0	3.0	2.5	2.5	0.6	0.6	1.0
1988					5.2	4.8	4.1	3.8	3.0	3.0	0.8	0.7	1.2
1989						4.4	3.6	3.4	2.5	2.5	0.0	0.1	0.7
1990							2.8	2.9	1.8	2.1	−0.8	−0.6	0.1
1991								2.9	1.3	1.8	−1.7	−1.3	−0.3
1992									−0.2	1.3	−3.2	−2.3	−0.9
1993										2.8	−4.6	−2.9	−1.1
1994											−11.5	−5.7	−2.4
1995												0.5	2.5
1996													4.6

Gross domestic product (volume)
Produit intérieur brut (volume)

	1985	1986	1987	1988	1989	1990	1991	1992	1993	1994	1995	1996	1997
1984	2.8	−0.5	0.2	0.5	1.2	1.9	2.2	2.4	2.3	2.5	1.7	2.0	2.4
1985		−3.8	−1.0	−0.2	0.8	1.7	2.1	2.3	2.3	2.5	1.6	1.9	2.3
1986			1.9	1.6	2.4	3.1	3.3	3.4	3.2	3.3	2.2	2.5	2.9
1987				1.2	2.7	3.5	3.7	3.7	3.4	3.5	2.3	2.6	3.0
1988					4.2	4.6	4.5	4.3	3.8	3.9	2.4	2.7	3.2
1989						5.1	4.6	4.3	3.7	3.9	2.1	2.5	3.1
1990							4.2	3.9	3.3	3.5	1.5	2.1	2.8
1991								3.6	2.8	3.3	0.9	1.7	2.6
1992									2.0	3.2	−0.0	1.2	2.4
1993										4.4	−1.0	1.0	2.5
1994											−6.2	−0.7	1.8
1995												5.2	6.1
1996													7.0

Gross domestic product (implicit price deflator)
Produit intérieur brut (prix implicite)

	1985	1986	1987	1988	1989	1990	1991	1992	1993	1994	1995	1996	1997
1984	56.5	64.8	86.7	89.8	75.0	66.2	59.2	52.8	47.2	42.8	42.3	41.2	39.3
1985		73.6	104.0	102.5	80.0	68.2	59.7	52.3	46.1	41.3	41.0	39.9	38.0
1986			139.7	118.7	82.2	66.9	57.0	49.0	42.6	37.7	37.8	36.9	35.2
1987				99.5	58.9	47.9	41.3	35.5	30.7	27.3	28.5	28.7	27.6
1988					26.5	27.3	26.0	23.0	20.1	18.1	20.7	21.8	21.5
1989						28.1	25.7	21.8	18.6	16.5	19.8	21.1	20.8
1990							23.3	18.7	15.6	13.7	18.2	20.0	19.8
1991								14.4	11.9	10.7	16.9	19.4	19.3
1992									9.5	8.9	17.8	20.6	20.3
1993										8.3	22.2	24.6	23.1
1994											37.9	33.7	28.5
1995												29.6	24.1
1996													18.8

Private final consumption expenditure (volume)
Consommation finale privée (volume)

	1985	1986	1987	1988	1989	1990	1991	1992	1993	1994	1995	1996	1997
1984	3.6	0.3	0.2	0.6	1.9	2.6	2.9	3.1	2.9	3.1	1.9	1.9	2.3
1985		−2.8	−1.5	−0.4	1.5	2.4	2.8	3.1	2.9	3.1	1.7	1.8	2.1
1986			−0.1	0.8	2.9	3.8	4.0	4.1	3.7	3.8	2.2	2.2	2.6
1987				1.8	4.5	5.1	5.0	5.0	4.4	4.4	2.5	2.5	2.9
1988					7.3	6.9	6.1	5.8	4.9	4.8	2.7	2.6	3.0
1989						6.4	5.5	5.3	4.3	4.4	1.9	1.9	2.5
1990							4.7	4.7	3.6	3.8	1.0	1.2	1.9
1991								4.7	3.1	3.6	0.1	0.5	1.5
1992									1.5	3.0	−1.3	−0.5	0.9
1993										4.6	−2.7	−1.1	0.7
1994											−9.5	−3.8	−0.6
1995												2.2	4.3
1996													6.3

Private final consumption expenditure (implicit price deflator)
Consommation finale privée (prix implicite)

	1985	1986	1987	1988	1989	1990	1991	1992	1993	1994	1995	1996	1997
1984	58.8	70.2	89.6	94.3	77.9	68.4	61.2	54.6	48.9	44.1	43.2	42.0	40.2
1985		82.5	107.1	107.8	83.0	70.4	61.6	54.0	47.7	42.6	41.7	40.5	38.7
1986			135.1	121.7	83.2	67.5	57.8	49.8	43.3	38.3	37.8	36.9	35.3
1987				109.1	61.8	49.5	42.8	36.8	32.0	28.2	28.9	28.9	28.0
1988					25.1	26.5	25.7	23.1	20.4	18.1	20.3	21.3	21.2
1989						27.8	26.1	22.4	19.2	16.8	19.5	20.8	20.8
1990							24.3	19.8	16.5	14.2	17.9	19.7	19.8
1991								15.4	12.7	11.0	16.3	18.8	19.0
1992									10.1	8.9	16.7	19.6	19.8
1993										7.6	20.1	23.0	22.3
1994											34.0	31.5	27.7
1995												29.0	24.6
1996													20.4

Government final consumption expenditure (volume)
Consommation des administrations publiques (volume)

	1985	1986	1987	1988	1989	1990	1991	1992	1993	1994	1995	1996	1997
1984	0.9	1.2	0.4	0.2	0.6	1.0	1.6	1.7	1.7	1.9	1.6	1.4	1.4
1985		1.5	0.1	−0.1	0.5	1.0	1.8	1.8	1.9	2.0	1.6	1.4	1.4
1986			−1.2	−0.9	0.2	0.9	1.8	1.8	1.9	2.0	1.6	1.4	1.4
1987				−0.5	0.8	1.7	2.6	2.4	2.4	2.5	2.0	1.7	1.7
1988					2.2	2.8	3.6	3.2	3.0	3.0	2.4	2.0	2.0
1989						3.3	4.4	3.5	3.2	3.2	2.4	2.0	1.9
1990							5.4	3.6	3.2	3.1	2.2	1.7	1.7
1991								1.9	2.1	2.4	1.4	1.0	1.1
1992									2.4	2.6	1.3	0.8	1.0
1993										2.9	0.7	0.3	0.6
1994											−1.3	−1.0	−0.1
1995												−0.7	0.5
1996													1.8

Government final consumption expenditure (implicit price deflator)
Consommation des administrations publiques (prix implicite)

	1985	1986	1987	1988	1989	1990	1991	1992	1993	1994	1995	1996	1997
1984	59.3	60.8	83.4	87.3	73.3	65.6	60.3	55.8	51.5	47.4	44.5	43.0	39.9
1985		62.4	96.9	97.8	77.0	66.9	60.5	55.3	50.5	46.1	43.1	41.6	38.4
1986			138.7	118.2	82.1	68.0	60.1	54.1	48.9	44.2	41.1	39.7	36.4
1987				99.5	59.0	49.5	44.9	41.2	37.6	34.2	32.1	31.6	29.0
1988					26.8	29.4	30.2	29.5	27.8	25.6	24.6	25.0	22.9
1989						32.1	32.0	30.4	28.0	25.4	24.2	24.7	22.4
1990							31.9	29.6	26.7	23.7	22.7	23.5	21.1
1991								27.3	24.2	21.1	20.4	21.9	19.3
1992									21.1	18.1	18.2	20.6	17.8
1993										15.2	16.8	20.4	17.0
1994											18.5	23.1	17.6
1995												27.9	17.1
1996													7.3

Gross fixed capital formation (volume)
Formation brute de capital fixe (volume)

	1985	1986	1987	1988	1989	1990	1991	1992	1993	1994	1995	1996	1997
1984	7.9	−2.5	−1.7	0.1	1.2	3.1	4.2	5.0	4.1	4.6	0.9	2.2	3.5
1985		−11.8	−6.1	−2.3	−0.4	2.2	3.6	4.6	3.7	4.2	0.3	1.7	3.1
1986			−0.1	2.8	3.8	6.0	7.0	7.6	6.1	6.4	1.7	3.1	4.6
1987				5.8	5.8	8.2	8.9	9.3	7.2	7.4	2.0	3.5	5.1
1988					5.8	9.4	9.9	10.1	7.5	7.6	1.4	3.2	5.0
1989						13.1	12.1	11.6	7.9	8.0	0.7	2.8	4.9
1990							11.0	10.9	6.2	6.8	−1.6	1.2	3.8
1991								10.8	3.9	5.4	−4.5	−0.7	2.7
1992									−2.5	2.8	−9.1	−3.3	1.1
1993										8.4	−12.3	−3.6	2.0
1994											−29.0	−9.1	−0.0
1995												16.4	18.6
1996													20.9

Gross fixed capital formation (implicit price deflator)
Formation brute de capital fixe (prix implicite)

	1985	1986	1987	1988	1989	1990	1991	1992	1993	1994	1995	1996	1997
1984	58.7	75.1	92.2	94.0	75.0	65.1	57.9	51.3	45.8	41.6	42.5	41.5	39.2
1985		93.1	111.5	107.4	79.4	66.4	57.8	50.3	44.3	39.8	41.0	40.0	37.7
1986			131.7	114.9	75.0	60.4	51.5	44.2	38.4	34.3	36.2	35.6	33.5
1987				99.3	52.1	41.9	36.3	31.1	27.0	24.2	27.4	27.7	26.3
1988					16.1	19.7	20.0	18.1	16.1	14.8	19.5	20.8	20.1
1989						23.4	22.0	18.7	16.1	14.6	20.1	21.5	20.6
1990							20.7	16.5	13.8	12.5	19.5	21.2	20.2
1991								12.4	10.4	9.9	19.2	21.3	20.1
1992									8.5	8.6	21.5	23.6	21.7
1993										8.8	28.6	29.2	25.3
1994											52.0	40.7	31.4
1995												30.3	22.1
1996													14.5

National disposable income (value)
Revenu national disponible (valeur)

	1985	1986	1987	1988	1989	1990	1991	1992	1993	1994	1995	1996	1997
1984	63.8	60.3	86.7	91.1	78.1	70.5	63.8	57.3	51.4	47.0	44.8	44.2	42.8
1985		56.8	99.4	101.2	81.8	71.9	63.8	56.4	49.9	45.2	43.0	42.5	41.2
1986			153.5	127.9	91.0	75.9	65.2	56.4	48.9	43.8	41.5	41.2	39.8
1987				104.9	65.8	55.7	48.4	42.0	36.3	32.6	31.6	32.3	31.7
1988					34.2	35.7	33.3	29.5	25.6	23.4	23.5	25.2	25.4
1989						37.2	32.9	28.0	23.5	21.3	21.8	24.0	24.4
1990							28.7	23.6	19.3	17.6	18.9	21.9	22.7
1991								18.7	14.9	14.2	16.6	20.6	21.7
1992									11.1	11.9	15.9	21.1	22.3
1993										12.8	18.4	24.6	25.2
1994											24.3	31.0	29.7
1995												38.0	32.5
1996													27.1

Compensation of employees (value)
Rémunération des salariés (valeur)

	1985	1986	1987	1988	1989	1990	1991	1992	1993	1994	1995	1996	1997
1984	60.9	63.6	83.1	86.5	73.7	66.5	61.5	56.6	51.7	47.6	44.1	42.7	41.4
1985		66.3	95.4	95.9	77.1	67.6	61.6	56.0	50.6	46.2	42.5	41.1	39.9
1986			129.5	112.6	80.8	68.0	60.6	54.3	48.5	43.8	40.1	38.8	37.7
1987				97.0	60.5	51.4	46.9	42.5	38.1	34.5	31.7	31.3	30.9
1988					30.8	32.7	33.2	31.4	28.6	26.2	24.4	24.8	25.0
1989						34.6	34.4	31.7	28.1	25.4	23.3	24.0	24.3
1990							34.3	30.2	26.0	23.2	21.2	22.3	22.9
1991								26.3	22.0	19.6	18.1	20.0	21.1
1992									18.0	16.5	15.6	18.5	20.2
1993										15.0	14.4	18.6	20.7
1994											13.8	20.5	22.7
1995												27.7	27.4
1996													27.1

UNITED STATES

ÉTATS-UNIS

Average per cent changes at annual rate

Variations moyennes en pourcentage aux taux annuels

G.D.P. per head (volume)
P.I.B. par tête (volume)

	1985	1986	1987	1988	1989	1990	1991	1992	1993	1994	1995	1996	1997
1984	2.4	2.2	2.0	2.2	2.3	1.9	1.3	1.4	1.4	1.5	1.5	1.6	1.7
1985		2.0	1.9	2.2	2.2	1.8	1.1	1.2	1.2	1.4	1.4	1.5	1.7
1986			1.8	2.3	2.3	1.8	1.0	1.1	1.1	1.3	1.4	1.5	1.7
1987				2.8	2.6	1.8	0.8	1.0	1.0	1.3	1.3	1.5	1.7
1988					2.3	1.2	0.1	0.5	0.7	1.0	1.1	1.3	1.5
1989						0.1	–1.0	–0.1	0.3	0.7	0.9	1.1	1.4
1990							–2.1	–0.2	0.3	0.9	1.0	1.3	1.6
1991								1.7	1.5	1.9	1.8	2.0	2.2
1992									1.4	2.0	1.9	2.1	2.3
1993										2.7	2.1	2.3	2.6
1994											1.6	2.1	2.6
1995												2.6	3.0
1996													3.5

Private final consumption expenditure per head (volume)
Consommation finale privée par tête (volume)

	1985	1986	1987	1988	1989	1990	1991	1992	1993	1994	1995	1996	1997
1984	3.6	3.1	2.8	2.8	2.6	2.2	1.6	1.7	1.7	1.8	1.8	1.8	1.9
1985		2.7	2.4	2.6	2.3	2.0	1.3	1.4	1.5	1.6	1.6	1.6	1.7
1986			2.1	2.5	2.2	1.8	1.1	1.2	1.3	1.4	1.5	1.5	1.7
1987				3.0	2.2	1.7	0.8	1.0	1.2	1.3	1.4	1.5	1.6
1988					1.4	1.0	0.1	0.5	0.8	1.1	1.2	1.3	1.5
1989						0.6	–0.6	0.2	0.6	1.0	1.1	1.3	1.5
1990							–1.7	0.0	0.7	1.1	1.3	1.4	1.6
1991								1.8	1.9	2.1	2.0	2.0	2.2
1992									2.0	2.2	2.1	2.1	2.2
1993										2.5	2.1	2.1	2.3
1994											1.8	1.9	2.3
1995												2.0	2.5
1996													2.9

Gross domestic product (volume)
Produit intérieur brut (volume)

	1985	1986	1987	1988	1989	1990	1991	1992	1993	1994	1995	1996	1997
1984	3.3	3.1	3.0	3.2	3.2	2.9	2.3	2.4	2.4	2.5	2.5	2.6	2.7
1985		2.9	2.8	3.1	3.2	2.8	2.1	2.2	2.3	2.4	2.4	2.5	2.6
1986			2.7	3.2	3.2	2.7	2.0	2.1	2.2	2.3	2.4	2.5	2.6
1987				3.8	3.5	2.7	1.8	2.0	2.1	2.3	2.3	2.5	2.6
1988					3.3	2.2	1.1	1.6	1.7	2.1	2.1	2.3	2.5
1989						1.2	0.1	1.0	1.3	1.8	1.9	2.2	2.4
1990							–1.0	0.9	1.4	2.0	2.1	2.3	2.6
1991								2.8	2.6	3.0	2.9	3.0	3.2
1992									2.4	3.1	2.9	3.1	3.2
1993										3.7	3.1	3.3	3.4
1994											2.6	3.1	3.4
1995												3.6	3.8
1996													3.9

Gross domestic product (implicit price deflator)
Produit intérieur brut (prix implicite)

	1985	1986	1987	1988	1989	1990	1991	1992	1993	1994	1995	1996	1997
1984	3.5	3.0	3.1	3.3	3.5	3.6	3.7	3.5	3.5	3.3	3.2	3.1	3.0
1985		2.4	2.9	3.2	3.5	3.7	3.7	3.5	3.4	3.3	3.2	3.0	2.9
1986			3.3	3.6	3.8	4.0	3.9	3.7	3.6	3.4	3.3	3.1	3.0
1987				3.8	4.1	4.2	4.1	3.8	3.6	3.4	3.3	3.0	2.9
1988					4.4	4.4	4.2	3.8	3.6	3.4	3.2	3.0	2.8
1989						4.3	4.1	3.6	3.4	3.2	3.0	2.7	2.6
1990							3.9	3.3	3.1	2.9	2.7	2.5	2.4
1991								2.7	2.7	2.5	2.4	2.2	2.2
1992									2.7	2.5	2.3	2.1	2.1
1993										2.2	2.1	1.9	1.9
1994											2.0	1.7	1.8
1995												1.5	1.7
1996													1.9

Private final consumption expenditure (volume)
Consommation finale privée (volume)

	1985	1986	1987	1988	1989	1990	1991	1992	1993	1994	1995	1996	1997
1984	4.5	4.1	3.7	3.8	3.5	3.2	2.6	2.7	2.7	2.8	2.8	2.8	2.8
1985		3.7	3.3	3.5	3.2	2.9	2.3	2.4	2.5	2.6	2.6	2.6	2.7
1986			3.0	3.5	3.1	2.7	2.0	2.2	2.3	2.5	2.5	2.5	2.6
1987				3.9	3.2	2.6	1.8	2.0	2.2	2.4	2.4	2.5	2.6
1988					2.4	2.0	1.1	1.6	1.9	2.1	2.2	2.3	2.4
1989						1.6	0.5	1.3	1.7	2.1	2.2	2.3	2.4
1990							–0.7	1.1	1.8	2.2	2.3	2.4	2.6
1991								2.9	3.0	3.1	3.1	3.0	3.1
1992									3.0	3.3	3.1	3.1	3.1
1993										3.5	3.1	3.1	3.2
1994											2.8	2.9	3.0
1995												3.0	3.2
1996													3.4

Private final consumption expenditure (implicit price deflator)
Consommation finale privée (prix implicite)

	1985	1986	1987	1988	1989	1990	1991	1992	1993	1994	1995	1996	1997
1984	3.6	3.2	3.4	3.6	3.8	4.0	4.0	3.9	3.8	3.6	3.5	3.4	3.3
1985		2.7	3.3	3.6	3.9	4.1	4.1	4.0	3.8	3.6	3.5	3.4	3.2
1986			3.9	4.0	4.3	4.5	4.4	4.2	4.0	3.7	3.6	3.4	3.3
1987				4.2	4.5	4.7	4.5	4.2	4.0	3.7	3.5	3.4	3.2
1988					4.9	4.9	4.6	4.2	3.9	3.7	3.5	3.3	3.1
1989						5.0	4.5	4.0	3.7	3.4	3.2	3.0	2.9
1990							4.0	3.6	3.3	3.0	2.9	2.7	2.6
1991								3.1	2.9	2.7	2.6	2.5	2.4
1992									2.7	2.5	2.4	2.3	2.2
1993										2.3	2.3	2.2	2.1
1994											2.2	2.1	2.0
1995												2.0	1.9
1996													1.9

Government final consumption expenditure (volume)
Consommation des administrations publiques (volume)

	1985	1986	1987	1988	1989	1990	1991	1992	1993	1994	1995	1996	1997
1984	4.6	4.2	3.8	3.3	3.0	2.9	2.5	2.2	1.8	1.6	1.5	1.4	1.4
1985		3.9	3.5	2.9	2.6	2.6	2.2	1.8	1.5	1.3	1.2	1.1	1.1
1986			3.0	2.4	2.2	2.2	1.9	1.5	1.1	1.0	0.9	0.8	0.8
1987				1.8	1.8	2.0	1.6	1.2	0.8	0.7	0.6	0.6	0.6
1988					1.8	2.1	1.5	1.0	0.6	0.5	0.4	0.4	0.5
1989						2.4	1.4	0.8	0.3	0.3	0.2	0.2	0.3
1990							0.4	–0.0	–0.4	–0.2	–0.2	–0.2	0.1
1991								–0.4	–0.7	–0.4	–0.4	–0.3	0.0
1992									–1.0	–0.4	–0.4	–0.2	0.1
1993										0.2	–0.0	0.1	0.4
1994											–0.2	–0.0	0.4
1995												0.2	0.8
1996													1.3

Government final consumption expenditure (implicit price deflator)
Consommation des administrations publiques (prix implicite)

	1985	1986	1987	1988	1989	1990	1991	1992	1993	1994	1995	1996	1997
1984	4.5	3.6	3.6	3.5	3.5	3.7	3.8	3.7	3.6	3.5	3.5	3.4	3.4
1985		2.7	3.2	3.2	3.3	3.6	3.7	3.6	3.5	3.4	3.4	3.4	3.3
1986			3.6	3.4	3.5	3.8	3.8	3.7	3.6	3.4	3.4	3.4	3.3
1987				3.1	3.4	3.9	3.9	3.7	3.6	3.4	3.4	3.4	3.3
1988					3.6	4.3	4.2	3.9	3.7	3.5	3.5	3.4	3.3
1989						4.9	4.4	4.0	3.7	3.4	3.4	3.4	3.3
1990							3.9	3.5	3.3	3.1	3.1	3.1	3.0
1991								3.1	3.0	2.8	2.9	3.0	2.9
1992									2.9	2.6	2.9	3.0	2.8
1993										2.3	2.9	3.0	2.8
1994											3.4	3.3	3.0
1995												3.2	2.8
1996													2.4

Gross fixed capital formation (volume)
Formation brute de capital fixe (volume)

	1985	1986	1987	1988	1989	1990	1991	1992	1993	1994	1995	1996	1997
1984	5.3	3.3	2.0	2.0	1.9	1.3	0.1	0.8	1.4	2.0	2.3	3.0	3.3
1985		1.4	0.3	0.9	1.1	0.5	–0.8	0.1	0.9	1.6	2.1	2.8	3.1
1986			–0.7	0.7	1.0	0.3	–1.2	–0.1	0.8	1.6	2.1	2.9	3.3
1987				2.1	1.9	0.7	–1.3	0.1	1.1	2.0	2.5	3.3	3.7
1988					1.6	–0.1	–2.4	–0.5	0.9	2.0	2.6	3.5	3.9
1989						–1.7	–4.4	–1.1	0.7	2.0	2.7	3.8	4.2
1990							–7.0	–0.8	1.5	3.0	3.6	4.7	5.0
1991								5.7	6.0	6.5	6.4	7.2	7.2
1992									6.3	6.9	6.7	7.6	7.5
1993										7.6	6.9	8.0	7.8
1994											6.2	8.2	7.8
1995												10.2	8.7
1996													7.1

Gross fixed capital formation (implicit price deflator)
Formation brute de capital fixe (prix implicite)

	1985	1986	1987	1988	1989	1990	1991	1992	1993	1994	1995	1996	1997
1984	1.5	2.1	2.4	2.6	2.7	2.7	2.6	2.3	2.2	2.2	2.0	1.6	1.5
1985		2.8	2.8	3.0	3.0	3.0	2.7	2.4	2.3	2.2	2.0	1.6	1.5
1986			2.9	3.1	3.1	3.0	2.7	2.4	2.2	2.2	1.9	1.5	1.4
1987				3.3	3.3	3.0	2.7	2.3	2.1	2.1	1.8	1.4	1.2
1988					3.2	2.9	2.5	2.0	1.9	1.9	1.6	1.1	1.0
1989						2.6	2.1	1.6	1.6	1.6	1.4	0.8	0.7
1990							1.7	1.1	1.2	1.3	1.1	0.6	0.5
1991								0.6	1.0	1.2	1.0	0.3	0.3
1992									1.5	1.6	1.1	0.3	0.2
1993										1.7	0.9	–0.1	–0.1
1994											0.2	–1.0	–0.7
1995												–2.2	–1.1
1996													–0.0

National disposable income (value)
Revenu national disponible (valeur)

	1985	1986	1987	1988	1989	1990	1991	1992	1993	1994	1995	1996	1997
1984	6.7	5.9	6.0	6.5	6.7	6.6	6.1	5.9	5.9	5.9	5.8	5.7	5.7
1985		5.1	5.6	6.4	6.7	6.6	6.0	5.8	5.8	5.8	5.7	5.6	5.7
1986			6.1	7.0	7.3	6.9	6.2	6.0	5.9	5.9	5.8	5.7	5.7
1987				7.9	7.9	7.2	6.2	5.9	5.9	5.9	5.7	5.7	5.7
1988					7.9	6.9	5.7	5.4	5.5	5.5	5.4	5.4	5.4
1989						5.9	4.6	4.6	4.9	5.0	5.0	5.0	5.1
1990							3.4	4.0	4.6	4.8	4.9	4.9	5.0
1991								4.6	5.2	5.3	5.2	5.2	5.3
1992									5.7	5.7	5.4	5.3	5.4
1993										5.7	5.3	5.2	5.3
1994											4.9	5.0	5.2
1995												5.0	5.4
1996													5.7

Compensation of employees (value)
Rémunération des salariés (valeur)

	1985	1986	1987	1988	1989	1990	1991	1992	1993	1994	1995	1996	1997
1984	7.5	6.8	7.0	7.2	7.0	6.9	6.3	6.2	6.1	6.0	5.9	5.8	5.9
1985		6.1	6.7	7.1	6.8	6.8	6.2	6.0	5.9	5.8	5.8	5.7	5.7
1986			7.3	7.6	7.1	6.9	6.2	6.0	5.9	5.8	5.7	5.6	5.7
1987				8.0	7.0	6.8	5.9	5.8	5.6	5.6	5.5	5.5	5.5
1988					6.0	6.3	5.2	5.3	5.2	5.2	5.2	5.2	5.3
1989						6.5	4.8	5.0	5.0	5.0	5.0	5.0	5.2
1990							3.1	4.3	4.5	4.7	4.8	4.8	5.0
1991								5.4	5.1	5.2	5.2	5.1	5.3
1992									4.8	5.0	5.1	5.0	5.3
1993										5.2	5.2	5.1	5.4
1994											5.2	5.1	5.5
1995												4.9	5.6
1996													6.3

JAPAN

JAPON

Average per cent changes at annual rate

Variations moyennes en pourcentage aux taux annuels

G.D.P. per head (volume)
P.I.B. par tête (volume)

	1985	1986	1987	1988	1989	1990	1991	1992	1993	1994	1995	1996	1997
1984	3.8	3.0	3.2	3.9	4.0	4.1	4.0	3.6	3.2	2.9	2.7	2.8	2.6
1985		2.3	3.0	3.9	4.0	4.2	4.0	3.6	3.1	2.8	2.6	2.7	2.5
1986			3.6	4.7	4.6	4.6	4.4	3.8	3.2	2.9	2.7	2.8	2.6
1987				5.7	5.1	5.0	4.6	3.8	3.2	2.8	2.5	2.7	2.5
1988					4.4	4.6	4.2	3.3	2.6	2.3	2.1	2.3	2.1
1989						4.7	4.1	3.0	2.2	1.9	1.7	2.0	1.8
1990							3.5	2.1	1.4	1.1	1.1	1.5	1.4
1991								0.7	0.4	0.4	0.5	1.2	1.1
1992									0.0	0.2	0.5	1.3	1.1
1993										0.4	0.7	1.7	1.4
1994											1.0	2.3	1.7
1995												3.7	2.1
1996													0.6

Private final consumption expenditure per head (volume)
Consommation finale privée par tête (volume)

	1985	1986	1987	1988	1989	1990	1991	1992	1993	1994	1995	1996	1997
1984	2.7	2.8	3.1	3.5	3.7	3.7	3.5	3.3	3.0	2.9	2.8	2.8	2.6
1985		2.9	3.3	3.8	3.9	3.9	3.7	3.4	3.1	2.9	2.8	2.8	2.6
1986			3.7	4.3	4.3	4.2	3.8	3.5	3.1	2.9	2.8	2.8	2.6
1987				4.8	4.6	4.4	3.8	3.4	3.0	2.8	2.6	2.7	2.5
1988					4.3	4.2	3.5	3.1	2.6	2.5	2.3	2.4	2.2
1989						4.0	3.1	2.7	2.2	2.1	2.0	2.1	1.9
1990							2.2	2.0	1.6	1.6	1.6	1.8	1.7
1991								1.7	1.3	1.4	1.5	1.7	1.6
1992									0.9	1.3	1.4	1.7	1.5
1993										1.7	1.6	2.0	1.7
1994											1.6	2.1	1.7
1995												2.7	1.7
1996													0.8

Gross domestic product (volume)
Produit intérieur brut (volume)

	1985	1986	1987	1988	1989	1990	1991	1992	1993	1994	1995	1996	1997
1984	4.4	3.6	3.8	4.4	4.5	4.6	4.5	4.0	3.6	3.3	3.1	3.2	3.0
1985		2.9	3.5	4.4	4.5	4.6	4.5	4.0	3.5	3.2	3.0	3.1	2.9
1986			4.2	5.2	5.1	5.1	4.8	4.2	3.6	3.2	3.0	3.1	2.9
1987				6.2	5.5	5.4	5.0	4.2	3.5	3.1	2.9	3.0	2.8
1988					4.8	5.0	4.6	3.7	3.0	2.6	2.4	2.6	2.4
1989						5.1	4.4	3.3	2.5	2.2	2.0	2.3	2.1
1990							3.8	2.4	1.7	1.4	1.4	1.9	1.7
1991								1.0	0.7	0.7	0.9	1.5	1.4
1992									0.3	0.5	0.8	1.6	1.4
1993										0.6	1.1	2.0	1.7
1994											1.5	2.7	2.1
1995												3.9	2.4
1996													0.8

Gross domestic product (implicit price deflator)
Produit intérieur brut (prix implicite)

	1985	1986	1987	1988	1989	1990	1991	1992	1993	1994	1995	1996	1997
1984	2.1	1.9	1.3	1.2	1.3	1.5	1.7	1.7	1.6	1.4	1.2	1.1	1.0
1985		1.7	0.9	0.8	1.1	1.4	1.6	1.6	1.5	1.3	1.1	1.0	1.0
1986			0.1	0.4	0.9	1.3	1.6	1.6	1.4	1.3	1.1	0.9	0.9
1987				0.7	1.4	1.7	1.9	1.9	1.7	1.5	1.2	1.0	1.0
1988					2.0	2.2	2.3	2.2	1.9	1.6	1.3	1.0	1.0
1989						2.3	2.5	2.2	1.8	1.5	1.1	0.9	0.9
1990							2.7	2.2	1.7	1.3	0.9	0.7	0.7
1991								1.7	1.2	0.8	0.5	0.3	0.3
1992									0.6	0.4	0.0	–0.1	0.1
1993										0.2	–0.2	–0.3	–0.1
1994											–0.6	–0.5	–0.2
1995												–0.5	0.1
1996													0.6

Private final consumption expenditure (volume)
Consommation finale privée (volume)

	1985	1986	1987	1988	1989	1990	1991	1992	1993	1994	1995	1996	1997
1984	3.3	3.4	3.7	4.1	4.2	4.2	4.0	3.7	3.5	3.3	3.2	3.2	3.0
1985		3.5	3.9	4.3	4.4	4.4	4.1	3.8	3.5	3.3	3.2	3.2	3.0
1986			4.2	4.7	4.8	4.7	4.2	3.9	3.5	3.3	3.1	3.1	2.9
1987				5.3	5.0	4.8	4.2	3.8	3.4	3.1	3.0	3.0	2.8
1988					4.8	4.6	3.9	3.4	3.0	2.8	2.7	2.7	2.5
1989						4.4	3.4	3.0	2.5	2.4	2.3	2.4	2.3
1990							2.5	2.3	1.9	1.9	1.9	2.1	2.0
1991								2.1	1.6	1.7	1.8	2.0	1.9
1992									1.2	1.5	1.7	2.0	1.8
1993										1.9	2.0	2.3	2.0
1994											2.1	2.5	2.0
1995												2.9	2.0
1996													1.1

Private final consumption expenditure (implicit price deflator)
Consommation finale privée (prix implicite)

	1985	1986	1987	1988	1989	1990	1991	1992	1993	1994	1995	1996	1997
1984	2.3	1.5	1.1	1.0	1.2	1.4	1.6	1.6	1.6	1.5	1.3	1.2	1.2
1985		0.7	0.6	0.5	0.9	1.2	1.4	1.5	1.5	1.4	1.2	1.1	1.1
1986			0.5	0.5	1.0	1.4	1.6	1.6	1.6	1.5	1.2	1.1	1.2
1987				0.5	1.3	1.7	1.9	1.9	1.8	1.6	1.3	1.2	1.2
1988					2.1	2.3	2.4	2.2	2.0	1.8	1.5	1.3	1.3
1989						2.6	2.5	2.3	2.0	1.8	1.4	1.2	1.2
1990							2.5	2.2	1.8	1.6	1.1	1.0	1.1
1991								1.9	1.5	1.3	0.8	0.7	0.8
1992									1.2	1.0	0.5	0.4	0.6
1993										0.7	0.1	0.1	0.5
1994											–0.5	–0.2	0.4
1995												0.1	0.9
1996													1.6

Government final consumption expenditure (volume)
Consommation des administrations publiques (volume)

	1985	1986	1987	1988	1989	1990	1991	1992	1993	1994	1995	1996	1997
1984	0.3	2.7	2.3	2.3	2.2	2.1	2.1	2.1	2.1	2.1	2.2	2.2	2.0
1985		5.1	3.3	3.0	2.7	2.5	2.4	2.3	2.3	2.3	2.4	2.4	2.1
1986			1.6	1.9	2.0	1.8	1.9	1.9	2.0	2.0	2.1	2.1	1.9
1987				2.3	2.2	1.9	1.9	1.9	2.0	2.1	2.2	2.1	1.9
1988					2.0	1.7	1.8	1.9	2.0	2.0	2.2	2.1	1.9
1989						1.5	1.7	1.8	1.9	2.0	2.2	2.1	1.9
1990							2.0	2.0	2.1	2.2	2.4	2.3	1.9
1991								2.0	2.2	2.2	2.5	2.3	1.9
1992									2.4	2.4	2.7	2.4	1.9
1993										2.4	2.8	2.4	1.8
1994											3.3	2.4	1.6
1995												1.5	0.7
1996													–0.1

Government final consumption expenditure (implicit price deflator)
Consommation des administrations publiques (prix implicite)

	1985	1986	1987	1988	1989	1990	1991	1992	1993	1994	1995	1996	1997
1984	3.9	2.1	1.5	1.4	2.0	2.5	2.8	2.8	2.6	2.3	2.1	2.0	1.9
1985		0.4	0.3	0.6	1.5	2.3	2.6	2.6	2.4	2.1	2.0	1.8	1.8
1986			0.2	0.8	1.9	2.7	3.1	3.0	2.7	2.4	2.1	2.0	1.9
1987				1.3	2.7	3.6	3.8	3.6	3.1	2.7	2.4	2.2	2.1
1988					4.1	4.7	4.7	4.1	3.5	2.9	2.5	2.3	2.1
1989						5.4	4.9	4.2	3.4	2.7	2.3	2.0	1.9
1990							4.5	3.5	2.7	2.0	1.7	1.4	1.4
1991								2.6	1.9	1.2	1.0	0.9	0.9
1992									1.1	0.4	0.4	0.4	0.6
1993										–0.2	0.1	0.2	0.5
1994											0.4	0.4	0.7
1995												0.4	0.9
1996													1.3

Gross fixed capital formation (volume)
Formation brute de capital fixe (volume)

	1985	1986	1987	1988	1989	1990	1991	1992	1993	1994	1995	1996	1997
1984	5.0	4.9	6.3	7.6	7.7	7.8	7.2	6.0	5.1	4.5	4.3	4.7	4.0
1985		4.8	6.9	8.4	8.4	8.4	7.5	6.2	5.1	4.5	4.2	4.7	4.0
1986			9.1	10.3	9.6	9.3	8.1	6.4	5.2	4.4	4.1	4.6	3.9
1987				11.5	9.8	9.4	7.8	5.9	4.5	3.8	3.5	4.2	3.4
1988					8.2	8.4	6.6	4.5	3.2	2.5	2.4	3.3	2.5
1989						8.5	5.8	3.3	2.0	1.4	1.5	2.6	1.8
1990							3.3	0.8	–0.1	–0.3	0.1	1.6	0.9
1991								–1.5	–1.7	–1.4	–0.6	1.3	0.5
1992									–2.0	–1.4	–0.3	2.1	0.9
1993										–0.8	0.5	3.4	1.6
1994											1.7	5.6	2.4
1995												9.5	2.8
1996													–3.5

Gross fixed capital formation (implicit price deflator)
Formation brute de capital fixe (prix implicite)

	1985	1986	1987	1988	1989	1990	1991	1992	1993	1994	1995	1996	1997
1984	0.7	–0.1	–0.3	–0.1	0.3	0.7	0.9	1.0	0.8	0.6	0.4	0.2	0.2
1985		–0.8	–0.8	–0.4	0.2	0.7	0.9	1.0	0.8	0.6	0.4	0.2	0.2
1986			–0.7	–0.2	0.5	1.1	1.3	1.3	1.1	0.8	0.5	0.3	0.3
1987				0.3	1.1	1.7	1.8	1.7	1.4	1.0	0.7	0.4	0.4
1988					1.9	2.4	2.3	2.1	1.6	1.1	0.7	0.4	0.4
1989						2.9	2.5	2.1	1.5	0.9	0.5	0.2	0.2
1990							2.2	1.7	1.1	0.4	0.0	–0.2	–0.2
1991								1.2	0.5	–0.2	–0.5	–0.7	–0.5
1992									–0.2	–0.9	–1.1	–1.2	–0.9
1993										–1.5	–1.5	–1.5	–1.1
1994											–1.5	–1.5	–0.9
1995												–1.6	–0.6
1996													0.3

National disposable income (value)
Revenu national disponible (valeur)

	1985	1986	1987	1988	1989	1990	1991	1992	1993	1994	1995	1996	1997
1984	6.8	5.6	5.3	5.7	5.8	6.0	6.1	5.6	5.0	4.6	4.2	4.2	4.0
1985		4.5	4.6	5.4	5.6	5.9	6.0	5.4	4.8	4.3	4.0	4.0	3.8
1986			4.7	5.8	6.0	6.2	6.3	5.6	4.9	4.3	3.9	3.9	3.7
1987				7.0	6.7	6.8	6.7	5.8	4.9	4.3	3.8	3.8	3.6
1988					6.4	6.7	6.6	5.5	4.5	3.8	3.4	3.5	3.2
1989						7.0	6.7	5.2	4.0	3.3	2.9	3.1	2.9
1990							6.4	4.3	3.1	2.4	2.1	2.4	2.3
1991								2.3	1.4	1.1	1.1	1.6	1.6
1992									0.6	0.5	0.6	1.5	1.5
1993										0.5	0.7	1.8	1.7
1994											0.8	2.4	2.1
1995												4.0	2.8
1996													1.6

Compensation of employees (value)
Rémunération des salariés (valeur)

	1985	1986	1987	1988	1989	1990	1991	1992	1993	1994	1995	1996	1997
1984	4.7	4.5	4.2	4.5	5.0	5.6	5.9	5.6	5.2	5.0	4.7	4.4	4.3
1985		4.2	3.9	4.5	5.1	5.8	6.1	5.7	5.3	5.0	4.7	4.4	4.3
1986			3.6	4.6	5.4	6.2	6.5	6.0	5.5	5.1	4.7	4.4	4.3
1987				5.6	6.4	7.0	7.2	6.5	5.8	5.3	4.8	4.5	4.3
1988					7.1	7.8	7.8	6.7	5.8	5.2	4.7	4.4	4.2
1989						8.4	8.1	6.5	5.5	4.9	4.3	4.0	3.9
1990							7.8	5.6	4.5	4.0	3.5	3.3	3.2
1991								3.5	2.9	2.8	2.5	2.4	2.5
1992									2.3	2.4	2.2	2.1	2.3
1993										2.5	2.1	2.1	2.3
1994											1.6	1.8	2.2
1995												2.0	2.4
1996													2.9

KOREA

CORÉE

Average per cent changes at annual rate

Variations moyennes en pourcentage aux taux annuels

G.D.P. per head (volume) / **P.I.B. par tête** (volume)

	1985	1986	1987	1988	1989	1990	1991	1992	1993	1994	1995	1996	1997
1984	5.5	7.9	8.8	9.1	8.4	8.4	8.3	7.8	7.5	7.4	7.5	7.3	7.1
1985		10.5	10.4	10.4	9.1	8.9	8.8	8.1	7.7	7.6	7.7	7.5	7.3
1986			10.4	10.3	8.6	8.6	8.5	7.7	7.3	7.3	7.4	7.2	7.0
1987				10.2	7.7	8.0	8.0	7.2	6.8	6.9	7.0	6.9	6.6
1988					5.3	6.9	7.3	6.5	6.1	6.3	6.5	6.5	6.2
1989						8.4	8.3	6.9	6.4	6.5	6.7	6.6	6.4
1990							8.1	6.1	5.7	6.0	6.4	6.3	6.1
1991								4.1	4.5	5.4	6.0	6.0	5.7
1992									4.8	6.0	6.6	6.4	6.1
1993										7.2	7.5	7.0	6.4
1994											7.8	6.9	6.1
1995												6.0	5.2
1996													4.5

Private final consumption expenditure per head (volume) / **Consommation finale privée par tête** (volume)

	1985	1986	1987	1988	1989	1990	1991	1992	1993	1994	1995	1996	1997
1984	5.4	6.2	6.5	6.9	7.4	7.8	7.9	7.6	7.3	7.2	7.2	7.0	6.[illegible]
1985		7.0	7.1	7.3	7.9	8.3	8.3	7.9	7.5	7.4	7.3	7.2	6.[illegible]
1986			7.1	7.5	8.2	8.6	8.5	8.1	7.6	7.4	7.4	7.2	6.[illegible]
1987				7.9	8.8	9.1	8.9	8.3	7.7	7.4	7.4	7.2	6.[illegible]
1988					9.7	9.6	9.3	8.3	7.6	7.4	7.3	7.1	6.[illegible]
1989						9.6	9.0	7.9	7.1	6.9	6.9	6.8	6.[illegible]
1990							8.5	7.0	6.3	6.2	6.4	6.3	5.[illegible]
1991								5.6	5.2	5.5	5.9	5.9	5.[illegible]
1992									4.7	5.4	6.0	5.9	5.[illegible]
1993										6.1	6.7	6.4	5.[illegible]
1994											7.2	6.5	5.[illegible]
1995												5.7	3.[illegible]
1996													2.[illegible]

Gross domestic product (volume) / **Produit intérieur brut** (volume)

	1985	1986	1987	1988	1989	1990	1991	1992	1993	1994	1995	1996	1997
1984	6.5	9.0	9.8	10.2	9.4	9.4	9.4	8.8	8.5	8.5	8.5	8.4	8.2
1985		11.6	11.5	11.4	10.2	10.0	9.9	9.2	8.7	8.7	8.7	8.6	8.3
1986			11.5	11.4	9.7	9.7	9.5	8.8	8.3	8.4	8.4	8.3	8.0
1987				11.3	8.8	9.0	9.1	8.2	7.8	7.9	8.1	7.9	7.7
1988					6.4	7.9	8.3	7.5	7.2	7.4	7.6	7.5	7.3
1989						9.5	9.3	7.9	7.3	7.6	7.8	7.7	7.4
1990							9.1	7.1	6.6	7.1	7.5	7.4	7.1
1991								5.1	5.4	6.5	7.1	7.1	6.8
1992									5.8	7.2	7.7	7.6	7.2
1993										8.6	8.8	8.2	7.5
1994											8.9	8.0	7.2
1995												7.1	6.3
1996													5.5

Gross domestic product (implicit price deflator) / **Produit intérieur brut** (prix implicite)

	1985	1986	1987	1988	1989	1990	1991	1992	1993	1994	1995	1996	1997
1984	4.6	4.6	4.7	5.2	5.3	6.0	6.6	6.5	6.4	6.3	6.2	6.0	5.[illegible]
1985		4.6	4.8	5.4	5.4	6.3	6.9	6.8	6.6	6.5	6.4	6.1	5.[illegible]
1986			5.0	5.9	5.7	6.7	7.4	7.2	6.9	6.7	6.6	6.3	5.[illegible]
1987				6.7	6.0	7.3	8.0	7.6	7.2	6.9	6.8	6.4	6.[illegible]
1988					5.3	7.6	8.4	7.8	7.3	7.0	6.8	6.4	5.[illegible]
1989						9.9	10.0	8.7	7.8	7.3	7.0	6.5	6.[illegible]
1990							10.1	8.1	7.1	6.7	6.5	5.9	5.[illegible]
1991								6.1	5.6	5.5	5.6	5.1	4.[illegible]
1992									5.1	5.3	5.4	4.9	4.[illegible]
1993										5.5	5.5	4.8	4.[illegible]
1994											5.6	4.5	3.[illegible]
1995												3.4	2.[illegible]
1996													2.[illegible]

Private final consumption expenditure (volume) / **Consommation finale privée** (volume)

	1985	1986	1987	1988	1989	1990	1991	1992	1993	1994	1995	1996	1997
1984	6.4	7.3	7.6	7.9	8.5	8.8	8.9	8.6	8.3	8.2	8.2	8.1	7.7
1985		8.1	8.1	8.4	9.0	9.3	9.4	9.0	8.5	8.4	8.4	8.3	7.8
1986			8.1	8.6	9.3	9.6	9.6	9.1	8.6	8.5	8.5	8.3	7.8
1987				9.0	9.9	10.1	10.0	9.3	8.7	8.5	8.5	8.3	7.8
1988					10.8	10.7	10.3	9.4	8.6	8.4	8.4	8.2	7.6
1989						10.7	10.1	8.9	8.1	8.0	8.0	7.9	7.2
1990							9.5	8.0	7.2	7.3	7.5	7.4	6.8
1991								6.6	6.1	6.6	7.0	7.0	6.3
1992									5.7	6.6	7.2	7.1	6.3
1993										7.6	7.9	7.5	6.4
1994											8.3	7.5	6.0
1995												6.8	4.9
1996													3.1

Private final consumption expenditure (implicit price deflator) / **Consommation finale privée** (prix implicite)

	1985	1986	1987	1988	1989	1990	1991	1992	1993	1994	1995	1996	1997
1984	3.9	2.8	3.0	3.6	4.0	4.9	5.5	5.5	5.5	5.5	5.5	5.5	5.[illegible]
1985		1.7	2.5	3.6	4.0	5.1	5.8	5.8	5.7	5.7	5.6	5.6	5.[illegible]
1986			3.3	4.5	4.8	6.0	6.6	6.5	6.2	6.2	6.1	6.0	5.[illegible]
1987				5.6	5.6	6.9	7.4	7.1	6.7	6.7	6.4	6.3	6.[illegible]
1988					5.5	7.5	8.0	7.5	6.9	6.8	6.5	6.4	6.[illegible]
1989						9.7	9.3	8.1	7.3	7.1	6.7	6.5	6.[illegible]
1990							9.0	7.4	6.5	6.5	6.1	6.0	5.[illegible]
1991								5.8	5.3	5.6	5.4	5.4	5.[illegible]
1992									4.8	5.6	5.3	5.3	5.[illegible]
1993										6.3	5.5	5.5	5.[illegible]
1994											4.7	5.1	4.[illegible]
1995												5.4	4.[illegible]
1996													4.[illegible]

Government final consumption expenditure (volume) / **Consommation des administrations publiques** (volume)

	1985	1986	1987	1988	1989	1990	1991	1992	1993	1994	1995	1996	1997
1984	4.8	6.6	6.4	6.8	7.2	7.2	7.3	7.4	6.9	6.6	6.1	6.2	6.2
1985		8.4	7.3	7.5	7.8	7.6	7.8	7.8	7.2	6.8	6.2	6.4	6.3
1986			6.1	7.1	7.6	7.5	7.7	7.6	7.0	6.6	6.0	6.2	6.1
1987				8.0	8.3	7.9	8.0	8.0	7.1	6.7	6.0	6.2	6.1
1988					8.6	7.9	8.1	7.9	6.9	6.5	5.7	6.0	5.9
1989						7.2	7.8	7.7	6.5	6.1	5.2	5.6	5.6
1990							8.5	8.0	6.3	5.8	4.8	5.3	5.4
1991								7.6	5.3	4.9	3.9	4.7	4.9
1992									3.0	3.6	2.8	4.0	4.3
1993										4.2	2.6	4.3	4.7
1994											1.0	4.4	4.8
1995												7.8	6.8
1996													5.7

Government final consumption expenditure (implicit price deflator) / **Consommation des administrations publiques** (prix implicite)

	1985	1986	1987	1988	1989	1990	1991	1992	1993	1994	1995	1996	1997
1984	7.8	7.1	6.9	7.2	8.0	8.5	9.1	9.1	8.9	8.8	8.9	8.8	8.[illegible]
1985		6.3	6.5	7.1	8.0	8.7	9.3	9.3	9.0	8.9	9.0	8.9	8.[illegible]
1986			6.7	7.4	8.6	9.2	9.9	9.8	9.4	9.2	9.3	9.1	8.[illegible]
1987				8.1	9.5	10.1	10.7	10.4	9.8	9.6	9.7	9.4	9.[illegible]
1988					10.9	11.1	11.5	11.0	[illegible]0.2	9.8	9.9	9.6	9.[illegible]
1989						11.4	11.9	11.1	[illegible]0.0	9.6	9.7	9.4	9.[illegible]
1990							12.4	10.9	9.5	9.2	9.4	9.0	8.[illegible]
1991								9.5	8.1	8.2	8.7	8.4	8.[illegible]
1992									6.8	7.5	8.4	8.1	7.[illegible]
1993										8.2	9.2	8.5	8.[illegible]
1994											10.2	8.7	7.[illegible]
1995												7.2	6.[illegible]
1996													6.[illegible]

Gross fixed capital formation (volume) / **Formation brute de capital fixe** (volume)

	1985	1986	1987	1988	1989	1990	1991	1992	1993	1994	1995	1996	1997
1984	4.3	7.4	10.5	11.3	12.2	14.4	14.1	12.1	11.4	11.4	11.4	11.1	9.9
1985		10.6	13.8	13.7	14.3	16.5	15.8	13.3	12.3	12.2	12.2	11.7	10.3
1986			17.0	15.3	15.5	18.0	16.9	13.8	12.5	12.4	12.3	11.8	10.3
1987				13.7	14.8	18.4	16.9	13.1	11.8	11.8	11.8	11.2	9.7
1988					15.9	20.8	18.0	13.0	11.4	11.5	11.5	10.9	9.2
1989						25.9	19.1	12.0	10.3	10.6	10.8	10.2	8.4
1990							12.6	5.7	5.6	7.1	8.0	7.8	6.1
1991								–0.8	2.2	5.3	6.8	6.9	5.1
1992									5.2	8.5	9.5	8.9	6.3
1993										11.8	11.7	10.2	6.6
1994											11.7	9.4	4.9
1995												7.1	1.6
1996													–3.5

Gross fixed capital formation (implicit price deflator) / **Formation brute de capital fixe** (prix implicite)

	1985	1986	1987	1988	1989	1990	1991	1992	1993	1994	1995	1996	1997
1984	5.0	4.5	4.1	4.7	4.6	5.6	6.3	6.4	6.1	5.7	5.7	5.5	5.6
1985		4.0	3.7	4.6	4.5	5.8	6.6	6.6	6.3	5.8	5.7	5.6	5.6
1986			3.3	4.8	4.6	6.2	7.1	7.0	6.6	6.0	5.9	5.7	5.8
1987				6.4	5.3	7.2	8.0	7.8	7.2	6.4	6.2	6.0	6.0
1988					4.3	7.6	8.6	8.2	7.3	6.4	6.2	6.0	6.0
1989						11.0	10.8	9.5	8.1	6.8	6.5	6.2	6.2
1990							10.6	8.7	7.1	5.7	5.7	5.4	5.6
1991								6.8	5.4	4.2	4.4	4.4	4.7
1992									4.0	2.9	3.7	3.8	4.3
1993										1.7	3.5	3.8	4.4
1994											5.3	4.8	5.3
1995												4.3	5.3
1996													6.3

National disposable income (value) / **Revenu national disponible** (valeur)

	1985	1986	1987	1988	1989	1990	1991	1992	1993	1994	1995	1996	1997
1984	10.6	14.0	15.3	16.2	15.3	16.2	16.8	16.1	15.6	15.5	15.3	14.9	14.4
1985		17.4	17.7	18.1	16.5	17.3	17.9	16.9	16.2	16.0	15.8	15.3	14.7
1986			18.0	18.4	16.2	17.3	17.9	16.8	16.0	15.9	15.7	15.1	14.4
1987				18.9	15.3	17.1	17.9	16.6	15.7	15.5	15.4	14.8	14.1
1988					11.8	16.2	17.6	16.1	15.0	15.0	14.9	14.3	13.5
1989						20.7	20.6	17.5	15.9	15.6	15.4	14.6	13.8
1990							20.4	15.9	14.3	14.4	14.3	13.6	12.8
1991								11.6	11.3	12.5	12.9	12.3	11.6
1992									11.1	12.9	13.3	12.5	11.6
1993										14.8	14.4	13.0	11.7
1994											14.1	12.1	10.7
1995												10.2	9.1
1996													7.9

Compensation of employees (value) / **Rémunération des salariés** (valeur)

	1985	1986	1987	1988	1989	1990	1991	1992	1993	1994	1995	1996	1997
1984	11.0	12.8	15.2	17.1	17.5	18.4	19.2	18.3	[illegible].4	16.9	16.9	16.6	15.9
1985		14.7	17.4	19.2	19.2	20.0	20.6	19.4	[illegible].2	17.6	17.5	17.1	16.3
1986			20.3	21.5	20.7	21.3	21.9	20.2	[illegible].7	18.0	17.8	17.3	16.4
1987				22.8	20.9	21.7	22.2	20.2	[illegible].4	17.7	17.5	17.0	16.0
1988					19.1	21.1	22.1	19.6	[illegible].6	16.8	16.7	16.3	15.3
1989						23.2	23.6	19.7	[illegible].2	16.4	16.4	15.9	14.8
1990							24.0	18.0	[illegible].3	14.8	15.0	14.8	13.7
1991								12.3	[illegible].1	11.8	12.9	13.0	12.1
1992									[illegible].9	11.6	13.1	13.2	12.0
1993										13.3	14.7	14.3	12.5
1994											16.2	14.8	12.3
1995												13.4	10.4
1996													7.5

AUSTRALIA[1]

Average per cent changes at annual rate

G.D.P. per head (volume) / P.I.B. par tête (volume)

	1985	1986	1987	1988	1989	1990	1991	1992	1993	1994	1995	1996	1997
1984	3.3	2.0	2.3	2.3	2.3	1.9	1.2	1.2	1.4	1.7	1.8	1.9	1.8
1985		0.7	1.8	1.9	2.0	1.6	0.9	1.0	1.2	1.5	1.7	1.7	1.7
1986			2.9	2.5	2.5	1.8	0.9	1.0	1.3	1.6	1.8	1.8	1.8
1987				2.1	2.3	1.4	0.4	0.6	1.0	1.5	1.6	1.7	1.7
1988					2.5	1.1	–0.2	0.2	0.8	1.4	1.6	1.7	1.6
1989						–0.3	–1.4	–0.5	0.4	1.1	1.4	1.5	1.5
1990							–2.6	–0.6	0.6	1.5	1.8	1.9	1.8
1991								1.5	2.2	2.9	2.9	2.8	2.6
1992									3.0	3.6	3.3	3.1	2.8
1993										4.2	3.5	3.1	2.7
1994											2.8	2.6	2.2
1995												2.4	1.9
1996													1.5

Gross domestic product (volume) / Produit intérieur brut (volume)

	1985	1986	1987	1988	1989	1990	1991	1992	1993	1994	1995	1996	1997
1984	4.7	3.4	3.8	3.8	3.9	3.4	2.7	2.7	2.9	3.1	3.2	3.2	3.2
1985		2.2	3.3	3.5	3.7	3.2	2.4	2.4	2.6	2.9	3.1	3.1	3.1
1986			4.4	4.1	4.2	3.4	2.4	2.5	2.7	3.0	3.1	3.2	3.2
1987				3.8	4.0	3.1	2.0	2.1	2.4	2.8	3.0	3.1	3.0
1988					4.2	2.7	1.3	1.7	2.1	2.7	2.9	3.0	2.9
1989						1.2	–0.1	0.8	1.6	2.4	2.6	2.8	2.8
1990							–1.3	0.7	1.8	2.7	2.9	3.1	3.0
1991								2.7	3.4	4.0	4.0	4.0	3.8
1992									4.0	4.7	4.5	4.3	4.0
1993										5.3	4.7	4.4	4.0
1994											4.1	3.9	3.5
1995												3.7	3.2
1996													2.8

Private final consumption expenditure (volume) / Consommation finale privée (volume)

	1985	1986	1987	1988	1989	1990	1991	1992	1993	1994	1995	1996	1997
1984	4.7	3.0	2.7	2.9	3.3	3.2	2.9	3.0	2.9	3.1	3.3	3.2	3.3
1985		1.2	1.6	2.3	3.0	2.9	2.6	2.7	2.7	2.9	3.1	3.1	3.1
1986			2.1	2.8	3.6	3.4	2.8	3.0	2.9	3.1	3.3	3.3	3.3
1987				3.6	4.4	3.8	3.0	3.1	3.1	3.3	3.5	3.4	3.4
1988					5.2	3.9	2.9	3.0	3.0	3.2	3.5	3.4	3.4
1989						2.6	1.7	2.3	2.4	2.8	3.2	3.2	3.2
1990							0.8	2.2	2.3	2.9	3.3	3.3	3.3
1991								3.6	3.1	3.6	3.9	3.8	3.7
1992									2.6	3.6	4.0	3.8	3.7
1993										4.6	4.7	4.2	4.0
1994											4.9	4.0	3.8
1995												3.1	3.3
1996													3.4

Government final consumption expenditure (volume) / Consommation des administrations publiques (volume)

	1985	1986	1987	1988	1989	1990	1991	1992	1993	1994	1995	1996	1997
1984	5.4	4.9	3.9	3.7	3.4	3.6	3.4	3.2	2.8	3.1	3.0	3.0	3.0
1985		4.4	3.2	3.1	2.9	3.2	3.1	2.9	2.5	2.8	2.8	2.8	2.8
1986			1.9	2.5	2.4	2.9	2.8	2.6	2.2	2.6	2.6	2.6	2.6
1987				3.0	2.7	3.2	3.1	2.8	2.3	2.7	2.7	2.7	2.7
1988					2.4	3.3	3.1	2.7	2.2	2.7	2.6	2.7	2.6
1989						4.2	3.4	2.8	2.1	2.7	2.7	2.7	2.7
1990							2.7	2.2	1.4	2.3	2.4	2.5	2.4
1991								1.7	0.8	2.2	2.3	2.4	2.4
1992									–0.1	2.5	2.5	2.6	2.6
1993										5.2	3.8	3.6	3.2
1994											2.4	2.8	2.6
1995												3.1	2.7
1996													2.3

Gross fixed capital formation (volume) / Formation brute de capital fixe (volume)

	1985	1986	1987	1988	1989	1990	1991	1992	1993	1994	1995	1996	1997
1984	9.9	3.5	3.6	4.5	5.5	3.1	1.2	1.4	1.6	2.6	2.7	3.0	3.6
1985		–2.5	0.5	2.8	4.4	1.8	–0.2	0.2	0.6	1.8	2.0	2.4	3.1
1986			3.6	5.5	6.9	2.9	0.3	0.7	1.1	2.3	2.5	2.9	3.6
1987				7.5	8.5	2.6	–0.5	0.1	0.7	2.2	2.4	2.8	3.6
1988					9.5	0.3	–3.0	–1.7	–0.6	1.3	1.7	2.2	3.2
1989						–8.2	–8.7	–5.2	–3.0	–0.3	0.4	1.2	2.4
1990							–9.3	–3.7	–1.3	1.8	2.2	2.9	4.0
1991								2.3	3.0	5.8	5.3	5.5	6.4
1992									3.7	7.6	6.3	6.3	7.3
1993										11.6	7.7	7.2	8.2
1994											3.9	5.1	7.0
1995												6.2	8.6
1996													11.1

National disposable income (value) / Revenu national disponible (valeur)

	1985	1986	1987	1988	1989	1990	1991	1992	1993	1994	1995	1996	1997
1984	9.8	8.8	10.3	11.0	11.1	10.1	8.8	8.3	8.0	7.9	7.8	7.7	7.5
1985		7.9	10.6	11.3	11.5	10.2	8.6	8.0	7.8	7.7	7.6	7.5	7.3
1986			13.3	13.1	12.7	10.8	8.7	8.1	7.7	7.7	7.6	7.5	7.3
1987				12.9	12.3	9.9	7.6	7.0	6.8	6.9	6.9	6.8	6.7
1988					11.8	8.4	5.9	5.6	5.7	5.9	6.0	6.1	6.0
1989						5.2	3.1	3.6	4.2	4.8	5.1	5.3	5.3
1990							1.0	2.9	3.9	4.7	5.1	5.3	5.4
1991								4.7	5.3	5.9	6.1	6.2	6.1
1992									5.9	6.5	6.6	6.6	6.4
1993										7.1	7.0	6.8	6.5
1994											6.9	6.7	6.3
1995												6.6	6.0
1996													5.4

1. These growth triangles are derived from data referring to calendar year.

AUSTRALIE[1]

Variations moyennes en pourcentage aux taux annuels

Private final consumption expenditure per head (volume) / Consommation finale privée par tête (volume)

	1985	1986	1987	1988	1989	1990	1991	1992	1993	1994	1995	1996	1997
1984	3.3	1.5	1.2	1.4	1.8	1.7	1.4	1.5	1.5	1.7	1.9	1.9	1.9
1985		–0.2	0.1	0.7	1.4	1.3	1.0	1.2	1.3	1.5	1.7	1.7	1.8
1986			0.5	1.2	1.9	1.7	1.3	1.5	1.5	1.7	1.9	1.9	2.0
1987				1.9	2.6	2.1	1.5	1.7	1.6	1.9	2.1	2.1	2.1
1988					3.4	2.3	1.4	1.6	1.6	1.9	2.2	2.1	2.1
1989						1.1	0.4	1.0	1.2	1.6	1.9	1.9	2.0
1990							–0.4	0.9	1.2	1.7	2.1	2.1	2.1
1991								2.3	2.0	2.5	2.8	2.6	2.5
1992									1.6	2.5	2.9	2.6	2.5
1993										3.5	3.6	3.0	2.8
1994											3.6	2.7	2.5
1995												1.8	2.0
1996													2.2

Gross domestic product (implicit price deflator) / Produit intérieur brut (prix implicite)

	1985	1986	1987	1988	1989	1990	1991	1992	1993	1994	1995	1996	1997
1984	5.6	6.2	6.8	7.3	7.3	6.9	6.2	5.6	5.1	4.7	4.5	4.3	4.1
1985		6.7	7.4	7.8	7.8	7.1	6.3	5.6	5.0	4.6	4.4	4.2	4.0
1986			8.0	8.4	8.1	7.2	6.2	5.4	4.8	4.3	4.1	3.9	3.7
1987				8.7	8.1	6.9	5.8	4.9	4.3	3.8	3.7	3.5	3.3
1988					7.6	6.1	4.8	3.9	3.4	3.0	2.9	2.8	2.8
1989						4.6	3.4	2.8	2.4	2.1	2.2	2.2	2.2
1990							2.3	1.9	1.7	1.5	1.7	1.8	1.8
1991								1.4	1.4	1.3	1.6	1.7	1.7
1992									1.3	1.2	1.6	1.8	1.8
1993										1.1	1.8	1.9	1.9
1994											2.5	2.3	2.2
1995												2.1	2.1
1996													2.0

Private final consumption expenditure (implicit price deflator) / Consommation finale privée (prix implicite)

	1985	1986	1987	1988	1989	1990	1991	1992	1993	1994	1995	1996	1997
1984	7.4	7.8	8.0	7.9	7.7	7.4	6.9	6.3	5.8	5.3	5.0	4.8	4.5
1985		8.2	8.3	8.1	7.8	7.4	6.8	6.1	5.6	5.1	4.8	4.5	4.3
1986			8.4	8.0	7.6	7.2	6.5	5.7	5.2	4.7	4.4	4.2	3.9
1987				7.7	7.2	6.9	6.1	5.2	4.7	4.2	3.9	3.7	3.5
1988					6.8	6.4	5.5	4.6	4.1	3.6	3.4	3.2	3.0
1989						6.1	4.9	3.9	3.4	2.9	2.8	2.7	2.5
1990							3.7	2.8	2.6	2.2	2.2	2.2	2.0
1991								2.0	2.0	1.7	1.8	1.9	1.8
1992									2.1	1.5	1.8	1.8	1.7
1993										1.0	1.6	1.8	1.7
1994											2.3	2.2	1.9
1995												2.0	1.7
1996													1.3

Government final consumption expenditure (implicit price deflator) / Consommation des administrations publiques (prix implicite)

	1985	1986	1987	1988	1989	1990	1991	1992	1993	1994	1995	1996	1997
1984	6.0	6.3	5.6	5.5	5.5	5.5	5.4	5.1	4.8	4.3	4.0	3.9	3.7
1985		6.6	5.4	5.4	5.4	5.5	5.3	4.9	4.7	4.1	3.8	3.7	3.5
1986			4.2	4.8	5.0	5.2	5.0	4.7	4.4	3.8	3.5	3.4	3.2
1987				5.4	5.4	5.5	5.2	4.7	4.4	3.7	3.4	3.3	3.1
1988					5.4	5.5	5.1	4.6	4.2	3.4	3.1	3.0	2.9
1989						5.7	5.0	4.3	4.0	3.0	2.8	2.7	2.6
1990							4.3	3.7	3.4	2.4	2.2	2.2	2.1
1991								3.0	2.9	1.7	1.7	1.8	1.7
1992									2.8	1.1	1.2	1.5	1.5
1993										–0.5	0.4	1.1	1.2
1994											1.4	1.9	1.7
1995												2.3	1.9
1996													1.5

Gross fixed capital formation (implicit price deflator) / Formation brute de capital fixe (prix implicite)

	1985	1986	1987	1988	1989	1990	1991	1992	1993	1994	1995	1996	1997
1984	8.7	9.9	9.0	8.2	7.9	7.1	6.1	5.4	5.1	4.6	4.2	3.7	3.2
1985		11.0	9.2	8.1	7.7	6.8	5.7	4.9	4.6	4.1	3.7	3.3	2.8
1986			7.3	6.7	6.6	5.8	4.7	3.9	3.7	3.3	3.0	2.5	2.1
1987				6.0	6.3	5.3	4.0	3.3	3.1	2.7	2.4	2.0	1.5
1988					6.6	5.0	3.4	2.6	2.6	2.2	1.9	1.5	1.1
1989						3.4	1.9	1.3	1.6	1.4	1.2	0.8	0.4
1990							0.4	0.3	1.0	0.9	0.8	0.4	–0.0
1991								0.1	1.3	1.0	0.8	0.4	–0.1
1992									2.5	1.4	1.1	0.4	–0.1
1993										0.4	0.4	–0.3	–0.8
1994											0.3	–0.6	–1.2
1995												–1.5	–1.9
1996													–2.3

Compensation of employees (value) / Rémunération des salariés (valeur)

	1985	1986	1987	1988	1989	1990	1991	1992	1993	1994	1995	1996	1997
1984	9.2	9.9	9.4	9.7	10.3	10.0	8.8	8.1	7.6	7.4	7.4	7.4	7.3
1985		10.6	9.5	9.9	10.6	10.2	8.7	7.9	7.4	7.2	7.3	7.2	7.1
1986			8.4	9.5	10.5	10.1	8.3	7.5	6.9	6.8	6.9	6.9	6.8
1987				10.7	11.6	10.6	8.3	7.3	6.7	6.6	6.7	6.7	6.6
1988					12.5	10.6	7.5	6.5	5.9	5.9	6.1	6.2	6.2
1989						8.7	5.1	4.5	4.3	4.6	5.1	5.4	5.4
1990							1.5	2.4	2.8	3.6	4.4	4.8	5.0
1991								3.4	3.5	4.3	5.1	5.5	5.6
1992									3.6	4.8	5.7	6.0	6.0
1993										6.0	6.8	6.8	6.6
1994											7.6	7.2	6.8
1995												6.9	6.4
1996													6.0

1. Ces triangles de croissance sont calculés à partir de données se référant aux années calendaires.

NEW ZEALAND

NOUVELLE-ZÉLANDE

Average per cent changes at annual rate

Variations moyennes en pourcentage aux taux annuels

	1985	1986	1987	1988	1989	1990	1991	1992	1993	1994	1995	1996	1997
1984	0.3	1.1	0.6	0.3	0.3	-0.0	-0.7	-0.6	0.1	0.4	0.6	0.6	0.7
1985		1.9	0.8	0.2	0.3	-0.1	-0.8	-0.7	0.0	0.5	0.6	0.7	0.7
1986			-0.4	-0.6	-0.2	-0.6	-1.4	-1.1	-0.3	0.3	0.5	0.5	0.6
1987				-0.8	-0.2	-0.6	-1.6	-1.3	-0.2	0.4	0.6	0.6	0.7
1988					0.5	-0.6	-1.9	-1.4	-0.1	0.6	0.8	0.8	0.8
1989						-1.6	-3.0	-2.0	-0.3	0.6	0.8	0.9	0.9
1990							-4.5	-2.2	0.2	1.1	1.3	1.3	1.2
1991								0.1	2.6	3.1	2.8	2.5	2.2
1992									5.1	4.6	3.7	3.1	2.7
1993										4.0	3.0	2.4	2.0
1994											2.1	1.6	1.4
1995												1.1	1.1
1996													1.0

G.D.P. per head (volume)
P.I.B. par tête (volume)

	1985	1986	1987	1988	1989	1990	1991	1992	1993	1994	1995	1996	1997
1984	0.9	2.5	2.2	2.0	1.6	1.1	0.2	0.0	0.3	0.7	0.9	1.0	1.1
1985		4.0	2.8	2.3	1.7	1.1	0.0	-0.1	0.2	0.7	0.9	1.0	1.1
1986			1.6	1.5	1.0	0.4	-0.7	-0.7	-0.3	0.3	0.5	0.7	0.8
1987				1.4	0.6	0.0	-1.3	-1.2	-0.7	0.1	0.4	0.6	0.7
1988					-0.1	-0.6	-2.2	-1.8	-1.1	-0.1	0.2	0.5	0.7
1989						-1.2	-3.2	-2.4	-1.3	-0.2	0.3	0.6	0.8
1990							-5.2	-3.0	-1.4	0.1	0.6	0.9	1.1
1991								-0.8	0.6	2.0	2.1	2.2	2.2
1992									2.0	3.3	3.1	2.9	2.7
1993										4.7	3.6	3.2	2.9
1994											2.6	2.5	2.3
1995												2.4	2.2
1996													2.0

Private final consumption expenditure per head (volume)
Consommation finale privée par tête (volume)

	1985	1986	1987	1988	1989	1990	1991	1992	1993	1994	1995	1996	1997
1984	0.8	1.4	1.1	0.7	0.7	0.5	0.3	0.4	1.0	1.5	1.6	1.7	1.8
1985		2.1	1.3	0.7	0.7	0.5	0.2	0.3	1.1	1.5	1.7	1.8	1.9
1986			0.4	0.0	0.3	0.1	-0.2	0.0	0.9	1.5	1.7	1.8	1.8
1987				-0.4	0.2	-0.0	-0.3	-0.0	1.0	1.6	1.9	2.0	2.0
1988					0.8	0.1	-0.3	0.1	1.3	1.9	2.2	2.3	2.3
1989						-0.6	-0.9	-0.2	1.4	2.2	2.4	2.5	2.4
1990							-1.2	-0.0	2.0	2.9	3.0	3.0	2.9
1991								1.2	3.7	4.3	4.1	3.8	3.6
1992									6.3	5.9	5.1	4.5	4.1
1993										5.4	4.5	3.9	3.5
1994											3.6	3.2	2.9
1995												2.7	2.5
1996													2.3

Gross domestic product (volume)
Produit intérieur brut (volume)

	1985	1986	1987	1988	1989	1990	1991	1992	1993	1994	1995	1996	1997
1984	14.2	16.3	14.9	13.2	11.6	10.1	8.8	7.9	7.2	6.7	6.2	5.8	5.4
1985		18.4	15.2	12.8	11.0	9.3	7.9	7.0	6.4	5.8	5.5	5.1	4.7
1986			12.2	10.2	8.6	7.1	5.9	5.3	4.8	4.4	4.1	3.8	3.5
1987				8.2	6.9	5.5	4.4	3.9	3.6	3.3	3.1	2.9	2.7
1988					5.6	4.1	3.2	2.9	2.7	2.5	2.4	2.3	2.1
1989						2.7	2.0	2.0	2.0	1.9	1.9	1.8	1.7
1990							1.3	1.6	1.7	1.7	1.8	1.7	1.3
1991								2.0	2.0	1.8	1.9	1.8	1.3
1992									1.9	1.8	1.8	1.7	1.5
1993										1.6	1.8	1.6	1.5
1994											2.0	1.7	1.4
1995												1.3	1.1
1996													0.9

Gross domestic product (implicit price deflator)
Produit intérieur brut (prix implicite)

	1985	1986	1987	1988	1989	1990	1991	1992	1993	1994	1995	1996	1997
1984	1.4	2.8	2.7	2.4	2.0	1.6	1.1	1.0	1.2	1.7	1.9	2.1	2.2
1985		4.2	3.3	2.8	2.2	1.7	1.1	0.9	1.2	1.8	2.0	2.2	2.3
1986			2.4	2.1	1.5	1.1	0.4	0.4	0.8	1.5	1.7	2.0	2.1
1987				1.7	1.0	0.6	-0.1	0.0	0.5	1.3	1.7	1.9	2.1
1988					0.3	0.0	-0.6	-0.4	0.3	1.2	1.6	1.9	2.1
1989						-0.3	-1.1	-0.7	0.3	1.4	1.9	2.2	2.3
1990							-2.0	-0.9	0.5	1.9	2.3	2.6	2.7
1991								0.3	1.7	3.2	3.4	3.5	3.5
1992									3.2	4.6	4.5	4.4	4.1
1993										6.1	5.1	4.7	4.4
1994											4.1	4.1	3.8
1995												4.1	3.7
1996													3.3

Private final consumption expenditure (volume)
Consommation finale privée (volume)

	1985	1986	1987	1988	1989	1990	1991	1992	1993	1994	1995	1996	1997
1984	16.6	15.0	13.6	11.8	10.8	9.9	8.8	7.8	7.1	6.6	6.2	5.8	5.4
1985		13.5	12.2	10.2	9.4	8.6	7.5	6.6	6.0	5.5	5.2	4.9	4.3
1986			10.9	8.6	8.0	7.4	6.3	5.5	5.0	4.6	4.4	4.1	3.3
1987				6.4	6.6	6.3	5.2	4.5	4.0	3.7	3.6	3.4	3.1
1988					6.9	6.2	4.8	4.0	3.6	3.3	3.2	3.0	2.7
1989						5.6	3.8	3.1	2.8	2.6	2.6	2.4	2.2
1990							2.2	1.9	1.8	1.8	2.0	1.9	1.3
1991								1.6	1.7	1.7	1.9	1.9	1.7
1992									1.8	1.8	2.1	2.0	1.7
1993										1.8	2.2	2.0	1.7
1994											2.7	2.2	1.7
1995												1.7	1.2
1996													0.8

Private final consumption expenditure (implicit price deflator)
Consommation finale privée (prix implicite)

	1985	1986	1987	1988	1989	1990	1991	1992	1993	1994	1995	1996	1997
1984	1.7	1.2	1.3	1.2	1.5	1.4	1.2	1.4	1.1	0.9	1.1	1.2	1.5
1985		0.7	1.0	1.1	1.4	1.3	1.1	1.3	1.0	0.8	1.0	1.1	1.5
1986			1.4	1.3	1.7	1.5	1.2	1.5	1.1	0.8	1.1	1.2	1.6
1987				1.2	1.9	1.5	1.1	1.5	1.0	0.8	1.0	1.1	1.6
1988					2.6	1.6	1.1	1.5	1.0	0.7	1.0	1.1	1.7
1989						0.7	0.3	1.2	0.6	0.3	0.7	0.9	1.6
1990							-0.0	1.5	0.6	0.2	0.7	1.0	1.7
1991								3.0	0.9	0.3	0.9	1.2	2.0
1992									-1.1	-1.0	0.3	0.8	1.8
1993										-0.9	0.9	1.4	2.5
1994											2.8	2.5	3.7
1995												2.3	4.1
1996													6.0

Government final consumption expenditure (volume)
Consommation des administrations publiques (volume)

	1985	1986	1987	1988	1989	1990	1991	1992	1993	1994	1995	1996	1997
1984	14.0	17.3	15.5	13.4	11.4	10.2	8.6	7.6	6.7	6.1	5.8	5.4	[illegible]
1985		20.8	16.2	13.3	10.8	9.4	7.8	6.7	5.9	5.3	5.0	4.7	[illegible]
1986			11.8	9.7	7.7	6.8	5.3	4.5	3.9	3.5	3.4	3.2	[illegible]
1987				7.6	5.7	5.1	3.8	3.1	2.6	2.3	2.3	2.3	[illegible]
1988					3.8	3.9	2.5	2.0	1.6	1.5	1.6	1.6	[illegible]
1989						4.0	1.9	1.4	1.1	1.0	1.3	1.3	[illegible]
1990							-0.1	0.1	0.2	0.3	0.7	0.9	[illegible]
1991								0.4	0.3	0.4	0.9	1.1	[illegible]
1992									0.3	0.4	1.1	1.3	[illegible]
1993										0.6	1.6	1.6	[illegible]
1994											2.5	2.2	[illegible]
1995												1.8	[illegible]
1996													[illegible]

Government final consumption expenditure (implicit price deflator)
Consommation des administrations publiques (prix implicite)

	1985	1986	1987	1988	1989	1990	1991	1992	1993	1994	1995	1996	1997
1984	6.9	0.4	1.4	-0.1	1.4	0.3	-2.5	-1.8	0.3	1.9	2.5	2.8	2.8
1985		-5.7	-1.2	-2.3	0.1	-1.0	-4.0	-2.9	-0.5	1.3	2.1	2.5	2.5
1986			3.5	-0.6	2.1	0.2	-3.7	-2.5	0.2	2.2	3.0	3.3	3.3
1987				-4.5	1.3	-0.9	-5.4	-3.6	-0.3	2.0	2.9	3.3	3.3
1988					7.5	0.9	-5.7	-3.4	0.6	3.2	4.0	4.3	4.2
1989						-5.2	-11.6	-6.8	-1.1	2.3	3.4	3.9	3.7
1990							-17.6	-7.6	0.3	4.3	5.3	5.5	5.1
1991								3.7	10.7	12.8	11.9	10.8	9.4
1992									18.2	17.7	14.8	12.6	10.6
1993										17.2	13.1	10.9	8.8
1994											9.2	7.8	6.2
1995												6.5	4.7
1996													2.9

Gross fixed capital formation (volume)
Formation brute de capital fixe (volume)

	1985	1986	1987	1988	1989	1990	1991	1992	1993	1994	1995	1996	1997
1984	12.1	10.8	8.7	6.7	6.0	5.2	4.7	4.4	4.1	3.9	3.6	3.1	2.4
1985		9.5	7.0	4.9	4.5	3.9	3.5	3.4	3.2	3.0	2.7	2.3	1.6
1986			4.6	2.7	2.9	2.6	2.4	2.4	2.3	2.2	2.0	1.6	0.9
1987				0.9	2.0	1.9	1.8	2.0	2.0	1.9	1.7	1.3	0.6
1988					3.2	2.5	2.1	2.3	2.2	2.1	1.8	1.4	0.5
1989						1.8	1.6	2.0	1.9	1.9	1.6	1.1	0.2
1990							1.5	2.1	2.0	1.9	1.6	1.0	0.0
1991								2.7	2.2	2.1	1.6	0.9	-0.2
1992									1.8	1.7	1.2	0.4	-0.8
1993										1.7	0.9	-0.0	-1.4
1994											0.2	-0.9	-2.5
1995												-1.9	-3.8
1996													-5.7

Gross fixed capital formation (implicit price deflator)
Formation brute de capital fixe (prix implicite)

	1985	1986	1987	1988	1989	1990	1991	1992	1993	1994	1995	1996	1997
1984	14.1	18.0	15.9	13.8	11.9	10.3	8.6	8.2	8.2	7.9	7.6	7.2	6.9
1985		22.0	16.8	13.7	11.3	9.5	7.7	7.3	7.4	7.2	7.0	6.6	6.3
1986			11.8	9.8	8.0	6.6	5.1	5.1	5.5	5.5	5.5	5.1	5.0
1987				7.9	6.1	4.9	3.4	3.8	4.5	4.7	4.7	4.4	4.4
1988					4.3	3.4	2.0	2.8	3.8	4.1	4.3	4.0	4.0
1989						2.5	0.8	2.2	3.7	4.1	4.3	3.9	3.9
1990							-0.8	2.1	4.1	4.5	4.6	4.2	4.1
1991								5.1	6.6	6.3	6.0	5.2	5.0
1992									8.2	6.9	6.3	5.2	5.0
1993										5.7	5.4	4.3	4.2
1994											5.1	3.6	3.7
1995												2.1	3.0
1996													4.0

National disposable income (value)
Revenu national disponible (valeur)

	1985	1986	1987	1988	1989	1990	1991	1992	1993	1994	1995	1996	1997
1984	17.8	18.6	16.5	13.4	11.4	9.6	8.0	7.3	7.0	6.9	6.8	6.8	6.5
1985		19.5	15.9	12.0	9.8	8.0	6.5	5.9	5.7	5.8	5.8	5.8	5.6
1986			12.4	8.5	6.7	5.3	4.0	3.7	3.8	4.2	4.4	4.5	4.4
1987				4.6	4.0	3.1	2.0	2.1	2.5	3.0	3.4	3.7	3.7
1988					3.4	2.3	1.2	1.5	2.0	2.8	3.2	3.6	3.6
1989						1.2	0.1	0.8	1.7	2.6	3.2	3.6	3.6
1990							-1.1	0.6	1.9	3.0	3.6	4.0	3.9
1991								2.4	3.4	4.4	4.8	5.0	4.8
1992									4.4	5.4	5.6	5.7	5.3
1993										6.4	6.2	6.2	5.5
1994											5.9	6.0	5.2
1995												6.1	4.9
1996													3.6

Compensation of employees (value)
Rémunération des salariés (valeur)

AUSTRIA AUTRICHE

Average per cent changes at annual rate

Variations moyennes en pourcentage aux taux annuels

G.D.P. per head (volume) / P.I.B. par tête (volume)

	1985	1986	1987	1988	1989	1990	1991	1992	1993	1994	1995	1996	1997
1984	2.1	2.2	2.0	2.2	2.5	2.7	2.6	2.3	2.0	2.0	2.0	1.9	2.0
1985		2.2	1.9	2.2	2.6	2.8	2.7	2.3	2.0	2.0	2.0	1.9	2.0
1986			1.5	2.2	2.7	2.9	2.8	2.3	1.9	1.9	1.9	1.9	1.9
1987				2.9	3.3	3.4	3.1	2.5	2.0	2.0	2.0	1.9	2.0
1988					3.6	3.6	3.2	2.4	1.8	1.9	1.9	1.8	1.9
1989						3.6	3.0	2.0	1.4	1.5	1.6	1.5	1.7
1990							2.3	1.2	0.6	1.0	1.2	1.2	1.4
1991								0.0	−0.2	0.5	0.9	1.0	1.2
1992									−0.5	0.8	1.1	1.2	1.5
1993										2.0	1.9	1.8	1.9
1994											1.8	1.7	1.9
1995												1.5	1.9
1996													2.4

Private final consumption expenditure per head (volume) / Consommation finale privée par tête (volume)

	1985	1986	1987	1988	1989	1990	1991	1992	1993	1994	1995	1996	1997
1984	1.8	1.9	2.2	2.4	2.6	2.6	2.5	2.4	2.1	2.0	2.1	2.1	2.0
1985		2.0	2.4	2.6	2.7	2.8	2.6	2.5	2.1	2.0	2.1	2.1	2.0
1986			2.8	2.9	3.0	2.9	2.7	2.5	2.1	2.0	2.1	2.1	2.0
1987				3.1	3.1	3.0	2.7	2.5	2.0	1.9	2.0	2.0	1.9
1988					3.1	2.9	2.5	2.3	1.8	1.7	1.8	1.9	1.7
1989						2.8	2.3	2.1	1.5	1.4	1.6	1.7	1.6
1990							1.7	1.7	1.0	1.1	1.4	1.5	1.4
1991								1.7	0.7	0.9	1.3	1.5	1.3
1992									−0.3	0.5	1.2	1.5	1.3
1993										1.3	2.0	2.1	1.7
1994											2.7	2.5	1.8
1995												2.3	1.4
1996													0.5

Gross domestic product (volume) / Produit intérieur brut (volume)

	1985	1986	1987	1988	1989	1990	1991	1992	1993	1994	1995	1996	1997
1984	2.2	2.3	2.1	2.4	2.7	3.0	3.1	2.9	2.6	2.6	2.5	2.5	2.5
1985		2.3	2.0	2.4	2.8	3.2	3.2	3.0	2.6	2.6	2.6	2.5	2.5
1986			1.7	2.4	3.0	3.4	3.4	3.1	2.7	2.7	2.6	2.5	2.5
1987				3.2	3.7	4.0	3.8	3.3	2.9	2.8	2.7	2.6	2.6
1988					4.2	4.4	4.1	3.4	2.8	2.8	2.7	2.5	2.5
1989						4.6	4.0	3.1	2.4	2.5	2.4	2.3	2.3
1990							3.4	2.4	1.8	1.9	2.0	1.9	2.0
1991								1.3	0.9	1.5	1.6	1.6	1.8
1992									0.5	1.5	1.7	1.7	1.9
1993										2.5	2.3	2.1	2.2
1994											2.1	1.8	2.1
1995												1.6	2.1
1996													2.5

Gross domestic product (implicit price deflator) / Produit intérieur brut (prix implicite)

	1985	1986	1987	1988	1989	1990	1991	1992	1993	1994	1995	1996	1997
1984	3.1	2.9	2.6	2.4	2.4	2.6	2.8	3.0	2.9	2.9	2.9	2.8	2.7
1985		2.7	2.4	2.1	2.3	2.5	2.7	2.9	2.9	2.9	2.8	2.8	2.6
1986			2.1	1.8	2.1	2.5	2.7	3.0	3.0	2.9	2.8	2.8	2.6
1987				1.6	2.2	2.6	2.9	3.2	3.1	3.1	2.9	2.8	2.7
1988					2.7	3.1	3.3	3.6	3.4	3.3	3.1	3.0	2.8
1989						3.4	3.6	3.8	3.6	3.4	3.2	3.0	2.8
1990							3.7	4.0	3.6	3.4	3.1	3.0	2.7
1991								4.3	3.6	3.3	3.0	2.8	2.6
1992									2.8	2.8	2.6	2.4	2.2
1993										2.8	2.4	2.3	2.1
1994											2.1	2.1	1.9
1995												2.1	1.7
1996													1.4

Private final consumption expenditure (volume) / Consommation finale privée (volume)

	1985	1986	1987	1988	1989	1990	1991	1992	1993	1994	1995	1996	1997
1984	1.9	2.0	2.3	2.6	2.8	3.0	2.9	2.9	2.7	2.6	2.6	2.6	2.5
1985		2.2	2.5	2.8	3.0	3.2	3.1	3.1	2.8	2.7	2.7	2.7	2.5
1986			2.9	3.1	3.3	3.4	3.3	3.2	2.9	2.7	2.8	2.7	2.5
1987				3.3	3.5	3.6	3.4	3.3	2.9	2.7	2.7	2.7	2.5
1988					3.7	3.7	3.4	3.3	2.8	2.6	2.6	2.6	2.4
1989						3.8	3.3	3.2	2.6	2.4	2.5	2.5	2.2
1990							2.8	2.9	2.2	2.1	2.2	2.3	2.0
1991								3.0	1.8	1.8	2.1	2.1	1.9
1992									0.7	1.2	1.8	1.9	1.7
1993										1.7	2.3	2.3	1.9
1994											2.9	2.6	2.0
1995												2.4	1.6
1996													0.7

Private final consumption expenditure (implicit price deflator) / Consommation finale privée (prix implicite)

	1985	1986	1987	1988	1989	1990	1991	1992	1993	1994	1995	1996	1997
1984	3.3	2.5	1.9	1.8	2.0	2.2	2.3	2.5	2.6	2.7	2.6	2.6	2.5
1985		1.7	1.2	1.3	1.7	2.0	2.2	2.4	2.5	2.6	2.5	2.5	2.5
1986			0.7	1.2	1.7	2.1	2.3	2.6	2.7	2.7	2.6	2.6	2.5
1987				1.6	2.2	2.6	2.7	2.9	3.0	3.0	2.8	2.8	2.7
1988					2.7	3.1	3.1	3.3	3.3	3.3	3.0	3.0	2.8
1989						3.5	3.2	3.5	3.4	3.4	3.1	3.0	2.9
1990							3.0	3.4	3.4	3.4	3.0	2.9	2.8
1991								3.9	3.6	3.5	3.0	2.9	2.7
1992									3.3	3.3	2.7	2.6	2.5
1993										3.3	2.4	2.4	2.3
1994											1.5	2.0	2.0
1995												2.5	2.2
1996													2.0

Government final consumption expenditure (volume) / Consommation des administrations publiques (volume)

	1985	1986	1987	1988	1989	1990	1991	1992	1993	1994	1995	1996	1997
1984	1.3	1.6	1.1	1.1	1.2	1.2	1.3	1.4	1.6	1.7	1.5	1.4	1.3
1985		1.8	1.0	1.1	1.1	1.2	1.3	1.4	1.6	1.7	1.5	1.4	1.4
1986			0.2	0.7	0.9	1.0	1.2	1.4	1.6	1.7	1.5	1.3	1.3
1987				1.1	1.3	1.3	1.5	1.6	1.8	1.9	1.6	1.5	1.4
1988					1.4	1.3	1.6	1.7	1.9	2.0	1.7	1.5	1.4
1989						1.3	1.7	1.8	2.1	2.1	1.8	1.5	1.5
1990							2.2	2.1	2.3	2.4	1.9	1.6	1.5
1991								2.0	2.4	2.4	1.8	1.5	1.4
1992									2.7	2.6	1.7	1.3	1.2
1993										2.5	1.2	0.8	0.9
1994											−0.0	0.0	0.3
1995												0.1	0.5
1996													0.9

Government final consumption expenditure (implicit price deflator) / Consommation des administrations publiques (prix implicite)

	1985	1986	1987	1988	1989	1990	1991	1992	1993	1994	1995	1996	1997
1984	5.2	4.9	4.5	3.9	4.0	4.1	4.4	4.6	4.6	4.5	4.4	4.2	3.9
1985		4.7	4.1	3.5	3.7	3.8	4.3	4.5	4.6	4.4	4.3	4.1	3.8
1986			3.6	2.9	3.3	3.6	4.2	4.5	4.6	4.4	4.3	4.0	3.7
1987				2.3	3.2	3.6	4.3	4.7	4.7	4.5	4.4	4.1	3.8
1988					4.2	4.3	5.0	5.3	5.2	4.9	4.7	4.3	3.9
1989						4.5	5.4	5.7	5.5	5.1	4.8	4.3	3.9
1990							6.4	6.3	5.8	5.2	4.8	4.3	3.8
1991								6.1	5.6	4.8	4.4	3.9	3.4
1992									5.0	4.2	3.8	3.3	2.9
1993										3.4	3.3	2.8	2.3
1994											3.2	2.5	2.0
1995												1.8	1.4
1996													1.0

Gross fixed capital formation (volume) / Formation brute de capital fixe (volume)

	1985	1986	1987	1988	1989	1990	1991	1992	1993	1994	1995	1996	1997
1984	6.9	4.6	4.6	5.1	5.4	5.6	5.7	5.0	4.2	4.6	4.3	4.2	4.1
1985		2.4	3.4	4.5	5.0	5.3	5.5	4.7	3.8	4.3	4.1	3.9	3.9
1986			4.4	5.6	5.8	6.0	6.1	5.1	4.0	4.6	4.3	4.1	4.0
1987				6.8	6.6	6.6	6.5	5.2	4.0	4.6	4.2	4.0	4.0
1988					6.3	6.4	6.4	4.8	3.4	4.2	3.9	3.7	3.7
1989						6.6	6.5	4.3	2.7	3.8	3.5	3.3	3.4
1990							6.3	3.2	1.4	3.1	2.9	2.8	2.9
1991								0.1	−0.9	2.1	2.0	2.1	2.4
1992									−2.0	3.1	2.7	2.6	2.8
1993										8.4	5.1	4.2	4.1
1994											1.9	2.2	2.7
1995												2.4	3.0
1996													3.6

Gross fixed capital formation (implicit price deflator) / Formation brute de capital fixe (prix implicite)

	1985	1986	1987	1988	1989	1990	1991	1992	1993	1994	1995	1996	1997
1984	2.0	2.2	2.0	1.8	1.9	2.0	2.3	2.5	2.4	2.3	2.3	2.2	2.2
1985		2.4	2.0	1.7	1.9	2.0	2.4	2.5	2.5	2.4	2.3	2.3	2.2
1986			1.6	1.4	1.8	2.0	2.4	2.6	2.5	2.4	2.3	2.3	2.2
1987				1.1	1.8	2.1	2.5	2.7	2.7	2.5	2.4	2.3	2.3
1988					2.6	2.6	3.0	3.2	3.0	2.7	2.6	2.5	2.4
1989						2.5	3.2	3.3	3.1	2.8	2.6	2.5	2.4
1990							3.9	3.7	3.3	2.8	2.6	2.5	2.4
1991								3.6	3.0	2.5	2.3	2.2	2.1
1992									2.4	1.9	1.9	1.8	1.8
1993										1.4	1.7	1.7	1.7
1994											1.9	1.8	1.7
1995												1.6	1.7
1996													1.7

National disposable income (value) / Revenu national disponible (valeur)

	1985	1986	1987	1988	1989	1990	1991	1992	1993	1994	1995	1996	1997
1984	5.5	5.1	4.7	4.6	5.1	5.7	5.9	5.8	5.5	5.5	5.3	5.1	5.0
1985		4.7	4.3	4.4	5.1	5.8	6.0	5.9	5.5	5.5	5.2	5.1	4.9
1986			3.9	4.2	5.2	6.0	6.2	6.1	5.6	5.6	5.3	5.1	5.0
1987				4.5	5.8	6.8	6.8	6.5	5.9	5.8	5.5	5.2	5.1
1988					7.2	7.9	7.6	7.0	6.1	6.0	5.6	5.3	5.1
1989						8.7	7.8	6.9	5.9	5.8	5.4	5.1	4.9
1990							6.9	6.1	5.0	5.1	4.7	4.5	4.3
1991								5.2	4.0	4.5	4.2	4.0	3.9
1992									2.8	4.1	3.8	3.7	3.7
1993										5.5	4.3	4.0	3.9
1994											3.2	3.2	3.4
1995												3.2	3.4
1996													3.7

Compensation of employees (value) / Rémunération des salariés (valeur)

	1985	1986	1987	1988	1989	1990	1991	1992	1993	1994	1995	1996	1997
1984	6.0	6.1	5.4	5.0	5.3	5.7	6.1	6.2	6.0	5.7	5.5	5.2	4.9
1985		6.2	5.1	4.7	5.1	5.6	6.1	6.2	6.0	5.7	5.5	5.1	4.8
1986			4.1	3.9	4.7	5.5	6.1	6.2	5.9	5.7	5.4	5.0	4.7
1987				3.7	5.0	6.0	6.6	6.6	6.2	5.9	5.6	5.1	4.8
1988					6.4	7.1	7.6	7.4	6.7	6.2	5.8	5.2	4.9
1989						7.9	8.2	7.7	6.8	6.2	5.8	5.1	4.7
1990							8.5	7.6	6.5	5.8	5.3	4.6	4.2
1991								6.6	5.5	4.9	4.5	3.9	3.5
1992									4.3	4.0	3.9	3.2	2.9
1993										3.8	3.6	2.8	2.6
1994											3.5	2.3	2.2
1995												1.2	1.6
1996													2.0

BELGIUM

BELGIQUE

Average per cent changes at annual rate

Variations moyennes en pourcentage aux taux annuels

	1985	1986	1987	1988	1989	1990	1991	1992	1993	1994	1995	1996	1997
1984	0.9	1.2	1.5	2.3	2.5	2.5	2.3	2.2	1.7	1.8	1.8	1.7	1.8
1985		1.4	1.8	2.7	2.9	2.9	2.6	2.4	1.8	1.9	1.9	1.8	1.9
1986			2.2	3.4	3.4	3.2	2.8	2.5	1.9	1.9	2.0	1.9	1.9
1987				4.6	4.0	3.6	3.0	2.6	1.8	1.9	1.9	1.8	1.9
1988					3.4	3.1	2.4	2.1	1.3	1.5	1.5	1.5	1.6
1989						2.7	2.0	1.7	0.8	1.1	1.2	1.2	1.4
1990							1.2	1.1	0.1	0.6	0.9	1.0	1.2
1991								1.0	-0.4	0.5	0.9	0.9	1.2
1992									-1.8	0.2	0.8	0.9	1.3
1993										2.2	2.2	1.8	2.1
1994											2.1	1.6	2.0
1995												1.1	1.9
1996													2.8

G.D.P. per head
(volume)
P.I.B. par tête
(volume)

	1985	1986	1987	1988	1989	1990	1991	1992	1993	1994	1995	1996	1997
1984	1.9	1.9	2.0	2.3	2.5	2.5	2.5	2.4	2.0	1.9	1.8	1.8	1.8
1985		2.0	2.0	2.4	2.7	2.7	2.6	2.5	2.0	1.9	1.8	1.8	1.8
1986			2.1	2.6	2.9	2.8	2.8	2.6	2.0	1.9	1.7	1.7	1.7
1987				3.1	3.3	3.1	2.9	2.7	1.9	1.9	1.7	1.7	1.7
1988					3.5	3.1	2.9	2.6	1.7	1.6	1.5	1.5	1.5
1989						2.6	2.5	2.3	1.3	1.3	1.2	1.2	1.3
1990							2.4	2.1	0.8	0.9	0.9	1.0	1.1
1991								1.8	0.0	0.4	0.5	0.7	0.9
1992									-1.7	-0.2	0.1	0.5	0.7
1993										1.3	1.0	1.2	1.3
1994											0.7	1.1	1.4
1995												1.6	1.7
1996													1.3

Private final consumption expenditure per head
(volume)
Consommation finale privée par tête
(volume)

	1985	1986	1987	1988	1989	1990	1991	1992	1993	1994	1995	1996	1997
1984	1.0	1.2	1.6	2.4	2.6	2.7	2.5	2.4	2.0	2.0	2.1	2.0	2.1
1985		1.5	1.9	2.8	3.0	3.0	2.8	2.6	2.1	2.1	2.2	2.1	2.2
1986			2.4	3.5	3.6	3.4	3.1	2.8	2.2	2.2	2.2	2.1	2.2
1987				4.7	4.2	3.8	3.2	2.9	2.1	2.2	2.2	2.1	2.2
1988					3.6	3.3	2.7	2.4	1.6	1.8	1.9	1.8	1.9
1989						3.0	2.3	2.0	1.2	1.4	1.6	1.5	1.7
1990							1.6	1.5	0.5	1.0	1.3	1.3	1.5
1991								1.5	0.0	0.9	1.2	1.2	1.5
1992									-1.5	0.5	1.1	1.2	1.5
1993										2.6	2.5	2.1	2.3
1994											2.3	1.8	2.2
1995												1.3	2.1
1996													3.0

Gross domestic product
(volume)
Produit intérieur brut
(volume)

	1985	1986	1987	1988	1989	1990	1991	1992	1993	1994	1995	1996	1997
1984	6.1	4.8	3.9	3.5	3.7	3.6	3.6	3.6	3.6	3.5	3.3	3.2	3.0
1985		3.6	2.9	2.7	3.1	3.1	3.1	3.2	3.3	3.2	3.0	2.9	2.8
1986			2.2	2.2	3.0	3.0	3.1	3.2	3.3	3.1	3.0	2.8	2.7
1987				2.1	3.4	3.3	3.3	3.4	3.5	3.3	3.1	2.9	2.7
1988					4.6	3.9	3.6	3.7	3.7	3.5	3.2	3.0	2.8
1989						3.1	3.1	3.3	3.5	3.2	2.9	2.8	2.5
1990							3.1	3.4	3.6	3.3	2.9	2.7	2.5
1991								3.7	3.8	3.3	2.8	2.6	2.4
1992									4.0	3.1	2.6	2.3	2.1
1993										2.3	1.9	1.8	1.7
1994											1.5	1.6	1.5
1995												1.6	1.5
1996													1.4

Gross domestic product
(implicit price deflator)
Produit intérieur brut
(prix implicite)

	1985	1986	1987	1988	1989	1990	1991	1992	1993	1994	1995	1996	1997
1984	2.0	2.0	2.1	2.4	2.6	2.7	2.7	2.7	2.2	2.1	2.0	2.0	2.0
1985		2.0	2.2	2.5	2.8	2.8	2.8	2.8	2.2	2.2	2.0	2.0	2.0
1986			2.3	2.7	3.1	3.0	3.0	2.9	2.3	2.2	2.0	2.0	2.0
1987				3.2	3.5	3.3	3.2	3.0	2.3	2.2	2.0	2.0	2.0
1988					3.7	3.3	3.2	2.9	2.1	2.0	1.8	1.8	1.9
1989						2.9	2.9	2.7	1.7	1.7	1.5	1.6	1.6
1990							2.9	2.5	1.2	1.3	1.2	1.3	1.4
1991								2.2	0.4	0.8	0.8	1.0	1.2
1992									-1.3	0.1	0.4	0.7	1.0
1993										1.6	1.2	1.4	1.6
1994											0.9	1.3	1.6
1995												1.8	1.9
1996													2.1

Private final consumption expenditure
(volume)
Consommation finale privée
(volume)

	1985	1986	1987	1988	1989	1990	1991	1992	1993	1994	1995	1996	1997
1984	5.7	3.4	3.0	2.6	2.8	2.9	3.0	2.9	2.9	2.9	2.8	2.8	2.[illegible]
1985		1.1	1.7	1.5	2.1	2.4	2.5	2.5	2.6	2.6	2.5	2.5	2.[illegible]
1986			2.3	1.7	2.5	2.7	2.8	2.7	2.8	2.8	2.7	2.7	2.[illegible]
1987				1.2	2.6	2.8	2.9	2.8	2.9	2.9	2.8	2.7	2.[illegible]
1988					4.0	3.6	3.5	3.2	3.2	3.1	3.0	2.9	2.[illegible]
1989						3.3	3.2	3.0	3.0	3.0	2.8	2.8	2.[illegible]
1990							3.2	2.8	2.9	2.9	2.7	2.7	2.[illegible]
1991								2.4	2.8	2.8	2.6	2.6	2.[illegible]
1992									3.2	3.0	2.7	2.6	2.[illegible]
1993										2.8	2.4	2.4	2.[illegible]
1994											2.1	2.2	2.[illegible]
1995												2.3	2.[illegible]
1996													1.[illegible]

Private final consumption expenditure
(implicit price deflator)
Consommation finale privée
(prix implicite)

	1985	1986	1987	1988	1989	1990	1991	1992	1993	1994	1995	1996	1997
1984	2.5	2.2	1.5	0.9	0.5	0.3	0.6	0.6	0.6	0.7	0.7	0.8	0.8
1985		1.9	1.0	0.4	0.0	-0.1	0.3	0.3	0.4	0.6	0.6	0.6	0.7
1986			0.1	-0.4	-0.6	-0.6	-0.0	0.0	0.2	0.4	0.4	0.5	0.5
1987				-0.9	-0.9	-0.8	-0.1	0.0	0.2	0.4	0.5	0.6	0.6
1988					-1.0	-0.7	0.2	0.3	0.5	0.7	0.7	0.8	0.8
1989						-0.5	0.8	0.7	0.8	1.0	0.9	1.0	1.0
1990							2.2	1.3	1.3	1.4	1.2	1.3	1.2
1991								0.4	0.8	1.1	1.0	1.1	1.0
1992									1.3	1.5	1.2	1.2	1.2
1993										1.7	1.2	1.2	1.1
1994											0.7	1.0	1.0
1995												1.4	1.1
1996													0.8

Government final consumption expenditure
(volume)
Consommation des administrations publiques
(volume)

	1985	1986	1987	1988	1989	1990	1991	1992	1993	1994	1995	1996	1997
1984	4.6	3.3	2.3	2.0	2.4	2.7	3.1	3.2	3.3	3.3	3.3	3.0	3.[illegible]
1985		2.0	1.2	1.1	1.9	2.4	2.8	3.0	3.2	3.1	3.1	2.9	2.[illegible]
1986			0.3	0.7	1.8	2.4	3.0	3.1	3.3	3.3	3.3	3.0	3.[illegible]
1987				1.0	2.6	3.1	3.7	3.7	3.8	3.7	3.6	3.3	3.[illegible]
1988					4.1	4.2	4.6	4.4	4.4	4.2	4.0	3.6	3.5
1989						4.3	4.8	4.4	4.5	4.2	4.0	3.5	3.[illegible]
1990							5.3	4.5	4.5	4.1	3.9	3.4	3.[illegible]
1991								3.7	4.2	3.8	3.6	3.0	3.0
1992									4.6	3.8	3.5	2.8	2.8
1993										3.0	3.0	2.2	2.4
1994											3.1	1.8	2.2
1995												0.6	1.8
1996													3.0

Government final consumption expenditure
(implicit price deflator)
Consommation des administrations publiques
(prix implicite)

	1985	1986	1987	1988	1989	1990	1991	1992	1993	1994	1995	1996	1997
1984	3.9	3.7	4.6	7.4	8.2	8.4	6.4	5.8	4.7	4.2	4.2	3.9	4.0
1985		3.5	4.9	8.6	9.3	9.3	6.9	6.1	4.8	4.2	4.2	3.9	4.0
1986			6.3	11.2	11.3	10.9	7.6	6.5	5.0	4.3	4.3	3.9	4.1
1987				16.4	13.8	12.4	7.9	6.5	4.8	4.1	4.1	3.7	3.8
1988					11.4	10.5	5.2	4.2	2.6	2.1	2.4	2.2	2.5
1989						9.6	2.2	1.9	0.5	0.4	1.0	0.9	1.5
1990							-4.7	-1.7	-2.4	-1.8	-0.6	-0.4	0.4
1991								1.3	-1.2	-0.8	0.4	0.4	1.2
1992									-3.6	-1.9	0.1	0.2	1.2
1993										-0.1	2.0	1.5	2.5
1994											4.2	2.3	3.3
1995												0.5	2.9
1996													5.4

Gross fixed capital formation
(volume)
Formation brute de capital fixe
(volume)

	1985	1986	1987	1988	1989	1990	1991	1992	1993	1994	1995	1996	1997
1984	3.6	2.4	1.9	1.9	2.4	2.5	2.4	2.5	2.4	2.4	2.3	2.2	2.1
1985		1.1	1.0	1.4	2.1	2.2	2.2	2.3	2.2	2.2	2.2	2.1	2.0
1986			1.0	1.5	2.5	2.5	2.4	2.5	2.4	2.4	2.3	2.2	2.0
1987				2.0	3.2	3.1	2.8	2.8	2.6	2.6	2.5	2.3	2.1
1988					4.4	3.6	3.1	3.0	2.8	2.7	2.5	2.3	2.2
1989						2.8	2.4	2.6	2.4	2.3	2.2	2.0	1.9
1990							2.1	2.5	2.2	2.2	2.1	1.9	1.8
1991								2.9	2.3	2.3	2.1	1.9	1.7
1992									1.6	1.9	1.9	1.6	1.5
1993										2.2	2.0	1.6	1.4
1994											1.8	1.3	1.1
1995												0.9	0.8
1996													0.8

Gross fixed capital formation
(implicit price deflator)
Formation brute de capital fixe
(prix implicite)

	1985	1986	1987	1988	1989	1990	1991	1992	1993	1994	1995	1996	1997
1984	7.2	6.4	5.8	5.9	6.5	6.4	6.2	6.0	5.8	5.7	5.6	5.3	5.3
1985		5.6	5.1	5.5	6.3	6.2	6.1	5.9	5.6	5.5	5.4	5.2	5.1
1986			4.6	5.5	6.6	6.4	6.2	5.9	5.6	5.5	5.4	5.1	5.1
1987				6.3	7.6	7.0	6.6	6.2	5.8	5.7	5.5	5.2	5.1
1988					8.9	7.3	6.7	6.1	5.7	5.6	5.4	5.1	5.0
1989						5.8	5.6	5.2	4.9	4.9	4.8	4.5	4.5
1990							5.4	5.0	4.6	4.7	4.6	4.3	4.4
1991								4.5	4.1	4.5	4.4	4.1	4.2
1992									3.7	4.4	4.3	4.0	4.1
1993										5.1	4.6	4.1	4.2
1994											4.2	3.5	3.9
1995												2.9	3.8
1996													4.6

National disposable income
(value)
Revenu national disponible
(valeur)

	1985	1986	1987	1988	1989	1990	1991	1992	1993	1994	1995	1996	1997
1984	5.5	5.0	4.2	4.1	4.3	5.0	5.3	5.3	5.0	4.8	4.7	4.4	4.3
1985		4.4	3.5	3.7	4.0	4.9	5.3	5.3	4.9	4.8	4.6	4.3	4.2
1986			2.5	3.3	3.9	5.0	5.5	5.4	5.0	4.8	4.6	4.3	4.2
1987				4.1	4.6	5.9	6.2	6.0	5.4	5.1	4.9	4.5	4.4
1988					5.1	6.7	7.0	6.5	5.7	5.3	5.0	4.6	4.4
1989						8.5	7.9	7.0	5.8	5.4	5.0	4.5	4.3
1990							7.4	6.3	5.0	4.6	4.3	3.9	3.8
1991								5.2	4.8	3.7	3.5	3.2	3.2
1992									4.4	3.0	3.0	2.7	2.8
1993										3.5	3.3	2.8	2.9
1994											3.0	2.4	2.7
1995												1.8	2.5
1996													3.2

Compensation of employees
(value)
Rémunération des salariés
(valeur)

G.D.P. per head (volume) / P.I.B. par tête (volume)

Year	1985	1986	1987	1988	1989	1990	1991	1992	1993	1994	1995	1996	1997
1984	..												
1985		..											
1986			..										
1987				..									
1988					..								
1989						..							
1990							-11.0	-7.3	-4.8	-2.8	-1.1	-0.2	-0.0
1991								-3.4	-1.5	0.0	1.6	2.1	1.9
1992									0.4	1.8	3.3	3.5	3.0
1993										3.2	4.8	4.5	3.7
1994											6.4	5.2	3.8
1995												4.1	2.6
1996													1.1

Private final consumption expenditure per head (volume) / Consommation finale privée par tête (volume)

Year	1985	1986	1987	1988	1989	1990	1991	1992	1993	1994	1995	1996	1997
1984	..												
1985		..											
1986			..										
1987				..									
1988					..								
1989						..							
1990							-28.1	-9.1	-5.1	-2.6	-0.7	0.6	0.8
1991								15.0	9.1	7.8	7.6	7.5	6.6
1992									3.5	4.4	5.3	5.8	5.0
1993										5.3	6.2	6.5	5.3
1994											7.0	7.1	5.3
1995												7.2	4.5
1996													1.9

Gross domestic product (volume) / Produit intérieur brut (volume)

Year	1985	1986	1987	1988	1989	1990	1991	1992	1993	1994	1995	1996	1997
1984	..												
1985		..											
1986			..										
1987				..									
1988					..								
1989						..							
1990							-11.5	-7.5	-4.9	-2.9	-1.1	-0.3	-0.1
1991								-3.3	-1.4	0.1	1.6	2.1	1.9
1992									0.6	1.9	3.4	3.5	3.0
1993										3.2	4.8	4.5	3.6
1994											6.3	5.1	3.7
1995												3.9	2.4
1996													1.0

Gross domestic product (implicit price deflator) / Produit intérieur brut (prix implicite)

Year	1985	1986	1987	1988	1989	1990	1991	1992	1993	1994	1995	1996	1997
1984	..												
1985		..											
1986			..										
1987				..									
1988					..								
1989						..							
1990							46.2	30.7	26.3	22.2	19.8	18.0	16.3
1991								16.8	17.4	15.1	13.9	13.0	11.0
1992									17.9	14.3	13.0	12.1	11.0
1993										10.8	10.6	10.2	9.3
1994											10.4	9.9	8.8
1995												9.4	8.0
1996													6.6

Private final consumption expenditure (volume) / Consommation finale privée (volume)

Year	1985	1986	1987	1988	1989	1990	1991	1992	1993	1994	1995	1996	1997
1984	..												
1985		..											
1986			..										
1987				..									
1988					..								
1989						..							
1990							-28.5	-9.3	-5.2	-2.6	-0.8	0.5	0.7
1991								15.1	9.2	7.9	7.7	7.6	6.6
1992									3.6	4.5	5.3	5.7	4.9
1993										5.4	6.2	6.5	5.3
1994											7.0	7.0	5.2
1995												7.1	4.4
1996													1.7

Private final consumption expenditure (implicit price deflator) / Consommation finale privée (prix implicite)

Year	1985	1986	1987	1988	1989	1990	1991	1992	1993	1994	1995	1996	1997
1984	..												
1985		..											
1986			..										
1987				..									
1988					..								
1989						..							
1990							56.2	32.1	23.6	19.9	17.6	16.0	14.8
1991								11.7	9.9	9.7	9.6	9.3	9.0
1992									8.2	8.7	8.9	8.7	8.5
1993										9.3	9.2	8.8	8.6
1994											9.2	8.6	8.3
1995												8.0	7.9
1996													7.9

Government final consumption expenditure (volume) / Consommation des administrations publiques (volume)

Year	1985	1986	1987	1988	1989	1990	1991	1992	1993	1994	1995	1996	1997
1984	..												
1985		..											
1986			..										
1987				..									
1988					..								
1989						..							
1990							-9.0	-6.1	-4.7	-4.1	-3.7	-2.5	-2.4
1991								-3.0	-2.4	-2.5	-2.4	-1.1	-1.3
1992									-1.8	-2.2	-2.1	-0.6	-0.9
1993										-2.6	-2.3	-0.2	-0.7
1994											-2.1	1.0	-0.1
1995												4.1	0.9
1996													-2.1

Government final consumption expenditure (implicit price deflator) / Consommation des administrations publiques (prix implicite)

Year	1985	1986	1987	1988	1989	1990	1991	1992	1993	1994	1995	1996	1997
1984	..												
1985		..											
1986			..										
1987				..									
1988					..								
1989						..							
1990							32.3	28.8	31.9	28.4	25.0	22.5	19.9
1991								25.3	31.7	27.1	23.3	20.6	17.9
1992									38.3	28.0	22.6	19.4	16.5
1993										18.4	15.4	13.7	11.6
1994											12.5	11.4	9.4
1995												10.4	7.9
1996													5.5

Gross fixed capital formation (volume) / Formation brute de capital fixe (volume)

Year	1985	1986	1987	1988	1989	1990	1991	1992	1993	1994	1995	1996	1997
1984	..												
1985		..											
1986			..										
1987				..									
1988					..								
1989						..							
1990							-17.7	-5.3	-6.1	-0.4	3.6	4.4	3.0
1991								8.9	0.3	6.2	9.7	9.5	6.9
1992									-7.7	4.8	10.0	9.6	6.6
1993										19.0	20.0	16.1	10.5
1994											21.0	14.7	7.7
1995												8.7	1.7
1996													-4.9

Gross fixed capital formation (implicit price deflator) / Formation brute de capital fixe (prix implicite)

Year	1985	1986	1987	1988	1989	1990	1991	1992	1993	1994	1995	1996	1997
1984	..												
1985		..											
1986			..										
1987				..									
1988					..								
1989						..							
1990							34.5	29.9	29.4	21.3	18.4	16.1	14.5
1991								25.4	26.9	17.2	14.7	12.7	11.5
1992									28.3	13.2	11.3	9.7	8.9
1993										-0.1	3.7	4.2	4.5
1994											7.6	6.4	6.0
1995												5.1	5.3
1996													5.4

National disposable income (value) / Revenu national disponible (valeur)

Year	1985	1986	1987	1988	1989	1990	1991	1992	1993	1994	1995	1996	1997
1984	..												
1985		..											
1986			..										
1987				..									
1988					..								
1989						..							
1990							..						
1991								..					
1992									16.7	14.9	17.5	16.6	..
1993										13.2	18.0	16.5	..
1994											23.0	18.2	..
1995												13.6	..
1996													..

Compensation of employees (value) / Rémunération des salariés (valeur)

Year	1985	1986	1987	1988	1989	1990	1991	1992	1993	1994	1995	1996	1997
1984	..												
1985		..											
1986			..										
1987				..									
1988					..								
1989						..							
1990							..						
1991								..					
1992									22.4	20.7	20.1	19.6	..
1993										18.9	18.9	18.7	..
1994											19.0	18.6	..
1995												18.1	..
1996													..

DENMARK

DANEMARK

Average per cent changes at annual rate

Variations moyennes en pourcentage aux taux annuels

G.D.P. per head (volume)
P.I.B. par tête (volume)

	1985	1986	1987	1988	1989	1990	1991	1992	1993	1994	1995	1996	1997
1984	4.2	3.9	2.6	2.2	1.8	1.7	1.6	1.5	1.4	1.8	1.9	2.0	2.0
1985		3.5	1.8	1.6	1.2	1.2	1.2	1.2	1.1	1.5	1.7	1.7	1.8
1986			0.2	0.6	0.5	0.6	0.7	0.8	0.7	1.3	1.5	1.6	1.7
1987				1.1	0.7	0.8	0.9	0.9	0.8	1.5	1.6	1.7	1.8
1988					0.2	0.6	0.8	0.8	0.8	1.5	1.7	1.8	1.9
1989						1.1	1.1	1.0	0.9	1.8	2.0	2.0	2.1
1990							1.1	1.0	0.9	2.0	2.1	2.2	2.3
1991								1.0	0.7	2.3	2.4	2.4	2.5
1992									0.5	2.9	2.9	2.8	2.8
1993										5.4	4.1	3.6	3.4
1994											2.8	2.6	2.7
1995												2.5	2.7
1996													2.9

Private final consumption expenditure per head (volume)
Consommation finale privée par tête (volume)

	1985	1986	1987	1988	1989	1990	1991	1992	1993	1994	1995	1996	1997
1984	4.9	5.3	2.9	1.9	1.4	1.2	1.3	1.4	1.3	1.9	2.0	2.0	2.1
1985		5.6	1.9	0.9	0.6	0.5	0.7	0.9	0.9	1.5	1.7	1.7	1.3
1986			–1.6	–1.3	–1.0	–0.7	–0.3	0.1	0.3	1.0	1.2	1.3	1.5
1987				–1.1	–0.7	–0.5	0.0	0.5	0.6	1.4	1.6	1.6	1.3
1988					–0.4	–0.1	0.4	0.9	0.9	1.8	2.0	2.0	2.1
1989						0.1	0.8	1.3	1.2	2.3	2.4	2.3	2.4
1990							1.5	1.9	1.6	2.9	2.8	2.7	2.3
1991								2.2	1.6	3.3	3.2	3.0	3.0
1992									1.0	3.8	3.5	3.1	3.1
1993										6.7	4.7	3.8	3.7
1994											2.8	2.4	2.7
1995												2.1	2.5
1996													3.2

Gross domestic product (volume)
Produit intérieur brut (volume)

	1985	1986	1987	1988	1989	1990	1991	1992	1993	1994	1995	1996	1997
1984	4.3	4.0	2.7	2.3	1.9	1.8	1.7	1.7	1.6	2.0	2.1	2.2	2.3
1985		3.6	2.0	1.7	1.3	1.3	1.3	1.3	1.3	1.7	1.9	2.0	2.1
1986			0.3	0.7	0.6	0.7	0.9	0.9	0.9	1.5	1.7	1.8	2.0
1987				1.2	0.7	0.9	1.0	1.1	1.0	1.7	1.9	2.0	2.1
1988					0.3	0.7	1.0	1.0	1.0	1.8	2.0	2.1	2.3
1989						1.2	1.3	1.3	1.2	2.1	2.3	2.4	2.5
1990							1.4	1.3	1.2	2.3	2.5	2.6	2.7
1991								1.3	1.1	2.6	2.8	2.8	2.9
1992									0.8	3.3	3.3	3.2	3.2
1993										5.8	4.5	4.0	3.9
1994											3.2	3.2	3.2
1995												3.2	3.2
1996													3.3

Gross domestic product (implicit price deflator)
Produit intérieur brut (prix implicite)

	1985	1986	1987	1988	1989	1990	1991	1992	1993	1994	1995	1996	1997
1984	4.3	4.4	4.5	4.2	4.4	4.2	4.0	3.8	3.4	3.2	3.1	3.0	2.3
1985		4.6	4.6	4.2	4.4	4.2	3.9	3.7	3.3	3.1	2.9	2.9	2.3
1986			4.7	4.0	4.4	4.1	3.8	3.5	3.1	2.9	2.8	2.7	2.5
1987				3.4	4.2	4.0	3.6	3.3	2.8	2.6	2.5	2.5	2.4
1988					5.1	4.3	3.7	3.3	2.7	2.5	2.4	2.4	2.3
1989						3.4	2.9	2.7	2.2	2.0	2.0	2.0	2.0
1990							2.5	2.4	1.7	1.7	1.7	1.7	1.3
1991								2.2	1.4	1.4	1.5	1.6	1.5
1992									0.5	1.0	1.2	1.4	1.5
1993										1.4	1.6	1.7	1.3
1994											1.7	1.8	[illegible]
1995												2.0	[illegible]
1996													[illegible]

Private final consumption expenditure (volume)
Consommation finale privée (volume)

	1985	1986	1987	1988	1989	1990	1991	1992	1993	1994	1995	1996	1997
1984	5.0	5.4	3.0	2.0	1.5	1.3	1.4	1.5	1.5	2.1	2.2	2.2	2.3
1985		5.7	2.1	1.0	0.7	0.6	0.8	1.0	1.1	1.7	1.9	2.0	2.1
1986			–1.5	–1.3	–1.0	–0.7	–0.2	0.3	0.4	1.2	1.5	1.6	1.8
1987				–1.0	–0.7	–0.4	0.2	0.6	0.8	1.6	1.8	1.9	2.1
1988					–0.3	–0.0	0.6	1.1	1.1	2.1	2.3	2.3	2.5
1989						0.3	1.0	1.5	1.5	2.6	2.7	2.7	2.8
1990							1.8	2.2	1.9	3.2	3.2	3.1	3.2
1991								2.6	2.0	3.7	3.5	3.4	3.4
1992									1.4	4.2	3.9	3.6	3.6
1993										7.1	5.1	4.3	4.1
1994											3.2	3.0	3.2
1995												2.7	3.2
1996													3.6

Private final consumption expenditure (implicit price deflator)
Consommation finale privée (prix implicite)

	1985	1986	1987	1988	1989	1990	1991	1992	1993	1994	1995	1996	1997
1984	4.3	3.6	3.9	3.9	4.1	3.9	3.7	3.4	3.1	3.1	2.9	2.8	2.7
1985		2.9	3.7	3.8	4.1	3.8	3.6	3.3	3.0	2.9	2.7	2.6	[illegible]
1986			4.6	4.3	4.5	4.1	3.8	3.3	3.0	2.9	2.7	2.6	[illegible]
1987				4.0	4.5	3.9	3.6	3.1	2.8	2.7	2.5	2.4	[illegible]
1988					5.0	3.8	3.4	2.9	2.5	2.5	2.3	2.2	[illegible]
1989						2.7	2.7	2.2	1.9	2.0	1.8	1.8	[illegible]
1990							2.7	1.9	1.6	1.8	1.7	1.7	1.7
1991								1.2	1.1	1.6	1.4	1.5	[illegible]
1992									1.1	1.8	1.5	1.5	1.7
1993										2.5	1.7	1.7	[illegible]
1994											0.9	1.3	[illegible]
1995												1.7	[illegible]
1996													[illegible]

Government final consumption expenditure (volume)
Consommation des administrations publiques (volume)

	1985	1986	1987	1988	1989	1990	1991	1992	1993	1994	1995	1996	1997
1984	2.5	1.5	1.8	1.6	1.1	0.9	0.8	0.8	1.2	1.4	1.5	1.5	1.6
1985		0.5	1.5	1.3	0.8	0.6	0.6	0.6	1.0	1.2	1.4	1.5	1.5
1986			2.5	1.7	0.8	0.6	0.6	0.6	1.1	1.3	1.5	1.5	1.6
1987				0.9	0.0	–0.1	0.1	0.3	0.9	1.2	1.3	1.4	1.5
1988					–0.8	–0.5	–0.1	0.1	0.9	1.2	1.4	1.5	1.6
1989						–0.3	0.2	0.4	1.3	1.6	1.8	1.9	1.9
1990							0.7	0.8	1.9	2.1	2.2	2.2	2.2
1991								0.9	2.5	2.6	2.5	2.5	2.5
1992									4.1	3.5	3.1	2.9	2.8
1993										2.9	2.6	2.6	2.5
1994											2.4	2.4	2.3
1995												2.4	2.3
1996													2.2

Government final consumption expenditure (implicit price deflator)
Consommation des administrations publiques (prix implicite)

	1985	1986	1987	1988	1989	1990	1991	1992	1993	1994	1995	1996	1997
1984	3.7	2.9	4.5	4.9	4.9	4.6	4.5	4.3	4.0	3.7	3.4	3.4	[illegible]
1985		2.0	4.9	5.3	5.2	4.8	4.7	4.4	4.0	3.6	3.4	3.3	[illegible]
1986			7.9	6.9	6.3	5.5	5.2	4.8	4.3	3.9	3.6	3.4	[illegible]
1987				6.0	5.4	4.7	4.5	4.2	3.7	3.3	3.0	3.0	2.9
1988					4.9	4.1	4.0	3.8	3.2	2.8	2.6	2.6	2.6
1989						3.4	3.6	3.4	2.8	2.4	2.3	2.3	[illegible]
1990							3.9	3.4	2.6	2.2	2.0	2.1	[illegible]
1991								3.0	2.0	1.7	1.6	1.7	1.8
1992									1.0	1.0	1.1	1.4	1.6
1993										1.0	1.2	1.5	1.8
1994											1.4	1.8	2.0
1995												2.3	[illegible]
1996													2.4

Gross fixed capital formation (volume)
Formation brute de capital fixe (volume)

	1985	1986	1987	1988	1989	1990	1991	1992	1993	1994	1995	1996	1997
1984	12.6	14.8	8.2	4.3	3.5	2.7	1.9	1.6	1.2	1.8	2.7	2.9	3.4
1985		17.1	6.2	1.7	1.3	0.9	0.3	0.1	–0.2	0.7	1.8	2.0	2.7
1986			–3.8	–5.2	–3.4	–2.8	–2.8	–2.5	–2.4	–1.2	0.2	0.6	1.5
1987				–6.6	–3.3	–2.5	–2.5	–2.2	–2.2	–0.9	0.7	1.1	2.0
1988					0.2	–0.3	–1.1	–1.1	–1.3	0.1	1.8	2.2	3.0
1989						–0.9	–1.8	–1.5	–1.6	0.1	2.0	2.4	3.4
1990							–2.7	–1.9	–1.9	0.4	2.6	3.0	4.0
1991								–1.0	–1.5	1.4	4.0	4.2	5.2
1992									–1.9	2.6	5.7	5.5	6.5
1993										7.4	9.8	8.1	8.7
1994											12.3	8.4	9.1
1995												4.8	7.6
1996													10.4

Gross fixed capital formation (implicit price deflator)
Formation brute de capital fixe (prix implicite)

	1985	1986	1987	1988	1989	1990	1991	1992	1993	1994	1995	1996	1997
1984	5.2	3.9	3.8	3.5	3.8	3.6	3.5	2.8	2.3	2.2	2.0	2.0	1.9
1985		2.6	3.1	2.9	3.5	3.3	3.2	2.5	2.0	1.8	1.7	1.7	1.6
1986			3.7	3.1	3.8	3.5	3.3	2.4	1.9	1.7	1.5	1.6	1.5
1987				2.6	3.8	3.4	3.2	2.2	1.6	1.5	1.3	1.4	1.3
1988					5.1	3.8	3.4	2.1	1.4	1.3	1.1	1.3	1.2
1989						2.6	2.6	1.1	0.5	0.5	0.4	0.7	0.7
1990							2.6	0.4	0.2	–0.0	0.0	0.4	0.4
1991								–1.8	–1.6	–0.8	–0.6	–0.0	0.1
1992									–1.4	–0.4	–0.2	0.4	0.5
1993										0.6	0.4	1.0	0.9
1994											0.1	1.2	1.0
1995												2.3	1.4
1996													0.5

National disposable income (value)
Revenu national disponible (valeur)

	1985	1986	1987	1988	1989	1990	1991	1992	1993	1994	1995	1996	1997
1984	8.3	9.7	7.7	7.0	6.5	6.2	5.8	5.6	5.2	5.5	5.5	5.4	5.4
1985		11.2	7.3	6.6	6.1	5.8	5.4	5.2	4.8	5.2	5.2	5.2	5.2
1986			3.6	4.3	4.4	4.5	4.2	4.2	3.9	4.5	4.6	4.6	4.6
1987				5.0	4.9	4.8	4.4	4.3	3.9	4.6	4.7	4.7	4.7
1988					4.7	4.7	4.2	4.1	3.7	4.5	4.6	4.6	4.7
1989						4.7	4.0	4.0	3.5	4.5	4.6	4.6	4.7
1990							3.3	3.6	3.1	4.4	4.6	4.6	4.7
1991								4.0	3.0	4.8	5.0	4.9	5.0
1992									2.0	5.3	5.3	5.1	5.2
1993										8.6	7.0	6.2	6.0
1994											5.3	4.9	5.1
1995												4.5	5.0
1996													5.5

Compensation of employees (value)
Rémunération des salariés (valeur)

	1985	1986	1987	1988	1989	1990	1991	1992	1993	1994	1995	1996	1997
1984	8.1	7.9	8.3	7.4	6.7	6.2	5.8	5.4	4.9	4.8	4.8	4.8	4.9
1985		7.7	8.4	7.2	6.3	5.8	5.4	5.1	4.5	4.4	4.5	4.5	4.7
1986			9.2	6.9	5.9	5.4	5.0	4.6	4.1	4.0	4.2	4.2	4.4
1987				4.7	4.3	4.1	3.9	3.7	3.3	3.3	3.5	3.6	3.9
1988					3.9	3.9	3.7	3.5	3.0	3.1	3.4	3.5	3.8
1989						3.9	3.6	3.4	2.8	2.9	3.3	3.5	3.8
1990							3.3	3.1	2.4	2.7	3.2	3.4	3.8
1991								3.0	1.9	2.5	3.2	3.4	3.9
1992									0.9	2.3	3.2	3.5	4.1
1993										3.6	4.4	4.4	4.9
1994											5.2	4.8	5.4
1995												4.5	5.5
1996													6.5

FINLAND

Average per cent changes at annual rate

	1985	1986	1987	1988	1989	1990	1991	1992	1993	1994	1995	1996	1997
1984	2.9	2.5	2.9	3.3	3.7	3.0	1.4	0.7	0.5	0.8	1.2	1.3	1.7
1985		2.0	2.9	3.5	3.9	3.0	1.2	0.4	0.2	0.6	1.0	1.2	1.6
1986			3.8	4.2	4.6	3.3	1.0	0.2	–0.1	0.4	0.9	1.1	1.5
1987				4.6	4.9	3.1	0.3	–0.6	–0.7	–0.1	0.5	0.8	1.3
1988					5.3	2.4	–1.1	–1.8	–1.8	–0.8	–0.1	0.3	0.9
1989						–0.4	–4.1	–4.1	–3.5	–2.0	–0.9	–0.3	0.4
1990							–7.6	–5.9	–4.5	–2.4	–1.0	–0.3	0.5
1991								–4.1	–2.9	–0.6	0.7	1.2	1.9
1992									–1.6	1.2	2.3	2.5	3.2
1993										4.1	4.4	4.0	4.4
1994											4.6	3.9	4.5
1995												3.2	4.4
1996													5.7

G.D.P. per head
(volume)
P.I.B. par tête
(volume)

	1985	1986	1987	1988	1989	1990	1991	1992	1993	1994	1995	1996	1997
1984	3.4	2.9	3.3	3.7	4.1	3.4	1.8	1.1	0.9	1.2	1.6	1.7	2.1
1985		2.4	3.2	3.8	4.3	3.4	1.6	0.8	0.6	1.0	1.4	1.6	2.0
1986			4.1	4.5	4.9	3.6	1.4	0.6	0.3	0.8	1.3	1.5	1.9
1987				4.9	5.3	3.5	0.7	–0.1	–0.3	0.4	1.0	1.2	1.7
1988					5.7	2.8	–0.6	–1.3	–1.3	–0.4	0.4	0.8	1.4
1989						0.0	–3.6	–3.6	–3.0	–1.5	–0.5	0.1	0.8
1990							–7.1	–5.3	–4.0	–1.9	–0.5	0.1	0.9
1991								–3.6	–2.4	–0.1	1.2	1.6	2.3
1992									–1.2	1.6	2.8	3.0	3.6
1993										4.5	4.8	4.4	4.8
1994											5.1	4.3	4.9
1995												3.6	4.8
1996													6.0

Gross domestic product
(volume)
Produit intérieur brut
(volume)

	1985	1986	1987	1988	1989	1990	1991	1992	1993	1994	1995	1996	1997
1984	3.7	3.9	4.3	4.5	4.5	3.7	2.6	1.7	1.1	1.2	1.5	1.7	1.8
1985		4.0	4.6	4.8	4.7	3.7	2.4	1.4	0.8	0.9	1.3	1.5	1.6
1986			5.2	5.2	4.9	3.6	2.1	0.9	0.4	0.6	1.0	1.2	1.4
1987				5.1	4.7	3.1	1.4	0.1	–0.4	–0.1	0.5	0.8	1.1
1988					4.3	2.1	0.2	–1.1	–1.5	–0.9	–0.2	0.3	0.6
1989						–0.0	–1.8	–2.9	–2.9	–1.9	–0.9	–0.3	0.2
1990							–3.6	–4.2	–3.8	–2.4	–1.0	–0.3	0.2
1991								–4.9	–3.9	–2.0	–0.4	0.4	0.9
1992									–2.9	–0.5	1.1	1.7	2.0
1993										1.9	3.2	3.3	3.3
1994											4.6	4.0	3.8
1995												3.5	3.4
1996													3.3

Private final consumption expenditure
(volume)
Consommation finale privée
(volume)

	1985	1986	1987	1988	1989	1990	1991	1992	1993	1994	1995	1996	1997
1984	4.5	3.8	4.0	3.5	3.3	3.4	3.3	2.6	1.7	1.5	1.5	1.7	1.6
1985		3.1	3.7	3.2	3.0	3.2	3.1	2.3	1.3	1.1	1.2	1.4	1.3
1986			4.3	3.3	3.0	3.2	3.0	2.1	1.0	0.9	1.0	1.2	1.2
1987				2.3	2.3	2.8	2.7	1.7	0.5	0.4	0.6	0.9	0.9
1988					2.3	3.1	2.9	1.6	0.2	0.1	0.3	0.7	0.7
1989						3.8	3.2	1.3	–0.4	–0.3	0.0	0.5	0.5
1990							2.5	0.1	–1.7	–1.4	–0.7	–0.1	0.1
1991								–2.2	–3.8	–2.6	–1.5	–0.6	–0.3
1992									–5.3	–2.8	–1.3	–0.1	0.0
1993										–0.3	0.8	1.6	1.4
1994											1.9	2.6	2.0
1995												3.4	2.1
1996													0.7

Government final consumption expenditure
(volume)
Consommation des administrations publiques
(volume)

	1985	1986	1987	1988	1989	1990	1991	1992	1993	1994	1995	1996	1997
1984	2.2	0.9	2.2	4.1	6.1	4.4	0.4	–1.9	–4.0	–3.6	–2.3	–1.5	–0.5
1985		–0.4	2.2	4.7	7.1	4.8	0.1	–2.5	–4.8	–4.2	–2.8	–1.9	–0.8
1986			4.9	7.3	9.8	6.1	0.2	–2.8	–5.4	–4.7	–3.0	–2.0	–0.8
1987				9.8	12.3	6.5	–0.9	–4.3	–7.0	–6.0	–4.0	–2.7	–1.3
1988					14.8	4.9	–4.2	–7.6	–10.0	–8.4	–5.8	–4.2	–2.5
1989						–4.1	–12.5	–14.0	–15.3	–12.4	–8.9	–6.7	–4.5
1990							–20.3	–18.6	–18.8	–14.4	–9.8	–7.1	–4.5
1991								–16.9	–18.0	–12.4	–7.0	–4.2	–1.6
1992									–19.2	–10.0	–3.4	–0.7	1.7
1993										0.2	5.6	6.3	7.7
1994											11.3	9.5	10.4
1995												7.8	10.0
1996													12.2

Gross fixed capital formation
(volume)
Formation brute de capital fixe
(volume)

	1985	1986	1987	1988	1989	1990	1991	1992	1993	1994	1995	1996	1997
1984	9.2	7.9	8.3	9.4	9.7	8.8	6.3	4.8	4.2	4.7	5.2	5.2	5.5
1985		6.7	7.9	9.5	9.8	8.7	5.8	4.2	3.6	4.2	4.8	4.9	5.2
1986			9.0	10.9	10.8	9.2	5.6	3.8	3.2	3.9	4.6	4.7	5.1
1987				12.8	11.8	9.2	4.7	2.8	2.3	3.2	4.0	4.2	4.7
1988					10.8	7.5	2.2	0.4	0.3	1.7	2.9	3.2	3.9
1989						4.4	–1.8	–2.8	–2.2	0.0	1.6	2.2	3.0
1990							–7.7	–6.3	–4.2	–1.1	1.0	1.8	2.8
1991								–4.8	–2.5	1.2	3.3	3.8	4.7
1992									–0.1	4.4	6.2	6.1	6.7
1993										9.1	9.5	8.2	8.5
1994											9.9	7.7	8.3
1995												5.6	7.5
1996													9.3

National disposable income
(value)
Revenu national disponible
(valeur)

FINLANDE

Variations moyennes en pourcentage aux taux annuels

	1985	1986	1987	1988	1989	1990	1991	1992	1993	1994	1995	1996	1997
1984	3.3	3.5	4.0	4.2	4.1	3.3	2.2	1.2	0.7	0.8	1.1	1.3	1.4
1985		3.7	4.3	4.5	4.3	3.3	2.1	1.0	0.4	0.5	0.9	1.1	1.2
1986			4.9	4.9	4.5	3.3	1.7	0.5	–0.1	0.1	0.6	0.8	1.0
1987				4.8	4.4	2.7	1.0	–0.3	–0.9	–0.5	0.0	0.4	0.6
1988					3.9	1.7	–0.3	–1.6	–2.0	–1.4	–0.6	–0.2	0.2
1989						–0.5	–2.3	–3.4	–3.4	–2.4	–1.3	–0.7	–0.3
1990							–4.1	–4.8	–4.3	–2.9	–1.5	–0.8	–0.2
1991								–5.4	–4.4	–2.5	–0.9	–0.1	0.4
1992									–3.4	–1.0	0.7	1.3	1.7
1993										1.5	2.8	2.9	2.9
1994											4.2	3.7	3.4
1995												3.1	3.1
1996													3.0

Private final consumption expenditure per head
(volume)
Consommation finale privée par tête
(volume)

	1985	1986	1987	1988	1989	1990	1991	1992	1993	1994	1995	1996	1997
1984	5.3	4.9	4.9	5.4	5.5	5.6	5.1	4.6	4.3	4.0	3.9	3.6	3.5
1985		4.6	4.6	5.4	5.6	5.6	5.1	4.5	4.2	3.9	3.7	3.5	3.4
1986			4.7	5.8	5.9	5.9	5.2	4.4	4.1	3.8	3.6	3.4	3.2
1987				7.0	6.6	6.3	5.3	4.4	4.1	3.7	3.5	3.2	3.1
1988					6.1	6.0	4.8	3.8	3.5	3.1	3.0	2.7	2.7
1989						5.8	4.1	3.0	2.8	2.5	2.5	2.3	2.3
1990							2.5	1.6	1.9	1.7	1.9	1.7	1.8
1991								0.7	1.5	1.5	1.7	1.5	1.6
1992									2.4	1.8	2.0	1.7	1.8
1993										1.3	1.9	1.5	1.7
1994											2.4	1.6	1.8
1995												0.8	1.5
1996													2.2

Gross domestic product
(implicit price deflator)
Produit intérieur brut
(prix implicite)

	1985	1986	1987	1988	1989	1990	1991	1992	1993	1994	1995	1996	1997
1984	5.6	4.4	4.1	4.2	4.4	4.6	4.8	4.7	4.6	4.3	3.9	3.8	3.6
1985		3.1	3.4	3.8	4.1	4.5	4.7	4.6	4.5	4.2	3.8	3.6	3.4
1986			3.6	4.1	4.4	4.8	5.0	4.8	4.7	4.3	3.9	3.6	3.4
1987				4.6	4.8	5.2	5.3	5.1	4.9	4.4	3.9	3.6	3.4
1988					5.0	5.5	5.5	5.2	5.0	4.4	3.8	3.5	3.3
1989						6.0	5.8	5.3	5.0	4.3	3.6	3.3	3.1
1990							5.6	4.9	4.6	3.8	3.1	2.9	2.7
1991								4.1	4.2	3.2	2.5	2.3	2.2
1992									4.2	2.8	1.9	1.9	1.8
1993										1.4	0.8	1.1	1.2
1994											0.3	1.0	1.1
1995												1.7	1.6
1996													1.5

Private final consumption expenditure
(implicit price deflator)
Consommation finale privée
(prix implicite)

	1985	1986	1987	1988	1989	1990	1991	1992	1993	1994	1995	1996	1997
1984	8.9	7.2	6.6	6.6	6.8	7.1	7.1	6.4	5.7	5.3	5.1	4.9	4.6
1985		5.5	5.4	5.8	6.2	6.8	6.8	6.1	5.3	4.9	4.7	4.5	4.3
1986			5.4	6.0	6.5	7.1	7.0	6.2	5.3	4.8	4.6	4.4	4.2
1987				6.5	7.1	7.7	7.4	6.3	5.2	4.8	4.6	4.3	4.1
1988					7.6	8.2	7.7	6.3	5.0	4.5	4.3	4.0	3.8
1989						8.9	7.8	5.8	4.3	3.9	3.7	3.5	3.3
1990							6.7	4.3	2.9	2.6	2.7	2.6	2.5
1991								2.0	1.0	1.3	1.8	1.8	1.9
1992									0.0	1.0	1.7	1.8	1.8
1993										1.9	2.5	2.4	2.3
1994											3.2	2.6	2.4
1995												2.1	2.1
1996													2.0

Government final consumption expenditure
(implicit price deflator)
Consommation des administrations publiques
(prix implicite)

	1985	1986	1987	1988	1989	1990	1991	1992	1993	1994	1995	1996	1997
1984	6.4	5.6	5.9	6.3	6.7	6.7	5.6	4.4	3.9	3.9	3.8	3.5	3.4
1985		4.8	5.6	6.2	6.8	6.8	5.5	4.1	3.6	3.6	3.6	3.3	3.1
1986			6.4	7.0	7.5	7.3	5.6	4.0	3.4	3.5	3.4	3.1	3.0
1987				7.5	8.0	7.5	5.4	3.5	2.9	3.1	3.1	2.8	2.6
1988					8.6	7.5	4.7	2.5	2.0	2.3	2.5	2.2	2.1
1989						6.5	2.8	0.5	0.4	1.1	1.5	1.3	1.3
1990							–0.8	–2.3	–1.5	–0.2	0.5	0.5	0.6
1991								–3.9	–1.9	0.1	0.8	0.7	0.9
1992									0.2	2.1	2.4	1.9	1.8
1993										4.0	3.6	2.5	2.2
1994											3.1	1.7	1.6
1995												0.3	0.9
1996													1.6

Gross fixed capital formation
(implicit price deflator)
Formation brute de capital fixe
(prix implicite)

	1985	1986	1987	1988	1989	1990	1991	1992	1993	1994	1995	1996	1997
1984	11.3	9.3	9.1	9.5	10.0	9.8	8.4	6.6	5.1	4.8	5.0	4.9	4.9
1985		7.2	8.0	8.9	9.6	9.5	7.9	5.9	4.4	4.1	4.4	4.4	4.4
1986			8.8	9.7	10.4	10.1	8.1	5.7	4.0	3.7	4.1	4.1	4.2
1987				10.6	11.2	10.5	7.9	5.1	3.2	3.0	3.5	3.6	3.7
1988					11.9	10.5	7.0	3.7	1.8	1.8	2.5	2.7	3.0
1989						9.1	4.7	1.1	–0.6	–0.1	1.0	1.5	1.9
1990							0.3	–2.7	–3.7	–2.2	–0.5	0.3	0.9
1991								–5.6	–5.6	–3.1	–0.7	0.3	1.0
1992									–5.7	–1.8	0.9	1.8	2.4
1993										2.2	4.4	4.4	4.5
1994											6.7	5.5	5.3
1995												4.3	4.6
1996													4.8

Compensation of employees
(value)
Rémunération des salariés
(valeur)

FRANCE

Average per cent changes at annual rate

FRANCE

Variations moyennes en pourcentage aux taux annuels

G.D.P. per head (volume) / **P.I.B. par tête** (volume)

	1985	1986	1987	1988	1989	1990	1991	1992	1993	1994	1995	1996	1997
1984	1.3	1.6	1.7	2.2	2.4	2.3	2.0	1.8	1.4	1.5	1.5	1.5	1.5
1985		1.9	1.8	2.4	2.7	2.5	2.1	1.9	1.4	1.5	1.5	1.5	1.5
1986			1.7	2.7	2.9	2.6	2.2	1.9	1.3	1.5	1.5	1.4	1.5
1987				3.7	3.5	2.9	2.3	1.9	1.3	1.4	1.5	1.4	1.5
1988					3.3	2.6	1.8	1.5	0.8	1.0	1.1	1.1	1.2
1989						1.8	1.0	0.8	0.2	0.6	0.8	0.8	0.9
1990							0.2	0.4	–0.4	0.3	0.6	0.6	0.8
1991								0.5	–0.6	0.3	0.7	0.7	0.9
1992									–1.8	0.2	0.7	0.8	1.0
1993										2.2	2.0	1.7	1.7
1994											1.7	1.4	1.5
1995												1.0	1.4
1996													1.9

Private final consumption expenditure per head (volume) / **Consommation finale privée par tête** (volume)

	1985	1986	1987	1988	1989	1990	1991	1992	1993	1994	1995	1996	1997
1984	1.6	2.4	2.3	2.3	2.3	2.2	2.0	1.8	1.6	1.5	1.5	1.5	1.4
1985		3.1	2.6	2.5	2.5	2.3	2.0	1.8	1.6	1.5	1.5	1.5	1.4
1986			2.1	2.3	2.2	2.1	1.8	1.6	1.3	1.3	1.3	1.3	1.2
1987				2.4	2.3	2.1	1.8	1.5	1.2	1.2	1.2	1.2	1.1
1988					2.2	2.0	1.5	1.3	1.0	1.0	1.0	1.1	1.0
1989						1.8	1.2	1.0	0.7	0.7	0.8	0.9	0.8
1990							0.6	0.7	0.3	0.5	0.6	0.7	0.7
1991								0.7	0.2	0.4	0.6	0.8	0.7
1992									–0.4	0.3	0.5	0.8	0.7
1993										0.9	1.0	1.2	0.9
1994											1.1	1.3	1.0
1995												1.5	0.9
1996													0.3

Gross domestic product (volume) / **Produit intérieur brut** (volume)

	1985	1986	1987	1988	1989	1990	1991	1992	1993	1994	1995	1996	1997
1984	1.8	2.1	2.2	2.7	2.9	2.8	2.5	2.3	1.9	2.0	2.0	2.0	2.0
1985		2.4	2.3	3.0	3.2	3.0	2.6	2.4	1.9	2.0	2.0	2.0	2.0
1986			2.2	3.2	3.5	3.2	2.7	2.4	1.9	2.0	2.0	1.9	2.0
1987				4.2	4.1	3.5	2.8	2.5	1.8	1.9	2.0	1.9	1.9
1988					3.9	3.1	2.3	2.0	1.4	1.6	1.7	1.6	1.7
1989						2.4	1.6	1.4	0.7	1.1	1.3	1.3	1.4
1990							0.8	0.9	0.2	0.8	1.1	1.1	1.3
1991								1.1	–0.1	0.8	1.1	1.2	1.4
1992									–1.3	0.7	1.2	1.2	1.4
1993										2.7	2.4	2.1	2.1
1994											2.2	1.8	1.9
1995												1.4	1.8
1996													2.3

Gross domestic product (implicit price deflator) / **Produit intérieur brut** (prix implicite)

	1985	1986	1987	1988	1989	1990	1991	1992	1993	1994	1995	1996	1997
1984	5.8	5.6	4.7	4.3	4.1	4.0	3.9	3.7	3.5	3.3	3.2	3.0	2.9
1985		5.3	4.1	3.8	3.7	3.6	3.5	3.4	3.2	3.1	2.9	2.8	2.6
1986			3.0	3.0	3.1	3.2	3.2	3.0	2.9	2.8	2.6	2.5	2.4
1987				3.1	3.2	3.2	3.2	3.0	2.9	2.8	2.6	2.5	2.3
1988					3.4	3.3	3.3	3.0	2.9	2.7	2.5	2.4	2.2
1989						3.2	3.3	2.9	2.8	2.6	2.4	2.2	2.1
1990							3.3	2.8	2.6	2.4	2.2	2.1	1.9
1991								2.2	2.3	2.1	2.0	1.8	1.7
1992									2.4	2.1	1.9	1.7	1.6
1993										1.7	1.6	1.5	1.4
1994											1.5	1.4	1.3
1995												1.3	1.2
1996													1.1

Private final consumption expenditure (volume) / **Consommation finale privée** (volume)

	1985	1986	1987	1988	1989	1990	1991	1992	1993	1994	1995	1996	1997
1984	2.1	2.8	2.8	2.8	2.8	2.7	2.5	2.4	2.1	2.0	2.0	2.0	1.9
1985		3.6	3.1	3.0	3.0	2.9	2.6	2.4	2.1	2.0	2.0	2.0	1.9
1986			2.6	2.8	2.8	2.7	2.4	2.2	1.9	1.8	1.8	1.8	1.7
1987				2.9	2.9	2.7	2.3	2.1	1.8	1.7	1.7	1.7	1.6
1988					2.8	2.6	2.1	1.9	1.5	1.5	1.5	1.5	1.5
1989						2.4	1.8	1.6	1.2	1.2	1.3	1.4	1.3
1990							1.2	1.2	0.8	1.0	1.1	1.2	1.1
1991								1.3	0.7	0.9	1.1	1.2	1.1
1992									0.1	0.7	1.0	1.2	1.1
1993										1.4	1.4	1.6	1.4
1994											1.5	1.7	1.4
1995												1.9	1.3
1996													0.7

Private final consumption expenditure (implicit price deflator) / **Consommation finale privée** (prix implicite)

	1985	1986	1987	1988	1989	1990	1991	1992	1993	1994	1995	1996	1997
1984	6.1	4.5	4.1	3.8	3.8	3.7	3.7	3.5	[illegible]	3.3	3.1	3.0	2.9
1985		3.0	3.2	3.1	3.3	3.2	3.3	3.1	[illegible]	2.9	2.8	2.7	2.6
1986			3.4	3.2	3.4	3.3	3.3	3.2	[illegible]	2.9	2.8	2.7	2.6
1987				3.0	3.4	3.3	3.3	3.1	[illegible]	2.9	2.7	2.6	2.5
1988					3.7	3.5	3.4	3.2	[illegible]	2.9	2.7	2.6	2.5
1989						3.2	3.3	3.0	[illegible]	2.7	2.5	2.4	2.3
1990							3.3	2.9	[illegible]	2.6	2.4	2.3	2.2
1991								2.4	[illegible]	2.3	2.2	2.1	2.0
1992									[illegible]	2.2	2.1	2.0	1.9
1993										2.1	1.9	1.9	1.8
1994											1.7	1.8	1.6
1995												2.0	1.6
1996													1.3

Government final consumption expenditure (volume) / **Consommation des administrations publiques** (volume)

	1985	1986	1987	1988	1989	1990	1991	1992	1993	1994	1995	1996	1997
1984	2.2	1.9	2.2	2.5	2.1	2.1	2.2	2.3	2.4	2.3	2.1	2.1	2.1
1985		1.6	2.2	2.6	2.1	2.1	2.2	2.3	2.5	2.3	2.1	2.1	2.1
1986			2.8	3.1	2.2	2.2	2.3	2.5	2.6	2.4	2.2	2.2	2.1
1987				3.4	1.9	2.0	2.2	2.4	2.6	2.4	2.1	2.1	2.0
1988					0.5	1.3	1.8	2.2	2.4	2.2	1.9	2.0	1.9
1989						2.0	2.4	2.7	2.9	2.5	2.1	2.2	2.0
1990							2.7	3.0	3.2	2.7	2.1	2.2	2.0
1991								3.3	3.4	2.6	2.0	2.1	1.9
1992									3.4	2.3	1.6	1.8	1.7
1993										1.1	0.6	1.3	1.2
1994											0.1	1.3	1.2
1995												2.5	1.8
1996													1.1

Government final consumption expenditure (implicit price deflator) / **Consommation des administrations publiques** (prix implicite)

	1985	1986	1987	1988	1989	1990	1991	1992	1993	1994	1995	1996	1997
1984	4.2	4.0	3.3	2.9	3.1	3.2	3.2	3.2	[illegible]	3.0	2.9	2.8	2.7
1985		3.7	2.8	2.5	2.9	3.0	3.0	3.0	[illegible]	2.8	2.8	2.7	2.6
1986			1.9	1.9	2.6	2.9	2.9	2.9	[illegible]	2.7	2.7	2.6	2.5
1987				1.9	2.9	3.2	3.2	3.2	[illegible]	2.8	2.8	2.7	2.5
1988					3.9	3.8	3.6	3.5	[illegible]	3.0	2.9	2.8	2.6
1989						3.7	3.4	3.3	[illegible]	2.8	2.8	2.6	2.4
1990							3.0	3.1	[illegible]	2.6	2.6	2.4	2.2
1991								3.1	[illegible]	2.4	2.4	2.3	2.1
1992									[illegible]	2.1	2.2	2.1	1.9
1993										1.4	2.0	1.9	1.7
1994											2.5	2.1	1.8
1995												1.7	1.4
1996													1.1

Gross fixed capital formation (volume) / **Formation brute de capital fixe** (volume)

	1985	1986	1987	1988	1989	1990	1991	1992	1993	1994	1995	1996	1997
1984	3.2	3.8	4.3	5.6	6.0	5.5	4.6	3.6	2.4	2.3	2.3	2.1	1.9
1985		4.5	4.9	6.4	6.7	5.9	4.9	3.7	2.3	2.2	2.2	2.0	1.8
1986			5.2	7.4	7.4	6.3	5.0	3.6	2.0	1.9	2.0	1.7	1.6
1987				9.6	8.6	6.6	4.9	3.2	1.5	1.4	1.6	1.3	1.2
1988					7.6	5.2	3.4	1.7	–0.1	0.1	0.5	0.4	0.3
1989						2.9	1.4	–0.2	–1.9	–1.3	–0.7	–0.6	–0.5
1990							–0.1	–1.7	–3.4	–2.3	–1.4	–1.2	–1.0
1991								–3.2	–5.0	–3.0	–1.7	–1.4	–1.1
1992									–6.9	–2.9	–1.1	–1.0	–0.7
1993										1.2	1.9	1.0	0.9
1994											2.6	1.0	0.8
1995												–0.6	–0.1
1996													0.3

Gross fixed capital formation (implicit price deflator) / **Formation brute de capital fixe** (prix implicite)

	1985	1986	1987	1988	1989	1990	1991	1992	1993	1994	1995	1996	1997
1984	4.4	3.9	3.4	3.3	3.2	3.1	3.2	2.9	[illegible]	2.4	2.2	2.1	2.0
1985		3.3	2.9	2.9	2.9	2.9	3.0	2.7	[illegible]	2.2	2.0	1.9	1.8
1986			2.5	2.7	2.7	2.8	2.9	2.6	[illegible]	2.0	1.9	1.7	1.6
1987				2.8	2.8	2.8	3.0	2.6	[illegible]	1.9	1.8	1.6	1.5
1988					2.8	2.8	3.0	2.5	[illegible]	1.8	1.6	1.5	1.4
1989						2.9	3.1	2.4	[illegible]	1.6	1.4	1.3	1.2
1990							3.4	2.2	[illegible]	1.3	1.1	1.0	1.0
1991								1.0	[illegible]	0.5	0.6	0.5	0.6
1992									[illegible]	0.3	0.4	0.4	0.5
1993										0.4	0.5	0.5	0.6
1994											0.6	0.5	0.6
1995												0.4	0.6
1996													0.9

National disposable income (value) / **Revenu national disponible** (valeur)

	1985	1986	1987	1988	1989	1990	1991	1992	1993	1994	1995	1996	1997
1984	7.9	8.0	7.1	7.2	7.2	6.8	6.4	6.0	5.4	5.3	5.2	5.0	4.9
1985		8.0	6.7	6.9	7.0	6.6	6.1	5.7	5.1	5.0	4.9	4.7	4.7
1986			5.4	6.4	6.6	6.3	5.8	5.3	4.7	4.7	4.6	4.4	4.4
1987				7.4	7.2	6.5	5.9	5.3	4.6	4.6	4.5	4.3	4.3
1988					7.1	6.1	5.4	4.8	4.0	4.1	4.1	3.9	3.9
1989						5.2	4.5	4.0	3.2	3.5	3.6	3.5	3.5
1990							3.8	3.4	2.6	3.1	3.3	3.2	3.3
1991								2.9	2.0	2.8	3.2	3.1	3.2
1992									1.1	2.8	3.2	3.1	3.2
1993										4.5	4.4	3.8	3.8
1994											4.2	3.4	3.6
1995												2.6	3.2
1996													3.8

Compensation of employees (value) / **Rémunération des salariés** (valeur)

	1985	1986	1987	1988	1989	1990	1991	1992	1993	1994	1995	1996	1997
1984	6.5	5.7	5.2	5.2	5.4	5.6	5.5	5.3	[illegible]	4.7	4.6	4.5	4.4
1985		4.9	4.5	4.8	5.2	5.5	5.4	5.1	[illegible]	4.5	4.4	4.3	4.2
1986			4.2	4.8	5.3	5.6	5.5	5.2	[illegible]	4.4	4.4	4.3	4.1
1987				5.5	5.9	6.1	5.8	5.4	[illegible]	4.5	4.4	4.3	4.1
1988					6.2	6.4	5.9	5.4	[illegible]	4.3	4.2	4.1	4.0
1989						6.6	5.7	5.1	[illegible]	3.9	3.9	3.8	3.7
1990							4.7	4.3	[illegible]	3.2	3.4	3.4	3.3
1991								3.9	[illegible]	2.7	3.0	3.1	3.0
1992									[illegible]	2.2	2.8	2.9	2.8
1993										2.4	3.2	3.3	3.1
1994											3.9	3.7	3.3
1995												3.4	3.0
1996													2.6

GERMANY[1]

ALLEMAGNE[1]

Average per cent changes at annual rate

Variations moyennes en pourcentage aux taux annuels

G.D.P. per head (volume)
P.I.B. par tête (volume)

	1985	1986	1987	1988	1989	1990	1991	1992	1993	1994	1995	1996	1997
1984	2.6	2.5	2.2	2.5	2.5	2.5	2.4	2.3	1.8	1.9	1.8	1.7	1.7
1985		2.5	2.1	2.4	2.5	2.5	2.4	2.3	1.7	1.8	1.7	1.6	1.7
1986			1.6	2.4	2.5	2.5	2.4	2.2	1.6	1.7	1.6	1.6	1.6
1987				3.1	2.9	2.7	2.6	2.3	1.6	1.7	1.6	1.6	1.6
1988					2.7	2.5	2.4	2.1	1.3	1.5	1.4	1.4	1.4
1989						2.3	2.2	1.9	1.0	1.3	1.2	1.2	1.3
1990							2.0	1.7	0.5	1.0	1.0	1.0	1.1
1991								1.4	–0.2	0.6	0.7	0.8	1.0
1992									–1.9	0.2	0.5	0.6	0.9
1993										2.4	1.7	1.4	1.6
1994											0.9	1.0	1.3
1995												1.0	1.5
1996													2.0

Private final consumption expenditure per head (volume)
Consommation finale privée par tête (volume)

	1985	1986	1987	1988	1989	1990	1991	1992	1993	1994	1995	1996	1997
1984	2.3	2.9	3.1	2.9	2.7	2.9	3.2	3.1	2.6	2.5	2.4	2.3	2.1
1985		3.6	3.5	3.1	2.9	3.1	3.4	3.2	2.7	2.5	2.4	2.3	2.1
1986			3.4	2.9	2.6	3.0	3.3	3.1	2.6	2.4	2.3	2.2	2.0
1987				2.3	2.2	2.8	3.3	3.0	2.4	2.2	2.1	2.0	1.9
1988					2.1	3.1	3.6	3.2	2.5	2.2	2.1	2.0	1.8
1989						4.0	4.4	3.6	2.5	2.2	2.1	2.0	1.8
1990							4.8	3.4	2.1	1.8	1.7	1.6	1.4
1991								2.0	0.7	0.8	1.0	1.0	0.9
1992									–0.6	0.2	0.6	0.8	0.7
1993										0.9	1.2	1.2	1.0
1994											1.5	1.4	1.0
1995												1.3	0.8
1996													0.3

Gross domestic product (volume)
Produit intérieur brut (volume)

	1985	1986	1987	1988	1989	1990	1991	1992	1993	1994	1995	1996	1997
1984	2.4	2.4	2.2	2.6	2.7	2.8	2.8	2.7	2.3	2.3	2.2	2.2	2.2
1985		2.5	2.1	2.6	2.8	2.9	2.9	2.8	2.3	2.3	2.2	2.1	2.1
1986			1.7	2.7	2.9	3.0	3.0	2.8	2.3	2.3	2.2	2.1	2.1
1987				3.7	3.6	3.5	3.3	3.1	2.4	2.4	2.3	2.1	2.2
1988					3.5	3.4	3.2	2.9	2.1	2.2	2.1	2.0	2.0
1989						3.2	3.0	2.8	1.8	1.9	1.8	1.7	1.8
1990							2.8	2.5	1.3	1.6	1.5	1.5	1.6
1991								2.2	0.5	1.2	1.2	1.2	1.4
1992									–1.2	0.7	0.9	1.0	1.2
1993										2.7	2.0	1.7	1.9
1994											1.2	1.2	1.6
1995												1.3	1.7
1996													2.2

Gross domestic product (implicit price deflator)
Produit intérieur brut (prix implicite)

	1985	1986	1987	1988	1989	1990	1991	1992	1993	1994	1995	1996	1997
1984	2.0	2.4	2.1	2.0	2.0	2.2	2.6	2.9	3.1	3.0	2.9	2.8	2.6
1985		2.7	2.2	2.0	2.0	2.3	2.7	3.1	3.2	3.1	3.0	2.8	2.7
1986			1.7	1.6	1.8	2.2	2.7	3.1	3.3	3.2	3.1	2.9	2.6
1987				1.5	1.8	2.3	2.9	3.4	3.5	3.4	3.2	3.0	2.7
1988					2.1	2.8	3.4	3.9	4.0	3.7	3.5	3.2	2.9
1989						3.4	4.1	4.6	4.4	4.0	3.7	3.3	3.0
1990							4.7	5.1	4.8	4.2	3.8	3.3	2.9
1991								5.6	4.8	4.0	3.5	3.0	2.6
1992									4.0	3.2	2.9	2.4	2.1
1993										2.4	2.3	1.9	1.6
1994											2.2	1.6	1.3
1995												1.0	0.8
1996													0.6

Private final consumption expenditure (volume)
Consommation finale privée (volume)

	1985	1986	1987	1988	1989	1990	1991	1992	1993	1994	1995	1996	1997
1984	2.0	2.8	3.0	3.0	3.0	3.3	3.6	3.5	3.1	2.9	2.8	2.7	2.6
1985		3.6	3.5	3.3	3.2	3.5	3.9	3.7	3.3	3.0	2.9	2.8	2.6
1986			3.5	3.2	3.1	3.5	3.9	3.7	3.2	3.0	2.8	2.7	2.5
1987				2.8	2.8	3.5	4.0	3.8	3.2	2.9	2.8	2.6	2.4
1988					2.8	3.9	4.4	4.0	3.2	2.9	2.8	2.6	2.4
1989						4.9	5.3	4.4	3.3	2.9	2.7	2.6	2.3
1990							5.6	4.2	2.8	2.4	2.3	2.2	1.9
1991								2.8	1.5	1.4	1.5	1.5	1.3
1992									0.1	0.7	1.1	1.2	1.0
1993										1.2	1.5	1.5	1.3
1994											1.8	1.7	1.3
1995												1.6	1.0
1996													0.5

Private final consumption expenditure (implicit price deflator)
Consommation finale privée (prix implicite)

	1985	1986	1987	1988	1989	1990	1991	1992	1993	1994	1995	1996	1997
1984	1.8	0.6	0.5	0.7	1.2	1.4	1.9	2.2	2.4	2.5	2.4	2.4	2.3
1985		–0.6	–0.1	0.4	1.0	1.3	1.9	2.3	2.5	2.5	2.5	2.4	2.4
1986			0.5	0.9	1.6	1.8	2.4	2.8	2.9	2.9	2.8	2.7	2.7
1987				1.3	2.1	2.2	2.9	3.2	3.4	3.3	3.1	3.0	2.9
1988					2.9	2.7	3.4	3.7	3.8	3.6	3.4	3.2	3.0
1989						2.4	3.6	4.0	4.0	3.8	3.4	3.2	3.1
1990							4.7	4.7	4.5	4.1	3.6	3.4	3.2
1991								4.7	4.4	3.9	3.4	3.1	2.9
1992									4.1	3.5	2.9	2.7	2.5
1993										3.0	2.4	2.2	2.2
1994											1.8	1.9	1.9
1995												2.0	1.9
1996													1.9

Government final consumption expenditure (volume)
Consommation des administrations publiques (volume)

	1985	1986	1987	1988	1989	1990	1991	1992	1993	1994	1995	1996	1997
1984	2.4	2.3	2.2	2.2	1.5	1.6	1.5	1.8	1.6	1.6	1.7	1.8	1.6
1985		2.3	2.2	2.2	1.3	1.5	1.4	1.8	1.5	1.6	1.6	1.7	1.5
1986			2.1	2.1	1.0	1.3	1.2	1.7	1.4	1.5	1.5	1.6	1.4
1987				2.2	0.4	1.1	1.0	1.6	1.3	1.4	1.5	1.6	1.4
1988					–1.3	0.5	0.6	1.5	1.1	1.2	1.3	1.5	1.3
1989						2.3	1.6	2.4	1.7	1.8	1.8	1.9	1.6
1990							0.8	2.4	1.5	1.6	1.7	1.9	1.5
1991								4.1	1.8	1.9	1.9	2.1	1.6
1992									–0.5	0.8	1.2	1.6	1.1
1993										2.1	2.1	2.3	1.5
1994											2.0	2.4	1.3
1995												2.7	1.0
1996													–0.7

Government final consumption expenditure (implicit price deflator)
Consommation des administrations publiques (prix implicite)

	1985	1986	1987	1988	1989	1990	1991	1992	1993	1994	1995	1996	1997
1984	2.2	2.1	2.2	2.0	2.3	2.5	3.2	3.6	3.6	3.4	3.3	3.0	2.8
1985		2.0	2.1	2.0	2.3	2.6	3.3	3.8	3.7	3.5	3.4	3.1	2.8
1986			2.2	1.9	2.3	2.7	3.6	4.1	4.0	3.7	3.5	3.2	2.9
1987				1.6	2.4	2.8	3.9	4.4	4.3	3.9	3.7	3.3	3.0
1988					3.2	3.4	4.7	5.1	4.8	4.3	4.0	3.5	3.1
1989						3.7	5.5	5.8	5.2	4.5	4.1	3.5	3.1
1990							7.3	6.9	5.7	4.7	4.2	3.5	3.0
1991								6.4	4.9	3.8	3.4	2.7	2.3
1992									3.5	2.5	2.4	1.8	1.5
1993										1.6	1.9	1.3	1.1
1994											2.2	1.1	0.9
1995												–0.0	0.2
1996													0.4

Gross fixed capital formation (volume)
Formation brute de capital fixe (volume)

	1985	1986	1987	1988	1989	1990	1991	1992	1993	1994	1995	1996	1997
1984	–0.0	1.8	2.0	2.6	3.2	4.2	5.0	4.8	3.6	3.6	3.2	2.9	2.6
1985		3.6	3.0	3.5	4.1	5.0	5.8	5.5	4.0	4.0	3.6	3.1	2.9
1986			2.5	3.5	4.2	5.4	6.3	5.8	4.1	4.0	3.6	3.1	2.8
1987				4.6	5.1	6.4	7.2	6.5	4.4	4.3	3.7	3.2	2.8
1988					5.6	7.3	8.1	7.0	4.3	4.2	3.6	3.0	2.6
1989						9.0	9.4	7.4	4.0	3.9	3.2	2.6	2.3
1990							9.8	6.6	2.4	2.7	2.1	1.6	1.4
1991								3.5	–1.1	0.4	0.3	0.0	0.0
1992									–5.6	–1.1	–0.8	–0.9	–0.7
1993										3.5	1.7	0.8	0.6
1994											–0.0	–0.6	–0.4
1995												–1.2	–0.6
1996													0.1

Gross fixed capital formation (implicit price deflator)
Formation brute de capital fixe (prix implicite)

	1985	1986	1987	1988	1989	1990	1991	1992	1993	1994	1995	1996	1997
1984	2.0	1.8	1.7	1.7	1.9	2.4	2.7	2.9	2.9	2.8	2.7	2.4	2.2
1985		1.6	1.5	1.6	1.9	2.5	2.8	3.0	3.1	2.9	2.7	2.4	2.2
1986			1.4	1.6	2.1	2.7	3.1	3.3	3.3	3.0	2.9	2.5	2.3
1987				1.8	2.4	3.2	3.5	3.7	3.6	3.3	3.0	2.6	2.4
1988					3.0	3.9	4.1	4.1	3.9	3.5	3.2	2.7	2.4
1989						4.8	4.6	4.5	4.2	3.6	3.3	2.7	2.4
1990							4.4	4.4	4.0	3.4	3.0	2.4	2.0
1991								4.4	3.8	3.0	2.6	2.0	1.6
1992									3.1	2.3	2.0	1.4	1.1
1993										1.5	1.4	0.8	0.6
1994											1.3	0.4	0.2
1995												–0.5	–0.3
1996													–0.1

National disposable income (value)
Revenu national disponible (valeur)

	1985	1986	1987	1988	1989	1990	1991	1992	1993	1994	1995	1996	1997
1984	4.4	5.1	4.6	4.8	5.1	5.4	5.6	5.9	5.4	5.4	5.2	4.9	4.8
1985		5.9	4.7	4.9	5.3	5.6	5.8	6.1	5.5	5.5	5.3	5.0	4.8
1986			3.6	4.4	5.1	5.5	5.8	6.1	5.5	5.4	5.2	4.9	4.7
1987				5.3	5.9	6.1	6.4	6.7	5.8	5.7	5.4	5.0	4.8
1988					6.5	6.5	6.8	7.0	5.9	5.7	5.4	5.0	4.8
1989						6.6	6.9	7.2	5.7	5.6	5.2	4.8	4.6
1990							7.3	7.5	5.5	5.3	4.9	4.5	4.3
1991								7.7	4.5	4.7	4.4	3.9	3.8
1992									1.5	3.2	3.0	3.0	3.0
1993										5.0	4.2	3.5	3.4
1994											3.4	2.8	2.9
1995												2.2	2.6
1996													3.0

Compensation of employees (value)
Rémunération des salariés (valeur)

	1985	1986	1987	1988	1989	1990	1991	1992	1993	1994	1995	1996	1997
1984	3.8	4.5	4.4	4.3	4.3	5.0	5.5	5.8	5.4	5.1	5.0	4.6	4.3
1985		5.2	4.7	4.4	4.5	5.2	5.8	6.1	5.6	5.3	5.1	4.7	4.3
1986			4.2	4.1	4.2	5.2	5.9	6.3	5.7	5.3	5.1	4.7	4.2
1987				4.0	4.2	5.5	6.3	6.7	5.9	5.4	5.2	4.7	4.3
1988					4.5	6.3	7.1	7.4	6.3	5.7	5.4	4.8	4.3
1989						8.2	8.4	8.3	6.8	5.9	5.5	4.8	4.3
1990							8.7	8.4	6.3	5.4	5.0	4.3	3.7
1991								8.2	5.1	4.3	4.1	3.4	2.9
1992									2.2	2.4	2.7	2.3	1.9
1993										2.6	3.0	2.3	1.8
1994											3.3	2.2	1.5
1995												1.0	0.6
1996													0.2

1. Data refer to Germany after unification.

1. Les données se réfèrent à l'Allemagne aprés l'unification.

GREECE

GRÈCE

Average per cent changes at annual rate

Variations moyennes en pourcentage aux taux annuels

G.D.P. per head (volume)
P.I.B. par tête (volume)

	1985	1986	1987	1988	1989	1990	1991	1992	1993	1994	1995	1996	1997
1984	2.7	2.0	1.1	1.8	2.1	1.6	1.7	1.5	1.1	1.1	1.2	1.3	1.4
1985		1.3	0.2	1.5	1.9	1.4	1.6	1.3	0.9	1.0	1.0	1.1	1.3
1986			–0.8	1.6	2.2	1.5	1.6	1.3	0.8	0.9	1.0	1.1	1.3
1987				4.1	3.7	2.2	2.2	1.8	1.1	1.2	1.2	1.3	1.5
1988					3.3	1.3	1.6	1.2	0.5	0.7	0.8	1.0	1.2
1989						–0.7	0.8	0.5	–0.2	0.2	0.4	0.7	1.0
1990							2.2	1.1	–0.0	0.4	0.7	0.9	1.2
1991								–0.0	–1.1	–0.2	0.3	0.7	1.1
1992									–2.2	–0.3	0.4	0.8	1.3
1993										1.6	1.7	1.9	2.2
1994											1.8	2.0	2.3
1995												2.2	2.6
1996													3.1

Private final consumption expenditure per head (volume)
Consommation finale privée par tête (volume)

	1985	1986	1987	1988	1989	1990	1991	1992	1993	1994	1995	1996	1997
1984	3.5	1.9	1.6	2.0	2.7	2.5	2.5	2.4	1.9	1.9	2.0	1.9	2.[illegible]
1985		0.3	0.6	1.5	2.5	2.3	2.3	2.2	1.7	1.7	1.8	1.8	1.[illegible]
1986			0.9	2.0	3.2	2.9	2.7	2.5	1.9	1.9	2.0	1.9	2.[illegible]
1987				3.2	4.4	3.5	3.1	2.8	2.1	2.0	2.1	2.1	2.[illegible]
1988					5.5	3.7	3.1	2.7	1.9	1.9	1.9	1.9	2.[illegible]
1989						1.9	1.9	1.8	1.0	1.1	1.4	1.4	1.[illegible]
1990							2.0	1.8	0.8	1.0	1.3	1.3	1.[illegible]
1991								1.7	0.1	0.6	1.1	1.2	1.[illegible]
1992									–1.3	0.1	0.9	1.1	1.[illegible]
1993										1.6	2.0	1.9	2.[illegible]
1994											2.5	2.1	2.[illegible]
1995												1.7	2.[illegible]
1996													2.[illegible]

Gross domestic product (volume)
Produit intérieur brut (volume)

	1985	1986	1987	1988	1989	1990	1991	1992	1993	1994	1995	1996	1997
1984	3.1	2.4	1.4	2.2	2.5	2.1	2.2	2.0	1.6	1.7	1.7	1.8	1.9
1985		1.6	0.6	1.9	2.3	1.9	2.1	1.9	1.4	1.5	1.6	1.6	1.8
1986			–0.5	2.0	2.6	1.9	2.2	1.9	1.4	1.5	1.6	1.6	1.8
1987				4.5	4.1	2.8	2.8	2.4	1.7	1.8	1.8	1.9	2.0
1988					3.8	1.9	2.3	1.9	1.2	1.3	1.4	1.6	1.7
1989						0.0	1.5	1.3	0.5	0.8	1.0	1.2	1.5
1990							3.1	1.9	0.7	1.0	1.2	1.4	1.7
1991								0.7	–0.5	0.4	0.8	1.1	1.4
1992									–1.6	0.2	0.8	1.2	1.6
1993										2.0	2.1	2.2	2.4
1994											2.1	2.2	2.5
1995												2.4	2.8
1996													3.2

Gross domestic product (implicit price deflator)
Produit intérieur brut (prix implicite)

	1985	1986	1987	1988	1989	1990	1991	1992	1993	1994	1995	1996	1997
1984	17.7	17.6	16.5	16.2	15.9	16.7	17.1	16.8	16.6	16.0	15.4	14.8	14.[illegible]
1985		17.5	15.9	15.8	15.4	16.5	17.0	16.7	16.4	15.8	15.2	14.5	13.[illegible]
1986			14.3	14.9	14.8	16.2	16.9	16.5	16.3	15.6	15.0	14.2	13.[illegible]
1987				15.6	15.0	16.8	17.6	17.0	16.6	15.8	15.0	14.2	13.[illegible]
1988					14.4	17.5	18.2	17.4	16.8	15.8	15.0	14.1	13.[illegible]
1989						20.6	20.2	18.4	17.4	16.1	15.0	14.0	13.[illegible]
1990							19.8	17.3	16.3	15.0	14.0	12.9	12.[illegible]
1991								14.8	14.7	13.5	12.6	11.6	10.[illegible]
1992									14.5	12.8	11.8	10.8	10.[illegible]
1993										11.2	10.5	9.6	8.[illegible]
1994											9.8	8.8	8.[illegible]
1995												7.9	7.[illegible]
1996													6.[illegible]

Private final consumption expenditure (volume)
Consommation finale privée (volume)

	1985	1986	1987	1988	1989	1990	1991	1992	1993	1994	1995	1996	1997
1984	3.9	2.3	1.9	2.3	3.1	3.0	3.0	2.9	2.5	2.4	2.5	2.4	2.4
1985		0.7	0.9	1.8	2.9	2.8	2.8	2.8	2.3	2.3	2.3	2.3	2.3
1986			1.2	2.4	3.6	3.3	3.2	3.1	2.5	2.5	2.5	2.4	2.5
1987				3.6	4.8	4.1	3.8	3.5	2.8	2.7	2.7	2.6	2.6
1988					6.1	4.3	3.8	3.5	2.6	2.5	2.5	2.5	2.5
1989						2.6	2.7	2.6	1.7	1.8	2.0	1.9	2.0
1990							2.8	2.6	1.5	1.6	1.8	1.8	1.9
1991								2.4	0.8	1.2	1.6	1.6	1.8
1992									–0.8	0.6	1.3	1.5	1.7
1993										2.0	2.4	2.2	2.3
1994											2.8	2.3	2.4
1995												1.9	2.2
1996													2.6

Private final consumption expenditure (implicit price deflator)
Consommation finale privée (prix implicite)

	1985	1986	1987	1988	1989	1990	1991	1992	1993	1994	1995	1996	1997
1984	18.3	20.2	18.7	17.5	16.7	17.2	17.6	17.3	17.0	16.4	15.7	15.0	14.[illegible]
1985		22.1	18.9	17.3	16.3	17.0	17.5	17.2	16.8	16.2	15.4	14.7	13.[illegible]
1986			15.7	15.0	14.5	15.8	16.6	16.4	16.1	15.5	14.7	14.0	13.[illegible]
1987				14.2	13.8	15.8	16.8	16.6	16.2	15.4	14.6	13.9	13.[illegible]
1988					13.5	16.6	17.7	17.2	16.6	15.6	14.6	13.8	12.[illegible]
1989						19.9	19.8	18.4	17.3	16.0	14.8	13.9	12.[illegible]
1990							19.7	17.7	16.5	15.1	13.8	12.9	11.[illegible]
1991								15.6	14.9	13.6	12.4	11.6	10.[illegible]
1992									14.2	12.6	11.3	10.6	9.[illegible]
1993										11.0	9.9	9.4	8.[illegible]
1994											8.8	8.6	7.[illegible]
1995												8.3	6.[illegible]
1996													5.[illegible]

Government final consumption expenditure (volume)
Consommation des administrations publiques (volume)

	1985	1986	1987	1988	1989	1990	1991	1992	1993	1994	1995	1996	1997
1984	3.2	1.2	1.1	2.2	2.9	2.5	1.9	1.3	1.4	1.2	1.6	1.5	1.4
1985		–0.8	0.0	1.9	2.8	2.3	1.7	1.0	1.2	0.9	1.4	1.4	1.2
1986			0.9	3.3	4.0	3.1	2.2	1.3	1.5	1.2	1.7	1.6	1.4
1987				5.7	5.6	3.9	2.5	1.4	1.6	1.2	1.8	1.7	1.5
1988					5.5	3.0	1.5	0.3	0.8	0.5	1.2	1.2	1.0
1989						0.6	–0.5	–1.3	–0.4	–0.5	0.5	0.6	0.4
1990							–1.5	–2.3	–0.7	–0.8	0.5	0.6	0.4
1991								–3.1	–0.3	–0.5	1.0	1.0	0.8
1992									2.6	0.8	2.4	2.0	1.5
1993										–1.1	2.2	1.8	1.3
1994											5.7	3.3	2.0
1995												1.0	0.3
1996													–0.4

Government final consumption expenditure (implicit price deflator)
Consommation des administrations publiques (prix implicite)

	1985	1986	1987	1988	1989	1990	1991	1992	1993	1994	1995	1996	1997
1984	22.9	18.5	16.9	17.2	17.7	18.2	18.2	17.8	[illegible].4	16.7	16.8	15.6	15.[illegible]
1985		14.2	14.0	15.3	16.4	17.2	17.4	17.1	[illegible].7	16.0	16.2	14.9	14.[illegible]
1986			13.8	15.9	17.1	18.0	18.1	17.6	[illegible].1	16.2	16.5	15.0	14.[illegible]
1987				18.1	18.9	19.4	19.2	18.4	[illegible].7	16.6	16.8	15.1	14.[illegible]
1988					19.6	20.1	19.5	18.4	[illegible].6	16.4	16.6	14.8	14.[illegible]
1989						20.6	19.4	18.1	[illegible].1	15.7	16.1	14.1	13.[illegible]
1990							18.3	16.8	[illegible].9	14.5	15.2	13.1	12.[illegible]
1991								15.3	[illegible].8	13.3	14.5	12.0	12.[illegible]
1992									[illegible].2	12.3	14.2	11.2	11.[illegible]
1993										10.4	14.2	10.3	10.[illegible]
1994											18.2	10.2	10.[illegible]
1995												2.7	7.[illegible]
1996													12.1

Gross fixed capital formation (volume)
Formation brute de capital fixe (volume)

	1985	1986	1987	1988	1989	1990	1991	1992	1993	1994	1995	1996	1997
1984	5.2	–0.7	–2.2	0.5	1.8	2.3	2.7	1.9	1.3	0.9	1.2	1.8	2.4
1985		–6.2	–5.7	–1.0	1.0	1.7	2.2	1.5	0.8	0.4	0.8	1.5	2.2
1986			–5.1	1.7	3.5	3.8	4.0	2.8	1.9	1.3	1.6	2.3	3.0
1987				8.9	8.0	7.0	6.4	4.4	3.1	2.2	2.5	3.2	3.8
1988					7.1	6.1	5.6	3.4	2.0	1.2	1.6	2.5	3.2
1989						5.0	4.9	2.1	0.7	–0.0	0.7	1.8	2.8
1990							4.8	0.7	–0.7	–1.2	–0.1	1.3	2.4
1991								–3.2	–3.3	–3.1	–1.3	0.6	2.1
1992									–3.5	–3.1	–0.7	1.6	3.1
1993										–2.7	0.7	3.3	4.9
1994											4.2	6.5	7.5
1995												8.8	9.2
1996													9.6

Gross fixed capital formation (implicit price deflator)
Formation brute de capital fixe (prix implicite)

	1985	1986	1987	1988	1989	1990	1991	1992	1993	1994	1995	1996	1997
1984	19.1	21.2	17.8	16.5	16.4	16.6	16.4	15.9	[illegible].4	14.5	13.9	13.2	12.5
1985		23.3	17.1	15.6	15.7	16.1	16.0	15.5	[illegible].9	14.1	13.4	12.6	11.9
1986			11.2	11.9	13.3	14.4	14.5	14.2	[illegible].8	12.9	12.3	11.6	11.0
1987				12.7	14.4	15.5	15.4	14.9	[illegible].2	13.2	12.4	11.7	10.9
1988					16.1	17.0	16.3	15.4	[illegible].5	13.3	12.4	11.5	10.7
1989						17.8	16.4	15.2	[illegible].1	12.7	11.8	10.9	10.1
1990							15.1	13.9	[illegible].9	11.5	10.6	9.8	9.0
1991								12.7	[illegible].9	10.3	9.6	8.8	8.0
1992									[illegible].0	9.1	8.5	7.8	7.1
1993										7.3	7.3	6.8	6.2
1994											7.3	6.5	5.8
1995												5.7	5.1
1996													4.5

National disposable income (value)
Revenu national disponible (valeur)

	1985	1986	1987	1988	1989	1990	1991	1992	1993	1994	1995	1996	1997
1984	19.2	21.0	19.4	20.8	20.3	20.7	21.2	20.6	19.6	19.0	18.3	17.5	16.9
1985		22.9	19.6	21.4	20.6	21.0	21.6	20.8	19.6	18.9	18.2	17.4	16.7
1986			16.4	20.7	19.9	20.6	21.3	20.4	19.2	18.5	17.6	16.8	16.1
1987				25.1	21.6	22.0	22.6	21.2	19.6	18.8	17.8	16.9	16.1
1988					18.3	20.5	21.7	20.3	18.6	17.7	16.8	15.9	15.1
1989						22.8	23.5	21.0	18.6	17.6	16.6	15.5	14.8
1990							24.2	20.1	17.3	16.4	15.3	14.4	13.7
1991								16.1	14.0	13.9	13.2	12.5	12.0
1992									11.9	12.8	12.3	11.6	11.2
1993										13.7	12.5	11.5	11.0
1994											11.3	10.5	10.1
1995												9.7	9.5
1996													9.4

Compensation of employees (value)
Rémunération des salariés (valeur)

	1985	1986	1987	1988	1989	1990	1991	1992	1993	1994	1995	1996	1997
1984	25.0	18.9	16.7	18.1	19.7	20.0	19.2	18.3	1[illegible].6	17.1	17.0	16.8	16.4
1985		13.0	12.8	15.8	18.4	19.1	18.3	17.3	1[illegible].7	16.3	16.2	16.0	15.7
1986			12.5	17.3	20.3	20.6	19.4	18.1	1[illegible].2	16.7	16.6	16.4	15.9
1987				22.3	24.3	23.5	21.1	19.2	1[illegible].0	17.3	17.1	16.8	16.3
1988					26.4	24.1	20.8	18.5	1[illegible].2	16.5	16.3	16.1	15.6
1989						21.7	18.0	16.0	1[illegible].0	14.6	14.7	14.7	14.3
1990							14.4	13.2	1[illegible].9	12.9	13.4	13.6	13.3
1991								11.9	1[illegible].1	12.4	13.1	13.4	13.1
1992									1[illegible].2	12.6	13.5	13.8	13.4
1993										13.0	14.2	14.3	13.6
1994											15.4	15.0	13.9
1995												14.6	13.1
1996													11.6

HUNGARY / HONGRIE

Average per cent changes at annual rate / Variations moyennes en pourcentage aux taux annuels

G.D.P. per head (volume) / P.I.B. par tête (volume)

	1985	1986	1987	1988	1989	1990	1991	1992	1993	1994	1995	1996	1997
1984	..	..	..	..	..	..	..	..	..	..	..	..	..
1985		..	..	..	..	..	..	..	..	..	..	..	..
1986			..	..	..	..	..	..	..	..	..	..	..
1987				..	..	..	..	..	..	..	..	..	..
1988					..	..	..	..	..	..	..	..	..
1989						..	..	..	..	..	..	..	..
1990							−11.7	−7.4	−5.1	−3.1	−2.1	−1.5	−0.6
1991								−2.9	−1.6	0.0	0.5	0.7	1.4
1992									−0.3	1.5	1.6	1.6	2.3
1993										3.3	2.5	2.3	2.9
1994											1.8	1.7	2.8
1995												1.7	3.3
1996													5.0

Private final consumption expenditure per head (volume) / Consommation finale privée par tête (volume)

	1985	1986	1987	1988	1989	1990	1991	1992	1993	1994	1995	1996	1997
1984	..	..	..	..	..	..	..	..	..	..	..	..	..
1985		..	..	..	..	..	..	..	..	..	..	..	..
1986			..	..	..	..	..	..	..	..	..	..	..
1987				..	..	..	..	..	..	..	..	..	..
1988					..	..	..	..	..	..	..	..	..
1989						..	..	..	..	..	..	..	..
1990							−5.4	−1.9	−0.1	0.1	−1.3	−1.6	−1.0
1991								1.6	2.7	1.9	−0.3	−0.8	−0.2
1992									3.7	2.1	−0.9	−1.4	−0.6
1993										0.5	−3.2	−3.1	−1.7
1994											−6.8	−4.8	−2.4
1995												−2.9	−0.1
1996													2.7

Gross domestic product (volume) / Produit intérieur brut (volume)

	1985	1986	1987	1988	1989	1990	1991	1992	1993	1994	1995	1996	1997
1984	..	..	..	..	..	..	..	..	..	..	..	..	..
1985		..	..	..	..	..	..	..	..	..	..	..	..
1986			..	..	..	..	..	..	..	..	..	..	..
1987				..	..	..	..	..	..	..	..	..	..
1988					..	..	..	..	..	..	..	..	..
1989						..	..	..	..	..	..	..	..
1990							−11.9	−7.6	−5.3	−3.3	−2.4	−1.8	−0.9
1991								−3.1	−1.8	−0.3	0.2	0.4	1.1
1992									−0.6	1.2	1.3	1.3	1.9
1993										2.9	2.2	1.9	2.6
1994											1.5	1.4	2.5
1995												1.3	2.9
1996													4.6

Gross domestic product (implicit price deflator) / Produit intérieur brut (prix implicite)

	1985	1986	1987	1988	1989	1990	1991	1992	1993	1994	1995	1996	1997
1984	..	..	..	..	..	..	..	..	..	..	..	..	..
1985		..	..	..	..	..	..	..	..	..	..	..	..
1986			..	..	..	..	..	..	..	..	..	..	..
1987				..	..	..	..	..	..	..	..	..	..
1988					..	..	..	..	..	..	..	..	..
1989						..	..	..	..	..	..	..	..
1990							25.4	23.4	22.7	21.9	22.6	22.4	21.8
1991								21.5	21.4	20.8	21.9	21.8	21.2
1992									21.3	20.4	22.1	21.9	21.2
1993										19.5	22.5	22.0	21.1
1994											25.6	23.3	21.7
1995												21.2	19.8
1996													18.5

Private final consumption expenditure (volume) / Consommation finale privée (volume)

	1985	1986	1987	1988	1989	1990	1991	1992	1993	1994	1995	1996	1997
1984	..	..	..	..	..	..	..	..	..	..	..	..	..
1985		..	..	..	..	..	..	..	..	..	..	..	..
1986			..	..	..	..	..	..	..	..	..	..	..
1987				..	..	..	..	..	..	..	..	..	..
1988					..	..	..	..	..	..	..	..	..
1989						..	..	..	..	..	..	..	..
1990							−5.5	−2.1	−0.3	−0.2	−1.6	−1.9	−1.3
1991								1.4	2.4	1.7	−0.6	−1.1	−0.6
1992									3.4	1.8	−1.2	−1.7	−0.9
1993										0.2	−3.5	−3.4	−2.0
1994											−7.1	−5.2	−2.7
1995												−3.2	−0.5
1996													2.3

Private final consumption expenditure (implicit price deflator) / Consommation finale privée (prix implicite)

	1985	1986	1987	1988	1989	1990	1991	1992	1993	1994	1995	1996	1997
1984	..	..	..	..	..	..	..	..	..	..	..	..	..
1985		..	..	..	..	..	..	..	..	..	..	..	..
1986			..	..	..	..	..	..	..	..	..	..	..
1987				..	..	..	..	..	..	..	..	..	..
1988					..	..	..	..	..	..	..	..	..
1989						..	..	..	..	..	..	..	..
1990							32.5	27.2	25.0	23.6	24.4	24.2	23.3
1991								22.1	21.4	20.7	22.4	22.6	21.8
1992									20.6	20.0	22.5	22.7	21.7
1993										19.4	23.5	23.4	22.0
1994											27.7	25.5	22.9
1995												23.3	20.5
1996													17.9

Government final consumption expenditure (volume) / Consommation des administrations publiques (volume)

	1985	1986	1987	1988	1989	1990	1991	1992	1993	1994	1995	1996	1997
1984	..	..	..	..	..	..	..	..	..	..	..	..	..
1985		..	..	..	..	..	..	..	..	..	..	..	..
1986			..	..	..	..	..	..	..	..	..	..	..
1987				..	..	..	..	..	..	..	..	..	..
1988					..	..	..	..	..	..	..	..	..
1989						..	..	..	..	..	..	..	..
1990							−2.7	−1.9	1.9	−0.5	−1.6	−1.7	−1.3
1991								−1.1	4.2	0.2	−1.3	−1.5	−1.1
1992									9.8	0.8	−1.4	−1.6	−1.1
1993										−7.4	−6.6	−5.2	−3.6
1994											−5.7	−4.0	−2.3
1995												−2.3	−0.6
1996													1.2

Government final consumption expenditure (implicit price deflator) / Consommation des administrations publiques (prix implicite)

	1985	1986	1987	1988	1989	1990	1991	1992	1993	1994	1995	1996	1997
1984	..	..	..	..	..	..	..	..	..	..	..	..	..
1985		..	..	..	..	..	..	..	..	..	..	..	..
1986			..	..	..	..	..	..	..	..	..	..	..
1987				..	..	..	..	..	..	..	..	..	..
1988					..	..	..	..	..	..	..	..	..
1989						..	..	..	..	..	..	..	..
1990							34.0	28.4	24.9	24.2	24.1	23.0	22.5
1991								23.0	20.6	21.1	21.8	20.9	20.6
1992									18.2	20.1	21.3	20.4	20.2
1993										22.0	22.9	21.1	20.7
1994											23.8	20.6	20.2
1995												17.5	18.4
1996													19.4

Gross fixed capital formation (volume) / Formation brute de capital fixe (volume)

	1985	1986	1987	1988	1989	1990	1991	1992	1993	1994	1995	1996	1997
1984	..	..	..	..	..	..	..	..	..	..	..	..	..
1985		..	..	..	..	..	..	..	..	..	..	..	..
1986			..	..	..	..	..	..	..	..	..	..	..
1987				..	..	..	..	..	..	..	..	..	..
1988					..	..	..	..	..	..	..	..	..
1989						..	..	..	..	..	..	..	..
1990							−10.4	−6.6	−3.8	0.0	−0.9	0.4	1.5
1991								−2.6	−0.3	3.8	1.7	2.7	3.7
1992									2.0	7.1	3.2	4.0	5.0
1993										12.5	3.7	4.7	5.7
1994											−4.3	1.0	3.6
1995												6.7	7.8
1996													8.8

Gross fixed capital formation (implicit price deflator) / Formation brute de capital fixe (prix implicite)

	1985	1986	1987	1988	1989	1990	1991	1992	1993	1994	1995	1996	1997
1984	..	..	..	..	..	..	..	..	..	..	..	..	..
1985		..	..	..	..	..	..	..	..	..	..	..	..
1986			..	..	..	..	..	..	..	..	..	..	..
1987				..	..	..	..	..	..	..	..	..	..
1988					..	..	..	..	..	..	..	..	..
1989						..	..	..	..	..	..	..	..
1990							22.9	18.8	16.6	16.6	18.4	19.2	18.9
1991								14.8	13.6	14.6	17.3	18.4	18.2
1992									12.3	14.4	18.2	19.3	18.9
1993										16.6	21.2	21.8	20.7
1994											26.1	24.4	22.0
1995												22.8	20.1
1996													17.4

National disposable income (value) / Revenu national disponible (valeur)

	1985	1986	1987	1988	1989	1990	1991	1992	1993	1994	1995	1996	1997
1984	..	..	..	..	..	..	..	..	..	..	..	..	..
1985		..	..	..	..	..	..	..	..	..	..	..	..
1986			..	..	..	..	..	..	..	..	..	..	..
1987				..	..	..	..	..	..	..	..	..	..
1988					..	..	..	..	..	..	..	..	..
1989						..	..	..	..	..	..	..	..
1990							..	..	..	..	..	..	..
1991								..	..	..	..	..	..
1992									..	..	..	..	..
1993										..	..	..	..
1994											..	..	..
1995												..	..
1996													..

Compensation of employees (value) / Rémunération des salariés (valeur)

	1985	1986	1987	1988	1989	1990	1991	1992	1993	1994	1995	1996	1997
1984	..	..	..	..	..	..	..	..	..	..	..	..	..
1985		..	..	..	..	..	..	..	..	..	..	..	..
1986			..	..	..	..	..	..	..	..	..	..	..
1987				..	..	..	..	..	..	..	..	..	..
1988					..	..	..	..	..	..	..	..	..
1989						..	..	..	..	..	..	..	..
1990							..	..	..	..	..	..	..
1991								..	..	..	..	..	..
1992									..	..	..	..	..
1993										..	..	..	..
1994											..	..	..
1995												..	..
1996													..

ICELAND

ISLANDE

Average per cent changes at annual rate

Variations moyennes en pourcentage aux taux annuels

G.D.P. per head (volume) / P.I.B. par tête (volume)

	1985	1986	1987	1988	1989	1990	1991	1992	1993	1994	1995	1996	1997
1984	2.4	3.9	5.0	3.3	2.4	2.1	1.8	1.0	0.8	1.0	1.0	1.3	1.5
1985		5.4	6.3	3.6	2.4	2.0	1.7	0.8	0.6	0.9	0.9	1.2	1.4
1986			7.2	2.7	1.5	1.2	0.9	0.0	–0.0	0.3	0.4	0.8	1.1
1987				–1.7	–1.3	–0.8	–0.6	–1.4	–1.2	–0.6	–0.4	0.1	0.5
1988					–0.9	–0.3	–0.2	–1.3	–1.1	–0.4	–0.3	0.4	0.7
1989						0.4	0.2	–1.4	–1.1	–0.3	–0.2	0.5	0.9
1990							–0.1	–2.3	–1.6	–0.5	–0.3	0.6	1.0
1991								–4.5	–2.3	–0.6	–0.3	0.7	1.2
1992									–0.2	1.3	1.1	2.0	2.3
1993										2.9	1.8	2.8	3.0
1994											0.6	2.7	3.0
1995												4.8	4.2
1996													3.6

Private final consumption expenditure per head (volume) / Consommation finale privée par tête (volume)

	1985	1986	1987	1988	1989	1990	1991	1992	1993	1994	1995	1996	1997
1984	3.4	4.7	7.9	4.5	2.4	2.0	2.1	1.1	0.3	0.4	0.7	1.1	1.4
1985		6.0	10.3	4.8	2.2	1.7	1.9	0.8	–0.0	0.1	0.5	0.9	1.3
1986			14.8	4.2	0.9	0.6	1.1	–0.1	–0.9	–0.6	–0.1	0.4	0.8
1987				–5.3	–5.3	–3.7	–2.1	–2.8	–3.2	–2.6	–1.9	–1.1	–0.4
1988					–5.3	–2.8	–1.0	–2.1	–2.8	–2.2	–1.3	–0.5	0.1
1989						–0.3	1.3	–1.0	–2.2	–1.5	–0.7	0.2	0.8
1990							2.9	–1.4	–2.8	–1.9	–0.7	0.3	1.0
1991								–5.6	–5.6	–3.4	–1.6	–0.2	0.7
1992									–5.6	–2.3	–0.3	1.1	1.9
1993										1.1	2.5	3.5	3.9
1994											3.8	4.7	4.9
1995												5.6	5.4
1996													5.2

Gross domestic product (volume) / Produit intérieur brut (volume)

	1985	1986	1987	1988	1989	1990	1991	1992	1993	1994	1995	1996	1997
1984	3.3	4.8	6.0	4.5	3.6	3.2	2.9	2.1	2.0	2.1	2.0	2.3	2.5
1985		6.3	7.4	4.8	3.7	3.2	2.8	1.9	1.8	2.0	1.9	2.2	2.4
1986			8.5	4.1	2.8	2.4	2.1	1.2	1.2	1.5	1.4	1.8	2.1
1987				–0.1	0.1	0.4	0.6	–0.2	0.0	0.5	0.6	1.1	1.4
1988					0.3	0.7	0.8	–0.2	0.0	0.6	0.7	1.3	1.6
1989						1.2	1.1	–0.4	–0.0	0.7	0.7	1.4	1.8
1990							1.1	–1.1	–0.4	0.6	0.7	1.5	1.9
1991								–3.3	–1.2	0.4	0.5	1.5	2.0
1992									1.0	2.3	1.9	2.8	3.1
1993										3.7	2.3	3.4	3.7
1994											1.0	3.3	3.7
1995												5.6	5.0
1996													4.4

Gross domestic product (implicit price deflator) / Produit intérieur brut (prix implicite)

	1985	1986	1987	1988	1989	1990	1991	1992	1993	1994	1995	1996	1997
1984	31.3	28.4	25.3	24.7	23.7	22.5	20.3	18.1	16.2	14.7	13.6	12.6	11.8
1985		25.5	22.5	22.6	21.9	20.9	18.6	16.3	14.5	13.0	11.9	11.0	10.3
1986			19.5	21.2	20.7	19.7	17.2	14.8	13.0	11.6	10.5	9.6	9.1
1987				22.8	21.3	19.8	16.7	13.9	11.9	10.5	9.5	8.6	8.1
1988					19.8	18.3	14.7	11.8	9.9	8.5	7.7	6.9	6.5
1989						16.9	12.2	9.3	7.5	6.4	5.8	5.2	5.0
1990							7.8	5.7	4.6	3.9	3.7	3.4	3.4
1991								3.6	3.0	2.7	2.7	2.5	2.7
1992									2.5	2.2	2.4	2.3	2.5
1993										2.0	2.4	2.2	2.5
1994											2.7	2.3	2.7
1995												1.9	2.6
1996													3.4

Private final consumption expenditure (volume) / Consommation finale privée (volume)

	1985	1986	1987	1988	1989	1990	1991	1992	1993	1994	1995	1996	1997
1984	4.2	5.6	9.0	5.6	3.6	3.1	3.2	2.2	1.5	1.5	1.7	2.1	2.4
1985		6.9	11.4	6.1	3.4	2.8	3.1	1.9	1.1	1.2	1.5	1.9	2.3
1986			16.2	5.7	2.3	1.9	2.3	1.1	0.3	0.5	0.9	1.4	1.9
1987				–3.8	–4.0	–2.5	–0.9	–1.6	–2.1	–1.5	–0.8	–0.1	0.5
1988					–4.2	–1.9	0.1	–1.1	–1.8	–1.2	–0.4	0.4	1.0
1989						0.5	2.3	–0.0	–1.1	–0.6	0.2	1.1	1.7
1990							4.1	–0.3	–1.7	–0.8	0.2	1.2	1.9
1991								–4.5	–4.5	–2.4	–0.8	0.6	1.5
1992									–4.5	–1.4	0.5	1.9	2.7
1993										1.9	3.0	4.1	4.6
1994											4.2	5.3	5.5
1995												6.4	6.2
1996													6.0

Private final consumption expenditure (implicit price deflator) / Consommation finale privée (prix implicite)

	1985	1986	1987	1988	1989	1990	1991	1992	1993	1994	1995	1996	1997
1984	32.6	26.2	22.7	23.4	23.3	22.2	19.9	17.9	16.3	14.8	13.5	12.5	11.7
1985		20.1	18.0	20.4	21.1	20.2	17.9	15.9	14.4	12.9	11.8	10.9	10.1
1986			15.9	20.5	21.4	20.2	17.4	15.2	13.6	12.1	10.9	10.0	9.2
1987				25.4	24.3	21.7	17.8	15.1	13.3	11.5	10.3	9.4	8.6
1988					23.3	20.0	15.4	12.6	11.0	9.4	8.3	7.5	6.9
1989						16.7	11.7	9.3	8.1	6.8	5.9	5.4	5.0
1990							6.9	5.8	5.4	4.4	3.9	3.6	3.4
1991								4.7	4.6	3.6	3.2	3.0	2.8
1992									4.6	3.1	2.7	2.6	2.4
1993										1.6	1.7	1.9	1.9
1994											1.8	2.1	2.0
1995												2.3	2.1
1996													1.8

Government final consumption expenditure (volume) / Consommation des administrations publiques (volume)

	1985	1986	1987	1988	1989	1990	1991	1992	1993	1994	1995	1996	1997
1984	6.5	6.9	6.8	6.2	5.6	5.4	5.1	4.3	4.1	4.0	3.8	3.5	3.5
1985		7.3	6.9	6.1	5.4	5.2	4.8	4.0	3.8	3.8	3.5	3.3	3.2
1986			6.5	5.6	4.7	4.6	4.3	3.5	3.3	3.3	3.1	2.9	2.9
1987				4.7	3.8	4.0	3.8	2.8	2.8	2.9	2.7	2.5	2.5
1988					3.0	3.7	3.5	2.4	2.4	2.6	2.4	2.2	2.3
1989						4.4	3.7	2.2	2.2	2.5	2.3	2.1	2.2
1990							3.2	1.1	1.5	2.1	1.9	1.8	1.9
1991								–0.8	0.7	1.7	1.6	1.5	1.7
1992									2.3	3.0	2.4	2.1	2.2
1993										3.7	2.5	2.0	2.1
1994											1.3	1.1	1.6
1995												1.0	1.8
1996													2.6

Government final consumption expenditure (implicit price deflator) / Consommation des administrations publiques (prix implicite)

	1985	1986	1987	1988	1989	1990	1991	1992	1993	1994	1995	1996	1997
1984	35.0	30.9	29.6	28.2	25.6	23.1	20.9	18.6	16.7	15.1	14.1	13.3	12.6
1985		27.0	27.1	26.0	23.4	20.8	18.6	16.4	14.6	13.1	12.2	11.6	10.9
1986			27.1	25.5	22.2	19.4	17.0	14.7	13.0	11.5	10.6	10.1	9.6
1987				23.9	19.8	16.9	14.6	12.4	10.8	9.4	8.7	8.4	7.9
1988					15.9	13.5	11.7	9.7	8.3	7.2	6.7	6.6	6.3
1989						11.2	9.7	7.7	6.5	5.5	5.3	5.3	5.2
1990							8.3	6.0	5.0	4.2	4.1	4.4	4.3
1991								3.7	3.4	2.8	3.1	3.6	3.7
1992									3.2	2.4	2.9	3.6	3.7
1993										1.7	2.8	3.7	3.8
1994											3.9	4.7	4.6
1995												5.6	4.9
1996													4.2

Gross fixed capital formation (volume) / Formation brute de capital fixe (volume)

	1985	1986	1987	1988	1989	1990	1991	1992	1993	1994	1995	1996	1997
1984	1.0	–0.3	5.7	4.2	1.7	1.9	1.9	0.2	–1.2	–1.2	–1.3	0.7	1.5
1985		–1.6	8.1	5.3	1.8	2.1	2.1	0.0	–1.5	–1.4	–1.6	0.7	1.5
1986			18.8	8.9	3.0	3.0	2.8	0.3	–1.5	–1.4	–1.6	0.9	1.8
1987				–0.2	–4.1	–1.8	–0.8	–3.0	–4.5	–4.0	–3.9	–0.9	0.3
1988					–7.9	–2.6	–1.1	–3.7	–5.3	–4.6	–4.4	–1.0	0.3
1989						3.0	2.5	–2.3	–4.7	–3.9	–3.8	0.1	1.4
1990							2.0	–4.8	–7.1	–5.6	–5.1	–0.4	1.2
1991								–11.3	–11.3	–8.0	–6.8	–0.9	1.0
1992									–11.4	–6.4	–5.2	1.9	3.7
1993										–1.1	–1.9	6.7	7.8
1994											–2.8	10.9	11.0
1995												26.5	18.6
1996													11.2

Gross fixed capital formation (implicit price deflator) / Formation brute de capital fixe (prix implicite)

	1985	1986	1987	1988	1989	1990	1991	1992	1993	1994	1995	1996	1997
1984	30.7	26.8	23.1	22.0	22.8	21.6	19.4	17.2	15.6	14.4	13.3	12.5	11.7
1985		23.0	19.5	19.2	20.9	19.9	17.6	15.4	13.9	12.7	11.7	11.0	10.2
1986			16.2	17.4	20.3	19.2	16.5	14.1	12.6	11.5	10.5	9.8	9.1
1987				18.7	22.4	20.2	16.6	13.7	12.1	10.8	9.8	9.2	8.5
1988					26.2	20.9	15.9	12.5	10.8	9.6	8.6	8.0	7.4
1989						15.9	11.1	8.3	7.3	6.5	5.9	5.7	5.2
1990							6.5	4.7	4.5	4.3	4.1	4.0	3.8
1991								3.0	3.5	3.6	3.5	3.6	3.3
1992									4.1	3.9	3.6	3.7	3.4
1993										3.7	3.4	3.6	3.3
1994											3.0	3.5	3.1
1995												4.0	3.1
1996													2.3

National disposable income (value) / Revenu national disponible (valeur)

	1985	1986	1987	1988	1989	1990	1991	1992	1993	1994	1995	1996	1997
1984	36.5	36.0	34.9	31.6	28.6	26.9	24.3	20.9	18.8	17.3	16.1	15.5	14.9
1985		35.5	34.1	30.0	26.7	25.1	22.4	18.9	16.7	15.4	14.2	13.7	13.3
1986			32.7	27.4	23.9	22.6	19.9	16.3	14.3	13.1	12.1	11.8	11.5
1987				22.2	19.7	19.4	16.9	13.3	11.5	10.5	9.8	9.7	9.5
1988					17.3	17.9	15.2	11.1	9.4	8.7	8.1	8.2	8.2
1989						18.6	14.1	9.2	7.6	7.0	6.6	6.9	7.1
1990							9.8	4.7	4.1	4.3	4.4	5.1	5.6
1991								–0.1	1.4	2.6	3.0	4.2	4.9
1992									2.9	3.9	4.1	5.3	5.9
1993										5.0	4.8	6.1	6.7
1994											4.5	6.7	7.3
1995												8.8	8.7
1996													8.5

Compensation of employees (value) / Rémunération des salariés (valeur)

	1985	1986	1987	1988	1989	1990	1991	1992	1993	1994	1995	1996	1997
1984	46.6	39.3	42.0	37.3	32.0	28.8	26.8	23.2	20.4	18.6	17.4	16.9	16.1
1985		32.4	39.8	34.3	28.5	25.5	23.7	20.2	17.4	15.8	14.9	14.5	13.9
1986			47.7	35.3	27.3	23.8	22.1	18.3	15.5	13.9	13.1	12.8	12.3
1987				23.9	18.1	16.8	16.4	13.1	10.8	9.8	9.3	9.5	9.3
1988					12.7	13.4	14.0	10.6	8.4	7.6	7.4	7.8	7.8
1989						14.1	14.6	9.9	6.3	6.6	6.6	7.1	7.2
1990							15.2	7.9	5.1	4.8	5.1	6.0	6.2
1991								1.1	0.5	1.5	2.7	4.3	4.8
1992									–0.2	1.8	3.3	5.1	5.5
1993										3.7	5.1	6.9	7.0
1994											6.4	8.6	8.1
1995												10.7	8.9
1996													7.2

IRELAND

Average per cent changes at annual rate

G.D.P. per head (volume)
P.I.B. par tête (volume)

	1985	1986	1987	1988	1989	1990	1991	1992	1993	1994	1995	1996	1997
1984	2.7	1.1	2.3	3.1	3.8	4.5	4.2	4.2	4.1	4.4	5.0	5.2	5.6
1985		–0.5	2.1	3.2	4.0	4.9	4.4	4.4	4.2	4.6	5.2	5.5	5.8
1986			4.6	5.1	5.5	6.3	5.4	5.2	4.9	5.2	5.9	6.1	6.4
1987				5.6	6.0	6.9	5.6	5.3	5.0	5.3	6.1	6.2	6.6
1988					6.4	7.5	5.6	5.2	4.8	5.3	6.1	6.3	6.7
1989						8.6	5.2	4.8	4.5	5.1	6.1	6.3	6.7
1990							2.0	3.0	3.1	4.2	5.6	5.9	6.4
1991								4.1	3.7	4.9	6.5	6.7	7.2
1992									3.3	5.4	7.3	7.4	7.8
1993										7.5	9.4	8.8	9.0
1994											11.3	9.4	9.5
1995												7.6	8.6
1996													9.6

Gross domestic product (volume)
Produit intérieur brut (volume)

	1985	1986	1987	1988	1989	1990	1991	1992	1993	1994	1995	1996	1997
1984	3.1	1.3	2.4	3.1	3.6	4.4	4.2	4.2	4.2	4.6	5.2	5.4	5.8
1985		–0.4	2.1	3.1	3.8	4.7	4.3	4.4	4.3	4.7	5.4	5.7	6.1
1986			4.7	4.9	5.2	6.0	5.3	5.2	5.0	5.4	6.1	6.3	6.7
1987				5.2	5.5	6.5	5.5	5.3	5.1	5.5	6.3	6.5	6.9
1988					5.8	7.1	5.6	5.4	5.0	5.5	6.4	6.6	7.1
1989						8.5	5.5	5.2	4.8	5.5	6.5	6.8	7.2
1990							2.5	3.6	3.7	4.8	6.1	6.5	7.1
1991								4.8	4.2	5.5	7.0	7.3	7.8
1992									3.7	5.9	7.8	7.9	8.5
1993										8.1	9.9	9.4	9.7
1994											11.8	10.0	10.2
1995												8.3	9.4
1996													10.6

Private final consumption expenditure (volume)
Consommation finale privée (volume)

	1985	1986	1987	1988	1989	1990	1991	1992	1993	1994	1995	1996	1997
1984	4.6	3.3	3.3	3.6	4.2	3.7	3.5	3.6	3.5	3.8	3.8	4.0	4.2
1985		2.0	2.7	3.3	4.1	3.5	3.3	3.5	3.3	3.7	3.7	3.9	4.1
1986			3.3	3.9	4.8	3.9	3.6	3.7	3.5	3.9	3.9	4.1	4.3
1987				4.5	5.5	4.1	3.6	3.8	3.6	4.0	4.0	4.2	4.4
1988					6.5	3.9	3.3	3.7	3.4	3.9	3.9	4.2	4.4
1989						1.4	1.8	2.7	2.6	3.3	3.5	3.8	4.1
1990							2.1	3.4	3.0	3.8	3.9	4.2	4.5
1991								4.6	3.5	4.4	4.3	4.7	4.9
1992									2.4	4.3	4.2	4.7	5.0
1993										6.3	5.2	5.5	5.7
1994											4.1	5.1	5.5
1995												6.1	6.2
1996													6.3

Government final consumption expenditure (volume)
Consommation des administrations publiques (volume)

	1985	1986	1987	1988	1989	1990	1991	1992	1993	1994	1995	1996	1997
1984	1.8	2.2	–0.2	–1.4	–1.4	–0.3	0.2	0.5	0.4	0.9	1.0	1.1	1.4
1985		2.6	–1.2	–2.5	–2.2	–0.7	–0.1	0.3	0.3	0.8	1.0	1.0	1.3
1986			–4.8	–4.9	–3.7	–1.5	–0.6	–0.1	–0.1	0.6	0.8	0.9	1.2
1987				–5.0	–3.1	–0.4	0.4	0.8	0.8	1.4	1.5	1.5	1.8
1988					–1.3	2.0	2.3	2.4	2.0	2.5	2.5	2.4	2.6
1989						5.4	4.2	3.6	2.8	3.2	3.1	2.9	3.1
1990							2.9	2.7	1.9	2.7	2.7	2.5	2.8
1991								2.4	1.4	2.6	2.6	2.4	2.8
1992									0.4	2.7	2.7	2.4	2.8
1993										5.0	3.8	3.0	3.5
1994											2.6	2.0	2.9
1995												1.5	3.1
1996													4.8

Gross fixed capital formation (volume)
Formation brute de capital fixe (volume)

	1985	1986	1987	1988	1989	1990	1991	1992	1993	1994	1995	1996	1997
1984	–7.7	–5.3	–3.9	–1.7	0.6	2.6	1.1	1.0	0.2	1.4	2.3	3.2	3.7
1985		–2.8	–2.0	0.4	2.7	4.8	2.7	2.3	1.3	2.4	3.3	4.2	4.8
1986			–1.1	2.0	4.6	6.8	3.8	3.1	1.9	3.1	4.0	4.9	5.5
1987				5.2	7.7	9.5	5.1	4.0	2.4	3.7	4.7	5.6	6.2
1988					10.1	11.8	5.0	3.7	1.8	3.5	4.6	5.7	6.3
1989						13.4	2.6	1.7	–0.2	2.2	3.7	5.1	5.8
1990							–7.2	–3.7	–4.3	–0.4	1.9	3.8	4.7
1991								–0.1	–2.8	1.9	4.3	6.1	6.9
1992									–5.4	3.0	5.8	7.7	8.3
1993										12.1	11.9	12.5	12.1
1994											11.7	12.7	12.1
1995												13.6	12.3
1996													10.9

National disposable income (value)
Revenu national disponible (valeur)

	1985	1986	1987	1988	1989	1990	1991	1992	1993	1994	1995	1996	1997
1984	8.3	7.4	7.1	7.2	7.8	8.2	7.9	7.5	7.4	7.4	7.6	7.8	7.9
1985		6.6	6.5	6.9	7.7	8.2	7.8	7.4	7.3	7.3	7.6	7.7	7.8
1986			6.4	7.0	8.1	8.6	8.1	7.5	7.4	7.3	7.7	7.8	7.9
1987				7.7	8.9	9.3	8.5	7.7	7.5	7.5	7.9	8.0	8.1
1988					10.2	10.1	8.8	7.8	7.5	7.4	7.9	8.1	8.2
1989						10.1	8.1	7.0	6.8	6.9	7.5	7.8	7.9
1990							6.1	5.4	5.8	6.1	7.0	7.4	7.6
1991								4.7	5.6	6.1	7.2	7.6	7.8
1992									6.5	6.8	8.1	8.3	8.5
1993										7.2	8.9	9.0	9.0
1994											10.6	9.9	9.6
1995												9.2	9.1
1996													9.0

IRLANDE

Variations moyennes en pourcentage aux taux annuels

Private final consumption expenditure per head (volume)
Consommation finale privée par tête (volume)

	1985	1986	1987	1988	1989	1990	1991	1992	1993	1994	1995	1996	1997
1984	4.2	3.1	3.2	3.6	4.3	3.8	3.5	3.6	3.4	3.6	3.6	3.8	3.9
1985		2.0	2.6	3.4	4.3	3.7	3.4	3.5	3.3	3.5	3.5	3.7	3.8
1986			3.3	4.1	5.1	4.2	3.7	3.7	3.5	3.7	3.7	3.9	4.0
1987				4.8	6.0	4.5	3.7	3.8	3.5	3.8	3.8	3.9	4.1
1988					7.2	4.3	3.4	3.5	3.2	3.6	3.6	3.8	4.0
1989						1.5	1.5	2.3	2.2	2.9	3.0	3.4	3.6
1990							1.5	2.7	2.5	3.3	3.3	3.7	3.9
1991								4.0	3.0	3.9	3.8	4.1	4.3
1992									2.0	3.8	3.7	4.2	4.4
1993										5.7	4.6	4.9	5.0
1994											3.6	4.5	4.8
1995												5.4	5.3
1996													5.3

Gross domestic product (implicit price deflator)
Produit intérieur brut (prix implicite)

	1985	1986	1987	1988	1989	1990	1991	1992	1993	1994	1995	1996	1997
1984	5.2	5.9	4.6	4.3	4.5	3.6	3.4	3.2	3.4	3.1	2.9	2.8	2.7
1985		6.6	4.4	4.0	4.4	3.3	3.1	3.0	3.1	2.9	2.7	2.6	2.5
1986			2.2	2.7	3.6	2.5	2.4	2.4	2.7	2.5	2.2	2.2	2.2
1987				3.2	4.4	2.6	2.4	2.4	2.7	2.5	2.3	2.2	2.2
1988					5.5	2.3	2.1	2.2	2.6	2.4	2.1	2.0	2.1
1989						–0.7	0.5	1.1	1.9	1.8	1.6	1.6	1.6
1990							1.7	2.0	2.8	2.4	2.0	1.9	2.0
1991								2.4	3.4	2.6	2.1	2.0	2.0
1992									4.5	2.8	2.0	1.9	2.0
1993										1.2	0.8	1.1	1.3
1994											0.5	1.0	1.4
1995												1.6	1.9
1996													2.2

Private final consumption expenditure (implicit price deflator)
Consommation finale privée (prix implicite)

	1985	1986	1987	1988	1989	1990	1991	1992	1993	1994	1995	1996	1997
1984	5.0	4.8	4.0	3.9	4.0	3.7	3.6	3.4	3.3	3.2	3.1	3.0	2.8
1985		4.6	3.5	3.6	3.7	3.4	3.3	3.2	3.0	3.0	2.9	2.8	2.6
1986			2.4	3.1	3.4	3.1	3.1	3.0	2.8	2.8	2.7	2.6	2.4
1987				3.8	4.0	3.3	3.2	3.1	2.9	2.9	2.8	2.6	2.5
1988					4.1	3.1	3.0	2.9	2.7	2.7	2.6	2.5	2.3
1989						2.1	2.5	2.5	2.4	2.4	2.4	2.2	2.1
1990							3.0	2.8	2.5	2.5	2.5	2.3	2.1
1991								2.6	2.2	2.4	2.3	2.1	1.9
1992									1.9	2.3	2.3	2.0	1.8
1993										2.8	2.5	2.1	1.8
1994											2.1	1.8	1.5
1995												1.4	1.1
1996													0.9

Government final consumption expenditure (implicit price deflator)
Consommation des administrations publiques (prix implicite)

	1985	1986	1987	1988	1989	1990	1991	1992	1993	1994	1995	1996	1997
1984	5.7	5.1	5.4	5.1	5.1	5.1	5.4	5.4	5.6	5.2	5.0	4.8	4.7
1985		4.6	5.3	4.9	5.0	5.0	5.3	5.4	5.6	5.2	4.9	4.7	4.7
1986			6.1	5.1	5.1	5.1	5.5	5.5	5.7	5.2	4.9	4.7	4.7
1987				4.2	4.6	4.8	5.3	5.4	5.7	5.1	4.8	4.6	4.5
1988					5.0	5.1	5.7	5.7	6.0	5.3	4.9	4.6	4.6
1989						5.1	6.1	5.9	6.2	5.3	4.9	4.6	4.5
1990							7.0	6.3	6.6	5.4	4.8	4.5	4.4
1991								5.5	6.4	4.8	4.3	4.0	4.0
1992									7.2	4.5	3.9	3.6	3.7
1993										1.8	2.2	2.4	2.8
1994											2.7	2.8	3.2
1995												2.8	3.4
1996													3.9

Gross fixed capital formation (implicit price deflator)
Formation brute de capital fixe (prix implicite)

	1985	1986	1987	1988	1989	1990	1991	1992	1993	1994	1995	1996	1997
1984	4.4	3.7	3.2	3.7	4.1	3.8	3.6	3.7	3.8	3.7	3.7	3.7	4.0
1985		3.1	2.7	3.5	4.0	3.7	3.5	3.6	3.8	3.6	3.6	3.7	3.9
1986			2.3	3.7	4.4	3.8	3.6	3.7	3.9	3.7	3.7	3.7	4.0
1987				5.1	5.4	4.4	3.9	4.0	4.1	3.9	3.9	3.9	4.2
1988					5.8	4.0	3.5	3.8	4.0	3.7	3.7	3.7	4.1
1989						2.3	2.4	3.1	3.5	3.3	3.4	3.4	3.9
1990							2.5	3.5	3.9	3.6	3.6	3.6	4.1
1991								4.5	4.7	3.9	3.9	3.9	4.4
1992									4.8	3.6	3.6	3.7	4.4
1993										2.5	3.1	3.3	4.2
1994											3.7	3.8	4.8
1995												3.8	5.4
1996													7.0

Compensation of employees (value)
Rémunération des salariés (valeur)

	1985	1986	1987	1988	1989	1990	1991	1992	1993	1994	1995	1996	1997
1984	7.2	7.0	6.4	5.9	6.0	6.4	6.4	6.5	6.7	6.7	6.8	6.9	7.2
1985		6.8	6.0	5.4	5.8	6.2	6.3	6.4	6.6	6.6	6.7	6.9	7.2
1986			5.2	4.7	5.4	6.1	6.2	6.4	6.6	6.6	6.7	6.9	7.2
1987				4.3	5.5	6.4	6.4	6.6	6.9	6.8	6.9	7.1	7.4
1988					6.7	7.4	7.1	7.2	7.4	7.2	7.3	7.4	7.7
1989						8.1	7.3	7.3	7.5	7.3	7.4	7.5	7.9
1990							6.5	7.0	7.3	7.1	7.2	7.5	7.8
1991								7.4	7.7	7.3	7.4	7.6	8.1
1992									8.1	7.2	7.4	7.7	8.2
1993										6.3	7.1	7.6	8.2
1994											7.8	8.2	8.8
1995												8.6	9.4
1996													10.2

ITALY

ITALIE

Average per cent changes at annual rate

Variations moyennes en pourcentage aux taux annuels

G.D.P. per head (volume) / P.I.B. par tête (volume)

	1985	1986	1987	1988	1989	1990	1991	1992	1993	1994	1995	1996	1997
1984	2.8	2.8	2.9	3.1	3.1	2.9	2.7	2.4	1.9	1.9	2.0	1.9	1.8
1985		2.8	3.0	3.3	3.2	2.9	2.6	2.3	1.8	1.8	1.9	1.8	1.8
1986			3.1	3.5	3.3	3.0	2.6	2.2	1.7	1.7	1.8	1.7	1.7
1987				3.8	3.3	2.9	2.5	2.1	1.5	1.5	1.7	1.5	1.5
1988					2.9	2.5	2.0	1.6	1.0	1.1	1.4	1.3	1.3
1989						2.1	1.6	1.2	0.5	0.8	1.1	1.0	1.1
1990							1.1	0.7	–0.0	0.5	0.9	0.9	0.9
1991								0.4	–0.6	0.3	0.9	0.8	0.9
1992									–1.5	0.2	1.0	0.9	1.0
1993										1.9	2.3	1.7	1.6
1994											2.8	1.6	1.5
1995												0.5	0.9
1996													1.3

Private final consumption expenditure per head (volume) / Consommation finale privée par tête (volume)

	1985	1986	1987	1988	1989	1990	1991	1992	1993	1994	1995	1996	1997
1984	3.1	3.6	3.9	4.0	3.9	3.7	3.5	3.2	2.4	2.2	2.2	2.1	2.1
1985		4.2	4.3	4.3	4.2	3.8	3.6	3.3	2.4	2.2	2.1	2.0	2.0
1986			4.3	4.4	4.1	3.7	3.5	3.1	2.1	1.9	1.8	1.8	1.8
1987				4.5	4.1	3.5	3.3	2.9	1.7	1.6	1.5	1.5	1.5
1988					3.6	3.0	2.9	2.4	1.2	1.1	1.1	1.1	1.2
1989						2.4	2.5	2.1	0.6	0.6	0.7	0.7	0.9
1990							2.6	1.9	–0.0	0.1	0.4	0.5	0.7
1991								1.2	–1.3	–0.7	–0.2	0.1	0.4
1992									–3.7	–1.6	–0.6	–0.2	0.2
1993										0.6	0.9	1.0	1.2
1994											1.3	1.1	1.5
1995												1.0	1.6
1996													2.1

Gross domestic product (volume) / Produit intérieur brut (volume)

	1985	1986	1987	1988	1989	1990	1991	1992	1993	1994	1995	1996	1997
1984	2.8	2.8	2.9	3.2	3.1	2.9	2.7	2.4	2.0	2.0	2.1	2.0	2.0
1985		2.8	3.0	3.3	3.2	3.0	2.7	2.4	1.9	1.9	2.0	1.9	1.9
1986			3.1	3.5	3.3	3.0	2.6	2.3	1.8	1.8	2.0	1.8	1.8
1987				3.9	3.4	3.0	2.5	2.1	1.6	1.7	1.8	1.7	1.7
1988					2.9	2.5	2.1	1.7	1.1	1.3	1.5	1.4	1.4
1989						2.2	1.6	1.3	0.7	1.0	1.3	1.2	1.2
1990							1.1	0.9	0.2	0.7	1.1	1.0	1.1
1991								0.6	–0.3	0.5	1.1	1.0	1.1
1992									–1.2	0.5	1.3	1.1	1.2
1993										2.2	2.6	1.9	1.8
1994											2.9	1.8	1.7
1995												0.7	1.1
1996													1.5

Gross domestic product (implicit price deflator) / Produit intérieur brut (prix implicite)

	1985	1986	1987	1988	1989	1990	1991	1992	1993	1994	1995	1996	1997
1984	9.0	8.4	7.6	7.4	7.2	7.3	7.3	7.0	[illegible]	6.4	6.3	6.1	5.9
1985		7.8	7.0	6.9	6.8	6.9	7.1	6.7	[illegible]	6.1	6.0	5.9	5.6
1986			6.1	6.5	6.4	6.7	6.9	6.5	[illegible]	5.9	5.8	5.7	5.4
1987				6.8	6.5	6.9	7.1	6.6	[illegible]	5.8	5.7	5.6	5.3
1988					6.3	7.0	7.2	6.6	[illegible]	5.7	5.6	5.5	5.2
1989						7.6	7.7	6.7	[illegible]	5.6	5.5	5.4	5.0
1990							7.7	6.2	[illegible]	5.0	5.0	5.0	4.7
1991								4.7	[illegible]	4.2	4.4	4.5	4.2
1992									[illegible]	3.9	4.3	4.5	4.1
1993										3.5	4.3	4.5	4.0
1994											5.1	5.0	4.2
1995												5.0	3.8
1996													2.6

Private final consumption expenditure (volume) / Consommation finale privée (volume)

	1985	1986	1987	1988	1989	1990	1991	1992	1993	1994	1995	1996	1997
1984	3.1	3.6	3.9	4.0	4.0	3.7	3.6	3.3	2.5	2.3	2.3	2.2	2.2
1985		4.2	4.3	4.4	4.2	3.8	3.6	3.3	2.4	2.3	2.2	2.1	2.1
1986			4.3	4.4	4.2	3.7	3.6	3.2	2.2	2.0	2.0	1.9	1.9
1987				4.6	4.1	3.5	3.3	2.9	1.8	1.7	1.7	1.6	1.7
1988					3.6	3.0	2.9	2.5	1.3	1.2	1.3	1.3	1.4
1989						2.5	2.6	2.2	0.7	0.8	0.9	0.9	1.1
1990							2.7	2.0	0.2	0.3	0.6	0.7	0.9
1991								1.3	–1.0	–0.4	0.0	0.3	0.6
1992									–3.4	–1.3	–0.4	0.0	0.5
1993										0.9	1.2	1.2	1.5
1994											1.4	1.3	1.7
1995												1.2	1.8
1996													2.4

Private final consumption expenditure (implicit price deflator) / Consommation finale privée (prix implicite)

	1985	1986	1987	1988	1989	1990	1991	1992	1993	1994	1995	1996	1997
1984	9.3	7.7	6.9	6.7	6.7	6.6	6.6	6.5	[illegible]	6.2	6.2	6.0	5.7
1985		6.2	5.8	5.8	6.0	6.1	6.2	6.1	[illegible]	5.9	5.9	5.7	5.4
1986			5.3	5.6	6.0	6.0	6.2	6.1	[illegible]	5.8	5.8	5.7	5.4
1987				5.9	6.3	6.3	6.4	6.3	[illegible]	5.9	5.9	5.7	5.4
1988					6.6	6.4	6.6	6.3	[illegible]	5.9	5.9	5.7	5.3
1989						6.2	6.6	6.3	[illegible]	5.8	5.8	5.6	5.2
1990							6.9	6.3	[illegible]	5.6	5.7	5.4	5.0
1991								5.6	[illegible]	5.2	5.4	5.2	4.7
1992									[illegible]	5.0	5.3	5.0	4.5
1993										4.6	5.2	4.9	4.3
1994											5.9	5.1	4.2
1995												4.3	3.4
1996													2.5

Government final consumption expenditure (volume) / Consommation des administrations publiques (volume)

	1985	1986	1987	1988	1989	1990	1991	1992	1993	1994	1995	1996	1997
1984	3.1	2.8	2.9	2.9	2.5	2.3	2.2	2.0	1.9	1.6	1.4	1.3	1.1
1985		2.5	2.8	2.8	2.3	2.1	2.0	1.9	1.7	1.5	1.2	1.1	1.0
1986			3.2	2.9	2.3	2.0	1.9	1.8	1.6	1.3	1.1	1.0	0.8
1987				2.7	1.8	1.6	1.6	1.5	1.3	1.1	0.8	0.7	0.6
1988					0.9	1.1	1.3	1.2	1.1	0.8	0.5	0.5	0.4
1989						1.2	1.4	1.3	1.1	0.8	0.5	0.4	0.3
1990							1.7	1.4	1.1	0.7	0.3	0.3	0.1
1991								1.2	0.8	0.3	–0.0	0.0	–0.1
1992									0.5	–0.1	–0.4	–0.3	–0.3
1993										–0.6	–0.8	–0.5	–0.5
1994											–1.1	–0.4	–0.5
1995												0.2	–0.3
1996													–0.7

Government final consumption expenditure (implicit price deflator) / Consommation des administrations publiques (prix implicite)

	1985	1986	1987	1988	1989	1990	1991	1992	1993	1994	1995	1996	1997
1984	9.5	8.2	8.3	8.6	8.2	9.1	8.8	8.3	[illegible]	7.2	6.7	6.8	6.6
1985		6.8	7.7	8.3	7.9	9.0	8.7	8.1	[illegible]	6.9	6.5	6.5	6.4
1986			8.7	9.0	8.3	9.5	9.1	8.3	[illegible]	6.9	6.4	6.5	6.4
1987				9.4	8.0	9.8	9.2	8.2	[illegible]	6.7	6.2	6.3	6.1
1988					6.7	10.1	9.2	8.0	[illegible]	6.2	5.7	5.9	5.8
1989						13.5	10.4	8.4	[illegible]	6.1	5.5	5.8	5.7
1990							7.4	5.9	[illegible]	4.4	4.0	4.5	4.6
1991								4.4	[illegible]	3.4	3.2	4.0	4.1
1992									[illegible]	2.9	2.8	3.9	4.1
1993										3.2	2.9	4.3	4.5
1994											2.6	4.9	4.9
1995												7.3	6.0
1996													4.8

Gross fixed capital formation (volume) / Formation brute de capital fixe (volume)

	1985	1986	1987	1988	1989	1990	1991	1992	1993	1994	1995	1996	1997
1984	0.5	1.3	2.3	3.4	3.6	3.6	3.2	2.6	0.7	0.7	1.3	1.2	1.2
1985		2.0	3.2	4.4	4.4	4.3	3.7	2.9	0.8	0.7	1.4	1.3	1.2
1986			4.4	5.6	5.2	4.8	4.0	3.0	0.6	0.6	1.3	1.2	1.1
1987				6.9	5.6	5.0	3.9	2.7	–0.0	0.0	0.9	0.8	0.8
1988					4.4	4.0	2.9	1.7	–1.4	–1.0	0.1	0.1	0.2
1989						3.6	2.2	0.9	–2.7	–2.1	–0.6	–0.5	–0.4
1990							0.8	–0.5	–4.8	–3.5	–1.5	–1.2	–0.9
1991								–1.8	–7.5	–4.9	–2.0	–1.5	–1.2
1992									–12.8	–6.4	–2.1	–1.5	–1.1
1993										0.5	3.7	2.6	2.1
1994											7.1	3.7	2.6
1995												0.4	0.5
1996													0.6

Gross fixed capital formation (implicit price deflator) / Formation brute de capital fixe (prix implicite)

	1985	1986	1987	1988	1989	1990	1991	1992	1993	1994	1995	1996	1997
1984	9.1	6.4	5.8	5.8	5.7	5.8	5.8	5.5	5.4	5.2	5.2	5.0	4.8
1985		3.8	4.2	4.7	4.9	5.2	5.2	5.0	5.0	4.8	4.8	4.7	4.4
1986			4.5	5.2	5.3	5.6	5.5	5.2	5.1	4.9	4.9	4.7	4.5
1987				5.9	5.6	5.9	5.8	5.4	5.3	5.0	5.0	4.8	4.5
1988					5.4	5.9	5.7	5.3	5.1	4.8	4.8	4.6	4.3
1989						6.5	5.9	5.2	5.1	4.7	4.8	4.5	4.2
1990							5.4	4.6	4.6	4.3	4.4	4.2	3.8
1991								3.9	4.2	3.9	4.2	4.0	3.6
1992									4.6	3.9	4.3	4.0	3.5
1993										3.3	4.2	3.8	3.3
1994											5.0	4.1	3.3
1995												3.1	2.4
1996													1.7

National disposable income (value) / Revenu national disponible (valeur)

	1985	1986	1987	1988	1989	1990	1991	1992	1993	1994	1995	1996	1997
1984	11.7	11.2	10.7	10.8	10.4	10.2	10.0	9.3	8.5	8.3	8.3	8.1	7.8
1985		10.7	10.2	10.5	10.1	10.0	9.7	9.0	8.1	7.9	8.0	7.8	7.5
1986			9.8	10.4	9.9	9.8	9.5	8.7	7.8	7.5	7.7	7.5	7.2
1987				10.9	9.9	9.8	9.4	8.4	7.4	7.2	7.4	7.2	7.0
1988					8.8	9.2	8.9	7.8	6.8	6.6	6.9	6.8	6.5
1989						9.5	8.9	7.5	6.2	6.2	6.6	6.5	6.3
1990							8.3	6.5	5.2	5.3	6.0	6.0	5.8
1991								4.7	3.7	4.4	5.4	5.5	5.4
1992									2.6	4.2	5.7	5.7	5.5
1993										5.8	7.3	6.7	6.3
1994											8.7	7.2	6.4
1995												5.7	5.3
1996													4.9

Compensation of employees (value) / Rémunération des salariés (valeur)

	1985	1986	1987	1988	1989	1990	1991	1992	1993	1994	1995	1996	1997
1984	11.7	9.8	9.4	9.6	9.5	10.0	9.9	9.3	8.3	7.6	7.3	7.2	7.0
1985		8.0	8.3	8.9	9.0	9.6	9.6	8.9	7.9	7.2	6.9	6.8	6.6
1986			8.6	9.3	9.4	10.0	9.9	9.1	7.9	7.1	6.7	6.7	6.5
1987				10.0	9.7	10.5	10.2	9.2	7.3	6.9	6.5	6.4	6.3
1988					9.5	10.8	10.3	9.0	7.4	6.3	6.0	6.0	5.9
1989						12.1	10.7	8.9	6.8	5.7	5.4	5.5	5.4
1990							9.4	7.3	[illegible]	4.2	4.2	4.5	4.5
1991								5.2	[illegible]	2.5	2.9	3.5	3.7
1992									[illegible]	1.2	2.1	3.1	3.4
1993										1.4	2.7	3.8	4.0
1994											4.0	5.0	4.9
1995												6.0	5.4
1996													4.7

LUXEMBOURG

Average per cent changes at annual rate

G.D.P. per head (volume) / P.I.B. par tête (volume)

	1985	1986	1987	1988	1989	1990	1991	1992	1993	1994	1995	1996	1997
1984	2.6	5.0	3.8	5.2	5.9	5.1	5.0	4.8	5.1	4.8	4.6	4.3	4.2
1985		7.5	4.4	6.1	6.7	5.6	5.5	5.1	5.4	5.1	4.8	4.5	4.3
1986			1.5	5.4	6.5	5.1	5.1	4.7	5.1	4.8	4.5	4.2	4.0
1987				9.5	9.1	6.4	6.0	5.3	5.7	5.2	4.9	4.5	4.3
1988					8.7	4.8	4.8	4.3	4.9	4.5	4.2	3.9	3.7
1989						1.1	2.9	2.9	4.0	3.7	3.5	3.2	3.1
1990							4.8	3.8	5.0	4.4	4.0	3.6	3.4
1991								2.9	5.1	4.3	3.8	3.3	3.1
1992									7.3	5.0	4.1	3.4	3.2
1993										2.7	2.5	2.2	2.2
1994											2.3	1.9	2.0
1995												1.6	1.9
1996													2.2

Gross domestic product (volume) / Produit intérieur brut (volume)

	1985	1986	1987	1988	1989	1990	1991	1992	1993	1994	1995	1996	1997
1984	2.9	5.3	4.3	5.8	6.6	5.8	5.9	5.7	6.0	5.9	5.7	5.4	5.3
1985		7.8	5.0	6.8	7.5	6.4	6.4	6.1	6.4	6.2	5.9	5.7	5.5
1986			2.3	6.3	7.5	6.1	6.1	5.8	6.2	6.0	5.7	5.5	5.3
1987				10.4	10.1	7.4	7.1	6.6	6.9	6.5	6.2	5.8	5.6
1988					9.8	5.9	6.0	5.6	6.2	5.9	5.6	5.3	5.1
1989						2.2	4.1	4.2	5.3	5.1	4.9	4.6	4.5
1990							6.1	5.3	6.4	5.9	5.4	5.0	4.8
1991								4.5	6.6	5.8	5.3	4.8	4.6
1992									8.7	6.4	5.5	4.9	4.7
1993										4.2	4.0	3.7	3.7
1994											3.8	3.4	3.5
1995												3.0	3.4
1996													3.7

Private final consumption expenditure (volume) / Consommation finale privée (volume)

	1985	1986	1987	1988	1989	1990	1991	1992	1993	1994	1995	1996	1997
1984	2.7	4.2	4.3	4.4	4.5	4.7	4.9	4.2	3.9	3.8	3.6	3.5	3.4
1985		5.7	5.1	5.0	5.0	5.1	5.3	4.4	4.1	3.9	3.7	3.6	3.5
1986			4.6	4.6	4.8	5.0	5.3	4.2	3.8	3.7	3.5	3.4	3.3
1987				4.6	4.8	5.1	5.4	4.1	3.7	3.5	3.4	3.2	3.2
1988					5.1	5.4	5.7	4.0	3.5	3.3	3.2	3.0	3.0
1989						5.7	6.0	3.6	3.1	3.0	2.9	2.8	2.8
1990							6.3	2.6	2.3	2.3	2.3	2.3	2.3
1991								−0.9	0.4	1.1	1.4	1.5	1.7
1992									1.7	2.1	2.2	2.1	2.2
1993										2.4	2.4	2.2	2.4
1994											2.4	2.1	2.4
1995												1.9	2.3
1996													2.8

Government final consumption expenditure (volume) / Consommation des administrations publiques (volume)

	1985	1986	1987	1988	1989	1990	1991	1992	1993	1994	1995	1996	1997
1984	2.0	2.3	3.1	3.6	3.6	3.6	3.6	3.3	3.4	3.2	3.1	3.2	3.2
1985		2.7	3.7	4.1	4.1	3.9	3.9	3.5	3.5	3.4	3.3	3.3	3.3
1986			4.7	4.8	4.5	4.2	4.1	3.7	3.7	3.5	3.3	3.3	3.4
1987				4.9	4.4	4.0	4.0	3.5	3.5	3.3	3.2	3.2	3.2
1988					3.9	3.5	3.6	3.1	3.2	3.0	2.9	3.0	3.1
1989						3.1	3.5	2.8	3.0	2.8	2.7	2.8	2.9
1990							3.9	2.7	3.0	2.8	2.7	2.8	2.9
1991								1.5	2.6	2.4	2.4	2.5	2.8
1992									3.7	2.8	2.6	2.8	3.0
1993										2.0	2.1	2.5	2.9
1994											2.2	2.8	3.1
1995												3.3	3.6
1996													3.9

Gross fixed capital formation (volume) / Formation brute de capital fixe (volume)

	1985	1986	1987	1988	1989	1990	1991	1992	1993	1994	1995	1996	1997
1984	−9.5	8.9	11.8	12.6	11.5	10.0	12.8	9.8	11.8	8.8	8.3	7.4	7.4
1985		31.0	24.3	21.1	17.4	14.3	17.0	12.9	14.7	11.0	10.2	9.1	9.0
1986			17.9	16.5	13.2	10.5	14.4	10.1	12.6	8.7	8.1	7.1	7.2
1987				15.0	11.0	8.1	13.6	8.6	11.7	7.5	7.0	6.0	6.2
1988					7.0	4.9	13.1	7.1	11.1	6.2	5.9	4.9	5.2
1989						2.7	16.2	7.1	12.1	6.1	5.7	4.6	5.0
1990							31.6	9.4	15.4	7.0	6.3	4.9	5.3
1991								−9.0	8.1	−0.2	0.7	0.2	1.5
1992									28.4	4.5	4.2	2.7	3.7
1993										−14.9	−6.1	−4.7	−1.7
1994											3.5	0.9	3.2
1995												−1.7	3.0
1996													8.0

National disposable income (value) / Revenu national disponible (valeur)

	1985	1986	1987	1988	1989	1990	1991	1992	1993	1994	1995	1996	1997
1984	7.0	7.6	5.2	6.3	7.7	7.9	8.0	7.3	6.6	6.4	6.2	5.9	6.0
1985		8.1	4.3	6.0	7.8	8.1	8.2	7.4	6.6	6.4	6.1	5.8	5.9
1986			0.5	5.0	7.7	8.1	8.2	7.2	6.4	6.1	5.9	5.6	5.7
1987				9.6	11.5	10.8	10.2	8.6	7.4	7.0	6.5	6.2	6.3
1988					13.4	11.3	10.3	8.4	6.9	6.5	6.1	5.7	5.9
1989						9.3	8.9	6.8	5.4	5.2	4.9	4.7	5.0
1990							8.4	5.5	4.1	4.2	4.1	3.9	4.4
1991								2.8	2.0	2.8	3.0	3.1	3.8
1992									1.3	2.9	3.1	3.1	4.0
1993										4.4	4.0	3.7	4.6
1994											3.6	3.4	4.7
1995												3.1	5.2
1996													7.3

LUXEMBOURG

Variations moyennes en pourcentage aux taux annuels

Private final consumption expenditure per head (volume) / Consommation finale privée par tête (volume)

	1985	1986	1987	1988	1989	1990	1991	1992	1993	1994	1995	1996	1997
1984	2.4	3.9	3.8	3.8	3.8	4.0	4.1	3.3	2.9	2.7	2.6	2.4	2.3
1985		5.4	4.6	4.3	4.2	4.3	4.4	3.4	3.0	2.8	2.6	2.4	2.3
1986			3.7	3.7	3.8	4.0	4.2	3.1	2.7	2.5	2.3	2.1	2.0
1987				3.8	3.9	4.1	4.3	2.9	2.5	2.3	2.1	1.9	1.9
1988					4.0	4.3	4.5	2.7	2.3	2.0	1.9	1.7	1.6
1989						4.6	4.8	2.3	1.8	1.6	1.5	1.4	1.4
1990							4.9	1.2	0.9	0.9	0.9	0.8	0.9
1991								−2.4	−1.0	−0.4	−0.1	0.0	0.2
1992									0.4	0.7	0.7	0.7	0.8
1993										0.9	0.9	0.7	0.9
1994											0.9	0.6	0.9
1995												0.4	0.9
1996													1.3

Gross domestic product (implicit price deflator) / Produit intérieur brut (prix implicite)

	1985	1986	1987	1988	1989	1990	1991	1992	1993	1994	1995	1996	1997
1984	3.0	2.9	2.2	1.8	2.2	2.4	2.2	2.5	2.3	2.6	2.4	2.2	2.3
1985		2.8	1.8	1.5	2.0	2.2	2.1	2.4	2.2	2.6	2.4	2.2	2.3
1986			0.9	0.8	1.7	2.1	2.0	2.4	2.1	2.5	2.3	2.1	2.2
1987				0.7	2.1	2.5	2.3	2.7	2.3	2.8	2.5	2.2	2.4
1988					3.5	3.4	2.8	3.2	2.7	3.1	2.8	2.4	2.5
1989						3.4	2.4	3.1	2.5	3.0	2.6	2.3	2.4
1990							1.5	2.9	2.2	2.9	2.5	2.1	2.3
1991								4.3	2.5	3.4	2.7	2.2	2.4
1992									0.7	3.0	2.2	1.7	2.0
1993										5.3	3.0	2.0	2.4
1994											0.7	0.4	1.4
1995												0.0	1.7
1996													3.5

Private final consumption expenditure (implicit price deflator) / Consommation finale privée (prix implicite)

	1985	1986	1987	1988	1989	1990	1991	1992	1993	1994	1995	1996	1997
1984	4.3	2.4	2.1	2.2	2.5	2.7	2.7	2.8	3.0	2.9	2.8	2.7	2.6
1985		0.5	1.0	1.6	2.1	2.4	2.5	2.6	2.8	2.7	2.7	2.6	2.4
1986			1.5	2.1	2.6	2.9	2.9	3.0	3.1	3.0	2.9	2.8	2.6
1987				2.8	3.2	3.4	3.2	3.3	3.4	3.3	3.1	2.9	2.7
1988					3.6	3.7	3.4	3.4	3.5	3.3	3.2	3.0	2.7
1989						3.8	3.3	3.3	3.5	3.3	3.1	2.9	2.6
1990							2.8	3.1	3.4	3.2	3.0	2.7	2.5
1991								3.4	3.8	3.3	3.0	2.7	2.4
1992									4.1	3.2	2.9	2.6	2.2
1993										2.3	2.2	2.0	1.7
1994											2.1	1.9	1.5
1995												1.6	1.3
1996													0.9

Government final consumption expenditure (implicit price deflator) / Consommation des administrations publiques (prix implicite)

	1985	1986	1987	1988	1989	1990	1991	1992	1993	1994	1995	1996	1997
1984	6.5	5.1	5.3	4.0	4.2	5.1	4.8	4.9	4.9	4.8	5.0	4.8	4.5
1985		3.8	4.8	3.2	3.7	4.9	4.5	4.7	4.7	4.6	4.9	4.7	4.4
1986			5.7	2.9	3.6	5.1	4.7	4.9	4.8	4.7	5.0	4.8	4.4
1987				0.2	2.6	5.0	4.4	4.7	4.6	4.5	4.9	4.7	4.3
1988					5.0	7.4	5.9	5.9	5.5	5.3	5.6	5.3	4.8
1989						9.9	6.3	6.1	5.7	5.3	5.7	5.3	4.7
1990							2.8	4.3	4.3	4.2	4.9	4.6	4.0
1991								5.9	5.1	4.7	5.4	4.9	4.2
1992									4.3	4.1	5.3	4.7	3.9
1993										3.9	5.8	4.8	3.8
1994											7.8	5.3	3.8
1995												2.8	1.9
1996													1.0

Gross fixed capital formation (implicit price deflator) / Formation brute de capital fixe (prix implicite)

	1985	1986	1987	1988	1989	1990	1991	1992	1993	1994	1995	1996	1997
1984	3.2	3.3	2.2	2.8	2.5	3.2	0.9	1.5	−0.1	1.0	1.4	1.5	1.9
1985		3.5	1.7	2.7	2.3	3.2	0.6	1.2	−0.5	0.8	1.2	1.3	1.8
1986			0.0	2.3	1.9	3.2	−0.0	0.8	−1.0	0.5	0.9	1.1	1.7
1987				4.6	2.9	4.3	−0.0	1.0	−1.2	0.5	1.0	1.2	1.8
1988					1.1	4.1	−1.5	0.1	−2.3	−0.2	0.5	0.8	1.5
1989						7.2	−2.8	−0.2	−3.1	−0.4	0.4	0.8	1.6
1990							−11.8	−3.7	−6.3	−2.2	−0.9	−0.3	0.8
1991								5.1	−3.5	1.2	2.1	2.2	3.1
1992									−11.3	−0.7	1.1	1.5	2.7
1993										11.3	7.9	6.2	6.5
1994											4.7	3.7	4.9
1995												2.8	5.1
1996													7.4

Compensation of employees (value) / Rémunération des salariés (valeur)

	1985	1986	1987	1988	1989	1990	1991	1992	1993	1994	1995	1996	1997
1984	6.2	7.5	7.5	7.4	8.3	8.7	9.1	9.0	8.8	8.6	8.3	7.9	7.9
1985		8.9	8.2	7.8	8.9	9.2	9.6	9.4	9.1	8.8	8.5	8.1	8.0
1986			7.4	7.2	8.8	9.3	9.7	9.4	9.1	8.8	8.4	8.0	8.0
1987				7.1	9.6	9.9	10.3	9.9	9.4	9.0	8.5	8.1	8.0
1988					12.2	11.3	11.3	10.6	9.9	9.4	8.7	8.2	8.1
1989						10.5	10.9	10.0	9.3	8.8	8.2	7.7	7.6
1990							11.4	9.8	8.9	8.4	7.7	7.2	7.2
1991								8.3	7.7	7.4	6.8	6.4	6.6
1992									7.1	7.0	6.4	5.9	6.2
1993										7.0	6.0	5.6	6.0
1994											5.1	4.9	5.7
1995												4.7	6.0
1996													7.3

Average per cent changes at annual rate

Variations moyennes en pourcentage aux taux annuels

G.D.P. per head (volume) / **P.I.B. par tête** (volume)

	1985	1986	1987	1988	1989	1990	1991	1992	1993	1994	1995	1996	1997
1984	2.6	2.4	1.8	1.9	2.3	2.5	2.3	2.2	2.0	2.0	2.0	2.1	2.1
1985		2.2	1.5	1.6	2.2	2.5	2.3	2.1	1.9	2.0	1.9	2.0	2.1
1986			0.7	1.3	2.2	2.5	2.3	2.1	1.8	1.9	1.9	2.0	2.1
1987				1.9	3.0	3.1	2.7	2.4	2.0	2.1	2.1	2.1	2.2
1988					4.1	3.7	3.0	2.5	2.0	2.1	2.1	2.2	2.3
1989						3.4	2.4	2.0	1.5	1.7	1.7	1.9	2.0
1990							1.4	1.4	0.9	1.3	1.4	1.6	1.8
1991								1.3	0.7	1.3	1.4	1.7	1.9
1992									0.0	1.3	1.5	1.8	2.0
1993										2.6	2.2	2.3	2.5
1994											1.7	2.2	2.5
1995												2.7	2.9
1996													3.1

Private final consumption expenditure per head (volume) / **Consommation finale privée par tête** (volume)

	1985	1986	1987	1988	1989	1990	1991	1992	1993	1994	1995	1996	1997
1984	2.4	2.2	2.2	1.7	1.9	2.2	2.2	2.1	1.9	1.9	1.9	1.9	1.9
1985		2.0	2.0	1.4	1.8	2.1	2.2	2.1	1.9	1.8	1.8	1.9	1.9
1986			2.1	1.1	1.7	2.2	2.2	2.1	1.8	1.8	1.8	1.8	1.9
1987				0.2	1.5	2.2	2.2	2.1	1.8	1.8	1.7	1.8	1.9
1988					2.9	3.2	2.9	2.6	2.1	2.0	2.0	2.0	[illegible]
1989						3.5	2.9	2.5	2.0	1.9	1.8	1.9	2.0
1990							2.3	2.0	1.4	1.5	1.5	1.6	[illegible]
1991								1.8	1.0	1.2	1.3	1.5	1.6
1992									0.3	0.9	1.1	1.4	1.6
1993										1.6	1.6	1.8	2.0
1994											1.5	1.9	[illegible]
1995												2.3	2.4
1996													2.5

Gross domestic product (volume) / **Produit intérieur brut** (volume)

	1985	1986	1987	1988	1989	1990	1991	1992	1993	1994	1995	1996	1997
1984	3.1	2.9	2.4	2.5	2.9	3.1	3.0	2.9	2.6	2.7	2.6	2.7	2.8
1985		2.8	2.1	2.3	2.9	3.1	3.0	2.8	2.6	2.6	2.6	2.7	2.7
1986			1.4	2.0	2.9	3.2	3.0	2.8	2.5	2.6	2.6	2.6	2.7
1987				2.6	3.6	3.8	3.4	3.1	2.7	2.8	2.7	2.8	2.9
1988					4.7	4.4	3.7	3.3	2.8	2.8	2.8	2.8	2.9
1989						4.1	3.2	2.8	2.3	2.5	2.4	2.5	2.7
1990							2.3	2.1	1.7	2.1	2.1	2.3	2.5
1991								2.0	1.4	2.0	2.1	2.3	2.5
1992									0.8	2.0	2.1	2.3	2.6
1993										3.2	2.7	2.9	3.1
1994											2.3	2.7	3.0
1995												3.1	3.4
1996													3.6

Gross domestic product (implicit price deflator) / **Produit intérieur brut** (prix implicite)

	1985	1986	1987	1988	1989	1990	1991	1992	1993	1994	1995	1996	1997
1984	1.8	0.9	0.4	0.6	0.7	1.0	1.2	1.4	1.4	1.5	1.5	1.5	1.6
1985		0.1	−0.3	0.2	0.4	0.8	1.1	1.3	1.4	1.5	1.5	1.5	1.6
1986			−0.7	0.2	0.6	1.0	1.3	1.5	1.6	1.6	1.7	1.7	[illegible]
1987				1.2	1.2	1.6	1.9	1.9	1.9	2.0	2.0	1.9	1.9
1988					1.2	1.8	2.1	2.1	2.1	2.1	2.1	2.0	2.0
1989						2.3	2.5	2.4	2.3	2.3	2.2	2.1	[illegible]
1990							2.7	2.5	2.3	2.3	2.2	2.1	[illegible]
1991								2.3	2.1	2.2	2.1	2.0	2.0
1992									1.9	2.1	2.0	1.9	2.0
1993										2.3	2.1	1.9	2.0
1994											1.8	1.7	1.8
1995												1.5	1.8
1996													2.2

Private final consumption expenditure (volume) / **Consommation finale privée** (volume)

	1985	1986	1987	1988	1989	1990	1991	1992	1993	1994	1995	1996	1997
1984	2.8	2.7	2.7	2.2	2.5	2.8	2.8	2.8	2.6	2.5	2.5	2.5	2.6
1985		2.6	2.7	2.1	2.4	2.8	2.8	2.8	2.6	2.5	2.5	2.5	2.5
1986			2.7	1.8	2.3	2.8	2.9	2.8	2.6	2.5	2.5	2.5	2.5
1987				0.8	2.2	2.8	2.9	2.8	2.5	2.5	2.4	2.5	2.5
1988					3.5	3.9	3.6	3.3	2.9	2.8	2.7	2.7	2.7
1989						4.2	3.7	3.3	2.7	2.6	2.5	2.5	2.6
1990							3.1	2.8	2.2	2.2	2.2	2.3	2.4
1991								2.5	1.8	1.9	1.9	2.1	2.2
1992									1.0	1.6	1.7	2.0	2.2
1993										2.2	2.1	2.3	2.5
1994											2.0	2.4	2.6
1995												2.7	2.9
1996													3.0

Private final consumption expenditure (implicit price deflator) / **Consommation finale privée** (prix implicite)

	1985	1986	1987	1988	1989	1990	1991	1992	1993	1994	1995	1996	1997
1984	2.4	1.3	0.9	0.8	0.9	1.1	1.4	1.6	1.7	1.8	1.8	1.7	1.8
1985		0.3	0.3	0.3	0.6	0.9	1.3	1.5	1.6	1.7	1.7	1.7	[illegible]
1986			0.2	0.4	0.7	1.0	1.5	1.7	1.8	1.9	1.9	1.8	1.8
1987				0.5	0.9	1.3	1.8	2.0	2.1	2.2	2.1	2.0	2.0
1988					1.2	1.7	2.2	2.4	2.4	2.4	2.3	2.2	2.2
1989						2.2	2.7	2.8	2.7	2.7	2.5	2.3	2.3
1990							3.2	3.2	2.8	2.8	2.5	2.4	2.3
1991								3.1	2.6	2.7	2.4	2.2	2.2
1992									2.1	2.5	2.1	2.0	2.0
1993										2.8	2.1	1.9	1.9
1994											1.4	1.5	[illegible]
1995												1.6	1.8
1996													2.0

Government final consumption expenditure (volume) / **Consommation des administrations publiques** (volume)

	1985	1986	1987	1988	1989	1990	1991	1992	1993	1994	1995	1996	1997
1984	2.4	3.0	2.9	2.5	2.3	2.2	2.1	2.0	2.0	1.8	1.7	1.7	1.7
1985		3.6	3.1	2.5	2.3	2.2	2.1	2.0	1.9	1.8	1.7	1.6	1.6
1986			2.6	2.0	1.9	1.8	1.8	1.7	1.7	1.6	1.5	1.5	1.5
1987				1.4	1.5	1.5	1.5	1.6	1.6	1.4	1.3	1.3	1.3
1988					1.5	1.6	1.6	1.6	1.6	1.4	1.3	1.3	1.3
1989						1.6	1.6	1.6	1.6	1.4	1.3	1.3	1.3
1990							1.5	1.6	1.6	1.3	1.2	1.2	1.3
1991								1.7	1.6	1.2	1.1	1.2	1.2
1992									1.5	1.0	1.0	1.0	1.1
1993										0.6	0.7	0.9	1.0
1994											0.8	1.0	1.2
1995												1.2	1.3
1996													1.5

Government final consumption expenditure (implicit price deflator) / **Consommation des administrations publiques** (prix implicite)

	1985	1986	1987	1988	1989	1990	1991	1992	1993	1994	1995	1996	1997
1984	−0.5	−1.4	−0.8	−0.8	−0.5	0.0	0.4	0.9	1.0	1.1	1.3	1.3	1.3
1985		−2.2	−0.9	−0.9	−0.5	0.1	0.6	1.1	1.2	1.3	1.5	1.4	1.5
1986			0.4	−0.2	0.1	0.7	1.2	1.6	1.7	1.7	1.9	1.8	1.8
1987				−0.8	−0.1	0.8	1.4	1.9	1.9	1.9	2.1	2.0	1.9
1988					0.7	1.6	2.1	2.5	2.5	2.3	2.5	2.3	2.2
1989						2.5	2.8	3.2	3.0	2.7	2.8	2.5	2.4
1990							3.1	3.5	3.1	2.7	2.9	2.5	2.4
1991								3.9	3.1	2.6	2.8	2.4	2.3
1992									2.3	1.9	2.4	2.1	2.0
1993										1.5	2.5	2.0	1.9
1994											3.4	2.2	2.1
1995												1.0	1.4
1996													1.8

Gross fixed capital formation (volume) / **Formation brute de capital fixe** (volume)

	1985	1986	1987	1988	1989	1990	1991	1992	1993	1994	1995	1996	1997
1984	7.0	7.0	4.9	4.8	4.8	4.3	3.7	3.3	2.6	2.6	2.8	3.0	3.3
1985		6.9	3.8	4.1	4.3	3.7	3.1	2.8	2.1	2.1	2.4	2.6	3.0
1986			0.9	2.7	3.4	3.0	2.4	2.1	1.4	1.5	1.9	2.2	2.6
1987				4.5	4.7	3.7	2.8	2.4	1.5	1.6	2.0	2.4	2.8
1988					4.9	3.3	2.2	1.8	0.9	1.1	1.6	2.1	2.6
1989						1.6	0.9	0.8	−0.1	0.4	1.1	1.7	2.3
1990							0.2	0.4	−0.7	0.0	1.0	1.7	2.4
1991								0.6	−1.1	−0.0	1.2	2.0	2.8
1992									−2.8	−0.3	1.4	2.4	3.2
1993										2.2	3.5	4.1	4.8
1994											4.8	5.1	5.7
1995												5.4	6.1
1996													6.8

Gross fixed capital formation (implicit price deflator) / **Formation brute de capital fixe** (prix implicite)

	1985	1986	1987	1988	1989	1990	1991	1992	1993	1994	1995	1996	1997
1984	1.2	0.5	0.9	1.1	1.2	1.4	1.5	1.5	1.5	1.5	1.4	1.4	1.5
1985		−0.1	0.7	1.1	1.3	1.4	1.5	1.6	1.6	1.5	1.4	1.5	1.5
1986			1.6	1.7	1.7	1.8	1.9	1.9	1.8	1.7	1.6	1.6	1.6
1987				1.7	1.8	1.9	1.9	1.9	1.8	1.7	1.6	1.6	1.6
1988					1.8	2.0	2.0	2.0	1.9	1.7	1.6	1.6	1.6
1989						2.1	2.1	2.1	1.9	1.7	1.6	1.6	1.6
1990							2.1	2.0	1.8	1.6	1.5	1.5	1.5
1991								2.0	1.6	1.4	1.3	1.4	1.4
1992									1.3	1.2	1.1	1.2	1.3
1993										1.0	1.0	1.2	1.3
1994											1.0	1.3	1.5
1995												1.6	1.7
1996													1.7

National disposable income (value) / **Revenu national disponible** (valeur)

	1985	1986	1987	1988	1989	1990	1991	1992	1993	1994	1995	1996	1997
1984	5.5	4.1	2.9	3.0	3.7	4.1	4.2	4.2	4.0	4.2	4.2	4.3	4.5
1985		2.8	1.6	2.1	3.3	3.8	3.9	4.0	3.8	4.1	4.1	4.2	4.4
1986			0.4	1.8	3.4	4.1	4.2	4.2	4.0	4.3	4.2	4.3	4.5
1987				3.2	5.0	5.4	5.2	4.9	4.6	4.8	4.7	4.8	5.0
1988					6.8	6.5	5.8	5.4	4.8	5.1	4.9	5.0	5.2
1989						6.2	5.3	4.9	4.4	4.8	4.6	4.7	5.0
1990							4.4	4.3	3.7	4.4	4.3	4.5	4.8
1991								4.1	3.4	4.4	4.3	4.5	4.8
1992									2.7	4.5	4.3	4.6	5.0
1993										6.3	5.1	5.2	5.6
1994											4.0	4.7	5.3
1995												5.4	6.0
1996													6.7

Compensation of employees (value) / **Rémunération des salariés** (valeur)

	1985	1986	1987	1988	1989	1990	1991	1992	1993	1994	1995	1996	1997
1984	3.5	4.0	3.8	3.5	3.4	3.8	4.1	4.3	4.1	3.9	3.9	3.9	3.9
1985		4.4	3.9	3.5	3.3	3.8	4.2	4.4	4.2	4.0	3.9	3.9	4.0
1986			3.4	3.0	3.0	3.7	4.2	4.4	4.2	3.9	3.8	3.8	3.9
1987				2.7	2.8	3.8	4.4	4.6	4.3	4.0	3.9	3.9	4.0
1988					2.9	4.4	4.9	5.1	4.7	4.2	4.1	4.0	4.1
1989						5.9	6.0	5.9	5.1	4.5	4.3	4.2	4.3
1990							6.0	5.9	4.9	4.1	4.0	3.9	4.1
1991								5.8	4.3	3.5	3.5	3.5	3.8
1992									2.8	2.4	2.7	3.0	3.4
1993										1.9	2.6	3.0	3.5
1994											3.3	3.5	4.0
1995												3.7	4.3
1996													5.0

NORWAY

NORVÈGE

Average per cent changes at annual rate

Variations moyennes en pourcentage aux taux annuels

G.D.P. per head (volume)
P.I.B. par tête (volume)

	1985	1986	1987	1988	1989	1990	1991	1992	1993	1994	1995	1996	1997
1984	4.9	4.1	3.2	2.2	1.9	1.8	2.0	2.0	2.1	2.3	2.4	2.6	2.6
1985		3.2	2.4	1.4	1.1	1.2	1.5	1.6	1.7	2.1	2.2	2.4	2.5
1986			1.5	0.4	0.5	0.8	1.1	1.4	1.5	1.9	2.1	2.3	2.4
1987				–0.6	–0.1	0.5	1.0	1.3	1.5	2.0	2.1	2.4	2.5
1988					0.5	1.1	1.6	1.9	1.9	2.4	2.5	2.8	2.8
1989						1.6	2.1	2.3	2.3	2.8	2.9	3.2	3.1
1990							2.6	2.6	2.5	3.1	3.1	3.4	3.3
1991								2.7	2.4	3.2	3.2	3.6	3.5
1992									2.1	3.5	3.4	3.8	3.6
1993										4.9	4.1	4.4	4.0
1994											3.3	4.1	3.7
1995												4.9	3.9
1996													2.9

Private final consumption expenditure per head (volume)
Consommation finale privée par tête (volume)

	1985	1986	1987	1988	1989	1990	1991	1992	1993	1994	1995	1996	1997
1984	9.0	6.8	4.0	2.3	1.7	1.4	1.4	1.4	1.4	1.6	1.7	1.9	2.0
1985		4.6	1.6	0.2	–0.1	–0.0	0.2	0.4	0.5	0.8	1.0	1.3	1.4
1986			–1.3	–1.9	–1.6	–1.1	–0.7	–0.3	–0.1	0.4	0.6	1.0	1.2
1987				–2.5	–1.8	–1.1	–0.6	–0.1	0.1	0.6	0.9	1.2	1.4
1988					–1.0	–0.3	0.1	0.5	0.7	1.1	1.4	1.7	1.9
1989						0.4	0.7	1.0	1.1	1.6	1.8	2.1	2.2
1990							1.0	1.3	1.4	1.9	2.1	2.4	2.5
1991								1.7	1.6	2.2	2.4	2.7	2.7
1992									1.5	2.5	2.6	3.0	3.0
1993										3.4	3.1	3.5	3.3
1994											2.9	3.5	3.3
1995												4.1	3.5
1996													2.9

Gross domestic product (volume)
Produit intérieur brut (volume)

	1985	1986	1987	1988	1989	1990	1991	1992	1993	1994	1995	1996	1997
1984	5.2	4.4	3.6	2.7	2.3	2.3	2.4	2.5	2.5	2.8	2.9	3.1	3.1
1985		3.6	2.8	1.8	1.6	1.7	1.9	2.1	2.2	2.5	2.7	2.9	3.0
1986			2.0	1.0	0.9	1.2	1.6	1.9	2.0	2.4	2.6	2.9	2.9
1987				–0.1	0.4	0.9	1.5	1.8	2.0	2.5	2.6	3.0	3.0
1988					0.9	1.4	2.0	2.3	2.4	2.9	3.0	3.3	3.4
1989						2.0	2.5	2.8	2.8	3.3	3.4	3.7	3.7
1990							3.1	3.2	3.0	3.6	3.7	4.0	3.9
1991								3.3	3.0	3.8	3.8	4.2	4.0
1992									2.7	4.1	4.0	4.4	4.2
1993										5.5	4.7	4.9	4.6
1994											3.8	4.7	4.3
1995												5.5	4.5
1996													3.4

Gross domestic product (implicit price deflator)
Produit intérieur brut (prix implicite)

	1985	1986	1987	1988	1989	1990	1991	1992	1993	1994	1995	1996	1997
1984	5.2	2.1	3.7	4.0	4.3	4.3	4.0	3.4	3.3	2.9	3.0	3.0	3.0
1985		–0.9	2.9	3.6	4.1	4.1	3.8	3.2	3.1	2.7	2.7	2.9	2.9
1986			6.9	5.9	5.9	5.4	4.8	3.9	3.6	3.2	3.1	3.2	3.2
1987				5.0	5.3	4.8	4.2	3.3	3.1	2.6	2.7	2.8	2.8
1988					5.7	4.8	4.0	2.9	2.7	2.2	2.4	2.6	2.6
1989						3.9	3.2	1.9	2.0	1.6	1.8	2.1	2.2
1990							2.4	1.0	1.4	1.0	1.4	1.9	2.0
1991								–0.4	0.8	0.5	1.1	1.7	1.9
1992									2.1	1.0	1.7	2.3	2.4
1993										–0.2	1.5	2.3	2.5
1994											3.1	3.6	3.3
1995												4.1	3.5
1996													2.8

Private final consumption expenditure (volume)
Consommation finale privée (volume)

	1985	1986	1987	1988	1989	1990	1991	1992	1993	1994	1995	1996	1997
1984	9.4	7.1	4.4	2.8	2.1	1.8	1.8	1.8	1.9	2.1	2.2	2.4	2.5
1985		5.0	2.0	0.7	0.3	0.4	0.6	0.8	1.0	1.3	1.5	1.8	1.9
1986			–0.8	–1.4	–1.2	–0.7	–0.3	0.1	0.4	0.9	1.1	1.5	1.7
1987				–2.0	–1.3	–0.7	–0.1	0.3	0.6	1.1	1.4	1.8	1.9
1988					–0.6	0.0	0.5	0.9	1.2	1.6	1.9	2.2	2.4
1989						0.7	1.1	1.5	1.6	2.1	2.3	2.7	2.7
1990							1.5	1.8	2.0	2.5	2.6	3.0	3.0
1991								2.2	2.2	2.8	2.9	3.3	3.3
1992									2.2	3.1	3.2	3.5	3.5
1993										4.0	3.7	4.0	3.9
1994											3.4	4.0	3.8
1995												4.7	4.0
1996													3.4

Private final consumption expenditure (implicit price deflator)
Consommation finale privée (prix implicite)

	1985	1986	1987	1988	1989	1990	1991	1992	1993	1994	1995	1996	1997
1984	5.9	6.3	6.8	6.6	6.3	6.0	5.7	5.3	4.9	4.6	4.4	4.1	4.0
1985		6.7	7.3	6.9	6.4	6.0	5.7	5.2	4.8	4.4	4.2	3.9	3.8
1986			7.8	6.9	6.2	5.8	5.4	5.0	4.5	4.1	3.9	3.7	3.6
1987				6.1	5.5	5.2	4.9	4.4	4.0	3.6	3.5	3.2	3.1
1988					4.8	4.8	4.5	4.0	3.6	3.2	3.1	2.9	2.8
1989						4.7	4.3	3.7	3.3	2.9	2.8	2.6	2.6
1990							3.9	3.3	2.8	2.4	2.4	2.3	2.3
1991								2.7	2.3	2.0	2.1	1.9	2.0
1992									2.0	1.6	1.9	1.8	1.9
1993										1.2	1.8	1.7	1.9
1994											2.4	1.9	2.1
1995												1.4	1.9
1996													2.5

Government final consumption expenditure (volume)
Consommation des administrations publiques (volume)

	1985	1986	1987	1988	1989	1990	1991	1992	1993	1994	1995	1996	1997
1984	2.4	2.1	2.9	2.2	2.1	2.6	2.8	3.1	3.0	2.9	2.6	2.7	2.7
1985		1.9	3.2	2.1	2.1	2.6	2.9	3.2	3.1	2.9	2.6	2.7	2.7
1986			4.6	2.2	2.1	2.8	3.1	3.5	3.3	3.0	2.7	2.8	2.8
1987				–0.1	0.9	2.2	2.7	3.3	3.1	2.8	2.5	2.6	2.6
1988					1.9	3.4	3.7	4.1	3.7	3.3	2.9	2.9	2.9
1989						4.9	4.6	4.9	4.2	3.6	3.0	3.1	3.1
1990							4.3	4.8	3.9	3.3	2.7	2.8	2.8
1991								5.3	3.7	2.9	2.3	2.5	2.6
1992									2.2	1.8	1.3	1.8	2.0
1993										1.4	0.8	1.6	2.0
1994											0.3	1.8	2.2
1995												3.2	3.1
1996													3.0

Government final consumption expenditure (implicit price deflator)
Consommation des administrations publiques (prix implicite)

	1985	1986	1987	1988	1989	1990	1991	1992	1993	1994	1995	1996	1997
1984	6.5	6.9	7.9	7.2	6.6	6.0	5.6	5.1	4.7	4.5	4.4	4.3	4.2
1985		7.4	8.6	7.5	6.7	5.9	5.5	5.0	4.5	4.3	4.2	4.1	4.0
1986			9.8	7.5	6.5	5.6	5.1	4.6	4.1	3.9	3.9	3.8	3.7
1987				5.4	4.8	4.2	4.0	3.6	3.2	3.1	3.2	3.2	3.1
1988					4.3	3.6	3.6	3.1	2.8	2.7	2.9	2.9	2.9
1989						3.0	3.2	2.7	2.4	2.4	2.6	2.7	2.7
1990							3.4	2.6	2.2	2.2	2.6	2.6	2.7
1991								1.7	1.6	1.8	2.4	2.5	2.5
1992									1.5	1.9	2.6	2.7	2.7
1993										2.3	3.1	3.1	3.0
1994											4.0	3.5	3.2
1995												3.0	2.9
1996													2.7

Gross fixed capital formation (volume)
Formation brute de capital fixe (volume)

	1985	1986	1987	1988	1989	1990	1991	1992	1993	1994	1995	1996	1997
1984	–4.0	1.7	1.2	0.5	–1.0	–2.7	–2.4	–2.5	–1.8	–1.2	–0.8	0.1	1.0
1985		7.6	3.9	2.0	–0.3	–2.5	–2.2	–2.3	–1.5	–0.8	–0.4	0.5	1.4
1986			0.3	–0.7	–2.8	–4.9	–4.0	–3.9	–2.7	–1.9	–1.3	–0.2	0.9
1987				–1.8	–4.4	–6.6	–5.1	–4.7	–3.2	–2.2	–1.5	–0.3	0.9
1988					–6.9	–8.9	–6.1	–5.4	–3.5	–2.2	–1.4	–0.1	1.2
1989						–10.8	–5.8	–4.9	–2.7	–1.3	–0.5	0.9	2.3
1990							–0.4	–1.8	0.2	1.3	1.7	3.0	4.3
1991								–3.1	0.6	1.9	2.2	3.7	5.1
1992									4.3	4.4	4.1	5.4	6.8
1993										4.5	3.9	5.8	7.5
1994											3.4	6.5	8.5
1995												9.6	11.1
1996													12.6

Gross fixed capital formation (implicit price deflator)
Formation brute de capital fixe (prix implicite)

	1985	1986	1987	1988	1989	1990	1991	1992	1993	1994	1995	1996	1997
1984	8.1	7.5	8.2	8.2	7.3	6.0	5.3	5.0	4.8	4.5	4.4	4.3	4.1
1985		7.0	8.3	8.2	7.1	5.6	4.9	4.5	4.3	4.1	4.1	3.9	3.8
1986			9.6	8.9	7.1	5.3	4.5	4.1	4.0	3.7	3.7	3.6	3.5
1987				8.1	5.8	3.9	3.2	3.1	3.1	2.9	3.0	3.0	2.9
1988					3.6	1.8	1.6	1.8	2.1	2.1	2.3	2.4	2.4
1989						0.1	0.6	1.2	1.7	1.8	2.1	2.2	2.2
1990							1.2	1.8	2.3	2.2	2.5	2.5	2.5
1991								2.5	2.8	2.5	2.9	2.8	2.7
1992									3.1	2.6	3.0	2.9	2.8
1993										2.0	2.9	2.8	2.7
1994											3.8	3.2	3.0
1995												2.6	2.5
1996													2.5

National disposable income (value)
Revenu national disponible (valeur)

	1985	1986	1987	1988	1989	1990	1991	1992	1993	1994	1995	1996	1997
1984	12.0	6.3	6.9	5.8	6.0	6.1	6.1	5.8	5.7	5.7	6.0	6.4	6.4
1985		0.9	4.5	3.8	4.5	5.0	5.1	5.0	4.9	5.1	5.4	5.9	6.0
1986			8.1	5.2	5.8	6.0	6.0	5.6	5.5	5.6	5.9	6.5	6.5
1987				2.5	4.6	5.3	5.4	5.2	5.1	5.2	5.6	6.3	6.3
1988					6.8	6.8	6.4	5.8	5.6	5.7	6.1	6.8	6.7
1989						6.8	6.3	5.5	5.3	5.5	5.9	6.8	6.7
1990							5.8	4.9	4.9	5.2	5.8	6.8	6.7
1991								4.0	4.4	5.0	5.8	6.9	6.9
1992									4.8	5.5	6.3	7.7	7.5
1993										6.2	7.1	8.7	8.2
1994											8.1	10.0	8.8
1995												11.9	9.2
1996													6.6

Compensation of employees (value)
Rémunération des salariés (valeur)

	1985	1986	1987	1988	1989	1990	1991	1992	1993	1994	1995	1996	1997
1984	10.9	11.9	12.1	10.6	8.6	7.8	7.4	6.9	6.4	6.2	6.2	6.3	6.4
1985		12.8	12.7	10.4	8.1	7.2	6.8	6.4	5.8	5.7	5.7	5.9	6.1
1986			12.5	9.3	6.6	5.9	5.6	5.3	4.8	4.9	5.0	5.2	5.5
1987				6.1	3.7	3.7	4.0	3.9	3.6	3.8	4.1	4.4	4.8
1988					1.3	2.5	3.3	3.4	3.1	3.4	3.8	4.2	4.6
1989						3.8	4.2	4.1	3.6	3.9	4.2	4.6	5.1
1990							4.7	4.3	3.5	3.9	4.3	4.8	5.3
1991								3.8	2.9	3.6	4.2	4.8	5.3
1992									2.1	3.5	4.3	5.1	5.7
1993										4.9	5.4	6.1	6.6
1994											5.9	6.7	7.1
1995												7.5	7.8
1996													8.1

POLAND

Average per cent changes at annual rate

G.D.P. per head (volume) / P.I.B. par tête (volume)

	1985	1986	1987	1988	1989	1990	1991	1992	1993	1994	1995	1996	1997
1984	..	..	..	..	..	..	..	..	..	..	..	..	..
1985		..	..	..	..	..	..	..	..	..	..	..	..
1986			..	..	..	..	..	..	..	..	..	..	..
1987				..	..	..	..	..	..	..	..	..	..
1988					..	..	..	..	..	..	..	..	..
1989						..	..	..	..	..	..	..	..
1990							−7.3	−2.6	−0.6	0.8	2.0	2.6	3.2
1991								2.3	2.9	3.6	4.4	4.7	5.1
1992									3.5	4.3	5.1	5.3	5.6
1993										5.0	5.9	6.0	6.2
1994											6.9	6.4	6.6
1995												6.0	6.4
1996													6.8

Gross domestic product (volume) / Produit intérieur brut (volume)

	1985	1986	1987	1988	1989	1990	1991	1992	1993	1994	1995	1996	1997
1984	..	..	..	..	..	..	..	..	..	..	..	..	..
1985		..	..	..	..	..	..	..	..	..	..	..	..
1986			..	..	..	..	..	..	..	..	..	..	..
1987				..	..	..	..	..	..	..	..	..	..
1988					..	..	..	..	..	..	..	..	..
1989						..	..	..	..	..	..	..	..
1990							−7.0	−2.3	−0.3	1.0	2.2	2.8	3.4
1991								2.6	3.2	3.9	4.7	4.9	5.3
1992									3.8	4.5	5.3	5.5	5.8
1993										5.2	6.1	6.1	6.3
1994											7.0	6.5	6.7
1995												6.1	6.5
1996													6.9

Private final consumption expenditure (volume) / Consommation finale privée (volume)

	1985	1986	1987	1988	1989	1990	1991	1992	1993	1994	1995	1996	1997
1984	..	..	..	..	..	..	..	..	..	..	..	..	..
1985		..	..	..	..	..	..	..	..	..	..	..	..
1986			..	..	..	..	..	..	..	..	..	..	..
1987				..	..	..	..	..	..	..	..	..	..
1988					..	..	..	..	..	..	..	..	..
1989						..	..	..	..	..	..	..	..
1990							6.6	4.6	4.8	4.7	4.5	5.2	5.5
1991								2.6	4.0	4.1	4.0	4.9	5.3
1992									5.4	4.9	4.5	5.5	5.8
1993										4.4	4.0	5.5	5.9
1994											3.6	6.1	6.4
1995												8.6	7.8
1996													7.1

Government final consumption expenditure (volume) / Consommation des administrations publiques (volume)

	1985	1986	1987	1988	1989	1990	1991	1992	1993	1994	1995	1996	1997
1984	..	..	..	..	..	..	..	..	..	..	..	..	..
1985		..	..	..	..	..	..	..	..	..	..	..	..
1986			..	..	..	..	..	..	..	..	..	..	..
1987				..	..	..	..	..	..	..	..	..	..
1988					..	..	..	..	..	..	..	..	..
1989						..	..	..	..	..	..	..	..
1990							9.6	7.8	6.2	5.2	4.7	4.5	4.3
1991								5.9	4.6	3.8	3.6	3.5	3.5
1992									3.2	2.7	2.8	2.9	3.0
1993										2.2	2.6	2.9	2.9
1994											2.9	3.2	3.2
1995												3.4	3.3
1996													3.1

Gross fixed capital formation (volume) / Formation brute de capital fixe (volume)

	1985	1986	1987	1988	1989	1990	1991	1992	1993	1994	1995	1996	1997
1984	..	..	..	..	..	..	..	..	..	..	..	..	..
1985		..	..	..	..	..	..	..	..	..	..	..	..
1986			..	..	..	..	..	..	..	..	..	..	..
1987				..	..	..	..	..	..	..	..	..	..
1988					..	..	..	..	..	..	..	..	..
1989						..	..	..	..	..	..	..	..
1990							−4.4	−1.1	0.2	2.4	5.1	7.6	9.3
1991								2.3	2.6	4.8	7.7	10.1	11.8
1992									2.9	6.0	9.5	12.2	13.8
1993										9.2	13.0	15.5	16.7
1994											16.9	18.8	19.4
1995												20.6	20.6
1996													20.6

National disposable income (value) / Revenu national disponible (valeur)

	1985	1986	1987	1988	1989	1990	1991	1992	1993	1994	1995	1996	1997
1984	..	..	..	..	..	..	..	..	..	..	..	..	..
1985		..	..	..	..	..	..	..	..	..	..	..	..
1986			..	..	..	..	..	..	..	..	..	..	..
1987				..	..	..	..	..	..	..	..	..	..
1988					..	..	..	..	..	..	..	..	..
1989						..	..	..	..	..	..	..	..
1990							..	..	..	..	..	..	..
1991								..	..	..	..	..	..
1992									..	..	..	..	..
1993										..	..	..	..
1994											..	..	..
1995												..	..
1996													..

POLOGNE

Variations moyennes en pourcentage aux taux annuels

Private final consumption expenditure per head (volume) / Consommation finale privée par tête (volume)

	1985	1986	1987	1988	1989	1990	1991	1992	1993	1994	1995	1996	1997
1984	..	..	..	..	..	..	..	..	..	..	..	..	..
1985		..	..	..	..	..	..	..	..	..	..	..	..
1986			..	..	..	..	..	..	..	..	..	..	..
1987				..	..	..	..	..	..	..	..	..	..
1988					..	..	..	..	..	..	..	..	..
1989						..	..	..	..	..	..	..	..
1990							6.3	4.2	4.5	4.5	4.3	5.0	5.2
1991								2.2	3.7	3.8	4.7	5.3	5.1
1992									5.1	4.7	4.3	5.3	5.6
1993										4.2	3.8	5.4	6.3
1994											3.5	6.0	6.3
1995												8.6	7.6
1996													7.0

Gross domestic product (implicit price deflator) / Produit intérieur brut (prix implicite)

	1985	1986	1987	1988	1989	1990	1991	1992	1993	1994	1995	1996	1997
1984	..	..	..	..	..	..	..	..	..	..	..	..	..
1985		..	..	..	..	..	..	..	..	..	..	..	..
1986			..	..	..	..	..	..	..	..	..	..	..
1987				..	..	..	..	..	..	..	..	..	..
1988					..	..	..	..	..	..	..	..	..
1989						..	..	..	..	..	..	..	..
1990							55.2	46.6	41.0	37.8	35.8	32.7	30.0
1991								38.5	34.5	32.4	31.3	28.7	26.2
1992									30.6	29.5	29.0	26.3	23.5
1993										28.4	28.3	24.9	22.5
1994											28.2	23.2	20.5
1995												18.5	16.6
1996													14.7

Private final consumption expenditure (implicit price deflator) / Consommation finale privée (prix implicite)

	1985	1986	1987	1988	1989	1990	1991	1992	1993	1994	1995	1996	1997
1984	..	..	..	..	..	..	..	..	..	..	..	..	..
1985		..	..	..	..	..	..	..	..	..	..	..	..
1986			..	..	..	..	..	..	..	..	..	..	..
1987				..	..	..	..	..	..	..	..	..	..
1988					..	..	..	..	..	..	..	..	..
1989						..	..	..	..	..	..	..	..
1990							67.8	55.5	47.0	43.1	40.0	36.3	33.0
1991								44.2	37.7	35.8	33.8	30.8	27.9
1992									31.4	31.7	30.5	27.6	24.9
1993										32.0	30.0	26.4	23.4
1994											27.9	23.7	20.6
1995												19.5	17.1
1996													14.7

Government final consumption expenditure (implicit price deflator) / Consommation des administrations publiques (prix implicite)

	1985	1986	1987	1988	1989	1990	1991	1992	1993	1994	1995	1996	1997
1984	..	..	..	..	..	..	..	..	..	..	..	..	..
1985		..	..	..	..	..	..	..	..	..	..	..	..
1986			..	..	..	..	..	..	..	..	..	..	..
1987				..	..	..	..	..	..	..	..	..	..
1988					..	..	..	..	..	..	..	..	..
1989						..	..	..	..	..	..	..	..
1990							53.9	39.9	33.2	30.7	30.9	29.1	27.4
1991								27.1	25.4	23.8	25.7	24.7	23.5
1992									23.7	22.1	25.3	24.1	22.7
1993										20.6	26.0	24.2	22.5
1994											31.7	26.1	23.1
1995												20.7	19.1
1996													17.4

Gross fixed capital formation (implicit price deflator) / Formation brute de capital fixe (prix implicite)

	1985	1986	1987	1988	1989	1990	1991	1992	1993	1994	1995	1996	1997
1984	..	..	..	..	..	..	..	..	..	..	..	..	..
1985		..	..	..	..	..	..	..	..	..	..	..	..
1986			..	..	..	..	..	..	..	..	..	..	..
1987				..	..	..	..	..	..	..	..	..	..
1988					..	..	..	..	..	..	..	..	..
1989						..	..	..	..	..	..	..	..
1990							40.3	29.5	27.9	27.4	26.4	24.8	23.1
1991								19.5	21.1	23.4	23.1	21.9	20.4
1992									21.6	25.4	24.4	22.5	20.6
1993										26.1	24.2	21.7	19.6
1994											22.3	19.6	17.5
1995												17.0	15.2
1996													13.5

Compensation of employees (value) / Rémunération des salariés (valeur)

	1985	1986	1987	1988	1989	1990	1991	1992	1993	1994	1995	1996	1997
1984	..	..	..	..	..	..	..	..	..	..	..	..	..
1985		..	..	..	..	..	..	..	..	..	..	..	..
1986			..	..	..	..	..	..	..	..	..	..	..
1987				..	..	..	..	..	..	..	..	..	..
1988					..	..	..	..	..	..	..	..	..
1989						..	..	..	..	..	..	..	..
1990							..	..	..	..	..	..	..
1991								..	..	..	..	..	..
1992									..	..	..	..	..
1993										..	..	..	..
1994											..	..	..
1995												..	..
1996													..

PORTUGAL

PORTUGAL

Average per cent changes at annual rate

Variations moyennes en pourcentage aux taux annuels

G.D.P. per head (volume)
P.I.B. par tête (volume)

	1985	1986	1987	1988	1989	1990	1991	1992	1993	1994	1995	1996	1997
1984	2.6	3.4	4.4	5.2	5.3	5.2	4.8	4.5	3.9	3.7	3.6	3.6	3.6
1985		4.1	5.3	6.1	6.0	5.7	5.2	4.8	4.0	3.8	3.7	3.7	3.6
1986			6.6	7.2	6.6	6.1	5.4	4.9	4.0	3.8	3.7	3.6	3.6
1987				7.8	6.6	6.0	5.1	4.6	3.6	3.4	3.3	3.3	3.3
1988					5.5	5.1	4.3	3.8	2.8	2.7	2.7	2.7	2.8
1989						4.8	3.7	3.3	2.2	2.1	2.2	2.3	2.5
1990							2.6	2.6	1.3	1.5	1.7	1.9	2.2
1991								2.6	0.6	1.1	1.5	1.8	2.1
1992									-1.2	0.4	1.1	1.6	2.0
1993										2.0	2.4	2.6	2.8
1994											2.7	2.9	3.1
1995												3.1	3.3
1996													3.5

Private final consumption expenditure per head (volume)
Consommation finale privée par tête (volume)

	1985	1986	1987	1988	1989	1990	1991	1992	1993	1994	1995	1996	1997
1984	0.5	3.0	3.8	4.6	4.3	4.6	4.5	4.5	4.1	3.9	3.7	3.6	3.5
1985		5.6	5.5	6.1	5.3	5.5	5.2	5.1	4.6	4.3	4.0	3.9	3.8
1986			5.5	6.3	5.2	5.5	5.2	5.0	4.5	4.2	3.9	3.7	3.6
1987				7.2	5.0	5.4	5.1	4.9	4.3	4.0	3.7	3.5	3.5
1988					2.9	4.6	4.4	4.4	3.8	3.5	3.2	3.1	3.1
1989						6.3	5.1	4.8	4.0	3.6	3.2	3.1	3.1
1990							4.0	4.1	3.2	2.9	2.6	2.6	2.6
1991								4.3	2.8	2.6	2.3	2.3	2.4
1992									1.4	1.7	1.6	1.8	2.0
1993										2.0	1.7	2.0	2.2
1994											1.5	1.9	2.2
1995												2.4	2.6
1996													2.8

Gross domestic product (volume)
Produit intérieur brut (volume)

	1985	1986	1987	1988	1989	1990	1991	1992	1993	1994	1995	1996	1997
1984	2.8	3.5	4.4	5.2	5.2	5.0	4.7	4.4	3.8	3.6	3.5	3.5	3.5
1985		4.1	5.3	6.0	5.8	5.5	5.0	4.6	3.9	3.7	3.6	3.6	3.6
1986			6.4	6.9	6.3	5.8	5.1	4.7	3.8	3.6	3.6	3.5	3.5
1987				7.5	6.3	5.7	4.8	4.4	3.4	3.3	3.2	3.2	3.2
1988					5.1	4.8	3.9	3.6	2.6	2.6	2.6	2.7	2.8
1989						4.4	3.4	3.1	2.0	2.1	2.2	2.3	2.5
1990							2.3	2.4	1.2	1.5	1.8	2.0	2.2
1991								2.5	0.7	1.2	1.6	1.9	2.2
1992									-1.1	0.6	1.3	1.8	2.2
1993										2.2	2.5	2.8	3.0
1994											2.9	3.0	3.2
1995												3.2	3.4
1996													3.7

Gross domestic product (implicit price deflator)
Produit intérieur brut (prix implicite)

	1985	1986	1987	1988	1989	1990	1991	1992	1993	1994	1995	1996	1997
1984	21.7	21.1	17.3	15.7	15.1	14.7	14.3	13.8	13.0	12.3	11.6	10.9	10.1
1985		20.5	15.2	13.8	13.5	13.3	13.1	12.7	11.9	11.3	10.6	9.9	9.2
1986			10.1	10.6	11.2	11.6	11.7	11.4	10.7	10.2	9.6	8.9	8.3
1987				11.2	11.8	12.1	12.1	11.7	10.9	10.2	9.5	8.8	8.1
1988					12.4	12.6	12.5	11.8	10.8	10.0	9.3	8.5	7.7
1989						12.8	12.5	11.6	10.4	9.6	8.8	7.9	7.2
1990							12.2	11.1	9.6	8.8	8.0	7.1	6.4
1991								10.0	8.3	7.6	7.0	6.2	5.5
1992									6.7	6.5	6.0	5.2	4.6
1993										6.3	5.7	4.7	4.1
1994											5.1	4.0	3.3
1995												2.8	2.4
1996													2.0

Private final consumption expenditure (volume)
Consommation finale privée (volume)

	1985	1986	1987	1988	1989	1990	1991	1992	1993	1994	1995	1996	1997
1984	0.7	3.1	3.8	4.6	4.2	4.5	4.4	4.3	4.0	3.8	3.6	3.5	3.5
1985		5.6	5.5	5.9	5.1	5.2	5.0	4.9	4.4	4.2	3.9	3.8	3.7
1986			5.3	6.1	4.9	5.2	4.9	4.8	4.3	4.0	3.8	3.6	3.6
1987				6.9	4.7	5.1	4.7	4.6	4.1	3.8	3.6	3.4	3.4
1988					2.6	4.2	4.0	4.1	3.6	3.3	3.1	3.0	3.0
1989						5.9	4.8	4.6	3.8	3.5	3.2	3.1	3.1
1990							3.7	4.0	3.1	2.9	2.6	2.6	2.7
1991								4.3	2.9	2.7	2.4	2.4	2.5
1992									1.5	1.9	1.8	2.0	2.2
1993										2.2	1.9	2.1	2.4
1994											1.6	2.1	2.4
1995												2.5	2.8
1996													3.0

Private final consumption expenditure (implicit price deflator)
Consommation finale privée (prix implicite)

	1985	1986	1987	1988	1989	1990	1991	1992	1993	1994	1995	1996	1997
1984	19.4	16.6	14.3	13.6	13.5	13.3	13.2	12.7	12.0	11.4	10.7	10.1	9.5
1985		13.8	11.9	11.7	12.1	12.2	12.2	11.8	11.1	10.5	9.9	9.3	8.7
1986			9.9	10.7	11.5	11.7	11.8	11.5	10.8	10.1	9.5	8.9	8.2
1987				11.5	12.3	12.4	12.3	11.8	10.9	10.1	9.4	8.7	8.0
1988					13.1	12.8	12.6	11.9	10.8	9.9	9.1	8.4	7.7
1989						12.4	12.3	11.4	10.2	9.3	8.4	7.7	7.0
1990							12.2	11.0	9.5	8.5	7.7	7.0	6.3
1991								9.7	8.1	7.3	6.6	6.0	5.3
1992									6.6	6.1	5.5	5.0	4.4
1993										5.6	5.0	4.5	3.9
1994											4.5	4.0	3.3
1995												3.6	2.8
1996													2.0

Government final consumption expenditure (volume)
Consommation des administrations publiques (volume)

	1985	1986	1987	1988	1989	1990	1991	1992	1993	1994	1995	1996	1997
1984	6.4	6.8	5.8	6.5	6.5	6.3	6.9	6.2	5.6	5.2	4.9	4.7	4.5
1985		7.2	5.5	6.5	6.5	6.3	7.0	6.1	5.4	5.1	4.8	4.5	4.3
1986			3.8	6.2	6.3	6.1	6.9	5.9	5.2	4.8	4.5	4.3	4.1
1987				8.6	7.6	6.9	7.7	6.4	5.4	4.9	4.6	4.3	4.1
1988					6.6	6.0	7.4	5.8	4.8	4.4	4.0	3.8	3.6
1989						5.4	7.8	5.5	4.4	3.9	3.6	3.4	3.3
1990							10.3	5.6	4.0	3.5	3.3	3.0	3.0
1991								1.1	1.0	1.4	1.6	1.7	1.8
1992									0.9	1.5	1.7	1.8	1.9
1993										2.1	2.1	2.1	2.2
1994											2.2	2.1	2.2
1995												2.0	2.2
1996													2.5

Government final consumption expenditure (implicit price deflator)
Consommation des administrations publiques (prix implicite)

	1985	1986	1987	1988	1989	1990	1991	1992	1993	1994	1995	1996	1997
1984	21.5	18.6	16.1	15.7	15.5	15.4	15.4	15.0	14.2	13.2	12.6	12.1	11.6
1985		15.8	13.6	13.8	14.0	14.3	14.5	14.1	13.4	12.3	11.7	11.3	10.8
1986			11.4	12.8	13.4	13.9	14.2	13.8	13.0	11.9	11.3	10.8	10.4
1987				14.3	14.5	14.7	14.9	14.3	13.3	12.0	11.3	10.8	10.3
1988					14.7	15.0	15.1	14.3	13.1	11.6	10.8	10.3	9.8
1989						15.2	15.4	14.2	12.7	11.0	10.2	9.7	9.3
1990							15.5	13.7	11.8	10.0	9.2	8.8	8.4
1991								11.9	10.1	8.2	7.7	7.5	7.3
1992									8.2	6.3	6.3	6.5	6.4
1993										4.5	5.4	5.9	5.9
1994											6.3	6.6	6.4
1995												6.8	6.4
1996													6.0

Gross fixed capital formation (volume)
Formation brute de capital fixe (volume)

	1985	1986	1987	1988	1989	1990	1991	1992	1993	1994	1995	1996	1997
1984	-3.5	3.4	8.1	9.7	8.6	8.5	7.7	7.4	5.8	5.5	5.5	5.5	5.9
1985		10.9	14.4	14.5	11.9	11.0	9.7	9.0	7.0	6.6	6.4	6.4	6.8
1986			18.0	16.4	12.3	11.1	9.5	8.7	6.5	6.1	5.9	5.9	6.4
1987				14.8	9.5	8.9	7.5	7.0	4.7	4.5	4.5	4.7	5.3
1988					4.4	6.0	5.2	5.1	2.8	2.9	3.1	3.5	4.3
1989						7.6	5.5	5.3	2.3	2.5	2.9	3.3	4.3
1990							3.5	4.1	0.6	1.3	2.0	2.6	3.8
1991								4.8	-0.8	0.6	1.6	2.4	3.9
1992									-6.0	-1.4	0.6	1.9	3.7
1993										3.4	4.1	4.6	6.3
1994											4.8	5.3	7.3
1995												5.7	8.5
1996													11.3

Gross fixed capital formation (implicit price deflator)
Formation brute de capital fixe (prix implicite)

	1985	1986	1987	1988	1989	1990	1991	1992	1993	1994	1995	1996	1997
1984	20.0	17.3	14.8	13.8	12.9	12.3	11.3	10.2	9.5	9.1	8.7	8.0	7.4
1985		14.7	12.3	11.8	11.2	10.8	9.9	8.8	8.3	8.0	7.6	7.0	6.4
1986			9.9	10.4	10.1	9.8	8.9	7.9	7.4	7.2	6.8	6.2	5.7
1987				10.9	10.2	9.8	8.7	7.5	7.0	6.8	6.4	5.8	5.3
1988					9.5	9.2	8.0	6.6	6.2	6.2	5.8	5.2	4.6
1989						9.0	7.2	5.7	5.4	5.5	5.2	4.6	4.0
1990							5.4	4.1	4.3	4.6	4.5	3.9	3.4
1991								2.7	3.7	4.4	4.2	3.6	3.0
1992									4.7	5.2	4.7	3.8	3.1
1993										5.7	4.8	3.6	2.7
1994											3.8	2.5	1.7
1995												1.2	0.6
1996													0.1

National disposable income (value)
Revenu national disponible (valeur)

	1985	1986	1987	1988	1989	1990	1991	1992	1993	1994	1995	1996	1997
1984	25.1	25.8	23.5	22.4	21.6	20.9	19.9	19.0	17.4	16.2	15.4	14.6	13.9
1985		26.5	22.7	21.6	20.7	20.1	19.1	18.2	16.5	15.3	14.5	13.7	13.0
1986			18.9	19.1	18.9	18.5	17.7	16.8	15.1	14.0	13.2	12.5	11.8
1987				19.4	18.8	18.4	17.3	16.4	14.5	13.3	12.5	11.8	11.1
1988					18.3	17.9	16.7	15.7	13.5	12.3	11.5	10.8	10.3
1989						17.5	15.8	14.8	12.3	11.1	10.4	9.8	9.3
1990							14.2	13.5	10.7	9.6	9.1	8.6	8.2
1991								12.7	8.9	8.1	7.8	7.5	7.2
1992									5.2	5.8	6.3	6.2	6.1
1993										6.4	6.8	6.6	6.4
1994											7.2	6.6	6.4
1995												6.1	6.0
1996													5.8

Compensation of employees (value)
Rémunération des salariés (valeur)

	1985	1986	1987	1988	1989	1990	1991	1992	1993	1994	1995	1996	1997
1984	20.5	20.4	19.0	18.4	18.3	18.8	19.1	18.6	16.9	15.5	14.6	13.9	13.2
1985		20.3	18.3	17.7	17.8	18.5	18.9	18.3	16.5	15.0	14.1	13.3	12.7
1986			16.3	16.4	17.0	18.0	18.6	18.0	16.0	14.3	13.4	12.6	12.0
1987				16.4	17.3	18.6	19.1	18.3	15.9	14.0	13.0	12.2	11.6
1988					18.2	19.7	20.1	18.8	15.8	13.7	12.5	11.7	11.0
1989						21.2	21.0	19.0	15.2	12.8	11.6	10.8	10.2
1990							20.9	17.9	13.3	10.8	9.8	9.2	8.7
1991								14.9	9.7	7.6	7.2	7.0	6.8
1992									4.8	4.1	4.7	5.1	5.2
1993										3.5	4.7	5.2	5.3
1994											6.0	6.1	6.0
1995												6.1	6.0
1996													5.8

SPAIN

ESPAGNE

Average per cent changes at annual rate

Variations moyennes en pourcentage aux taux annuels

G.D.P. per head (volume) / **P.I.B. par tête** (volume)

	1985	1986	1987	1988	1989	1990	1991	1992	1993	1994	1995	1996	1997
1984	1.3	2.1	3.2	3.6	3.8	3.8	3.5	3.1	2.6	2.6	2.6	2.5	2.6
1985		2.9	4.1	4.4	4.4	4.3	3.9	3.4	2.8	2.7	2.7	2.7	2.7
1986			5.4	5.2	4.9	4.6	4.1	3.5	2.8	2.7	2.7	2.6	2.7
1987				4.9	4.7	4.3	3.8	3.1	2.3	2.3	2.3	2.3	2.4
1988					4.5	4.1	3.4	2.7	1.8	1.9	2.0	2.0	2.2
1989						3.6	2.8	2.0	1.2	1.4	1.6	1.7	1.9
1990							2.1	1.3	0.4	0.8	1.2	1.3	1.6
1991								0.5	-0.5	0.4	0.9	1.2	1.6
1992									-1.4	0.3	1.1	1.4	1.8
1993										2.1	2.3	2.3	2.6
1994											2.6	2.4	2.7
1995												2.3	2.8
1996													3.4

Private final consumption expenditure per head (volume) / **Consommation finale privée par tête** (volume)

	1985	1986	1987	1988	1989	1990	1991	1992	1993	1994	1995	1996	1997
1984	1.6	2.3	3.4	3.7	4.0	4.0	3.8	3.5	2.9	2.7	2.5	2.5	2.5
1985		3.0	4.3	4.4	4.7	4.4	4.1	3.8	3.0	2.8	2.6	2.6	2.6
1986			5.5	5.1	5.2	4.8	4.4	4.0	3.0	2.7	2.6	2.5	2.6
1987				4.7	5.1	4.5	4.1	3.7	2.6	2.3	2.2	2.2	2.3
1988					5.4	4.5	3.9	3.4	2.2	2.0	1.9	1.9	2.0
1989						3.5	3.1	2.7	1.4	1.3	1.3	1.4	1.6
1990							2.7	2.3	0.7	0.7	0.9	1.0	1.3
1991								2.0	-0.2	0.1	0.4	0.7	1.1
1992									-2.4	-0.8	-0.1	0.4	0.9
1993										0.7	1.1	1.3	1.7
1994											1.4	1.6	2.1
1995												1.8	2.4
1996													3.0

Gross domestic product (volume) / **Produit intérieur brut** (volume)

	1985	1986	1987	1988	1989	1990	1991	1992	1993	1994	1995	1996	1997
1984	1.7	2.4	3.5	3.9	4.1	4.0	3.8	3.4	2.9	2.8	2.8	2.8	2.8
1985		3.2	4.4	4.7	4.7	4.5	4.1	3.6	3.0	2.9	2.9	2.9	2.9
1986			5.6	5.4	5.2	4.8	4.3	3.7	3.0	2.9	2.9	2.8	2.9
1987				5.2	4.9	4.5	4.0	3.3	2.5	2.5	2.5	2.5	2.6
1988					4.7	4.2	3.6	2.8	2.0	2.1	2.2	2.2	2.3
1989						3.7	3.0	2.2	1.4	1.5	1.7	1.8	2.0
1990							2.3	1.5	0.6	1.0	1.3	1.5	1.8
1991								0.7	-0.2	0.6	1.1	1.4	1.7
1992									-1.2	0.5	1.3	1.5	1.9
1993										2.3	2.5	2.5	2.7
1994											2.7	2.6	2.9
1995												2.4	3.0
1996													3.5

Gross domestic product (implicit price deflator) / **Produit intérieur brut** (prix implicite)

	1985	1986	1987	1988	1989	1990	1991	1992	1993	1994	1995	1996	1997
1984	7.7	9.4	8.2	7.5	7.5	7.4	7.4	7.3	7.0	6.7	6.5	6.2	5.9
1985		11.1	8.4	7.5	7.4	7.4	7.3	7.3	6.9	6.6	6.4	6.1	5.8
1986			5.8	5.8	6.2	6.5	6.6	6.6	6.3	6.0	5.9	5.6	5.3
1987				5.7	6.4	6.7	6.8	6.8	6.4	6.0	5.9	5.6	5.2
1988					7.1	7.2	7.2	7.1	6.5	6.1	5.9	5.6	5.2
1989						7.3	7.2	7.1	6.4	5.9	5.7	5.4	4.9
1990							7.1	7.0	6.1	5.6	5.4	5.0	4.6
1991								6.9	5.6	5.1	5.0	4.6	4.2
1992									4.3	4.2	4.4	4.1	3.7
1993										4.0	4.4	4.0	3.5
1994											4.8	4.0	3.3
1995												3.2	2.6
1996													2.0

Private final consumption expenditure (volume) / **Consommation finale privée** (volume)

	1985	1986	1987	1988	1989	1990	1991	1992	1993	1994	1995	1996	1997
1984	2.0	2.6	3.7	4.0	4.3	4.2	4.0	3.8	3.1	2.9	2.8	2.7	2.7
1985		3.3	4.5	4.7	4.9	4.7	4.4	4.1	3.2	3.0	2.8	2.8	2.8
1986			5.8	5.4	5.5	5.0	4.6	4.2	3.2	2.9	2.8	2.7	2.7
1987				4.9	5.3	4.7	4.3	3.9	2.8	2.5	2.4	2.4	2.4
1988					5.7	4.6	4.1	3.6	2.4	2.2	2.1	2.1	2.2
1989						3.6	3.3	2.9	1.6	1.5	1.5	1.6	1.7
1990							2.9	2.6	0.9	0.9	1.1	1.2	1.5
1991								2.2	-0.0	0.3	0.6	0.9	1.2
1992									-2.2	-0.7	0.1	0.6	1.1
1993										0.9	1.2	1.5	1.9
1994											1.6	1.8	2.2
1995												2.0	2.5
1996													3.1

Private final consumption expenditure (implicit price deflator) / **Consommation finale privée** (prix implicite)

	1985	1986	1987	1988	1989	1990	1991	1992	1993	1994	1995	1996	1997
1984	7.1	8.3	7.4	6.8	6.8	6.7	6.7	6.6	6.5	6.4	6.2	6.0	5.7
1985		9.4	7.5	6.7	6.7	6.6	6.6	6.6	6.4	6.3	6.1	5.9	5.6
1986			5.7	5.4	5.8	6.0	6.0	6.1	6.0	5.9	5.8	5.5	5.2
1987				5.0	5.8	6.0	6.1	6.2	6.1	5.9	5.8	5.5	5.2
1988					6.6	6.6	6.5	6.5	6.3	6.1	5.9	5.6	5.2
1989						6.5	6.4	6.4	6.2	5.9	5.7	5.4	5.0
1990							6.4	6.4	6.1	5.8	5.6	5.2	4.8
1991								6.4	6.0	5.6	5.4	5.0	4.6
1992									5.6	5.2	5.0	4.6	4.2
1993										4.9	4.8	4.3	3.9
1994											4.7	4.0	3.5
1995												3.4	3.0
1996													2.5

Government final consumption expenditure (volume) / **Consommation des administrations publiques** (volume)

	1985	1986	1987	1988	1989	1990	1991	1992	1993	1994	1995	1996	1997
1984	6.0	5.7	6.7	6.1	6.5	6.5	6.4	6.1	5.7	5.1	4.8	4.4	4.2
1985		5.4	7.1	6.1	6.6	6.6	6.4	6.1	5.6	5.0	4.6	4.3	4.0
1986			8.9	6.4	7.0	6.9	6.7	6.2	5.7	4.9	4.5	4.2	3.9
1987				4.0	6.1	6.3	6.1	5.7	5.1	4.3	4.0	3.7	3.4
1988					8.3	7.5	6.8	6.1	5.4	4.4	4.0	3.6	3.4
1989						6.6	6.1	5.4	4.6	3.6	3.3	3.0	2.8
1990							5.6	4.8	4.0	2.9	2.7	2.4	2.2
1991								4.0	3.2	2.0	2.0	1.8	1.7
1992									2.4	1.0	1.3	1.2	1.2
1993										-0.3	0.7	0.8	0.9
1994											1.8	1.4	1.4
1995												0.9	1.2
1996													1.4

Government final consumption expenditure (implicit price deflator) / **Consommation des administrations publiques** (prix implicite)

	1985	1986	1987	1988	1989	1990	1991	1992	1993	1994	1995	1996	1997
1984	7.9	8.1	7.3	6.6	6.6	6.7	6.8	7.1	6.7	6.3	6.1	6.0	5.6
1985		8.3	7.0	6.1	6.2	6.4	6.6	7.0	6.6	6.1	6.0	5.8	5.4
1986			5.7	5.1	5.5	6.0	6.3	6.8	6.3	5.9	5.7	5.5	5.2
1987				4.5	5.5	6.1	6.5	7.0	6.4	5.9	5.7	5.5	5.1
1988					6.5	6.9	7.1	7.7	6.8	6.1	5.9	5.7	5.2
1989						7.3	7.5	8.1	6.9	6.1	5.8	5.6	5.0
1990							7.6	8.4	6.8	5.8	5.5	5.3	4.7
1991								9.2	6.3	5.1	5.0	4.8	4.2
1992									3.5	3.2	3.6	3.7	3.2
1993										2.8	3.6	3.8	3.2
1994											4.4	4.3	3.3
1995												4.2	2.7
1996													1.3

Gross fixed capital formation (volume) / **Formation brute de capital fixe** (volume)

	1985	1986	1987	1988	1989	1990	1991	1992	1993	1994	1995	1996	1997
1984	6.1	8.0	10.0	10.9	11.5	10.6	9.3	7.5	5.3	5.0	5.3	5.0	5.0
1985		9.9	12.0	12.6	12.8	11.6	9.8	7.7	5.2	4.9	5.2	4.9	4.9
1986			14.0	14.0	13.8	12.0	9.8	7.3	4.6	4.3	4.7	4.4	4.5
1987				13.9	13.7	11.3	8.8	6.0	3.1	3.0	3.6	3.4	3.5
1988					13.6	10.1	7.2	4.1	1.0	1.3	2.2	2.1	2.4
1989						6.6	4.1	1.2	-1.9	-1.0	0.5	0.6	1.1
1990							1.6	-1.5	-4.6	-2.8	-0.7	-0.4	0.4
1991								-4.4	-7.5	-4.3	-1.3	-0.8	0.2
1992									-10.5	-4.2	-0.2	0.2	1.1
1993										2.5	5.4	4.0	4.3
1994											8.2	4.7	4.8
1995												1.3	3.2
1996													5.1

Gross fixed capital formation (implicit price deflator) / **Formation brute de capital fixe** (prix implicite)

	1985	1986	1987	1988	1989	1990	1991	1992	1993	1994	1995	1996	1997
1984	6.7	6.3	5.8	5.9	5.7	5.8	5.6	5.3	5.3	5.1	5.0	4.8	4.5
1985		5.9	5.3	5.6	5.5	5.6	5.5	5.1	5.1	4.9	4.9	4.6	4.4
1986			4.7	5.4	5.4	5.5	5.4	5.0	5.0	4.8	4.7	4.5	4.2
1987				6.1	5.7	5.7	5.5	5.1	5.0	4.8	4.7	4.4	4.2
1988					5.3	5.6	5.3	4.8	4.8	4.6	4.6	4.2	4.0
1989						5.8	5.3	4.6	4.7	4.5	4.4	4.1	3.8
1990							4.9	4.0	4.3	4.2	4.2	3.8	3.5
1991								3.2	4.1	3.9	4.0	3.6	3.3
1992									4.9	4.3	4.2	3.7	3.3
1993										3.7	3.9	3.3	2.9
1994											4.1	3.1	2.7
1995												2.0	1.9
1996													1.9

National disposable income (value) / **Revenu national disponible** (valeur)

	1985	1986	1987	1988	1989	1990	1991	1992	1993	1994	1995	1996	1997
1984	9.7	12.7	12.7	12.4	12.4	12.2	11.8	11.2	10.3	9.7	9.7	9.3	9.0
1985		15.7	14.3	13.3	13.1	12.7	12.1	11.4	10.3	9.7	9.7	9.3	8.9
1986			12.8	12.1	12.2	11.9	11.4	10.7	9.6	9.0	9.1	8.7	8.3
1987				11.4	11.9	11.6	11.1	10.3	9.1	8.5	8.6	8.2	7.9
1988					12.5	11.8	11.0	10.0	8.6	8.0	8.2	7.8	7.5
1989						11.0	10.3	9.2	7.6	7.1	7.5	7.1	6.9
1990							9.5	8.4	6.5	6.1	6.8	6.5	6.3
1991								7.2	5.1	5.1	6.2	5.9	5.8
1992									2.9	4.0	5.8	5.6	5.6
1993										5.0	7.3	6.5	6.2
1994											9.6	7.3	6.6
1995												4.9	5.1
1996													5.3

Compensation of employees (value) / **Rémunération des salariés** (valeur)

	1985	1986	1987	1988	1989	1990	1991	1992	1993	1994	1995	1996	1997
1984	10.5	11.6	11.7	11.8	12.0	12.4	12.3	11.8	10.9	10.0	9.5	9.2	8.9
1985		12.7	12.3	12.2	12.2	12.8	12.6	12.0	10.9	9.9	9.4	9.1	8.8
1986			11.9	11.9	12.2	12.8	12.6	11.8	10.7	9.6	9.1	8.7	8.4
1987				11.9	12.3	13.1	12.8	11.8	10.4	9.2	8.7	8.4	8.1
1988					12.8	13.7	13.1	11.8	10.2	8.8	8.3	8.0	7.7
1989						14.7	13.2	11.5	9.5	8.0	7.5	7.3	7.1
1990							11.7	9.9	7.8	6.4	6.2	6.1	6.0
1991								8.0	5.9	4.7	4.8	5.0	5.1
1992									3.8	3.1	3.8	4.2	4.5
1993										2.3	3.7	4.4	4.7
1994											5.1	5.4	5.5
1995												5.7	5.7
1996													5.6

SWEDEN

SUÈDE

Average per cent changes at annual rate

Variations moyennes en pourcentage aux taux annuels

G.D.P. per head (volume) / **P.I.B. par tête** (volume)

	1985	1986	1987	1988	1989	1990	1991	1992	1993	1994	1995	1996	1997
1984	1.8	1.9	2.2	2.1	2.0	1.8	1.3	0.8	0.4	0.7	0.9	0.9	1.0
1985		2.0	2.4	2.2	2.1	1.8	1.2	0.7	0.3	0.5	0.8	0.8	0.9
1986			2.8	2.3	2.1	1.7	1.0	0.5	0.0	0.3	0.7	0.7	0.8
1987				1.8	1.7	1.3	0.6	0.0	–0.4	–0.0	0.4	0.5	0.6
1988					1.7	1.1	0.2	–0.4	–0.9	–0.3	0.2	0.3	0.5
1989						0.5	–0.6	–1.1	–1.5	–0.7	–0.0	0.1	0.3
1990							–1.7	–1.9	–2.2	–1.0	–0.1	0.1	0.3
1991								–2.0	–2.4	–0.8	0.3	0.4	0.6
1992									–2.8	–0.1	1.0	1.1	1.2
1993										2.6	3.0	2.4	2.2
1994											3.4	2.2	2.1
1995												1.1	1.4
1996													1.7

Gross domestic product (volume) / **Produit intérieur brut** (volume)

	1985	1986	1987	1988	1989	1990	1991	1992	1993	1994	1995	1996	1997
1984	1.9	2.1	2.5	2.4	2.4	2.2	1.7	1.3	0.9	1.2	1.4	1.4	1.4
1985		2.3	2.7	2.6	2.5	2.3	1.7	1.3	0.8	1.1	1.4	1.4	1.4
1986			3.1	2.7	2.6	2.3	1.6	1.1	0.6	0.9	1.3	1.3	1.3
1987				2.3	2.3	2.0	1.2	0.7	0.2	0.6	1.0	1.1	1.1
1988					2.4	1.9	0.9	0.3	–0.2	0.4	0.9	0.9	1.0
1989						1.4	0.1	–0.4	–0.9	–0.0	0.6	0.7	0.8
1990							–1.1	–1.3	–1.6	–0.4	0.5	0.6	0.8
1991								–1.4	–1.8	–0.1	0.9	1.0	1.1
1992									–2.2	0.5	1.6	1.6	1.6
1993										3.3	3.6	2.8	2.6
1994											3.9	2.6	2.3
1995												1.3	1.5
1996													1.8

Private final consumption expenditure (volume) / **Consommation finale privée** (volume)

	1985	1986	1987	1988	1989	1990	1991	1992	1993	1994	1995	1996	1997
1984	2.7	3.5	3.9	3.5	3.0	2.5	2.2	1.8	1.2	1.3	1.2	1.2	1.3
1985		4.4	4.5	3.8	3.1	2.4	2.2	1.7	1.0	1.1	1.1	1.1	1.2
1986			4.6	3.5	2.7	1.9	1.7	1.2	0.6	0.7	0.7	0.8	0.9
1987				2.4	1.8	1.1	1.0	0.5	–0.1	0.2	0.3	0.4	0.5
1988					1.2	0.4	0.6	0.1	–0.6	–0.2	–0.0	0.1	0.3
1989						–0.4	0.3	–0.3	–1.0	–0.4	–0.2	–0.0	0.2
1990							0.9	–0.2	–1.2	–0.5	–0.2	0.0	0.3
1991								–1.4	–2.2	–0.9	–0.5	–0.1	0.2
1992									–3.1	–0.7	–0.2	0.2	0.5
1993										1.8	1.3	1.3	1.5
1994											0.8	1.0	1.4
1995												1.3	1.7
1996													2.0

Government final consumption expenditure (volume) / **Consommation des administrations publiques** (volume)

	1985	1986	1987	1988	1989	1990	1991	1992	1993	1994	1995	1996	1997
1984	2.2	1.7	1.5	1.2	1.4	1.6	1.8	1.6	1.4	1.2	1.0	0.9	0.7
1985		1.3	1.1	0.9	1.2	1.5	1.7	1.5	1.3	1.1	0.9	0.8	0.5
1986			1.0	0.8	1.2	1.6	1.8	1.5	1.3	1.1	0.8	0.7	0.5
1987				0.6	1.4	1.8	2.0	1.6	1.4	1.1	0.8	0.7	0.4
1988					2.1	2.4	2.5	1.9	1.5	1.2	0.9	0.7	0.4
1989						2.6	2.7	1.8	1.4	1.0	0.6	0.5	0.2
1990							2.8	1.4	1.0	0.6	0.3	0.2	–0.1
1991								–0.0	0.1	–0.2	–0.4	–0.3	–0.6
1992									0.2	–0.2	–0.5	–0.4	–0.7
1993										–0.7	–0.8	–0.6	–1.0
1994											–0.9	–0.6	–1.1
1995												–0.2	–1.1
1996													–2.1

Gross fixed capital formation (volume) / **Formation brute de capital fixe** (volume)

	1985	1986	1987	1988	1989	1990	1991	1992	1993	1994	1995	1996	1997
1984	5.2	2.7	4.5	5.0	6.3	5.4	3.2	1.4	–0.9	–0.6	0.5	0.8	0.3
1985		0.3	4.2	5.0	6.5	5.5	2.9	0.8	–1.6	–1.2	0.1	0.4	–0.1
1986			8.2	7.4	8.7	6.8	3.5	0.9	–1.9	–1.4	0.0	0.4	–0.1
1987				6.6	9.0	6.3	2.3	–0.5	–3.5	–2.7	–1.0	–0.4	–0.9
1988					11.3	6.2	0.9	–2.2	–5.4	–4.2	–2.0	–1.3	–1.7
1989						1.3	–3.9	–6.3	–9.2	–7.0	–4.0	–3.0	–3.2
1990							–8.9	–9.9	–12.4	–9.0	–5.1	–3.7	–3.8
1991								–10.8	–14.1	–9.0	–4.1	–2.6	–3.0
1992									–17.2	–8.1	–1.8	–0.4	–1.3
1993										2.0	7.0	5.9	3.1
1994											12.4	8.0	3.5
1995												3.7	–0.6
1996													–4.8

National disposable income (value) / **Revenu national disponible** (valeur)

	1985	1986	1987	1988	1989	1990	1991	1992	1993	1994	1995	1996	1997
1984	8.6	9.3	9.1	8.9	9.0	9.0	8.7	7.3	6.4	6.5	6.6	6.3	6.1
1985		10.1	9.4	9.0	9.1	9.1	8.7	7.2	6.1	6.2	6.4	6.1	5.9
1986			8.6	8.4	8.8	8.9	8.5	6.7	5.6	5.8	6.0	5.7	5.5
1987				8.2	8.9	9.0	8.4	6.3	5.1	5.4	5.7	5.4	5.2
1988					9.6	9.4	8.5	5.8	4.5	4.9	5.4	5.0	4.9
1989						9.2	8.0	4.6	3.2	4.0	4.7	4.4	4.3
1990							6.8	2.4	1.3	2.7	3.8	3.6	3.6
1991								–1.9	–1.3	1.4	3.1	3.0	3.1
1992									–0.7	3.0	4.8	4.2	4.1
1993										7.0	7.6	5.9	5.3
1994											8.3	5.4	4.8
1995												2.6	3.1
1996													3.7

Private final consumption expenditure per head (volume) / **Consommation finale privée par tête** (volume)

	1985	1986	1987	1988	1989	1990	1991	1992	1993	1994	1995	1996	1997
1984	2.5	3.3	3.6	3.2	2.7	2.0	1.8	1.3	0.7	0.8	0.7	0.7	0.8
1985		4.2	4.2	3.4	2.7	1.9	1.6	1.1	0.5	0.6	0.5	0.6	0.7
1986			4.2	3.1	2.2	1.3	1.1	0.6	–0.0	0.1	0.1	0.2	0.4
1987				2.0	1.2	0.4	0.4	–0.1	–0.7	–0.4	–0.4	–0.2	0.0
1988					0.5	–0.4	–0.1	–0.6	–1.2	–0.8	–0.7	–0.5	–0.2
1989						–1.3	–0.5	–1.0	–1.6	–1.1	–0.9	–0.6	–0.3
1990							0.3	–0.8	–1.8	–1.1	–0.8	–0.5	–0.1
1991								–2.0	–2.8	–1.5	–1.1	–0.6	–0.2
1992									–3.6	–1.3	–0.8	–0.3	0.1
1993										1.1	0.7	0.8	1.1
1994											0.3	0.7	1.1
1995												1.1	1.5
1996													2.0

Gross domestic product (implicit price deflator) / **Produit intérieur brut** (prix implicite)

	1985	1986	1987	1988	1989	1990	1991	1992	1993	1994	1995	1996	1997
1984	6.6	6.7	6.1	6.2	6.5	6.9	7.0	6.3	5.8	5.5	5.3	5.0	4.7
1985		6.9	5.8	6.0	6.5	7.0	7.1	6.2	5.7	5.4	5.2	4.8	4.5
1986			4.8	5.6	6.4	7.0	7.1	6.1	5.6	5.2	5.0	4.6	4.3
1987				6.5	7.3	7.8	7.7	6.4	5.7	5.3	5.1	4.6	4.3
1988					8.0	8.4	8.2	6.3	5.6	5.1	4.9	4.4	4.0
1989						8.8	8.2	5.8	5.0	4.5	4.3	3.9	3.5
1990							7.6	4.3	3.7	3.4	3.5	3.0	2.8
1991								1.0	1.8	2.0	2.4	2.2	2.0
1992									2.6	2.5	2.9	2.4	2.2
1993										2.5	3.1	2.4	2.1
1994											3.7	2.3	2.0
1995												1.0	1.1
1996													1.2

Private final consumption expenditure (implicit price deflator) / **Consommation finale privée** (prix implicite)

	1985	1986	1987	1988	1989	1990	1991	1992	1993	1994	1995	1996	1997
1984	7.0	6.1	5.9	6.0	6.2	6.8	7.3	6.6	6.5	6.2	5.8	5.4	5.2
1985		5.2	5.4	5.6	6.0	6.7	7.3	6.6	6.5	6.1	5.7	5.3	5.0
1986			5.6	5.8	6.2	7.1	7.8	6.8	6.7	6.2	5.8	5.3	5.0
1987				6.1	6.5	7.7	8.3	7.1	6.8	6.3	5.8	5.3	5.0
1988					7.0	8.5	9.1	7.3	7.0	6.3	5.8	5.2	4.9
1989						9.9	10.1	7.4	7.0	6.2	5.6	4.9	4.6
1990							10.3	6.2	6.0	5.2	4.7	4.1	3.9
1991								2.2	3.9	3.6	3.4	2.9	2.8
1992									5.7	4.3	3.8	3.1	2.9
1993										3.0	2.8	2.3	2.3
1994											2.7	1.9	2.0
1995												1.2	1.7
1996													2.2

Government final consumption expenditure (implicit price deflator) / **Consommation des administrations publiques** (prix implicite)

	1985	1986	1987	1988	1989	1990	1991	1992	1993	1994	1995	1996	1997
1984	5.9	6.1	5.4	5.4	6.1	7.1	6.6	6.0	5.4	5.2	5.0	4.9	4.8
1985		6.3	5.2	5.3	6.2	7.4	6.7	6.0	5.3	5.1	4.9	4.8	4.7
1986			4.1	4.8	6.1	7.7	6.7	6.0	5.2	4.9	4.7	4.7	4.6
1987				5.5	7.2	8.9	7.4	6.3	5.4	5.1	4.8	4.8	4.6
1988					8.8	10.6	8.1	6.5	5.3	5.0	4.7	4.7	4.5
1989						12.4	7.7	5.8	4.5	4.2	4.1	4.1	4.0
1990							3.1	2.6	2.0	2.3	2.5	2.8	2.9
1991								2.1	1.4	2.0	2.3	2.7	2.8
1992									0.7	1.9	2.4	2.8	3.0
1993										3.2	3.2	3.6	3.6
1994											3.3	3.8	3.7
1995												4.3	3.9
1996													3.5

Gross fixed capital formation (implicit price deflator) / **Formation brute de capital fixe** (prix implicite)

	1985	1986	1987	1988	1989	1990	1991	1992	1993	1994	1995	1996	1997
1984	6.7	5.7	5.2	5.6	6.1	6.2	6.0	5.0	4.6	4.1	3.9	3.6	3.3
1985		4.8	4.5	5.2	5.9	6.1	5.9	4.7	4.3	3.8	3.7	3.3	3.0
1986			4.2	5.4	6.3	6.4	6.1	4.7	4.3	3.7	3.5	3.2	2.9
1987				6.7	7.4	7.1	6.6	4.8	4.3	3.6	3.4	3.1	2.8
1988					8.1	7.4	6.6	4.4	3.8	3.1	3.0	2.6	2.3
1989						6.6	5.9	3.1	2.7	2.1	2.2	1.9	1.6
1990							5.2	1.4	1.5	1.1	1.3	1.1	1.0
1991								–2.2	–0.3	–0.3	0.3	0.3	0.3
1992									1.6	0.7	1.2	0.9	0.8
1993										–0.2	1.0	0.7	0.5
1994											2.2	1.2	0.8
1995												0.1	0.1
1996													0.1

Compensation of employees (value) / **Rémunération des salariés** (valeur)

	1985	1986	1987	1988	1989	1990	1991	1992	1993	1994	1995	1996	1997
1984	9.0	9.3	8.9	9.0	9.8	10.2	9.5	8.1	6.9	6.6	6.4	6.3	6.0
1985		9.6	8.9	9.0	9.9	10.5	9.6	7.9	6.7	6.3	6.1	6.1	5.8
1986			8.2	8.7	10.1	10.7	9.5	7.7	6.3	5.9	5.7	5.7	5.5
1987				9.2	11.0	11.5	9.9	7.5	5.9	5.6	5.4	5.5	5.2
1988					12.8	12.7	10.1	7.1	5.3	5.0	4.9	5.0	4.7
1989						12.5	8.8	5.3	3.5	3.5	3.6	3.9	3.8
1990							5.2	1.9	0.6	1.3	1.9	2.6	2.6
1991								–1.3	–1.6	0.1	1.1	2.1	2.2
1992									–1.8	0.8	1.9	2.9	2.9
1993										3.4	3.8	4.5	4.1
1994											4.2	5.1	4.3
1995												6.0	4.3
1996													2.7

SWITZERLAND

SUISSE

Average per cent changes at annual rate

Variations moyennes en p-urcentage aux taux annue s

G.D.P. per head (volume)
P.I.B. par tête (volume)

	1985	1986	1987	1988	1989	1990	1991	1992	1993	1994	1995	1996	1997
1984	3.0	2.0	1.3	1.6	2.0	2.1	1.5	1.2	0.9	0.8	0.7	0.6	0.7
1985		1.0	0.5	1.1	1.7	1.9	1.3	0.9	0.7	0.6	0.5	0.4	0.5
1986			0.0	1.2	1.9	2.1	1.3	0.9	0.6	0.5	0.4	0.4	0.5
1987				2.3	2.9	2.8	1.6	1.1	0.7	0.6	0.5	0.4	0.5
1988					3.5	3.1	1.4	0.8	0.4	0.3	0.2	0.2	0.3
1989						2.6	0.3	–0.2	–0.4	–0.4	–0.3	–0.3	–0.1
1990							–1.9	–1.5	–1.4	–1.1	–0.9	–0.8	–0.5
1991								–1.1	–1.1	–0.8	–0.6	–0.6	–0.2
1992									–1.1	–0.6	–0.5	–0.4	–0.0
1993										–0.2	–0.1	–0.2	0.3
1994											–0.1	–0.2	0.4
1995												–0.4	0.6
1996													1.7

Private final consumption expenditure per head (volume)
Consommation finale privée par tête (volume)

	1985	1986	1987	1988	1989	1990	1991	1992	1993	1994	1995	1996	1997
1984	1.2	1.5	1.5	1.3	1.4	1.2	1.1	0.8	0.6	0.5	0.5	0.5	[illegible]
1985		1.7	1.6	1.4	1.4	1.2	1.1	0.8	0.5	0.5	0.4	0.4	[illegible]
1986			1.5	1.2	1.3	1.0	0.9	0.6	0.3	0.3	0.3	0.3	[illegible]
1987				0.9	1.2	0.9	0.8	0.5	0.1	0.1	0.1	0.1	[illegible]
1988					1.6	0.8	0.7	0.3	–0.0	0.0	0.0	0.0	[illegible]
1989						0.1	0.3	–0.1	–0.4	–0.3	–0.3	–0.2	[illegible]
1990							0.6	–0.2	–0.6	–0.4	–0.3	–0.2	[illegible]
1991								–0.9	–1.2	–0.7	–0.5	–0.4	[illegible]
1992									–1.5	–0.6	–0.4	–0.3	[illegible]
1993										0.3	0.1	0.2	[illegible]
1994											–0.1	0.1	[illegible]
1995												0.2	[illegible]
1996													[illegible]

Gross domestic product (volume)
Produit intérieur brut (volume)

	1985	1986	1987	1988	1989	1990	1991	1992	1993	1994	1995	1996	1997
1984	3.4	2.5	1.9	2.2	2.6	2.8	2.3	2.0	1.7	1.6	1.5	1.4	1.4
1985		1.6	1.2	1.8	2.4	2.7	2.1	1.8	1.5	1.4	1.3	1.2	1.2
1986			0.7	1.9	2.7	3.0	2.2	1.8	1.5	1.4	1.3	1.1	1.2
1987				3.1	3.7	3.7	2.6	2.0	1.6	1.5	1.3	1.2	1.2
1988					4.3	4.0	2.4	1.8	1.3	1.2	1.1	0.9	1.0
1989						3.7	1.4	0.9	0.6	0.6	0.6	0.5	0.6
1990							–0.8	–0.5	–0.5	–0.2	–0.1	–0.1	0.2
1991								–0.1	–0.3	–0.0	0.1	0.1	0.4
1992									–0.5	0.0	0.2	0.1	0.5
1993										0.5	0.5	0.3	0.7
1994											0.6	0.3	0.7
1995												–0.0	0.8
1996													1.7

Gross domestic product (implicit price deflator)
Produit intérieur brut (prix implicite)

	1985	1986	1987	1988	1989	1990	1991	1992	1993	1994	1995	1996	1997
1984	2.4	2.7	2.7	2.8	2.8	3.1	3.5	3.4	3.3	3.1	3.0	2.7	[illegible]
1985		3.1	2.9	2.9	2.9	3.2	3.7	3.5	3.4	3.2	3.0	2.8	[illegible]
1986			2.7	2.8	2.9	3.2	3.8	3.6	3.5	3.2	3.0	2.7	[illegible]
1987				2.8	3.0	3.4	4.0	3.8	3.6	3.3	3.0	2.7	[illegible]
1988					3.1	3.7	4.4	4.0	3.7	3.4	3.1	2.7	[illegible]
1989						4.3	5.1	4.3	3.9	3.5	3.1	2.7	[illegible]
1990							6.0	4.4	3.8	3.3	2.8	2.4	[illegible]
1991								2.7	2.7	2.4	2.0	1.7	[illegible]
1992									2.7	2.2	1.8	1.5	[illegible]
1993										1.6	1.4	1.1	[illegible]
1994											1.1	0.8	[illegible]
1995												0.4	[illegible]
1996													[illegible]

Private final consumption expenditure (volume)
Consommation finale privée (volume)

	1985	1986	1987	1988	1989	1990	1991	1992	1993	1994	1995	1996	1997
1984	1.6	2.0	2.1	2.0	2.0	1.9	1.9	1.7	1.4	1.3	1.3	1.2	1.2
1985		2.3	2.3	2.1	2.1	2.0	1.9	1.7	1.3	1.3	1.2	1.2	1.2
1986			2.2	2.0	2.1	1.9	1.8	1.5	1.2	1.2	1.1	1.0	1.1
1987				1.7	2.0	1.8	1.7	1.4	1.0	1.0	1.0	0.9	1.0
1988					2.3	1.8	1.8	1.3	0.9	0.9	0.9	0.8	0.9
1989						1.2	1.5	1.0	0.5	0.6	0.6	0.6	0.7
1990							1.7	0.9	0.3	0.5	0.5	0.5	0.6
1991								0.1	–0.4	0.1	0.2	0.3	0.4
1992									–0.9	0.1	0.2	0.3	0.5
1993										1.0	0.8	0.7	0.8
1994											0.5	0.6	0.8
1995												0.6	0.9
1996													1.2

Private final consumption expenditure (implicit price deflator)
Consommation finale privée (prix implicite)

	1985	1986	1987	1988	1989	1990	1991	1992	1993	1994	1995	1996	1997
1984	3.3	2.3	2.0	2.0	2.2	2.7	3.2	3.3	3.3	3.1	3.0	2.8	[illegible]
1985		1.3	1.4	1.6	1.9	2.6	3.1	3.3	3.3	3.1	2.9	2.8	[illegible]
1986			1.5	1.7	2.1	2.9	3.5	3.6	3.6	3.3	3.1	2.9	[illegible]
1987				1.9	2.5	3.4	4.0	4.1	3.9	3.5	3.3	3.1	[illegible]
1988					3.0	4.1	4.7	4.6	4.3	3.8	3.5	3.2	[illegible]
1989						5.2	5.6	5.1	4.7	4.0	3.6	3.2	[illegible]
1990							6.0	5.1	4.5	3.7	3.3	2.9	[illegible]
1991								4.2	3.8	2.9	2.6	2.3	[illegible]
1992									3.4	2.3	2.1	1.8	[illegible]
1993										1.1	1.4	1.3	[illegible]
1994											1.7	1.4	[illegible]
1995												1.1	[illegible]
1996													[illegible]

Government final consumption expenditure (volume)
Consommation des administrations publiques (volume)

	1985	1986	1987	1988	1989	1990	1991	1992	1993	1994	1995	1996	1997
1984	3.3	3.3	2.7	3.2	3.6	3.9	3.8	3.4	3.0	2.9	2.6	2.5	2.3
1985		3.3	2.4	3.1	3.7	4.0	3.9	3.5	3.0	2.9	2.6	2.4	2.2
1986			1.6	3.0	3.8	4.2	4.0	3.5	3.0	2.8	2.5	2.4	2.1
1987				4.5	4.9	5.1	4.7	3.9	3.2	3.0	2.6	2.4	2.2
1988					5.3	5.4	4.7	3.7	2.9	2.8	2.3	2.2	1.9
1989						5.4	4.4	3.2	2.3	2.3	1.9	1.7	1.5
1990							3.4	2.1	1.3	1.5	1.2	1.1	0.9
1991								0.8	0.3	0.9	0.6	0.7	0.5
1992									–0.2	0.9	0.5	0.7	0.5
1993										2.1	0.9	1.0	0.7
1994											–0.2	0.4	0.2
1995												1.0	0.4
1996													–0.2

Government final consumption expenditure (implicit price deflator)
Consommation des administrations publiques (prix implicite)

	1985	1986	1987	1988	1989	1990	1991	1992	1993	1994	1995	1996	1997
1984	3.2	2.4	1.9	2.2	2.5	3.0	3.4	3.5	3.1	2.8	2.6	2.4	[illegible]
1985		1.7	1.3	1.8	2.3	2.9	3.4	3.5	3.1	2.8	2.5	2.4	[illegible]
1986			0.9	1.9	2.5	3.3	3.7	3.8	3.3	2.9	2.6	2.4	[illegible]
1987				3.0	3.4	4.1	4.5	4.4	3.7	3.2	2.8	2.6	[illegible]
1988					3.8	4.6	5.0	4.8	3.8	3.3	2.8	2.6	[illegible]
1989						5.4	5.6	5.1	3.8	3.1	2.7	2.4	[illegible]
1990							5.7	4.9	3.3	2.6	2.1	1.9	[illegible]
1991								4.1	2.1	1.5	1.2	1.1	[illegible]
1992									0.2	0.3	0.3	0.4	[illegible]
1993										0.4	0.4	0.5	[illegible]
1994											0.3	0.5	[illegible]
1995												0.7	[illegible]
1996													[illegible]

Gross fixed capital formation (volume)
Formation brute de capital fixe (volume)

	1985	1986	1987	1988	1989	1990	1991	1992	1993	1994	1995	1996	1997
1984	2.8	4.1	4.1	5.1	5.1	4.9	3.8	2.4	1.8	2.3	2.2	1.8	1.8
1985		5.4	4.7	5.8	5.7	5.3	3.9	2.3	1.7	2.2	2.2	1.7	1.7
1986			4.0	6.0	5.8	5.3	3.6	1.8	1.2	1.8	1.8	1.4	1.4
1987				8.1	6.7	5.7	3.5	1.4	0.7	1.5	1.6	1.1	1.1
1988					5.3	4.6	2.0	–0.2	–0.7	0.5	0.7	0.2	0.4
1989						3.8	0.4	–2.0	–2.1	–0.5	–0.1	–0.5	–0.2
1990							–2.9	–4.7	–4.1	–1.5	–0.9	–1.2	–0.8
1991								–6.6	–4.7	–1.1	–0.4	–0.8	–0.5
1992									–2.7	1.8	1.8	0.6	0.8
1993										6.5	4.1	1.8	1.7
1994											1.8	–0.5	0.2
1995												–2.7	–0.6
1996													1.5

Gross fixed capital formation (implicit price deflator)
Formation brute de capital fixe (prix implicite)

	1985	1986	1987	1988	1989	1990	1991	1992	1993	1994	1995	1996	1997
1984	3.4	2.4	2.0	2.4	2.8	2.8	2.7	2.2	1.8	1.4	1.0	0.7	[illegible]
1985		1.4	1.3	2.1	2.7	2.7	2.6	2.1	1.6	1.2	0.8	0.5	[illegible]
1986			1.1	2.4	3.1	3.0	2.8	2.2	1.7	1.2	0.7	0.4	[illegible]
1987				3.6	4.2	3.7	3.2	2.4	1.7	1.2	0.6	0.3	[illegible]
1988					4.7	3.7	3.1	2.1	1.4	0.8	0.2	–0.1	[illegible]
1989						2.8	2.3	1.2	0.6	0.0	–0.5	–0.8	[illegible]
1990							1.9	0.5	–0.2	–0.6	–1.1	–1.4	[illegible]
1991								–0.9	–1.2	–1.5	–1.9	–2.0	[illegible]
1992									–1.4	–1.7	–2.2	–2.3	[illegible]
1993										–2.0	–2.6	–2.6	[illegible]
1994											–3.1	–2.9	[illegible]
1995												–2.6	[illegible]
1996													[illegible]

National disposable income (value)
Revenu national disponible (valeur)

	1985	1986	1987	1988	1989	1990	1991	1992	1993	1994	1995	1996	1997
1984	5.3	4.5	3.9	4.5	4.8	5.2	5.1	4.7	4.5	4.2	4.2	3.9	3.8
1985		3.7	3.2	4.2	4.7	5.2	5.1	4.6	4.4	4.1	4.1	3.7	3.7
1986			2.7	4.5	5.1	5.6	5.4	4.8	4.5	4.1	4.1	3.8	3.7
1987				6.4	6.3	6.6	6.1	5.2	4.8	4.4	4.3	3.9	3.8
1988					6.3	6.7	5.9	4.9	4.5	4.0	4.0	3.6	3.6
1989						7.1	5.8	4.5	4.1	3.6	3.6	3.2	3.2
1990							4.4	3.2	3.1	2.7	2.9	2.5	2.7
1991								1.9	2.4	2.1	2.5	2.2	2.4
1992									2.9	2.2	2.7	2.2	2.5
1993										1.6	2.7	2.0	2.4
1994											3.8	2.2	2.7
1995												0.7	2.1
1996													3.5

Compensation of employees (value)
Rémunération des salariés (valeur)

	1985	1986	1987	1988	1989	1990	1991	1992	1993	1994	1995	1996	1997
1984	6.1	6.2	5.8	6.0	6.2	6.7	6.8	6.3	5.7	5.2	4.9	4.6	[illegible]
1985		6.3	5.7	5.9	6.3	6.8	6.9	6.4	5.7	5.1	4.8	4.4	[illegible]
1986			5.1	5.7	6.2	6.9	7.0	6.4	5.6	5.0	4.7	4.2	[illegible]
1987				6.3	6.8	7.6	7.5	6.6	5.6	4.9	4.6	4.1	[illegible]
1988					7.3	8.2	7.9	6.7	5.5	4.7	4.4	3.9	[illegible]
1989						9.1	8.2	6.5	5.1	4.2	3.9	3.4	[illegible]
1990							7.4	5.3	3.8	3.0	2.9	2.5	[illegible]
1991								3.2	2.0	1.6	1.8	1.5	[illegible]
1992									0.8	0.8	1.3	1.1	[illegible]
1993										0.9	1.6	1.2	[illegible]
1994											2.3	1.3	[illegible]
1995												0.4	[illegible]
1996													[illegible]

TURKEY

TURQUIE

Average per cent changes at annual rate

Variations moyennes en pourcentage aux taux annuels

G.D.P. per head (volume)
P.I.B. par tête (volume)

	1985	1986	1987	1988	1989	1990	1991	1992	1993	1994	1995	1996	1997
1984	1.7	3.2	4.5	3.3	2.3	3.0	2.4	2.6	3.0	1.9	2.2	2.5	2.7
1985		4.7	5.9	3.9	2.4	3.2	2.5	2.7	3.1	1.9	2.3	2.5	2.8
1986			7.1	3.5	1.6	2.9	2.1	2.4	2.9	1.6	2.0	2.3	2.6
1987				−0.1	−1.0	1.5	0.9	1.5	2.2	0.8	1.4	1.8	2.2
1988					−1.9	2.3	1.2	1.9	2.7	1.0	1.6	2.0	2.5
1989						6.7	2.8	3.2	3.9	1.6	2.2	2.6	3.0
1990							−1.0	1.5	3.0	0.3	1.3	2.0	2.5
1991								4.0	5.0	0.8	1.9	2.6	3.1
1992									6.1	−0.8	1.2	2.2	2.9
1993										−7.1	−1.1	1.0	2.1
1994											5.3	5.3	5.4
1995												5.2	5.5
1996													5.8

Private final consumption expenditure per head (volume)
Consommation finale privée par tête (volume)

	1985	1986	1987	1988	1989	1990	1991	1992	1993	1994	1995	1996	1997
1984	−3.1	0.2	−0.7	−0.8	−1.3	0.6	0.6	0.7	1.3	0.5	0.7	1.2	1.6
1985		3.5	0.5	0.0	−0.8	1.4	1.3	1.3	1.9	0.9	1.1	1.6	2.0
1986			−2.5	−1.7	−2.2	0.8	0.8	0.9	1.7	0.5	0.8	1.4	1.9
1987				−1.0	−2.1	1.9	1.6	1.6	2.4	1.0	1.2	1.8	2.3
1988					−3.2	3.4	2.5	2.2	3.1	1.3	1.6	2.2	2.7
1989						10.5	5.5	4.1	4.7	2.2	2.4	3.0	3.4
1990							0.7	1.0	2.8	0.3	0.8	1.8	2.4
1991								1.3	3.9	0.1	0.8	2.0	2.7
1992									6.6	−0.5	0.7	2.1	3.0
1993										−7.1	−2.2	0.7	2.1
1994											3.0	4.8	5.4
1995												6.7	6.6
1996													6.6

Gross domestic product (volume)
Produit intérieur brut (volume)

	1985	1986	1987	1988	1989	1990	1991	1992	1993	1994	1995	1996	1997
1984	4.2	5.6	6.9	5.7	4.6	5.3	4.7	4.9	5.2	4.1	4.4	4.6	4.8
1985		7.0	8.2	6.2	4.7	5.6	4.8	4.9	5.3	4.1	4.4	4.6	4.9
1986			9.5	5.7	3.9	5.2	4.3	4.6	5.1	3.7	4.1	4.4	4.7
1987				2.1	1.2	3.8	3.1	3.7	4.4	2.9	3.4	3.8	4.2
1988					0.3	4.7	3.4	4.0	4.8	3.0	3.6	4.0	4.4
1989						9.3	5.0	5.3	6.0	3.6	4.2	4.6	5.0
1990							0.9	3.4	4.9	2.2	3.2	3.8	4.4
1991								6.0	7.0	2.7	3.8	4.4	4.9
1992									8.0	1.1	3.1	4.0	4.7
1993										−5.5	0.7	2.7	3.9
1994											7.2	7.1	7.2
1995												7.0	7.3
1996													7.5

Gross domestic product (implicit price deflator)
Produit intérieur brut (prix implicite)

	1985	1986	1987	1988	1989	1990	1991	1992	1993	1994	1995	1996	1997
1984	53.1	44.3	40.6	47.3	52.6	53.5	54.2	55.4	56.7	61.1	63.3	64.5	65.7
1985		36.0	34.8	45.5	52.4	53.6	54.4	55.7	57.2	62.0	64.4	65.6	66.8
1986			33.6	50.4	58.3	58.3	58.4	59.3	60.5	65.6	67.9	68.9	70.0
1987				69.4	72.4	67.5	65.3	65.0	65.5	70.8	72.7	73.3	74.1
1988					75.5	66.6	64.0	63.9	64.7	71.0	73.2	73.8	74.6
1989						58.3	58.5	60.3	62.1	70.1	72.9	73.6	74.5
1990							58.8	61.3	63.4	73.2	75.9	76.3	77.0
1991								63.7	65.7	78.3	80.5	80.0	80.2
1992									67.8	86.1	86.5	84.3	83.7
1993										106.5	96.6	90.1	87.9
1994											87.2	82.5	82.2
1995												77.8	79.7
1996													81.5

Private final consumption expenditure (volume)
Consommation finale privée (volume)

	1985	1986	1987	1988	1989	1990	1991	1992	1993	1994	1995	1996	1997
1984	−0.6	2.6	1.6	1.5	1.0	2.9	2.9	2.9	3.5	2.6	2.8	3.3	3.7
1985		5.8	2.7	2.2	1.4	3.6	3.5	3.4	4.1	3.0	3.2	3.6	4.0
1986			−0.3	0.4	−0.0	3.1	3.0	3.0	3.8	2.6	2.9	3.4	3.9
1987				1.2	0.1	4.2	3.9	3.7	4.5	3.1	3.3	3.8	4.3
1988					−1.0	5.8	4.8	4.4	5.2	3.4	3.6	4.2	4.6
1989						13.1	7.8	6.2	6.8	4.3	4.4	4.9	5.4
1990							2.7	3.0	4.8	2.2	2.7	3.6	4.3
1991								3.2	5.9	2.0	2.7	3.8	4.6
1992									8.6	1.4	2.5	4.0	4.8
1993										−5.4	−0.4	2.5	3.9
1994											4.8	6.6	7.2
1995												8.5	8.4
1996													8.4

Private final consumption expenditure (implicit price deflator)
Consommation finale privée (prix implicite)

	1985	1986	1987	1988	1989	1990	1991	1992	1993	1994	1995	1996	1997
1984	50.9	40.2	43.0	46.8	53.6	54.6	55.4	56.7	57.7	62.2	64.7	65.0	66.2
1985		30.4	39.3	45.5	54.2	55.3	56.2	57.5	58.5	63.5	66.2	66.3	67.6
1986			48.8	53.8	63.1	62.3	62.0	62.6	63.0	68.2	70.7	70.4	71.4
1987				58.9	70.8	67.1	65.5	65.5	65.5	71.1	73.7	73.0	73.9
1988					83.7	71.3	67.7	67.2	66.9	73.3	75.9	74.8	75.6
1989						59.8	60.2	62.0	63.0	71.3	74.6	73.6	74.7
1990							60.7	63.1	64.0	74.2	77.7	76.0	76.9
1991								65.6	65.7	79.0	82.3	79.3	79.7
1992									65.9	86.1	88.2	82.9	82.7
1993										108.9	100.5	88.9	87.2
1994											92.4	79.7	80.5
1995												67.8	74.8
1996													82.1

Government final consumption expenditure (volume)
Consommation des administrations publiques (volume)

	1985	1986	1987	1988	1989	1990	1991	1992	1993	1994	1995	1996	1997
1984	14.1	11.7	10.9	7.8	6.4	6.6	6.2	5.9	6.2	4.9	5.1	5.4	5.3
1985		9.2	9.3	5.8	4.5	5.2	4.9	4.7	5.2	4.0	4.2	4.6	4.6
1986			9.4	4.1	3.0	4.2	4.1	4.0	4.7	3.3	3.7	4.2	4.2
1987				−1.1	−0.1	2.5	2.8	3.0	3.9	2.5	3.0	3.6	3.7
1988					0.8	4.3	4.1	4.0	4.9	3.1	3.6	4.2	4.2
1989						8.0	5.8	5.1	5.9	3.5	4.1	4.7	4.6
1990							3.7	3.6	5.3	2.5	3.3	4.2	4.2
1991								3.6	6.1	2.1	3.2	4.3	4.2
1992									8.6	1.3	3.1	4.4	4.4
1993										−5.5	0.5	3.1	3.4
1994											6.8	7.7	6.5
1995												8.6	6.3
1996													4.1

Government final consumption expenditure (implicit price deflator)
Consommation des administrations publiques (prix implicite)

	1985	1986	1987	1988	1989	1990	1991	1992	1993	1994	1995	1996	1997
1984	40.0	36.9	29.7	38.8	51.4	56.9	59.3	61.1	62.0	64.1	65.0	66.8	69.0
1985		33.9	24.8	38.4	54.3	60.5	62.8	64.3	64.9	67.0	67.7	69.5	71.7
1986			16.3	40.7	61.8	68.0	69.2	70.0	69.9	71.7	71.9	73.5	75.6
1987				70.1	90.9	89.8	85.9	83.5	81.0	81.5	80.6	81.4	83.0
1988					114.2	100.6	91.4	87.0	83.2	83.5	82.1	82.8	84.5
1989						87.8	81.0	78.7	76.2	77.9	77.2	78.7	81.1
1990							74.4	74.3	72.5	75.5	75.2	77.3	80.2
1991								74.2	71.6	75.9	75.4	77.9	81.2
1992									69.1	76.8	75.8	78.8	82.6
1993										84.8	79.3	82.2	86.1
1994											73.9	80.8	86.6
1995												88.0	93.2
1996													98.6

Gross fixed capital formation (volume)
Formation brute de capital fixe (volume)

	1985	1986	1987	1988	1989	1990	1991	1992	1993	1994	1995	1996	1997
1984	11.5	9.9	20.6	14.8	12.1	12.8	10.9	10.3	12.0	8.8	8.9	9.3	9.7
1985		8.4	25.4	15.9	12.3	13.0	10.8	10.2	12.1	8.5	8.6	9.1	9.6
1986			45.1	19.8	13.6	14.2	11.3	10.5	12.6	8.6	8.6	9.2	9.7
1987				−1.0	0.6	5.4	4.2	4.6	7.9	4.1	4.8	5.8	6.6
1988					2.2	8.8	6.0	6.1	9.8	5.0	5.6	6.6	7.5
1989						15.9	7.9	7.4	11.8	5.6	6.2	7.3	8.2
1990							0.4	3.4	10.5	3.2	4.4	5.9	7.1
1991								6.4	15.9	4.1	5.4	7.1	8.3
1992									26.4	3.0	5.0	7.2	8.7
1993										−16.0	−4.2	1.5	4.7
1994											9.1	11.6	12.7
1995												14.1	14.5
1996													14.8

Gross fixed capital formation (implicit price deflator)
Formation brute de capital fixe (prix implicite)

	1985	1986	1987	1988	1989	1990	1991	1992	1993	1994	1995	1996	1997
1984	64.7	59.1	36.3	47.0	47.6	48.0	50.5	51.8	52.8	58.2	59.9	61.1	62.4
1985		53.7	24.0	41.5	43.7	44.8	48.2	50.1	51.4	57.5	59.4	60.8	62.3
1986			−0.0	35.8	40.5	42.7	47.1	49.5	51.1	57.9	60.1	61.6	63.1
1987				84.4	66.5	60.7	62.1	62.0	61.8	68.6	69.8	70.4	71.2
1988					50.3	50.0	55.3	56.9	57.7	66.1	67.8	68.7	69.8
1989						49.7	57.8	59.1	59.6	69.5	70.9	71.5	72.5
1990							66.3	64.0	63.0	74.8	75.5	75.5	76.0
1991								61.8	61.4	77.8	77.8	77.4	77.6
1992									60.9	86.3	83.5	81.5	81.0
1993										115.7	95.9	88.9	86.4
1994											78.0	76.8	77.5
1995												75.6	77.3
1996													79.0

National disposable income (value)
Revenu national disponible (valeur)

	1985	1986	1987	1988	1989	1990	1991	1992	1993	1994	1995	1996	1997
1984	59.5	52.0	49.3	54.5	59.4	61.7	61.3	62.8	64.9	67.4	70.4	72.0	73.7
1985		44.8	44.5	52.9	59.3	62.1	61.6	63.3	65.5	68.3	71.5	73.2	75.0
1986			44.2	57.2	64.5	66.7	65.2	66.7	68.7	71.5	74.7	76.3	78.0
1987				71.3	75.7	75.0	70.9	71.5	73.2	75.8	79.0	80.3	81.8
1988					80.2	76.9	70.8	71.6	73.6	76.5	80.1	81.4	83.0
1989						73.6	66.2	68.8	72.0	75.8	80.1	81.6	83.4
1990							59.1	66.5	71.4	76.3	81.4	83.0	84.8
1991								74.2	77.9	82.5	87.5	88.2	89.5
1992									81.8	86.8	92.1	91.9	92.7
1993										92.0	97.5	95.3	95.6
1994											103.2	97.0	96.8
1995												91.0	93.6
1996													96.2

Compensation of employees (value)
Rémunération des salariés (valeur)

	1985	1986	1987	1988	1989	1990	1991	1992	1993	1994	1995	1996	1997
1984	55.7	49.1	51.3	57.9	64.9	69.7	72.2	72.2	72.7	71.6	71.8	74.6	76.1
1985		42.8	49.2	58.6	67.3	72.7	75.1	74.7	75.0	73.4	73.5	76.4	77.9
1986			55.8	67.2	76.4	81.1	82.4	80.7	80.1	77.7	77.3	80.2	81.5
1987				79.4	87.7	90.4	89.7	86.1	84.5	81.0	80.2	83.1	84.3
1988					96.4	96.1	93.3	87.8	85.6	81.3	80.3	83.6	84.8
1989						95.8	91.7	85.1	82.9	78.4	77.7	81.8	83.4
1990							87.7	79.9	78.9	74.3	74.3	79.6	81.8
1991								72.5	74.6	70.1	71.1	78.0	80.8
1992									76.7	68.9	70.7	79.4	82.5
1993										61.4	67.8	80.3	83.9
1994											74.3	90.6	92.1
1995												108.4	101.7
1996													95.2

UNITED KINGDOM

ROYAUME-UNI

Average per cent changes at annual rate

Variations moyennes en pourcentage aux taux annuels

G.D.P. per head (volume)
P.I.B. par tête (volume)

	1985	1986	1987	1988	1989	1990	1991	1992	1993	1994	1995	1996	1997
1984	3.2	3.6	3.9	4.1	3.7	3.0	2.2	1.9	1.8	2.0	2.1	2.1	2.1
1985		4.1	4.3	4.4	3.8	3.0	2.1	1.7	1.7	1.9	2.0	2.0	2.1
1986			4.5	4.6	3.7	2.7	1.7	1.3	1.3	1.7	1.7	1.8	1.9
1987				4.7	3.3	2.2	1.0	0.6	0.8	1.3	1.4	1.5	1.6
1988					1.8	0.9	–0.2	–0.4	0.1	0.7	0.9	1.1	1.3
1989						0.0	–1.2	–1.1	–0.4	0.5	0.8	1.0	1.2
1990							–2.4	–1.6	–0.5	0.6	0.9	1.1	1.4
1991								–0.9	0.4	1.6	1.8	1.8	2.0
1992									1.7	2.8	2.7	2.5	2.6
1993										4.0	3.2	2.8	2.8
1994											2.4	2.2	2.5
1995												2.0	2.5
1996													3.0

Private final consumption expenditure per head (volume)
Consommation finale privée par tête (volume)

	1985	1986	1987	1988	1989	1990	1991	1992	1993	1994	1995	1996	1997
1984	3.5	5.0	5.0	5.6	5.0	4.2	3.2	2.7	2.7	2.7	2.5	2.6	2.7
1985		6.5	5.8	6.3	5.4	4.3	3.2	2.6	2.6	2.6	2.4	2.5	2.6
1986			5.0	6.1	5.0	3.8	2.5	2.0	2.0	2.1	2.0	2.1	2.3
1987				7.2	5.0	3.4	1.9	1.4	1.5	1.7	1.6	1.8	2.0
1988					2.9	1.5	0.1	–0.0	0.4	0.8	0.8	1.1	1.5
1989						0.3	–1.2	–0.9	–0.2	0.3	0.5	0.9	1.3
1990							–2.6	–1.5	–0.3	0.4	0.6	1.0	1.5
1991								–0.4	0.9	1.4	1.4	1.7	2.1
1992									2.2	2.3	2.0	2.3	2.7
1993										2.4	1.9	2.3	2.8
1994											1.4	2.2	2.9
1995												3.1	3.7
1996													4.2

Gross domestic product (volume)
Produit intérieur brut (volume)

	1985	1986	1987	1988	1989	1990	1991	1992	1993	1994	1995	1996	1997
1984	3.5	4.0	4.2	4.4	4.0	3.4	2.6	2.2	2.2	2.4	2.4	2.4	2.5
1985		4.4	4.6	4.7	4.1	3.3	2.4	2.0	2.0	2.3	2.3	2.3	2.4
1986			4.8	4.9	4.0	3.1	2.0	1.6	1.7	2.0	2.1	2.1	2.2
1987				5.0	3.6	2.5	1.4	1.0	1.2	1.6	1.7	1.8	2.0
1988					2.2	1.3	0.2	0.0	0.4	1.1	1.3	1.4	1.6
1989						0.4	–0.8	–0.7	–0.0	0.8	1.1	1.3	1.6
1990							–2.0	–1.3	–0.2	0.9	1.3	1.5	1.7
1991								–0.5	0.8	1.9	2.1	2.2	2.4
1992									2.1	3.2	3.0	2.9	3.0
1993										4.3	3.5	3.1	3.2
1994											2.8	2.5	2.8
1995												2.3	2.8
1996													3.4

Gross domestic product (implicit price deflator)
Produit intérieur brut (prix implicite)

	1985	1986	1987	1988	1989	1990	1991	1992	1993	1994	1995	1996	1997
1984	5.9	4.5	4.7	5.0	5.4	5.6	5.7	5.6	5.3	4.9	4.7	4.6	4.4
1985		3.2	4.1	4.7	5.3	5.5	5.7	5.6	5.3	4.8	4.6	4.5	4.3
1986			5.0	5.5	6.1	6.1	6.2	6.0	5.6	5.1	4.8	4.6	4.4
1987				6.1	6.6	6.5	6.5	6.1	5.6	5.1	4.7	4.5	4.3
1988					7.1	6.8	6.7	6.2	5.6	4.9	4.5	4.3	4.1
1989						6.4	6.5	5.9	5.2	4.5	4.1	4.0	3.8
1990							6.6	5.6	4.8	4.0	3.7	3.6	3.4
1991								4.6	3.9	3.1	3.0	3.0	2.9
1992									3.2	2.4	2.4	2.6	2.6
1993										1.6	2.0	2.4	2.4
1994											2.4	2.7	2.7
1995												3.0	2.8
1996													2.5

Private final consumption expenditure (volume)
Consommation finale privée (volume)

	1985	1986	1987	1988	1989	1990	1991	1992	1993	1994	1995	1996	1997
1984	3.8	5.3	5.3	5.9	5.3	4.5	3.5	3.1	3.0	3.0	2.9	2.9	3.1
1985		6.8	6.1	6.6	5.7	4.7	3.5	3.0	2.9	2.9	2.8	2.8	3.0
1986			5.3	6.4	5.3	4.1	2.8	2.3	2.4	2.4	2.3	2.5	2.6
1987				7.5	5.3	3.7	2.2	1.8	1.9	2.0	2.0	2.1	2.4
1988					3.2	1.9	0.5	0.4	0.8	1.1	1.2	1.5	1.8
1989						0.6	–0.8	–0.6	0.2	0.7	0.9	1.2	1.7
1990							–2.2	–1.1	0.1	0.7	0.9	1.4	1.8
1991								–0.1	1.2	1.7	1.7	2.1	2.5
1992									2.5	2.6	2.3	2.6	3.0
1993										2.8	2.3	2.7	3.1
1994											1.7	2.6	3.3
1995												3.5	4.0
1996													4.6

Private final consumption expenditure (implicit price deflator)
Consommation finale privée (prix implicite)

	1985	1986	1987	1988	1989	1990	1991	1992	1993	1994	1995	1996	1997
1984	5.3	4.6	4.5	4.7	4.9	5.0	5.4	5.3	5.1	4.8	4.6	4.4	4.3
1985		4.0	4.2	4.5	4.8	5.0	5.4	5.3	5.1	4.8	4.6	4.4	4.2
1986			4.3	4.7	5.1	5.2	5.7	5.6	5.2	4.9	4.6	4.4	4.2
1987				5.0	5.5	5.5	6.0	5.8	5.4	4.9	4.6	4.4	4.2
1988					5.9	5.7	6.3	6.0	5.5	4.9	4.6	4.3	4.1
1989						5.5	6.5	6.0	5.4	4.7	4.4	4.1	3.9
1990							7.5	6.3	5.3	4.5	4.1	3.9	3.6
1991								5.0	4.2	3.5	3.3	3.2	3.0
1992									3.4	2.8	2.7	2.7	2.6
1993										2.2	2.4	2.5	2.4
1994											2.6	2.6	2.4
1995												2.6	2.3
1996													2.1

Government final consumption expenditure (volume)
Consommation des administrations publiques (volume)

	1985	1986	1987	1988	1989	1990	1991	1992	1993	1994	1995	1996	1997
1984	–0.1	0.8	0.8	0.8	0.9	1.2	1.4	1.2	1.0	1.2	1.2	1.3	1.2
1985		1.6	1.3	1.1	1.2	1.4	1.6	1.4	1.2	1.3	1.3	1.4	1.3
1986			1.0	0.8	1.0	1.4	1.6	1.3	1.1	1.3	1.3	1.4	1.3
1987				0.7	1.1	1.5	1.8	1.4	1.1	1.3	1.3	1.4	1.3
1988					1.4	2.0	2.2	1.6	1.2	1.4	1.4	1.5	1.4
1989						2.5	2.6	1.7	1.2	1.4	1.4	1.5	1.4
1990							2.6	1.2	0.8	1.1	1.1	1.4	1.2
1991								–0.1	–0.1	0.6	0.8	1.1	1.0
1992									–0.2	1.0	1.1	1.4	1.2
1993										2.2	1.7	1.9	1.5
1994											1.3	1.8	1.3
1995												2.4	1.3
1996													0.2

Government final consumption expenditure (implicit price deflator)
Consommation des administrations publiques (prix implicite)

	1985	1986	1987	1988	1989	1990	1991	1992	1993	1994	1995	1996	1997
1984	5.8	5.8	6.0	6.2	6.4	6.7	6.8	6.7	6.5	6.1	5.7	5.4	5.1
1985		5.8	6.2	6.4	6.6	6.9	6.9	6.9	6.6	6.1	5.7	5.4	5.1
1986			6.5	6.7	6.9	7.2	7.2	7.0	6.7	6.1	5.7	5.3	5.0
1987				6.8	7.0	7.4	7.3	7.1	6.7	6.1	5.6	5.2	4.8
1988					7.2	7.7	7.5	7.2	6.7	6.0	5.4	5.0	4.6
1989						8.2	7.7	7.2	6.6	5.7	5.1	4.7	4.3
1990							7.1	6.7	6.0	5.1	4.5	4.1	3.8
1991								6.4	5.5	4.4	3.9	3.5	3.2
1992									4.6	3.5	3.1	2.8	2.6
1993										2.3	2.3	2.2	2.1
1994											2.3	2.1	2.0
1995												2.0	1.8
1996													1.7

Gross fixed capital formation (volume)
Formation brute de capital fixe (volume)

	1985	1986	1987	1988	1989	1990	1991	1992	1993	1994	1995	1996	1997
1984	4.2	3.4	5.7	7.7	7.3	5.4	3.2	2.6	2.4	2.6	2.5	2.4	2.6
1985		2.6	6.4	8.8	8.1	5.7	3.0	2.3	2.1	2.4	2.3	2.2	2.5
1986			10.3	12.1	10.0	6.5	3.1	2.3	2.1	2.4	2.3	2.2	2.5
1987				13.9	9.9	5.2	1.3	0.8	0.8	1.3	1.3	1.3	1.7
1988					6.0	1.1	–2.5	–2.3	–1.7	–0.7	–0.4	–0.1	0.5
1989						–3.5	–6.5	–4.9	–3.5	–2.0	–1.4	–1.0	–0.2
1990							–9.5	–5.5	–3.5	–1.6	–1.0	–0.5	0.3
1991								–1.5	–0.4	1.1	1.2	1.3	2.0
1992									0.6	2.5	2.1	2.1	2.7
1993										4.3	2.9	2.5	3.2
1994											1.5	1.6	2.8
1995												1.8	3.5
1996													5.2

Gross fixed capital formation (implicit price deflator)
Formation brute de capital fixe (prix implicite)

	1985	1986	1987	1988	1989	1990	1991	1992	1993	1994	1995	1996	1997
1984	5.6	5.0	4.9	5.4	6.1	6.0	5.2	4.1	3.7	3.5	3.8	3.8	3.6
1985		4.4	4.6	5.4	6.2	6.1	5.1	3.9	3.4	3.3	3.6	3.6	3.4
1986			4.7	5.8	6.8	6.5	5.2	3.9	3.3	3.1	3.5	3.5	3.3
1987				6.9	7.8	7.1	5.4	3.7	3.1	2.9	3.4	3.4	3.2
1988					8.7	7.2	4.9	2.9	2.3	2.3	2.9	3.0	2.8
1989						5.7	3.0	1.0	0.8	1.0	2.0	2.2	2.1
1990							0.4	–1.2	–0.8	–0.1	1.2	1.6	1.6
1991								–2.8	–1.4	–0.3	1.5	1.9	1.8
1992									0.1	1.0	2.9	3.1	2.7
1993										1.9	4.4	4.1	3.4
1994											6.9	5.2	3.8
1995												3.5	2.4
1996													1.2

National disposable income (value)
Revenu national disponible (valeur)

	1985	1986	1987	1988	1989	1990	1991	1992	1993	1994	1995	1996	1997
1984	9.2	8.6	9.0	9.5	9.5	8.9	8.4	7.9	7.7	7.5	7.3	7.2	7.1
1985		8.1	8.9	9.7	9.6	8.8	8.2	7.8	7.5	7.4	7.1	7.0	6.9
1986			9.6	10.4	10.1	9.0	8.3	7.7	7.4	7.3	7.0	6.9	6.8
1987				11.2	10.3	8.8	7.9	7.3	7.0	6.9	6.7	6.6	6.6
1988					9.3	7.6	6.9	6.4	6.2	6.2	6.0	6.0	6.1
1989						5.9	5.7	5.4	5.4	5.6	5.5	5.6	5.7
1990							5.4	5.2	5.3	5.6	5.4	5.5	5.6
1991								5.0	5.2	5.6	5.4	5.5	5.7
1992									5.5	6.0	5.6	5.6	5.8
1993										6.4	5.6	5.7	5.9
1994											4.8	5.3	5.7
1995												5.9	6.1
1996													6.4

Compensation of employees (value)
Rémunération des salariés (valeur)

	1985	1986	1987	1988	1989	1990	1991	1992	1993	1994	1995	1996	1997
1984	8.5	8.2	8.3	9.0	9.4	9.7	9.0	8.3	7.6	7.2	7.0	6.8	6.8
1985		7.9	8.1	9.2	9.7	9.9	9.1	8.2	7.5	7.1	6.8	6.7	6.6
1986			8.4	9.9	10.3	10.4	9.3	8.3	7.5	7.0	6.7	6.5	6.5
1987				11.4	11.2	11.1	9.6	8.3	7.3	6.8	6.5	6.3	6.3
1988					11.1	10.9	9.0	7.5	6.5	6.0	5.8	5.7	5.8
1989						10.7	7.9	6.3	5.4	5.1	5.0	5.0	5.2
1990							5.2	4.2	3.7	3.7	3.9	4.0	4.4
1991								3.2	2.9	3.2	3.5	3.8	4.3
1992									2.6	3.2	3.6	4.0	4.5
1993										3.8	4.1	4.4	4.9
1994											4.5	4.7	5.3
1995												5.0	5.7
1996													6.5

Comparative tables based on exchange rates
Tableaux comparatifs basés sur les taux de change

The statistics for Germany in this publication refer to Germany after unification. Official data for Germany after unification are available only from 1991 onwards. In this publication, the secretariat has estimated some national accounts aggregates for the whole of Germany back to 1960 in order to calculate the various zones totals. These estimates are based on statistics published by Deutsches Institut für Wirtschaftsforschung for period 1989-90 and by the East German Statistical Office in 1990 for period 1980-89. They are also based on the ratios of the aggregates of West Germany and the whole of Germany.

Les statistiques concernant l'Allemagne dans cette publication se réfèrent à l'Allemagne après l'unification. Des données officielles pour l'Allemagne après l'unification ne sont disponibles qu'à partir de 1991. Dans cette publication, le secrétariat a estimé certains agrégats des comptes nationaux pour l'Allemagne dans son ensemble depuis 1960 afin de calculer les différentes zones. Ces estimations sont basées sur des statistiques publiées par Deutsches Institut für Wirtschaftsforschung pour la période 1989-90 et par l'Office Statistique de l'Allemagne de l'Est en 1990 pour la période 1980-89. Elles sont aussi basées sur les rapports des agrégats de l'Allemagne occidentale et de l'Allemagne dans son ensemble.

CALCULATION PROCEDURES

The following points should be borne in mind in using the tables in Part VI of this volume.

a) The various aggregates shown in tables 1 to 18 have been calculated by three different methods: *at current prices and 1990 exchange rates* (Tables 1-6); *at 1990 prices and 1990 exchange rates* (Tables 7-12); and *at current prices and current exchange rates* (Tables 13-18). By using 1990 exchange rates throughout, the year to year movements in the data for a given country or group of countries shown in Tables 1-6 are determined entirely by movements in the national data at current prices. Year to year movements in the data in Tables 13 to 18, however, are liable to be strongly influenced by fluctuations in exchange rates as well as by movements in the national data at current prices. The data in Tables 13 to 18 are, therefore, only suitable for comparisons between countries within a single year, and not for comparisons between years for the same country, or group of countries.

b) In the tables giving *volume and price indices* all series are shown with 1990 = 100. In practice many countries use a year before 1990 as their base year for calculating volume and price indices, and the indices shown for these countries (and for groups of countries) are therefore based on the relative prices or quantities of years prior to 1990. The base years used by Member countries are indicated in the country tables where they differ from 1990.

c) the volume indices for *groups of countries* are arithmetic, weighted averages of the component indices using as weights the 1990 value of the aggregate concerned (GDP, private final consumption expenditure, etc.) expressed in US dollars at 1990 exchange rates. The price indices for *groups of countries* are harmonic weighted averages of the component indices using as weights the current value of the aggregate concerned, expressed in US dollars at 1990 exchange rates. It should be noted that the product of these two weighted volume and price indices for groups of countries does not correspond with the aggregates shown at current prices and exchange rates, but correspond with the aggregates shown at current prices and 1990 exchange rates.

Data for Korea, Czech Republic, Hungary and Poland have not been included in area total. Data for Australia are based on calendar year.

MÉTHODES DE CALCUL

Il est nécessaire de souligner les points suivants pour l'utilisation des tableaux de cette sixième partie.

a) les différents agrégats montrés dans les tableaux 1 à 18 ont été calculés de trois façons differentes: *aux prix courants et taux de change de 1990* (tableaux 1-6), *aux prix de 1990 et taux de change de 1990* (tableaux 7-12) et *aux prix courants et taux de change courants* (tableaux 13-18). En utilisant les taux de change de 1990 sur toute la période, les variations d'une année sur l'autre, pour un pays ou groupe de pays, des series montrées dans les tableaux 1-6 sont déterminées exclusivement par les mouvements des données nationales à prix courants. Par contre les variations calculées à partir des données des tableaux 13-18 sont susceptibles d'être aussi largement influencées par les fluctuations des taux de change que par les mouvements des données nationales à prix courants. Ainsi les données des tableaux 13-18 doivent être utilisées uniquement pour des comparaisons entre pays pour une année particulière, et non pour des comparaisons dans le temps pour le même pays ou groupe de pays.

b) Les tableaux d'*indices de volume et de prix* sont montrés avec 1990 = 100. En réalité beaucoup de pays utilisent une année antérieure à 1990 comme année de base pour calculer leurs indices de volume et de prix ; et donc les indices montrés pour ces pays (et groupe de pays) sont basés sur des quantités et prix relatifs différents de 1990. Les années de base utilisées par les pays membres sont précisées dans les tableaux quand elles diffèrent de 1990.

c) Les indices de volume concernant les *groupes de pays* sont obtenus comme moyennes arithmétiques des indices par pays pondérés par la valeur en 1990 de l'agrégat concerné (PIB, Consommation finale privée, etc.), exprimée en dollars É-U aux taux de change de 1990. Les indices de prix concernant les *groupes de pays* sont obtenus comme moyennes harmoniques des indices par pays pondérés par la valeur courante de l'agrégat concerné exprimée en dollars É-U aux taux de change de 1990. Il faut noter que le produit de ces deux indices pondérés de volume et de prix ne correspond pas aux agrégats montrés aux prix courants et taux de change courants, mais correspond aux agrégats montrés aux prix courants et taux de change de 1990.

Les données de la Corée, de la République tchèque, de la Hongrie et de la Pologne n'ont pas été intégrées aux totaux par zones. Les données de l'Australie sont établies sur une base calendaire.

COMPARATIVE TABLES BASED ON EXCHANGE RATES
TABLEAUX COMPARATIFS BASÉS SUR LES TAUX DE CHANGE

1. Gross domestic product - at current prices and 1990 exchange rates (billions of US dollars)

	1960	1961	1962	1963	1964	1965	1966	1967	1968	1969	1970	1971	1972	1973	1974	1975	1976	1977	1978
Canada	33.77	35.00	37.97	40.75	44.65	49.22	55.07	59.17	64.57	71.03	76.37	83.35	93.06	109.23	130.39	146.93	169.33	187.09	2[illegible]7.41
Mexico	0.06	0.06	0.07	0.08	0.09	0.10	0.11	0.12	0.13	0.15	0.18	0.19	0.22	0.27	0.36	0.44	0.54	0.73	0.93
United States	511.70	529.40	569.50	600.80	645.70	700.90	768.50	812.10	887.30	958.10	1008.90	1096.10	1205.80	1348.30	1457.60	[illegible]585.50	1771.40	1973.80	22[illegible]9.00
Japan	110.58	133.55	151.55	173.45	204.03	226.99	263.62	308.93	365.88	429.78	506.56	557.37	638.13	776.97	927.16	[illegible]024.43	1150.45	1282.01	14[illegible]1.73
Korea	..	..	..	..	..	..	..	..	..	..	3.92	4.84	5.95	7.66	10.83	14.55	19.90	25.52	[illegible]4.46
Australia	11.69	11.83	12.71	13.93	15.30	16.56	17.60	19.33	21.18	23.54	25.98	29.21	32.64	38.50	46.19	55.06	64.70	71.26	[illegible]8.99
New Zealand	1.70	1.74	1.88	2.04	2.23	2.42	2.51	2.60	2.75	3.06	3.42	4.02	4.60	5.38	5.87	6.63	8.06	8.93	[illegible]0.12
Austria	14.67	16.28	17.30	18.65	20.42	22.20	24.18	25.72	27.63	30.17	33.85	37.79	43.19	48.94	55.71	59.09	65.27	72.20	[illegible]6.24
Belgium	16.72	17.76	18.98	20.42	22.85	24.91	26.74	28.66	30.65	34.00	37.80	41.41	46.36	52.68	61.78	68.38	77.71	84.05	[illegible]0.26
Czech Republic	..	..	..	..	..	..	..	..	..	..	..	..	..	..	..	..	..	..	..
Denmark	6.80	7.54	8.50	9.05	10.34	11.61	12.75	14.01	15.58	17.73	19.59	21.66	24.90	28.55	31.98	35.72	41.49	46.13	[illegible]1.43
Finland	4.24	4.80	5.14	5.58	6.30	6.97	7.47	8.19	9.39	10.72	11.96	13.14	15.33	18.66	23.55	26.98	30.51	33.62	[illegible]7.21
France	55.21	60.23	67.25	75.40	83.64	90.03	97.47	105.28	114.43	130.48	145.73	162.38	181.43	207.49	239.28	269.57	312.30	352.19	4[illegible]0.82
Germany	210.08	230.19	250.38	265.36	291.61	318.66	338.84	343.08	370.11	414.28	468.65	520.32	571.25	636.57	682.84	712.48	777.63	829.54	8[illegible]0.78
Greece	0.80	0.91	0.96	1.07	1.21	1.37	1.53	1.65	1.79	2.04	2.28	2.52	2.89	3.70	4.31	5.13	6.30	7.36	8.87
Hungary	..	..	..	..	..	..	..	..	..	..	..	..	..	..	..	..	..	..	..
Iceland	0.00	0.00	0.00	0.00	0.00	0.00	0.00	0.00	0.01	0.01	0.01	0.01	0.01	0.02	0.03	0.04	0.05	0.08	0.12
Ireland	1.09	1.17	1.27	1.37	1.56	1.66	1.74	1.91	2.15	2.48	2.80	3.20	3.86	4.66	5.16	6.55	8.03	9.85	[illegible]1.67
Italy	20.68	23.00	25.84	29.60	32.40	34.86	37.77	41.61	45.10	49.79	56.03	60.93	66.56	80.63	101.82	115.67	145.72	177.54	2[illegible]9.50
Luxembourg	0.86	0.86	0.91	0.97	1.11	1.16	1.22	1.23	1.34	1.55	1.82	1.85	2.09	2.54	3.09	2.86	3.30	3.39	3.71
Netherlands	24.74	26.12	28.12	30.51	35.90	40.10	43.66	47.90	53.11	60.15	67.50	76.05	85.93	98.06	111.28	122.53	140.33	153.15	1[illegible]5.07
Norway	5.93	6.47	6.97	7.48	8.23	9.08	9.80	10.72	11.44	12.46	14.34	16.00	17.67	20.08	23.29	26.69	30.65	34.38	[illegible]8.25
Poland	..	..	..	..	..	..	..	..	..	..	..	..	..	..	..	..	..	..	..
Portugal	0.57	0.62	0.66	0.71	0.77	0.86	0.95	1.06	1.17	1.28	1.43	1.60	1.86	2.27	2.73	3.03	3.77	5.03	6.32
Spain	6.71	7.69	8.97	10.60	11.86	13.75	15.96	18.07	20.40	23.36	25.80	29.12	34.17	41.20	50.45	59.24	71.29	90.45	1[illegible]0.71
Sweden	12.32	13.41	14.54	15.74	17.55	19.31	21.01	22.80	24.20	26.28	29.43	31.82	34.82	38.74	43.76	51.40	58.13	63.22	[illegible]0.48
Switzerland	28.44	32.00	35.48	39.02	43.25	46.32	49.74	53.54	57.17	61.95	69.01	78.39	88.83	98.99	107.39	106.67	108.05	110.96	1[illegible]5.44
Turkey	0.03	0.03	0.03	0.04	0.04	0.04	0.05	0.05	0.06	0.07	0.08	0.10	0.12	0.15	0.20	0.26	0.33	0.42	0.63
United Kingdom	45.91	48.69	51.17	54.24	59.28	63.86	67.98	71.56	77.54	83.45	91.64	102.25	114.49	131.53	148.64	187.51	221.94	258.63	2[illegible]8.56
OECD - Total[1]	1125.32	1209.34	1316.16	1416.85	1560.31	1702.95	1866.28	1999.32	2205.11	2447.90	2701.15	2970.78	3310.20	3794.12	4264.87	[illegible]678.77	5267.26	5856.02	65[illegible]4.23
OECD - Europe[2]	455.82	497.76	542.48	585.80	648.32	706.76	758.86	797.06	863.29	962.25	1079.74	1200.53	1335.75	1515.46	1697.30	[illegible]859.79	2102.79	2332.19	25[illegible]6.06
EU15	421.41	459.26	499.99	539.26	596.80	651.32	699.27	732.74	794.61	887.76	996.31	1106.04	1229.13	1396.23	1566.40	[illegible]726.13	1963.71	2186.35	24[illegible]1.62

2. Private final consumption expenditure - at current prices and 1990 exchange rates (billions of US dollars)

	1960	1961	1962	1963	1964	1965	1966	1967	1968	1969	1970	1971	1972	1973	1974	1975	1976	1977	1978
Canada	21.53	21.91	23.36	24.86	26.64	28.83	31.45	33.93	36.95	40.22	42.37	46.11	51.60	59.04	68.79	79.53	90.54	101.00	1[illegible]2.87
Mexico	0.05	0.05	0.05	0.06	0.07	0.07	0.08	0.09	0.10	0.11	0.13	0.15	0.16	0.20	0.25	0.31	0.38	0.50	0.63
United States	327.80	338.00	358.90	378.20	406.10	438.20	475.00	501.20	550.60	595.50	637.30	690.20	757.20	836.80	914.00	[illegible]08.40	1126.60	1252.60	13[illegible]6.80
Japan	64.89	76.19	87.39	102.02	117.60	132.88	152.92	175.46	200.11	229.99	264.75	298.57	344.64	416.52	503.57	585.42	661.54	739.53	8[illegible]4.44
Korea	..	..	..	..	..	..	..	..	..	..	2.92	3.65	4.39	5.33	7.62	10.26	13.03	15.90	[illegible]0.89
Australia	7.41	7.55	8.06	8.67	9.37	10.06	10.74	11.71	12.76	14.03	15.48	17.21	19.05	22.04	26.46	32.17	37.74	42.14	[illegible]7.24
New Zealand	1.15	1.18	1.24	1.34	1.44	1.56	1.67	1.73	1.83	1.99	2.23	2.52	2.84	3.27	3.72	4.25	4.89	5.46	6.16
Austria	8.72	9.53	10.28	11.13	11.94	13.09	13.97	15.02	16.01	17.03	18.43	20.64	23.32	26.19	29.67	33.05	36.82	41.05	[illegible]2.00
Belgium	11.58	12.06	12.66	13.72	14.66	16.02	17.11	18.07	19.56	21.19	22.69	25.07	28.04	32.10	37.21	42.20	47.81	52.58	[illegible]6.20
Czech Republic	..	..	..	..	..	..	..	..	..	..	..	..	..	..	..	..	..	..	..
Denmark	3.98	4.43	4.98	5.25	5.89	6.46	7.18	7.94	8.67	9.63	10.63	11.43	12.56	14.71	16.44	18.73	22.20	24.82	[illegible]7.32
Finland	2.58	2.85	3.15	3.45	3.93	4.32	4.60	5.01	5.48	6.19	6.77	7.35	8.64	10.27	12.50	15.04	17.19	19.00	[illegible]1.02
France	32.98	36.12	40.35	45.58	49.79	53.12	57.45	62.20	67.88	77.06	84.40	93.87	104.73	118.45	137.66	158.35	182.46	205.15	2[illegible]2.13
Germany	117.87	129.18	140.48	148.71	160.17	176.71	188.68	193.87	206.29	226.97	253.01	280.54	310.01	339.95	366.05	400.21	433.42	467.90	4[illegible]7.95
Greece	0.67	0.73	0.77	0.83	0.93	1.04	1.15	1.25	1.34	1.47	1.65	1.79	1.98	2.44	3.04	3.61	4.32	5.05	6.02
Hungary	..	..	..	..	..	..	..	..	..	..	..	..	..	..	..	..	..	..	..
Iceland	0.00	0.00	0.00	0.00	0.00	0.00	0.00	0.00	0.00	0.00	0.00	0.01	0.01	0.01	0.02	0.02	0.03	0.04	0.07
Ireland	0.86	0.91	0.98	1.04	1.16	1.22	1.29	1.37	1.57	1.78	1.98	2.24	2.58	3.09	3.63	4.32	5.33	6.50	7.65
Italy	12.28	13.43	15.16	17.73	19.22	20.56	22.67	25.11	26.80	29.39	33.22	36.31	39.93	48.65	61.19	71.61	88.54	106.62	1[illegible]3.79
Luxembourg	0.52	0.55	0.58	0.62	0.70	0.75	0.79	0.81	0.86	0.92	1.02	1.13	1.25	1.38	1.59	1.85	2.08	2.25	2.39
Netherlands	14.51	15.63	17.02	18.90	21.38	23.89	25.99	28.21	30.84	35.29	39.56	44.10	49.41	55.77	63.34	72.03	82.67	91.79	1[illegible]0.03
Norway	3.39	3.69	3.97	4.22	4.59	4.90	5.25	5.70	6.09	6.79	7.45	8.29	9.10	10.09	11.44	13.43	15.49	17.98	[illegible]9.15
Poland	..	..	..	..	..	..	..	..	..	..	..	..	..	..	..	..	..	..	..
Portugal	0.42	0.45	0.45	0.49	0.52	0.58	0.64	0.69	0.79	0.88	0.93	1.08	1.18	1.46	1.96	2.32	2.80	3.59	4.26
Spain	4.68	5.29	6.06	7.27	8.09	9.49	10.89	12.21	13.60	15.03	16.69	18.89	22.03	26.43	32.70	38.45	47.26	59.36	[illegible]1.34
Sweden	7.31	7.87	8.45	9.09	9.79	10.77	11.69	12.61	13.36	14.42	15.67	16.88	18.58	20.50	23.38	26.66	30.83	33.80	[illegible]7.46
Switzerland	17.40	19.11	21.33	23.16	25.28	27.20	29.33	31.51	33.58	36.39	39.87	44.67	50.68	56.79	62.16	64.34	66.49	69.29	[illegible]1.26
Turkey	0.02	0.02	0.03	0.03	0.03	0.03	0.04	0.04	0.05	0.05	0.06	0.07	0.09	0.11	0.15	0.19	0.23	0.30	[illegible].46
United Kingdom	30.29	31.85	33.76	35.85	38.26	40.70	43.03	45.22	48.63	51.61	56.23	63.06	71.33	81.56	94.07	[illegible]15.76	134.54	153.81	1[illegible]7.42
OECD - Total[1]	692.88	738.55	799.42	862.23	937.55	1022.48	1113.61	1190.95	1303.73	1433.95	1572.51	1732.17	1930.96	2187.81	2474.98	[illegible]92.26	3142.16	3502.09	38[illegible].05
OECD - Europe[2]	270.05	293.67	320.42	347.08	376.33	410.87	441.74	466.82	501.38	552.11	610.26	677.41	755.46	849.94	958.19	[illegible]82.17	1220.48	1360.87	14[illegible]7.91
EU15	249.24	270.86	295.10	319.66	346.43	378.73	407.12	429.57	461.67	508.87	562.88	624.38	695.58	782.95	[illegible]84.43	[illegible]04.19	1138.25	1273.25	14[illegible].98

3. Government final consumption expenditure - at current prices and 1990 exchange rates (billions of US dollars)

	1960	1961	1962	1963	1964	1965	1966	1967	1968	1969	1970	1971	1972	1973	1974	1975	1976	1977	1978
Canada	4.84	5.66	6.09	6.48	7.07	7.75	9.11	10.60	12.03	13.62	15.82	17.45	19.36	21.95	26.62	32.34	37.13	42.10	4[illegible].30
Mexico	0.00	0.00	0.00	0.01	0.01	0.01	0.01	0.01	0.01	0.01	0.01	0.01	0.02	0.02	0.03	0.04	0.05	0.07	[illegible].09
United States	84.90	91.90	99.70	103.70	108.50	114.40	133.20	151.40	164.40	174.30	186.40	196.40	212.50	229.10	256.50	[illegible]87.90	311.20	339.40	37[illegible].40
Japan	8.85	10.25	12.07	14.30	16.24	18.58	21.09	23.55	27.17	31.48	37.68	44.35	52.05	64.48	84.54	[illegible]02.84	113.39	126.00	1[illegible].42
Korea	..	..	..	..	..	..	..	..	..	..	0.37	0.47	0.60	0.65	1.05	1.60	2.17	2.75	3.59
Australia	1.30	1.42	1.52	1.61	1.83	2.10	2.33	2.68	2.98	3.21	3.56	4.10	4.59	5.56	7.20	9.46	11.33	12.68	1[illegible].28
New Zealand	0.18	0.19	0.21	0.22	0.25	0.30	0.35	0.33	0.36	0.38	0.46	0.53	0.61	0.70	0.86	1.03	1.16	1.41	[illegible].72
Austria	1.93	2.08	2.25	2.51	2.75	3.00	3.34	3.79	4.13	4.60	5.03	5.65	6.39	7.47	8.88	10.31	11.65	12.66	13.89
Belgium	2.07	2.12	2.33	2.65	2.86	3.18	3.50	3.85	4.16	4.62	5.07	5.83	6.71	7.64	9.05	11.18	12.67	13.98	15.56
Czech Republic	..	..	..	..	..	..	..	..	..	..	..	..	..	..	..	..	..	..	..
Denmark	0.92	1.11	1.32	1.43	1.64	1.93	2.23	2.55	2.96	3.41	3.99	4.70	5.41	6.20	7.63	8.96	10.20	11.25	1[illegible].85
Finland	0.51	0.56	0.64	0.75	0.85	0.95	1.07	1.22	1.43	1.55	1.73	1.99	2.34	2.80	3.58	4.60	5.50	6.21	[illegible].78
France	7.85	8.66	9.77	11.08	12.15	12.93	13.85	14.93	16.92	19.05	21.42	24.23	26.96	30.79	36.77	44.71	52.85	60.52	7[illegible].46
Germany	28.83	32.62	37.65	42.32	44.25	49.64	53.77	57.05	58.96	66.36	75.87	90.34	100.51	116.23	135.48	[illegible]49.71	158.11	167.57	18[illegible].36
Greece	0.07	0.07	0.08	0.09	0.10	0.11	0.13	0.15	0.16	0.18	0.20	0.22	0.25	0.30	0.42	0.55	0.67	0.83	[illegible].00
Hungary	..	..	..	..	..	..	..	..	..	..	..	..	..	..	..	..	..	..	..
Iceland	0.00	0.00	0.00	0.00	0.00	0.00	0.00	0.00	0.00	0.00	0.00	0.00	0.00	0.00	0.00	0.01	0.01	0.01	[illegible].02
Ireland	0.13	0.14	0.15	0.17	0.20	0.22	0.23	0.24	0.28	0.32	0.39	0.47	0.57	0.70	0.85	1.17	1.39	1.61	[illegible].91
Italy	2.53	2.80	3.24	3.95	4.47	5.07	5.40	5.76	6.28	6.81	7.42	9.04	10.26	11.84	14.27	16.59	19.86	24.98	3[illegible].31
Luxembourg	0.07	0.07	0.08	0.10	0.10	0.11	0.12	0.13	0.14	0.14	0.16	0.18	0.21	0.24	0.30	0.36	0.41	0.46	[illegible].49
Netherlands	3.02	3.32	3.72	4.26	5.07	5.64	6.29	7.07	7.66	8.74	10.05	11.77	13.16	14.77	17.48	20.60	23.41	25.77	2[illegible].34
Norway	0.74	0.80	0.94	1.04	1.15	1.32	1.46	1.67	1.83	2.03	2.35	2.77	3.10	3.54	4.12	4.98	5.92	6.71	[illegible].56
Poland	..	..	..	..	..	..	..	..	..	..	..	..	..	..	..	..	..	..	..
Portugal	0.06	0.07	0.08	0.08	0.09	0.10	0.11	0.13	0.14	0.15	0.18	0.20	0.23	0.27	0.36	0.42	0.48	0.65	[illegible].81
Spain	0.56	0.63	0.73	0.89	0.97	1.16	1.39	1.70	1.86	2.14	2.44	2.80	3.25	3.91	4.99	6.19	8.04	10.39	1[illegible].19
Sweden	1.98	2.16	2.47	2.75	3.05	3.47	4.02	4.50	5.03	5.52	6.41	7.26	8.03	8.92	10.30	12.41	14.67	17.63	1[illegible].96
Switzerland	2.46	3.03	3.52	4.03	4.43	4.76	5.08	5.40	5.81	6.38	7.09	8.38	9.48	10.90	12.24	13.19	13.94	14.09	1[illegible].55
Turkey	0.00	0.00	0.00	0.00	0.00	0.00	0.00	0.00	0.01	0.01	0.01	0.01	0.01	0.02	0.02	0.03	0.04	0.06	[illegible].08
United Kingdom	7.53	8.12	8.70	9.29	9.90	10.87	11.85	13.10	13.93	14.55	16.42	18.75	21.43	24.47	30.46	42.01	49.20	53.61	6[illegible].62
OECD - Total[1]	161.35	177.80	197.26	213.68	227.92	247.60	279.93	311.81	338.64	369.58	410.18	457.43	507.42	572.83	672.96	[illegible]31.59	863.28	950.65	104[illegible].48
OECD - Europe[2]	61.27	68.37	77.67	87.38	94.03	104.46	113.84	123.24	131.69	146.58	166.25	194.59	218.29	251.01	297.22	[illegible]47.98	389.02	428.98	47[illegible].77
EU15	58.06	64.54	73.21	82.31	88.44	98.37	107.29	116.17	124.04	138.16	156.80	183.42	205.70	236.54	280.82	[illegible]29.77	369.11	408.11	45[illegible].57

1. Excluding Korea Czech Republic Hungary and Poland.
2. Excluding Czech Republic Hungary and Poland.

Produit intérieur brut - aux prix courants et taux de change de 1990 (milliards de dollars É-U) 1.

1979	1980	1981	1982	1983	1984	1985	1986	1987	1988	1989	1990	1991	1992	1993	1994	1995	1996	1997	
236.97	266.56	304.89	321.16	347.30	379.69	409.89	432.09	471.27	516.32	554.04	572.67	576.38	589.12	611.35	643.21	674.51	692.14	721.15	Canada
1.22	1.69	2.32	3.71	6.78	11.17	17.97	30.02	73.28	148.01	195.14	262.71	337.46	400.10	446.63	504.93	653.14	890.21	1131.45	Mexique
2488.00	2709.00	3039.30	3158.90	3412.90	3786.40	4048.20	4268.10	4528.10	4878.80	5260.90	5554.10	5710.90	6027.70	6341.60	6722.90	7033.60	7390.60	7824.00	États-Unis
1530.12	1658.79	1781.64	1868.92	1946.04	2075.72	2212.99	2316.85	2415.63	2582.87	2762.61	2970.09	3165.27	3253.13	3283.25	3310.04	3337.39	3452.32	3501.46	Japon
44.36	53.90	67.33	77.32	90.70	104.00	115.95	135.27	158.43	188.11	210.76	253.67	304.81	339.65	377.45	432.31	497.31	550.77	594.82	Corée
91.04	103.35	117.30	129.76	141.92	162.27	179.44	195.73	220.81	249.25	279.42	295.61	298.54	310.83	327.75	348.96	372.26	394.17	413.26	Australie
11.81	13.72	16.64	18.74	20.78	23.47	27.02	32.65	36.77	39.65	42.22	43.10	43.12	44.49	48.22	51.64	54.56	56.80	58.61	Nouvelle-Zélande
83.19	89.37	95.14	102.13	108.83	114.25	120.42	126.57	131.41	137.71	147.47	159.50	171.14	180.94	186.93	196.98	205.31	212.99	221.37	Autriche
96.53	104.99	109.38	118.41	125.35	135.04	144.66	152.16	159.16	170.25	184.55	196.13	205.55	216.31	221.59	232.48	241.43	248.52	259.61	Belgique
..	..	..	..	..	..	..	..	..	..	..	27.40	35.45	40.05	47.48	54.32	63.78	72.48	78.01	République tchèque
57.30	61.74	67.35	76.71	84.66	93.37	101.59	110.08	115.60	120.91	127.43	133.36	138.59	143.47	145.45	156.05	163.79	172.38	181.46	Danemark
43.30	50.05	56.67	63.71	71.04	79.66	86.73	92.85	101.18	113.60	127.37	134.81	128.38	124.70	126.17	133.64	143.81	150.13	162.71	Finlande
455.64	515.73	581.20	665.90	735.77	801.04	863.16	930.95	980.05	1053.22	1131.19	1195.43	1244.42	1285.43	1299.67	1357.07	1407.16	1445.60	1494.33	France
963.58	1021.59	1064.31	1102.02	1157.53	1216.05	1269.15	1336.93	1382.20	1453.50	1536.27	1640.06	1766.14	1905.39	1958.06	2059.87	2130.80	2180.75	2242.95	Allemagne
10.91	13.07	15.66	19.67	23.52	29.07	35.27	42.13	47.91	57.84	68.73	82.91	102.39	118.39	133.34	151.30	169.60	187.35	206.62	Grèce
..	..	..	..	..	..	..	..	..	..	..	35.78	39.53	46.56	56.14	69.06	88.00	108.06	133.88	Hongrie
0.17	0.28	0.43	0.68	1.17	1.53	2.07	2.77	3.59	4.40	5.29	6.25	6.81	6.82	7.06	7.46	7.75	8.34	9.00	Islande
13.67	16.16	19.61	23.11	25.52	28.33	30.72	32.59	34.86	37.87	42.28	45.53	47.47	50.91	55.14	60.29	67.70	74.45	84.18	Irlande
256.93	321.62	384.82	452.49	527.18	603.30	676.14	749.76	820.27	909.79	994.88	1093.95	1191.53	1254.06	1293.96	1367.72	1479.22	1563.00	1628.14	Italie
4.03	4.39	4.68	5.24	5.77	6.39	6.78	7.50	7.75	8.62	9.79	10.35	11.14	12.14	13.30	14.59	15.25	15.72	16.87	Luxembourg
175.70	187.64	196.71	204.87	212.72	222.80	233.69	240.46	242.09	251.34	266.32	283.67	297.96	310.88	319.32	337.34	351.27	367.58	389.35	Pays-Bas
42.15	50.04	57.02	63.05	69.85	78.64	87.06	89.32	97.46	102.18	109.01	115.45	121.96	125.39	131.59	138.59	148.37	162.95	173.30	Norvège
..	..	..	..	..	..	..	..	..	..	..	58.98	85.14	120.99	163.98	221.48	303.90	381.91	468.16	Pologne
7.98	10.09	12.06	14.86	18.49	22.62	28.31	35.51	41.59	49.69	58.73	69.13	79.37	89.50	94.44	102.62	110.96	117.75	124.56	Portugal
129.51	150.04	168.70	195.17	222.99	252.63	276.66	317.11	354.58	393.97	441.89	491.94	538.85	579.83	597.96	635.82	684.56	723.44	764.19	Espagne
78.99	89.72	98.28	107.46	120.35	134.71	146.42	160.04	172.94	188.30	208.25	229.76	244.53	243.58	244.34	258.68	278.76	285.23	293.79	Suède
120.67	129.64	139.28	146.58	151.25	161.29	170.75	178.87	185.12	196.32	211.14	228.41	240.18	246.45	251.80	257.32	261.65	262.57	266.68	Suisse
1.09	2.01	3.03	4.02	5.33	8.43	13.45	19.58	28.64	49.54	87.14	150.68	241.55	419.13	759.73	1482.93	2975.67	5662.76	11053.99	Turquie
351.27	410.59	451.50	494.06	538.94	576.80	632.43	681.19	749.13	834.12	913.11	975.51	1019.06	1060.08	1116.30	1183.34	1245.60	1312.66	1391.43	Royaume-Uni
7251.77	7981.86	8787.92	9361.32	10081.95	11004.68	11820.96	12581.81	13401.39	14548.07	15765.17	16941.12	17928.70	18998.79	20014.95	21715.77	24214.14	28030.43	34614.45	OCDE - Total[1]
2892.61	3228.75	3525.83	3860.14	4206.23	4565.96	4925.46	5306.37	5655.52	6133.18	6670.84	7242.83	7797.02	8373.41	8956.15	10134.10	12088.68	15154.19	20964.51	OCDE - Europe[2]
2728.53	3046.79	3326.07	3645.81	3978.63	4316.06	4652.12	5015.82	5340.71	5780.74	6258.26	6742.04	7186.52	7575.62	7805.97	8247.80	8695.24	9057.56	9461.55	UE15

Consommation finale privée - aux prix courants et taux de change de 1990 (milliards de dollars É-U) 2.

1979	1980	1981	1982	1983	1984	1985	1986	1987	1988	1989	1990	1991	1992	1993	1994	1995	1996	1997	
126.15	141.82	160.31	172.01	188.50	205.55	224.32	242.49	262.30	283.95	306.95	323.85	334.37	345.14	359.46	372.87	384.84	399.48	422.81	Canada
0.80	1.07	1.46	2.23	4.02	6.87	11.29	20.03	47.01	100.11	134.36	182.79	237.91	287.32	321.12	361.28	438.03	577.50	739.53	Mexique
1556.90	1720.60	1902.40	2034.60	2226.70	2432.30	2633.70	2803.90	2998.60	3247.40	3486.70	3720.50	3844.50	4079.80	4318.40	4569.40	4802.40	5043.00	5311.80	États-Unis
898.39	976.06	1035.96	1110.81	1171.96	1233.73	1303.68	1358.60	1422.45	1504.52	1608.47	1721.72	1808.76	1880.62	1924.88	1976.34	2006.52	2067.00	2123.41	Japon
27.36	34.74	43.30	48.93	54.95	61.38	67.86	74.63	83.41	96.03	112.22	136.19	162.54	183.30	203.07	232.22	263.38	296.45	319.00	Corée
53.17	60.78	69.24	78.48	86.95	95.21	107.05	117.26	129.69	144.66	162.48	176.95	185.09	195.41	204.66	216.13	231.97	244.07	255.79	Australie
7.19	8.45	9.92	11.35	12.36	14.07	16.63	19.66	22.33	24.18	25.92	27.30	27.33	27.85	29.25	31.59	33.75	35.71	37.19	Nouvelle-Zélande
45.70	49.23	53.25	57.84	63.06	65.50	68.93	71.59	74.22	77.93	82.96	89.09	94.37	100.94	105.02	110.35	115.24	120.97	124.23	Autriche
61.39	67.06	72.26	79.11	83.85	89.46	96.48	99.49	104.07	108.72	117.27	124.67	132.37	138.53	141.09	147.35	151.75	158.06	164.22	Belgique
..	..	..	..	..	..	..	..	..	..	..	14.57	16.28	20.94	23.47	27.03	31.57	36.51	40.07	République tchèque
30.59	32.62	35.70	39.93	43.73	48.09	52.67	57.28	59.02	60.73	63.55	65.43	68.36	70.98	72.74	79.80	83.13	86.86	91.93	Danemark
23.88	27.08	30.67	35.11	39.13	43.19	47.31	50.74	55.32	60.83	66.58	70.55	71.85	71.17	71.99	74.39	77.99	82.04	86.09	Finlande
264.82	303.62	350.25	404.17	447.28	486.90	527.26	562.47	596.76	632.55	674.30	712.28	744.80	772.79	791.35	819.25	845.85	878.47	895.81	France
535.93	574.14	607.97	632.33	661.78	692.34	718.81	740.29	769.49	801.98	848.84	912.44	1009.04	1086.51	1132.16	1179.66	1222.55	1266.52	1296.77	Allemagne
7.20	8.79	11.01	13.80	16.35	19.59	24.08	29.60	34.68	41.02	49.38	60.74	74.77	88.53	100.31	113.63	127.05	140.17	151.69	Grèce
..	..	..	..	..	..	..	..	..	..	..	17.32	21.68	26.85	33.51	40.08	47.58	56.76	68.47	Hongrie
0.10	0.16	0.26	0.41	0.70	0.96	1.33	1.70	2.29	2.76	3.26	3.83	4.26	4.26	4.26	4.41	4.68	5.09	5.50	Islande
9.18	10.94	13.30	14.21	15.65	17.14	18.82	20.08	21.25	23.05	25.55	26.45	27.81	29.85	31.13	34.00	36.12	38.85	41.67	Irlande
152.83	195.74	234.39	277.45	320.23	367.64	414.35	458.37	503.72	557.71	616.13	670.74	736.23	787.99	802.49	846.73	909.37	959.28	1006.38	Italie
2.60	2.88	3.18	3.53	3.84	4.15	4.44	4.71	5.00	5.38	5.85	6.42	7.02	7.19	7.61	7.98	8.34	8.64	8.96	Luxembourg
107.31	114.17	117.83	123.21	127.95	131.98	138.89	142.91	147.14	149.18	156.23	166.45	177.08	187.22	193.15	202.89	209.89	218.95	230.12	Pays-Bas
21.00	23.43	26.49	29.74	32.85	36.04	41.73	46.75	49.98	51.95	54.12	57.05	60.11	63.09	65.76	69.19	73.24	77.75	82.39	Norvège
..	..	..	..	..	..	..	..	..	..	..	28.62	51.20	75.71	104.87	144.59	191.61	248.77	305.51	Pologne
5.34	6.73	8.32	10.25	12.71	15.84	19.05	22.90	26.50	31.59	36.69	43.64	50.79	58.09	62.83	67.81	71.99	76.44	80.33	Portugal
84.19	99.37	112.47	128.74	145.34	162.36	177.37	200.50	224.22	247.02	278.29	307.09	336.19	365.70	377.52	399.51	424.92	448.02	473.61	Espagne
41.41	46.18	51.62	57.45	62.42	68.22	74.96	82.34	90.87	98.73	106.90	117.03	130.32	131.33	134.55	140.99	145.90	149.54	155.93	Suède
75.33	80.80	86.21	91.50	95.50	99.63	104.61	108.48	112.50	116.67	122.93	130.90	141.08	147.24	150.85	154.11	157.59	160.18	163.09	Suisse
0.81	1.62	2.16	2.95	3.96	6.37	9.56	13.18	19.56	31.45	57.17	103.33	170.54	291.44	524.92	1037.42	2092.24	3809.53	7520.81	Turquie
210.58	244.72	272.41	298.89	327.43	350.69	383.49	426.08	468.14	528.65	578.03	613.75	645.53	677.38	717.76	754.29	787.46	835.76	892.70	Royaume-Uni
4322.81	4798.07	5269.04	5710.09	6194.23	6693.82	7220.81	7701.41	8247.14	8932.69	9668.93	10435.01	11120.46	11896.38	12645.24	13771.36	15442.81	17887.87	22362.74	OCDE - Total[1]
1680.20	1889.28	2089.75	2300.61	2503.74	2706.11	2924.15	3139.46	3364.75	3627.88	3944.04	4281.89	4682.49	5080.24	5487.49	6243.75	7545.31	9521.11	13472.23	OCDE - Europe[2]
1582.95	1783.27	1974.63	2176.01	2370.73	2563.10	2766.92	2969.34	3180.42	3425.06	3706.56	3986.79	4306.50	4574.22	4741.70	4978.62	5217.56	5468.55	5700.44	UE15

Consommation finale des administrations publiques - aux prix courants et taux de change de 1990 (milliards de dollars É-U) 3.

1979	1980	1981	1982	1983	1984	1985	1986	1987	1988	1989	1990	1991	1992	1993	1994	1995	1996	1997	
50.61	57.44	65.49	74.50	80.02	84.09	90.90	95.55	101.10	109.69	118.77	129.88	139.11	144.68	145.92	144.95	146.19	144.29	143.91	Canada
0.12	0.17	0.24	0.38	0.58	1.00	1.61	2.66	6.27	12.45	16.14	22.03	30.63	39.73	49.27	58.37	68.26	86.65	94.65	Mexique
410.30	463.20	516.90	567.80	612.20	658.50	719.50	767.70	819.70	860.20	907.20	974.90	1016.80	1043.30	1062.70	1089.90	1124.60	1163.00	1206.10	États-Unis
148.40	162.77	176.70	185.07	193.36	203.39	211.93	223.68	227.75	236.09	250.53	268.02	285.62	298.79	309.22	315.92	327.50	333.95	337.69	Japon
4.42	6.24	7.85	8.92	9.80	10.39	11.73	13.53	15.32	17.89	21.53	25.70	31.32	36.89	40.62	45.81	50.99	58.95	66.25	Corée
15.62	18.15	20.91	23.80	26.60	29.72	33.22	36.99	39.29	42.65	46.03	50.68	54.32	56.86	58.40	61.11	63.46	66.95	69.51	Australie
1.98	2.47	2.98	3.32	3.49	3.78	4.38	5.33	6.04	6.58	7.00	7.33	7.32	7.57	7.50	7.48	7.89	8.21	8.91	Nouvelle-Zélande
15.10	16.25	17.72	19.45	20.71	21.81	23.25	24.79	25.72	26.60	28.11	29.74	32.35	35.03	37.78	40.01	41.28	42.07	42.85	Autriche
16.79	18.45	20.02	21.14	21.80	22.89	24.55	25.51	25.63	25.65	26.45	27.46	29.55	30.75	32.57	34.10	35.37	36.07	37.45	Belgique
..	..	..	..	..	..	..	..	..	..	..	5.27	6.35	7.71	10.48	12.09	13.31	15.30	15.80	République tchèque
14.64	16.81	19.08	22.10	23.69	24.64	26.21	26.86	29.70	31.77	33.06	34.08	35.63	37.03	38.93	40.45	41.97	43.96	45.99	Danemark
7.69	8.99	10.51	11.99	13.72	15.39	17.51	19.05	20.94	22.81	25.11	28.39	31.05	30.98	29.34	29.82	31.33	33.07	34.00	Finlande
80.19	93.53	109.27	128.79	143.63	156.89	167.17	176.21	184.50	194.37	203.12	214.94	227.54	242.49	257.63	264.20	271.13	282.63	288.88	France
194.93	212.38	225.79	231.99	239.67	248.93	260.45	271.85	283.56	294.59	299.97	318.27	344.56	381.47	392.92	407.61	424.92	436.40	435.35	Allemagne
1.26	1.51	1.99	2.55	3.13	4.02	5.09	5.77	6.62	8.27	10.44	12.66	14.75	16.49	19.32	21.10	26.36	27.33	30.52	Grèce
..	..	..	..	..	..	..	..	..	..	..	7.78	10.15	12.35	16.03	18.12	21.16	24.28	29.34	Hongrie
0.03	0.05	0.07	0.12	0.21	0.25	0.36	0.49	0.67	0.87	1.04	1.20	1.34	1.38	1.46	1.53	1.61	1.72	1.84	Islande
2.37	3.08	3.74	4.38	4.73	5.07	5.46	5.86	5.91	5.85	6.07	6.73	7.41	8.01	8.62	9.21	9.71	10.13	11.03	Irlande
38.00	48.17	62.67	73.87	87.53	99.72	112.61	123.23	138.19	155.27	167.18	192.11	209.72	221.53	228.18	234.10	237.57	255.40	265.76	Italie
0.55	0.62	0.69	0.73	0.77	0.83	0.90	0.96	1.07	1.12	1.22	1.39	1.48	1.59	1.72	1.82	2.01	2.13	2.24	Luxembourg
30.92	32.62	33.98	35.50	36.39	36.17	36.83	37.31	38.46	38.70	39.56	41.23	43.16	45.59	47.34	48.34	50.41	51.54	53.22	Pays-Bas
8.12	9.37	10.86	12.19	13.51	14.50	15.80	17.29	19.84	20.89	22.21	23.98	25.87	27.73	28.75	29.81	31.08	33.05	34.96	Norvège
..	..	..	..	..	..	..	..	..	..	..	11.04	18.62	25.07	32.01	39.46	53.48	66.77	80.87	Pologne
1.02	1.36	1.68	2.05	2.59	3.14	4.06	5.04	5.83	7.23	8.84	10.75	13.69	15.49	16.91	18.04	19.61	21.36	23.22	Portugal
16.08	19.57	23.11	27.16	32.01	35.59	40.73	46.50	53.48	58.12	67.02	76.66	87.13	99.02	104.97	107.55	114.29	120.23	123.46	Espagne
22.67	26.26	29.06	31.70	34.76	37.74	40.85	43.96	46.19	49.04	54.51	62.87	66.63	68.01	68.61	70.31	71.92	74.86	75.91	Suède
15.31	16.17	17.60	19.05	20.31	21.20	22.61	23.73	24.31	26.18	28.61	31.81	34.77	36.48	36.49	37.39	37.43	38.07	37.51	Suisse
0.13	0.17	0.33	0.38	0.56	0.75	1.20	1.76	2.24	3.77	8.14	16.52	29.86	53.89	98.93	172.74	320.95	655.23	1355.15	Turquie
70.36	88.79	100.38	109.49	119.38	126.48	133.70	143.73	154.62	166.33	180.82	200.60	220.44	234.23	244.68	255.90	265.03	276.61	282.08	Royaume-Uni
1163.16	1318.34	1471.79	1609.49	1735.34	1856.51	2000.89	2131.82	2267.65	2405.10	2557.17	2784.23	2990.75	3178.11	3328.16	3501.77	3771.85	4244.92	5042.18	OCDE - Total[1]
536.14	614.14	688.57	754.62	819.08	876.02	939.34	999.91	1067.49	1137.44	1211.50	1331.38	1456.94	1587.18	1695.16	1824.03	2033.96	2441.87	3181.42	OCDE - Europe[2]
512.56	588.38	659.71	722.88	784.50	839.32	899.37	956.63	1020.43	1085.73	1151.50	1257.88	1365.10	1467.70	1529.54	1582.57	1642.89	1713.81	1751.96	UE15

1. Non compris la Corée la République tchèque la Hongrie et la Pologne.
2. Non compris la République tchèque la Hongrie et la Pologne.

4. Gross fixed capital formation - at current prices and 1990 exchange rates (billions of US dollars)

	1960	1961	1962	1963	1964	1965	1966	1967	1968	1969	1970	1971	1972	1973	1974	1975	1976	1977	1978
Canada	7.67	7.59	7.99	8.54	9.99	11.69	13.61	13.97	14.24	15.67	16.43	18.63	20.59	24.84	30.87	35.99	40.14	43.19	47.12
Mexico	0.01	0.01	0.01	0.01	0.02	0.02	0.02	0.02	0.03	0.03	0.03	0.03	0.04	0.05	0.07	0.09	0.11	0.14	0.19
United States	91.70	92.80	100.70	108.80	119.90	133.90	144.60	146.90	162.10	177.20	180.10	201.30	230.60	263.00	276.10	281.10	319.90	383.20	461.60
Japan	32.03	42.59	48.79	54.76	64.66	67.56	79.85	98.67	121.33	148.08	179.87	190.88	217.72	282.74	322.50	332.45	358.76	386.64	429.22
Korea	..	..	..	..	..	..	..	..	..	..	0.98	1.09	1.23	1.83	2.92	3.88	5.08	7.22	11.20
Australia	2.90	2.89	3.09	3.41	3.93	4.46	4.68	4.98	5.54	6.13	6.73	7.68	8.09	9.33	10.83	13.04	15.51	16.97	18.92
New Zealand	0.36	0.40	0.39	0.43	0.50	0.55	0.59	0.56	0.54	0.64	0.78	0.90	1.12	1.31	1.61	1.94	2.11	2.11	2.31
Austria	3.40	3.96	4.14	4.51	5.01	5.63	6.25	6.35	6.59	7.02	8.12	9.77	12.11	12.95	14.68	14.62	15.77	18.20	17.77
Belgium	3.22	3.66	4.03	4.21	5.10	5.55	6.11	6.55	6.57	7.22	8.56	9.12	9.87	11.24	13.99	15.30	17.02	18.04	19.38
Czech Republic	..	..	..	..	..	..	..	..	..	..	..	..	..	..	..	..	..	..	..
Denmark	1.68	2.01	2.25	2.28	2.91	3.21	3.52	3.89	4.18	4.99	5.54	6.01	7.00	8.10	8.79	8.63	10.92	11.67	12.78
Finland	1.20	1.34	1.42	1.43	1.59	1.83	1.98	2.06	2.17	2.55	3.14	3.61	4.28	5.38	7.02	8.50	8.56	9.16	8.95
France	11.52	13.27	14.93	17.33	19.91	21.81	24.01	26.08	27.77	31.80	35.43	40.08	44.89	52.37	61.73	65.07	74.79	80.68	89.70
Germany	50.39	57.16	63.61	66.92	76.50	82.11	85.04	78.19	81.76	95.13	117.83	134.30	143.25	150.16	145.67	143.42	154.54	166.03	181.42
Greece	0.19	0.20	0.24	0.25	0.31	0.36	0.41	0.41	0.51	0.62	0.66	0.78	0.99	1.28	1.18	1.32	1.65	2.08	2.62
Hungary	..	..	..	..	..	..	..	..	..	..	..	..	..	..	..	..	..	..	..
Iceland	0.00	0.00	0.00	0.00	0.00	0.00	0.00	0.00	0.00	0.00	0.00	0.00	0.00	0.01	0.01	0.01	0.01	0.02	0.03
Ireland	0.15	0.19	0.22	0.26	0.31	0.34	0.33	0.37	0.44	0.56	0.62	0.73	0.89	1.14	1.23	1.44	1.95	2.36	3.13
Italy	5.39	6.16	7.05	8.20	8.30	7.75	8.19	9.36	10.56	12.08	13.81	14.60	15.43	20.07	26.42	28.85	34.84	41.99	48.15
Luxembourg	0.16	0.19	0.21	0.26	0.34	0.29	0.29	0.27	0.27	0.31	0.38	0.48	0.53	0.63	0.69	0.72	0.74	0.77	0.81
Netherlands	6.11	6.64	7.05	7.43	9.38	10.33	11.73	12.93	14.61	15.13	17.88	19.75	20.75	23.18	25.00	26.41	27.92	33.00	35.99
Norway	1.69	1.90	1.99	2.16	2.25	2.51	2.75	3.12	3.01	2.97	3.73	4.66	4.81	5.76	6.97	8.94	10.91	12.51	11.92
Poland	..	..	..	..	..	..	..	..	..	..	..	..	..	..	..	..	..	..	..
Portugal	0.15	0.16	0.16	0.19	0.19	0.22	0.26	0.31	0.28	0.32	0.36	0.43	0.55	0.67	0.78	0.86	1.04	1.46	1.94
Spain	1.38	1.65	1.95	2.33	2.80	3.42	4.00	4.56	5.23	6.06	6.71	6.93	8.51	10.87	14.09	15.62	17.73	21.60	25.03
Sweden	2.77	3.10	3.44	3.79	4.28	4.74	5.17	5.62	5.75	6.06	6.58	6.94	7.67	8.42	9.33	10.67	12.22	13.24	13.59
Switzerland	7.32	9.09	10.61	12.14	13.77	13.79	14.13	14.47	15.15	16.57	19.70	23.78	27.34	30.16	30.69	26.57	23.07	23.87	25.65
Turkey	0.00	0.00	0.00	0.01	0.01	0.01	0.01	0.01	0.01	0.01	0.01	0.02	0.02	0.03	0.04	0.05	0.08	0.09	0.12
United Kingdom	7.51	8.43	8.71	9.13	10.87	11.77	12.54	13.69	15.10	15.68	17.29	19.34	21.20	26.15	31.07	37.35	43.51	48.01	55.15
OECD - Total [1]	238.92	265.40	292.99	318.79	362.84	393.87	430.10	453.33	503.75	572.83	650.30	720.76	808.26	949.83	1 041.36	1 078.95	1 193.80	1 337.06	1 513.45
OECD - Europe [2]	104.24	119.11	132.02	142.83	163.84	175.68	186.74	188.22	199.97	225.08	266.36	301.34	330.10	368.57	399.39	414.34	457.26	504.80	554.09
EU15	95.23	108.11	119.41	128.51	147.80	159.38	169.85	170.62	181.80	205.53	242.92	272.88	297.93	332.61	361.68	378.77	423.18	468.31	516.38

5. Exports of goods and services - at current prices and 1990 exchange rates (billions of US dollars)

	1960	1961	1962	1963	1964	1965	1966	1967	1968	1969	1970	1971	1972	1973	1974	1975	1976	1977	1978
Canada	5.78	6.27	6.81	7.48	8.69	9.23	10.78	12.14	13.85	15.27	17.25	18.02	20.32	25.49	32.22	33.22	37.77	43.67	52.27
Mexico	0.01	0.01	0.01	0.01	0.01	0.01	0.01	0.01	0.01	0.01	0.01	0.02	0.02	0.02	0.03	0.03	0.05	0.08	0.10
United States	26.80	27.30	28.70	30.80	34.70	36.70	40.50	43.00	47.40	51.40	59.10	62.30	70.10	93.70	124.90	137.00	147.80	157.50	184.60
Japan	11.84	12.37	14.27	15.65	19.34	23.83	27.84	29.77	36.94	45.29	54.74	65.28	67.54	77.98	126.10	131.10	155.96	167.88	156.98
Korea	..	..	..	..	..	..	..	..	..	..	0.55	0.75	1.18	2.26	3.01	4.04	6.17	8.06	10.21
Australia	1.60	1.87	1.90	2.22	2.42	2.42	2.52	2.80	2.87	3.36	3.86	4.17	4.86	5.89	6.97	8.25	9.73	10.89	11.60
New Zealand	0.37	0.39	0.41	0.51	0.51	0.51	0.55	0.51	0.64	0.75	0.77	0.93	1.16	1.34	1.26	1.59	2.25	2.46	2.80
Austria	3.47	3.81	4.20	4.56	4.94	5.44	5.92	6.29	6.93	8.36	10.27	11.31	12.88	14.59	17.96	18.38	20.78	22.60	24.69
Belgium	6.40	7.03	7.82	8.64	9.85	10.59	11.83	12.39	13.93	16.81	19.41	20.70	23.37	28.90	37.32	35.86	43.10	45.60	47.18
Czech Republic	..	..	..	..	..	..	..	..	..	..	..	..	..	..	..	..	..	..	..
Denmark	2.22	2.29	2.46	2.78	3.13	3.45	3.69	3.88	4.37	4.95	5.56	6.08	6.86	8.29	10.33	10.93	12.17	13.52	14.54
Finland	0.95	1.02	1.09	1.13	1.27	1.41	1.49	1.62	2.13	2.59	3.07	3.20	3.91	4.75	6.49	6.48	7.73	9.67	11.26
France	8.00	8.44	8.69	9.56	10.64	11.99	13.04	13.93	15.18	18.41	23.03	26.67	30.33	36.47	49.52	51.38	61.15	72.15	81.81
Germany	37.23	38.76	40.58	44.20	49.14	53.68	60.59	65.43	73.77	83.85	92.62	100.84	109.97	129.80	168.38	164.19	186.42	197.26	206.15
Greece	0.06	0.07	0.07	0.08	0.09	0.10	0.13	0.14	0.13	0.15	0.18	0.20	0.26	0.41	0.54	0.67	0.86	0.96	1.21
Hungary	..	..	..	..	..	..	..	..	..	..	..	..	..	..	..	..	..	..	..
Iceland	0.00	0.00	0.00	0.00	0.00	0.00	0.00	0.00	0.00	0.00	0.00	0.00	0.00	0.01	0.01	0.01	0.02	0.02	0.04
Ireland	0.33	0.39	0.39	0.44	0.50	0.55	0.62	0.69	0.80	0.89	0.99	1.11	1.28	1.70	2.11	2.68	3.57	4.67	5.59
Italy	2.70	3.08	3.42	3.76	4.34	5.21	5.81	6.29	7.19	8.25	9.26	10.36	11.83	14.05	20.59	23.83	32.22	41.62	49.58
Luxembourg	0.74	0.74	0.72	0.74	0.86	0.92	0.93	0.95	1.07	1.29	1.60	1.61	1.71	2.24	3.13	2.62	2.87	2.90	3.07
Netherlands	11.45	11.52	12.23	13.29	15.16	16.68	17.67	18.84	21.13	24.82	29.36	33.53	37.52	45.09	58.27	59.32	69.46	70.68	72.40
Norway	2.18	2.30	2.39	2.62	3.01	3.29	3.56	4.00	4.40	4.70	5.34	5.73	6.41	7.80	9.60	9.95	11.23	12.20	13.96
Poland	..	..	..	..	..	..	..	..	..	..	..	..	..	..	..	..	..	..	..
Portugal	0.09	0.09	0.11	0.12	0.18	0.21	0.23	0.26	0.27	0.29	0.32	0.37	0.47	0.56	0.67	0.57	0.60	0.85	1.17
Spain	0.60	0.65	0.79	0.87	1.11	1.20	1.51	1.65	2.30	2.82	3.42	4.14	4.98	5.99	7.26	8.00	9.78	13.09	16.78
Sweden	2.79	2.95	3.14	3.40	3.86	4.16	4.43	4.74	5.14	5.91	7.01	7.65	8.32	10.49	13.93	14.30	15.89	17.11	19.66
Switzerland	7.89	8.68	9.52	10.37	11.47	12.59	13.83	14.75	16.68	19.17	21.39	23.08	25.75	28.95	33.04	31.69	34.34	38.47	38.31
Turkey	0.00	0.00	0.00	0.00	0.00	0.00	0.00	0.00	0.00	0.00	0.00	0.00	0.01	0.01	0.01	0.01	0.02	0.02	0.03
United Kingdom	9.61	10.04	10.30	10.86	11.50	12.25	13.21	13.70	16.63	18.57	21.16	23.72	24.90	31.17	41.62	48.62	63.35	77.84	85.14
OECD - Total [1]	143.13	150.06	160.02	174.13	196.73	216.43	240.68	257.79	293.74	337.91	389.73	431.02	474.75	575.68	772.28	800.70	929.10	1 023.73	1 100.90
OECD - Europe [2]	96.74	101.86	107.92	117.46	131.06	143.73	158.48	169.55	192.03	221.82	253.99	280.30	310.75	371.26	480.80	489.50	575.54	641.25	692.56
EU15	86.66	90.87	96.01	104.47	116.57	127.84	141.09	150.79	170.95	197.95	227.25	251.49	278.58	334.49	438.13	447.83	529.95	590.53	640.22

6. Imports of goods and services - at current prices and 1990 exchange rates (billions of US dollars)

	1960	1961	1962	1963	1964	1965	1966	1967	1968	1969	1970	1971	1972	1973	1974	1975	1976	1977	1978
Canada	6.25	6.44	6.90	7.19	8.16	9.29	10.76	11.53	13.06	15.20	15.28	16.63	19.48	23.94	32.06	35.89	39.06	44.09	51.61
Mexico	0.01	0.01	0.01	0.01	0.01	0.01	0.01	0.01	0.02	0.02	0.02	0.02	0.02	0.03	0.04	0.05	0.06	0.09	0.12
United States	22.80	22.70	25.00	26.10	28.10	31.50	37.10	39.90	46.60	50.50	55.80	62.30	74.20	91.20	127.50	122.70	151.10	182.40	212.30
Japan	11.33	14.50	14.03	17.07	19.70	20.66	23.72	29.08	32.85	38.45	48.24	50.10	52.80	77.78	133.00	130.67	146.74	146.88	132.43
Korea	..	..	..	..	..	..	..	..	..	..	0.93	1.24	1.46	2.48	4.20	5.27	6.53	8.21	11.39
Australia	1.97	1.79	1.91	2.07	2.48	2.87	2.69	3.03	3.35	3.48	3.83	4.16	3.96	4.93	7.76	7.82	9.58	11.54	12.90
New Zealand	0.41	0.42	0.40	0.46	0.49	0.57	0.60	0.52	0.59	0.68	0.88	0.90	1.02	1.33	1.99	2.05	2.42	2.61	2.77
Austria	3.58	3.77	3.97	4.38	4.94	5.57	6.25	6.49	7.00	8.00	9.94	11.05	12.64	14.41	18.14	18.01	21.75	24.49	24.66
Belgium	6.55	7.20	7.85	8.88	9.97	10.64	12.07	12.33	13.85	16.49	18.55	19.87	21.85	27.87	37.14	35.79	43.04	46.46	48.22
Czech Republic	..	..	..	..	..	..	..	..	..	..	..	..	..	..	..	..	..	..	..
Denmark	2.35	2.45	2.78	2.80	3.39	3.68	3.95	4.23	4.66	5.42	6.26	6.59	6.82	8.98	11.46	11.45	14.36	15.47	15.91
Finland	0.98	1.07	1.15	1.13	1.39	1.53	1.61	1.69	1.98	2.49	3.22	3.44	3.87	4.87	7.35	8.09	8.32	9.08	9.73
France	6.86	7.35	8.06	9.29	10.79	11.19	12.77	13.64	15.23	19.09	22.27	24.90	28.44	34.66	51.92	48.16	63.44	71.72	76.47
Germany	32.44	34.10	37.80	40.59	45.15	53.09	55.50	54.03	61.54	73.36	84.13	92.58	99.65	112.89	140.70	145.42	170.75	179.58	186.06
Greece	0.11	0.13	0.14	0.16	0.20	0.24	0.24	0.25	0.28	0.32	0.36	0.40	0.49	0.79	0.94	1.17	1.39	1.58	1.86
Hungary	..	..	..	..	..	..	..	..	..	..	..	..	..	..	..	..	..	..	..
Iceland	0.00	0.00	0.00	0.00	0.00	0.00	0.00	0.00	0.00	0.00	0.00	0.00	0.00	0.01	0.01	0.02	0.02	0.02	0.04
Ireland	0.39	0.45	0.48	0.54	0.61	0.70	0.73	0.75	0.94	1.11	1.21	1.34	1.49	2.02	2.85	3.08	4.20	5.56	6.73
Italy	2.79	3.11	3.58	4.46	4.33	4.44	5.16	5.90	6.29	7.61	9.15	9.88	11.29	15.58	24.78	23.97	33.97	39.78	44.93
Luxembourg	0.62	0.68	0.71	0.74	0.85	0.91	0.90	0.85	0.93	1.06	1.35	1.53	1.57	1.91	2.47	2.48	2.66	2.75	2.99
Netherlands	11.04	11.52	12.15	13.53	15.91	16.97	18.30	19.29	21.18	24.98	30.54	33.80	35.28	42.10	55.40	55.41	64.94	68.98	72.39
Norway	2.19	2.37	2.44	2.65	2.90	3.23	3.54	4.01	4.02	4.28	5.29	5.95	6.03	7.57	9.79	11.08	13.27	14.86	13.68
Poland	..	..	..	..	..	..	..	..	..	..	..	..	..	..	..	..	..	..	..
Portugal	0.12	0.15	0.14	0.16	0.21	0.24	0.26	0.28	0.31	0.33	0.40	0.46	0.54	0.69	1.04	0.89	1.05	1.52	1.85
Spain	0.49	0.70	0.97	1.22	1.44	1.92	2.30	2.28	2.74	3.26	3.67	3.89	4.91	6.32	9.69	10.27	12.95	14.93	15.91
Sweden	2.87	2.89	3.09	3.36	3.82	4.32	4.58	4.75	5.19	6.01	7.18	7.29	7.81	9.44	14.27	14.41	16.86	18.17	18.96
Switzerland	7.96	9.59	10.71	11.55	12.81	12.96	13.79	14.49	15.82	18.43	22.49	24.22	26.50	29.99	35.02	28.81	30.96	35.76	35.65
Turkey	0.00	0.00	0.00	0.00	0.00	0.00	0.00	0.00	0.00	0.00	0.00	0.01	0.01	0.01	0.02	0.03	0.04	0.04	0.05
United Kingdom	10.25	10.19	10.38	11.06	12.52	12.80	13.28	14.43	17.23	18.18	20.30	22.23	24.97	34.34	48.99	51.82	65.75	75.85	81.03
OECD - Total [1]	134.38	143.58	154.63	169.39	190.16	209.35	230.12	243.78	275.65	318.76	370.37	403.55	445.64	553.65	774.32	769.53	918.67	1 014.22	1 069.30
OECD - Europe [2]	91.61	97.72	106.39	116.49	131.23	144.45	155.23	159.70	179.18	210.44	246.32	269.45	294.16	354.44	471.96	470.35	569.71	626.60	657.17
EU15	81.46	85.75	93.23	102.29	115.52	128.26	137.90	141.19	159.33	187.73	218.53	239.27	261.62	316.87	427.12	430.42	525.43	575.91	607.75

1. Excluding Korea Czech Republic Hungary and Poland.
2. Excluding Czech Republic Hungary and Poland.

Formation brute de capital fixe - aux prix courants et taux de change de 1990 (milliards de dollars É-U) 4.

1979	1980	1981	1982	1983	1984	1985	1986	1987	1988	1989	1990	1991	1992	1993	1994	1995	1996	1997	
54.71	62.51	75.00	70.33	70.80	74.24	82.50	88.55	101.48	114.56	124.85	120.84	111.71	108.89	107.52	118.15	116.00	121.00	135.90	Canada
0.28	0.40	0.59	0.82	1.14	1.93	3.30	5.62	13.00	27.42	33.66	46.97	62.95	78.41	82.91	97.72	105.49	159.98	221.45	Mexique
529.20	547.30	603.20	590.10	629.50	734.50	785.50	818.20	835.50	881.60	924.60	932.50	882.10	937.50	1011.70	1106.40	1176.90	1269.30	1359.50	États-Unis
484.64	523.66	544.98	550.69	544.79	574.98	608.05	631.94	684.80	765.64	844.49	942.51	994.53	991.26	969.91	948.21	950.42	1024.39	991.41	Japon
14.94	17.28	18.89	22.02	26.77	30.21	33.11	38.11	46.04	55.70	67.29	94.06	117.20	124.20	135.95	154.54	181.79	203.02	208.18	Corée
21.33	24.95	30.19	32.83	32.33	36.92	44.12	47.75	53.11	60.50	70.63	67.05	61.05	62.58	66.51	74.53	77.73	81.31	88.22	Australie
2.43	2.84	3.94	4.64	5.14	5.96	7.15	7.38	7.98	7.69	8.53	8.23	6.88	7.33	8.81	10.50	11.48	12.00	11.65	Nouvelle-Zélande
19.41	21.58	22.73	22.27	23.10	23.78	25.92	27.19	28.83	31.14	33.95	37.11	41.01	42.52	42.67	46.91	48.73	50.73	53.46	Autriche
19.78	22.01	19.79	20.21	19.81	21.12	22.75	23.81	25.55	30.33	35.27	39.74	38.68	40.34	39.53	40.37	42.80	43.38	46.08	Belgique
..	..	..	..	..	..	..	..	..	..	..	7.55	8.36	11.41	13.52	16.07	20.93	23.91	23.97	République tchèque
13.72	13.31	12.08	14.12	15.53	18.41	21.80	26.19	26.13	25.03	26.37	26.82	26.76	26.01	25.16	27.21	30.58	32.78	36.41	Danemark
10.08	12.74	14.33	16.12	18.19	19.10	20.77	21.68	24.20	23.58	35.61	36.39	28.79	23.00	18.62	19.40	22.25	24.07	27.42	Finlande
101.94	118.59	128.65	142.19	148.68	154.33	166.25	179.52	193.70	213.23	241.41	255.52	263.88	258.10	240.83	244.63	252.48	251.97	254.91	France
206.34	227.43	228.54	223.43	234.54	240.15	244.84	257.64	267.82	285.03	310.05	354.25	406.01	439.03	427.68	449.44	455.28	447.75	447.43	Allemagne
3.47	3.89	4.29	4.83	5.87	6.61	8.28	9.58	10.11	12.41	15.44	19.10	23.03	25.13	26.92	28.10	31.42	36.14	41.41	Grèce
..	..	..	..	..	..	..	..	..	..	..	7.52	8.27	9.25	10.60	13.90	16.76	21.98	28.07	Hongrie
0.04	0.07	0.11	0.17	0.25	0.33	0.44	0.53	0.73	0.87	1.01	1.20	1.31	1.19	1.10	1.13	1.13	1.49	1.69	Islande
4.04	4.48	5.63	5.93	5.72	5.88	5.66	5.68	5.74	6.35	7.39	8.58	8.15	8.51	8.44	9.69	11.23	13.25	15.72	Irlande
59.16	78.71	92.67	101.82	112.43	127.56	139.86	148.16	161.64	182.95	201.29	222.05	235.91	240.55	219.32	227.70	256.13	265.04	271.19	Italie
0.89	1.08	1.08	1.19	1.11	1.16	1.09	1.47	1.74	2.09	2.26	2.49	2.89	2.76	3.15	2.98	3.23	3.26	3.79	Luxembourg
37.66	40.12	38.46	38.17	39.66	42.45	45.96	49.07	50.29	53.48	57.16	59.28	60.66	62.23	61.30	63.27	66.97	71.73	77.92	Pays-Bas
12.61	13.48	15.44	17.19	19.46	20.76	21.55	24.82	27.30	28.98	27.97	24.95	25.15	24.98	26.87	28.65	30.75	34.59	39.93	Norvège
..	..	..	..	..	..	..	..	..	..	..	12.38	16.61	20.31	26.05	35.87	51.30	72.38	99.02	Pologne
2.33	3.16	4.08	5.06	5.92	5.85	6.77	8.61	11.16	14.21	16.25	19.06	20.79	22.39	22.02	24.08	26.20	28.03	31.23	Portugal
27.88	33.04	36.58	41.83	45.97	45.88	53.06	61.77	73.75	89.11	106.61	120.29	128.19	126.45	118.71	126.16	142.19	146.92	157.25	Espagne
15.53	17.98	18.48	13.95	22.35	25.14	28.21	29.65	33.44	38.03	45.79	49.42	47.37	41.33	34.76	35.35	40.61	42.17	40.19	Suède
27.30	31.97	34.83	35.08	36.98	39.22	41.71	44.61	46.90	52.53	57.91	61.80	61.17	56.60	54.29	56.66	55.86	52.93	52.21	Suisse
0.21	0.32	0.58	0.77	1.01	1.60	2.93	4.89	7.09	12.93	19.87	34.46	57.56	99.06	201.45	365.06	709.29	1420.82	2920.44	Turquie
65.57	73.80	73.34	73.59	86.32	97.98	107.81	115.47	133.45	162.52	187.23	191.02	173.56	166.27	167.43	178.01	193.08	203.53	216.65	Royaume-Uni
1720.53	1879.42	2009.60	2039.35	2126.60	2325.84	2496.29	2639.79	2825.45	3132.21	3435.60	3681.65	3770.10	3892.42	3987.59	4330.32	4858.24	5838.55	7543.46	OCDE - Total[1]
627.96	717.76	751.70	789.94	842.90	893.31	965.68	1040.35	1129.58	1274.81	1428.83	1563.54	1650.87	1706.45	1740.23	1974.81	2420.22	3170.57	4735.32	OCDE - Europe[2]
587.80	671.91	700.74	736.73	785.19	835.39	899.05	965.50	1047.56	1179.49	1322.07	1441.12	1505.69	1524.63	1456.52	1523.29	1623.18	1660.75	1721.05	UE15

Exportations de biens et services - aux prix courants et taux de change de 1990 (milliards de dollars É-U) 5.

1979	1980	1981	1982	1983	1984	1985	1986	1987	1988	1989	1990	1991	1992	1993	1994	1995	1996	1997	
64.03	75.15	82.52	82.83	88.88	109.42	116.75	121.33	127.55	139.53	143.76	149.50	146.55	161.63	187.60	223.25	257.85	273.79	293.17	Canada
0.14	0.22	0.29	0.68	1.53	2.30	3.29	6.18	16.96	29.50	37.07	48.87	55.23	60.97	68.10	84.96	198.68	289.00	342.46	Mexique
227.00	277.30	301.10	280.30	272.90	298.30	297.00	314.10	357.70	438.70	500.90	548.20	592.20	629.50	647.80	708.50	804.20	856.00	945.70	États-Unis
177.00	227.13	262.29	272.05	271.25	311.25	319.82	263.07	250.08	258.88	292.51	317.15	322.69	326.96	305.25	306.72	313.51	343.26	389.06	Japon
12.35	18.29	24.50	26.52	32.14	36.91	39.52	50.91	63.65	72.24	68.99	75.54	85.81	98.10	110.44	130.16	164.41	178.36	226.72	Corée
15.41	17.60	17.60	19.91	20.66	24.55	30.19	31.81	37.08	41.48	45.23	49.59	53.23	57.19	62.35	65.23	72.64	78.30	87.43	Australie
3.58	4.18	4.92	5.53	6.27	7.89	8.32	9.02	9.94	10.77	11.43	11.91	12.93	14.25	15.10	16.21	16.36	16.43	16.81	Nouvelle-Zélande
28.82	32.21	35.58	37.42	39.09	43.22	47.72	45.44	45.99	51.96	58.89	64.06	68.14	69.62	69.18	73.78	79.24	86.97	93.34	Autriche
55.04	59.81	67.80	78.56	86.42	99.65	102.71	98.54	99.41	112.46	130.10	133.59	136.84	139.98	137.40	150.90	161.43	169.05	189.31	Belgique
..	..	..	..	..	..	..	..	..	..	..	16.16	20.26	22.00	24.76	28.75	35.75	38.72	44.90	République tchèque
17.05	20.54	25.04	28.38	31.31	34.87	37.90	35.88	36.98	40.15	44.70	47.78	51.56	52.39	51.48	55.37	57.91	60.83	65.27	Danemark
13.74	16.60	18.92	19.82	21.64	24.63	25.64	25.01	26.17	28.44	30.52	31.08	28.58	33.55	41.70	47.74	54.20	57.26	64.78	Finlande
96.77	111.00	131.17	145.14	165.40	193.44	206.40	197.25	202.26	224.29	259.14	269.59	282.46	291.65	285.82	309.28	331.11	348.50	398.23	France
225.53	252.05	285.93	308.46	313.87	349.68	387.09	379.40	377.72	404.26	454.36	457.21	450.03	453.23	431.74	468.49	508.28	536.09	601.46	Allemagne
1.48	2.13	2.51	2.81	3.62	4.90	5.81	7.33	9.13	10.70	12.51	13.94	16.53	20.03	21.17	24.63	26.86	29.64	32.45	Grèce
..	..	..	..	..	..	..	..	..	..	..	10.09	12.95	14.64	14.82	19.97	30.29	39.15	56.78	Hongrie
0.06	0.10	0.15	0.21	0.46	0.58	0.84	1.06	1.23	1.40	1.82	2.14	2.16	2.09	2.33	2.70	2.77	3.03	3.28	Islande
6.53	7.69	9.13	10.67	12.85	16.20	17.81	17.16	19.61	22.58	26.73	26.72	28.05	31.19	36.37	41.76	50.87	56.70	67.05	Irlande
62.62	70.40	89.85	103.52	115.93	136.93	154.28	151.13	159.43	173.19	199.01	219.23	226.55	246.65	296.71	333.79	410.29	417.32	444.84	Italie
3.62	3.84	4.00	4.61	5.14	6.38	7.27	7.40	7.48	8.54	9.77	10.13	10.79	11.48	12.37	13.68	13.99	14.33	15.38	Luxembourg
84.15	95.88	111.31	114.44	117.90	133.28	142.09	121.89	120.41	131.94	147.00	153.62	160.96	161.94	161.00	172.68	186.48	198.02	217.87	Pays-Bas
16.80	21.64	24.83	26.31	29.48	34.03	37.55	31.00	31.92	34.16	41.96	46.93	49.21	47.94	50.47	53.23	56.46	66.18	71.50	Norvège
..	..	..	..	..	..	..	..	..	..	..	16.90	20.03	28.68	37.61	53.25	78.71	94.83	118.40	Pologne
1.98	2.53	2.87	3.60	5.31	7.73	9.69	10.80	13.31	16.08	20.16	23.47	24.59	25.53	25.89	29.81	34.22	36.42	39.14	Portugal
19.38	23.41	29.84	35.62	45.78	57.53	62.86	62.95	68.63	74.31	79.96	83.93	92.31	102.22	116.16	141.69	164.14	184.05	216.87	Espagne
23.74	26.44	29.42	34.59	42.79	48.97	51.68	52.57	56.17	60.77	66.65	68.74	68.29	67.85	79.96	94.23	114.11	114.06	128.64	Suède
40.32	45.05	49.74	50.07	51.65	57.98	64.08	64.15	65.16	70.54	79.55	82.82	84.02	87.94	90.20	91.42	91.80	94.68	106.38	Suisse
0.04	0.11	0.26	0.49	0.70	1.37	2.21	2.70	4.46	9.24	14.12	20.02	33.43	60.32	103.88	316.79	591.91	1219.91	2717.26	Turquie
98.48	112.04	120.45	129.95	142.62	163.64	182.04	174.66	189.90	191.53	216.93	237.71	239.78	254.38	286.47	315.30	356.39	387.74	399.11	Royaume-Uni
1283.32	1505.05	1707.52	1795.96	1893.45	2168.72	2321.03	2231.84	2334.69	2585.39	2924.77	3117.91	3237.09	3410.49	3586.49	4142.14	4955.68	5937.54	7946.78	OCDE - Total[1]
796.16	903.47	1038.80	1134.67	1231.95	1415.02	1545.66	1486.33	1535.38	1666.53	1893.87	1992.69	2054.26	2159.99	2300.30	2737.27	3292.45	4080.75	5872.15	OCDE - Europe[2]
738.94	836.57	963.83	1057.59	1149.67	1321.05	1440.98	1387.41	1432.60	1551.19	1756.42	1840.78	1885.44	1961.70	2053.42	2273.13	2549.52	2696.95	2973.73	UE15

Importations de biens et services - aux prix courants et taux de change de 1990 (milliards de dollars É-U) 6.

1979	1980	1981	1982	1983	1984	1985	1986	1987	1988	1989	1990	1991	1992	1993	1994	1995	1996	1997	
62.85	70.42	80.59	70.61	77.91	96.35	107.64	117.61	122.32	135.91	144.11	149.14	150.33	164.28	188.09	216.83	237.86	247.14	281.35	Canada
0.18	0.27	0.37	0.47	0.78	1.30	2.26	4.90	11.92	27.44	37.20	51.77	65.04	81.11	85.64	109.33	181.28	270.02	342.81	Mexique
252.70	293.80	317.80	303.20	328.60	405.10	417.20	452.20	507.90	553.20	589.70	628.60	622.30	669.00	719.30	812.10	904.50	965.70	1059.60	États-Unis
190.82	241.98	248.13	257.90	236.61	254.61	245.40	171.22	174.01	200.74	253.94	296.10	270.19	254.79	230.29	237.49	264.33	324.76	347.51	Japon
15.30	22.29	27.86	28.50	32.57	36.79	38.04	42.90	51.37	57.32	63.28	76.89	93.32	101.50	108.75	133.32	169.67	200.14	231.03	Corée
15.02	18.23	20.87	23.56	22.61	27.84	34.45	36.53	38.64	43.46	51.72	51.65	51.06	57.08	63.04	68.88	76.98	77.87	84.65	Australie
3.73	4.34	5.47	6.16	6.60	8.67	9.13	9.09	9.33	9.30	11.30	11.60	11.40	12.95	13.48	15.00	15.61	15.94	16.54	Nouvelle-Zélande
29.16	33.92	36.81	35.79	37.68	43.06	47.49	44.33	45.51	51.24	57.47	62.00	66.67	67.90	67.95	74.14	80.08	88.11	94.77	Autriche
57.22	63.16	70.38	80.80	85.72	98.58	100.78	94.31	95.75	107.39	125.13	129.24	132.07	133.51	129.04	140.95	150.89	158.69	177.55	Belgique
..	..	..	..	..	..	..	..	..	..	..	15.40	17.41	21.31	24.19	29.91	38.57	43.80	49.18	République tchèque
18.98	21.54	24.92	28.49	30.06	34.20	38.14	36.96	35.36	36.67	40.76	41.02	43.41	42.91	41.58	47.02	51.37	53.07	59.19	Danemark
13.06	17.00	18.11	19.29	21.28	22.53	24.75	23.51	25.57	28.73	32.95	33.11	29.40	31.88	34.90	39.24	42.13	44.87	50.38	Finlande
94.05	117.31	136.77	157.85	166.64	188.23	200.65	187.65	200.97	223.61	257.66	269.92	278.12	274.28	257.98	279.70	297.77	310.76	339.38	France
220.54	257.70	280.03	284.81	292.82	322.96	348.08	319.21	318.28	340.11	384.38	402.51	451.43	453.79	420.73	455.48	491.53	509.66	567.50	Allemagne
2.35	2.92	3.62	4.80	6.02	7.41	9.84	11.07	12.96	14.89	18.88	23.27	27.65	31.41	33.91	36.32	42.36	46.06	49.55	Grèce
..	..	..	..	..	..	..	..	..	..	..	8.81	13.33	14.76	19.43	24.45	32.22	41.38	58.07	Hongrie
0.06	0.10	0.15	0.25	0.43	0.58	0.83	0.96	1.27	1.44	1.70	2.05	2.24	2.09	2.10	2.31	2.48	2.98	3.22	Islande
8.72	9.83	11.85	12.35	13.60	16.35	17.31	16.42	17.67	19.72	23.75	24.04	24.95	26.33	29.16	34.09	40.81	45.04	52.09	Irlande
59.95	79.65	98.08	109.65	113.31	139.41	157.47	140.84	155.29	172.20	200.60	218.84	226.10	246.76	252.34	282.70	347.77	335.62	374.38	Italie
3.43	3.84	4.11	4.66	5.09	6.23	6.87	6.96	7.33	8.29	9.32	9.97	10.99	10.83	11.31	12.01	12.56	12.72	13.54	Luxembourg
85.02	96.74	104.31	105.47	109.61	121.61	130.87	112.82	113.99	122.12	136.61	140.49	146.84	147.82	141.41	151.11	163.02	173.28	190.57	Pays-Bas
15.77	18.55	20.59	22.99	23.83	26.90	31.01	34.07	34.06	34.70	37.93	39.36	39.36	39.27	41.80	44.60	47.55	52.16	59.27	Norvège
..	..	..	..	..	..	..	..	..	..	..	12.68	21.66	26.82	36.02	50.94	74.67	105.50	141.59	Pologne
2.72	3.82	4.91	6.02	7.34	9.20	10.55	11.49	15.49	20.41	23.92	28.50	30.90	32.78	33.09	37.52	41.87	45.09	49.98	Portugal
18.99	26.89	33.30	39.31	47.63	52.23	57.49	56.21	68.04	78.70	94.38	100.56	109.26	118.34	119.49	140.59	163.44	178.21	207.70	Espagne
24.54	28.14	29.62	35.18	40.23	44.05	49.20	47.48	52.93	57.67	65.51	67.89	64.50	63.80	71.21	83.42	96.17	94.85	108.04	Suède
40.91	49.37	51.05	49.42	51.72	58.42	63.39	62.18	63.65	69.67	79.96	81.64	80.71	79.32	77.78	79.91	81.31	83.71	94.54	Suisse
0.08	0.24	0.38	0.59	0.87	1.63	2.50	3.11	5.09	8.70	15.49	26.47	40.18	72.70	146.96	302.28	724.61	1575.76	3359.15	Turquie
97.14	102.81	107.62	120.80	138.12	155.16	176.06	179.95	199.17	222.60	254.65	264.37	251.51	268.76	300.63	326.75	364.78	397.88	405.70	Royaume-Uni
1318.00	1562.56	1709.83	1780.42	1865.10	2152.60	2289.37	2181.08	2332.49	2588.92	2949.03	3154.09	3226.60	3383.68	3513.20	4029.78	4923.05	6109.93	8388.95	OCDE - Total[1]
792.70	933.52	1036.61	1118.53	1191.99	1358.73	1473.29	1389.53	1468.37	1618.88	1861.07	1965.24	2056.29	2144.48	2213.37	2570.15	3242.49	4208.51	6256.49	OCDE - Europe[2]
735.88	865.26	964.43	1045.28	1115.14	1271.20	1375.56	1289.21	1364.30	1504.36	1725.98	1815.72	1893.80	1951.10	1944.73	2141.05	2386.54	2493.90	2740.31	UE15

1. Non compris la Corée la République tchèque la Hongrie et la Pologne.
2. Non compris la République tchèque la Hongrie et la Pologne.

7. Gross domestic product - at the price levels and exchange rates of 1990 (billions of US dollars)

	1960	1961	1962	1963	1964	1965	1966	1967	1968	1969	1970	1971	1972	1973	1974	1975	1976	1977	1978
Canada	174.57	180.06	192.39	202.12	215.43	229.47	244.58	251.71	265.04	278.98	286.18	302.12	318.08	340.86	354.79	362.80	382.67	395.53	411.53
Mexico	61.89	64.37	67.31	72.34	80.03	85.23	90.48	95.85	102.80	108.77	115.91	120.75	130.99	142.01	150.69	159.14	165.89	171.60	185.76
United States	2233.00	2288.00	2406.20	2501.80	2641.40	2789.30	2955.20	3035.70	3163.00	3247.40	3254.40	3348.00	3519.10	3701.40	3686.70	3671.50	3850.50	4014.60	4213.50
Japan	479.96	537.76	585.67	635.30	709.48	750.77	830.64	922.70	1041.57	1171.53	1296.98	1357.92	1472.17	1590.43	1570.94	1619.51	1683.88	1757.81	1850.48
Korea	..	..	..	..	..	..	..	..	..	..	51.30	55.65	58.34	65.80	71.11	75.83	84.75	93.50	102.27
Australia	93.49	93.14	99.07	105.61	112.25	118.49	121.83	130.28	137.90	146.26	155.07	164.25	170.60	179.63	182.46	187.55	194.53	196.47	202.29
New Zealand	20.81	21.99	22.46	23.87	25.05	26.65	28.31	27.01	27.00	29.75	29.33	30.85	32.18	34.46	36.51	36.09	36.97	35.17	35.31
Austria	56.16	59.14	60.56	63.03	66.83	68.75	72.62	74.81	78.15	83.06	88.98	93.52	99.33	104.19	108.29	107.90	112.84	118.12	117.69
Belgium	72.52	76.13	80.08	83.60	89.41	92.62	95.49	99.19	103.33	110.17	116.99	121.38	127.76	135.59	141.28	139.40	147.28	148.21	152.42
Czech Republic	..	..	..	..	..	..	..	..	..	..	..	..	..	..	..	..	..	..	..
Denmark	56.75	60.37	63.79	64.20	70.15	73.34	75.35	77.93	81.03	86.15	87.90	90.24	95.00	98.45	97.53	96.89	103.16	104.84	106.38
Finland	44.24	47.60	49.02	50.63	53.28	56.11	57.44	58.68	60.03	65.79	70.71	72.19	77.70	82.91	85.42	86.40	86.04	86.25	83.05
France	408.83	431.34	460.12	484.73	516.32	540.99	569.20	595.89	621.26	664.69	702.79	736.80	769.55	811.43	835.21	829.39	865.24	897.54	922.45
Germany	654.66	684.96	716.91	737.08	786.18	828.27	851.38	848.76	895.04	961.82	1010.26	1041.15	1085.41	1137.14	1139.35	1125.10	1184.99	1218.71	1255.23
Greece	21.41	23.80	24.16	26.61	28.81	31.51	33.43	35.27	37.62	41.34	44.63	47.81	52.05	55.86	53.83	57.09	60.72	62.80	67.01
Hungary	..	..	..	..	..	..	..	..	..	..	..	..	..	..	..	..	..	..	..
Iceland	1.64	1.64	1.78	1.96	2.15	2.31	2.51	2.48	2.35	2.40	2.58	2.92	3.10	3.31	3.50	3.52	3.73	4.06	4.30
Ireland	13.32	13.98	14.43	15.12	15.69	16.00	16.14	17.07	18.48	19.56	20.08	20.78	22.13	23.17	24.16	25.53	25.88	28.01	30.02
Italy	353.75	382.78	406.53	429.34	441.34	455.77	483.05	517.72	551.61	585.24	616.32	628.00	646.37	688.66	720.95	705.48	751.32	773.03	801.35
Luxembourg	3.67	3.81	3.86	3.99	4.31	4.39	4.44	4.45	4.63	5.10	5.18	5.32	5.67	6.14	6.40	5.98	6.13	6.23	6.48
Netherlands	104.61	104.92	112.10	116.17	125.78	132.38	136.01	143.19	152.38	162.18	171.41	178.65	184.56	193.21	200.88	200.69	210.97	215.86	220.95
Norway	38.04	40.43	41.57	43.14	45.30	47.70	49.50	52.60	53.79	56.21	57.34	59.96	63.06	65.65	69.06	71.94	76.84	79.59	83.20
Poland	..	..	..	..	..	..	..	..	..	..	..	..	..	..	..	..	..	..	..
Portugal	17.19	18.13	19.34	20.48	21.83	23.46	24.41	26.26	28.59	29.19	31.85	33.97	36.69	40.80	41.26	39.47	42.19	44.56	45.81
Spain	126.64	141.63	155.72	170.67	179.73	190.97	204.80	213.69	227.79	248.08	258.61	270.64	292.69	315.49	333.22	335.02	346.09	355.92	361.12
Sweden	98.59	104.19	108.62	114.41	122.21	126.89	129.54	133.90	138.77	145.72	155.15	156.62	160.20	166.56	171.89	176.28	178.14	175.30	178.37
Switzerland	103.85	112.27	117.65	123.39	129.88	134.01	137.31	141.50	146.58	154.84	164.71	171.43	176.91	182.31	184.96	171.49	169.08	173.20	173.91
Turkey	35.06	35.66	37.83	41.40	43.11	44.24	49.42	51.64	55.10	58.03	60.87	64.26	69.03	71.29	75.27	80.67	89.11	92.15	93.53
United Kingdom	467.58	479.61	485.98	505.21	530.66	545.46	556.64	569.50	592.20	604.35	618.61	631.72	654.07	698.05	688.57	687.77	703.21	718.46	744.07
OECD - Total[1]	5742.22	6007.73	6333.15	6636.18	7056.62	7415.06	7819.73	8127.79	8586.03	9066.62	9422.86	9751.24	10264.43	10869.00	10963.13	10982.61	11477.43	11873.99	12351.83
OECD - Europe[2]	2678.50	2822.40	2960.06	3095.14	3272.98	3415.15	3548.70	3664.54	3848.73	4083.94	4284.99	4427.34	4621.30	4880.20	4981.04	4946.02	5162.98	5302.80	5452.85
EU15	2499.90	2632.39	2761.23	2885.25	3052.53	3186.89	3309.95	3416.31	3590.91	3812.46	3999.49	4128.77	4309.20	4557.65	4648.25	4618.39	4824.21	4953.81	5097.91

8. Private final consumption expenditure - at the price levels and exchange rates of 1990 (billions of US dollars)

	1960	1961	1962	1963	1964	1965	1966	1967	1968	1969	1970	1971	1972	1973	1974	1975	1976	1977	1978
Canada	105.03	106.28	111.71	116.30	122.48	129.72	136.17	141.08	147.20	154.24	156.79	166.39	177.78	190.02	199.83	208.29	219.43	225.77	233.38
Mexico	45.87	47.72	49.50	52.51	58.47	62.51	65.73	70.07	74.92	79.95	85.04	89.48	95.52	101.86	107.11	113.23	118.37	120.78	130.63
United States	1344.70	1373.30	1435.60	1488.10	1572.30	1664.20	1751.90	1804.50	1901.10	1972.20	2022.80	2092.60	2211.80	2314.10	2301.90	2349.60	2472.60	2569.60	2676.80
Japan	319.37	352.60	379.21	412.55	457.03	483.36	531.84	587.11	637.22	703.14	755.25	796.74	868.26	944.73	943.93	985.50	1014.16	1055.06	1110.48
Korea	..	..	..	..	..	..	..	..	..	..	33.81	36.78	38.57	41.82	44.64	46.92	50.80	53.49	58.02
Australia	58.40	58.18	61.80	65.55	69.02	71.68	74.31	78.36	82.65	87.59	92.00	95.57	99.70	106.13	110.01	114.45	117.73	119.21	123.22
New Zealand	14.45	14.67	15.23	16.29	16.88	17.85	18.60	17.84	18.27	19.28	20.19	20.28	21.71	23.54	24.49	24.31	23.51	22.75	23.16
Austria	31.96	33.60	34.71	36.63	37.89	39.76	41.48	42.93	44.65	45.96	47.87	51.09	54.19	57.10	58.81	60.72	63.48	66.97	65.89
Belgium	49.06	49.87	51.81	54.15	55.57	57.95	59.45	61.14	64.38	67.81	70.78	74.26	78.66	85.07	87.45	88.20	92.69	95.13	97.50
Czech Republic	..	..	..	..	..	..	..	..	..	..	..	..	..	..	..	..	..	..	..
Denmark	33.01	35.44	37.53	37.54	40.49	41.88	43.67	44.94	45.80	48.69	50.39	50.01	50.84	53.30	51.78	53.68	57.91	58.53	58.97
Finland	22.53	24.25	25.71	26.84	28.33	29.91	30.67	31.32	31.34	34.70	37.33	37.95	41.14	43.58	44.36	45.76	46.15	45.69	46.78
France	244.02	258.53	276.79	295.88	312.54	325.07	340.78	358.14	372.39	394.86	411.69	430.96	451.04	473.03	478.87	490.88	513.53	527.38	546.22
Germany	321.72	341.32	360.68	370.77	390.60	417.39	430.41	435.34	455.79	492.14	529.99	559.11	585.15	602.40	605.37	624.44	648.97	678.43	703.45
Greece	15.90	16.98	17.70	18.60	20.23	21.78	23.25	24.70	26.40	28.03	30.50	32.19	34.44	37.07	37.32	39.36	41.45	43.34	45.81
Hungary	..	..	..	..	..	..	..	..	..	..	..	..	..	..	..	..	..	..	..
Iceland	0.93	0.93	1.03	1.14	1.25	1.34	1.52	1.54	1.46	1.39	1.61	1.89	2.02	2.13	2.35	2.12	2.24	2.53	2.75
Ireland	10.43	10.76	11.13	11.60	12.10	12.19	12.38	12.84	13.99	14.74	14.59	15.06	15.84	16.98	17.26	17.40	17.89	19.10	20.84
Italy	180.57	194.07	207.94	227.22	234.75	242.41	259.77	278.94	293.36	312.71	336.50	348.56	361.01	385.02	399.51	402.38	422.68	436.14	448.75
Luxembourg	2.04	2.14	2.23	2.34	2.55	2.65	2.70	2.70	2.81	2.96	3.14	3.32	3.48	3.68	3.84	4.05	4.17	4.27	4.39
Netherlands	56.10	56.03	62.64	67.06	71.01	76.32	78.75	83.03	88.50	95.49	102.55	105.94	109.65	114.03	118.25	122.15	128.63	134.55	140.42
Norway	23.29	24.64	25.40	26.26	27.24	27.91	28.92	30.02	31.13	33.52	33.51	35.05	36.08	37.13	38.56	40.54	43.00	45.98	45.23
Poland	..	..	..	..	..	..	..	..	..	..	..	..	..	..	..	..	..	..	..
Portugal	12.79	13.66	13.95	14.89	14.68	15.34	15.48	16.25	20.57	21.48	22.05	24.85	25.85	28.96	31.78	31.50	32.60	32.79	32.12
Spain	81.80	90.79	98.77	109.93	114.64	122.43	131.27	139.17	147.49	158.04	165.41	173.85	188.28	202.97	213.32	217.16	229.32	232.76	234.85
Sweden	59.68	62.85	64.94	67.81	70.52	73.52	74.95	76.66	79.81	83.35	86.26	86.34	89.30	91.61	94.70	97.35	101.40	100.34	99.63
Switzerland	58.71	62.71	66.72	69.94	73.24	75.78	78.04	80.32	83.44	87.99	92.72	97.13	102.41	105.24	104.73	101.67	102.75	105.86	108.21
Turkey	28.85	29.13	31.41	34.52	34.86	35.75	39.01	40.21	43.14	45.43	46.44	50.62	53.89	54.67	50.42	54.62	59.81	71.55	72.96
United Kingdom	276.57	282.68	289.26	301.52	310.71	315.35	320.84	328.58	337.74	339.80	349.65	360.71	383.01	403.97	398.12	396.76	398.67	397.30	418.53
OECD - Total[1]	3397.78	3543.13	3733.39	3925.95	4149.37	4364.07	4591.88	4787.76	5045.55	5325.49	5565.06	5799.95	6141.05	6478.32	6524.06	686.11	6973.14	7211.84	7490.99
OECD - Europe[2]	1509.97	1590.38	1680.34	1774.65	1853.18	1934.75	2013.33	2088.79	2184.20	2309.09	2432.99	2538.89	2666.28	2797.94	2836.79	890.73	3007.34	3098.66	3193.33
EU15	1398.19	1472.97	1555.78	1642.78	1716.59	1793.96	1865.84	1936.68	2025.03	2140.78	2258.72	2354.20	2471.87	2598.77	2640.73	691.78	2799.54	2872.73	2964.16

9. Government final consumption expenditure - at the price levels and exchange rates of 1990 (billions of US dollars)

	1960	1961	1962	1963	1964	1965	1966	1967	1968	1969	1970	1971	1972	1973	1974	1975	1976	1977	1978
Canada	36.35	41.09	42.98	44.40	46.77	48.91	53.24	57.95	61.74	64.35	69.98	72.86	75.10	78.65	83.54	89.28	91.01	95.19	96.77
Mexico	3.10	3.34	3.84	4.32	4.84	5.01	5.43	5.79	6.40	6.68	7.24	8.00	9.08	9.99	10.62	12.12	12.89	12.75	14.01
United States	504.00	526.30	547.90	554.60	563.70	574.30	633.90	684.80	701.40	701.90	695.40	677.90	680.10	673.30	689.90	704.10	707.70	719.70	734.10
Japan	71.82	76.05	82.63	89.49	92.42	95.96	101.42	105.44	112.19	118.82	127.28	137.51	144.34	152.14	151.50	170.58	177.79	185.21	194.86
Korea	..	..	..	..	..	..	..	..	..	..	9.04	9.64	10.04	10.01	11.12	12.00	12.37	13.09	14.28
Australia	12.50	13.25	13.78	14.31	15.47	17.13	18.24	20.04	21.44	21.91	22.68	23.44	24.30	26.13	27.79	30.18	31.99	32.70	34.45
New Zealand	3.27	3.32	3.49	3.61	3.74	4.07	4.48	4.26	4.36	4.38	4.57	4.68	4.96	5.16	5.59	5.86	5.82	6.05	6.34
Austria	13.63	13.88	14.21	14.77	15.50	15.61	16.34	16.99	17.52	17.92	18.51	19.12	19.90	20.50	21.67	22.53	23.49	24.15	24.35
Belgium	10.55	10.75	11.67	13.02	13.57	14.32	15.00	15.85	16.40	17.43	17.97	18.97	20.08	21.16	21.88	22.86	23.71	24.24	25.71
Czech Republic	..	..	..	..	..	..	..	..	..	..	..	..	..	..	..	..	..	..	..
Denmark	11.13	11.72	12.88	13.25	14.21	14.70	15.55	16.73	17.52	18.71	20.00	21.09	22.30	23.19	24.00	24.49	25.58	26.19	27.82
Finland	7.42	7.86	8.48	9.07	9.26	9.69	10.14	10.60	11.22	11.60	12.23	12.94	13.94	14.72	15.38	16.45	17.39	18.12	18.78
France	82.87	86.84	90.94	94.01	97.92	101.07	103.81	108.23	114.30	119.01	123.99	128.87	133.41	137.92	139.60	145.72	151.77	155.39	163.27
Germany	128.85	136.77	149.72	158.96	161.85	169.76	175.23	181.61	182.62	190.57	198.76	208.85	217.60	228.44	237.62	246.79	250.47	253.77	263.55
Greece	2.81	2.93	3.13	3.26	3.56	3.88	4.13	4.48	4.54	4.88	5.17	5.43	5.74	6.13	6.87	7.69	8.08	8.61	8.91
Hungary	..	..	..	..	..	..	..	..	..	..	..	..	..	..	..	..	..	..	..
Iceland	0.20	0.20	0.22	0.23	0.25	0.27	0.29	0.31	0.33	0.34	0.37	0.40	0.46	0.50	0.54	0.59	0.62	0.63	0.68
Ireland	2.33	2.37	2.45	2.55	2.62	2.72	2.75	2.87	3.04	3.25	3.62	3.93	4.22	4.51	4.85	5.27	5.41	5.52	5.96
Italy	76.15	79.49	82.58	86.12	89.76	93.32	97.01	101.26	106.51	109.49	112.31	117.82	123.54	127.02	130.23	133.52	136.58	140.62	145.30
Luxembourg	0.56	0.56	0.58	0.61	0.61	0.62	0.66	0.69	0.72	0.75	0.78	0.80	0.83	0.86	0.90	0.93	0.95	0.98	1.00
Netherlands	18.77	19.30	19.94	20.88	21.24	21.57	21.94	22.47	22.96	23.99	25.44	26.55	26.76	26.98	27.57	28.70	29.88	30.90	32.08
Norway	6.06	6.46	6.77	7.22	7.68	8.40	8.65	9.47	9.86	10.34	10.99	11.65	12.18	12.84	13.36	14.21	15.26	16.02	16.87
Poland	..	..	..	..	..	..	..	..	..	..	..	..	..	..	..	..	..	..	..
Portugal	1.28	1.63	1.76	1.82	1.94	2.08	2.19	2.43	2.64	2.73	2.92	3.11	3.37	3.64	4.27	4.55	4.87	5.44	5.68
Spain	17.53	18.49	19.74	21.65	21.92	22.70	23.15	23.70	24.15	25.21	26.66	27.80	29.25	31.12	34.01	35.78	38.25	39.74	41.89
Sweden	22.55	23.32	24.79	27.14	27.95	29.29	30.91	32.35	34.54	36.35	39.29	40.15	41.13	42.18	43.48	45.52	47.12	48.53	50.13
Switzerland	10.76	12.62	13.66	14.85	15.24	15.94	16.26	16.51	17.15	17.99	18.85	19.96	20.53	21.03	21.38	21.52	22.12	22.21	22.65
Turkey	2.48	2.67	2.78	3.01	3.24	3.40	3.65	3.96	4.23	4.51	4.67	4.95	5.32	5.77	6.25	7.64	8.86	9.20	8.94
United Kingdom	112.01	115.96	119.51	123.31	125.47	129.10	132.81	140.28	140.98	138.54	140.99	145.28	151.69	158.44	161.30	170.08	172.30	169.37	173.09
OECD - Total[1]	1158.98	1217.16	1280.43	1326.47	1360.76	1403.81	1497.19	1589.06	1638.77	1671.66	1710.65	1742.06	1790.15	1832.30	1884.11	1966.96	2009.91	2051.24	2117.15
OECD - Europe[2]	527.94	553.80	585.81	615.74	633.81	658.44	680.47	710.79	731.24	753.61	783.52	817.66	852.27	886.94	915.17	954.84	982.70	999.64	1036.63
EU15	508.43	531.86	562.39	590.43	607.40	630.44	651.62	680.53	699.66	720.43	748.63	780.70	813.79	846.80	873.64	910.86	935.84	951.58	987.49

1. Excluding Korea Czech Republic Hungary and Poland.
2. Excluding Czech Republic Hungary and Poland.

Produit intérieur brut - aux niveaux de prix et taux de change de 1990 (milliards de dollars É-U) 7.

1979	1980	1981	1982	1983	1984	1985	1986	1987	1988	1989	1990	1991	1992	1993	1994	1995	1996	1997	
428.63	434.37	447.86	434.21	446.85	472.47	498.02	511.07	531.90	557.76	571.25	572.67	561.73	566.85	581.17	603.93	616.73	624.31	647.38	Canada
202.76	219.64	238.96	237.27	227.07	235.25	241.77	232.69	237.01	239.96	250.04	262.71	273.80	283.74	289.27	302.04	283.42	298.09	318.97	Mexique
4319.40	4294.50	4367.00	4278.50	4424.30	4691.90	4845.90	4987.10	5121.30	5314.30	5489.10	5554.10	5498.50	5653.20	5790.40	6004.50	6158.80	6378.70	6629.50	États-Unis
1951.96	2006.96	2070.59	2133.89	2183.44	2268.98	2368.90	2437.49	2538.87	2696.14	2826.41	2970.09	3082.89	3114.40	3124.10	3144.24	3190.50	3315.66	3343.73	Japon
109.57	106.63	113.24	121.84	135.85	147.63	157.30	175.47	195.69	217.74	231.65	253.67	276.84	290.86	307.59	333.98	363.83	389.53	411.00	Corée
211.44	216.13	224.00	222.79	224.96	241.65	252.98	258.53	270.01	280.34	292.19	295.61	291.74	299.63	311.74	328.34	341.65	354.33	364.10	Australie
36.03	36.28	38.04	38.75	39.82	41.78	42.10	42.98	43.16	42.99	43.36	43.10	42.57	43.08	45.81	48.27	50.01	51.38	52.56	Nouvelle-Zélande
124.11	126.98	126.85	129.27	132.90	133.34	136.33	139.52	141.87	146.36	152.55	159.50	164.96	167.17	168.03	172.30	175.85	178.73	183.27	Autriche
155.99	162.97	160.94	163.21	163.20	167.23	168.91	171.44	175.48	183.77	190.36	196.13	199.27	202.24	199.29	204.41	209.19	211.89	218.25	Belgique
..	..	..	..	..	..	..	..	..	..	..	27.40	24.25	23.45	23.59	24.34	25.89	26.90	27.17	République tchèque
110.15	109.67	108.69	111.97	114.79	119.83	124.97	129.52	129.91	131.42	131.76	133.36	135.22	136.94	138.10	146.04	150.74	155.53	160.69	Danemark
94.18	99.20	101.05	104.33	107.15	110.38	114.10	116.81	121.59	127.56	134.79	134.81	125.28	120.83	119.41	124.84	131.16	135.82	143.99	Finlande
950.24	962.87	969.04	990.51	998.32	1011.33	1029.78	1054.30	1078.00	1123.69	1167.49	1195.43	1204.74	1217.46	1201.75	1233.88	1260.51	1278.26	1307.35	France
1308.26	1321.09	1327.59	1320.16	1347.25	1388.14	1420.83	1456.66	1481.22	1535.30	1588.71	1640.06	1686.65	1723.77	1703.38	1749.66	1770.94	1793.63	1833.12	Allemagne
69.48	70.70	70.74	71.02	71.30	73.26	75.55	76.78	76.42	79.82	82.89	82.91	85.47	86.08	84.67	86.40	88.21	90.31	93.17	Grèce
..	..	..	..	..	..	..	..	..	..	..	35.78	31.52	30.55	30.38	31.27	31.74	32.16	33.64	Hongrie
4.51	4.77	4.97	5.08	4.97	5.18	5.35	5.68	6.17	6.16	6.18	6.25	6.32	6.11	6.17	6.40	6.46	6.82	7.12	Islande
30.94	31.90	32.96	33.71	33.63	35.09	36.18	36.02	37.70	39.67	41.97	45.53	46.68	48.91	50.72	54.81	61.28	66.33	73.40	Irlande
847.34	877.26	881.41	885.45	896.24	919.26	945.09	971.93	1002.02	1040.79	1070.78	1093.95	1106.40	1112.66	1099.80	1123.67	1156.71	1164.36	1181.92	Italie
6.64	6.69	6.65	6.73	6.93	7.36	7.57	8.16	8.35	9.22	10.13	10.35	10.98	11.47	12.47	13.00	13.49	13.90	14.41	Luxembourg
225.87	228.59	227.43	224.79	228.63	236.15	243.42	250.12	253.66	260.29	272.47	283.67	290.11	295.99	298.24	307.86	314.80	324.63	336.45	Pays-Bas
86.80	91.10	91.98	92.14	95.40	101.00	106.27	110.08	112.31	112.19	113.22	115.45	119.05	122.94	126.30	133.24	138.36	145.93	150.96	Norvège
..	..	..	..	..	..	..	..	..	..	..	58.98	54.86	56.30	58.44	61.48	65.81	69.80	74.58	Pologne
48.40	50.62	51.44	52.53	52.44	51.46	52.90	55.09	58.61	63.00	66.23	69.13	70.75	72.53	71.73	73.33	75.42	77.82	80.68	Portugal
361.27	369.25	368.79	374.48	382.58	388.32	394.90	407.54	430.53	452.75	474.20	491.94	503.10	506.55	500.66	511.93	525.84	538.55	557.57	Espagne
185.22	188.31	188.28	190.17	193.50	201.34	205.22	209.93	216.53	221.41	226.67	229.76	227.19	223.96	218.99	226.29	235.21	238.20	242.39	Suède
178.24	186.44	189.38	186.66	187.61	193.29	199.89	203.15	204.64	211.01	220.17	228.41	226.58	226.29	225.20	226.40	227.65	227.56	231.53	Suisse
92.95	90.68	95.08	98.47	103.36	110.30	114.97	123.04	134.71	137.57	137.91	150.68	152.07	161.17	174.14	164.64	176.48	188.84	203.05	Turquie
764.59	752.05	742.25	753.74	780.50	800.01	828.24	864.67	905.84	950.97	971.69	975.51	956.23	951.14	970.71	1012.61	1040.47	1064.57	1100.51	Royaume-Uni
12795.41	12939.02	13131.98	13139.85	13447.16	14004.30	14460.16	14860.30	15317.81	15964.43	16532.53	16941.12	17068.31	17355.13	17512.25	18003.04	18399.87	18924.16	19476.06	OCDE - Total[1]
5645.17	5731.13	5745.54	5794.43	5900.72	6052.27	6210.49	6390.43	6575.56	6832.93	7060.19	7242.83	7317.06	7394.23	7369.76	7571.71	7758.76	7901.68	8119.82	OCDE - Europe[2]
5282.67	5358.14	5364.12	5412.08	5509.37	5642.50	5784.00	5948.48	6117.72	6366.01	6582.71	6742.04	6813.04	6877.71	6837.95	7041.04	7209.81	7332.52	7527.16	UE15

Consommation finale privée - aux niveaux de prix et taux de change de 1990 (milliards de dollars É-U) 8.

1979	1980	1981	1982	1983	1984	1985	1986	1987	1988	1989	1990	1991	1992	1993	1994	1995	1996	1997	
239.55	244.39	248.35	242.05	249.38	260.70	274.14	284.89	296.34	309.20	319.79	323.85	319.29	325.00	331.05	341.29	346.99	355.04	369.70	Canada
142.18	152.90	164.17	160.12	151.54	156.47	162.04	157.45	157.24	160.09	171.75	182.79	191.34	200.30	203.23	212.54	192.32	196.59	209.05	Mexique
2741.30	2744.00	2786.00	2813.40	2940.50	3083.90	3222.50	3340.90	3439.90	3575.50	3660.80	3720.50	3696.20	3803.90	3919.90	4055.90	4169.30	4292.50	4438.00	États-Unis
1182.51	1195.06	1212.63	1265.47	1307.73	1342.06	1386.57	1435.14	1495.57	1574.67	1649.60	1721.72	1765.06	1801.67	1822.66	1857.60	1896.08	1951.27	1972.05	Japon
62.70	62.43	65.42	69.54	75.94	81.90	87.18	94.24	101.92	111.06	123.08	136.19	149.10	158.95	167.97	180.66	195.63	208.93	215.44	Corée
126.46	130.79	136.36	140.03	142.04	146.27	153.18	155.08	158.26	163.89	172.39	176.95	178.45	184.79	189.62	198.29	208.02	214.55	221.93	Australie
23.05	22.99	23.46	23.14	23.86	24.78	25.12	26.17	26.81	27.28	27.37	27.30	26.75	26.84	27.70	29.38	30.59	31.83	32.88	Nouvelle-Zélande
68.76	69.84	70.43	72.23	75.82	74.82	76.24	77.90	80.17	82.82	85.87	89.09	91.63	94.35	95.01	96.67	99.45	101.86	102.57	Autriche
102.50	104.94	104.63	106.54	105.60	106.29	108.41	110.63	113.13	116.79	121.10	124.67	128.23	131.09	129.34	131.44	132.57	134.96	137.75	Belgique
..	..	..	..	..	..	..	..	..	..	..	14.57	10.42	12.00	12.43	13.10	14.01	15.01	15.27	République tchèque
59.78	57.58	56.25	57.06	58.54	60.52	63.52	67.17	66.16	65.48	65.27	65.43	66.59	68.30	69.26	74.15	76.54	78.64	81.47	Danemark
49.13	50.20	50.87	53.36	55.00	56.73	58.85	61.20	64.38	67.69	70.58	70.55	68.01	64.70	62.82	64.01	66.95	69.27	71.58	Finlande
561.47	567.30	577.58	596.18	600.89	605.99	618.69	640.91	657.80	677.00	695.85	712.28	720.66	729.96	730.42	740.37	751.59	765.63	771.06	France
726.73	735.77	733.81	726.47	736.72	751.86	767.14	794.60	822.12	845.52	869.59	912.44	963.37	990.58	991.95	1003.92	1022.38	1038.54	1043.37	Allemagne
47.01	47.09	48.05	49.92	50.05	50.90	52.89	53.24	53.89	55.81	59.21	60.74	62.46	63.95	63.45	64.74	66.53	67.78	69.52	Grèce
..	..	..	..	..	..	..	..	..	..	..	17.32	16.36	16.58	17.16	17.19	15.97	15.46	15.82	Hongrie
2.83	2.93	3.11	3.26	3.08	3.19	3.33	3.56	4.13	3.98	3.81	3.83	3.99	3.81	3.64	3.71	3.86	4.11	4.35	Islande
21.77	21.86	22.23	20.66	20.84	21.26	22.23	22.68	23.43	24.49	26.08	26.45	27.01	28.27	28.94	30.75	32.00	33.94	36.08	Irlande
479.68	509.39	516.77	522.66	526.16	539.22	555.97	579.21	604.27	631.78	654.60	670.74	688.57	697.85	674.29	680.08	689.92	697.93	714.38	Italie
4.55	4.68	4.76	4.78	4.80	4.87	5.00	5.28	5.53	5.78	6.07	6.42	6.83	6.76	6.88	7.04	7.21	7.35	7.55	Luxembourg
143.66	143.12	138.88	138.24	139.55	141.21	145.19	148.96	153.04	154.33	159.71	166.45	171.61	175.95	177.71	181.63	185.34	190.32	196.06	Pays-Bas
47.13	48.07	48.13	48.64	49.54	51.11	55.89	58.66	58.19	57.00	56.64	57.05	57.88	59.18	60.45	62.85	65.00	68.03	70.36	Norvège
..	..	..	..	..	..	..	..	..	..	..	28.62	30.52	31.30	32.98	34.44	35.68	38.76	41.50	Pologne
32.12	33.32	34.29	35.10	34.59	33.57	33.80	35.69	37.59	40.17	41.23	43.64	45.24	47.17	47.88	48.95	49.73	50.99	52.54	Portugal
237.91	242.82	239.94	239.62	240.16	239.81	244.57	252.68	267.32	280.45	296.31	307.09	315.97	322.96	315.80	318.67	323.73	330.13	340.39	Espagne
102.04	101.22	100.96	101.69	99.67	101.14	103.85	108.44	113.39	116.15	117.50	117.03	118.11	116.45	112.89	114.90	115.79	117.30	119.66	Suède
109.59	112.47	113.66	114.05	115.38	116.88	118.79	121.55	124.21	126.35	129.31	130.90	133.12	133.30	132.11	133.44	134.17	134.92	136.53	Suisse
72.09	76.34	70.54	75.38	80.46	86.98	86.45	91.49	91.21	92.31	91.36	103.33	106.13	109.55	118.96	112.56	118.01	128.02	138.76	Turquie
436.79	436.60	437.05	441.24	461.22	470.53	488.60	522.06	549.70	591.04	610.06	613.75	600.36	599.80	614.79	631.90	642.93	665.25	695.91	Royaume-Uni
7760.60	7855.67	7942.92	8051.28	8273.11	8531.08	8832.96	9155.56	9463.78	9845.58	10161.86	10435.01	10552.84	10786.47	10930.73	11196.80	11426.99	11726.74	12033.51	OCDE - Total[1]
3305.54	3365.54	3371.94	3407.08	3458.07	3516.89	3609.40	3755.92	3889.66	4034.95	4160.16	4281.89	4375.74	4443.97	4436.59	4501.80	4583.70	4684.97	4789.90	OCDE - Europe[2]
3073.90	3125.73	3136.50	3165.75	3209.62	3258.73	3344.95	3480.66	3611.92	3755.31	3879.03	3986.79	4074.63	4138.14	4121.42	4189.24	4262.67	4349.89	4439.89	UE15

Consommation finale des administrations publiques - aux niveaux de prix et taux de change de 1990 (milliards de dollars É-U) 9.

1979	1980	1981	1982	1983	1984	1985	1986	1987	1988	1989	1990	1991	1992	1993	1994	1995	1996	1997	
97.93	101.23	102.77	104.97	106.82	108.08	112.77	114.91	116.55	121.90	125.31	129.88	133.57	134.95	134.60	132.24	131.69	129.96	129.88	Canada
15.36	16.82	18.55	18.93	19.44	20.72	20.91	21.22	20.96	20.86	21.31	22.03	23.22	23.65	24.22	24.91	24.58	24.40	24.85	Mexique
743.70	755.80	765.30	784.30	800.40	820.90	858.70	891.90	919.10	935.20	951.90	974.90	978.40	974.10	964.00	966.20	963.80	965.80	978.50	États-Unis
203.05	209.37	218.78	225.15	230.88	236.31	236.99	249.18	253.07	258.97	264.08	268.02	273.36	278.71	285.27	292.09	301.73	306.36	305.90	Japon
14.43	15.40	16.14	16.28	16.75	16.96	17.78	19.27	20.45	22.09	23.98	25.70	27.87	29.99	30.90	32.20	32.53	35.08	37.09	Corée
34.85	36.22	37.49	37.36	39.31	41.09	43.32	45.24	46.12	47.51	48.65	50.68	52.06	52.92	52.85	55.60	56.94	58.70	60.03	Australie
6.25	6.31	6.42	6.46	6.64	6.76	6.87	6.92	7.02	7.10	7.28	7.33	7.33	7.55	7.47	7.40	7.61	7.78	8.25	Nouvelle-Zélande
25.19	25.73	26.21	27.01	27.48	27.69	28.06	28.57	28.63	28.96	29.37	29.74	30.40	31.02	31.86	32.65	32.64	32.67	32.96	Autriche
26.35	26.86	27.04	26.67	26.74	26.91	27.57	28.09	28.12	27.87	27.60	27.46	28.06	28.16	28.51	28.99	29.18	29.59	29.83	Belgique
..	..	..	..	..	..	..	..	..	..	..	5.27	4.80	4.65	4.57	4.45	4.36	4.54	4.44	République tchèque
29.45	30.71	31.52	32.49	32.47	32.34	33.15	33.32	34.14	34.46	34.17	34.08	34.31	34.60	36.01	37.06	37.93	38.85	39.69	Danemark
19.47	20.28	21.11	21.81	22.63	23.25	24.30	25.05	26.12	26.71	27.34	28.39	29.10	28.46	26.95	26.87	27.37	28.30	28.51	Finlande
168.24	172.29	177.58	184.10	187.68	189.90	194.14	197.33	202.75	209.57	210.69	214.94	220.83	228.20	236.06	238.73	238.98	245.04	247.75	France
272.42	279.51	283.03	281.15	282.50	288.59	295.41	302.17	308.38	315.25	311.10	318.27	320.98	334.03	332.46	339.52	346.23	355.68	353.27	Allemagne
9.43	9.45	10.09	10.32	10.61	10.93	11.28	11.19	11.29	11.93	12.59	12.66	12.47	12.09	12.41	12.27	12.97	13.09	13.04	Grèce
..	..	..	..	..	..	..	..	..	..	..	7.78	7.57	7.49	8.23	7.62	7.18	7.02	7.10	Hongrie
0.72	0.73	0.79	0.83	0.87	0.88	0.93	1.00	1.07	1.12	1.15	1.20	1.24	1.23	1.26	1.30	1.32	1.33	1.37	Islande
6.23	6.67	6.70	6.91	6.89	6.84	6.97	7.15	6.80	6.46	6.38	6.73	6.92	7.09	7.12	7.48	7.67	7.79	8.16	Irlande
149.28	152.36	155.66	159.48	164.47	167.98	173.21	177.46	183.14	188.07	189.80	192.11	195.29	197.54	198.44	197.26	195.13	195.56	194.13	Italie
1.02	1.05	1.06	1.08	1.10	1.12	1.15	1.18	1.23	1.29	1.34	1.39	1.44	1.46	1.52	1.55	1.58	1.63	1.70	Luxembourg
33.20	33.66	34.60	35.39	36.19	36.19	37.05	38.38	39.39	39.95	40.57	41.23	41.87	42.57	43.20	43.45	43.80	44.34	44.99	Pays-Bas
17.64	18.61	19.54	19.88	20.43	20.59	21.08	21.48	22.46	22.43	22.86	23.98	25.02	26.36	26.92	27.30	27.38	28.26	29.10	Norvège
..	..	..	..	..	..	..	..	..	..	..	11.04	12.10	12.82	13.23	13.52	13.91	14.39	14.85	Pologne
6.05	6.53	6.89	7.15	7.42	7.43	7.91	8.48	8.80	9.56	10.19	10.75	11.85	11.98	12.09	12.34	12.61	12.86	13.18	Portugal
43.65	45.17	46.78	49.29	51.21	52.48	55.64	58.63	63.83	66.40	71.91	76.66	80.94	84.21	86.23	85.94	87.50	88.33	89.54	Espagne
52.50	53.67	54.88	55.41	55.87	57.09	58.35	59.08	59.65	60.00	61.27	62.87	64.61	64.59	64.71	64.28	63.67	63.56	62.25	Suède
22.89	23.11	23.69	23.95	24.85	25.29	26.12	26.98	27.40	28.64	30.17	31.81	32.89	33.15	33.08	33.76	33.68	34.04	33.95	Suisse
8.72	7.11	10.58	9.46	11.03	11.24	12.82	14.01	15.33	15.17	15.29	16.52	17.12	17.74	19.26	18.20	19.44	21.11	21.98	Turquie
176.35	179.41	179.87	181.44	185.26	186.82	186.68	189.75	191.59	192.93	195.64	200.60	205.77	205.56	205.19	209.73	212.38	217.42	217.94	Royaume-Uni
2169.92	2218.67	2266.94	2310.99	2359.18	2407.40	2481.40	2558.67	2622.94	2678.32	2717.98	2784.23	2829.05	2861.92	2871.68	2897.11	2917.82	2952.45	2970.75	OCDE - Total[1]
1068.79	1092.92	1117.62	1133.82	1155.69	1173.54	1201.83	1229.30	1260.12	1286.77	1299.44	1331.38	1361.11	1390.03	1403.27	1418.68	1431.47	1459.45	1463.34	OCDE - Europe[2]
1018.82	1043.36	1063.02	1079.70	1098.50	1115.55	1140.87	1165.83	1193.86	1219.41	1229.97	1257.88	1284.84	1311.56	1322.76	1338.12	1349.65	1374.71	1376.94	UE15

1. Non compris la Corée la République tchèque la Hongrie et la Pologne.
2. Non compris la République tchèque la Hongrie et la Pologne.

10. Gross fixed capital formation - at the price levels and exchange rates of 1990 (billions of US dollars)

	1960	1961	1962	1963	1964	1965	1966	1967	1968	1969	1970	1971	1972	1973	1974	1975	1976	1977	1978
Canada	28.41	28.31	29.45	30.62	34.56	38.43	42.49	42.54	42.93	45.20	45.39	48.87	50.86	55.62	59.40	62.64	65.41	66.78	69.04
Mexico	10.35	10.45	10.68	12.09	14.71	15.30	16.79	18.73	20.58	21.99	23.77	23.37	26.23	30.09	32.47	35.48	35.64	33.25	38.29
United States	392.30	397.60	427.20	459.10	499.30	543.50	565.70	556.60	587.20	603.70	581.80	613.40	672.20	723.50	679.10	611.20	657.40	730.60	804.00
Japan	94.10	116.09	132.49	148.31	171.60	179.52	204.74	241.83	291.29	346.26	404.68	423.73	466.46	520.40	476.13	472.89	486.61	500.47	540.14
Korea											9.03	9.30	9.42	12.03	13.81	14.87	17.99	23.14	31.10
Australia	23.50	23.08	24.37	26.54	29.91	32.85	33.56	34.59	37.23	39.76	41.83	44.50	43.87	46.28	44.93	44.76	46.76	46.33	47.84
New Zealand	3.70	4.03	3.91	4.32	4.89	5.21	5.55	5.04	4.29	4.93	5.37	5.68	6.67	7.47	7.98	7.55	6.94	6.18	5.88
Austria	11.31	12.74	13.08	13.53	14.83	15.60	16.98	16.99	17.48	18.34	20.14	22.91	25.69	25.78	26.81	25.48	26.45	28.89	26.69
Belgium	14.27	16.04	16.98	17.01	19.50	20.31	21.69	22.32	22.04	23.22	25.17	24.70	25.53	27.33	29.22	28.58	29.82	29.84	30.66
Czech Republic																			
Denmark	12.64	14.40	15.36	14.99	18.51	19.38	20.20	21.29	21.68	24.24	24.77	25.25	27.59	28.54	26.02	22.79	26.70	26.04	26.33
Finland	13.73	14.99	15.07	14.62	15.51	17.13	17.80	17.58	18.78	18.78	21.12	21.92	23.35	25.34	26.22	27.78	25.35	24.66	22.88
France	77.29	85.69	92.96	101.13	111.73	119.53	128.21	135.94	143.45	156.60	163.84	175.08	185.05	198.32	200.01	186.31	191.87	189.19	192.69
Germany	175.38	186.72	193.84	196.18	218.23	228.45	231.10	214.91	221.97	243.20	264.96	280.57	288.09	287.29	259.28	245.37	254.16	263.19	273.93
Greece	6.19	6.69	7.26	7.65	9.24	10.42	10.75	10.58	12.84	15.23	15.02	17.13	19.77	21.28	15.84	15.97	16.96	18.27	19.37
Hungary																			
Iceland	0.43	0.33	0.38	0.50	0.59	0.58	0.67	0.75	0.69	0.52	0.56	0.80	0.81	0.99	1.06	0.97	0.94	1.05	0.99
Ireland	1.77	2.07	2.38	2.66	2.95	3.26	3.16	3.37	3.82	4.60	4.45	4.85	5.23	6.07	5.36	5.17	5.87	6.11	7.26
Italy	98.22	109.58	120.28	130.00	122.44	112.14	116.99	130.72	144.83	156.06	160.80	159.58	160.94	174.49	177.89	165.31	163.57	165.82	156.80
Luxembourg	0.96	1.04	1.12	1.28	1.57	1.35	1.28	1.18	1.13	1.25	1.34	1.48	1.59	1.78	1.65	1.53	1.47	1.46	1.48
Netherlands	25.21	26.73	27.64	27.95	33.30	35.07	37.89	41.10	45.68	44.66	48.02	48.75	47.64	49.63	47.64	45.57	44.57	48.92	50.09
Norway	10.71	12.03	12.50	12.97	13.40	14.31	15.16	16.94	16.43	15.02	17.25	20.49	19.65	22.23	23.47	26.26	28.92	29.97	26.61
Poland																			
Portugal	5.03	5.34	5.39	6.18	6.46	7.14	8.38	8.87	8.04	8.76	9.77	10.73	12.18	13.34	12.42	11.01	11.10	12.43	13.21
Spain	21.20	25.01	27.84	31.03	35.68	41.54	46.98	49.82	54.53	59.98	62.03	60.17	68.72	77.65	82.47	78.75	78.12	77.42	75.33
Sweden	20.59	22.24	24.25	25.24	27.15	28.25	29.54	31.12	31.32	32.66	33.73	33.53	34.93	35.86	34.77	35.35	36.51	35.44	33.01
Switzerland	23.35	27.02	29.78	31.96	34.57	33.72	33.44	33.49	34.52	36.57	39.83	43.76	45.94	47.27	45.26	39.11	35.00	35.57	37.74
Turkey	4.86	5.03	5.37	5.62	5.78	5.92	7.24	7.70	8.74	9.29	10.55	9.70	11.54	12.49	18.79	19.61	23.46	18.40	15.26
United Kingdom	74.14	81.38	81.94	83.08	96.83	101.84	104.44	113.57	120.68	119.98	123.01	125.28	125.01	133.16	129.93	127.35	129.48	127.17	130.00
OECD - Total [1]	1149.65	1234.61	1320.92	1404.57	1543.23	1630.74	1720.74	1777.56	1910.06	2050.81	2149.22	2246.24	2395.52	2572.31	2464.12	2343.30	2429.09	2523.47	2656.53
OECD - Europe [2]	597.28	655.06	692.82	723.60	788.27	815.94	851.90	878.24	926.54	988.96	1046.37	1086.68	1129.24	1188.94	1164.11	1108.78	1130.34	1139.86	1157.35
EU15	557.93	610.65	644.79	672.55	733.92	761.40	795.39	819.35	866.17	927.56	978.18	1011.94	1051.30	1105.86	1075.54	1022.82	1042.01	1054.87	1070.74

11. Exports of goods and services - at the price levels and exchange rates of 1990 (billions of US dollars)

	1960	1961	1962	1963	1964	1965	1966	1967	1968	1969	1970	1971	1972	1973	1974	1975	1976	1977	1978
Canada	22.57	24.10	25.19	27.44	31.20	32.61	37.06	40.93	46.16	49.88	54.55	56.94	61.79	68.30	66.52	62.22	68.86	74.16	82.15
Mexico	4.92	5.32	5.72	6.13	6.62	7.17	7.80	7.59	8.44	9.49	10.34	10.74	12.51	14.22	14.25	12.98	15.14	17.35	19.36
United States	104.30	105.10	111.10	118.60	133.00	136.70	146.30	150.80	163.50	171.50	186.40	188.80	204.90	240.40	263.70	262.80	270.90	274.60	330.90
Japan	17.72	18.65	21.85	23.37	28.45	35.18	41.17	43.94	54.45	65.77	77.28	89.64	93.33	98.22	120.95	119.80	139.68	156.07	155.68
Korea											4.23	5.17	7.03	10.84	10.80	12.82	17.74	21.44	24.53
Australia	8.70	10.76	10.84	11.66	12.25	12.76	12.78	14.70	15.10	16.56	19.00	20.89	22.20	22.18	21.28	23.05	25.09	25.18	26.17
New Zealand	3.39	3.69	3.71	4.14	4.00	4.14	4.48	4.44	5.04	5.70	5.74	6.16	6.29	6.17	6.00	6.76	7.51	7.51	7.69
Austria	8.24	8.70	9.56	10.24	10.81	11.58	12.36	13.07	14.18	16.68	19.43	20.67	22.77	24.01	26.58	25.94	28.81	30.11	32.41
Belgium	22.98	25.09	27.63	29.90	32.72	34.71	37.38	38.97	43.73	50.43	55.09	57.57	63.93	72.96	75.67	69.40	78.33	80.00	81.83
Czech Republic																			
Denmark	10.60	11.06	11.60	12.76	13.85	14.94	15.52	16.13	17.63	18.71	19.76	20.86	22.03	23.75	24.58	24.14	25.13	26.16	26.47
Finland	7.12	7.49	8.02	8.19	8.67	9.15	9.74	10.32	11.35	13.25	14.41	14.23	16.29	17.47	17.36	14.94	16.73	19.34	21.21
France	38.99	40.99	41.71	44.66	47.63	53.11	56.62	60.75	66.47	76.92	89.32	98.50	110.25	122.35	134.42	133.75	144.74	156.51	156.91
Germany	87.77	92.19	94.69	102.16	110.62	117.67	129.52	139.55	157.27	171.87	183.72	191.73	204.84	226.51	253.73	237.66	260.60	270.84	276.00
Greece	1.06	1.21	1.33	1.42	1.44	1.62	2.18	2.29	2.27	2.60	2.92	3.27	4.02	4.96	4.96	5.49	6.39	6.50	7.57
Hungary																			
Iceland	0.55	0.54	0.65	0.70	0.74	0.79	0.84	0.74	0.69	0.81	0.94	0.87	0.99	1.08	1.05	1.08	1.22	1.33	1.53
Ireland	2.35	2.75	2.73	2.99	3.23	3.52	3.90	4.30	4.68	4.90	5.82	6.06	6.28	6.96	7.01	7.54	8.15	9.30	10.44
Italy	27.60	31.67	34.95	37.21	41.23	49.47	55.01	58.95	67.13	75.02	79.39	84.90	91.47	96.79	104.84	106.06	119.40	131.77	144.96
Luxembourg	2.42	2.50	2.46	2.56	2.90	3.07	3.06	3.12	3.45	3.93	4.28	4.45	4.69	5.34	5.91	4.98	5.03	5.24	5.39
Netherlands	27.01	27.65	29.37	31.13	34.65	37.27	39.21	41.81	47.15	54.20	60.63	67.09	73.76	82.69	84.83	82.17	90.29	88.69	91.64
Norway	8.84	9.48	10.07	10.90	11.78	12.44	13.14	14.24	15.34	16.15	16.17	16.35	18.66	20.20	20.34	20.97	23.33	24.18	26.20
Poland																			
Portugal	2.95	2.87	3.42	3.45	5.46	6.08	7.08	7.33	7.00	7.29	7.17	7.88	9.34	9.73	8.20	6.92	6.92	7.33	8.00
Spain	8.15	8.80	9.92	10.31	12.88	13.75	15.88	15.15	17.94	20.77	24.50	27.98	31.73	34.91	34.56	34.42	36.14	40.51	44.85
Sweden	15.28	16.07	17.37	18.64	20.89	22.05	23.12	24.40	26.25	29.26	31.79	33.31	35.26	40.09	42.22	38.30	39.96	40.64	43.70
Switzerland	19.87	21.46	22.79	23.98	25.51	27.44	28.86	29.85	32.84	37.22	39.76	41.31	43.94	47.39	47.88	44.73	48.90	53.65	55.64
Turkey	1.69	1.72	1.82	1.99	2.08	2.13	2.38	2.58	2.58	2.76	3.16	3.64	4.17	4.90	4.44	4.74	5.86	3.99	5.08
United Kingdom	67.58	69.76	70.88	74.32	77.12	80.51	84.71	85.56	96.44	105.36	111.08	118.61	119.61	133.90	143.17	138.55	150.68	160.50	163.10
OECD - Total [1]	522.65	549.62	579.39	618.84	679.72	729.86	790.09	831.53	927.16	1027.03	1122.64	1192.46	1285.04	1425.48	1534.45	1489.38	1623.78	1711.35	1847.47
OECD - Europe [2]	361.05	381.99	400.98	427.50	464.21	501.31	540.51	569.12	634.47	708.13	769.34	819.28	884.01	975.99	1041.75	1001.78	1096.59	1156.48	1255.52
EU15	330.10	348.79	365.64	389.93	424.11	458.51	495.29	521.71	583.03	651.19	709.31	757.11	816.25	902.42	968.04	930.26	1017.29	1073.35	1157.07

12. Imports of goods and services - at the price levels and exchange rates of 1990 (billions of US dollars)

	1960	1961	1962	1963	1964	1965	1966	1967	1968	1969	1970	1971	1972	1973	1974	1975	1976	1977	1978
Canada	20.37	20.42	20.87	21.23	23.92	27.15	30.80	32.49	35.85	40.49	39.76	42.37	48.47	55.51	61.71	60.47	65.25	65.88	69.58
Mexico	9.40	8.77	8.74	9.31	11.64	12.05	12.06	13.07	10.44	14.26	15.52	14.81	16.32	19.05	22.91	23.01	23.24	20.87	25.43
United States	117.40	116.10	127.60	128.50	134.00	146.60	170.10	182.80	210.20	224.10	231.80	242.40	266.40	278.10	269.40	235.30	279.80	306.70	334.00
Japan	25.21	31.87	31.50	37.65	42.82	45.21	50.72	62.24	69.80	79.37	97.51	104.38	115.34	143.41	149.41	134.03	142.98	148.83	159.11
Korea											6.89	8.27	8.36	11.34	13.34	13.72	17.08	20.62	26.33
Australia	12.10	10.88	11.70	12.72	15.23	17.25	15.95	17.80	19.73	20.17	21.01	21.10	19.19	23.22	28.63	24.11	26.96	27.04	28.23
New Zealand	3.78	3.81	3.73	4.28	4.49	5.23	5.54	4.52	4.51	5.00	5.99	5.87	6.42	7.79	8.83	6.92	6.82	6.90	7.01
Austria	9.20	9.45	9.89	10.84	12.02	13.28	14.66	14.99	16.08	17.53	20.50	21.79	24.44	26.77	28.62	27.29	32.04	34.02	34.06
Belgium	24.07	25.80	27.92	30.33	33.02	35.19	38.68	39.29	43.89	50.69	54.24	56.22	61.60	73.04	76.27	69.34	77.93	81.65	83.83
Czech Republic																			
Denmark	12.24	12.78	14.49	14.33	17.14	18.31	19.31	20.18	21.16	23.94	26.17	25.98	26.37	29.73	28.60	27.23	31.47	31.48	31.52
Finland	7.04	7.61	8.04	7.81	9.42	10.20	10.56	10.53	10.12	12.37	14.88	14.79	15.41	17.42	18.59	18.69	18.39	18.91	17.60
France	34.34	36.72	39.19	44.71	51.46	52.62	58.18	63.00	71.12	85.01	90.34	96.81	109.82	125.20	128.77	117.75	139.90	141.83	147.30
Germany	68.71	73.99	82.20	86.22	94.22	107.63	110.54	109.13	123.49	144.49	177.29	193.19	204.39	214.36	215.11	217.85	240.78	248.95	262.63
Greece	2.17	2.45	2.69	3.11	3.58	4.34	4.32	4.63	5.10	5.90	6.26	6.74	7.78	10.28	8.61	9.15	9.71	10.49	11.24
Hungary																			
Iceland	0.46	0.42	0.50	0.59	0.67	0.72	0.83	0.88	0.80	0.69	0.88	1.10	1.11	1.33	1.50	1.31	1.26	1.52	1.57
Ireland	3.07	3.49	3.68	4.07	4.60	5.10	5.28	5.48	6.34	7.19	7.81	8.17	8.58	10.22	9.98	8.95	10.28	11.64	13.47
Italy	28.61	32.53	37.39	45.82	43.00	43.86	50.01	56.76	60.10	71.69	83.17	85.43	93.54	101.44	106.22	92.50	103.77	105.51	111.60
Luxembourg	2.41	2.59	2.67	2.76	3.13	3.27	3.19	3.04	3.31	3.68	4.38	4.73	4.86	5.41	5.72	5.21	5.27	5.25	5.61
Netherlands	26.13	27.80	29.60	32.50	37.33	39.62	42.41	45.10	50.97	58.17	66.71	70.79	74.18	82.35	81.65	78.33	86.26	88.75	94.34
Norway	10.66	11.75	12.38	13.12	14.05	15.32	16.51	18.45	18.86	19.20	21.81	23.21	22.97	26.29	27.53	29.44	33.07	34.20	33.57
Poland																			
Portugal	3.54	4.42	4.04	4.44	5.63	6.17	6.69	6.29	8.37	9.00	10.40	11.65	13.13	13.75		10.28	10.63	11.91	11.93
Spain	4.74	6.65	8.94	11.04	12.48	16.58	19.80	19.15	20.71	24.02	25.81	25.99	32.31	37.70	40.72	40.35	44.31	41.87	41.45
Sweden	18.91	18.95	20.02	21.45	23.53	26.19	27.30	27.97	30.29	34.19	37.74	36.48	37.93	40.56	44.60	43.05	46.93	45.16	42.59
Switzerland	15.31	18.35	20.27	21.26	23.10	23.11	23.92	24.89	26.96	30.44	34.67	36.83	39.50	42.07	41.66	35.27	39.87	43.56	43.32
Turkey	2.36	2.51	3.05	3.52	2.77	2.75	3.44	3.17	3.73	3.80	4.64	5.08	6.05	7.25	7.57	9.69	9.89		13.58
United Kingdom	72.22	71.71	73.21	76.27	84.54	85.49	87.59	93.93	101.39	104.35	109.71	115.41	126.25	140.82	141.96	132.12	138.39	140.38	145.51
OECD - Total [1]	534.45	561.82	604.31	647.88	707.79	763.25	828.40	879.76	973.32	1089.74	1207.70	1270.09	1380.89	1532.45	1568.32	1456.48	1624.99	1681.93	1783.33
OECD - Europe [2]	346.19	369.97	400.16	434.19	475.68	509.75	543.22	566.84	622.78	706.36	796.10	839.15	908.74	1005.37	1027.43	972.64	1079.95	1105.71	1140.98
EU15	317.41	336.95	363.96	395.70	435.10	467.86	498.52	519.46	572.44	652.23	734.10	772.93	839.11	928.43	949.17	898.13	996.06	1017.05	1053.94

1. Excluding Korea Czech Republic Hungary and Poland.
2. Excluding Czech Republic Hungary and Poland.

Formation brute de capital fixe - aux niveaux de prix et taux de change de 1990 (milliards de dollars É-U) 10.

1979	1980	1981	1982	1983	1984	1985	1986	1987	1988	1989	1990	1991	1992	1993	1994	1995	1996	1997	
74.75	82.10	92.41	81.49	81.75	83.78	92.37	97.36	107.81	118.37	125.40	120.84	116.58	115.09	111.81	119.70	116.32	121.93	135.79	Canada
46.05	52.92	61.51	51.18	36.71	39.07	42.14	37.16	37.12	39.26	41.52	46.97	52.14	57.79	56.33	61.05	43.35	50.45	61.01	Mexique
837.00	776.40	769.80	707.30	751.30	862.70	908.60	921.00	914.20	933.70	948.70	932.50	867.60	916.90	974.80	1048.70	1113.70	1227.80	1315.40	États-Unis
571.98	569.78	582.80	581.53	575.18	599.78	629.72	659.95	720.26	802.83	868.88	942.51	973.39	958.35	939.65	932.57	948.82	1039.41	1002.73	Japon
34.11	30.46	29.33	32.57	38.19	42.00	43.83	48.49	56.72	64.49	74.72	94.06	105.93	105.09	110.60	123.61	138.07	147.85	142.63	Corée
49.63	52.19	57.12	55.54	50.85	55.83	61.36	59.84	61.99	66.65	73.00	67.05	60.81	62.24	64.55	72.03	74.86	79.50	88.32	Australie
5.67	5.58	6.74	7.20	7.67	8.10	8.66	8.17	8.46	8.08	8.68	8.23	6.78	7.03	8.31	9.74	10.63	11.32	11.65	Nouvelle-Zélande
27.97	29.08	28.83	26.70	26.80	26.83	28.69	29.38	30.67	32.77	34.82	37.11	39.46	39.51	38.72	41.97	42.78	43.82	45.41	Autriche
29.83	31.51	26.42	25.34	23.85	24.45	25.42	26.31	27.96	32.54	36.24	39.74	37.88	38.37	37.00	36.96	38.50	38.69	40.79	Belgique
..	..	..	..	..	..	..	..	..	..	..	7.55	6.21	6.76	6.24	7.43	8.99	9.77	9.29	République tchèque
26.22	22.91	18.51	19.82	20.19	22.79	25.65	30.04	28.91	26.99	27.05	26.82	26.09	25.83	25.33	27.21	30.54	31.99	35.34	Danemark
23.48	26.06	26.39	27.75	28.77	28.18	28.81	28.69	30.09	33.05	37.94	36.39	29.02	24.12	19.49	19.52	21.72	23.42	26.27	Finlande
198.81	204.33	200.35	197.25	190.24	185.71	191.60	200.21	210.66	230.78	248.34	255.52	255.15	247.10	230.06	232.75	238.72	237.35	238.08	France
292.18	298.60	285.79	270.68	278.07	277.10	277.06	286.97	294.07	307.56	324.88	354.25	388.88	402.67	380.28	393.71	393.60	388.92	389.15	Allemagne
21.07	19.71	18.23	17.88	17.65	16.65	17.51	16.42	15.59	16.97	18.19	19.10	20.01	19.37	18.70	18.18	18.96	20.63	22.61	Grèce
..	..	..	..	..	..	..	..	..	..	..	7.52	6.73	6.55	6.69	7.52	7.20	7.68	8.36	Hongrie
0.98	1.11	1.13	1.13	0.98	1.08	1.09	1.07	1.27	1.27	1.17	1.20	1.23	1.09	0.96	0.95	0.93	1.17	1.30	Islande
8.25	7.86	8.61	8.32	7.55	7.36	6.79	6.60	6.52	6.87	7.56	8.58	7.95	7.95	7.51	8.43	9.41	10.70	11.86	Irlande
175.47	190.18	184.34	175.24	173.46	179.39	180.27	183.93	192.02	205.22	214.27	222.05	223.92	219.82	191.66	192.63	206.27	207.09	208.28	Italie
1.54	1.73	1.60	1.59	1.41	1.41	1.27	1.67	1.97	2.27	2.43	2.49	3.28	2.98	3.83	3.26	3.37	3.32	3.58	Luxembourg
49.33	49.23	44.35	42.49	43.57	46.08	49.32	52.71	53.19	55.59	58.34	59.28	59.39	59.76	58.10	59.38	62.24	65.58	70.03	Pays-Bas
27.12	26.51	27.52	27.72	29.22	29.49	28.32	30.49	30.60	30.04	27.98	24.95	24.85	24.08	25.12	26.26	27.14	29.76	33.52	Norvège
..	..	..	..	..	..	..	..	..	..	..	12.38	11.83	12.11	12.46	13.60	15.90	19.19	23.13	Pologne
13.03	14.14	14.92	15.26	14.17	11.71	11.29	12.52	14.77	16.96	17.72	19.06	19.72	20.67	19.43	20.08	21.05	22.25	24.78	Portugal
72.02	72.52	70.69	72.19	70.47	65.59	69.58	76.47	87.20	99.32	112.81	120.29	122.24	116.80	104.54	107.19	116.03	117.55	123.48	Espagne
34.49	35.68	33.55	33.25	33.61	36.01	37.87	37.99	41.11	43.83	48.80	49.42	45.03	40.16	33.25	33.89	38.08	39.50	37.62	Suède
39.66	43.60	44.39	42.64	44.31	46.39	47.70	50.29	52.30	56.52	59.52	61.80	60.03	56.07	54.56	58.13	59.16	57.53	58.40	Suisse
15.68	13.05	17.18	16.20	16.62	16.77	18.69	20.26	29.40	29.10	29.74	34.46	34.61	36.81	46.51	39.08	42.66	48.66	55.87	Turquie
134.66	127.43	115.22	121.46	127.57	138.98	144.85	148.59	163.96	186.73	197.93	191.02	172.95	170.41	171.50	178.95	181.56	184.83	194.47	Royaume-Uni
2776.86	2754.22	2738.38	2627.15	2651.95	2811.20	2934.62	3024.10	3162.10	3383.25	3571.90	3681.65	3648.98	3670.97	3621.99	3742.32	3860.39	4103.17	4235.76	OCDE - Total[1]
1191.79	1215.23	1168.00	1142.90	1148.49	1161.95	1191.77	1240.62	1312.26	1414.37	1505.71	1563.54	1571.69	1553.58	1466.55	1498.53	1552.71	1572.77	1620.85	OCDE - Europe[2]
1108.35	1130.96	1077.79	1055.22	1057.37	1063.22	1095.97	1138.50	1198.70	1297.44	1387.31	1441.12	1450.97	1435.52	1339.40	1374.11	1422.82	1435.64	1471.75	UE15

Exportations de biens et services - aux niveaux de prix et taux de change de 1990 (milliards de dollars É-U) 11.

1979	1980	1981	1982	1983	1984	1985	1986	1987	1988	1989	1990	1991	1992	1993	1994	1995	1996	1997	
85.01	86.37	89.48	88.03	94.02	111.72	117.99	124.30	128.59	141.05	142.59	149.50	152.95	165.08	185.00	206.99	226.11	239.13	258.37	Canada
21.72	23.04	25.71	31.31	35.56	37.59	35.91	37.93	41.52	43.92	46.40	48.87	51.34	53.90	58.26	68.63	89.36	105.64	119.35	Mexique
327.50	357.80	362.50	329.40	312.70	332.60	336.80	359.40	394.60	456.70	508.60	548.20	581.30	619.10	638.80	695.80	791.50	888.10	1001.70	États-Unis
162.38	189.95	213.77	215.77	226.03	259.48	273.59	258.02	256.63	271.86	296.69	317.15	333.79	350.26	354.98	371.28	391.42	405.10	449.00	Japon
24.92	26.91	31.02	32.43	38.74	41.73	43.63	55.21	67.17	75.60	72.53	75.54	84.47	93.75	104.35	121.57	150.72	170.32	210.54	Corée
29.03	28.67	27.72	30.09	28.63	33.21	36.93	38.66	43.12	44.25	45.73	49.59	56.17	59.08	63.49	69.22	72.54	80.61	89.76	Australie
8.03	8.28	8.47	8.61	9.13	9.99	10.15	10.62	11.39	11.47	11.19	11.91	13.02	13.35	14.41	15.62	16.03	16.65	17.10	Nouvelle-Zélande
36.26	38.16	40.09	40.73	42.21	44.88	48.07	46.94	48.40	53.34	59.39	64.06	67.85	68.98	68.09	71.92	76.58	83.73	89.43	Autriche
87.55	87.02	90.15	92.42	94.75	100.94	101.24	103.94	108.48	118.38	128.10	133.59	137.80	142.60	141.66	153.53	162.72	166.28	178.15	Belgique
..	..	..	..	..	..	..	..	..	..	..	16.16	15.45	16.50	17.74	17.77	20.62	21.74	23.96	République tchèque
28.68	30.16	32.64	33.45	35.08	36.29	38.09	38.11	40.04	43.15	45.00	47.78	51.13	50.88	50.94	55.11	57.71	60.13	62.73	Danemark
22.95	24.90	26.20	25.93	26.45	27.78	28.08	28.42	29.20	30.28	30.66	31.08	29.02	31.92	37.26	42.21	45.66	48.48	54.71	Finlande
178.89	183.46	190.51	188.38	195.21	208.43	212.00	208.96	214.20	231.45	256.46	269.59	280.84	294.76	291.46	310.22	328.98	346.50	391.27	France
290.51	305.54	327.77	341.59	341.28	367.67	394.62	392.48	394.41	414.62	455.15	457.21	443.98	442.61	420.49	453.55	483.50	508.33	564.68	Allemagne
8.07	8.63	8.12	7.54	8.14	9.52	9.64	10.99	12.75	13.89	14.53	13.94	14.46	15.98	15.41	16.38	16.53	17.05	17.94	Grèce
..	..	..	..	..	..	..	..	..	..	..	10.09	9.78	9.99	8.97	10.21	11.57	12.54	16.08	Hongrie
1.62	1.67	1.72	1.56	1.74	1.78	1.97	2.09	2.16	2.08	2.14	2.14	2.02	1.98	2.12	2.33	2.28	2.51	2.65	Islande
11.12	11.82	12.06	12.72	14.05	16.38	17.46	17.97	20.43	22.27	24.57	26.72	28.13	31.94	35.01	39.97	47.79	53.43	62.48	Irlande
156.07	143.15	150.41	149.25	154.05	166.25	172.06	173.36	181.01	190.05	204.66	219.23	219.51	234.34	257.33	283.71	317.89	315.84	336.27	Italie
5.91	5.82	5.54	5.53	5.82	6.87	7.52	7.77	8.11	9.07	9.80	10.13	10.80	11.32	11.63	12.14	12.67	12.96	13.56	Luxembourg
98.45	100.59	102.46	101.57	104.79	112.70	118.44	120.61	125.48	136.75	145.84	153.62	160.84	165.46	167.99	179.20	191.13	201.08	214.60	Pays-Bas
26.82	28.07	28.55	28.59	30.60	33.02	35.41	36.20	36.60	38.93	43.21	46.93	49.78	52.37	54.03	58.74	61.27	67.30	71.20	Norvège
..	..	..	..	..	..	..	..	..	..	..	16.90	16.62	18.41	19.00	21.49	26.56	29.86	33.02	Pologne
10.63	10.87	10.38	10.87	12.35	13.78	14.70	15.70	17.46	18.88	21.34	23.47	24.08	25.25	24.34	26.46	28.88	31.82	34.48	Portugal
47.36	48.45	52.43	55.03	60.51	67.58	69.38	70.66	75.14	78.95	81.31	83.93	90.53	97.22	105.49	123.13	135.45	149.82	171.92	Espagne
46.38	46.09	47.04	49.77	54.63	58.36	59.18	61.39	64.00	65.60	67.64	68.74	67.14	68.72	73.97	84.29	95.18	100.98	113.89	Suède
57.01	59.90	62.47	59.86	60.34	64.86	70.08	69.79	71.39	76.06	81.10	82.82	81.12	83.54	84.77	86.26	87.67	89.87	97.94	Suisse
4.73	4.52	7.39	9.90	11.20	14.05	13.78	13.08	16.53	19.57	19.52	20.02	20.76	23.05	24.82	28.59	30.87	37.65	44.85	Turquie
169.29	169.03	167.63	169.21	172.56	183.94	194.69	203.39	215.19	216.32	226.46	237.71	236.18	246.45	255.04	278.74	300.32	321.20	346.84	Royaume-Uni
1921.98	2001.96	2091.21	2087.08	2131.83	2319.67	2417.81	2450.77	2556.82	2748.89	2968.09	3117.91	3204.54	3350.15	3436.78	3734.04	4070.03	4350.17	4804.86	OCDE - Total[1]
1288.32	1307.84	1363.55	1383.88	1425.76	1535.09	1606.43	1621.84	1680.96	1779.65	1916.88	1992.69	2015.97	2089.37	2121.83	2306.50	2483.08	2614.94	2869.58	OCDE - Europe[2]
1198.13	1213.68	1263.43	1283.97	1321.87	1421.38	1485.18	1500.68	1554.28	1643.00	1770.91	1840.78	1862.29	1928.44	1956.09	2130.58	2300.99	2417.62	2652.95	UE15

Importations de biens et services - aux niveaux de prix et taux de change de 1990 (milliards de dollars É-U) 12.

1979	1980	1981	1982	1983	1984	1985	1986	1987	1988	1989	1990	1991	1992	1993	1994	1995	1996	1997	
75.26	79.08	87.40	73.46	81.59	96.43	105.05	114.05	120.49	137.20	145.83	149.14	153.92	163.56	176.87	193.12	206.10	216.69	245.83	Canada
33.03	43.56	51.28	31.87	21.10	24.86	27.59	25.49	26.81	36.65	43.23	51.77	59.63	71.32	72.65	88.09	74.84	91.90	112.15	Mexique
338.40	323.30	339.70	339.40	382.50	476.10	509.10	542.90	571.20	591.10	609.70	628.60	620.30	665.20	725.30	816.90	902.30	1012.90	1153.60	États-Unis
179.66	165.72	166.40	162.30	157.37	173.83	171.41	174.75	191.38	231.44	274.43	296.10	286.88	284.87	284.13	309.29	353.35	394.00	393.34	Japon
29.41	27.98	29.60	30.41	34.03	36.55	36.34	42.85	51.23	57.86	67.27	76.89	91.68	96.37	102.83	125.15	152.65	175.25	181.83	Corée
28.87	30.26	33.20	34.98	31.33	37.76	39.81	37.66	38.36	44.67	53.78	51.65	50.45	54.41	57.29	66.09	72.80	79.94	91.15	Australie
7.89	7.35	8.15	8.27	8.21	9.15	9.29	9.48	10.30	10.22	11.64	11.60	11.16	11.99	12.94	14.79	15.85	16.95	17.76	Nouvelle-Zélande
38.03	40.38	40.07	38.20	40.37	44.43	47.16	45.79	48.28	53.29	57.76	62.00	65.99	67.18	66.74	72.27	77.30	84.03	89.43	Autriche
91.34	88.77	87.02	88.01	86.84	92.33	92.55	96.72	102.62	112.62	123.21	129.24	132.89	138.36	137.33	147.15	154.28	157.70	167.66	Belgique
..	..	..	..	..	..	..	..	..	..	..	15.40	12.77	15.59	17.21	18.55	22.64	25.56	27.28	République tchèque
33.08	30.84	30.32	31.47	32.02	33.77	36.50	38.97	38.19	38.76	40.40	41.02	42.60	42.67	42.17	47.75	52.91	55.10	59.28	Danemark
20.74	22.47	21.55	22.03	22.70	23.07	24.55	25.18	27.51	30.57	33.30	33.11	29.23	29.55	29.77	33.58	35.92	37.56	41.50	Finlande
163.01	169.67	169.43	175.49	171.59	175.66	184.14	196.75	213.37	233.65	254.24	269.92	277.44	281.16	271.79	290.72	305.79	315.69	341.36	France
286.78	296.98	288.78	285.72	290.57	303.45	316.70	324.57	338.30	354.88	382.64	402.51	441.28	450.16	423.38	456.15	489.37	503.66	544.60	Allemagne
12.04	11.08	11.49	12.29	13.10	13.13	14.81	15.37	17.92	19.35	21.40	23.27	24.67	23.98	24.03	24.32	26.58	27.93	29.39	Grèce
..	..	..	..	..	..	..	..	..	..	..	8.81	9.29	9.31	11.19	12.18	12.10	12.90	16.19	Hongrie
1.61	1.66	1.78	1.77	1.60	1.74	1.91	1.92	2.37	2.26	2.03	2.05	2.17	2.00	1.82	1.90	1.97	2.30	2.50	Islande
15.34	14.65	14.90	14.44	15.11	16.60	17.14	18.10	19.22	20.16	22.88	24.04	24.36	26.03	27.63	31.42	36.08	40.10	45.99	Irlande
125.07	131.62	129.19	129.43	125.65	140.96	147.98	154.37	172.95	183.42	199.95	218.84	226.01	242.74	221.48	236.65	259.34	255.01	285.40	Italie
5.97	6.21	6.03	6.01	6.09	6.93	7.41	7.69	8.27	8.95	9.54	9.97	10.87	10.78	11.09	11.07	11.49	11.61	12.21	Luxembourg
99.88	100.19	94.24	93.82	97.52	102.36	108.84	112.70	117.39	126.31	134.83	140.49	146.28	149.30	146.18	156.01	167.70	176.52	188.97	Pays-Bas
30.08	30.89	31.34	32.96	31.96	33.81	36.82	41.15	38.48	37.58	38.39	39.36	39.43	39.71	41.47	43.50	45.96	49.79	55.93	Norvège
..	..	..	..	..	..	..	..	..	..	..	12.68	16.44	16.72	18.93	21.06	26.19	33.52	39.61	Pologne
13.43	14.36	14.70	15.27	14.33	13.69	13.88	16.23	19.97	23.56	25.01	28.50	30.58	33.85	32.73	35.66	38.44	41.33	45.65	Portugal
46.18	47.67	45.66	47.83	47.68	46.82	50.58	57.88	69.52	79.55	93.29	100.56	109.62	117.22	111.12	123.73	137.32	147.42	165.45	Espagne
47.65	47.86	45.30	46.66	47.03	49.54	52.97	55.35	59.61	62.79	67.43	67.89	64.55	65.29	63.66	72.03	79.39	82.34	91.96	Suède
51.63	55.35	53.55	52.53	55.43	60.05	62.25	67.31	71.48	75.19	79.61	81.64	80.30	76.90	76.94	83.04	87.31	89.64	96.13	Suisse
6.10	10.32	11.61	12.57	14.70	17.59	16.43	15.85	19.50	18.62	19.90	26.47	25.09	27.82	37.78	29.52	38.25	46.10	56.44	Turquie
159.76	154.21	149.82	157.21	167.12	183.77	188.34	201.25	217.54	245.10	263.21	264.37	250.81	268.05	276.36	291.84	304.04	330.22	360.60	Royaume-Uni
1910.83	1924.43	1932.88	1913.98	1963.49	2177.83	2283.20	2397.48	2561.03	2777.92	3007.62	3154.09	3206.51	3344.11	3372.65	3676.59	3974.68	4266.43	4694.27	OCDE - Total[1]
1247.72	1275.16	1246.76	1263.70	1281.40	1359.70	1420.95	1493.14	1602.49	1726.63	1869.01	1965.24	2024.18	2092.77	2043.47	2188.31	2349.44	2454.04	2680.44	OCDE - Europe[2]
1158.30	1176.95	1148.48	1163.87	1177.72	1246.51	1303.55	1366.91	1470.66	1592.99	1729.08	1815.72	1877.20	1946.34	1885.45	2030.35	2175.95	2266.21	2469.45	UE15

1. Non compris la Corée la République tchèque la Hongrie et la Pologne.
2. Non compris la République tchèque la Hongrie et la Pologne.

13. Gross domestic product - at current prices and current exchange rates (billions of US dollars)

	1960	1961	1962	1963	1964	1965	1966	1967	1968	1969	1970	1971	1972	1973	1974	1975	1976	1977	1978
Canada	40.63	40.31	41.40	43.98	48.18	53.12	59.44	63.86	69.69	76.66	85.06	96.31	109.69	127.43	155.56	168.54	200.37	205.27	[illegible]12.16
Mexico	13.42	14.56	15.70	17.47	20.63	22.47	24.97	27.31	30.24	33.43	39.61	43.69	50.35	61.60	80.22	98.08	99.21	91.19	[illegible]14.25
United States	511.70	529.40	569.50	600.80	645.70	700.90	768.50	812.10	887.30	958.10	1008.90	1096.10	1205.80	1348.30	1457.60	[illegible]585.50	1771.40	1973.80	2[illegible]29.00
Japan	44.47	53.71	60.95	69.76	82.06	91.29	106.03	124.25	147.16	172.86	203.74	231.02	304.76	414.05	459.61	499.77	561.70	691.30	[illegible]71.32
Korea	..	..	..	..	..	..	..	..	..	..	8.92	9.86	10.72	13.61	18.95	21.27	29.11	37.32	50.39
Australia	16.77	16.97	18.23	19.99	21.95	23.76	25.26	27.74	30.39	33.77	37.28	42.39	49.86	70.04	84.93	92.34	101.28	101.22	[illegible]15.83
New Zealand	4.00	4.07	4.38	4.76	5.19	5.64	5.84	5.94	5.16	5.74	6.42	7.65	9.21	12.25	13.76	13.34	13.45	14.53	17.58
Austria	6.42	7.12	7.57	8.16	8.93	9.71	10.58	11.25	12.08	13.19	14.80	17.21	21.24	28.42	33.88	38.57	41.37	49.67	59.59
Belgium	11.17	11.87	12.69	13.65	15.27	16.65	17.87	19.16	20.48	22.72	25.26	28.32	35.20	45.16	53.01	62.13	67.27	78.36	95.78
Czech Republic	..	..	..	..	..	..	..	..	..	..	..	..	..	..	..	..	..	..	..
Denmark	6.09	6.76	7.61	8.10	9.26	10.41	11.42	12.46	12.86	14.63	16.17	18.07	22.17	29.21	32.47	38.47	42.48	47.56	57.71
Finland	5.06	5.74	6.14	6.67	7.53	8.32	8.92	9.08	8.55	9.76	10.89	12.01	14.14	18.68	23.86	28.05	30.18	31.90	34.56
France	60.90	66.43	74.18	83.16	92.25	99.30	107.50	116.12	126.21	136.79	142.87	159.53	195.85	253.45	270.66	342.47	355.84	390.31	[illegible]83.61
Germany	80.82	92.21	101.14	107.19	117.79	128.72	136.87	138.58	149.50	169.75	206.89	240.83	289.46	384.84	426.35	467.90	498.98	577.18	[illegible]16.54
Greece	4.24	4.79	5.09	5.68	6.38	7.26	8.07	8.72	9.47	10.75	12.06	13.33	15.25	19.79	22.77	25.39	27.35	31.68	38.27
Hungary	..	..	..	..	..	..	..	..	..	..	..	..	..	..	..	..	..	..	..
Iceland	0.26	0.26	0.29	0.34	0.44	0.53	0.64	0.63	0.48	0.42	0.53	0.67	0.84	1.15	1.51	1.40	1.67	2.20	2.51
Ireland	1.85	1.99	2.15	2.31	2.63	2.80	2.95	3.18	3.12	3.60	4.06	4.71	5.83	6.91	7.29	8.76	8.73	10.39	13.53
Italy	39.70	44.09	49.53	56.74	62.11	66.83	72.41	79.76	86.46	95.44	107.41	117.76	136.74	165.70	187.58	212.28	209.75	241.06	[illegible]95.76
Luxembourg	0.58	0.58	0.61	0.65	0.74	0.77	0.81	0.82	0.90	1.04	1.21	1.27	1.58	2.17	2.65	2.60	2.85	3.16	3.93
Netherlands	11.86	13.03	14.15	15.35	18.06	20.17	21.96	24.10	26.72	30.26	33.95	39.54	48.75	63.87	75.38	88.22	96.65	113.63	[illegible]38.93
Norway	5.20	5.67	6.11	6.56	7.21	7.96	8.58	9.39	10.03	10.92	12.57	14.22	16.78	21.80	26.32	31.97	35.16	40.43	45.68
Poland	..	..	..	..	..	..	..	..	..	..	..	..	..	..	..	..	..	..	..
Portugal	2.85	3.06	3.26	3.53	3.83	4.28	4.69	5.24	5.80	6.36	7.08	8.05	9.81	13.18	15.29	16.90	17.76	18.72	20.52
Spain	11.39	13.06	15.23	18.01	20.15	23.37	27.11	29.87	29.71	34.02	37.57	42.72	54.20	72.08	89.15	105.18	108.61	121.38	[illegible]47.19
Sweden	14.10	15.34	16.64	18.01	20.08	22.10	24.04	26.09	27.69	30.07	33.67	36.81	43.27	52.51	58.35	73.26	78.99	83.50	92.32
Switzerland	9.04	10.16	11.27	12.39	13.74	14.72	15.80	17.01	18.16	19.68	21.92	26.34	32.31	43.45	50.07	57.41	60.05	64.13	89.69
Turkey	13.67	7.84	9.11	10.53	11.24	12.03	14.28	15.92	17.65	19.58	17.91	17.09	21.55	27.07	37.34	46.67	53.39	60.88	67.21
United Kingdom	72.40	76.77	80.68	85.53	93.48	100.70	107.20	111.30	104.81	112.79	123.86	140.13	161.04	181.49	195.70	233.60	224.60	254.08	[illegible]22.42
OECD - Total[1]	988.59	1045.79	1133.60	1219.31	1334.85	1453.78	1591.75	1699.89	1840.61	2022.33	2211.69	2455.78	2855.70	3464.61	3861.31	[illegible]338.32	4709.09	5297.53	6[illegible]35.98
OECD - Europe[2]	357.59	386.77	423.44	462.55	511.13	556.61	601.72	638.69	670.67	741.78	830.69	938.62	1126.03	1430.93	1609.63	[illegible]881.25	1961.67	2220.21	2[illegible]25.84
EU15	329.43	362.83	396.66	432.72	478.49	521.38	562.41	595.74	624.35	691.17	777.76	880.29	1054.54	1337.46	1494.39	[illegible]743.30	1811.41	2052.56	2[illegible]20.75

14. Private final consumption expenditure - at current prices and current exchange rates (billions of US dollars)

	1960	1961	1962	1963	1964	1965	1966	1967	1968	1969	1970	1971	1972	1973	1974	1975	1976	1977	1978
Canada	25.91	25.23	25.47	26.83	28.75	31.12	33.95	36.62	39.88	43.41	47.19	53.28	60.82	68.88	82.06	91.23	107.14	110.81	[illegible]15.45
Mexico	10.46	11.31	12.18	13.16	15.60	16.60	18.50	20.22	22.60	24.63	29.14	32.72	36.98	44.41	57.30	68.93	69.08	61.84	77.18
United States	327.80	338.00	358.90	378.20	406.10	438.20	475.00	501.20	550.60	595.50	637.30	690.20	757.20	836.80	914.00	[illegible]008.40	1126.60	1252.60	1[illegible]36.80
Japan	26.10	30.64	35.15	41.03	47.30	53.44	61.51	70.57	80.48	92.50	106.48	123.75	164.60	221.96	249.63	285.60	322.99	398.78	[illegible]50.36
Korea	..	..	..	..	..	..	..	..	..	..	6.66	7.45	7.90	9.47	13.33	15.01	19.05	23.24	30.55
Australia	10.64	10.84	11.56	12.43	13.45	14.44	15.42	16.80	18.31	20.13	22.20	24.98	29.10	40.10	48.66	53.96	59.08	59.86	59.27
New Zealand	2.70	2.76	2.89	3.13	3.35	3.64	3.89	3.96	3.43	3.75	4.19	4.80	5.70	7.44	8.71	8.56	8.16	8.88	10.70
Austria	3.81	4.17	4.49	4.87	5.22	5.72	6.11	6.57	7.00	7.45	8.06	9.40	11.47	15.21	18.05	21.58	23.33	28.24	32.88
Belgium	7.74	8.06	8.46	9.17	9.80	10.71	11.44	12.07	13.07	14.16	15.16	17.14	21.29	27.53	31.93	38.35	41.39	49.02	59.63
Czech Republic	..	..	..	..	..	..	..	..	..	..	..	..	..	..	..	..	..	..	..
Denmark	3.57	3.97	4.46	4.71	5.28	5.79	6.43	7.06	7.15	7.95	8.77	9.54	11.19	15.05	16.69	20.18	22.73	25.59	30.66
Finland	3.08	3.41	3.76	4.12	4.69	5.17	5.49	5.55	4.98	5.64	6.17	6.72	7.97	10.28	12.67	15.63	17.00	18.03	19.52
France	36.38	39.83	44.50	50.27	54.92	58.59	63.36	68.60	74.86	80.78	82.74	92.22	113.06	144.69	155.71	201.17	207.90	227.35	230.07
Germany	45.35	51.75	56.74	60.07	64.70	71.38	76.21	78.31	83.33	93.00	111.69	129.85	157.09	205.52	228.55	262.83	278.11	325.56	400.55
Greece	3.55	3.83	4.05	4.40	4.89	5.50	6.08	6.58	7.09	7.75	8.70	9.44	10.44	13.08	16.07	17.87	18.74	21.75	25.99
Hungary	..	..	..	..	..	..	..	..	..	..	..	..	..	..	..	..	..	..	..
Iceland	0.17	0.16	0.18	0.22	0.27	0.31	0.39	0.40	0.31	0.25	0.32	0.41	0.50	0.65	0.89	0.81	0.94	1.24	1.42
Ireland	1.45	1.53	1.65	1.76	1.97	2.07	2.18	2.29	2.28	2.59	2.88	3.29	3.90	4.57	5.13	5.78	5.79	6.85	8.87
Italy	23.59	25.75	29.06	33.99	36.85	39.41	43.46	48.14	51.37	56.34	63.68	70.18	82.02	99.97	112.72	131.41	127.44	144.77	1[illegible]4.76
Luxembourg	0.35	0.37	0.39	0.42	0.47	0.50	0.53	0.54	0.58	0.62	0.68	0.77	0.95	1.19	1.36	1.68	1.80	2.10	2.54
Netherlands	6.95	7.80	8.56	9.51	10.75	12.02	13.07	14.19	15.51	17.75	19.90	22.93	28.03	36.33	42.90	51.87	56.94	68.10	[illegible]4.18
Norway	2.97	3.23	3.48	3.70	4.02	4.29	4.60	4.99	5.34	5.95	6.53	7.37	8.64	10.95	12.93	16.09	17.77	21.15	[illegible]2.87
Poland	..	..	..	..	..	..	..	..	..	..	..	..	..	..	..	..	..	..	..
Portugal	2.06	2.23	2.25	2.43	2.59	2.88	3.16	3.40	3.94	4.36	4.63	5.45	6.24	8.47	11.01	12.92	13.20	13.35	[illegible]3.83
Spain	7.95	8.98	10.29	12.35	13.74	16.12	18.49	20.18	19.80	21.89	24.30	27.72	34.93	46.25	57.78	68.28	72.00	79.65	[illegible]4.86
Sweden	8.36	9.00	9.67	10.40	11.20	12.32	13.38	14.42	15.28	16.50	17.93	19.53	23.09	27.78	31.17	38.00	41.89	44.63	[illegible]9.06
Switzerland	5.53	6.07	6.78	7.36	8.03	8.64	9.32	10.01	10.67	11.56	12.67	15.01	18.44	24.93	28.98	34.63	36.95	40.05	[illegible]5.36
Turkey	10.78	6.10	7.34	8.53	8.71	9.28	10.70	11.78	13.11	14.61	13.04	12.87	16.11	19.65	27.43	33.79	36.94	43.11	[illegible]9.63
United Kingdom	47.76	50.23	53.24	56.53	60.33	64.19	67.86	70.33	65.73	69.76	76.00	86.42	100.33	112.53	123.85	144.22	136.15	151.10	1[illegible]1.60
OECD - Total[1]	624.99	655.25	705.49	759.58	822.96	892.33	970.52	1034.80	1116.70	1218.81	1330.34	1475.98	1710.09	2044.20	2296.18	[illegible]633.74	2850.07	3204.39	38[illegible]8.05
OECD - Europe[2]	221.38	236.47	259.34	284.79	308.42	334.89	362.26	385.43	401.40	438.90	483.85	546.26	655.69	824.62	935.82	117.07	1157.02	1311.62	15[illegible]8.28
EU15	201.94	220.90	241.57	264.98	287.40	312.36	337.25	358.24	371.98	406.53	451.29	510.60	612.00	768.44	865.59	[illegible]031.75	1064.42	1206.08	14[illegible]9.00

15. Government final consumption expenditure - at current prices and current exchange rates (billions of US dollars)

	1960	1961	1962	1963	1964	1965	1966	1967	1968	1969	1970	1971	1972	1973	1974	1975	1976	1977	1978
Canada	5.83	6.51	6.64	6.99	7.63	8.37	9.83	11.44	12.99	14.70	17.62	20.17	22.81	25.61	31.76	37.10	43.94	46.19	[illegible]6.85
Mexico	0.76	0.84	0.99	1.15	1.33	1.42	1.64	1.81	2.09	2.32	2.60	3.01	3.92	5.11	6.63	9.14	9.86	8.86	1.27
United States	84.90	91.90	99.70	103.70	108.50	114.40	133.20	151.40	164.40	174.30	186.40	196.40	212.50	229.10	256.50	287.90	311.20	339.40	3[illegible]0.40
Japan	3.56	4.12	4.85	5.75	6.53	7.47	8.48	9.47	10.93	12.66	15.15	18.38	24.86	34.36	41.91	50.17	55.36	67.94	[illegible]3.86
Korea	..	..	..	..	..	..	..	..	..	..	0.84	0.96	1.08	1.15	1.83	2.34	3.18	4.02	5.25
Australia	1.87	2.04	2.18	2.31	2.63	3.02	3.35	3.85	4.28	4.60	5.11	5.95	7.02	10.12	13.24	15.86	17.74	18.02	[illegible]0.93
New Zealand	0.42	0.45	0.49	0.51	0.57	0.70	0.81	0.76	0.67	0.72	0.86	1.01	1.22	1.60	2.02	2.08	1.93	2.29	2.99
Austria	0.84	0.91	0.98	1.10	1.20	1.31	1.46	1.66	1.80	2.01	2.20	2.57	3.14	4.34	5.40	6.73	7.38	8.71	[illegible]0.88
Belgium	1.39	1.41	1.56	1.77	1.91	2.12	2.34	2.58	2.78	3.09	3.39	3.98	5.10	6.55	7.76	10.16	10.97	13.04	[illegible]6.52
Czech Republic	..	..	..	..	..	..	..	..	..	..	..	..	..	..	..	..	..	..	..
Denmark	0.83	1.00	1.18	1.28	1.47	1.73	2.00	2.27	2.44	2.82	3.29	3.92	4.82	6.35	7.75	9.66	10.44	11.60	[illegible]4.42
Finland	0.60	0.67	0.77	0.89	1.02	1.14	1.28	1.35	1.31	1.41	1.57	1.82	2.16	2.80	3.63	4.78	5.44	5.89	6.30
France	8.66	9.55	10.78	12.22	13.40	14.26	15.28	16.46	18.67	19.97	21.00	23.80	29.10	37.62	41.59	56.80	60.21	67.07	[illegible]5.02
Germany	11.09	13.07	15.21	17.09	17.88	20.05	21.72	23.04	23.81	27.19	33.49	41.81	50.93	70.26	84.59	98.32	101.45	116.59	1[illegible]5.08
Greece	0.35	0.38	0.42	0.45	0.53	0.60	0.67	0.80	0.86	0.97	1.08	1.18	1.31	1.60	2.23	2.73	2.92	3.58	4.32
Hungary	..	..	..	..	..	..	..	..	..	..	..	..	..	..	..	..	..	..	..
Iceland	0.03	0.03	0.03	0.04	0.05	0.06	0.07	0.08	0.06	0.05	0.07	0.09	0.12	0.16	0.24	0.23	0.26	0.34	0.41
Ireland	0.22	0.24	0.26	0.28	0.34	0.37	0.38	0.41	0.40	0.47	0.57	0.69	0.86	1.04	1.20	1.56	1.51	1.70	2.22
Italy	4.87	5.37	6.22	7.58	8.56	9.71	10.35	11.04	12.04	13.05	14.23	17.47	21.08	24.32	26.29	30.45	28.59	33.91	[illegible]2.79
Luxembourg	0.05	0.05	0.06	0.07	0.07	0.07	0.08	0.08	0.09	0.10	0.11	0.13	0.16	0.21	0.26	0.33	0.36	0.42	0.52
Netherlands	1.45	1.65	1.87	2.14	2.55	2.84	3.17	3.56	3.85	4.39	5.06	6.12	7.47	9.62	11.84	14.83	16.13	19.12	[illegible]3.85
Norway	0.65	0.70	0.83	0.91	1.01	1.16	1.28	1.46	1.61	1.78	2.06	2.47	2.95	3.84	4.66	5.97	6.79	7.89	9.03
Poland	..	..	..	..	..	..	..	..	..	..	..	..	..	..	..	..	..	..	..
Portugal	0.28	0.35	0.39	0.40	0.43	0.47	0.53	0.63	0.70	0.76	0.90	1.01	1.21	1.56	1.99	2.34	2.25	2.43	2.64
Spain	0.96	1.07	1.23	1.51	1.65	1.97	2.37	2.82	2.71	3.11	3.55	4.11	5.16	6.85	8.82	10.99	12.26	13.95	[illegible]7.54
Sweden	2.27	2.47	2.82	3.15	3.49	3.97	4.59	5.15	5.76	6.32	7.33	8.40	9.97	12.08	13.74	17.69	19.93	23.28	[illegible]6.15
Switzerland	0.78	0.96	1.12	1.28	1.41	1.51	1.61	1.71	1.85	2.03	2.25	2.82	3.45	4.79	5.71	7.10	7.75	8.15	[illegible]1.31
Turkey	1.03	0.68	0.73	0.83	0.97	1.07	1.24	1.41	1.59	1.74	1.65	1.68	2.26	3.04	3.81	5.33	6.67	8.44	[illegible]3.20
United Kingdom	11.87	12.81	13.73	14.65	15.60	17.14	18.68	20.37	18.83	19.67	22.20	25.69	30.14	33.76	40.11	52.34	49.79	52.66	[illegible]6.47
OECD - Total[1]	145.55	159.25	175.01	188.05	200.73	216.93	246.41	275.61	296.51	320.23	353.75	394.66	453.72	536.69	623.65	740.57	791.13	881.48	10[illegible]3.95
OECD - Europe[2]	48.21	53.39	60.16	67.64	73.53	81.55	89.10	96.88	101.16	110.93	126.01	149.75	181.39	230.79	271.61	338.32	351.09	398.77	4[illegible].65
EU15	45.72	51.01	57.46	64.59	70.10	77.76	84.89	92.22	96.05	105.33	119.98	142.70	172.61	218.96	257.19	319.70	329.63	373.95	4[illegible]3.71

1. Excluding Korea Czech Republic Hungary and Poland.
2. Excluding Czech Republic Hungary and Poland.

Produit intérieur brut - aux prix et taux de change courants (milliards de dollars É-U) 13.

1979	1980	1981	1982	1983	1984	1985	1986	1987	1988	1989	1990	1991	1992	1993	1994	1995	1996	1997	
236.03	266.00	296.72	303.73	328.80	342.07	350.25	362.83	414.68	489.50	545.99	572.67	586.98	568.68	552.93	549.55	573.44	592.29	607.69	Canada
149.94	207.22	266.67	185.22	158.72	187.26	196.69	138.01	149.55	183.14	222.98	262.71	314.45	363.61	403.20	420.78	286.17	329.47	402.11	Mexique
2488.00	2709.00	3039.30	3158.90	3412.90	3786.40	4048.20	4268.10	4528.10	4878.80	5260.90	5554.10	5710.90	6027.70	6341.60	6722.90	7033.60	7390.60	7824.00	États-Unis
1010.98	1059.26	1169.69	1086.40	1186.34	1265.34	1343.25	1990.61	2418.14	2918.25	2899.38	2970.09	3402.12	3719.07	4275.01	4688.97	5137.36	4595.16	4190.24	Japon
64.86	62.80	69.98	74.85	82.75	91.32	94.32	108.61	136.32	182.01	222.15	253.67	294.18	307.94	332.82	380.82	456.36	484.57	442.54	Corée
130.37	150.75	172.68	168.61	163.79	182.43	160.54	167.62	198.07	249.47	283.05	295.61	297.92	292.43	285.51	326.84	353.50	395.16	392.92	Australie
20.23	22.39	24.19	23.57	23.28	22.31	22.38	28.60	36.38	43.54	42.32	43.10	41.69	40.06	43.68	51.32	60.02	65.44	64.96	Nouvelle-Zélande
70.76	78.54	67.92	68.07	68.88	64.92	66.17	94.26	118.18	126.81	126.73	159.50	166.65	187.21	182.71	196.08	231.55	228.74	206.23	Autriche
110.03	119.98	98.45	86.61	81.92	78.10	81.42	113.83	142.46	154.74	156.52	196.13	201.15	224.84	214.05	232.21	273.68	268.24	242.51	Belgique
..	..	..	..	..	..	..	..	..	..	..	27.40	26.85	29.85	34.44	39.90	50.82	56.46	52.04	République tchèque
67.40	67.79	58.51	56.98	57.29	55.79	59.33	84.20	104.59	111.16	107.88	133.36	134.08	147.09	138.83	151.83	180.93	183.97	170.03	Danemark
42.50	51.31	50.21	50.53	48.76	50.68	53.51	70.03	88.01	103.84	113.49	134.81	121.38	106.44	84.45	97.83	125.92	124.96	119.83	Finlande
583.18	664.59	582.34	551.73	525.70	499.13	523.10	731.91	887.86	962.76	965.45	1195.43	1201.01	1322.22	1249.66	1330.99	1535.09	1538.80	1394.12	France
849.42	908.10	760.90	733.77	732.49	690.39	696.54	994.77	1242.50	1337.22	1320.29	1640.06	1719.51	1971.38	1913.54	2050.91	2402.29	2341.55	2089.89	Allemagne
46.71	48.61	44.80	46.67	42.34	40.88	40.48	47.70	56.08	64.63	67.08	82.91	89.05	98.45	92.20	98.86	116.05	123.37	119.95	Grèce
..	..	..	..	..	..	..	..	..	..	..	35.78	33.43	37.25	38.60	41.51	44.25	44.74	45.30	Hongrie
2.85	3.37	3.50	3.20	2.75	2.81	2.91	3.92	5.41	5.97	5.40	6.25	6.73	6.91	6.09	6.22	6.98	7.31	7.40	Islande
16.92	20.08	19.09	19.83	19.17	18.57	19.64	26.51	31.32	34.87	36.23	45.53	46.19	52.37	49.23	54.51	65.62	72.02	77.16	Irlande
370.49	449.91	405.58	400.83	415.85	411.40	424.25	602.55	758.26	837.44	868.72	1093.95	1150.70	1219.15	985.15	1016.26	1087.99	1213.67	1145.37	Italie
4.60	5.02	4.21	3.83	3.77	3.70	3.81	5.61	6.94	7.83	8.30	10.35	10.91	12.62	12.84	14.58	17.29	16.97	15.76	Luxembourg
159.49	171.86	143.56	139.71	135.72	126.44	128.12	178.72	217.62	231.55	228.67	283.67	290.20	321.93	313.07	337.51	398.37	397.03	363.35	Pays-Bas
52.10	63.42	62.19	61.15	59.93	60.32	63.39	75.61	90.55	98.14	98.83	115.45	117.76	126.31	116.11	122.93	146.60	158.15	153.36	Norvège
..	..	..	..	..	..	..	..	..	..	..	58.98	76.48	84.36	86.00	92.60	119.05	134.57	135.62	Pologne
23.25	28.73	27.93	26.66	23.79	22.02	23.68	33.84	42.08	49.21	53.17	69.13	78.32	94.51	83.73	88.13	104.68	108.82	101.29	Portugal
196.66	213.31	186.27	181.09	158.47	160.19	165.84	230.81	292.72	344.75	380.51	491.94	528.59	577.31	478.96	483.82	559.63	582.21	532.03	Espagne
109.06	125.56	114.88	101.23	92.90	96.39	100.72	132.98	161.44	181.90	191.19	229.76	239.33	247.56	185.81	198.43	231.30	251.75	227.75	Suède
100.82	107.47	98.51	100.29	100.10	95.36	96.54	138.14	172.46	186.38	179.30	228.41	232.68	243.47	236.73	261.36	307.39	295.12	255.27	Suisse
91.74	68.79	71.04	64.55	61.68	59.99	67.23	75.73	87.17	90.85	107.14	150.68	151.04	159.10	180.42	130.65	169.32	181.46	189.88	Turquie
418.96	537.38	510.96	486.06	460.07	432.08	457.07	562.35	689.45	835.62	841.40	975.51	1012.16	1047.80	942.88	1019.90	1107.04	1153.37	1282.86	Royaume-Uni
7352.48	8148.45	8280.08	8109.23	8365.40	8754.96	9195.08	11159.22	12940.00	14528.36	15110.92	16941.12	17851.50	19178.20	19368.37	20653.37	22511.81	22615.64	22175.96	OCDE - Total[1]
3316.93	3733.82	3310.84	3182.80	3091.58	2969.15	3073.77	4203.45	5195.09	5765.67	5856.30	7242.83	7497.44	8166.65	7466.45	7893.01	9067.72	9247.52	8694.04	OCDE - Europe[2]
3069.43	3490.76	3075.60	2953.60	2867.13	2750.67	2843.70	3910.06	4839.51	5384.33	5465.63	6742.04	6989.23	7630.87	6927.10	7371.85	8437.43	8605.48	8088.14	UE15

Consommation finale privée - aux prix et taux de change courants (milliards de dollars É-U) 14.

1979	1980	1981	1982	1983	1984	1985	1986	1987	1988	1989	1990	1991	1992	1993	1994	1995	1996	1997	
125.65	141.52	156.02	162.68	178.46	185.18	191.67	203.62	230.81	269.20	302.49	323.85	340.52	333.16	325.10	318.58	327.17	341.85	356.29	Canada
98.78	131.40	167.30	111.20	94.14	115.11	123.66	92.06	95.95	123.87	153.53	182.79	221.69	261.11	289.89	301.07	191.92	213.73	262.82	Mexique
1556.90	1720.60	1902.40	2034.60	2226.70	2432.30	2633.70	2803.90	2998.60	3247.40	3486.70	3720.50	3844.50	4079.80	4318.40	4569.40	4802.40	5043.00	5311.80	États-Unis
593.58	623.29	680.13	645.71	714.44	752.07	791.31	1167.29	1423.92	1699.88	1688.10	1721.72	1944.11	2149.98	2506.32	2799.66	3088.71	2751.25	2541.10	Japon
40.01	40.47	45.00	47.37	50.13	53.90	55.20	59.93	71.76	92.91	118.29	136.19	156.87	166.19	179.05	204.56	241.70	260.82	237.33	Corée
76.14	88.65	101.93	101.99	100.35	107.03	95.77	100.42	116.33	144.79	164.60	176.95	184.70	183.85	178.28	202.43	220.28	244.68	243.20	Australie
12.32	13.80	14.43	14.27	13.84	13.37	13.77	17.23	22.09	26.55	25.99	27.30	26.43	25.07	26.49	31.39	37.13	41.14	41.22	Nouvelle-Zélande
38.87	43.26	38.02	38.55	39.91	37.22	37.88	53.32	66.75	71.76	71.30	89.09	91.90	104.44	102.65	109.84	129.97	129.92	115.74	Autriche
69.97	76.64	65.03	57.86	54.80	51.74	54.30	74.43	93.15	98.81	99.46	124.67	129.54	144.00	136.28	147.18	172.02	170.60	153.41	Belgique
..	..	..	..	..	..	..	..	..	..	..	14.57	12.33	15.61	17.02	19.86	25.15	28.44	26.73	République tchèque
35.98	35.81	31.02	29.66	29.59	28.74	30.76	43.82	53.40	55.83	53.80	65.43	66.13	72.77	69.43	77.64	91.83	92.70	86.14	Danemark
23.44	27.76	27.18	27.85	26.86	27.48	29.19	38.27	48.12	55.60	59.33	70.55	67.93	60.75	48.19	54.45	68.29	68.29	63.40	Finlande
338.95	391.26	350.94	334.87	319.57	303.38	319.54	442.21	540.62	578.22	575.50	712.28	718.82	794.91	760.90	803.51	922.75	935.10	835.73	France
472.44	510.36	434.65	421.04	418.78	393.07	394.50	550.83	691.72	737.82	729.51	912.44	982.40	1124.14	1106.42	1174.53	1378.32	1359.91	1208.28	Allemagne
30.83	32.71	31.50	32.76	29.42	27.55	27.64	33.52	40.59	45.83	48.19	60.74	65.02	73.62	69.36	74.25	86.93	92.31	88.06	Grèce
..	..	..	..	..	..	..	..	..	..	..	17.32	18.33	21.48	23.04	24.09	23.93	23.50	23.17	Hongrie
1.64	1.94	2.07	1.93	1.65	1.76	1.86	2.41	3.45	3.74	3.34	3.83	4.21	4.32	3.67	3.67	4.22	4.46	4.52	Islande
11.36	13.59	12.94	12.19	11.76	11.23	12.03	16.33	19.09	21.23	21.90	26.45	27.06	30.71	27.79	30.74	35.02	37.58	38.19	Irlande
220.38	273.82	247.03	245.78	252.60	250.70	259.99	368.37	465.64	513.36	538.00	670.74	711.00	766.06	610.97	629.15	668.85	744.88	707.97	Italie
2.97	3.29	2.86	2.58	2.51	2.40	2.50	3.53	4.48	4.89	4.96	6.42	6.87	7.47	7.35	7.97	9.45	9.32	8.37	Luxembourg
97.41	104.57	85.99	84.02	81.63	74.90	76.15	106.22	132.27	137.43	134.15	166.45	172.47	193.87	189.37	203.00	238.03	236.48	214.75	Pays-Bas
25.96	29.69	28.89	28.85	28.18	27.64	30.39	39.58	46.44	49.90	49.07	57.05	58.04	63.55	58.03	61.37	72.37	75.46	72.91	Norvège
..	..	..	..	..	..	..	..	..	..	..	28.62	45.99	52.79	55.00	60.45	75.07	87.66	88.51	Pologne
15.55	19.17	19.28	18.38	16.35	15.43	15.94	21.82	26.82	31.29	33.21	43.64	50.11	61.34	55.70	58.23	67.92	70.64	65.32	Portugal
127.84	141.27	124.18	119.45	103.29	102.95	106.33	145.93	185.10	216.16	239.63	307.09	329.79	364.11	302.39	304.00	347.37	360.55	329.73	Espagne
57.17	64.62	60.34	54.12	48.19	48.81	51.57	68.41	84.83	95.37	98.15	117.03	127.54	133.47	102.32	108.15	121.06	131.98	120.88	Suède
62.94	66.99	60.97	62.61	63.20	58.90	59.15	83.77	104.80	110.76	104.39	130.90	136.67	145.46	141.83	156.53	185.14	180.04	156.11	Suisse
68.41	55.63	50.74	47.31	45.79	45.34	47.76	50.99	59.52	57.69	70.29	103.33	106.64	110.62	124.66	91.40	119.05	122.08	129.19	Turquie
251.16	320.29	308.28	294.05	279.51	262.70	277.16	351.74	430.85	529.59	532.63	613.75	641.16	669.54	606.25	650.11	699.86	734.34	823.05	Royaume-Uni
4416.65	4931.93	5004.12	4984.29	5181.55	5377.01	5684.50	6880.01	7985.34	8926.96	9288.19	10435.01	11055.24	11958.11	12168.04	12968.26	14086.05	14192.31	13978.18	OCDE - Total[1]
1953.27	2212.67	1981.91	1913.85	1853.61	1771.95	1834.61	2495.49	3097.65	3415.28	3466.79	4281.89	4493.30	4925.14	4523.55	4745.73	5418.45	5556.65	5221.75	OCDE - Europe[2]
1794.32	2058.42	1839.25	1773.15	1714.78	1638.30	1695.46	2318.74	2883.43	3193.19	3239.71	3986.79	4187.74	4601.19	4195.37	4432.75	5037.68	5174.61	4859.03	UE15

Consommation finale des administrations publiques - aux prix et taux de change courants (milliards de dollars É-U) 15.

1979	1980	1981	1982	1983	1984	1985	1986	1987	1988	1989	1990	1991	1992	1993	1994	1995	1996	1997	
50.41	57.32	63.73	70.46	75.76	75.76	77.68	80.23	88.96	103.99	117.04	129.88	141.67	139.66	131.97	123.85	124.28	123.48	121.27	Canada
14.76	20.25	27.97	18.88	13.60	16.84	17.68	12.23	12.80	15.41	18.44	22.03	28.55	36.11	44.47	48.64	29.91	32.07	33.64	Mexique
410.30	463.20	516.90	567.80	612.20	653.50	719.50	767.70	819.70	860.20	907.20	974.90	1016.80	1043.30	1062.70	1089.90	1124.60	1163.00	1206.10	États-Unis
98.05	103.94	116.01	107.58	117.87	123.98	128.64	192.19	227.98	266.74	262.94	268.02	307.00	341.59	402.62	447.54	504.13	444.50	404.12	Japon
6.47	7.27	8.16	8.64	8.94	9.12	9.55	10.86	13.18	17.31	22.69	25.70	30.23	33.45	35.81	40.36	46.79	51.86	49.29	Corée
22.36	26.48	30.78	30.92	30.70	33.41	29.72	31.68	35.25	42.69	46.63	50.68	54.20	53.50	50.87	57.24	60.26	67.12	66.08	Australie
3.39	4.03	4.33	4.18	3.91	3.59	3.63	4.67	5.98	7.22	7.02	7.33	7.08	6.81	6.80	7.43	8.67	9.46	9.87	Nouvelle-Zélande
12.84	14.28	12.65	12.96	13.11	12.40	12.77	18.46	23.13	24.50	24.16	29.74	31.50	36.24	36.93	39.83	46.55	45.18	39.92	Autriche
19.14	21.08	18.02	15.46	14.25	13.24	13.81	19.08	22.94	23.31	22.44	27.46	28.91	31.96	31.46	34.06	40.09	38.93	34.99	Belgique
..	..	..	..	..	..	..	..	..	..	..	5.27	4.81	5.75	7.60	8.88	10.61	11.92	10.54	République tchèque
17.22	18.46	16.58	16.41	16.03	14.72	15.31	20.55	26.87	29.21	27.98	34.08	34.48	37.96	37.16	39.35	46.36	46.92	43.10	Danemark
7.55	9.22	9.31	9.51	9.42	9.79	10.80	14.37	18.21	20.85	22.38	28.39	29.36	26.44	19.64	21.82	27.43	27.53	25.04	Finlande
102.64	120.52	109.49	106.71	102.62	97.76	101.31	138.54	167.14	177.68	173.36	214.94	219.60	249.43	247.72	259.12	295.78	300.85	269.51	France
171.84	188.79	161.42	154.47	151.66	141.32	142.94	202.28	254.90	271.02	257.80	318.27	335.47	394.68	383.99	405.83	479.06	468.58	405.64	Allemagne
5.40	5.63	5.70	6.05	5.64	5.65	5.85	6.53	7.75	9.24	10.19	12.66	12.83	13.71	13.36	13.79	18.04	18.00	17.72	Grèce
..	..	..	..	..	..	..	..	..	..	..	7.78	8.58	9.88	11.02	10.89	10.64	10.05	9.93	Hongrie
0.49	0.56	0.59	0.56	0.49	0.46	0.51	0.70	1.01	1.17	1.06	1.20	1.32	1.40	1.25	1.28	1.45	1.51	1.51	Islande
2.93	3.82	3.64	3.76	3.55	3.32	3.49	4.77	5.31	5.39	5.20	6.73	7.21	8.24	7.69	8.33	9.41	9.80	10.11	Irlande
54.79	67.38	66.05	65.43	69.04	68.00	70.66	99.03	127.74	142.92	145.98	192.11	202.53	215.37	173.72	173.94	174.74	198.32	186.96	Italie
0.62	0.71	0.62	0.53	0.50	0.48	0.51	0.72	0.95	1.02	1.04	1.39	1.45	1.65	1.66	1.82	2.28	2.30	2.09	Luxembourg
28.07	29.87	24.80	24.21	23.22	20.53	20.19	27.73	34.58	35.65	33.97	41.23	42.04	47.21	46.42	48.37	57.17	55.67	49.67	Pays-Bas
10.04	11.87	11.84	11.83	11.59	11.12	11.51	14.64	18.44	20.06	20.13	23.98	24.98	27.93	25.36	26.44	30.71	32.07	30.93	Norvège
..	..	..	..	..	..	..	..	..	..	..	11.04	16.73	17.48	16.79	16.50	20.95	23.53	23.43	Pologne
2.98	3.86	3.88	3.68	3.33	3.06	3.40	4.80	5.90	7.16	8.01	10.75	13.50	16.36	14.99	15.50	18.50	19.74	18.88	Portugal
24.42	27.82	25.52	25.20	22.75	22.57	24.42	33.85	44.15	50.86	57.71	76.66	85.48	98.59	84.08	81.84	93.43	96.76	85.95	Espagne
31.30	36.75	33.97	29.87	26.83	27.01	28.10	36.52	43.12	47.37	50.04	62.87	65.22	69.11	52.17	53.94	59.67	66.07	58.85	Suède
12.79	13.41	12.45	13.03	13.44	12.53	12.78	18.33	22.65	24.85	24.30	31.81	33.69	36.03	34.30	37.98	43.97	42.79	35.90	Suisse
10.55	5.79	7.74	6.11	6.45	5.36	6.01	6.81	6.82	6.92	10.01	16.52	18.67	20.46	23.50	15.22	18.26	21.00	23.28	Turquie
83.91	116.21	113.60	107.72	101.91	94.74	96.63	118.65	142.30	166.63	166.62	200.60	218.95	231.52	206.67	220.56	235.54	243.04	260.07	Royaume-Uni
1198.77	1371.26	1397.60	1413.32	1449.88	1476.15	1557.83	1875.05	2164.59	2362.08	2421.64	2784.23	2962.47	3185.26	3141.52	3273.60	3550.30	3574.69	3441.20	OCDE - Total[1]
599.51	696.03	637.88	613.50	595.83	564.06	581.00	786.36	973.92	1065.82	1062.38	1331.38	1407.18	1564.30	1442.09	1499.01	1698.44	1735.07	1600.12	OCDE - Europe[2]
565.64	664.41	605.26	581.96	563.87	534.59	550.19	745.88	925.01	1012.82	1006.87	1257.88	1328.52	1478.48	1357.67	1418.10	1604.05	1637.70	1508.49	UE15

1. Non compris la Corée la République tchèque la Hongrie et la Pologne.
2. Non compris la République tchèque la Hongrie et la Pologne.

16. Gross fixed capital formation - at current prices and current exchange rates (billions of US dollars)

	1960	1961	1962	1963	1964	1965	1966	1967	1968	1969	1970	1971	1972	1973	1974	1975	1976	1977	1978
Canada	9.22	8.75	8.71	9.22	10.79	12.62	14.69	15.08	15.37	16.91	18.29	21.52	24.27	28.97	36.82	41.29	47.50	47.39	48.19
Mexico	2.24	2.26	2.41	2.86	3.49	3.89	4.42	5.20	5.77	6.39	7.79	7.74	9.42	11.72	15.72	20.71	20.58	17.66	23.73
United States	91.70	92.80	100.70	108.80	119.90	133.90	144.60	146.90	162.10	177.20	180.10	201.30	230.60	263.00	276.10	281.10	319.90	383.20	[illegible]61.60
Japan	12.88	17.13	19.63	22.03	26.01	27.17	32.12	39.69	48.80	59.56	72.34	79.11	103.98	150.68	159.87	162.19	175.17	208.49	[illegible]95.32
Korea	..	..	..	..	..	..	..	..	..	..	2.24	2.21	2.22	3.26	5.11	5.67	7.43	10.55	16.37
Australia	4.17	4.15	4.43	4.89	5.64	6.40	6.71	7.15	7.95	8.79	9.66	11.15	12.35	16.97	19.92	21.87	24.29	24.11	27.74
New Zealand	0.85	0.94	0.91	1.01	1.17	1.28	1.38	1.29	1.01	1.20	1.46	1.72	2.25	2.97	3.77	3.90	3.52	3.44	4.02
Austria	1.49	1.73	1.81	1.97	2.19	2.46	2.73	2.78	2.88	3.07	3.55	4.45	5.96	7.52	8.93	9.54	9.99	12.52	13.91
Belgium	2.15	2.45	2.70	2.82	3.41	3.71	4.09	4.38	4.39	4.83	5.72	6.24	7.49	9.64	12.00	13.90	14.73	16.82	20.56
Czech Republic	..	..	..	..	..	..	..	..	..	..	..	..	..	..	..	..	..	..	..
Denmark	1.51	1.80	2.02	2.05	2.60	2.88	3.16	3.46	3.45	4.12	4.57	5.01	6.24	8.29	8.93	9.29	11.18	12.03	14.34
Finland	1.43	1.60	1.69	1.71	1.90	2.19	2.36	2.28	1.97	2.33	2.86	3.30	3.95	5.38	7.12	8.83	8.47	8.69	8.31
France	12.70	14.63	16.47	19.11	21.96	24.05	26.48	28.76	30.63	33.34	34.74	39.38	48.46	63.98	69.82	82.66	85.21	89.41	[illegible]08.23
Germany	19.39	22.90	25.69	27.03	30.90	33.17	34.35	31.58	33.03	38.98	52.02	62.16	72.59	90.78	90.96	94.18	99.16	115.52	[illegible]45.93
Greece	0.99	1.08	1.26	1.35	1.65	1.93	2.15	2.18	2.70	3.26	3.51	4.14	5.21	6.83	6.24	6.51	7.15	8.97	11.29
Hungary	..	..	..	..	..	..	..	..	..	..	..	..	..	..	..	..	..	..	..
Iceland	0.08	0.06	0.07	0.10	0.13	0.14	0.18	0.20	0.15	0.11	0.13	0.20	0.24	0.36	0.50	0.45	0.47	0.60	0.61
Ireland	0.26	0.31	0.37	0.44	0.52	0.58	0.57	0.62	0.63	0.81	0.89	1.08	1.34	1.69	1.74	1.93	2.12	2.49	3.62
Italy	10.34	11.82	13.51	15.71	15.91	14.85	15.70	17.94	20.24	23.15	26.47	28.21	31.69	41.25	48.67	52.94	50.15	57.01	67.97
Luxembourg	0.11	0.13	0.14	0.18	0.23	0.20	0.20	0.18	0.18	0.21	0.25	0.33	0.40	0.54	0.59	0.66	0.64	0.72	0.86
Netherlands	2.93	3.31	3.54	3.74	4.72	5.19	5.90	6.50	7.35	7.61	8.99	10.27	11.77	15.10	16.93	19.01	19.23	24.49	30.29
Norway	1.48	1.67	1.75	1.90	1.97	2.20	2.41	2.73	2.64	2.60	3.27	4.14	4.57	6.26	7.88	10.71	12.52	14.71	14.23
Poland	..	..	..	..	..	..	..	..	..	..	..	..	..	..	..	..	..	..	..
Portugal	0.72	0.78	0.80	0.92	0.96	1.07	1.29	1.53	1.41	1.58	1.80	2.18	2.91	3.88	4.36	4.80	4.88	5.44	6.28
Spain	2.35	2.80	3.31	3.95	4.77	5.82	6.80	7.53	7.62	8.83	9.77	10.16	13.50	19.02	24.89	27.74	27.02	28.98	33.28
Sweden	3.17	3.54	3.93	4.34	4.90	5.42	5.92	6.43	6.57	6.93	7.52	8.02	9.54	11.41	12.44	15.22	16.60	17.49	17.30
Switzerland	2.32	2.89	3.37	3.86	4.38	4.38	4.49	4.60	4.81	5.26	6.26	7.99	9.95	13.24	14.31	14.30	12.82	13.79	19.93
Turkey	2.17	1.23	1.37	1.51	1.63	1.74	2.26	2.59	3.04	3.39	3.30	2.88	3.75	4.88	6.96	9.21	12.33	13.67	12.44
United Kingdom	11.85	13.30	13.73	14.40	17.14	18.56	19.78	21.29	20.41	21.20	23.37	26.51	29.82	36.08	40.90	46.53	44.03	47.16	59.56
OECD - Total[1]	198.52	214.04	234.33	255.87	288.86	315.83	344.72	362.85	395.12	441.65	488.66	549.21	652.23	820.42	896.38	959.48	1029.67	1174.81	1[illegible]50.04
OECD - Europe[2]	77.45	88.02	97.54	107.07	121.87	130.56	140.81	147.55	154.12	171.60	199.01	226.66	269.37	346.11	384.18	428.43	438.71	490.52	[illegible]89.43
EU15	71.40	82.18	90.98	99.70	113.76	122.09	131.47	137.44	143.48	160.23	186.05	211.45	250.87	321.37	354.53	393.76	400.57	447.75	[illegible]42.23

17. Exports of goods and services - at current prices and current exchange rates (billions of US dollars)

	1960	1961	1962	1963	1964	1965	1966	1967	1968	1969	1970	1971	1972	1973	1974	1975	1976	1977	1978
Canada	6.95	7.22	7.43	8.08	9.38	9.96	11.63	13.10	14.95	16.48	19.21	20.82	23.95	29.74	38.44	38.11	44.70	47.91	53.46
Mexico	1.40	1.51	1.65	1.79	1.94	2.11	2.30	2.31	2.62	3.10	3.10	3.38	4.11	5.24	6.82	6.84	8.52	9.52	12.10
United States	26.80	27.30	28.70	30.80	34.70	36.70	40.50	43.00	47.40	51.40	59.10	62.30	70.10	93.70	124.90	137.00	147.80	157.50	[illegible]84.60
Japan	4.76	4.98	5.74	6.29	7.78	9.59	11.20	11.97	14.86	18.22	22.02	27.06	32.26	41.56	62.51	63.96	76.15	90.53	[illegible]08.00
Korea	..	..	..	..	..	..	..	..	..	..	1.25	1.52	2.13	4.01	5.27	5.91	9.03	11.79	14.93
Australia	2.29	2.68	2.72	3.19	3.48	3.47	3.62	4.02	4.12	4.82	5.54	6.06	7.42	10.72	12.82	13.83	15.23	15.47	17.01
New Zealand	0.88	0.92	0.96	1.18	1.19	1.20	1.28	1.17	1.19	1.41	1.45	1.77	2.33	3.04	2.96	3.20	3.75	4.00	4.86
Austria	1.52	1.66	1.84	2.00	2.16	2.38	2.59	2.75	3.03	3.65	4.49	5.15	6.34	8.47	10.92	12.00	13.17	15.55	19.33
Belgium	4.28	4.70	5.22	5.77	6.58	7.08	7.91	8.28	9.31	11.23	12.97	14.16	17.74	24.78	32.02	32.58	37.31	42.52	50.06
Czech Republic	..	..	..	..	..	..	..	..	..	..	..	..	..	..	..	..	..	..	..
Denmark	1.99	2.05	2.21	2.49	2.80	3.09	3.30	3.45	3.60	4.08	4.59	5.07	6.11	8.48	10.49	11.77	12.46	13.94	16.31
Finland	1.14	1.22	1.30	1.35	1.52	1.68	1.78	1.79	1.94	2.36	2.80	2.92	3.60	4.75	6.57	6.73	7.64	9.18	10.45
France	8.83	9.31	9.58	10.55	11.74	13.23	14.38	15.37	16.74	19.30	22.58	26.20	32.74	44.55	56.01	65.28	69.67	79.96	98.70
Germany	14.32	15.53	16.39	17.85	19.85	21.68	24.47	26.43	29.80	34.36	40.89	46.67	55.72	78.47	105.13	107.83	119.62	137.25	[illegible]65.83
Greece	0.30	0.35	0.38	0.44	0.45	0.51	0.71	0.72	0.71	0.81	0.94	1.07	1.39	2.19	2.85	3.33	3.74	4.15	5.24
Hungary	..	..	..	..	..	..	..	..	..	..	..	..	..	..	..	..	..	..	..
Iceland	0.11	0.10	0.13	0.14	0.16	0.19	0.21	0.17	0.15	0.18	0.23	0.25	0.29	0.40	0.47	0.46	0.57	0.71	0.90
Ireland	0.56	0.66	0.67	0.75	0.84	0.94	1.06	1.16	1.16	1.29	1.44	1.63	1.94	2.52	2.98	3.59	3.88	4.93	6.49
Italy	5.19	5.90	6.56	7.22	8.32	9.98	11.13	12.06	13.78	15.81	17.75	20.02	24.30	28.87	37.94	43.73	46.38	56.51	70.00
Luxembourg	0.49	0.49	0.48	0.50	0.57	0.62	0.62	0.64	0.71	0.86	1.07	1.10	1.30	1.92	2.69	2.38	2.48	2.71	3.25
Netherlands	5.49	5.75	6.15	6.69	7.63	8.39	8.89	9.47	10.63	12.48	14.77	17.43	21.29	29.37	39.47	42.71	47.84	52.44	60.94
Norway	1.91	2.01	2.10	2.29	2.64	2.88	3.12	3.51	3.85	4.12	4.68	5.09	6.09	8.46	10.85	11.92	12.88	14.35	16.66
Poland	..	..	..	..	..	..	..	..	..	..	..	..	..	..	..	..	..	..	..
Portugal	0.46	0.46	0.56	0.62	0.90	1.05	1.17	1.31	1.33	1.43	1.58	1.85	2.45	3.23	3.77	3.16	2.84	3.16	3.79
Spain	1.02	1.11	1.35	1.48	1.89	2.04	2.57	2.72	3.34	4.10	4.98	6.07	7.89	10.48	12.83	14.21	14.90	17.56	22.31
Sweden	3.20	3.38	3.59	3.89	4.41	4.76	5.07	5.42	5.88	6.76	8.02	8.85	10.34	14.22	18.58	20.39	21.59	22.60	25.75
Switzerland	2.51	2.76	3.02	3.29	3.65	4.00	4.39	4.69	5.30	6.09	6.79	7.75	9.37	12.71	15.41	17.06	19.08	22.24	29.77
Turkey	0.62	0.36	0.41	0.48	0.51	0.55	0.65	0.69	0.69	0.74	0.78	0.87	1.20	1.77	2.15	2.35	2.87	2.33	2.97
United Kingdom	15.16	15.83	16.24	17.12	18.14	19.31	20.83	21.31	22.48	25.11	28.60	32.50	35.02	43.00	54.80	60.57	64.11	76.46	[illegible]1.94
OECD - Total[1]	112.17	118.22	125.38	136.26	153.23	167.38	185.35	197.51	219.57	250.21	290.38	326.07	385.28	512.64	674.38	724.99	799.17	903.48	1[illegible]30.72
OECD - Europe[2]	69.09	73.62	78.18	84.93	94.77	104.36	114.83	121.93	134.44	154.77	179.96	204.68	245.12	328.65	425.93	462.05	503.03	578.55	[illegible]0.68
EU15	63.94	68.39	72.52	78.72	87.82	96.74	106.46	112.88	124.44	143.64	167.46	190.72	228.18	305.30	397.05	430.26	467.64	538.92	[illegible]50.39

18. Imports of goods and services - at current prices and current exchange rates (billions of US dollars)

	1960	1961	1962	1963	1964	1965	1966	1967	1968	1969	1970	1971	1972	1973	1974	1975	1976	1977	1978
Canada	7.51	7.42	7.52	7.76	8.81	10.03	11.61	12.44	14.09	16.40	17.02	19.22	22.96	27.94	38.25	41.17	46.22	48.38	[illegible]2.79
Mexico	1.97	1.95	1.99	2.19	2.56	2.70	2.84	3.11	3.56	3.90	4.46	4.45	5.19	6.80	9.90	11.01	11.43	10.88	[illegible]4.72
United States	22.80	22.70	25.00	26.10	28.10	31.50	37.10	39.90	46.60	50.50	55.80	62.30	74.20	91.20	127.50	122.70	151.10	182.40	[illegible]2.30
Japan	4.56	5.83	5.64	6.86	7.92	8.31	9.54	11.70	13.21	15.46	19.40	20.77	25.22	41.45	65.93	63.75	71.65	79.20	[illegible]1.11
Korea	..	..	..	..	..	..	..	..	..	..	2.12	2.53	2.63	4.41	7.35	7.70	9.55	12.01	[illegible]6.66
Australia	2.83	2.56	2.75	2.97	3.56	4.12	3.86	4.35	4.81	4.99	5.49	6.03	6.05	8.96	14.27	13.12	14.99	16.40	[illegible]8.92
New Zealand	0.97	0.97	0.92	1.07	1.13	1.32	1.41	1.19	1.11	1.28	1.65	1.71	2.04	3.03	4.67	4.12	4.04	4.25	4.82
Austria	1.57	1.65	1.73	1.92	2.16	2.44	2.73	2.84	3.06	3.50	4.35	5.03	6.22	8.37	11.04	11.76	13.79	16.85	[illegible]9.31
Belgium	4.38	4.81	5.25	5.93	6.66	7.11	8.07	8.24	9.25	11.02	12.40	13.59	16.59	23.90	31.86	32.52	37.26	43.32	[illegible]1.17
Czech Republic	..	..	..	..	..	..	..	..	..	..	..	..	..	..	..	..	..	..	..
Denmark	2.10	2.20	2.49	2.51	3.04	3.30	3.54	3.76	3.84	4.47	5.16	5.50	6.07	9.18	11.64	12.33	14.70	15.95	[illegible]7.86
Finland	1.17	1.28	1.37	1.35	1.66	1.83	1.92	1.87	1.80	2.27	2.93	3.14	3.57	4.87	7.44	8.41	8.23	8.62	9.08
France	7.57	8.10	8.88	10.25	11.90	12.34	14.08	15.04	16.80	20.02	21.83	24.47	30.70	42.34	58.72	61.19	72.28	79.48	[illegible]2.27
Germany	12.48	13.66	15.27	16.40	18.24	21.44	22.42	21.82	24.86	30.06	37.14	42.85	50.49	68.25	87.85	95.50	109.57	124.95	1[illegible]9.66
Greece	0.60	0.67	0.73	0.87	1.03	1.25	1.29	1.34	1.48	1.71	1.89	2.09	2.60	4.25	4.97	5.81	6.01	6.81	8.02
Hungary	..	..	..	..	..	..	..	..	..	..	..	..	..	..	..	..	..	..	..
Iceland	0.12	0.10	0.12	0.14	0.17	0.18	0.21	0.22	0.19	0.17	0.22	0.29	0.30	0.43	0.61	0.57	0.56	0.73	0.83
Ireland	0.66	0.76	0.81	0.91	1.04	1.19	1.23	1.26	1.36	1.61	1.76	1.97	2.25	2.99	4.02	4.12	4.56	5.86	7.81
Italy	5.36	5.96	6.87	8.55	8.29	8.51	9.89	11.31	12.05	14.58	17.54	19.10	23.19	32.01	45.64	43.99	48.90	54.02	[illegible]3.44
Luxembourg	0.42	0.45	0.47	0.49	0.57	0.61	0.60	0.57	0.62	0.71	0.90	1.05	1.19	1.63	2.12	2.25	2.30	2.56	3.18
Netherlands	5.29	5.75	6.11	6.81	8.00	8.54	9.20	9.70	10.65	12.57	15.36	17.57	20.01	27.42	37.52	39.90	44.72	51.18	[illegible]0.92
Norway	1.92	2.08	2.14	2.32	2.54	2.83	3.11	3.51	3.53	3.75	4.63	5.29	5.73	8.21	11.06	13.26	15.22	17.47	[illegible]6.34
Poland	..	..	..	..	..	..	..	..	..	..	..	..	..	..	..	..	..	..	..
Portugal	0.61	0.76	0.69	0.77	1.03	1.21	1.31	1.39	1.56	1.64	1.97	2.33	2.82	4.00	5.81	4.99	4.93	5.64	6.01
Spain	0.84	1.20	1.64	2.07	2.44	3.27	3.91	3.78	3.98	4.75	5.34	5.71	7.78	11.06	17.12	18.24	19.73	20.04	[illegible]1.15
Sweden	3.28	3.30	3.53	3.85	4.37	4.95	5.24	5.44	5.93	6.88	8.21	8.44	9.70	12.80	19.03	20.54	22.91	23.99	[illegible]4.83
Switzerland	2.53	3.05	3.40	3.67	4.07	4.12	4.38	4.60	5.02	5.86	7.15	8.14	9.64	13.16	16.33	15.51	17.21	20.67	[illegible]7.70
Turkey	0.79	0.47	0.61	0.75	0.60	0.62	0.78	0.73	0.87	0.90	1.04	1.34	1.84	2.40	4.16	5.26	5.73	6.28	5.02
United Kingdom	16.16	16.06	16.36	17.44	19.74	20.19	20.94	22.45	23.29	24.57	27.44	30.46	35.13	47.38	64.50	64.56	66.54	74.51	[illegible]7.50
OECD - Total[1]	108.48	113.74	122.31	133.93	149.65	163.89	181.21	192.56	213.55	243.56	281.11	312.83	371.49	504.04	701.98	716.56	814.59	920.43	10[illegible]6.75
OECD - Europe[2]	67.84	72.31	78.49	86.98	97.56	105.92	114.85	119.87	130.16	151.03	177.28	198.36	235.84	324.66	441.45	460.69	515.16	578.92	6[illegible]2.09
EU15	62.49	66.61	72.22	80.10	90.18	98.17	106.37	110.81	120.55	140.35	164.23	183.31	218.33	300.45	409.28	426.08	476.45	533.77	6[illegible]2.20

1. Excluding Korea Czech Republic Hungary and Poland.
2. Excluding Czech Republic Hungary and Poland.

Formation brute de capital fixe - aux prix et taux de change courants (milliards de dollars É-U) 16.

1979	1980	1981	1982	1983	1984	1985	1986	1987	1988	1989	1990	1991	1992	1993	1994	1995	1996	1997	
54.49	62.38	72.99	66.51	67.03	66.89	70.49	74.36	89.30	108.61	123.04	120.84	113.77	105.11	97.24	100.94	98.61	103.54	114.52	Canada
34.62	49.34	67.67	40.89	26.78	32.31	36.12	25.84	26.54	33.92	38.46	46.97	58.65	71.26	74.84	81.44	46.22	59.21	78.70	Mexique
529.20	547.30	603.20	590.10	629.50	734.50	785.50	818.20	835.50	881.60	924.60	932.50	882.10	937.50	1011.70	1106.40	1176.90	1269.30	1359.50	États-Unis
320.21	334.40	357.80	320.12	332.12	350.50	369.08	542.96	685.51	865.05	886.30	942.51	1068.95	1133.24	1262.88	1343.23	1463.02	1363.50	1186.43	Japon
21.85	20.13	19.63	21.32	24.42	26.53	26.94	30.60	39.62	53.90	70.93	94.06	113.11	112.61	119.87	136.14	166.82	178.62	154.88	Corée
30.54	36.40	44.44	42.67	37.31	41.51	39.47	40.89	47.64	60.55	71.55	67.05	60.92	58.87	57.94	69.81	73.81	81.51	83.88	Australie
4.16	4.63	5.72	5.83	5.75	5.67	5.92	6.46	7.90	8.45	8.55	8.23	6.65	6.60	7.98	10.44	12.63	13.83	12.91	Nouvelle-Zélande
16.51	18.97	16.23	14.84	14.62	13.51	14.25	20.25	25.93	28.68	29.18	37.11	39.94	43.99	41.70	46.70	54.96	54.48	49.80	Autriche
22.55	25.15	17.82	14.78	12.95	12.22	12.80	17.81	22.87	27.57	29.91	39.74	37.85	41.93	38.19	40.32	48.51	46.83	43.05	Belgique
..	..	..	..	..	..	..	..	..	..	..	7.55	6.33	8.50	9.80	11.81	16.67	18.62	15.99	République tchèque
16.14	14.61	10.49	10.49	10.51	11.00	12.73	20.03	23.64	23.01	22.32	26.82	25.89	26.67	24.02	26.47	33.78	34.99	34.11	Danemark
9.89	13.06	12.69	12.79	12.49	12.15	12.81	16.35	21.05	26.12	31.73	36.39	27.22	19.63	12.46	14.20	19.49	20.04	20.20	Finlande
130.47	152.82	128.90	117.81	106.23	96.16	100.75	141.14	175.48	199.49	206.04	255.52	254.68	265.48	231.56	239.93	275.44	268.21	237.82	France
181.89	202.16	163.39	148.77	148.42	136.34	134.38	191.70	240.75	262.23	266.46	354.25	395.30	454.24	417.95	447.48	513.29	480.76	416.90	Allemagne
14.87	14.48	12.29	11.47	10.57	9.30	9.51	10.85	11.84	13.86	15.07	19.10	20.03	20.90	18.61	18.36	21.50	23.80	24.04	Grèce
..	..	..	..	..	..	..	..	..	..	..	7.52	7.00	7.40	7.29	8.35	8.43	9.10	9.50	Hongrie
0.67	0.86	0.86	0.79	0.60	0.61	0.62	0.75	1.10	1.17	1.03	1.20	1.29	1.21	0.95	0.94	1.02	1.30	1.39	Islande
5.00	5.56	5.48	5.09	4.30	3.85	3.62	4.62	5.16	5.84	6.33	8.58	7.93	8.76	7.53	8.76	10.88	12.82	14.41	Irlande
85.31	110.11	97.67	90.20	88.68	86.98	87.76	119.07	149.42	168.40	175.76	222.05	227.83	233.85	166.98	169.19	188.39	205.80	190.78	Italie
1.02	1.23	0.97	0.87	0.73	0.67	0.61	1.10	1.56	1.90	1.92	2.49	2.83	2.87	3.04	2.98	3.66	3.52	3.54	Luxembourg
34.18	36.74	28.07	26.03	25.30	24.09	25.20	36.47	45.21	49.27	49.08	59.28	59.08	64.44	60.10	63.30	75.95	77.47	72.71	Pays-Bas
15.58	17.09	16.83	16.67	16.70	15.92	15.69	21.01	25.37	27.84	25.35	24.95	24.28	25.16	23.71	25.42	30.39	33.57	35.33	Norvège
..	..	..	..	..	..	..	..	..	..	..	12.38	14.92	14.16	13.66	15.00	20.10	25.50	28.69	Pologne
6.78	9.00	9.45	9.08	7.61	5.69	5.66	8.20	11.29	14.07	14.71	19.06	20.52	23.64	19.53	20.68	24.71	25.91	25.39	Portugal
42.34	46.97	40.39	38.81	32.67	29.73	31.81	44.96	60.89	77.98	91.80	120.29	125.75	125.90	95.08	96.00	116.24	118.23	109.48	Espagne
21.45	25.16	21.61	18.80	17.26	17.99	19.41	24.64	31.22	36.74	42.04	49.42	46.36	42.00	26.43	27.12	33.70	37.22	31.16	Suède
22.81	26.50	24.63	24.00	24.48	23.19	23.58	34.45	43.69	49.87	49.18	61.80	59.26	55.91	51.04	57.55	65.63	59.49	49.98	Suisse
17.67	10.93	13.72	12.43	11.66	11.37	14.66	18.90	21.57	23.72	24.43	34.46	35.99	37.60	47.84	32.16	40.36	45.53	50.17	Turquie
78.20	96.59	83.00	78.30	73.69	73.40	77.92	95.33	122.82	162.82	172.53	191.02	172.39	164.35	141.42	153.42	171.60	178.83	199.74	Royaume-Uni
1696.54	1862.45	1856.31	1718.14	1717.93	1815.55	1910.34	2336.34	2733.22	3158.76	3307.37	3681.65	3775.45	3971.12	3940.74	4203.24	4600.68	4619.70	4445.94	OCDE - Total [1]
723.32	828.01	704.49	652.03	619.44	584.17	603.76	827.63	1040.84	1200.58	1254.87	1563.54	1584.40	1658.54	1428.14	1490.99	1729.49	1728.80	1609.99	OCDE - Europe [2]
666.60	772.63	648.44	598.13	566.02	533.08	549.21	752.52	949.11	1097.98	1154.88	1441.12	1463.58	1538.66	1304.60	1374.91	1592.09	1588.91	1473.12	UE15

Exportations de biens et services - aux prix et taux de change courants (milliards de dollars É-U) 17.

1979	1980	1981	1982	1983	1984	1985	1986	1987	1988	1989	1990	1991	1992	1993	1994	1995	1996	1997	
63.78	75.00	80.31	78.33	84.14	98.58	99.76	101.88	112.24	132.28	141.67	149.50	149.25	156.02	169.67	190.74	219.21	234.30	247.05	Canada
16.97	26.33	32.94	33.70	35.79	38.62	35.98	28.40	34.60	36.50	42.36	48.87	51.46	55.41	61.48	70.80	87.05	106.96	121.71	Mexique
227.00	277.30	301.10	280.30	272.90	298.30	297.00	314.10	357.70	438.70	500.90	548.20	592.20	629.50	647.80	708.50	804.20	856.00	945.70	États-Unis
116.94	145.04	172.20	158.14	165.36	189.74	194.13	226.03	250.34	292.49	306.99	317.15	346.84	373.79	397.46	434.49	482.60	456.89	465.59	Japon
18.05	21.31	25.46	25.67	29.32	32.42	32.15	40.88	54.77	69.90	72.72	75.54	82.82	88.94	97.38	114.66	150.87	156.92	168.68	Corée
22.07	25.68	25.91	25.87	23.85	27.59	27.01	27.24	33.26	41.52	45.82	49.59	53.12	53.81	54.31	61.10	68.98	78.50	83.12	Australie
6.13	6.82	7.16	6.95	7.02	7.50	6.89	7.90	9.83	11.83	11.45	11.91	12.51	12.83	13.68	16.11	18.00	18.93	18.63	Nouvelle-Zélande
24.51	28.31	25.40	24.94	24.74	24.56	26.22	33.84	41.36	47.84	50.61	64.06	66.35	72.04	67.61	73.44	89.36	93.40	86.96	Autriche
62.74	68.35	61.03	57.46	56.48	57.63	57.81	73.72	88.98	102.21	110.33	133.59	133.92	145.50	132.72	150.72	182.99	182.47	176.84	Belgique
..	..	..	..	..	..	..	..	..	..	..	16.16	15.34	16.40	17.96	21.12	28.48	30.16	29.95	République tchèque
20.05	22.56	21.76	21.08	21.19	20.84	22.14	27.45	33.46	36.91	37.84	47.78	49.89	53.72	49.13	53.87	63.97	64.92	61.16	Danemark
13.49	17.02	16.77	15.72	14.85	15.67	15.82	18.86	22.76	26.00	27.20	31.08	27.03	28.64	27.91	34.94	47.46	47.66	47.71	Finlande
123.86	143.04	131.43	120.26	118.18	120.53	125.09	155.08	183.24	205.02	221.17	269.59	272.60	299.99	274.82	303.34	361.21	370.97	371.53	France
198.81	224.05	204.42	205.39	198.62	198.52	212.45	282.30	339.54	371.92	390.48	457.21	438.15	468.93	421.92	466.46	573.04	575.62	560.41	Allemagne
6.35	7.91	7.18	6.67	6.52	6.89	6.67	8.30	10.69	11.96	12.21	13.94	14.38	16.65	14.64	16.09	18.38	19.52	18.84	Grèce
..	..	..	..	..	..	..	..	..	..	..	10.09	10.95	11.71	10.19	12.01	15.24	16.21	19.21	Hongrie
1.06	1.18	1.19	1.01	1.07	1.07	1.18	1.51	1.85	1.90	1.86	2.14	2.13	2.11	2.01	2.25	2.49	2.66	2.69	Islande
8.08	9.56	8.88	9.15	9.66	10.62	11.38	13.96	17.62	20.80	22.90	26.72	27.29	32.09	32.47	37.76	49.31	54.84	61.46	Irlande
90.30	98.49	94.70	91.70	91.45	93.38	96.81	121.46	147.38	159.41	173.78	219.23	218.79	239.79	225.90	248.02	301.78	324.05	312.93	Italie
4.13	4.38	3.60	3.37	3.36	3.69	4.09	5.53	6.69	7.77	8.29	10.13	10.55	11.93	11.95	13.67	15.86	15.47	14.37	Luxembourg
76.39	87.82	81.23	78.04	75.22	75.64	77.90	90.59	108.24	121.55	126.22	153.62	156.76	167.69	157.85	172.77	211.48	213.88	203.31	Pays-Bas
20.76	27.43	27.08	25.51	25.29	26.10	27.34	26.24	29.65	32.82	38.04	46.93	47.52	48.29	44.54	47.21	55.79	64.23	63.28	Norvège
..	..	..	..	..	..	..	..	..	..	..	16.90	17.99	19.99	19.73	22.26	30.83	33.42	34.30	Pologne
5.77	7.22	6.65	6.46	6.84	7.52	8.11	10.30	13.47	15.92	18.25	23.47	24.26	26.96	22.95	25.60	32.29	33.66	31.83	Portugal
29.43	33.28	32.95	33.05	32.54	36.48	37.68	45.82	56.66	65.03	68.85	83.93	90.55	101.78	93.04	107.81	134.19	148.11	150.98	Espagne
32.78	36.99	34.39	32.59	33.03	35.04	35.55	43.68	52.43	58.70	61.19	68.74	66.84	68.96	60.81	72.29	94.68	100.67	99.73	Suède
33.69	37.34	35.18	34.26	34.19	34.28	36.23	49.54	60.71	66.97	67.55	82.82	81.39	86.88	84.80	92.86	107.84	106.41	101.83	Suisse
3.48	3.73	5.99	7.84	8.05	9.75	11.04	10.44	13.58	16.95	17.36	20.02	20.91	22.90	24.67	27.91	33.68	39.09	46.68	Turquie
117.46	146.64	136.32	127.84	121.75	122.59	131.56	144.18	174.77	191.87	199.89	237.71	238.15	251.44	241.97	271.75	316.74	340.69	367.97	Royaume-Uni
1326.01	1561.45	1555.73	1485.64	1472.07	1561.11	1605.82	1868.35	2201.06	2514.86	2703.22	3117.91	3192.82	3427.62	3336.10	3700.51	4372.56	4549.88	4662.30	OCDE - Total [1]
873.12	1005.29	936.12	902.34	883.01	900.78	945.04	1162.80	1403.09	1561.54	1654.02	1992.69	1987.45	2146.27	1991.71	2218.76	2692.54	2798.31	2780.50	OCDE - Europe [2]
814.14	935.60	866.69	833.72	814.42	829.59	869.26	1075.07	1297.29	1442.91	1529.21	1840.78	1835.50	1986.09	1835.70	2048.53	2492.74	2585.91	2566.03	UE15

Importations de biens et services - aux prix et taux de change courants (milliards de dollars É-U) 18.

1979	1980	1981	1982	1983	1984	1985	1986	1987	1988	1989	1990	1991	1992	1993	1994	1995	1996	1997	
62.60	70.28	78.43	66.78	73.76	86.81	91.98	98.76	107.64	128.85	142.01	149.14	153.09	158.57	170.12	185.26	202.22	211.49	237.09	Canada
21.79	32.68	41.92	23.22	18.17	21.74	24.70	22.53	24.33	33.95	42.50	51.77	60.60	73.71	77.31	91.11	79.43	99.93	121.83	Mexique
252.70	293.80	317.80	303.20	328.60	405.10	417.20	452.20	507.90	553.20	589.70	628.60	622.30	669.00	719.30	812.10	904.50	965.70	1059.60	États-Unis
126.08	154.52	162.91	149.92	144.24	155.21	148.95	147.11	174.19	226.81	266.51	296.10	290.41	291.28	299.85	336.43	406.89	432.27	415.87	Japon
22.38	25.97	28.95	27.59	29.71	32.31	30.94	34.45	44.20	55.46	66.70	76.89	90.07	92.03	95.89	117.44	155.70	176.08	171.89	Corée
21.51	26.59	30.72	30.62	26.10	31.29	30.82	31.28	34.66	43.50	52.39	51.65	50.95	53.70	54.92	64.51	73.11	78.06	80.48	Australie
6.39	7.08	7.95	7.74	7.34	8.24	7.57	7.97	9.23	10.21	11.33	11.60	11.02	11.66	12.21	14.91	17.17	18.36	18.33	Nouvelle-Zélande
24.81	29.81	26.27	23.85	23.85	24.47	26.10	33.01	40.93	47.18	49.38	62.00	64.92	70.25	66.42	73.80	90.31	94.63	88.29	Autriche
65.22	72.18	63.34	59.10	56.03	57.01	56.72	70.55	85.71	97.61	106.12	129.24	129.24	138.78	124.64	140.79	171.04	171.28	165.86	Belgique
..	..	..	..	..	..	..	..	..	..	..	15.40	13.18	15.88	17.55	21.97	30.73	34.12	32.81	République tchèque
22.33	23.65	21.65	21.16	20.34	20.44	22.27	28.27	31.99	33.71	34.50	41.02	42.00	44.00	39.68	45.75	56.74	56.64	55.46	Danemark
12.82	17.43	16.05	15.30	14.61	14.33	15.27	17.73	22.24	26.27	29.36	33.11	27.80	27.21	23.36	28.72	36.89	37.35	37.11	Finlande
120.37	151.17	137.04	130.79	119.06	117.29	121.60	147.53	182.07	204.41	219.91	269.92	268.42	282.13	248.05	274.33	324.84	330.79	316.62	France
194.42	229.07	200.20	189.64	185.30	183.36	191.04	237.51	286.11	312.90	330.34	402.51	439.51	469.50	411.17	453.50	554.16	547.24	528.78	Allemagne
10.04	10.85	10.34	11.39	10.83	10.41	11.29	12.54	15.17	16.64	18.43	23.27	24.05	26.12	23.45	23.73	28.99	30.33	28.76	Grèce
..	..	..	..	..	..	..	..	..	..	..	8.81	11.27	11.81	13.36	14.69	16.20	17.13	19.65	Hongrie
1.03	1.18	1.24	1.16	1.02	1.07	1.17	1.36	1.91	1.96	1.74	2.05	2.21	2.12	1.81	1.92	2.24	2.61	2.65	Islande
10.79	12.21	11.53	10.60	10.22	10.71	11.07	13.36	15.87	18.16	20.35	24.04	24.28	27.09	26.03	30.83	39.55	43.57	47.74	Irlande
86.45	111.42	103.37	97.13	89.38	95.07	98.81	113.18	143.55	158.50	175.16	218.84	218.35	239.89	192.11	210.06	255.79	260.61	263.37	Italie
3.92	4.39	3.70	3.41	3.33	3.60	3.87	5.21	6.56	7.53	7.90	9.97	10.76	11.25	10.92	11.99	14.24	13.73	12.65	Luxembourg
77.18	88.61	76.13	71.93	69.93	69.02	71.75	83.85	102.46	112.51	117.30	140.49	143.01	153.07	138.64	151.19	184.87	187.16	177.84	Pays-Bas
19.50	23.51	22.46	22.30	20.44	20.63	22.58	28.84	31.64	33.33	34.39	39.36	38.00	39.55	36.89	39.56	46.98	50.62	52.45	Norvège
..	..	..	..	..	..	..	..	..	..	..	12.68	19.46	18.70	18.89	21.30	29.25	37.17	41.02	Pologne
7.93	10.88	11.37	10.80	9.45	8.96	8.83	10.95	15.67	20.21	21.65	28.50	30.49	34.61	29.33	32.22	39.50	41.67	40.64	Portugal
28.84	38.22	36.76	36.47	33.85	33.12	34.46	40.91	56.16	68.87	81.27	100.56	107.18	117.83	95.71	106.98	133.61	143.41	144.61	Espagne
33.87	39.38	34.62	33.14	31.06	31.52	33.84	39.45	49.41	55.71	60.15	67.89	63.13	64.84	54.15	63.99	79.80	83.71	83.76	Suède
34.18	40.93	36.11	33.82	34.23	34.54	35.84	48.02	59.30	66.15	67.90	81.64	78.19	78.36	73.13	81.17	95.52	94.09	90.49	Suisse
6.34	8.09	8.93	9.44	10.02	11.59	12.49	12.01	15.48	15.95	19.05	26.47	25.13	27.60	34.90	26.63	41.23	50.50	57.70	Turquie
115.86	134.56	121.79	118.84	117.90	123.72	127.24	148.55	183.30	223.00	234.65	264.37	249.80	265.65	253.93	281.62	324.20	349.60	374.04	Royaume-Uni
1366.96	1632.48	1582.63	1481.75	1459.09	1579.23	1627.46	1852.70	2203.49	2517.11	2734.02	3154.09	3174.85	3377.77	3218.03	3583.10	4203.82	4395.35	4502.01	OCDE - Total [1]
875.88	1047.53	942.90	900.27	860.83	870.84	906.24	1092.85	1345.55	1520.59	1629.58	1965.24	1986.47	2119.85	1884.33	2078.78	2520.51	2589.54	2568.80	OCDE - Europe [2]
814.84	973.82	874.18	833.55	795.12	803.02	834.16	1002.62	1237.22	1403.21	1506.49	1815.72	1842.94	1972.22	1737.61	1929.50	2334.54	2391.73	2365.51	UE15

1. Non compris la Corée la République tchèque la Hongrie et la Pologne.
2. Non compris la République tchèque la Hongrie et la Pologne.

19. Gross domestic product per head - at current prices and 1990 exchange rates (US dollars)

	1960	1961	1962	1963	1964	1965	1966	1967	1968	1969	1970	1971	1972	1973	1974	1975	1976	1977	1978
Canada	1890	1919	2043	2153	2314	2505	2751	2904	3119	3382	3586	3784	4176	4842	5700	6331	7200	7862	8629
Mexico	2	2	2	2	2	2	3	3	3	3	4	4	4	5	6	8	9	12	15
United States	2832	2882	3053	3175	3365	3607	3910	4087	4421	4727	4920	5278	5745	6363	6816	7341	8124	8962	10014
Japan	1186	1419	1596	1809	2106	2317	2667	3092	3620	4200	4884	5321	6010	7151	8417	9186	10202	11258	12284
Korea	..	..	..	..	..	..	..	..	..	..	121	147	178	225	312	412	555	701	932
Australia	1108	1098	1157	1244	1340	1422	1484	1601	1722	1875	2027	2235	2454	2851	3366	3963	4610	5021	5501
New Zealand	717	716	756	804	861	918	935	953	999	1100	1212	1404	1579	1812	1938	2146	2587	2855	3233
Austria	2081	2297	2427	2599	2827	3053	3303	3486	3727	4055	4533	5038	5725	6452	7331	7796	8627	9541	10082
Belgium	1834	1937	2059	2200	2440	2625	2813	2999	3196	3537	3922	4281	4775	5409	6325	6981	7921	8557	9182
Czech Republic	..	..	..	..	..	..	..	..	..	..	..	..	..	..	..	..	..	..	..
Denmark	1484	1635	1829	1931	2191	2442	2658	2895	3202	3624	3975	4364	4987	5685	6339	7059	8179	9067	10076
Finland	956	1077	1145	1235	1385	1526	1630	1778	2030	2318	2597	2850	3304	4000	5021	5727	6455	7094	7830
France	1209	1305	1431	1576	1730	1847	1983	2125	2293	2593	2870	3168	3509	3981	4561	5115	5903	6627	7509
Germany	2891	3140	3386	3560	3890	4212	4446	4493	4833	5370	6031	6641	7257	8062	8646	9055	9929	10613	11408
Greece	96	108	114	127	142	161	177	189	205	232	260	286	325	414	481	568	687	791	941
Hungary	..	..	..	..	..	..	..	..	..	..	..	..	..	..	..	..	..	..	..
Iceland	9	10	12	14	17	20	24	24	25	31	39	49	61	84	121	170	237	339	520
Ireland	385	416	449	479	543	576	605	657	738	849	948	1074	1278	1518	1651	2061	2489	3010	3520
Italy	412	455	508	577	627	669	719	787	847	930	1041	1127	1224	1473	1848	2086	2615	3173	3731
Luxembourg	2745	2720	2829	2990	3372	3490	3646	3658	3991	4594	5345	5411	6014	7226	8710	7978	9128	9380	10235
Netherlands	2155	2245	2383	2550	2961	3262	3506	3803	4174	4673	5180	5764	6446	7297	8217	8970	10189	11053	11842
Norway	1655	1791	1916	2041	2228	2438	2610	2831	2997	3236	3697	4098	4492	5069	5844	6662	7612	8505	9422
Poland	..	..	..	..	..	..	..	..	..	..	..	..	..	..	..	..	..	..	..
Portugal	66	71	76	81	88	98	108	120	133	146	164	185	216	263	311	333	403	532	662
Spain	219	249	288	337	374	429	492	550	614	696	762	852	991	1184	1435	1668	1984	2487	3010
Sweden	1648	1783	1923	2070	2291	2497	2691	2898	3058	3298	3659	3929	4287	4761	5363	6274	7070	7663	8517
Switzerland	5304	5805	6262	6740	7347	7794	8296	8831	9324	9973	11011	12358	13877	15369	16624	16657	17061	17568	18228
Turkey	1	1	1	1	1	1	2	2	2	2	2	3	3	4	5	6	8	10	15
United Kingdom	877	922	960	1011	1098	1175	1244	1302	1404	1505	1647	1828	2041	2340	2643	3335	3948	4603	5315
OECD - Total[1]	1624	1722	1850	1966	2138	2305	2497	2646	2888	3171	3458	3757	4140	4688	5219	5670	6325	6969	7694
OECD - Europe[2]	1293	1397	1507	1610	1765	1906	2028	2113	2271	2511	2795	3081	3402	3832	4269	4651	5232	5774	6370
EU15	1335	1442	1556	1663	1826	1976	2106	2193	2364	2625	2927	3228	3567	4030	4502	4943	5605	6219	6894

20. Gross domestic product per head - at the price levels and exchange rates of 1990 (US dollars)

	1960	1961	1962	1963	1964	1965	1966	1967	1968	1969	1970	1971	1972	1973	1974	1975	1976	1977	1978
Canada	9769	9873	10353	10677	11168	11681	12220	12352	12803	13284	13438	13717	14273	15109	15510	15632	16271	16622	17121
Mexico	1741	1754	1777	1850	1982	2044	2100	2154	2236	2290	2363	2382	2500	2623	2695	2760	2792	2805	2951
United States	12359	12456	12899	13220	13765	14355	15035	15277	15759	16023	15871	16122	16766	17467	17239	17000	17660	18228	18930
Japan	5146	5715	6166	6625	7322	7665	8402	9234	10305	11450	12505	12963	13865	14637	14261	14522	14932	15436	16102
Korea	..	..	..	..	..	..	..	..	..	..	1591	1693	1741	1929	2050	2149	2364	2568	2766
Australia	8864	8644	9018	9433	9831	10173	10268	10790	11212	11651	12098	12570	12823	13301	13296	13499	13863	13844	14088
New Zealand	8754	9061	9037	9407	9677	10113	10553	9903	9804	10703	10402	10773	11046	11599	12043	11692	11866	11244	11286
Austria	7968	8345	8494	8785	9252	9455	9919	10141	10540	11162	11916	12468	13167	13734	14251	14237	14914	15607	15563
Belgium	7954	8306	8687	9006	9545	9761	10044	10379	10774	11461	12139	12549	13159	13923	14463	14232	15012	15089	15505
Czech Republic	..	..	..	..	..	..	..	..	..	..	..	..	..	..	..	..	..	..	..
Denmark	12388	13090	13727	13705	14862	15418	15708	16105	16649	17614	17833	18183	19031	19604	19333	19148	20335	20604	20843
Finland	9985	10670	10915	11194	11713	12293	12538	12741	12978	14229	15352	15652	16745	17768	18209	18337	18205	18199	18526
France	8949	9344	9790	10129	10679	11095	11578	12026	12446	13210	13842	14376	14885	15569	15921	15738	16353	16888	17282
Germany	9008	9343	9696	9888	10488	10949	11171	11114	11687	12468	13001	13289	13789	14402	14426	14300	15131	15591	16076
Greece	2571	2834	2860	3138	3385	3685	3881	4046	4304	4712	5076	5414	5856	6257	6007	6311	6624	6747	7106
Hungary	..	..	..	..	..	..	..	..	..	..	..	..	..	..	..	..	..	..	..
Iceland	9331	9167	9765	10595	11399	12039	12824	12470	11670	11829	12649	14163	14822	15607	16267	16147	16953	18283	19210
Ireland	4699	4961	5100	5305	5479	5562	5596	5887	6344	6686	6808	6978	7318	7541	7734	8035	8018	8560	9059
Italy	7047	7574	7990	8377	8541	8746	9198	9787	10362	10931	11451	11614	11886	12578	13082	12725	13484	13815	14279
Luxembourg	11680	12013	12024	12323	13130	13222	13288	13277	13791	15077	15244	15558	16346	17503	18035	16662	16990	17256	17910
Netherlands	9110	9016	9499	9710	10373	10769	10920	11367	11974	12598	13153	13540	13845	14378	14832	14692	15317	15578	15851
Norway	10612	11184	11423	11765	12264	12812	13191	13897	14085	14597	14781	15363	16033	16575	17330	17954	19086	19686	20494
Poland	..	..	..	..	..	..	..	..	..	..	..	..	..	..	..	..	..	..	..
Portugal	1992	2081	2222	2338	2480	2663	2777	2990	3252	3325	3653	3929	4251	4725	4713	4340	4510	4712	4793
Spain	4141	4583	4998	5430	5662	5952	6311	6505	6853	7391	7634	7916	8484	9063	9481	9433	9630	9787	9819
Sweden	13180	13855	14364	15046	15951	16406	16593	17016	17539	18288	19291	19341	19725	20470	21062	21518	21666	21246	21555
Switzerland	19368	20369	20764	21315	22062	22549	22900	23339	23904	24926	26283	27026	27638	28304	28632	26779	26699	27422	27460
Turkey	1263	1254	1298	1385	1408	1409	1535	1564	1627	1672	1710	1758	1841	1854	1928	2016	2178	2206	2194
United Kingdom	8928	9082	9119	9421	9829	10036	10187	10362	10725	10897	11120	11295	11660	12416	12244	12232	12509	12786	13245
OECD - Total[1]	8287	8557	8901	9207	9670	10037	10464	10757	11244	11743	12064	12332	12836	13431	13416	13308	13782	14131	14567
OECD - Europe[2]	7596	7924	8221	8506	8912	9208	9483	9714	10125	10656	11093	11363	11769	12339	12527	12368	12847	13129	13432
EU15	7917	8266	8591	8895	9339	9668	9967	10222	10684	11271	11752	12050	12504	13156	13359	13224	13769	14092	14454

21. Gross domestic product per head - at current prices and current exchange rates (US dollars)

	1960	1961	1962	1963	1964	1965	1966	1967	1968	1969	1970	1971	1972	1973	1974	1975	1976	1977	1978
Canada	2274	2210	2228	2323	2498	2704	2970	3134	3366	3650	3994	4373	4922	5649	6800	7262	8520	8626	8827
Mexico	378	397	414	447	511	539	580	614	658	704	807	862	961	1138	1435	1701	1670	1491	1815
United States	2832	2882	3053	3175	3365	3607	3910	4087	4421	4727	4920	5278	5745	6363	6816	7341	8124	8962	10014
Japan	477	571	642	728	847	932	1073	1243	1456	1689	1964	2205	2870	3811	4172	4481	4981	6070	8452
Korea	..	..	..	..	..	..	..	..	..	..	277	300	320	399	546	603	812	1025	1363
Australia	1590	1575	1660	1785	1923	2040	2129	2297	2471	2690	2909	3244	3748	5186	6189	6646	7218	7132	8066
New Zealand	1682	1676	1763	1874	2006	2139	2178	2178	1875	2066	2275	2672	3162	4123	4540	4323	4315	4645	5620
Austria	910	1004	1061	1137	1236	1335	1444	1525	1630	1773	1982	2295	2816	3746	4459	5089	5467	6564	7394
Belgium	1226	1295	1376	1470	1631	1755	1880	2005	2136	2364	2621	2928	3625	4638	5427	6343	6857	7978	9744
Czech Republic	..	..	..	..	..	..	..	..	..	..	..	..	..	..	..	..	..	..	..
Denmark	1329	1465	1638	1730	1963	2188	2381	2575	2642	2990	3280	3641	4441	5816	6437	7603	8373	9347	11308
Finland	1143	1286	1368	1475	1654	1824	1948	1971	1848	2110	2365	2604	3047	4003	5087	5952	6387	6732	7271
France	1333	1439	1578	1738	1908	2037	2187	2344	2529	2718	2814	3113	3788	4863	5159	6499	6725	7344	9060
Germany	1112	1258	1368	1438	1571	1702	1796	1815	1952	2200	2662	3074	3677	4874	5398	5947	6371	7384	9177
Greece	510	570	602	670	749	849	937	1001	1083	1226	1372	1510	1715	2216	2541	2807	2984	3403	4058
Hungary	..	..	..	..	..	..	..	..	..	..	..	..	..	..	..	..	..	..	..
Iceland	1499	1436	1580	1857	2322	2761	3249	3161	2389	2069	2575	3246	4008	5432	7030	6437	7570	9923	11186
Ireland	651	705	760	812	919	975	1024	1097	1071	1231	1376	1581	1929	2248	2334	2756	2704	3174	4081
Italy	791	872	974	1107	1202	1282	1379	1508	1624	1783	1996	2178	2514	3026	3404	3829	3765	4308	5267
Luxembourg	1835	1818	1891	1998	2254	2333	2437	2445	2667	3070	3573	3700	4566	6195	7472	7249	7902	8746	10861
Netherlands	1033	1120	1199	1283	1490	1641	1763	1913	2099	2351	2606	2997	3657	4753	5566	6458	7017	8201	9967
Norway	1451	1569	1679	1788	1952	2137	2287	2481	2626	2836	3240	3643	4268	5504	6604	7978	8732	10000	11250
Poland	..	..	..	..	..	..	..	..	..	..	..	..	..	..	..	..	..	..	..
Portugal	330	352	374	403	436	486	534	597	660	725	812	932	1137	1527	1746	1859	1898	1980	2146
Spain	373	423	489	573	635	728	835	909	894	1013	1109	1250	1571	2071	2536	2962	3022	3338	4002
Sweden	1885	2040	2200	2368	2621	2857	3079	3316	3499	3773	4186	4545	5327	6453	7150	8943	9607	10120	11156
Switzerland	1685	1844	1989	2141	2334	2476	2635	2806	2962	3168	3498	4153	5048	6746	7752	8965	9482	10154	14163
Turkey	492	276	312	352	367	383	444	482	521	564	503	468	575	704	956	1166	1305	1458	1576
United Kingdom	1382	1454	1514	1595	1731	1853	1962	2025	1898	2034	2226	2506	2871	3228	3480	4155	3995	4522	5739
OECD - Total[1]	1427	1489	1593	1692	1829	1968	2130	2250	2410	2619	2832	3106	3571	4281	4725	5258	5655	6304	7531
OECD - Europe[2]	1014	1086	1176	1271	1392	1501	1608	1693	1764	1936	2150	2409	2868	3618	4048	4704	4881	5497	6715
EU15	1043	1139	1234	1334	1464	1582	1694	1783	1858	2043	2285	2569	3060	3861	4295	4993	5170	5839	7147

1. Excluding Korea Czech Republic Hungary and Poland.
2. Excluding Czech Republic Hungary and Poland.

Produit intérieur brut par tête - aux prix courants et taux de change de 1990 (dollars É-U) 19.

1979	1980	1981	1982	1983	1984	1985	1986	1987	1988	1989	1990	1991	1992	1993	1994	1995	1996	1997	
9761	10839	12245	12743	13643	14773	15800	16489	17750	19198	20236	20606	20497	20641	21120	21986	22775	23095	23811	Canada
19	25	34	53	95	153	240	394	941	1864	2409	3181	4014	4678	5134	5707	7218	9675	12093	Mexique
11055	11896	13216	13605	14566	16020	16976	17736	18649	19912	21270	22224	22605	23600	24568	25790	26727	27831	29326	États-Unis
13204	14202	15144	15778	16318	17295	18327	19070	19786	21066	22438	24042	25543	26167	26335	26489	26578	27429	27753	Japon
1182	1414	1739	1966	2273	2574	2841	3282	3806	4475	4965	5917	7045	7779	8568	9684	11028	12093	12933	Corée
6272	7033	7860	8546	9220	10416	11366	12220	13577	15077	16618	17323	17273	17767	18551	19544	20598	21526	22300	Australie
3763	4363	5271	5887	6443	7205	8257	9963	11130	11952	12679	12817	12401	12662	13567	14336	14924	15293	15584	Nouvelle-Zélande
11020	11839	12570	13480	14382	15391	15890	16680	17296	18084	19254	20637	21904	22863	23392	24530	25514	26429	27424	Autriche
9813	10662	11100	12007	12704	13380	14644	15388	16075	17171	18582	19690	20553	21534	21975	22981	23817	24468	25499	Belgique
..	..	..	..	..	..	..	..	..	..	..	2644	3439	3882	4596	5256	6174	7026	7571	République tchèque
11197	12051	13150	14989	16554	18264	19865	21496	22548	23569	24830	25945	26889	27750	28031	29980	31330	32760	34341	Danemark
9087	10471	11805	13198	14629	16318	17694	18879	20515	22968	25659	27037	25605	24732	24904	26267	28154	29294	31655	Finlande
8500	9572	10727	12220	13433	14558	15613	16760	17556	18768	20048	21070	21811	22404	22543	23438	24204	24765	25499	France
12337	13047	13572	14068	14817	15621	16341	17209	17785	18607	19526	20665	22081	23642	24120	25299	26093	26628	27335	Allemagne
1143	1355	1610	2009	2389	2938	3551	4227	4791	5763	6812	8160	9992	11469	12847	14512	16223	17884	19703	Grèce
..	..	..	..	..	..	..	..	..	..	..	3452	3820	4509	5454	6730	8603	10601	13184	Hongrie
762	1218	1877	2902	4940	6399	8607	11383	14585	17613	20900	24518	26400	26139	26738	28060	29016	30991	33202	Islande
4059	4752	5696	6640	7281	8027	8675	9201	9839	10724	12046	12985	13463	14345	15476	16826	18817	20561	23026	Irlande
4562	5699	6810	7997	9310	10649	11930	13229	14473	16049	17545	19281	20992	22056	22681	23910	25815	27240	28306	Italie
11110	12058	12817	14325	15759	17471	18466	20390	20889	23036	25905	27083	28797	30890	33405	36122	37204	37793	39979	Luxembourg
12520	13263	13807	14315	14805	15447	16130	16507	16509	17029	17939	18979	19774	20477	20884	21932	22722	23680	24946	Pays-Bas
10349	12247	13907	15323	16921	18996	20964	21436	23276	24275	25788	27223	28615	29257	30517	31956	34037	37196	39341	Norvège
..	..	..	..	..	..	..	..	..	..	..	1547	2226	3154	4264	5746	7875	9889	12113	Pologne
826	1033	1224	1500	1857	2264	2827	3547	4161	4985	5910	6984	8041	9071	9559	10363	11190	11861	12524	Portugal
3490	4000	4470	5144	5849	6600	7201	8229	9178	10176	11391	12662	13845	14865	15299	16241	17459	18422	19434	Espagne
9524	10796	11812	12908	14449	16158	17535	19121	20593	22321	24520	26822	28378	28102	28027	29460	31580	32262	33211	Suède
19000	20304	21664	22666	23333	24795	26133	27213	27969	29429	31406	33609	34946	35496	36028	36566	36952	36956	37502	Suisse
25	45	67	86	111	172	267	381	545	922	1588	2681	4215	7177	12771	24482	48270	90322	173410	Turquie
6246	7289	8012	8773	9560	10208	11157	11982	13141	14593	15919	16947	17628	18275	19183	20264	21254	22324	23580	Royaume-Uni
8475	9235	10081	10651	11383	12333	13148	13888	14681	15811	16989	18094	18984	19942	20833	22433	24809	28515	35007	OCDE - Total[1]
7088	7865	8541	9307	10099	10917	11724	12573	13339	14385	15550	16765	17927	19122	20319	22866	27138	33858	46621	OCDE - Europe[2]
7710	8573	9330	10206	11120	12046	12962	13947	14819	15991	17245	18495	19623	20586	21113	22232	23368	24275	25288	UE15

Produit intérieur brut par tête - aux niveaux de prix et taux de change de 1990 (dollars É-U) 20.

1979	1980	1981	1982	1983	1984	1985	1986	1987	1988	1989	1990	1991	1992	1993	1994	1995	1996	1997	
17656	17662	17986	17229	17554	18383	19197	19503	20034	20738	20865	20606	19976	19860	20077	20643	20823	20832	21375	Canada
3132	3289	3496	3392	3174	3216	3236	3051	3045	3021	3087	3181	3257	3317	3325	3414	3132	3240	3409	Mexique
19193	18858	18990	18427	18882	19852	20321	20723	21092	21689	22192	22224	21764	22134	22433	23034	23403	24020	24849	États-Unis
16845	17183	17600	18015	18308	18905	19618	20063	20795	21990	22957	24042	24878	25051	25059	25162	25408	26343	26503	Japon
2919	2797	2924	3098	3404	3654	3855	4258	4702	5181	5457	5917	6398	6661	6982	7481	8068	8553	8936	Corée
14566	14708	15011	14673	14615	15512	16024	16140	16602	16958	17378	17323	16879	17127	17645	18389	18905	19351	19647	Australie
11483	11540	12050	12176	12342	12824	12867	13117	13064	12962	13020	12817	12245	12260	12888	13401	13680	13835	13975	Nouvelle-Zélande
16440	16821	16760	17064	17563	17612	17991	18387	18672	19220	19918	20637	21114	21124	21028	21457	21853	22177	22705	Autriche
15857	16551	16332	16550	16540	16942	17098	17338	17724	18534	19166	19690	19925	20134	19763	20207	20636	20862	21437	Belgique
..	..	..	..	..	..	..	..	..	..	..	2644	2352	2273	2283	2355	2506	2608	2636	République tchèque
21527	21407	21221	21878	22447	23441	24437	25293	25338	25618	25675	25945	26235	26488	26613	28058	28833	29557	30411	Danemark
19765	20753	21052	21614	22066	22610	23276	23751	24654	25790	27153	27037	24986	23965	23571	24537	25677	26502	28013	Finlande
17726	17871	17885	18177	18227	18379	18627	18980	19311	20024	20692	21070	21115	21220	20844	21311	21681	21899	22308	France
16750	16872	16930	16853	17245	17832	18294	18750	19059	19654	20193	20665	21087	21388	20983	21489	21686	21901	22341	Allemagne
7277	7332	7271	7254	7241	7403	7605	7703	7641	7953	8215	8160	8341	8340	8158	8287	8438	8620	8884	Grèce
..	..	..	..	..	..	..	..	..	..	..	3452	3046	2959	2951	3048	3103	3155	3312	Hongrie
19965	20926	21536	21718	20981	21665	22193	23390	25079	24656	24427	24518	24501	23408	23370	24043	24197	25365	26282	Islande
9188	9379	9572	9687	9594	9944	10216	10169	10641	11234	11958	12985	13240	13781	14234	15298	17031	18319	20076	Irlande
15046	15545	15597	15650	15827	16226	16676	17149	17680	18360	18883	19281	19493	19569	19278	19643	20187	20292	20548	Italie
18280	18383	18231	18387	18937	20109	20639	22178	22512	24651	26792	27083	28377	29191	31336	32166	32897	33408	34151	Luxembourg
16094	16157	15964	15706	15912	16373	16801	17171	17298	17635	18353	18979	19254	19496	19506	20015	20362	20913	21557	Pays-Bas
21312	22296	22434	22391	23111	24397	25590	26417	26824	26654	26785	27223	27933	28684	29291	30721	31742	33311	34270	Norvège
..	..	..	..	..	..	..	..	..	..	..	1547	1435	1468	1520	1595	1706	1807	1930	Pologne
5009	5182	5221	5300	5268	5151	5284	5503	5864	6320	6665	6984	7167	7351	7260	7406	7606	7839	8112	Portugal
9736	9844	9772	9869	10036	10144	10279	10575	11144	11694	12224	12662	12926	12986	12809	13076	13411	13714	14179	Espagne
22332	22658	22630	22844	23233	24150	24577	25081	25784	26245	26689	26822	26365	25838	25119	25771	26647	26942	27401	Suède
28065	29200	29458	28864	28943	29713	30593	30906	30917	31630	32748	33609	32967	32593	32222	32173	32150	32029	32559	Suisse
2135	2040	2088	2109	2159	2248	2286	2292	2563	2561	2512	2681	2654	2760	2927	2718	2863	3012	3185	Turquie
13595	13351	13172	13384	13844	14158	14611	15209	15889	15637	16941	16947	16541	16397	16682	17341	17754	18105	18650	Royaume-Uni
14953	14971	15064	14950	15183	15695	16084	16403	16780	17350	17816	18094	18073	18217	18228	18598	18852	19251	19697	OCDE - Total[1]
13833	13960	13918	13971	14167	14471	14782	15141	15508	16026	16458	16765	16824	16886	16720	17084	17418	17654	18057	OCDE - Europe[2]
14926	15077	15046	15150	15398	15749	16116	16540	16975	17610	18139	18495	18603	18690	18495	18979	19376	19652	20118	UE15

Produit intérieur brut par tête - aux prix et taux de change courants (dollars É-U) 21.

1979	1980	1981	1982	1983	1984	1985	1986	1987	1988	1989	1990	1991	1992	1993	1994	1995	1996	1997	
9722	10816	11916	12052	12917	13309	13501	13846	15619	18200	19942	20606	20874	19924	19101	18784	19362	19764	20064	Canada
2316	3103	3901	2648	2218	2560	2632	1809	1921	2306	2753	3181	3741	4251	4634	4756	3163	3581	4298	Mexique
11055	11896	13216	13605	14566	16020	16976	17736	18649	19912	21270	22224	22605	23600	24568	25790	26727	27831	29326	États-Unis
8724	9069	9942	9172	9947	10543	11124	16385	19806	23801	23549	24042	27454	29915	34291	37524	40912	36509	33212	Japon
1728	1647	1807	1903	2074	2260	2311	2635	3275	4330	5233	5917	6799	7052	7555	8531	10120	10639	9622	Corée
8981	10259	11571	11104	10640	11710	10168	10464	12178	15090	16834	17323	17237	16715	16161	18305	19561	21580	21202	Australie
6446	7123	7664	7405	7215	6846	6840	8729	11009	13125	12710	12817	11991	11399	12289	14248	16416	17620	17272	Nouvelle-Zélande
9374	10404	8973	8984	9103	8575	8732	12422	15554	16652	16546	20637	21330	23655	22865	24419	28775	28384	25549	Autriche
11186	12184	9990	8782	8303	7912	8241	11512	14389	15607	15759	19690	20113	22383	21226	22955	26998	26409	23820	Belgique
..	..	..	..	..	..	..	..	..	..	..	2644	2604	2893	3334	3861	4919	5473	5050	République tchèque
13171	13233	11424	11133	11202	10914	11602	16442	20400	21669	21020	25945	26015	28451	26754	29170	34608	34963	32179	Danemark
8919	10734	10460	10469	10042	10381	10915	14239	17845	20995	22862	27037	24209	21110	16670	19227	24652	24383	23314	Finlande
10879	12335	10748	10125	9598	9071	9462	13176	15905	17156	17111	21070	21050	23046	21675	22988	26404	26362	23789	France
10875	11597	9703	9367	9376	8869	8968	12804	15987	17119	16781	20665	21498	24460	23572	25189	29418	28592	25470	Allemagne
4892	5041	4605	4767	4300	4131	4075	4786	5607	6440	6648	8160	8690	9537	8883	9482	11101	11777	11438	Grèce
..	..	..	..	..	..	..	..	..	..	..	3452	3231	3608	3749	4045	4326	4390	4461	Hongrie
12594	14794	15147	13695	11591	11768	12086	16141	21978	23866	21355	24518	26081	26474	23052	23382	26142	27162	27292	Islande
5022	5904	5543	5698	5470	5261	5546	7485	8839	9877	10322	12985	13101	14757	13816	15214	18239	19889	21104	Irlande
6578	7972	7177	7084	7344	7262	7486	10632	13379	14773	15320	19281	20273	21442	17268	17766	18988	21151	19913	Italie
12664	13780	11536	10477	10299	10104	10393	15253	18698	20937	21970	27083	28181	32109	32267	36080	42173	40791	37346	Luxembourg
11365	12147	10076	9762	9446	8766	8843	12269	14841	15688	15403	18979	19259	21205	20475	21943	25768	25577	23280	Pays-Bas
12792	15521	15168	14861	14517	14570	15264	18146	21625	23317	23380	27223	27630	29470	26927	28344	33632	36100	34815	Norvège
..	..	..	..	..	..	..	..	..	..	..	1547	2000	2199	2236	2402	3085	3485	3509	Pologne
2406	2941	2835	2690	2390	2205	2366	3380	4211	4937	5351	6984	7934	9579	8474	8900	10557	10962	10184	Portugal
5300	5687	4935	4773	4157	4185	4317	5989	7577	8904	9809	12662	13582	14800	12254	12358	14273	14826	13530	Espagne
13149	15107	13808	12160	11154	11562	12062	15887	19224	21562	22512	26822	27774	28560	21313	22598	26204	28475	25746	Suède
15875	16832	15322	15509	15442	14659	14775	21016	26056	27938	26670	33609	33854	35067	33872	37141	43411	41536	35897	Suisse
2107	1548	1560	1382	1289	1223	1337	1472	1658	1691	1952	2681	2636	2724	3033	2157	2747	2894	2979	Turquie
7450	9540	9067	8631	8161	7647	8063	9891	12094	14619	14669	16947	17509	18064	16203	17466	18890	19615	21740	Royaume-Uni
8592	9428	9498	9227	9445	9812	10227	12317	14175	15789	16284	18094	18902	20130	20160	21336	23065	23007	22428	OCDE - Total[1]
8128	9095	8020	7674	7423	7099	7316	9959	12253	13523	13651	16765	17239	18650	16939	17809	20356	20661	19334	OCDE - Europe[2]
8673	9822	8627	8268	8013	7677	7923	10872	13429	14894	15061	18495	19085	20736	18736	19871	22675	23063	21617	UE15

1. Non compris la Corée la République tchèque la Hongrie et la Pologne.
2. Non compris la République tchèque la Hongrie et la Pologne.

22. **Private final consumption expenditure per head** - at current prices and 1990 exchange rates (US dollars)

	1960	1961	1962	1963	1964	1965	1966	1967	1968	1969	1970	1971	1972	1973	1974	1975	1976	1977	1978
Canada	1205	1201	1257	1313	1381	1468	1572	1665	1785	1915	1989	2093	2316	2617	3007	3427	3850	4244	4696
Mexico	1	1	1	1	2	2	2	2	2	2	3	3	3	4	5	5	6	8	10
United States	1814	1840	1924	1998	2116	2255	2417	2522	2743	2938	3108	3324	3608	3949	4274	4669	5167	5687	6275
Japan	696	810	920	1064	1214	1357	1547	1756	1980	2248	2553	2850	3246	3833	4571	5249	5866	6494	7087
Korea	..	..	..	..	..	..	..	..	..	..	91	111	131	156	220	291	363	437	565
Australia	703	701	734	774	821	864	906	970	1037	1118	1207	1317	1432	1632	1928	2316	2689	2969	3290
New Zealand	484	485	499	529	556	593	623	635	663	718	792	880	976	1100	1226	1377	1569	1745	1968
Austria	1237	1344	1441	1551	1653	1800	1908	2036	2159	2288	2468	2752	3091	3452	3905	4361	4866	5425	5554
Belgium	1270	1315	1373	1478	1565	1689	1800	1890	2040	2204	2354	2592	2888	3297	3810	4309	4873	5353	5717
Czech Republic	..	..	..	..	..	..	..	..	..	..	..	..	..	..	..	..	..	..	..
Denmark	869	960	1071	1122	1249	1359	1497	1641	1780	1970	2157	2303	2517	2930	3258	3702	4376	4878	5352
Finland	582	639	701	763	864	947	1004	1087	1184	1339	1471	1594	1862	2201	2666	3191	3637	4009	4423
France	722	782	859	952	1030	1089	1168	1255	1360	1531	1662	1831	2026	2273	2624	3005	3449	3860	4349
Germany	1622	1762	1900	1995	2137	2336	2476	2539	2694	2942	3256	3581	3938	4306	4635	5087	5534	5986	6377
Greece	81	86	91	98	109	122	134	143	153	167	187	202	222	274	339	400	471	543	639
Hungary	..	..	..	..	..	..	..	..	..	..	..	..	..	..	..	..	..	..	..
Iceland	6	6	7	9	11	12	15	15	16	19	24	30	36	48	71	99	134	191	295
Ireland	303	321	345	365	405	425	447	474	539	609	672	752	854	1005	1162	1359	1652	1986	2309
Italy	245	266	298	346	372	394	432	475	503	549	617	672	734	888	1110	1292	1589	1905	2204
Luxembourg	1653	1727	1795	1918	2132	2265	2365	2410	2569	2736	3011	3309	3594	3940	4479	5140	5763	6231	6614
Netherlands	1263	1343	1442	1580	1763	1943	2086	2240	2424	2742	3036	3342	3707	4150	4677	5273	6002	6624	7176
Norway	944	1020	1090	1152	1241	1315	1398	1505	1594	1762	1921	2124	2313	2547	2871	3352	3847	4448	4717
Poland	..	..	..	..	..	..	..	..	..	..	..	..	..	..	..	..	..	..	..
Portugal	48	52	52	56	59	66	72	78	90	100	107	125	137	169	224	255	299	379	446
Spain	153	171	194	231	255	296	335	372	409	448	493	553	639	759	930	1083	1315	1632	1940
Sweden	977	1047	1118	1196	1278	1392	1498	1602	1688	1810	1948	2085	2288	2520	2865	3254	3749	4096	4526
Switzerland	3245	3467	3764	4001	4295	4578	4892	5197	5476	5858	6362	7042	7918	8817	9623	10047	10499	10970	11252
Turkey	1	1	1	1	1	1	1	1	1	1	2	2	2	3	4	5	6	7	11
United Kingdom	578	603	633	668	709	749	787	823	881	931	1011	1127	1272	1451	1673	2059	2393	2737	3158
OECD - Total[1]	1000	1052	1124	1196	1285	1384	1490	1576	1707	1857	2013	2191	2415	2703	3029	3384	3773	4168	4571
OECD - Europe[2]	766	824	890	954	1025	1108	1180	1237	1319	1441	1580	1739	1924	2149	2410	2706	3037	3369	3690
EU15	789	851	918	986	1060	1149	1226	1285	1374	1504	1654	1822	2018	2260	2542	2875	3249	3622	3939

23. **Private final consumption expenditure per head** - at the price levels and exchange rates of 1990 (US dollars)

	1960	1961	1962	1963	1964	1965	1966	1967	1968	1969	1970	1971	1972	1973	1974	1975	1976	1977	1978
Canada	5877	5828	6011	6143	6349	6604	6804	6923	7111	7344	7362	7554	7978	8423	8736	8974	9330	9488	9709
Mexico	1291	1301	1307	1343	1448	1499	1526	1575	1630	1683	1733	1765	1823	1881	1916	1963	1992	1974	2075
United States	7443	7476	7696	7863	8194	8565	8913	9081	9472	9731	9865	10077	10538	10920	10764	10879	11340	11667	12026
Japan	3425	3747	3993	4302	4717	4935	5380	5876	6305	6872	7282	7606	8177	8694	8569	8837	8993	9265	9663
Korea	..	..	..	..	..	..	..	..	..	..	1049	1119	1151	1226	1287	1330	1417	1469	1569
Australia	5537	5400	5625	5854	6045	6153	6263	6490	6719	6977	7178	7314	7494	7859	8017	8238	8389	8400	8582
New Zealand	6077	6046	6130	6422	6521	6776	6934	6540	6635	6937	7159	7080	7453	7925	8077	7874	7546	7273	7401
Austria	4534	4740	4869	5106	5245	5468	5666	5820	6022	6176	6411	6811	7184	7528	7740	8012	8391	8850	8713
Belgium	5381	5440	5620	5834	5932	6108	6253	6397	6713	7054	7344	7677	8102	8736	8953	9005	9447	9685	9919
Czech Republic	..	..	..	..	..	..	..	..	..	..	..	..	..	..	..	..	..	..	..
Denmark	7207	7684	8076	8015	8577	8803	9103	9287	9411	9954	10224	10077	10184	10614	10263	10609	11414	11504	11554
Finland	5086	5436	5725	5935	6227	6553	6695	6799	6774	7505	8104	8230	8866	9341	9456	9710	9766	9641	9343
France	5342	5600	5889	6183	6464	6667	6932	7228	7460	7847	8109	8409	8724	9076	9128	9315	9706	9923	10233
Germany	4427	4656	4878	4974	5211	5518	5647	5701	5952	6380	6820	7136	7434	7630	7665	7937	8286	8679	9309
Greece	1909	2022	2095	2193	2377	2547	2699	2834	3020	3195	3468	3645	3874	4151	4164	4351	4521	4657	4358
Hungary	..	..	..	..	..	..	..	..	..	..	..	..	..	..	..	..	..	..	..
Iceland	5280	5179	5650	6188	6601	6996	7764	7763	7274	6835	7891	9156	9680	10052	10928	9742	10177	11388	12298
Ireland	3680	3816	3933	4071	4223	4240	4291	4428	4803	5039	4947	5059	5238	5525	5524	5476	5542	5838	6289
Italy	3597	3840	4087	4433	4543	4652	4946	5273	5511	5841	6252	6446	6639	7032	7249	7258	7586	7795	7991
Luxembourg	6493	6750	6961	7213	7780	7994	8076	8049	8371	8755	9237	9699	10022	10478	10826	11270	11559	11824	12139
Netherlands	4886	4815	5308	5605	5857	6209	6323	6591	6955	7418	7869	8029	8226	8486	8732	8942	9339	9710	10074
Norway	6495	6817	6980	7162	7375	7497	7705	7933	8151	8703	8639	8980	9175	9374	9676	10116	10680	11373	11141
Poland	..	..	..	..	..	..	..	..	..	..	..	..	..	..	..	..	..	..	..
Portugal	1482	1568	1603	1699	1668	1742	1762	1850	2340	2447	2529	2875	2995	3354	3630	3463	3484	3468	3361
Spain	2675	2938	3170	3498	3612	3816	4045	4237	4437	4708	4883	5085	5458	5831	6069	6115	6381	6400	6386
Sweden	7979	8358	8587	8917	9204	9506	9600	9742	10087	10461	10725	10662	10995	11258	11604	11884	12332	12161	12040
Switzerland	10950	11377	11775	12082	12441	12751	13016	13248	13607	14165	14794	15313	16000	16339	16212	15876	16225	16761	17087
Turkey	1040	1024	1077	1155	1138	1139	1212	1218	1274	1308	1304	1385	1437	1422	1292	1365	1462	1713	1711
United Kingdom	5281	5353	5428	5623	5755	5802	5872	5979	6117	6127	6285	6450	6828	7185	7079	7057	7092	7071	7450
OECD - Total[1]	4904	5046	5247	5447	5686	5907	6145	6337	6607	6898	7125	7335	7680	8005	7984	8102	8373	8582	8835
OECD - Europe[2]	4282	4465	4667	4877	5046	5217	5380	5537	5746	6025	6298	6516	6790	7074	7134	7229	7483	7672	7866
EU15	4428	4625	4840	5065	5252	5442	5619	5795	6025	6329	6637	6871	7173	7502	7590	7708	7990	8172	8404

24. **Private final consumption expenditure per head** - at current prices and current exchange rates (US dollars)

	1960	1961	1962	1963	1964	1965	1966	1967	1968	1969	1970	1971	1972	1973	1974	1975	1976	1977	1978
Canada	1450	1384	1370	1417	1490	1584	1696	1797	1927	2067	2216	2419	2729	3053	3587	3931	4556	4657	4803
Mexico	294	308	322	337	386	398	429	454	492	519	594	645	706	820	1025	1195	1163	1011	1226
United States	1814	1840	1924	1998	2116	2255	2417	2522	2743	2938	3108	3324	3608	3949	4274	4669	5167	5687	6275
Japan	280	326	370	428	488	546	622	706	796	904	1027	1181	1550	2043	2266	2561	2864	3502	4876
Korea	..	..	..	..	..	..	..	..	..	..	207	227	236	278	384	425	531	638	826
Australia	1009	1006	1053	1111	1178	1240	1299	1392	1488	1604	1732	1912	2187	2969	3546	3884	4210	4218	4824
New Zealand	1137	1137	1162	1232	1295	1382	1451	1450	1245	1347	1486	1675	1956	2503	2872	2774	2617	2839	3421
Austria	541	588	630	678	723	787	834	890	944	1001	1079	1254	1520	2005	2375	2847	3084	3732	4349
Belgium	849	879	918	988	1046	1129	1203	1263	1363	1473	1573	1772	2193	2827	3268	3915	4218	4991	6066
Czech Republic	..	..	..	..	..	..	..	..	..	..	..	..	..	..	..	..	..	..	..
Denmark	779	860	959	1005	1119	1218	1341	1460	1469	1625	1780	1921	2241	2997	3308	3988	4480	5029	6006
Finland	695	764	837	911	1032	1132	1199	1205	1078	1219	1339	1457	1717	2202	2701	3317	3598	3804	4107
France	796	863	947	1050	1136	1202	1289	1384	1500	1605	1630	1799	2187	2776	2968	3817	3929	4278	5247
Germany	624	706	767	806	863	944	1000	1025	1088	1206	1437	1657	1996	2603	2894	3340	3551	4165	5130
Greece	426	457	479	518	574	644	706	755	811	884	989	1069	1174	1465	1793	1976	2045	2336	2756
Hungary	..	..	..	..	..	..	..	..	..	..	..	..	..	..	..	..	..	..	..
Iceland	961	889	986	1170	1427	1635	1996	2022	1528	1233	1582	1981	2396	3073	4146	3737	4278	5592	6348
Ireland	513	544	584	618	686	719	756	791	782	884	975	1106	1289	1488	1643	1818	1794	2094	2677
Italy	470	509	571	663	713	756	828	910	965	1052	1183	1298	1508	1826	2045	2370	2287	2587	3112
Luxembourg	1105	1154	1200	1282	1425	1514	1580	1611	1717	1829	2012	2263	2728	3378	3843	4670	4989	5810	7018
Netherlands	605	670	725	795	887	978	1050	1127	1219	1379	1527	1738	2103	2703	3168	3797	4134	4915	6039
Norway	828	894	956	1009	1088	1153	1226	1319	1397	1545	1683	1888	2197	2765	3244	4015	4413	5230	5633
Poland	..	..	..	..	..	..	..	..	..	..	..	..	..	..	..	..	..	..	..
Portugal	239	257	259	278	295	327	359	387	448	496	531	630	723	981	1258	1421	1411	1412	1446
Spain	260	291	330	393	433	502	570	614	596	652	717	811	1013	1329	1644	1922	2004	2190	2579
Sweden	1118	1197	1279	1368	1462	1593	1714	1833	1931	2071	2229	2411	2843	3415	3820	4638	5095	5409	5929
Switzerland	1031	1101	1196	1271	1364	1454	1554	1651	1740	1861	2021	2366	2880	3870	4487	5407	5835	6341	8742
Turkey	388	215	252	285	284	296	332	357	387	421	366	352	430	511	703	844	903	1032	1164
United Kingdom	912	951	999	1054	1117	1181	1242	1280	1190	1258	1366	1545	1789	2002	2202	2565	2422	2689	3411
OECD - Total[1]	902	933	992	1054	1128	1208	1299	1370	1462	1579	1703	1867	2139	2526	2810	3191	3422	3813	4515
OECD - Europe[2]	628	664	720	783	840	903	968	1022	1056	1145	1253	1402	1670	2085	2353	2793	2879	3247	3937
EU15	640	694	752	817	879	948	1016	1072	1107	1202	1326	1490	1776	2218	2488	2954	3038	3431	4165

1. Excluding Korea Czech Republic Hungary and Poland.
2. Excluding Czech Republic Hungary and Poland.

Consommation finale privée par tête - aux prix courants et taux de change de 1990 (dollars É-U) 22.

1979	1980	1981	1982	1983	1984	1985	1986	1987	1988	1989	1990	1991	1992	1993	1994	1995	1996	1997	
5196	5767	6438	6825	7405	7997	8647	9254	9879	10558	11211	11653	11891	12092	12418	12745	12994	13330	13960	Canada
12	16	21	32	56	94	151	263	604	1261	1659	2213	2830	3359	3691	4083	4841	6277	7904	Mexique
6918	7556	8273	8763	9503	10291	11044	11651	12350	13254	14097	14887	15217	15974	16730	17529	18248	18990	19910	États-Unis
7753	8357	8805	9378	9827	10279	10797	11183	11651	12271	13064	13937	14596	15127	15440	15816	15979	16423	16830	Japon
729	911	1118	1244	1377	1519	1663	1811	2004	2285	2644	3177	3757	4198	4609	5202	5841	6509	6936	Corée
3663	4136	4640	5169	5649	6111	6780	7321	7974	8750	9664	10369	10709	11170	11584	12105	12836	13329	13803	Australie
2291	2689	3143	3565	3831	4318	5081	6001	6759	7288	7785	8118	7860	7925	8230	8769	9232	9614	9888	Nouvelle-Zélande
6054	6522	7035	7634	8333	8552	9096	9435	9769	10234	10832	11527	12079	12755	13142	13742	14321	15011	15391	Autriche
6241	6810	7333	8022	8498	9063	9766	10062	10511	10965	11808	12516	13236	13791	13991	14566	14970	15562	16130	Belgique
..	..	..	..	..	..	..	..	..	..	..	1406	1579	2029	2272	2615	3056	3539	3888	République tchèque
5977	6367	6970	7802	8551	9407	10299	11186	11512	11838	12382	12729	13263	13729	14018	15331	15902	16507	17398	Danemark
5012	5666	6390	7273	8059	8847	9651	10317	11217	12299	13414	14150	14329	14115	14210	14620	15268	16008	16748	Finlande
4940	5635	6464	7417	8166	8849	9537	10126	10690	11272	11951	12555	13054	13469	13726	14149	14549	15049	15286	France
6862	7332	7753	8072	8471	8894	9255	9529	9901	10267	10789	11497	12615	13481	13946	14488	14971	15465	15804	Allemagne
754	912	1132	1410	1660	1980	2424	2970	3467	4087	4894	5978	7296	8577	9665	10899	12153	13381	14465	Grèce
..	..	..	..	..	..	..	..	..	..	..	1671	2095	2600	3255	3906	4651	5568	6743	Hongrie
440	702	1111	1750	2969	4011	5499	7004	9315	11054	12902	15016	16517	16325	16129	16574	17524	18933	20280	Islande
2726	3215	3863	4083	4466	4857	5315	5668	5997	6528	7280	7544	7887	8411	8736	9488	10040	10728	11397	Irlande
2714	3468	4148	4904	5655	6490	7311	8088	8888	9838	10865	11822	12971	13859	14066	14802	15870	16718	17496	Italie
7166	7899	8701	9633	10481	11328	12092	12806	13484	14378	15480	16807	18129	18290	19125	19746	20342	20765	21226	Luxembourg
7647	8070	8271	8609	8905	9151	9587	9811	10034	10107	10524	11136	11752	12332	12633	13191	13576	14105	14744	Pays-Bas
5157	5734	6460	7228	7957	8705	10049	11220	11937	12342	12803	13451	14104	14721	15250	15953	16803	17746	18704	Norvège
..	..	..	..	..	..	..	..	..	..	..	751	1339	1973	2727	3751	4966	6442	7905	Pologne
552	689	845	1034	1276	1586	1903	2287	2652	3170	3692	4409	5145	5887	6360	6848	7260	7700	8077	Portugal
2269	2649	2980	3393	3812	4241	4617	5203	5804	6380	7174	7904	8638	9375	9659	10205	10837	11409	12044	Espagne
4993	5556	6205	6901	7494	8183	8977	9837	10821	11703	12587	13662	15123	15151	15434	16056	16529	16914	17627	Suède
11861	12655	13410	14149	14733	15316	16010	16503	16996	17488	18285	19261	20526	21206	21584	21900	22255	22545	22934	Suisse
19	36	48	63	83	130	190	256	372	586	1042	1839	2976	4990	8824	17127	33940	60763	117983	Turquie
3744	4344	4834	5307	5808	6206	6765	7494	8212	9249	10078	10663	11167	11678	12334	12917	13437	14213	15128	Royaume-Uni
5052	5552	6044	6497	6994	7502	8031	8501	9034	9708	10419	11145	11775	12487	13162	14226	15822	18197	22616	OCDE - Total[1]
4117	4602	5062	5547	6011	6470	6960	7438	7936	8509	9194	9911	10766	11602	12450	14088	16939	21273	29959	OCDE - Europe[2]
4473	5018	5539	6091	6626	7154	7710	8256	8825	9474	10214	10937	11759	12430	12825	13420	14022	14656	15236	UE15

Consommation finale privée par tête - aux niveaux de prix et taux de change de 1990 (dollars É-U) 23.

1979	1980	1981	1982	1983	1984	1985	1986	1987	1988	1989	1990	1991	1992	1993	1994	1995	1996	1997	
9867	9937	9974	9605	9796	10143	10567	10872	11162	11496	11680	11653	11355	11387	11436	11666	11716	11847	12206	Canada
2197	2290	2402	2289	2118	2139	2169	2064	2020	2016	2120	2213	2276	2342	2336	2402	2125	2137	2234	Mexique
12181	12050	12115	12117	12550	13048	13513	13883	14167	14593	14801	14887	14630	14893	15186	15559	15843	16164	16635	États-Unis
10205	10232	10307	10684	10965	11182	11483	11813	12250	12843	13398	13937	14244	14492	14620	14866	15100	15503	15631	Japon
1671	1638	1690	1768	1903	2027	2136	2287	2449	2642	2899	3177	3446	3640	3813	4047	4338	4587	4684	Corée
8712	8900	9138	9222	9227	9389	9702	9682	9731	9914	10253	10369	10325	10562	10733	11106	11510	11717	11976	Australie
7345	7313	7432	7269	7395	7607	7678	7986	8114	8224	8219	8118	7695	7637	7793	8157	8366	8569	8742	Nouvelle-Zélande
9108	9251	9305	9534	10019	9882	10060	10266	10551	10876	11211	11527	11728	11922	11890	12039	12359	12639	12707	Autriche
10420	10657	10618	10803	10703	10768	10974	11188	11426	11779	12193	12516	12822	13051	12827	12994	13078	13288	13530	Belgique
..	..	..	..	..	..	..	..	..	..	..	1406	1011	1163	1203	1267	1356	1455	1482	République tchèque
11683	11239	10982	11150	11447	11838	12421	13116	12904	12765	12717	12729	12920	13210	13347	14247	14641	14945	15418	Danemark
10310	10502	10597	11054	11326	11620	12005	12444	13054	13686	14219	14150	13564	12831	12399	12582	13106	13517	13927	Finlande
10474	10529	10660	10941	10971	11013	11191	11538	11783	12064	12333	12555	12631	12723	12669	12787	12928	13116	13157	France
9305	9396	9358	9274	9430	9658	9877	10228	10578	10824	11053	11497	12044	12291	12219	12330	12520	12681	12716	Allemagne
4924	4883	4939	5099	5083	5144	5324	5341	5389	5561	5868	5978	6095	6196	6113	6210	6364	6470	6629	Grèce
..	..	..	..	..	..	..	..	..	..	..	1671	1581	1606	1667	1675	1562	1517	1558	Hongrie
12533	12843	13458	13944	12992	13361	13809	14642	16802	15905	15061	15016	15454	14595	13781	13932	14468	15272	16069	Islande
6463	6428	6457	5937	5945	6024	6279	6403	6614	6935	7431	7544	7661	7965	8122	8582	8893	9372	9868	Irlande
8517	9026	9145	9238	9292	9518	9810	10220	10662	11145	11544	11822	12131	12273	11819	11889	12041	12163	12420	Italie
12533	12850	13038	13053	13117	13307	13624	14360	14897	15457	16070	16807	17638	17209	17278	17435	17586	17661	17898	Luxembourg
10237	10116	9748	9659	9712	9791	10021	10226	10436	10456	10758	11136	11389	11589	11623	11808	11988	12261	12562	Pays-Bas
11571	11765	11740	11819	12000	12345	13457	14078	13897	13543	13401	13451	13580	13807	14020	14492	14911	15528	15972	Norvège
..	..	..	..	..	..	..	..	..	..	..	751	798	816	858	894	925	1004	1074	Pologne
3325	3412	3481	3541	3475	3361	3376	3565	3761	4030	4149	4409	4583	4780	4846	4943	5015	5136	5283	Portugal
6411	6473	6358	6315	6300	6265	6366	6557	6920	7244	7638	7904	8118	8279	8080	8140	8256	8407	8656	Espagne
12303	12180	12135	12215	11967	12131	12437	12956	13502	13768	13835	13662	13706	13435	12949	13085	13118	13267	13527	Suède
17256	17615	17679	17635	17800	17967	18180	18493	18766	18940	19234	19261	19368	19199	18903	18963	18947	18989	19200	Suisse
1656	1718	1549	1615	1681	1773	1718	1779	1735	1719	1664	1839	1852	1876	2000	1858	1914	2042	2177	Turquie
7767	7751	7756	7835	8181	8327	8619	9183	9642	10340	10636	10663	10385	10340	10565	10821	10970	11314	11793	Royaume-Uni
9069	9089	9111	9161	9341	9561	9825	10106	10367	10700	10951	11145	11174	11322	11377	11567	11708	11930	12170	OCDE - Total[1]
8100	8198	8168	8215	8303	8409	8591	8899	9174	9464	9698	9911	10061	10149	10065	10157	10290	10467	10652	OCDE - Europe[2]
8685	8795	8798	8862	8971	9095	9320	9678	10022	10388	10689	10937	11126	11245	11147	11292	11456	11658	11867	UE15

Consommation finale privée par tête - aux prix et taux de change courants (dollars É-U) 24.

1979	1980	1981	1982	1983	1984	1985	1986	1987	1988	1989	1990	1991	1992	1993	1994	1995	1996	1997	
5176	5755	6266	6455	7011	7205	7389	7771	8693	10009	11048	11653	12109	11673	11231	10889	11047	11407	11764	Canada
1526	1968	2447	1590	1316	1574	1655	1207	1233	1560	1895	2213	2637	3053	3332	3403	2121	2323	2809	Mexique
6918	7556	8273	8763	9503	10291	11044	11651	12350	13254	14097	14887	15217	15974	16730	17529	18248	18990	19910	États-Unis
5122	5336	5781	5451	5991	6266	6553	9608	11663	13864	13711	13937	15688	17294	20104	22404	24597	21859	20141	Japon
1066	1062	1162	1204	1256	1334	1353	1454	1724	2211	2787	3177	3626	3806	4064	4582	5360	5727	5160	Corée
5245	6033	6830	6717	6519	6870	6066	6269	7153	8758	9789	10369	10686	10508	10091	11337	12189	13362	13123	Australie
3925	4390	4570	4484	4291	4103	4210	5258	6686	8004	7804	8118	7600	7135	7454	8715	10155	11076	10959	Nouvelle-Zélande
5149	5731	5022	5088	5275	4916	4999	7026	8786	9423	9309	11527	11762	13196	12846	13679	16151	16121	14338	Autriche
7113	7783	6600	5867	5554	5241	5496	7527	9408	9966	10014	12516	12953	14335	13515	14549	16970	16796	15068	Belgique
..	..	..	..	..	..	..	..	..	..	..	1406	1196	1513	1648	1921	2435	2757	2594	République tchèque
7031	6991	6055	5795	5787	5621	6015	8556	10415	10883	10482	12729	12832	14076	13380	14916	17566	17617	16302	Danemark
4920	5808	5662	5769	5532	5629	5954	7781	9758	11242	11952	14150	13548	12048	9512	10702	13369	13325	12335	Finlande
6323	7262	6477	6145	5835	5513	5780	7961	9684	10304	10200	12555	12599	13855	13198	13878	15872	16020	14261	France
6049	6518	5543	5375	5361	5049	5079	7090	8900	9445	9272	11497	12282	13948	13629	14425	16879	16605	14726	Allemagne
3229	3392	3237	3346	2988	2784	2782	3363	4058	4566	4777	5978	6346	7132	6683	7121	8316	8811	8397	Grèce
..	..	..	..	..	..	..	..	..	..	..	1671	1772	2081	2238	2348	2339	2306	2282	Hongrie
7277	8526	8963	8257	6966	7376	7721	9931	14037	14978	13183	15016	16317	16534	13906	13811	15788	16594	16670	Islande
3373	3994	3759	3504	3355	3183	3398	4612	5388	6012	6238	7544	7675	8652	7799	8579	9732	10378	10446	Irlande
3913	4852	4372	4344	4461	4425	4587	6500	8216	9056	9488	11822	12527	13473	10709	10998	11673	12982	12308	Italie
8168	9027	7831	7046	6850	6551	6805	9580	12069	13068	13128	16807	17742	19012	18473	19723	23059	22412	19828	Luxembourg
6941	7391	6036	5871	5682	5193	5256	7292	9020	9311	9036	11136	11446	12770	12385	13198	15397	15234	13759	Pays-Bas
6375	7267	7045	7011	6827	6677	7317	9498	11091	11854	11608	13451	13618	14828	13457	14150	16603	17224	16552	Norvège
..	..	..	..	..	..	..	..	..	..	..	751	1203	1376	1430	1568	1945	2270	2290	Pologne
1609	1962	1957	1854	1642	1545	1592	2180	2683	3139	3342	4409	5076	6217	5638	5881	6849	7116	6568	Portugal
3445	3766	3290	3148	2709	2689	2767	3787	4791	5583	6177	7904	8473	9334	7736	7765	8859	9181	8385	Espagne
6893	7776	7253	6501	5785	5855	6176	8173	10101	11305	11556	13662	14801	15398	11736	12317	13715	14928	13665	Suède
9910	10491	9484	9681	9750	9055	9052	12745	15834	16603	15528	19261	19885	20950	20293	22244	26145	25340	21953	Suisse
1571	1252	1114	1013	957	924	949	991	1132	1074	1281	1839	1861	1894	2095	1509	1931	1947	2027	Turquie
4466	5686	5471	5221	4958	4649	4889	6187	7557	9265	9286	10663	11091	11543	10418	11133	11942	12489	13948	Royaume-Uni
5162	5707	5740	5671	5850	6026	6323	7594	8748	9702	10009	11145	11706	12552	12665	13397	14432	14438	14137	OCDE - Total[1]
4786	5390	4801	4615	4450	4237	4367	5913	7306	8010	8081	9911	10331	11248	10263	10708	12164	12415	11612	OCDE - Europe[2]
5070	5792	5159	4964	4793	4573	4724	6447	8001	8833	8927	10937	11435	12503	11347	11949	13539	13868	12987	UE15

1. Non compris la Corée la République tchèque la Hongrie et la Pologne.
2. Non compris la République tchèque la Hongrie et la Pologne.

25. Gross domestic product - volume indices (1990 = 100)

	1960	1961	1962	1963	1964	1965	1966	1967	1968	1969	1970	1971	1972	1973	1974	1975	1976	1977	1978
Canada	30.5	31.4	33.6	35.3	37.6	40.1	42.7	44.0	46.3	48.7	50.0	52.8	55.5	59.5	62.0	63.4	66.8	69.1	71.9
Mexico	23.6	24.5	25.6	27.5	30.5	32.4	34.4	36.5	39.1	41.4	44.1	46.0	49.9	54.1	57.4	60.6	63.1	65.3	70.7
United States	40.2	41.2	43.3	45.0	47.6	50.2	53.2	54.7	56.9	58.5	58.6	60.3	63.4	66.6	66.4	66.1	69.3	72.3	75.9
Japan	16.2	18.1	19.7	21.4	23.9	25.3	28.0	31.1	35.1	39.4	43.7	45.7	49.6	53.5	52.9	54.5	56.7	59.2	62.3
Korea	..	..	..	..	..	..	..	..	..	..	20.2	21.9	23.0	25.9	28.0	29.9	33.4	36.9	40.3
Australia	31.6	31.5	33.5	35.7	38.0	40.1	41.2	44.1	46.7	49.5	52.5	55.6	57.7	60.8	61.7	63.4	65.8	66.5	68.4
New Zealand	48.3	51.0	52.1	55.4	58.1	61.8	65.7	62.7	62.6	69.0	68.1	71.6	74.6	80.0	84.7	83.7	85.8	81.6	81.9
Austria	35.2	37.1	38.0	39.5	41.9	43.1	45.5	46.9	49.0	52.1	55.8	58.6	62.3	65.3	67.9	67.7	70.7	74.1	73.8
Belgium	37.0	38.8	40.8	42.6	45.6	47.2	48.7	50.6	52.7	56.2	59.6	61.9	65.1	69.1	72.0	71.1	75.1	75.6	77.7
Czech Republic	..	..	..	..	..	..	..	..	..	..	..	..	..	..	..	..	..	..	..
Denmark	42.6	45.3	47.8	48.1	52.6	55.0	56.5	58.4	60.8	64.6	65.9	67.7	71.2	73.8	73.1	72.7	77.4	78.6	79.8
Finland	32.8	35.3	36.4	37.6	39.5	41.6	42.6	43.5	44.5	48.8	52.5	53.5	57.6	61.5	63.4	64.1	63.8	64.0	65.3
France	34.2	36.1	38.5	40.5	43.2	45.3	47.6	49.8	52.0	55.6	58.8	61.6	64.4	67.9	69.9	69.4	72.4	75.1	77.2
Germany	39.9	41.8	43.7	44.9	47.9	50.5	51.9	51.8	54.6	58.6	61.6	63.5	66.2	69.3	69.5	68.6	72.3	74.3	76.5
Greece	25.8	28.7	29.1	32.1	34.7	38.0	40.3	42.5	45.4	49.9	53.8	57.7	62.8	67.4	64.9	68.9	73.2	75.7	80.8
Hungary	..	..	..	..	..	..	..	..	..	..	..	..	..	..	..	..	..	..	..
Iceland	26.3	26.2	28.4	31.3	34.5	37.0	40.2	39.7	37.5	38.4	41.3	46.7	49.5	52.9	55.9	56.3	59.7	64.9	68.8
Ireland	29.3	30.7	31.7	33.2	34.5	35.1	35.4	37.5	40.6	43.0	44.1	45.6	48.6	50.9	53.1	56.1	56.9	61.5	65.9
Italy	32.3	35.0	37.2	39.2	40.3	41.7	44.2	47.3	50.4	53.5	56.3	57.4	59.1	63.0	65.9	64.5	68.7	70.7	73.3
Luxembourg	35.4	36.8	37.3	38.6	41.6	42.4	42.9	43.0	44.8	49.3	50.1	51.4	54.8	59.4	61.9	57.8	59.3	60.2	62.7
Netherlands	36.9	37.0	39.5	41.0	44.3	46.7	47.9	50.5	53.7	57.2	60.4	63.0	65.1	68.1	70.8	70.7	74.4	76.1	77.9
Norway	33.0	35.0	36.0	37.4	39.2	41.3	42.9	45.6	46.6	48.7	49.7	51.9	54.6	56.9	59.8	62.3	66.6	68.9	72.1
Poland	..	..	..	..	..	..	..	..	..	..	..	..	..	..	..	..	..	..	..
Portugal	24.9	26.2	28.0	29.6	31.6	33.9	35.3	38.0	41.4	42.2	46.1	49.1	53.1	59.0	59.7	57.1	61.0	64.5	66.3
Spain	25.7	28.8	31.7	34.7	36.5	38.8	41.6	43.4	46.3	50.4	52.6	55.0	59.5	64.1	67.7	68.1	70.4	72.3	73.4
Sweden	42.9	45.3	47.3	49.8	53.2	55.2	56.4	58.3	60.4	63.4	67.5	68.2	69.7	72.5	74.8	76.7	77.5	76.3	77.6
Switzerland	45.5	49.2	51.5	54.0	56.9	58.7	60.1	62.0	64.2	67.8	72.1	75.1	77.5	79.8	81.0	75.1	74.0	75.8	76.1
Turkey	23.3	23.7	25.1	27.5	28.6	29.4	32.8	34.3	36.6	38.5	40.4	42.6	45.8	47.3	50.0	53.5	59.1	61.2	62.1
United Kingdom	47.9	49.2	49.8	51.8	54.4	55.9	57.1	58.4	60.7	62.0	63.4	64.8	67.0	71.6	70.6	70.5	72.1	73.6	76.3
OECD - Total[1]	33.9	35.5	37.4	39.2	41.7	43.8	46.2	48.0	50.7	53.5	55.6	57.6	60.6	64.2	64.7	64.8	67.7	70.1	72.9
OECD - Europe[2]	37.0	39.0	40.9	42.7	45.2	47.2	49.0	50.6	53.1	56.4	59.2	61.1	63.8	67.4	68.8	68.3	71.3	73.2	75.3
EU15	37.1	39.0	41.0	42.8	45.3	47.3	49.1	50.7	53.3	56.5	59.3	61.2	63.9	67.6	68.9	68.5	71.6	73.5	75.6

26. Private final consumption expenditure - volume indices (1990 = 100)

	1960	1961	1962	1963	1964	1965	1966	1967	1968	1969	1970	1971	1972	1973	1974	1975	1976	1977	1978
Canada	32.4	32.8	34.5	35.9	37.8	40.1	42.0	43.6	45.5	47.6	48.4	51.4	54.9	58.7	61.7	64.3	67.8	69.7	72.1
Mexico	25.1	26.1	27.1	28.7	32.0	34.2	36.0	38.3	41.0	43.7	46.5	49.0	52.3	55.7	58.6	61.9	64.8	66.1	71.5
United States	36.1	36.9	38.6	40.0	42.3	44.7	47.1	48.5	51.1	53.0	54.4	56.2	59.4	62.2	61.9	63.2	66.5	69.1	71.9
Japan	18.5	20.5	22.0	24.0	26.5	28.1	30.9	34.1	37.0	40.8	43.9	46.3	50.4	54.9	54.8	57.2	58.9	61.3	64.5
Korea	..	..	..	..	..	..	..	..	..	..	24.8	27.0	28.3	30.7	32.8	34.5	37.3	39.3	42.6
Australia	33.0	32.9	34.9	37.0	39.0	40.5	42.0	44.3	46.7	49.5	52.0	54.0	56.3	60.0	62.2	64.7	66.5	67.4	69.6
New Zealand	52.9	53.7	55.8	59.7	61.8	65.4	68.1	65.3	66.9	70.6	73.9	74.3	79.5	86.2	89.7	89.0	86.1	83.3	84.8
Austria	35.9	37.7	39.0	41.1	42.5	44.6	46.6	48.2	50.1	51.6	53.7	57.3	60.8	64.1	66.0	68.2	71.3	75.2	74.0
Belgium	39.4	40.0	41.6	43.4	44.6	46.5	47.7	49.0	51.6	54.4	56.8	59.6	63.1	68.2	70.2	70.8	74.3	76.3	73.2
Czech Republic	..	..	..	..	..	..	..	..	..	..	..	..	..	..	..	..	..	..	..
Denmark	50.5	54.2	57.4	57.4	61.9	64.0	66.7	68.7	70.0	74.4	77.0	76.4	77.7	81.5	79.1	82.0	88.5	89.5	90.1
Finland	31.9	34.4	36.4	38.0	40.1	42.4	43.5	44.4	44.4	49.2	52.9	53.8	58.3	61.8	62.9	64.9	65.4	64.8	66.3
France	34.3	36.3	38.9	41.5	43.9	45.6	47.8	50.3	52.3	55.4	57.8	60.5	63.3	66.4	67.2	68.9	72.1	74.0	76.7
Germany	35.3	37.4	39.5	40.6	42.8	45.7	47.2	47.7	50.0	53.9	58.1	61.3	64.1	66.0	66.3	68.4	71.1	74.4	77.1
Greece	26.2	28.0	29.1	30.6	33.3	35.9	38.3	40.7	43.5	46.2	50.2	53.0	56.7	61.0	61.4	64.8	68.2	71.4	75.4
Hungary	..	..	..	..	..	..	..	..	..	..	..	..	..	..	..	..	..	..	..
Iceland	24.3	24.2	26.9	29.9	32.6	35.1	39.7	40.3	38.2	36.2	42.0	49.3	52.8	55.7	61.4	55.5	58.5	66.0	71.9
Ireland	39.4	40.7	42.1	43.9	45.7	46.1	46.8	48.5	52.9	55.7	55.2	57.0	59.9	64.2	65.2	65.8	67.6	72.2	78.8
Italy	26.9	28.9	31.0	33.9	35.0	36.1	38.7	41.6	43.7	46.6	50.2	52.0	53.8	57.4	59.6	60.0	63.0	65.0	66.9
Luxembourg	31.8	33.3	34.8	36.4	39.7	41.3	42.0	42.0	43.8	46.1	48.9	51.7	54.2	57.3	59.9	63.0	65.0	66.5	68.4
Netherlands	33.7	33.7	37.6	40.3	42.7	45.9	47.3	49.9	53.2	57.4	61.6	63.6	65.9	68.5	71.0	73.4	77.3	80.8	84.4
Norway	40.8	43.2	44.5	46.0	47.8	48.9	50.7	52.6	54.6	58.8	58.7	61.4	63.3	65.1	67.6	71.1	75.4	80.6	79.3
Poland	..	..	..	..	..	..	..	..	..	..	..	..	..	..	..	..	..	..	..
Portugal	29.3	31.3	32.0	34.1	31.6	35.2	35.5	37.2	47.1	49.2	50.5	56.9	59.2	66.3	72.8	72.2	74.7	75.1	73.6
Spain	26.6	29.6	32.2	35.8	37.3	39.9	42.7	45.3	48.0	51.5	53.9	56.6	61.3	66.1	69.5	70.7	74.7	75.8	76.5
Sweden	51.0	53.7	55.5	57.9	60.3	62.8	64.0	65.5	68.2	71.2	73.7	73.8	76.3	78.3	80.9	83.2	86.6	85.7	85.1
Switzerland	44.9	47.9	51.0	53.4	56.0	57.9	59.6	61.4	63.7	67.2	70.8	74.2	78.2	80.4	80.0	77.7	78.5	80.9	82.7
Turkey	27.9	28.2	30.4	33.4	33.7	34.6	37.7	38.9	41.7	44.0	44.9	49.0	52.1	52.9	48.8	52.9	57.9	69.2	70.6
United Kingdom	45.1	46.1	47.1	49.1	50.6	51.4	52.3	53.5	55.0	55.4	57.0	58.8	62.4	65.8	64.9	64.6	65.0	64.7	68.2
OECD - Total[1]	32.6	34.0	35.8	37.6	39.8	41.8	44.0	45.9	48.4	51.0	53.3	55.6	58.9	62.1	62.5	64.1	66.8	69.1	71.8
OECD - Europe[2]	35.3	37.1	39.2	41.4	43.3	45.2	47.0	48.8	51.0	53.9	56.8	59.3	62.3	65.3	66.3	67.5	70.2	72.4	74.6
EU15	35.1	36.9	39.0	41.2	43.1	45.0	46.8	48.6	50.8	53.7	56.7	59.1	62.0	65.2	66.2	67.5	70.2	72.1	74.3

27. Government final consumption expenditure - volume indices (1990 = 100)

	1960	1961	1962	1963	1964	1965	1966	1967	1968	1969	1970	1971	1972	1973	1974	1975	1976	1977	1978
Canada	28.0	31.6	33.1	34.2	36.0	37.7	41.0	44.6	47.5	49.5	53.9	56.1	57.8	60.6	64.3	68.7	70.1	73.3	74.5
Mexico	14.1	15.2	17.4	19.6	22.0	22.7	24.7	26.3	29.1	30.3	32.9	36.3	41.2	45.4	48.2	55.0	58.5	57.9	63.6
United States	51.7	54.0	56.2	56.9	57.8	58.9	65.0	70.2	71.9	72.0	71.3	69.5	69.8	69.1	70.8	72.2	72.6	73.8	75.3
Japan	26.8	28.4	30.8	33.4	34.5	35.8	37.8	39.3	41.9	44.3	47.5	51.3	53.9	56.8	56.5	63.6	66.3	69.1	72.7
Korea	..	..	..	..	..	..	..	..	..	..	35.2	37.5	39.1	39.0	43.3	46.7	48.1	50.9	55.6
Australia	24.7	26.2	27.2	28.2	30.5	33.8	36.0	39.5	42.3	43.2	44.7	46.3	48.0	51.6	54.8	59.6	63.1	64.5	68.0
New Zealand	44.6	45.3	47.6	49.2	51.0	55.4	61.1	58.1	59.4	59.8	62.3	63.8	67.7	70.4	76.2	79.9	79.3	82.5	86.4
Austria	45.8	46.7	47.8	49.7	52.1	52.5	54.9	57.1	58.9	60.3	62.2	64.3	66.9	68.9	72.9	75.8	79.0	81.2	81.9
Belgium	38.4	39.1	42.5	47.4	49.4	52.2	54.6	57.7	59.7	63.5	65.5	69.1	73.1	77.0	79.7	83.3	86.3	88.3	93.6
Czech Republic	..	..	..	..	..	..	..	..	..	..	..	..	..	..	..	..	..	..	..
Denmark	32.7	34.4	37.8	38.9	41.7	43.1	45.6	49.1	51.4	54.9	58.7	61.9	65.4	68.0	70.4	71.8	75.1	76.9	81.6
Finland	26.2	27.7	29.9	32.0	32.6	34.2	35.7	37.3	39.5	40.9	43.1	45.6	49.1	51.9	54.2	57.9	61.3	63.8	66.1
France	38.6	40.4	42.3	43.7	45.6	47.0	48.3	50.4	53.2	55.4	57.7	60.0	62.1	64.2	64.9	67.8	70.6	72.3	76.0
Germany	40.5	43.0	47.0	49.9	50.9	53.3	55.1	57.1	57.4	59.9	62.4	65.6	68.4	71.8	74.7	77.5	78.7	79.7	82.8
Greece	22.2	23.2	24.7	25.7	28.1	30.7	32.6	35.4	35.8	38.6	40.9	42.9	45.3	48.4	54.2	60.7	63.8	68.0	70.4
Hungary	..	..	..	..	..	..	..	..	..	..	..	..	..	..	..	..	..	..	..
Iceland	16.6	17.0	18.1	19.3	21.1	22.5	24.3	26.2	27.7	28.5	31.1	33.4	38.3	41.5	45.0	49.2	51.7	52.8	56.6
Ireland	34.6	35.3	36.4	37.9	39.0	40.4	40.9	42.7	45.2	48.3	53.8	58.4	62.8	67.0	72.1	78.4	80.4	82.1	88.6
Italy	39.6	41.4	43.0	44.8	46.7	48.6	50.5	52.7	55.4	57.0	58.5	61.3	64.3	66.1	67.8	69.5	71.1	73.2	75.6
Luxembourg	40.2	40.7	41.6	44.1	43.7	44.8	47.4	49.4	52.2	53.9	56.1	57.8	60.2	62.2	64.6	66.7	68.6	70.6	71.8
Netherlands	45.5	46.8	48.4	50.6	51.5	52.3	53.2	54.5	55.7	58.2	61.7	64.4	64.9	65.4	66.9	69.6	72.5	74.9	77.8
Norway	25.3	26.9	28.2	30.1	32.0	35.0	36.1	39.5	41.1	43.1	45.8	48.6	50.8	53.6	55.7	59.3	63.7	66.8	70.4
Poland	..	..	..	..	..	..	..	..	..	..	..	..	..	..	..	..	..	..	..
Portugal	11.9	15.1	16.4	16.9	18.1	19.4	20.4	22.6	24.5	25.4	27.2	28.9	31.4	33.8	39.7	42.3	45.3	50.6	52.9
Spain	22.9	24.1	25.8	28.2	28.6	29.6	30.2	30.9	31.5	32.9	34.8	36.3	38.2	40.6	44.4	46.7	49.9	51.8	54.3
Sweden	35.9	37.1	39.4	43.2	44.5	46.6	49.2	51.4	54.9	57.8	62.5	63.9	65.4	67.1	69.2	72.4	74.9	77.2	79.7
Switzerland	33.8	39.7	42.9	46.7	47.9	50.1	51.1	51.9	53.9	56.6	59.3	62.7	64.5	66.1	67.2	67.7	69.5	69.8	71.2
Turkey	15.0	16.1	16.8	18.2	19.6	20.6	22.1	24.0	25.6	27.3	28.3	30.0	32.2	34.9	37.8	46.3	53.7	55.7	54.1
United Kingdom	55.8	57.8	59.6	61.5	62.5	64.4	66.2	69.9	70.3	69.1	70.3	72.4	75.6	79.0	80.4	84.8	85.9	84.4	86.3
OECD - Total[1]	41.6	43.7	46.0	47.6	48.9	50.4	53.8	57.1	58.9	60.0	61.4	62.6	64.3	65.8	67.7	70.6	72.2	73.7	76.0
OECD - Europe[2]	39.7	41.6	44.0	46.2	47.6	49.5	51.1	53.4	54.9	56.6	58.8	61.4	64.0	66.6	68.7	71.7	73.8	75.1	77.9
EU15	40.4	42.3	44.7	46.9	48.3	50.1	51.8	54.1	55.6	57.3	59.5	62.1	64.7	67.3	69.5	72.4	74.4	75.6	78.5

1. Excluding Korea Czech Republic Hungary and Poland.
2. Excluding Czech Republic Hungary and Poland.

Produit intérieur brut - indices de volume (1990 = 100) 25.

1979	1980	1981	1982	1983	1984	1985	1986	1987	1988	1989	1990	1991	1992	1993	1994	1995	1996	1997	
74.8	75.8	78.2	75.8	78.0	82.5	87.0	89.2	92.9	97.4	99.8	100.0	98.1	99.0	101.5	105.5	107.7	109.0	113.0	Canada
77.2	83.6	91.0	90.3	86.4	89.5	92.0	88.6	90.2	91.3	95.2	100.0	104.2	108.0	110.1	115.0	107.9	113.5	121.4	Mexique
77.8	77.3	78.6	77.0	79.7	84.5	87.2	89.8	92.2	95.7	98.8	100.0	99.0	101.8	104.3	108.1	110.9	114.8	119.4	États-Unis
65.7	67.6	69.7	71.8	73.5	76.4	79.8	82.1	85.5	90.8	95.2	100.0	103.8	104.9	105.2	105.9	107.4	111.6	112.6	Japon
43.2	42.0	44.6	48.0	53.6	58.2	62.0	69.2	77.1	85.8	91.3	100.0	109.1	114.7	121.3	131.7	143.4	153.6	162.0	Corée
71.5	73.1	75.8	75.4	76.1	81.7	85.6	87.5	91.3	94.8	98.8	100.0	98.7	101.4	105.5	111.1	115.6	119.9	123.2	Australie
83.6	84.2	88.3	89.9	92.4	96.9	97.7	99.7	100.1	99.7	100.6	100.0	98.8	100.0	106.3	112.0	116.0	119.2	121.9	Nouvelle-Zélande
77.8	79.6	79.5	81.0	83.3	83.6	85.5	87.5	88.9	91.8	95.6	100.0	103.4	104.8	105.3	108.0	110.2	112.1	114.9	Autriche
79.5	83.1	82.1	83.2	83.2	85.3	86.1	87.4	89.5	93.7	97.1	100.0	101.6	103.1	101.6	104.2	106.7	108.0	111.3	Belgique
..	..	..	..	..	..	..	..	..	..	..	100.0	88.5	85.6	86.1	88.9	94.5	98.2	99.2	République tchèque
82.6	82.2	81.5	84.0	86.1	89.9	93.7	97.1	97.4	98.5	98.8	100.0	101.4	102.7	103.6	109.5	113.0	116.6	120.5	Danemark
69.9	73.6	75.0	77.4	79.5	81.9	84.6	86.6	90.2	94.6	100.0	100.0	92.9	89.6	88.6	92.6	97.3	100.8	106.8	Finlande
79.5	80.5	81.1	82.9	83.5	84.6	86.1	88.2	90.2	94.0	97.7	100.0	100.8	101.8	100.5	103.2	105.4	106.9	109.4	France
79.8	80.6	80.9	80.5	82.1	84.6	86.6	88.8	90.3	93.6	96.9	100.0	102.8	105.1	103.9	106.7	108.0	109.4	111.8	Allemagne
83.8	85.3	85.3	85.7	86.0	88.4	91.1	92.6	92.2	96.3	100.0	100.0	103.1	103.8	102.1	104.2	106.4	108.9	112.4	Grèce
..	..	..	..	..	..	..	..	..	..	..	100.0	88.1	85.4	84.9	87.4	88.7	89.9	94.0	Hongrie
72.2	76.3	79.6	81.3	79.5	82.8	85.5	90.9	98.7	98.6	98.8	100.0	101.1	97.7	98.7	102.3	103.3	109.1	113.9	Islande
68.0	70.1	72.4	74.0	73.9	77.1	79.5	79.1	82.8	87.1	92.2	100.0	102.5	107.4	111.4	120.4	134.6	145.7	161.2	Irlande
77.5	80.2	80.6	80.9	81.9	84.0	86.4	88.8	91.6	95.1	97.9	100.0	101.1	101.7	100.5	102.7	105.7	106.4	108.0	Italie
64.1	64.7	64.3	65.0	67.0	71.1	73.2	78.9	80.7	89.1	97.9	100.0	106.1	110.9	120.5	125.6	130.4	134.3	139.3	Luxembourg
79.6	80.6	80.2	79.2	80.6	83.2	85.8	88.2	89.4	91.8	96.1	100.0	102.3	104.3	105.1	108.5	111.0	114.4	118.6	Pays-Bas
75.2	78.9	79.7	79.8	82.6	87.5	92.0	95.3	97.3	97.2	98.1	100.0	103.1	106.5	109.4	115.4	119.8	126.4	130.8	Norvège
..	..	..	..	..	..	..	..	..	..	..	100.0	93.0	95.5	99.1	104.2	111.6	118.4	126.5	Pologne
70.0	73.2	74.4	76.0	75.9	74.4	76.5	79.7	84.8	91.1	95.8	100.0	102.3	104.9	103.8	106.1	109.1	112.6	116.7	Portugal
73.4	75.1	75.0	76.1	77.8	78.9	80.3	82.8	87.5	92.0	96.4	100.0	102.3	103.0	101.8	104.1	106.9	109.5	113.3	Espagne
80.6	82.0	81.9	82.8	84.2	87.6	89.3	91.4	94.2	96.4	98.7	100.0	98.9	97.5	95.3	98.5	102.4	103.7	105.5	Suède
78.0	81.6	82.9	81.7	82.1	84.6	87.5	88.9	89.6	92.4	96.4	100.0	99.2	99.1	98.6	99.1	99.7	99.6	101.4	Suisse
61.7	60.2	63.1	65.3	68.6	73.2	76.3	81.7	89.4	91.3	91.5	100.0	100.9	107.0	115.6	109.3	117.1	125.3	134.8	Turquie
78.4	77.1	76.1	77.3	80.0	82.0	84.9	88.6	92.9	97.5	99.6	100.0	98.0	97.5	99.5	103.8	106.7	109.1	112.8	Royaume-Uni
75.5	76.4	77.5	77.6	79.4	82.7	85.4	87.7	90.4	94.2	97.6	100.0	100.8	102.4	103.4	106.3	108.6	111.7	115.0	OCDE - Total[1]
77.9	79.1	79.3	80.0	81.5	83.6	85.7	88.2	90.8	94.3	97.5	100.0	101.0	102.1	101.8	104.5	107.1	109.1	112.1	OCDE - Europe[2]
78.4	79.5	79.6	80.3	81.7	83.7	85.8	88.2	90.7	94.4	97.6	100.0	101.1	102.0	101.4	104.4	106.9	108.8	111.6	UE15

Consommation finale privée - indices de volume (1990 = 100) 26.

1979	1980	1981	1982	1983	1984	1985	1986	1987	1988	1989	1990	1991	1992	1993	1994	1995	1996	1997	
74.0	75.5	76.7	74.7	77.0	80.5	84.6	88.0	91.5	95.5	98.7	100.0	98.6	100.4	102.2	105.4	107.1	109.6	114.2	Canada
77.8	83.6	89.8	87.6	82.9	85.6	88.6	86.1	86.0	87.6	94.0	100.0	104.7	109.6	111.2	116.3	105.2	107.5	114.4	Mexique
73.7	73.8	74.9	75.6	79.0	82.9	86.6	89.8	92.5	96.1	98.4	100.0	99.3	102.2	105.4	109.0	112.1	115.4	119.3	États-Unis
68.7	69.4	70.4	73.5	76.0	77.9	80.5	83.4	86.9	91.5	95.8	100.0	102.5	104.6	105.9	107.9	110.1	113.3	114.5	Japon
46.0	45.8	48.0	51.1	55.8	60.1	64.0	69.2	74.8	81.6	90.4	100.0	109.5	116.7	123.3	132.7	143.7	153.4	158.2	Corée
71.5	73.9	77.1	79.1	80.3	82.7	86.6	87.6	89.4	92.6	97.4	100.0	100.8	104.4	107.2	112.1	117.6	121.2	125.4	Australie
84.4	84.2	85.9	84.8	87.4	90.8	92.0	95.9	98.2	99.9	100.3	100.0	98.0	98.3	101.5	107.6	112.0	116.6	120.4	Nouvelle-Zélande
77.2	78.4	79.1	81.1	85.1	84.0	85.6	87.4	90.0	93.0	96.4	100.0	102.8	105.9	106.6	108.5	111.6	114.3	115.1	Autriche
82.2	84.2	83.9	85.5	84.7	85.3	87.0	88.7	90.7	93.7	97.1	100.0	102.9	105.2	103.7	105.4	106.3	108.3	110.5	Belgique
..	..	..	..	..	..	..	..	..	..	..	100.0	71.5	82.4	85.3	89.9	96.2	103.0	104.8	République tchèque
91.4	88.0	86.0	87.2	89.5	92.5	97.1	102.7	101.1	100.1	99.8	100.0	101.8	104.4	105.9	113.3	117.0	120.2	124.5	Danemark
69.6	71.2	72.1	75.6	78.0	80.4	83.4	86.7	91.3	95.9	100.0	100.0	96.4	91.7	89.0	90.7	94.9	98.2	101.5	Finlande
78.8	79.6	81.1	83.7	84.4	85.1	86.9	90.0	92.4	95.0	97.7	100.0	101.2	102.5	102.5	103.9	105.5	107.5	108.3	France
79.6	80.6	80.4	79.6	80.7	82.4	84.1	87.1	90.1	92.7	95.3	100.0	105.6	108.6	108.7	110.0	112.0	113.8	114.3	Allemagne
77.4	77.5	79.1	82.2	82.4	83.8	87.1	87.7	88.7	91.9	97.5	100.0	102.8	105.3	104.5	106.6	109.5	111.6	114.5	Grèce
..	..	..	..	..	..	..	..	..	..	..	100.0	94.5	95.8	99.1	99.3	92.3	89.3	91.4	Hongrie
74.0	76.5	81.2	85.2	80.4	83.4	86.9	92.9	107.9	103.8	99.5	100.0	104.1	99.5	95.0	96.8	100.9	107.3	113.7	Islande
82.3	82.6	84.0	78.1	78.8	80.4	84.1	85.7	88.6	92.6	98.6	100.0	102.1	106.9	109.4	116.3	121.0	128.3	136.4	Irlande
71.5	75.9	77.0	77.9	78.4	80.4	82.9	86.4	90.1	94.2	97.6	100.0	102.7	104.0	100.5	101.4	102.9	104.1	106.5	Italie
70.9	72.9	74.1	74.4	74.8	75.9	77.9	82.3	86.1	90.0	94.6	100.0	106.3	105.3	107.1	109.7	112.3	114.4	117.6	Luxembourg
86.3	86.0	83.4	83.0	83.8	84.8	87.2	89.5	91.9	92.7	95.9	100.0	103.1	105.7	106.8	109.1	111.3	114.3	117.8	Pays-Bas
82.6	84.3	84.4	85.3	86.8	89.6	98.0	102.8	102.0	99.9	99.3	100.0	101.5	103.7	106.0	110.2	113.9	119.3	123.3	Norvège
..	..	..	..	..	..	..	..	..	..	..	100.0	106.6	109.4	115.2	120.4	124.7	135.4	145.0	Pologne
73.6	76.4	78.6	80.4	79.3	76.9	77.4	81.8	86.1	92.0	94.5	100.0	103.7	108.1	109.7	112.2	113.9	116.8	120.4	Portugal
77.5	79.1	78.1	78.0	78.2	78.1	79.6	82.3	87.0	91.3	96.5	100.0	102.9	105.2	102.8	103.8	105.4	107.5	110.8	Espagne
87.2	86.5	86.3	86.9	85.2	86.4	88.7	92.7	96.9	99.2	100.4	100.0	100.9	99.5	96.5	98.2	98.9	100.2	102.2	Suède
83.7	85.9	86.8	87.1	88.1	89.3	90.8	92.9	94.9	96.5	98.8	100.0	101.7	101.8	100.9	101.9	102.5	103.1	104.3	Suisse
69.8	73.9	68.3	72.9	77.9	84.2	83.7	88.5	88.3	89.3	88.4	100.0	102.7	106.0	115.1	108.9	114.2	123.9	134.3	Turquie
71.2	71.1	71.2	71.9	75.1	76.7	79.6	85.1	89.6	96.3	99.4	100.0	97.8	97.7	100.2	103.0	104.8	108.4	113.4	Royaume-Uni
74.4	75.3	76.1	77.2	79.3	81.8	84.6	87.7	90.7	94.4	97.4	100.0	101.1	103.4	104.8	107.3	109.5	112.4	115.3	OCDE - Total[1]
77.2	78.6	78.7	79.6	80.8	82.1	84.3	87.7	90.8	94.2	97.2	100.0	102.2	103.8	103.6	105.1	107.0	109.4	111.9	OCDE - Europe[2]
77.1	78.4	78.7	79.4	80.5	81.7	83.9	87.3	90.6	94.2	97.3	100.0	102.2	103.8	103.4	105.1	106.9	109.1	111.4	UE15

Consommation finale des administrations publiques - indices de volume (1990 = 100) 27.

1979	1980	1981	1982	1983	1984	1985	1986	1987	1988	1989	1990	1991	1992	1993	1994	1995	1996	1997	
75.4	77.9	79.1	80.8	82.2	83.2	86.8	88.5	89.7	93.9	96.5	100.0	102.8	103.9	103.6	101.8	101.4	100.1	100.0	Canada
69.7	76.4	84.2	85.9	88.3	94.1	94.9	96.3	95.2	94.7	96.8	100.0	105.4	107.4	110.0	113.1	111.6	110.8	112.8	Mexique
76.3	77.5	78.5	80.4	82.1	84.2	88.1	91.5	94.3	95.9	97.6	100.0	100.4	99.9	98.9	99.1	98.9	99.1	100.4	États-Unis
75.8	78.1	81.6	84.0	86.1	88.2	88.4	93.0	94.4	96.6	98.5	100.0	102.0	104.0	106.4	109.0	112.6	114.3	114.1	Japon
56.2	59.9	62.8	63.4	65.2	66.0	69.2	75.0	79.6	86.0	93.3	100.0	108.5	116.7	120.2	125.3	126.6	136.5	144.3	Corée
68.8	71.5	74.0	73.7	77.6	81.1	85.5	89.3	91.0	93.7	96.0	100.0	102.7	104.4	104.3	109.7	112.3	115.8	118.5	Australie
85.3	86.0	87.6	88.1	90.5	92.2	93.8	94.4	95.7	96.8	99.3	100.0	100.0	102.9	101.8	100.9	103.7	106.1	112.5	Nouvelle-Zélande
84.7	86.5	88.1	90.8	92.4	93.1	94.4	96.1	96.3	97.4	98.8	100.0	102.2	104.3	107.1	109.8	109.7	109.9	110.8	Autriche
95.9	97.8	98.5	97.1	97.4	98.0	100.4	102.3	102.4	101.5	100.5	100.0	102.2	102.5	103.8	105.6	106.3	107.7	108.6	Belgique
..	..	..	..	..	..	..	..	..	..	..	100.0	91.0	88.2	86.7	84.4	82.7	86.1	84.2	République tchèque
86.4	90.1	92.5	95.3	95.3	94.9	97.3	97.7	100.2	101.1	100.3	100.0	100.7	101.5	105.7	108.7	111.3	114.0	116.4	Danemark
68.6	71.5	74.4	76.8	79.7	81.9	85.6	88.3	92.0	94.1	96.3	100.0	102.5	100.2	94.9	94.6	96.4	99.7	100.4	Finlande
78.3	80.2	82.6	85.6	87.3	88.3	90.3	91.8	94.3	97.5	98.0	100.0	102.7	106.2	109.8	111.1	111.2	114.0	115.3	France
85.6	87.8	88.9	88.3	88.8	90.7	92.8	94.9	96.9	99.1	97.7	100.0	100.8	105.0	104.5	106.7	108.8	111.8	111.0	Allemagne
74.5	74.6	79.7	81.5	83.8	86.3	89.1	88.4	89.1	94.3	99.4	100.0	98.5	95.5	98.0	96.9	102.4	103.4	103.0	Grèce
..	..	..	..	..	..	..	..	..	..	..	100.0	97.3	96.3	105.7	97.9	92.3	90.2	91.3	Hongrie
59.7	60.9	65.5	69.4	72.6	73.0	77.8	83.4	88.9	93.0	95.8	100.0	103.2	102.3	104.6	108.5	109.9	111.0	113.9	Islande
92.7	99.2	99.6	102.8	102.4	101.7	103.6	106.3	101.1	96.1	94.9	100.0	102.9	105.4	105.8	111.2	114.1	115.7	121.2	Irlande
77.7	79.3	81.0	83.0	85.6	87.4	90.2	92.4	95.3	97.9	98.8	100.0	101.7	102.8	103.3	102.7	101.6	101.8	101.1	Italie
73.4	75.7	76.8	77.9	79.4	81.1	82.7	84.9	88.9	93.3	97.0	100.0	103.9	105.4	109.3	111.5	114.0	117.7	122.3	Luxembourg
80.5	81.6	83.9	85.8	87.8	87.8	89.9	93.1	95.5	96.9	98.4	100.0	101.5	103.2	104.8	105.4	106.2	107.5	109.1	Pays-Bas
73.5	77.6	81.5	82.9	85.2	85.9	87.9	89.6	93.7	93.6	95.4	100.0	104.3	109.9	112.3	113.8	114.2	117.9	121.4	Norvège
..	..	..	..	..	..	..	..	..	..	..	100.0	109.6	116.1	119.8	122.5	126.0	130.4	134.5	Pologne
56.3	60.8	64.1	66.5	69.0	69.2	73.6	78.9	81.9	88.9	94.8	100.0	110.3	111.5	112.5	114.8	117.3	119.7	122.7	Portugal
56.9	58.9	61.0	64.3	66.8	68.5	72.6	76.5	83.3	86.6	93.8	100.0	105.6	109.8	112.5	112.1	114.1	115.2	116.8	Espagne
83.5	85.4	87.3	88.1	88.9	90.8	92.8	94.0	94.9	95.4	97.5	100.0	102.8	102.7	102.9	102.2	101.3	101.1	99.0	Suède
72.0	72.7	74.5	75.3	78.1	79.5	82.1	84.8	86.1	90.0	94.8	100.0	103.4	104.2	104.0	106.1	105.9	107.0	106.7	Suisse
52.8	43.1	64.1	57.3	66.8	68.0	77.6	84.8	92.8	91.8	92.6	100.0	103.7	107.4	116.6	110.2	117.7	127.8	133.1	Turquie
87.9	89.4	89.7	90.4	92.4	93.1	93.1	94.6	95.5	96.2	97.5	100.0	102.6	102.5	102.3	104.6	105.9	108.4	108.6	Royaume-Uni
77.9	79.7	81.4	83.0	84.7	86.5	89.1	91.9	94.2	96.2	97.6	100.0	101.6	102.8	103.1	104.1	104.8	106.0	106.7	OCDE - Total[1]
80.3	82.1	83.9	85.2	86.8	88.1	90.3	92.3	94.6	96.6	97.6	100.0	102.2	104.4	105.4	106.6	107.5	109.6	109.9	OCDE - Europe[2]
81.0	82.9	84.5	85.8	87.3	88.7	90.7	92.7	94.9	96.9	97.8	100.0	102.1	104.3	105.2	106.4	107.3	109.3	109.5	UE15

1. Non compris la Corée la République tchèque la Hongrie et la Pologne.
2. Non compris la République tchèque la Hongrie et la Pologne.

28. Gross fixed capital formation - volume indices (1990 = 100)

	1960	1961	1962	1963	1964	1965	1966	1967	1968	1969	1970	1971	1972	1973	1974	1975	1976	1977	1978
Canada	23.5	23.4	24.4	25.3	28.6	31.8	35.2	35.2	35.5	37.4	37.6	40.4	42.1	46.0	49.2	51.8	54.1	55.3	57.1
Mexico	22.0	22.2	22.7	25.7	31.3	32.6	35.7	39.9	43.8	46.8	50.6	49.7	55.8	64.1	69.1	75.5	75.9	70.8	81.5
United States	42.1	42.6	45.8	49.2	53.5	58.3	60.7	59.7	63.0	64.7	62.4	65.8	72.1	77.6	72.8	65.5	70.5	78.3	86.2
Japan	10.0	12.3	14.1	15.7	18.2	19.0	21.7	25.7	30.9	36.7	42.9	45.0	49.5	55.2	50.5	50.2	51.6	53.1	57.3
Korea										9.6	9.9	10.0	12.8	14.7	15.8	19.1	24.6	33.1	
Australia	35.0	34.4	36.3	39.6	44.4	49.0	50.0	51.6	55.5	59.3	62.4	66.4	65.4	69.0	67.0	66.8	69.7	69.1	71.3
New Zealand	45.0	48.9	47.5	52.5	59.4	63.3	67.5	61.2	52.1	60.0	65.2	69.1	81.1	90.8	96.9	91.7	84.3	75.1	71.4
Austria	30.5	34.3	35.3	36.5	40.0	42.0	45.8	45.8	47.1	49.4	54.3	61.7	69.2	69.5	72.2	68.7	71.3	77.8	71.9
Belgium	35.9	40.4	42.7	42.8	49.1	51.1	54.6	56.2	55.5	58.4	63.4	62.1	64.3	68.8	73.5	72.2	75.0	75.1	77.2
Czech Republic																			
Denmark	47.1	53.7	57.3	55.9	69.0	72.3	75.3	79.4	80.9	90.4	92.4	94.2	102.9	106.4	97.0	85.0	99.6	97.1	98.2
Finland	37.7	41.2	41.4	40.2	42.6	47.1	48.9	48.4	45.8	51.6	58.0	60.2	64.2	69.6	72.1	76.3	69.7	67.8	62.9
France	30.2	33.5	36.4	39.6	43.7	46.8	50.2	53.2	56.1	61.3	64.1	68.5	72.4	77.6	78.3	72.9	75.1	74.0	75.4
Germany	49.5	52.7	54.7	55.4	61.6	64.5	65.2	60.7	62.7	68.7	74.8	79.2	81.3	81.1	73.2	69.3	71.7	74.3	77.3
Greece	32.4	35.0	38.0	40.1	48.4	54.6	56.3	55.4	67.2	79.8	78.7	89.7	103.5	111.4	82.9	83.1	88.8	95.7	101.4
Hungary																			
Iceland	35.8	27.6	31.7	41.5	49.2	48.6	56.0	62.5	57.0	43.5	46.6	66.4	66.9	82.0	88.5	80.7	78.5	87.5	62.6
Ireland	20.7	24.1	27.7	31.0	34.4	38.0	36.9	39.4	44.6	53.7	51.9	56.5	60.9	70.8	62.6	60.3	68.5	71.3	34.7
Italy	44.2	49.3	54.2	58.5	55.1	50.5	52.7	58.9	65.2	70.3	72.4	71.9	72.5	78.6	80.1	74.4	73.7	74.7	75.1
Luxembourg	38.4	41.9	45.1	51.5	62.9	54.2	51.4	47.3	45.3	50.1	53.9	59.6	63.8	71.3	66.4	61.4	58.8	58.8	59.4
Netherlands	42.5	45.1	46.6	47.2	56.2	59.2	63.9	69.3	77.1	75.3	81.0	82.2	80.4	83.7	80.4	76.9	75.2	82.5	84.5
Norway	42.9	48.2	50.1	52.0	53.7	57.4	60.8	67.9	65.8	60.2	69.1	82.1	78.7	89.5	94.0	105.2	115.9	120.1	106.6
Poland																			
Portugal	26.4	28.0	28.3	32.4	33.9	37.4	44.0	46.5	42.2	46.0	51.3	56.3	63.9	70.0	65.1	57.8	58.2	65.2	69.3
Spain	17.6	20.8	23.1	25.8	29.7	34.5	39.1	41.4	45.3	49.9	51.6	50.0	57.1	64.6	68.6	65.5	64.9	64.4	62.6
Sweden	41.7	45.0	47.8	51.1	54.9	57.2	59.8	63.0	63.4	66.1	68.2	67.8	70.7	72.6	70.4	72.5	73.9	71.7	66.8
Switzerland	37.8	43.7	48.2	51.7	55.9	54.6	54.1	54.2	55.9	59.2	64.5	70.8	74.3	76.5	73.2	63.3	56.6	57.6	61.1
Turkey	14.1	14.6	15.6	16.3	16.8	17.2	21.0	22.4	25.4	27.0	30.6	28.1	33.5	36.3	54.5	56.9	68.1	53.4	44.3
United Kingdom	38.8	42.6	42.9	43.5	50.7	53.3	54.7	59.5	63.2	62.8	64.4	65.6	65.4	69.7	68.0	66.7	67.8	66.6	68.6
OECD - Total [1]	31.2	33.5	35.9	38.2	41.9	44.3	46.7	48.3	51.9	55.7	58.4	61.0	65.1	69.9	66.9	63.6	66.0	68.5	72.2
OECD - Europe [2]	38.2	41.9	44.3	46.3	50.4	52.2	54.5	56.2	59.3	63.3	66.9	69.5	72.2	76.0	74.5	70.9	72.3	72.9	73.6
EU15	38.7	42.4	44.7	46.7	50.9	52.8	55.2	56.9	60.1	64.4	67.9	70.2	73.0	76.7	74.6	71.0	72.3	73.2	74.3

29. Exports of goods and services - volume indices (1990 = 100)

	1960	1961	1962	1963	1964	1965	1966	1967	1968	1969	1970	1971	1972	1973	1974	1975	1976	1977	1978
Canada	15.1	16.1	16.8	18.4	20.9	21.8	24.8	27.4	30.9	33.4	36.5	38.1	41.3	45.7	44.5	41.6	46.1	49.6	54.9
Mexico	10.1	10.9	11.7	12.6	13.5	14.7	16.0	15.5	17.3	19.4	21.2	22.0	25.6	29.1	29.2	26.6	31.0	35.5	39.6
United States	19.0	19.2	20.3	21.6	24.3	24.9	26.7	27.5	29.8	31.3	34.0	34.4	37.4	43.9	48.1	47.9	49.4	50.1	54.9
Japan	5.6	5.9	6.9	7.4	9.0	11.1	13.0	13.9	17.2	20.7	24.4	28.3	29.4	31.0	38.1	37.8	44.0	49.2	49.1
Korea											5.6	6.8	9.3	14.4	14.3	17.0	23.5	28.4	32.5
Australia	17.6	21.7	21.9	23.5	24.7	25.7	25.8	29.6	30.5	33.4	38.3	42.1	44.8	44.7	42.9	46.5	50.6	50.8	52.8
New Zealand	28.5	31.0	31.2	34.7	33.6	34.7	37.6	37.3	42.3	47.9	48.2	51.7	52.8	51.8	50.4	56.8	63.1	63.1	64.5
Austria	12.9	13.6	14.9	16.0	16.9	18.1	19.3	20.4	22.1	26.0	30.3	32.3	35.5	37.5	41.5	40.5	45.0	47.0	50.6
Belgium	17.2	18.8	20.7	22.4	24.5	26.0	28.0	29.2	32.7	37.8	41.2	43.1	47.9	54.6	56.6	51.9	58.6	59.9	61.3
Czech Republic																			
Denmark	22.2	23.1	24.3	26.7	29.0	31.3	32.5	33.8	36.9	39.2	41.4	43.7	46.1	49.7	51.4	50.5	52.6	54.8	55.4
Finland	22.9	24.1	25.8	26.4	27.9	29.5	31.3	33.2	36.5	42.6	46.4	45.8	52.4	56.2	55.9	48.1	53.8	62.2	68.2
France	14.5	15.2	15.5	16.6	17.7	19.7	21.0	22.5	24.7	28.5	33.1	36.5	40.9	45.4	49.9	49.6	53.7	58.1	61.9
Germany	19.2	20.2	20.7	22.3	24.2	25.7	28.3	30.5	34.4	37.6	40.2	41.9	44.8	49.5	55.5	52.0	57.0	59.2	60.9
Greece	7.6	8.7	9.5	10.2	10.3	11.7	15.7	16.5	16.3	18.7	21.0	23.5	28.8	35.6	35.6	39.4	45.8	46.7	54.3
Hungary																			
Iceland	25.4	25.4	30.4	32.7	34.4	36.9	39.4	34.4	32.2	37.8	44.0	40.4	46.2	50.3	48.9	50.2	56.8	61.8	77.2
Ireland	8.8	10.3	10.2	11.2	12.1	13.2	14.6	16.1	17.5	18.3	21.8	22.7	23.5	26.1	26.2	28.2	30.5	34.8	39.1
Italy	12.6	14.4	15.9	17.0	18.8	22.6	25.1	26.9	30.6	34.2	36.2	38.7	41.7	44.2	47.8	48.4	54.5	60.1	66.1
Luxembourg	23.9	24.7	24.3	25.3	28.6	30.3	30.2	30.8	34.1	38.8	42.3	43.9	46.3	52.7	58.4	49.2	49.7	51.8	55.2
Netherlands	17.6	18.0	19.1	20.3	22.6	24.3	25.5	27.2	30.7	35.3	39.5	43.7	48.0	53.8	55.2	53.5	58.8	57.7	58.7
Norway	18.8	20.2	21.5	23.2	25.1	26.5	28.0	30.4	32.7	34.4	34.5	34.8	39.8	43.0	43.3	44.7	49.7	51.5	55.8
Poland																			
Portugal	12.6	12.2	14.6	14.7	23.3	25.9	30.2	31.2	30.2	31.0	30.5	33.6	39.8	41.4	34.9	29.5	29.5	31.2	34.1
Spain	9.7	10.5	11.8	12.3	15.3	16.4	18.9	18.1	21.4	24.7	29.2	33.3	37.8	41.6	41.2	41.0	43.1	48.3	52.4
Sweden	22.2	23.4	25.3	27.1	30.4	32.1	33.6	35.5	38.2	42.6	46.3	48.5	51.3	58.3	61.4	55.7	58.1	59.0	53.6
Switzerland	24.0	25.9	27.5	29.0	30.8	33.1	34.8	36.0	39.6	44.9	48.0	49.9	53.1	57.2	57.8	54.0	59.0	64.8	67.2
Turkey	8.4	8.6	9.1	10.0	10.4	10.6	11.9	12.9	12.9	13.8	15.8	18.2	20.9	24.5	22.2	23.7	29.3	19.9	15.4
United Kingdom	28.4	29.3	29.8	31.3	32.4	33.9	35.6	36.0	40.6	44.3	46.7	49.9	50.3	56.3	60.2	58.3	63.4	67.5	68.6
OECD - Total [1]	16.8	17.6	18.6	19.8	21.8	23.4	25.3	26.7	29.7	32.9	36.0	38.2	41.2	45.7	49.2	47.8	52.1	54.9	58.0
OECD - Europe [2]	18.1	19.2	20.1	21.5	23.3	25.2	27.1	28.6	31.8	35.5	38.6	41.1	44.4	49.0	52.3	50.3	55.0	58.0	61.0
EU15	17.9	18.9	19.9	21.2	23.0	24.9	26.9	28.3	31.7	35.4	38.5	41.1	44.3	49.0	52.6	50.5	55.3	58.3	61.2

30. Imports of goods and services - volume indices (1990 = 100)

	1960	1961	1962	1963	1964	1965	1966	1967	1968	1969	1970	1971	1972	1973	1974	1975	1976	1977	1978
Canada	13.7	13.7	14.0	14.2	16.0	18.2	20.7	21.8	24.0	27.1	26.7	28.4	32.5	37.2	41.4	40.5	43.8	44.2	45.7
Mexico	18.2	16.9	16.9	18.0	22.5	23.3	23.3	25.3	20.2	27.5	30.0	28.6	31.5	36.8	44.3	44.4	44.9	40.3	42.1
United States	18.7	18.5	20.3	20.4	21.3	23.3	27.1	29.1	33.4	35.7	36.9	38.6	42.4	44.2	42.9	37.4	44.5	48.8	53.1
Japan	8.5	10.8	10.6	12.7	14.5	15.3	17.1	21.0	23.6	26.8	32.9	35.3	39.0	48.4	50.5	45.3	48.3	50.3	53.7
Korea											9.0	10.8	10.9	14.7	17.4	17.8	22.2	26.8	33.2
Australia	23.4	21.1	22.7	24.6	29.5	33.4	30.9	34.5	38.2	39.1	40.7	40.8	37.1	45.0	55.4	46.7	52.2	52.4	53.7
New Zealand	32.6	32.9	32.2	36.9	38.7	45.1	47.8	38.9	38.9	43.1	51.6	50.6	55.4	67.2	76.1	59.7	58.8	59.5	60.5
Austria	14.8	15.2	16.0	17.5	19.4	21.4	23.7	24.2	25.9	28.3	33.1	35.1	39.4	43.2	46.2	44.0	51.7	54.9	58.9
Belgium	18.6	20.0	21.6	23.5	25.5	27.2	29.9	30.4	34.0	39.2	42.0	43.5	47.7	56.5	59.0	53.7	60.3	63.2	68.9
Czech Republic																			
Denmark	29.8	31.2	35.3	34.9	41.8	44.7	47.1	49.2	51.6	58.4	63.8	63.3	64.3	72.5	69.7	66.4	76.7	76.7	77.8
Finland	21.3	23.0	24.3	23.6	28.5	30.8	31.9	31.8	30.6	37.4	44.9	44.7	46.6	52.6	56.1	56.4	55.5	54.8	54.1
France	12.7	13.6	14.5	16.6	19.1	19.5	21.6	23.3	26.4	31.5	33.5	35.9	40.7	46.4	47.7	43.6	51.8	52.5	54.6
Germany	17.1	18.4	20.4	21.4	23.4	26.7	27.5	27.1	30.7	35.9	44.0	48.0	50.8	53.3	53.4	54.1	59.8	61.9	64.2
Greece	9.3	10.5	11.6	13.3	15.4	18.6	18.6	19.9	21.9	25.3	26.9	28.9	33.4	44.2	37.0	39.3	41.7	45.1	48.3
Hungary																			
Iceland	22.2	20.2	24.3	28.9	32.8	35.1	40.2	42.8	39.0	33.7	43.0	53.6	53.9	64.9	73.0	53.7	61.3	74.0	76.7
Ireland	12.8	14.5	15.3	16.9	19.1	21.2	22.0	22.8	26.4	29.9	32.5	34.0	35.7	42.5	41.5	37.3	42.8	48.4	54.0
Italy	13.1	14.9	17.1	20.9	19.6	20.0	22.9	25.9	27.5	32.8	38.0	39.0	42.7	46.4	48.5	42.3	47.4	48.2	51.0
Luxembourg	24.2	26.0	26.8	27.7	31.4	32.8	32.0	30.5	33.2	37.0	44.0	47.5	48.7	54.2	57.4	52.2	52.8	52.6	56.3
Netherlands	18.6	19.8	21.1	23.1	26.6	28.2	30.2	32.1	36.3	41.4	47.5	50.4	52.8	58.6	58.1	55.8	61.4	63.2	67.2
Norway	27.1	29.8	31.4	33.3	35.7	38.9	42.0	46.9	47.9	48.8	55.4	59.0	58.4	66.8	69.9	74.8	84.0	86.9	75.1
Poland																			
Portugal	12.4	15.5	14.2	15.6	19.8	21.7	23.5	22.1	29.4	31.6	31.9	36.5	40.9	46.1	48.3	36.1	37.3	41.8	41.9
Spain	4.7	6.6	8.9	11.0	12.4	16.5	19.7	19.0	20.6	23.9	25.7	25.8	32.1	37.5	40.5	40.1	44.1	41.6	41.2
Sweden	27.9	27.9	29.5	31.6	34.7	38.6	40.2	41.2	44.6	50.4	55.6	53.7	55.9	59.8	65.7	53.4	69.1	66.5	62.9
Switzerland	18.8	22.5	24.8	26.0	28.3	28.3	29.3	30.5	33.0	37.3	42.5	45.1	48.4	51.5	51.0	43.2	48.8	53.4	56.2
Turkey	8.9	9.5	11.5	13.3	10.5	10.4	13.0	12.0	14.1	14.4	17.5	19.2	22.9	27.4	28.6	32.1	36.6	35.5	24.8
United Kingdom	27.3	27.1	27.7	28.9	32.0	32.3	33.1	35.5	38.4	39.5	41.5	43.7	47.8	53.3	53.7	50.0	52.3	53.1	55.1
OECD - Total [1]	16.9	17.8	19.2	20.5	22.4	24.2	26.3	27.9	30.9	34.5	38.3	40.3	43.8	48.6	49.7	46.2	51.5	53.3	55.9
OECD - Europe [2]	17.6	18.8	20.4	22.1	24.2	25.9	27.6	28.8	31.7	35.9	40.5	42.7	46.2	51.2	52.3	49.5	55.0	56.3	58.1
EU15	17.5	18.6	20.0	21.8	24.0	25.8	27.5	28.6	31.5	35.9	40.4	42.6	46.2	51.1	52.3	49.5	54.9	56.0	58.1

1. Excluding Korea Czech Republic Hungary and Poland.
2. Excluding Czech Republic Hungary and Poland.

Formation brute de capital fixe - indices de volume (1990 = 100) 28.

1979	1980	1981	1982	1983	1984	1985	1986	1987	1988	1989	1990	1991	1992	1993	1994	1995	1996	1997	
61.9	67.9	76.5	67.4	67.6	69.3	76.4	80.6	89.2	98.0	103.8	100.0	96.5	95.2	92.5	99.1	96.3	100.9	112.4	Canada
98.0	112.7	131.0	109.0	78.1	83.2	89.7	79.1	79.0	83.6	88.4	100.0	111.0	123.0	119.9	130.0	92.3	107.4	129.9	Mexique
89.8	83.3	82.6	75.8	80.6	92.5	97.4	98.8	98.0	100.1	101.7	100.0	93.0	98.3	104.5	112.5	119.4	131.7	141.1	États-Unis
60.7	60.5	61.8	61.7	61.0	63.6	66.8	70.0	76.4	85.2	92.2	100.0	103.3	101.7	99.7	98.9	100.7	110.3	106.4	Japon
36.3	32.4	31.2	34.6	40.6	44.7	46.6	51.5	60.3	68.6	79.4	100.0	112.6	111.7	117.6	131.4	146.8	157.2	151.6	Corée
74.0	77.8	85.2	82.8	75.8	83.3	91.5	89.2	92.5	99.4	108.9	100.0	90.7	92.8	96.3	107.4	111.6	118.6	131.7	Australie
68.8	67.8	81.8	87.5	93.2	98.5	105.3	99.3	102.8	98.1	105.5	100.0	82.4	85.4	100.9	118.3	129.2	137.5	141.5	Nouvelle-Zélande
75.4	78.3	77.7	71.9	72.2	72.3	77.3	79.2	82.6	88.3	93.8	100.0	106.3	106.4	104.3	113.1	115.3	118.1	122.4	Autriche
75.1	79.3	66.5	63.8	60.0	61.5	64.0	66.2	70.4	81.9	91.2	100.0	95.3	96.6	93.1	93.0	96.9	97.4	102.6	Belgique
..	..	..	..	..	..	..	..	..	..	..	100.0	82.3	89.6	82.7	98.5	119.1	129.4	123.1	République tchèque
97.8	85.4	69.0	73.9	75.3	85.0	95.7	112.0	107.8	100.6	100.9	100.0	97.3	96.3	94.5	101.5	113.9	119.3	131.8	Danemark
64.5	71.6	72.5	76.3	79.1	77.4	79.2	78.8	82.7	90.8	104.2	100.0	79.7	66.3	53.6	53.6	59.7	64.4	72.2	Finlande
77.8	80.0	78.4	77.2	74.5	72.7	75.0	78.4	82.4	90.3	97.2	100.0	99.9	96.7	90.0	91.1	93.4	92.9	93.2	France
82.5	84.3	80.7	76.4	78.5	78.2	78.2	81.0	83.0	86.8	91.7	100.0	109.8	113.7	107.3	111.1	111.1	109.8	109.9	Allemagne
110.4	103.2	95.5	93.6	92.4	87.2	91.7	86.0	81.6	88.9	95.2	100.0	104.8	101.5	97.9	95.2	99.3	108.0	118.4	Grèce
..	..	..	..	..	..	..	..	..	..	..	100.0	89.6	87.2	89.0	100.1	95.8	102.2	111.2	Hongrie
81.2	92.5	93.6	93.6	81.7	89.4	90.3	88.9	105.6	105.4	97.1	100.0	102.0	90.6	80.2	79.4	77.1	97.6	108.5	Islande
96.2	91.7	100.4	97.0	88.0	85.8	79.2	77.0	76.1	80.1	88.2	100.0	92.8	92.7	87.6	98.3	109.8	124.7	138.3	Irlande
79.0	85.6	83.0	78.9	78.1	80.8	81.2	82.8	86.5	92.4	96.5	100.0	100.8	99.0	86.3	86.7	92.9	93.3	93.8	Italie
61.6	69.5	64.3	64.0	56.5	56.6	51.2	67.1	79.1	91.0	97.4	100.0	131.6	119.7	153.7	130.9	135.5	133.2	143.8	Luxembourg
83.2	83.0	74.8	71.7	73.5	77.7	83.2	88.9	89.7	93.8	98.4	100.0	100.2	100.8	98.0	100.2	105.0	110.6	118.1	Pays-Bas
108.7	106.2	110.3	111.1	117.1	118.2	113.5	122.2	122.6	120.4	112.1	100.0	99.6	96.5	100.7	105.2	108.8	119.3	134.3	Norvège
..	..	..	..	..	..	..	..	..	..	..	100.0	95.6	97.8	100.7	109.9	128.5	155.0	186.8	Pologne
68.3	74.2	78.3	80.0	74.3	61.4	59.2	65.7	77.5	89.0	92.9	100.0	103.5	108.4	101.9	105.3	110.4	116.7	130.0	Portugal
59.9	60.3	58.8	60.0	58.6	54.5	57.8	63.6	72.5	82.6	93.8	100.0	101.6	97.1	86.9	89.1	96.5	97.7	102.7	Espagne
69.8	72.2	67.9	67.3	68.0	72.9	76.6	76.9	83.2	88.7	98.7	100.0	91.1	81.2	67.3	68.6	77.1	79.9	76.1	Suède
64.2	70.5	71.8	69.0	71.7	75.1	77.2	81.4	84.6	91.5	96.3	100.0	97.1	90.7	88.3	94.1	95.7	93.1	94.5	Suisse
45.5	37.9	49.9	47.0	48.2	48.7	54.3	58.8	85.3	84.4	86.3	100.0	100.4	106.8	135.0	113.4	123.8	141.2	162.1	Turquie
70.5	66.7	60.3	63.6	66.8	72.8	75.8	77.8	85.8	97.8	103.6	100.0	90.5	89.2	89.8	93.7	95.0	96.8	101.8	Royaume-Uni
75.4	74.8	74.4	71.4	72.0	76.4	79.7	82.1	85.9	91.9	97.0	100.0	99.1	99.7	98.4	101.6	104.9	111.4	115.1	OCDE - Total[1]
76.2	77.7	74.7	73.1	73.5	74.3	76.2	79.3	83.9	90.5	96.3	100.0	100.5	99.4	93.8	95.8	99.3	100.6	103.7	OCDE - Europe[2]
76.9	78.5	74.8	73.2	73.4	74.1	76.0	79.0	83.2	90.0	96.3	100.0	100.7	99.6	92.9	95.4	98.7	99.6	102.1	UE15

Exportations de biens et services - indices de volume (1990 = 100) 29.

1979	1980	1981	1982	1983	1984	1985	1986	1987	1988	1989	1990	1991	1992	1993	1994	1995	1996	1997	
56.9	57.8	59.9	58.9	62.9	74.7	78.9	83.1	86.0	94.3	95.4	100.0	102.3	110.4	123.7	138.5	151.2	160.0	172.8	Canada
44.4	47.2	52.6	64.1	72.8	76.9	73.5	77.6	85.0	89.9	95.0	100.0	105.1	110.3	119.2	140.5	182.9	216.2	244.2	Mexique
59.7	65.3	66.1	60.1	57.0	60.7	61.4	65.6	72.0	83.3	92.8	100.0	106.0	112.9	116.5	126.9	144.4	162.0	182.7	États-Unis
51.2	59.9	67.4	68.0	71.3	81.8	86.3	81.4	80.9	85.7	93.6	100.0	105.2	110.4	111.9	117.1	123.4	127.7	141.6	Japon
33.0	35.6	41.1	42.9	51.3	55.2	57.8	73.1	88.9	100.1	96.0	100.0	111.8	124.1	138.1	160.9	199.5	225.5	278.7	Corée
58.5	57.8	55.9	60.7	57.7	67.0	74.5	78.0	86.9	89.2	92.2	100.0	113.3	119.1	128.0	139.6	146.3	162.5	181.0	Australie
67.4	69.6	71.2	72.3	76.7	83.9	85.3	89.2	95.7	96.4	94.0	100.0	109.3	112.1	121.0	131.2	134.6	139.8	143.6	Nouvelle-Zélande
56.6	59.6	62.6	63.6	65.9	70.1	75.0	73.3	75.6	83.3	92.7	100.0	105.9	107.7	106.3	112.3	119.6	130.7	139.6	Autriche
65.5	65.1	67.5	69.2	70.9	75.6	75.8	77.8	81.2	88.6	95.9	100.0	103.1	106.7	106.0	114.9	121.8	124.5	133.4	Belgique
..	..	..	..	..	..	..	..	..	..	..	100.0	95.6	102.1	109.8	110.0	127.6	134.5	148.3	République tchèque
60.0	63.1	68.3	70.0	73.4	76.0	79.7	79.7	83.8	90.3	94.2	100.0	107.0	106.5	106.6	115.3	120.8	125.8	131.3	Danemark
73.8	80.1	84.3	83.4	85.1	89.4	90.4	91.5	93.9	97.4	98.7	100.0	93.4	102.7	119.9	135.8	146.9	156.0	176.0	Finlande
66.4	68.1	70.7	69.9	72.4	77.3	78.6	77.5	79.5	85.9	95.1	100.0	104.2	109.3	108.1	115.1	122.0	128.5	145.1	France
63.5	66.8	71.7	74.7	74.6	80.4	86.3	85.8	86.3	90.7	99.5	100.0	97.1	96.8	92.0	99.2	105.7	111.2	123.5	Allemagne
57.9	61.9	58.3	54.1	58.4	68.3	69.1	78.9	91.5	99.7	104.2	100.0	103.7	114.6	110.5	117.5	118.6	122.3	128.7	Grèce
..	..	..	..	..	..	..	..	..	..	..	100.0	96.9	99.0	88.9	101.1	114.7	124.3	159.4	Hongrie
75.7	77.7	80.2	73.0	81.0	83.0	92.1	97.6	100.8	97.2	100.0	100.0	94.1	92.3	98.8	108.7	106.3	116.9	123.5	Islande
41.6	44.3	45.1	47.6	52.6	61.3	65.4	67.2	76.5	83.4	92.0	100.0	105.3	119.6	131.0	149.6	178.9	200.0	233.9	Irlande
71.2	65.3	68.6	68.1	70.3	75.8	78.5	79.1	82.6	86.7	93.4	100.0	100.1	106.9	117.4	129.4	145.0	144.1	153.4	Italie
58.3	57.5	54.7	54.6	57.4	67.8	74.3	76.7	80.1	89.5	96.7	100.0	106.7	111.8	114.8	119.9	125.1	128.0	133.9	Luxembourg
64.1	65.5	66.7	66.1	68.2	73.4	77.1	78.5	81.7	89.0	94.9	100.0	104.7	107.7	109.4	116.6	124.4	130.9	139.7	Pays-Bas
57.2	59.8	60.8	60.9	65.2	70.4	75.5	77.1	78.0	83.0	92.1	100.0	106.1	111.6	115.1	125.2	130.6	143.4	151.7	Norvège
..	..	..	..	..	..	..	..	..	..	..	100.0	98.3	108.9	112.5	127.2	157.2	176.7	195.5	Pologne
45.3	46.3	44.2	46.3	52.6	58.7	62.6	66.9	74.4	80.5	90.9	100.0	102.6	107.6	103.7	112.8	123.1	135.6	146.9	Portugal
56.4	57.7	62.5	65.6	72.1	80.5	82.7	84.2	89.5	94.1	96.9	100.0	107.9	115.8	125.7	146.7	161.4	178.5	204.8	Espagne
67.5	67.0	68.4	72.4	79.5	84.9	86.1	89.3	93.1	95.4	98.4	100.0	97.7	100.0	107.6	122.6	138.5	146.9	165.7	Suède
68.8	72.3	75.4	72.3	72.9	78.3	84.6	84.3	86.2	91.8	97.9	100.0	97.9	100.9	102.4	104.2	105.9	108.5	118.3	Suisse
23.6	22.6	36.9	49.5	56.0	70.2	68.8	65.3	82.6	97.8	97.5	100.0	103.7	115.1	124.0	142.8	154.2	188.1	224.0	Turquie
71.2	71.1	70.5	71.2	72.6	77.4	81.9	85.6	90.5	91.0	95.3	100.0	99.4	103.7	107.3	117.3	126.3	135.1	145.9	Royaume-Uni
61.6	64.2	67.1	66.9	68.4	74.4	77.5	78.6	82.0	88.2	95.2	100.0	102.8	107.4	110.2	119.8	130.5	139.5	154.1	OCDE - Total[1]
64.7	65.6	68.4	69.4	71.5	77.0	80.6	81.4	84.4	89.3	96.2	100.0	101.2	104.9	106.5	115.7	124.6	131.2	144.0	OCDE - Europe[2]
65.1	65.9	68.6	69.8	71.8	77.2	80.7	81.5	84.4	89.3	96.2	100.0	101.2	104.8	106.3	115.7	125.0	131.3	144.1	UE15

Importations de biens et services - indices de volume (1990 = 100) 30.

1979	1980	1981	1982	1983	1984	1985	1986	1987	1988	1989	1990	1991	1992	1993	1994	1995	1996	1997	
50.5	53.0	58.6	49.3	54.7	64.7	70.4	76.5	80.8	92.0	97.8	100.0	103.2	109.7	118.6	129.5	138.2	145.3	164.8	Canada
63.8	84.1	99.1	61.6	40.8	48.0	53.3	49.2	51.8	70.8	83.5	100.0	115.2	137.8	140.3	170.2	144.6	177.5	216.6	Mexique
53.8	51.4	54.0	54.0	60.8	75.7	81.0	86.4	90.9	94.0	97.0	100.0	98.7	105.8	115.4	130.0	143.5	161.1	183.5	États-Unis
60.7	56.0	56.2	54.8	53.1	58.7	57.9	59.0	64.6	78.2	92.7	100.0	96.9	96.2	96.0	104.5	119.3	133.1	132.8	Japon
38.3	36.4	38.5	39.5	44.3	47.5	47.3	55.7	66.6	75.3	87.5	100.0	119.2	125.3	133.7	162.8	198.5	227.9	236.5	Corée
55.9	58.6	64.3	67.7	60.7	73.1	77.1	72.9	74.3	86.5	104.1	100.0	97.7	105.4	110.9	128.0	141.0	154.8	176.5	Australie
68.0	63.3	70.3	71.3	70.7	78.9	80.1	81.7	88.8	88.1	100.4	100.0	96.2	103.3	111.6	127.5	136.7	146.1	153.1	Nouvelle-Zélande
61.3	65.1	64.6	61.6	65.1	71.7	76.1	73.9	77.9	86.0	93.2	100.0	106.5	108.4	107.7	116.6	124.7	135.5	144.2	Autriche
70.7	68.7	67.3	68.1	67.2	71.4	71.6	74.8	79.4	87.1	95.3	100.0	102.8	107.1	106.3	113.9	119.4	122.0	129.7	Belgique
..	..	..	..	..	..	..	..	..	..	..	100.0	82.9	101.2	111.8	120.4	147.0	165.9	177.1	République tchèque
80.7	75.2	73.9	76.7	78.1	82.3	89.0	95.0	93.1	94.5	98.5	100.0	103.9	104.0	102.8	116.4	129.0	134.3	144.5	Danemark
62.6	67.9	65.1	66.5	68.6	69.7	74.1	76.1	83.1	92.3	100.6	100.0	88.3	89.2	89.9	101.4	108.5	113.4	125.3	Finlande
60.4	62.9	62.8	65.0	63.6	65.1	68.2	72.9	79.0	86.6	94.2	100.0	102.8	104.2	100.7	107.7	113.3	117.0	126.5	France
71.2	73.8	71.7	71.0	72.2	75.4	78.7	80.6	84.0	88.2	95.1	100.0	109.6	111.8	105.2	113.3	121.6	125.1	135.3	Allemagne
51.7	47.6	49.4	52.8	56.3	56.4	63.6	66.0	77.0	83.2	92.0	100.0	106.0	103.1	103.2	104.5	114.2	120.0	126.3	Grèce
..	..	..	..	..	..	..	..	..	..	..	100.0	105.4	105.7	127.1	138.3	137.3	146.4	183.8	Hongrie
78.6	80.9	86.7	86.2	77.8	84.9	92.9	93.8	115.6	110.3	99.0	100.0	105.7	97.3	88.9	92.6	96.1	112.1	121.6	Islande
63.8	60.9	62.0	60.1	62.9	69.0	71.3	75.3	80.0	83.9	95.2	100.0	101.4	108.3	114.9	130.7	150.1	166.8	191.3	Irlande
57.2	60.1	59.0	59.1	57.4	64.4	67.6	70.5	79.0	83.8	91.4	100.0	103.3	110.9	101.2	108.1	118.5	116.5	130.4	Italie
59.9	62.2	60.5	60.3	61.0	69.5	74.4	77.2	82.9	89.7	95.7	100.0	109.0	108.2	111.2	111.0	115.3	116.4	122.5	Luxembourg
71.1	71.3	67.1	66.8	69.4	72.9	77.5	80.2	83.6	89.9	96.0	100.0	104.1	106.3	104.0	111.0	119.4	125.6	134.5	Pays-Bas
76.4	78.5	79.6	83.8	81.2	85.9	93.6	104.6	97.8	95.5	97.5	100.0	100.2	100.9	105.4	110.5	116.8	126.5	142.1	Norvège
..	..	..	..	..	..	..	..	..	..	..	100.0	129.6	131.8	149.2	166.0	206.5	264.3	312.3	Pologne
47.1	50.4	51.6	53.6	50.3	48.0	48.7	56.9	70.1	82.7	87.7	100.0	107.3	118.8	114.8	125.1	134.8	145.0	160.1	Portugal
45.9	47.4	45.4	47.6	47.4	46.6	50.3	57.6	69.1	79.1	92.8	100.0	109.0	116.6	110.5	123.0	136.6	146.6	164.5	Espagne
70.2	70.5	66.7	68.7	69.3	73.0	78.0	81.5	87.8	92.5	99.3	100.0	95.1	96.2	93.8	106.1	116.9	121.3	135.5	Suède
63.2	67.8	65.6	64.3	67.9	73.5	76.2	82.4	87.6	92.1	97.5	100.0	98.4	94.2	94.2	101.7	106.9	109.8	117.7	Suisse
23.0	39.0	43.9	47.5	55.5	66.5	62.1	59.9	73.7	70.3	75.2	100.0	94.8	105.1	142.8	111.5	144.5	174.2	213.3	Turquie
60.4	58.3	56.7	59.5	63.2	69.5	71.2	76.1	82.3	92.7	99.6	100.0	94.9	101.4	104.5	110.4	115.0	124.9	136.4	Royaume-Uni
60.6	61.0	61.3	60.7	62.3	69.0	72.4	76.0	81.2	88.1	95.4	100.0	101.7	106.0	106.9	116.6	126.0	135.3	148.8	OCDE - Total[1]
63.5	64.9	63.4	64.3	65.2	69.2	72.3	76.0	81.5	87.9	95.1	100.0	103.0	106.5	104.0	111.4	119.5	124.9	136.4	OCDE - Europe[2]
63.8	64.8	63.3	64.1	64.9	68.7	71.8	75.3	81.0	87.7	95.2	100.0	103.4	107.2	103.8	111.8	119.8	124.8	136.0	UE15

1. Non compris la Corée la République tchèque la Hongrie et la Pologne.
2. Non compris la République tchèque la Hongrie et la Pologne.

31. Gross domestic product - price indices (1990 = 100)

	1960	1961	1962	1963	1964	1965	1966	1967	1968	1969	1970	1971	1972	1973	1974	1975	1976	1977	1978
Canada	19.3	19.4	19.7	20.2	20.7	21.4	22.5	23.5	24.4	25.5	26.7	27.6	29.3	32.0	36.8	40.5	44.2	47.3	50.4
Mexico	0.1	0.1	0.1	0.1	0.1	0.1	0.1	0.1	0.1	0.1	0.2	0.2	0.2	0.2	0.2	0.3	0.3	0.4	0.5
United States	22.9	23.1	23.7	24.0	24.4	25.1	26.0	26.8	28.1	29.5	31.0	32.7	34.3	36.4	39.5	43.2	46.0	49.2	52.9
Japan	23.0	24.8	25.9	27.3	28.8	30.2	31.7	33.5	35.1	36.7	39.1	41.0	43.3	48.9	59.0	63.3	68.3	72.9	76.3
Korea	..	..	..	..	..	..	..	..	..	..	7.6	8.7	10.2	11.6	15.2	19.2	23.5	27.3	33.7
Australia	12.5	12.7	12.8	13.2	13.6	14.0	14.4	14.8	15.4	16.1	16.8	17.8	19.1	21.4	25.3	29.4	33.3	36.3	39.0
New Zealand	8.2	7.9	8.4	8.5	8.9	9.1	8.9	9.6	10.2	10.3	11.6	13.0	14.3	15.6	16.1	18.4	21.8	25.4	28.6
Austria	26.1	27.5	28.6	29.6	30.6	32.3	33.3	34.4	35.4	36.3	38.0	40.4	43.5	47.0	51.4	54.8	57.8	61.1	64.8
Belgium	23.1	23.3	23.7	24.4	25.6	26.9	28.0	28.9	29.7	30.9	32.3	34.1	36.3	38.9	43.7	49.0	52.8	56.7	59.2
Czech Republic	..	..	..	..	..	..	..	..	..	..	..	..	..	..	..	..	..	..	..
Denmark	12.0	12.5	13.3	14.1	14.7	15.8	16.9	18.0	19.2	20.6	22.3	24.0	26.2	29.0	32.8	36.9	40.2	44.0	48.3
Finland	9.6	10.1	10.5	11.0	11.8	12.4	13.0	14.0	15.6	16.3	16.9	18.2	19.7	22.5	27.6	31.2	35.5	39.0	42.3
France	13.5	14.0	14.6	15.6	16.2	16.6	17.1	17.7	18.4	19.6	20.7	22.0	23.6	25.6	28.6	32.5	36.1	39.2	43.5
Germany	32.1	33.6	34.9	36.0	37.1	38.5	39.8	40.4	41.4	43.1	46.4	50.0	52.6	56.0	59.9	63.3	65.6	68.1	71.0
Greece	3.8	3.8	4.0	4.0	4.2	4.4	4.6	4.7	4.8	4.9	5.1	5.3	5.5	6.6	8.0	9.0	10.4	11.7	13.2
Hungary	..	..	..	..	..	..	..	..	..	..	..	..	..	..	..	..	..	..	..
Iceland	0.1	0.1	0.1	0.1	0.2	0.2	0.2	0.2	0.2	0.3	0.3	0.3	0.4	0.5	0.7	1.1	1.4	1.9	2.7
Ireland	8.2	8.4	8.8	9.0	9.9	10.4	10.8	11.2	11.6	12.7	13.9	15.4	17.5	20.1	21.4	25.6	31.0	35.2	38.9
Italy	5.8	6.0	6.4	6.9	7.3	7.6	7.8	8.0	8.2	8.5	9.1	9.7	10.3	11.7	14.1	16.4	19.4	23.0	26.1
Luxembourg	23.5	22.6	23.5	24.3	25.7	26.4	27.4	27.6	28.9	30.5	35.1	34.8	36.8	41.3	48.3	47.9	53.7	54.4	57.1
Netherlands	23.7	24.9	25.1	26.3	28.5	30.3	32.1	33.5	34.9	37.1	39.4	42.6	46.6	50.8	55.4	61.1	66.5	70.9	74.7
Norway	15.6	16.0	16.8	17.3	18.2	19.0	19.8	20.4	21.3	22.2	25.0	26.7	28.0	30.6	33.7	37.1	39.9	43.2	46.0
Poland	..	..	..	..	..	..	..	..	..	..	..	..	..	..	..	..	..	..	..
Portugal	3.3	3.4	3.4	3.5	3.5	3.7	3.9	4.0	4.1	4.4	4.5	4.7	5.1	5.6	6.6	7.7	8.9	11.3	13.8
Spain	5.3	5.4	5.8	6.2	6.6	7.2	7.8	8.5	9.0	9.4	10.0	10.8	11.7	13.1	15.1	17.7	20.6	25.4	30.7
Sweden	12.5	12.9	13.4	13.8	14.4	15.2	16.2	17.0	17.4	18.0	19.0	20.3	21.7	23.3	25.5	29.2	32.6	36.1	39.5
Switzerland	27.4	28.5	30.2	31.6	33.3	34.6	36.2	37.8	39.0	40.0	41.9	45.7	50.2	54.3	58.1	62.2	63.9	64.1	66.4
Turkey	0.1	0.1	0.1	0.1	0.1	0.1	0.1	0.1	0.1	0.1	0.1	0.2	0.2	0.2	0.3	0.3	0.4	0.5	0.7
United Kingdom	9.8	10.2	10.5	10.7	11.2	11.7	12.2	12.6	13.1	13.8	14.8	16.2	17.5	18.8	21.6	27.3	31.6	36.0	40.1
OECD - Total[1]	19.6	20.1	20.8	21.4	22.1	23.0	23.9	24.6	25.7	27.0	28.7	30.5	32.2	34.9	38.9	42.6	45.9	49.3	52.8
OECD - Europe[2]	17.0	17.6	18.3	18.9	19.8	20.7	21.4	21.8	22.4	23.6	25.2	27.1	28.9	31.1	34.1	37.6	40.7	44.0	47.4
EU15	16.9	17.4	18.1	18.7	19.6	20.4	21.1	21.4	22.1	23.3	24.9	26.8	28.5	30.6	33.7	37.4	40.7	44.1	47.7

32. Private final consumption expenditure - price indices (1990 = 100)

	1960	1961	1962	1963	1964	1965	1966	1967	1968	1969	1970	1971	1972	1973	1974	1975	1976	1977	1978
Canada	20.5	20.6	20.9	21.4	21.7	22.2	23.1	24.1	25.1	26.1	27.0	27.7	29.0	31.1	34.4	38.2	41.3	44.7	48.4
Mexico	0.1	0.1	0.1	0.1	0.1	0.1	0.1	0.1	0.1	0.1	0.2	0.2	0.2	0.2	0.2	0.3	0.3	0.4	0.5
United States	24.4	24.6	25.0	25.4	25.8	26.3	27.1	27.8	29.0	30.2	31.5	33.0	34.2	36.2	39.7	42.9	45.6	48.7	52.2
Japan	20.3	21.6	23.0	24.7	25.7	27.5	28.8	29.9	31.4	32.7	35.1	37.5	39.7	44.1	53.3	59.4	65.2	70.1	73.3
Korea	..	..	..	..	..	..	..	..	..	..	8.6	9.9	11.4	12.7	17.1	21.9	25.6	29.7	36.0
Australia	12.7	13.0	13.0	13.2	13.6	14.0	14.5	14.9	15.4	16.0	16.8	18.0	19.1	20.8	24.1	28.1	32.1	35.3	38.3
New Zealand	8.0	8.0	8.1	8.2	8.5	8.8	9.0	9.7	10.0	10.3	11.1	12.4	13.1	13.9	15.2	17.5	20.8	24.0	26.6
Austria	27.3	28.4	29.6	30.4	31.5	32.9	33.7	35.0	35.9	37.0	38.5	40.4	43.0	45.9	50.5	54.4	58.0	61.3	63.7
Belgium	23.6	24.2	24.4	25.3	26.4	27.7	28.8	29.5	30.4	31.2	32.1	33.8	35.7	37.7	42.6	47.8	51.6	55.3	57.6
Czech Republic	..	..	..	..	..	..	..	..	..	..	..	..	..	..	..	..	..	..	..
Denmark	12.1	12.5	13.3	14.0	14.6	15.4	16.4	17.7	18.9	19.8	21.1	22.9	24.7	27.6	31.7	34.9	38.3	42.4	46.3
Finland	11.4	11.8	12.2	12.9	13.9	14.5	15.0	16.0	17.5	17.8	18.1	19.4	21.0	23.6	28.2	32.9	37.2	41.6	44.9
France	13.5	14.0	14.6	15.4	15.9	16.3	16.9	17.4	18.2	19.5	20.5	21.8	23.2	25.0	28.7	32.3	35.5	38.9	42.5
Germany	36.6	37.8	38.9	40.1	41.0	42.3	43.8	44.5	45.3	46.1	47.7	50.2	53.0	56.4	60.5	64.1	66.8	69.0	70.8
Greece	4.2	4.3	4.3	4.5	4.6	4.8	4.9	5.0	5.1	5.2	5.4	5.6	5.7	6.6	8.1	9.2	10.4	11.7	13.2
Hungary	..	..	..	..	..	..	..	..	..	..	..	..	..	..	..	..	..	..	..
Iceland	0.1	0.1	0.1	0.1	0.2	0.2	0.2	0.2	0.2	0.3	0.3	0.3	0.4	0.5	0.7	1.0	1.3	1.7	2.4
Ireland	8.2	8.4	8.8	9.0	9.6	10.0	10.4	10.7	11.2	12.1	13.6	14.9	16.3	18.2	21.0	24.8	29.8	34.0	36.7
Italy	6.8	6.9	7.3	7.8	8.2	8.5	8.7	9.0	9.1	9.4	9.9	10.4	11.1	12.6	15.3	17.8	20.9	24.4	27.6
Luxembourg	25.5	25.6	25.8	26.6	27.4	28.3	29.3	29.9	30.7	31.3	32.6	34.1	35.9	37.6	41.4	45.6	49.9	52.7	54.5
Netherlands	25.9	27.9	27.2	28.2	30.1	31.3	33.0	34.0	34.8	37.0	38.6	41.6	45.1	48.9	53.6	59.0	64.3	68.2	71.2
Norway	14.5	15.0	15.6	16.1	16.8	17.5	18.2	19.0	19.6	20.3	22.2	23.7	25.2	27.2	29.7	33.1	36.0	39.1	42.3
Poland	..	..	..	..	..	..	..	..	..	..	..	..	..	..	..	..	..	..	..
Portugal	3.2	3.3	3.3	3.3	3.6	3.8	4.1	4.2	3.9	4.1	4.2	4.4	4.6	5.0	6.2	7.4	8.6	10.9	13.3
Spain	5.7	5.8	6.1	6.6	7.1	7.7	8.3	8.8	9.2	9.5	10.1	10.9	11.7	13.0	15.3	17.7	20.6	25.5	30.4
Sweden	12.2	12.5	13.0	13.4	13.9	14.6	15.6	16.4	16.7	17.3	18.2	19.6	20.8	22.4	24.7	27.4	30.4	33.7	37.6
Switzerland	29.6	30.5	32.0	33.1	34.5	35.9	37.6	39.2	40.2	41.4	43.0	46.0	49.5	54.0	59.4	63.3	64.7	65.4	65.8
Turkey	0.1	0.1	0.1	0.1	0.1	0.1	0.1	0.1	0.1	0.1	0.1	0.1	0.2	0.2	0.3	0.3	0.4	0.4	0.6
United Kingdom	11.0	11.3	11.7	11.9	12.3	12.9	13.4	13.8	14.4	15.2	16.1	17.5	18.6	20.2	23.6	29.2	33.7	38.7	42.4
OECD - Total[1]	20.4	20.8	21.4	22.0	22.6	23.4	24.3	24.9	25.8	26.9	28.3	29.9	31.4	33.8	37.9	41.8	45.1	48.6	51.7
OECD - Europe[2]	17.9	18.5	19.1	19.6	20.3	21.2	21.9	22.3	23.0	23.9	25.1	26.7	28.3	30.4	33.8	37.4	40.6	43.9	46.9
EU15	17.8	18.4	19.0	19.5	20.2	21.1	21.8	22.2	22.8	23.8	24.9	26.5	28.1	30.1	33.5	37.3	40.7	44.3	47.5

33. Government final consumption expenditure - price indices (1990 = 100)

	1960	1961	1962	1963	1964	1965	1966	1967	1968	1969	1970	1971	1972	1973	1974	1975	1976	1977	1978
Canada	13.3	13.8	14.2	14.6	15.1	15.8	17.1	18.3	19.5	21.2	22.6	24.0	25.8	27.9	31.9	36.2	40.8	44.2	47.3
Mexico	0.1	0.1	0.1	0.1	0.1	0.1	0.1	0.1	0.1	0.2	0.2	0.2	0.2	0.2	0.3	0.3	0.4	0.6	0.7
United States	16.8	17.5	18.2	18.7	19.2	19.9	21.0	22.1	23.4	24.8	26.8	29.0	31.2	34.0	37.2	40.9	44.0	47.2	50.5
Japan	12.3	13.5	14.6	16.0	17.6	19.4	20.8	22.3	24.2	26.5	29.6	32.3	36.1	42.4	55.8	60.3	63.8	68.0	70.0
Korea	..	..	..	..	..	..	..	..	..	..	4.1	4.9	6.0	6.5	9.4	13.4	17.6	21.0	25.2
Australia	10.4	10.7	11.0	11.2	11.9	12.3	12.8	13.4	13.9	14.6	15.7	17.5	18.9	21.3	25.9	31.3	35.4	38.8	41.4
New Zealand	5.5	5.7	6.0	6.1	6.6	7.4	7.7	7.8	8.2	8.8	10.1	11.3	12.3	13.6	15.4	17.6	19.9	23.3	27.1
Austria	14.1	15.0	15.8	17.0	17.8	19.2	20.5	22.3	23.5	25.7	27.2	29.6	32.1	36.4	41.0	45.8	49.6	52.4	57.1
Belgium	19.7	19.7	20.0	20.3	21.1	22.2	23.4	24.3	25.4	26.5	28.2	30.7	33.4	36.1	41.4	48.9	53.4	57.7	60.5
Czech Republic	..	..	..	..	..	..	..	..	..	..	..	..	..	..	..	..	..	..	..
Denmark	8.3	9.5	10.2	10.8	11.5	13.1	14.3	15.2	16.9	18.2	20.0	22.3	24.2	26.8	31.8	36.6	39.9	43.0	46.2
Finland	6.8	7.2	7.6	8.2	9.2	9.8	10.5	11.5	12.8	13.4	14.1	15.4	16.8	19.0	23.3	28.0	31.6	34.3	36.1
France	9.5	10.0	10.7	11.8	12.4	12.8	13.3	13.8	14.8	16.0	17.3	18.8	20.2	22.3	26.3	30.7	34.8	38.9	43.2
Germany	22.4	23.9	25.1	26.6	27.3	29.2	30.7	31.4	32.3	34.8	38.2	43.3	46.2	50.9	57.0	60.7	63.1	66.0	68.4
Greece	2.4	2.5	2.5	2.6	2.8	2.9	3.1	3.4	3.6	3.7	3.9	4.1	4.3	4.9	6.1	7.2	8.3	9.7	11.2
Hungary	..	..	..	..	..	..	..	..	..	..	..	..	..	..	..	..	..	..	..
Iceland	0.1	0.1	0.1	0.1	0.1	0.2	0.2	0.2	0.2	0.2	0.3	0.3	0.4	0.5	0.8	1.0	1.3	1.8	2.8
Ireland	5.6	5.9	6.2	6.5	7.6	7.9	8.3	8.5	9.1	9.9	10.9	11.9	13.4	15.5	17.5	22.1	25.7	29.1	32.1
Italy	3.3	3.5	3.9	4.6	5.0	5.4	5.6	5.7	5.9	6.2	6.6	7.7	8.3	9.3	11.0	12.4	14.5	17.8	20.9
Luxembourg	12.8	12.9	14.5	16.5	16.7	17.3	17.9	18.3	18.9	19.4	20.8	22.9	24.9	28.1	33.5	39.2	43.3	46.6	49.3
Netherlands	16.1	17.2	18.6	20.4	23.9	26.2	28.7	31.5	33.4	36.4	39.5	44.3	49.2	54.7	63.4	71.8	78.4	83.4	83.4
Norway	12.2	12.5	13.9	14.4	15.0	15.7	16.9	17.6	18.6	19.6	21.4	23.8	25.5	27.6	30.9	35.1	38.8	41.9	44.3
Poland	..	..	..	..	..	..	..	..	..	..	..	..	..	..	..	..	..	..	..
Portugal	4.4	4.4	4.4	4.5	4.5	4.6	4.8	5.3	5.4	5.6	6.3	6.4	6.8	7.4	8.3	9.2	9.8	12.0	14.3
Spain	3.2	3.4	3.7	4.1	4.4	5.1	6.0	7.2	7.7	8.5	9.2	10.1	11.1	12.6	14.7	17.3	21.0	26.1	31.5
Sweden	8.8	9.2	9.9	10.1	10.9	11.8	13.0	13.9	14.6	15.2	16.3	18.1	19.5	21.1	23.7	27.3	31.1	36.3	39.3
Switzerland	22.9	24.0	25.7	27.1	29.0	29.9	31.2	32.7	33.9	35.5	37.6	42.0	46.2	51.9	57.3	61.3	63.0	63.5	64.2
Turkey	0.1	0.1	0.1	0.1	0.1	0.1	0.1	0.1	0.1	0.1	0.2	0.2	0.2	0.3	0.3	0.4	0.5	0.6	0.9
United Kingdom	6.7	7.0	7.3	7.5	7.9	8.4	8.9	9.3	9.9	10.5	11.6	12.9	14.1	15.4	18.9	24.7	28.6	31.7	35.0
OECD - Total[1]	13.9	14.6	15.4	16.1	16.7	17.6	18.7	19.6	20.7	22.1	24.0	26.3	28.3	31.3	35.7	39.7	43.0	46.3	49.5
OECD - Europe[2]	11.6	12.3	13.3	14.2	14.8	15.9	16.7	17.3	18.0	19.5	21.2	23.8	25.6	28.3	32.5	36.4	39.6	42.9	46.2
EU15	11.4	12.1	13.0	13.9	14.6	15.6	16.5	17.1	17.7	19.2	20.9	23.5	25.3	27.9	32.1	36.2	39.4	42.9	46.2

1. Excluding Korea Czech Republic Hungary and Poland.
2. Excluding Czech Republic Hungary and Poland.

Produit intérieur brut - indices de prix (1990 = 100) 31.

1979	1980	1981	1982	1983	1984	1985	1986	1987	1988	1989	1990	1991	1992	1993	1994	1995	1996	1997	
55.3	61.4	68.1	74.0	77.7	80.4	82.3	84.5	88.6	92.6	97.0	100.0	102.6	103.9	105.2	106.5	109.4	110.9	111.4	Canada
0.6	0.8	1.0	1.6	3.0	4.7	7.4	12.9	30.9	61.7	78.0	100.0	123.3	141.0	154.4	167.2	230.5	298.6	354.7	Mexique
57.6	63.1	69.6	73.8	77.1	80.7	83.5	85.6	88.4	91.8	95.8	100.0	103.9	106.6	109.5	112.0	114.2	115.9	118.0	États-Unis
78.4	82.7	86.0	87.6	89.1	91.5	93.4	95.1	95.1	95.8	97.7	100.0	102.7	104.5	105.1	105.3	104.6	104.1	104.7	Japon
40.5	50.6	59.5	63.5	66.8	70.4	73.7	77.1	81.0	86.4	91.0	100.0	110.1	116.8	122.7	129.4	136.7	141.4	144.7	Corée
43.1	47.8	52.4	58.2	63.1	67.2	70.9	75.7	81.8	88.9	95.6	100.0	102.3	103.7	105.1	106.3	109.0	111.2	113.5	Australie
32.8	37.8	43.7	48.4	52.2	56.2	64.2	76.0	85.2	92.2	97.4	100.0	101.3	103.3	105.3	107.0	109.1	110.5	111.5	Nouvelle-Zélande
67.0	70.4	75.0	79.0	81.9	85.7	88.3	90.7	92.6	94.1	96.7	100.0	103.7	108.2	111.2	114.3	116.8	119.2	120.8	Autriche
61.9	64.4	68.0	72.6	76.8	80.7	85.6	88.8	90.7	92.6	96.9	100.0	103.1	107.0	111.2	113.7	115.4	117.3	118.9	Belgique
..	..	..	..	..	..	..	..	..	..	..	100.0	146.2	170.8	201.3	223.1	246.4	269.4	287.2	République tchèque
52.0	56.3	62.0	68.5	73.7	77.9	81.3	85.0	89.0	92.0	96.7	100.0	102.5	104.8	105.3	106.9	108.7	110.8	112.9	Danemark
46.0	50.5	56.1	61.1	66.3	72.2	76.0	79.5	83.2	89.1	94.5	100.0	102.5	103.2	105.7	107.0	109.6	110.5	113.0	Finlande
47.9	53.6	60.0	67.2	73.7	79.2	83.8	88.3	90.9	93.7	96.9	100.0	103.3	105.6	108.1	110.0	111.6	113.1	114.3	France
73.7	77.3	80.2	83.5	85.9	87.6	89.3	91.8	93.3	94.7	96.7	100.0	104.7	110.5	115.0	117.7	120.3	121.6	122.4	Allemagne
15.7	18.5	22.1	27.7	33.0	39.7	46.7	54.9	62.7	72.5	82.9	100.0	119.8	137.5	157.5	175.1	192.3	207.5	221.8	Grèce
..	..	..	..	..	..	..	..	..	..	..	100.0	125.4	152.4	184.8	220.8	277.3	336.0	398.0	Hongrie
3.8	5.8	8.7	13.4	23.5	29.5	38.8	48.7	58.2	71.4	85.6	100.0	107.8	111.7	114.4	116.7	119.9	122.2	126.3	Islande
44.2	50.7	59.5	68.5	75.9	80.7	84.9	90.5	92.5	95.5	100.7	100.0	101.7	104.1	108.7	110.0	110.5	112.2	114.7	Irlande
30.3	36.7	43.7	51.1	58.8	65.6	71.5	77.1	81.9	87.4	92.9	100.0	107.7	112.7	117.7	121.7	127.9	134.2	137.8	Italie
60.8	65.6	70.3	77.9	83.2	86.9	89.5	91.9	92.8	93.4	96.7	100.0	101.5	105.8	106.6	112.3	113.1	113.1	117.1	Luxembourg
77.8	82.1	86.5	91.1	93.0	94.3	96.0	96.1	95.4	96.6	97.7	100.0	102.7	105.0	107.1	109.6	111.6	113.2	115.7	Pays-Bas
48.6	54.9	62.0	68.4	73.2	77.9	81.9	81.1	86.8	91.1	96.3	100.0	102.4	102.0	104.2	104.0	107.2	111.7	114.8	Norvège
..	..	..	..	..	..	..	..	..	..	..	100.0	155.2	214.9	280.6	360.2	461.8	547.1	627.7	Pologne
16.5	19.9	23.4	28.3	35.3	44.0	53.5	64.4	71.0	78.9	88.7	100.0	112.2	123.4	131.7	139.9	147.1	151.3	154.4	Portugal
35.8	40.6	45.7	52.1	58.3	65.1	70.1	77.8	82.4	87.0	93.2	100.0	107.1	114.5	119.4	124.2	130.2	134.3	137.1	Espagne
42.6	47.6	52.2	56.5	62.2	66.9	71.3	76.2	79.9	85.0	91.9	100.0	107.6	108.8	111.6	114.3	118.5	119.7	121.2	Suède
67.7	69.5	73.5	78.5	80.6	83.4	85.4	88.1	90.5	93.0	95.9	100.0	106.0	108.9	111.8	113.7	114.9	115.4	115.2	Suisse
1.2	2.2	3.2	4.1	5.2	7.6	11.7	15.9	21.3	36.0	63.2	100.0	158.8	260.1	436.3	900.7	1686.2	2998.7	5443.9	Turquie
45.9	54.6	60.8	65.5	69.1	72.1	76.4	78.8	82.7	87.7	94.0	100.0	106.6	111.5	115.0	116.9	119.7	123.3	126.4	Royaume-Uni
56.7	61.7	66.9	71.2	75.0	78.6	81.7	84.7	87.5	91.1	95.4	100.0	105.0	109.5	114.3	120.6	131.6	148.1	177.7	OCDE - Total[1]
51.2	56.3	61.4	66.6	71.3	75.4	79.3	83.0	86.0	89.8	94.5	100.0	106.6	113.2	121.5	133.8	155.8	191.8	258.2	OCDE - Europe[2]
51.7	56.9	62.0	67.4	72.2	76.5	80.4	84.3	87.3	90.8	95.1	100.0	105.5	110.1	114.2	117.1	120.6	123.5	125.7	UE15

Consommation finale privée - indices de prix (1990 = 100) 32.

1979	1980	1981	1982	1983	1984	1985	1986	1987	1988	1989	1990	1991	1992	1993	1994	1995	1996	1997	
52.7	58.0	64.6	71.1	75.6	78.8	81.8	85.1	88.5	91.8	96.0	100.0	104.7	106.2	108.6	109.3	110.9	112.5	114.4	Canada
0.6	0.7	0.9	1.4	2.7	4.4	7.0	12.7	29.9	62.5	78.2	100.0	124.3	143.4	158.0	170.0	227.8	293.8	353.8	Mexique
56.8	62.7	68.3	72.3	75.7	78.9	81.7	83.9	87.2	90.8	95.2	100.0	104.0	107.3	110.2	112.7	115.2	117.5	119.7	États-Unis
76.0	81.7	85.4	87.8	89.6	91.9	94.0	94.7	95.1	95.5	97.5	100.0	102.5	104.4	105.6	106.4	105.8	105.9	107.7	Japon
43.6	55.6	66.2	70.4	72.4	74.9	77.8	79.2	81.8	86.5	91.2	100.0	109.0	115.3	120.9	128.5	134.6	141.9	148.1	Corée
42.0	46.5	50.8	56.0	61.2	65.1	69.9	75.6	81.9	88.3	94.3	100.0	103.7	105.7	107.9	109.0	111.5	113.8	115.3	Australie
31.2	36.8	42.3	49.0	51.8	56.8	66.2	75.1	83.3	88.6	94.7	100.0	102.2	103.8	105.6	107.5	110.4	112.2	113.1	Nouvelle-Zélande
66.5	70.5	75.6	80.1	83.2	87.5	90.4	91.9	92.6	94.1	96.6	100.0	103.0	107.0	110.5	114.1	115.9	118.8	121.1	Autriche
59.9	63.9	69.1	74.3	79.4	84.2	89.0	89.9	92.0	93.1	96.8	100.0	103.2	105.7	109.1	112.1	114.5	117.1	119.2	Belgique
..	..	..	..	..	..	..	..	..	..	..	100.0	156.2	174.5	188.8	206.4	225.3	243.3	262.4	République tchèque
51.2	56.6	63.5	70.0	74.7	79.5	82.9	85.3	89.2	92.7	97.4	100.0	102.7	103.9	105.0	107.6	108.6	110.5	112.8	Danemark
48.6	54.0	60.3	65.8	71.2	76.1	80.4	82.9	85.9	89.9	94.3	100.0	105.6	110.0	114.6	116.2	116.5	118.4	120.3	Finlande
47.2	53.5	60.6	67.8	74.4	80.3	85.2	87.8	90.7	93.4	96.9	100.0	103.3	105.9	108.3	110.7	112.5	114.7	116.2	France
73.7	78.0	82.9	87.0	89.8	92.1	93.7	93.2	93.6	94.9	97.6	100.0	104.7	109.7	114.1	117.5	119.6	122.0	124.3	Allemagne
15.3	18.7	22.9	27.7	32.7	38.5	45.5	55.6	64.3	73.5	83.4	100.0	119.7	138.4	158.1	175.5	191.0	206.8	218.2	Grèce
..	..	..	..	..	..	..	..	..	..	..	100.0	132.5	161.9	195.3	233.2	297.8	367.1	432.7	Hongrie
3.5	5.5	8.3	12.5	22.9	30.0	39.8	47.8	55.4	69.5	85.7	100.0	106.9	111.9	117.0	119.0	121.1	124.0	126.2	Islande
42.2	50.0	59.8	68.8	75.1	80.6	84.6	88.5	90.7	94.1	98.0	100.0	103.0	105.6	107.6	110.6	112.9	114.5	115.5	Irlande
31.9	38.4	45.4	53.1	60.9	68.2	74.5	79.1	83.4	88.3	94.1	100.0	106.9	112.9	119.0	124.5	131.8	137.4	140.9	Italie
57.2	61.5	66.7	73.8	79.9	85.1	88.8	89.2	90.5	93.0	96.3	100.0	102.8	106.3	110.7	113.3	115.7	117.6	118.6	Luxembourg
74.7	79.8	84.8	89.1	91.7	93.5	95.7	95.9	96.1	96.7	97.8	100.0	103.2	106.4	108.7	111.7	113.2	115.0	117.4	Pays-Bas
44.6	48.7	55.0	61.2	66.3	70.5	74.7	79.7	85.9	91.1	95.5	100.0	103.9	106.6	108.8	110.1	112.7	114.3	117.1	Norvège
..	..	..	..	..	..	..	..	..	..	..	100.0	167.8	241.9	318.0	419.8	537.1	641.8	736.2	Pologne
16.6	20.2	24.3	29.2	36.7	47.2	56.4	64.1	70.5	78.6	89.0	100.0	112.2	123.2	131.2	138.5	144.8	149.9	152.9	Portugal
35.4	40.9	46.9	53.7	60.5	67.7	72.5	79.3	83.9	88.1	93.9	100.0	106.4	113.2	119.5	125.4	131.3	135.7	139.1	Espagne
40.6	45.6	51.1	56.5	62.6	67.5	72.2	75.9	80.1	85.0	91.0	100.0	110.3	112.8	119.2	122.7	126.0	127.5	130.3	Suède
68.7	71.8	75.8	80.2	82.8	85.2	88.1	89.2	90.6	92.3	95.1	100.0	106.0	110.5	114.2	115.5	117.5	118.7	119.4	Suisse
1.1	2.1	3.1	3.9	4.9	7.3	11.1	14.4	21.4	34.1	62.6	100.0	160.7	266.0	441.3	921.7	1773.0	2975.6	5420.0	Turquie
48.2	56.1	62.3	67.7	71.0	74.5	78.5	81.6	85.2	89.4	94.7	100.0	107.5	112.9	116.7	119.4	122.5	125.6	128.3	Royaume-Uni
55.7	61.1	66.3	70.9	74.9	78.5	81.7	84.1	87.1	90.7	95.1	100.0	105.4	110.3	115.7	123.0	135.1	152.5	185.8	OCDE - Total[1]
50.8	56.1	62.0	67.5	72.4	76.9	81.0	83.6	86.5	89.9	94.8	100.0	107.0	114.3	123.7	138.7	164.6	203.2	281.3	OCDE - Europe[2]
51.5	57.1	63.0	68.7	73.9	78.7	82.7	85.3	88.1	91.2	95.6	100.0	105.7	110.5	115.1	118.8	122.4	125.7	128.4	UE15

Consommation finale des administrations publiques - indices de prix (1990 = 100) 33.

1979	1980	1981	1982	1983	1984	1985	1986	1987	1988	1989	1990	1991	1992	1993	1994	1995	1996	1997	
51.7	56.7	63.7	71.0	74.9	77.8	80.6	83.1	86.7	90.0	94.8	100.0	104.1	107.2	108.4	109.6	111.0	111.0	110.8	Canada
0.8	1.0	1.3	2.0	3.0	4.8	7.7	12.5	29.9	59.7	75.7	100.0	131.9	168.0	203.4	234.3	277.6	355.1	380.9	Mexique
55.2	61.3	67.5	72.4	76.5	80.2	83.8	86.1	89.2	92.0	95.3	100.0	103.9	107.1	110.2	112.8	116.7	120.4	123.3	États-Unis
73.1	77.7	80.8	82.2	83.7	86.1	89.4	89.8	90.0	91.2	94.9	100.0	104.5	107.2	108.4	108.2	108.5	109.0	110.4	Japon
30.6	40.5	48.6	54.8	58.5	61.2	66.0	70.2	74.9	81.0	89.8	100.0	112.4	123.0	131.4	142.3	156.7	168.1	178.6	Corée
44.8	50.1	55.8	63.7	67.7	72.3	76.7	81.8	85.2	89.8	94.6	100.0	104.3	107.4	110.5	109.9	111.4	114.0	115.8	Australie
31.6	39.1	46.3	51.4	52.7	55.9	63.7	77.0	86.1	92.6	96.1	100.0	99.9	100.2	100.5	101.1	103.7	105.5	108.0	Nouvelle-Zélande
59.9	63.2	67.6	72.0	75.4	78.8	82.8	86.8	89.8	91.9	95.7	100.0	106.4	112.9	118.6	122.6	126.5	128.8	130.0	Autriche
63.7	68.7	74.1	79.3	81.5	85.1	89.0	90.8	91.1	92.0	95.8	100.0	105.3	109.2	114.2	117.6	121.2	121.9	125.5	Belgique
..	..	..	..	..	..	..	..	..	..	..	100.0	132.3	165.8	229.3	271.5	305.3	337.1	355.6	République tchèque
49.7	54.7	60.6	68.0	73.0	76.2	79.1	80.6	87.0	92.2	96.7	100.0	103.9	107.0	108.1	109.1	110.6	113.2	115.9	Danemark
39.5	44.3	49.8	55.0	60.6	66.2	72.1	76.0	80.1	85.4	91.9	100.0	106.7	108.9	108.9	111.0	114.5	116.9	119.3	Finlande
47.7	54.3	61.5	70.0	76.5	82.6	86.1	89.3	91.0	92.7	96.4	100.0	103.0	106.3	109.1	110.7	113.5	115.3	116.6	France
71.6	76.0	79.8	82.5	84.8	86.3	88.2	90.0	92.0	93.4	96.4	100.0	107.3	114.2	118.2	120.1	122.7	122.7	123.2	Allemagne
13.4	16.0	19.7	24.7	29.5	36.7	45.2	51.6	58.7	69.3	82.9	100.0	118.3	136.4	155.8	172.0	203.3	208.8	234.0	Grèce
..	..	..	..	..	..	..	..	..	..	..	100.0	134.0	164.9	194.9	237.9	294.5	346.0	413.1	Hongrie
4.1	6.2	9.2	14.3	23.7	28.8	38.8	49.3	62.7	77.6	90.0	100.0	108.3	112.3	115.8	117.8	122.3	129.2	134.6	Islande
38.0	46.1	55.8	63.3	68.6	74.1	78.4	82.0	86.9	90.6	95.1	100.0	107.0	112.9	121.1	123.2	126.6	130.1	135.3	Irlande
25.5	31.6	40.3	46.3	53.2	59.4	65.0	69.4	75.5	82.6	88.1	100.0	107.4	112.1	115.0	118.7	121.7	130.6	136.9	Italie
53.6	59.1	64.8	67.6	70.0	74.0	78.8	81.8	86.5	86.7	91.0	100.0	102.8	108.8	113.5	117.9	127.1	130.6	131.9	Luxembourg
93.2	96.9	98.2	100.3	100.6	100.0	99.4	97.2	97.6	96.9	97.5	100.0	103.1	107.1	109.6	111.3	115.1	116.2	118.3	Pays-Bas
46.0	50.3	55.6	61.3	66.1	70.4	75.0	80.5	88.4	93.1	97.1	100.0	103.4	105.2	106.8	109.2	113.5	116.9	120.1	Norvège
..	..	..	..	..	..	..	..	..	..	..	100.0	153.9	195.6	242.0	291.8	384.3	463.9	544.7	Pologne
16.9	20.8	24.3	28.7	34.9	42.3	51.3	59.4	66.2	75.7	86.8	100.0	115.5	129.3	139.9	146.2	155.5	166.1	176.1	Portugal
36.8	43.3	49.4	55.1	62.5	67.8	73.2	79.3	83.8	87.5	93.2	100.0	107.6	117.6	121.7	125.1	130.6	136.1	137.9	Espagne
43.2	48.9	52.9	57.2	62.2	66.1	70.0	74.4	77.4	81.7	89.0	100.0	103.1	105.3	106.0	109.4	113.0	117.8	121.9	Suède
66.9	70.0	74.3	79.5	81.7	83.8	86.5	88.0	88.7	91.4	94.9	100.0	105.7	110.0	110.3	110.7	111.1	111.9	110.5	Suisse
1.4	2.4	3.1	4.0	5.1	6.7	9.4	12.6	14.6	24.9	53.2	100.0	174.4	303.7	513.6	949.3	1651.2	3104.5	6166.5	Turquie
39.9	49.5	55.8	60.3	64.4	67.7	71.6	75.7	80.7	86.2	92.4	100.0	107.1	114.0	119.2	122.0	124.8	127.2	129.4	Royaume-Uni
53.6	59.4	64.9	69.6	73.6	77.1	80.6	83.3	86.5	89.8	94.1	100.0	105.7	111.0	115.9	120.9	129.3	143.8	169.7	OCDE - Total[1]
50.2	56.2	61.6	66.6	70.9	74.6	78.2	81.3	84.7	88.4	93.2	100.0	107.0	114.2	120.8	128.6	142.1	167.3	217.4	OCDE - Europe[2]
50.3	56.4	62.1	67.0	71.4	75.2	78.8	82.1	85.5	89.0	93.6	100.0	106.2	111.9	115.6	118.3	121.7	124.7	127.2	UE15

1. Non compris la Corée la République tchèque la Hongrie et la Pologne.
2. Non compris la République tchèque la Hongrie et la Pologne.

34. Gross fixed capital formation - prices indices (1990 = 100)

	1960	1961	1962	1963	1964	1965	1966	1967	1968	1969	1970	1971	1972	1973	1974	1975	1976	1977	1978
Canada	27.0	26.8	27.1	27.9	28.9	30.4	32.0	32.8	33.2	34.7	36.2	38.1	40.5	44.7	52.0	57.5	61.4	64.7	68.2
Mexico	0.1	0.1	0.1	0.1	0.1	0.1	0.1	0.1	0.1	0.1	0.1	0.1	0.2	0.2	0.2	0.3	0.3	0.4	0.5
United States	23.4	23.3	23.6	23.7	24.0	24.6	25.6	26.4	27.6	29.4	31.0	32.8	34.3	36.4	40.7	46.0	48.7	52.5	57.4
Japan	34.0	36.7	36.8	36.9	37.7	37.6	39.0	40.8	41.7	42.8	44.4	45.0	46.7	54.3	67.7	70.3	73.7	77.3	79.5
Korea	..	..	..	..	..	..	..	..	..	..	10.9	11.7	13.1	15.2	21.2	26.1	28.2	31.2	36.0
Australia	12.4	12.5	12.7	12.8	13.2	13.6	13.9	14.4	14.9	15.4	16.1	17.3	18.4	20.2	24.1	29.1	33.2	36.6	39.5
New Zealand	9.8	9.9	10.0	10.0	10.3	10.6	10.7	11.2	12.6	13.0	14.5	15.9	16.8	17.5	20.2	25.7	30.4	34.2	39.4
Austria	30.0	31.1	31.7	33.3	33.8	36.1	36.8	37.4	37.7	38.3	40.3	42.6	47.1	50.2	54.8	57.4	59.6	63.0	66.6
Belgium	22.6	22.8	23.7	24.8	26.2	27.3	28.2	29.3	29.8	31.1	34.0	36.9	38.6	41.1	47.9	53.3	57.1	60.5	63.2
Czech Republic	..	..	..	..	..	..	..	..	..	..	..	..	..	..	..	..	..	..	..
Denmark	13.3	13.9	14.7	15.2	15.7	16.6	17.4	18.3	19.3	20.6	22.4	23.8	25.4	28.4	33.8	37.9	40.9	44.8	48.5
Finland	8.7	9.0	9.4	9.8	10.2	10.7	11.1	11.7	13.0	13.6	14.9	16.5	18.3	21.2	26.8	30.6	33.8	37.1	39.1
France	14.9	15.5	16.1	17.1	17.8	18.2	18.7	19.2	19.4	20.3	21.6	22.9	24.3	26.4	30.9	34.9	39.0	42.6	46.6
Germany	28.7	30.6	32.8	34.1	35.1	35.9	36.8	36.4	36.8	39.1	44.5	47.9	49.7	52.3	56.2	58.4	60.8	63.1	66.2
Greece	3.0	3.0	3.3	3.3	3.4	3.5	3.8	3.9	4.0	4.1	4.4	4.6	5.0	6.0	7.5	8.3	9.7	11.4	13.5
Hungary	..	..	..	..	..	..	..	..	..	..	..	..	..	..	..	..	..	..	..
Iceland	0.1	0.1	0.1	0.1	0.2	0.2	0.2	0.2	0.2	0.3	0.3	0.4	0.5	0.6	0.8	1.2	1.6	1.9	2.9
Ireland	8.6	9.0	9.3	9.7	10.5	10.5	10.6	11.0	11.4	12.2	13.9	15.1	17.0	18.8	22.9	27.9	33.2	38.7	43.0
Italy	5.5	5.6	5.9	6.3	6.8	6.9	7.0	7.2	7.3	7.7	8.6	9.1	9.6	11.5	14.9	17.5	21.3	25.3	28.9
Luxembourg	17.1	18.2	19.0	20.6	21.6	21.8	23.0	22.6	23.8	25.1	28.4	32.1	33.1	35.3	41.7	47.1	50.8	52.6	54.7
Netherlands	24.3	24.8	25.5	26.6	28.2	29.4	31.0	31.5	32.0	33.9	37.2	40.5	43.6	46.7	52.5	58.0	62.6	67.5	71.8
Norway	15.7	15.8	16.0	16.7	16.8	17.6	18.2	18.4	18.3	19.8	21.6	22.7	24.5	25.8	29.7	34.0	37.7	41.7	44.8
Poland	..	..	..	..	..	..	..	..	..	..	..	..	..	..	..	..	..	..	..
Portugal	2.9	2.9	3.0	3.0	3.0	3.0	3.1	3.5	3.5	3.6	3.7	4.0	4.5	5.0	6.3	7.8	9.3	11.7	14.7
Spain	6.5	6.6	7.0	7.5	7.9	8.2	8.5	9.1	9.6	10.1	10.8	11.5	12.4	14.0	17.1	19.8	22.7	27.9	33.2
Sweden	13.5	13.9	14.5	15.0	15.8	16.8	17.5	18.1	18.3	18.6	19.5	20.7	22.0	23.5	26.8	29.8	33.5	37.4	41.2
Switzerland	31.3	33.6	35.6	38.0	39.8	40.9	42.3	43.2	43.9	45.3	49.5	54.3	59.5	63.8	67.8	67.9	65.9	67.1	68.0
Turkey	0.1	0.1	0.1	0.1	0.1	0.1	0.1	0.1	0.1	0.1	0.1	0.2	0.2	0.2	0.2	0.3	0.3	0.5	0.8
United Kingdom	10.1	10.4	10.6	11.0	11.2	11.6	12.0	12.1	12.5	13.1	14.1	15.4	17.0	19.6	23.9	29.3	33.6	37.8	42.1
OECD - Total[1]	20.8	21.5	22.2	22.7	23.5	24.2	25.0	25.5	26.4	27.9	30.3	32.1	33.7	36.9	42.3	46.0	49.1	53.0	57.0
OECD - Europe[2]	17.5	18.2	19.1	19.7	20.8	21.5	21.9	21.4	21.6	22.8	25.5	27.7	29.2	31.0	34.3	37.4	40.5	44.3	48.1
EU15	17.1	17.7	18.5	19.1	20.1	20.9	21.4	20.8	21.0	22.2	24.8	27.0	28.3	30.1	33.6	37.0	40.6	44.4	48.2

35. Exports of goods and services - prices indices (1990 = 100)

	1960	1961	1962	1963	1964	1965	1966	1967	1968	1969	1970	1971	1972	1973	1974	1975	1976	1977	1978
Canada	25.6	26.0	27.1	27.3	27.8	28.3	29.1	29.6	30.0	30.6	31.6	31.6	32.9	37.3	48.4	53.4	54.9	58.9	63.6
Mexico	0.1	0.1	0.1	0.1	0.1	0.1	0.1	0.1	0.1	0.1	0.1	0.1	0.1	0.2	0.2	0.2	0.3	0.4	0.5
United States	25.7	26.0	25.8	26.0	26.1	26.8	27.7	28.5	29.0	30.0	31.7	33.0	34.2	39.0	47.4	52.1	54.6	57.4	61.3
Japan	66.8	66.3	65.3	67.0	68.0	67.7	67.6	67.8	67.8	68.9	70.8	72.8	72.4	79.4	104.3	109.4	111.7	107.6	100.8
Korea	..	..	..	..	..	..	..	..	..	..	13.0	14.4	16.9	20.8	27.9	31.5	34.8	37.6	41.6
Australia	18.3	17.4	17.5	19.1	19.8	18.9	19.7	19.1	19.0	20.3	20.3	20.0	21.9	26.6	32.7	35.8	38.8	43.3	44.3
New Zealand	11.1	10.7	11.1	12.3	12.7	12.4	12.3	11.6	12.6	13.2	13.5	15.1	18.5	21.7	21.1	23.5	29.9	32.8	36.4
Austria	42.2	43.7	43.9	44.6	45.8	47.0	47.9	48.1	48.9	50.1	52.9	54.7	56.6	60.8	67.6	70.9	72.1	75.1	76.2
Belgium	27.9	28.0	28.3	28.9	30.1	30.5	31.6	31.8	31.9	33.3	35.2	36.0	36.6	39.6	49.3	51.7	55.0	57.0	57.7
Czech Republic	..	..	..	..	..	..	..	..	..	..	..	..	..	..	..	..	..	..	..
Denmark	21.0	20.7	21.2	21.8	22.6	23.1	23.7	24.0	24.8	26.4	28.1	29.1	31.2	34.9	42.0	45.3	48.5	51.7	54.9
Finland	13.4	13.7	13.6	13.8	14.7	15.4	15.3	15.7	18.8	19.6	21.3	22.5	24.0	27.2	37.4	43.4	46.2	50.0	53.1
France	20.5	20.6	20.8	21.4	22.3	22.6	23.0	22.9	22.8	23.9	25.8	27.1	27.5	29.8	36.8	38.4	42.2	46.1	49.0
Germany	42.4	42.0	42.9	43.3	44.4	45.6	46.8	46.9	46.9	48.8	50.4	52.6	53.7	57.3	66.4	69.1	71.5	72.8	74.0
Greece	5.4	5.4	5.5	5.9	6.0	5.9	6.1	6.0	5.9	5.9	6.1	6.2	6.6	8.3	10.9	12.3	13.5	14.8	16.0
Hungary	..	..	..	..	..	..	..	..	..	..	..	..	..	..	..	..	..	..	..
Iceland	0.1	0.1	0.1	0.1	0.2	0.2	0.2	0.2	0.2	0.3	0.4	0.4	0.4	0.6	0.8	1.1	1.5	1.8	2.7
Ireland	14.2	14.2	14.4	14.7	15.4	15.7	16.0	16.1	17.1	18.2	17.1	18.3	20.4	24.4	30.1	35.6	43.8	50.2	53.6
Italy	9.8	9.7	9.8	10.1	10.5	10.5	10.6	10.7	10.7	11.0	11.7	12.2	12.9	14.5	19.6	22.5	27.0	31.6	34.2
Luxembourg	30.5	29.6	29.1	29.0	29.7	30.1	30.4	30.5	30.9	32.9	37.2	36.2	36.5	41.9	53.0	52.5	57.0	55.4	56.9
Netherlands	42.4	41.7	41.6	42.7	43.8	44.8	45.1	45.1	44.8	45.8	48.4	50.0	50.9	54.5	68.7	72.2	76.9	79.7	79.0
Norway	24.7	24.2	23.7	24.0	25.5	26.5	27.1	28.1	28.7	29.1	33.1	35.0	34.4	38.6	47.2	47.5	48.1	50.5	53.3
Poland	..	..	..	..	..	..	..	..	..	..	..	..	..	..	..	..	..	..	..
Portugal	3.1	3.2	3.3	3.6	3.3	3.5	3.3	3.6	3.8	3.9	4.5	4.7	5.0	5.7	8.2	8.2	8.7	11.6	14.6
Spain	7.3	7.4	8.0	8.4	8.6	8.7	9.5	10.9	12.8	13.6	13.9	14.8	15.7	17.2	21.0	23.3	27.1	32.3	37.4
Sweden	18.3	18.4	18.1	18.2	18.5	18.9	19.2	19.4	19.6	20.2	22.1	23.0	23.6	26.2	33.0	37.3	39.8	42.2	45.0
Switzerland	39.7	40.5	41.8	43.2	45.0	45.9	47.9	49.4	50.8	51.5	53.8	55.9	58.6	61.1	69.0	70.9	70.2	71.7	68.9
Turkey	0.1	0.1	0.1	0.1	0.1	0.1	0.1	0.1	0.1	0.1	0.1	0.1	0.2	0.2	0.3	0.3	0.3	0.4	0.5
United Kingdom	14.2	14.4	14.5	14.6	14.9	15.2	15.6	16.0	17.2	17.6	19.0	20.0	20.8	23.3	29.1	35.1	42.0	48.5	52.2
OECD - Total[1]	27.4	27.3	27.6	28.1	28.9	29.7	30.5	31.0	31.7	32.9	34.7	36.1	36.9	40.4	50.3	53.8	57.2	59.8	60.9
OECD - Europe[2]	26.8	26.7	26.9	27.5	28.2	28.7	29.3	29.8	30.3	31.3	33.0	34.2	35.2	38.0	46.2	48.9	52.5	55.4	57.0
EU15	26.3	26.1	26.3	26.8	27.5	27.9	28.5	28.9	29.3	30.4	32.0	33.2	34.1	37.1	45.3	48.1	52.1	55.0	56.8

36. Imports of goods and services - prices indices (1990 = 100)

	1960	1961	1962	1963	1964	1965	1966	1967	1968	1969	1970	1971	1972	1973	1974	1975	1976	1977	1978
Canada	30.7	31.5	33.0	33.9	34.1	34.2	34.9	35.5	36.4	37.5	38.4	39.2	40.2	43.1	52.0	59.4	59.9	66.9	74.2
Mexico	0.1	0.1	0.1	0.1	0.1	0.1	0.1	0.1	0.2	0.1	0.1	0.1	0.1	0.2	0.2	0.2	0.3	0.4	0.5
United States	19.4	19.6	19.6	20.3	21.0	21.5	21.8	21.8	22.2	22.5	24.1	25.7	27.9	32.8	47.3	52.1	54.0	59.5	63.6
Japan	45.0	45.5	44.5	45.3	46.0	45.7	46.8	46.7	47.1	48.4	49.5	48.0	45.8	54.2	89.0	97.5	102.6	98.7	83.2
Korea	..	..	..	..	..	..	..	..	..	..	13.5	15.0	17.5	21.9	31.5	38.4	38.2	39.8	43.3
Australia	16.3	16.4	16.3	16.3	16.3	16.6	16.9	17.0	17.0	17.2	18.2	19.7	20.6	21.2	27.1	32.5	35.5	42.7	45.7
New Zealand	10.9	10.9	10.6	10.7	10.8	10.9	10.9	11.5	13.1	13.6	14.7	15.3	15.9	17.1	22.6	29.6	35.5	37.9	39.5
Austria	39.0	39.8	40.1	40.4	41.1	41.9	42.6	43.3	43.5	45.7	48.5	50.7	51.7	53.8	63.4	66.0	67.9	72.0	72.4
Belgium	27.2	27.9	28.1	29.3	30.2	30.3	31.2	31.4	31.5	32.5	34.2	35.4	35.5	38.2	48.7	51.6	55.2	56.9	57.5
Czech Republic	..	..	..	..	..	..	..	..	..	..	..	..	..	..	..	..	..	..	..
Denmark	19.2	19.2	19.2	19.5	19.8	20.1	20.4	20.9	22.0	22.6	23.9	25.4	25.9	30.2	40.1	42.0	45.6	49.1	50.5
Finland	13.9	14.1	14.3	14.5	14.8	15.0	15.2	16.0	19.6	20.1	21.6	23.2	25.1	27.9	39.5	43.3	45.3	50.0	55.6
France	20.0	20.0	20.6	20.8	21.0	21.3	21.9	21.6	21.4	22.5	24.6	25.7	25.9	27.7	40.3	40.9	45.3	50.6	51.9
Germany	47.2	46.1	46.0	47.1	47.9	49.3	50.2	49.5	49.8	50.8	47.5	47.9	48.8	52.7	65.4	66.8	70.9	72.1	70.8
Greece	5.3	5.2	5.1	5.3	5.5	5.5	5.6	5.5	5.5	5.5	5.7	5.9	6.3	7.7	10.9	12.8	14.3	15.1	16.6
Hungary	..	..	..	..	..	..	..	..	..	..	..	..	..	..	..	..	..	..	..
Iceland	0.2	0.2	0.2	0.2	0.2	0.2	0.2	0.2	0.2	0.4	0.4	0.4	0.4	0.5	0.7	1.2	1.4	1.6	2.4
Ireland	12.7	12.9	13.0	13.2	13.4	13.7	13.8	13.7	14.8	15.4	15.5	16.4	17.3	19.7	28.5	34.4	40.9	47.7	50.0
Italy	9.8	9.5	9.6	9.7	10.1	10.1	10.3	10.4	10.5	10.6	11.0	11.6	12.1	15.4	23.3	25.9	32.7	37.7	40.3
Luxembourg	25.8	26.2	26.4	26.7	27.3	27.8	28.1	28.0	28.0	28.8	30.8	32.4	32.3	35.2	43.1	47.5	50.5	52.4	53.3
Netherlands	42.2	41.4	41.1	41.6	42.6	42.8	43.2	42.8	41.6	42.9	45.8	47.7	47.6	51.1	67.8	70.7	75.3	77.7	76.7
Norway	20.5	20.2	19.8	20.2	20.6	21.1	21.5	21.7	21.3	22.3	24.2	25.6	26.3	28.8	35.6	37.6	40.1	43.4	46.3
Poland	..	..	..	..	..	..	..	..	..	..	..	..	..	..	..	..	..	..	..
Portugal	3.4	3.5	3.4	3.5	3.7	4.0	4.0	4.5	3.8	3.7	4.4	4.4	4.6	5.2	7.5	8.7	9.8	12.7	15.5
Spain	10.4	10.6	10.8	11.0	11.5	11.6	11.6	11.9	13.2	13.6	14.2	15.0	15.2	16.8	23.8	25.5	29.2	35.7	38.4
Sweden	15.2	15.2	15.4	15.7	16.2	16.5	16.8	17.0	17.1	17.6	19.0	20.0	20.6	23.3	32.0	33.5	35.9	40.2	44.4
Switzerland	52.0	52.3	52.8	54.3	55.5	56.1	57.6	58.2	58.7	60.5	64.9	65.8	67.1	71.3	84.1	81.7	77.6	82.1	73.8
Turkey	0.1	0.1	0.1	0.1	0.1	0.1	0.1	0.1	0.1	0.1	0.1	0.2	0.2	0.2	0.3	0.3	0.4	0.5	0.7
United Kingdom	14.2	14.2	14.2	14.5	14.8	15.0	15.2	15.4	17.0	17.4	18.5	19.3	19.8	24.4	34.5	39.2	47.5	54.0	55.6
OECD - Total[1]	25.1	25.6	25.6	26.1	26.9	27.4	27.8	27.7	28.3	29.3	30.7	31.8	32.3	36.1	49.4	52.8	56.5	60.3	60.6
OECD - Europe[2]	26.5	26.4	26.6	26.8	27.6	28.3	28.6	28.2	28.8	29.8	30.9	32.1	32.4	35.3	45.9	48.4	52.8	56.7	57.6
EU15	25.7	25.4	25.6	25.9	26.5	27.4	27.7	27.2	27.8	28.8	29.8	31.0	31.2	34.1	45.0	47.9	52.8	56.6	57.6

1. Excluding Korea Czech Republic Hungary and Poland.
2. Excluding Czech Republic Hungary and Poland.

34

Formation brute de capital fixe - indices de prix (1990 = 100) 34.

1979	1980	1981	1982	1983	1984	1985	1986	1987	1988	1989	1990	1991	1992	1993	1994	1995	1996	1997	
73.2	76.1	81.2	86.3	86.6	83.6	89.3	90.9	94.1	96.8	99.6	100.0	95.8	94.6	96.2	98.7	99.7	99.2	100.1	Canada
0.6	0.8	1.0	1.6	3.1	4.9	7.8	15.1	35.0	69.8	81.1	100.0	120.7	135.7	147.2	160.1	243.4	317.1	363.0	Mexique
63.2	70.5	78.4	83.4	83.8	85.1	86.5	88.8	91.4	94.4	97.5	100.0	101.7	102.2	103.8	105.5	105.7	103.4	103.4	États-Unis
84.7	91.9	93.5	94.7	94.7	95.9	96.6	95.8	95.1	95.4	97.2	100.0	102.2	103.4	103.2	101.7	100.2	98.6	98.9	Japon
43.8	56.7	64.4	67.6	70.1	71.9	75.6	78.6	81.2	86.4	90.1	100.0	110.6	118.2	122.9	125.0	131.7	137.3	146.0	Corée
43.0	47.8	52.8	59.1	63.6	63.1	71.9	79.8	85.7	90.8	96.7	100.0	100.4	100.5	103.0	103.5	103.8	102.3	99.9	Australie
42.8	50.8	58.4	64.4	67.0	73.6	82.5	90.3	94.4	95.2	98.3	100.0	101.5	104.2	106.1	107.9	108.0	106.0	100.0	Nouvelle-Zélande
69.4	74.2	78.9	83.4	86.2	83.6	90.4	92.5	94.0	95.1	97.5	100.0	103.9	107.6	110.2	111.8	113.9	115.8	117.7	Autriche
66.3	69.8	74.9	79.8	83.1	83.4	89.5	90.5	91.4	93.2	97.3	100.0	102.1	105.1	106.8	109.2	111.2	112.1	113.0	Belgique
..	..	..	..	..	..	..	..	..	..	..	100.0	134.5	168.7	216.5	216.3	232.8	244.7	257.9	République tchèque
52.3	58.1	65.3	71.3	76.9	80.8	85.0	87.2	90.4	92.7	97.5	100.0	102.6	100.7	99.4	100.0	100.1	102.5	103.0	Danemark
42.9	48.9	54.3	58.1	63.2	67.8	72.1	75.6	80.4	86.5	93.9	100.0	99.2	95.4	95.5	99.4	102.4	102.8	104.4	Finlande
51.3	58.0	64.2	72.1	78.2	83.1	86.8	89.7	92.0	94.6	97.2	100.0	103.4	104.4	104.7	105.1	105.8	106.2	107.1	France
70.6	76.2	80.0	82.5	84.3	86.7	88.4	89.8	91.1	92.7	95.4	100.0	104.4	109.0	112.5	114.2	115.7	115.1	115.0	Allemagne
16.5	19.8	23.6	27.0	33.3	39.7	47.3	58.3	64.9	73.1	84.9	100.0	115.1	129.7	144.0	154.5	165.8	175.2	183.1	Grèce
..	..	..	..	..	..	..	..	..	..	..	100.0	122.9	141.2	158.5	184.8	233.0	286.2	335.9	Hongrie
4.1	6.3	9.5	14.8	25.9	30.9	40.3	49.6	57.6	68.4	86.3	100.0	106.5	109.6	114.1	118.4	122.0	126.8	129.7	Islande
48.9	56.9	65.4	71.3	75.8	80.0	83.4	86.0	88.0	92.4	97.7	100.0	102.5	107.1	112.3	115.0	119.3	123.9	132.5	Irlande
33.7	41.4	50.3	58.1	64.8	71.1	77.6	80.6	84.2	89.2	93.9	100.0	105.4	109.4	114.4	118.2	124.2	128.0	130.2	Italie
58.1	62.4	67.4	74.6	79.0	82.6	85.3	88.2	88.2	92.3	93.3	100.0	88.2	92.7	82.2	91.5	95.7	98.4	105.7	Luxembourg
76.3	81.5	86.7	89.8	91.0	92.1	93.2	93.1	94.6	96.2	98.0	100.0	102.1	104.1	105.5	106.6	107.6	109.4	111.3	Pays-Bas
46.5	50.9	56.1	62.0	66.6	70.4	76.1	81.4	89.2	96.5	99.9	100.0	101.2	103.7	107.0	109.1	113.3	116.2	119.1	Norvège
..	..	..	..	..	..	..	..	..	..	..	100.0	140.3	167.7	209.1	263.7	322.6	377.3	428.1	Pologne
17.8	22.4	27.3	33.2	41.8	50.0	59.9	68.8	75.5	83.8	91.7	100.0	105.4	108.3	113.4	119.9	124.5	126.0	126.0	Portugal
38.7	45.6	51.7	57.9	65.2	71.5	76.3	80.8	84.6	89.7	94.5	100.0	104.9	108.3	113.5	117.7	122.6	125.0	127.3	Espagne
45.0	50.4	55.1	60.0	66.5	69.8	74.5	78.1	81.4	86.8	93.8	100.0	105.2	102.9	104.5	104.3	106.6	106.8	106.8	Suède
68.8	73.3	78.5	82.3	83.5	84.6	87.5	88.7	89.7	92.9	97.3	100.0	101.9	100.9	99.5	97.5	94.4	92.0	89.4	Suisse
1.3	2.4	3.4	4.8	6.1	9.5	15.7	24.1	24.1	44.4	66.8	100.0	166.3	269.1	433.1	934.1	1 662.9	2 920.1	5 226.8	Turquie
48.7	57.9	63.7	65.5	67.7	70.5	74.4	77.7	81.4	87.0	94.6	100.0	100.4	97.6	97.6	99.5	106.3	110.1	111.4	Royaume-Uni
62.0	68.2	73.4	77.6	80.2	82.8	85.1	87.3	89.4	92.6	96.2	100.0	103.3	106.0	110.1	115.7	125.8	142.3	178.1	OCDE - Total[1]
52.7	59.1	64.4	69.1	73.4	77.3	81.0	83.9	86.1	90.1	94.9	100.0	105.0	109.8	118.7	131.8	155.9	201.6	292.1	OCDE - Europe[2]
53.0	59.4	65.0	69.8	74.3	78.3	82.0	84.8	87.4	90.9	95.3	100.0	103.8	106.2	108.7	110.9	114.1	115.7	116.9	UE15

35

Exportations de biens et services - indices de prix (1990 = 100) 35.

1979	1980	1981	1982	1983	1984	1985	1986	1987	1988	1989	1990	1991	1992	1993	1994	1995	1996	1997	
75.3	87.0	92.2	94.1	94.5	97.9	98.9	97.6	99.2	98.9	100.8	100.0	95.8	97.9	101.4	107.9	114.0	114.5	113.5	Canada
0.6	0.9	1.1	2.2	4.3	6.1	9.2	16.3	40.8	67.2	79.9	100.0	107.6	113.1	116.9	123.8	222.3	273.6	286.9	Mexique
69.3	77.5	83.1	85.1	87.3	89.7	88.2	87.4	90.6	96.1	98.5	100.0	101.9	101.7	101.4	101.8	101.6	96.4	94.4	États-Unis
109.0	119.6	122.7	126.1	120.0	120.0	116.9	102.0	97.4	95.2	98.6	100.0	96.7	93.3	86.0	82.6	80.1	84.7	86.7	Japon
49.5	68.0	79.0	81.8	83.0	88.5	90.6	92.2	94.8	95.6	95.1	100.0	101.6	104.6	105.8	107.1	109.1	104.7	107.7	Corée
53.1	61.4	63.5	66.2	72.2	73.9	81.8	82.3	86.0	93.7	98.9	100.0	94.8	96.8	98.2	94.2	100.1	97.1	97.4	Australie
44.6	50.4	58.1	64.2	68.7	79.0	82.0	85.0	87.2	93.9	102.1	100.0	99.4	106.8	104.8	103.8	102.1	98.7	98.3	Nouvelle-Zélande
79.5	84.4	88.7	91.9	92.6	96.3	99.3	96.8	95.0	97.4	99.2	100.0	100.4	100.9	101.6	102.6	103.5	103.9	104.4	Autriche
62.9	68.7	75.2	85.0	91.2	98.7	101.5	94.8	91.6	95.0	101.6	100.0	99.3	98.2	97.0	98.3	99.2	101.7	106.3	Belgique
..	..	..	..	..	..	..	..	..	..	..	100.0	131.1	133.4	139.6	161.8	173.3	178.1	187.4	République tchèque
59.4	68.1	76.7	84.9	89.3	96.1	99.5	94.2	92.4	93.0	99.3	100.0	100.8	103.0	101.1	100.5	100.4	101.2	104.0	Danemark
59.9	66.7	72.2	76.5	81.8	88.7	91.3	88.0	89.6	93.9	99.5	100.0	98.5	105.1	111.9	113.1	118.7	118.1	118.4	Finlande
54.1	60.5	68.9	77.0	84.7	92.8	97.4	94.4	94.4	96.9	101.0	100.0	100.6	98.9	98.1	99.7	100.6	100.6	101.8	France
77.6	82.5	87.2	90.3	92.0	95.1	98.1	96.7	95.8	97.5	99.8	100.0	101.4	102.4	102.7	103.3	105.1	105.5	106.5	Allemagne
18.4	24.6	30.9	37.3	44.5	51.5	60.3	66.7	71.6	77.0	86.1	100.0	114.4	125.4	137.4	150.3	162.5	173.8	180.8	Grèce
..	..	..	..	..	..	..	..	..	..	..	100.0	132.4	146.6	165.2	195.7	261.7	312.1	353.0	Hongrie
4.0	5.8	8.5	13.7	26.4	32.6	42.4	50.8	56.9	67.3	85.0	100.0	106.9	105.5	109.9	116.0	121.4	121.1	123.8	Islande
58.7	65.0	75.7	83.8	91.5	98.9	102.0	95.5	96.0	101.4	108.8	100.0	99.7	97.7	103.9	104.5	106.4	106.1	107.3	Irlande
40.1	49.2	59.7	69.4	75.3	82.4	89.7	87.2	88.1	91.1	97.2	100.0	103.2	105.3	115.3	117.7	129.1	132.1	132.3	Italie
61.3	65.9	72.2	83.4	88.3	93.0	96.6	95.2	92.2	94.2	99.8	100.0	99.9	101.4	106.3	112.7	110.4	110.5	113.4	Luxembourg
85.5	95.3	108.6	112.7	112.5	118.3	120.0	101.1	96.0	96.5	100.8	100.0	100.1	97.9	95.8	96.4	97.6	98.5	101.5	Pays-Bas
62.6	77.1	87.0	92.0	96.3	103.1	106.0	85.6	87.2	87.8	97.1	100.0	98.9	91.5	93.4	90.6	92.1	98.3	100.4	Norvège
..	..	..	..	..	..	..	..	..	..	..	100.0	120.5	155.8	197.9	247.7	296.4	317.6	358.5	Pologne
18.6	23.3	27.6	33.1	43.0	56.0	65.9	68.8	76.2	85.1	94.4	100.0	102.1	101.1	106.4	112.6	118.5	114.5	113.5	Portugal
40.9	48.3	56.9	64.7	75.7	85.1	90.6	89.1	91.3	94.1	98.3	100.0	102.0	105.2	110.1	115.1	121.2	122.8	126.1	Espagne
51.2	57.4	62.5	69.5	78.3	83.9	87.3	85.6	87.8	92.6	98.5	100.0	101.7	98.7	108.1	111.8	119.9	113.0	113.0	Suède
70.7	75.2	79.6	83.6	85.6	89.4	91.4	91.9	91.3	92.7	98.1	100.0	103.6	105.3	106.4	106.0	104.7	105.4	108.6	Suisse
0.9	2.4	3.5	4.9	6.2	9.8	16.0	20.6	27.0	47.2	72.3	100.0	161.0	261.7	418.6	1 108.2	1 917.5	3 240.5	6 059.1	Turquie
58.2	66.3	71.9	76.8	82.7	89.0	93.5	85.9	88.2	88.5	95.8	100.0	101.5	103.2	112.3	113.1	118.7	120.7	115.1	Royaume-Uni
66.8	75.2	81.7	86.1	88.8	93.5	96.0	91.1	91.3	94.1	98.5	100.0	101.0	101.8	104.4	110.9	121.8	136.5	165.4	OCDE - Total[1]
61.8	69.1	76.2	82.0	86.4	92.2	96.2	91.6	91.3	93.6	98.8	100.0	101.9	103.4	108.4	118.7	132.6	156.1	204.6	OCDE - Europe[2]
61.7	68.9	76.3	82.4	87.0	92.9	97.0	92.5	92.2	94.4	99.2	100.0	101.2	101.7	105.0	106.7	110.8	111.6	112.1	UE15

Importations de biens et services - indices de prix (1990 = 100) 36.

1979	1980	1981	1982	1983	1984	1985	1986	1987	1988	1989	1990	1991	1992	1993	1994	1995	1996	1997	
83.5	89.0	92.2	96.1	95.5	99.9	102.5	103.1	101.5	99.1	98.8	100.0	97.7	100.4	106.3	112.3	115.4	114.0	114.5	Canada
0.5	0.6	0.7	1.5	3.7	5.2	8.2	19.2	44.5	74.9	86.0	100.0	109.1	113.7	117.9	124.1	242.2	293.8	305.7	Mexique
74.7	90.9	93.6	89.3	85.9	85.1	81.9	83.3	88.9	93.6	96.7	100.0	100.3	100.6	99.2	99.4	100.2	95.3	91.9	États-Unis
106.2	146.0	149.1	158.9	150.4	146.5	143.2	98.0	90.9	86.7	92.5	100.0	94.2	89.4	81.1	76.8	74.8	82.4	88.3	Japon
52.0	79.7	94.1	93.7	95.7	100.7	104.7	100.1	100.3	99.1	94.1	100.0	101.8	105.3	105.8	106.5	111.2	114.2	127.1	Corée
52.0	60.2	62.9	67.4	72.2	73.7	86.5	97.0	100.7	97.3	96.2	100.0	101.2	104.9	110.0	104.2	105.8	97.4	92.9	Australie
47.3	59.1	67.1	74.4	80.4	94.8	98.3	95.9	90.5	90.9	97.1	100.0	102.1	108.1	104.1	101.4	98.5	94.0	93.1	Nouvelle-Zélande
76.7	84.0	91.9	93.7	93.3	96.9	100.7	96.8	94.3	96.1	99.5	100.0	101.0	101.1	101.8	102.6	103.6	104.9	106.0	Autriche
62.6	71.1	80.9	91.8	98.7	106.8	108.9	97.5	93.3	95.4	101.6	100.0	99.4	96.5	94.0	95.8	97.8	100.6	105.9	Belgique
..	..	..	..	..	..	..	..	..	..	..	100.0	136.3	136.7	140.5	161.2	170.4	171.4	180.3	République tchèque
57.4	69.8	82.2	90.5	93.9	101.3	104.5	94.8	92.6	94.6	100.9	100.0	101.9	100.6	98.6	98.5	97.1	96.3	99.8	Danemark
63.0	75.7	84.0	87.6	93.7	97.6	100.8	93.4	93.0	94.0	99.0	100.0	100.6	107.9	117.2	116.8	117.3	119.5	121.4	Finlande
57.7	69.1	80.7	89.9	97.1	107.2	109.0	95.4	94.2	95.7	101.3	100.0	100.2	97.6	94.9	96.2	97.4	98.4	99.4	France
76.9	86.8	97.0	99.7	100.8	106.4	109.9	98.3	94.1	95.8	100.5	100.0	102.3	100.8	99.4	99.9	100.4	101.2	104.2	Allemagne
19.5	26.3	31.5	39.0	45.9	56.4	66.4	72.0	72.3	76.9	88.2	100.0	112.1	131.0	141.2	149.4	159.4	164.9	168.6	Grèce
..	..	..	..	..	..	..	..	..	..	..	100.0	143.6	158.6	173.6	200.6	266.4	320.7	358.6	Hongrie
3.9	5.8	8.6	13.9	27.2	33.4	43.8	49.8	53.5	63.8	83.8	100.0	103.3	104.7	115.2	121.6	126.0	129.7	129.1	Islande
56.8	67.1	79.6	85.5	90.0	98.5	101.0	90.7	91.9	97.8	103.8	100.0	102.4	101.1	105.5	108.5	113.1	112.3	113.2	Irlande
47.9	60.5	75.9	84.7	90.2	98.9	106.4	91.2	89.8	93.9	100.3	100.0	100.0	101.7	113.9	119.5	134.1	131.6	131.2	Italie
57.5	61.9	68.1	77.5	83.7	89.9	92.7	90.5	88.6	92.6	97.7	100.0	101.1	100.4	102.0	108.4	109.3	109.6	110.9	Luxembourg
85.1	96.6	110.7	112.4	112.4	118.8	120.2	100.1	97.1	96.7	101.3	100.0	100.4	99.0	96.7	96.9	97.2	98.2	100.8	Pays-Bas
52.4	60.1	65.7	69.8	74.6	79.6	84.2	82.8	88.5	92.4	98.8	100.0	99.8	98.9	100.8	102.5	103.5	104.7	106.0	Norvège
..	..	..	..	..	..	..	..	..	..	..	100.0	131.8	160.4	190.3	241.8	285.1	314.7	357.5	Pologne
20.3	26.6	33.4	39.5	51.2	67.2	76.0	70.8	77.5	86.6	95.6	100.0	101.1	96.8	101.1	105.2	108.9	109.1	109.5	Portugal
41.1	56.4	72.9	82.2	99.9	111.6	113.7	97.1	97.9	98.9	101.2	100.0	99.7	101.0	107.5	113.6	119.0	120.9	125.5	Espagne
51.5	58.8	65.4	75.4	85.5	88.9	92.9	85.8	88.8	91.8	97.1	100.0	99.9	97.7	111.9	115.8	121.1	115.2	117.5	Suède
79.2	89.2	95.3	94.1	93.3	97.3	101.8	92.4	89.0	92.7	100.4	100.0	100.5	103.1	101.1	96.2	93.1	93.4	98.3	Suisse
1.2	2.3	3.3	4.7	5.9	9.3	15.2	19.6	26.1	46.7	77.9	100.0	160.2	261.3	389.0	1 024.1	1 894.5	3 418.2	5 951.4	Turquie
60.8	66.7	71.8	76.8	82.6	89.9	93.5	89.4	91.6	90.8	96.7	100.0	100.3	100.3	108.8	112.0	120.0	120.5	112.5	Royaume-Uni
69.0	81.2	88.5	93.0	95.0	98.8	100.3	91.0	91.1	93.2	98.1	100.0	100.6	101.2	104.2	109.6	123.9	143.2	178.7	OCDE - Total[1]
63.5	73.2	83.1	88.5	93.0	99.9	103.7	93.1	91.6	93.8	99.6	100.0	101.6	102.5	108.3	117.4	138.0	171.5	233.4	OCDE - Europe[2]
63.5	73.5	84.0	89.8	94.7	102.0	105.5	94.3	92.8	94.4	99.8	100.0	100.9	100.2	103.1	105.5	109.7	110.0	111.0	UE15

1. Non compris la Corée la République tchèque la Hongrie et la Pologne.
2. Non compris la République tchèque la Hongrie et la Pologne.

PART SEVEN

Comparative tables based on PPPs
Tableaux comparatifs basés sur les PPA

The statistics for Germany in this publication refer to Germany after unification. Official data for Germany after unification are available only from 1991 onwards. In this publication, the secretariat has estimated some national accounts aggregates for the whole of Germany back to 1960 in order to calculate the various zones totals. These estimates are based on statistics published by Deutsches Institut fur Wirtschaftsforschung for period 1989-90 and by the East German Statistical Office in 1990 for period 1980-89. They are also based on the ratios of the aggregates of West Germany and the whole of Germany.

Les statistiques concernant l'Allemagne dans cette publication se réfèrent à l'Allemagne après l'unification. Des données officielles pour l'Allemagne après l'unification ne sont disponibles qu'à partir de 1991. Dans cette publication, le secrétariat a estimé certains agrégats des comptes nationaux pour l'Allemagne dans son ensemble depuis 1960 afin de calculer les différentes zones. Ces estimations sont basées sur des statistiques publiées par Deutsches Institut fur Wirtschaftsforschung pour la période 1989-90 et par l'Office Statistique de l'Allemagne de l'Est en 1990 pour la période 1980-89. Elles sont aussi basées sur les rapports des agrégats de l'Allemagne occidentale et de l'Allemagne dans son ensemble.

CALCULATION PROCEDURES

The data in this section have been converted to United States dollars using purchasing power parities (PPPs) for GDP rather than the exchange rates used in earlier parts of this volume. PPPs are the rates of currency conversion that equalise the purchasing power of different countries by eliminating differences in price levels between countries. When converted by means of PPPs, the expenditures on GDP for different countries are in effect expressed at the same set of prices so that comparisons between countries reflect only differences in the volume of goods and services purchased.

The PPP converted data and the exchange rate converted data in the tables are shown in US dollars, but the choice of currency unit in both cases is purely a matter of convention which has no effect on comparisons between countries.

1990, 1993, 1996: PPPs for all OECD countries except those listed below are triennial benchmark results calculated jointly by the OECD and the Statistical Office of the European Communities (Eurostat). For Mexico, Korea, Czech Republic, Hungary and Poland, the PPPs for 1990 and 1993 are OECD estimates. for Korea the PPPs for 1996 are also OECD estimates.

1970 to 1989: The 1990 PPPs were backdated to 1970 using each country's rate of inflation relative to that of the United States. Specifically, country k's PPP for year t was obtained by multiplying its 1990 PPP by Ikt divided by Iust where Ik is the GDP price index based on 1990 for country k and Ius is the GDP price index based on 1990 for the United States. As changes in PPPs depend directly on relative rates of inflation in different countries, this method produces robust estimates for years other than the base year provided they are not too remote from the base morning.

1991, 1992, 1994 and 1995: Since 1991, Eurostat has calculated annual PPPs for EU Member States and a number of other European OECD countries. In 1991, Eurostat calculated PPPs for the twelve EU Member States plus Austria, Sweden and Switzerland; in 1992, Eurostat calculated PPPs for the same 15 countries plus Finland; and in 1994 and 1995, Eurostat calculated PPPs for the 15 EU Member States plus Iceland, Norway, Poland and Switzerland. PPPs for the countries not covered by Eurostat are OECD estimates.

1997: PPPs for all countries are OECD estimates.

The time series of real values for private final consumption expenditure, government final consumption expenditure and gross fixed capital formation have been derived using the general GDP PPPs and not the PPPs specific to these aggregates.

Data for Korea, Czech Republic, Hungary and Poland have not been included in area total. Data for Australia are based on calendar year.

MÉTHODES DE CALCUL

Les données de la présente section ont été converties en dollars des États-Unis au moyen des parités de pouvoir d'achat (PPA) pour le PIB et non des taux de change comme dans les précédentes parties du présent volume. Les PPA sont les taux de conversion monétaire qui permettent d'exprimer dans une unité commune les pouvoirs d'achat des différentes monnaies en éliminant les différences de niveaux de prix existant entre les pays. Les dépenses imputées au PIB, pour les différents pays, converties en utilisant les PPA sont en effet exprimées en fonction d'une même structure de prix internationaux si bien que les écarts entre pays reflètent uniquement les différences de volume de biens et services achetés.

Les données converties au moyen des PPA et celles converties en utilisant les taux de change sont exprimées en dollars É-U mais, dans les deux cas, le choix de l'unité monétaire est une convention qui n'affecte en aucune façon les comparaisons entre pays.

1990, 1993, 1996 : les PPA pour tous les pays de l'OCDE, à l'exception de ceux énumérés ci-dessous, sont les résultats, pour ces années de référence des calculs triennaux effectués par l'Office Statistique des Communautés Européennes (Eurostat). Pour le Mexique, la Corée, la République tchèque, la Hongrie et la Pologne, les PPA pour 1990 et 1993 sont des estimations de l'OCDE; les PPA de 1996 pour la Corée sont aussi des estimations de l'OCDE.

1970-1989 : les PPA de 1990 du PIB ont été extrapolées jusqu'en 1970 en utilisant les taux d'inflation de chaque pays rapportés à celui des États-Unis. Plus précisément la PPA du pays k pour l'année t a été obtenue en multipliant sa PPA de 1990 par le rapport Ikt/Iust où Ik est l'indice de prix du PIB du pays k sur la base 1990 et Ius l'indice de prix du PIB des États-Unis sur la base 1990. Les variations des PPA dépendant directement des taux d'inflation relatifs des différents pays, cette méthode permet d'obtenir des estimations fiables pour les années autres que l'année de base à condition quelles ne soient pas trop éloignées de cette année de base.

1991, 1992, 1994 et 1995 : Depuis 1991, Eurostat calcule des parités annuelles pour les États Membres de l'UE et pour plusieurs autres pays européens. En 1991, Eurostat a calculé des données annuelles pour les 12 États Membres des communautés, plus l'Autriche, la Suède et la Suisse; en 1992, la Finlande a été associée à ces calculs; en 1994 et 1995, Eurostat a calculé des PPA pour les 15 pays de l'UE plus l'Islande, la Norvège, la Pologne et la Suisse. Les PPA pour les pays non couverts par Eurostat sont des estimations de l'OCDE.

1997 : Les PPA pour tous les pays sont des estimations de l'OCDE.

Les séries chronologiques de valeurs réelles pour la consommation finale privée, la consommation finale des administrations publiques et la formation brute de capital fixe ont été calculées en utilisant la PPA du PIB et non leurs PPA respectives.

Les données de la Corée, de la République tchèque, de la Hongrie et de la Pologne n'ont pas été intégrées aux totaux par zones. Les données de l'Australie sont établies sur une base calendaire.

COMPARATIVE TABLES BASED ON PPPs
TABLEAUX COMPARATIFS BASÉS SUR LES PPA

1.

Gross domestic product - at current prices and current PPPs (billions US dollars)

	1960	1961	1962	1963	1964	1965	1966	1967	1968	1969	1970	1971	1972	1973	1974	1975	1976	1977	1978	1979
Canada	..	..	..	..	..	..	..	..	..	..	79.4	88.6	97.6	111.2	125.6	140.3	157.6	174.1	194.9	221.1
Mexico	..	..	..	..	..	..	..	..	..	..	65.9	72.5	82.3	94.9	109.3	126.0	140.0	154.7	180.2	214.2
United States	..	..	..	..	..	..	..	..	..	..	1008.9	1096.1	1205.8	1348.3	1457.6	1585.5	1771.4	1973.8	2229.0	2488.0
Japan	..	..	..	..	..	..	..	..	..	..	298.1	329.6	374.0	429.5	460.5	518.5	574.3	640.7	725.7	833.6
Korea	..	..	..	..	..	..	..	..	..	..	20.9	24.0	26.3	31.5	37.0	43.1	51.3	60.5	71.2	83.0
Australia	..	..	..	..	..	..	..	..	..	..	44.4	49.7	54.0	60.4	66.6	74.8	82.7	89.2	98.8	112.5
New Zealand	..	..	..	..	..	..	..	..	..	..	9.5	10.5	11.5	13.1	15.0	16.2	17.7	18.0	19.5	21.6
Austria	..	..	..	..	..	..	..	..	..	..	22.3	24.8	27.6	30.7	34.7	37.7	42.0	47.0	50.4	57.9
Belgium	..	..	..	..	..	..	..	..	..	..	30.7	33.7	37.1	41.8	47.3	51.0	57.4	61.7	68.3	76.1
Czech Republic	..	..	..	..	..	..	..	..	..	..	..	..	..	..	..	..	..	..	..	..
Denmark	..	..	..	..	..	..	..	..	..	..	18.0	19.5	21.4	23.6	25.4	27.6	31.3	34.0	37.1	41.8
Finland	..	..	..	..	..	..	..	..	..	..	13.1	14.2	15.9	18.1	20.2	22.3	23.7	25.4	27.9	32.5
France	..	..	..	..	..	..	..	..	..	..	179.4	198.6	217.1	243.3	271.9	294.9	327.7	363.3	401.8	450.6
Germany	..	..	..	..	..	..	..	..	..	..	242.4	263.8	287.8	320.5	348.6	376.0	421.8	463.7	513.8	583.1
Greece	..	..	..	..	..	..	..	..	..	..	15.6	17.6	20.1	22.9	24.0	27.8	31.4	34.8	39.9	45.1
Hungary	..	..	..	..	..	..	..	..	..	..	..	..	..	..	..	..	..	..	..	..
Iceland	..	..	..	..	..	..	..	..	..	..	0.6	0.7	0.7	0.9	1.0	1.1	1.2	1.4	1.6	1.8
Ireland	..	..	..	..	..	..	..	..	..	..	5.5	6.0	6.6	7.4	8.4	9.7	10.4	12.1	13.9	15.6
Italy	..	..	..	..	..	..	..	..	..	..	161.1	173.3	186.7	211.5	240.3	256.9	291.4	320.4	357.6	411.5
Luxembourg	..	..	..	..	..	..	..	..	..	..	1.4	1.5	1.6	1.9	2.1	2.2	2.4	2.6	2.9	3.2
Netherlands	..	..	..	..	..	..	..	..	..	..	44.7	49.2	53.2	59.2	66.8	72.9	81.6	89.3	98.3	109.4
Norway	..	..	..	..	..	..	..	..	..	..	11.4	12.6	13.9	15.4	17.6	20.0	22.7	25.2	28.3	32.2
Poland	..	..	..	..	..	..	..	..	..	..	..	..	..	..	..	..	..	..	..	..
Portugal	..	..	..	..	..	..	..	..	..	..	13.6	15.3	17.3	20.4	22.4	23.4	25.7	30.1	33.3	38.3
Spain	..	..	..	..	..	..	..	..	..	..	74.6	82.5	93.4	107.0	122.6	134.7	143.2	162.9	177.8	193.7
Sweden	..	..	..	..	..	..	..	..	..	..	30.5	32.5	34.8	38.5	43.1	48.3	52.0	54.6	59.8	67.6
Switzerland	..	..	..	..	..	..	..	..	..	..	32.3	35.5	38.3	42.0	46.2	46.8	49.2	53.8	58.1	64.9
Turkey	..	..	..	..	..	..	..	..	..	..	33.0	36.8	41.4	45.4	52.1	61.0	71.7	79.3	86.6	93.7
United Kingdom	..	..	..	..	..	..	..	..	..	..	179.3	193.4	209.6	237.8	254.6	277.7	302.5	330.3	368.0	411.8
OECD - Total [1]	..	..	..	..	..	..	..	..	..	..	2615.6	2858.2	3149.7	3545.7	3883.8	4253.1	4732.2	5242.4	5873.8	6421.9
OECD - Europe [2]	..	..	..	..	..	..	..	..	..	..	1109.4	1211.3	1324.5	1488.3	1649.2	1791.7	1995.5	2191.8	2425.6	2730.9
EU15	..	..	..	..	..	..	..	..	..	..	1032.1	1125.7	1230.2	1384.7	1532.4	1662.9	1850.6	2032.1	2250.9	2538.3

2.

Gross domestic product per head - at current prices and current PPPs (US dollars)

	1960	1961	1962	1963	1964	1965	1966	1967	1968	1969	1970	1971	1972	1973	1974	1975	1976	1977	1978	1979
Canada	..	..	..	..	..	..	..	..	..	..	3730	4021	4379	4928	5491	6045	6623	7318	8110	9107
Mexico	..	..	..	..	..	..	..	..	..	..	1343	1430	1571	1752	1954	2186	2356	2529	2863	3309
United States	..	..	..	..	..	..	..	..	..	..	4920	5278	5745	6363	6816	7341	8324	8962	10014	11055
Japan	..	..	..	..	..	..	..	..	..	..	2874	3146	3522	3953	4180	4649	5033	5626	6315	7193
Korea	..	..	..	..	..	..	..	..	..	..	649	729	785	925	1066	1221	1431	1661	1926	2213
Australia	..	..	..	..	..	..	..	..	..	..	3464	3801	4058	4475	4855	5384	5800	6287	6883	7749
New Zealand	..	..	..	..	..	..	..	..	..	..	3359	3674	3943	4402	4960	5260	5617	5759	6220	6891
Austria	..	..	..	..	..	..	..	..	..	..	2991	3306	3654	4051	4563	4979	5556	6214	6667	7569
Belgium	..	..	..	..	..	..	..	..	..	..	3188	3480	3819	4296	4844	5206	5800	6284	6948	7737
Czech Republic	..	..	..	..	..	..	..	..	..	..	..	..	..	..	..	..	..	..	..	..
Denmark	..	..	..	..	..	..	..	..	..	..	3642	3922	4296	4705	5036	5448	6114	6674	7265	8170
Finland	..	..	..	..	..	..	..	..	..	..	2850	3069	3436	3876	4312	4743	5006	5359	5869	6818
France	..	..	..	..	..	..	..	..	..	..	3533	3875	4199	4669	5182	5595	6114	6836	7527	8406
Germany	..	..	..	..	..	..	..	..	..	..	3119	3367	3656	4060	4414	4779	5346	5932	6581	7166
Greece	..	..	..	..	..	..	..	..	..	..	1771	1995	2259	2566	2674	3068	3441	3735	4232	4719
Hungary	..	..	..	..	..	..	..	..	..	..	..	..	..	..	..	..	..	..	..	..
Iceland	..	..	..	..	..	..	..	..	..	..	2766	3271	3582	4010	4536	4918	5551	6340	7168	8112
Ireland	..	..	..	..	..	..	..	..	..	..	1849	2001	2196	2406	2678	3039	3221	3687	4198	4536
Italy	..	..	..	..	..	..	..	..	..	..	2993	3206	3434	3863	4361	4633	5220	5727	6369	7307
Luxembourg	..	..	..	..	..	..	..	..	..	..	3980	4290	4717	5370	6005	6060	6553	7145	7979	8468
Netherlands	..	..	..	..	..	..	..	..	..	..	3430	3728	3990	4405	4932	5336	5972	6442	7053	7797
Norway	..	..	..	..	..	..	..	..	..	..	2948	3235	3534	3884	4408	4987	5663	6226	6974	7797
Poland	..	..	..	..	..	..	..	..	..	..	..	..	..	..	..	..	..	..	..	..
Portugal	..	..	..	..	..	..	..	..	..	..	1557	1768	2002	2366	2562	2577	2882	3185	3485	3965
Spain	..	..	..	..	..	..	..	..	..	..	2203	2412	2706	3073	3489	3792	4123	4479	4835	5220
Sweden	..	..	..	..	..	..	..	..	..	..	3791	4014	4285	4727	5279	5891	6313	6622	7229	8155
Switzerland	..	..	..	..	..	..	..	..	..	..	5150	5592	5985	6516	7155	7309	7763	8521	9181	10217
Turkey	..	..	..	..	..	..	..	..	..	..	927	1007	1104	1182	1334	1523	1753	1898	2030	2152
United Kingdom	..	..	..	..	..	..	..	..	..	..	3223	3458	3736	4229	4527	4939	5383	5878	6551	7322
OECD - Total [1]	..	..	..	..	..	..	..	..	..	..	3349	3615	3939	4381	4753	5154	5669	6239	6927	7739
OECD - Europe [2]	..	..	..	..	..	..	..	..	..	..	2872	3109	3373	3763	4148	4481	4963	5427	5975	6692
EU15	..	..	..	..	..	..	..	..	..	..	3033	3285	3570	3997	4404	4762	5281	5781	6382	7172

3.

Gross domestic product per head - indices using current PPPs (OECD = 100)

	1960	1961	1962	1963	1964	1965	1966	1967	1968	1969	1970	1971	1972	1973	1974	1975	1976	1977	1978	1979
Canada	..	..	..	..	..	..	..	..	..	..	111	111	111	112	116	117	118	117	117	118
Mexico	..	..	..	..	..	..	..	..	..	..	40	40	40	40	41	42	41	41	41	43
United States	..	..	..	..	..	..	..	..	..	..	147	146	146	145	143	142	147	144	145	143
Japan	..	..	..	..	..	..	..	..	..	..	86	87	89	90	88	90	89	90	91	93
Korea	..	..	..	..	..	..	..	..	..	..	19	20	20	21	22	24	25	27	28	29
Australia	..	..	..	..	..	..	..	..	..	..	103	105	103	102	102	104	104	101	99	100
New Zealand	..	..	..	..	..	..	..	..	..	..	100	102	100	100	104	102	100	92	90	89
Austria	..	..	..	..	..	..	..	..	..	..	89	91	93	92	96	97	98	100	96	98
Belgium	..	..	..	..	..	..	..	..	..	..	95	96	97	98	102	101	103	101	100	100
Czech Republic	..	..	..	..	..	..	..	..	..	..	..	..	..	..	..	..	..	..	..	..
Denmark	..	..	..	..	..	..	..	..	..	..	109	108	109	107	106	106	108	107	105	106
Finland	..	..	..	..	..	..	..	..	..	..	85	85	87	88	91	92	88	86	85	88
France	..	..	..	..	..	..	..	..	..	..	105	107	107	107	109	109	109	110	109	109
Germany	..	..	..	..	..	..	..	..	..	..	93	93	93	93	93	93	95	95	95	96
Greece	..	..	..	..	..	..	..	..	..	..	53	55	57	59	56	60	60	60	61	61
Hungary	..	..	..	..	..	..	..	..	..	..	..	..	..	..	..	..	..	..	..	..
Iceland	..	..	..	..	..	..	..	..	..	..	83	90	91	92	95	95	97	102	103	105
Ireland	..	..	..	..	..	..	..	..	..	..	55	55	56	55	56	59	57	59	61	60
Italy	..	..	..	..	..	..	..	..	..	..	89	89	87	88	92	90	92	92	92	94
Luxembourg	..	..	..	..	..	..	..	..	..	..	119	119	120	123	126	118	116	115	115	110
Netherlands	..	..	..	..	..	..	..	..	..	..	102	103	101	101	104	104	104	103	102	101
Norway	..	..	..	..	..	..	..	..	..	..	88	90	90	89	93	97	99	100	101	101
Poland	..	..	..	..	..	..	..	..	..	..	..	..	..	..	..	..	..	..	..	..
Portugal	..	..	..	..	..	..	..	..	..	..	46	49	51	54	54	50	50	51	50	51
Spain	..	..	..	..	..	..	..	..	..	..	66	67	69	70	73	74	72	72	70	67
Sweden	..	..	..	..	..	..	..	..	..	..	113	111	109	108	111	114	111	106	104	105
Switzerland	..	..	..	..	..	..	..	..	..	..	154	155	152	149	151	142	136	137	133	132
Turkey	..	..	..	..	..	..	..	..	..	..	28	28	28	27	28	30	31	30	29	28
United Kingdom	..	..	..	..	..	..	..	..	..	..	96	96	95	97	95	96	95	94	95	95
OECD - Total [1]	..	..	..	..	..	..	..	..	..	..	100	100	100	100	100	100	100	100	100	100
OECD - Europe [2]	..	..	..	..	..	..	..	..	..	..	86	86	86	86	87	87	87	87	86	86
EU15	..	..	..	..	..	..	..	..	..	..	91	91	91	91	93	92	93	93	92	93

1. Excluding Korea, Czech Republic, Hungary and Poland.
2. Excluding Czech Republic, Hungary and Poland.

Produit intérieur brut - aux prix et PPA courants (milliards de dollars É-U) 1.

1980	1981	1982	1983	1984	1985	1986	1987	1988	1989	1990	1991	1992	1993	1994	1995	1996	1997	
245.4	279.1	287.1	308.7	341.4	372.5	391.7	421.1	458.5	490.3	512.8	522.4	536.3	564.8	600.0	663.4	681.3	719.7	Canada
254.1	305.0	321.3	321.3	348.2	370.4	365.2	384.3	404.0	439.5	481.8	503.4	558.1	592.1	623.9	619.2	660.7	720.2	Mexique
2709.0	3039.3	3158.9	3412.9	3786.4	4048.2	4268.1	4528.1	4878.8	5260.9	5554.1	5710.9	6027.7	6341.6	6722.9	7033.6	7390.6	7824.0	États-Unis
938.6	1068.4	1168.0	1248.7	1357.5	1467.1	1546.6	1664.2	1835.0	2008.3	2201.9	2373.9	2503.3	2579.3	2653.9	2862.7	3018.2	3100.4	Japon
88.5	103.7	118.4	137.9	156.8	172.9	197.6	227.7	263.1	292.2	333.8	365.2	410.5	451.7	495.0	570.3	619.5	665.8	Corée
125.9	144.0	151.9	160.3	180.1	195.2	204.4	220.5	237.7	258.7	273.0	279.9	290.4	310.3	334.2	369.3	388.6	406.8	Australie
23.8	27.6	29.8	32.0	35.1	36.6	38.3	39.8	41.1	43.3	44.9	46.2	49.3	53.5	57.6	62.2	64.4	67.1	Nouvelle-Zélande
64.9	71.5	77.3	83.0	87.1	92.2	96.7	101.6	108.8	118.4	129.2	137.3	147.2	153.3	160.9	169.3	178.3	186.3	Autriche
87.1	94.9	102.1	106.6	114.3	119.5	124.3	131.4	142.9	154.5	166.1	175.4	191.3	198.5	208.3	218.7	225.5	236.6	Belgique
..	..	..	..	..	..	..	..	..	..	110.5	98.0	101.4	106.1	110.6	124.4	131.1	134.8	République tchèque
45.6	49.8	54.5	58.3	63.7	68.8	73.0	75.7	79.5	83.2	87.9	93.5	97.1	102.5	110.9	120.0	128.1	134.8	Danemark
37.5	42.1	46.1	49.5	53.4	57.1	59.9	64.4	70.1	77.4	80.7	77.9	75.0	79.3	83.1	93.4	97.5	105.3	Finlande
500.1	555.3	602.1	634.0	671.9	708.3	742.9	784.7	849.3	921.2	984.2	1041.0	1090.8	1076.7	1115.7	1181.4	1197.8	1247.8	France
644.9	715.0	754.2	804.2	866.9	918.5	964.7	1013.4	1090.7	1178.3	1269.1	1363.3	1490.5	1504.5	1608.3	1701.3	1737.9	1809.2	Allemagne
50.2	55.4	59.0	61.9	66.6	71.1	74.0	76.1	82.5	89.4	93.3	100.7	110.4	114.7	122.2	131.9	138.8	145.9	Grèce
..	..	..	..	..	..	..	..	..	..	86.6	76.5	79.4	82.1	85.3	91.6	94.1	100.3	Hongrie
2.1	2.4	2.6	2.7	2.9	3.2	3.4	3.8	4.0	4.2	4.4	4.6	4.8	5.0	5.2	5.9	6.3	6.7	Islande
17.6	20.1	21.8	22.7	24.8	26.5	27.0	29.2	31.9	35.2	39.9	43.1	48.3	50.9	57.1	64.2	66.9	75.4	Irlande
466.6	517.2	551.2	582.9	625.5	665.7	701.3	747.0	805.6	865.3	922.3	976.1	1030.1	1010.7	1068.6	1138.7	1183.0	1223.1	Italie
3.6	3.9	4.2	4.5	5.0	5.3	5.9	6.2	7.1	8.2	8.7	9.4	10.4	11.2	12.2	13.1	13.2	14.0	Luxembourg
121.3	133.1	139.6	148.3	160.3	171.0	180.0	188.6	201.0	219.6	238.6	248.5	265.1	272.4	289.2	314.3	327.4	345.6	Pays-Bas
37.0	41.2	43.8	47.3	52.4	57.1	60.6	63.9	66.3	69.8	74.3	79.5	87.4	92.2	95.1	101.2	111.9	117.9	Norvège
..	..	..	..	..	..	..	..	..	..	185.9	173.3	190.3	205.6	210.3	252.9	265.9	289.4	Pologne
43.9	49.2	53.3	55.6	57.1	60.8	64.8	71.2	79.5	87.3	95.0	102.9	110.4	115.1	123.9	132.3	137.1	144.8	Portugal
216.8	238.9	257.4	274.7	291.7	307.1	324.7	354.4	386.9	423.1	457.9	497.6	515.0	521.1	534.2	569.4	596.2	628.8	Espagne
75.3	83.1	89.0	94.6	103.0	108.7	113.9	121.4	128.9	137.7	145.7	145.6	147.2	147.1	154.7	168.9	174.4	180.8	Suède
74.3	83.3	87.1	91.5	98.6	105.5	109.9	114.4	122.4	133.4	144.4	149.6	158.3	164.1	170.4	180.1	177.7	184.2	Suisse
100.1	115.8	127.2	139.5	155.7	168.0	184.2	208.4	221.0	231.3	263.6	276.3	298.2	330.9	319.8	346.5	376.1	412.0	Turquie
443.6	483.0	520.4	563.0	603.7	647.0	691.9	748.9	816.3	870.8	912.1	903.9	969.6	986.4	1032.3	1068.6	1147.9	1208.7	Royaume-Uni
7329.1	8218.6	8709.9	9308.9	10153.4	10851.4	11417.4	12162.7	13150.0	14209.2	15186.2	15862.9	16812.3	17378.1	18264.7	19329.5	20226.3	21246.1	OCDE - Total[1]
3032.3	3355.3	3592.9	3825.1	4104.7	4361.3	4603.1	4904.7	5294.7	5708.3	6117.5	6426.2	6847.1	6936.5	7272.2	7719.1	8022.4	8408.0	OCDE - Europe[2]
2818.8	3112.6	3332.2	3544.1	3795.0	4027.4	4245.0	4514.2	4881.1	5269.7	5630.9	5916.2	6298.4	6344.4	6681.7	7085.5	7350.3	7687.2	UE15

Produit intérieur brut par tête - aux prix et PPA courants (dollars É-U) 2.

1980	1981	1982	1983	1984	1985	1986	1987	1988	1989	1990	1991	1992	1993	1994	1995	1996	1997	
9977	11209	11391	12125	13284	14361	14947	15862	17048	17907	18452	18579	18790	19511	20508	22400	22735	23761	Canada
3805	4462	4593	4490	4761	4957	4788	4938	5087	5426	5834	5988	6525	6805	7052	6843	7181	7697	Mexique
11896	13216	13605	14566	16020	16976	17736	18649	19912	21270	22224	22605	23600	24568	25790	26727	27831	29326	États-Unis
8036	9081	9861	10470	11311	12150	12730	13631	14967	16312	17824	19156	20136	20689	21238	22797	23980	24574	Japon
2322	2678	3010	3455	3880	4238	4795	5470	6259	6882	7787	8440	9402	10253	11088	12648	13602	14477	Corée
8569	9649	10006	10413	11562	12364	12758	13558	14379	15383	16000	16192	16598	17565	18715	20437	21223	21949	Australie
7584	8737	9365	9919	10781	11198	11695	12033	12396	13000	13352	13291	14041	15043	15997	17000	17345	17846	Nouvelle-Zélande
8593	9446	10202	10971	11510	12171	12744	13369	14289	15459	16712	17576	18600	19183	20039	21041	22129	23077	Autriche
8844	9629	10351	10808	11582	12100	12569	13275	14414	15561	16679	17540	19047	19686	20595	21577	22205	23242	Belgique
..	..	..	..	..	..	..	..	..	..	10660	9508	9830	10273	10696	12037	12709	13087	République tchèque
8897	9730	10643	11408	12464	13450	14262	14760	15495	16213	17094	18133	18780	19744	21303	22946	24345	25514	Danemark
7841	8775	9558	10194	10928	11646	12174	13056	14180	15586	16193	15543	14885	15646	16339	18293	19030	20488	Finlande
9281	10248	11049	11576	12211	12811	13374	14057	15135	16327	17347	18245	19011	18676	19270	20321	20520	21293	France
8235	9118	9628	10294	11136	11826	12417	13040	13963	14976	15991	17045	18493	18532	19753	20834	21221	22049	Allemagne
5207	5697	6030	6288	6726	7153	7422	7606	8220	8864	9187	9828	10691	11047	11724	12613	13253	13912	Grèce
..	..	..	..	..	..	..	..	..	..	8359	7396	7687	7976	8313	8951	9236	9875	Hongrie
9311	10572	11310	11416	12332	13077	14120	15641	15966	16513	17294	17949	18326	18793	19456	22203	23533	24836	Islande
5182	5836	6265	6483	7029	7476	7624	8241	9034	10039	11375	12214	13597	14290	15934	17854	18484	20634	Irlande
8268	9153	9742	10294	11041	11746	12374	13180	14211	15259	16257	17197	18117	17717	18681	19872	20616	21265	Italie
9766	10686	11433	12302	13667	14520	15985	16763	19060	21626	22809	24378	26551	28176	30174	31858	31807	33119	Luxembourg
8572	9345	9753	10324	11113	11805	12360	12864	13617	14795	15962	16491	17463	17817	18801	20327	21089	22142	Pays-Bas
9047	10044	10634	11468	12665	13751	14543	15257	15741	16514	17512	18663	20393	21389	21936	23209	25547	26771	Norvège
..	..	..	..	..	..	..	..	..	..	4876	4532	4961	5345	5455	6554	6884	7487	Pologne
4494	4995	5379	5586	5715	6068	6474	7128	7976	8782	9600	10428	11190	11651	12508	13344	13816	14562	Portugal
5781	6331	6783	7206	7621	7993	8425	9173	9994	10906	11787	12784	13204	13333	13646	14521	15183	15990	Espagne
9061	9985	10692	11362	12356	13016	13608	14453	15275	16217	17004	16891	16979	16870	17615	19139	19730	20439	Suède
11642	12958	13469	14111	15155	16153	16717	17277	18353	19837	21242	21762	22801	23480	24212	25428	25015	25902	Suisse
2252	2542	2724	2914	3174	3340	3582	3965	4114	4213	4691	4822	5105	5562	5280	5620	5999	6463	Turquie
7875	8572	9240	9986	10683	11413	12171	13136	14282	15182	15847	15636	16715	16951	17678	18233	19521	20483	Royaume-Uni
8480	9428	9910	10510	11379	12070	12602	13324	14291	15312	16220	16796	17647	18088	18868	19804	20576	21487	OCDE - Total[1]
7386	8128	8663	9184	9814	10381	10906	11568	12419	13306	14160	14776	15637	15737	16408	17329	17924	18698	OCDE - Europe[2]
7932	8731	9328	9905	10592	11222	11803	12526	13502	14521	15447	16154	17116	17160	18011	19042	19699	20546	UE15

Produit intérieur brut par tête - indices en utilisant les PPA courantes (OCDE = 100) 3.

1980	1981	1982	1983	1984	1985	1986	1987	1988	1989	1990	1991	1992	1993	1994	1995	1996	1997	
118	119	115	115	117	119	119	119	119	117	114	111	106	108	109	113	110	111	Canada
45	47	46	43	42	41	38	37	36	35	36	36	37	38	37	35	35	36	Mexique
140	140	137	139	141	141	141	140	139	139	137	135	134	136	137	135	135	136	États-Unis
95	96	100	100	99	101	101	102	105	107	110	114	114	114	113	115	117	114	Japon
27	28	30	33	34	35	38	41	44	45	48	50	53	57	59	64	66	67	Corée
101	102	101	99	102	102	101	102	101	100	99	96	94	97	99	103	103	102	Australie
89	93	94	94	95	93	93	90	87	85	82	79	80	83	85	86	84	83	Nouvelle-Zélande
101	100	103	104	101	101	101	100	100	101	103	105	105	106	106	106	108	107	Autriche
104	102	104	103	102	100	100	100	101	102	103	104	108	109	109	109	108	108	Belgique
..	..	..	..	..	..	..	..	..	..	66	57	56	57	57	61	62	61	République tchèque
105	103	107	109	110	111	113	111	108	106	105	108	106	109	113	116	118	119	Danemark
92	93	96	97	96	96	97	98	99	102	100	93	84	86	87	92	92	95	Finlande
109	109	111	110	107	106	106	106	106	107	107	109	108	103	102	103	100	99	France
97	97	97	98	98	98	99	98	98	98	99	101	105	102	105	105	103	103	Allemagne
61	60	61	60	59	59	59	57	58	58	57	59	61	61	62	64	64	65	Grèce
..	..	..	..	..	..	..	..	..	..	52	44	44	44	44	45	45	46	Hongrie
110	112	114	109	108	108	112	117	112	108	107	107	104	104	103	112	114	116	Islande
61	62	63	62	62	62	60	62	63	66	70	73	77	79	84	90	90	96	Irlande
97	97	98	98	97	97	98	99	99	100	100	102	103	98	99	100	100	99	Italie
115	113	115	117	120	120	127	126	133	141	141	145	150	156	160	161	155	154	Luxembourg
101	99	98	98	98	98	98	97	95	97	98	98	99	99	100	103	102	103	Pays-Bas
107	107	107	109	111	114	115	115	110	108	108	111	116	118	116	117	124	125	Norvège
..	..	..	..	..	..	..	..	..	..	30	27	28	30	29	33	33	35	Pologne
53	53	54	53	50	50	51	53	56	57	59	62	63	64	66	67	67	68	Portugal
68	67	68	69	67	66	67	69	70	71	73	76	75	74	72	73	74	74	Espagne
107	106	108	108	109	108	108	108	107	106	105	101	96	93	93	97	96	95	Suède
137	137	136	134	133	134	133	130	128	130	131	130	129	130	128	128	122	121	Suisse
27	27	27	28	28	28	28	30	29	28	29	29	29	31	28	28	29	30	Turquie
93	91	93	95	94	95	97	99	100	99	98	93	95	94	94	92	95	95	Royaume-Uni
100	100	100	100	100	100	100	100	100	100	100	100	100	100	100	100	100	100	OCDE - Total[1]
87	86	87	87	86	86	87	87	87	87	87	88	89	87	87	87	87	87	OCDE - Europe[2]
94	93	94	94	93	93	94	94	94	95	95	96	97	95	95	96	96	96	UE15

1. Non compris la Corée, la République tchèque, la Hongrie et la Pologne.
2. Non compris la République tchèque, la Hongrie et la Pologne.

4.
Private final consumption expenditure - at current prices and current PPPs (billions US dollars)

	1960	1961	1962	1963	1964	1965	1966	1967	1968	1969	1970	1971	1972	1973	1974	1975	1976	1977	1978	1979
Canada	..	..	..	..	..	..	..	..	..	..	44.1	49.0	54.1	60.1	66.3	75.9	84.3	94.0	106.1	117.7
Mexico	..	..	..	..	..	..	..	..	..	..	48.5	54.3	60.5	68.4	78.0	88.6	97.5	104.9	121.7	141.1
United States	..	..	..	..	..	..	..	..	..	..	637.3	690.2	757.2	836.8	914.0	1008.4	1126.6	1252.6	1396.8	1556.9
Japan	..	..	..	..	..	..	..	..	..	..	155.8	176.6	202.0	230.2	250.1	296.3	330.2	369.6	418.7	489.4
Korea	..	..	..	..	..	..	..	..	..	..	15.6	18.1	19.4	21.9	26.0	30.4	33.6	37.7	43.2	51.2
Australia	..	..	..	..	..	..	..	..	..	..	26.4	29.3	31.5	34.6	38.2	43.7	48.2	52.8	59.1	65.7
New Zealand	..	..	..	..	..	..	..	..	..	..	6.2	6.6	7.1	7.9	9.5	10.4	10.7	11.0	11.8	13.2
Austria	..	..	..	..	..	..	..	..	..	..	12.2	13.5	14.9	16.4	18.5	21.1	23.7	26.7	27.8	31.8
Belgium	..	..	..	..	..	..	..	..	..	..	18.4	20.4	22.4	25.5	28.5	31.5	35.3	38.6	42.5	48.4
Czech Republic	..	..	..	..	..	..	..	..	..	..	..	..	..	..	..	..	..	..	..	..
Denmark	..	..	..	..	..	..	..	..	..	..	9.7	10.3	10.8	12.2	13.1	14.5	16.7	18.3	19.7	22.3
Finland	..	..	..	..	..	..	..	..	..	..	7.4	7.9	9.0	10.0	10.7	12.5	13.4	14.4	15.8	17.9
France	..	..	..	..	..	..	..	..	..	..	103.9	114.8	125.3	138.9	156.4	173.2	191.5	211.6	232.7	261.9
Germany	..	..	..	..	..	..	..	..	..	..	130.8	142.2	156.2	171.2	186.9	211.2	235.1	261.5	287.2	324.3
Greece	..	..	..	..	..	..	..	..	..	..	11.2	12.5	13.7	15.1	16.9	19.5	21.5	23.9	27.1	29.7
Hungary	..	..	..	..	..	..	..	..	..	..	..	..	..	..	..	..	..	..	..	..
Iceland	..	..	..	..	..	..	..	..	..	..	0.3	0.4	0.4	0.5	0.6	0.6	0.7	0.8	0.9	1.1
Ireland	..	..	..	..	..	..	..	..	..	..	3.9	4.2	4.4	4.9	5.9	6.4	6.9	8.0	9.1	10.5
Italy	..	..	..	..	..	..	..	..	..	..	95.5	103.3	112.0	127.6	144.4	159.0	177.1	192.4	211.3	244.8
Luxembourg	..	..	..	..	..	..	..	..	..	..	0.8	0.9	1.0	1.0	1.1	1.4	1.5	1.7	1.9	2.1
Netherlands	..	..	..	..	..	..	..	..	..	..	26.2	28.5	30.6	33.7	38.0	42.9	48.1	53.5	59.6	66.3
Norway	..	..	..	..	..	..	..	..	..	..	5.9	6.5	7.2	7.7	8.6	10.1	11.5	13.2	14.2	16.0
Poland	..	..	..	..	..	..	..	..	..	..	..	..	..	..	..	..	..	..	..	..
Portugal	..	..	..	..	..	..	..	..	..	..	8.9	10.3	11.0	13.1	16.2	17.9	19.8	21.5	22.5	25.6
Spain	..	..	..	..	..	..	..	..	..	..	48.3	53.5	60.2	68.6	79.5	87.4	93.3	106.9	114.6	125.9
Sweden	..	..	..	..	..	..	..	..	..	..	16.2	17.2	18.6	20.4	23.0	25.0	27.6	29.2	31.8	35.5
Switzerland	..	..	..	..	..	..	..	..	..	..	18.6	20.2	21.9	24.1	26.8	28.2	29.3	33.6	35.9	40.5
Turkey	..	..	..	..	..	..	..	..	..	..	24.0	27.7	30.9	33.0	38.3	44.1	48.6	56.1	63.9	69.9
United Kingdom	..	..	..	..	..	..	..	..	..	..	110.0	119.3	130.6	147.4	161.1	171.5	181.4	196.4	218.7	246.9
OECD - Total[1]	..	..	..	..	..	..	..	..	..	..	1570.7	1719.7	1893.5	2109.4	2330.4	2601.3	2881.5	3193.2	3551.4	4005.9
OECD - Europe[2]	..	..	..	..	..	..	..	..	..	..	652.4	713.8	781.1	871.3	974.3	1077.9	1190.9	1308.3	1437.1	1621.9
EU15	..	..	..	..	..	..	..	..	..	..	603.5	658.9	720.7	806.1	900.1	994.9	1098.8	1204.6	1322.2	1494.5

5.
Private final consumption expenditure per head - at current prices and current PPPs (US dollars)

	1960	1961	1962	1963	1964	1965	1966	1967	1968	1969	1970	1971	1972	1973	1974	1975	1976	1977	1978	1979
Canada	..	..	..	..	..	..	..	..	..	..	2069	2224	2428	2664	2897	3272	3544	3950	4413	4848
Mexico	..	..	..	..	..	..	..	..	..	..	988	1071	1154	1263	1396	1536	1640	1715	1934	2180
United States	..	..	..	..	..	..	..	..	..	..	3108	3324	3608	3949	4274	4669	5147	5687	6275	6918
Japan	..	..	..	..	..	..	..	..	..	..	1502	1685	1902	2119	2270	2657	2938	3246	3643	4223
Korea	..	..	..	..	..	..	..	..	..	..	485	551	578	643	750	862	977	1035	1168	1365
Australia	..	..	..	..	..	..	..	..	..	..	2063	2240	2369	2562	2782	3146	3445	3718	4117	4526
New Zealand	..	..	..	..	..	..	..	..	..	..	2195	2304	2439	2672	3138	3375	3440	3520	3787	4196
Austria	..	..	..	..	..	..	..	..	..	..	1628	1806	1973	2168	2431	2785	3141	3533	3673	4213
Belgium	..	..	..	..	..	..	..	..	..	..	1913	2107	2310	2618	2918	3213	3590	3931	4326	4920
Czech Republic	..	..	..	..	..	..	..	..	..	..	..	..	..	..	..	..	..	..	..	..
Denmark	..	..	..	..	..	..	..	..	..	..	1977	2070	2168	2425	2588	2857	3238	3591	3859	4361
Finland	..	..	..	..	..	..	..	..	..	..	1614	1717	1937	2133	2289	2643	2823	3029	3316	3761
France	..	..	..	..	..	..	..	..	..	..	2046	2240	2424	2666	2981	3287	3617	3982	4359	4886
Germany	..	..	..	..	..	..	..	..	..	..	1684	1815	1984	2168	2366	2684	3002	3346	3679	4152
Greece	..	..	..	..	..	..	..	..	..	..	1277	1414	1546	1696	1886	2160	2385	2564	2874	3115
Hungary	..	..	..	..	..	..	..	..	..	..	..	..	..	..	..	..	..	..	..	..
Iceland	..	..	..	..	..	..	..	..	..	..	1699	1997	2142	2269	2675	2855	3100	3573	4068	4687
Ireland	..	..	..	..	..	..	..	..	..	..	1310	1400	1468	1593	1885	2005	2141	2432	2753	3114
Italy	..	..	..	..	..	..	..	..	..	..	1774	1911	2060	2331	2621	2868	3171	3439	3763	4346
Luxembourg	..	..	..	..	..	..	..	..	..	..	2242	2623	2818	2928	3088	3904	4151	4746	5156	5720
Netherlands	..	..	..	..	..	..	..	..	..	..	2010	2162	2294	2505	2807	3137	3491	3861	4274	4762
Norway	..	..	..	..	..	..	..	..	..	..	1531	1677	1820	1951	2165	2510	2851	3257	3492	3935
Poland	..	..	..	..	..	..	..	..	..	..	..	..	..	..	..	..	..	..	..	..
Portugal	..	..	..	..	..	..	..	..	..	..	1017	1196	1273	1521	1845	1969	2121	2271	2349	2652
Spain	..	..	..	..	..	..	..	..	..	..	1425	1565	1744	1972	2261	2462	2731	2939	3116	3393
Sweden	..	..	..	..	..	..	..	..	..	..	2019	2130	2287	2501	2820	3055	3351	3540	3842	4275
Switzerland	..	..	..	..	..	..	..	..	..	..	2975	3187	3415	3738	4141	4409	4771	5321	5667	6378
Turkey	..	..	..	..	..	..	..	..	..	..	675	758	825	858	980	1103	1215	1344	1499	1605
United Kingdom	..	..	..	..	..	..	..	..	..	..	1978	2132	2327	2622	2865	3049	3262	3496	3893	4390
OECD - Total[1]	..	..	..	..	..	..	..	..	..	..	2011	2175	2368	2607	2852	3152	3470	3800	4188	4681
OECD - Europe[2]	..	..	..	..	..	..	..	..	..	..	1689	1832	1989	2203	2450	2696	2966	3239	3540	3974
EU15	..	..	..	..	..	..	..	..	..	..	1773	1923	2091	2327	2587	2849	3139	3427	3749	4223

6.
Private final consumption expenditure per head - indices using current PPPs (OECD = 100)

	1960	1961	1962	1963	1964	1965	1966	1967	1968	1969	1970	1971	1972	1973	1974	1975	1976	1977	1978	1979
Canada	..	..	..	..	..	..	..	..	..	..	103	102	103	102	102	104	103	104	105	104
Mexico	..	..	..	..	..	..	..	..	..	..	49	49	49	48	49	49	47	45	46	47
United States	..	..	..	..	..	..	..	..	..	..	155	153	152	151	150	148	149	150	150	148
Japan	..	..	..	..	..	..	..	..	..	..	75	77	80	81	80	84	84	85	87	90
Korea	..	..	..	..	..	..	..	..	..	..	24	25	24	25	26	27	27	27	28	29
Australia	..	..	..	..	..	..	..	..	..	..	103	103	100	98	98	100	99	98	98	97
New Zealand	..	..	..	..	..	..	..	..	..	..	109	106	103	103	110	107	99	93	90	90
Austria	..	..	..	..	..	..	..	..	..	..	81	83	83	83	85	88	90	93	88	90
Belgium	..	..	..	..	..	..	..	..	..	..	95	97	98	100	102	102	104	103	103	105
Czech Republic	..	..	..	..	..	..	..	..	..	..	..	..	..	..	..	..	..	..	..	..
Denmark	..	..	..	..	..	..	..	..	..	..	98	95	92	93	91	91	95	94	92	93
Finland	..	..	..	..	..	..	..	..	..	..	80	79	82	82	80	84	81	80	79	80
France	..	..	..	..	..	..	..	..	..	..	102	103	102	102	105	104	104	105	104	104
Germany	..	..	..	..	..	..	..	..	..	..	84	83	84	83	83	85	87	88	88	89
Greece	..	..	..	..	..	..	..	..	..	..	64	65	65	65	66	69	68	67	69	67
Hungary	..	..	..	..	..	..	..	..	..	..	..	..	..	..	..	..	..	..	..	..
Iceland	..	..	..	..	..	..	..	..	..	..	84	92	90	87	94	91	90	94	97	100
Ireland	..	..	..	..	..	..	..	..	..	..	65	64	62	61	66	64	62	64	66	67
Italy	..	..	..	..	..	..	..	..	..	..	88	88	87	89	92	91	92	91	90	93
Luxembourg	..	..	..	..	..	..	..	..	..	..	111	121	119	112	108	124	120	125	123	122
Netherlands	..	..	..	..	..	..	..	..	..	..	100	99	97	96	98	100	101	102	102	102
Norway	..	..	..	..	..	..	..	..	..	..	76	77	77	75	76	80	82	86	83	84
Poland	..	..	..	..	..	..	..	..	..	..	..	..	..	..	..	..	..	..	..	..
Portugal	..	..	..	..	..	..	..	..	..	..	51	55	54	58	65	62	61	60	56	57
Spain	..	..	..	..	..	..	..	..	..	..	71	72	74	76	79	78	79	77	74	72
Sweden	..	..	..	..	..	..	..	..	..	..	100	98	97	96	99	97	97	93	92	91
Switzerland	..	..	..	..	..	..	..	..	..	..	148	147	144	143	145	140	138	140	135	136
Turkey	..	..	..	..	..	..	..	..	..	..	34	35	35	33	34	35	35	35	36	34
United Kingdom	..	..	..	..	..	..	..	..	..	..	98	98	98	101	100	97	94	92	93	94
OECD - Total[1]	..	..	..	..	..	..	..	..	..	..	100	100	100	100	100	100	100	100	100	100
OECD - Europe[2]	..	..	..	..	..	..	..	..	..	..	84	84	84	85	86	86	85	85	85	85
EU15	..	..	..	..	..	..	..	..	..	..	88	88	88	89	91	90	90	90	90	90

1. Excluding Korea, Czech Republic, Hungary and Poland.
2. Excluding Czech Republic, Hungary and Poland.

Consommation finale privée - aux prix et PPA courants (milliards de dollars É-U) 4.

1980	1981	1982	1983	1984	1985	1986	1987	1988	1989	1990	1991	1992	1993	1994	1995	1996	1997	
130.5	146.8	153.8	167.5	184.8	203.9	219.8	234.4	252.2	271.6	290.0	303.1	314.2	332.1	347.8	378.5	393.2	*421.9*	Canada
161.1	191.4	192.9	190.5	214.0	232.9	243.6	246.6	273.3	302.6	335.2	354.9	400.8	425.7	446.4	415.3	428.6	*470.7*	Mexique
1720.6	1902.4	2034.6	2226.7	2432.3	2633.7	2803.9	2998.6	3247.4	3486.7	3720.5	3844.5	4079.8	4318.4	4569.4	4802.4	5043.0	*5311.8*	États-Unis
552.3	621.2	694.2	752.0	806.9	864.3	906.9	980.0	1068.9	1169.3	1276.4	1356.5	1447.2	1512.2	1584.6	1721.1	1807.1	*1880.2*	Japon
57.0	*66.7*	*74.9*	*83.5*	*92.5*	*101.2*	*109.0*	*119.9*	*134.3*	*155.6*	*179.2*	*194.7*	*221.5*	*243.0*	*265.9*	*302.1*	*333.4*	*357.1*	*Corée*
74.1	85.0	91.9	98.2	105.7	116.4	122.4	129.5	138.0	150.4	163.4	173.5	182.6	193.8	207.0	230.2	240.6	*251.8*	Australie
14.7	16.4	18.0	19.0	21.1	22.6	23.1	24.1	25.1	26.6	28.4	29.3	30.9	32.4	35.2	38.4	40.5	*42.6*	Nouvelle-Zélande
35.7	40.0	43.8	48.1	50.0	52.8	54.7	57.4	61.6	66.6	72.1	75.7	82.1	86.1	90.1	95.0	101.3	*104.5*	Autriche
55.6	62.7	68.2	71.3	75.7	79.7	81.3	85.9	91.3	98.2	105.6	113.0	122.5	126.4	132.1	137.5	143.4	*149.7*	Belgique
..	..	..	..	..	..	..	..	..	..	58.8	45.0	53.0	52.5	55.0	61.6	66.0	*69.3*	République tchèque
24.1	26.4	28.4	30.1	32.8	35.7	38.0	38.6	39.9	41.5	43.1	46.1	48.0	51.2	56.7	60.9	64.5	*68.3*	Danemark
20.3	22.8	25.4	27.3	28.9	31.1	32.7	35.2	37.6	40.4	42.3	43.6	42.8	45.2	46.3	50.7	53.3	*55.7*	Finlande
294.4	334.6	365.4	385.4	408.4	432.6	448.8	477.8	510.1	549.1	586.4	623.0	655.8	655.6	673.6	710.2	727.9	*748.0*	France
362.4	408.4	432.8	459.8	493.5	520.2	534.2	564.2	601.8	651.0	706.1	778.9	849.9	869.9	921.1	976.2	1009.3	*1046.0*	Allemagne
33.8	39.0	41.4	43.0	44.9	48.5	52.0	55.1	58.5	64.3	68.4	73.5	82.5	86.3	91.8	98.8	103.9	*107.1*	Grèce
..	..	..	..	..	..	..	..	..	..	41.9	42.0	45.8	49.0	49.5	49.5	49.4	*51.3*	Hongrie
1.2	1.4	1.6	1.6	1.8	2.0	2.1	2.5	2.5	2.6	2.7	2.9	3.0	3.0	3.1	3.6	3.9	*4.1*	Islande
11.9	13.6	13.4	13.9	15.0	16.2	16.6	17.8	19.4	21.3	23.2	25.2	28.3	28.7	32.2	34.3	34.9	*37.3*	Irlande
284.0	315.0	338.0	354.1	381.2	407.9	428.8	458.7	493.8	535.9	565.5	603.1	647.3	626.8	661.6	700.0	726.0	*756.0*	Italie
2.3	2.6	2.8	3.0	3.2	3.5	3.7	4.0	4.4	4.9	5.4	5.9	6.2	6.4	6.7	7.1	7.3	*7.4*	Luxembourg
73.8	79.7	83.9	89.2	95.0	101.6	107.0	114.7	119.3	128.9	140.0	147.7	159.7	164.8	173.9	187.8	195.0	*204.3*	Pays-Bas
17.3	19.1	20.6	22.3	24.0	27.4	31.7	32.8	33.7	34.7	36.7	39.2	44.0	46.1	47.5	49.9	53.4	*56.1*	Norvège
..	..	..	..	..	..	..	..	..	..	90.2	104.2	119.1	131.5	137.3	159.5	173.2	*188.8*	Pologne
29.3	34.0	36.8	38.2	40.0	40.9	41.8	45.4	50.5	54.5	60.0	65.9	71.7	76.6	81.8	85.8	89.0	*93.4*	Portugal
143.6	159.3	169.8	179.1	187.5	196.9	205.3	224.1	242.6	266.4	285.9	310.4	324.8	329.0	335.7	353.4	369.2	*389.7*	Espagne
38.8	43.6	47.6	49.1	52.2	55.6	58.6	63.8	67.6	70.7	74.2	77.6	79.3	81.0	84.3	88.4	91.5	*96.0*	Suède
46.3	51.6	54.4	57.8	60.9	64.7	66.6	69.5	72.8	77.6	82.7	87.9	94.6	98.3	102.0	108.4	108.4	*112.6*	Suisse
80.9	82.7	93.2	103.6	117.7	119.4	124.1	142.3	140.3	151.7	180.8	195.1	207.3	228.6	223.7	243.6	253.0	*280.3*	Turquie
264.4	291.4	314.8	342.0	367.0	392.3	432.8	468.0	517.4	551.2	573.9	572.6	619.6	634.2	658.0	675.5	730.8	*775.5*	Royaume-Uni
4473.4	4991.3	5367.7	5772.9	6244.5	6702.9	7080.5	7570.9	8169.8	8818.8	9469.0	9949.1	10624.8	11058.9	11612.5	12253.1	12819.3	*13471.0*	OCDE - Total[1]
1820.1	2028.1	2182.3	2318.9	2479.8	2629.1	2760.8	2957.7	3165.0	3411.6	3655.0	3887.3	4169.4	4244.3	4422.1	4667.2	4866.2	*5092.1*	OCDE - Europe[2]
1674.4	1873.3	2012.5	2133.7	2275.3	2415.7	2536.2	2710.7	2915.8	3145.0	3352.0	3562.3	3820.5	3868.3	4045.8	4261.6	4447.5	*4639.0*	UE15

Consommation finale privée par tête - aux prix et PPA courants (dollars É-U) 5.

1980	1981	1982	1983	1984	1985	1986	1987	1988	1989	1990	1991	1992	1993	1994	1995	1996	1997	
5308	5894	6101	6581	7191	7859	8388	8828	9376	9921	10435	10778	11008	11472	11889	12780	13122	*13931*	Canada
2413	2799	2757	2663	2926	3117	3194	3168	3441	3736	4059	4222	4686	4893	5046	4589	4659	*5031*	Mexique
7556	8273	8763	9503	10291	11044	11651	12350	13254	14097	14887	15217	15974	16730	17529	18248	18990	*19910*	États-Unis
4728	5280	5861	6306	6723	7158	7465	8027	8718	9497	10332	10947	11641	12129	12681	13706	14357	*14902*	Japon
1496	*1723*	*1905*	*2093*	*2290*	*2480*	*2646*	*2880*	*3195*	*3665*	*4180*	*4501*	*5074*	*5516*	*5956*	*6699*	*7321*	*7764*	*Corée*
5039	5696	6052	6380	6783	7376	7643	7963	8345	8945	9577	10039	10435	10968	11591	12735	13141	*13585*	Australie
4673	5210	5670	5898	6462	6892	7044	7307	7559	7982	8457	8424	8788	9125	9785	10516	10903	*11323*	Nouvelle-Zélande
4733	5287	5778	6357	6599	6967	7208	7551	8086	8697	9335	9692	10376	10777	11225	11810	12569	*12951*	Autriche
5649	6361	6915	7230	7672	8069	8218	8680	9204	9888	10602	11296	12198	12534	13054	13562	14122	*14703*	Belgique
..	..	..	..	..	..	..	..	..	..	5669	4367	5140	5078	5322	5958	6401	*6721*	République tchèque
4700	5158	5539	5893	6420	6974	7421	7536	7783	8085	8387	8944	9291	9874	10894	11646	12267	*12926*	Danemark
4242	4750	5267	5616	5925	6352	6653	7139	7593	8148	8475	8698	8495	8927	9094	9921	10399	*10840*	Finlande
5464	6176	6706	7037	7422	7826	8080	8559	9090	9733	10336	10920	11429	11371	11633	12215	12470	*12764*	France
4628	5208	5525	5885	6340	6698	6876	7259	7704	8275	8897	9738	10545	10716	11312	11954	12325	*12748*	Allemagne
3503	4005	4232	4370	4533	4883	5215	5505	5829	6369	6730	7176	7995	8311	8805	9449	9916	*10214*	Grèce
..	..	..	..	..	..	..	..	..	..	4046	4056	4433	4760	4825	4840	4851	*5051*	Hongrie
5366	6256	6819	6862	7729	8355	8688	9990	10020	10194	10592	11230	11446	11336	11492	13409	14377	*15170*	Islande
3506	3958	3852	3976	4253	4580	4697	5023	5499	6067	6609	7156	7972	8067	8985	9527	9645	*10213*	Irlande
5032	5575	5974	6253	6728	7198	7565	8094	8712	9450	9968	10626	11384	10988	11565	12217	12653	*13144*	Italie
6397	7254	7689	8182	8861	9508	10040	10820	11896	12923	14155	15347	15721	16131	16494	17419	17476	*17584*	Luxembourg
5216	5598	5866	6210	6583	7016	7346	7819	8082	8679	9366	9801	10516	10777	11308	12146	12561	*13087*	Pays-Bas
4236	4665	5017	5393	5804	6592	7612	7825	8003	8199	8653	9199	10261	10689	10951	11458	12189	*12728*	Norvège
..	..	..	..	..	..	..	..	..	..	2366	2726	3104	3418	3561	4132	4484	*4886*	Pologne
2998	3448	3708	3839	4003	4084	4175	4543	5071	5485	6061	6672	7263	7751	8265	8658	8969	*9391*	Portugal
3829	4221	4474	4697	4898	5125	5327	5800	6266	6868	7358	7976	8327	8418	8574	9013	9403	*9910*	Espagne
4664	5245	5717	5893	6257	6664	7001	7594	8009	8325	8661	9002	9154	9290	9601	10017	10344	*10848*	Suède
7256	8020	8408	8910	9361	9896	10138	10499	10907	11550	12173	12782	13622	14067	14501	15315	15260	*15840*	Suisse
1821	1816	1997	2164	2399	2373	2412	2707	2612	2764	3217	3405	3550	3843	3694	3952	4036	*4397*	Turquie
4693	5172	5590	6067	6495	6921	7613	8209	9052	9611	9970	9905	10681	10899	11269	11527	12429	*13141*	Royaume-Uni
5176	5726	6107	6513	6998	7455	7815	8294	8879	9503	10113	10535	11152	11511	11996	12554	13041	*13624*	OCDE - Total[1]
4434	4913	5262	5568	5929	6258	6541	6976	7424	7953	8460	8938	9522	9629	9978	10477	10872	*11324*	OCDE - Europe[2]
4711	5255	5633	5964	6351	6731	7052	7522	8066	8666	9196	9727	10382	10463	10905	11453	11920	*12399*	UE15

Consommation finale privée par tête - indices en utilisant les PPA courantes (OCDE = 100) 6.

1980	1981	1982	1983	1984	1985	1986	1987	1988	1989	1990	1991	1992	1993	1994	1995	1996	1997	
103	103	100	101	103	105	107	106	106	104	103	102	99	100	99	102	101	*102*	Canada
47	49	45	41	42	42	41	38	39	39	40	40	42	43	42	37	36	*37*	Mexique
146	144	143	146	147	148	149	149	149	148	147	144	143	145	146	145	146	*146*	États-Unis
91	92	96	97	96	96	96	97	98	100	102	104	104	105	106	109	110	*109*	Japon
29	*30*	*31*	*32*	*33*	*33*	*34*	*35*	*36*	*39*	*41*	*43*	*45*	*48*	*50*	*53*	*56*	*57*	*Corée*
97	99	99	98	97	99	98	96	94	94	95	95	94	95	97	101	101	*100*	Australie
90	91	93	90	92	92	90	88	85	84	84	80	79	79	82	84	84	*83*	Nouvelle-Zélande
91	92	95	98	94	93	92	91	91	92	92	92	93	94	94	94	96	*95*	Autriche
109	111	113	111	110	108	105	105	104	104	105	107	109	109	109	108	108	*108*	Belgique
..	..	..	..	..	..	..	..	..	..	56	41	46	44	44	47	49	*49*	République tchèque
91	90	91	90	92	94	95	91	88	85	83	85	83	86	91	93	94	*95*	Danemark
82	83	86	86	85	85	85	86	86	86	84	83	76	78	76	79	80	*80*	Finlande
106	108	110	108	106	105	103	103	102	102	102	104	102	99	97	97	96	*94*	France
89	91	90	90	91	90	88	88	87	87	88	92	95	93	94	95	95	*94*	Allemagne
68	70	69	67	65	66	67	66	66	67	67	68	72	72	73	75	76	*75*	Grèce
..	..	..	..	..	..	..	..	..	..	40	39	40	41	40	39	37	*37*	Hongrie
104	109	112	105	110	112	111	120	113	107	105	107	103	98	96	107	110	*111*	Islande
68	69	63	61	61	61	60	61	62	64	65	68	71	70	75	76	74	*75*	Irlande
97	97	98	96	96	97	97	98	98	99	99	101	102	95	96	97	97	*96*	Italie
124	127	126	126	127	128	128	130	134	136	140	146	141	140	137	139	134	*129*	Luxembourg
101	98	96	95	94	94	94	94	91	91	93	93	94	94	94	97	96	*96*	Pays-Bas
82	81	82	83	83	88	97	94	90	86	86	87	92	93	91	91	93	*93*	Norvège
..	..	..	..	..	..	..	..	..	..	23	26	28	30	30	33	34	*36*	Pologne
58	60	61	59	57	55	53	55	57	58	60	63	65	67	69	69	69	*69*	Portugal
74	74	73	72	70	69	68	70	71	72	73	76	75	73	71	72	72	*73*	Espagne
90	92	94	90	89	89	90	92	90	88	86	85	82	81	80	80	79	*80*	Suède
140	140	138	137	134	133	130	127	123	122	120	121	122	122	121	122	117	*116*	Suisse
35	32	33	33	34	32	31	33	29	29	32	32	32	33	31	31	31	*32*	Turquie
91	90	92	93	93	93	97	99	102	101	99	94	96	95	94	92	95	*96*	Royaume-Uni
100	100	100	100	100	100	100	100	100	100	100	100	100	100	100	100	100	*100*	OCDE - Total[1]
86	86	86	85	85	84	84	84	84	84	84	85	85	84	83	83	83	*83*	OCDE - Europe[2]
91	92	92	91	91	90	90	91	91	91	91	92	93	91	91	91	91	*91*	UE15

1. Non compris la Corée, la République tchèque, la Hongrie et la Pologne.
2. Non compris la République tchèque, la Hongrie et la Pologne.

7.

Government final consumption expenditure - at current prices and current PPPs (billions US dollars)

	1960	1961	1962	1963	1964	1965	1966	1967	1968	1969	1970	1971	1972	1973	1974	1975	1976	1977	1978	1979
Canada	..	..	..	..	..	..	..	..	..	..	16.5	18.5	20.3	22.3	25.6	30.9	34.6	39.2	43.0	47.2
Mexico	..	..	..	..	..	..	..	..	..	..	4.3	5.0	6.4	7.9	9.0	11.7	13.9	15.0	17.8	21.1
United States	..	..	..	..	..	..	..	..	..	..	186.4	196.4	212.5	229.1	256.5	287.9	311.2	339.4	370.4	410.3
Japan	..	..	..	..	..	..	..	..	..	..	22.2	26.2	30.5	35.6	42.0	52.1	55.6	63.0	70.1	80.8
Korea	..	..	..	..	..	..	..	..	..	..	2.0	2.3	2.7	2.7	3.6	4.7	5.6	6.5	7.4	8.3
Australia	..	..	..	..	..	..	..	..	..	..	6.1	7.0	7.6	8.7	10.4	12.8	14.5	15.9	17.9	19.3
New Zealand	..	..	..	..	..	..	..	..	..	..	1.3	1.4	1.5	1.7	2.2	2.5	2.5	2.8	3.3	3.6
Austria	..	..	..	..	..	..	..	..	..	..	3.3	3.7	4.1	4.7	5.5	6.6	7.5	8.2	9.2	10.5
Belgium	..	..	..	..	..	..	..	..	..	..	4.1	4.7	5.4	6.1	6.9	8.3	9.4	10.3	11.8	13.2
Czech Republic	..	..	..	..	..	..	..	..	..	..										
Denmark	..	..	..	..	..	..	..	..	..	..	3.7	4.2	4.7	5.1	6.1	6.9	7.7	8.3	9.3	10.7
Finland	..	..	..	..	..	..	..	..	..	..	1.9	2.1	2.4	2.7	3.1	3.8	4.3	4.7	5.1	5.8
France	..	..	..	..	..	..	..	..	..	..	26.4	29.6	32.3	36.1	41.8	48.9	55.5	62.4	70.6	79.3
Germany	..	..	..	..	..	..	..	..	..	..	39.2	45.8	50.6	58.5	69.2	79.0	85.8	93.7	104.0	118.0
Greece	..	..	..	..	..	..	..	..	..	..	1.4	1.6	1.7	1.9	2.3	3.0	3.4	3.9	4.5	5.2
Hungary	..	..	..	..	..	..	..	..	..	..										
Iceland	..	..	..	..	..	..	..	..	..	..	0.1	0.1	0.1	0.1	0.2	0.2	0.2	0.2	0.3	0.3
Ireland	..	..	..	..	..	..	..	..	..	..	0.8	0.9	1.0	1.1	1.4	1.7	1.8	2.0	2.3	2.7
Italy	..	..	..	..	..	..	..	..	..	..	21.3	25.7	28.8	31.0	33.7	36.8	39.7	45.1	51.7	60.9
Luxembourg	..	..	..	..	..	..	..	..	..	..	0.1	0.1	0.2	0.2	0.2	0.3	0.3	0.3	0.4	0.4
Netherlands	..	..	..	..	..	..	..	..	..	..	6.7	7.6	8.1	8.9	10.5	12.3	13.6	15.0	16.9	19.3
Norway	..	..	..	..	..	..	..	..	..	..	1.9	2.2	2.4	2.7	3.1	3.7	4.4	4.9	5.6	6.2
Poland	..	..	..	..	..	..	..	..	..	..										
Portugal	..	..	..	..	..	..	..	..	..	..	1.7	1.9	2.1	2.4	2.9	3.2	3.4	3.9	4.3	4.9
Spain	..	..	..	..	..	..	..	..	..	..	7.1	7.9	8.9	10.2	12.1	14.1	15.7	18.7	21.2	24.0
Sweden	..	..	..	..	..	..	..	..	..	..	6.6	7.4	8.0	8.9	10.1	11.7	13.1	15.2	16.9	19.4
Switzerland	..	..	..	..	..	..	..	..	..	..	3.3	3.8	4.1	4.6	5.3	5.8	6.3	6.8	7.3	8.2
Turkey	..	..	..	..	..	..	..	..	..	..	3.0	3.6	4.3	5.1	5.3	7.0	9.0	11.0	10.6	10.8
United Kingdom	..	..	..	..	..	..	..	..	..	..	32.1	35.5	39.2	44.2	52.2	62.2	67.1	68.5	74.7	82.5
OECD - Total[1]	..	..	..	..	..	..	..	..	..	..	401.5	443.1	487.3	540.0	617.6	713.4	782.3	858.5	949.2	1064.7
OECD - Europe[2]	..	..	..	..	..	..	..	..	..	..	164.7	188.5	208.5	234.6	271.8	315.5	349.0	383.2	426.7	482.3
EU15	..	..	..	..	..	..	..	..	..	..	156.4	178.9	197.5	222.0	258.0	298.8	329.1	360.2	402.9	456.8

8.

Government final consumption expenditure per head - at current prices and current PPPs (US dollars)

	1960	1961	1962	1963	1964	1965	1966	1967	1968	1969	1970	1971	1972	1973	1974	1975	1976	1977	1978	1979
Canada	..	..	..	..	..	..	..	..	..	..	773	842	911	990	1121	1331	1471	1647	1791	1945
Mexico	..	..	..	..	..	..	..	..	..	..	88	98	122	145	161	204	231	246	282	326
United States	..	..	..	..	..	..	..	..	..	..	909	946	1012	1081	1199	1333	1427	1541	1664	1823
Japan	..	..	..	..	..	..	..	..	..	..	214	250	287	328	381	467	507	553	610	693
Korea	..	..	..	..	..	..	..	..	..	..	61	71	79	78	103	135	157	179	201	221
Australia	..	..	..	..	..	..	..	..	..	..	475	533	571	647	757	925	1025	1119	1244	1329
New Zealand	..	..	..	..	..	..	..	..	..	..	452	483	523	574	727	820	815	909	1057	1154
Austria	..	..	..	..	..	..	..	..	..	..	445	494	541	618	728	868	992	1089	1215	1392
Belgium	..	..	..	..	..	..	..	..	..	..	428	490	553	623	709	851	955	1046	1198	1346
Czech Republic	..	..	..	..	..	..	..	..	..	..	..	..	..	..	..	..	..	..	..	..
Denmark	..	..	..	..	..	..	..	..	..	..	742	851	933	1022	1201	1367	1515	1628	1816	2087
Finland	..	..	..	..	..	..	..	..	..	..	412	465	525	581	655	808	905	990	1070	1211
France	..	..	..	..	..	..	..	..	..	..	519	578	624	693	796	928	1047	1175	1323	1479
Germany	..	..	..	..	..	..	..	..	..	..	505	585	643	741	876	1004	1099	1198	1332	1510
Greece	..	..	..	..	..	..	..	..	..	..	158	177	194	208	262	330	363	422	478	546
Hungary	..	..	..	..	..	..	..	..	..	..	..	..	..	..	..	..	..	..	..	..
Iceland	..	..	..	..	..	..	..	..	..	..	356	435	528	572	720	799	851	988	1185	1384
Ireland	..	..	..	..	..	..	..	..	..	..	259	292	323	361	441	542	555	602	688	803
Italy	..	..	..	..	..	..	..	..	..	..	396	476	529	567	611	665	713	806	921	1081
Luxembourg	..	..	..	..	..	..	..	..	..	..	354	426	470	513	583	767	824	962	1058	1201
Netherlands	..	..	..	..	..	..	..	..	..	..	511	577	611	663	775	897	985	1084	1211	1372
Norway	..	..	..	..	..	..	..	..	..	..	483	561	620	685	781	931	1091	1214	1378	1521
Poland	..	..	..	..	..	..	..	..	..	..	..	..	..	..	..	..	..	..	..	..
Portugal	..	..	..	..	..	..	..	..	..	..	199	221	248	280	334	356	362	413	449	508
Spain	..	..	..	..	..	..	..	..	..	..	208	232	257	292	345	396	465	515	576	648
Sweden	..	..	..	..	..	..	..	..	..	..	825	916	988	1088	1243	1423	1595	1847	2048	2340
Switzerland	..	..	..	..	..	..	..	..	..	..	529	598	639	718	816	904	1002	1082	1157	1296
Turkey	..	..	..	..	..	..	..	..	..	..	86	99	116	133	136	174	219	263	248	248
United Kingdom	..	..	..	..	..	..	..	..	..	..	578	634	699	787	928	1107	1193	1218	1330	1467
OECD - Total[1]	..	..	..	..	..	..	..	..	..	..	514	560	609	667	756	865	939	1022	1119	1244
OECD - Europe[2]	..	..	..	..	..	..	..	..	..	..	426	484	531	593	684	789	868	949	1051	1182
EU15	..	..	..	..	..	..	..	..	..	..	460	522	573	641	742	856	939	1025	1142	1291

9.

Government final consumption expenditure per head - indices using current PPPs (OECD = 100)

	1960	1961	1962	1963	1964	1965	1966	1967	1968	1969	1970	1971	1972	1973	1974	1975	1976	1977	1978	1979
Canada	..	..	..	..	..	..	..	..	..	..	150	150	149	148	148	154	156	161	160	156
Mexico	..	..	..	..	..	..	..	..	..	..	17	18	20	22	21	24	25	24	25	26
United States	..	..	..	..	..	..	..	..	..	..	177	169	166	162	159	154	152	151	149	147
Japan	..	..	..	..	..	..	..	..	..	..	42	45	47	49	50	54	53	54	55	56
Korea	..	..	..	..	..	..	..	..	..	..	12	13	13	12	14	16	17	18	18	18
Australia	..	..	..	..	..	..	..	..	..	..	92	95	94	97	100	107	110	110	111	107
New Zealand	..	..	..	..	..	..	..	..	..	..	88	86	86	86	96	95	87	89	94	93
Austria	..	..	..	..	..	..	..	..	..	..	87	88	89	93	96	100	106	107	109	112
Belgium	..	..	..	..	..	..	..	..	..	..	83	87	91	93	94	98	102	102	107	108
Czech Republic	..	..	..	..	..	..	..	..	..	..	..	..	..	..	..	..	..	..	..	..
Denmark	..	..	..	..	..	..	..	..	..	..	144	152	153	153	159	158	161	159	162	168
Finland	..	..	..	..	..	..	..	..	..	..	80	83	86	87	87	94	96	97	96	97
France	..	..	..	..	..	..	..	..	..	..	101	103	102	104	105	107	112	115	118	119
Germany	..	..	..	..	..	..	..	..	..	..	98	104	106	111	116	116	117	117	119	121
Greece	..	..	..	..	..	..	..	..	..	..	31	32	32	31	35	38	39	41	43	44
Hungary	..	..	..	..	..	..	..	..	..	..	..	..	..	..	..	..	..	..	..	..
Iceland	..	..	..	..	..	..	..	..	..	..	69	78	87	86	95	92	91	97	106	111
Ireland	..	..	..	..	..	..	..	..	..	..	50	52	53	54	58	63	59	59	61	65
Italy	..	..	..	..	..	..	..	..	..	..	77	85	87	85	81	77	76	79	82	87
Luxembourg	..	..	..	..	..	..	..	..	..	..	69	76	77	77	77	89	87	94	94	97
Netherlands	..	..	..	..	..	..	..	..	..	..	99	103	100	99	103	104	105	106	108	110
Norway	..	..	..	..	..	..	..	..	..	..	94	100	102	103	103	108	116	119	123	122
Poland	..	..	..	..	..	..	..	..	..	..	..	..	..	..	..	..	..	..	..	..
Portugal	..	..	..	..	..	..	..	..	..	..	39	39	41	42	44	41	39	40	40	41
Spain	..	..	..	..	..	..	..	..	..	..	41	41	42	44	46	46	50	50	51	52
Sweden	..	..	..	..	..	..	..	..	..	..	161	163	162	163	164	165	170	181	183	188
Switzerland	..	..	..	..	..	..	..	..	..	..	103	107	105	108	108	105	107	106	103	104
Turkey	..	..	..	..	..	..	..	..	..	..	17	18	19	20	18	20	23	26	22	20
United Kingdom	..	..	..	..	..	..	..	..	..	..	112	113	115	118	123	128	127	119	119	118
OECD - Total[1]	..	..	..	..	..	..	..	..	..	..	100	100	100	100	100	100	100	100	100	100
OECD - Europe[2]	..	..	..	..	..	..	..	..	..	..	83	86	87	89	90	91	92	93	94	95
EU15	..	..	..	..	..	..	..	..	..	..	89	93	94	96	98	99	100	100	102	104

1. Excluding Korea, Czech Republic, Hungary and Poland.
2. Excluding Czech Republic, Hungary and Poland.

Consommation finale des administrations publiques - aux prix et PPA courants (milliards de dollars É-U) 7.

1980	1981	1982	1983	1984	1985	1986	1987	1988	1989	1990	1991	1992	1993	1994	1995	1996	1997	
52.9	59.9	66.6	71.1	75.6	82.6	86.6	90.3	97.4	105.1	116.3	126.1	131.7	134.8	135.2	143.8	142.0	143.6	Canada
24.8	32.0	32.8	27.5	31.3	33.3	32.4	32.9	34.0	36.3	40.4	45.7	55.4	65.3	72.1	64.7	64.3	60.2	Mexique
463.2	516.9	567.8	612.2	658.5	719.5	767.7	819.7	860.2	907.2	974.9	1016.8	1043.3	1062.7	1089.9	1124.6	1163.0	1206.1	États-Unis
92.1	106.0	115.7	124.1	133.0	140.5	149.3	156.9	167.7	182.1	198.7	214.2	229.9	242.9	253.3	280.9	292.0	299.0	Japon
10.2	*12.1*	*13.7*	*14.9*	*15.7*	*17.5*	*19.8*	*22.0*	*25.0*	*29.8*	*33.8*	*37.5*	*44.6*	*48.6*	*52.5*	*58.5*	*66.3*	*74.2*	*Corée*
22.1	25.7	27.9	30.0	33.0	36.1	38.6	39.2	40.7	42.6	46.8	50.9	53.1	55.3	58.5	63.0	66.0	68.4	Australie
4.3	4.9	5.3	5.4	5.7	5.9	6.3	6.5	6.8	7.2	7.6	7.8	8.4	8.3	8.3	9.0	9.3	10.2	Nouvelle-Zélande
11.8	13.3	14.7	15.8	16.6	17.8	18.9	19.9	21.0	22.6	24.1	26.0	28.5	31.0	32.7	34.0	35.2	36.1	Autriche
15.3	17.4	18.2	18.5	19.4	20.3	20.8	21.2	21.5	22.2	23.3	25.2	27.2	29.2	30.6	32.0	32.7	34.1	Belgique
..	..	..	..	..	..	..	..	..	..	21.3	17.5	19.5	23.4	24.6	26.0	27.7	27.3	République tchèque
12.4	14.1	15.7	16.3	16.8	17.7	17.8	19.4	20.9	21.6	22.5	24.0	25.1	27.4	28.7	30.7	32.7	34.2	Danemark
6.7	7.8	8.7	9.6	10.3	11.5	12.3	13.3	14.1	15.3	17.0	18.8	18.6	18.4	18.5	20.4	21.5	22.0	Finlande
90.7	104.4	116.4	123.8	131.6	137.2	140.6	147.7	156.7	165.4	177.0	190.3	205.8	213.4	217.2	227.6	234.2	241.2	France
134.1	151.7	158.8	166.5	177.4	188.5	196.2	207.9	221.1	230.1	246.3	266.0	298.4	301.9	318.2	339.3	347.8	351.2	Allemagne
5.8	7.1	7.6	8.2	9.2	10.3	10.1	10.5	11.8	13.6	14.3	14.5	15.4	16.6	17.0	20.5	20.3	21.6	Grèce
..	..	..	..	..	..	..	..	..	..	18.8	19.6	21.1	23.5	22.4	22.0	21.2	22.0	Hongrie
0.3	0.4	0.5	0.5	0.5	0.6	0.6	0.7	0.8	0.8	0.8	0.9	1.0	1.0	1.1	1.2	1.3	1.4	Islande
3.4	3.8	4.1	4.2	4.4	4.7	4.9	5.0	4.9	5.1	5.9	6.7	7.6	8.0	8.7	9.2	9.1	9.9	Irlande
69.9	84.2	90.0	96.8	103.4	110.9	115.3	125.8	137.5	145.4	162.0	171.8	182.0	178.2	182.9	182.9	193.3	199.7	Italie
0.5	0.6	0.6	0.6	0.7	0.7	0.8	0.9	0.9	1.0	1.2	1.3	1.4	1.5	1.5	1.7	1.8	1.9	Luxembourg
21.1	23.0	24.2	25.4	26.0	27.0	27.9	30.0	30.9	32.6	34.7	36.0	38.9	40.4	41.4	45.1	45.9	47.2	Pays-Bas
6.9	7.8	8.5	9.2	9.7	10.4	11.7	13.0	13.5	14.2	15.4	16.9	19.3	20.1	20.5	21.2	22.7	23.8	Norvège
..	..	..	..	..	..	..	..	..	..	34.8	37.9	39.4	40.1	37.5	44.5	46.5	50.0	Pologne
5.9	6.8	7.4	7.8	7.9	8.7	9.2	10.0	11.6	13.1	14.8	17.7	19.1	20.6	21.8	23.4	24.9	27.0	Portugal
28.3	32.7	35.8	39.4	41.1	45.2	47.6	53.4	57.1	64.2	71.4	80.5	88.0	91.5	90.4	95.1	99.1	101.6	Espagne
22.0	24.6	26.3	27.3	28.9	30.3	31.3	32.4	33.6	36.0	39.9	39.7	41.1	41.3	42.0	43.6	45.8	46.7	Suède
9.3	10.5	11.3	12.3	13.0	14.0	14.6	15.0	16.3	18.1	20.1	21.7	23.4	23.8	24.8	25.8	25.8	25.9	Suisse
8.4	12.6	12.1	14.6	13.9	15.0	16.6	16.3	16.8	21.6	28.9	34.2	38.3	43.1	37.3	37.4	43.5	50.5	Turquie
95.9	107.4	115.3	124.7	132.4	136.8	146.0	154.6	162.8	172.4	187.6	195.5	214.2	216.2	223.2	227.4	241.9	245.0	Royaume-Uni
1208.1	1375.7	1492.1	1591.8	1700.3	1825.4	1924.0	2042.7	2160.7	2295.8	2491.6	2649.2	2815.1	2893.0	2976.0	3104.4	3216.0	3308.4	OCDE - Total[1]
548.7	630.3	676.1	721.5	763.2	807.4	843.2	897.1	953.9	1015.3	1106.9	1187.6	1293.2	1323.6	1358.6	1418.4	1479.4	1520.9	OCDE - Europe[2]
523.8	598.9	643.8	685.0	726.2	767.5	799.7	852.0	906.4	960.5	1041.6	1114.0	1211.1	1235.6	1275.1	1332.9	1386.1	1419.3	UE15

Consommation finale des administrations publiques par tête - aux prix et PPA courants (dollars É-U) 8.

1980	1981	1982	1983	1984	1985	1986	1987	1988	1989	1990	1991	1992	1993	1994	1995	1996	1997	
2150	2408	2642	2794	2942	3185	3305	3403	3622	3839	4185	4484	4614	4657	4622	4855	4740	4742	Canada
372	468	468	385	428	445	424	423	428	449	489	544	648	751	815	715	699	644	Mexique
2034	2248	2445	2613	2786	3017	3190	3376	3511	3668	3901	4025	4085	4117	4181	4273	4379	4521	États-Unis
789	901	976	1040	1108	1164	1229	1285	1368	1479	1608	1729	1849	1948	2027	2237	2320	2370	Japon
269	*312*	*347*	*373*	*388*	*429*	*480*	*529*	*595*	*703*	*789*	*867*	*1021*	*1103*	*1175*	*1297*	*1456*	*1612*	*Corée*
1505	1720	1835	1952	2118	2289	2411	2413	2461	2534	2743	2946	3036	3130	3277	3484	3605	3692	Australie
1364	1563	1660	1668	1736	1816	1908	1977	2056	2155	2271	2256	2388	2341	2317	2457	2507	2712	Nouvelle-Zélande
1563	1760	1943	2088	2198	2350	2496	2617	2761	2947	3116	3322	3601	3877	4071	4230	4371	4467	Autriche
1554	1763	1848	1880	1963	2053	2107	2138	2172	2230	2335	2521	2708	2893	3021	3161	3223	3353	Belgique
..	..	..	..	..	..	..	..	..	..	2052	1702	1893	2267	2379	2512	2683	2650	République tchèque
2423	2757	3066	3193	3289	3470	3480	3793	4072	4206	4369	4663	4847	5284	5522	5879	6208	6467	Danemark
1409	1627	1799	1969	2111	2352	2498	2701	2847	3073	3410	3759	3698	3639	3645	3985	4192	4281	Finlande
1683	1927	2137	2260	2392	2481	2531	2646	2793	2932	3119	3336	3586	3702	3752	3916	4012	4116	France
1712	1934	2027	2131	2279	2427	2525	2675	2830	2924	3103	3325	3702	3719	3909	4155	4247	4280	Allemagne
603	725	781	838	929	1033	1017	1051	1175	1346	1403	1416	1489	1601	1635	1960	1933	2055	Grèce
..	..	..	..	..	..	..	..	..	..	1818	1899	2039	2278	2182	2152	2075	2164	Hongrie
1532	1768	1984	2016	2034	2286	2520	2916	3144	3233	3322	3534	3704	3874	3999	4626	4861	5082	Islande
987	1112	1187	1201	1259	1329	1370	1398	1397	1441	1681	1906	2139	2233	2435	2561	2515	2704	Irlande
1238	1491	1590	1709	1825	1956	2034	2220	2425	2564	2855	3027	3200	3124	3197	3192	3369	3471	Italie
1381	1577	1592	1645	1779	1937	2053	2308	2482	2703	3058	3240	3481	3646	3770	4197	4317	4394	Luxembourg
1490	1614	1690	1766	1804	1861	1918	2044	2097	2198	2320	2389	2561	2642	2694	2917	2957	3027	Pays-Bas
1694	1913	2057	2217	2335	2496	2816	3107	3218	3364	3637	3960	4510	4673	4718	4861	5181	5400	Norvège
..	..	..	..	..	..	..	..	..	..	913	991	1028	1043	972	1153	1204	1293	Pologne
604	695	742	781	794	870	919	999	1161	1322	1492	1798	1937	2086	2199	2358	2507	2715	Portugal
754	867	944	1035	1074	1177	1236	1384	1474	1654	1837	2067	2255	2341	2308	2424	2523	2583	Espagne
2652	2953	3155	3281	3462	3631	3738	3860	3978	4245	4653	4603	4740	4737	4788	4938	5178	5281	Suède
1452	1637	1750	1895	1992	2139	2218	2269	2447	2688	2958	3151	3375	3402	3518	3637	3627	3643	Suisse
189	277	258	305	283	299	322	310	313	394	514	596	656	724	615	606	694	792	Turquie
1703	1906	2048	2212	2343	2413	2568	2711	2848	3006	3259	3382	3693	3715	3823	3879	4114	4152	Royaume-Uni
1398	1578	1698	1797	1906	2030	2124	2238	2348	2474	2661	2805	2955	3011	3074	3181	3272	3346	OCDE - Total[1]
1337	1527	1630	1732	1825	1922	1998	2116	2237	2367	2562	2731	2953	3003	3065	3184	3305	3382	OCDE - Europe[2]
1474	1680	1802	1914	2027	2139	2224	2364	2507	2647	2857	3042	3291	3342	3437	3582	3715	3793	UE15

Consommation finale des administrations publiques par tête - indices en utilisant les PPA courantes (OCDE = 100) 9.

1980	1981	1982	1983	1984	1985	1986	1987	1988	1989	1990	1991	1992	1993	1994	1995	1996	1997	
154	153	156	155	154	157	156	152	154	155	157	160	156	155	150	153	145	142	Canada
27	30	28	21	22	22	20	19	13	18	18	19	22	25	27	22	21	19	Mexique
146	142	144	145	146	149	150	151	150	148	147	143	138	137	136	134	134	135	États-Unis
56	57	58	58	58	57	58	57	58	60	60	62	63	65	66	70	71	71	Japon
19	*20*	*20*	*21*	*20*	*21*	*23*	*24*	*25*	*28*	*30*	*31*	*35*	*37*	*38*	*41*	*44*	*48*	*Corée*
108	109	108	109	111	113	114	108	105	102	103	105	103	104	107	110	110	110	Australie
98	99	98	93	91	89	90	88	88	87	85	80	81	78	75	77	77	81	Nouvelle-Zélande
112	112	114	116	115	116	118	117	118	119	117	118	122	129	132	133	134	134	Autriche
111	112	109	105	103	101	99	96	92	90	88	90	92	96	98	99	99	100	Belgique
..	..	..	..	..	..	..	..	..	..	77	61	64	75	77	79	82	79	République tchèque
173	175	181	178	173	171	164	169	173	170	164	166	164	175	180	185	190	193	Danemark
101	103	106	110	111	116	118	121	121	124	128	134	125	121	119	125	128	128	Finlande
120	122	126	126	126	122	119	118	119	119	117	119	121	123	122	123	123	123	France
122	123	119	119	120	120	119	120	121	118	117	119	125	124	127	131	130	128	Allemagne
43	46	46	47	49	51	48	47	50	54	53	50	50	53	53	62	59	61	Grèce
..	..	..	..	..	..	..	..	..	..	68	68	69	76	71	68	63	65	Hongrie
110	112	117	112	107	113	119	130	134	131	125	126	125	129	130	145	149	152	Islande
71	70	70	67	66	65	65	62	59	58	63	68	72	74	79	81	77	81	Irlande
89	94	94	95	96	96	96	99	103	104	107	108	108	104	104	100	103	104	Italie
99	100	94	92	93	95	97	103	106	109	115	116	118	121	123	132	132	131	Luxembourg
107	102	100	98	95	92	90	91	89	89	87	85	87	88	88	92	90	90	Pays-Bas
121	121	121	123	123	123	133	139	137	136	137	141	153	155	153	153	158	161	Norvège
..	..	..	..	..	..	..	..	..	..	34	35	35	35	32	36	37	39	Pologne
43	44	44	43	42	43	43	45	49	53	56	64	66	69	72	74	77	81	Portugal
54	55	56	58	56	58	58	62	63	67	69	74	76	78	75	76	77	77	Espagne
190	187	186	183	182	179	176	173	169	172	175	164	160	157	156	155	158	158	Suède
104	104	103	105	105	105	104	101	104	109	111	112	114	113	114	114	111	109	Suisse
14	18	15	17	15	15	15	14	13	16	19	21	22	24	20	19	21	24	Turquie
122	121	121	123	123	119	121	121	121	122	122	121	125	123	124	122	126	124	Royaume-Uni
100	100	100	100	100	100	100	100	100	100	100	100	100	100	100	100	100	100	OCDE - Total[1]
96	97	96	96	96	95	94	95	95	96	96	97	100	100	100	100	101	101	OCDE - Europe[2]
105	106	106	107	106	105	105	106	107	107	107	108	111	111	112	113	114	113	UE15

1. Non compris la Corée, la République tchèque, la Hongrie et la Pologne.
2. Non compris la République tchèque, la Hongrie et la Pologne.

10. Gross fixed capital formation - at current prices and current PPPs (billions US dollars)

	1960	1961	1962	1963	1964	1965	1966	1967	1968	1969	1970	1971	1972	1973	1974	1975	1976	1977	1978	1979
Canada	..	..	..	..	..	..	..	..	..	..	17.1	19.8	21.6	25.3	29.7	34.4	37.4	40.2	44.3	51.0
Mexico	..	..	..	..	..	..	..	..	..	..	13.0	12.8	15.4	18.1	21.4	26.6	29.0	30.0	37.4	49.5
United States	..	..	..	..	..	..	..	..	..	..	180.1	201.3	230.6	263.0	276.1	281.1	319.9	383.2	461.6	529.2
Japan	..	..	..	..	..	..	..	..	..	..	105.8	112.9	127.6	156.3	160.2	168.3	179.1	193.2	220.7	264.0
Korea	..	..	..	..	..	..	..	..	..	..	*5.3*	*5.4*	*5.4*	*7.6*	*10.0*	*11.5*	*13.1*	*17.1*	*23.1*	*28.0*
Australia	..	..	..	..	..	..	..	..	..	..	11.5	13.1	13.4	14.6	15.6	17.7	19.8	21.3	23.7	26.3
New Zealand	..	..	..	..	..	..	..	..	..	..	2.2	2.4	2.8	3.2	4.1	4.7	4.6	4.3	4.5	4.4
Austria	..	..	..	..	..	..	..	..	..	..	5.4	6.4	7.7	8.1	9.1	9.3	10.2	11.9	11.8	13.5
Belgium	..	..	..	..	..	..	..	..	..	..	7.0	7.4	7.9	8.9	10.7	11.4	12.6	13.3	14.7	15.6
Czech Republic	..	..	..	..	..	..	..	..	..	..	..	..	..	..	..	..	..	..	..	..
Denmark	..	..	..	..	..	..	..	..	..	..	5.1	5.4	6.0	6.7	7.0	6.7	8.2	8.6	9.2	10.0
Finland	..	..	..	..	..	..	..	..	..	..	3.4	3.9	4.4	5.2	6.0	7.0	6.7	6.9	6.7	7.6
France	..	..	..	..	..	..	..	..	..	..	43.6	49.0	53.7	61.4	70.1	71.2	78.5	83.2	89.9	100.8
Germany	..	..	..	..	..	..	..	..	..	..	60.9	68.1	72.2	75.6	74.4	75.7	83.8	92.8	104.6	124.9
Greece	..	..	..	..	..	..	..	..	..	..	4.5	5.5	6.9	7.9	6.6	7.1	8.2	9.8	11.8	14.3
Hungary	..	..	..	..	..	..	..	..	..	..	..	..	..	..	..	..	..	..	..	..
Iceland	..	..	..	..	..	..	..	..	..	..	0.1	0.2	0.2	0.3	0.3	0.3	0.3	0.4	0.4	0.4
Ireland	..	..	..	..	..	..	..	..	..	..	1.2	1.4	1.5	1.8	2.0	2.1	2.5	2.9	3.7	4.6
Italy	..	..	..	..	..	..	..	..	..	..	39.7	41.5	43.3	52.7	62.4	64.1	69.7	75.8	82.2	94.8
Luxembourg	..	..	..	..	..	..	..	..	..	..	0.3	0.4	0.4	0.5	0.5	0.5	0.5	0.6	0.6	0.7
Netherlands	..	..	..	..	..	..	..	..	..	..	11.8	12.8	12.8	14.0	15.0	15.7	16.2	19.2	21.4	23.5
Norway	..	..	..	..	..	..	..	..	..	..	3.0	3.7	3.8	4.4	5.3	6.7	8.1	9.2	8.8	9.6
Poland	..	..	..	..	..	..	..	..	..	..	..	..	..	..	..	..	..	..	..	..
Portugal	..	..	..	..	..	..	..	..	..	..	3.5	4.1	5.1	6.0	6.4	6.7	7.3	8.8	10.2	11.2
Spain	..	..	..	..	..	..	..	..	..	..	19.4	19.6	23.3	28.2	34.2	35.5	36.9	38.9	40.2	41.7
Sweden	..	..	..	..	..	..	..	..	..	..	6.8	7.1	7.7	8.4	9.2	10.0	10.9	11.4	11.5	13.3
Switzerland	..	..	..	..	..	..	..	..	..	..	9.2	10.8	11.8	12.8	13.2	11.7	10.5	11.6	12.9	14.7
Turkey	..	..	..	..	..	..	..	..	..	..	6.1	6.2	7.2	8.2	9.7	12.0	16.6	17.8	16.0	18.0
United Kingdom	..	..	..	..	..	..	..	..	..	..	33.8	36.6	38.8	47.3	53.2	55.3	59.3	61.3	68.0	76.9
OECD - Total[1]	..	..	..	..	..	..	..	..	..	..	594.5	652.3	726.1	838.8	902.5	941.9	1 036.9	1 156.4	1 316.8	1 520.6
OECD - Europe[2]	..	..	..	..	..	..	..	..	..	..	264.9	290.0	314.8	358.4	395.3	409.1	447.1	484.3	524.7	596.1
EU15	..	..	..	..	..	..	..	..	..	..	246.5	269.2	291.8	332.7	366.8	378.4	411.5	445.4	486.6	553.3

11. Gross fixed capital formation per head - at current prices and current PPPs (US dollars)

	1960	1961	1962	1963	1964	1965	1966	1967	1968	1969	1970	1971	1972	1973	1974	1975	1976	1977	1978	1979
Canada	..	..	..	..	..	..	..	..	..	..	802	899	969	1 121	1 300	1 481	1 589	1 689	1 842	2 102
Mexico	..	..	..	..	..	..	..	..	..	..	264	253	294	333	383	461	489	490	595	764
United States	..	..	..	..	..	..	..	..	..	..	878	969	1 099	1 241	1 291	1 302	1 467	1 740	2 074	2 351
Japan	..	..	..	..	..	..	..	..	..	..	1 020	1 078	1 202	1 438	1 454	1 509	1 588	1 697	1 920	2 273
Korea	..	..	..	..	..	..	..	..	..	..	*163*	*164*	*162*	*221*	*288*	*326*	*365*	*470*	*626*	*745*
Australia	..	..	..	..	..	..	..	..	..	..	898	999	1 005	1 085	1 139	1 275	1 413	1 497	1 649	1 815
New Zealand	..	..	..	..	..	..	..	..	..	..	764	825	962	1 067	1 358	1 537	1 489	1 364	1 423	1 416
Austria	..	..	..	..	..	..	..	..	..	..	718	855	1 024	1 072	1 203	1 232	1 342	1 567	1 554	1 790
Belgium	..	..	..	..	..	..	..	..	..	..	722	766	813	917	1 097	1 165	1 281	1 349	1 492	1 586
Czech Republic	..	..	..	..	..	..	..	..	..	..	..	..	..	..	..	..	..	..	..	..
Denmark	..	..	..	..	..	..	..	..	..	..	1 030	1 088	1 209	1 335	1 385	1 316	1 622	1 689	1 805	1 956
Finland	..	..	..	..	..	..	..	..	..	..	748	844	959	1 117	1 286	1 493	1 408	1 460	1 412	1 587
France	..	..	..	..	..	..	..	..	..	..	859	957	1 039	1 179	1 337	1 351	1 483	1 566	1 684	1 881
Germany	..	..	..	..	..	..	..	..	..	..	784	869	917	958	942	962	1 070	1 187	1 340	1 599
Greece	..	..	..	..	..	..	..	..	..	..	516	620	772	886	733	787	897	1 057	1 248	1 502
Hungary	..	..	..	..	..	..	..	..	..	..	..	..	..	..	..	..	..	..	..	..
Iceland	..	..	..	..	..	..	..	..	..	..	680	969	1 028	1 256	1 504	1 588	1 550	1 729	1 744	1 908
Ireland	..	..	..	..	..	..	..	..	..	..	407	458	504	589	639	669	783	884	1 125	1 369
Italy	..	..	..	..	..	..	..	..	..	..	737	768	796	962	1 132	1 155	1 251	1 354	1 464	1 683
Luxembourg	..	..	..	..	..	..	..	..	..	..	834	1 104	1 190	1 330	1 339	1 526	1 488	1 626	1 742	1 962
Netherlands	..	..	..	..	..	..	..	..	..	..	908	968	964	1 041	1 108	1 150	1 179	1 388	1 538	1 671
Norway	..	..	..	..	..	..	..	..	..	..	767	942	961	1 115	1 319	1 670	2 011	2 265	2 173	2 362
Poland	..	..	..	..	..	..	..	..	..	..	..	..	..	..	..	..	..	..	..	..
Portugal	..	..	..	..	..	..	..	..	..	..	397	480	595	696	730	732	784	925	1 067	1 156
Spain	..	..	..	..	..	..	..	..	..	..	573	574	674	811	974	1 000	1 026	1 070	1 093	1 124
Sweden	..	..	..	..	..	..	..	..	..	..	847	875	944	1 027	1 126	1 224	1 328	1 387	1 394	1 604
Switzerland	..	..	..	..	..	..	..	..	..	..	1 470	1 696	1 842	1 986	2 045	1 820	1 658	1 833	2 040	2 312
Turkey	..	..	..	..	..	..	..	..	..	..	171	170	192	213	249	300	405	426	376	414
United Kingdom	..	..	..	..	..	..	..	..	..	..	608	654	692	841	946	984	1 055	1 091	1 210	1 367
OECD - Total[1]	..	..	..	..	..	..	..	..	..	..	761	825	908	1 037	1 104	1 141	1 245	1 376	1 553	1 777
OECD - Europe[2]	..	..	..	..	..	..	..	..	..	..	686	744	802	906	994	1 023	1 112	1 199	1 293	1 461
EU15	..	..	..	..	..	..	..	..	..	..	724	786	847	960	1 054	1 083	1 175	1 267	1 380	1 563

12. Gross fixed capital formation per head - indices using current PPPs (OECD = 100)

	1960	1961	1962	1963	1964	1965	1966	1967	1968	1969	1970	1971	1972	1973	1974	1975	1976	1977	1978	1979
Canada	..	..	..	..	..	..	..	..	..	..	105	109	107	108	118	130	128	123	119	118
Mexico	..	..	..	..	..	..	..	..	..	..	35	31	32	32	35	40	39	36	38	43
United States	..	..	..	..	..	..	..	..	..	..	115	118	121	120	117	114	118	126	134	132
Japan	..	..	..	..	..	..	..	..	..	..	134	131	132	139	132	132	128	123	124	128
Korea	..	..	..	..	..	..	..	..	..	..	*21*	*20*	*18*	*21*	*26*	*29*	*29*	*34*	*40*	*42*
Australia	..	..	..	..	..	..	..	..	..	..	118	121	111	105	103	112	113	109	106	102
New Zealand	..	..	..	..	..	..	..	..	..	..	100	100	106	103	123	135	120	99	92	80
Austria	..	..	..	..	..	..	..	..	..	..	94	104	113	103	109	108	108	114	100	101
Belgium	..	..	..	..	..	..	..	..	..	..	95	93	90	88	99	102	103	98	96	89
Czech Republic	..	..	..	..	..	..	..	..	..	..	..	..	..	..	..	..	..	..	..	..
Denmark	..	..	..	..	..	..	..	..	..	..	135	132	133	129	125	115	130	123	116	110
Finland	..	..	..	..	..	..	..	..	..	..	98	102	106	108	116	131	113	106	91	89
France	..	..	..	..	..	..	..	..	..	..	113	116	114	114	121	118	119	114	108	106
Germany	..	..	..	..	..	..	..	..	..	..	103	105	101	92	85	84	86	86	86	90
Greece	..	..	..	..	..	..	..	..	..	..	68	75	85	85	66	69	72	77	80	85
Hungary	..	..	..	..	..	..	..	..	..	..	..	..	..	..	..	..	..	..	..	..
Iceland	..	..	..	..	..	..	..	..	..	..	89	117	113	121	136	139	124	126	112	107
Ireland	..	..	..	..	..	..	..	..	..	..	54	56	55	57	58	59	63	64	72	77
Italy	..	..	..	..	..	..	..	..	..	..	97	93	88	93	102	101	100	98	94	95
Luxembourg	..	..	..	..	..	..	..	..	..	..	110	134	131	128	121	134	120	118	112	110
Netherlands	..	..	..	..	..	..	..	..	..	..	119	117	106	100	100	101	95	101	99	94
Norway	..	..	..	..	..	..	..	..	..	..	101	114	106	108	119	146	162	165	140	133
Poland	..	..	..	..	..	..	..	..	..	..	..	..	..	..	..	..	..	..	..	..
Portugal	..	..	..	..	..	..	..	..	..	..	52	58	66	67	66	64	63	67	69	65
Spain	..	..	..	..	..	..	..	..	..	..	75	70	74	78	88	88	82	78	70	63
Sweden	..	..	..	..	..	..	..	..	..	..	111	106	104	99	102	107	107	101	90	90
Switzerland	..	..	..	..	..	..	..	..	..	..	193	206	203	192	185	159	133	133	131	130
Turkey	..	..	..	..	..	..	..	..	..	..	22	21	21	21	23	26	33	31	24	23
United Kingdom	..	..	..	..	..	..	..	..	..	..	80	79	76	81	86	86	85	79	78	77
OECD - Total[1]	..	..	..	..	..	..	..	..	..	..	100	100	100	100	100	100	100	100	100	100
OECD - Europe[2]	..	..	..	..	..	..	..	..	..	..	90	90	88	87	90	90	89	87	83	82
EU15	..	..	..	..	..	..	..	..	..	..	95	95	93	93	95	95	94	92	89	88

1. Excluding Korea, Czech Republic, Hungary and Poland.
2. Excluding Czech Republic, Hungary and Poland.

Formation brute de capital fixe - aux prix et PPA courants (milliards de dollars É-U) — 10.

1980	1981	1982	1983	1984	1985	1986	1987	1988	1989	1990	1991	1992	1993	1994	1995	1996	1997	
57.5	68.7	62.9	62.9	66.8	75.0	80.3	90.7	101.7	110.5	108.2	101.3	99.1	99.3	110.2	114.1	119.1	135.6	Canada
60.5	77.4	70.9	54.2	60.1	68.0	68.4	68.2	74.8	75.8	86.1	93.9	109.4	109.9	120.8	100.0	118.7	141.0	Mexique
547.3	603.2	590.1	629.5	734.5	785.5	818.2	835.5	881.6	924.6	932.5	882.1	937.5	1011.7	1106.4	1176.9	1269.3	1359.5	États-Unis
296.3	326.8	344.2	349.6	376.0	403.1	421.8	471.8	544.0	613.9	698.8	745.9	762.8	762.0	760.2	815.2	895.6	877.8	Japon
28.4	29.1	33.7	40.7	45.5	49.4	55.7	66.2	77.9	93.3	123.8	140.4	150.1	162.7	176.9	208.5	228.4	233.0	Corée
30.4	37.1	38.4	36.5	41.0	48.0	49.9	53.0	57.7	65.4	61.9	57.2	58.5	63.0	71.4	77.1	80.2	86.8	Australie
4.9	6.5	7.4	7.9	8.9	9.7	8.7	8.6	8.0	8.7	8.6	7.4	8.1	9.8	11.7	13.1	13.6	13.3	Nouvelle-Zélande
15.7	17.1	16.9	17.6	18.1	19.9	20.8	22.3	24.6	27.3	30.1	32.9	34.6	35.0	38.3	40.2	42.5	45.0	Autriche
18.3	17.2	17.4	16.9	17.9	18.8	19.5	21.1	25.5	29.5	33.7	33.0	35.7	35.4	36.2	38.8	39.4	42.0	Belgique
..	..	..	..	..	..	..	..	..	..	30.4	23.1	28.9	30.2	32.7	40.8	43.2	41.4	République tchèque
9.8	8.9	10.0	10.7	12.6	14.8	17.4	17.1	16.5	17.2	17.7	18.0	17.6	17.7	19.3	22.4	24.4	27.0	Danemark
9.5	10.7	11.7	12.7	12.8	13.7	14.0	15.4	17.6	21.6	21.8	17.5	13.8	11.7	12.1	14.5	15.6	17.7	Finlande
115.0	122.9	128.6	128.1	129.5	136.4	143.2	155.1	176.0	196.6	210.4	220.7	219.0	199.5	201.1	212.0	208.8	212.9	France
143.6	153.5	152.9	162.9	171.2	177.2	185.9	196.4	213.9	237.8	274.1	313.4	343.4	328.6	350.9	363.5	356.8	360.9	Allemagne
15.0	15.2	14.5	15.5	15.1	16.7	16.8	16.1	17.7	20.1	21.5	22.6	23.4	23.1	22.7	24.4	26.8	29.2	Grèce
..	..	..	..	..	..	..	..	..	..	18.2	16.0	15.8	15.5	17.2	17.4	19.1	21.0	Hongrie
0.5	0.6	0.7	0.6	0.6	0.7	0.7	0.8	0.8	0.8	0.8	0.9	0.8	0.8	0.8	0.9	1.1	1.3	Islande
4.9	5.8	5.6	5.1	5.2	4.9	4.7	4.8	5.3	6.2	7.5	7.4	8.1	7.8	9.2	10.7	11.9	14.1	Irlande
114.2	124.5	124.0	124.3	132.2	137.7	138.6	147.2	162.0	175.1	187.2	193.3	197.6	171.3	177.9	197.2	200.6	203.7	Italie
0.9	0.9	0.9	0.9	0.9	0.9	1.2	1.4	1.7	1.9	2.1	2.4	2.4	2.7	2.5	2.8	2.7	3.1	Luxembourg
25.9	26.0	26.0	27.7	30.5	33.6	36.7	39.2	42.8	47.1	49.9	50.6	53.1	52.3	54.2	59.9	63.9	69.2	Pays-Bas
10.0	11.1	11.9	13.2	13.8	14.1	16.8	17.9	18.8	17.9	16.1	16.4	17.4	18.8	19.7	21.0	23.8	27.2	Norvège
..	..	..	..	..	..	..	..	..	..	39.0	33.8	32.0	32.7	34.1	42.7	50.4	61.2	Pologne
13.8	16.6	18.2	17.8	14.8	14.5	15.7	19.1	22.7	24.1	26.2	27.0	27.6	26.8	29.1	31.2	32.7	36.3	Portugal
47.8	51.8	55.2	56.6	54.1	58.9	63.2	73.7	87.5	102.1	112.0	118.4	112.3	103.5	106.0	118.3	121.1	129.4	Espagne
15.1	15.6	16.5	17.6	19.2	20.9	21.1	23.5	26.0	30.3	31.3	28.2	25.0	20.9	21.1	24.6	25.8	24.7	Suède
18.3	20.8	20.8	22.4	24.0	25.8	27.4	29.0	32.8	36.6	39.1	38.1	36.4	35.4	37.5	38.4	35.8	36.1	Suisse
15.9	22.4	24.5	26.4	29.5	36.6	46.0	51.6	57.7	52.7	60.3	65.9	70.5	87.7	78.7	82.6	94.4	108.8	Turquie
79.7	78.5	83.8	90.2	102.5	110.3	117.3	133.4	159.1	178.6	178.6	153.9	152.1	147.9	155.3	165.6	178.0	188.2	Royaume-Uni
1670.7	1839.9	1854.0	1907.6	2091.9	2245.6	2354.2	2512.7	2776.7	3022.4	3216.4	3248.4	3366.1	3382.7	3553.3	3765.3	4002.5	4191.0	OCDE - Total [1]
673.7	720.2	740.2	767.0	804.6	856.3	907.0	984.9	1108.9	1223.5	1320.2	1360.6	1390.7	1327.0	1372.6	1468.9	1506.0	1576.9	OCDE - Europe [2]
629.0	665.3	682.2	704.5	736.7	779.1	816.1	885.7	998.9	1115.4	1204.0	1239.4	1265.7	1184.3	1235.9	1326.0	1350.9	1403.5	UE15

Formation brute de capital fixe par tête - aux prix et PPA courants (dollars É-U) — 11.

1980	1981	1982	1983	1984	1985	1986	1987	1988	1989	1990	1991	1992	1993	1994	1995	1996	1997	
2340	2757	2495	2472	2598	2890	3063	3416	3783	4035	3894	3601	3473	3431	3767	3852	3974	4478	Canada
906	1132	1014	758	821	910	896	876	942	936	1043	1117	1279	1263	1365	1105	1291	1507	Mexique
2403	2623	2541	2687	3108	3294	3400	3441	3598	3738	3731	3491	3671	3919	4244	4472	4780	5096	États-Unis
2537	2778	2906	2931	3133	3338	3472	3864	4437	4986	5656	6019	6136	6112	6084	6492	7115	6958	Japon
744	751	857	1020	1127	1210	1351	1590	1853	2197	2887	3245	3438	3693	3964	4623	5014	5067	Corée
2069	2483	2532	2372	2631	3040	3113	3261	3490	3888	3629	3311	3342	3565	3997	4267	4378	4686	Australie
1568	2067	2318	2452	2738	2962	2642	2612	2405	2627	2549	2121	2312	2749	3254	3578	3665	3548	Nouvelle-Zélande
2075	2257	2225	2329	2396	2620	2737	2933	3232	3560	3889	4212	4371	4378	4772	4994	5271	5573	Autriche
1854	1743	1767	1706	1812	1903	1967	2131	2568	2974	3379	3301	3552	3512	3576	3825	3876	4126	Belgique
..	..	..	..	..	..	..	..	..	..	2937	2241	2801	2925	3165	3949	4192	4022	République tchèque
1918	1745	1959	2093	2457	2887	3393	3336	3207	3355	3437	3501	3405	3416	3714	4284	4630	5119	Danemark
1995	2219	2419	2610	2619	2789	2843	3123	3567	4357	4371	3485	2746	2309	2372	2831	3051	3453	Finlande
2134	2268	2359	2339	2353	2468	2579	2778	3136	3484	3708	3869	3817	3461	3474	3646	3577	3632	France
1833	1958	1952	2086	2199	2281	2393	2527	2738	3022	3454	3918	4261	4048	4310	4452	4357	4398	Allemagne
1551	1562	1482	1570	1531	1680	1688	1606	1763	1991	2116	2210	2270	2230	2177	2337	2557	2788	Grèce
..	..	..	..	..	..	..	..	..	..	1756	1548	1527	1506	1673	1705	1879	2070	Hongrie
2368	2599	2779	2482	2675	2761	2707	3189	3142	3145	3327	3444	3207	2931	2946	3243	4202	4673	Islande
1436	1676	1609	1453	1459	1379	1328	1357	1514	1755	2142	2098	2273	2186	2562	2961	3289	3853	Irlande
2023	2204	2192	2195	2334	2430	2445	2597	2858	3087	3300	3405	3475	3003	3110	3441	3496	3542	Italie
2403	2466	2593	2371	2487	2329	3139	3759	4627	4998	5492	6322	6045	6672	6164	6747	6605	7433	Luxembourg
1833	1827	1817	1925	2117	2322	2522	2672	2898	3175	3336	3357	3496	3420	3526	3875	4115	4431	Pays-Bas
2438	2719	2900	3195	3344	3404	4042	4274	4465	4237	3785	3849	4062	4368	4535	4811	5422	6168	Norvège
..	..	..	..	..	..	..	..	..	..	1024	884	833	849	884	1106	1305	1584	Pologne
1408	1690	1833	1788	1477	1451	1570	1912	2281	2430	2648	2732	2799	2717	2935	3150	3289	3651	Portugal
1273	1373	1454	1486	1414	1533	1641	1908	2260	2631	2882	3041	2879	2647	2708	3016	3083	3290	Espagne
1816	1878	1985	2110	2306	2508	2521	2795	3085	3565	3658	3272	2881	2400	2407	2788	2917	2796	Suède
2871	3240	3223	3450	3686	3946	4169	4377	4911	5441	5748	5542	5236	5063	5332	5429	5042	5071	Suisse
358	491	525	551	601	728	894	981	1074	961	1073	1149	1207	1475	1300	1340	1505	1707	Turquie
1415	1392	1488	1599	1815	1946	2063	2340	2783	3113	3103	2663	2622	2542	2659	2826	3027	3189	Royaume-Uni
1933	2111	2110	2154	2344	2498	2598	2753	3018	3257	3435	3439	3533	3521	3671	3858	4072	4239	OCDE - Total [1]
1641	1745	1785	1841	1924	2038	2149	2323	2601	2852	3056	3128	3176	3011	3097	3297	3365	3507	OCDE - Europe [2]
1770	1866	1910	1969	2056	2171	2269	2458	2763	3074	3303	3384	3439	3203	3331	3564	3620	3751	UE15

Formation brute de capital fixe par tête - indices en utilisant les PPA courantes (OCDE = 100) — 12.

1980	1981	1982	1983	1984	1985	1986	1987	1988	1989	1990	1991	1992	1993	1994	1995	1996	1997	
121	131	118	115	111	116	118	124	125	124	113	105	98	97	103	100	98	106	Canada
47	54	48	35	35	36	34	32	31	29	30	32	36	36	37	29	32	36	Mexique
124	124	120	125	133	132	131	125	119	115	109	102	104	111	116	116	117	120	États-Unis
131	132	138	136	134	134	134	140	147	153	165	175	174	174	166	168	175	164	Japon
39	36	41	47	48	48	52	58	61	67	84	94	97	105	108	120	123	120	Corée
107	118	120	110	112	122	120	118	116	119	106	96	95	101	109	111	108	111	Australie
81	98	110	114	117	119	102	95	80	81	74	62	65	78	89	93	90	84	Nouvelle-Zélande
107	107	105	108	102	105	105	107	107	109	113	122	124	124	130	129	129	131	Autriche
96	83	84	79	77	76	76	77	85	91	98	96	101	100	97	99	95	97	Belgique
..	..	..	..	..	..	..	..	..	..	85	65	79	83	86	102	103	95	République tchèque
99	83	93	97	105	116	131	121	106	103	100	102	96	97	101	111	114	121	Danemark
103	105	115	121	112	112	109	113	118	134	127	101	78	66	65	73	75	81	Finlande
110	107	112	109	100	99	99	101	104	107	108	112	108	98	95	95	88	86	France
95	93	93	97	94	91	92	92	91	93	101	114	121	115	117	115	107	104	Allemagne
80	74	70	73	65	67	65	58	58	61	62	64	64	63	59	61	63	66	Grèce
..	..	..	..	..	..	..	..	..	..	51	45	43	43	46	44	46	49	Hongrie
123	123	132	115	114	111	104	116	104	97	97	100	91	83	80	84	103	110	Islande
74	79	76	67	62	55	51	49	50	54	62	61	64	62	70	77	81	91	Irlande
105	104	104	102	100	97	94	94	95	95	96	99	98	85	85	89	86	84	Italie
124	117	123	110	106	93	121	137	153	153	160	184	171	189	168	175	162	175	Luxembourg
95	87	86	89	90	93	97	97	96	97	97	98	99	97	96	100	101	105	Pays-Bas
126	129	137	148	143	136	156	155	148	130	110	112	115	124	124	125	133	146	Norvège
..	..	..	..	..	..	..	..	..	..	30	26	24	24	24	29	32	37	Pologne
73	80	87	83	63	58	60	69	76	75	77	79	79	77	80	82	81	86	Portugal
66	65	69	69	60	61	63	69	75	81	84	88	81	75	74	78	76	78	Espagne
94	89	94	98	98	100	97	102	102	109	106	95	82	68	66	72	72	66	Suède
149	154	153	160	157	158	160	159	163	167	167	161	148	144	145	141	124	120	Suisse
19	23	25	26	26	29	34	36	36	29	31	33	34	42	35	35	37	40	Turquie
73	66	71	74	77	78	79	85	92	96	90	77	74	72	72	73	74	75	Royaume-Uni
100	100	100	100	100	100	100	100	100	100	100	100	100	100	100	100	100	100	OCDE - Total [1]
85	83	85	85	82	82	83	84	86	88	89	91	90	86	84	85	83	83	OCDE - Europe [2]
92	88	91	91	88	87	87	89	92	94	96	98	97	91	91	92	89	89	UE15

1. Non compris la Corée, la République tchèque, la Hongrie et la Pologne.
2. Non compris la République tchèque, la Hongrie et la Pologne.

PART EIGHT

Appendix
Annexe

The statistics for Germany in this publication refer to Germany after unification. Official data for Germany after unification are available only from 1991 onwards. In this publication, the secretariat has estimated some national accounts aggregates for the whole of Germany back to 1960 in order to calculate the various zones totals. These estimates are based on statistics published by Deutsches Institut fur Wirtschaftsforschung for period 1989-90 and by the East German Statistical Office in 1990 for period 1980-89. They are also based on the ratios of the aggregates of West Germany and the whole of Germany.

Les statistiques concernant l'Allemagne dans cette publication se réfèrent à l'Allemagne après l'unification. Des données officielles pour l'Allemagne après l'unification ne sont disponibles qu'à partir de 1991. Dans cette publication, le secrétariat a estimé certains agrégats des comptes nationaux pour l'Allemagne dans son ensemble depuis 1960 afin de calculer les différentes zones. Ces estimations sont basées sur des statistiques publiées par Deutsches Institut fur Wirtschaftsforschung pour la période 1989-90 et par l'Office Statistique de l'Allemagne de l'Est en 1990 pour la période 1980-89. Elles sont aussi basées sur les rapports des agrégats de l'Allemagne occidentale et de l'Allemagne dans son ensemble.

POPULATION

Population is defined as all nationals present in or temporarely absent from the country and aliens permanently settled in the country. For further details see Labour force statistics, OECD. Data for Korea, Czech Republic, Hungary and Poland have not been included in area total. Data for Germany refer to Germany after unification.

EXCHANGE RATES

The exchange rates have been calculated by the International Monetary Fund, and are published in International Financial Statistics. They are par or market rates averaged over the year. The exchange rates shown for Germany refer to the Deutsche Mark.

PURCHASING POWER PARITIES FOR GDP

PPPs are the rates of currency conversion that equalise the purchasing power of different countries by eliminating differences in price levels between countries. When converted by means of PPPs, the expenditures on GDP for different countries are in effect expressed at the same set of prices so that comparisons between countries reflect only differences in the volume of goods and services purchased.

1990, 1993, 1996: PPPs for all OECD countries except those listed below are triennial benchmark results calculated jointly by the OECD and the Statistical Office of the European Communities (Eurostat). For Mexico, Korea, Czech Republic, Hungary and Poland, the PPPs for 1990 and 1993 are OECD estimates. for Korea the PPPs for 1996 are also OECD estimates.

1970 to 1989: The 1990 PPPs were backdated to 1970 using each country's rate of inflation relative to that of the United States. Specifically, country k's PPP for year t was obtained by multiplying its 1990 PPP by Ikt divided by Iust where Ik is the GDP price index based on 1990 for country k and Ius is the GDP price index based on 1990 for the United States. As changes in PPPs depend directly on relative rates of inflation in different countries, this method produces robust estimates for years other than the base year provided they are not too remote from the base morning.

1991, 1992, 1994 and 1995: Since 1991, Eurostat has calculated annual PPPs for EU Member States and a number of other European OECD countries. In 1991, Eurostat calculated PPPs for the twelve EU Member States plus Austria, Sweden and Switzerland; in 1992, Eurostat calculated PPPs for the same 15 countries plus Finland; and in 1994 and 1995, Eurostat calculated PPPs for the 15 EU Member States plus Iceland, Norway, Poland and Switzerland. PPPs for the countries not covered by Eurostat are OECD estimates.

1997: PPPs for all countries are OECD estimates.

POPULATION

La population est définie comme l'ensemble des nationaux présents ou temporairement absents du pays et des étrangers établis en permanence dans le pays. Pour plus de détails, se reporter aux Statistiques de la population active, OCDE. Les données de la Corée, de la République tchèque, de la Hongrie et de la Pologne n'ont pas été intégrées aux totaux par zones. Les données de l'Allemagne se réfèrent à l'Allemagne après l'unification.

TAUX DE CHANGE

Les taux de change sont calculés par le Fonds Monétaire International et publiés dans International Financial Statistics. Ce taux est une moyenne sur l'année du taux du marché/parité ou taux central. Le taux de change montré pour l'Allemagne se réfère au Deutsche Mark.

PARITÉS DE POUVOIR D'ACHAT DU PIB

Les PPA sont les taux de conversion monétaire qui permettent d'exprimer dans une unité commune les pouvoirs d'achat des différentes monnaies en éliminant les différences de niveaux de prix existant entre les pays. Les dépenses imputées au PIB, pour les différents pays, converties en utilisant les PPA sont en effet exprimées en fonction d'une même structure de prix internationaux si bien que les écarts entre pays reflètent uniquement les différences de volume de biens et services achetés.

1990, 1993, 1996 : les PPA pour tous les pays de l'OCDE, à l'exception de ceux énumérés ci-dessous, sont les résultats, pour ces années de référence des calculs triennaux effectués par l'Office Statistique des Communautés Européennes (Eurostat). Pour le Mexique, la Corée, la République tchèque, la Hongrie et la Pologne, les PPA pour 1990 et 1993 sont des estimations de l'OCDE. les PPA de 1996 pour la Corée sont aussi des estimations de l'OCDE.

1970-1989 : les PPA de 1990 du PIB ont été extrapolées jusqu'en 1970 en utilisant les taux d'inflation de chaque pays rapportés à celui des États-Unis. Plus précisément la PPA du pays k pour l'année t a été obtenue en multipliant sa PPA de 1990 par le rapport Ikt/Iust où Ik est l'indice de prix du PIB du pays k sur la base 1990 et Ius l'indice de prix du PIB des États-Unis sur la base 1990. Les variations des PPA dépendant directement des taux d'inflation relatifs des différents pays, cette méthode permet dobtenir des estimations fiables pour les années autres que lannée de base à condition quelles ne soient pas trop éloignées de cette année de base.

1991, 1992, 1994 et 1995 : Depuis 1991, Eurostat calcule des parités annuelles pour les États Membres de l'UE et pour plusieurs autres pays européens. En 1991, Eurostat a calculé des données annuelles pour les 12 États Membres des communautés, plus l'Autriche, la Suède et la Suisse ; en 1992, la Finlande a été associée à ces calculs ; en 1994 et 1995, Eurostat a calculé des PPA pour les 15 pays de l'UE plus l'Islande, la Norvège, la Pologne et la Suisse. Les PPA pour les pays non couverts par Eurostat sont des estimations de l'OCDE.

1997 : Les PPA pour tous les pays sont des estimations de l'OCDE.

1. Population - mid-year estimates in thousands

	1960	1961	1962	1963	1964	1965	1966	1967	1968	1969	1970	1971	1972	1973	1974	1975	1976	1977	1978
Canada	17870	18238	18583	18931	19290	19644	20015	20378	20701	21001	21297	22026	22285	22560	22875	23209	23518	23796	24036
Mexico	35540*	36690*	37880*	39100*	40380*	41700*	43080*	44500*	45970*	47490*	49060*	50700*	52400*	54150*	55910*	57670*	59420*	61180*	62940*
United States	180671	183691	186538	189242	191889	194303	196560	198712	200706	202677	205052	207661	209896	211909	213854	215973	218035	220239	222585
Japan	93260	94100	94980	95890	96900	97950	98860	99920	101070	102320	103720	104750	106180	108660	110160	111520	112770	113880	114920
Korea	..	..	..	..	..	..	28960	30130	30840	31540	32240	32880	33510	34103	34692	35281	35849	36412	36969
Australia	10547	10774	10986	11196	11418	11648	11865	12074	12300	12553	12817	13067	13304	13505	13723	13893	14033	14192	14359
New Zealand	2377	2427	2485	2537	2589	2635	2683	2728	2754	2780	2820	2864	2913	2971	3032	3087	3116	3128	3129
Austria	7048	7087	7130	7175	7224	7271	7322	7377	7415	7441	7467	7501	7544	7586	7599	7579	7566	7568	7562
Belgium	9118	9166	9218	9283	9367	9488	9508	9557	9590	9613	9638	9673	9709	9738	9768	9795	9811	9822	9830
Czech Republic	..	..	..	..	..	9785	9826	9854	9878	9897	9805	9831	9868	9922	9989	10062	10128	10189	10246
Denmark	4581	4612	4647	4684	4720	4757	4797	4839	4867	4891	4929	4963	4992	5022	5045	5060	5073	5088	5104
Finland	4430	4461	4491	4523	4549	4564	4581	4606	4626	4624	4606	4612	4640	4666	4691	4712	4726	4739	4753
France	45684	46163	46998	47854	48348	48758	49164	49548	49915	50318	50772	51251	51701	52118	52460	52699	52909	53145	53376
Germany	72674	73310	73939	74544	74963	75647	76214	76368	76584	77143	77709	78345	78715	78956	78979	78679	78317	78165	78082
Greece	8327	8398	8448	8480	8510	8551	8614	8716	8741	8773	8793	8831	8889	8929	8962	9046	9167	9308	9430
Hungary	9984	10030	10063	10091	10124	10153	10185	10224	10264	10303	10337	10365	10394	10426	10472	10532	10589	10638	10674
Iceland	176	179	182	185	189	192	196	199	201	203	204	206	209	212	215	218	220	222	224
Ireland	2834	2819	2830	2850	2864	2876	2884	2900	2913	2926	2950	2978	3024	3073	3124	3177	3228	3272	3314
Italy	50200	50536	50879	51252	51675	52112	52519	52901	53236	53538	53822	54073	54381	54751	55111	55441	55718	55955	56155
Luxembourg	314	317	321	324	328	332	334	335	336	338	340	342	347	351	355	359	361	361	362
Netherlands	11483	11637	11801	11964	12125	12293	12455	12597	12726	12873	13032	13194	13330	13438	13543	13660	13773	13856	13939
Norway	3585	3615	3639	3667	3694	3723	3753	3785	3819	3851	3879	3903	3933	3961	3985	4007	4026	4043	4060
Poland	..	..	..	..	..	..	31540	31750	32080	32300	32526	32800	33070	33371	33691	34022	34362	34698	35010
Portugal	8630*	8710*	8700*	8760*	8800*	8810*	8790*	8780*	8790*	8780*	8720*	8644	8631	8634	8755	9094	9356	9456	9355
Spain	30583	30904	31158	31430	31741	32085	32453	32850	33240	33566	33876	34190	34498	34810	35147	35515	35937	36367	36778
Sweden	7480	7520	7562	7604	7662	7734	7807	7869	7912	7968	8043	8098	8122	8137	8161	8192	8222	8251	8275
Switzerland	5362	5512	5666	5789	5887	5943	5996	6063	6132	6212	6267	6343	6401	6441	6460	6404	6333	6316	6333
Turkey	27755	28447	29156	29883	30628	31391	32192	33013	33855	34719	35605	36554	37502	38451	39037	40026	40916	41769	42641
United Kingdom	52373	52807	53292	53625	53991	54350	54643	54959	55214	55461	55632	55928	56097	56223	56236	56226	56216	56190	56178
OECD - Total[1]	692902	702120	711509	720772	729731	738757	747285	755574	763613	772059	781050	790697	799643	809252	817187	825241	832767	840308	847924
OECD - Europe[2]	352637	356200	360057	363876	367265	370877	374222	377262	380112	383238	386284	389629	392665	395497	397633	399889	401875	403893	405955
EU15	315759	318447	321414	324352	326867	329628	332085	334202	336105	338253	340329	342623	344620	346432	347936	349234	350380	351543	352697

2. Exchange rates - national currency per US dollar

	1960	1961	1962	1963	1964	1965	1966	1967	1968	1969	1970	1971	1972	1973	1974	1975	1976	1977	1978
Canada	0.970	1.013	1.070	1.081	1.081	1.081	1.081	1.081	1.081	1.081	1.048	1.010	0.990	1.000	0.978	1.017	0.986	1.063	1.141
Mexico	0.012	0.012	0.012	0.012	0.012	0.012	0.012	0.012	0.012	0.012	0.012	0.012	0.012	0.012	0.012	0.012	0.015	0.023	0.023
United States	1.000	1.000	1.000	1.000	1.000	1.000	1.000	1.000	1.000	1.000	1.000	1.000	1.000	1.000	1.000	1.000	1.000	1.000	1.000
Japan	360.000	360.000	360.000	360.000	360.000	360.000	360.000	360.000	360.000	360.000	360.000	349.330	303.170	271.700	292.080	296.790	296.550	268.510	210.440
Korea	..	..	..	..	..	..	271.340	270.520	276.650	288.160	310.560	347.150	392.890	398.320	404.470	484.000	484.000	484.000	484.000
Australia	0.893	0.893	0.893	0.893	0.893	0.893	0.893	0.893	0.893	0.893	0.893	0.883	0.839	0.704	0.697	0.764	0.818	0.902	0.874
New Zealand	0.714	0.716	0.719	0.719	0.719	0.719	0.719	0.734	0.893	0.893	0.893	0.881	0.837	0.737	0.715	0.832	1.005	1.030	0.964
Austria	26.000	26.000	26.000	26.000	26.000	26.000	26.000	26.000	26.000	26.000	26.000	24.960	23.115	19.580	18.692	17.417	17.940	16.527	14.522
Belgium	50.000	50.000	50.000	50.000	50.000	50.000	50.000	50.000	50.000	50.000	50.000	48.870	44.015	38.976	38.951	35.779	38.605	35.843	31.492
Czech Republic	..	..	..	..	..	..	..	..	..	..	..	..	..	..	..	..	..	..	..
Denmark	6.907	6.907	6.907	6.907	6.907	6.907	6.907	6.956	7.500	7.500	7.500	7.417	6.949	6.049	6.095	5.746	6.045	6.003	5.515
Finland	3.200	3.200	3.200	3.200	3.200	3.200	3.200	3.450	4.200	4.200	4.200	4.184	4.146	3.821	3.774	3.679	3.864	4.029	4.117
France	4.937	4.937	4.937	4.937	4.937	4.937	4.937	4.937	4.937	5.194	5.554	5.543	5.044	4.458	4.814	4.286	4.779	4.914	4.513
Germany	4.200	4.033	4.000	4.000	4.000	4.000	4.000	4.000	4.000	3.943	3.660	3.491	3.189	2.673	2.588	2.460	2.518	2.322	2.009
Greece	30.000	30.000	30.000	30.000	30.000	30.000	30.000	30.000	30.000	30.000	30.000	30.000	30.000	29.625	30.000	32.051	36.518	36.838	36.745
Hungary	..	..	..	..	..	..	..	..	60.000	60.000	60.000	59.822	55.260	48.966	46.752	43.971	41.575	40.961	37.911
Iceland	0.344	0.401	0.430	0.430	0.430	0.430	0.430	0.442	0.622	0.880	0.880	0.880	0.883	0.901	1.000	1.537	1.822	1.989	2.711
Ireland	0.357	0.357	0.357	0.357	0.357	0.357	0.357	0.362	0.417	0.417	0.417	0.411	0.400	0.408	0.428	0.452	0.557	0.573	0.522
Italy	623.990	625.000	625.000	625.000	625.000	625.000	625.000	625.000	625.000	625.000	625.000	619.930	583.220	583.000	650.340	652.850	832.340	882.390	848.660
Luxembourg	50.000	50.000	50.000	50.000	50.000	50.000	50.000	50.000	50.000	50.000	50.000	48.870	44.015	38.976	38.951	35.779	38.605	35.843	31.492
Netherlands	3.800	3.650	3.620	3.620	3.620	3.620	3.620	3.620	3.620	3.620	3.620	3.502	3.209	2.796	2.688	2.529	2.644	2.454	2.164
Norway	7.143	7.143	7.143	7.143	7.143	7.143	7.143	7.143	7.143	7.143	7.143	7.042	6.588	5.766	5.540	5.227	5.457	5.323	5.242
Poland	..	..	..	..	..	..	0.000	0.000	0.000	0.000	0.000	0.000	0.000	0.000	0.000	0.000	0.000	0.000	0.000
Portugal	28.750	28.750	28.750	28.750	28.750	28.750	28.750	28.750	28.750	28.750	28.750	28.312	27.054	24.515	25.408	25.553	30.229	38.277	43.937
Spain	60.000	60.000	60.000	60.000	60.000	60.000	60.000	61.667	70.000	70.000	70.000	69.469	64.271	58.260	57.686	57.407	66.903	75.962	76.668
Sweden	5.173	5.173	5.173	5.173	5.173	5.173	5.173	5.173	5.173	5.173	5.173	5.117	4.762	4.367	4.439	4.152	4.356	4.482	4.518
Switzerland	4.373	4.373	4.373	4.373	4.373	4.373	4.373	4.373	4.373	4.373	4.373	4.134	3.819	3.165	2.979	2.581	2.500	2.403	1.788
Turkey	4.867	9.000	9.000	9.000	9.000	9.000	9.000	9.000	9.000	9.000	11.500	14.917	14.150	14.150	13.927	14.442	16.053	18.002	24.282
United Kingdom	0.357	0.357	0.357	0.357	0.357	0.357	0.357	0.362	0.417	0.417	0.417	0.411	0.400	0.408	0.428	0.452	0.557	0.573	0.522

3. Purchasing power parities for GDP - national currency per US dollar

	1960	1961	1962	1963	1964	1965	1966	1967	1968	1969	1970	1971	1972	1973	1974	1975	1976	1977	1978
Canada	..	..	..	..	..	..	..	..	..	..	1.12	1.10	1.11	1.15	1.21	1.22	1.25	1.25	1.24
Mexico	..	..	..	..	..	..	..	..	..	..	0.0075	0.0075	0.0076	0.0081	0.0092	0.0097	0.0109	0.0133	0.0145
United States	..	..	..	..	..	..	..	..	..	..	1.00	1.00	1.00	1.00	1.00	1.00	1.00	1.00	1.00
Japan	..	..	..	..	..	..	..	..	..	..	246	245	247	262	292	286	290	290	282
Korea	..	..	..	..	..	..	..	..	..	..	132	143	160	172	207	239	275	299	343
Australia	..	..	..	..	..	..	..	..	..	..	0.75	0.75	0.77	0.82	0.89	0.94	1.00	1.02	1.02
New Zealand	..	..	..	..	..	..	..	..	..	..	0.60	0.64	0.67	0.69	0.55	0.68	0.76	0.83	0.87
Austria	..	..	..	..	..	..	..	..	..	..	17.2	17.3	17.8	18.1	18.3	17.8	17.7	17.5	17.2
Belgium	..	..	..	..	..	..	..	..	..	..	41.1	41.1	41.8	42.1	43.6	44.8	45.2	45.5	44.2
Czech Republic	..	..	..	..	..	..	..	..	..	..	..	..	..	..	..	..	..	..	..
Denmark	..	..	..	..	..	..	..	..	..	..	6.75	6.89	7.18	7.48	7.79	8.02	8.21	8.41	8.58
Finland	..	..	..	..	..	..	..	..	..	..	3.48	3.55	3.68	3.95	4.45	4.62	4.92	5.06	5.10
France	..	..	..	..	..	..	..	..	..	..	4.42	4.45	4.55	4.64	4.79	4.98	5.19	5.28	5.43
Germany	..	..	..	..	..	..	..	..	..	..	3.12	3.19	3.21	3.21	3.17	3.06	2.98	2.89	2.80
Greece	..	..	..	..	..	..	..	..	..	..	23.2	22.7	22.8	25.6	28.5	28.3	31.8	33.6	35.2
Hungary	..	..	..	..	..	..	..	..	..	..	..	..	..	..	..	..	..	..	..
Iceland	..	..	..	..	..	..	..	..	..	..	0.82	0.87	0.99	1.22	1.55	2.01	2.51	3.11	4.23
Ireland	..	..	..	..	..	..	..	..	..	..	0.310	0.325	0.352	0.381	0.373	0.410	0.466	0.494	0.507
Italy	..	..	..	..	..	..	..	..	..	..	417	421	427	457	508	530	599	664	702
Luxembourg	..	..	..	..	..	..	..	..	..	..	44.9	42.2	42.6	45.0	48.5	47.0	46.3	43.9	42.9
Netherlands	..	..	..	..	..	..	..	..	..	..	2.75	2.82	2.94	3.02	3.03	3.06	3.13	3.12	3.06
Norway	..	..	..	..	..	..	..	..	..	..	7.85	7.93	7.96	8.17	8.30	8.36	8.44	8.55	8.46
Poland	..	..	..	..	..	..	..	..	..	..	..	..	..	..	..	..	..	..	..
Portugal	..	..	..	..	..	..	..	..	..	..	15.0	14.9	15.4	15.8	17.3	18.4	20.1	23.8	27.1
Spain	..	..	..	..	..	..	..	..	..	..	35.2	36.0	37.3	39.3	41.9	44.8	49.0	56.6	63.5
Sweden	..	..	..	..	..	..	..	..	..	..	5.71	5.79	5.92	5.96	6.01	6.10	6.62	6.85	6.97
Switzerland	..	..	..	..	..	..	..	..	..	..	2.97	3.07	3.22	3.28	3.23	3.37	3.05	2.86	2.76
Turkey	..	..	..	..	..	..	..	..	..	..	6.2	6.9	7.4	8.4	10.0	11.0	11.9	13.8	18.9
United Kingdom	..	..	..	..	..	..	..	..	..	..	0.288	0.298	0.308	0.312	0.329	0.350	0.413	0.441	0.457

1. Excluding Korea Czech Republic Hungary and Poland.
2. Excluding Czech Republic Hungary and Poland.

Population - estimations au milieu de l'année en milliers

1.

1979	1980	1981	1982	1983	1984	1985	1986	1987	1988	1989	1990	1991	1992	1993	1994	1995	1996	1997	
24277	24593	24900	25202	25456	25702	25942	26204	26550	26895	27379	27791	28120	28542	28947	29256	29617	29969	30287	Canada
64730*	66780*	68360*	69950*	71550*	73140*	74720*	76280*	77840*	79420*	81000*	82589	84065	85533	87000	88473	90487	92007	93561	Mexique
225055	227726	229966	232188	234307	236348	238466	240651	242804	245021	247342	249911	252643	255407	258120	260682	263168	265557	266792	États-Unis
115880	116800	117650	118450	119260	120020	120750	121490	122090	122610	123120	123540	123920	124320	124670	124960	125570	125864	126166	Japon
37534	38124	38723	39326	39910	40406	40806	41214	41622	42031	42449	42869	43268	43664	44056	44642	45093	45545	45991	Corée
14516	14695	14923	15184	15393	15579	15788	16018	16264	16532	16814	17065	17284	17495	17667	17855	18072	18311	18532	Australie
3138	3144	3157	3183	3226	3258	3272	3277	3304	3317	3330	3363	3477	3514	3554	3602	3656	3714	3761	Nouvelle-Zélande
7549	7549	7569	7576	7567	7571	7578	7588	7598	7615	7659	7729	7813	7914	7991	8030	8047	8059	8072	Autriche
9837	9847	9854	9862	9867	9871	9879	9888	9901	9915	9932	9961	10001	10045	10084	10116	10137	10157	10181	Belgique
10297	10327	10303	10314	10323	10331	10337	10341	10349	10356	10362	10363	10309	10318	10331	10336	10331	10316	10304	République tchèque
5117	5123	5122	5118	5114	5112	5114	5121	5127	5130	5132	5140	5154	5170	5189	5205	5228	5262	5284	Danemark
4765	4780	4800	4827	4856	4882	4902	4918	4932	4946	4964	4986	5014	5042	5066	5088	5108	5125	5140	Finlande
53606	53880	54182	54492	54772	55026	55284	55547	55824	56118	56423	56735	57055	57374	57654	57900	58138	58372	58604	France
78104	78303	78418	78335	78122	77846	77668	77690	77718	78115	78677	79364	79984	80595	81180	81422	81661	81896	82053	Allemagne
9548	9643	9729	9790	9847	9896	9934	9967	10001	10037	10090	10161	10247	10322	10379	10426	10454	10476	10487	Grèce
10698	10707	10700	10683	10656	10620	10579	10534	10486	10443	10398	10365	10346	10324	10294	10261	10229	10193	10155	Hongrie
226	228	231	234	237	239	241	243	246	250	253	255	258	261	264	266	267	269	271	Islande
3368	3401	3443	3480	3505	3529	3541	3542	3543	3531	3510	3506	3526	3549	3563	3583	3598	3621	3656*	Irlande
56318	56434	56510	56579	56626	56652	56674	56675	56674	56688	56705	56737	56760	56859	57050	57204	57300	57380	57520	Italie
363	364	365	366	366	366	367	368	371	374	378	382	387	393	398	404	410	416	422	Luxembourg
14034	14148	14247	14312	14368	14423	14488	14567	14664	14760	14846	14947	15068	15182	15290	15381	15460	15523	15608	Pays-Bas
4073	4086	4100	4115	4128	4140	4153	4167	4187	4209	4227	4241	4262	4286	4312	4337	4359	4381	4405	Norvège
35256	35578	35902	36227	36571	36914	37203	37456	37664	37862	37963	38119	38245	38365	38459	38544	38588	38618	38650	Pologne
9662	9767	9851	9912	9955	9989	10011	10011	9994	9968	9937	9899	9871	9867	9880	9902	9916	9927	9946	Portugal
37108	37510	37741	37944	38123	38279	38420	38537	38632	38717	38792	38851	38920	39008	39086	39150	39210	39270	39323	Espagne
8294	8311	8320	8325	8329	8337	8350	8370	8398	8436	8493	8566	8617	8668	8718	8781	8827	8841	8846	Suède
6351	6385	6429	6467	6482	6505	6534	6573	6619	6671	6723	6796	6873	6943	6989	7037	7081	7105	7111	Suisse
43531	44439	45540	46688	47864	49070	50306	51433	52561	53715	54893	56203	57305	58401	59491	60573	61646	62695	63745	Turquie
56240	56330	56352	56318	56377	56506	56685	56852	57009	57158	57358	57561	57808	58006	58191	58395	58606	58801	59009	Royaume-Uni
855690	864266	871759	878897	885697	892286	899067	905977	912851	920148	927977	936279	944432	952696	960733	968028	976023	982998	988782	OCDE - Total[1]
408094	410528	412803	414740	416505	418239	420129	422057	423999	426353	428992	432020	434923	437885	440775	443200	445453	447576	449683	OCDE - Europe[2]
353913	355390	356503	357236	357794	358285	358895	359641	360386	361508	362896	364525	366225	367994	369719	370987	372100	373126	374151	UE15

Taux de change - monnaie nationale par dollar É-U

2.

1979	1980	1981	1982	1983	1984	1985	1986	1987	1988	1989	1990	1991	1992	1993	1994	1995	1996	1997	
1.171	1.169	1.199	1.234	1.232	1.295	1.365	1.389	1.326	1.231	1.184	1.167	1.146	1.209	1.290	1.366	1.372	1.363	1.385	Canada
0.023	0.023	0.025	0.056	0.120	0.168	0.257	0.612	1.378	2.273	2.461	2.813	3.018	3.095	3.116	3.375	6.419	7.599	7.914	Mexique
1.000	1.000	1.000	1.000	1.000	1.000	1.000	1.000	1.000	1.000	1.000	1.000	1.000	1.000	1.000	1.000	1.000	1.000	1.000	États-Unis
219.140	226.740	220.540	249.080	237.510	237.520	238.540	168.520	144.640	128.150	137.960	144.790	134.710	126.650	111.200	102.210	94.060	108.780	120.990	Japon
484.000	607.430	681.030	731.080	775.750	805.980	870.020	881.450	822.570	731.470	671.460	707.760	733.350	780.650	802.670	803.450	771.270	804.450	951.290	Corée
0.895	0.878	0.870	0.986	1.110	1.140	1.432	1.496	1.428	1.280	1.265	1.281	1.284	1.362	1.471	1.368	1.349	1.278	1.347	Australie
0.978	1.027	1.153	1.333	1.497	1.764	2.023	1.913	1.695	1.526	1.672	1.676	1.734	1.862	1.851	1.687	1.524	1.455	1.512	Nouvelle-Zélande
13.368	12.938	15.927	17.059	17.963	20.009	20.689	15.267	12.642	12.348	13.231	11.370	11.676	10.989	11.632	11.422	10.081	10.587	12.204	Autriche
29.319	29.242	37.129	45.691	51.132	57.784	59.378	44.672	37.334	36.768	39.404	33.418	34.148	32.150	34.596	33.456	29.480	30.961	35.774	Belgique
..	14.840	..	..	..	..	16.000	..	..	..	..	21.145	27.920	28.370	29.153	28.785	26.541	27.145	31.698	République tchèque
5.261	5.636	7.123	8.332	9.145	10.357	10.596	8.091	6.840	6.731	7.310	6.189	6.396	6.036	6.484	6.361	5.602	5.799	6.604	Danemark
3.895	3.730	4.315	4.820	5.570	6.010	6.198	5.070	4.396	4.183	4.291	3.824	4.044	4.479	5.712	5.224	4.367	4.594	5.191	Finlande
4.254	4.226	5.435	6.572	7.621	8.739	8.985	6.926	6.011	5.957	6.380	5.445	5.642	5.294	5.663	5.552	4.991	5.115	5.837	France
1.833	1.818	2.260	2.427	2.553	2.846	2.944	2.171	1.797	1.756	1.880	1.616	1.660	1.562	1.653	1.623	1.433	1.505	1.734	Allemagne
37.038	42.617	55.408	66.803	88.064	112.717	138.119	139.981	135.430	141.861	162.417	158.514	182.266	190.624	229.250	242.603	231.663	240.711	273.058	Grèce
35.578	32.532	34.314	36.631	42.671	48.042	50.119	45.832	46.971	50.413	59.066	63.206	74.735	78.988	91.933	105.160	125.681	152.647	186.789	Hongrie
3.526	4.798	7.224	12.351	24.843	31.694	41.508	41.104	38.677	43.014	57.042	58.284	58.996	57.546	67.603	69.944	64.692	66.500	70.904	Islande
0.489	0.487	0.621	0.705	0.805	0.923	0.946	0.743	0.673	0.656	0.706	0.605	0.621	0.588	0.677	0.669	0.624	0.625	0.660	Irlande
830.860	856.450	1136.760	1352.510	1518.850	1756.960	1909.440	1490.810	1296.070	1301.620	1372.090	1198.100	1240.610	1232.410	1573.670	1612.440	1628.930	1542.950	1703.100	Italie
29.319	29.242	37.129	45.691	51.132	57.784	59.378	44.672	37.334	36.768	39.404	33.418	34.148	32.150	34.596	33.456	29.480	30.961	35.774	Luxembourg
2.006	1.988	2.495	2.670	2.854	3.209	3.321	2.450	2.026	1.977	2.121	1.821	1.870	1.758	1.857	1.820	1.606	1.686	1.951	Pays-Bas
5.064	4.939	5.740	6.454	7.296	8.161	8.597	7.395	6.737	6.517	6.904	6.260	6.483	6.214	7.094	7.058	6.335	6.450	7.073	Norvège
0.004	0.004	0.005	0.008	0.009	0.011	0.015	0.018	0.027	0.043	0.144	0.950	1.058	1.363	1.811	2.272	2.425	2.696	3.279	Pologne
48.924	50.062	61.546	79.473	110.780	146.390	170.395	149.587	140.882	143.954	157.458	142.555	144.482	134.998	160.800	165.993	151.106	154.244	175.313	Portugal
67.125	71.702	92.322	109.859	143.430	160.761	170.044	140.048	123.478	116.487	118.378	101.934	103.912	102.379	127.260	133.958	124.689	126.662	146.414	Espagne
4.287	4.230	5.063	6.283	7.667	8.272	8.604	7.124	6.340	6.127	6.447	5.919	6.047	5.824	7.783	7.716	7.133	6.706	7.635	Suède
1.663	1.676	1.964	2.030	2.099	2.350	2.457	1.799	1.491	1.463	1.636	1.389	1.434	1.406	1.478	1.368	1.182	1.236	1.451	Suisse
31.078	76.038	111.219	162.553	225.457	366.678	521.983	674.512	857.216	1422.350	2121.680	2608.640	4171.820	6872.420	10984.600	29608.700	45845.100	81404.900	151865.000	Turquie
0.472	0.430	0.498	0.572	0.660	0.752	0.779	0.682	0.612	0.562	0.611	0.563	0.567	0.570	0.667	0.653	0.634	0.641	0.611	Royaume-Uni

Parités de pouvoir d'achat du PIB - monnaie nationale par dollar É-U

3.

1979	1980	1981	1982	1983	1984	1985	1986	1987	1988	1989	1990	1991	1992	1993	1994	1995	1996	1997	
1.25	1.27	1.27	1.31	1.31	1.30	1.28	1.29	1.31	1.31	1.32	1.30	1.29	1.28	1.26	1.25	1.19	1.19	*1.17*	Canada
0.0160	0.0188	0.0214	0.0325	0.0593	0.0902	0.136	0.231	0.536	1.03	1.25	1.53	1.89	2.02	2.12	2.28	2.97	3.79	*4.42*	Mexique
1.00	1.00	1.00	1.00	1.00	1.00	1.00	1.00	1.00	1.00	1.00	1.00	1.00	1.00	1.00	1.00	1.00	1.00	*1.00*	États-Unis
266	256	241	232	226	221	218	217	210	204	199	195	193	188	184	181	169	166	*164*	Japon
378	*431*	*460*	*462*	*466*	*469*	*475*	*484*	*492*	*506*	*511*	*538*	*591*	*586*	*591*	*618*	*617*	*629*	*632*	*Corée*
1.04	1.05	1.04	1.09	1.13	1.15	1.18	1.23	1.28	1.34	1.38	1.39	1.37	1.37	1.35	1.34	1.29	1.30	*1.30*	Australie
0.92	0.96	1.01	1.05	1.09	1.12	1.24	1.43	1.55	1.62	1.63	1.61	1.56	1.51	1.51	1.50	1.47	1.48	*1.46*	Nouvelle-Zélande
16.3	15.7	15.1	15.0	14.9	14.9	14.8	14.9	14.7	14.4	14.2	14.0	14.2	14.0	13.9	13.9	13.8	13.6	*13.5*	Autriche
42.4	40.3	38.5	38.8	39.3	39.5	40.4	40.9	40.5	39.8	39.9	39.5	39.2	37.8	37.3	37.3	36.9	36.8	*36.7*	Belgique
..	..	..	..	..	..	..	..	..	..	..	5.24	7.65	8.35	9.46	10.4	10.8	11.7	12.2	République tchèque
8.48	8.38	8.36	8.72	8.98	9.07	9.14	9.33	9.45	9.41	9.48	9.39	9.18	9.14	8.79	8.71	8.45	8.33	*8.33*	Danemark
5.10	5.11	5.14	5.23	5.49	5.71	5.81	5.93	6.01	6.19	6.29	6.38	6.30	6.35	6.09	6.15	5.88	5.89	*5.91*	Finlande
5.51	5.62	5.70	6.02	6.32	6.49	6.64	6.82	6.80	6.75	6.69	6.61	6.51	6.42	6.57	6.62	6.49	6.57	*6.52*	France
2.67	2.56	2.41	2.35	2.33	2.27	2.23	2.24	2.20	2.15	2.11	2.09	2.09	2.07	2.10	2.07	2.02	2.03	*2.00*	Allemagne
38.4	41.3	44.8	52.8	60.2	69.2	78.7	90.3	99.8	111	122	141	161	170	184	196	204	214	*224*	Grèce
..	..	..	..	..	..	..	..	..	..	..	26.1	32.6	37.1	43.2	51.2	60.7	72.6	84.4	Hongrie
5.47	7.62	10.4	15.0	25.2	30.2	38.4	47.0	54.3	64.3	73.8	82.6	85.7	83.1	82.9	84.1	76.2	76.8	*77.9*	Islande
0.529	0.554	0.590	0.641	0.679	0.690	0.702	0.730	0.722	0.718	0.725	0.690	0.666	0.638	0.655	0.638	0.637	0.673	*0.675*	Irlande
748	826	891	984	1084	1156	1217	1281	1316	1353	1378	1421	1463	1459	1534	1533	1556	1583	*1595*	Italie
41.9	41.3	40.1	41.9	42.8	42.7	42.5	42.6	41.6	40.4	40.0	39.7	39.5	38.9	39.6	40.0	39.0	39.7	*40.3*	Luxembourg
2.92	2.82	2.69	2.67	2.61	2.53	2.49	2.43	2.34	2.28	2.21	2.16	2.18	2.14	2.13	2.12	2.04	2.04	*2.05*	Pays-Bas
8.20	8.47	8.67	9.02	9.24	9.39	9.54	9.23	9.55	9.65	9.78	9.73	9.60	8.98	8.93	9.12	9.18	9.11	*9.20*	Norvège
..	..	..	..	..	..	..	..	..	..	..	0.301	0.467	0.604	0.758	1.00	1.14	1.36	1.54	Pologne
29.7	32.8	34.9	39.7	47.4	56.5	66.4	78.1	83.2	89.1	95.9	104	110	116	117	118	120	122	*123*	Portugal
68.1	70.5	72.0	77.3	82.7	88.3	91.8	99.6	102	104	106	110	110	115	117	121	123	124	*124*	Espagne
6.91	7.05	7.00	7.15	7.53	7.74	7.97	8.32	8.43	8.65	8.95	9.34	9.94	9.80	9.83	9.90	9.77	9.68	*9.62*	Suède
2.58	2.42	2.32	2.34	2.30	2.27	2.25	2.26	2.25	2.23	2.20	2.20	2.23	2.16	2.13	2.10	2.02	2.05	*2.01*	Suisse
30.4	52.3	68.2	82.5	99.7	141	209	277	359	585	983	1491	2280	3667	5990	12096	22405	39275	*69997*	Turquie
0.480	0.521	0.526	0.535	0.539	0.538	0.551	0.554	0.563	0.575	0.591	0.602	0.635	0.616	0.637	0.646	0.656	0.644	*0.648*	Royaume-Uni

1. Non compris la Corée la Républicue tchèque la Hongrie et la Pologne.
2. Non compris la République tchèque la Hongrie e: la Pologne.

Did you Know?

This publication is available in electronic form

Many OECD publications and data sets are now available in electronic form to suit your needs at affordable prices. For our statistical publications we use powerful software platforms (Ivation's Beyond 20/20 or STATWISE) that allow you to get the maximum value from the data. Other publications are available using the simple Acrobat/PDF presentation. **Delivery platforms** range from magnetic tape through CD-Rom and diskettes to online via internet. **Stand alone and network** versions are offered for many titles.

For more information about electronic editions of this publication, or to ask for a catalogue of all our electronic publications, contact your nearest OECD Centre (see overleaf).

Le saviez-vous ?

La version électronique de cette publication est disponible !

Désormais, afin de mieux répondre à vos besoins, un grand nombre de publications et de données de l'OCDE sont disponibles sous forme électronique à des prix très abordables. Nos études statistiques sont présentées sur des logiciels puissants (Beyond 20/20 ou Statwise) permettant d'optimiser les données au maximum. Certaines publications sont également disponibles sur Acrobat/PDF. Par ailleurs, **un éventail très large de supports** vous est proposé : bande magnétique, Cédérom, disquette et interrogation en ligne via Internet. De nombreux titres sont également proposés en **versions monoposte et réseau.**

Pour de plus amples informations sur les versions électroniques de cette publication ou pour obtenir le catalogue de nos éditions électroniques, n'hésitez pas à contacter le Centre OCDE le plus proche (voir verso).

OECD-OCDE

A POTENT INSTRUMENT OF GLOBAL CHANGE
UN INSTUMENT PUISSANT DE CHANGEMENT ET DE REFORME DANS LE MONDE

Where to send your request:

Où envoyer votre demande:

In Austria, Germany and Switzerland / En Allemagne, en Autriche et en Suisse

OECD Centre Bonn / Centre OCDE de Bonn
August-Bebel-Allee 6,
D-53175 Bonn
Tel.: (49-228) 959 1215
Fax: (49-228) 959 1218
E-mail: bonn.contact@oecd.org
Internet: www.oecd.org/bonn

In Latin America / En Amérique latine

OECD Centre Mexico / Centre OCDE de Mexico
Edificio INFOTEC
Av. San Fernando No. 37
Col. Toriello Guerra
Tlalpan C.P. 14050,
Mexico D.F.
Tel.: (525) 528 10 38
Fax: (525) 606 13 07
E-mail: mexico.contact@oecd.org

Internet: rtn.net.mx/ocde/

In the United States / Aux États-Unis

OECD Center Washington / Centre OCDE de Washington
2001 L Street N.W., Suite 650
Washington, DC 20036-4922
Tel.: (202) 785 6323
Toll free / Numéro vert : (800) 456-6323
Fax: (202) 785 0350
E-mail: washington.contact@oecd.org
Internet: www.oecdwash.org

In Asia / En Asie

OECD Centre Tokyo / Centre OCDE de Tokyo
Landic Akasaka Bldg.
2-3-4 Akasaka, Minato-ku,
Tokyo 107-0052
Tel.: (81-3) 3586 2016
Fax: (81-3) 3584 7929
E-mail : center@oecdtokyo.org
Internet: www.oecdtokyo.org

In the rest of the world / Dans le reste du monde
OECD Paris Centre / Centre OCDE de Paris
2 rue André-Pascal, 75775 Paris Cedex 16, France
Orders / Commandes : Fax: 33 (0)1 49 10 42 76

Enquiries / Renseignements : Tel: 33 (0)1 45 24 81 22 Fax: 33 (0) 1 45 24 19 50
E-mail : sales@oecd.org

Online Ordering: www.oecd.org/publications *(secure payment with credit card)*
Commande en ligne : www.oecd.org/publications *(paiement sécurisé par carte de crédit)*

OECD Main Switchboard / Standard OCDE : 33 (0) 1 45 24 82 00

Internet: www.oecd.org

OECD PUBLICATIONS, 2, rue André-Pascal, 75775 PARIS CEDEX 16
PRINTED IN FRANCE
(30 99 01 3P) ISBN 92-64-05840-0 – No. 50480 1999